Conversations

CONVERSATIONS

Readings for Writing

second edition

Jack Selzer

The Pennsylvania State University

MACMILLAN PUBLISHING COMPANY

NEW YORK

Editor: Eben W. Ludlow.
Production Supervisor: Kelly Ricci
Production Manager: Aliza Greenblatt
Cover Designer: Hothouse Designs
Cover Art: Piñeiro Design Associates

This book was set in 10 pt. Aster by AmeriComp and printed and bound by R. R. Donnelley & Sons.
The cover was printed by New England Book Components.

Printed in the United States of America

Macmillan Publishing Company
866 Third Avenue, New York, New York 10022

Macmillan Publishing Company is part of the Maxwell Communication Group of Companies.

Library of Congress Cataloging-in-Publication Data
Conversations : readings for writing / [compiled by] Jack Selzer. — 2nd ed.
p. cm.
Includes index.
ISBN 0-02-408961-3
1. College readers. 2. English language—Rhetoric. I. Selzer, Jack.
PE1417.C6545 1994
808′.0427—dc20 93-17555
CIP

Printing: 1 2 3 4 5 6 7 Year: 4 5 6 7 8 9 0

(*Copy credits information continues on page 1069, which constitutes a continuation of the copyright page*)

For Molly and Maggie:
Their Book

Preface

> Imagine that you enter a parlor. You come late. When you arrive, others have long preceded you, and they are engaged in a heated discussion, a discussion too heated for them to pause and tell you exactly what it is about. In fact, the discussion had already begun long before any of them got there, so that no one present is qualified to retrace for you all the steps that had gone before. You listen for a while, until you decide that you have caught the tenor of the argument; then you put in your oar. Someone answers; you answer him; another comes to your defense; another aligns himself against you, to either the embarrassment or gratification of your opponent, depending upon the quality of your ally's assistance.

This well-known passage from Kenneth Burke's *Philosophy of Literary Form* explains the basic metaphor and the socio-rhetorical orientation of this anthology of readings for college composition courses. *Conversations* contains conversations: public discourse on contemporary issues that is calculated to engage students' interests, to encourage and empower their own contributions to contemporary civic discussions, and to represent a broad cross-section of the kinds of conversational styles and genres that are available to writers at the end of the twentieth century.

What's Different About *Conversations*?

Conversations encourages student writing on important current civic issues. The premise of this reader is that writing is less a private act of making personal meaning out of nothing than it is a public and social act of making meaning within a specific rhetorical situation—a specific situation that guides and shapes the meaning-making activity. To put the matter more simply, writing emerges from other writing, other discourse. Though nearly every anthology claims to encourage student responses, those readers just as often actually intimidate students because they present only one or two authoritative voices on a given issue and because those voices are given little context outside the anthology; the student reads an essay by Booth or Didion or Baldwin or Woolf or some other eloquent writer, and says to himself or herself, "Gee, that sure seems right to me. How could I disagree with such an expert?" Therefore, instead of one or two authoritative items on an issue or a topic, this reader contains "conversations" on public issues or topics, conversations-with-contexts that will seem less intimidating and therefore invite student responses.

In fact, the book will encourage students to adopt a social and rhetorical model—a "conversation model"—for their own writing: Instead of seeing writing merely as private or as debate or point-counterpoint, students should sense that "people are talking about this issue—and I'd like to get in on the talk somewhere." The conversation metaphor does not mean that students should "write like they talk" (since conversational informality is not always appropriate in public discourse); rather, the metaphor simply implies that students should see writing as a response to other writing, a response that they make after considering the implications and importance of what they have read and heard. Students should be encouraged to cooperate as well as to compete with other writers, to address subissues as well as the main chance, to seek consensus and new syntheses as often as victory.

Thus *Conversations* is organized around focused, topical contemporary public issues (e.g., censorship, what to do about public education, gender at work, affirmative action, legalization of drugs, abortion), each within seven larger thematic groupings (education, language, gender, media, civil liberties and civil rights, crime and punishment, and science and society) that lend additional historical and conceptual perspective to those contemporary issues. *Intertextuality* would be the buzzword from contemporary critical theory: The book includes items that "talk to each other" both directly and indirectly. Some pieces speak directly and explicitly to each other (as in the case of the discussion of 2 Live Crew's rap lyrics, or Milton Friedman's exchange with

William Bennett about the legalization of drugs, or the conversation among John Wallace, Robert Nadeau, and Nat Hentoff on censoring *Huckleberry Finn*). Some pieces refer only indirectly to others, as in the sections on education, genetic engineering, and affirmative action. Still other items comment on selections in other sections of *Conversations*: e.g., selections on education comment on those on language and race; the section on pornography is informed by the sections on gender and the causes of crime; the items on gay rights are related to the section on AIDS. And so forth. There is certainly no reason why the selections in this anthology cannot be read individually as they are in other books, without reference to other selections, especially because the headnotes orient readers to each item. And there is certainly no reason why the selections could not be read in some other order. Nevertheless, *Conversations* does give students a particular incentive to write because it establishes contexts for writing.

The conversation model should make the book suitable to a range of courses in writing. There is plenty of expository prose here: e.g., comparisons of all kinds; a careful analysis of the language of men and women by Deborah Tannen; Tom Regan's analysis of the religious grounds for animal rights; Mia Klein Anderson's study of the rhetoric of Martin Luther King, Jr.; cool descriptions of schools, men and women, novels and movies, campus politics, television, and a hanging; expositions of the reasons why women are excluded from science and why people commit crimes; and lots of et cetera. The "modes of exposition" are illustrated by numerous selections, as the alternate table of contents makes clear. But *Conversations* will also accommodate courses with an argumentative edge, for this book includes a fair proportion of explicitly or implicitly argumentative writing and tends to encourage a broadly argumentative approach to all discourse. In short, the conversation metaphor implies an inclusive approach to prose, one that subsumes and includes exposition as well as argument, dialogue as well as dialectic. *Conversations* includes not only Edward Fiske's prescriptions for the high school classroom, but Theodore Sizer's descriptions as well. It includes not only partisan arguments for and against gun control, but also a careful analysis of the issue by Leonard Kriegel. It includes not only impassionate pro and con arguments on capital punishment, abortion, animal rights, and the "mommy track" for business executives, but also dispassionate analyses of language issues, the appeal of rap music, affirmative action, and more.

Consequently—and this is another notable feature of *Conversations*—this anthology includes a very broad range of genres; the book tries to represent as fully as possible the full spectrum of the "universe of discourse." True, essays are prominent in *Conversations*—familiar and formal essays, academic as well as nonacademic ones—because the essay is a common and important genre and because the form has important correspondences with other genres (e.g., the letter, the sermon, the report, the news story). But essays are not so prominent here as to exclude other genres. Students will find other ways of engaging in public discourse as well: through fiction, poetry, drama, letters of various kinds, public oratory, interviews, congressional hearings and reports, cartoons, advertisements, journals—and more. The occasions for public discourse are many and various. Students and their teachers will find news stories and movie reviews, rhetorical analyses and studies of cultural artifacts, parodies and satires, letters to the editor and counterresponses, and laws and constitutional amendments.

And they will hear a range of voices as well. *Conversations* assumes that students are ready, willing, and able to engage in civic, public discourse, but that does not preclude the possibility for personal inventiveness. Indeed, *Conversations* is committed to the proposition that there are many possible rhetorical stances, that there is no one correct way to address a reader. This anthology therefore exposes students to as many rhetorical choices as possible—from the studied erudition of John Simon to the semiformal, "objective" voice associated with the academy; from the conversational informality of E. B. White, Garrison Keillor, and Deborah Tannen to satiric invective by Judy Syfers and Lewis Grizzard; from the thrilling oratory of Sojourner Truth to the careful reasoning of Evelyn Fox Keller; from *Rolling Stone*, *Ms.*, *Mother Jones*, and *The Village Voice* to *Esquire*, *The New Yorker*, and *The American Scholar*; from Jamaica Kincaid, Stephen Jay Gould, and James Baldwin to George Orwell, Robert Bly, Richard Rodriguez, and Andrea Dworkin. Students will encounter mainstream texts and dissenting views, conventional rhetorical maneuvers and startlingly inventive ones. They will hear from famous professional writers and anonymous but eloquent fellow citizens; from public figures and fellow students (a half dozen student contributions are included); from women and men; from majority and minority voices. *Conversations* gives students a better chance to find their own voices because they've experienced a full range of possible voices in their reading.

"A rhetorician," says Kenneth Burke in "Rhetoric—Old and New," "is like one voice in a dialogue. Put several such voices together, with each voicing its own special assertion, let them act upon one another in cooperative competition, and you get a dialectic that, properly developed, can lead to views transcending the limitations of each." Fostering that "cooperative competition" is the aim of *Conversations*.

Editorial Apparatus

Substantial editorial assistance has been provided to the users of *Conversations*. The book's Introduction orients students to social motives for writing and domesticates for them the metaphor of conversation. It also introduces students to the notion of critical or rhetorical reading, so that they might have a practical means of approaching every item in *Conversations*—and so that they might understand better how careful reading habits can reinforce effective writing habits. In addition, a headnote is provided for each selection so that students can orient themselves to the rhetoric of each piece. The headnotes provide background on the author (especially when prior knowledge about the author affects one's response to an item), on the topic of the selection (when the matter requires any explanation), and on the specific occasion for the piece (especially on when and where it was originally published). The assumption of most anthologies is that the original context of an essay or story—or whatever—doesn't matter much, or that the anthology itself comprises the context. *Conversations* assumes instead that careful reading must take into account the original circumstances that prompted a given piece of writing. Writing, after all, most often emerges from other writing, so situating each item by means of the headnotes is essential to the concept of *Conversations*. Finally, each part of the book includes an introduction to the particular issues under discussion in that part. In sum, the editorial apparatus ensures that the selections in *Conversations* can be used in any order that a teacher or student might want.

Otherwise, the text of *Conversations* assumes that students are already quite capable readers. On the grounds that students and teachers can handle things on their own and can appropriate readings to their own ends, the book includes no questions at the end of each selection, no suggestions for writing assignments or class discussions, no exercises, and few footnotes. Space that might have been devoted to those matters is given instead to additional selections so that teachers might have as many selections as possible from which to choose.

Instructor's Manual

Teachers who do want additional background on unfamiliar readings or specific suggestions for making the most of *Conversations* will find plenty of help in the detailed Instructor's Manual compiled by Robert Davis, Eva Elsmere Aldrich, and me. The manual contains further information on writers, overviews, and minianalyses of each selection, questions for discussion, and ideas for writing assignments. It also offers pointers for teaching each "conversation"—for how particular selections can be used with other selections. Together, the editorial apparatus and the Instructor's Manual are designed to help *Conversations* engage the intelligence and passions of students and teachers, without getting in the way of either.

Acknowledgments

There may be only one name on the cover of this book, but it too is the product of a conversation—many conversations, in fact—with a number of people who collaborated on its development and production. My greatest debt is to those who assisted me in finding appropriate selections. Rosa Eberly of Penn State, Dawn Keetley (now of the University of Wisconsin), Tom Buckley (now of the University of Texas), and Jay Shuchter deserve special mention; but lots of others affected the outcome: Paul Klemp (University of Wisconsin—Eau Claire); Linda Ferreira-Buckley (University of Texas); Tony O'Keeffe (Bellarmine College); Debra Journet (University of Louisville); and Jim Brasfield, Bob Burkholder, Deb Clarke, Christopher Clausen, Mel

DeYoung, Claudia Limbert, Nancy Lowe, Steve Mastrofski, Jeff Purvis, David Randall, Linda Selzer, and Cynthia Miecznikowski Sheard (all of Penn State). Several reviewers of the book made excellent suggestions: Stephen Behrendt, University of Nebraska; John Bodnar, Prince George's Community College; Kitty Dean, Nassau Community College; John Dick, University of Texas at El Paso; Jack Dodds, Harper College; Robert Funk, Eastern Illinois University, Paula Gillespie, Marquette University; Dona Hickey, University of Richmond; Robert Lesman, Northern Virginia Community College; Gerald Levin, University of Akron; George Otte, Baruch College, CUNY; and Richard Zbaracki, Iowa State University. The second edition in particular profited from advice from Eugene Antonio, Georgia Institute of Technology; Philip Auslander, Georgia Institute of Technology; Margaret T. Banocy-Payne, Tallahassee Community College; Vivian R. Brown, Laredo Junior College; Wyeth O. Burgess, Georgia Institute of Technology; Christine Cetrulo, University of Kentucky; John Cooper, University of Kentucky; Lester Faigley, University of Texas at Austin; Ann George, The Pennsylvania State University; JoEllen Hall, California State University, Chico; Douglas D. Hesse, Illinois State University; Missy James, Tallahassee Community College; Keith Kroll, Kalamazoo Valley Community College; Lia Kushnir, University of New Orleans; Steven Lynn, University of South Carolina–Columbia; Margaret Mahoney, Iowa State University; James May, Pennsylvania State University, DuBois Campus; James C. McDonald, University of Southwestern Louisiana; Robert Miedel, La Salle University; Gordon M. Pradl, New York University; David Ragsdale, Kingwood College; Gerald Richman, Suffolk University; Patricia Roberts, The University of North Carolina at Greensboro; Joan Samuelson, Kingwood College; Sheila Schwartz, Cleveland State University; Carol A. Senf, Georgia Institute of Technology; Carolyn H. Smith, University of Florida; Scott F. Stoddart, Nova University; Gloria J. Underwood, University of South Carolina–Columbia; and Richard Vela, Pembroke State University. Other colleagues across the country and at Penn State—particularly Davida Charney, Christina Haas, John Harwood, Jennifer Jackson, Nancy Lowe, Marie Secor, and Jeff Walker—stimulate my thinking on a daily basis. Peggy Keating and Suzanne Marcum worked diligently to secure permissions, and Todd Post and Keith Waddle did research for many of the headnotes. And twenty teachers at Penn State tested a prototype of the first edition in their classes during the fall semester of 1989.

Thanks too to those on the production end of things. Kim Witherite Keller and especially Kathy Leitzell efficiently and cheerfully produced much of the manuscript; they helped me out of a thousand small scrapes to boot. Another thousand that I don't even know about were taken care of by Nancy Cooperman (at Macmillan) and Betsy Keefer and Durrae Johanek for the first edition. The second edition profited from the expertise of Kristin Miller, Kathy Riley-King, and Kelly Ricci of Spectrum Publisher Services. Eben Ludlow has been an ideal editor: full of excellent suggestions, encouraging without ever being overbearing, supportive at every turn. His confidence in this project brought it into being. I won't forget it.

J. S.

Contents

I. EDUCATION

III. GENDER

IV. MEDIA

V. CIVIL LIBERTIES AND CIVIL RIGHTS

eight clergymen urge an end to those demonstrations.

MARTIN LUTHER KING, JR., Letter from Birmingham Jail (letter/essay) **673**

The Nobel-Prize-winning civil rights leader defends civil disobedience and articulates—from his jail cell—the thinking behind civil rights demonstrations.

MIA KLEIN ANDERSON, The *Other* Beauty of Martin Luther King, Jr.'s "Letter from Birmingham Jail" (essay) **690**

A stylistic analysis of King's letter reveals his rhetorical artistry.

LEWIS H. VAN DUSEN, JR., Civil Disobedience: Destroyer of Democracy (essay) **700**

Civil disobedience "is an assault on our democratic society," argues a successful lawyer.

WOODY ALLEN, A Brief, Yet Helpful, Guide to Civil Disobedience (essay) **707**

"It is well known that Mahatma Gandhi's insistence on eating his salads untossed shamed the British government into concessions."

Affirmative Action **711**

KURT VONNEGUT, JR., Harrison Bergeron (fiction) **711**

"The year was 2081, and everybody was finally equal," thanks to the Handicapper General.

PAUL R. SPICKARD, Why I Believe in Affirmative Action (essay) **717**

Denied several jobs by affirmative action efforts, a white male nevertheless contends that affirmative action is good social policy—and a scriptural imperative.

VII. SCIENCE AND SOCIETY

Rhetorical Contents

Journal and Personal Report

Description and Narration

Process

Illustration, Example

Comparison and Contrast

Analysis

Cause and Effect

Definition

Argument: Categorical Proposition ("X is in fact Y")

Argument: Evaluation

Argument: Proposal

Argument: Refutation

Irony and Satire

Introduction

Why Write?

Why do people write?

For lots of reasons, of course. Sometimes the impulse to write derives from a personal need. The motive to write can come from within. Everyone needs to sort out feelings at one time or another or to make some personal sense of the world and its parts, and a good way to do such sorting is by writing. If you keep a diary or journal, or if you've shared your most intimate feelings through correspondence with a trusted friend, or if you've written essays—or notes toward an essay—in order to explore possible explanations for things, then you know what it means to write for personal reasons. (A root meaning of the word *essay* is "to try out, to experiment.") People do need a means of expressing powerful feelings and personal insights, and writing seems to provide just the tranquility required for a gathering of thoughts.

Other times the world itself motivates a writer. We seem to have a need to note our observations about the world, especially if those observations are indeed noteworthy—if they seem special or unique in some way. Sometimes this process of "taking note" is relatively formalized, as when a scientist records observations in a log of some kind or when the president at the end of a day records significant details for future reference or when you keep score at a baseball game or when a reporter transcribes "just the facts" into a news article. But just as often it is something less formal—when you take notes for a course, for instance, or when I write something in my journal about the life and times of my two children. The drive "to hold the mirror up to nature," as Hamlet called it, to record our understanding about the way of the world, accounts for much of the prose we encounter and produce each day.

The motive to write can also derive from one's vocation. In other words, some people write because it's their life's work. They are professional writers—poets, news reporters, novelists, technical writers, screenwriters. And they are semiprofessional writers, people who don't think of themselves as writers but who indeed spend a large amount of their time writing—police officers, engineers, college professors, lawyers, physicians, corporate managers, teachers, and so forth. (You'd be surprised at how much time such people spend on the writing required by their jobs.) Professional writers and professionals who write sometimes put words onto paper for the reasons named in the previous paragraphs—to express personal feelings or ideas, or to record their impressions or interpretations of their workaday worlds. But they also often think in terms of a particular kind of writing—a genre—when they compose: Newspaper employees think of themselves as writing news stories or editorials; poets set out to write poems; engineers or police officers think of the reports they have to turn in; lawyers have to produce those legal briefs next week. Their sense of completing a particular genre can sometimes take precedence over other motives.

Of course all these motives to write are legitimate, and seldom do these motives exist in a pure state. It is probably better to think of motives to write, instead of *a* motive, and to think of primary and secondary motives, instead of a single, all-consuming aim. When John Milton wrote *Paradise Lost,* for instance, he was certainly out to record his assessment of the nature of things and to express his most personal thoughts—and to write an epic. When Henry David Thoreau wrote *Walden,* he certainly had personal motives—the book originated in his daily journals—but he wanted "to hold the mirror up to nature" as well (the very title of *Walden* suggests that Thoreau was attempting to record his close observations of nature).

But *Walden* and *Paradise Lost* are "public" documents, too—attempts to sway public opinion and public behavior. Thoreau advertised *Walden,* after all, as his attempt to "brag as lustily as Chanticleer [the rooster] in the morning, if only to wake my neighbor up." He wanted to awaken his fellow citizens to nature and to persuade them to renew their own lives after his own example and experience. Milton's stated purpose—"to justify the ways of God to man"—was just as social. He wanted to change how people conceive of their relation to God, and to detail his vision of the heroic life to be lived by every wayfaring Christian. Writing to persuade, to have an effect on the thinking of others, does not preclude writing to discover or writing to record or writing in a particular genre. Indeed, writing to persuade nearly always means writing *about something* in a *particular genre* for reasons that are *intensely personal.* But writing to persuade does mean writing something that has designs on the hearts or minds (or both) of particular readers. It is writing that is calculated to have an effect on a real reader. This goes for John Milton and Joan Didion, and it goes for you, too.

For though a writer may work in private, a writer is never really alone. A writer out "to wake people up" or "to justify the ways of God" to men and women is obviously anything but working privately, for the writer out to persuade is inherently social. But every other kind of writing is social as well. The engineer who writes a report on a project is out to influence the project's managers. A physician's report on a patient is used by other caregivers in the short run and long run to direct medical attention in a specific way. The lawyer's brief is meant to sway judges. The movie reviewer's account is designed to direct people to (or away from) the film. Even private writing is often quite public in fact. The letters in which you pour out your feelings get read by sympathetic and responsive friends. The essays you write to discover your version of the truth become written attempts to convert readers to that version. Even journal entries that no one but you will read are shaped to an extent by what society considers to be noteworthy and by what a different "you" will want to read a few years from now; and the very words you choose to use reflect a vocabulary you share with others and learn from others. Writing is a social act. It is a primary means for touching others, and reading what others have written is a primary way of being touched in turn. The words you read and write are surrounded and shaped by the words and attitudes and beliefs of the many people who share your society, your "social context." People may write to express themselves, or to complete a particular kind of writing, or to say something about their world—or some combination of these—but in some sense they do so in order to have an effect on someone else.

In fact, usually writing emerges quite specifically in response to other writing. When you write, your reasons for writing are nearly always related to the people around you and what they have said or written themselves. A friend expects a letter; a supervisor at work has asked for a report; a professor assigns a paper; a job is advertised that requires a written application; a story or an editorial is printed in a local paper or national magazine that arouses your ire; an encouraging teacher or a moving story inspires you to write a journal entry or your own story. That is why this book is titled *Conversations.* It assumes that your writing emerges from other writing or from other speech, and that other writing is likely to follow in response to your own. You want to stay in touch, answer a friend's questions, ask your own questions, and maybe gossip or otherwise entertain along the way, so you return a friend's letter; you expect a response in a week or two. You've listened to a controversy or witnessed some expression of confusion in one of your classes, so you write a paper to straighten things out; you anticipate an argument, a counterresponse (or assent and praise) in turn. You want the person who takes your job to have an easier time than you did, so you rewrite the directions on how to do it; you figure the next person will make further revisions next year. Your cousin asks you how you like your school, so you write to encourage her to join you there next year; you end by asking her to let you know if she needs more information. Writing is engaging in conversation. To get in on it, you have to know what others have said about the matter at hand, and you must be able to anticipate possible responses.

This collection of readings comprises "public conversations"—conversations on public issues that concern American society (in general and within your local community) in the last decade of the twentieth century. Not every burning issue is represented here, of course; that would be impossible. But this book does include conversations—give-and-take discussions—on many matters that concern you and your community today. What do you want to get out of your years in college? What kind of experience should your college or university be providing? What changes ought to be made to improve American secondary schools? Should English be our official or semiofficial national language? What does it (or should it) mean to be a woman or a man these days? Should women be treated differently on the job? Do the news media control elections? Does television promote violence or make people passive? How good is a particular film or recording artist? Should pornography be banned or regulated? Should certain books be kept out of the curriculum? Is affirmative action legitimate? Should abortion remain legal? Should the ownership of handguns be restricted? What are the causes and cures of crime? Is capital punishment ever justified? Should drugs be legalized? Do animals have rights? Is mercy killing ever legitimate? How should we fight AIDS? And so forth. This book assumes that you'll want to get in on some of these conversations, that you'll want to contribute to resolving some of those questions either nationally or within your own community.

For while there is plenty of discussion of these matters in the national media, there is plenty of local discussion as well. What you read here about the reform of secondary education or the control of the curriculum probably frames in many ways discussions of particular school matters in your local community. What you read here about race on campus or animal rights probably is relevant to what is happening someplace on your own campus. What you read here about gender issues will be relevant to your campus (do many women major in science or engineering at your school?), your community (does your town have adequate child-care facilities?), your job (how are women treated where you work?), even your own family (are family chores apportioned in stereotypical ways?). Sometimes you will want to be involved in a debate over The Larger Issue—for instance, should pornography be banned? Other times you'll want to take up more local concerns or subissues: Should x-rated films be shown on your campus? Does pornography demean women—or men? Is a particular item really pornographic? How might pornography be defined? Democracy can be seen as a sometimes messy but always spirited exchange of ideas on how we should conduct ourselves as a society and as individual communities. The readings here are designed to introduce you to public conversations going on in our democracy, and to encourage you to contribute in some way to those conversations yourself. Even if these particular issues do not always engage you personally, they should provide you with models of how to engage in public discussions when an issue does concern you.

There are plenty of ways to make such contributions. The contents to follow will introduce you to many different genres, many different kinds of writing. Essays are most prominent because the essay is a common genre and because the essay (or article) has important analogs with other forms, like the letter, the sermon, the report, or the editorial. But you will see other ways of engaging in public discourse as well—through fiction, poetry, speeches, plays, interviews, cartoons, and advertisements, for instance. There are news stories and movie reviews, personal letters and letters to the editor and counterresponses, parodies and satires, explanations and analyses and outright arguments. As you think about what to contribute to discussions going on around you, you'll need to think about how to contribute, too—in what form, in what manner.

Indeed there are as many ways of addressing issues as reasons for doing so. Do you want to be formal, less formal, or downright intimate with your reader? Do you want to present yourself as something of an expert on the matter in question, or as someone on the same level as your readers? Do you want to speak dispassionately, or do you want to let your feelings show? Do you want to be explicit in stating your purpose, or less direct? Do you want to compose sentences that are careful and complex and qualified, or ones that are direct and emphatic? You'll see a broad range of tactics illustrated in the following pages, a broad range that will represent the possible ways of engaging in public discourse. You'll encounter mainstream, classic items—and dissenting views. You'll see conventional presentations and startingly inventive ones. You'll see how famous professional writers earned their fame, and you'll hear from anonymous but just-as-eloquent fellow citizens and fellow students. You'll hear from women as well as men, from majority as well as minority voices. The idea is to give you a better chance of finding your voice in a given circumstance by exposing you to a full range of possible voices in your reading. The idea is to empower you to engage in civic discourse—now, today—on the issues that concern you and your community.

How to Read This Book—And an Example

As the previous section explains, an answer to the question "Why write?" ultimately depends on several factors: on the writer's personal needs and motives, on the state of the world or issues within our world, on a genre or form of writing that a writer may be drawn or compelled toward, and on a reader or a community of readers that the writer wants to influence. Many times all those factors, in combination, are involved in the decision to write.

All those factors, in combination, are also involved in decisions on *how* to write. Effective writers consider what they want to accomplish (aim), on what subject or issue, in what genre, for which particular readers. A writer's decisions on those matters compose what rhetoricians call a writer's "rhetorical stance"—what *you* decide to say to *someone* on a given *issue* in a particular *genre.* But the matter might be put more simply: Your decisions about how to write at a given time are colored by the *occasion* for that writing and your attitude toward that occasion. A football coach will prepare his team for a game by considering the opponent's strengths and weaknesses (audience), by thinking about his own aims (to win, of course, but also perhaps "to establish our running game" or "to get some experience for our younger players"), by assessing his own team's strengths, and so forth. Writers devise their own game plans as well, based on aim, issue, genre, and audience.

But what does all of that have to do with reading—with reading in general and reading this book in particular? When you read this book, try to distinguish between two kinds of reading that in practice usually go on together whenever you engage yourself with a particular document.

In the first kind of reading, think of yourself as part of each writer's intended audience—as someone who the writer actually hoped would read and respond to his or her message. In other words, in this first kind of reading, read as you normally read the things that are directed to you every day: as you would read a newspaper or an article in your favorite magazine or a personal letter from a friend. Read as if the writer has written just for you, and react accordingly. In most cases this will be quite easy to do, for most of the items in *Conversations* (e.g., the articles on abortion by Sallie Tisdale and Mike Royko, the exchange on pornography between John Irving and Andrea Dworkin) are directed to the American public—people like you—and were written quite recently in magazines and newspapers that you read yourself. In some other cases you will feel more remote from an article because it was written some time ago (e.g., Clarence Darrow's address to the prisoners in Cook County Jail or Martin Luther King, Jr.'s "Letter from Birmingham

Jail") or because it is not on a topic that has interested you, but even then you can behave as a member of the writer's intended audience and react to the selection as if the piece were written directly to you.

In the second kind of reading—let's call it "critical reading" or "rhetorical reading"—you read a document not as the intended reader but as a student of it, as someone studying it to understand and appreciate its tactics. Since you are probably reading this book as part of a writing course, as a critical reader encountering the selections in *Conversations* you should remember your role as student and try to use the readings to advance your sophistication as a writer and an analyst of writing. Although you normally read as a writer's intended audience, when you read critically you try to get some distance on the experience; it's almost as if you are eavesdropping on what someone is saying to someone else, with the purpose of understanding better how it is said. When you read critically you not only react to the message, but you also appreciate *how* the writer is conveying that message to his or her intended audience, whether that intended audience includes you or not. For example, as a critical reader you try to consider how Sallie Tisdale's content, arrangement, and style advance her aims, or how Martin Luther King, Jr., and Clarence Darrow adapted their presentations to the particular situations in which they found themselves. Again, let me emphasize that normally in the act of reading you read critically as well as for content, and the two activities aren't really separable. But for the sake of your progress in writing, here in this introduction to *Conversations* it is important to emphasize critical reading.

Critical readers—readers committed to understanding how prose works—must attend to the same matters that writers attend to: shaping an idea to an audience in a particular form for a specific purpose. When you read each item in this book, therefore, read with those matters in mind. Read the headnotes carefully, for the headnotes are designed to orient you to the original situation in which the writers found themselves: You'll hear about the writer's audience in the headnote, you'll learn more about the writer (especially when the writer is well-known enough that prior reputation affects the reading experience), and you'll learn anything else necessary to orient you to the original occasion of each selection. That way, you'll be in a position to read critically. When you do, consider the issue of course; consider what the writer has to offer on a given subject. But also consider the writer's purpose, the limitations (or opportunities) that a given genre exerts, and the way the item is adapted by the writer to specific readers' knowledge, attitudes, and needs. Consider how those matters affect *what* is said (what rhetoricians call "invention"—the art of discovering what information and arguments will affect readers), in what *order* it is said (or arrangement), and *how* it is said (style and tone). Reading, like writing, is a social and rhetorical activity. It involves not simply passively decoding a message but actively understanding the designs the message has for the reader and how it is calculated to achieve its effects.

Let me offer an extended example of critical reading. The first item in this book is E. B. White's short essay, "Education." What is its purpose? (If you haven't read "Education" yet, take five minutes to do so now; that way, you can more easily follow the rest of this introduction.) White wrote the essay half a century ago, but you probably find it to be interesting still, in part at least because it concerns a perennial American question: What should our schools be like? Is education better carried out in large, fully equipped, but relatively impersonal settings, or in smaller but intensely personal, teacher-dominated schools? Which should count for more: the efficiencies of an educational system that is "progressive" (the word comes from paragraph two), or the personal traits of the individual classroom teacher? The essay is a personal one, in that it is the education of his son that White is "worried about"; yet it is public matter, too. After all, as the headnote indicates, White published it in *The New Yorker*, a magazine with a readership wide and influential, and far more national than its name implies.

What is White's position on the issue? At first it might seem that the author takes no sides, that he simply wants to describe objectively the two alternatives and to record his son's experiences in each circumstance. He gives equal time to each school, he spends the same amount of space on concrete details about each, and he seems in firm control of his personal biases ("I have always rather favored public schools"). Through his light and comic tone White implies that all will be well for his son—and our children—in either circumstance, that the two schools each are to be neither favored nor feared by us. "All one can say is that the situation is different" (paragraph four), not better, in the two places.

Or is it? Many readers—myself among them—contend that "Education" is less an objective, neutral appraisal than it is a calculated argument that subtly favors the country school. To such readers, White's objective pose is only that—a created pose, an attempt to create a genial, sympathetic, and trustworthy speaker. By caring so obviously for his son (final paragraph), by confessing his biases, and by treating both schools with distance and detachment and reliable detail, White creates what rhetoricians call "ethos"—that quality of a piece of writing that persuades through the character of the speaker or writer. By poking gentle humor at just about everything—his son "the scholar"; his wife the prim graduate of Miss Winsor's private schools; himself "the victim of a young ceramist"; and, of course, both schools—White makes himself seem enormously sympathetic and trustworthy: fair-minded and unflappable, balanced and detached.

But is this reliable speaker arguing or describing? Those who see the essay as an argument for the ways of the country school can point to the emotional aspects of the essay—to its pathos, in other words. The image of the one-room schoolhouse, for instance, is imprinted in positive terms on the American psyche, and White exploits that image for his argumentative purposes. The "scholar" walks miles through the snow to get his education; like the schoolhouse itself, he has the self-reliance and weather-resistance to care for himself and to fit into a class with children both younger and older; and he learns a practical curriculum—there is "no time at all for the esoteric"—"just as fast and as hard as he can." It is all Abraham Lincoln and "The Waltons," isn't it? And the teacher who presides over the country school appeals to the reader's emotions as only The Fairy Tale Mother can. This teacher-mother is not only "a guardian of their health, their clothes, their habits . . . and their snowball engagements," but "she has been doing this sort of Augean task for twenty years, and is both kind and wise. She cooks for the children on the stove that heats the room, and she can cool their passions or warm their soup with equal competence."

No such individual Fairy Tale Mother presides over the city school. Instead, that school is presided over by a staff of Educational Professionals—a bus driver, half a dozen anonymous teachers, a nurse, an athletic instructor, dietitians.

The school itself is institutional, regimented, professionalized. There the scholar is "worked on," "supervised," "pulled." Like the one-room schoolhouse, the regimented institution is ingrained in the American psyche. But in this case the emotional appeal is negative, for "The System" is something that Americans instinctively resist. True, the city school is no prison, and true, the scholar in this school learns "to read with a gratifying discernment." But the accomplishments remain rather abstract. Faced with such an education, such a school, no wonder the students literally become ill. At least that is the implication of the end of paragraph three, where the account of the city school is concluded with an account of the networks of professional physicians that discuss diseases that never seem to appear in the country schools.

For these reasons many readers see "Education" as an argument against the city school and an endorsement of the country one. They see the essay as a comparison with an aim like most comparison essays: to show a preference. The evaluative aim is carried out by reference to specific criteria, namely that schools are better if they are less structured and if they make students want to attend (because motivated students learn better); a structured, supervised curriculum and facilities are inferior to a personalized, unstructured environment that makes students love school. Days at the country school pass "just like lightning"; to attend the country school the boy is willing literally to walk through snowdrifts, while to get to the city school he must be escorted to the bus stop—or be "pulled" there. The country school is full of "surprises" and "individual instruction," while the city school is full of supervision; there are no surprises in the "progressive" school. In a real sense, therefore, White persuades not only by the force of his personality or through emotional appeals but also through hard evidence, what rhetoricians call "logos." "Education" amounts to an argument by example wherein the single case—the boy scholar—stands for many such cases. This case study persuades like other case studies: by being presented as representative. White creates through his unnamed son, who is described as typical in every way, a representative example that stands for the education of Everychild. The particular details provided in the essay become not mere "concrete description" but hard evidence, good reasons, summoned to support White's implicit thesis. The logic of the piece seems to go something like this: "Country schools are a bit superior to city ones. They make up for what they lack in facilities with a more personal, less authoritarian atmosphere that children respond to."

E. B. White, then, wins his reader's assent by means of ethos, pathos, and logos. But the country-school approach is also reinforced by the essay's arrangement. Notice, for example, that the essay begins and ends with favorable accounts of the country school. In other words, the emphatic first and final positions of the essay are reserved for the virtues of country schools, while the account of the city school is buried in the unemphatic middle of the essay. The article could easily have begun with the second paragraph (wouldn't sentence two of paragraph two have made a successful opener?), but such a strategy would have promoted the value of the city school. By choosing to add the loving vignette of the Fairy Tale Teacher in his opening paragraph, White disposes his readers to favor country schools from the very start. Notice too that the comparison of the two schools in the body of "Education" proceeds from city to country. Again, it didn't have to be so; White could have discussed the country school first, or he could have gone back and forth from city to country more often (adopting what some handbooks call an "alternating" method of comparison as opposed to the "divided" pattern that White actually did use). By choosing to deal first with the city school, all in one lump, and then to present the country school in another lump, White furthered his persuasive aim. After all, most "preference comparisons" move from the inferior item to the superior one. In other words, writers of comparisons usually move from "this one is good" to "but this other one is even better," rather than vice versa. So when White opts to deal first with the city schools, he subtly reinforces his persuasive end through very indirect means. White's arrangement serves his purpose in two ways, then: it permits him to end with the item he wishes to prefer; and it permits him to add an introductory paragraph that places his country school in that favorable spot as well.

Even the arrangement of details within White's individual paragraphs serves his goals. It appears that the central paragraphs (three, four, and five) are arranged chronologically, that details in those paragraphs are arranged according to the rhythm of the school day. But a closer examination shows that paragraph three closes on a note of sickness.

That detail could have come earlier in the paragraph, but White places the negative detail in the emphatic final position. Similarly, the two paragraphs on the country school are manipulated for rhetorical ends. Why does White divide the account of the country school into two paragraphs? (After all, he dealt with the city school in one paragraph.) By doing so he is able to give special emphasis to the first sentence of one of his paragraphs, "There is no supervised play," highlighting thereby a key difference between the two schools.

A critical reading of "Education" must also consider expression, those sentence and word choices that are sometimes equated with the style of a particular essay or author. Like most rhetoricians, I personally resist the idea that "style is the person"—that style is something inherent in a writer, that it amounts to a sort of genetic code or set of fingerprints that are idiosyncratic to each person, that it is possible to speak generically of Didion's style or Martin Luther King's style or E. B. White's style. It has always seemed to me more appropriate to think of style as characteristic of a particular *occasion* for writing, as something that is as appropriate to reader and subject and genre as it is to a particular author. Words and sentences are chosen in response to rhetorical and social circumstances, and those words and sentences change as the occasion changes. If it is possible to characterize E. B. White's style or Hemingway's style in general (and I'm not sure even of that), then it is so only with respect to certain kinds of writing that they did again and again and again. For when those writers found themselves writing outside *The New Yorker* (in White's case) or outside fiction (in Hemingway's), they did indeed adopt different stylistic choices. It is probably wiser to focus not on the apparent idiosyncrasies associated with a Didion or a King or a Hemingway or an E. B. White, but on the particular word and sentence choices at work in a particular rhetorical situation.

Take the case at hand. What stylistic choices are worthy of note in "Education"? How has White chosen particular sentence patterns and words in order to further the aims of his essay?

The sentences of White's essay are certainly appropriate for public discourse. There are roughly a thousand words and fifty sentences in "Education," so average sentence length comes to about twenty words. Many are shorter than twenty words, though (the shortest is five words), and only one forty-three-word sentence seems particularly long. The result is that this essay can probably be readily comprehended by most adults, without its sentences creating the impression of superficiality or childishness. (The sentences in White's book for children *Charlotte's Web,* by contrast, have an average length of about twelve words.)

Moreover, White's sentences are unpretentious. They move in conventional ways—from subjects and verbs to objects and modifiers. There are no sentence inversions (violations of the normal subject/verb/object order), few distracting interrupters (the parentheses and the "I suspect" in that one long sentence in paragraph two are exceptions), and few lengthy opening sentence modifiers that keep us too long from subjects and verbs. Not only that, the sentences are simple and unpretentious in another sense: White comparatively rarely uses subordinate (or modifying) clauses—clauses containing a subject and verb and beginning with "who" or "although" or "that" or "because" or the like. I count only two such modifying (or dependent) clauses in the first and third paragraphs, for instance, and just five in the second; if you don't think that is a low number, compare it to a six-hundred-word sample of your own prose. When White does add length to a sentence, he does it not by adding complex clauses that modify other clauses, but by adding independent clauses (ones that begin with "and" or "but") and by adding phrases and modifiers in parallel series. Some examples? The children's teacher is a guardian "of their health, their clothes, their habits, their mothers, and their snowball engagements"; the boy "learned fast, kept well, and we were satisfied"; the bus "would sweep to a halt, open its mouth, suck the boy in, and spring away." And so forth. The "ands" make White's essay informal and conversational, never remote or scholarly or full of disclaimers and qualifiers.

White uses relatively simple sentence patterns in "Education," then, but his prose is still anything but simple. Some of his sentences are beautifully parallel: "she can cool their passions or warm their soup"; "she conceives their costumes, cleans up their noses, and shares their confidences"; "in a cinder court he played games supervised by an athletic instructor, and in a cafeteria he ate lunch worked out by a dietitian"; "when the snow is deep or the motor is dead"; "rose hips in fall, snowballs in winter." These precise, mirror-image parallel structures are known as isocolons to rhetoricians. White delights in them and in the artful informality they create. He uses parallel structures and relentless coordination—"and" after "and" after "and"—to make his prose accessible to a large audience of appreciative readers. And he uses those lists of specific items in parallel series to give his writing its remarkably concrete, remarkably vivid quality.

That brings us to White's word choices. They too contributed to White's purposes. Remember the sense of detachment and generosity in White's narrative voice, the ethos of involvement and detachment apparent in the speaker? In large measure that is the result of White's word choices. For instance, White has the ability to attach mock-heroic terminology to his descriptions so that he comes across as balanced and wise, as someone who doesn't take himself or his world too seriously. The boy is a "scholar" who "sallied forth" on a "journey" to school or to "make Indian weapons of a semi-deadly nature." The gentle hyperbole fits in well with the classical allusion inherent in the word "Augean" (one of Hercules' labors was to clean the Augean stables): there is a sophistication and worldly wisdom in the speaker's voice that qualifies him to speak on this subject. And remember the discussion of whether White's aim was purely descriptive or more argumentative in character? White's metaphors underscore his argumentative aim: the city school bus "was as punctual as death," a sort of macabre monster that "would sweep to a halt, open its mouth, suck the boy in, and spring away with an angry growl"; or it is "like a train picking up a bag of mail." At the country school, by contrast, the day passes "just like lightning." If the metaphors do not provide enough evidence of White's persuasive aim, consider the connotations of words—their emotional charges, that is—that are associated with the city school: "regimented," "supervised," "worked on," "uniforms," "fevers." And then compare these with the connotation of some words White associates with the country school: "surprises," a "bungalow," "weather-resistant," "individual instruction," "guardian," and so forth. The diction and sentence choices made by White indeed do reinforce his argumentative purpose.

This analysis by no means exhausts the full measure of rhetorical sophistication that E. B. White brings to the composition of "Education." You may have noticed other tactics at work, or you might disagree with some of the generalizations presented here. But the purpose of this discussion is not to detail the rhetoric of White's "Education." It is merely to illustrate a method of critical reading that you might employ as you read the selections in this book and the public rhetoric that you encounter in your life each day. The point has been to encourage you to read not just for *what* is said—though this is crucial—but for *how* it is said as well. For reading is as "rhetorical" an activity as writing. It depends on an appreciation of how writer, subject, and reader are all "negotiated" through a particular document.

If you read for "how" as well as "what," the distinction between the two may begin to shorten for you. Appreciation of the rhetoric of public discourse can make you more skeptical of the arguments presented to you and to other citizens. It can make you a reader less likely to be won over on slender grounds, more likely to remain the doubter than the easy victim or trusting soul who accepts all arguments at face value. Whether you decide to take part in any of the particular "conversations" captured in this book or not, therefore, your thinking can be stimulated by critical reading.

Not only that, you'll find yourself growing as a writer; if you read critically, you'll begin to adopt and adapt for your own purposes the best rhetorical maneuvers on display in this book and elsewhere. What is a particular writer's real aim? What evidence is used to win the assent of readers? How does a particular writer establish credibility? What kind of emotional and logical appeals are at work in a given circumstance? How does the arrangement of a presentation influence its reception? How can sentence style and word choices sustain a writer's aim? By asking and answering questions like these, you can gain confidence as reader and writer. By becoming better able to understand and appreciate the conversations going on around you, you'll learn to make more powerful and sophisticated contributions to the discussions that most engage you personally. Critical reading of the selections in this book can make you a better writer, a better citizen.

I.

EDUCATION

Introduction

Americans have always been passionate about issues related to education. Why? For one thing, education issues affect every American in a personal way. True, there is a strong anti-intellectual strain in American life; but it is also true that Americans pursue with a passion the ideal of "education for all," both as a means of self-improvement and as the source of the enlightened citizenry required by democratic institutions. For another thing, education issues are decided locally and immediately. The decentralized nature of our educational "system" (American education is hardly as monolithic as the term "system" implies) encourages continuing and passionate public discussion among citizens interested in shaping the policies and practices of local schools. (About 93% of the $425 billion spent on American primary and secondary education in 1991 came from state and local governments. Incidentally, Americans spend more per capita on education than all but three other Western nations.)

Portions of three current discussions related to education are included in this part of *Conversations*. (In addition, education issues are taken up more tangentially elsewhere in the book in the parts on language, gender, media, and civil liberties.) The first—"What to Do About the Schools?"—concerns proposals for improving public education, particularly secondary education. In the past decade, particularly in response to the economic crises of the early 1980s and early 1990s, a number of committees and commissions launched well-publicized reform efforts aimed at everything from teacher education and school governance to classroom climate and the curriculum—at everything from competency testing and conduct codes to the size of schools and the wisdom of "tracking." Those calls for reform can be seen in the selections included here. Should schools be large, centralized, efficient, and comprehensive? Or should they be smaller and more personal—have all the advantages of small size? Is discipline a problem, and (if so) how can it be improved? Or does an overemphasis on discipline make schools confining and constricting—places that value order and conformity over independence and freedom of inquiry? What about the curriculum—should it emphasize mastery of bodies of knowledge, "what every educated person needs to know"? Or instead should it emphasize learning skills—

problem-solving ability, flexibility, independent thinking, and resourcefulness? Should the way schools are funded be reconsidered, to even out differences between the "haves" and the "have nots"? Or would that undermine a cornerstone of our educational tradition, local control? Should schools be "privatized"? Could citizens through some sort of voucher system be given more choice over which school to attend? Or would that tend to widen the gap in educational opportunities now available to rich and poor? And finally, what about the teachers? Should they be given better pay and more responsibility for what goes on in the classroom? Or should we continue to honor top-down administrative mechanisms for ensuring competency and consistency and currency?

The second set of readings address the question, "What Is College For?" No doubt on your own campus you have listened in on discussions of this topic in one form or another, and no doubt you have given your own educational goals considerable thought. In broad terms, the question can be posed this way: Is college an occasion for personal growth and general intellectual development? Or is it a means to economic advancement? If college should foster both general education and professional specialization, then in what proportions should it do so? And through what means? Is college designed for the intellectual elite who are sophisticated enough to pursue truly advanced learning, or is it something that ought to be within the reach of most high school graduates? Does college offer a critical perspective on our institutions and habits? Or is it merely a way of socializing students into willing servants of the status quo?

That last question introduces the final group of readings, on the question of so-called "political correctness." Political correctness is usually used to denote efforts of various kinds to create a more hospitable atmosphere on campus for women and minorities—people whose presence on campus has been increasingly visible in the past few decades. Such efforts may take the form of conduct codes, curricular reforms (for example, insistence that course syllabi reflect the experiences of women and minorities, or perhaps a requirement that students take some kind of course that investigates issues related to ethnic diversity or gender or multiculturalism), or other efforts to encourage toleration and awareness on campus. But in its effort to encourage "doing the right thing" on campus and in society, especially on issues of race and gender, are universities going too far?

Are the first-amendment right to free speech and the university's avowed openness to diverse opinions and free exchange being dampened by political proselytizing on behalf of women and minorities? Is that what is going on—political proselytizing, rather than teaching? Are curricular changes long overdue, or are they politically motivated assaults on mainstream culture? Is "political correctness" a bad thing, merely a liberal fashion, or is it a code word used by conservatives to undermine the efforts of those who simply want to mitigate the oppression and repression experienced by racial minorities, women, and homosexuals?

Some of these ideas are developed further in part V of *Conversations,* which considers issues of civil liberties and civil rights. But here the emphasis is on education in general and college education in particular. The readings you encounter should give you a better understanding of the issues that you and your classmates are grappling with right now. As you read, remember that the perennial nature of debates about education can be frustrating, especially to educational leaders. But the very relentlessness of the debates probably brings out the best feature of a democratic society: the freedom of citizens to shape policy through open and public exchange.

WHAT TO DO ABOUT THE SCHOOLS?

E. B. White

Education

E. B. White (1899–1985), who contributed regularly to The New Yorker *and whose work has been collected into several books, was perhaps America's most popular essayist. You may also know him as the author of the children's classic* Charlotte's Web *(1952). First published in 1939 in* Harper's *and in White's* One Man's Meat, *the following comparison of two educational philosophies remains relevant half a century later.*

I have an increasing admiration for the teacher in the country school where we have a third-grade scholar in attendance. She not only undertakes to instruct her charges in all the subjects of the first three grades, but she manages to function quietly and effectively as a guardian of their health, their clothes, their habits, their mothers, and their snowball engagements. She has been doing this sort of Augean task for twenty years, and is both kind and wise. She cooks for the children on the stove that heats the room, and she can cool their passions or warm their soup with equal competence. She conceives their costumes, cleans up their messes, and shares their confidences. My boy already regards his teacher as his great friend, and I think tells her a great deal more than he tells us. 1

The shift from city school to country school was something we worried about quietly all last summer. I have always rather favored public school over private school, if only because in public school you meet a greater variety of children. This bias of mine, I suspect, is partly an attempt to justify my own past (I never knew anything but public schools) and partly an involuntary defense against getting kicked in the shins by a young ceramist on his way to the kiln. My wife was unacquainted with public schools, never 2 having been exposed (in her early life) to anything more public than the washroom of Miss Winsor's. Regardless of our backgrounds, we both knew that the change in schools was something that concerned not us but the scholar himself. We hoped it would work out all right. In New York our son went to a medium-priced private institution with semi-progressive ideas of education, and modern plumbing. He learned fast, kept well, and we were satisfied. It was an electric, colorful, regimented existence with moments of pleasurable pause and giddy incident. The day the Christmas angel fainted and had to be carried out by one of the Wise Men was educational in the highest sense of the term. Our scholar gave imitations of it around the house for weeks afterward, and I doubt if it ever goes completely out of his mind.

3 His days were rich in formal experience. Wearing overalls and an old sweater (the accepted uniform of the private seminary), he sallied forth at morn accompanied by a nurse or a parent and walked (or was pulled) two blocks to a corner where the school bus made a flag stop. This flashy vehicle was as punctual as death: seeing us waiting at the cold curb, it would sweep to a halt, open its mouth, suck the boy in, and spring away with an angry growl. It was a good deal like a train picking up a bag of mail. At school the scholar was worked on for six or seven hours by half a dozen teachers and a nurse, and was revived on orange juice in mid-morning. In a cinder court he played games supervised by an athletic instructor, and in a cafeteria he ate lunch worked out by a dietitian. He soon learned to read with gratifying facility and discernment and to make Indian weapons of a semi-deadly nature. Whenever one of his classmates fell low of a fever the news was put on the wires and there were breathless phone calls to physicians, discussing periods of incubation and allied magic.

4 In the country all one can say is that the situation is different, and somehow more casual. Dressed in corduroys, sweatshirt, and short rubber boots, and carrying a tin dinner pail, our scholar departs at the crack of dawn for the village school, two and a half miles down the road, next to the cemetery. When the road is open and the car will start, he makes the journey by motor, courtesy of his old man. When the snow is deep or the motor is dead or both, he makes it on the hoof. In the afternoons he walks or hitches all or part of the way home in fair weather, gets transported

in foul. The schoolhouse is a two-room frame building, bungalow type, shingles stained a burnt brown with weather-resistant stain. It has a chemical toilet in the basement and two teachers above the stairs. One takes the first three grades, the other the fourth, fifth, and sixth. They have little or no time for individual instruction, and no time at all for the esoteric. They teach what they know themselves, just as fast and as hard as they can manage. The pupils sit still at their desks in class, and do their milling around outdoors during recess.

There is no supervised play. They play cops and robbers 5
(only they call it "Jail") and throw things at one another—snowballs in winter, rose hips in fall. It seems to satisfy them. They also construct darts, pinwheels, and "pick-up-sticks" (jackstraws), and the school itself does a brisk trade in penny candy, which is for sale right in the classroom and which contains "surprises." The most highly prized surprise is a fake cigarette, made of cardboard, fiendishly lifelike.

The memory of how apprehensive we were at the begin- 6
ning is still strong. The boy was nervous about the change too. The tension, on that first fair morning in September when we drove him to school, almost blew the windows out of the sedan. And when later we picked him up on the road, wandering along with his little blue lunch-pail, and got his laconic report "All right" in answer to our inquiry about how the day had gone, our relief was vast. Now, after almost a year of it, the only difference we can discover in the two school experiences is that in the country he sleeps better at night—and *that* probably is more the air than the education. When grilled on the subject of school-in-country vs. school-in-city, he replied that the chief difference is that the day seems to go so much quicker in the country. "Just like lightning," he reported.

John Chubb and Terry Moe

The Private vs. Public Debate

Chubb, a fellow at the Brookings Institute (an officially neutral but politically liberal Washington, DC, research institute devoted to the study of public-policy issues), and Mr. Moe, a professor at Stanford University with a special interest in education, contributed this essay to The Wall Street Journal *in July 1991. They are the authors of several books, including* Politics, Markets, and America's Schools, *published by the Brookings Institute in 1990. That book recommends fundamental institutional changes in America's schools—in particular, a greater reliance on choice and free-market mechanisms for the schools.*

1 The Bush administration wants Congress to enact legislation to encourage state and local authorities to provide parents with choice among and between public and private schools. Opponents of the administration's proposal generally accept the expansion of public school choice but vehemently oppose public support for private school options. Most of the reasons for this opposition are familiar—private schools are said to succeed, for example, through selective admissions and expulsions. But in recent days, opponents have come up with a fresh justification: Private schools are no better than public schools—so why add private schools to the public educational menu?

2 This is an important argument—indeed, far more important than its proponents seem to realize—for if there are no differences between public and private schools, there is little reason to support educational choice of any kind, private or public. Private schools, subject to the daily discipline of parental choice, are the best test of the argument that choice enhances school performance. If private schools fail this test, why subject public schools to the same ineffective discipline?

3 The test that private schools (religious and nonreligious) are now said to have failed is the mathematics exam of the recent National Assessment of Educational Progress. Testifying before the House Education and Labor Committee, Al Shanker, president of the American Federation of Teachers, charged that students in private schools performed scarcely

better than students in public schools: both need great improvement. Mr. Shanker is right about the widespread need for improvement but wrong about the differences between public and private performance—on the NAEP and in general.

Dropout Rates

Public and private math scores on the NAEP are close only in the 12th grade, after public schools have lost a large portion of their least successful students as dropouts and gained a large number of students from private elementary and middle schools (one-third of whose students go to public high schools). Among fourth- and eighth-graders, scores are not close. Private schools place 10 to 15 percentage points more students at grade-appropriate levels than public schools do. 4

Some may say that these differences are not large, but the NAEP is but one measure of how schools perform. Consider dropout rates. According to a recent national survey, the sophomore-to-senior-year dropout rate is 24% in public schools vs. 12% in private schools. Or take the results of college admissions testing. A little over a third of all public school seniors take the SAT: In 1990 they had an average score of 896. About two-thirds of all private school seniors take the SAT; yet this more inclusive group scored an average 932—12 percentiles higher than the score for public school students. 5

Experiences after high school are also revealing. Public high schools send fewer than 30% of their graduates directly on to four-year colleges. Six years later, only about 13% of public school graduates have earned bachelor's degrees; among black and Hispanic graduates, only about 9%. Private schools send roughly half of their graduates directly to four-year colleges; 31% of all of their graduates and more than a quarter of their black and Hispanic graduates hold bachelor's degrees six years later. 6

To be sure, private schools have certain advantages over public schools. Nearly twice as many private school students as public school students come from families that are college educated, and less than half as many private school students come from families that are financially poor. Private schools also get to select their students 7 (though most are not very selective) and can expel students more easily than public schools can (though public schools actually lose or get rid of more problem students). In light of all this, it is somewhat surprising to note that private schools are more likely than public schools to be racially mixed.

8 Some will argue that school composition—students and parents—rather than school quality can account for any and all differences between the outcomes of public and private schooling. However, there are lots of differences between public and private schools not easily explained by differences between students. For example, teachers in private schools seem to work with more dedication: A recent survey found that 40% of private school teachers go a whole semester without missing a day of school; only 20% of the teachers in public schools have the same exemplary record. Teachers in private schools also report spending about 15% more time outside of school preparing lessons, helping students, meeting with parents, and otherwise trying to do a good job.

9 Private schools, which generally have smaller budgets than public schools, spend relatively more of their financial resources directly on instruction. Public schools spend relatively more of theirs on administration. Private schools are far more successful at encouraging students to take academic track coursework: An average student is twice as likely to be placed in a "college prep" program in a private school as in a public school. Private schools also do a much better job of promoting parent involvement. Indeed, private schools get more participation out of parents of lower socioeconomic status than public schools get out of parents of higher socioeconomic status—even though participation rapidly increases with socioeconomic status.

10 Private schools, in short, do many of the things that school reformers believe are important for school success: They emphasize academic instruction and achievement, get teachers and students to work hard, and get parents involved. The question that should be on the minds of policy makers is not *whether* private schools do these things but *why* they do them—or, more precisely, why they are more likely than public schools to do them.

11 In a recent study of 500 high schools, we concluded that the differences between public and private schools have a lot to do with the differences between politics and markets—

especially with the absence or presence of choice. Private educators, trying to succeed in a market where parents can take or leave their schools, are compelled to organize their schools in ways that are most sensitive to and most effective in meeting parent and student demands.

Generally, this means concentrating resources at the 12
school level, where they can make the most difference. It means vesting greater authority in teachers, who are in the best position to understand the diverse needs of families and students, and who can be expected to work with greater dedication if trusted to do so. It also means focusing sharply on the tangible results, like academic achievement, and involving parents—who, after all, are doing the choosing—deeply in the school.

Market Pressures

Public educators have their schools organized for them by 13
federal, state, and local authorities pressured by countless groups with legitimate but conflicting interest in school policy. Generally, these conflicts are resolved through bureaucratic solutions that, despite the best intentions of everyone concerned, tend to rob schools of critical authority, divert schools from their core academic mission, discourage bold leadership from principals, make a mockery of teacher professionalism, drive a wedge between schools and parents (who become just another political interest), and provide accountability for following rules—not for producing results.

Public schools could—and would—do things differently if 14
they were subject to different pressures. The lesson of public-private comparisons is not that private schools are better than public schools. It is that market pressures encourage the development of better schools than political pressures do.

Choice, then, is essential. However, the issue that Con- 15
gress and the administration should be worrying about is not whether choice should include private schools (though with appropriate ground rules, private school participation would enhance market pressures). The key issue is whether choice plans provide all schools—be they public or private—the political autonomy and economic interest to focus, reorganize, compete and improve.

Jonathan Kozol
A Tale of Two Schools: How Poor Children Are Lost to the World

The following article was published in The Los Angeles Times *in October 1991; it amounts to an excerpt from Mr. Kozol's polemical book* Savage Inequalities: Children in America's Schools, *published in the same year. In 1964 Mr. Kozol, a teacher at the time at an inner-city school in Boston, had described in* Death at an Early Age *the terrible conditions that he found in schools in poor neighborhoods.* Savage Inequalities *emerged from his visits twenty-five years later to similar schools in places like Camden, NJ; Bronx, NY; East St. Louis, IL; and Washington, DC—and from his conviction that the gap between schools for the rich and those for the poor in America has only been widening, not narrowing.*

1 New Trier's physical setting might well make the students of Du Sable High School envious. The Chicago suburb school is, says a student, "a maple land of beauty and civility." While Du Sable is sited on one crowded Chicago city block, New Trier students have the use of 27 acres. While Du Sable's science students have to settle for makeshift equipment, New Trier's students have superior labs and up-to-date technology. One wing of the school, a physical-education center that includes three separate gyms, also contains a fencing room, a wrestling room and studios for dance instruction. In all, the school has seven gyms as well as an Olympic pool.

2 "This is a school with a lot of choices," says one student at New Trier; and this hardly seems an overstatement if one studies the curriculum. Courses in music, art and drama are so varied and abundant that students can virtually major in these subjects in addition to their academic programs. The modern and classical language department offers Latin and six other foreign languages. In a senior literature class, students are reading Nietzsche, Darwin, Plato, Freud and Goethe.

3 Average class size is 24 children; classes for slower learners hold 15.

4 The wealth of New Trier's geographical district provides

$340,000 worth of taxable property for each child; Chicago's property wealth affords only one-fifth this much. Nonetheless, *Town and Country,* which profiled the school, gives New Trier's parents credit for a "willingness to pay enough . . . in taxes" to make this one of the state's best-funded schools. New Trier, according to the magazine, is "a striking example of what is possible when citizens want to achieve the best for their children." Families move here "seeking the best," and their children "make good use" of what they're given. Both statements may be true, but *Town and Country* flatters the privileged for having privilege but terms it aspiration.

"Competition is the lifeblood of New Trier," *Town and* 5
Country writes. But there is one kind of competition that these children will not need to face. They will not compete against the children who attended Du Sable.

Conditions at Du Sable High School, which I visited in 6
1990, seem in certain ways to be improved. Improvement, however, is a relative term. Du Sable is better than it was three or four years ago. It is still a school that would be shunned—or, probably, shut down—if it were serving a white middle-class community. The building, a three-story Tudor structure, is in fairly good repair and, in this respect, contrasts with its immediate surroundings, which are almost indescribably despairing. The school, whose student population is 100% black, has no campus and no schoolyard, but there is at least a full-sized playing field and track. Overcrowding is not a problem. Much to the reverse, it is uncomfortably empty. Built in 1935 and holding some 4,500 students in past years, its student population is now fewer than 1,600. Of these students, according to data provided by the school, 646 are "chronic truants."

The graduation rate is 25%. Of those who get to senior 7
year, only 17% are in a college-preparation program. Twenty percent are in the general curriculum, a stunning 63% in vocational classes.

A vivid sense of loss is felt by standing in the cafeteria in 8
early spring, when students file in to choose their courses for the following year. "These are the ninth graders," says a supervising teacher; but, of the official freshman class of some 600 children, only 350 fill the room. An hour later the 11th graders come to choose their classes: I count at most 170 students.

The faculty includes some excellent teachers, but there 9

are others, says the principal, who don't belong in education. "I can't do anything with them but I'm not allowed to fire them," he says.

10 In a 12th-grade English class, the students are learning to pronounce a list of words. The words are not derived from any context; they are simply written on a list. A tall boy struggles to read "fastidious," "gregarious," "auspicious," "fatuous." When he struggles to pronounce "egregious," I ask him if he knows its meaning. It turns out that he has no idea. The teacher never asks the children to write the words or use them in a sentence. The lesson baffles me. It may be that these are words that will appear on a required test that states impose now in the name of "raising standards," but it all seems dreamlike and surreal.

11 After lunch, I talk with a group of students who are hoping to go on to college but do not seem sure of what they'll need to do to make this possible. Only one out of five seniors in the group has filed an application, and it is already April. Pamela, the one who did apply, however, tells me she neglected to submit her grades and college-entrance test results and therefore has to start again. The courses she is taking seem to rule out application to a four-year college. She tells me she is taking Spanish, literature, physical education, Afro-American history and a class she terms "job strategy." When I ask her what this is, she says, "It teaches how to dress and be on time and figure your deductions." She's a bright, articulate student, and it seems quite sad that she has not had any of the richness of curriculum that would have been given to her at a high school like New Trier.

12 The children in the group seem not just lacking in important, useful information that would help them to achieve their dreams, but, in a far more drastic sense, cut off and disconnected from the outside world. In talking of some recent news events, they speak of Moscow and Berlin, but all but Pamela are unaware that Moscow is the capital of the Soviet Union or that Berlin is in Germany. Several believe that Jesse Jackson is the mayor of New York City. Listening to their guesses and observing their confusion, I am thinking of the students at New Trier High. These children live in truly separate worlds. What do they have in common? Yet the kids before me seem so innocent and spiritually clean and also—most of all—so vulnerable. It's as if they have been stripped of all the armament—the reference points, the

facts, the reasoning, the elemental weapons—that suburban children take for granted.

"It took an extraordinary combination of greed, racism, political cowardice and public apathy," writes James D. Squires, the former editor of the Chicago Tribune, "to let the public schools in Chicago get so bad." He speaks of the schools as a costly result of "the political orphaning of the urban poor . . . daytime warehouses for inferior students . . . a bottomless pit." 13

The results of these conditions are observed in thousands of low-income children in Chicago, who are virtually disjoined from the worldview, even from the basic reference points, of the American experience. A 16-year-old girl who has dropped out discusses her economic prospects with a TV interviewer. 14

"How much money would you like to make in a year?" asks the reporter. 15

"About $2,000," she replies. 16

The reporter looks bewildered by this answer. This teenage girl, he says, "has no clue that $2,000 a year isn't enough to survive anywhere in America, not even in her world." 17

John Gatto

I May Be a Teacher, but I'm Not an Educator

Mr. Gatto had just been named Teacher of the Year in the state of New York (by the State Education Department) when he contributed the following essay to The Wall Street Journal *in July 1991.*

I've taught public school for 26 years but I just can't do it anymore. For years I asked the local school board and superintendent to let me teach a curriculum that doesn't hurt kids, but they had other fish to fry. So I'm going to quit, I think. 1

I've come slowly to understand what it is I really teach: a 2 curriculum of confusion, class position, arbitrary justice, vulgarity, rudeness, disrespect for privacy, indifference to quality, and utter dependency. I teach how to fit into a world I don't want to live in.

3 I just can't do it anymore. I can't train children to wait to be told what to do; I can't train people to drop what they are doing when a bell sounds; I can't persuade children to feel some justice in their class placement when there isn't any, and I can't persuade children to believe teachers have valuable secrets they can acquire by becoming our disciples. That isn't true.

4 Government schooling is the most radical adventure in history. It kills the family by monopolizing the best times of childhood and by teaching disrespect for home and parents.

5 An exaggeration? Hardly. Parents aren't meant to participate in our form of schooling, rhetoric to the contrary. My orders as schoolteacher are to make children fit an animal training system, not to help each find his or her personal path.

6 The whole blueprint of school procedure is Egyptian, not Greek or Roman. It grows from the faith that human value is a scarce thing, represented symbolically by the narrow peak of a pyramid.

7 That idea passed into American history through the Puritans. It found its "scientific" presentation in the bell curve, along which talent supposedly apportions itself by some Iron Law of biology.

8 It's a religious idea and school is its church. New York City hires me to be a priest. I offer rituals to keep heresy at bay. I provide documentation to justify the heavenly pyramid.

9 Socrates foresaw that if teaching became a formal profession something like this would happen. Professional interest is best served by making what is easy to do seem hard; by subordinating laity to priesthood. School has become too vital a jobs project, contract-giver and protector of the social order, to allow itself to be "re-formed." It has political allies to guard its marches.

10 That's why reforms come and go—without changing much. Even reformers can't imagine school much different.

11 David learns to read at age four; Rachel, at age nine. In normal development, when both are 13, you can't tell which one learned first—the five-year spread means nothing at all. But in school I will label Rachel "learning disabled" and slow David down a bit, too.

For a paycheck, I adjust David to depend on me to tell him when to go and stop. He won't outgrow that dependency. I identify Rachel as discount merchandise, "special education." After a few months she'll be locked into her place forever. 12

In 26 years of teaching rich kids and poor I almost never met a "learning disabled" child; hardly ever met a "gifted and talented" one, either. Like all school categories, these are sacred myths, created by the human imagination. They derive from questionable values we never examine because they preserve the temple of schooling. 13

That's the secret behind short-answer tests, bells, uniform time blocks, age grading, standardization, and all the rest of the school religion punishing our nation. 14

There isn't a right way to become educated; there are as many ways as fingerprints. We don't need state-certified teachers to make education happen—that probably guarantees it *won't*. 15

How much more evidence is necessary? Good schools don't need more money or a longer year; they need real free-market choices, variety that speaks to every need and runs risks. We don't need a national curriculum, or national testing either. Both initiatives arise from ignorance of how people learn, or deliberate indifference to it. 16

I can't teach this way any longer. If you hear of a job where I don't have to hurt kids to make a living, let me know. Come fall I'll be looking for work, I think. 17

Theodore Sizer

Horace's Compromise

Born in 1932, Theodore Sizer now chairs the education department at Brown University. His book Horace's Compromise: The Dilemma of the American High School, *published in 1984, offered a program of reform for America's high schools; the book described the frustrations (and their sources) of a fictional but representative English teacher, Horace Smith, who was forced to compromise his best educational instincts in the face of a fragmented and fragmenting high school system. In 1992 Mr. Sizer wrote* Horace's School, *which proposes a series of solutions to Horace's problems and those of his fictional Franklin High School. Sizer has pioneered the Coalition of Essential Schools, which now has more than four-hundred-member schools. The following is the first chapter from* Horace's School.

1 Meet Horace Smith, fifty-nine, a veteran English teacher at Franklin High. Among parents and graduates, he is widely considered a star faculty member of this inner suburban high school of 1350 pupils. Certainly he is respected by his colleagues; they find him the professional's professional, even to a fault. While many of the faculty who are his age are already considering retirement, thanks to the state's generous annuity plan, Horace is not. He believes—perversely, he often thinks—that Franklin High is not nearly what it could be. He wants to stay on and make it better.

2 The good light in which the community sees the school is not deserved, he feels. Franklin is a caring place, but the kids worry Horace. Many are lively, well intentioned, and adept at cranking out acceptable test scores, but they are without the habits of serious thought, respectful skepticism, and curiosity about much of what lies beyond their immediate lives. They lack assurance, skill, and interest in confronting the stuff of Franklin's curriculum and committing their God-given minds to strenuous use.

3 Sure, they rack up lists of "extracurriculars" to dazzle university admissions officers, but even when they show a dash of substance, too many of them lack style, that gossamer quality which separates the interesting person from the conventional one. They get top grades on the English Advanced Placement exams, but never read a serious piece of fiction outside or beyond school. They score high on the social studies tests, but later will vote for political candidates on impulse, if they vote at all.

4 The kids play a game with school, making deals with us, striking bargains. What will be on the test, Mr. Smith? Will this count in the grade, Mr. Smith? How many pages must this be, Mr. Smith? When do we have to read this by, Mr. Smith? If we do this, will you ease up on that? They all ought to be ambassadors, Horace thinks, wheeler-dealers striking bargains and making treaties. However, the treaties will be ones to lessen work, lessen the pain of thinking anew, lessen anything that may get into the way of having a happy time after school. Treaties to protect the Good Life. Horace

snorts at himself: What a cynic I am. Aren't we adults that way too, excessively so? What are all of us coming to?

Many of Horace's colleagues find his criticism harsh, but 5
he persists. We do not know the half of what these kids can do, he contends. But, his friends retort, can one school turn them around? The whole society is soft. The kids' culture is defined by MTV and cravings created by national merchandise. Even their parents do not want the school to change much. Get Susie into a good college, they say. And if we do, they love us. If we do not, they blame us. But *style*? Come on, Horace.

Horace understands the familiar lament. And he knows 6
that Franklin hasn't many of the searing problems swamping the nearby city schools. For kids in those schools, there's not even a question of developing style; sheer survival is their task. He also remembers the exceptional kids he taught who did have fresh, inquiring, informed minds, and thoughtful hearts too. Why can't we have more kids like those, he wonders. Schools can help shape them, or at the least encourage those happy tendencies. Why must schooling, and its typical products, be so mindless? It need not be so. And though the culture out there may be inattentive, the school—even Franklin High School—can do something about it.

That, Horace knows, is a presumption. Who are teachers 7
to set standards? Who says that they have a corner on wisdom? Horace worries about this. The schools should reflect what the culture wants, and if the culture is careless, then the school can be careless.

But, then, what is the role of the teacher? Merely to be the 8
agent of the culture? No, Horace says, we must try to be better than that. And, contrary to conventional wisdom, most parents are our allies. What they want, at heart, is more than a ticket for their offspring to a prestigious college. They want that, yes, but they want more; and it is by an alliance of aware and demanding teachers, parents, and adolescents that a better school can be molded, a thoughtful place to teach thoughtful young citizens.

A thoughtful place. Horace hesitates on this, because he 9
knows from decades of experience that Franklin is, if nothing else, unexamined. Like most high schools, it just rolls on, fettered by routines of long standing. The result is a cacophony of jumbled practices, orchestrated only by a

complex computer-driven schedule whose instrument is a bell system and whose ushers are assistant principals.

10 The faculty itself, he muses, is hardly thoughtful about its own situation. The status quo is never challenged. We have curriculum committees that talk only about revising the accepted subjects, never pondering what the curriculum could be. We have committees on schedule changes that never ask the basic questions about the uses of time. We "restructure" while assuming that all the existing building materials and architectural commitments—physical and intellectual—will remain as they are.

11 Horace knows that the status quo *is* the problem. It forces him to compromise in ways that cripple his teaching, his ability to create thoughtful students. Compromises are always necessary in the real world, Horace admits; and the issue, then, is which compromises will serve the students best. Only by examining the existing compromises, however painful that may be, and moving beyond them to better compromises, can one form a more thoughtful school. And only in thoughtful schools can thoughtful students be hatched.

12 Horace's complaints are many and fundamental. It would be easier if the system were basically sound, but the lamentable truth is that it is not, and that the complex routines of schools are all related. Question one, and you question all.

13 Take Horace's student load. Officially it should be 120, five classes of twenty-four students each, the "contract ratio" for English teachers. This year it is 132. Horace's courses are popular, and he has difficulty saying no to eager kids, particularly those who have studied with him before. Horace knows that he should insist on a writing assignment from every one of those youngsters every day, or at least every other day, and that he should promptly read, comment on, and return these papers. But with 120? Impossible. Spending just five out-of-class minutes per week looking at the work of each student and, at least once a month, talking privately with the youngster would total ten hours—ten hours of enervating work, two hours every evening, Monday through Friday, week after week. And this in addition to all the rest he has to do outside those contact hours in class with the kids, not to mention his evening work at the family's liquor store to help meet the household bills. So, like most English teachers, he does not do the

careful reading and criticizing he knows is so valuable for students.

Accordingly, Horace recognizes that he does not know 14
many of his kids well enough to understand really how their minds work, how and why they make mistakes, what motivates them, what stars they seek to reach or whether each hankers after a star at all. Yes, most are acquaintances; they hail him in the hallways. But does he know them well enough to teach them powerfully, know the ways of their minds and moods? No, not even close. Horace compromises. He gets to know a few students well, usually those who interest him especially or who press themselves to his attention. The kids in the middle remain a genial blur. Indeed, Horace wryly admits most of them cherish their anonymity. If Mr. Smith really knows me, then he'd find out that . . .

During the school day, the students come to Horace by 15
"classes," ninth grade, tenth grade, and the rest. A student is in a particular class on the basis of her or his birthday. To be out of step, sixteen in the ninth grade or fourteen in the eleventh grade, is cause for comment, usually contemptuous. Dummy. Nerd. One of *those* kids. The assumption behind the system is that kids of the same age are essentially alike, more or less teachable in the same ways and properly held to similar standards. Franklin High School splits each grade into three lumps, honors, college prep, and regular, as well as special needs. But the prevailing, and overwhelming, characterization of students is by grade level. Teachers ask, *What's your name? What grade are you in?* The answers provide the two critical labels. Because all the kids in each grade have experienced, it is presumed, the same number of hours of schooling, they should, save at the extremes, all know the same things.

Horace knows better. Young people grow intellectually, 16
physically, and socially at different rates, often with mysterious spurts and stops along the way. Some kids excel at language and flounder in mathematics; the hotshot in one area is not necessarily great in another. Further, not all kids pay attention at school at any given moment, for benign or deplorable reasons. So by their high school years the youngster's potential and actual school performance often diverge: "ninth grade" is an administratively useful concept, but one that tells a teacher far less about a student's intellectual and emotional development than the grouping would suggest.

17 One copes, however, largely by not being careful, by deliberately not attending to the record and specialness and stage of growth and disposition of each youngster. They are all *ninth-graders.* Treat them the same—same curriculum, same textbook, same pedagogy, same tests, same standards, same everything.

18 It defies common sense, Horace knows. Age grading hurts some kids, swelling the heads of those who appear, for whatever obvious or mysterious reasons, to be "swift" and humiliating the "slow." Pigeonholing honors, regular, and special needs students sets up the self-fulfilling prophecies. *Oh no, Mr. Smith, I couldn't take AP English. I'm not an honors student. . . .* Every year Horace sees the swift kid who plugs hard, with the confidence of being perceived as honors quality, and the slow youngster who ignores his talents, giving up, acting up, not caring, finding school a place of unrelieved and anticipated failure.

19 Franklin High School uses plenty of public relations talk about "taking each child individually," but the school's practices belie the boast. For example, there is virtually no attempt, Horace ruefully recalls, to get thorough information to a student's new teacher about the youngster's history in school. Students do have files someplace, Horace knows. Teachers don't read them, though, and are not encouraged to do so. In any event, there are too many to absorb. May as well treat 'em all the same. Or accept someone else's judgment about how swift a kid is, and go with it. Expect more, or expect less. Compromise with your common sense: the kids are different, but we can't admit it, even to ourselves.

20 The curriculum does not help. Franklin High School has a statement of goals, but it is as vague as it is hortatory and conventional. The goals connect only rhetorically with the formal Course of Study. The latter is laid out by course and grade and is usually cast as a list of ideas, classics to be read, facts, skills, procedures, and qualities of character to be read, facts, skills, procedures, and qualities of character to be admired, opportunities to stock one's mind. Simply, the curriculum, however artfully described, is a listing of what the *teachers* will do, what "things" the kids will be "exposed" to. The students remain invisible, lumped in their age-graded cohorts, ready to watch the teachers' parade of things.

21 Horace knows this is backward. What counts is what the

students do, as Horace has learned from the Theater Club plays he directs. The members know what the "target" is. Others find targets in some of the more imaginative Advanced Placement courses. But there are few such compelling ends in view in the core curriculum; the destinations are clearly cast in terms of what the students should be able to do. Except for aiming to help students pass the tests, the formal Course of Study Guide says little about what the material *means*. We teachers are "to cover" the Lake poets, and the students should then be able to answer questions about them. How the students are to *use* the experience is not addressed. This is as depressing as it is confusing, but Horace continues to compromise. We will all read *Hamlet* during the spring term, and there will be one test for all eleventh-graders . . . .

Franklin's "goal statement" talks of graduates able to "function in society and the economy as useful citizens." Horace would put that as "making sense of the world." Either way, it assumes that Franklin alumni will see which issues are of consequence to themselves and others, will be competent to analyze these situations, to sort them out, and will be both able and disposed to do something about them. Some would say that this means that graduates should be interested in learning and practiced in teaching themselves, able to figure out their world and motivated to do something about it. 22

Fine, Horace thinks. But how is the school's curriculum organized? By subjects, most of which are poorly defined and each of which is planned in almost total isolation from the others. The stuff of these subjects is offered up to students in fifty-two-minute slivers of time, rapid fire. 23

Horace wonders whether this gives kids practice in making sense of the world. Even the teachers in the English Department can't agree on what their subject really is; the mathematics sequence has no planned connection with science courses; and the teachers of literature, art, music, and drama pay attention only to each art separately. Making sense is tough even for adults; despite its goal statement, Franklin gives students little practice in the craft. Indeed, the high school's presentation of the curriculum guarantees superficiality. 24

These realities sting Horace, but he goes along. He compromises. The faculty doesn't like to hear any sort of fundamental criticism. We're tired of being the butt of all 25 the griping, they say. Furthermore, this list of subjects is what the colleges want. A likely story, Horace thinks. Do the colleges want kids schooled in intellectual chaos?

26 Give a little, get along, compromise. Yes, sometimes there is electricity in the classrooms, but not often enough. The kids compromise too, taking what is offered, observing that to which they are exposed, more or less cranking out the tests, and then forgetting most of it. Feeling good is important, not only about oneself but also about the school. Franklin Pride.

27 Horace remembers a devilish experiment that a visiting consultant recently suggested: give students a test they took twelve to fifteen months earlier, and see how they perform. What had they retained? Horace winces at the thought. Kids forget so much so quickly. It is better that school accentuate the immediate, the stuff of the last unit, rather than instill intellectual habits. Horace plays the game too. Last year's English is expected to be gone, and if we hold a student responsible for it, we are "unfair." And so we stress the immediate.

28 All this is agonizing for Horace. He resents his compromises, and derides himself for making them. Some respected colleagues share his frustration, but they know that an honest evaluation of the school's compromises will open a Pandora's box. Everything in the school affects everything else. That finely tuned complexity which is the daily schedule cannot withstand more than trivial adjustments, and more than trivial adjustments are needed to improve Franklin High. The ultimate frustration for Horace is that even if a corps of like-minded, risk-taking colleagues evolved an ambitious, sensible new plan for Franklin, they would not have the authority to act on it. The major elements of schooling are controlled outside the teachers' world. The state, or its contractor firms, writes the tests. The state mandates when each subject is to be taught; it and the district control that key coinage of school, the time of teachers and students. Evaluations of school and teachers, the union contract, the departmental divisions, all run according to traditional formulas.

29 Horace knows that he has limited control over his own destiny. Others would have to affirm his intention to teach with better compromises, to organize his and the students' work along more sensible lines. Obviously, they don't trust

us, Horace thinks. The folk higher up are sure they know better. We always have to ask permission. Teachers with hall passes not to the bathroom but to better schools, he snorts to himself. Of all Horace's feelings about his work, this is the most bitter.

David P. Gardner et al.

A Nation at Risk

In 1981, Secretary of Education T. H. Bell created the National Commission on Excellence in Education and directed it to report within eighteen months on the quality of education in American schools. Sparked by a widespread public perception that "something is wrong" with our educational system, the Commission (chaired by David P. Gardner, president of the University of California, and comprising eighteen teachers, school administrators, university presidents, and distinguished public officials and business leaders) created a national stir with its final report, "A Nation at Risk," reprinted (with some small omissions) below. A decade later the report continues to provide a context for discussions of educational reform in the United States.

Our Nation is at risk. Our once unchallenged preeminence 1
in commerce, industry, science, and technological innovation is being overtaken by competitors throughout the world. This report is concerned with only one of the many causes and dimensions of the problem, but it is the one that undergirds American prosperity, security, and civility. We report to the American people that while we can take justifiable pride in what our schools and colleges have historically accomplished and contributed to the United States and the well-being of its people, the educational foundations of our society are presently being eroded by a rising tide of mediocrity that threatens our very future as a Nation and a people. What was unimaginable a generation ago has begun to occur—others are matching and surpassing our educational attainments.

2 If an unfriendly foreign power had attempted to impose on America the mediocre educational performance that exists today, we might well have viewed it as an act of war. As it stands, we have allowed this to happen to ourselves. We have even squandered the gains in student achievement made in the wake of the Sputnik challenge. Moreover, we have dismantled essential support systems which helped make those gains possible. We have, in effect, been committing an act of unthinking, unilateral educational disarmament.

3 Our society and its educational institutions seem to have lost sight of the basic purposes of schooling, and of the high expectations and disciplined effort needed to attain them. This report, the result of 18 months of study, seeks to generate reform of our educational system in fundamental ways and to renew the Nation's commitment to schools and colleges of high quality throughout the length and breadth of our land.

4 That we have compromised this commitment is, upon reflection, hardly surprising, given the multitude of often conflicting demands we have placed on our Nation's schools and colleges. They are routinely called on to provide solutions to personal, social, and political problems that the home and other institutions either will not or cannot resolve. We must understand that these demands on our schools and colleges often exact an educational cost as well as a financial one.

5 On the occasion of the Commission's first meeting, President Reagan noted the central importance of education in American life when he said: "Certainly there are few areas of American life as important to our society, to our people, and to our families as our schools and colleges." This report, therefore, is as much an open letter to the American people as it is a report to the Secretary of Education. We are confident that the American people, properly informed, will do what is right for their children and for the generations to come.

The Risk

6 History is not kind to idlers. The time is long past when America's destiny was assured simply by an abundance of

natural resources and inexhaustible human enthusiasm, and by our relative isolation from the malignant problems of older civilizations. The world is indeed one global village. We live among determined, well-educated, and strongly motivated competitors. We compete with them for international standing and markets, not only with products but also with the ideas of our laboratories and neighborhood workshops. America's position in the world may once have been reasonably secure with only a few exceptionally well-trained men and women. It is no longer.

The risk is not only that the Japanese make automobiles 7
more efficiently than Americans and have government subsidies for development and export. It is not just that the South Koreans recently built the world's most efficient steel mill, or that American machine tools, once the pride of the world, are being displaced by German products. It is also that these developments signify a redistribution of trained capability throughout the globe. Knowledge, learning, information, and skilled intelligence are the new raw materials of international commerce and are today spreading throughout the world as vigorously as miracle drugs, synthetic fertilizers, and blue jeans did earlier. If only to keep and improve on the slim competitive edge we still retain in world markets, we must dedicate ourselves to the reform of our educational system for the benefit of all—old and young alike, affluent and poor, majority and minority. Learning is the indispensable investment required for success in the "information age" we are entering.

Our concern, however, goes well beyond matters such 8
as industry and commerce. It also includes the intellectual, moral, and spiritual strengths of our people which knit together the very fabric of our society. The people of the United States need to know that individuals in our society who do not possess the levels of skill, literacy, and training essential to this new era will be effectively disenfranchised, not simply from the material rewards that accompany competent performance, but also from the chance to participate fully in our national life. A high level of shared education is essential to a free, democratic society and to the fostering of a common culture, especially in a country that prides itself on pluralism and individual freedom.

For our country to function, citizens must be able to reach 9 some common understandings on complex issues, often on short notice and on the basis of conflicting or incomplete evidence. Education helps form these common understandings, a point Thomas Jefferson made long ago in his justly famous dictum:

> I know no safe depository of the ultimate powers of the society but the people themselves; and if we think them not enlightened enough to exercise their control with a wholesome discretion, the remedy is not to take it from them but to inform their discretion.

10 Part of what is at risk is the promise first made on this continent: All, regardless of race or class or economic status, are entitled to a fair chance and to the tools for developing their individual powers of mind and spirit to the utmost. This promise means that all children by virtue of their own efforts, competently guided, can hope to attain the mature and informed judgment needed to secure gainful employment and to manage their own lives, thereby serving not only their own interests but also the progress of society itself.

Indicators of the Risk

11 The educational dimensions of the risk before us have been amply documented in testimony received by the Commission. For example:

- International comparisons of student achievement, completed a decade ago, reveal that on 19 academic tests American students were never first or second and, in comparison with other industrialized nations, were last seven times.
- Some 23 million American adults are functionally illiterate by the simplest tests of everyday reading, writing, and comprehension.
- About 13 percent of all 17-year-olds in the United States can be considered functionally illiterate. Functional illiteracy among minority youth may run as high as 40 percent.

- Average achievement of high school students on most standardized tests is now lower than 26 years ago when Sputnik was launched.
- Over half the population of gifted students do not match their tested ability with comparable achievement in school.
- The College Board's Scholastic Aptitude Tests (SAT) demonstrate a virtually unbroken decline from 1963 to 1980. Average verbal scores fell over 50 points and average mathematics scores dropped nearly 40 points.
- College Board achievement tests also reveal consistent declines in recent years in such subjects as physics and English.
- Both the number and proportion of students demonstrating superior achievement on the SATs (i.e., those with scores of 650 or higher) have also dramatically declined.
- There was a steady decline in science achievement scores of U.S. 17-year-olds as measured by national assessments of science in 1969, 1973, and 1977.
- Between 1975 and 1980, remedial mathematics courses in public 4-year colleges increased by 72 percent and now constitute one-quarter of all mathematics courses taught in those institutions.
- Average tested achievement of students graduating from college is also lower.
- Business and military leaders complain that they are required to spend millions of dollars on costly remedial education and training programs in such basic skills as reading, writing, spelling, and computation. The Department of the Navy, for example, reported to the Commission that one-quarter of its recent recruits cannot read at the ninth grade level, the minimum needed simply to understand written safety instructions. Without remedial work they cannot even begin, much less complete, the sophisticated training essential in much of the modern military.

These deficiencies come at a time when the demand for 12
highly skilled workers in new fields is accelerating rapidly. For example:

- Computers and computer-controlled equipment are penetrating every aspect of our lives—homes, factories, and offices.
- One estimate indicates that by the turn of the century millions of jobs will involve laser technology and robotics.
- Technology is radically transforming a host of other occupations. They include health care, medical science, energy production, food processing, construction, and the building, repair, and maintenance of sophisticated scientific, educational, military, and industrial equipment.

13 Analysts examining these indicators of student performance and the demands for new skills have made some chilling observations. Educational researcher Paul Hurd concluded at the end of a thorough national survey of student achievement that within the context of the modern scientific revolution, "We are raising a new generation of Americans that is scientifically and technologically illiterate." In a similar vein, John Slaughter, a former Director of the National Science Foundation, warned of "a growing chasm between a small scientific and technological elite and a citizenry ill-informed, indeed uninformed, on issues with a science component."

14 But the problem does not stop there, nor do all observers see it the same way. Some worry that schools may emphasize such rudiments as reading and computation at the expense of other essential skills such as comprehension, analysis, solving problems, and drawing conclusions. Still others are concerned that an over-emphasis on technical and occupational skills will leave little time for studying the arts and humanities that so enrich daily life, help maintain civility, and develop a sense of community. Knowledge of the humanities, they maintain, must be harnessed to science and technology if the latter are to remain creative and humane, just as the humanities need to be informed by science and technology if they are to remain relevant to the human condition. Another analyst, Paul Copperman, has drawn a sobering conclusion. Until now, he has noted:

> Each generation of Americans has outstripped its parents in education, in literacy, and in economic attainment. For the first time in the history of our country, the educational skills

of one generation will not surpass, will not equal, will not even approach, those of their parents.

It is important, of course, to recognize that *the average citizen* today is better educated and more knowledgeable than the average citizen of a generation ago—more literate, and exposed to more mathematics, literature, and science. The positive impact of this fact on the well-being of our country and the lives of our people cannot be overstated. Nevertheless, *the average graduate* of our schools and colleges today is not as well-educated as the average graduate of 25 or 35 yeas ago, when a much smaller proportion of our population completed high school and college. The negative impact of this fact likewise cannot be overstated. 15

Hope and Frustration

Statistics and their interpretation by experts show only 16 the surface dimension of the difficulties we face. Beneath them lies a tension between hope and frustration that characterizes current attitudes about education at every level.

We have heard the voices of high school and college 17 students, school board members, and teachers; of leaders of industry, minority groups, and higher education; of parents and State officials. We could hear the hope evident in their commitment to quality education and in their descriptions of outstanding programs and schools. We could also hear the intensity of their frustration, a growing impatience with shoddiness in many walks of American life, and the complaint that this shoddiness is too often reflected in our schools and colleges. Their frustration threatens to overwhelm their hope.

What lies behind this emerging national sense of frustra- 18 tion can be described as both a dimming of personal expectations and the fear of losing a shared vision for America.

On the personal level the student, the parent, and the 19 caring teacher all perceive that a basic promise is not being kept. More and more young people emerge from high school ready neither for college nor for work. This predicament becomes more acute as the knowledge base continues its rapid expansion, the number of traditional jobs shrinks, and new jobs demand greater sophistication and preparation.

20 On a broader scale, we sense that this undertone of frustration has significant political implications, for it cuts across ages, generations, races, and political and economic groups. We have come to understand that the public will demand that educational and political leaders act forcefully and effectively on these issues. Indeed, such demands have already appeared and could well become a unifying national preoccupation. This unity, however, can be achieved only if we avoid the unproductive tendency of some to search for scapegoats among the victims, such as the beleaguered teachers.

21 On the positive side is the significant movement by political and educational leaders to search for solutions—so far centering largely on the nearly desperate need for increased support for the teaching of mathematics and science. This movement is but a start on what we believe is a larger and more educationally encompassing need to improve teaching and learning in fields such as English, history, geography, economics, and foreign languages. We believe this movement must be broadened and directed toward reform and excellence throughout education.

Excellence in Education

22 We define "excellence" to mean several related things. At the level of the *individual learner,* it means performing on the boundary of individual ability in ways that test and push back personal limits, in school and in the workplace. Excellence characterizes a *school or college* that sets high expectations and goals for all learners, then tries in every way possible to help students reach them. Excellence characterizes a *society* that has adopted these policies, for it will then be prepared through the education and skill of its people to respond to the challenges of a rapidly changing world. Our Nation's people and its schools and colleges must be committed to achieving excellence in all these senses.

23 We do not believe that a public commitment to excellence and educational reform must be made at the expense of a strong public commitment to the equitable treatment of our diverse population. The twin goals of equity and high-quality schooling have profound and practical meaning for

our economy and society, and we cannot permit one to yield to the other either in principle or in practice. To do so would deny young people their chance to learn and live according to their aspirations and abilities. It also would lead to a generalized accommodation to mediocrity in our society on the one hand or the creation of an undemocratic elitism on the other.

Our goal must be to develop the talents of all to their 24
fullest. Attaining that goal requires that we expect and assist all students to work to the limits of their capabilities. We should expect schools to have genuinely high standards rather than minimum ones, and parents to support and encourage their children to make the most of their talents and abilities.

The search for solutions to our educational problems 25
must also include a commitment to life-long learning. The task of rebuilding our system of learning is enormous and must be properly understood and taken seriously: Although a million and a half new workers enter the economy each year from our schools and colleges, the adults working today will still make up about 75 percent of the workforce in the year 2000. These workers, and new entrants into the workforce, will need further education and retraining if they—and we as a Nation—are to thrive and prosper.

The Learning Society

In a world of ever-accelerating competition and change in 26
the conditions of the workplace, of ever-greater danger, and of ever-larger opportunities for those prepared to meet them, educational reform should focus on the goal of creating a Learning Society. At the heart of such a society is the commitment to a set of values and to a system of education that affords all members the opportunity to stretch their minds to full capacity, from early childhood through adulthood, learning more as the world itself changes. Such a society has as a basic foundation the idea that education is important not only because of what it contributes to one's career goals but also because of the value it adds to the general quality of one's life. Also at the heart of the Learning Society are educational opportunities extending far beyond the traditional institutions of learning,

our schools and colleges. They extend into homes and workplaces; into libraries, art galleries, museums, and science centers; indeed, into every place where the individual can develop and mature in work and life. In our view, formal schooling in youth is the essential foundation for learning throughout one's life. But without life-long learning, one's skills will become rapidly dated.

27 In contrast to the ideal of the Learning Society, however, we find that for too many people education means doing the minimum work necessary for the moment, then coasting through life on what may have been learned in its first quarter. But this should not surprise us because we tend to express our educational standards and expectations largely in terms of "minimum requirements." And where there should be a coherent continuum of learning, we have none, but instead an often incoherent, outdated patchwork quilt. Many individual, sometimes heroic, examples of schools and colleges of great merit do exist. Our findings and testimony confirm the vitality of a number of notable schools and programs, but their very distinction stands out against a vast mass shaped by tensions and pressures that inhibit systematic academic and vocational achievement for the majority of students. In some metropolitan areas basic literacy has become the goal rather than the starting point. In some colleges maintaining enrollments is of greater day-to-day concern than maintaining rigorous academic standards. And the ideal of academic excellence as the primary goal of schooling seems to be fading across the board in American education.

28 Thus, we issue this call to all who care about America and its future: to parents and students; to teachers, administrators, and school board members; to colleges and industry; to union members and military leaders; to governors and State legislators; to the President; to members of Congress and other public officials; to members of learned and scientific societies; to the print and electronic media; to concerned citizens everywhere. America is at risk.

Recommendations

29 In light of the urgent need for improvement, both immediate and long term, this Commission has agreed on a set of

recommendations that the American people can begin to act on now, that can be implemented over the next several years, and that promise lasting reform. The topics are familiar; there is little mystery about what we believe must be done. Many schools, districts, and States are already giving serious and constructive attention to these matters, even though their plans may differ from our recommendations in some details.

We wish to note that we refer to public, private, and 30
parochial schools and colleges alike. All are valuable national resources. Examples of actions similar to those recommended below can be found in each of them.

We must emphasize that the variety of student aspirations, 31
abilities, and preparation requires that appropriate content be available to satisfy diverse needs. Attention must be directed to both the nature of the content available and to the needs of particular learners. The most gifted students, for example, may need a curriculum enriched and accelerated beyond even the needs of other students of high ability. Similarly, educationally disadvantaged students may require special curriculum materials, smaller classes, or individual tutoring to help them master the material presented. Nevertheless, there remains a common expectation: We must demand the best effort and performance from all students, whether they are gifted or less able, affluent or disadvantaged, whether destined for college, the farm, or industry.

Our recommendations are based on the beliefs that every- 32
one can learn, that everyone is born with an *urge* to learn which can be nurtured, that a solid high school education is within the reach of virtually all, and that life-long learning will equip people with the skills required for new careers and for citizenship.

Recommendation A: Content. **We recommend** *that State* 33
and local high school graduation requirements be strengthened and that, at a minimum, all *students seeking a diploma be required to lay the foundations in the Five New Basics by taking the following curriculum during their 4 years of high school: (a) 4 years of English; (b) 3 years of mathematics; (c) 3 years of science; (d) 3 years of social studies; and (e) one-half year of computer science. For the college-bound, 2 years of foreign language in high school are strongly recommended in addition to those taken earlier.*

34 *Recommendation B: Standards and Expectations.* **We recommend** *that schools, colleges, and universities adopt more rigorous and measurable standards, and higher expectations, for academic performance and student conduct, and that 4-year colleges and universities raise their requirements for admission. This will help students do their best educationally with challenging materials in an environment that supports learning and authentic accomplishment.*

35 *Recommendation C: Time.* **We recommend** *significantly more time be devoted to learning the New Basics. This will require more effective use of the existing school day, a longer school day, or a lengthened school year.*

36 *Recommendation D: Teaching.* **This recommendation** *consists of seven parts. Each is intended to improve the preparation of teachers or to make teaching a more rewarding and respected profession. Each of the seven stands on its own and should not be considered solely as an implementing recommendation.*

1. Persons preparing to teach should be required to meet high educational standards, to demonstrate an aptitude for teaching, and to demonstrate competence in an academic discipline. Colleges and universities offering teacher preparation programs should be judged by how well their graduates meet these criteria.
2. Salaries for the teaching profession should be increased and should be professionally competitive, market-sensitive, and performance-based. Salary, promotion, tenure, and retention decisions should be tied to an effective evaluation system that includes peer review so that superior teachers can be rewarded, average ones encouraged, and poor ones either improved or terminated.
3. School boards should adopt an 11-month contract for teachers. This would ensure time for curriculum and professional development, programs for students with special needs, and a more adequate level of teacher compensation.
4. School boards, administrators, and teachers should cooperate to develop career ladders for teachers that

distinguish among the beginning instructor, the experienced teacher, and the master teacher.

5. Substantial nonschool personnel resources should be employed to help solve the immediate problem of the shortage of mathematics and science teachers. Qualified individuals including recent graduates with mathematics and science degrees, graduate students, and industrial and retired scientists could, with appropriate preparation, immediately begin teaching in these fields. A number of our leading science centers have the capacity to begin educating and retraining teachers immediately. Other areas of critical teacher need, such as English, must also be addressed.
6. Incentives, such as grants and loans, should be made available to attract outstanding students to the teaching profession, particularly in those areas of critical shortage.
7. Master teachers should be involved in designing teacher preparation programs and in supervising teachers during their probationary years.

America Can Do It

Despite the obstacles and difficulties that inhibit the 37
pursuit of superior educational attainment, we are confident, with history as our guide, that we can meet our goal. The American educational system has responded to previous challenges with remarkable success. In the 19th century our land-grant colleges and universities provided the research and training that developed our Nation's natural resources and the rich agricultural bounty of the American farm. From the late 1800s through mid-20th century, American schools provided the educated workforce needed to seal the success of the Industrial Revolution and to provide the margin of victory in two world wars. In the early part of this century and continuing to this very day, our schools have absorbed vast waves of immigrants and educated them and their children to productive citizenship. Similarly, the Nation's Black colleges have provided opportunity and undergraduate education to the vast majority of college-educated Black Americans.

38 More recently, our institutions of higher education have provided the scientists and skilled technicians who helped us transcend the boundaries of our planet. In the last 30 years, the schools have been a major vehicle for expanded social opportunity, and now graduate 75 percent of our young people from high school. Indeed, the proportion of Americans of college age enrolled in higher education is nearly twice that of Japan and far exceeds other nations such as France, West Germany, and the Soviet Union. Moreover, when international comparisons were last made a decade ago, the top 9 percent of American students compared favorably in achievement with their peers in other countries.

39 In addition, many large urban areas in recent years report that average student achievement in elementary schools is improving. More and more schools are also offering advanced placement programs and programs for gifted and talented students, and more and more students are enrolling in them.

40 We are the inheritors of a past that gives us every reason to believe that we will succeed.

A Final Word

41 This is not the first or only commission on education, and some of our findings are surely not new, but old business that now at last must be done. For no one can doubt that the United States is under challenge from many quarters.

42 Children born today can expect to graduate from high school in the year 2000. We dedicate our report not only to these children, but also to those now in school and others to come. We firmly believe that a movement of America's schools in the direction called for by our recommendations will prepare these children for far more effective lives in a far stronger America.

43 Our final word, perhaps better characterized as a plea, is that all segments of our population give attention to the implementation of our recommendations. Our present plight did not appear overnight, and the responsibility for our current situation is widespread. Reform of our educational system will take time and unwavering commitment. It will require equally widespread, energetic, and dedicated

action. For example, we call upon the National Academy of Sciences, National Academy of Engineering, Institute of Medicine, Science Service, National Science Foundation, Social Science Research Council, American Council of Learned Societies, National Endowment for the Humanities, National Endowment for the Arts, and other scholarly, scientific, and learned societies for their help in this effort. Help should come from students themselves; from parents, teachers, and school boards; from colleges and universities; from local, State, and Federal officials; from teachers' and administrators' organizations; from industrial and labor councils; and from other groups with interest in and responsibility for educational reform.

It is their America, and the America of all of us, that is at risk; it is to each of us that this imperative is addressed. It is by our willingness to take up the challenge, and our resolve to see it through, that America's place in the world will be either secured or forfeited. Americans have succeeded before and so we shall again. 44

Charles Dickens

What Is a Horse?

Was Charles Dickens (1812–1870) the greatest English novelist? This selection from the opening pages of Hard Times *(1854) illustrates Dickens' satiric edge; designed as a commentary on a "mechanical" system of education devised during the industrial revolution, it may also offer perspective on the schools of today.*

Thomas Gradgrind, sir. A man of realities. A man of fact and calculations. A man who proceeds upon the principle that two and two are four, and nothing over, and who is not to be talked into allowing for anything over. Thomas Gradgrind, sir—peremptorily Thomas—Thomas Gradgrind. With a rule and a pair of scales, and the multiplication table always in his pocket, sir, ready to weigh and measure any parcel of human nature, and tell you exactly what it comes 1 to. It is a mere question of figures, case of simple arithmetic. You might hope to get some other nonsensical belief into the head of George Gradgrind, or Augustus Gradgrind, or John Gradgrind, or Joseph Gradgrind (all suppositious, nonexistent persons), but into the head of Thomas Gradgrind—no sir!

2 In such terms Mr Gradgrind always mentally introduced himself, whether to his private circle of acquaintance, or to the public in general. In such terms, no doubt, substituting the words 'boys and girls', for 'sir', Thomas Gradgrind now presented Thomas Gradgrind to the little pitchers before him, who were to be filled so full of facts.

3 Indeed, as he eagerly sparkled at them from the cellarage before mentioned, he seemed a kind of cannon loaded to the muzzle with facts, and prepared to blow them clean out of the regions of the childhood at one discharge. He seemed a galvanizing apparatus, too, charged with a grim mechanical substitute for the tender young imaginations that were to be stormed away.

4 'Girl number twenty,' said Mr Gradgrind, squarely pointing with his square forefinger, 'I don't know that girl. Who is that girl?'

5 'Sissy Jupe, sir,' explained number twenty, blushing, standing up, and curtseying.

6 'Sissy is not a name,' said Mr Gradgrind. 'Don't call yourself Sissy. Call yourself Cecilia.'

7 'It's father as calls me Sissy, sir,' returned the young girl in a trembling voice, and with another curtsey.

8 'Then he has no business to do it,' said Mr Gradgrind. 'Tell him he mustn't. Cecilia Jupe. Let me see. What is your father?'

9 'He belongs to the horse-riding, if you please, sir.'

10 Mr Gradgrind frowned, and waved off the objectionable calling with his hand.

11 'We don't want to know anything about that, here. You mustn't tell us about that, here. Your father breaks horses, don't he?'

12 'If you please, sir, when they can get any to break, they do break horses in the ring, sir.'

13 'You mustn't tell us about the ring, here. Very well, then. Describe your father as a horsebreaker. He doctors sick horses, I dare say?'

14 'Oh yes, sir.'

15 'Very well, then. He is a veterinary surgeon, a farrier and horsebreaker. Give me your definition of a horse.'

(Sissy Jupe thrown into the greatest alarm by this demand.) 16

'Girl number twenty unable to define a horse!' said Mr Gradgrind, for the general behoof of all the little pitchers. 'Girl number twenty possessed of no facts, in reference to one of the commonest of animals! Some boy's definition of a horse. Bitzer, yours.' 17

The square finger, moving here and there, lighted suddenly on Bitzer, perhaps because he chanced to sit in the same ray of sunlight which, darting in at one of the bare windows of the intensely whitewashed room, irradiated Sissy. For, the boys and girls sat on the face of the inclined plane in two compact bodies, divided up the centre by a narrow interval; and Sissy, being at the corner of a row on the sunny side, came in for the beginning of a sunbeam, of which Bitzer, being at the corner of a row on the other side, a few rows in advance, caught the end. But, whereas the girl was so dark-eyed and dark-haired, that she seemed to receive a deeper and more lustrous colour from the sun when it shone upon her, the boy was so light-eyed and light-haired that the self-same rays appeared to draw out of him what little colour he ever possessed. His cold eyes would hardly have been eyes, but for the short ends of lashes which, by bringing them into immediate contrast with something paler than themselves, expressed their form. His short-cropped hair might have been a mere continuation of the sandy freckles on his forehead and face. His skin was so unwholesomely deficient in the natural tinge, that he looked as though, if he were cut, he would bleed white. 18

'Bitzer,' said Thomas Gradgrind. 'Your definition of a horse.' 19

'Quadruped. Graminivorous. Forty teeth, namely twenty-four grinders, four eye-teeth, and twelve incisive. Sheds coat in the spring; in marshy countries, sheds hoofs, too. Hoofs hard, but requiring to be shod with iron. Age known by marks in mouth.' Thus (and much more) Bitzer. 20

'Now girl number twenty,' said Mr Gradgrind. 'You know what a horse is.' 21

Edward Fiske

The Learning Crisis

Mr. Fiske, a journalist who writes about education issues for The New York Times, *was assisted by Sally Read and Craig Sautter in composing his 1991 book* Smart Schools, Smart Kids: Why Do Some Schools Work, *an account of "new" public schools being created in the past few years—schools that might be models for additional changes. For according to Mr. Fiske, "anything short of fundamental structural change [in our system of education] is futile. The renewal of public education in this country requires a frontal assault on* every *aspect of schooling." The following comes from the introductory chapter to* Smart Schools.

1 Morris Jefferson was an academic failure in a school where academic failure was commonplace. A sprawling one-story brick building in a barrio on the northwestern outskirts of Houston, the Hollibrook Elementary School sits across the street from a run-down public housing project where the roofs leak and the potholes in the street are large enough to swallow a tricycle. Almost all of the school's one thousand students are poor members of minority groups who live in homes where a language other than English is spoken. The typical Hollibrook student entered kindergarten ill prepared for academic work and, year by year, slipped farther and farther below grade level. When it came to standardized test scores, Hollibrook was the caboose of the Spring Branch School District.

2 As a second-grader, Morris was traveling the familiar route. Tall and skinny, with olive skin, big brown eyes, and dark hair cut in bangs over his forehead, he showed a wry sense of humor and a talent for goofy drawings but little enthusiasm for sitting quietly and listening to teachers talk. He neglected his homework assignments and picked fights with classmates. A standardized reading test put him at only the 8th percentile nationally, and by the end of the 1989 school year he had failed to master the full list of "competencies" that the state of Texas requires for promotion to third grade. Morris was, as educators like to put it, "retained."

3 By September, though, just as Morris was gearing up for

his second shot at second grade, major changes were taking place at Hollibrook. The school had a new principal, Suzanne Still, a former special-education teacher whose years of working with struggling young people had convinced her that *all* students, including the Morris Jeffersons of the world, could learn more than most public schools either encourage or expect. One of her first acts was to tack a small sign above the door to her office: "A good principal always remembers what it was like." She then set out to overhaul Hollibrook around principles that were the exact opposite of most of those held dear by the state of Texas, the Spring Branch School District, and a century of American public school tradition.

4 Instead of putting every student in a class with peers of like ability, as had been the practice for years, she grouped them randomly, even allowing children in various grades to work together in a multiage "pod." Two second-grade teachers got the go-ahead to combine their classes and do team teaching, while three others took on a group of second-graders and agreed to stay with them until they graduate in 1993. Spanish-speaking students worked side by side with Anglos. The school day was no longer divided into regular forty-five- or seventy-two-minute periods, and teachers were encouraged to disregard artificial distinctions between the various academic areas. Students wrote while they were doing math, learned spelling from the social studies teacher, and read for the first half hour of every school day.

5 Whereas Texas expects its teachers to take their state-approved basal readers and textbooks in hand, start on page one, and work their way through to the last chapter, Still told her faculty to use whatever teaching resources they wanted. Gone, too, was the requirement that teachers file the educational equivalent of flight plans (otherwise known as planning books) so that the principal or a visiting inspector from the State Education Department in Austin could quickly ascertain that on Thursday at 10:15 A.M. "Miss Burpee in 5B" is doing simple division. As a teacher, Still recalls, she "always preferred to work for someone who thought that I had a brain and could think." So at Hollibrook decisions on everything from the hiring of new teachers to the choosing of curriculum materials are now made by committees dominated by teachers. Perhaps most important, Hollibrook adopted the principle of "accelerated learning," which asserts that if students are having difficulty,

teachers should give them *more* academic stimulation, not plunk them in "remedial" classes, slow down the learning process, and condemn them to perpetual failure.

6 Cumulatively the changes at Hollibrook constituted a frontal assault on just about every aspect of traditional school management—how to manage a school, treat teachers, deal with students, organize instruction, and manage time. It was also politically risky. To deal with the threat that some inspector from the state or local school district might show up and call teachers on some technicality, Hollibrook set up an early warning system. Whenever such a visitor showed up at the front office, one of the secretaries unobtrusively meandered over to the nearest classroom, stuck her head in the door and spoke the code word, "Bluebird." The teacher immediately dropped what she was doing and sent a student on the rounds of the other classrooms, like a modern-day Paul Revere, spreading word of the impending danger.

7 "Bluebird."

8 "OK."

9 "Bluebird."

10 "Thanks."

11 "Bluebird."

12 "Got it."

13 Within minutes, students who were reading on their own in the halls would be recalled to their desks. Officially sanctioned textbooks were pulled from their hiding places in closets and opened prominently on the teachers' desks. To the untrained eye, Hollibrook had become a model of educational orthodoxy.

14 The turnaround at Hollibrook was virtually immediate. By the fall of 1990 students at Hollibrook were performing at the national and district average, and in math they were even higher. Vandalism and fights in the halls became a rarity. Attendance reached a lofty 96 percent, and more than 1,000 parents show up for regular conferences with their children's teachers. Most significant, the average student in Hollibrook is now making *more* than a full year's progress in basic academic subjects—this in a school where two-thirds of a year's progress would be considered respectable.

15 The success stories include Morris Jefferson, who was assigned to the team-taught second grade. The two teachers, Joy Campbell and Marylou Bland, tried everything they could think of to get Morris and the other students actively

involved in their own learning. Instead of having students simply read stories about the circus and answer questions, they had them do research on elephants and clowns, give reports, and make costumes. The teachers also noticed that Morris became engaged whenever the topic under discussion involved science, so they began building on this strength. Soon he was introducing fourth-grade words such as *predator* and *camouflage* to his classmates. One night at the end of the school year Bland was sitting at home thumbing through a report on the reading-test scores of her students. She was dumbfounded to see that Morris's had jumped from the 8th to the 86th percentile."I was so excited that I called his mother at ten P.M. to tell her the news," she said. "We cried."

The story of what Hollibrook calls its renaissance is dramatic but by no means unique. In recent years a growing number of farsighted and courageous educators like Suzanne Still have become alarmed at the way public schools are failing America's children. They have begun to question traditional theories of learning and notions of how to run schools and to put their ideas into action. In many cases their ideas have been embraced by entire districts and even states. They have become the pioneers in a transformation of virtually all of the fundamental structures of American public education. 16

The failures of the current system are well documented. The 1983 federal report by the National Commission on Excellence in Education, "A Nation at Risk," warned of a "rising tide of mediocrity that threatens our very future as a nation and a people." Since then our national senses have been numbed by one horror story after another about the abysmal ignorance of our young people. It would be comforting to say that such findings resulted from the well-publicized problems of inner-city and rural schools, but we would be kidding ourselves. Even our *best* schools are failing to meet minimal international standards. Extrapolation of data from the National Assessment of Educational Progress shows that only 5 percent of the graduates of American high schools can read at a level that would qualify them for a spot in a university in Europe. And when they get to a college in this country, the overwhelming majority of these graduates start off studying what their European counterparts learned in high school. Some high schools 17 never graduate 50 percent of their students. By some estimates, 50 percent of those who enroll in college never get degrees.

18 The country is paying a terrible price for the failure of its public schools—economically and socially. Study after study has described the "mismatch" that exists between the needs of employers and the skills of available workers. The head of the Federal Reserve Bank of Boston once observed that New England's so-called economic miracle came to a grinding halt not because employers were not ready to invest in new factories but because they feared that they would not be able to find workers to run them. Yet he spoke from a city where thousands of persons are unemployed. American companies spend an estimated $20 billion a year—and colleges and universities spend billions more—on remedial education programs to teach what should have been learned years before. "Business is having to do the schools' project-recall work for them," grumbled David Kearns, the former chairman of the Xerox Corporation who joined the Bush administration as deputy secretary of education earlier this year. Louis V. Gerstner, Jr., of RJR Nabisco, Inc., was equally blunt. "Every corporate chief in the country now faces an annual crop of entrants to the labor force that every year contains a higher proportion of functional illiterates," he said. "The results of this educational drought go straight to the bottom line—lost customers, poor product quality, lost shipments, garbled paperwork."

19 The social cost is equally devastating. More than a quarter of students who start out in American high schools fail to graduate with their classes. (Given the job prospects for high school dropouts, that's the equivalent of driving 7,800 school buses a year, or 43 buses every school day—with a different group of passengers each—up to the welfare office.) Economically the 1980s was a decade when the rich got richer and the poor got poorer. Study after study has documented the widening earnings gap between the well educated and poorly educated. The Economic Policy Institute, for example, found that between 1979 and 1987 the wages of working male college graduates rose by 7 percent in real dollars while the wages of those with only a high school diploma fell by a comparable amount. We are moving toward becoming a nation of educational haves and have-nots. Such a situation may be tolerable in England or other countries where rigid class structures are the norm, but in

this country it is not only morally wrong but tantamount to planting a social time bomb.

We live in an increasingly competitive global economy, one where information is power and where, as Shoshana Zuboff of the Harvard Business School put it, "learning is the new form of labor." Samuel M. Ehrenhalt, the regional commissioner of the United States Bureau of Labor Statistics in New York, noted the "historic moment in American economic development" that occurred in the late 1980s when the number of professional, managerial, and technical workers exceeded the number of blue-collar workers for the first time. The shift ended an era that began in the early days of the twentieth century, when manual workers succeeded farm workers as the largest group of employees. "Now, three-quarters of a century later, the blue-collar preeminence is giving way to the quintessential workers of the new economy," he said. "Their stock in trade is knowledge, their working tools, above all, ideas. With the changes in the industrial structure of the 1980s, these occupations comprise the prime growth field of the American labor force." 20

Gone are the days when a young person could drop out of school and get a job with his father at the local meatpacking plant. Jobs of the future will require higher levels of mathematics, better reading skills, and a greater capacity for high-level thinking. Paul O'Neill, the chief executive officer of Alcoa, argues that American industry is, in effect, rolling back one of the fundamentals of the Industrial Revolution. "Instead of dumbing-down production, business is evolving a high-tech version of preindustrial craftsmanship," he said. "This time the artisans are using their heads, not their hands." Consider, for example, the task of repairing textile machinery. In the past a semiliterate worker could look inside a loom, see how the parts fit together, diagnose the problem, and fix it. Today the comparable machine is full of nonobservable microprocessors and other electronic equipment. To diagnose and fix the new machines, technicians must be able to represent the workings symbolically in their minds through the use of complicated manuals, diagrams, and updates provided by the manufacturer. The entire process has been moved to a higher level of abstraction—one that requires a whole different level of educational preparation. 21

In its report "A Nation Prepared: Teachers for the 21st Century," the Carnegie Forum on Education and the Econ- 22 omy, based in Rochester, New York, described what goes on at the Samsung Electronics plant outside of Seoul, Korea, which produces home video recorders for sale in the United States. The line workers at that plant, who are better educated than their American counterparts, work twelve hours a day, 363 days a year, for $3,000 a year. American firms cannot compete with the Samsungs of the world in their terms. American industry must shift its focus from rote, low-wage operations to those requiring a better-educated workforce. The choice is either to transform ourselves into a high-skill, high-wage economy or see a rapid deterioration of our standard of living. "America must leave the routine work of the world to others," says Marc Tucker, president of the National Center on Education and the Economy. "We must become a nation that thinks for a living. We must become smarter than the rest of the world."

23 The consequences of becoming a learning society are enormous, for it means that for the first time schools have been given the job of producing the *capital* on which the country depends. Yet unless drastic changes are made, American public schools are going to get worse. The fastest-growing segments of the school population are precisely those students with whom schools have been least successful in the past. Between 1970 and 1980 the proportion of minority students in American public schools rose from 21 to 27 percent, and by the year 2020 it is expected that such students will represent almost half of all students—something that has already happened in California and Texas. Between 1979 and 1983 the proportion of students living in poverty rose from 16 to 22 percent, and this, too, is projected to increase.

24 Outside pressures are making it increasingly difficult for schools even to hold their own. In its new report, "The Condition of Teaching, 1990," the Carnegie Foundation for the Advancement of Teaching provided vivid firsthand documentation of the difficulties that teachers confront. "Today's children are living with many more stresses than children of a decade or even five years ago," wrote one teacher. "Single-parent families, dual-employed parents, unemployment and teen parents have produced children with little or no coping skills, and parents are too busy, too uneducated themselves, to help." Another commented that "the quality of life for my students" is her biggest problem. "Divorce, substance abuse and plain loneliness leave stu-

dents with very little curiosity, very little interest in learning," she said. "The biggest battle I have as a teacher is getting kids to care about their own intellect." Ernest L. Boyer, president of the foundation, drew the inevitable conclusion. "The problems of society are washing over schools, dramatically distracting and even damaging the children and reducing their motivation and capacity to learn," he said. "Unless prospects for success improve, not only the schools but the very future of our nation is imperiled."

The failure of our public schools has, of course, not gone unnoticed. Largely because of the political impact of "A Nation at Risk," the 1980s was an era of feverish educational reform efforts. Legislatures and state boards of education in every state moved aggressively to tighten the course requirements for a high school diploma, raise teacher salaries, and set new standards for those entering the teaching profession. Tennessee enacted merit pay for teachers. New Jersey allowed liberal arts graduates without education degrees to become teachers. Everyone had new standardized tests—for teachers as well as students. Over the decade spending for elementary and secondary education rose by one-third. But then a funny thing happened. In April 1988, five years after "A Nation at Risk," President Reagan hosted a ceremony in the East Room of the White House to celebrate this flurry of school-reform efforts. Leading politicians and educators, as well as those in the national media who cover education, used the occasion to reflect on the accomplishments of school reform. And we came to a startling conclusion: 25

There *weren't* any. 26

To be sure, standardized reading and math scores were up slightly—but mostly in the lower grades and in the most primitive academic skills. In November 1990 the Policy Information Center of the Educational Testing Service issued a report summarizing the results of what it terms the "education reform decade" of the 1980s. The report looked at achievement test results ranging across all major curriculum areas, starting with reading, where it found "no gains in average reading proficiency." The researchers identified "some improvement" in average math proficiency, but "none at the higher level we associate with having taken several years of high school math." Not surprisingly, American students were still "bringing up the rear in science achieve- 27 ment." As for writing, the study concluded: "Our students are poor writers, and they are not improving. They don't much like to write, and they like it less as they go through school." The only big increase, the study found, came in time in front of the tube. "Television watching increased substantially in the 1980s," the researchers said. Some good news came in the form of a narrowing of the gap between seventeen-year-old black and white students. But even this good news was tempered, for the gains came "more at the basic and middle ranges . . . than at the top." At the academic level required for moving on to college, the black-white gap widened, and there was no narrowing of the chasm between whites and Hispanics. "A Nation at Risk" and the reforms associated with it had done little if anything to help the Morris Jeffersons of the world, who themselves were "at risk."

28 With the wisdom of hindsight, the reason became clear: The reforms inspired by "A Nation at Risk" contained no new ideas! They called for more of the same: more core academic courses, more standardized tests, a longer school year, more money for teachers. By the end of the 1980s it was evident that the existing system of public education had been pushed to its limits and that more of the same would not make any difference. School reformers in the 1980s tried to squeeze more juice out of the orange. It took five years to realize that we were not dealing with an orange. We were holding a lemon.

29 The reforms of the 1980s were doomed from the outset because they asked American public schools to do something they were never designed to do, never did do, and never could do. We have been asking schools to prepare students—*all* students—for demanding, fast-changing jobs of the future with rigid structures and teaching methods designed for the factories of the early industrial age. We have been asking a nineteenth-century institution to educate people for life in the twenty-first century. Public schools as currently organized are as archaic as a turn-of-the-century Model T Ford rattling down a thruway.

30 Public schools are nineteenth-century institutions because they were organized around an industrial model that prevailed at the turn of the century. Mass production sought to reduce as many elements of the manufacturing process as possible to simple, repetitive tasks that could be handled by workers who were easily trained and, for all practical

purposes, interchangeable. A relatively small group of people—perhaps 20 percent—did the thinking for the entire enterprise. Industry embraced the principles of managerial theorists of the day such as Frederick Winslow Taylor, who spoke of "scientific management" and the "one best system" to solve any organizational problem. He called for a centralized, hierarchical style of management and preached the value of standardization, a rigid sense of time, and an accountability system based on loyalty to the system. As agents of the state, public schools did their part to reinforce these values. They organized themselves to turn out a few well-trained "thinkers" and large numbers of ordinary workers with the knowledge and skills to do their own jobs. In their own functioning as educational institutions, schools also embraced the values of centralization, standardization, and bureaucratic accountability.

In recent years many of the same American companies 31
that gave birth to this old industrial model have been abandoning it. Corporations such as Ford, Xerox, and Motorola have recognized that, given the complexity of new production processes and the need to introduce new products more frequently, they must abandon the old hierarchical structures. They have decentralized and trimmed their management structures and reorganized their workplaces around teams of workers, each given responsibility for organizing and carrying out their assignments, whether they be assembling lawn mowers or processing insurance claims. They had adopted more flexible work schedules and developed new standards of quality control. To pull this off, they have poured billions of dollars into educational programs aimed at equipping workers to learn new skills, solve problems, and take a more active role in promoting the economic and other goals of the enterprise.

It is now time for schools to do the same. It is no longer 32
possible to run an effective system of public education under the old values of centralized authority, standardization, and bureaucratic accountability any more than it is possible to run *any* large institution effectively in this fashion. Moreover, the "product" that schools must turn out is changing, and the traditional structures are as ill suited to meeting the new market demands as a buggy factory would be to turning out jet aircraft. The "thinking society" of the twenty-first century can no longer be content with graduates trained to take in and recycle information handed out by

teachers and other authority figures. Today's students must be taught to think for themselves and to generate new information. But you cannot say: "We will lecture to you about how to be creative, and then we will measure your creativity with this multiple-choice test." We need a whole new approach to designing and running schools.

33 Technology has given us the concept of the "smart machine"—one that, instead of simply repeating the same operation over and over in rote fashion, is capable of receiving new information and altering its actions accordingly. The emerging global economy requires workers who are "smart" in the same sense: workers who can analyze new situations, come up with creative solutions, and take responsibility for decisions relating to the performance of their jobs. The functioning of a modern democracy requires citizens with similar skills, and to produce "smart" workers and "smart" citizens, we need "smart" schools and "smart" kids.

34 This transformation of American public schools from nineteenth-century institutions into schools that reflect the values of twenty-first-century economic, political, and social life is well under way. Teachers, administrators, parents, and political leaders are questioning the old way of doing things. Although full-fledged smart schools do not yet exist, every one of the ingredients for creating them—new ways of managing school systems, running schools, organizing classrooms, using time, measuring results, and so forth—exists somewhere in the United States. Somewhere some public school or group of teachers within a school is turning every one of the elements of the factory-model school on its head. Thus far, most of these modern-day Horace Manns are working in isolation, and by themselves none of their new ideas is powerful enough to transform American public schools. But put together, these bold experiments can bring about the smart schools that American students need if they are to be prepared for the twenty-first century.

A selection from his popular collection School is Hell *(1987), this cartoon by Matt Groening (born 1954) captures some of the feelings students associate with high school. Groening also developed the television series "The Simpsons." For another example of his work,* *see page 452.*

Jerome Stern

What They Learn in School

Jerome Stern teaches English at Florida State University. This "monologue" aired March 17, 1989 on National Public Radio's "All Things Considered." It was later reprinted in Harper's *magazine.*

1 In the schools now, they want them to know all about marijuana, crack, heroin, and amphetamines,
2 Because then they won't be interested in marijuana, crack, heroin, and amphetamines,
3 But they don't want to tell them anything about sex because if the schools tell them about sex, then they will be interested in sex,
4 But if the schools don't tell them anything about sex,
5 Then they will have high morals and no one will get pregnant, and everything will be all right,
6 And they do want them to know a lot about computers so they will outcompete the Japanese,
7 But they don't want them to know anything about real science because then they will lose their faith and become secular humanists,
8 And they do want them to know all about this great land of ours so they will be patriotic,
9 But they don't want them to learn about the tragedy and pain in its real history because then they will be critical about this great land of ours and we will be passively taken over by a foreign power,
10 And they want them to learn how to think for themselves so they can get good jobs and be successful,
11 But they don't want them to have books that confront them with real ideas because that will confuse their values,
12 And they'd like them to be good parents,
13 But they can't teach them about families because that takes them back to how you get to be a family,
14 And they want to warn them about how not to get AIDS
15 But that would mean telling them how not to get AIDS,
16 And they'd like them to know the Constitution,
17 But they don't like some of those amendments except when they are invoked by the people they agree with,
18 And they'd like them to vote,

But they don't want them to discuss current events because 19
it might be controversial and upset them and make them
want to take drugs, which they already have told them all
about,

And they want to teach them the importance of morality, 20

But they also want them to learn that Winning is not 21
everything—it is the Only Thing,

And they want them to be well-read, 22

But they don't want them to read Chaucer or Shakespeare or 23
Aristophanes or Mark Twain or Ernest Hemingway or
John Steinbeck, because that will corrupt them,

And they don't want them to know anything about art 24
because that will make them weird,

But they do want them to know about music so they can 25
march in the band,

And they mainly want to teach them not to question, not to 26
challenge, not to imagine, but to be obedient and behave
well so that they can hold them forever as children to their
bosoms as the second millennium lurches toward its
panicky close.

WHAT'S COLLEGE FOR?

Alice Walker
Everyday Use
for your grandmama

Alice Walker (born 1944) is an essayist, poet, feminist, and activist, but she is best known for her Pulitzer-Prize-winning third novel The Color Purple *(1982). Asked why she writes, she once explained, "I'm really paying homage to people I love, the people who are thought to be dumb and backward but who were the ones who first taught me to see beauty." "Everyday Use" appeared in her acclaimed collection of stories,* In Love and Trouble, *published in 1973.*

1 I will wait for her in the yard that Maggie and I made so clean and wavy yesterday afternoon. A yard like this is more comfortable than most people know. It is not just a yard. It is like an extended living room. When the hard clay is swept clean as a floor and the fine sand around the edges lined with tiny, irregular grooves anyone can come and sit and look up into the elm tree and wait for the breezes that never come inside the house.

2 Maggie will be nervous until after her sister goes: she will stand hopelessly in corners homely and ashamed of the burn scars down her arms and legs, eyeing her sister with a mixture of envy and awe. She thinks her sister has held life always in the palm of one hand, that "no" is a word the world never learned to say to her.

3 You've not doubt seen those TV shows where the child who has "made it" is confronted, as a surprise, by her own mother and father, tottering in weakly from backstage. (A pleasant surprise, of course: What would they do if parent and child came on the show only to curse out and insult each other?) On TV mother and child embrace and smile

into each other's faces. Sometimes the mother and father weep, the child wraps them in her arms and leans across the table to tell how she would not have made it without their help. I have seen these programs.

Sometimes I dream a dream in which Dee and I are suddenly brought together on a TV program of this sort. Out of a dark and soft-seated limousine I am ushered into a bright room filled with many people. There I meet a smiling, gray, sporty man like Johnny Carson who shakes my hand and tells me what a fine girl I have. Then we are on the stage and Dee is embracing me with tears in her eyes. She pins on my dress a large orchid, even though she has told me once that she thinks orchids are tacky flowers. 4

In real life I am a large, big-boned woman with rough, man-working hands. In the winter I wear flannel nightgowns to bed and overalls during the day. I can kill and clean a hog as mercilessly as a man. My fat keeps me hot in zero weather. I can work outside all day, breaking ice to get water for washing; I can eat pork liver cooked over the open fire minutes after it comes steaming from the hog. One winter I knocked a bull calf straight in the brain between the eyes with a sledge hammer and had the meat hung up to chill before nightfall. But of course all this does not show on television. I am the way my daughter would want me to be: a hundred pounds lighter, my skin like an uncooked barley pancake. My hair glistens in the hot bright lights. Johnny Carson has much to do to keep up with my quick and witty tongue. 5

But that is a mistake. I know even before I wake up. Who ever knew a Johnson with a quick tongue? Who can even imagine me looking a strange white man in the eye? It seems to me I have talked to them always with one foot raised in flight, and my head turned in whichever way is farthest from them. Dee, though. She would always look anyone in the eye. Hesitation was no part of her nature. 6

"How do I look, Mama?" Maggie says, showing just enough of her thin body enveloped in pink skirt and red blouse for me to know she's there, almost hidden by the door. 7

"Come out into the yard," I say. 8

Have you ever seen a lame animal, perhaps a dog run over by some careless person rich enough to own a car, sidle up to someone who is ignorant enough to be kind to him? That 9 is the way my Maggie walks. She has been like this, chin on chest, eyes on ground, feet in shuffle, ever since the fire that burned the other house to the ground.

10 Dee is lighter than Maggie, with nicer hair and a fuller figure. She's a woman now, though sometimes I forget. How long ago was it that the other house burned? Ten, twelve years? Sometimes I can still hear the flames and feel Maggie's arms sticking to me, her hair smoking and her dress falling off her in little black papery flakes. Her eyes seemed stretched open, blazed open by the flames reflected in them. And Dee. I see her standing off under the sweet gum tree she used to dig gum out of: a look of concentration on her face as she watched the last dingy gray board of the house fall in toward the red-hot brick chimney. Why don't you do a dance around the ashes? I'd wanted to ask her. She hated the house that much.

11 I used to think she hated Maggie, too. But that was before we raised the money, the church and me, to send her to Augusta to school. She used to read to us without pity; forcing words, lies, other folks' habits, whole lives upon us two, sitting trapped and ignorant underneath her voice. She washed us in a river of make-believe, burned us with a lot of knowledge we didn't necessarily need to know. Pressed us to her with the serious way she read, to shove us away at just the moment, like dimwits, we seemed about to understand.

12 Dee wanted nice things. A yellow organdy dress to wear to her graduation from high school; black pumps to match a green suit she'd made from an old suit somebody gave me. She was determined to stare down any disaster in her efforts. Her eyelids would not flicker for minutes at a time. Often I fought off the temptation to shake her. At sixteen she had a style of her own: and knew what style was.

13 I never had an education myself. After second grade the school was closed down. Don't ask me why: in 1927 colored asked fewer questions than they do now. Sometimes Maggie reads to me. She stumbles along good-naturedly but can't see well. She knows she is not bright. Like good looks and money, quickness passed her by. She will marry John Thomas (who has mossy teeth in an earnest face) and then I'll be free to sit here and I guess just sing church songs to myself. Although I never was a good singer. Never could carry a tune. I was always better at a man's job. I used to love to milk till I was hooked in the side in '49. Cows are

soothing and slow and don't bother you, unless you try to milk them the wrong way.

I have deliberately turned my back on the house. It is three rooms, just like the one that burned, except the roof is tin; they don't make shingle roofs anymore. There are no real windows, just some holes cut in the sides, like the portholes in a ship, but not round and not square, with rawhide holding the shutters up on the outside. This house is in a pasture, too, like the other one. No doubt when Dee sees it she will want to tear it down. She wrote me once that no matter where we "choose" to live, she will manage to come see us. But she will never bring her friends. Maggie and I thought about this and Maggie asked me, "Mama, when did Dee ever *have* any friends?" 14

She had a few. Furtive boys in pink shirts hanging about on washday after school. Nervous girls who never laughed. Impressed with her they worshiped the well-turned phrase, the cute shape, the scalding humor that erupted like bubbles in lye. She read to them. 15

When she was courting Jimmy T she didn't have much time to pay to us, but turned all her faultfinding power on him. He *flew* to marry a cheap gal from a family of ignorant flashy people. She hardly had time to recompose herself. 16

When she comes I will meet—but there they are! 17

Maggie attempts to make a dash for the house, in her shuffling way, but I stay her with my hand. "Come back here," I say. And she stops and tries to dig a well in the sand with her toe. 18

It is hard to see them clearly through the strong sun. But even the first glimpse of leg out of the car tells me it is Dee. Her feet were always neat-looking, as if God himself had shaped them with a certain style. From the other side of the car comes a short, stocky man. Hair is all over his head a foot long and hanging from his chin like a kinky mule tail. I hear Maggie suck in her breath. "Uhnnnh," is what it sounds like. Like when you see the wriggling end of a snake just in front of your foot on the road. "Uhnnnh." 19

Dee next. A dress down to the ground, in this hot weather. A dress so loud it hurts my eyes. There are yellows and oranges enough to throw back the light of the sun. I feel my whole face warming from the heat waves it throws out. Earrings gold, too, and hanging down to her shoulders. Bracelets dangling and making noises when she moves her 20 arm up to shake the folds of the dress out of her armpits. The dress is loose and flows, and as she walks closer, I like it. I hear Maggie go "Uhnnnh" again. It is her sister's hair. It stands straight up like the wool on a sheep. It is black as night and around the edges are two long pigtails that rope about like small lizards disappearing behind the ears.

21 "Wa-su-zo-Tean-o!" she says, coming on in that gliding way the dress makes her move. The short stocky fellow with the hair to his navel is all grinning and he follows up with "Asalamalakim, my mother and sister!" He moves to hug Maggie but she falls back, right up against the back of my chair. I feel her trembling there and when I look up I see the perspiration falling off her chin.

22 "Don't get up," says Dee. Since I am stout it takes something of a push. You can see me trying to move a second or two before I make it. She turns, showing white heels through her sandals, and goes back to the car. Out she peeks next with a Polaroid. She stoops down quickly and lines up picture after picture of me sitting there in front of the house with Maggie cowering behind me. She never takes a shot without making sure the house is included. When a cow comes nibbling around the edge of the yard she snaps it and me and Maggie *and* the house. Then she puts the Polaroid in the back seat of the car, and comes up and kisses me on the forehead.

23 Meanwhile Asalamalakim is going through the motions with Maggie's hand. Maggie's hand is as limp as a fish, and probably as cold, despite the sweat, and she keeps trying to pull it back. It looks like Asalamalakim wants to shake hands but wants to do it fancy. Or maybe he don't know how people shake hands. Anyhow, he soon gives up on Maggie.

24 "Well," I say. "Dee."

25 "No, Mama," she says. "Not 'Dee,' Wangero Leewanika Kemanjo!"

26 "What happened to 'Dee'?" I wanted to know.

27 "She's dead." Wangero said. "I couldn't bear it any longer being named after the people who oppress me."

28 "You know as well as me you was named after your aunt Dicie," I said. Dicie is my sister. She named Dee. We called her "Big Dee" after Dee was born.

29 "But who was *she* named after?" asked Wangero.

30 "I guess after Grandma Dee," I said.

31 "And who was she named after?" asked Wangero.

32 "Her mother," I said, and saw Wangero was getting tired.

"That's about as far back as I can trace it," I said. Though, in fact, I probably could have carried it back beyond the Civil War through the branches.

"Well," said Asalamalakim, "there you are." 33

"Uhnnnh," I heard Maggie say. 34

"There I was not," I said, "before 'Dicie' cropped up in our family, so why should I try to trace it that far back?" 35

He just stood there grinning, looking down on me like somebody inspecting a Model A car. Every once in a while he and Wangero sent eye signals over my head. 36

"How do you pronounce this name?" I asked. 37

"You don't have to call me by it if you don't want to," said Wangero. 38

"Why shouldn't I?" I asked. "If that's what you want us to call you, we'll call you." 39

"I know it might sound awkward at first," said Wangero. 40

"I'll get used to it," I said. "Ream it out again." 41

Well, soon we got the name out of the way. Asalamalakim had a name twice as long and three times as hard. After I tripped over it two or three times he told me to just call him Hakim-a-barber. I wanted to ask him was he a barber, but I didn't really think he was, so I didn't ask. 42

"You must belong to those beef-cattle peoples down the road," I said. They said "Asalamalakim" when they met you, too, but they didn't shake hands. Always too busy: feeding the cattle, fixing the fences, putting up salt-lick shelters, throwing down hay. When the white folks poisoned some of the herd the men stayed up all night with rifles in their hands. I walked a mile and a half just to see the sight. 43

Hakim-a-barber said, "I accept some of their doctrines, but farming and raising cattle is not my style." (They didn't tell me, and I didn't ask, whether Wangero [Dee] had really gone and married him.) 44

We sat down to eat and right away he said he didn't eat collards and pork was unclean. Wangero, though, went on through the chitlins and corn bread, the greens and everything else. She talked a blue streak over the sweet potatoes. Everything delighted her. Even the fact that we still used the benches her daddy made for the table when we couldn't afford to buy chairs. 45

"Oh, Mama!" she cried. Then turned to Hakim-a-barber. "I never knew how lovely these benches are. You can feel the rump prints," she said, running her hands underneath her and along the bench. Then she gave a sigh and her hand 46 closed over Grandma Dee's butter dish. "That's it!" she said. "I knew there was something I wanted to ask you if I could have." She jumped up from the table and went over in the corner where the churn stood, the milk in it clabber by now. She looked at the churn and looked at it.

47 "This churn top is what I need," she said. "Didn't Uncle Buddy whittle it out of a tree you all used to have?"

48 "Yes," I said.

49 "Uh huh," she said happily. "And I want the dasher, too."

50 "Uncle Buddy whittle that, too?" asked the barber.

51 Dee (Wangero) looked up at me.

52 "Aunt Dee's first husband whittle the dash," said Maggie so low you almost couldn't hear her. "His name was Henry, but they called him Stash."

53 "Maggie's brain is like an elephant's," Wangero said, laughing. "I can use the churn top as a centerpiece for the alcove table," she said, sliding a plate over the churn, "and I'll think of something artistic to do with the dasher."

54 When she finished wrapping the dasher the handle stuck out. I took it for a moment in my hands. You didn't even have to look close to see where hands pushing the dasher up and down to make butter had left a kind of sink in the wood. In fact, there were a lot of small sinks; you could see where thumbs and fingers had sunk into the wood. It was beautiful light yellow wood, from a tree that grew in the yard where Big Dee and Stash had lived.

55 After dinner Dee (Wangero) went to the trunk at the foot of my bed and started rifling through it. Maggie hung back in the kitchen over the dishpan. Out came Wangero with two quilts. They had been pieced by Grandma Dee and then Big Dee and me had hung them on the quilt frames on the front porch and quilted them. One was in the Lone Star pattern. The other was Walk Around the Mountain. In both of them were scraps of dresses Grandma Dee had worn fifty and more years ago. Bits and pieces of Grandpa Jarrell's Paisley shirts. And one teeny faded blue piece, about the size of a penny matchbox, that was from Great Grandpa Ezra's uniform that he wore in the Civil War.

56 "Mama," Wangero said sweet as a bird. "Can I have these old quilts?"

57 I heard something fall in the kitchen, and a minute later the kitchen door slammed.

58 "Why don't you take one or two of the others?" I asked.

"These old things was just done by me and Big Dee from some tops your grandma pieced before she died."

"No," said Wangero. "I don't want those. They are stitched 59
around the borders by machine."

"That'll make them last better," I said. 60

"That's not the point," said Wangero. "These are all pieces 61
of dresses Grandma used to wear. She did all this stitching by hand. Imagine!" She held the quilts securely in her arms, stroking them.

"Some of the pieces, like those lavender ones, come from 62
old clothes her mother handed down to her," I said, moving up to touch the quilts. Dee (Wangero) moved back just enough so that I couldn't reach the quilts. They already belonged to her.

"Imagine!" she breathed again, clutching them closely to 63
her bosom.

"The truth is," I said, "I promised to give them quilts to 64
Maggie, for when she marries John Thomas."

She gasped like a bee had stung her. 65

"Maggie can't appreciate these quilts!" she said. "She'd 66
probably be backward enough to put them to everyday use."

"I reckon she would," I said. "God knows I been saving 'em 67
for long enough with nobody using 'em. I hope she will!" I didn't want to bring up how I had offered Dee (Wangero) a quilt when she went away to college. Then she had told me they were old-fashioned, out of style.

"But they're *priceless!*" she was saying now, furiously; for 68
she has a temper. "Maggie would put them on the bed and in five years they'd be in rags. Less than that!"

"She can always make some more," I said. "Maggie knows 69
how to quilt."

Dee (Wangero) looked at me with hatred. "You just will 70
not understand. The point is these quilts, *these* quilts!"

"Well," I said, stumped. "What would *you* do with them?" 71

"Hang them," she said. As if that was the only thing you 72
could do with quilts.

Maggie by now was standing in the door. I could almost 73
hear the sound her feet made as they scraped over each other.

"She can have them, Mama," she said, like somebody used 74
to never winning anything, or having anything reserved for her. "I can 'member Grandma Dee without the quilts."

I looked at her hard. She had filled her bottom lip with 75

checkerberry snuff and it gave her face a kind of dopey, hangdog look. It was Grandma Dee and Big Dee who taught her how to quilt herself. She stood there with her scarred hands hidden in the folds of her skirt. She looked at her sister with something like fear but she wasn't mad at her. This was Maggie's portion. This was the way she knew God to work.

76 When I looked at her like that something hit me in the top of my head and ran down to the soles of my feet. Just like when I'm in church and the spirit of God touches me and I get happy and shout. I did something I never had done before: hugged Maggie to me, then dragged her on into the room, snatched the quilts out of Miss Wangero's hands and dumped them into Maggie's lap. Maggie just sat there on my bed with her mouth open.

77 "Take one or two of the others," I said to Dee.

78 But she turned without a word and went out to Hakim-a-barber.

79 "You just don't understand," she said, as Maggie and I came out to the car.

80 "What don't I understand?" I wanted to know.

81 "Your heritage," she said. And then she turned to Maggie, kissed her, and said, "You ought to try to make something of yourself, too, Maggie. It's really a new day for us. But from the way you and Mama still live you'd never know it."

82 She put on some sunglasses that hid everything above the tip of her nose and her chin.

83 Maggie smiled; maybe at the sunglasses. But a real smile, not scared. After we watched the car dust settle I asked Maggie to bring me a dip of snuff. And then the two of us sat there just enjoying, until it was time to go in the house and go to bed.

bell hooks

Pedagogy and Political Commitment: A Comment

bell hooks teaches at Oberlin College in Ohio. You will learn more about her by reading the following essay, which is a chapter in her book Talking Back: Thinking Feminist, Thinking Black *(1989), one of her five books on race, gender, politics, and culture.*

Education is a political issue for exploited and oppressed people. The history of slavery in the United States shows that black people regarded education—book learning, reading, and writing—as a political necessity. Struggle to resist white supremacy and racist attacks informed black attitudes toward education. Without the capacity to read and write, to think critically and analytically, the liberated slave would remain forever bound, dependent on the will of the oppressor. No aspect of black liberation struggled in the United States has been as charged with revolutionary fervor as the effort to gain access to education at all levels. 1

From slavery to the present, education has been revered in black communities, yet it has also been suspect. Education represented a means of radical resistance but it also led to caste/class divisions between the educated and the uneducated, as it meant the learned black person could more easily adopt the values and attitudes of the oppressor. Education could help one assimilate. If one could not become the white oppressor, one could at least speak and think like him or her, and in some cases the educated black person assumed the role of mediator—explaining uneducated black folks to white folks. 2

Given this history, many black parents have encouraged children to acquire an education while simultaneously warning us about the danger of education. One very real danger, as many black parents traditionally perceived it, was that the learned black person might lose touch with the concrete reality of everyday black experience. Books and ideas were important but not important enough to become barriers between the individual and community participation. Education was considered to have the potential to 3 alienate one from community and awareness of our collective circumstance as black people. In my family, it was constantly emphasized that too much book learning could lead to madness. Among everyday black folks, madness was deemed to be any loss of one's ability to communicate effectively with others, one's ability to cope with practical affairs.

4 These ambivalent attitudes toward education have made it difficult for black students to adapt and succeed in educational settings. Many of us have found that to succeed at the very education we had been encouraged to seek would be most easily accomplished if we separated ourselves from the experience of black folk, the underprivileged experience of the black underclass that was our grounding reality. This ambivalent stance toward education has had a tremendous impact on my psyche. Within the working-class black community where I grew up, I learned to be suspicious of education and suspicious of white folks. I went for my formative educational years to all-black schools. In those schools, I learned about the reality of white people but also about the reality of black people, about our history. We were taught in those schools to be proud of ourselves as black people and to work for the uplift of our race.

5 Experiencing as I did an educational environment structured to meet our needs as black people, we were deeply affected when those schools ceased to exist and we were compelled to attend white schools instead. At the white school, we were no longer people with a history, a culture. We did not exist as anything other than primitives and slaves. School was no longer the place where one learned how to use education as a means to resist white-supremacist oppression. Small wonder that I spent my last few years of high school depressed about education, feeling as though we had suffered a grave loss, that the direction had shifted, the goals had changed. We were no longer taught by people who spoke our language, who understood our culture; we were taught by strangers. And further, we were dependent on those strangers for evaluation, for approval. We learned not to challenge their racism since they had power over us. Although we were told at home that we were not to openly challenge whites, we were also told not to learn to think like them.

6 Within this atmosphere of ambivalence toward education, I, who had been dubbed smart, was uncertain about whether

or not I wanted to go to college. School was an oppressive drag. Yet the fate of smart black women had already been decided; we would be schoolteachers. At the private, mostly white women's college where I spent my first year, I was an outsider. Determined to stay grounded in the reality of southern black culture, I kept myself aloof from the social practices of the white women with whom I lived and studied. They, in their turn, perceived me as hostile and alien. I, who had always been a member of a community, was now a loner. One of my white teachers suggested to me that the alienation I experienced was caused by being at a school that was not intellectually challenging, that I should go to Stanford where she had gone.

My undergraduate years at Stanford were difficult ones. 7
Not only did I feel myself alienated from the white people who were my peers and teachers, but I met black people who were different, who did not think the way I did about black culture or black life—who seemed in some ways as strange to me as white people. I had known black people from different classes in my hometown, but we still experienced much the same reality, shared similar world views. It was different at Stanford. I was in an environment where black people's class backgrounds and their values were radically different than my own.

To overcome my feelings of isolation, I bonded with 8
workers, with black women who labored as maids, as secretaries. With them I felt at home. During holiday break, I would stay in their homes. Yet being with them was not the same as being home. In their houses I was an honored guest, someone to be looked up to, because I was getting a college education. My undergraduate years at Stanford were spent struggling to find meaning and significance in education. I had to succeed. I could not let my family or the race down. And so I graduated in English. I had become an English major for the same reason that hundreds of students of all races become English majors: I like to read. Yet I did not fully understand that the study of literature in English departments would really mean the study of works by white males.

It was disheartening for me and other non-white students 9
to face the extent to which education in the university was not the site of openness and intellectual challenge we had longed for. We hated the racism, the sexism, the domination. I began to have grave doubts about the future. Why was I

working to be an academic if I did not see people in that environment who were opposing domination? Even those very few concerned professors who endeavored to make courses interesting, to create a learning atmosphere, rarely acknowledged destructive and oppressive aspects of authoritarian rule in and outside the classroom. Whether one took courses from professors with feminist politics or marxist politics, their presentations of self in the classroom never differed from the norm. This was especially so with marxist professors. I asked one of these professors, a white male, how he could expect students to take his politics seriously as a radical alternative to a capitalist structure if we found marxist professors to be even more oppressively authoritarian than other professors. Everyone seemed reluctant to talk about the fact that professors who advocated radical politics rarely allowed their critique of domination and oppression to influence teaching strategies. The absence of any model of a professor who was combining a radical politic opposing domination with practice of that politic in the classroom made me feel wary about my ability to do differently. When I first began to teach, I tried not to emulate my professors in any way. I devised different strategies and approaches that I felt were more in keeping with my politics. Reading the work of Paulo Freire greatly influenced my sense that much was possible in the classroom setting, that one did not simply need to conform.

10 In the introduction to a conversation with Paulo Freire published in *idac*, emphasis is placed on an educative process that is not based on an authoritarian, dominating model where knowledge is transferred from a powerful professor to a powerless student. Education, it was suggested, could be a space for the development of critical consciousness, where there could be dialogue and mutual growth of both student and professor:

> If we accept education in this richer and more dynamic sense of acquiring a critical capacity and intervention in reality, we immediately know that there is no such thing as neutral education. All education has an intention, a goal, which can only be political. Either it mystifies reality by rendering it impenetrable and obscure—which leads people to a blind march through incomprehensible labyrinths—or it unmasks the economic and social structures which are determining the relationships of exploitation and oppression among per-

> sons, knocking down labyrinths and allowing people to walk their own road. So we find ourselves confronted with a clear option: to educate for liberation or to educate for domination.

In retrospect, it seems that my most radical professors were still educating for domination. And I wondered if this was so because we could not imagine how to educate for liberation in the corporate university. In Freire's case, he speaks as a white man of privilege who stands and acts in solidarity with oppressed and exploited groups, especially in their efforts to establish literacy programs that emphasize education for critical consciousness. In my case, as a black woman from a working-class background, I stand and act as a member of an oppressed, exploited group who has managed to acquire a degree of privilege. While I choose to educate for liberation, the site of my work has been within the walls of universities peopled largely by privileged white students and a few non-white students. Within those walls, I have tried to teach literature and Women's Studies courses in a way that does not reinforce structures of domination: imperialism, racism, sexism, and class exploitation.

I do not pretend that my approach is politically neutral, 11
yet this disturbs students who have been led to believe that all education within the university should be "neutral." On the first day of classes, I talk about my approach, about the ways the class may be different from other classes as we work to create strategies of learning to meet our needs—and of course we must discover together what those needs are. Even though I explain that the class will be different, students do not always take it seriously. One central difference is that all students are expected to contribute to class discussion, if not spontaneously, then through the reading of paragraphs and short papers. In this way, every student makes a contribution, every student's voice is heard. Despite the fact that this may be stated at the onset of class, written clearly on the syllabus, students will complain and whine about having to speak. It is only recently that I have begun to see much of the complaining as "change back" behavior. Students and teachers find it hard to shift their paradigms even though they have been longing for a different approach.

Struggling to educate for liberation in the corporate 12
university is a process that I have found enormously stressful. Implementing new teaching strategies that aim to sub-

vert the norm, to engage students fully, is really a difficult task. Unlike the oppressed or colonized, who may begin to feel as they engage in education for critical consciousness a newfound sense of power and identity that frees them from colonization of the mind, that liberates, privileged students are often downright unwilling to acknowledge that their minds have been colonized, that they have been learning how to be oppressors, how to dominate, or at least how to passively accept the domination of others. This past teaching year, a student confronted me (a black male student from a middle-class urban experience) in class with the question of what I expected from them (like his tone of voice was: did I have the right to expect anything). Seriously, he wanted to know what I wanted from them. I told him and the class that I thought the most important learning experience that could happen in our classroom was that students would learn to think critically and analytically, not just about the required books, but about the world they live in. Education for critical consciousness that encourages all students—privileged or non-privileged—who are seeking an entry into class privilege rather than providing a sense of freedom and release, invites critique of conventional expectations and desires. They may find such an experience terribly threatening. And even though they may approach the situation with great openness, it may still be difficult, and even painful.

13 This past semester, I taught a course on black women writers in which students were encouraged to think about the social context in which literature emerges, the impact of politics of domination—racism, sexism, class exploitation—on the writing. Students stated quite openly and honestly that reading the literature in the context of class discussion was making them feel pain. They complained that everything was changing for them, that they were seeing the world differently, and seeing things in that world that were painful to face. Never before had a group of students so openly talked about the way in which learning to see the world critically was causing pain. I did not belittle their pain or try to rationalize it. Initially, I was uncertain about how to respond and just asked us all to think about it. Later, we discussed the way in which all their comments implied that to experience pain is bad, an indication that something is wrong. We talked about changing how we perceive pain, about our society's approach to pain, consid-

ering the possibility that this pain could be a constructive sign of growth. I shared with them my sense that the experience should not be viewed as static, that at another point the knowledge and new perspectives they had might lead to clarity and a greater sense of well-being.

Education for liberation can work in the university setting 14
but it does not lead students to feel they are enjoying class or necessarily feeling positive about me as a teacher. One aspect of radical pedagogy that has been difficult for me is learning to cope with not being seen positively by students. When one provides an experience of learning that is challenging, possibly threatening, it is not entertainment, or necessarily a fun experience, though it can be. If one primary function of such a pedagogy is to prepare students to live and act more fully in the world, then it is usually when they are in that context, outside the classroom, that they most feel and experience the value of what they have shared and learned. For me, this often means that most positive feedback I receive as a teacher comes after students have left the class and rarely during it.

Recently talking with a group of students and faculty at 15
Duke University, we focussed on the issue of exposure and vulnerability. One white male professor, who felt his politics to be radical, his teaching to be an education for liberation, his teaching strategies subversive, felt it was important that no one in the university's bureaucratic structure know what was happening in the classroom. Fear of exposure may lead teachers with radical visions to suppress insight, to follow set norms. Until I came to teach at Yale, no one outside my classes had paid much attention to what was going on inside them. At Yale, students talked a lot outside about my classes, about what happens in them. This was very difficult for me as I felt both exposed and constantly scrutinized. I was certainly subjected to much critical feedback both from students in my classes and faculty and students who heard about them. Their responses forced recognition of the way in which teaching that is overtly political, especially if it radically challenges the status quo, requires acknowledgement that to choose education as the practice of freedom is to take a political stance that may have serious consequences.

Despite negative feedback or pressures, the most reward- 16
ing aspect of such teaching is to influence the way students mature and grow intellectually and spiritually. For those

students who wish to try to learn in a new way but who have fears, I try to reassure them that their involvement in different types of learning experiences need not threaten their security in other classes; it will not destroy the backing system of education, so they need not panic. Of course, if all they can do is panic, then that is a sign that the course is not for them. My commitment to education as the practice of freedom is strengthened by the large number of students who take my courses and, by doing so, affirm their longing to learn in a new way. Their testimony confirms that education as the practice of liberation does take place in university settings, that our lives are transformed there, that there we do meaningful radical political work.

Adrienne Rich

Claiming an Education

"Claiming an Education" is the transcript of a talk first given to new students at Douglass College, the Women's College of Rutgers University, on September 6, 1977; later it was included in Adrienne Rich's book On Lies, Secrets, and Silence. *Rich (born 1929) is a noted teacher, essayist, and feminist who won the National Book Award for poetry in 1974.*

1 For this convocation, I planned to separate my remarks into two parts: some thoughts about you, the women students here, and some thoughts about us who teach in a women's college. But ultimately, those two parts are indivisible. If university education means anything beyond the processing of human beings into expected roles, through credit hours, tests, and grades (and I believe that in a women's college especially it *might* mean much more), it implies an ethical and intellectual contract between teacher and student. This contract must remain intuitive, dynamic, unwritten; but we must turn to it again and again if learning is to be reclaimed from the depersonalizing and cheapening pressures of the present-day academic scene.

2 The first thing I want to say to you who are students is

that you cannot afford to think of being here to *receive* an education; you will do much better to think of yourselves as being here to *claim* one. One of the dictionary definitions of the verb "to claim" is: *to take as the rightful owner; to assert in the face of possible contradiction.* "To receive" is *to come into possession of; to act as receptacle or container for; to accept as authoritative or true.* The difference is that between acting and being acted-upon, and for women it can literally mean the difference between life and death.

One of the devastating weaknesses of university learning, of the store of knowledge and opinion that has been handed down through academic training, has been its almost total erasure of women's experience and thought from the curriculum, and its exclusion of women as members of the academic community. Today, with increasing numbers of women students in nearly every branch of higher learning, we still see very few women in the upper levels of faculty and administration in most institutions. Douglass College itself is a women's college in a university administered overwhelmingly by men, who in turn are answerable to the state legislature, again composed predominantly of men. But the most significant fact for you is that what you learn here, the very texts you read, the lectures you hear, the way your studies are divided into categories and fragmented one from the other—all this reflects, to a very large degree, neither objective reality, nor an accurate picture of the past, nor a group of rigorously tested observations about human behavior. What you can learn here (and I mean not only at Douglass but any college in any university) is how *men* have perceived and organized their experience, their history, their ideas of social relationships, good and evil, sickness and health, etc. When you read or hear about "great issues," "major texts," "the mainstream of Western thought," you are hearing about what men, above all white men, in their male subjectivity, have decided is important. 3

Black and other minority people have for some time recognized that their racial and ethnic experience was not accounted for in the studies broadly labeled human; and that even the sciences can be racist. For many reasons, it has been more difficult for women to comprehend our exclusion, and to realize that even the sciences can be sexist. For one thing, it is only within the last hundred years that higher education has grudgingly been opened up to women at all, even to white, middle-class women. And many of us have 4 found ourselves poring eagerly over books with titles like: *The Descent of Man; Man and His Symbols; Irrational Man; The Phenomenon of Man; The Future of Man; Man and the Machine; From Man to Man; May Man Prevail?; Man, Science and Society;* or *One-Dimensional Man*—books pretending to describe a "human" reality that does not include over one-half the human species.

5 Less than a decade ago, with the rebirth of a feminist movement in this country, women students and teachers in a number of universities began to demand and set up women's studies courses—to *claim* a woman-directed education. And, despite the inevitable accusations of "unscholarly," "group therapy," "faddism," etc., despite backlash and budget cuts, women's studies are still growing, offering to more and more women a new intellectual grasp on their lives, new understanding of our history, a fresh vision of the human experience, and also a critical basis for evaluating what they hear and read in other courses, and in the society at large.

6 But my talk is not really about women's studies, much as I believe in their scholarly, scientific, and human necessity. While I think that any Douglass student has everything to gain by investigating and enrolling in women's studies courses, I want to suggest that there is a more essential experience that you owe yourself, one which courses in women's studies can greatly enrich, but which finally depends on you, in all your interactions with yourself and your world. This is the experience of *taking responsibility toward yourself*. Our upbringing as women has so often told us that this should come second to our relationships and responsibilities to other people. We have been offered ethical models of the self-denying wife and mother; intellectual models of the brilliant but slapdash dilettante who never commits herself to anything the whole way, or the intelligent woman who denies her intelligence in order to seem more "feminine," or who sits in passive silence even when she disagrees inwardly with everything that is being said around her.

7 Responsibility to yourself means refusing to let others do your thinking, talking, and naming for you; it means learning to respect and use your own brains and instincts; hence, grappling with hard work. It means that you do not treat your body as a commodity with which to purchase superficial intimacy or economic security; for our bodies and minds are inseparable in this life, and when we allow our

bodies to be treated as objects, our minds are in mortal danger. It means insisting that those to whom you give your friendship and love are able to respect your mind. It means being able to say, with Charlotte Brontë's *Jane Eyre:* "I have an inward treasure born with me, which can keep me alive if all the extraneous delights should be withheld or offered only at a price I cannot afford to give."

Responsibility to yourself means that you don't fall for shallow and easy solutions—predigested books and ideas, weekend encounters guaranteed to change your life, taking "gut" courses instead of ones you know will challenge you, bluffing at school and life instead of doing solid work, marrying early as an escape from real decisions, getting pregnant as an evasion of already existing problems. It means that you refuse to sell your talents and aspirations short, simply to avoid conflict and confrontation. And this, in turn, means resisting the forces in society which say that women should be nice, play safe, have low professional expectations, drown in love and forget about work, live through others, and stay in the places assigned to us. It means that we insist on a life of meaningful work, insist that work be as meaningful as love and friendship in our lives. It means, therefore, the courage to be "different"; not to be continuously available to others when we need time for ourselves and our work; to be able to demand of others—parents, friends, roommates, teachers, lovers, husbands, children—that they respect our sense of purpose and our integrity as persons. Women everywhere are finding the courage to do this, more and more, and we are finding that courage both in our study of women in the past who possessed it, and in each other as we look at other women for comradeship, community, and challenge. The difference between a life lived actively, and a life of passive drifting and dispersal of energies, is an immense difference. Once we begin to feel committed to our lives, responsible to ourselves, we can never again be satisfied with the old, passive way. 8

Now comes the second part of the contract. I believe that in a women's college you have the right to expect your faculty to take you seriously. The education of women has been a matter of debate for centuries, and old, negative attitudes about women's role, women's ability to think and take leadership, are still rife both in and outside the university. Many male professors (and I don't mean only at 9

Douglass) still feel that teaching in a women's college is a second-rate career. Many tend to eroticize their women students—to treat them as sexual objects—instead of demanding the best of their minds. (At Yale a legal suit [*Alexander* v. *Yale*] has been brought against the university by a group of women students demanding a stated policy against sexual advances toward female students by male professors.) Many teachers, both men and women, trained in the male-centered tradition, are still handing the ideas and texts of that tradition on to students without teaching them to criticize its antiwoman attitudes, its omission of women as part of the species. Too often, all of us fail to teach the most important thing, which is that clear thinking, active discussion, and excellent writing are all necessary for intellectual freedom, and that these require *hard work*. Sometimes, perhaps in discouragement with a culture which is both anti-intellectual and antiwoman, we may resign ourselves to low expectations for our students before we have given them half a chance to become more thoughtful, expressive human beings. We need to take to heart the words of Elizabeth Barrett Browning, a poet, a thinking woman, and a feminist, who wrote in 1845 of her impatience with studies which cultivate a "passive recipiency" in the mind, and asserted that "women want to be made to *think actively:* their apprehension is quicker than that of men, but their defect lies for the most part in the logical faculty and in the higher mental activities." Note that she implies a defect which can be remedied by intellectual training, *not* an inborn lack of ability.

10 I have said that the contract on the student's part involves that you demand to be taken seriously so that you can also go on taking yourself seriously. This means seeking out criticism, recognizing that the most affirming thing anyone can do for you is demand that you push yourself further, show you the range of what you *can* do. It means rejecting attitudes of "take-it-easy," "why-be-so-serious," "why-worry-you'll-probably-get-married-anyway." It means assuming your share of responsibility for what happens in the classroom, because that affects the quality of your daily life here. It means that the student sees herself engaged *with* her teachers in an active, ongoing struggle for real education. But for her to do this, her teachers must be committed to the belief that women's minds and experience are intrinsically valuable and indispensable to any civilization worthy the

name; that there is no more exhilarating and intellectually fertile place in the academic world today than a women's college—*if* both students and teachers in large enough numbers are trying to fulfill this contract. The contract is really a pledge of mutual seriousness about women, about language, ideas, methods, and values. It is our shared commitment toward a world in which the inborn potentialities of so many women's minds will no longer be wasted, raveled-away, paralyzed, or denied.

Garry B. Trudeau

Doonesbury

Garry B. Trudeau (born 1948) is one of America's most influential (and controversial) political and social commentators. His vehicle is the comic strip "Doonesbury," which appears in more than 850 newspapers and whose readership may top 100 million people. For examples of his work, see pages 94, 170, and 1001 of this book.

Doonesbury
G. B. TRUDEAU
..AND FOR TOMORROW, I WANT YOU TO WRITE AN ESSAY ON THE TOPIC OF INDEPENDENT THOUGHT.
SCRIBBLE! SCRIBBLE! SCRIBBLE! SCRIBBLE!
EVERYONE GOT THAT?
BAA! BAA! BAA! BAA, SIR! BAA!
..AND IN MY VIEW, JEFFERSON'S DEFENSE OF THESE BASIC RIGHTS LACKED CONVICTION. OKAY, ANY DISCUSSION OF WHAT I'VE COVERED SO FAR?
SCRIBBLE! SCRIBBLE! SCRIBBLE! SCRIBBLE!
OF COURSE NOT. YOU'RE TOO BUSY GETTING IT ALL DOWN.
LET ME JUST ADD THAT PERSONALLY I BELIEVE THE BILL OF RIGHTS TO BE A SILLY, INCONSEQUENTIAL RECAPITULATION OF TRUTHS ALREADY FOUND IN THE CON-STITUTION. ANY COMMENT?
SCRIBBLE! SCRIBBLE! SCRIBBLE!
NO, SCRATCH THAT! THE CONSTITUTION ITSELF SHOULD NEVER HAVE BEEN RATIFIED! IT'S A DANGEROUS DOCUMENT! ALL POWER SHOULD REST WITH THE EXECUTIVE! WHAT DO YOU THINK OF THAT?
SCRATCH! SCRATCH! SCRATCH! SCRATCH!
JEFFERSON WAS THE ANTICHRIST! DEMOCRACY IS FASCISM! BLACK IS WHITE! NIGHT IS DAY!
SCRIBBLE! SCRIBBLE! SCRIBBLE! SCRIBBLE! SCRIBBLE!
TEACHING IS DEAD.
BOY, THIS COURSE IS REALLY GETTING INTEREST-ING.
YOU SAID IT. I DIDN'T KNOW HALF THIS STUFF.

Christopher Jester

Not Just a Diploma Factory

A version of the following essay appeared in 1989 in The Daily Collegian, *the student newspaper at Penn State. Its author, Christopher Jester, was at the time a student majoring in international politics and minoring in Russian. He is now serving as a first lieutenant in the Air Force in Germany, where he lives with his wife (a native of Germany) and son, but he plans to leave the Air Force soon and take a job in government, ideally somewhere in Europe.*

During the 1988 presidential campaign, George Bush 1
acknowledged the current crisis in the American education system and pledged to be the "education president." So far Bush has done little to back up that promise, but the situation is beginning to attract more and more attention. Test scores are dropping and dropout rates in high schools are on the rise. Illiteracy rates are climbing. Our universities' graduate programs are becoming increasingly populated by better-educated foreign students. Each new report brings more evidence of our educational decline, often with shocking examples of ignorance.

Americans seem to show no interest in learning anything 2
beyond what they need to know. Few bother to learn another language, try to understand another nation's culture, or study an opposing point of view. Due to our complacency and ethnocentric isolation we have fallen behind educationally. We prefer the easy entertainment of television to reading. We have been described as a nation with blinders on—which is as apparent in schools' curricula as in television. Instant gratification seems to be the requirement in every aspect of society from music videos to political campaigns. The majority of Americans lack an understanding of who we are, where we've been, the world around us, or our place in its history.

Such deficiencies have been addressed in the recent books 3
Cultural Literacy by E. D. Hirsch and *The Closing of the American Mind* by Allan Bloom. Hirsch and Bloom both claim that our schools fail to provide well-prepared students to universities, because the schools fail to teach common, basic knowledge. Hirsch goes into great depth to document

modern high school students' lack of intergenerational and "national cultural" information. Bloom also laments the self-centeredness of today's students and associates their inability to think in a broad, contextual way with either an existential nihilism or a sense of detachment and atomization. He sees universities' specialized divisions as "competing and contradictory" and states that students have forgotten that individual areas of study are only parts of a whole.

4 University of Virginia professor Richard Rorty puts forth his own theory of the American education process in the essay "The Opening of American Minds," which appeared in the July 1988 *Harper's*. He describes the current situation as a compromise between liberal and conservative education theories, with the right mainly controlling pre-university education and the left, for the most part, in control at universities.

5 According to Rorty, primary and secondary schools exist to develop the basic concepts, accepted ideas, and commonly believed moral and political assumptions of society—what can be referred to as the socialization process. Post-secondary education, in Rorty's scenario, urges students to question the conventional wisdom, consider opposing ideas, look critically at social deficiencies, and search for alternative solutions, with the ultimate goal of improving society for the next generation. The problem is that universities are failing both in providing a forum for divergent opinions and in providing students a comparative base of beliefs and knowledge to reshape on their own into an informed opinion and self-image, what Rorty calls "self-individualization."

6 It is hard to determine whether universities or the students themselves are to blame for this problem. Last fall, I had a lower-level political science class with an excellent professor who energetically encouraged his class to look critically at our political system and see how it differs from standard perceptions. All the students did was whine about how it was too much work to do all of the readings and out-of-class assignments. I heard a few people discuss the idea of dropping the class and taking it when they thought they would have someone easier. Even classmates I've had in 400-level classes seem just as averse to doing any substantive work. In general, today's Reagan-generation college students, weaned on television's fast-moving images and

short attention span, can easily be described as pleasure seeking, apolitical, and uninformed.

The typical student apparently thinks mainly of getting a 7
good job that pays well as soon after graduation as possible. The most important aspect of the average senior year involves putting together a slick resume, buying an interview suit, and worrying about on-campus recruiters and rejection letters. The standard measure of success among peers and even parents is the size of the expected starting salary. A desire to learn or quest for knowledge takes second place to a preoccupation with money and career.

The atmosphere on campus and in town can hardly be 8
described as intellectual. A walk down College Avenue reveals an overabundance of trendy clothing stores, gift shops, bars, and other places for spending money. Where there used to be a used-book store, there is now a Subway. More telling is the on-campus bookstore where the majority of available space is devoted to Penn State clothes and memorabilia or leather briefcases and corporate-looking appointment books. Oh, and they sell books, too.

Penn State just doesn't provide an environment very 9
conducive to the kinds of discourse Rorty feels a university should provide; instead it merely continues the socialization process, replete with fraternity parties and football games. Students learn what will help them later in life, such as what car to own, how to dress for success, and what music, magazines, and ideas are politically correct. This information on safe displays of status and inoffensive, socially acceptable behavior is provided in college-oriented marketing such as free magazines and bookstore advertising. Much of this socialization process tells us the only way to be happy and successful is to make a lot of money. Penn State mainly serves as a huge vocational school selling very expensive pieces of paper that form the primary ingredient of a resume and serve as tickets to good careers.

Penn State essentially pumps out hordes of careerist, 10
consumerist, educated elites—yuppies—instead of enabling students to think critically, analytically, or independently. The 1988 senior class exemplified this attitude with their class gift—the computerized career placement and interview center. The colleges of Business Administration, Engineering, and Science together dominate the College of Liberal Arts, and the College of Arts and Architecture has a comparatively modest presence on campus.

11 With such emphasis placed on specialization and a career-oriented curriculum, majors in the liberal arts are frowned upon as not "practical" enough—as in "What kind of job can you get with that?" Liberal arts majors, especially philosophy majors, are frequently the object of derision. A question often posed to English or foreign language majors is "What are you going to do, teach?"—with the tone implying the lack of respect (or monetary rewards) associated with teaching. If any given major doesn't appear to lead to a lucrative career, then it is regarded as a waste of time by many Penn Staters.

12 The overemphasis on specialized career training discourages broad conceptual thinking about changing world relationships or social and economic structures; it makes it difficult to develop a philosophy for living. The dominance of business and engineering breeds homogeneity and deprives students of the diversity that serves as an integral part of outside-the-classroom education.

13 Robert Reich points out the fallacy of this career-track thinking with his advice on preparing for future careers. Students' emphasis on "practical" majors is misguided: "The courses to which they now gravitate—finance, law, accounting, management, and other practical arts—may be helpful to understand how a particular job is *now* done (or, more accurately, how your instructors did it years ago when they held such jobs or studied the people who held them), but irrelevant to how such a job *will* be done."

14 Reich stresses the need to learn how to define problems, conceptualize and analyze information, communicate with colleagues to achieve solutions, and convince others. These skills cannot be learned in a strictly career-oriented course. "To the extent to which they can be found in universities at all," Reich writes, "they're more likely to be found in subjects such as history, literature, philosophy, or anthropology—in which students can witness how others have grappled for centuries with the challenge of living good and productive lives."

Lester Krogh

Overselling of American Universities

Lester Krogh, retired senior vice president for research and development at 3M Corporation, is particularly interested in the role universities can play in economic development. He contributed the following article to The Atlanta Constitution *in March 1991.*

The ivy-covered walls are growing a different kind of green these days. Increasingly, American universities are selling their wares. 1

Corporations are making arrangements with universities for patentable ideas and trained workers. Federal and state governments are turning to them for extension services and to develop new ideas for industry. Foreign governments and companies seek early access to research findings and training for their students. 2

Many universities, in turn, aggressively market an ever-broader range of services. Georgia Tech advises local businesses through its Industrial Extension Service. Worcester Polytechnic Institute's Manufacturing Engineering Applications Center develops products for subscribers. Stanford University and the University of California at Berkeley maintain active industrial affiliate programs. Examples abound. 3

Many of these arrangements provide valuable educational opportunities. Yet if universities become too eager in their pursuit of new revenues, they could lose sight of their main mission—the training of the next generation. That would be disastrous. 4

As Princeton University president Harold Shapiro notes, universities only recently have been expected to make a dollars-and-cents contribution to economic growth. Over the past eight centuries, their main product has been their graduates, who influence the economy through their daily working lives. The day-to-day job of education is less glamorous than campus research that wins Nobel Prizes, but it represents technology transfer at its most profound. 5

There are many reasons why university administrators have begun marketing new services. They are struggling with post-baby boom enrollment declines, rapidly rising 6 administrative and facilities costs, and shrinking pools of government support.

7 Nonetheless, at least some universities are now in danger of becoming victims of their own sales pitches. They endlessly cite a few notable successes—Silicon Valley in California, Boston's Route 128 and Research Triangle Park in North Carolina—as evidence of the economic leverage of their own proposals. These marketers risk becoming mercenaries if they advertise too direct a relationship between higher education and higher profits.

8 For professors, the pursuit of new sources of research funding may be the inevitable outgrowth of a "justify your existence" mentality. This mindset has helped make teaching careers so unattractive that U.S.-born professors are now a rarity in some disciplines. Teaching has taken a back seat to research because it simply doesn't pay for universities or professors. This shift away from teaching threatens to prevent our daughters, sons, employees and other students from getting full value from their education—and from our education dollars.

9 Make no mistake; university research is essential for generating new ideas, discoveries and technologies. But it is not a surefire ticket to prosperity. The openness of our university system is essential to intellectual vitality. Yet it also ensures that research findings, in many cases funded by our government, can be picked up easily by foreign companies. There is no guarantee that the benefits of university research will remain in the United States. We can be much more certain that our students—the real product of our colleges and universities—will invest their careers in our economy.

10 The real return on our personal and collective investments in universities is the career-long contributions of our graduates. We cannot put too high a value on their training, and we must not forget that the university's focus should be on people, not profit.

This ad for Hofstra University appeared in several magazines and newspapers in 1989 and 1990. What does it say about what Hofstra University is for?

What does it take to be the best?

Determination and hard work, at any age, can lead to being the best.
Hofstra University, just 50 years old, is already among the top ten percent of American colleges and universities in almost all academic criteria and resources.
Professionally accredited programs in such major areas as business, engineering, law, psychology and education.
A library with over 1.1 million volumes *on campus*—a collection larger than that of 95% of American universities.
Record enrollments with students from 31 states and 59 countries—with a student-faculty ratio of only 17 to 1.
The largest, most sophisticated non-commercial television facility in the East. A high technology undergraduate teaching resource with broadcast-quality production capability.
A ranking in *Barron's Guide to the Most Prestigious Colleges*—one of only 262 colleges and universities chosen from almost 4,000.
At Hofstra, determination, inspiration and hard work are qualities our faculty demands in itself and instills in our students.
These qualities are what it takes to be the best. In anything.

HOFSTRA UNIVERSITY

WE TEACH SUCCESS.

50th Anniversary
Hempstead, L.I., New York 11550

Babson College placed this ad in several publications in 1990. What does it imply about the purpose of a college education?

A BUSINESS MOVE FEW COLLEGES COULD DUPLICATE.

William F. Glavin
Vice Chairman, Xerox Corporation

William F. Glavin
President, Babson College

Now there's a business college being run by a business executive. William F. Glavin, the former Vice Chairman of Xerox, is the new President of Babson College.

While some colleges might consider that highly unusual, to us it's simply business as usual.

You see, at Babson, students discover an environment that's more like a hot company than a cold classroom. Our nationally respected professors are experts at translating blackboard theory into boardroom reality. And we encourage an entrepreneurial spirit that tends to stick with people for life.

That's why it's not surprising that such a high percentage of Babson graduates go on to become Presidents, CEOs, or owners of their own companies. Today, they're men and women who run all types of businesses: from family operations to Fortune 500 corporations like Pepsi Cola and Dun & Bradstreet.

So you could say, by naming Bill Glavin President, we are simply practicing what we teach.

For complete information on our undergraduate, full or part-time graduate MBA, or executive programs, call (617) 239-4317. Or write the Office of Admissions, Nichols-M, Babson College, Babson Park, Wellesley, MA 02157.

BABSON COLLEGE
EXECUTIVE THINKING

Aram Bakshian, Jr.

Just Say No to College

Aram Bakshian, Jr., (born 1944) is a member of the National Council for the Humanities; he served as communications expert in the Reagan administration. You'll learn more about him and his background when you read the following essay, which appeared in The American Spectator *(a monthly magazine that reviews politics and current affairs from a resolutely conservative perspective) in November 1991.*

Few things in life are worth standing in line for, especially on a sweltering summer day in Washington, D.C. Higher education certainly didn't seem like one of them in September of 1963, when, overcome by the dinginess of George Washington University's downtown campus, and the industrial-strength effluvium issuing from long queues of nervous, sweaty registering freshmen, I made what may well have been the defining choice of my life. Anticipating Nancy Reagan by twenty years, I "just said no"—in my case, to that most mind-bending of hallucinogens, a second-rate liberal arts degree. It meant chucking a generously apportioned yet unappetizing academic scholarship, but my mind was made up: rather than go to college, I would get an education. 1

More immediately, I decided to abandon campus and walk a few blocks to the old Circle Theatre on Pennsylvania Avenue. By happy chance, Lucino Visconti's exquisite film adaptation of Giuseppe di Lampedusa's *The Leopard* was playing and the erratic air conditioning system was working that afternoon; two auspicious omens in a row convinced me that I had made the right decision. As I watched the world-weary patrician hero turning his back on the gilded sham of *risorgimento* Italy, I felt a smug kinship, excusable, perhaps, in one still in his teens. 2

From elementary school onward, I had always learned more from independent reading and conversation than from the standard gruel dispensed in class, taking to heart the Shakespearean admonition that 3

> No profit grows where is no pleasure ta'en; in brief, sir, study what you most affect. . . .

and agreeing with Sydney Smith (to the aggravation of innumerable family members over the years) that there is "no furniture so charming as books." So much so that, from junior high school onward, I regularly played hooky to visit the vast, fusty second-hand bookstores that still dotted the Washington landscape in the 1950s and 1960s. Nearly all of them, Lowdermilk's, Pearlman's, Estate, Savile, and Park Books, are gone now.

4 Today's book fanciers, usually forced to choose between overpriced antiquarian dealers and chain retailers limited to standard current titles, would be amazed at how far—and wide—a few dollars could go in those literary old curiosity shops. Nicely bound broken sets of the collected works of Voltaire could be bought for all of seventy-five cents a volume, and Homer, Plato, Thucydides, Xenophon, Le Sage, Clarendon, Cervantes, Marcus Aurelius, Gibbon, Macaulay, Carlyle, Thackeray, Dickens, Sterne, Smollett, Daudet, de Maupassant, Surtees, Suetonius, Sheridan, Aristophanes, Chaucer, Emerson, Parkman, Pascal, Molière, Madame de Sévign, St. Simon, Pepys, Pope, Johnson, Boswell, Montaigne, Dryden, Goldsmith, Goethe, Byron, Tennyson, Kipling, de Ligne, Luther, and Dante, not to mention more recent and routine titles, could be had for a song, sometimes in morocco or calf.

5 "Good as it is to inherit a library, it is better to collect one," wrote Augustine Birrell, and at that time, even a newspaper carrier turned copyboy like myself could afford to start. The very act of working to pay for each volume seemed to quicken one's appetite for reading it, a principle that probably applies to students who have to work for their tuition. Serving as a copyboy, first at the (now-defunct) *National Observer* and then at the (now-unrecognizable) *U.S. News & World Report,* also meant access to good reference libraries and interesting conversation with the less stuffy writers and editors. One of the earliest pleasures of my own writing career came when, a few years after I had left the *National Observer,* I appeared in its pages as a book critic and was able to renew earlier acquaintances on a more equal footing.

6 Reading, writing, and intelligent discussion are the keys to a good liberal arts education in academia; I simply sought, and was lucky enough to find, the same essentials in the outside world without being subjected to the nuisance of gym, the irrelevance of Geology I, and the forced purchase

of dozens of badly written textbooks, as expensive as they were worthless.

This is *not* to say that I owe nothing to formal education. 7
Several inspiring elementary and secondary school teachers tolerated my maverick streak and encouraged my interests in history and literature. As a day student at a cozy if somewhat down-at-the-heels little academy called Woodward Prep, I even learned the elements of real, as opposed to apparent, political power: control communications and law enforcement and it doesn't matter who is president. This is as true of countries as of student councils, as I would later observe in the Nixon and Ford White Houses before becoming director of speechwriting for Ronald Reagan, a President who knew a thing or two about communicating.

Editing the school newspaper and literary supplement 8
and commanding the hall monitors meant real power and real rewards: extensive writing on the topics of one's choosing, more free time and fewer scheduled classes, and the ability to slip out for an illicit beer (I was tall for my age) with the connivance of one's subordinate hall monitors.

At the same time, a curriculum that still included Latin 9
meant an early grounding in the fundamental structure of languages that would make later acquisition of rudimentary French and German easier. How Latin came to be dropped by some high schools as "irrelevant" baffles me to this day; it is the most practical subject many secondary school students will ever study. Given a little Latin, years later you will be able to get the gist of street signs, simple news clips, and broadcasts in Spanish, Italian, Portuguese, and in a pinch, even Romanian.

This is particularly true in my case, since Don Manuel 10
Castello, Woodward Prep's Latin and French master, taught both languages with a thick Spanish accent. When asked about this, the headmaster's wife dismissed the matter with a phrase echoed thirty years later by Sybil Fawlty explaining the foibles of another Manuel, this time a waiter: "It's all right. He's from Barcelona."

Unlike the author of a recent best-seller, I do not claim 11
that everything I needed to know I had already learned in kindergarten. But I can honestly say that everything I needed to learn—in school, that is—I knew by the twelfth grade. While my own curiosity deserves some of the credit,

so does a motley but worthy crew of teachers, not one of whom was an education major.

12 They included a deaf, dentured retired colonel, Merritt Booth, who taught algebra and geometry with the logic and precision they deserved; a dedicated young English teacher named Bill Gaull who, while working his way through law school, took the trouble to encourage bright students to read non-syllabus authors like Fielding and Tolstoy; a one-legged Seventh Day Adventist history master named Donald F. Haynes who, although somewhere to the right of the John Birch Society, graded fairly and taught passionately; and a wonderful 76-year-old chemistry teacher, "Doc" Valaer, whose enthusiasm for his subject was such that, although a teetotaler, he had written a book entitled *Wines of the World,* painstakingly analyzing their chemical compositions without tasting any of them.

13 My graduate and post-graduate teachers, while more famous, have all been untenured and unofficial: editors, authors, politicians, journalists, artists, and a widening circle of interesting friends. We didn't need classrooms; sometimes we didn't even need face-to-face meetings. One of my earliest literary mentors was the late Frank Meyer, who edited the arts and manners section of *National Review* from the magazine's founding until his death in the early 1970s. Although we struck up a strong intellectual friendship during hundreds of hours of phone conversations, we never met. The only time we were in the same room together was at his funeral in Woodstock, New York, yet Frank's disembodied voice during our long-distance dialogues on everything from the ideals of the Founding Fathers to the foibles of King Farouk was an important part of my education.

14 A twenty-year association with the British magazine *History Today,* beginning with its founding editors, poet-biographer Peter Quennell and the late Alan Hodge who, among other things, was one of the two ghostwriters for Winston Churchill, I've been lucky enough to know, has been an unending source of new ideas, friendships, and interests. Similarly, collaborating with Viennese composer Robert Stolz (1880–1975) on his memoirs was the equivalent of several years of post-graduate study on the musical, theatrical, intellectual, political, and social history of *Mitteleuropa* under a man who had known or met everyone from the last two Hapsburg emperors to Brahms, Bruckner, Johann and Richard Strauss, Lehar, and Puccini to Charlie

Chaplin, Albert Einstein, Eleanor Roosevelt, Marshal Tito, Marlene Dietrich, and Marilyn Monroe, a rather fascinating mixed bag.

The odds are that I would have missed out on most of 15
these opportunities if I had kept my scholarship at George Washington University and followed the oft-trodden rut of academia, where as early an observer as William Penn remarked that "much reading is an oppression of the mind, and extinguishes the natural candle, which is the reason of so many useless scholars in the world." At the very worst, I might have ended up as a tenured, politically correct hack . . . perhaps even a registered Democrat.

Just thinking about *that* makes me shudder. Fortunately, 16
all I had to do was just say no.

W. D. Snodgrass

The Examination

W. D. Snodgrass (born 1926), educated at Geneva College and the University of Iowa, teaches at the University of Delaware. His book of poetry Heart's Needle *won the Pulitzer Prize in 1960.*

Under the thick beams of that swirly smoking light, 1
The black robes are clustering, huddled in together.
Hunching their shoulders, they spread short, broad sleeves like night-
Black grackles' wings; then they reach bone-yellow leather-

y fingers, each to each. And are prepared. Each turns 2
His single eye—or since one can't discern their eyes,
That reflective single, moon-pale disc which burns
Over each brow—to watch this uncouth shape that lies

Strapped to their table. One probes with his ragged nails 3
The slate-sharp calf, explores the thigh and the lean thews

Of the groin. Others raise, red as piratic sails,
His wing, stretching, trying the pectoral sinews.

4 One runs his finger down the whet of that cruel
Golden beak, lifts back the horny lids from the eyes,
Peers down in one bright eye malign as a jewel,
And steps back suddenly. "He is anaesthetized?"

5 "He is. He is. Yes. Yes." The tallest of them, bent
Down by the head, rises: "This drug possesses powers
Sufficient to still all gods in this firmament.
This is Garuda who was fierce. He's yours for hours.

6 "We shall continue, please." Now, once again, he bends
To the skull, and its clamped tissues. Into the cran-
ial cavity, he plunges both of his hands
Like obstetric forceps and lifts out the great brain,

7 Holds it aloft, then gives it to the next who stands
Beside him. Each, in turn, accepts it, although loath,
Turns it this way, that way, feels it between his hands
Like a wasp's nest or some sickening outsized growth.

8 They must decide what thoughts each part of it must think;
They tap at, then listen beside, each suspect lobe;
Next, with a crow's quill dipped into India ink,
Mark on its surface, as if on a map or globe,

9 Those dangerous areas which need to be excised.
They rinse it, then apply antiseptics to it;
Now silver saws appear which, inch by inch, slice
Through its ancient folds and ridges, like thick suet.

10 It's rinsed, dried, and daubed with thick salves. The smoky saws
Are scrubbed, resterilized, and polished till they gleam.
The brain is repacked in its case. Pinched in their claws,
Glimmering needles stitch it up, that leave no seam.

11 Meantime, one of them has set blinders to the eyes,
Inserting light packing beneath each of the ears,
And calked the nostrils in. One, with thin twine, ties
The genitals off. With long wood-handled shears,

Another chops pinions out of the scarlet wings. 12
It's hoped that with disuse he will forget the sky
Or, at least, in time, learn, among other things,
To fly no higher than his superiors fly.

Well; that's a beginning. The next time, they can split 13
His tongue and teach him to talk correctly, can give
Him opinions on fine books and choose clothing fit
For the integrated area where he'll live.

Their candidate may live to give them thanks one day. 14
He will recover and may hope for such success.
He might return to join their ranks. Bowing away,
They nod, whispering, "One of ours; one of ours. Yes. Yes."

Louis Menard

What Are Universities For?

Louis Menard teaches English at Queens College and at the Graduate Center of the City University of New York. The winner of prestigious fellowships and an expert on English and American writers of the first half of the twentieth century, he often writes articles on current cultural affairs such as the following one, which appeared in Harper's Magazine *(a prestigious forum for discussions of American politics and culture) in December of 1991. The article appeared in the same issue as the one by Rosa Ehrenreich that appears on page 179.*

Several times in the last few years I have taught a course called Introduction to Poetry. The class was always overenrolled; I usually spent the beginning of the first few meetings turning students away. Its popularity had nothing to do with me—I was one of many instructors, teaching one of many sections, and all the sections were overenrolled. Introduction to Poetry was popular because it happened to satisfy three requirements: It was a prerequisite for English department courses; it could be used as the final installment in a sequence of composition courses all students had to 1 take; and, as a "humanities" elective, it satisfied a college-wide distribution requirement.

2 There are 18,000 students at my school, which is one campus of a public university. Most of them are pursuing careers in fields remote from literature; many know English only as a second language. These students approach a course on poetry with the same sense of dread with which most English majors might approach an advanced course in statistics. Other students, though, are eager to take an English course—not because they hope to acquire an appreciation of poetry, but because they believe it will enhance their communications skills and help them get into law school. And there are a few students who want to become English majors because English literature is their primary academic interest.

3 All of these types of students have turned up in every section of Introduction to Poetry, so I found myself trying to teach some of my students how to write a grammatical sentence, to introduce others to the academic study of literature, and to give the rest of them—though most were essentially unacquainted with serious literary culture—exposure to the best that has been thought and said in the world. For the majority of the students, of course (as they were not shy about making me aware), the principal object was to secure the passing grade needed to fulfill whatever requirement happened to apply in their case. You could walk away from a session of Introduction to Poetry feeling that whatever the current public debate over the university was about—"political correctness," deconstruction, "multiculturalism," the canon—what you had just spent the last hour or so doing had very little to do with it. Ideology was about as remote a presence in an Introduction to Poetry classroom as leather bindings.

4 In all the uproar over the academy—which entered the mainstream of public debate in 1987 with Allan Bloom's best-selling *The Closing of the American Mind,* and which has produced, more recently, Roger Kimball's *Tenured Radicals,* Dinesh D'Souza's *Illiberal Education* (also a best-seller), cover stories in almost every news and opinion magazine of note, and even some observations in a commencement address last spring by President Bush—no one has bothered to ask what practical effect the so-called politicization of the humanities has actually had on the undergraduate mind. Seventy-four percent of the nation's

freshman class last year described themselves, in a poll conducted by the American Council on Education, as politically middle-of-the-road or conservative. When they were asked why they chose to attend college, the most popular answer, picked by 78 percent, was to "get a better job" followed by to "make more money" (73 percent). Asked to name an objective they considered "essential or very important," 74 percent chose "being very well-off financially"; second place went to "raising a family," named by 70 percent (an answer almost equally popular among male and female students).

There is no evidence I know of to suggest that in four 5
years spent trying to win the grades and recommendations needed for jobs or for admission to graduate or professional school, these students become radicalized, or are in any way deflected from the social mainstream, by the few humanities courses they are required to take. Students enrolled in Introduction to Poetry would learn just as much about poetry from a professor who thought Milton was a sexist as they would from one who didn't—which is to say, in either case, that they would have had to read and talk for a few hours about a writer of whom they would otherwise remain essentially ignorant. The professor's political slant, if it can be ferreted out, makes a difference to most students only insofar as it might determine the kind of questions likely to turn up on an exam. The effect the course might have on those students' good opinion of Milton—or of any other poet they are likely to be required to read—is a microscopic influence, rapidly diminishing to zero as college recedes behind them, on their ultimate sense of things.

The educational ethos is different at a selective, residen- 6
tial, private college. There students are likely to be better primed to become personally engaged with the course material; they are also likely to feel the loss of income higher education represents less acutely, which enables them to enter into the spirit of their instruction with their eyes a little less fixed on the bottom line. Students at elite colleges identify much more strongly with their professors: They want to argue the nuances and to pick up the insights. But in the end the practical impact is much the same. Anyone who has taught literature at such a school knows the phenomenon: The brightest students happily learn the most advanced styles of contemporary critical theory, with all of their radical political implications, and then they apply,

with equal good cheer, to business school. Whatever subversiveness they have ingested has mostly served to give them a kind of superior intellectual sophistication that they are right to feel is not in the least bit incompatible with professional success on Wall Street or Madison Avenue.

7 Academic thought may have been heading left in the last ten years or so, in other words, but college students themselves have been heading straight into the mainstream. Even comfortably middle-class students feel an economic imperative almost unknown to middle-class students of twenty years ago. When I was a freshman, in 1969, I didn't have a thought in my head about how I was eventually going to support myself. I suppose I imagined that I would just hitchhike around the country with my guitar (which I didn't know how to play) reciting my poetry (which I didn't know how to write).

8 In the 1990s, though, young people in the middle class are perfectly alive to the fact that they go to college because they have to; young people not in the middle class continue to go to college for the reason they always have, which is to get into the middle class. It seems to me that there is every good reason to challenge these students for a semester or two to think with a little balanced skepticism about the conventional wisdom of the society they are so anxious to join. But whether they're being taught skepticism or not, literature classes are the last places students are likely to be getting their values. Madonna has done more to affect the way young people think about sexuality than all the academic gender theorists put together. Perhaps D'Souza should write a book about her.

9 It's easier, of course, to attack Catharine Stimpson, the former dean of graduate school at Rutgers and former president of the Modern Language Association, who has become one of the point persons in the defense of new academic trends. Stimpson doesn't appear on MTV, so there isn't a tidal wave of popular sentiment to overcome before one can take her to task. But the lack of a mass following ought to be a clue to the extent of Stimpson's, or any other academic's, real influence on the culture at large. A group of literature professors calling themselves Teachers for a Democratic Culture has come together this fall to launch a counteroffensive against the attack on "political correctness." I suspect that it's a little late in the day for a counteroffensive: The center on this issue has already been

grabbed. But one of the arguments this new group wants to make is that the whole situation has been exaggerated. I think it's a just complaint.

It isn't hard to guess the motives behind the controversy 10
in its present melodramatic mode. It is always tempting to blame bad conditions on bad ideas, and it must seem to conservatives that since liberal and leftist thinking has been driven out of nearly every other part of American life, the pitiful remnant of left-wing ideology that has taken refuge in university literature departments must be the reason social problems so disobligingly persist. It is the good fortune of conservatives that this is a view that meets exactly the belief of some of the professors being attacked, which is that they are in possession of the one ground—the humanities curriculum of American colleges—on which real social change might be accomplished. The American media, for their rather inflammatory part, are always happy to find an occasion not to appear too liberal, and the excesses of "political correctness" are the perfect thing to get noisily to the right of. The whole controversy is marvelously apt in a country that no longer shows any interest in publicly funded social programs; for whichever political faction wins control of the undergraduate reading list, no taxpayer dollars will have been spent.

This doesn't mean that there's not a crisis. But the issue is 11
not whether (in the words of some of the demonstrators against Stanford's core curriculum a few years ago) Western culture's got to go. Western culture, whether it's in good odor at the Modern Language Association these days or not, we're stuck with. The real issue concerns the role of higher education in American life. Too many people are fighting over how much T. S. Eliot versus how much Alice Walker young minds ought to be exposed to, and not enough people are asking why undergraduate English courses should be bearing the load of this debate in the first place. What is it we are expecting colleges to do that makes the particular mix of the reading lists in literature courses seem to spell the difference between—well, between culture and anarchy?

Matthew Arnold is, indeed, the name most frequently 12
associated with the traditional idea of liberal arts education that the new wave of "politicization" in the academy is supposed to be wrecking. But the liberal arts component of higher education belongs to what is in some ways the least

salient of the university's social functions. In fact, the Arnoldian program of using humanistic studies as a means of moral instruction, far from being the most venerable of the university's activities, entered the modern university almost as an afterthought.

13 The modern university in America is defined by two features, both of which date from the late nineteenth century: the existence of an elective curriculum for undergraduates and the existence of a graduate school, which trains the people who teach the undergraduates. The elective system was not designed to disseminate culture. When Charles William Eliot instituted the first elective system, at Harvard in 1883, his idea was to allow college students to "track" themselves in the direction of their future careers—not to acquire a common culture, but to specialize according to individual needs. Eliot believed that college ought to play a vocational role, to serve a frankly utilitarian function. His faith in the real-world utility of academic studies was great enough, in fact, to allow him, in 1901, to praise the assembled scholars of the Modern Language Association, virtually all of whom were philologists, by telling them that their work enjoyed "a vital connection with the industrial and commercial activities of the day."

14 At the same time, Eliot saw the need to provide specialists to train college students, and in 1890 he established the Harvard Graduate School of Arts and Sciences, modeled on the first research institution in the country, Johns Hopkins (founded in 1876). The principal function of the graduate school is the production of teachers, whom it certifies with the doctoral degree, to staff the modern college; but it also produces scholarly research, and the research ideal is expressly nonutilitarian. The researcher cannot be influenced by what the world will find profitable: The goal is knowledge for its own sake, without regard for "the industrial and commercial activities of the day."

15 So there was already in the modern university, as Eliot and the other late-nineteenth-century pioneers of higher education helped to create it, a contradiction between what professors do, which is to follow their research interests, and what their students do, which is to prepare for careers outside the academy—to pursue "education for experience," as Eliot called it. There is no reason, of course, as William James complained in 1903 in an essay called "The Ph.D. Octopus," why the possession of a doctorate, earned by

scholarship, should serve as a credential for teaching undergraduates; yet these separate functions were made to complement each other, and by the end of the nineteenth century the ideals of research and of vocational training had achieved such an ascendancy in American universities that a reaction against them occurred on behalf of what was called, by many of its champions, "liberal culture." This reaction is the origin of the idea that college is the place of future social leaders to be exposed to, in Arnold's phrase, "the study of perfection." The liberal arts "tradition" that the new scholarship is accused of trashing, in other words, is not even a century old.

The "true aim of culture," wrote Hiram Corson, the 16
chairman of the Cornell English department and a proponent of "liberal culture," in 1894, is "to induce soul states or conditions, soul attitudes, to attune the inward forces to the idealized forms of nature and of human life produced by art, and not to make the head a cockloft for storing away the trumpery of barren knowledge." This ideal is both anti-utilitarian and anti-research, and the reaction on its behalf was successful enough to lead, in 1909, to Eliot's replacement as president of Harvard by A. Lawrence Lowell—a member of the faculty who, many years before, had opposed the institution of the elective system. Thus emerged the third mission of the modern academy: the liberalization, through exposure to art, literature, and philosophy, of the undergraduate mind.

Although no school was ever purely one type or another, 17
universities before 1910 could be distinguished according to their leading educational ideals: Harvard was utilitarian, for example; Johns Hopkins, Clark, and Chicago were research institutions. Schools like Princeton and Yale tended to resist both these trends. But after 1910 (as Laurence Veysey explains in *The Emergence of the American University*) there was a shift. Educators stopped arguing about ideals; the various versions of what properly constituted higher education were no longer regarded as conflicting. The university learned to accommodate divergent views of its purpose, and the goal of the people who administered universities became not the defense of an educational philosophy but the prosperity of the institution. And the prosperity of the institution depended on its being, to as great an extent as it found possible, all things to all people.

This is how a pedagogical portmanteau like Introduction 18

to Poetry could come into being—a single course on a specific subject expected to serve, all at the same time, a utilitarian function (by training students how to read and write), a research function (by preparing future English majors for the scholarly study of literature), and a liberal arts function (by exposing students to the leavening influence of high culture).

19 Even at schools where there is no actual Introduction to Poetry course, the overall effect of the undergraduate curriculum is the same. Students in the humanities are expected to major in a field—French, say, or religion—that will provide them with a lot of knowledge most of which will be useful only in the unlikely event they decide to enter graduate school and become professors themselves. At the same time, they are required to fulfill "distribution" requirements designed to expose them to smatterings of learning in every major area—with the vague idea that this contributes to something approximating genuine well-roundedness, and thus serves a "liberalizing" function. And there is the expectation, now almost universal, that beyond college lies professional school, for which some practical training will be useful.

20 It's possible to argue that these three educational functions—scholarly, vocational, and liberalizing—are only three ways of looking at the same thing, which is the exposure to knowledge. For higher education in any field certainly can serve, simultaneously, all three purposes: pure speculation, practical application, and general enlightenment. Even so, there needs to be a consensus that these benefits are worth pursuing, and that the traditional structure of the university provides the best means of doing so, in order for the system to work effectively. Three recent developments, none of them having to do explicitly with politics—illiberal or not—seem to me to have undermined this consensus.

21 The first is the major demographic change in the undergraduate population over the last twenty years, a change that reflects both a significant increase in the proportion of people who attend college (from 1970 to 1988, the percentage of Americans who had completed four years of college doubled) and a significant increase on most campuses in the proportion of students who are not white or not male. This means that the average college class is not the relatively

homogeneous group, culturally and socio-economically speaking, it once was: The level of preparation among students differs more widely, and their interests and assumptions differ as well.

Since the whole idea of liberal arts education is to use 22
literature and philosophy as a way of learning how to value one's interests and assumptions, it is (or it ought to be) obviously absurd to insist that books that served this function when the audience was predominantly made up of young middle-class white men can serve the same function now that the audience is more diverse. When Columbia College admitted women for the first time, in 1983, it was suddenly realized by the faculty that the reading list for Humanities A, the famous great books course required of all students, had never included a book by a woman. Though for years it had been advertised as representing the best that the educated person needed to know, the list was changed: Sappho and Jane Austen became great writers. It took some fancy rhetoric to explain why this adjustment didn't amount to a confession that "the great books" is really just a grand name for "the books that will expose students to ideas we want them at the moment to be talking about." And that is part of the problem; for since so much has been emotionally (and, I think, mistakenly) invested in the traditional great books curriculum, changes can't happen without resentment and reaction.

The second development putting pressure on traditional 23
educational ideals is the spread of critical theory as a kind of interdisciplinary currency in university humanities departments. For contemporary critical theory—in particular post-structuralist theories, emphasizing the indeterminacy of meaning, and ideological theories, emphasizing the social construction of values—rejects precisely the belief on which the professional apparatus of the university (graduate exams, dissertation defenses, tenure review, publication in refereed journals, and so forth) depends: the belief that the pursuit of knowledge is a disinterested activity whose results can be evaluated objectively by other trained specialists in one's field. "What's really going on" in the production of knowledge is now regarded, by these new theoretical lights, as not a disinterested enterprise at all but an effort to make the views of a particular class of people prevail.

This rejection of the positivistic model of knowledge 24
production has helped to turn the system of professional

rewards, always an arena for academic politics, into an arena for real-world politics as well. Critical theorists whose work attacks the traditional premises of scholarship are invited into humanities departments for the good marketing reason that their work is where the action is today: Every graduate program wants a prominent profile. But the system whose principles those professors teach one another to regard with skepticism remains, except that it has been thoroughly corrupted. It is now regarded as legitimate by some professors to argue that the absence of a political intention or multicultural focus in another professor's work constitutes a prima facie disqualification for professional advancement. And why not, if all scholarship is at bottom political anyway?

25 Finally, there has been a change in the role of college in the preparation of young people for careers outside the academy. Although the number of bachelor's degrees awarded each year has been increasing steadily—by 28 percent between 1970 and 1989—the number of professional degrees has been increasing at a much greater rate. The material value of a B.A. is a function of supply: The greater the number of people who have one, the less a B.A. is worth in the marketplace. Particularly for students interested in "being very well-off financially" (74 percent, according to the American Council of Education survey), it has now become imperative not to stop with the B.A. but to proceed to professional school; and the number of M.B.A.'s awarded between 1970 and 1989 therefore increased by 239 percent, the number of M.D.'s by 88 percent, the number of law degrees by 143 percent. Increases in advanced degrees in architecture, engineering, and a number of other nonacademic professional fields were similarly dramatic.

26 This wave of professionalism has transformed the experience of college. The academic demands on undergraduates are in a sense now more real, since good grades are essential for getting over the hurdle to the next degree program; but the content is somehow less real, since most students now perceive that the education that matters to them will take place after college is finished. This helps to explain the phenomenon of the undergraduate whiz in Foucauldian analysis who goes merrily on to a career in corporate finance.

27 These various challenges to the established design of higher education present difficulties that have little to do

with politics. Perhaps the university will find a way to muddle through them, but muddling alone is not likely to be very effective. For it is not only a philosophical idea about education that is being thrown into doubt by these recent developments. It is also the institutional structure of the university itself.

I happen to think, for example—and without putting any 28
political valuation on the judgment—that contemporary theoretical skepticism about the positivistic nature of "knowledge" in fields like literature is perfectly justified. It is absurd to treat literary criticism as a species of scientific inquiry; the professional system of rewards in the humanistic disciplines is essentially bogus and leads mostly to intellectual conformity, predictable "demonstrations" of theoretical points, and a panicky desire to please one's elders and superiors. But what university is about to tear down the bureaucratic system of professional advancement in the humanities? How would departments administer themselves without the fiction that they were engaged in the production of real knowledge about real specialities?

Similarly, the undergraduate major seems to me an insti- 29
tution that is at best pedagogically inefficient (why should students going on to law school have to pass a course of what amounts to pre-professional training for graduate school in English or some other academic discipline?) and at worst a contributor to the perpetuation of a fundamentally arbitrary definition of knowledge. The modern academic discipline is only as old as the modern university: Before the 1800s, no one imagined that history, political science, economics, anthropology, and sociology constituted distant areas of study, each with its own theoretical and methodological traditions. Nor was it imagined by most people that "literature" was a discriminable area of human endeavor that must be talked about exclusively in literary-critical (as opposed to sociological or ethical or theological) terms.

But these distinctions have become institutionalized in 30
the form of academic departments; the people who work in those departments have professionalized themselves to keep out "unqualified" practitioners; and the professions run the fields, monopolizing both instruction and scholarship. It seems to me that a college student today might want, in four years, to acquire knowledge about American culture, about American politics and law, and about capitalism. What a

student who bothers to seek out knowledge in these areas is likely to get are courses introducing him or her to the academic specialities of American studies, political science, and economics. Though there is no reason why every undergraduate should not receive it, a practical introduction to the law or to business must usually wait until law school or business school, since that is where the specialists are. Because there are no instructors who are not certified members of an academic discipline, there is very little genuinely general education going on in American colleges.

31 These problems are severe enough, but they don't explain completely why the university is in such a bad way right now. Questions about educational philosophy must eventually have educational answers; the contemporary university, though, has reached beyond the purview of education, and it has thereby become entangled in problems it lacks the means to resolve. Universities can decide the things people ought to know, and they can decide how those things should be taught. But universities cannot arbitrate disputes about democracy and social justice, or govern the manner in which people relate socially to one another, or police attitudes; and that is what they are being asked to do today.

32 To some extent this overreaching is the fault of the society as a whole, which is happy to turn over to educators problems it lacks the will (and, it believes, the means) to address politically. It is easier to integrate a reading list, or even a dormitory, than it is to integrate a suburban neighborhood. But to some extent it is the consequence of the university's own indiscriminate appetite, whose history begins in the 1960s.

33 The contention that the current problems in the academy are the natural outcome of Sixties radicalism is common to many of the recent attacks on higher education—it can be found in Bloom's, Kimball's, and D'Souza's books. I think the claim is basically false, and that (as Camille Paglia argued in a long diatribe on the subject last spring in the journal *Arion*) the humorless ethos of the politically correct humanities department could not be more antithetical to the spirit of the 1960s. Even the most callow radicalism of that era has nothing to do with the sort of doctrinaire political attitudes critics of the contemporary academy complain about. Are the people who are so eager to censor "fighting words" on campus today the same people who

went around in 1968 calling anyone wearing a uniform or a necktie a "pig"? If they are the same people, they've left their radicalism behind.

There is one thing, however, that the present situation 34
does owe to the 1960s, and that is the belief that the university is a miniature reproduction of the society as a whole. That idea dominates, for example, the Port Huron Statement, the manifesto of the New Left drafted by Tom Hayden and endorsed by the Students for a Democratic Society in 1962. But it is not only a leftist idea; for the postwar university has always been eager to incorporate every new intellectual and cultural development that has come its way.

The university is, in fact, expressly designed to do this: It 35
can accommodate almost any interest by creating a new course, a new program, a new studies center. It has managed, for instance, to institutionalize activities like painting and creative writing, not traditionally thought to require academic preparation, by devising M.F.A. programs—which, in turn, provide a place on university faculties for practicing painters and writers. When new scholarly movements emerged—Third World Studies, Women's Studies—the university was quick to establish research centers and institutes to house them. Degrees are now offered in almost everything. There are few intellectual activities left that do not have an academic incarnation.

The problems begin when this process of absorption 36
extends beyond the intellectual realm. In the late 1960s, serious attention began to be paid by university administrators to the quality of campus life. This, too, was in part a response to student protest: Everyone agreed, for example, that one of the lessons of the crisis that led to the shutdown of Columbia in 1968 was that the college had to become less like a corporation and more like a community. But it was also natural that, as higher education became accessible to (and desired by) a greater variety of people in the postwar boom years, the university would evolve in this direction of its own accord.

This development of the university as a social microcosm 37
has been guided in most places by the view (which originated with the students themselves) that there should be available within the walls of the academy the full range of experiences available (or ideally available) outside. The initial breakthrough was a purely middle-class phenome-

non: the liberalization of parietal restrictions. (In the late 1960s, to give an idea of the magnitude of the change that has taken place, a student at Barnard, a sophisticated school in a sophisticated city, was expelled for sharing an apartment with her boyfriend *off campus*.) The eventual abandonment of regulations governing relations between the sexes was followed by the sexual integration of many traditionally single-sex schools (Princeton, Yale, Dartmouth, Vassar), and by the recruitment of ethnic minorities in the interest (among other things) of social diversity on campus.

38 This enormous and successful engulfment of intellectual and social variety, coming on top of the shocks to the system's *academic* identity, is what has given the university its present headache. The university has become, at last, too many things to too many people. It now reproduces all the conflicts of the culture at large; but it reproduces them, as it were, in vitro. For unlike the society it simulates, the university is unequipped, both administratively and philosophically, to deal with conflicts that cannot be treated simply as conflicts of ideas. It has the machinery needed to arbitrate the sorts of disagreements that arise naturally in the pursuit of the university's traditional educational goals; but it is not designed to arbitrate among antagonistic interest groups, or to discover ways of correcting inequities and attitudes that persist in the society as a whole.

39 The reason is that the university is required, by its accommodationist philosophy, to give equal protection to every idea and point of view anyone chooses to express. This is, of course, an indispensable principle of intellectual freedom. But when the issue is political, when it involves the distribution of power, accommodationism fails. For power is a zero-sum game. In the real world, interest groups vie against one another for resources in the knowledge that one group gains by taking from other groups. Political and legal institutions exist to mediate these struggles.

40 In the university, though, no one has ever needed to cede ground to someone else, since conflict has always been avoided by expanding the playing field. But this strategy doesn't work when the stakes are not simply intellectual. As long as the activities of the Gay Student Alliance and the Bible Study Group remain merely academic, they can coexist. Once those groups become versions of their real-world counterparts—once they become actively political—there is

no way to keep both of them happy. But who in the university wants to have to choose between them? In the nonacademic world, pluralism means a continual struggle over the distribution of a single pie. In the academic world (and the Democratic Party), it means trying to give every group a pie of its own.

Yet somehow it is expected that, once they are relocated 41
to a campus, differences that have proved intractable elsewhere will be overcome, both in the classroom and in the student union. This insistence, on the part of academics and nonacademics alike, on making higher education the site for political and social disputes of all types, and on regarding the improvement of social relations and the mediation of political differences as one of higher education's proper functions, has produced ridiculous distortions. Thus we have a debate, for example, in which the economic rights of women are argued about in terms of reading lists for introductory literature courses—as though devoting fewer class hours to male authors might be counted a blow against discrimination in the workplace. And outside the classroom, in the dorms and the dean's office, the university has managed to become a laboratory for the study and cure of social problems like date rape.

There are as well the notorious speech codes and disci- 42
plinary procedures aimed at enforcing campus "civility." These are mostly the results of hasty attempts to jury-rig disciplinary systems whose need had not been felt until it became commonly assumed that how students addressed one another was a matter college administrators ought to be concerned about. That the president of the university should have become the leading figure and spokesperson in the incident in which a Brown undergraduate was expelled for drunkenly shouting insults at no one in particular is an indication not only that the university doesn't know how seriously it is supposed to be taking these sorts of "problems" but that it has no appropriate administrative apparatus for dealing with them either.

And there is, to take a final example, the notion—much 43
less prevalent than the critics of political correctness claim, but present nonetheless—that the undergraduate curriculum should include courses whose purpose is, in effect, to cheerlead for civil and sexual rights. There is no doubt that many civil and sexual rights remain to be secured in this country; there is no doubt that scandalous inequities persist

unattended to. But English professors are not experts on these matters. They are taught how to identify tropes, not how to eliminate racist attitudes. To turn their courses into classes on (say) Post-Colonial Literature with the idea of addressing with some degree of insight the problem of ethnocentrism is to ask someone equipped to catch butterflies to trap an elephant.

44 This is done, usually, by pretending the butterfly is an elephant—by loading up a poem with so much ideological baggage that it can pass for an instrument of oppression. Poems won't bear the weight; most works of literature are designed to deflect exactly this kind of attention and to confute efforts to assign them specific political force. If literature is taught honestly from an ideological perspective—if what a book seems to say about the relations of power among people is made the focus of classroom discussion—students are just being led around the mulberry bush. It's not that the spirit of great literature is being dishonored, for literature can surely be talked about ideologically; it's that a false impression is being created among students that unhappiness whose amelioration lies in real-world political actions is being meaningfully addressed by classroom debates about the representation of the Other in the work of Herman Melville.

45 Professors should not be regarded as the people in possession of the "correct" views on subjects of public concern. But the idea that they ought to be has become an illusion shared by academics and their critics alike. When George Will wrote last spring in *Newsweek* that the task faced by Secretary of Defense Dick Cheney was less urgent than the one confronting his wife, Lynne, who is the director of the National Endowment for the Humanities, he sounded clearly the note of hysteria that has come to dominate debate about higher education in America. Mrs. Cheney, Will suggested, "is secretary of domestic defense. The foreign adversaries her husband, Dick, must keep at bay are less dangerous, in the long run, than the domestic forces with which she must deal. Those forces are fighting against the conservation of the common culture that is the nation's social cement."

46 This is witch-hunt talk; but it repeats an error found in less partisan writing as well, which is that the care of "the common culture" is the responsibility of college professors. Professors are people trained to *study* culture, not to *con-*

serve it (whatever that would mean). Their purview is limited by the kind of work, always highly specialized and narrowly defined, professionals in their disciplines have traditionally done. It is no favor to these people to regard them as the guardians of our culture or as experts on ministering to its self-inflicted wounds. Nor is it a favor to the culture to hand it over to academics for its nourishment and protection.

Social and political controversies have swamped the academy for two reasons: because universities, unwilling to define their mission in specific terms and eager to accommodate everything that comes along, could not find a rationale for keeping those controversies at bay; and because there has been so little serious intellectual debate in the rest of American society in the last ten years. There have been no real ideas argued in American politics, for instance, since Ronald Reagan showed that ideas were overrated. And intellectual journalism has become dominated by position-taking—the point-counterpoint syndrome, which permits just two points of view to every pre-packaged "issue." 47

It is almost certain that one of the effects of the public scrutiny of what professors do will be to turn the academy into another bastion of intellectual predictability. I'm not sure that hasn't happened already. But if not, the only way to prevent it is for the university to renounce the role of model community and arbiter of social disputes that it has assumed, to ignore the impulse to regulate attitudes and expressions that are the epiphenomena of problems far outside the college walls, to stop trying to set up academic housing for every intellectual and political interest group that comes along, and to restrict itself to the business of imparting some knowledge to the people who need it. 48

POLITICAL CORRECTNESS

Eugene Genovese

Heresy, Yes—Sensitivity, No

Eugene Genovese (born in 1930 in Brooklyn) is Distinguished Scholar-in-Residence at The University Center in Georgia; he has been on the faculty at Rutgers, Yale, Columbia, Rochester, and other universities. Frequently honored for his outstanding scholarship in history, he has dedicated his career to a better understanding of slavery in America. Among his many books are Roll, Jordan, Roll: The World the Slaves Made, *the product of a decade of scholarship, and his recent* The Slaveholders' Dilemma: Freedom and Progress in Southern Political Thought *(1991). The following book review (and more than a book review) of Dinesh D'Souza's* Illiberal Education *appeared in* The New Republic, *a magazine of public affairs considered middle of the road in outlook, in April 1991.*

1 Were today's universities the places of higher education that they jocularly pretend to be, we would have had a vigorous debate on the issues raised by Allan Bloom's *The Closing of the American Mind.* Instead, with some notable exceptions, the left settled for the denunciations and the right for hosannas. Now we have another chance. Dinesh D'Souza's *Illiberal Education* recounts, in a manner both responsible and chilling, the atrocities that ravage our campuses. Whatever your politics, read it.

2 A domestic policy adviser in the Reagan White House and a frequent contributor to *National Review* and other satanic organs, D'Souza speaks from the right. He also speaks for sanity, and, rare among right-wingers, he displays a deep appreciation of the travails of black students. Nothing comes through this powerful yet restrained book more clearly than its protest against the betrayal of black youth by the demagogues who claim to support them. D'Souza shows that blacks are paying the highest price for the degradation

of our campuses and the prostitution of higher education. Thus he pointedly exposes what few right-wingers wish to notice: the increase in flagrantly racist assaults, physical and other, on black students.

The atrocities documented here include the silencing of professors accused of "insensitivity" because they dare to ask students to read racist material in appropriate courses. (By extension, a professor ought not to assign *Mein Kampf* in a course on Nazi Germany since it might offend the sensibilities of Jewish students.) And they include the repression of professors and students who take unpopular stands against quotas, affirmative action, busing, abortion, homosexuality, and much else. Clearly, they have no right to present views offensive to those who accept the reigning pieties in universities committed to "diversity." D'Souza's account makes stomach-turning reading. And I have a suspicion that he is pulling his punches, lest he be accused of exaggeration. 3

As one who saw his professors fired during the McCarthy era, and who had to fight, as a pro-Communist Marxist, for his own right to teach, I fear that our conservative colleagues are today facing a new McCarthyism in some ways more effective and vicious than the old. Are conservatives only getting, then, a dose of their own medicine? In fact, they are not. The right did not rule our campuses during the McCarthy era. Most of the purges of those years were conducted by administrators and faculties who loudly proclaimed their own liberalism—by the same kind of people, that is, who are enforcing "political correctness" today. Yet few of the culprits were then, or are now, "liberals." 4

The principled liberals on our campuses constitute about the same proportion of the center as principled people do of the left and the right. All political camps have principled people, careerists, and thugs. D'Souza seems to appreciate this distinction. He largely avoids liberal-bashing and appeals instead to honest people across the spectrum to stand up for the principles that they profess in common. He warns of the few who have a totalitarian agenda, but wisely he concentrates his fire on those who appease them. 5

In these matters, as in others, Harvard, led by Derek Bok, strives mightily to be No. 1. Harvard seems determined to lead in high comedy, too, though Stephan Thernstrom and other members of its faculty who have been savaged for political incorrectness in the classroom may be forgiven if 6 they do not appreciate the humor. To wit: dining hall workers held a "Back to the Fifties Party," and a dean denounced them for being nostalgic about a decade in which segregation still prevailed. A professor assigned a film in which a black maid appeared, and he was forced to cancel its screening, since blacks should not be shown in such jobs. A new president at Radcliffe declined to identify herself as a feminist, and local feminists, disgracing an admirable cause, denounced her for "doing violence to herself."

7 The Harvard administration more or less upheld Thernstrom's academic freedom; it did not fire him for having introduced pro-slavery and racist documents in his course on "The Peopling of America," which he co-taught with the distinguished historian Bernard Bailyn. Significantly, the students who complained about Thernstrom's "racial insensitivity" did not bother to confront him, as academic protocol, not to mention common courtesy, would require. Instead, they took their complaint to the administration and the press. In the event, the dean of the college, without mentioning Thernstrom by name, gravely announced his stern disapproval of "prejudice, harassment, and discrimination," and warned professors to watch their mouths, lest they offend the sensibilities of their students. In effect, the Harvard administration acknowledged Thernstrom's right to behave in a manner that embarrassed the university and ought to make him ashamed of himself. No doubt Bok and most of his deans disapprove of the excesses that accompany the struggle for diversity, sensitivity, and a radiant future for the peoples. They are merely doing their best to create an atmosphere in which professors who value their reputations and their perquisites learn to censor themselves.

8 The manner in which some of the administrators of our universities choose to fight racial discrimination is marvelous to behold. Having decided that a democratic admissions policy required roughly proportionate representation of blacks, Hispanics, and whites, the University of California, Berkeley, coolly discriminated against Asians. Nearly 30 percent of the Asian high school graduates from California qualified for admission to Berkeley, compared with about 15 percent of the whites, 6 percent of the Hispanics, and 4 percent of the blacks. Yet according to Berkeley's own weighted index, blacks were admitted with scores of 4800 out of 8000, whereas whites needed at least 7000. Asians

needed at least 7000 just to have a 50 percent chance of admission.

But Asian students, as is well known, offend the sensibilities of true egalitarians and democrats by displaying a passion for hard work, and by having strong and supportive families. Could America have been built if it had relied on such perverse people? Or more precisely, it must have relied on such people, which would explain its emergence as a racist, sexist, homophobic, imperialist country. Either way, a sensitive person must see that the fight against racism demands the exclusion of Asians in favor of people with safer credentials. How could we demonstrate that Asians are no better motivated and self-disciplined than the rest of us if we let them demonstrate that they are? And if we let them demonstrate that they are better motivated, how could we ever be sure that they are not also smarter? 9

The Asian community counterattacked and forced Berkeley to modify its policies. Still, three trifles must be noted. First, the administrators, with little or no protest from the faculty, repeatedly lied about their discriminatory policy until they were caught red-handed, and then they solemnly announced that they were shocked to learn of their own "insensitivity" to Asians. Second, nobody has yet explained how, if discrimination against Asians were necessary to fight white racism (never mind the blatant imbecility of the proposition), the university could eliminate such discrimination without succumbing to precisely that white racism. Third, how could the university now admit more Asians without further reducing the quota for white students, including deserving poor and working-class white students? 10

To right old wrongs, our leading universities are now trying to buy black students and professors, of whom there are demonstrably not enough qualified ones to go around, even in Afro-American history. In consequence, they accept some who could not compete on merit, but who might do well at a university of the second rank; and the universities of the second rank accept those who belong in universities of the third rank; and the universities of the third rank accept available warm bodies. At all levels, many black students who cannot compete receive passing grades while being treated with contempt. And so frustration, resentment, and anger build among them, and among the white 11 students, too, who have been shunted aside to facilitate this charade. The dropout rate for black students would rank as a scandal, if anything any longer ranked as a scandal.

12 At all levels, moreover, qualified black students and professors are made to look like charity cases. A number of blacks today rank among the finest American historians in the country, and many are honored for their achievements. But those well-deserved honors often stick in the craw of their recipients, who can never be sure that the honors are not merely awarded to fill quotas. And if mature and accomplished professors suffer from this outrage, how must gifted black students feel about their situation?

13 Does affirmative action, then, undermine academic standards? Not necessarily, according to D'Souza, who sharply attacks its present form, and offers an alternative to which we shall return. Affirmative action cannot explain the decline in academic standards, which began well before it. The damning indictment of the long-practiced discrimination against women and blacks, moreover, properly focused on the lowering of academic standards made inevitable by a talent pool restricted to white males. By insisting that qualified women and blacks be given due consideration, affirmative action properly implemented ought to replace mediocre professors with superior ones.

14 Unfortunately D'Souza sidesteps this larger issue. Still, it will emerge quickly if his book receives the attention it deserves. The decline in academic standards has proceeded in tandem with the radical egalitarian conviction that everyone is fit for, and has a right to, a college education. As a consequence of this conviction, even our finest colleagues have had to struggle constantly to do more than teach at a high school level, since most of their students are certainly unprepared and probably unqualified. We have transformed our colleges from places of higher learning into places for the technical training of poorly prepared young men and women who need a degree to get a job in a college-crazy society. An example: the "democratization" of the history curriculum has led to the abolition of required courses in Western civilization and, in American history, of the introductory courses that serve as prerequisites for ostensibly advanced courses on, say, the Civil War. Which means that every such course must be reduced to an introductory course, since the professor cannot assume that his students know the difference between John C. Calhoun and Henry

Clay, or know about Nullification and the Wilmot Proviso, or about anything else for that matter.

D'Souza recognizes as ghastly the conditions that are 15
keeping blacks off the fabled "level playing field," but he sensibly insists that universities cannot do much to correct those conditions without pointlessly ruining themselves. Still, D'Souza himself continues to preach "equality of opportunity," even though conservatives like Richard Weaver and M. E. Bradford, not to mention a few liberals, have exploded it as a cruel hoax. If, as should be obvious, some people, black or white, begin with less cultural advantage, less preparation, and less talent than others, "equality of opportunity" can only result in the perpetuation of the initial levels of inequality.

The problems posed by D'Souza range well beyond the 16
horror stories and lead directly to the essential purposes of liberal education, and to the alarming assault on Western civilization—on the civilization, not just on the courses on the civilization. D'Souza, a man of color born in India, is no mindless celebrant of Western virtues and values. He advocates a curriculum that includes attention to the rest of the world. And he argues well that those who denigrate the Western also denigrate the non-Western: they have no interest in teaching the *Analects,* the Ramayana, or the Koran, but prefer instead to peddle what usually turns out to be little more than recent non-Western versions of their favorite radical Western ideologies.

The point deserves pausing over. It is almost always the 17
case that those who denigrate Western civilization do not tolerate those who teach the entire truth about Asia and Africa, about Hinduism and Islam, which have also had a history of racism, sexism, class exploitation, imperialism, and murderous violence. It does not occur to them (or does it?) that they thereby rob their Asian and African American students of a chance to learn the specifics, and the complexities, of the history of their own forebears. They leave their Asian and African American students bereft of a full appreciation of the glory and the shame, the virtue and the vice, that go into the making of everything human.

The campaign for "political correctness" invites ugly tac- 18
tics that could never be sustained, however, without the complicity of the very administrators and the very faculty

members at whom they are directed. At Stanford, students seized the office of President Donald Kennedy, making demands, some constructive and some preposterous. Kennedy bravely announced: "The university will not negotiate on issues of substance in response to unlawful coercion." The next day under unlawful coercion, he entered into negotiations, and he caved in to the demands. (Come to think of it, did he mean that he might negotiate on issues of procedure under unlawful coercion? Did he mean to endorse lawful coercion? Never mind: we don't expect university presidents to speak English these days.)

19 Administrators capitulate to terrorists primarily because they are damage control experts obsessed with the smart move. When terrorists threaten to trash them as racists, sexists, homophobes, and enemies of the people, the smart move is to capitulate, for the administrators have nothing to lose save honor; and since the poststructuralists on their faculties have nicely deconstructed honor, they need pay it no mind. Who could blame administrators for not wanting to face demonstrators who denounce them as criminals? Besides, the national academic establishments and most of the media will commend them for their statesmanship in defusing confrontation, for opening new lines of communication, for showing compassion and sensitivity.

20 A university president who negotiates with storm troopers who have occupied any part of his campus, much less his own office, should be fired. But first we must do our best to save all such quivering time-servers from themselves. To that end, I offer the Law of Liberation through Counterterror: *In every such political struggle, honorable men and women can defeat terrorism only by unleashing counterterrorism against cowardly administrators and their complicit faculty.* Of course, we must obey this law in a humane spirit, for the purpose of liberating these benighted souls to realize their own inner wills. Like loving parents, we must accept the disagreeable duty to inflict excruciating pain on ourselves by whipping our errant children for their own good.

21 After all, our campus heroes do not wish to face demonstrators of another kind: those who, closer to the truth, trash them as front men for a new McCarthyism, as hypocrites who preach diversity and practice totalitarianism, as cowards, whores, and rogues. Let us, then, drive into their brains the terrifying recognition that counter-

terrorists will (figuratively) draw their blood for every concession made to terrorists; that administrators who deftly avoid calls for their ouster from the one side will face such calls from the other side; that, whatever they do, they will suffer hard blows; and that, despite every smart move known to God and man, they will find no place to hide from any war that the terrorists unleash. All, again, for their own good. By raising the price of sleaziness as high as the price of a staunch defense of their campuses, we shall liberate administrators to stand on their own professed principles, secure in the knowledge that they have nothing left to lose.

The surrender of the administrators is not hard to understand, at least in one respect. Who wants to be accused of insensitivity? The answer is, those who recognize "sensitivity" as a code word for the promulgation of a demagogic political program. At Brooklyn College, which I attended in the late 1940s, everyone took for granted that students ought to challenge their professors and each other. Professors acted as if they were paid to assault their students' sensibilities, to offend their most cherished values. The classroom was an ideological war zone. And self-respecting students returned the blows. In this way we had a chance to acquire a first-rate education, that is, to learn to sustain ourselves in combat against dedicated but overworked professors who lacked the time and the "tolerance" to worry about our "feelings." 22

I learned my lessons well, and so I routinely assign books that contradict the point of view presented in my own classroom. I insist only that students challenge my point of view in accordance with the canons of (Southern) courtesy, and in obedience to a rule: lay down plausible premises, argue logically, appeal to evidence. If they say things that offend others, the offended ones are invited to reply, fiercely but in accordance with the same courtesy and in obedience to the same rule. I know no other way to show students, white or black, male or female, the respect that ought to be shown in a place of intellectual and ideological contention. Thus I submit the First Law of College Teaching: *Any professor who, subject to the restraints of common sense and common decency, does not seize every opportunity to offend the sensibilities of his students is insulting and cheating them, and is no college professor at all.* 23

* * *

24 *Illiberal Education* pays much less attention to gender than to race, and displays less knowledge of the issues, the personalities, and the circumstances of women's studies in this country. Yet a larger problem affects D'Souza's treatment of both race and gender: he falls into the trap of condemning black studies and women's studies programs out of hand. D'Souza simply ignores the record of the best of those programs in enriching the college curriculum. He acknowledges excellent scholarship in black studies, but he wrongly asserts that it emanates from scholars in traditional departments. His assertion is anyway beside the point.

25 The demand for separate programs arose because the traditional departments were ignoring, and even condemning, significant subject matter. In this respect, the history of these programs does not differ markedly from the history of area studies, religious studies, Jewish studies, or film studies, some of which also arose in response to political pressures. In principle, we should emphatically welcome black studies and women's studies programs or departments as a legitimate means of promoting scholarship about valuable subjects long and stupidly ignored. In practice, moreover, some of these programs have functioned admirably, as have such centers for the promotion of scholarship as the Carter Woodson Center at the University of Virginia, which offers scholars in black studies an opportunity to pursue their research in an institution that upholds high standards and is open to diverse viewpoints. I very much doubt that D'Souza's blanket condemnation of these academic innovations would apply, after careful investigation, to the women's studies program at Emory University, say, or to a number of other black studies and women's studies programs.

26 If many such programs have little intellectual merit and are principally engaged in political indoctrination, there are exceptions, and they prove that the result is not fated. D'Souza is right to charge that the culpable programs arose from the cynicism (not to mention the racism and the sexism) of administrations and faculties that refused to hold them to proper academic standards. As a result, large numbers of excellent professors in black studies programs and women's studies programs have been left to the mercies of campus politicians who are uninterested in academic standards and hostile to academic freedom.

27 I know of no women's studies program that has a con-

servative or anti-feminist faculty member, although I know of at least one such program that would like to. The problem is not only that many programs are run by professors who, supported by administrators, apply ideological standards in the recruitment of faculty. The problem is also that professors of a more conservative disposition whose work includes subject matter appropriate to women's studies normally want nothing to do with programs that they view as inescapably political. Accepting exclusion, they do not fight for their right to participate and to teach from their own point of view.

When has a conservative or an anti-feminist professor 28
applied for a job in a women's studies program? Such an applicant would be rejected in most places. But if that is the case, then the issue of "discrimination" ought to be joined precisely on grounds of a commitment to "diversity." No university should tolerate a program or a department of any kind that applies political and ideological criteria in hiring and promotions (as many history departments now do). I do not underestimate the magnitude of the task that faces those who would fight this battle. Still, if principled liberals and leftists do inhabit our campuses, as we must hope that they do, then surely they can be rallied to the defense of the academic freedom of their conservative colleagues.

In discussing present trends, D'Souza presents two expla- 29
nations that, while not mutually exclusive, coexist uneasily. He excoriates administrators for succumbing to pressure from those who have sectarian agendas, but he also argues that administrators are imposing their own ideological agendas. He shows that "a revolution from above" is occurring at such leading universities as Harvard, Berkeley, Stanford, and Wisconsin, and that it is spreading; but the burden of his evidence suggests that the greater problem remains the general capitulation to destructive political pressures.

The capitulation has some high-minded alibis. D'Souza 30
mentions them, but he does not probe adequately. The principal alibi stresses the moral imperative of submission to the will of "the community," which is necessary, it is claimed, for the maintenance of a democratic society. The university, this song goes, has no right to exist as an ivory tower, oblivious to the needs and the aspirations of a democratic people. None can object, of course, when the choice is posed so starkly, though it might be recalled that

Southern universities long justified segregation as an accommodation to the prevailing sentiments of their communities. To pose it so starkly, however, is to talk nonsense.

31 Intellectual work in general, and higher education in particular, depend upon academic freedom, which depends upon a wide swath of autonomy, of detachment, for the university. The university must be ready, therefore, to stand against the community, and to protect those who challenge the attitudes and the sensibilities that prevail in the community. Neither academic freedom nor the autonomy of the university should be defended as absolutes. Some measure of accommodation to the larger society is always necessary and proper, and the gray area will always be a battleground. Still, a university worthy of the name must, so far as practicable, recognize its duty to protect those who defy the political consensus of the moment.

32 That is, it must recognize itself as an institution in constant and principled tension with the community in which it resides. When the New Left of the 1960s demanded that the universities become responsive to the community, it ironically advanced the work begun by its Establishment enemies. Long before the hysterical response to Sputnik, the universities had been under pressure to serve the interests of communities attuned to the government and big business. All that the New Left did was to define "community" to suit its own ideas and interests. Like its enemies, it insisted on an engaged academy and poured contempt on the ideal of the university as an autonomous institution.

33 D'Souza's book contains telling quotations from campus zealots on the problem of "politicization." The universities have always been political, they argue. Indeed, everything has a political dimension—and so the only issue is what kind of politics are to be imposed. There is a grain of truth here, but carried to its logical conclusion it would transform every institution into an instrument of political correctness. And that, to speak precisely, is totalitarianism.

34 D'Souza makes too many concessions to democratic and egalitarian dogmas for my taste. He responds to these arguments weakly, by arguing that the politicization of the universities is leading to their domination by coalitions of ideological minorities. No doubt it is. But the danger would be even greater if the universities were to succumb to an ideological majority. The hard truth is that academic freedom—the real work of scholarship—requires a willing-

ness to set limits to the claims of democracy. It requires a strong dose of hierarchical authority within institutions that must be able to defy a democratic consensus. Sooner or later we shall have to face this fact, or be defeated by those who seek the total politicization of our campuses.

D'Souza ends his book constructively, with three propos- 35
als to promote academic standards and academic freedom and simultaneously to do justice to genuinely disadvantaged youth. His first, and most significant, is his call for "non-racial affirmative action." With this idea, he risks the ire of many on the right. He notes that the rising tide of white racism among students is being fueled by discrimination against qualified white students in favor of less qualified black students who receive financial support despite coming from affluent families. Recognizing that most qualified black students, like many qualified white students, need financial support, he proposes to subsidize according to a combination of demonstrated merit and need. An advocate of "individualism," D'Souza insists that his program promotes "equality of opportunity" and rejects categorization by group. Surely he jests. For his program implies a collectivism that merely replaces "race" with "class." At least it promises to attack racial injustice, since the correlation of race and lower class among blacks is, as he takes pains to show, strikingly high.

His second proposal is for "choice without separation." 36
It's not exactly clear what this slogan means. It originates in a critique of black separatism that I find sadly wrongheaded. D'Souza, fearful of ghettoization and the institutionalization of racial oppression in a new form, seems alarmed at the very idea of separate black professional and extracurricular organizations. He lashes out, therefore, at everything that hints of black separatism, of any kind of separatism. But he is uncritically assimilating the black experience in America to the general "ethnic" experience, and he is thereby missing its uniqueness. Blacks did not bring a distinct culture from Africa as, say, Italian-Americans or Polish-Americans did from their homelands; they forged a new and powerful culture of their own. Afro-American culture has grown out of a forced emigration from Africa, out of resistance to slavery, and out of enforced segregation, and for those reasons it has imparted to many black people a sense of being "a nation within a nation," to invoke a term that dates from early

colonial times and was popularized by W. E. B. DuBois. The attendant problems of analysis, not to mention politics, are extraordinarily complex. And for just that reason they ought long ago to have been made the center of discussion on our campuses, in and out of black studies programs.

37 D'Souza's third proposal offers an intriguing curriculum reform that would expose students "to the basic issues of equality and human difference, through a carefully chosen set of classic texts that deal powerfully with those issues." Briefly, he aims at grounding American students in the Western experience that has constituted the foundation of our society and culture, but in a way that promotes comparison and contrast with the civilizations of the rest of the world and appreciates their contribution to our own national development. This proposal is unobjectionable, but it is not very original. In fact, an increasing number of principled professors are in fact promoting "World Civilization" in the manner D'Souza recommends—that is, by introducing African, Asian, and Latin American cultural studies without denigrating Western civilization.

38 *Illiberal Education* invites cooperation in a common effort in defense of the campus. Occasionally D'Souza descends into biased and irritating attacks on the left and center, with sweeping and one-sided characterizations of Marxism and Marxists, liberalism and liberals. (He does not do justice to the literary critic Henry Louis Gates, Jr. or the historian Linda Kerber, among others.) Yet on the whole he makes a good effort to be fair, to focus on issues, to avoid ad hominem attacks, and to check his own political passions. He acknowledges, however grudgingly, the commitment of certain Marxists, feminists, proponents of black studies, and others to academic freedom and to scholarly integrity. This book could open a salutary national debate. But the cause it champions will go down, unless it is supported by a substantial portion of the left and the center.

39 For this is not an issue only of the right, not least for a practical reason: there are not nearly enough conservatives on our campuses to do more than fight a rearguard action. Indeed, the predicament of the right should give many on the left a sense of déjà vu, and a good laugh. Opposition to campus atrocities attracts two kinds of right-wingers: those who defend academic freedom and academic standards on principle, and those interested in using the issue as a

"transmission belt" for recruitment into their "movement." The former, I mean the principled defenders of the academy, understand that they must cooperate with those whom they oppose on other issues. The latter, I mean the sectarians, do everything possible to identify the academic cause with their own partisan politics and slander all liberals and leftists as complicit in the new wave of campus barbarism. Looking beyond the immediate struggle, they fear nothing so much as the dissolution of the reigning isms, and the redrawing of political lines in a manner that brings together the healthiest elements of long-warring political camps.

The sectarians are correct to fear the consecration of the 40
campuses to a vigorous political debate under conditions of real mutual respect and genuine academic freedom. Such a debate would undermine all the sectarianisms. It would encourage new political formations to meet the challenges of a new era. And so it should: the defense of academic freedom requires an all-out counterattack by a coalition that cuts across all the lines of politics, race, and gender. It is time to close ranks.

John Taylor

Are You Politically Incorrect?

John Taylor writes frequently for New York *magazine; indeed, he is a contributing editor for it.* New York *magazine could be described as a sort of* Time *or* Newsweek *for New Yorkers: published weekly, it covers the current events and contemporary cultural affairs that are particularly interesting to people in the New York metropolitan area. The following article appeared in* New York *in January 1991.*

"Racist." 1

"Racist!" 2

"The man is a racist!" 3

"A *racist!*" 4

Such denunciations, hissed in tones of self-righteousness 5
and contempt, vicious and vengeful, furious, smoking with hatred—such denunciations haunted Stephan Thernstrom

for weeks. Whenever he walked through the campus that spring, down Harvard's brick paths, under the arched gates, past the fluttering elms, he found it hard not to imagine the pointing fingers, the whispers. Racist. There goes *the racist.* It was hellish, this persecution. Thernstrom couldn't sleep. His nerves were frayed, his temper raw. He was making his family miserable. And the worst thing was that he didn't know who was calling him a racist, or why.

6 Thernstrom, 56, a professor at Harvard University for 25 years, is considered one of the preeminent scholars of the history of race relations in America. He has tenure. He has won prizes and published numerous articles and four books and edited the *Harvard Encyclopedia of American Ethnic Groups*. For several years, Thernstrom and another professor, Bernard Bailyn, taught an undergraduate lecture course on the history of race relations in the United States called "Peopling of America." Bailyn covered the Colonial era. Thernstrom took the class up to the present.

7 Both professors are regarded as very much in the academic mainstream, their views grounded in extensive research on their subject, and both have solid liberal democratic credentials. But all of a sudden, in the fall of 1987, articles began to appear in the *Harvard Crimson* accusing Thernstrom and Bailyn of "racial insensitivity" in "Peopling of America." The sources for the articles were anonymous, the charges vague, but they continued to be repeated, these ringing indictments.

8 Finally, through the intervention of another professor, two students from the lecture course came forward and identified themselves as the sources for the articles. When asked to explain their grievances, they presented the professors with a six-page letter. Bailyn's crime had been to read from the diary of a southern planter without giving equal time to the recollections of a slave. This, to the students, amounted to a covert defense of slavery. Bailyn, who has won two Pulitzer Prizes, had pointed out during the lecture that no journals, diaries, or letters written by slaves had ever been found. He had explained to the class that all they could do was read the planter's diary and use it to speculate about the experience of slaves. But that failed to satisfy the complaining students. Since it was impossible to give equal representation to the slaves, Bailyn ought to have dispensed with the planter's diary altogether.

Thernstom's failures, according to the students, were almost systematic. He had, to begin with, used the word *Indians* instead of *Native Americans.* Thernstrom tried to point out that he had said very clearly in class that *Indian* was the word most Indians themselves use, but that was irrelevant to the students. They considered the word racist. Thernstrom was also accused of referring to an "Oriental religion." The word *Oriental,* with its imperialist overtones, was unacceptable. Thernstrom explained that he had used the word as an adjective, not as a noun, but the students weren't buying any wriggling, sophistic evasions like that. 9

Even worse, they continued, Thernstrom had assigned a book to the class that mentioned that some people regarded affirmative action as preferential treatment. That was a racist opinion. But most egregiously, Thernstrom had endorsed, in class, Patrick Moynihan's emphasis on the breakup of the black family as a cause of persistent black poverty. That was a racist idea. 10

All of these words and opinions and ideas and historical approaches were racist. *Racist!* They would not be tolerated. 11

The semester was pretty much over by then. But during the spring, when Thernstrom sat down to plan the course for the following year, he had to think about how he would combat charges of racism should they crop up again. And they assuredly would. All it took was one militant student, one word like *Oriental* taken out of context, one objection that a professor's account of slavery was insufficiently critical or that, in discussing black poverty, he had raised the "racist" issue of welfare dependency. And a charge of racism, however unsubstantiated, leaves a lasting impression. "It's like being called a Commie in the fifties," Thernstrom says. "Whatever explanation you offer, once accused, you're always suspect." 12

He decided that to protect himself in case he was misquoted or had comments taken out of context, he would need to tape all his lectures. Then he decided he would have to tape his talks with students in his office. He would, in fact, have to tape everything he said on the subject of race. It would require a tape-recording system worthy of the Nixon White House. Microphones everywhere, the reels turning constantly. That was plainly ridiculous. Thernstrom instead decided it would be easier just to drop the course altogether. "Peopling of America" is no longer offered at Harvard. 13

The New Fundamentalism

14 When the Christian-fundamentalist uprising began in the late seventies, Americans on the left sneered at the Bible thumpers who tried to ban the teaching of evolution in public schools, at the troglodtyes who wanted to remove *The Catcher in the Rye* from public libraries. They heaped scorn on the evangelists who railed against secular humanism and the pious hypocrites who tried to legislate patriotism and Christianity through school prayer and the Pledge of Allegiance. This last effort was considered particularly heinous. Those right-wing demagogues were interfering with individual liberties! They were trying to indoctrinate the children! It was scandalous and outrageous, and unconstitutional too.

15 But curiously enough, in the past few years, a new sort of fundamentalism has arisen precisely among those people who were the most appalled by Christian fundamentalism. And it is just as demagogic and fanatical. The new fundamentalists are an eclectic group; they include multiculturalists, feminists, radical homosexuals, Marxists, New Historicists. What unites them—as firmly as the Christian fundamentalists are united in the belief that the Bible is the revealed word of God—is their conviction that Western culture and American society are thoroughly and hopelessly racist, sexist, oppressive. "Racism and sexism are pervasive in America and fundamentally present in all American institutions," declares a draft report on "race and gender enrichment" at Tulane University. A 1989 report by a New York State Board of Education task force was even more sweeping: "Intellectual and educational oppression . . . has characterized the culture and institutions of the United States and the European American world for centuries."

16 The heart of the new fundamentalists' argument is not just that, as most everyone would agree, racism and sexism historically have existed within political systems designed to promote individual liberties. They believe that the doctrine of individual liberties *itself* is inherently oppressive. At the University of Pennsylvania, an undergraduate on the "diversity education committee" wrote a memo to committee members describing her "deep regard for the individual and my desire to protect the freedoms of all members of society." The tone was earnest and sincere. The young woman clearly considered herself an idealist of the Jeffersonian persuasion.

Individual freedom, she seemed to indicate, was a concept to be cherished above all else.

But in the prevailing climate, Thomas Jefferson and all the Founding Fathers are in disrepute. (The Constitution, according to the 1989 New York State report, is "the embodiment of the White Male with Property Model.") One college administrator had no patience with the young woman's naïve and bourgeois sentiments. He returned her memo with the word *individual* underlined. "This is a 'RED FLAG' phrase today, which many consider RACIST," the administrator wrote. "Arguments that champion the individual over the group ultimately privilege the 'INDIVIDUALS' belonging to the largest or dominant group." 17

Defenders of Western culture try to point out that other civilizations—from the Islamic and the Hindu to the Confucian and the Buddhist—are rife with racism and sexism. They find it odd that while Eastern Europeans are rushing to embrace Western democracy, while the pro-democracy movement in China actually erected a replica of the Statue of Liberty in Tiananmen Square, this peculiar intellectual cult back in the States continues to insist that Western values are the source of much of the world's evil. 18

But one of the marvels of the new fundamentalism is the rationale it has concocted for dismissing all dissent. Just as Christian fundamentalists attack nonbelievers as agents of Satan, so the politically correct dismiss their critics as victims of, to use the famous Marxist phrase, "false consciousness." Anyone who disagrees is simply too soaked in the oppressors' propaganda to see the truth. "Racism and sexism are subtle and, for the most part, subconscious or at least subsurface," the Tulane report continues. "It is difficult for us to see and overcome racism and sexism because we are all a product of the problem, i.e., we are all the progeny of a racist and sexist society." 19

This circular reasoning enables the new fundamentalists to attack not just the opinions of their critics but the right of their critics to disagree. Alternate viewpoints are simply not allowed. Though there was little visible protest when Louis Farrakhan was invited to speak at the University of Wisconsin, students at the University of Northern Colorado practically rioted when Linda Chavez, a Hispanic member of the Reagan administration who opposes affirmative action and believes immigrants should be encouraged to learn English, was asked to talk. The invitation was withdrawn. 20

Last February, Patrick Moynihan declared during a lecture at Vassar that America was "a model of a reasonably successful multiethnic society." Afterward, he got into an argument with a black woman who disagreed with him, and when she claimed the senator had insulted her, militant students occupied a school building until Moynihan returned his lecture fee. "The disturbing factor in the success of totalitarianism is . . . the true selflessness of its adherents," Hannah Arendt wrote in *The Origins of Totalitarianism.* "The fanaticized members can be reached by neither experience nor argument."

21 It is this sort of demand for intellectual conformity, enforced with harassment and intimidation, that has led some people to compare the atmosphere in universities today to that of Germany in the thirties. "It's fascism of the left," says Camille Paglia, a professor at the University of the Arts in Philadelphia and the author of *Sexual Personae.* "These people behave like the Hitler Youth."

22 It reminds others of America in the fifties. "This sort of atmosphere, where a few highly mobilized radical students can intimidate everyone else, is quite new," Thernstrom says. "This is a new McCarthyism. It's more frightening than the old McCarthyism, which had no support in the academy. Now the enemy is within. There are students and faculty who have no belief in freedom of speech."

23 And it reminds still others of China during the Cultural Revolution of the sixties, when thought criminals were paraded through towns in dunce caps. "In certain respects, the University of Pennsylvania has become like the University of Peking," says Alan Kors, a professor of history.

24 Indeed, schools like Berkeley and Carleton require courses in race relations, sometimes called "oppression studies." A proposed course book for a required writing seminar at the University of Texas contains, instead of models of clarity like E. B. White, essays such as "is not so gd [*sic*] to be born a girl," by Ntozake Shange. Many schools—including Stanford, Pennsylvania, and the University of Wisconsin—have adopted codes of conduct that require students who deviate from politically correct thinking to undergo thought reform. When a student at the University of Michigan read a limerick that speculated jokingly about the homosexuality of a famous athlete, he was required to attend gay-sensitivity sessions and publish a piece of self-criticism in the student newspaper called "Learned My Lesson."

But is any of this so awful? In the minds of its advocates, 25
thought reform is merely a well-intentioned effort to help stop the spread of the racial tensions that have proliferated in universities in recent years. "I don't know of any institution that is saying you have to adore everyone else," says Catharine Stimpson, dean of the graduate school at Rutgers. "They are saying you have to learn to live with everyone. They are taking insulting language seriously. That's a good thing. They're not laughing off anti-Semitic and homophobic graffiti."

After all, it is said, political indoctrination of one sort or 26
another has always taken place at universities. Now that process is simply being made overt. And anyway, all these people complaining about the loss of academic freedom and the decline in standards are only trying to disguise their own efforts to retain power. "The attack on diversity is a rhetorical strategy by neoconservatives who have their own political agenda," says Stimpson. "Under the guise of defending objectivity and intellectual rigor, which is a lot of mishmash, they are trying to preserve the cultural and political supremacy of white heterosexual males."

Everything Is Political

If the debate over what students should be taught has 27
become an openly political power struggle, that is only because, to the politically correct, *everything* is political. And nothing is more political, in their view, than the humanities, where much of the recent controversy has been centered.

For most of the twentieth century, professors in the 28
humanities modeled themselves on their counterparts in the natural sciences. They thought of themselves as specialists in the disinterested pursuit of the truth. Their job, in the words of T. S. Eliot, was "the elucidation of art and the correction of taste," and to do so they concentrated on what Matthew Arnold called "the best that has been thought and written."

That common sense of purpose began to fracture in the 29
sixties. The generation of professors now acquiring prominence and power at universities—Elaine Showalter, the head of the English department at Princeton; Donna Shalala, chancellor of the University of Wisconsin; James Freedman, the president of Dartmouth—came of age during

that period. They witnessed its upheavals and absorbed its political commitments.

30 And by and large, they have retained them. Which means that, though much of the country subsequently rejected the political vision of the sixties, it has triumphed at the universities. "If the undergraduate population has moved quietly to the right in recent years, the men and women who are paid to introduce students to the great works and ideas of our civilization have by and large remained true to the emancipationist ideology of the sixties," writes Roger Kimball in his book, *Tenured Radicals.* The professors themselves eagerly admit this. "I see my scholarship as an extension of my political activism," said Annette Kolodny, a former Berkeley radical and now the dean of the humanities faculty at the University of Arizona.

31 In the view of such activists, the universities were hardly the havens of academic independence they pretended to be. They had hopelessly compromised their integrity by accepting contracts from the Pentagon, but those alliances with the reviled "military-industrial Establishment" were seen as merely one symptom of a larger conspiracy by white males. Less obviously, but more insidiously, they had appointed themselves guardians of the culture and compiled the list of so-called Great Books as a propaganda exercise to reinforce the notion of white-male superiority. "The canon of great literature was created by high-Anglican ass----s to underwrite their social class," Stanley Hauerwas, a professor at Duke's Divinity School, put it recently.

32 Several schools of French critical theory that became fashionable during the seventies provided the jargon for this critique. Semiotics and Lacanian psychoanalysis argued that language and art conveyed subliminal cultural prejudices, power configurations, metaphoric representations of gender. Deconstruction declared that texts, to use the preferred word, had no meaning outside themselves. "There is no such thing as literal meaning . . . there is no such thing as intrinsic merit," wrote Stanley Fish, the head of Duke's English department.

33 That being the case, any attempt to assign meaning to art, literature, or thought, to interpret it and evaluate it, was nothing more than an exercise in political power by the individual with the authority to impose his or her view. It then followed that the only reason to require students to read certain books is not to "correct taste" or because the

books were "the best that has been thought or written" but because they promoted politically correct viewpoints. That ideological emphasis also applied to scholarship generally. "If the work doesn't have a strong political thrust, I don't see how it matters," said Eve Sedgwick, a professor of English at Duke and the author of such papers as "Jane Austen and the Masturbating Girl."

This agenda can produce a rather remarkable, not to say outré, reading list. Catharine Stimpson has declared that her ideal curriculum would contain the little-known book *Stars in My Pocket Like Grains of Sand*. "Like many contemporary speculative fictions," Stimpson wrote, "*Stars in My Pocket* finds conventional heterosexuality absurd. The central characters are two men, Rat Korga and Marq Dyeth, who have a complex but ecstatic affair. Marq is also the product of a rich 'nurture stream.' His ancestry includes both humans and aliens. His genetic heritage blends differences. In a sweet scene, he sees three of his mothers." 34

Ethnic and Ideological Purity

The multicultural and ethnic-studies programs now in place at most universities tend to divide humanity into five groups—whites, blacks, Native Americans, Hispanics, and Asians. (Homosexuals and feminists are usually included on the grounds that, though they are not a distinct ethnic group, they, too, have been oppressed by the "whitemale," to use the neologism of black literature professor Houston Baker, and prevented from expressing their "otherness.") These are somewhat arbitrary categories, and, in fact, the new fundamentalists have two contradictory views about just what constitutes an ethnic group and who can belong. 35

On the one hand, there is a reluctance to confer ethnic status on certain groups. At the University of Washington, a student-faculty Task Force on Ethnicity denied Jews, Italians, and Irish-Americans certification as ethnic groups. Status as an oppressed ethnic group is guarded even more jealously. The Washington task force also decided that a required ethnic-studies program exploring the pervasiveness of racism in America would not take up the subject of anti-Semitism. The reason, *Commentary* quoted professor Johnnella Butler as having said, was that "anti-Semitism is not institutionalized in this country." 36

37 At the same time, the racial credentials of people aspiring to membership in the officially sanctioned ethnic categories are examined with an attention to detail associated with apartheid. Recently, a Hispanic who had been turned down for an affirmative-action promotion in the San Francisco fire department filed a complaint because the person who got the job instead was from Spain rather than Latin America. Colleges are becoming equally obsessed with such distinctions. Three years ago, the faculty at Hampshire College in Amherst began interviewing candidates for a professorship in Latin American literature. The professor, of course, needed to be Latin. *Pure* Latin. One woman who applied for the job was turned down because, though she was Argentine, she had, like many Argentines, Jewish and Italian blood, and thus her Third World ethnicity was considered insufficiently pure. Her heritage made her, in the words of one faculty member, "Eurocentric."

38 But even as these standards become increasingly exacting, more and more groups are clamoring for oppressed status. While supporters of American involvement in the Vietnam War were denounced as "war criminals" at the University of Michigan in the sixties, the school now counts Vietnam veterans as an oppressed group. In fact, the politically correct have concluded that virtually *any*one with *any* sort of trait, anxiety, flaw, impediment, or unusual sexual preference qualifies for membership in an oppressed group. This past fall, a handout from the Office of Student Affairs at Smith College explained that many people are *unaware* they are oppressed, though with help they are finding out: "As groups of people begin the process of realizing that they are oppressed, and why, new words tend to be created to express the concepts that the existing language cannot."

39 This obsessive tendency to see oppression everywhere is creating a sort of New Age caste system. The Smith handout listed various categories of oppression that ranged from "classism" and "ageism" to "ableism" (identified as "oppression of the differently abled by the temporarily able") and "lookism," which was revealed to be "the construction of a standard for beauty/attractiveness; and oppression through stereotypes and generalizations of both those who do not fit that standard and those who do." Heightism may be next. In a joke now making the rounds, short people are demanding to be known as "the vertically challenged."

40 But joking isn't allowed! Even the most harmless, light-

hearted remarks can lead to virulent denunciations. In October, Roderick Nash, a professor at the University of California at Santa Barbara, pointed out during a lecture on environmental ethics that there is a movement to start referring to pets as animal companions. (Apparently, domesticated animals are offended by the word *pet.*) Nash then made some sort of off-the-cuff observation about how women who pose for *Penthouse* are still called Pets (and not *Penthouse* Animal Companions). Inevitably, several female students filed a formal sexual-harassment complaint against him. Susan Rode, one of the signers, said, "Maybe this will make more people aware in other classes and make other faculty watch what they say."

Indeed, making people *watch what they say* is the central preoccupation of politically correct students. Stephan Thernstrom is not the only professor who has been forced to give up a course on race relations. Reynolds Farley, one of the leading scholars on race relations, dropped a course he had taught for nearly ten years at the University of Michigan after he was accused of racial insensitivity for reading Malcolm X's description of himself as a pimp and a thief and for discussing the southern defense of slavery. "Given the climate at Michigan," Farley said, "I could be hassled for anything I do or don't say in that class." 41

Watch what you say: And it's not enough just to avoid racism. One must display absolute ideological purity. The search committee at Hampshire College also considered a highly qualified Chicano candidate for the Latin American–literature post. Unfortunately for him, in his dissertation on Chicano literature he drew parallels between Shakespeare and Mexican writers. This demonstrated dangerous "Eurocentric" tendencies. Certain faculty members, doubting the candidate's ethnic purity as well, wondered whether someone of Mexican heritage was *really* Latin American. They thought a Puerto Rican might be better. He didn't get the job. 42

It was finally offered to Norman Holland, who seemed both ethnically and ideologically pure. But this past summer, Holland's contract was not renewed, and Holland claims it is because he also was branded "Eurocentric." Though the school's official position is that Holland was an ineffective teacher, two of the professors who reviewed his work insinuated that he had a European bias. Holland, one professor declared, had "focused mainly on Western Europe 43 to the exclusion of cultural issues Third World students perceive as uniquely relevant." "I suppose I committed certain kinds of sins," says Holland. "When I was teaching *One Hundred Years of Solitude,* I would talk about colonial rape, but I would also talk about how the novel originated in Europe and how García Márquez was working in that tradition and addressing ideas in Proust and Joyce. I didn't limit myself to considering it as a sociological document."

The Gender Feminists and Date Rape

44 "Misogynistic!"

45 "Patriarchal!"

46 "Gynophobic!"

47 "Phallocentric!"

48 Last fall, Camille Paglia attended a lecture by a "feminist theorist" from a large Ivy League university who had set out to "decode" the subliminal sexual oppressiveness in fashion photography. The feminist theorist stood at the front of the room showing slides of fashion photography and cosmetics ads and exposing, in the style of Lacanian psychoanalysis, their violent sexism. She had selected a Revlon ad of a woman with a heavily made-up face who was standing up to her chin in a pool of water. When it came up on the screen, she exclaimed, "Decapitation!"

49 She showed a picture of a black woman who was wearing aviator goggles and had the collar of her turtleneck sweater pulled up. "Strangulation!" she shouted. "Bondage!"

50 It went on like this for the entire lecture. When it was over, Paglia, who considers herself a feminist, stood up and made an impassioned speech. She declared that the fashion photography of the past 40 years is great art, that instead of decapitation she saw the birth of Venus, instead of strangulation she saw references to King Tut. But political correctness has achieved a kind of exquisitely perfect rigidity among the group known as the gender feminists, and she was greeted, she says, "with gasps of horror and angry murmuring. It's a form of psychosis, this slogan-filled machinery. The radical feminists have contempt for values other than their own, and they're inspiring in students a resentful attitude toward the world."

51 Indeed, the central tenet of gender feminism is that Western society is organized around a "sex/gender system."

What defines the system, according to Sandra Harding, a professor of philosophy at the University of Delaware and one of its exponents, is "male dominance made possible by men's control of women's productive and reproductive labor."

The primary arena for this dominance is, of course, the 52
family, which Alison Jaggar, a professor at the University of Cincinnati and the head of the American Philosophical Association's Committee on the Status of Women in Philosophy, sees as "a cornerstone of women's oppression." The family, in Jaggar's view, "enforces heterosexuality" and "imposes the prevailing masculine and feminine character structures on the next generation."

This position makes gender feminists, as Christina Som- 53
mers has written in an article in *Public Affairs Quarterly*, from which some of these quotes were taken, "oddly unsympathetic to the women whom they claim to represent." But that poses no problem. Women who have decided to get married and raise families, women who want to become mothers, are, naturally, victims of false consciousness. The radical feminists are fond of quoting Simone de Beauvoir, who said, "No woman should be authorized to stay at home and raise children . . . precisely because if there is such a choice, too many women will make that one."

Jaggar, for one, would like to abolish the family altogether 54
and create a society where, with the aid of technology, "one woman could inseminate another, . . . men . . . could lactate, . . . and fertilized ova could be transferred into women's or even men's bodies." All that is preventing this, according to the gender feminists, is "phallocentricity" and "androcentricity," the view that society is organized around the male and his sexual organs. The feminists, ablaze with revolutionary rhetoric, have set out to overthrow this system. "What we feminists are doing," the philosopher Barbara Minnich has said, "is comparable to Copernicus shattering our geocentricity, Darwin shattering our species-centricity. We are shattering androcentricity, and the change is as fundamental, as dangerous, as exciting."

But unlike the pre-Copernican view that the Earth was at 55
the center of the universe, androcentricity is not, in the view of the gender feminists, merely a flawed theory. It is a moral evil, dedicated to the enslavement of women. And since most of Western culture, according to this view, has been a testament to "male power and transcendence," it is similar

to evil and must be discarded. This includes not only patriarchal books like the Bible and sexist subjects like traditional history, with its emphasis on great men and great deeds, but also the natural sciences and even the very process of analytical thinking itself. "To know is to f---" has become a radical-feminist rallying cry. Indeed, scientific inquiry itself is seen as "the rape of nature." A project sponsored by the state of New Jersey to integrate these views into college campuses has issued a set of "feminist scholarship guidelines" that declares "mind was male. Nature was female, and knowledge was created as an act of aggression—a passive nature had to be interrogated, unclothed, penetrated, and compelled by man to reveal her secrets."

56 To certain women, however, this is just a veiled restatement of the old idea that women don't make good scientists. "As as liberal feminist, I encourage women to study science," says Christina Sommers. "I'm not impugning science itself as hostile to the female sensibility."

57 But it is not just the coldly analytical and dualistic structures of male thinking that the gender feminists find so contemptible. It is males themselves, or at least heterosexual males. After all, heterosexuality is responsible for the subjugation of women, and so, in the oppressive culture of the West, any woman who goes on a date with a man is a prostitute. "Both man and woman might be outraged at the description of their candlelight dinner as prostitution," Jaggar has written. "But the radical feminist argues this outrage is simply due to the participants' failure or refusal to perceive the social context in which the dinner occurs." In other words, they are victims of—what else?—false consciousness.

58 This eagerness to see all women as victims, to describe all male behavior with images of rape and violation, may shed some light on the phenomenon of date rape, a legitimate issue that has been exaggerated and distorted by a small group with a specific political agenda. As with the hysteria a few years ago over the sexual abuse of children, endless talk shows, television news stories, and magazine articles have been devoted to date rape, often describing it as "an epidemic" that, as the Chicago *Tribune* put it, "makes women campus prisoners" and forces them, as at Brown, to list supposed rapists on bathroom walls.

59 Much of this discussion starts off with the claim that one

in four female students is raped by a date. The figure seems staggeringly high, and debate tends to focus on whether actual rape or merely the reporting of rape is on the rise. But the journalist Stephanie Gutmann has pointed out in *Reason* magazine the gross statistical flaws in the survey of date rape that produced this figure. According to Gutmann, "the real story about campus date rape is not that there's been any significant increase of rape on college campuses, at least of the acquaintance type, but that the word *rape* is being stretched to encompass any type of sexual interaction."

In fact, rape under the new definition does not have to 60
involve physical assault at all. Andrea Parrot, a professor at Cornell who has promoted the idea of the date-rape epidemic, has declared that "any sexual intercourse without mutual desire is a form of rape." In other words, a woman is being raped if she has sex when not in the mood, even if she fails to inform her partner of that fact. As a former director of Columbia's date-rape-education program told Gutmann, "Every time you have an act of intercourse, there must be explicit consent, and if there's no explicit consent, then it's rape. . . . Stone silence throughout an entire physical encounter with someone is not explicit consent." And rape is no longer limited to actual intercourse. A training manual at Swarthmore College states that "acquaintance rape . . . spans a spectrum of incidents and behaviors ranging from crimes legally defined as rape to verbal harassment and inappropriate innuendo."

It is no surprise then that Catherine Nye, a University of 61
Chicago psychologist interviewed by Gutmann, found that 43 percent of the women in a widely cited rape study "had not realized they had been raped." In other words, they were victims of, yes, false consciousness. But by the definition of the radical feminists, all sexual encounters that involve any confusion or ambivalence constitute rape. "Ordinary bungled sex—the kind you regret in the morning or even during—is being classified as rape," Gutmann says. "Bad or confused feelings after sex become someone else's fault." Which is fine with the feminists. "In terms of making men nervous or worried about overstepping their bounds, I don't think that's a bad thing," Parrot said. Indeed,since it encourages a general suspicion of all men, it's a good thing. As Parrot has put it, "Since you can't tell who has the potential for rape simply by looking, be on your guard with every man."

Afrocentrism

62 For all their fury, the gender feminists are surpassed in ideological rage by an even more extreme wing of the politically correct: the Afrocentrists. Afrocentrists argue that not only is Western culture oppressive, it isn't even really *Western.* Key accomplishments, from mathematics and biology to architecture and medicine, were in fact the work of Africans. "Very few doctors, African-American or otherwise in America, are aware of the fact that when they take their medical oath, the hypocratic [*sic*] oath, they actually swear to Imhotep, the African God of Medicine," Asa Hilliard, a professor of Afro-American history at Georgia State, has written.

63 The theory that Africa was the true source of Western civilization hinges on the claim that the ancient Egyptians were black. "The first 12 dynasties plus dynasties 18 and 25 were native-black-African dynasties," Hilliard has asserted. Traditional Egyptologists generally believe that while blacks, from Nubia to the south, were active in Egyptian society, ancient Egyptians, like their contemporary counterparts, tended to be of Semitic stock. But to the Afrocentrists, that explanation is merely part of the long-running conspiracy by Western whites to deny the African contribution to civilization.

64 The conspiracy began, in the Afrocentric view, when the ancient Greeks "stole" African philosophy and science from the Egyptians. To claim European credit for these discoveries, Romans and, later, Christians burned the library of Alexandria in Egypt. The conspiracy has continued ever since. Napoleon's soldiers shot off the nose and lips of the Sphinx to obliterate its Negroid features. Beethoven and Robert Browning were actually blacks whose ethnicity has been hidden. "African history has been lost, stolen, destroyed, and suppressed," Hilliard maintains.

65 Leonard Jeffries, chairman of the black-studies department at City College and one of the most extreme exponents of Afrocentrism, has worked up a sort of anthropological model to explain why Europeans have oppressed Africans. The human race, according to Jeffries, is divided into the "ice people" and the "sun people." The ethnic groups descended from the ice people are materialistic, selfish, and violent, while those descended from the sun people are

nonviolent, cooperative, and spiritual. In addition, blacks are biologically superior to whites, Jeffries maintains, because they have more melanin, and melanin regulates intellect and health.

Despite the spiritual benevolence one might expect from a "sun person," Jeffries is known for making the sort of hostile denunciations that, if he were at the other end of the political spectrum, would no doubt provoke howls of indignation. According to Fred Rueckher, a white student who took his course, Jeffries attacked black males for succumbing to the "white pussy syndrome," that is, pursuing white women. He called Diana Ross an "international whore" for her involvement with white men. And he applauded the destruction of the Challenger space shuttle because it would deter white people from "spreading their filth throughout the universe." 66

Jeffries's wild remarks are excused by the politically correct on the grounds that to be a racist, you have to have "institutional power," and since blacks do not have "institutional power," they cannot be considered racist. The somewhat flimsy propositions of Afrocentrism are excused with equal finesse. First of all, since everything is political, there has never been disinterested scholarship, only power plays by various groups to justify their own claims. And even if there are some holes in Afrocentrism, the approach is useful because it raises the "self-esteem" of black students. 67

Such was the reasoning of the New York State Board of Education's Task Force on Minorities, to which Leonard Jeffries was a consultant. Its report suggested that "all curricular materials [including math and science] be prepared on the basis of multicultural contributions." As a result, the report said, children from minority cultures "will have higher self-esteem and self-respect, while children from European cultures will have a less arrogant perspective." The notion has already been put into effect in public schools in Portland, Indianapolis, and Washington, D.C., where students are taught subjects like Yoruba mathematics and ancient-Egyptian astronomy. 68

The idea that the "self-esteem" of students—rather than historical relevance—should be the basis for including material in textbooks does have its critics. Among the most prominent is Diane Ravitch, who has said the idea "that children can learn only from the experiences of people from the same race" represents a sort of "racial fundamentalism." 69

The success of Chinese students in math is due not to numbers but to hard work. If the "self-esteem" model had any validity, Italian-American students—the descendants of Caesar and Michelangelo—would excel in school, but in fact they have the highest dropout rate of any white group in New York City schools. By promoting a brand of history "in which everyone is either a descendant of victims or oppressors," Ravitch has declared, "ancient hatreds are fanned and re-created in each new generation."

70 Ravitch naturally was branded a racist for this position. Participants at a recent Afrocentrism conference in Atlanta derided her as "Miss Daisy." She has been attacked in the *City Sun* and on black television and radio programs. As a result, she has received so many threats that when we first agreed to meet, she was afraid to tell me where she lived. "They've written saying things like 'We're going to get you, bitch. We're going to beat your white ass.' "

Moonies in the Classroom

71 The supreme irony of the new fundamentalism is that the generation that produced the free-speech movement in Berkeley and rebelled against the idea of *in loco parentis*—that university administrators should act as surrogate parents—is now trying to restrict speech and control the behavior of a new generation of students. The enterprise is undertaken to combat racism, of course, and it is an article of faith among the politically correct that the current climate of racial hostility can be traced to the Reagan and Bush presidencies, to conservative-Republican efforts to gut civil-rights legislation and affirmative-action programs. However true that may be, scholars like Shelby Steele, a black essayist and English professor, have also argued that the separatist movements at universities—black dorms, Native-American student centers, gay-studies programs, the relentless harping on "otherness"—have heightened tensions and contributed to the culture of victimization. "If you sensitize people from day one to look at everything in terms of race and sex, eventually they will see racism and sexism at the root of everything," says Alan Kors. "But not all the problems and frustrations in life are due to race and gender."

72 Furthermore, they say, instead of increasing self-esteem,

schools that offer an Afrocentric education will only turn out students who are more resentful, and incompetent, than ever. Indeed, while the more rabid Afrocentrics have claimed that crack and AIDS are conspiracies by whites to eliminate blacks, it could just as easily be argued that white indulgence of Afrocentric education represents a conspiracy to provide blacks with a useless education that will keep them out of the job market.

Of course, to make such a statement is invariably to 73
provoke a charge of racism. But part of the problem with this reaction is that it trivializes the debate. In fact, it makes debate impossible. But that is just as well, according to the new fundamentalists. Debate, and the analytic thinking it requires, is oppressive. It's logocentric. It favors the articulate at the expense of the inarticulate. It forces people to make distinctions, and since racism is the result of distinctions, they should be discouraged. "I have students tell me they don't need to study philosophy because it's patriarchal and logocentric," says Christina Sommers. "They're unteachable and scary. It's like having a Moonie in the classroom."

Resistance to this sort of robotic sloganeering is begin- 74
ning. "Today, routinized righteous indignation has been substituted for rigorous criticism," Henry Louis Gates, a black English professor at Duke, recently declared. Some professors are actually arguing that colleges should begin to emphasize what whites, homosexuals, minorities, and women have in common rather than dwelling constantly on "difference." In November, writing in the *Stanford Daily* about a proposal to require Stanford students to take a course in diversity, David Kennedy, chairman of American studies at Stanford and previously a champion of multiculturalism, said, "I worry that the proposal will add to the already considerable weight that Stanford culture places on racial and ethnic divisiveness, rather than shared participation. I question whether this is socially wise and, further, whether it is intellectually true to the lived experience of members of this society."

A few emboldened administrators are actually suggesting 75
that it is not unreasonable for Western culture to enjoy a certain prominence at American colleges. In an address to incoming Yale students in September, Donald Kagan, dean of the college, encouraged them to center their undergraduate studies around Western culture. He argued that the

West "has asserted the claims of the individual against those of the state, limiting its power and creating a realm of privacy into which it cannot penetrate." The West's tradition of civil liberties has produced "a tolerance and respect for diversity unknown in most cultures."

76 But many of the Yale freshmen—or "freshpeople," as the *Yale Daily News* puts it—considered the dean's statements "quite disturbing." And the dean was denounced with the obligatory mind-numbing litany.

77 "Paternalistic!"

78 "Racist!"

79 "Fascist!"

Campus Speech Code

In the late 1980s hundreds of colleges and universities enacted speech codes for their campuses, codes that spell out disciplinary measures appropriate for students and faculty who use racist or discriminatory language. Such codes are widely defended as ensuring hospitable environments for minorities (and hence reinforcing the Constitution's fourteenth-amendment guarantee of equal protection under the law). But they have also been widely criticized (particularly for restraining first-amendment guarantees of free speech). Here is one such code, enacted by the University of Connecticut. Its wording, influenced by an earlier version that was challenged in court, was collaboratively written by a federal judge, the university's attorney, and a representative of the American Civil Liberties Union.

1 An action which disrupts or impairs the purposes of the University and its community is subject to penalty under the *Student Conduct Code.* This is the *general principle* for determining whether a violation has occurred even if the action does not violate criminal law. Behaviors which violate the *Student Conduct Code* may also violate criminal or civil law and as such be subject to proceedings under the legal system.

2 Students at The University of Connecticut are subject to the provisions of the *Student Conduct Code* while on University premises or University-related premises or when involved with off-campus University activities. A student who is found guilty of misconduct or is found guilty of being

an accessory to misconduct shall be subject to the penalties authorized by this Code:

Students alleged to have committed the following acts are 3
subject to disciplinary procedures of this Code:

1. Academic Misconduct. (See Section XI of this Code for penalties and procedures related to academic misconduct.)
2. Disruption of Classes, Seminars, Research Projects, or Activities of the University.
3. Actual or Threatened Physical Assault or Injury to Persons.
4. Actual or Threatened Sexual Assault—This includes, but is not limited to, unwanted sexual touching even between acquaintances.
5. Harassment and/or Intimidation—Engaging in conduct which threatens to cause physical harm to persons or damage to their property; making unwelcome sexual advances or requests for sexual favors. This also covers harassment or intimidation of persons involved in a University disciplinary hearing and of persons in authority who are in the process of discharging their responsibilities.

   The face-to-face use of "fighting words" by students to harass any person(s) on University property or on other property to which the *Student Conduct Code* applies is prohibited. "Fighting words" are those personally abusive epithets which, when directly addressed to any ordinary person are, in the context used and as a matter of common knowledge, inherently likely to provoke an immediate violent reaction, whether or not they actually do so. Such words include, but are not limited to, those terms widely recognized to be derogatory references to race, ethnicity, religion, sex, sexual orientation, disability, and other personal characteristics.
6. Disorderly Conduct—Conduct causing inconvenience and/or annoyance which includes any action which can reasonably be expected to disturb the academic pursuits or to interfere with or infringe upon the privacy, rights, privileges, health or safety of members of the University community.
7. Manufacture, Distribution, Sale, Use, Offer for Sale, or Possession of Drugs or Narcotics, or Drug

Paraphernalia—The manufacture, distribution, sale, use, offer for sale, or possession of drug paraphernalia or of any illegal drug or narcotic, including barbiturates, hallucinogens, amphetamines, cocaine, opium, heroin, marijuana, or any other substance not chemically distinguishable from them except as authorized by medical prescription.

8. Behavior or Activity Which Endangers the Safety of Oneself or Others. . . .

University Commission on Racial/Ethnic Diversity

Terminology Guidelines

The following guidelines were drafted in 1989 after university president Dr. Bryce Jordan of Penn State asked the university's Commission on Racial/Ethnic Diversity (made up of faculty, community leaders, administrators, and students) for suggestions about appropriate terminology to use in reference to various racial and ethnic minorities.

Introduction

1 The Penn State Commission on Racial/Ethnic Diversity was appointed in 1989 as a University-wide advisory body to the President in matters relating to cultural diversity. One of its first charges was to research and identify appropriate terminology for use in official University communications. Subsequently, the Commission formed the Terminology Committee, which conducted the necessary research and submitted its findings for further review by the Commission.

2 This pamphlet includes commentaries that appear under the following headings: African/Black Americans; American Indians/Alaskan Natives; Asian & Pacific Americans; and Latino/Hispanic Americans. This terminology refers to individuals who are born or naturalized United States citizens

or permanent U.S. residents. Understandably, these racial/ethnic terminologies are constantly in flux, influenced by such factors as historical period, geographic region, political orientation, racial/ethnic consciousness, and individual preference. Researchers suggest that using self-defined references for specific groups is important because those terms usually correspond to important aspects of groups' self-concepts and hold different meanings for different groups and within groups. In making its final recommendations, the Commission considered these variables, as well as contemporary group preferences.

The racial/ethnic groups in this brochure are presented alphabetically. The recommendations should serve as guidelines in the use of various racial/ethnic designations within the Penn State community and will be subject to periodic reviews and updates. They do not affect racial/ethnic classifications mandated by state and federal agencies, nor do the recommendations require changes in the organizational title of any University student, staff member, or faculty association. 3

African/Black Americans

As early as the eighteenth century, people of African descent began to critically assess and challenge various racial designations that had either been assigned to them by Europeans or were self-determined in the course of their separation from Africa. For more than three hundred years, the popularity of designations such as *African, Colored, Afro, Negro,* and *Black* rose and fell depending on the political climate and development of the race consciousness within the Black community.[1] During this period, it was not surprising to find even two or more of these terms used in the same writing, despite the author's stated preference for a particular designation. Consensus achieved at one stage gave rise to further debate and resolution at another. 4

During the latter half of the 1980s, this controversy regarding appropriate terminology once again emerged with renewed vigor and continues. The crux of the debate concerns the use of the term *African American,* as opposed to *Black* or *Afro-American.* As in the past, the current dispute is influenced by political, cultural, and socio-psychological 5 factors, as well as the continued struggle for due recognition and full equality within the social structure.

6 The issue has seemingly come full circle in that one of the earliest controversies in African American history involved efforts to abolish use of the then-popular term *African.* As St. Clair Drake explains:

> During the first two hundred years of their existence as a racial and ethnic group in . . . the United States of America, there was a tendency for Negroes to refer to themselves as "Africans." In the early nineteenth century, however, free Negroes . . . sensed a danger in continued use of the term, since white friends and foes alike were supporting "colonization societies" and exerting pressure upon freedmen to leave the country for settlement in Africa. . . . Leaders among the freedmen felt that they might be told to "go back to Africa" if they continued to call themselves "African."[2]

7 Nowadays, however, those who advocate the use of the term *African American* argue that this designation identifies Americans of African descent within the context of their historical, cultural, and national origins and shared experiences.[3] Even in the late 1960s, many preferred the term *Afro-American* to *Black American,* not only because of its unequivocal link to Africa, but also because it avoided any reference to color.[4]

8 On the other hand, advocates of *Black American* (which, incidentally, was second only to *African* as a preferred racial designation during the eighteen century[5]) argue on behalf of the racial pride and consciousness this term denotes. The rebirth of this term during the mid-sixties was, in fact, part of a broader social movement characterized by a renewed cultural linkage and political solidarity with African nations and peoples. This linkage found expression not only in language, but also in dress, personal names, music, art, literature, and the emergence of Black Studies in higher education. It was also accompanied by the virtual demise of the term *Negro.*

9 As the linkage to Africa became more pronounced in the 1970s and beyond, the term *Afro-American* grew in popularity, along with the practice of using *Afro-American* and *Black American* interchangeably. Today, *African American* has all but overtaken its *Afro-* predecessor in such areas as popular literature, the news media, academic circles, and the polit-

ical arena. According to recent surveys, however, the vast majority of African Americans prefer *Black American.*

More than twenty years ago, Lerone Bennett noted: 10

> [A]ll black people are affected in the deepest reaches of their being by the collective label. . . . [T]he quest for the right name is the most sophisticated level of finding and projecting one's identity.[6]

Beyond the issue of identity and ethnic consciousness, the 11
general acceptance of a "collective label" would aid in political unity and reduce the possibility of division among people who share a common African ancestry. As the search continues, it is also important to recognize the individual's right to self-identify.

Given this background and in light of current trends, 12
African/Black Americans is recommended as the preferred designation for use at Penn State. It is also acceptable to use *African Americans* and *Black Americans* interchangeably, where appropriate. It is inappropriate to refer to African/Black Americans as *Negroes* or *colored.*

Notes

1. For an in-depth discussion of the historical evolution of various racial designations, see Sterling Stuckey, "Identity and Ideology: The Name Controversy," in his book *Slave Culture: Nationalist Theory & the Foundations of Black Americans* (New York: Oxford University Press, 1987), 193–244.
2. St. Claire Drake, "Negro Americans and the African Interest," in *The American Negro Reference Book,* John P. Davis, ed. (Englewood Cliffs, New Jersey: 1966), 662–750. Also see *Minutes of the Proceedings of the National Negro Convention, 1830–1864.* Howard Bell, ed. (New York: Arno Press, Inc., 1969) Convention Minutes, 1835, 14–15.
3. Molefi K. Asante, *Afrocentricity* (New Jersey: African World Press, 1988), 67; Edward Braxton, "Loaded Terms: What's In A Name," *Commonweal* 116, no. 11 (June 2, 1989), 328–329; "From 'Black' to 'African American'?" *Newsweek* 113 (Jan. 2, 1989), 2; Lawrence W. Young, "Nobody Knows My Name," *Centre Daily Times* (State College, Pennsylvania: Oct. 11, 1990), 6A.
4. Lerone Bennett, Jr., "What's In A Name: Negro vs. Afro-American vs. Black," *Ebony* 23 (November, 1967): 46–54.
5. Mary Frances Berry and John Blassingame, *Long Memory: The Black Experience In America* (New York: Oxford University Press, 1982), 393.
6. Bennett, "What's In A Name," 54.

American Indians/Alaskan Natives

13 It is recommended that *American Indian/Alaskan Native* be the first term used to refer to individuals or groups of individuals who are members or descendants of members of American Indian tribes or Alaskan Native villages. The term is appropriate when the name of the specific tribe or Alaskan Native village of the individual is not known to the writer or when the group consists of members of multiple tribes and/or Alaskan Native villages. Each of the words in the *American Indian/Alaskan Native* terminology should be capitalized.

14 After the first use of the term *American Indian/Alaskan Native,* shortened versions may be used: *American Indian, Native American, Indian,* and *Alaskan Native* whenever Alaskan Natives (Indian, Inuit, Yupik, Aleut) are included in the subject group. The term *Native* may be used to refer to American Indians when the meaning is clearly established. If the subject individual and/or group has a known preference for one of these shortened terms, the subject's preferred term should be used. Various American Indian/Alaskan Native individuals and groups have concerns about the appropriateness, connotation, clarity, and the political and historical implications of the various commonly used terms. For example, *Native American* is a broad term that includes Native Hawaiians and native people of Samoa, in addition to Indians and Alaskan Natives. Many people of many ethnic and racial groups in the United States consider themselves to be native Americans. In the context of the diverse population in our society, the term *Native American* does not clearly distinguish people from India and American Indians.

15 Whenever possible, the name of the specific tribe or Alaskan Native village of the individual or group should be used. Variations exist in the exact name, the manner or combining of, and the spelling of names among tribes and villages. The usage and spelling approved by the tribe or village government should be used. Spellings are published by the Bureau of Indian Affairs, *Reference Encyclopedia of the American Indian* (Rye, New York: Todd Publications), and in various tribal publications.

16 The term *Indian* should always be capitalized. When the

terms *tribe, nation,* or *village* are a formal part of a name, they should be capitalized also (e.g., Winnebago Tribe of Nebraska, Choctaw Nation of Oklahoma, Napakiak Native Village). The term *Indian Country* is generally used by the tribes and the United States government to refer to tribal lands within tribal jurisdiction. *Indian Nations* is a general term used widely by both the tribes and the federal government.

Indians should not be referred to in the past tense unless explicitly appropriate for the meaning of the sentence. Indians should not be uniformly referred to as "descendants" of American Indians, which implies that all of the real American Indians are dead. Referring to Indian heritage is generally inappropriate as a means of identifying a person as an Indian. 17

Some unacceptable terms for use in referring to Indians are *hostiles, savages, injuns, redskins, skins, breeds, half-breeds, squaws,* and *papoose.* 18

Reference

The Color of Federal Regulation 34, Chapter 2, Part 250.4 (Nov. 1, 1989).

Asian & Pacific Americans

Asian and Pacific American is the recommended term for referring to individuals who were born in the United States, are naturalized U.S. citizens, or are permanent residents. This term is preferred to the federal category *Asian & Pacific Islander.* The term *Asian* may be used to refer to international students coming from Asian countries if the country of origin is not known. 19

Although Asian Americans share many common values, they spring from a vast mosaic of cultures quite distinct from one another. After the end of World War II, the breakup of former colonial empires gave birth to several independent nation-states. Henceforth, most Asian Americans tend to identify themselves with their nationalities. In the 1990 census, for instance, one can distinguish twelve major nationalities among Asians: the Chinese, the Filipinos, the Japanese, the Asian Indians, the Koreans, the Vietnamese, the Laotians, the Thais, the Cambodians (also called 20

Kampucheans, a term that derives from the name of the former kingdom of Kampuchea), the Pakistanis, the Indonesians, and the Hmongs. The Hmongs, who came from the mountains of Laos, North Vietnam, and Thailand, prefer this term to *Miao,* by which they are also known. Miao means "cat" and in Hmong culture, cats are not welcome in anyone's home. The Hmong people were resettled in America in the aftermath of the Vietnam War. They are often associated with Indochinese refugees who inhabited the countries of Vietnam, Laos, and Cambodia. These three states with quite distinctive cultures formed what was known as French Indochina.

21 Asian newcomers speak hundreds of languages and dialects. They may transmit their diverse culture by means as ancient as the oral traditions of preliterate societies. For contrast, they may use Hangul, a modern method of writing developed by a royal commission in the fifteenth century, but only officially adopted by the Korean government at the end of World War II. When most Asian American ethnic groups communicate cross-culturally in America, the only real language—as one would expect—is English.

22 Along with possessing dimensions that define ethnicity and cultural identity, Asian Americans are affiliated with many international faiths, from Buddhism to Zoroastrian. And while they often identify themselves by their country of origin, many (e.g., the people of Vietnam with Chinese ancestry) choose to identify themselves by country of ancestry.

23 Also based on the 1990 census data, one notes three major groups among the Pacific Islanders: the Polynesians, who include the Hawaiians, the Samoans, the Tongans; the Micronesians, comprising the Guamanians; and the Melanesians, including the Fijans.

24 Since each individual has the right to self-identify, it is best to refer to him/her with whichever term he/she prefers. It is possible that some Asians are inclined to be called simply Americans. The majority, however, want to pay homage to their ancestry. The country of their forebearers will be used to qualify their Americanism. We often see or hear, among others, the terms *Vietnamese Americans, Chinese Americans, Japanese Americans* in the media.

25 Terms deemed offensive are *coolie, Asiatic,* and *Oriental.*

References

"Asian and Pacific Americans Behind the Myths," 1989, *Change, The Magazine of Higher Learning.*

Dictionary of Asian American History. 1986. New York: Greenwood Press.

Miller, Wayne Charles. 1976. *Handbook of American Minorities.* Ithaca, New York: New York University Press.

Momeni, Jamshid A. 1984. *Demography of Racial and Ethnic Minorities in the United States.* Westport, Connecticut: Greenwood Press.

Takaki, Ronald, ed. 1987. *From Different Shores.* New York: Oxford University Press Inc.

We, the Asian and Pacific Islander Americans. 1988. U.S. Department of Commerce, Bureau of the Census.

Wynar, Lubomyr Roman. 1975. *Encyclopedia Directory of Ethnic Organizations in the United States.* Littleton, Colorado: Libraries Unlimited.

Yun, Grace, ed. 1989. *A Look Beyond the Model Minority Image: Critical Issues in Asian America.* San Mateo, California: JACP Inc.

Latino/Hispanic Americans

Latino and *Hispanic* are terms used to refer to an ethnic category and not to denote race. Latinos/Hispanics are a racially mixed group that includes combinations of European White, African Black, and Native inhabitants of the Americas. Latinos/Hispanics identify with each other because they share common cultural values. Racial characteristics are less important. *Latinos* is perhaps the most generic term currently used in the literature and accepted by subgroups belonging to the broad category identified as Hispanic by the federal government. 26

In a recent *Hispanic Link Weekly Report,* Ortiz and Brownstein-Santiago acknowledge that this ethnic group identifies with a number of general terms, such as *Latino, Hispanic, Spanish-speaking, Latin, Spanish, Latin American,* and *Chicano,* as well as various specific designations that reflect country of origin. Those designations often are quoted in Spanish *(Mejicanos, Puertorriqueños, Cubanos, Salvadoreños,* etc.). In specific areas, Latinos/Hispanics might use additional identifying terms, such as *Nuyoricans,* to denote ties to country of origin as well as to place of birth or areas of settlement. Often, researchers will address a 27 specific subgroup and the name of that subgroup will be used in the study. Yet some Latino/Hispanic advocacy groups, especially those publishing literature in higher education in the southwest and other parts of the country, stress the importance of a unifying terminology to prevent divergent traditions from keeping these groups apart, and to provide identity and strength to the various subgroups. It is important to understand that terminologies used to identify people in racial/ethnic groups in the United States evolve over time and often reflect subtle dimensions. The term *Chicano* is a case in point.

28 Villanueva (1980) and Galarza (1972) trace the history of the terms *Chicano* and *Pocho* to class distinctions that were established in the barrios of California during the first decade of the twentieth century. The term *Pocho* evolved through the decades to currently denote "Americanized" Mexican Americans in California. In the same evolutionary way, during the 1950s, for many Mexican Americans the term *Chicano* became one of pride, solidarity, and often political activism. *Chicano* was meant to encompass all residents of the United States who are of Mexican background, whether new arrivals or U.S. born, whether seasonal workers or middle-class residents.

29 In the same vein, while various explanations are given for the origin of the term *Hispanic,* it apparently became the official term used by the government after a decision by the Office of Management and Budget in 1978 to operationalize a designation for "a person of Mexican, Puerto Rican, Cuban, Central or South American, or the Spanish culture or origin, regardless of race" (*Federal Register,* 1978, p. 19269). Although the term is not universally accepted, *Hispanic* is the one used by government institutions such as the Bureau of the Census, as well as the news media and many researchers. Clearly, the term *Hispanic* refers to individuals who have disparate migrational and sociodemographic characteristics.

30 *Latino* is the term more recently proposed. Etymologically, the term *Latino* comes from *Latin* and probably began as a reference to people of countries that are Latin but do not use Spanish as their primary language (for example, Portugal or Italy). In the United States, the word was used as early as 1939, specifically to refer to Latin American U.S. inhabitants, regardless of the language spoken.

31 While Latinos might use among themselves various terms

for purposes of general or more specific identification, there is merit in using the general term *Latinos/Hispanics* when attempting to collectively address this significant group of U.S. citizens and residents. The combined term *Latinos/Hispanics* collectively refers to Mexican Americans, Puerto Ricans, Cuban Americans, and to persons who trace their origins to other Latin American countries or to any of the regions of Spain.

References

Camarillo, A. 1986. *Latinos in the United States, A Historical Bibliography.* Santa Barbara, California: ABC-CLIO.

Fairchild, H. H., and J. A. Cozens. 1981. "Chicano, Hispanic, or Mexican American: What's in a Name?" *Hispanic Journal of Behavioral Science:* 191–198.

Federal Register. May 4, 1978. Washington, D.C.: Government Printing Office.

Galarza, E. 1972. *Barrio Boy.* Ballantine Books.

Hayes-Bautista, D. E., and J. Chapa. 1987. "Latino terminology: Conceptual bases for standardized terminology." *American Journal of Public Health* 77:61–68.

Marín, G. 1984. "Stereotyping Hispanics: The differential effect of research methods, label and degree of contact." *International Journal of Intercultural Relations* 8:17–27.

Marín, G., and B. VanOss Marín. 1991. *Research with Hispanic Populations.* Newbury Park, California: Sage Publications, Inc.

Ortiz, V., and Ch. Brownstein-Santiago. 1990. "Unifying Label Vital for Latino Empowerment." *Hispanic Link Weekly Report.*

The Oxford English Dictionary, second edition, *Latino.*

Rose, P. 1990. *They and We.* New York: McGraw-Hill Publishing.

Solís, D. 1990. "We Will Get Together." *Intercambios Femeniles.*

Treviño, F. 1987. "Standardized Terminology for Hispanic Populations." *American Journal of Public Health* 77 (1): 69–72.

Villanueva, T. 1980. *Chicanos. Antología Histórica y Literaria.* Mexico: Fondo de Cultural Económica

Population reports: 1960, 1979, 1982, 1985.

For information on Mr. Trudeau and his comic strip, see pages 94 and 1001.

DOONESBURY BY GARRY TRUDEAU

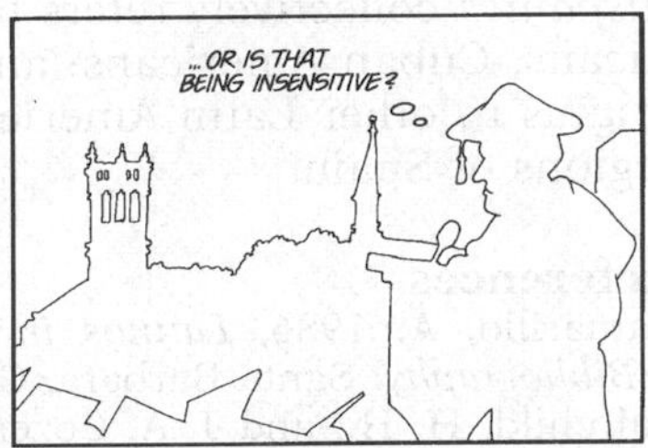

Emily Tsao

Thoughts of an Oriental Girl

Emily Tsau was a sophomore at Yale University when she contributed the following essay to The Washington Post *(the most important daily newspaper published in our nation's capital) in September 1991.*

I am an Oriental girl. Excuse me, I forgot to use my politically correct dictionary. Let me rephrase that, I am an Asian-American woman. Yes, that sounds about right. Excuse me again; I mean politically correct. 1

When I first stepped onto the campus scene last year, I, like many other anxious freshmen, wanted to fit in. I wanted to wear the right clothes, carry the right bookbag and, most important, say the right things. Speaking to upperclassmen, however, I realized that I had no command of the proper "PC" language. 2

Girls, it became clear, were to be called women. Freshmen who were girls were to be called freshwomen. Mixed groups of both sexes were to be labeled freshpeople, and upperclassmen were to be referred to as upperclasspeople. Orientals were to be called Asian Americans, blacks were to be called African Americans and Hispanics Latinos. 3

To me, most of this seemed pointless. Being called a girl doesn't bother me. I'm 18 years old. My mom is a woman. I'm her kid. I don't expect her to refer to me as a woman. 4

I have always referred to my female friends as girls, and still do. I want my boyfriend to call me his girlfriend, not his woman friend. 5

My friends and I refer to the male students at college as boys or guys. Never men. Kevin Costner and Robert Redford are men. Men don't drink themselves sick at keg parties every weekend, ask Dad for money, or take laundry home to Mom. 6

For 12 years of high school and grade school, the female students were always girls and the males were boys. Why does going to college with these same peers suddenly make me a woman and the boys men? I certainly don't feel much older or wiser than I did last year. When people refer to me as a woman, I turn around to see who might be standing behind me. 7

8 Another fad now is for people to spell women with a "y" in place of the "e"—"womyn." These people want to take the "men" out of "women." Next perhaps they'll invent "femyle."

9 I've always been gender conscious with my language when it seemed logical. In third grade I referred to the mailman as a mailperson because our mail was sometimes delivered by a woman. I don't think I ever said mailwoman, though, because it just didn't sound right.

10 From elementary through high school, I told people I was Chinese, and if I wanted to refer to all Asians, I used the word "Orientals." I guess I was young and foolish and didn't know any better.

11 At college I was told that the proper label for me was Asian American, that "Oriental" was a word to describe furniture, not people. But what is the difference? All Asians are still being clumped together, even though each group—Chinese, Korean, Japanese, Indians, Vietnamese and Filipinos, to name just a few—comes from a different country with a different language and culture.

12 The new "PC" term to describe Asian Americans and all other minorities is "people of color." The reason, I am told, is that the "minority" population has grown to be the majority. But even if that's true, the phrase seems contradictory. Since many African Americans no longer want to be referred to as blacks, why should the term for minorities once again refer to skin color? The same is true for Asians, most of whom find the label "yellow" more offensive than Oriental. And isn't white also a color?

13 As long as we're throwing out all the old labels, why not replace "white" with "European American." Wasps could be EAASPS (European-American Anglo Saxon Protestants). Well, maybe not. Minority groups want new labels to give themselves a more positive image, but unless the stereotypes disappear as well, is it really going to help very much?

14 Look at the word "sophomore," which comes from Greek roots meaning "wise fool." PC-conscious sophomores ought to revolt against this offensive phrase. I, however, will not be among them. Changing the world won't make me any smarter, humbler or wiser.

Richard Goldstein

The Politics of Political Correctness

Richard Goldstein, an executive editor for The Village Voice, *wrote the following analysis in June 1991.* The Village Voice *is a weekly newspaper for New Yorkers that has a decidedly liberal and irreverent tone. It reports on current events (national and local) and very thoroughly covers contemporary culture—films, books, music, dance, and so forth.*

When Carol Iannone, a frequent contributor to *Commentary,* was nominated to head the National Endowment for the Humanities, senators Edward Kennedy and Claiborne Pell put the appointment on hold. They were concerned about a piece in which Iannone called praise for Alice Walker's *The Color Purple* "less a recognition of literary achievement than some official act of reparation." Instead of defending the nominee's views on minority cultures—surely a valid issue for someone who would be dispensing federal grants to scholars—the current NEH chair, Lynn Cheney, chose to rail against "a classic example of political correctness—to oppose someone's ideological position, and then make inflammatory and irresponsible charges." The *New York Post* soon joined in, with an editorial excoriating "Literature's PC cops": "It's clear enough what is going on here. Various liberal groups are trying to chill discussion about a number of issues in the country by imposing a standard of 'political correctness.'" 1

The phrase has given conservatives, neo and trad, an excuse to avoid hard questions about race and gender. Now they can obscure all sorts of bigotry by accusing the left of practicing a new form of McCarthyism. And opponents of affirmative action have a new basis for defending hiring policies that exclude women and minorities: they're resisting intimidation. When Robert Brustein, artistic director of the American Repertory Theater, was attacked by *The Boston Globe* for running a largely white institution, he responded in *The New Republic* by deriding "the context of contemporary political correctness," which leads to inappropriate "inquiries into the racial, religious, political, and sexual background" of personnel. "To play this numbers game is to distract attention from the primary purpose of cultural 2 institutions, which is to create works of art with high standards," Brustein writes. This from the man who once suggested (also in *The New Republic*) that Harvey Fierstein got a Tony Award for *Torch Song Trilogy* because he won "the AIDS sympathy vote."

3 In this incarnation, politically correct stands for an undue attention to racial and gender parity. But the phrase has also become a way to chill any discussion of racism or sexism in cultural works. Congressional conservatives erupted last month over an exhibition of frontier art at the Smithsonian that included interpretive texts analyzing the racial and sexual politics of these familiar images. Though he defended the show's right to federal funding, *New York Times* critic Michael Kimmelman derided "art-historical revisionism of the kind that has given rise to the phrase political correctness." Kimmelman doesn't say whether he objects to the excesses of this approach or to any attempt at all to elucidate the politics of culture, especially when doing so might tread on hallowed ground, such as the American West. The p.c. label lets this critic off the hook. Is there racism in the representation of Indians? P.c. renders the question moot.

4 A handy phrase, indeed—as John Taylor demonstrated in his recent *New York* article, which featured the face of a bemused preppy, obscured by the question: "Are you politically correct?" For Taylor, the term describes everything about race and sex that would terrify the "young traditionalists" who are that magazine's demographic base. The proliferation of "oppression studies," campus codes against offensive speech, references to masturbation in academic papers, and "the phenomenon of date rape" all come under Taylor's fire. To deflect doubts about his authority to make such charges, he invokes the sacred name of Camille Paglia, whose book, *Sexual Personae,* is a tribute to the traditional view of gender as destiny. It is Paglia who tells the readers of *New York* that "radical feminists have contempt for values other than their own, and they're inspiring in students a resentful attitude toward the world."

5 Op-editors can count on Paglia to rail against p.c. But most of the other attacks have come from straight white males. Many are straight white *liberal* males. Indeed, the attack on p.c. has brought men of the left and right together in a new Popular Front. Just think: in *The New Republic,* Eugene Genovese, the Marxist historian of slavery, marches

hand in hand with Dinesh D'Souza, former editor of the race-baiting *Dartmouth Review*. It was during D'Souza's tenure that the *Review* ran an interview with an ex-official of the Ku Klux Klan, illustrated by a staged photo of a black student hanging from a tree. D'Souza also ran a fictional colloquium in which an affirmative-action candidate declared: "Now we be comin' to Dartmut and be up over our 'fros in studies, but we still be graduatin' Phi Beta Kappa."

6 Perhaps Genovese can be forgiven his myopia, since none of this is revealed in D'Souza's *Illiberal Education,* the book that put political correctness on the think-tank agenda. Nor does the scant jacket blurb explain that the author, during his tenure as a domestic policy analyst at the Reagan White House, came up with the bright idea of shifting federal funds from abortion clinics to adoption services. These biases are masked by D'Souza's background (Genovese calls him "a man of color who was born in India"), and by his insistence on referring to his ideas as "liberal." Neocons often use that word, in its Burkean sense, to describe politics that predate by centuries contemporary standards of social justice. Many white liberals have become incapable of seeing beneath the surface of this claim to the churning waters that often lie beneath.

7 Which is why, I suspect, Genovese can remark in his review of D'Souza's book that the author "displays a deep appreciation of the travails of black students." Though he chides D'Souza for his "sweeping and one-sided characterizations of Marxism and Marxists, liberalism and liberals," Genovese is otherwise glad to join in the bashing. Having asserted that "the campaign for 'political correctness' " is a threat to the integrity of universities, he calls on "honorable men and women [to] defeat terrorism . . . by unleashing counterterrorism against cowardly administrators and complicit faculty. . . . The hard truth is that academic freedom . . . requires a strong dose of hierarchical authority within institutions that must be able to defy a democratic consensus." To achieve this goal, Genovese envisions "the redrawing of political lines in a manner that brings together the healthiest elements of long-warring political camps."

8 Healthy elements? Hierarchical authority? These buzzwords reveal more about the mindset of many men on the left than any politically correct analysis can. Examining Genovese's discourse, one can glimpse the enduring rigidities of orthodox Marxism, with its insistence that class is the

only valid basis of struggle. This fear of racial and sexual pluralism, built into Marxism by its founder's hostility toward Jews and homosexuals (not to mention social democrats), persists on the left, fueling the ongoing struggle between political and cultural radicals. Ever since the '60s, the New Left has battled against its elders to broaden the base of progressive politics, and over the past 20 years feminism and gay liberation have sharpened that conflict. By now, a social conservative like Genovese has more in common with Dinesh D'Souza (who proposes that affirmative action programs be organized around class rather than race) than he does with radical feminists.

9 "What a pity we cannot . . . restore a genuine core curriculum to our schools," Genovese wrote last year in *Commentary*. "For then we might be able to require a four-semester sequence in Christian theology or at least in common decency and good sense. As it is, the rot deepens; we are being overwhelmed by drugs; mass-homelessness; the poisoning of our children with pornography, perversion, and impossible aspirations." So much for bread and roses.

10 The movement for cultural and sexual pluralism has forced liberals and leftists alike to make a choice between the old politics of dialectical materialism and new, often foreboding, modes of discourse and analysis—not to mention behavior. A similar challenge has gone out to men and women in all walks of society—and a similar backlash is the result. The sexist tropes of metal and rap, the rise of the psychokiller in movies and lately literature; these are the cultural components of a male revanchism that finds its political expression in the current conservative hegemony.

11 Liberals, of course, are not one of Poppy's constituencies. But they have an infinitely greater capacity than even Republicans to hide their sexual and racial fears behind a patina of high principle. When the consequences of that denial are identified as bigotry, liberals explode. Twenty years of such pent-up fury is being unleashed in the attack on political correctness. That's why this right-wing critique has such broad appeal. A similar gap between ideals and anxieties is what has driven so many blue-collar voters into the arms of the Republicans. It's a bromide of the '80s that "a neoconservative is a liberal who's been mugged," and this group of affluent intellectuals perceives the emergence of racial and sexual minorities in precisely such threatening terms.

12 "A new McCarthyism, in some ways more effective and

vicious than the old," Genovese cries. But as he might well remember, it was precisely the willingness of liberals to form an alliance with the right that enabled anticommunists to purge the universities of political radicals in the '50s. McCarthy could not have prevailed without the complicity of the left, and it's entirely possible that history will repeat itself in the current attack on p.c. This time around, the temptation to purge radicals may be even greater, because the "threat" involves nothing so tangible as communism, but regions of the psyche where one's nightmares about sexual and racial otherness abide.

The straight white male is being asked to give up the power to mistake his perceptions for reality. To forgo pleasure in a culture that glorifies his own image at everyone else's expense. To suffer the intrusion of otherness into what was once his exclusive representational domain. To question all practices that express dominance over any living thing. Meanwhile, Poppy says to those weary—or wary—of this herculean task: Make war, eat meat, be free. This conflation of liberty with the preservation of privilege is a secret weapon in the right's arsenal, far more tempting—even to many liberals—than the left's insistence on self-restraint in the name of justice. 13

The line between civility and oppression will always be argued, even among the politically correct. But the current critique—encompassing everything from multicultural curricula to date rape, from affirmative action to gay dances—is an assault on diversity itself. This attack announces a new alignment in American politics, between social conservatives of the left and right. 14

There's nothing new about male bonding, of course. But in the past, *all* politics was male, and alliances were forged by class, region, or religious affinities. Only now is it possible to construct an alignment of threatened men that transcends the old categories of the cold war. What is currently referred to as "the gender gap" may actually signal the emergence of a white male voting bloc, as an inevitable reaction to the autonomy of women, gays, and people of color. This is a powerful force, and its claim to reason and rectitude is made with all the authority men are so skillful at mustering. Yet underlying its morality of freedom and individuality is terror of a world where endlessly changing affinities and alliances determine social reality—not a simple consensus among dudes. 15

16 To understand the fear of pluralism is also to see D'Souza's program for what it is. On the op-ed page of the *Wall Street Journal,* he recently called for a return to "liberal education." His formula for achieving that is revealing: "Universities should [refuse] to recognize or fund any group that is racially separatist." Sounds progressive, until D'Souza gets into particulars. "Universities would not permit a Black Students Association, but they would permit a W. E. B. Du Bois Society based on interest in [his] writings. . . . This principle could extend beyond race, so that universities would decline to fund a homosexual association, but would fund a Sappho Society." His rationale: "The consolidation of identity based on race or sexuality may be a project that some students ardently seek, but it is not always consistent with the mission of universities."

17 Here is a program to intrude on the autonomy of universities in the name of academic freedom. No longer would students be invited to form their own campus societies. No longer would administrators be empowered to hire faculty on the basis of racial, sexual, or ideological balance. Tampering with the curriculum, so that it includes contemporary works by women, gays, and people of color, would be tantamount to treason against the West. D'Souza suggests introducing students to the *classical* tradition in other cultures, but no attempt would be made to convey current reality—especially in regard to groups whose experience was unaddressed in literature until this generation. And no course of study would explore the mass culture that is so powerful a determinant of values in American life. The university would return to the hermetic state it occupied in the '50s, when men were men, women were women, and everyone was white or stayed out of sight.

18 The restoration of America as a peaceable kingdom run by straight white males (and administered by those who identify with them) is a goal many might embrace if it were presented in more "progressive" terms. Which is what the attack on political correctness achieves. Its appeal to liberals reflects the perception that the right is less threatening than radical feminists, queer nationals, black separatists, and animal liberationists. In reality, of course, the fundamental threat to freedom comes *from* the right. And once you size up Poppy against p.c., the choice becomes clear. Even at its most ridiculous, political correctness stems from the impulse to create an etiquette of relations among people of

difference. And even at its most tempting, political incorrectness is the liberalism of fools.

Rosa Ehrenreich

What Campus Radicals?

Rosa Ehrenreich completed her studies at Harvard in 1991, just before she published the following essay in Harper's, *a monthly magazine on American politics and culture. (The essay appeared in the same issue as the one by Louis Menard, on page 109.)*

A national survey of college administrators released last summer found that "political correctness" is not the campus issue it has been portrayed to be by pundits and politicians of the political right. During the 1990–91 academic year, according to the survey's findings, faculty members complained of pressure from students and fellow professors to alter the political and cultural content of their courses at only 5 *percent* of all colleges. So much for the influence of the radicals, tenured or otherwise. 1

The survey's findings came as no real surprise to me. The hegemony of the "politically correct" is not a problem at Harvard, where I've just completed my undergraduate education, or at any other campus I visited during my student years. But then none among those who have escalated the P.C. debate in the past year—Dinesh D'Souza and Roger Kimball, George Will and George Bush, *Time* and *New York* magazines—is actually interested in what is happening on the campuses. In all the articles and op-ed pieces published on P.C., multiculturalism, etc., very few student voices have been heard. To be a liberal arts student with progressive politics today is at once to be at the center of a raging national debate and to be completely on the sidelines, watching others far from campus describe you and use you for their own ends. 2

For instance: During the spring semester of my freshman year at Harvard, Stephen Thernstrom, an American history 3 professor, was criticized by several black students for making "racially insensitive" comments during lectures. The incident made the *Harvard Crimson* for a few days, then blew over after a week or so and was quickly forgotten by most students. It continued a kind of mythic afterlife, however, in the P.C. debate. Here is how it was described last January in a *New York* magazine cover story by John Taylor on, in the author's words, the "moonies in the classroom" propagating the "new fundamentalism":

> "Racist." "Racist!" "The man is a racist!" "A *racist!*"
>
> Such denunciations, hissed in tones of self-righteousness and contempt, vicious and vengeful, furious, smoking with hatred—such denunciations haunted Stephen Thernstrom for weeks. Whenever he walked through the campus that spring, down Harvard's brick paths, under the arched gates, past the fluttering elms, he found it hard not to imagine the pointing fingers, the whispers.

4 The operative word here is "imagine." Taylor seriously distorted what actually happened. In February of 1988, several black female students told classmates that they had been disturbed by some "racially insensitive" comments made by Professor Thernstrom. Thernstrom, they said, had spoken approvingly of Jim Crow laws, and had said that black men, harboring feelings of inadequacy, beat their female partners. The students, fearing for their grades should they anger Professor Thernstrom by confronting him with their criticisms—this is not an unusual way for college students to think things through, as anyone who's been an undergraduate well knows—never discussed the matter with him. They told friends, who told friends, and the *Crimson* soon picked up word of the incident and ran an article.

5 Professor Thernstrom, understandably disturbed to learn of the matter in the *Crimson,* wrote a letter protesting that no student had ever approached him directly with such criticisms. He also complained that the students' vague criticisms about "racial insensitivity" had "launched a witch-hunt" that would have "chilling effect[s] upon freedom of expression." Suddenly, Professor Thernstrom was to be understood as a victim, falsely smeared with the charge of racism. But no one had ever accused him of any such thing. "I do not charge that [Thernstrom] is a racist," Wendi Grantham, one of the students who criticized Thernstrom,

wrote to the *Crimson* in response to his letter. Grantham believed the professor gave "an incomplete and over-simplistic presentation of the information. . . . I am not judging [his] character; I am simply asking questions about his presentation of the material. . . ." As for the professor's comment that the criticisms were like a "witch-hunt," Grantham protested that Thernstrom had "turned the whole situation full circle, proclaimed himself victim, and resorted to childish name-calling and irrational comparisons. . . . 'witch-hunt' [is] more than a little extreme. . . ." But vehement, even hysterical language is more and more used to demonize students who question and comment. Terms like "authoritarian" and "Hitler youth" have been hurled at students who, like Grantham, dare to express any sort of criticism of the classroom status quo.

In my four years as a student at Harvard, I found few signs of a new fascism of the left. For that matter, there are few signs of the left at all. The Harvard-Radcliffe Democratic Socialists Club collapsed due to lack of members, as did the left-wing newspaper, the *Subterranean Review*. As to the neoconservative charge that the traditional political left has been supplanted by a feminist-gay-multicultural left: In my senior year the African-American Studies department and the Women's Studies committee each had so few faculty that the same woman served as chair of both. I got through thirty-two courses at Harvard, majoring in the history and literature of England and America, without ever being required to read a work by a black woman writer, and of my thirty-two professors only two were women. I never even *saw* a black or Hispanic professor. (Fewer than 10 percent of tenured professors at Harvard are women, and fewer than 7 percent are members of minorities.) 6

Perhaps, as some conservatives have maintained, even a few radical professors can reach hundreds of students, bending their minds and sending them, angry and politicized, out into society upon graduation. To cure such fears, drop by Harvard's Office of Career Services. Most staffers there spend their days advising those who would be corporate execs, financial consultants, and investment bankers. Nearly 20 percent of the class of 1990 planned to go to law school. This compares with 10 percent who claimed that they would eventually go into government or one of what Career Services calls the "helping professions." 7

8 President Bush, speaking at the University of Michigan's commencement exercises last spring, went on about radical extremists on campus. It would be interesting to know how he calculated this rise in radicalism. Two thirds of Harvard students wholeheartedly supported the Gulf War, according to one *Crimson* poll. That's more support for the war than was found in the country at large. And during my years at Harvard I found that most women on campus, including those who consider themselves politically liberal, would not willingly identify themselves as feminists.

9 The very notion of "politicization" makes most Harvard students nervous. I discovered this in the fall of 1989, when I was elected president of Harvard's community service organization, Phillips Brooks House Association. I had been reckless enough to suggest that volunteers would benefit from having some awareness of the social and political issues that affected the communities in which they did their volunteer work. I was promptly attacked in the *Crimson* for trying to inappropriately "politicize" public service. The paper also suggested that under my leadership volunteer training might mimic a "party line," with Brooks House as a "central planning office." This used to be called red-baiting. (So much for the liberal campus media.)

10 Meanwhile—and unremarked upon by D'Souza, et al.—the campus right thrives nationally. Two new right-wing vehicles have popped up on Harvard's campus in recent years. The Association Against Learning in the Absence of Religion and Morality (AALARM) initially made a splash with its uninhibited gay-bashing. The magazine *Peninsula,* closely tied to AALARM, bears an uncanny editorial resemblance to the notorious *Dartmouth Review,* claims to uphold Truth, and has a bizarre propensity for centerfold spreads of mangled fetuses. And older, more traditional conservative groups have grown stronger and more ideological. The Harvard Republican Club, once a stodgy and relatively inactive group, suffered a rash of purges and resignations as more moderate members were driven out by the far right. It is inactive no more.

11 There *are* those on the left who are intolerant and who could stand to lighten up a bit—these are the activists whom *progressive* and *liberal* students mockingly called "politically correct" years before the right appropriated the term, with a typical lack of irony. But on the whole, intolerance at

Harvard—and, I suspect, elsewhere—is the province mostly of extreme conservatism. Posters put up at Harvard by the Bisexual, Gay and Lesbian Students Association are routinely torn down. I don't recall any Republican Club posters being ripped up or removed.

The day after the bombing started in Iraq, I went to an event advertised as "a non-partisan rally to support our troops," sponsored by the Republican Club. After the scheduled speakers—and several other non-scheduled speakers—had finished, I tried to speak. The rally organizers promptly turned off the microphone. I kept speaking, saying that I supported the troops but not the war. I added that I had been disturbed to hear it said by rally organizers—and applauded by the audience—that the time for debate was over. In a democracy, I said, the time for debate is never over. 12

I would have gone on, but at this point a group of men in the audience felt the need to demonstrate their conviction that there should be no debate. They began to loudly chant "victory" over and over, quite effectively drowning me out. By way of contrast, supporters of the war were listened to in polite silence by the crowd at an anti-war rally the next day. 13

In the classroom, too, right-wing political views are heard without disruption. One of Harvard's largest core courses, taken by nearly half of all undergraduates while I was there, is Social Analysis 10, Principles of Economics. It was taught, during my undergrad years, by two of President Reagan's top economic advisers, Martin Feldstein and Larry Lindsay. Students did not rise up *en masse* to protest the course's right-wing political bias; instead, they sat scribbling feverishly in their notebooks: Ec-10 had a notoriously steep grading curve. (No one seemed worried that each year some 750 innocent Harvard students were being lectured to by the engineers of what George Bush, in one of his more forthright moments, once referred to as "voodoo economics.") 14

There are many other politically conservative professors at Harvard whose courses are quite popular—Richard Pipes on Russian history and Samuel P. Huntington on modern democracy, to name two of the most prominent—and in their classrooms, as in all undergrad classrooms I was in, free and open discussion did quite well. I took many classes in which fearless conservatives rushed to take part in entirely civil discussions about the efficacy and justice of 15 affirmative action, about whether books like *Uncle Tom's Cabin* and Frederick Douglass's autobiography are "really *literature,*" as opposed to just interesting historical documents, and about whether it's at all fair or even interesting to condemn Jefferson for owning slaves even as he decried slavery. These are all valid questions, and all sides deserve a hearing—which, in my experience, is exactly what they always got.

16 And my experience was not unique. Most other Harvard students seemed to agree that there's no such thing as a cadre of P.C. thought police. Last winter the Republican Club laid huge sheets of poster board across several dining-hall tables and put up a sign asking students to scribble down their responses to the question "Is there free speech at Harvard?" The vast majority of students wrote things like "What's the big deal? Of course there's free speech here." And the lively, cheerful discussion going on among the students gathered around the tables attested to that fact.

17 Conservatives like D'Souza and Kimball charge that traditional Western culture courses barely exist anymore at schools like Harvard, because of some mysterious combination of student pressure and the multiculturalist, post-structuralist tendencies of radical professors. Writing in the *Atlantic Monthly* last year, Caleb Nelson, a former editor of the conservative *Harvard Salient,* complained that in the 1989–90 Harvard course catalogue:

> No core Literature and Arts course lists any of the great nineteenth-century British novelists among the authors studied, nor does any list such writers as Virgil, Milton, and Dostoevsky. In the core's history areas even students who. . . took every single course would not focus on any Western history before the Middle Ages, nor would they study the history of the Enlightenment, the Renaissance, the American Civil War, or a host of other topics that one might expect a core to cover.

18 Nelson's major complaint is that Harvard is not properly educating all of its students. I agree with him here; in Caleb Nelson, Harvard has let us all down by producing a student so poorly educated that he's unable even to read the course catalogue. I have the 1989–90 catalogue in front of me as I write, and a quick sampling of some of the entries gives us,

from the Literature and Arts and the Historical Study sections of the core curriculum, the following courses: Chaucer, Shakespeare, The Bible and Its Interpreters, Classical Greek Literature and 5th-Century Athens, The Rome of Augustus, The British Empire, The Crusades, The Protestant Reformation. Perhaps Chaucer and Shakespeare are somehow, to Caleb Nelson, not "such writers" as Milton and Dostoevsky and the Protestant Reformation is a historically trivial topic.

Nelson also worries that students will have "no broad look at . . . philosophy"—by which he really means Western philosophy. Yet in the Moral Reasoning section of the core, seven of the ten courses listed have at least four of the following authors on their primary reading lists: Plato, Aristotle, Thucydides, Machiavelli, Locke, Kant, Rousseau, Hume, Mill, Nietzsche, Marx, and Weber. There is one course devoted to a non-Western philosopher: Confucius. The remaining two Moral Reasoning courses focus, respectively, on the writings of "Aristotle . . . [and] Maimonides," and of "Jesus as presented in the Gospels." 19

These courses are far more representative of those taken by most Harvard undergraduates than the titillating and much denounced 1991 English course on Cross-Dressing and Cultural Anxiety—a graduate seminar listed in the course catalogue but ultimately never held. But then, if you are a right-winger looking for something to replace the commies on campus—remember them?—you aren't going to sell books or raise funds or win votes complaining about undergrads studying Confucian Humanism and Moral Community. 20

Many of the loudest complainers about P.C. thought police are those who are doing their best to curb free expression in other areas. It doesn't appear to bother Dinesh D'Souza that the word "abortion" cannot be uttered at a federally funded family clinic. More broadly, the brouhaha about political conformity on campus serves as a perfect smoke screen, masking from Americans—from ourselves—the rigid political conformity *off* campus: the blandness of our political discourse, the chronic silence in Washington on domestic matters, the same faces returned to office each year, the bipartisanship that keeps problems from becoming issues. During the Gulf War, the number of huge yellow bouquets in public places rivaled the number of larger-than- 21 life photos of Saddam Hussein displayed on Iraqi billboards. Patriotically correct.

22 The campuses are no more under siege by radicals than is the society at large. It has been clever of the Kimballs and D'Souzas to write as if it were so. It is always clever of those in ascendance to masquerade as victims. Rebecca Walkowitz, the newly elected president of the *Harvard Crimson,* understands perfectly how this dynamic works. Referring to the 1988 incident involving Professor Thernstrom and several of his black students, Walkowitz has said: "People call the *Crimson* and ask what we 'did to that man.' It's important to remember who has the power here, because it's not students. Who would dare criticize a professor for political reasons now? In addition to fearing for your grade, you'd fear being pilloried in the national press."

II.

LANGUAGE

Introduction

People used to think of language as being ideologically neutral—as a sort of transparent window through which ideas are conveyed. Now many people agree that language is not transparent but colored by ideological and cultural biases. Far from being neutral, language is a product (as well as a producer) of culture and inevitably reflects (as well as shapes) that particular culture. The three issues included in this part of *Conversations*—"Should There Be a 'Standard' English?"; "Should We Have a National Language?"; and "Is English Sexist?"—share the assumption that language is culture-bound, that social issues inevitably mingle with language issues.

The first section includes five items that explore relationships between language and power, particularly about the ideology of standard English. Is Black English a robust dialect that proceeds according to normal conventions of sound and structure? Or is it (especially in its written form) a substandard dialect that impedes communications and clouds thinking? Do Black English and other "nonstandard" dialects empower their users as fully as any other language, or do they undermine literacy, lessen their users' chances for success in the main streams of American life, and keep their users politically and socially marginalized?

Next come six items that are generally related to those in the previous section, items that consider language against the backdrop of America's ethnic diversity. Should our public policies enforce English as our national language and discourage the use of other tongues? For many years federal, state, and local governments, for instance, have supported the policy of giving students schoolwork in their native languages—English for most, but Spanish and Chinese and many other languages as well—so that students with limited proficiency in English would not fall behind in other subjects while they mastered English "as a second language." In 1974, Congress required schools to promote knowledge of students' native languages and cultures as well as to promote growth in English. But in the past decade the policy of bilingual education has come under fire. Some educators have contended that bilingual programs do not work well or that they are too expensive. Other critics, noting the importance of English as a unifying force in American society, contend that, because they interfere with students' mastery of English, bilingual programs prevent non-English-speaking citizens from assuming a central role in American life. As a result, some citizens in more than two dozen states have even advocated—and in some cases passed—laws designating English as "the official language" of the United States. They argue partly on the grounds of cost (bilingual equipment, bilingual ballots, bilingual forms and signs and menus all cost money), partly to promote a more unified nation, partly to avoid the possibility that states in the Southwest might become Spanish-speaking "American Quebecs." Their opponents contend that creating English as an official language would foster intolerance and bigotry, would compromise the civil rights of citizens who have not mastered English, and would compromise the richness of our nation's ethnic diversity.

Power is also at the heart of feminist critiques of the English language. As the four selections printed in this part disclose, the English language can favor some groups at the expense of others—particularly men at the expense of women. To what extent does English, as the product of a culture dominated by males, demean and delimit women? To what extent does English perpetuate outworn cultural assumptions about women? In other words, to what extent is English itself sexist? And what can be done about it? Those are the questions taken up in the final section of this part of *Conversations*.

Most citizens in this country have been proud of the metaphor of America as a melting pot—a place where immigrants are assimilated into the fabric of American life and American language. Recently another metaphor has been proposed: America as a salad bowl, as a place where immigrant citizens become American but still contribute their unique cultural flavors to the mix. Whatever the metaphor, language will continue to be an area where differences between individuals and their society are negotiated, where conflicts between "American society" and its diverse individuals are adjudicated. In other words, language itself will remain an issue.

SHOULD THERE BE—OR CAN THERE BE—A "STANDARD" ENGLISH?

Barbara Mellix

From Outside, In

You will learn a lot about Barbara Mellix from reading the following essay, which was published in The Georgia Review *in the summer of 1987, just after Ms. Mellix completed her masters' degree in creative writing at the University of Pittsburgh.* The Georgia Review *is a journal for academics and quasi-academics that includes scholarly articles, fiction, poetry, and book reviews.*

1 Two years ago, when I started writing this paper, trying to bring order out of chaos, my ten-year-old daughter was suffering from an acute attack of boredom. She drifted in and out of the room complaining that she had nothing to do, no one to "be with" because none of her friends were at home. Patiently I explained that I was working on something special and needed peace and quiet, and I suggested that she paint, read, or work with her computer. None of these interested her. Finally, she pulled up a chair to my desk and watched me, now and then heaving long, loud sighs. After two or three minutes (nine or ten sighs), I lost my patience. "Looka here, Allie," I said, "you too old for this kinda carryin' on. I done told you this is important. You wronger than dirt to be in here haggin' me like this and you know it. Now git on outta here and leave me off before I put my foot all the way down."

2 I was at home, alone with my family, and my daughter understood that this way of speaking was appropriate in that context. She knew, as a matter of fact, that it was almost inevitable; when I get angry at home, I speak some of my finest, most cherished black English. Had I been speaking to my daughter in this manner in certain other environments, she would have been shocked and probably worried that I had taken leave of my sense of propriety.

Like my children, I grew up speaking what I considered two distinctly different languages—black English and standard English (or as I thought of them then, the ordinary everyday speech of "country" coloreds and "proper" English)—and in the process of acquiring these languages, I developed an understanding of when, where, and how to use them. But unlike my children, I grew up in a world that was primarily black. My friends, neighbors, minister, teachers—almost everybody I associated with every day—were black. And we spoke to one another in our own special language: *That sho is a pretty dress you got on. If she don't soon leave me off I'm gon tell her head a mess. I was so mad I could'a pissed a blue nail. He all the time trying to low-rate somebody. Ain't that just about the nastiest thing you ever set ears on?* 3

Then there were the "others," the "proper" blacks, transplanted relatives and one-time friends who came home from the city for weddings, funerals, and vacations. And the whites. To these we spoke standard English. "Ain't?" my mother would yell at me when I used the term in the presence of "others." "You *know* better than that." And I would hang my head in shame and say the "proper" word. 4

I remember one summer sitting in my grandmother's house in Greeleyville, South Carolina, when it was full of the chatter of city relatives who were home on vacation. My parents sat quietly, only now and then volunteering a comment or answering a question. My mother's face took on a strained expression when she spoke. I could see that she was being careful to say just the right words in just the right way. Her voice sounded thick, muffled. And when she finished speaking, she would lapse into silence, her proper smile on her face. My father was more articulate, more aggressive. He spoke quickly, his words sharp and clear. But he held his proud head higher, a signal that he, too, was uncomfortable. My sisters and brothers and I stared at our aunts, uncles, and cousins, speaking only when prompted. Even then, we hesitated, formed our sentences in our minds, then spoke softly, shyly. 5

My parents looked small and anxious during those occasions, and I waited impatiently for leave-taking when we would mock our relatives the moment we were out of their hearing. "Reeely," we would say to one another, flexing our wrists and rolling our eyes, "how dooo you stan' this heat? Chile, it just too hy*ooo*-mid for words." Our relatives had made us feel "country," and this was our way of regaining 6 pride in ourselves while getting a little revenge in the bargain. The words bubbled in our throats and rolled across our tongues, a balming.

7 As a child I felt this same doubleness in uptown Greeleyville where the whites lived. "Ain't that a pretty dress you're wearing!" Toby, the town policeman, said to me one day when I was fifteen. "Thank you very much," I replied, my voice barely audible in my own ears. The words felt wrong in my mouth, rigid, foreign. It was not that I had never spoken that phrase before—it was common in black English, too—but I was extremely conscious that this was an occasion for proper English. I had taken out my English and put it on as I did my church clothes, and I felt as if I were wearing my Sunday best in the middle of the week. It did not matter that Toby had not spoken grammatically correct English. He was white and could speak as he wished. I had something to prove. Toby did not.

8 Speaking standard English to whites was our way of demonstrating that we knew their language and could use it. Speaking it to standard-English-speaking blacks was our way of showing them that we, as well as they, could "put on airs." But when we spoke standard English, we acknowledged (to ourselves and to others—but primarily to ourselves) that our customary way of speaking was inferior. We felt foolish, embarrassed, somehow diminished because we were ashamed to be our real selves. We were reserved, shy in the presence of those who owned and/or spoke *the* language.

9 My parents never set aside time to drill us in standard English. Their forms of instruction were less formal. When my father was feeling particularly expansive, he would regale us with tales of his exploits in the outside world. In almost flawless English, complete with dialogue and flavored with gestures and embellishment, he told us about his attempt to get a haircut at a white barbershop; his refusal to acknowledge one of the town merchants until the man addressed him as "Mister"; the time he refused to step off the sidewalk uptown to let some whites pass; his airplane trip to New York City (to visit a sick relative) during which the stewardesses and porters—recognizing that he was a "gentleman"—addressed him as "Sir." I did not realize then—nor, I think, did my father—that he was teaching us, among other things, standard English and the relationship between language and power.

10 My mother's approach was different. Often, when one of

us said, "I'm gon wash off my feet," she would say, "And what will you walk on if you wash them off?" Everyone would laugh at the victim of my mother's "proper" mood. But it was different when one of us children was in a proper mood. "You think you are so superior," I said to my oldest sister one day when we were arguing and she was winning. "Superior!" my sister mocked. "You mean I'm acting 'biggidy'?" My sisters and brothers sniggered, then joined in teasing me. Finally, my mother said, "Leave your sister alone. There's nothing wrong with using proper English." There was a half-smile on her face. I had gotten "uppity," had "put on airs" for no good reason. I was at home, alone with the family, and I hadn't been prompted by one of my mother's proper moods. But there was also a proud light in my mother's eyes; her children were learning English very well.

Not until years later, as a college student, did I begin to 11
understand our ambivalence toward English, our scorn of it, our need to master it, to own and be owned by it—an ambivalence that extended to the public school classroom. In our school, where there were no whites, my teacher taught standard English but used black English to do it. When my grammar-school teachers wanted us to write, for example, they usually said something like, "I want y'all to write five sentences that make a statement. Anybody git done before the rest can color." It was probably almost those exact words that led me to write these sentences in 1953 when I was in the second grade:

> The white clouds are pretty.
> There are only 15 people in our room.
> We will go to gym.
> We have a new poster.
> We may go out doors.

Second grade came after "Little First" and "Big First," so by then I knew the implied rules that accompanied all writing assignments. Writing was an occasion for proper English. I was not to write in the way we spoke to one another: The white clouds pretty; There ain't but fifteen people in our room; We going to gym; We got a new poster; We can go out in the yard. Rather I was to use the language of "other": clouds *are,* there *are,* we *will,* we *have,* we *may*.

12 My sentences were short, rigid, perfunctory, like the letters my mother wrote to relatives:

> Dear Papa,
>
> How are you? How is Mattie? Fine I hope. We are fine. We will come to see you Sunday. Cousin Ned will give us a ride.
>
> Love,
> Daughter

The language was not ours. It was something from outside us, something we used for special occasions.

13 But my coloring on the other side of that second-grade paper is different. I drew three hearts and a sun. The sun has a smiling face that radiates and envelopes everything it touches. And although the sun and the world are enclosed in a circle, the colors I used—red, blue, green, purple, orange, yellow, black—indicate that I was less restricted with drawing and coloring than I was with writing standard English. My valentines were not just red. My sun was not just a yellow ball in the sky.

14 By the time I reached the twelfth grade, speaking and writing standard English had taken on new importance. Each year, about half of the newly graduated seniors of our school moved to large cities—particularly in the North—to live with relatives and find work. Our English teacher constantly corrected our grammar: "Not 'ain't,' but 'isn't.'" We seldom wrote papers, and even those few were usually plot summaries of short stories. When our teacher returned the papers, she usually lectured on the importance of using standard English: "I *am*; you *are*; he, she, or it *is*," she would say, writing on the chalkboard as she spoke. "How you gon git a job talking about 'I is,' or 'I isn't' or 'I ain't'?"

15 In Pittsburgh, where I moved after graduation, I watched my aunt and uncle—who had always spoken standard English when in Greeleyville—switch from black English to standard English to a mixture of the two, according to where they were or who they were with. At home and with certain close relatives, friends, and neighbors, they spoke black English. With those less close, they spoke a mixture. In public and with strangers, they generally spoke standard English.

16 In time, I learned to speak standard English with ease and to switch smoothly from black to standard or a mixture, and back again. But no matter where I was, no matter what the

situation or occasion, I continued to write as I had in school:

> Dear Mommie,
> How are you? How is everybody else? Fine I hope. I am fine. So are Aunt and Uncle. Tell everyone I said hello. I will write again soon.
> Love,
> Barbara

At work, at a health insurance company, I learned to write letters to customers. I studied form letters and letters written by co-workers, memorizing the phrases and the ways in which they were used. I dictated:

> Thank you for your letter of January 5. We have made the changes in your coverage you requested. Your new premium will be $150 every three months. We are pleased to have been of service to you.

In a sense, I was proud of the letters I wrote for the company: they were proof of my ability to survive in the city, the outside world—an indication of my growing mastery of English. But they also indicate that writing was still mechanical for me, something that didn't require much thought.

Reading also became a more significant part of my life during those early years in Pittsburgh. I had always liked reading, but now I devoted more and more of my spare time to it. I read romances, mysteries, popular novels. Looking back, I realize that the books I liked best were simple, unambiguous: good versus bad and right versus wrong with right rewarded and wrong punished, mysteries unraveled and all set right in the end. It was how I remembered life in Greeleyville. 17

Of course I was romanticizing. Life in Greeleyville had not become very uncomplicated. Back there I had been—first as a child, then as a young woman with limited experience in the outside world—living in a relatively closed-in society. But there were implicit and explicit principles that guided our way of life and shaped our relationships with one another and the people outside—principles that a newcomer would find elusive and baffling. In Pittsburgh, I had matured, become more experienced. I had worked at three 18 different jobs, associated with a wider range of people, married, had children. This new environment with different prescripts for living required that I speak standard English much of the time and slowly, imperceptibly, I had ceased seeing a sharp distinction between myself and "others." Reading romances and mysteries, characterized by dichotomy, was a way of shying away from change, from the person I was becoming.

19 But that other part of me—that part which took great pride in my ability to hold a job writing business letters—was increasingly drawn to the new developments in my life and the attending possibilities, opportunities for even greater change. If I could write letters for a nationally known business, could I not also do something better, more challenging, more important? Could I not, perhaps, go to college and become a school teacher? For years, afraid and a little embarrassed, I did no more than imagine this different me, this possible me. But sixteen years after coming north, when my youngest daughter entered kindergarten, I found myself unable—or unwilling—to resist the lure of possibility. I enrolled in my first college course: Basic Writing, at the University of Pittsburgh.

20 For the first time in my life, I was required to write extensively about myself. Using the most formal English at my command, I wrote these sentences near the beginning of the term:

> One of my duties as a homemaker is simply picking up after others. A day seldom passes that I don't search for a mislaid toy, book, or gym shoe, etc. I change the Ty-D-Bol, fight "ring around the collar," and keep our laundry smelling "April fresh." Occasionally, I settle arguments between my children and suggest things to do when they're bored. Taking telephone messages for my oldest daughter is my newest (and sometimes most aggravating) chore. Hanging the toilet paper roll is my most insignificant.

My concern was to use "appropriate" language, to sound as if I belonged in a college classroom. But I felt separate from the language—as if it did not and could not belong to me. I couldn't think and feel genuinely in that language, couldn't make it express what I thought and felt about being a housewife. A part of me resented, among other things, being judged by such things as the appearance of my family's laundry and toilet bowl, but in that language I could only imagine and write about a conventional housewife.

21 For the most part, the remainder of the term was a period of adjustment, a time of trying to find my bearings as a student in a college composition class, to learn to shut out my black English whenever I composed, and to prevent it from creeping into my formulations; a time for trying to grasp the language of the classroom and reproduce it in my prose; for trying to talk about myself in that language, reach others through it. Each experience of writing was like standing naked and revealing my imperfection, my "otherness." And each new assignment was another chance to make myself over in language, reshape myself, make myself "better" in my rapidly changing image of a student in a college composition class.

22 But writing became increasingly unmanageable as the term progressed, and by the end of the semester, my sentences sounded like this:

> My excitement was soon dampened, however, by what seemed like a small voice in the back of my head saying that I should be careful with my long awaited opportunity. I felt frustrated and this seemed to make it difficult to concentrate.

There is a poverty of language in these sentences. By this point, I knew that the clichéd language of my Housewife essay was unacceptable, and I generally recognized trite expressions. At the same time, I hadn't yet mastered the language of the classroom, hadn't yet come to see it as belonging to me. Most notable is the lifelessness of the prose, the apparent absence of a person behind the words. I wanted those sentences—and the rest of the essay—to convey the anguish of yearning to, at once, become something more and yet remain the same. I had the sensation of being split in two, part of me going into a future the other part didn't believe possible. As that person, the student writer at that moment, I was essentially mute. I could not—in the process of composing—use the language of the old me, yet I couldn't imagine myself in the language of "others."

23 I found this particularly discouraging because at midsemester I had been writing in a much different way. Note the language of this introduction to an essay I had written then, near the middle of the term:

> Pain is a constant companion to the people in "Footwork." Their jobs are physically damaging. Employers are insensitive to their feelings and in many cases add to their problems. The general public wounds them further by treating them with disgrace because of what they do for a living. Although the workers are as diverse as they are similar, there is a definite link between them. They suffer a great deal of abuse.

The voice here is stronger, more confident, appropriating terms like "physically damaging," "wounds them further," "insensitive," "diverse"—terms I couldn't have imagined using when writing about my own experience—and shaping them into sentences like, "Although the workers are as diverse as they are similar, there is a definite link between them." And there is the sense of a personality behind the prose, someone who sympathizes with the workers: "The general public wounds them further by treating them with disgrace because of what they do for a living."

24 What caused these differences? I was, I believed, explaining other people's thoughts and feelings, and I was free to move about in the language of "others" so long as I was speaking *of* others. I was unaware that I was transforming into my best classroom language my own thoughts and feelings about people whose experiences and ways of speaking were in many ways similar to mine.

25 The following year, unable to turn back or let go of what had become something of an obsession with language (and hoping to catch and hold the sense of control that had eluded me in Basic Writing), I enrolled in a research writing course. I spent most of the term learning how to prepare for and write a research paper. I chose sex education as my subject and spent hours in libraries, searching for information, reading, taking notes. Then (not without messiness and often-demoralizing frustration) I organized my information into categories, wrote a thesis statement, and composed my paper—a series of paraphrases and quotations spaced between carefully constructed transitions. The process and results felt artificial, but as I would later come to realize I was passing through a necessary stage. My sentences sounded like this:

> This reserve becomes understandable with examination of who the abusers are. In an overwhelming number of cases, they are people the victims know and trust. Family members,

> relatives, neighbors and close family friends commit seventy-five percent of all reported sex crimes against children, and parents, parent substitutes and relatives are the offenders in thirty to eighty percent of all reported cases. While assault by strangers does occur, it is less common, and is usually a single episode. But abuse by family members, relatives and acquaintances may continue for an extended period of time. In cases of incest, for example, children are abused repeatedly for an average of eight years. In such cases, "the use of physical force is rarely necessary because of the child's trusting, dependent relationship with the offender. The child's cooperation is often facilitated by the adult's position of dominance, an offer of material goods, a threat of physical violence, or a misrepresentation of moral standards."

The completed paper gave me a sense of profound satis- 26
faction, and I read it often after my professor returned it. I know now that what I was pleased with was the language I used and the professional voice it helped me maintain. "Use better words," my teacher had snapped at me one day after reading the notes I'd begun accumulating from my research, and slowly I began taking on the language of my sources. In my next set of notes, I used the word "vacillating"; my professor applauded. And by the time I composed the final draft, I felt at ease with terms like "overwhelming number of cases," "single episode," and "reserve," and I shaped them into sentences similar to those of my "expert" sources.

If I were writing the paper today, I would of course do 27
some things differently. Rather than open with an anecdote—as my teacher suggested—I would begin simply with a quotation that caught my interest as I was researching my paper (and which I scribbled, without its source, in the margin of my notebook): "Truth does not do so much good in the world as the semblance of truth does evil." The quotation felt right because it captured what was for me the central idea of my essay—an idea that emerged gradually during the making of my paper—and expressed it in a way I would like to have said it. The anecdote, a hypothetical situation I invented to conform to the information in the paper, felt forced and insincere because it represented—to a great degree—my teacher's understanding of the essay, *her* idea of what in it was most significant. Improving upon my previous experiences with writing, I was beginning to think and feel in the language I used, to find my own voices in it,

to sense that how one speaks influences how one means. But I was not yet secure enough, comfortable enough with the language to trust my intuition.

28 Now that I know that to seek knowledge, freedom, and autonomy means always to be in the concentrated process of becoming—always to be venturing into new territory, feeling one's way at first, then getting one's balance, negotiating, accommodating, discovering one's self in ways that previously defined "others"—I sometimes get tired. And I ask myself why I keep on participating in this highbrow form of violence, this slamming against perplexity. But there is no real futility in the question, no hint of that part of the old me who stood outside standard English, hugging to herself a disabling mistrust of a language she thought could not represent a person with her history and experience. Rather, the question represents a person who feels the consequence of her education, the weight of her possibilities as a teacher and writer and human being, a voice in society. And I would not change that person, would not give back the good burden that accompanies my growing expertise, my increasing power to shape myself in language and share that self with "others."

29 "To speak," says Frantz Fanon, "means to be in a position to use a certain syntax, to grasp the morphology of this or that language, but it means above all to assume a culture, to support the weight of a civilization."* To write means to do the same, but in a more profound sense. However, Fanon also says that to achieve mastery means to "get" to a position of power, to "grasp," to "assume." This, I have learned—both as a student and subsequently as a teacher—can involve tremendous emotional and psychological conflict for those attempting to master academic discourse. Although as a beginning student writer I had a fairly good grasp of ordinary spoken English and was proficient at what Labov calls "code switching" (and what John Baugh in *Black Street Speech* terms "style shifting"), when I came face to face with the demands of academic writing, I grew increasingly self-conscious, constantly aware of my status as a black and a speaker of one of the many black English vernaculars, a traditional outsider. For the first time, I experienced my sense of doubleness as something menacing, a built-in

* *Black Skin, White Masks* (1952; rpt. New York: Grove Press, 1967), pp. 17–18.

enemy. Whenever I turned inward for salvation, the balm so available during my childhood, I found instead this new fragmentation which spoke to me in many voices. It was the voice of my desire to prosper, but at the same time it spoke of what I had relinquished and could not regain: a safe way of being, a state of powerlessness which exempted me from responsibility for who I was and might be. And it accused me of betrayal, of turning away from blackness. To recover balance, I had to take on the language of the academy, the language of "others." And to do that, I had to learn to imagine myself a part of the culture of that language, and therefore someone free to manage that language, to take liberties with it. Writing and rewriting, practicing, experimenting, I came to comprehend more fully the generative power of language. I discovered—with the help of some especially sensitive teachers—that through writing one can continually bring new selves into being, each with new responsibilities and difficulties, but also with new possibilities. Remarkable power, indeed. I write and continually give birth to myself.

Rachel L. Jones

What's Wrong with Black English

Rachel L. Jones contributed this essay to the "My Turn" column in Newsweek *in 1982, while she was a sophomore at Southern Illinois University. She currently writes for* The River Front Times, *a weekly newspaper in St. Louis.*

William Labov, a noted linguist, once said about the use of black English, "It is the goal of most black Americans to acquire full control of the standard language without giving up their own culture." He also suggested that there are certain advantages to having two ways to express one's feelings. I wonder if the good doctor might also consider the goals of those black Americans who have full control of standard English but who are every now and then troubled by that colorful grammar-to-the-winds patois that is black English. Case in point—me. 1

2 I'm a 21-year-old black born to a family that would probably be considered lower-middle class—which in my mind is a polite way of describing a condition only slightly better than poverty. Let's just say we rarely if ever did the winter-vacation thing in the Caribbean. I've often had to defend my humble beginnings to a most unlikely group of people for an even less likely reason. Because of the way I talk, some of my black peers look at me sideways and ask, "Why do you talk like you're white?"

3 The first time it happened to me I was nine years old. Cornered in the school bathroom by the class bully and her sidekick, I was offered the opportunity to swallow a few of my teeth unless I satisfactorily explained why I always got good grades, why I talked "proper" or "white." I had no ready answer for her, save the fact that my mother had from the time I was old enough to talk stressed the importance of reading and learning, or that L. Frank Baum and Ray Bradbury were my closest companions. I read all my older brothers' and sisters' literature textbooks more faithfully than they did, and even lightweights like the Bobbsey Twins and Trixie Belden were allowed into my bookish inner circle. I don't remember exactly what I told those girls, but I somehow talked my way out of a beating.

4 I was reminded once again of my "white pipes" problem while apartment hunting in Evanston, Illinois, last winter. I doggedly made out lists of available places and called all around. I would immediately be invited over—and immediately turned down. The thinly concealed looks of shock when the front door opened clued me in, along with the flustered instances of "just getting off the phone with the girl who was ahead of you and she wants the rooms." When I finally found a place to live, my roommate stirred up old memories when she remarked a few months later, "You know, I was surprised when I first saw you. You sounded white over the phone." Tell me another one, sister.

5 I should've asked her a question I've wanted an answer to for years: how does one "talk white"? The silly side of me pictures a rabid white foam spewing forth when I speak. I don't use Valley Girl jargon, so that's not what's meant in my case. Actually, I've pretty much deduced what people mean when they say that to me, and the implications are really frightening.

6 It means that I'm articulate and well-versed. It means that I can talk as freely about John Steinbeck as I can about Rick

James. It means that "ain't" and "he be" are not staples of my vocabulary and are only used around family and friends. (It is almost Jekyll and Hyde-ish the way I can slip out of academic abstractions into a long, lean, double-negative-filled dialogue, but I've come to terms with that aspect of my personality.) As a child, I found it hard to believe that's what people meant by "talking proper"; that would've meant that good grades and standard English were equated with white skin, and that went against everything I'd ever been taught. Running into the same type of mentality as an adult has confirmed the depressing reality that for many blacks, standard English is not only unfamiliar, it is socially unacceptable.

James Baldwin once defended black English by saying it 7
had added "vitality to the language," and even went so far as to label it a language in its own right, saying, "Language [i.e., black English] is a political instrument" and a "vivid and crucial key to identity." But did Malcolm X urge blacks to take power in this country, "any way y'all can"? Did Martin Luther King Jr. say to blacks, "I has been to the mountaintop, and I done seed the Promised Land"? Toni Morrison, Alice Walker and James Baldwin did not achieve their eloquence, grace and stature by using only black English in their writing. Andrew Young, Tom Bradley and Barbara Jordan did not acquire political power by saying, "Y'all crazy if you ain't gon vote for me." They all have full command of standard English, and I don't think that knowledge takes away from their blackness or commitment to black people.

I know from experience that it's important for black 8
people, stripped of culture and heritage, to have something they can point to and say, "This is ours, *we* can comprehend it, *we* alone can speak it with a soulful flourish." I'd be lying if I said that the rhythms of my people caught up in "some serious rap" don't sound natural and right to me sometimes. But how heartwarming is it for those same brothers when they hit the pavement searching for employment? Studies have proven that the use of ethnic dialects decreases power in the marketplace. "I be" is acceptable on the corner, but not with the boss.

Am I letting capitalistic, European-oriented thinking fog 9
the issue? Am I selling out blacks to an ideal of assimilating, being as much like whites as possible? I have not formed a personal political ideology, but I do know this: it hurts me to

hear black children use black English, knowing that they will be at yet another disadvantage in an educational system already full of stumbling blocks. It hurts me to sit in lecture halls and hear fellow black students complain that the professor "be tripping dem out using big words dey can't understand." And what hurts most is to be stripped of my own blackness simply because I know my way around the English language.

10 I would have to disagree with Labov in one respect. My goal is not so much to acquire full control of both standard and black English, but to one day see more black people less dependent on a dialect that excludes them from full participation in the world we live in. I don't think I talk white, I think I talk right.

Geneva Smitherman

White English in Blackface, or Who Do I Be?

Geneva Smitherman is a professor of linguistics at Michigan State University. Her contention printed here, that Black English is not slang but a dialect of English that follows careful rules, first appeared in The Black Scholar *in 1973.*

1 Bin nothin in a long time lit up the English teaching profession like the current hassle over Black English. One finds beaucoup sociolinguistic research studies and language projects for the "disadvantaged" on the scene in nearly every sizable black community in the country.[1] And

[1] For examples of such programs see *Non-Standard Dialect*, Board of Education of the City of New York (National Council of Teachers of English, 1968); San-Su C. Lin, *Pattern Practices in the Teaching of Standard English to Students with a Non-Standard Dialect* (USOE Project 1339, 1965); Arno Jewett, Joseph Mersand, Doris Gunderson, *Improving English Skills of Culturally Different Youth in Large Cities* (U.S. Department of

educators from K-Grad. School bees debating whether: (1) blacks should learn and use only standard white English (hereafter referred to as WE); (2) blacks should command both dialects, i.e., be bidialectal (hereafter BD); (3) blacks should be allowed (??????) to use standard Black English (hereafter BE or BI). The appropriate choice having everything to do with American political reality, which is usually ignored, and nothing to do with the educational process, which is usually claimed. I say without qualification that we cannot talk about the Black Idiom apart from Black Culture and the Black Experience. Nor can we specify educational goals for blacks apart from considerations about the structure of (white) American society.

And we black folks is not gon take all that weight, for no 2
one has empirically demonstrated that linguistic/stylistic features of BE impede educational progress in communication skills, or any other area of cognitive learning. Take reading. It's don been charged, but not actually verified, that BE interferes with mastery of reading skills.[2] Yet beyond pointing out the gap between the young brother/sistuh's phonological and syntactical patterns and those of the usually-middle-class-WE-speaking-teacher, this claim has not been validated. The distance between the two systems is, after all, short and is illuminated only by the fact that reading is taught *orally*. (Also get to the fact that preceding generations of BE-speaking folks learned to read, despite the many classrooms in which the teacher spoke a dialect different from that of their students.)

For example, a student who reads *den* for *then* probably 3
pronounces initial/th/as /d/ in most words. Or the one who reads *doing* for *during* probably deletes intervocalic and final /r/ in most words. So it is not that such students can't read, they is simply employing the black phonological system. In the reading classrooms of today, what we bees needin is teachers with the proper attitudinal orientation who thus can distinguish actual reading problems from mere dialect differences. Or take the writing of an essay. The

Health, Education and Welfare, 1964); *Language Programs for the Disadvantaged* (NCTE, 1965).

[2] See for example, Joan Baratz and Roger Shuy, ed., *Teaching Black Children to Read* (Center for Applied Linguistics, 1969); A. L. Davis, ed., *On the Dialects of Children* (NCTE, 1968); Eldonna L. Evertts, ed., *Dimensions of Dialect* (NCTE, 1967).

only percentage in writing a paper with WE spelling, punctuation, and usage is in maybe eliciting a positive *attitudinal* response from a prescriptivist middle-class-aspirant-teacher. Dig on the fact that sheer "correctness" does not a good writer make. And is it any point in dealing with the charge of BE speakers being "nonverbal" or "linguistically deficient" in oral communication skills—behind our many Raps who done disproved that in living, vibrant colors?[3]

4 What linguists and educators need to do at this juncture is to take serious cognizance of the Oral Tradition in Black Culture. The uniqueness of this verbal style requires a language competence/performance model to fit the black scheme of things. Clearly BI speakers possess rich communication skills (i.e., are highly *competent* in using language), but as yet there bees no criteria (evaluative, testing, or other instrument of measurement), based on black communication patterns, wherein BI speakers can demonstrate they competence (i.e., *performance*). Hence brothers and sisters fail on language performance tests in English classrooms. Like, to amplify on what Nikki [Giovanni] said, that's why we always lose, not only cause we don't know the rules, but it ain't even our game.

5 We can devise a performance model only after an analysis of the components of BI. Now there do be linguists who supposedly done did this categorization and definition of BE.[4] But the descriptions are generally confining, limited as they are to discrete linguistic units. One finds simply ten to fifteen patterns cited, as for example, the most frequently listed one, the use of *be* as finite verb, contrasting with its deletion: (a) *The coffee be cold* contrasts with (b) *The coffee cold*, the former statement denoting a continuing state of affairs, the latter applying to the present moment only. (Like if you the cook, (a) probably get you fired, and (b) only get you talked about.) In WE no comparable grammatical

[3] For the most racist and glaring of these charges, see Fred Hechinger, ed., *Pre-School Education Today* (Doubleday, 1966); for an excellent rebuttal, see William Labov, *Nonstandard English* (NCTE, 1970); for a complete overview of the controversy and issues involved as well as historical perspective and rebuttal to the non-verbal claim, see my "Black Idiom and White Institutions," *Negro American Literature Forum*, Fall 1971.

[4] The most thorough and scholarly of these, though a bit overly technical, is Walter Wolfram, *Detroit Negro Speech* (Center for Applied Linguistics, 1969).

distinction exists and *The coffee is cold* would be used to indicate both meanings. However, rarely does one find an investigation of the total vitality of black expressive style, a style inextricable from the Black Cultural Universe, for after all, BI connects with Black Soul and niggers is more than deleted copulas.[5]

The Black Idiom should be viewed from two important perspectives: linguistic and stylistic. The linguistic dimension is comprised of the so-called nonstandard features of phonology and syntax (patterns like *dis heah* and *The coffee be cold*), and a lexicon generally equated with "slang" or hip talk. The stylistic dimension has to do with *rapping, capping, jiving*, etc., and with features such as cadence, rhythm, resonance, gestures, and all those other elusive, difficult-to-objectify elements that make up what is considered a writer or speaker's "style." While I am separating linguistic and stylistic features, I have done so only for the purpose of simplifying the discussion since the BI speaker runs the full gamut of both dimensions in any given speech event. 6

I acknowledge from the bell that we's dealing with a dialect structure which is a subsystem of the English language; thus BE and WE may not appear fundamentally different. Yet, though black folks speak English, it do seem to be an entirely different lingo altogether. But wherein lies the uniqueness? Essentially in language, as in other areas of Black Culture, we have the problem of isolating those elements indigenous to black folks from those cultural aspects shared with white folks. Anthropologist Johnnetta Cole suggests that Black Culture has three dimensions: (1) those elements shared with mainstream America; (2) those elements shared with all oppressed peoples; (3) those elements peculiar to the black condition in America.[6] Applying her concepts to language, I propose the accompanying schematic representation. 7

Referring to the first column, contemporary BE is simply 8

[5] Kochman is one linguist who done gone this route; see for instance his "Rapping in the Black Ghetto," *Trans-action*, February 1969. However, he makes some black folks mad because of what one of my students called his "superfluity," and others shame cause of his exposure of our "bad" street elements. Kochman's data: jam up with mutafuckas and pussy-copping raps collected from Southside Chicago.

[6] Johnnetta B. Cole, "Culture: Negro, Black and Nigger," *The Black Scholar*, June 1970.

FEATURES SHARED WITH MAINSTREAM AMERICA	FEATURES SHARED WITH ALL OPPRESSED PEOPLES	FEATURES UNIQUE TO BLACK AMERICANS
Linguistic 1. British/American English lexicon 2. Most aspects of British/American English phonology and syntax	*Linguistic* 1. Superimpositions of dominant culture's language on native language, yielding 2. Pidginized form of dominant culture's language, subject to becoming extinct, due to 3. Historical evolution, linguistic leveling out in direction of dominant culture's dialect	*Linguistic* Unique meanings attributed to certain English lexical items *Stylistic* Unique communication patterns and rhetorical flourishes

one of the many dialects of contemporary American English, and it is most likely the case that the linguistic patterns of BE differ from those of WE in surface structure only. There's no essential linguistic difference between *dis heah* and *this here*, and from a strictly linguistic point of view, *God don't never change* can be written *God doesn't ever change* (though definitely not from a socio-cultural/political perspective, as Baraka quite rightly notes).[7] Perhaps we could make a case for deep structure difference in the BE use of *be* as finite verb (refer to *The coffee be cold* example above), but we be hard pressed to find any other examples,

[7] Imamu Baraka, "Expressive Language," *Home*, pp. 166–172.

and even in this case, we could posit that the copula exists in the deep structure, and is simply deleted by some low-level phonological deletion rule, dig: The coffee is cold . . . The coffee's cold . . . The coffee cold. My conclusion at this point is that despite the claims of some highly respected Creole linguists (with special propers to bad Sistuh Beryl Bailey),[8] the argument for deep structure differences between contemporary BE and WE syntax cannot pass the test of rigorous transformational analysis.

Referring to the second column, we note the psychological tendency of oppressed people to adopt the modes of behavior and expression of their oppressors (also, during the African slave trade, the functional necessity of pidginized forms of European language). Not only does the conqueror force his victims into political subjugation, he also coerces them into adopting his language and doles out special rewards to those among the oppressed who best mimic his language and cultural style. In the initial language contact stage, the victims attempt to assemble the new language into their native linguistic mold, producing a linguistic mixture that is termed *pidgin*. In the next stage, the pidgin may develop into a Creole, a highly systematic, widely used mode of communication among the oppressed, characterized by a substratum of patterns from the victim's language with an overlay of forms from the oppressor's language. As the oppressed people's identification with the victor's culture intensifies, the pidgin/Creole begins to lose its linguistic currency and naturally evolves in the direction of the victor's language. Reconstructing the linguistic history of BE, we theorize that it followed a similar pattern; due to the radically different condition of black oppression in America, the process of *de-creolization* is nearly complete and has been for perhaps over a hundred years. 9

The most important features of BI are, of course, those referred to in column three, for they point us toward the linguistic uniqueness and cultural significance of the Oral Tradition in the Black Experience. It should be clear that all along I been talkin about that Black Experience associated with the grass-roots black folks, the masses, the sho-nuff 10

[8] See her "Toward a New Perspective in Negro English Dialectology," *American Speech* (1965); and "Language and Communicative Styles of Afro-American Children in the United States," *Florida FL Reporter* 7 (Spring/Summer 1969).

niggers—in short, all those black folks who do not aspire to white middle-class American standards.

11 Within this tradition, language is used as a teaching/socializing force and as a means of establishing one's reputation via his verbal competence. Black talk is never meaningless cocktail chit-chat but a functional dynamic that is simultaneously a mechanism for acculturation and information-passing and a vehicle for achieving group recognition. Black communication is highly verbal and highly stylized; it is a performance before a black audience who become both observers and participants in the speech event. Whether it be through a slapping of hands ("giving five" or "giving skin"), Amen's, or Right on's, the audience influences the direction of a given rap and at the same time acknowledges or withholds its approval, depending on the linguistic skill and stylistic ingenuity of the speaker. I mean like a Brother is only as bad as his rap bees.

I. Toward a Black Language Model: Linguistic

12 While we concede that black people use the vocabulary of the English language, certain words are always selected out of that lexicon and given a special black semantic slant. So though we rappin bout the same language, the reality referents are different. As one linguist has suggested, the proper question is not what do words mean but what do the users of the words mean? These words may be associated with and more frequently used in black street culture but not necessarily. *Muthafucka* has social boundaries, but not *nigger*.

13 Referring to the lexicon of BI, then, the following general principles obtain:

14 1. The words given the special black slant exist in a dynamic state. The terms are discarded when they move into the white mainstream. (Example: One no longer speaks of a "hip" brother; now he is a "togetha" brother.) This was/is necessitated by our need to have a code that was/is undecipherable by foreigners (i.e., whites).

15 2. In BI, the concept of denotation vs. connotation does not apply.

16 3. What does apply is shades of meaning along the connotative spectrum. For example, depending on contex-

tual environment, the word *bad* can mean extraordinary; beautiful; good; versatile; or a host of other terms of positive value. Dig it; after watching a Sammy Davis performance, a BI speaker testified: "Sammy sho did some *bad* stuff," i.e., extraordinary stuff. Or upon observing a beautiful sister: "She sho is *bad*," i.e., beautiful, pretty, or good-looking. Or, noticing how a brother is dressed: "You sho got on some *bad* shit," i.e., *good* shit = attractively dressed.

Note that the above examples are all in the category of *approbation*. It is necessary to rap about *denigration* as well, since certain words in the black lexicon can frequently be used both ways. Consider the word *nigger*, for instance. "He's my main nigger" means my best friend (hence, approbation); "The nigger ain't shit," means he's probably lazy, trifling, scheming, wrong-doing, or a host of other *denigrating* terms, depending on the total context of the utterance. 17

4. Approbation and denigration relate to the semantic level; we can add two other possible functions of the same word on the grammatical level: *intensification* and *completion*. Slide back to *nigger* for a minute, and dig that often the word is void of real meaning and simply supplies the sentence with a subject. "Niggers was getting out of there left and right, then the niggers was running, and so the niggers said . . ." etc., etc., my main point being that a steady stream of overuse means neither denigration nor approbation. Some excellent illustrations of this function of the word are to be found in *Manchild in the Promised Land*, where you can observe the word used in larger contexts. 18

To give you a most vivid illustration, consider the use of what WE labels "obscenities." From the streets of Detroit: (a) "That's a bad *muthafucka*." Referring to a Cadillac Eldorado, obviously indicating approval. (b) "He's a no-good *muthafucka*." Referring to a person who has just "put some game" on the speaker, obviously indicating disapproval. (c) "You *muthafuckin* right I wasn't gon let him do that." Emphasizing how correct the listener's assessment is, obviously using the term as a grammatical intensifier, modifying "right." (d) "We wasn't doin nothing, just messing round and *shit*." Though a different "obscenity," the point is nonetheless illustrated, "shit" being used neutrally, as an expletive (filler) to complete the sentence pattern; semanti- 19 cally speaking, it is an empty word in this contextual environment.

20 Where I'm comin from is that the lexicon of BI, consisting of certain specially selected words, requires a unique scheme of analysis to account for the diverse range and multiplicity of meanings attributed to these words. While there do be some dictionaries of Afro-American "slang," they fail to get at the important question: what are the psycho-cultural processes that guide our selection of certain words out of the thousands of possible words in the Anglo-Saxon vocabulary? Like, for instance, Kochman[9] has suggested that we value action in the black community, and so those words that have action implied in them, we take and give positive meanings to, such as *swing, game, hip, hustle,* etc.; whereas words of implied stasis are taken and given negative connotations, such as *lame, square, hung-up, stiffin and jivin*, etc. At any rate, what I've tried to lay here are some suggestions in this particular linguistic dimension; the definitive word on black lexicon is yet to be given.

21 I shall go on to discuss the stylistic dimension of black communication patterns, where I have worked out a more definitive model.

II. Toward a Black Language Model: Stylistic

22 Black verbal style exists on a sacred-secular continuum, as represented by the accompanying scheme. The model allows us to account for the many individual variations in black speech, which can all be located at some point along the continuum.

23 The sacred style is rural and Southern. It is the style of the black preacher and that associated with the black church tradition. It tends to be more emotive and highly charged than the secular style. It is also older in time. However, though I've called it "sacred," it abounds in secularisms. Black church service tends to be highly

[9] See Thomas Kochman, "The Kinetic Element in Black Idiom," paper read at the American Anthropological Association Convention, Seattle, Washington, 1968; also his *Rappin' and Stylin' Out: Communication in Urban Black America*.

SACRED	*SECULAR*
Political Rap Style	*Political Rap Style*
Examples: Jesse Jackson	Examples: Malcom X
Martin Luther King	Rap Brown
Political Literary Style	*Political Literary Style*
Examples: Barbara Ann Teer's	Examples: Don Lee
National Black Theater	Last Poets
Nikki Giovanni's "Truth Is on Its Way"	

informal, and it ain't nothin for a preacher to get up in the pulpit and, say, show off what he's wearing: "Y'all didn't notice the new suit I got on today, did y'all? Ain the Lord good to us. . . ."

The secular style is urban and Northern, but since it probably had its beginnings in black folk tales and proverbs, its *roots* are Southern and rural. This is the street culture; the style found in barbershops and on street corners in the black ghettos of American cities. It tends to be more cool, more emotionally restrained than sacred style. It is newer and younger in time and only fully evolved as a distinct style with the massive wave of black migration to the cities. 24

Both sacred and secular styles share the following characteristics: 25

1. *Call and Response*. This is basic black oral tradition. The speaker's solo voice alternates or is intermingled with the audience's response. In the sacred style, the minister is urged by the congregation's Amen's, That's right, Reverend's, or Preach Reverend's. One also hears occasional Take your time's when the preacher is initiating his sermon, the congregation desiring to savor every little bit of this good message they bout to hear. (In both sacred and secular political rap styles, the "Preach Reverend" is transposed to "Teach Brother.") In the secular style, the response can take the form of a back-and-forth banter between the speaker and various members of the audience. Or the audience might manifest its response in giving skin (fives) when a really down verbal point is scored. Other approval responses 26

include laughter and phrases like "Oh, you mean, nigger," "Get back, nigger," "Git down, baby," etc.

27 2. *Rhythmic Pattern*. I refer to cadence, tone, and musical quality. This is a pattern that is lyrical, sonorous, and generally emphasizing sound apart from sense. It is often established through repetition, either of certain sounds or words. The preacher will get a rhythm going, conveying his message through sound rather than depending on sheer semantic import. "I-I-I-I-I-Oh-I-I-Oh, yeah, Lord-I-I-heard the voice of Jesus saying. . . ." Even though the secular style is characterized by rapidity, as in the toasts (narrative tales of bad niggers and they exploits like Stag-O-Lee, or bad animals and they trickeration, like the Signifying Monkey), the speaker's voice tone still has that rhythmic, musical quality, just with a faster tempo.

28 3. *Spontaneity*. Generally, the speaker's performance is improvisational, with the rich interaction between speaker and audience dictating and/or directing the course and outcome of the speech event. Since the speaker does not prepare a formal document, his delivery is casual, nondeliberate, and uncontrived. He speaks in a lively, conversational tone, and with an ever-present quality of immediacy. All emphasis is on process, movement, and creativity of the moment. The preacher says "Y'all don wont to hear dat, so I'm gon leave it lone," and his audience shouts, "Naw, tell it Reverend, tell it!," and he does. Or, like, once Malcolm [X] mentioned the fact of his being in prison, and sensing the surprise of his audience, he took advantage of the opportunity to note that all black people were in prison: "That's what American means: prison."

29 4. *Concreteness*. The speaker's imagery and ideas center around the empirical world, the world of reality, and the contemporary Here and Now. Rarely does he drift off into esoteric abstractions; his metaphors and illustrations are commonplace and grounded in everyday experience. Perhaps because of his concreteness, there is a sense of identification with the event being described or narrated, as in the secular style where the toast-teller's identity merges with that of the protagonist of his tale, and he becomes Stag-O-Lee or Shine; or when the preacher assumes the voice of God or the personality of a Biblical character. Even the experience of being saved takes on a presentness and rootedness in everyday life: "I first met God in 1925. . . ."

5. *Signifying.* This is a technique of talking about the 30
entire audience or some member of the audience either to initiate verbal "war" or to make a point hit home. The interesting thang bout this rhetorical device is that the audience is not offended and realizes—naw, expects—the speaker to launch this offensive to achieve this desired effect. "Pimp, punk, prostitute, Ph.D.—all the P's—you still in slavery!" announces the Reverend Jesse Jackson. Malcolm puts down the nonviolent movement with: "In a revolution, you swinging, not singing." (Notice the characteristic rhythmic pattern in the above examples—the alliterative poetic effect of Jackson's statement and the rhyming device in Malcolm's.)

An analysis of black expressive style, such as presented here, should facilitate the construction of a performance instrument to measure the degree of command of the style of any given BI speaker. Linguists and educators sincerely interested in black education might be about the difficult, complex business of devising such a "test," rather than establishing linguistic remediation programs to correct a nonexistent remediation. Like in any other area of human activity, some BI rappers are better than others, and today's most effective black preachers, leaders, politicians, writers are those who rap in the black expressive style, appropriating the ritual framework of the Oral Tradition as vehicle for the conveyance of they political ideologies. Which brings me back to what I said from Jump Street. The real heart of this language controversy relates to/is the underlying political nature of the American educational system. Brother Frantz Fanon is highly instructive at this point. From his "Negro and Language," in *Black Skin, White Masks:*

> I ascribe a basic importance to the phenomenon of language. . . . To speak means . . . above all to assume a culture, to support the weight of a civilization. . . . Every dialect is a way of thinking. . . . And the fact that the newly returned [i.e., from white schools] Negro adopts a language different from that of the group into which he was born is evidence of a dislocation, a separation. . . .

In showing why the "Negro adopts such a position . . . with respect to European languages," Fanon continues:

> It is because he wants to emphasize the rupture that has now occurred. He is incarnating a new type of man that he

> imposes on his associates and his family. And so his old mother can no longer understand him when he talks to her about his *duds*, the family's *crummy joint*, the *dump* . . . all of it, of course, tricked out with the appropriate accent.
>
> In every country of the world, there are climbers, 'the ones who forget who they are,' and in contrast to them, 'the ones who remember where they came from.' The Antilles Negro who goes home from France expresses himself in the dialect if he wants to make it plain that nothing has changed.

31 As black people go moving on up toward separation and cultural nationalism, the question of the moment is not which dialect, but which culture, not whose vocabulary but whose values, not *I am* vs. *I be*, but WHO DO I BE?

John Simon

Why Good English Is Good for You

John Simon (born 1925) has reviewed theater and film for several magazines. An eloquent—and sometimes merciless—critic of the misuse of language, for many years he wrote a language column for Esquire. *Several of those columns were collected in* Paradigms Lost, *a book about the "decline of literacy." This essay is from that 1976 collection.*

1 What's good English to you that . . . you should grieve for it? What good is correct speech and writing, you may ask, in an age in which hardly anyone seems to know, and no one seems to care? Why shouldn't you just fling bloopers, bloopers riotously with the throng, and not stick out from the rest like a sore thumb by using the language correctly? Isn't grammar really a thing of the past, and isn't the new idea to communicate in *any* way as long as you can make yourself understood?

2 The usual, basic defense of good English (and here, again, let us not worry about nomenclature—for all I care, you may call it "Standard English," "correct American," or anything else) is that it helps communication, that it is perhaps even a *sine qua non* of mutual understanding. Although this is a crude truth of sorts, it strikes me as, in some ways, both

more and less than the truth. Suppose you say, "Everyone in their right mind would cross on the green light" or "Hopefully, it won't rain tomorrow"; chances are very good that the person you say this to will understand you, even though you are committing obvious solecisms or creating needless ambiguities. Similarly, if you write in a letter, "The baby has finally ceased it's howling" (spelling *its* as *it's*), the recipient will be able to figure out what was meant. But "figuring out" is precisely what a listener or reader should not have to do. There is, of course, the fundamental matter of courtesy to the other person, but it goes beyond that: why waste time on unscrambling simple meaning when there are more complex questions that should receive our undivided attention? If the many cooks had to worry first about which out of a large number of pots had no leak in it, the broth, whether spoiled or not, would take forever to be ready.

It is, I repeat, only initially a matter of clarity. It is also a 3
matter of concision. Space today is as limited as time. If you have only a thousand words in which to convey an important message, it helps to know that "overcomplicated" is correct and "overly complicated" is incorrect. Never mind the grammatical explanations; the two extra characters and one space between words are reason enough. But what about the more advanced forms of word-mongering that hold sway nowadays? Take redundancy, like the "hopes and aspirations" of Jimmy Carter, quoted by Edwin Newman as having "a deeply profound religious experience"; or elaborate jargon, as when Charles G. Walcutt, a graduate professor of English at CUNY, writes (again as quoted by Newman): "The colleges, trying to remediate increasing numbers of . . . illiterates up to college levels, are being high-schoolized"; or just obfuscatory verbiage of the pretentious sort, such as this fragment from a letter I received: "It is my impression that effective inte*r*personal verbal communication depends on prior effective intr*a*-personal verbal communication." What this means is that if you think clearly, you can speak and write clearly—except if you are a "certified speech and language pathologist," like the writer of the letter I quote. (By the way, she adds the letters Ph.D. after her name, though she is not even from Germany, where *Herr* and *Frau Doktor* are in common, not to say, vulgar, use.)

But except for her ghastly verbiage, our certified language
pathologist (whatever that means) is perfectly right: there is 4
a close connection between the ability to think and the ability to use English correctly. After all, we think in words,

we conceptualize in words, we work out our problems inwardly with words, and using them correctly is comparable to a craftsman's treating his tools with care, keeping his materials in good shape. Would you trust a weaver who hangs her wet laundry on her loom, or lets her cats bed down in her yarn? The person who does not respect words and their proper relationships cannot have much respect for ideas—very possibly cannot have ideas at all. My quarrel is not so much with minor errors that we fall into from time to time even if we know better as it is with basic sloppiness or ignorance or defiance of good English.

5 Training yourself to speak and write correctly—and I say "training yourself" because nowadays, unfortunately, you cannot depend on other people or on institutions to give you the proper training, for reasons I shall discuss later—training yourself, then, in language, means developing at the very least two extremely useful faculties: your sense of discipline and your memory. Discipline because language is with us always, as nothing else is: it follows us much as, in the old morality play, Good Deeds followed Everyman, all the way to the grave; and, if the language is written, even beyond. Let me explain: if you can keep an orderly apartment, if you can see to it that your correspondence and bill-paying are attended to regularly, if your diet and wardrobe are maintained with the necessary care—good enough; you are a disciplined person.

6 But the preliminary discipline underlying all others is nevertheless your speech: the words that come out of you almost as frequently and—if you are tidy—as regularly as your breath. I would go so far as to say that, immediately after your bodily functions, language is first, unless you happen to be an ascetic, an anchorite, or a stylite; but unless you are a styl*ite*, you had better be a styl*ist*.

7 Most of us—almost all—must take in and give out language as we do breath, and we had better consider the seriousness of language pollution as second only to air pollution. For the linguistically disciplined, to misuse or mispronounce a word is an unnecessary and unhealthy contribution to the surrounding smog. To have taught ourselves not to do this, or—being human and thus also imperfect—to do it as little as possible, means deriving from every speaking moment the satisfaction we get from a cap that snaps on to a container perfectly, an elevator that stops flush with the landing, a roulette ball that comes to rest exactly on the number on which we have placed our bet. It gives us the pleasure of hearing or seeing our words—

because they are abiding by the rules—snapping, sliding, falling precisely into place, expressing with perfect lucidity and symmetry just what we wanted them to express. This is comparable to the satisfaction of the athlete or ballet dancer or pianist finding his body or legs or fingers doing his bidding with unimpeachable accuracy.

And if someone now says that "in George Eliot's lesser novels, she is not completely in command" is perfectly comprehensible even if it is ungrammatical, the "she" having no antecedent in the nominative (*Eliot's* is a genitive), I say, "Comprehensible, perhaps, but lopsided," for the civilized and orderly mind does not feel comfortable with that "she"—does not hear that desired and satisfying click of correctness—unless the sentence is restructured as "George Eliot, in her lesser novels, is not . . ." or in some similar way. In fact, the fully literate ear can be thrown by this error in syntax; it may look for the antecedent of that "she" elsewhere than in the preceding possessive case. Be that as it may, playing without rules and winning—in this instance, managing to communicate without using good English—is no more satisfactory than winning in a sport or game by accident or by disregarding the rules: which is really cheating. 8

The second faculty good speech develops is, as I have mentioned before, our memory. Grammar and syntax are partly logical—and to that extent they are also good exercisers and developers of our logical faculty—but they are also partly arbitrary, conventional, irrational. For example, the correct "compared to" and "contrasted with" could, from the logical point of view, just as well be "contrasted to" and "compared with" ("compared with," of course, is correct, but in a different sense from the one that concerns us here, namely, the antithesis of "contrasted with"). And, apropos *different*, logic would have to strain desperately to explain the exclusive correctness of "different from," given the exclusive correctness of "other than," which would seem to justify "different than," jarring though that is to the cultivated ear. 9

But there it is: some things are so because tradition, usage, the best speakers and writers, the grammar books and dictionaries have made them so. There may even exist some hidden historical explanation: something, perhaps, in the Sanskrit, Greek, Latin, or other origins of a word or construction that you and I may very easily never know. We can, however, memorize; and memorization can be a wonderfully useful thing—surely the Greeks were right to consider Mnemosyne (memory) the mother of the Muses, for 10 without her there would be no art and no science. And what better place to practice one's mnemonic skills than in the study of one's language?

11 There is something particularly useful about speaking correctly and precisely because language is always there as a foundation—or, if you prefer a more fluid image, an undercurrent—beneath what is going on. Now, it seems to me that the great difficulty of life lies in the fact that we must almost always do two things at a time. If, for example, we are walking and conversing, we must keep our mouths as well as feet from stumbling. If we are driving while listening to music, we must not allow the siren song of the cassette to prevent us from watching the road and the speedometer (otherwise the less endearing siren of the police car or the ambulance will follow apace). Well, it is just this sort of bifurcation of attention that care for precise, clear expression fosters in us. By learning early in life to pay attention to both what we are saying and to how we are saying it, we develop the much-needed life skill of doing two things simultaneously.

12 Put another way, we foster our awareness of, and ability to deal with, form and content. If there is any verity that modern criticism has fought for, it is the recognition of that indissolubility of content and form. Criticism won the battle, won it so resoundingly that this oneness has become a contemporary commonplace. And shall the fact that form *is* content be a platitude in all the arts but go unrecognized in the art of self-expression, whether in conversation or correspondence, or whatever form of spoken or written utterance a human being resorts to? Accordingly, you are going to be judged, whether you like it or not, by the correctness of your thinking; there are some people to whose ear bad English is as offensive as gibberish, or as your picking your nose in public would be to their eyes and stomachs. The fact that people of linguistic sensibilities may be a dying breed does not mean that they are wholly extinct, and it is best not to take any unnecessary chances.

13 To be sure, if you are a member of a currently favored minority, many of your linguistic failings may be forgiven you—whether rightly or wrongly is not my concern here. But if you cannot change your sex or color to the one that is getting preferential treatment—Bakke case or no Bakke case—you might as well learn good English and profit by it in your career, your social relations, perhaps even in your basic self-confidence. That, if you will, is the ultimate

practical application of good English; but now let me tell you about the ultimate impractical one, which strikes me as being possibly even more important.

Somewhere in the prose writings of Charles Péguy, who was a very fine poet and prose writer—and, what is perhaps even more remarkable, as good a human being as he was an artist—somewhere in those writings is a passage about the decline of pride in workmanship among French artisans, which, as you can deduce, set in even before World War I, wherein Péguy was killed. In the passage I refer to, Péguy bemoans the fact that cabinetmakers no longer finish the backs of furniture—the sides that go against the wall—in the same way as they do the exposed sides. What is not seen was just as important to the old artisans as what is seen—it was a moral issue with them. And so, I think, it ought to be with language. Even if no one else notices the niceties, the precision, the impeccable sense of grammar and syntax you deploy in your utterances, you yourself should be aware of them and take pride in them as in pieces of work well done. 14

Now, I realize that there are two possible reactions among you to what I have said up to this point. Some of you will say to yourselves: what utter nonsense! Language is a flexible, changing, living organism that belongs to the people who speak it. It has always been changed according to the ways in which people chose to speak it, and the dictionaries and books on grammar had to, and will have to, adjust themselves to the people and not the other way around. For isn't it the glory of language that it keeps throwing up new inventions as surf tosses out differently polished pebbles and bits of bottle glass onto the shore, and that in this inexhaustible variety, in this refusal to kowtow to dry-as-dust scholars, lies its vitality, its beauty? 15

Others among you, perhaps few in number, will say to yourselves: quite so, there is such a thing as Standard English, or purity of speech, or correctness of expression—something worth safeguarding and fostering; but how the devil is one to accomplish that under the prevailing conditions: in a democratic society full of minorities that have their own dialects or linguistic preferences, and in a world in which television, advertising, and other mass media manage daily to corrupt the language a little further? Let me try to answer the first group first, and then come back to the questions of the second. 16

Of course language is, and must be, a living organism to 17

the extent that new inventions, discoveries, ideas enter the scene and clamor rightfully for designations. Political, social, and psychological changes may also affect our mode of expression, and new words or phrases may have to be found to reflect what we might call historical changes. It is also quite natural for slang terms to be invented, become popular, and, in some cases, remain permanently in the language. It is perhaps equally inevitable (though here we are on more speculative ground) for certain words to become obsolescent and obsolete, and drop out of the language. But does that mean that grammar and syntax have to keep changing, that pronunciations and meanings of words must shift, that more complex or elegant forms are obliged to yield to simpler or cruder ones that often are not fully synonymous with them and not capable of expressing certain fine distinctions? Should, for instance, "terrestrial" disappear entirely in favor of "earthly," or are there shades of meaning involved that need to remain available to us? Must we sacrifice "notwithstanding" because we have "in spite of" or "despite"? Need we forfeit "jettison" just because we have "throw overboard"? And what about "disinterested," which is becoming a synonym for "uninterested," even though that means something else, and though we have no other word for "disinterested"?

18 "Language has *always* changed," say these people, and they might with equal justice say that there has always been war or sickness or insanity. But the truth is that some sicknesses that formerly killed millions have been eliminated, that some so-called insanity can today be treated, and that just because there have always been wars does not mean that someday a cure cannot be found even for that scourge. And if it cannot, it is only by striving to put an absolute end to war, by pretending that it can be licked, that we can at least partly control it. Without such assumptions and efforts, the evil would be so widespread that, given our current weaponry, we would no longer be here to worry about the future of language.

19 But we are here, and having evolved linguistically this far, and having the means—books of grammar, dictionaries, education for all—to arrest unnecessary change, why not endeavor with might and mind to arrest it? Certain cataclysms cannot be prevented: earthquakes and droughts, for example, can scarcely, if at all, be controlled; but we can prevent floods, for which purpose we have invented dams. And dams are precisely what we can construct to prevent

floods of ignorance from eroding our language, and, beyond that, to provide irrigation for areas that would otherwise remain linguistically arid.

For consider that what some people are pleased to call 20
linguistic evolution was almost always a matter of ignorance prevailing over knowledge. There is no valid reason, for example, for the word *nice* to have changed its meaning so many times—except ignorance of its exact definition. Had the change never occurred, or had it been stopped at any intermediate stage, we would have had just as good a word as we have now and saved some people a heap of confusion along the way. But if *nice* means what it does today—and it has two principal meanings, one of them, as in "nice distinction," alas, obsolescent—let us, for heaven's sake, keep it where it is, now that we have the means with which to hold it there.

If, for instance, we lose the accusative case *whom*—and we 21
are in great danger of losing it—our language will be the poorer for it. Obviously, "The man, whom I had never known, was a thief" means something other than "The man who I had never known was a thief." Now, you can object that it would be just a easy in the first instance to use some other construction; but what happens if *this* one is used incorrectly? Ambiguity and confusion. And why should we lose this useful distinction? Just because a million or ten million or a billion people less educated than we are cannot master the difference? Surely it behooves us to try to educate the ignorant up to our level rather than to stultify ourselves down to theirs. Yes, you say, but suppose they refuse to or are unable to learn? In that case, I say, there is a doubly good reason for not going along with them. Ah, you reply, but they are the majority, and we must accept their way or, if the revolution is merely linguistic, lose our "credibility" (as the current parlance, rather confusingly, has it) or, if the revolution is political, lose our heads. Well, I consider a sufficient number of people to be educable enough to be capable of using *who* and *whom* correctly, and to derive satisfaction from this capability—a sufficient number, I mean, to enable us to preserve *whom*, and not to have to ask "for who the bells tolls."

The main problem with education, actually, is not those 22
who need it and cannot get it, but those who should impart it and, for various reasons, do not. In short, the enemies of education are the educators themselves: miseducated, underpaid, overburdened, and intimidated teachers (frightened because, though the pen is supposed to be mightier than the sword, the switchblade is surely more powerful

than the ferule), and professors who—because they are structural linguists, democratic respecters of alleged minority rights, or otherwise misguided folk—believe in the sacrosanct privilege of any culturally underprivileged minority or majority to dictate its ignorance to the rest of the world. For, I submit, an English improvised by slaves and other strangers to the culture—to whom my heart goes out in every human way—under dreadfully deprived conditions can nowise equal an English that the best literary and linguistic talents have, over the centuries, perceptively and painstakingly brought to a high level of excellence.

23 So my answer to the scoffers in this or any audience is, in simplest terms, the following: contrary to popular misconception, language does not belong to the people, or at least not in the sense in which *belong* is usually construed. For things can rightfully belong only to those who invent or earn them. But we do not know who invented language: is it the people who first made up the words for *father* and *mother*, for *I* and *thou*, for *hand* and *foot*; or is it the people who evolved the subtler shadings of language, its poetic variety and suggestiveness, but also its unambiguousness, its accurate and telling details? Those are two very different groups of people and two very different languages, and I, as you must have guessed by now, consider the latter group at least as important as the former. As for *earning* language, it has surely been earned by those who have striven to learn it properly, and here even economic and social circumstances are but an imperfect excuse for bad usage; history is full of examples of people rising from humble origins to learn, against all kinds of odds, to speak and write correctly—even brilliantly.

24 *Belong*, then, should be construed in the sense that parks, national forests, monuments, and public utilities are said to belong to the people: available for properly respectful use but not for defacement and destruction. And all that we propose to teach is how to use and enjoy the gardens of language to their utmost aesthetic and salubrious potential. Still, I must now address myself to the group that, while agreeing with my aims, despairs of finding practical methods for their implementation.

25 True enough, after a certain age speakers not aware of Standard English or not exceptionally gifted will find it hard or impossible to change their ways. Nevertheless, if there were available funds for advanced methods in teaching; if teachers themselves were better trained and paid, and had smaller classes and more assistants; if, furthermore, college

entrance requirements were heightened and the motivation of students accordingly strengthened; if there were no structural linguists and National Councils of Teachers of English filling instructors' heads with notions about "Students' Rights to Their Own Language" (they have every right to it as a *second* language, but none as a *first*); if teachers in all disciplines, including the sciences and social sciences, graded on English usage as well as on specific proficiencies; if aptitude tests for various jobs stressed good English more than they do; and, above all, if parents were better educated and more aware of the need to set a good example to their children, and to encourage them to learn correct usage, the situation could improve enormously.

Clearly, to expect all this to come to pass is utopian; some of it, however, is well within the realm of possibility. For example, even if parents do not speak very good English, many of them at least can manage an English that is good enough to correct a very young child's mistakes; in other words, most adults can speak a good enough four-year-old's idiom. They would thus start kids on the right path; the rest could be done by the schools. 26

But the problem is what to do in the most underprivileged homes: those of blacks, Hispanics, immigrants from various Asian and European countries. This is where day-care centers could come in. If the fathers and mothers could be gainfully employed, their small children would be looked after by day-care centers where—is this asking too much?—good English could be inculcated in them. The difficulty, of course, is what to do about the discrepancy the little ones would note between the speech of the day-care people and that of their parents. Now, it seems to me that small children have a far greater ability to learn things, including languages, than some people give them credit for. Much of it is indeed rote learning, but, where languages are concerned, that is one of the basic learning methods even for adults. There is no reason for not teaching kids another language, to wit, Standard English, and turning this, if desirable, into a game: "At home you speak one way; here we have another language," at which point the instructor can make up names and explanations for Standard English that would appeal to pupils of that particular place, time, and background. 27

At this stage of the game, as well as later on in school, care should be exercised to avoid insulting the language spoken in the youngsters' homes. There must be ways to convey that both home and school languages have their validity and uses 28 and that knowing both enables one to accomplish more in life. This would be hard to achieve if the children's parents were, say, militant blacks of the Geneva Smitherman sort, who execrate Standard English as a weapon of capitalist oppression against the poor of all races, colors, and religions. But, happily, there is evidence that most black, Hispanic, and other non-Standard English–speaking parents want their children to learn correct English so as to get ahead in the world.

29 Yet how do we defend ourselves against the charge that we are old fogeys who cannot emotionally adjust to the new directions an ever-living and changing language must inevitably take? Here I would want to redefine or, at any rate, clarify, what "living and changing" means, and also explain where we old fogeys stand. Misinformed attacks on Old Fogeydom, I have noticed, invariably represent us as people who shudder at a split infinitive and would sooner kill or be killed than tolerate a sentence that ends with a preposition. Actually, despite all my travels through Old Fogeydom, I have yet to meet one inhabitant who would not stick a preposition onto the tail of a sentence; as for splitting infinitives, most of us O.F.'s are perfectly willing to do that, too, but tactfully and sparingly, where it feels right. There is no earthly reason, for example "to dangerously live," when "to live dangerously" sounds so much better; but it does seem right to say (and write) "What a delight to sweetly breathe in your sleeping lover's breath"; that sounds smoother, indeed sweeter, than "to breathe in sweetly" or "sweetly to breathe in." But infinitives begging to be split are relatively rare; a sensitive ear, a good eye for shades of meaning will alert you whenever the need to split arises; without that ear and eye, you had better stick to the rules.

30 About the sense in which language is, and must be, alive, let me speak while donning another of my several hats—actually it is not a hat but a cap, for there exists in Greenwich Village an inscription on a factory that reads "CRITIC CAPS." So with my drama critic's cap on, let me present you with an analogy. The world theater today is full of directors who wreak havoc on classic plays to demonstrate their own ingenuity, their superiority, as it were, to the author. These directors—aborted playwrights, for the most part—will stage productions of *Hamlet* in which the prince is a woman, a flaming homosexual, or a one-eyed hunchback.

Well, it seems to me that the same spirit prevails in our approach to linguistics, with every newfangled, ill-informed, know-nothing construction, definition, pronunciation enshrined by the joint efforts of structural linguists, permissive dictionaries, and allegedly democratic but actually demagogic educators. What really makes a production of, say, *Hamlet* different, and therefore alive, is that the director, while trying to get as faithfully as possible at Shakespeare's meanings, nevertheless ends up stressing things in the play that strike him most forcefully; and the same individuality in production design and performances (the Hamlet of Gielgud versus the Hamlet of Olivier, for instance—what a world of difference!) further differentiates one production from another, and bestows on each its particular vitality. So, too, language remains alive because each speaker (or writer) can and must *within the framework of accepted grammar, syntax, and pronunciation*, produce a style that is his very own, that is as personal as his posture, way of walking, mode of dress, and so on. It is such stylistic differences that make a person's—or a nation's—language flavorous, pungent, alive, and all this without having to play fast and loose with the existing rules. 31

But to have this, we need, among other things, good teachers and, beyond them, enlightened educators. I shudder when I read in the *Birmingham* (Alabama) *Post-Herald* on October 6, 1978, an account of a talk given to eight hundred English teachers by Dr. Alan C. Purves, vice-president of the National Council of Teachers of English. Dr. Purves is quoted as saying things like "We are in a situation with respect to reading where . . . ," and culminating in the following truly horrifying sentence: "I am going to suggest that when we go back to the basics, I think what we should be dealing with is our charge to help students to be more proficient in producing meaningful language—language that says what it means." Notice all the deadwood, the tautology, the anacoluthon in the first part of that sentence; but notice especially the absurdity of the latter part, in which the dubious word "meaningful"—a poor relation of "significant"—is thought to require explaining to an audience of English teachers. 32

Given such leadership from the N.C.T.E., the time must be at hand when we shall hear—not just "Don't ask for who the bell rings" (*ask not* and *tolls* being, of course, archaic, elitist language), but also "It rings for you and I." 33

Gary Larson grew up in Tacoma, Washington, and graduated from Washington State University. "The Far Side" is one of America's most popular (and offbeat) cartoons.

THE FAR SIDE By GARY LARSON

"Ha! The idiots spelled 'surrender' with only one 'r'!"

SHOULD WE HAVE A NATIONAL LANGUAGE?

Richard Rodriguez

Aria: A Memoir of a Bilingual Childhood

Richard Rodriguez, born in 1944 into a Spanish-speaking, Mexican-American family, was educated at Stanford, Columbia, and Berkeley. Many of his eloquent essays—like the ones in his 1992 book Days of Obligation: An Argument with My Mexican Father*—mix memoir and argument, and many measure the gains and losses that result when English replaces Spanish that is spoken at home. This essay, first published in the magazine* The American Scholar *(1981), was incorporated into his acclaimed book* Hunger of Memory *(1982).*

I remember, to start with, that day in Sacramento, in a California now nearly thirty years past, when I first entered a classroom—able to understand about fifty stray English words. The third of four children, I had been preceded by my older brother and sister to a neighborhood Roman Catholic school. But neither of them had revealed very much about their classroom experiences. They left each morning and returned each afternoon, always together, speaking Spanish as they climbed the five steps to the porch. And their mysterious books, wrapped in brown shopping-bag paper, remained on the table next to the door, closed firmly behind them. 1

An accident of geography sent me to a school where all my classmates were white and many were the children of doctors and lawyers and business executives. On that first day of school, my classmates must certainly have been uneasy to find themselves apart from their families, in the first institution of their lives. But I was astonished. I was fated to be the "problem student" in class. 2

The nun said, in a friendly but oddly impersonal voice: "Boys and girls, this is Richard Rodriguez." (I heard her 3 sound it out: *Rich-heard Road-ree-guess*.) It was the first time I had heard anyone say my name in English. "Richard," the nun repeated more slowly, writing my name down in her book. Quickly I turned to see my mother's face dissolve in a watery blur behind the pebbled-glass door.

4 Now, many years later, I hear of something called "bilingual education"—a scheme proposed in the late 1960s by Hispanic-American social activists, later endorsed by a congressional vote. It is a program that seeks to permit non-English-speaking children (many from lower class homes) to use their "family language" as the language of school. Such, at least, is the aim its supporters announce. I hear them, and am forced to say no: It is not possible for a child, any child, ever to use his family's language in school. Not to understand this is to misunderstand the public uses of schooling and to trivialize the nature of intimate life.

5 Memory teaches me what I know of these matters. The boy reminds the adult. I was a bilingual child, but of a certain kind: "socially disadvantaged," the son of working-class parents, both Mexican immigrants.

6 In the early years of my boyhood, my parents coped very well in America. My father had steady work. My mother managed at home. They were nobody's victims. When we moved to a house many blocks from the Mexican-American section of town, they were not intimidated by those two or three neighbors who initially tried to make us unwelcome. ("Keep your brats away from my sidewalk!") But despite all they achieved, or perhaps because they had so much to achieve, they lacked any deep feeling of ease, of belonging in public. They regarded the people at work or in crowds as being very distant from us. Those were the others, *los gringos*. That term was interchangeable in their speech with another, even more telling: *los americanos*.

7 I grew up in a house where the only regular guests were my relations. On a certain day, enormous families of relatives would visit us, and there would be so many people that the noise and the bodies would spill out to the backyard and onto the front porch. Then for weeks no one would come. (If the doorbell rang, it was usually a salesman.) Our house stood apart–gaudy yellow in a row of white bungalows. We were the people with the noisy dog, the people who raised chickens. We were the foreigners on the block. A few neighbors would smile and wave at us. We waved back. But

until I was seven years old, I did not know the name of the old couple living next door or the names of the kids living across the street.

In public, my father and mother spoke a hesitant, accented, and not always grammatical English. And then they would have to strain, their bodies tense, to catch the sense of what was rapidly said by *los gringos*. At home, they returned to Spanish. The language of their Mexican past sounded in counterpoint to the English spoken in public. The words would come quickly, with ease. Conveyed through those sounds was the pleasing, soothing, consoling reminder that one was at home. 8

During those years when I was first learning to speak, my mother and father addressed me only in Spanish; in Spanish I learned to reply. By contrast, English (*inglés*) was the language I came to associate with gringos, rarely heard in the house. I learned my first words of English overhearing my parents speaking to strangers. At six years of age, I knew just enough words for my mother to trust me on errands to stores one block away—but no more. 9

I was then a listening child, careful to hear the very different sounds of Spanish and English. Wide-eyed with hearing, I'd listen to sounds more than to words. First, there were English (gringo) sounds. So many words still were unknown to me that when the butcher or the lady at the drugstore said something, exotic polysyllabic sounds would bloom in the midst of their sentences. Often the speech of people in public seemed to me very loud, booming with confidence. The man behind the counter would literally ask, "What can I do for you?" But by being so firm and clear, the sound of his voice said that he was a gringo; he belonged in public society. There were also the high, nasal notes of middle-class American speech—which I rarely am conscious of hearing today because I hear them so often, but could not stop hearing when I was a boy. Crowds at Safeway or at bus stops were noisy with the birdlike sounds of *los gringos*. I'd move away from them all—all the chirping chatter above me. 10

My own sounds I was unable to hear, but I knew that I spoke English poorly. My words could not extend to form complete thoughts. And the words I did speak I didn't know well enough to make distinct sounds. (Listeners would usually lower their heads to hear better what I was trying to say.) But it was one thing for *me* to speak English with 11 difficulty; it was more troubling to hear my parents speaking in public: their high-whining vowels and guttural consonants; their sentences that got stuck with "eh" and "ah" sounds; the confused syntax; the hesitant rhythm of sounds so different from the way gringos spoke. I'd notice, moreover, that my parents' voices were softer than those of gringos we would meet.

12 I am tempted to say now that none of this mattered. (In adulthood I am embarrassed by childhood fears.) And, in a way, it didn't matter very much that my parents could not speak English with ease. Their linguistic difficulties had no serious consequences. My mother and father made themselves understood at the county hospital clinic and at government offices. And yet, in another way, it mattered very much. It was unsettling to hear my parents struggle with English. Hearing them, I'd grow nervous, and my clutching trust in their protection and power would be weakened.

13 There were many times like the night at a brightly lit gasoline station (a blaring white memory) when I stood uneasily hearing my father talk to a teenage attendant. I do not recall what they were saying, but I cannot forget the sounds my father made as he spoke. At one point his words slid together to form one long word—sounds as confused as the threads of blue and green oil in the puddle next to my shoes. His voice rushed through what he had left to say. Toward the end, he reached falsetto notes, appealing to his listener's understanding. I looked away at the lights of passing automobiles. I tried not to hear any more. But I heard only too well the attendant's reply, his calm, easy tones. Shortly afterward, headed for home, I shivered when my father put his hand on my shoulder. The very first chance that I got, I evaded his grasp and ran on ahead into the dark, skipping with feigned boyish exuberance.

14 But then there was Spanish: *español,* the language rarely heard away from the house; *español,* the language which seemed to me therefore a private language, my family's language. To hear its sounds was to feel myself specially recognized as one of the family, apart from *los otros.* A simple remark, an inconsequential comment could convey that assurance. My parents would say something to me and I would feel embraced by the sounds of their words. Those sounds said: *I am speaking with ease in Spanish. I am addressing you in words I never use with los gringos. I*

recognize you as someone special, close, like no one outside. You belong with us. In the family. Ricardo.

15 At the age of six, well past the time when most middle-class children no longer notice the difference between sounds uttered at home and words spoken in public, I had a different experience. I lived in a world compounded of sounds. I was a child longer than most. I lived in a magical world, surrounded by sounds both pleasing and fearful. I shared with my family a language enchantingly private—different from that used in the city around us.

16 Just opening or closing the screen door behind me was an important experience. I'd rarely leave home all alone or without feeling reluctance. Walking down the sidewalk, under the canopy of tall trees, I'd warily notice the (suddenly) silent neighborhood kids who stood warily watching me. Nervously, I'd arrive at the grocery store to hear there the sounds of the gringo, reminding me that in this so-big world I was a foreigner. But if leaving home was never routine, neither was coming back. Walking toward our house, climbing the steps from the sidewalk, in summer when the front door was open, I'd hear voices beyond the screen door talking in Spanish. For a second or two I'd stay, linger there listening. Smiling, I'd hear my mother call out, saying in Spanish, "Is that you, Richard?" Those were her words, but all the while her sounds would assure me: *You are home now. Come closer inside. With us. "Sí,"* I'd reply.

17 Once more inside the house, I would resume my place in the family. The sounds would grow harder to hear. Once more at home, I would grow less conscious of them. It required, however, no more than the blurt of the doorbell to alert me all over again to listen to sounds. The house would turn instantly quiet while my mother went to the door. I'd hear her hard English sounds. I'd wait to hear her voice turn to soft-sounding Spanish, which assured me, as surely as did the clicking tongue of the lock on the door, that the stranger was gone.

18 Plainly it is not healthy to hear such sounds often. It is not healthy to distinguish public from private sounds so easily. I remained cloistered by sounds, timid and shy in public, too dependent on the voices at home. And yet I was a very happy child when I was at home. I remember many nights when my father would come back from work, and I'd hear him call out to my mother in Spanish, sounding relieved. In Spanish, his voice would sound the light and free notes that he never

could manage in English. Some nights I'd jump up just hearing his voice. My brother and I would come running into the room where he was with our mother. Our laughing (so deep was the pleasure!) became screaming. Like others who feel the pain of public alienation, we transformed the knowledge of our public separateness into a consoling reminder of our intimacy. Excited, our voices joined in a celebration of sounds. *We are speaking now the way we never speak out in public—we are together,* the sounds told me. Some nights no one seemed willing to loosen the hold that sounds had on us. At dinner we invented new words that sounded Spanish, but made sense only to us. We pieced together new words by taking, say, an English verb and giving it Spanish endings. My mother's instructions at bedtime would be lacquered with mock-urgent tones. Or a word like *sí,* sounded in several notes, would convey added measures of feeling. Tongues lingered around the edges of words, especially fat vowels, and we happily sounded that military drum roll, the twirling roar of the Spanish *r*. Family language, my family's sounds: the voices of my parents and sisters and brother. Their voices insisting: *You belong here. We are family members. Related. Special to one another. Listen!* Voices singing and sighing, rising and straining, then surging, teeming with pleasure which burst syllables into fragments of laughter. At times it seemed there was steady quiet only when, from another room, the rustling whispers of my parents faded and I edged closer to sleep.

19 Supporters of bilingual education imply today that students like me miss a great deal by not being taught in their family's language. What they seem not to recognize is that, as a socially disadvantaged child, I regarded Spanish as a private language. It was a ghetto language that deepened and strengthened my feeling of public separateness. What I needed to learn in school was that I had the right, and the obligation, to speak the public language. The odd truth is that my first-grade classmates could have become bilingual, in the conventional sense of the word, more easily than I. Had they been taught early (as upper middle-class children often are taught) a "second language" like Spanish or French, they could have regarded it simply as another public language. In my case, such bilingualism could not have been so quickly achieved. What I did not believe was that I could speak a single public language.

20 Without question, it would have pleased me to have heard

my teachers address me in Spanish when I entered the classroom. I would have felt much less afraid. I would have imagined that my instructors were somehow "related" to me; I would indeed have heard their Spanish as my family's language. I would have trusted them and responded with ease. But I would have delayed—postponed for how long?—having to learn the language of public society. I would have evaded—and for how long?—learning the great lesson of school: that I had a public identity.

Fortunately, my teachers were unsentimental about their responsibility. What they understood was that I needed to speak public English. So their voices would search me out, asking me questions. Each time I heard them I'd look up in surprise to see a nun's face frowning at me. I'd mumble, not really meaning to answer. The nun would persist. "Richard, stand up. Don't look at the floor. Speak up. Speak to the entire class, not just to me!" But I couldn't believe English could be my language to use. (In part, I did not want to believe it.) I continued to mumble. I resisted the teacher's demands. (Did I somehow suspect that once I learned this public language my family life would be changed?) Silent, waiting for the bell to sound, I remained dazed, diffident, afraid. 21

Because I wrongly imagined that English was intrinsically a public language and Spanish was intrinsically private, I easily noted the difference between classroom language and the language at home. At school, words were directed to a general audience of listeners. ("Boys and girls . . .") Words were meaningfully ordered. And the point was not self-expression alone, but to make oneself understood by many others. The teacher quizzed: "Boys and girls, why do we use that word in this sentence? Could we think of a better word to use there? Would the sentence change its meaning if the words were differently arranged? Isn't there a better way of saying much the same thing?" (I couldn't say. I wouldn't try to say.) 22

Three months passed. Five. A half year. Unsmiling, ever watchful, my teachers noted my silence. They began to connect my behavior with the slow progress my brother and sisters were making. Until, one Saturday morning, three nuns arrived at the house to talk to our parents. Stiffly they sat on the blue living-room sofa. From the doorway of another room, spying on the visitors, I noted the incongruity, the clash of two worlds, the faces and voices of school 23 intruding upon the familiar setting of home. I overheard one voice gently wondering, "Do your children speak only Spanish at home, Mrs. Rodriguez?" While another voice added, "That Richard especially seems so timid and shy."

24 *That Rich-heard!*

25 With great tact, the visitors continued, "Is it possible for you and your husband to encourage your children to practice their English when they are home?" Of course my parents complied. What would they not do for their children's well-being? And how could they question the Church's authority which those women represented? In an instant they agreed to give up the language (the sounds) which had revealed and accentuated our family's closeness. The moment after the visitors left, the change was observed. "*Ahora,* speak to us only *en inglés,*" my father and mother told us.

26 At first, it seemed a kind of game. After dinner each night, the family gathered together to practice "our" English. It was still then *inglés,* a language foreign to us, so we felt drawn to it as strangers. Laughing, we would try to define words we could not pronounce. We played with strange English sounds, often overanglicizing our pronunciations. And we filled the smiling gaps of our sentences with familiar Spanish sounds. But that was cheating, somebody shouted, and everyone laughed.

27 In school, meanwhile, like my brother and sisters, I was required to attend a daily tutoring session. I needed a full year of this special work. I also needed my teachers to keep my attention from straying in class by calling out, "*Rich-heard*"—their English voices slowly loosening the ties to my other name, with its three notes, *Ri-car-do*. Most of all, I needed to hear my mother and father speak to me in a moment of seriousness in "broken"—suddenly heartbreaking—English. This scene was inevitable. One Saturday morning I entered the kitchen where my parents were talking, but I did not realize that they were talking in Spanish until, the moment they saw me, their voices changed and they began speaking English. The gringo sounds they uttered startled me. Pushed me away. In that moment of trivial misunderstanding and profound insight, I felt my throat twisted by unsounded grief. I simply turned and left the room. But I had no place to escape to where I could grieve in Spanish. My brother and sisters were speaking English in another part of the house.

28 Again and again in the days following, as I grew increas-

ingly angry, I was obliged to hear my mother and father encouraging me: "Speak to us *en inglés*." Only then did I determine to learn classroom English. Thus, sometime afterward it happened: one day in school, I raised my hand to volunteer an answer to a question. I spoke out in a loud voice and I did not think it remarkable when the entire class understood. That day I moved very far from being the disadvantaged child I had been only days earlier. Taken hold at last was the belief, the calming assurance, that I *belonged* in public.

Shortly after, I stopped hearing the high, troubling sounds 29
of *los gringos*. A more and more confident speaker of English, I didn't listen to how strangers sounded when they talked to me. With so many English-speaking people around me, I no longer heard American accents. Conversations quickened. Listening to persons whose voices sounded eccentrically pitched, I might note their sounds for a few seconds, but then I'd concentrate on what they were saying. Now when I heard someone's tone of voice—angry or questioning or sarcastic or happy or sad—I didn't distinguish it from the words it expressed. Sound and word were thus tightly wedded. At the end of each day I was often bemused, and always relieved, to realize how "soundless," though crowded with words, my day in public had been. An eight-year-old boy, I finally came to accept what had been technically true since my birth: I was an American citizen.

But diminished by then was the special feeling of close- 30
ness at home. Gone was the desperate, urgent, intense feeling of being at home among those with whom I felt intimate. Our family remained a loving family, but one greatly changed. We were no longer so close, no longer bound tightly together by the knowledge of our separateness from *los gringos*. Neither my older brother nor my sisters rushed home after school any more. Nor did I. When I arrived home, often there would be neighborhood kids in the house. Or the house would be empty of sounds.

Following the dramatic Americanization of their children, 31
even my parents grew more publicly confident—especially my mother. First she learned the names of all the people on the block. Then she decided we needed to have a telephone in our house. My father, for his part, continued to use the word gringo, but it was no longer charged with bitterness or distrust. Stripped of any emotional content, the word simply became a name for those Americans not of Hispanic de-

scent. Hearing him, sometimes, I wasn't sure if he was pronouncing the Spanish word *gringo*, or saying gringo in English.

32 There was a new silence at home. As we children learned more and more English, we shared fewer and fewer words with our parents. Sentences needed to be spoken slowly when one of us addressed our mother or father. Often the parent wouldn't understand. The child would need to repeat himself. Still the parent misunderstood. The young voice, frustrated, would end up saying, "Never mind"—the subject was closed. Dinners would be noisy with the clinking of knives and forks against dishes. My mother would smile softly between her remarks; my father, at the other end of the table, would chew and chew his food while he stared over the heads of his children.

33 My mother! My father! After English became my primary language, I no longer knew what words to use in addressing my parents. The old Spanish words (those tender accents of sound) I had earlier used—*mamá* and *papá*—I couldn't use any more. They would have been all-too-painful reminders of how much had changed in my life. On the other hand, the words I heard neighborhood kids call their parents seemed equally unsatisfactory. "Mother" and "father," "ma," "papa," "pa," "dad," "pop" (how I hated the all-American sound of that last word)—all these I felt were unsuitable terms of address for *my* parents. As a result, I never used them at home. Whenever I'd speak to my parents, I would try to get their attention by looking at them. In public conversations, I'd refer to them as my "parents" or my "mother" and "father."

34 My mother and father, for their part, responded differently, as their children spoke to them less. My mother grew restless, seemed troubled and anxious at the scarceness of words exchanged in the house. She would question me about my day when I came home from school. She smiled at my small talk. She pried at the edges of my sentences to get me to say something more. ("What . . . ?") She'd join conversations she overheard, but her intrusions often stopped her children's talking. By contrast, my father seemed to grow reconciled to the new quiet. Though his English somewhat improved, he tended more and more to retire into silence. At dinner he spoke very little. One night his children and even his wife helplessly giggled at his garbled English pronunciation of the Catholic "Grace Before Meals." There-

after he made his wife recite the prayer at the start of each meal, even on formal occasions when there were guests in the house.

Hers became the public voice of the family. On official business it was she, not my father, who would usually talk to strangers on the phone or in stores. We children grew so accustomed to his silence that years later we would routinely refer to his "shyness." (My mother often tried to explain: both of his parents died when he was eight. He was raised by an uncle who treated him as little more than a menial servant. He was never encouraged to speak. He grew up alone—a man of few words.) But I realized my father was not shy whenever I'd watch him speaking Spanish with relatives. Using Spanish, he was quickly effusive. Especially when talking with other men, his voice would spark, flicker, flare alive with varied sounds. In Spanish he expressed ideas and feelings he rarely revealed when speaking English. With firm Spanish sounds he conveyed a confidence and authority that English would never allow him. 35

The silence at home, however, was not simply the result of fewer words passing between parents and children. More profound for me was the silence created by inattention to sounds. At about the time I no longer bothered to listen with care to the sounds of English in public, I grew careless about listening to the sounds made by the family when they spoke. Most of the time I would hear someone speaking at home and didn't distinguish his sounds from the words people uttered in public. I didn't even pay much attention to my parents' accented and ungrammatical speech—at least not at home. Only when I was with them in public would I become alert to their accents. But even then their sounds caused me less and less concern. For I was growing increasingly confident of my own public identity. 36

I would have been happier about my public success had I not recalled, sometimes, what it had been like earlier, when my family conveyed its intimacy through a set of conveniently private sounds. Sometimes in public, hearing a stranger, I'd hark back to my lost past. A Mexican farm worker approached me one day downtown. He wanted directions to some place. *"Hijito, . . ."* he said. And his voice stirred old longings. Another time I was standing beside my mother in the visiting room of a Carmelite convent, before the dense screen which rendered the nuns shadowy figures. I heard several of them speaking Spanish in their busy, 37 singsong, overlapping voices, assuring my mother that yes, yes, we were remembered, all our family was remembered, in their prayers. Those voices echoed faraway family sounds. Another day a dark-faced old woman touched my shoulder lightly to steady herself as she boarded a bus. She murmured something to me I couldn't quite comprehend. Her Spanish voice came near, like the face of a never-before-seen relative in the instant before I was kissed. That voice, like so many of the Spanish voices I'd hear in public, recalled the golden age of my childhood.

38 Bilingual educators say today that children lose a degree of "individuality" by becoming assimilated into public society. (Bilingual schooling is a program popularized in the seventies, that decade when middle-class "ethnics" began to resist the process of assimilation—the "American melting pot.") But the bilingualists oversimplify when they scorn the value and necessity of assimilation. They do not seem to realize that a person is individualized in two ways. So they do not realize that, while one suffers a diminished sense of *private* individuality by being assimilated into public society, such assimilation makes possible the achievement of *public* individuality.

39 Simplistically again, the bilingualists insist that a student should be reminded of his difference from others in mass society, of his "heritage." But they equate mere separateness with individuality. The fact is that only in private—with intimates—is separateness from the crowd a prerequisite for individuality; an intimate "tells" me that I am unique, unlike all others, apart from the crowd. In public, by contrast, full individuality is achieved, paradoxically, by those who are able to consider themselves members of the crowd. Thus it happened for me. Only when I was able to think of myself as an American, no longer an alien in gringo society, could I seek the rights and opportunities necessary for full public individuality. The social and political advantages I enjoy as a man began on the day I came to believe that my name is indeed *Rich-heard Road-ree-guess*. It is true that my public society today is often impersonal; in fact, my public society is usually mass society. But despite the anonymity of the crowd, and despite the fact that the individuality I achieve in public is often tenuous—because it depends on my being one in a crowd—I celebrate the day I acquired my new name. Those middle-class ethnics who

scorn assimilation seem to me filled with decadent self-pity, obsessed by the burden of public life. Dangerously, they romanticize public separateness and trivialize the dilemma of those who are truly socially disadvantaged.

40 If I rehearse here the changes in my private life after my Americanization, it is finally to emphasize a public gain. The loss implies the gain. The house I returned to each afternoon was quiet. Intimate sounds no longer greeted me at the door. Inside there were other noises. The telephone rang. Neighborhood kids ran past the door of the bedroom where I was reading my schoolbooks—covered with brown shopping-bag paper. Once I learned the public language, it would never again be easy for me to hear intimate family voices. More and more of my day was spent hearing words, not sounds. But that may only be a way of saying that on the day I raised my hand in class and spoke loudly to an entire roomful of faces, my childhood started to end.

Victor Villanueva, Jr.

Whose Voice Is It Anyway? Rodriguez' Speech in Retrospect

Victor Villaneuva, Jr., who teaches at Northern Arizona University, tells a lot about himself in the following essay, which he wrote in 1988 for English Journal, *a magazine for high school and elementary school English teachers.*

1 During the 1986 annual conference of the NCTE (National Council of Teachers of English) I attended a luncheon sponsored by the secondary section. Richard Rodriguez, author of *Hunger of Memory,* was the guest speaker. He spoke of how he came to be an articulate speaker of this standard dialect, and he spoke of the conclusions concerning language that his experiences had brought him to. He was impressive. I was taken by his quiet eloquence. His stage presence recalled Olivier's Hamlet. He spoke well. But for all his eloquence and his studied stage presence, I was

nevertheless surprised by the audience's response, an enthusiastic, uncritical acceptance, marked by a long, loud standing ovation. I was surprised because he had blurred distinctions between language and culture, between his experiences and those more typical of the minority in America, between the history of the immigrant and that of the minority, in a way that I had thought would raise more than a few eyebrows. Yet all he raised was the audience to its feet.

2 In retrospect, I think I can understand the rave reception. The message he so softly delivered relieved us all of some anxiety. Classroom teachers' shoulders stoop under the weight of the paper load. They take 150 students through writing and grammar, spelling and punctuation. Within those same forty-five-minute spurts they also work on reading: drama, poetry, literature, the great issues in literature. After that, there's the writers' club or the school paper or the yearbook, coaching volleyball or producing the school play. And throughout it all, they are to remain sensitive to the language of the nonstandard or non-English speaker. They are not really told how—just "be sensitive," while parents, the media, sometimes it seems the whole world, shake their fingers at them for not doing something about America's literacy problems. Richard Rodriguez told the teachers to continue to be sensitive but to forget about doing anything special. The old ways may be painful, but they really are best. There is a kind of violence to the melting pot, he said, but it is necessary. He said that this linguistic assimilation is like alchemy, initially destructive perhaps but magical, creating something new and greater than what was. Do as you have always done. And the teachers sighed.

3 Richard Rodriguez is the authority, after all: a bilingual child of immigrant parents, a graduate of two of the nation's more prestigious schools, Stanford and Berkeley, an English teacher, the well-published author of numerous articles and a well-received, well-anthologized book. He knows. And he says that the teachers who insisted on a particular linguistic form can be credited with his fame. But what is it, really, that has made him famous? He is a fine writer; of that there can be no doubt. But it is his message that has brought him fame, a message that states that the minority is no different than any other immigrant who came to this country not knowing its culture or its language, leaving much of the old country behind to become part of this new one, and in

becoming part of America subtly changing what it means to be American. The American who brought his beef and pudding from England became the American of frankfurter, the bologna sandwich, pizza. Typically American foods—like typical Americans—partake of the world.

At the luncheon, Richard Rodriguez spoke of a TV ad for Mexican-style Velveeta, "the blandest of American cheeses," he called it, now speckled with peppers. This cultural contrast, said Rodriguez, demonstrated how Mexico—no less than England or Germany—is part of America. 4

But I think it shows how our times face a different kind of assimilation. Let's put side for the moment questions as to why, if Mexicans really are being assimilated, they have taken so much longer than other groups, especially since Mexicans were already part of the West and Southwest when the West and Southwest became part of America. Let's look, rather, at the hyphen in Mexican-Velveeta. Who speaks of a German-American sausage, for instance? It's a hot dog. Yet tacos remain ethnic, sold under a mock Spanish mission bell or a sombrero. You will find refried beans under "ethnic foods" in the supermarket, not among other canned beans, though items as foreign-sounding as sauerkraut are simply canned vegetables. Mexican foods, even when Americanized as the taco salad or Mexican-Velveeta, remain distinctly Mexican.[1] 5

And like the ethnic food, some ethnic minorities have not been assimilated in the way the Ellis Islanders were. The fires of the melting pot have cooled. No more soup. America's more a stew today. The difference is the difference between the immigrant and the minority, a difference having to do with how each, the immigrant and the minority, came to be Americans, the difference between choice and colonization. Those who emigrated from Europe chose to leave unacceptable conditions in search of better. Choice, I realize, is a tricky word in this context: religious persecution, debtor's prison, potato famine, fascism, foreign take- 6

[1] Mexican food is not the only ethnic food on the market, of course. Asian and Mediterranean foods share the shelves. But this too is telling, since Asians alone had had restricted access to the US before the country ended its Open Door Immigration Policy. When the US closed its doors in 1924, it was to regulate the flow of less desirable "new immigrants"—the Eastern and Southern Europeans who remain "ethnic" to this day. See Oscar Handlin's *Race in American Life*, New York: Anchor, 1957.

over, when compared with a chance at prosperity and self-determination, don't seem to make for much of a choice; yet most people apparently remained in their homelands despite the intolerable, while the immigrants did leave, and in leaving chose to sever ties with friends and families, created a distance between themselves and their histories, cultures, languages. There is something heroic in this. It's a heroism shared by the majority of Americans.

7 But choice hardly entered into most minorities' decisions to become American. Most of us recognize this when it comes to Blacks or American Indians. Slavery, forcible displacement, and genocide are fairly clear-cut. Yet the circumstances by which most minorities became Americans are no less clear-cut. The minority became an American almost by default, as part of the goods in big-time real estate deals or as some of the spoils of war. What is true for the Native American applies to the Alaska Native, the Pacific Islander (including the Asian), Mexican-Americans, Puerto Ricans. Puerto Rico was part of Christopher Columbus' great discovery, Arawaks and Boriquens among his "Indians," a real-estate coup for the Queen of Spain. Then one day in 1898, the Puerto Ricans who had for nearly four hundred years been made proud to be the offspring of Spain, so much so that their native Arawak and Boricua languages and ways were virtually gone, found themselves the property of the United States, property without the rights and privileges of citizenship until—conveniently—World War I. But citizenship notwithstanding, Puerto Rico remains essentially a colony today.[2]

8 One day in 1845 and in 1848 other descendants of Spain who had all but lost their Indian identities found themselves Americans. These were the long-time residents and landowners of the Republic of Texas and the California Republic: the area from Texas to New Mexico, Arizona, Utah, and California. Residents in the newly established US territories were given the option to relocate to Mexico or to remain on their native lands, with the understanding that should they remain they would be guaranteed American Constitutional rights. Those who stayed home saw their rights not very

[2] Nor is it a simple matter of Puerto Rico's deciding whether it wants to remain a commonwealth, gaining statehood, or independence. The interests of US industry, of the US military, and the social and economic ramifications of Puerto Rico's widespread poverty complicate matters.

scrupulously guarded, falling victim over time to displacement, dislocation, and forced expatriation. There is something tragic in losing a long-established birthright, tragic but not heroic—especially not heroic to those whose ancestors had fled their homelands rather than acknowledge external rule.

The immigrant gave up much in the name of freedom— 9
and for the sake of dignity. For the Spanish-speaking minority in particular, the freedom to be American without once again relinquishing one's ancestry is also a matter of dignity.

This is not to say that Richard Rodriguez forfeited his 10
dignity in choosing not to be Ricardo. The Mexican's status includes not only the descendants of the West and Southwest, Spanish-speaking natives to America, but also immigrants and the descendants of immigrants. Richard Rodriguez is more the immigrant than the minority. His father, he told us, had left his native Mexico for Australia. He fell in love along the way, eventually settling with wife and family in Sacramento. America was not his father's first choice for a new home perhaps, but he did choose to leave his homeland in much the same way European immigrants had. The Rodriguezes no doubt felt the immigrants' hardships, the drive to assimilate, a drive compounded perhaps by the association in their and others' minds between them and the undocumented migrant worker or between them and the minority.

And it is this confusion of immigrant and minority in 11
Richard Rodriguez with which we must contend. His message rings true to the immigrant heritage of his audience because it happens to be the immigrant's story. It is received as if it were a new story because it is confused with this story of the minority. The complexities of the minority are rendered simple—not easy, but easily understood.

Others tell the story of the minority. I think, for instance, 12
of Piri Thomas and Tato Laviera, since theirs are stories of Puerto Ricans. My own parents had immigrated to New York from Puerto Rico, though not in the way of most. My mother, an American, a US citizen like all Puerto Ricans, fair-skinned and proud of her European descent, had been sold into servitude to a wealthy Chicago family. My father, recently discharged from the US Army, followed my mother, rescued his sweetheart, and together they fled to New York. I was born a year later, 1948.

13 My mother believed in the traditional idea of assimilation. She and my father would listen to the radio shows in English and try to read the American newspapers. They spoke to me in two languages from the start. The local parochial school's tuition was a dollar a month, so I was spared PS 168. Rodriguez tells of nuns coming to his home to suggest that the family speak English at home. For Rodriguez this was something of a turning point in his life; intimacy lost, participation in the public domain gained. A public language would dominate, the painful path to his assimilation, the path to his eventual success. A nun spoke to my parents, too, when I was in kindergarten. I spoke with an accent, they were told. They should speak to me in English. My mother could only laugh: my English was as it was *because* they spoke to me in English. The irony reinforced our intimacy while I continued to learn the "public language."

14 There is more to assimilating than learning the language. I earned my snacks at the Saturday matinee by reading the credits on the screen. I enjoyed parsing sentences, was good at it too. I was a Merriam-Webster spelling bee champ. I was an "A" student who nevertheless took a special Saturday course on how to do well on the standardized test that would gain me entry to the local Catholic high school. I landed in the public vo-tech high school, slotted for a trade. Jarapolk, whose parents had fled the Ukraine, made the good school; so did Marie Engels, the daughter of German immigrants. Lana Walker, a Black girl whose brains I envied, got as far as the alternate list. I don't recall any of the Black or Puerto Rican kids from my class getting in. I never finished high school, despite my being a bright boy who knew the public language intimately.

15 I don't like thinking minorities were intentionally excluded from the better school. I would prefer to think minorities didn't do as well because we were less conscious than the immigrants of the cultural distances we had to travel to be truly Americans. We were Americans, after all, not even seeing ourselves as separated by language by the time most of us got to the eighth grade. I spoke Spanglish at home, a hybrid English and Spanish common to New York Puerto Ricans; I spoke the Puerto Rican version of Black English in the streets, and as far as I knew, I spoke something close to the standard dialect in the classroom. We thought ourselves Americans, assimilated. We didn't

know about cultural bias in standardized tests. I still don't do well on standardized tests.

A more pointed illustration of the difference between the minority and the immigrant comes by way of a lesson from my father. I was around ten. We went uptown one day, apartment hunting. I don't recall how he chose the place. He asked about an apartment in his best English, the sounds of a Spanish speaker attempting his best English. No vacancies. My father thanked the man, then casually slipped into the customary small talk of the courteous exit. During the talk my father mentioned our coming from Spain. By the end of the chat a unit became available. Maybe my father's pleasing personality had gained us entry. More likely, Puerto Rican stereotypes had kept us out. The immigrant could enter where the minority could not. My father's English hadn't improved in the five minutes it had taken for the situation to change. 16

Today I sport a doctorate in English from a major university, study and teach rhetoric at another university, do research in and teach composition, continue to enjoy and teach English literature. I live in an all-American city in the heart of America. And I know I am not quite assimilated. In one weekend I was asked if I was Iranian one day and East Indian the next. "No," I said. "You have an accent," I was told. Yet tape recordings and passing comments throughout the years have told me that though there is a "back East" quality to my voice, there isn't much of New York to it anymore, never mind the Black English of my younger years or the Spanish of my youngest. My "accent" was in my not sounding midwestern, which does have a discernible, though not usually a pronounced, regional quality. And my "accent," I would guess, was in my "foreign" features (which pale alongside the brown skin of Richard Rodriguez). 17

Friends think I make too much of such incidents. Minority hypersensitivity, they say. They desensitize me (and display their liberal attitudes) with playful jabs at Puerto Ricans: greasy hair jokes, knife-in-pocket jokes, spicy food jokes (and Puerto Ricans don't even eat hot foods, unless we're eating Mexican or East Indian foods). If language alone were the secret to assimilation, the rate of Puerto Rican and Mexican success would be greater, I would think. So many Mexican-Americans and Puerto Ricans remain in the barrios—even those who are monolingual, who have never known Spanish. If language alone were the secret, wouldn't 18 the secret have gotten out long before Richard Rodriguez recorded his memoirs? In fact, haven't we always worked with the assumption that language learning—oral and written—is the key to parity, even as parity continues to elude so many?

19 I'm not saying the assumption is wrong. I think teachers are right to believe in the potential power of language. We want our students to be empowered. That's why we read professional journals. That's why we try to accommodate the pronouncements of linguists. That's why we listen to the likes of Richard Rodriguez. But he spoke more of the English teacher's power than the empowerment of the student. "Listen to the sound of my voice," he said. He asked the audience to forget his brown skin and listen to his voice, his "unaccented voice." "This is your voice," he told the teachers. Better that we, teachers at all levels, give students the means to find their own voices, voices that don't have to ask that we ignore what we cannot ignore, voices that speak of their brown or yellow or red or black skin with pride and without need for bravado or hostility, voices that can recognize and exploit the conventions we have agreed to as the standards of written discourse—without necessarily accepting the ideology of those for whom the standard dialect is the language of home as well as commerce, for whom the standard dialect is as private as it is public, to use Rodriguez' terms.

20 Rodriguez said at the luncheon that he was not speaking of pedagogy as much as of ideology. He was. It is an ideology which grew out of the memoirs of an immigrant boy confronting contrasts, a child accommodating his circumstances. He remembers a brown boy in a white middle-class school and is forced to say no to bilingual education. His classmates were the descendants of other immigrants, the products of assimilation, leading him to accept the traditional American ideology of a multiculturalism that manifests as one new culture and language, a culture and language which encompasses and transcends any one culture. I remember a brown boy among other brown boys and girls, blacks, and olives, and variations on white, and must agree with Richard that bilingualism in the classroom would have been impractical. But my classmates were in the process of assimilation—Polish, German, Ukrainian, and Irish children, the first of their families to enter American schools; my classmates were also Black and Puerto Rican. It

seemed to this boy's eyes that the immigrants would move on but the minority would stay, that the colonized do not melt. Today I do not hear of the problems in educating new immigrants, but the problems of Black literacy continue to make the news. And I hear of an eighty per cent dropout rate among Puerto Ricans in Boston, of Mexicans in the Rio Grande Valley where the dropout rate exceeds seventy per cent, of places where English and the education system do not address the majority—Spanish speakers for whom menial labor has been the tradition and is apparently the future. I must ask how bilingual education in such situations. One person's experiences must remain one person's, applicable to many others, perhaps, but not all others. Simple, monolithic, universal solutions simply can't work in a complex society.

When it comes to the nonstandard speaker, for instance, we are torn between the findings of linguists and the demands of the marketplace. Our attempts at preparing students for the marketplace only succeed in alienating nonstandard speakers, we are told. Our attempts at accommodating their nonstandard dialects, we fear, only succeed in their being barred from the marketplace. So we go back to the basics. Or else we try to change their speech without alienating them, in the process perhaps sensing that our relativism might smack of condescension. Limiting the student's language to the playground and home still speaks of who's right and who's wrong, who holds the power. I would rather we left speaking dialects relatively alone (truly demonstrating a belief in the legitimacy of the nonstandard). The relationship between speaking and writing is complex, as the debate sparked by Thomas Farrell has made clear. My own research and studies, as well as my personal experiences, suggest that exposure to writing and reading affects speaking. My accent changes, it seems, with every book I read. We don't have to give voices to students. If we give them pen and paper and have them read the printed page aloud, no matter what their grade, they'll discover their own voices. 21

And if we let the printed page offer a variety of world views, of ideologies, those voices should gather the power we wish them to have. Booker T. Washington, Martin Luther King, Jr., W. E. B. DuBois all wrote with eloquence. Each presents a different world view. Maxine Hong Kingston's "voice" resounds differently from Frank Chin's. Er- 22 nesto Galarza saw a different world than Richard Rodriguez. Rodriguez' is only one view, one voice. Yet it's his voice which seems to resound the loudest. Rodriguez himself provided the reason why this is so. He said at the luncheon that the individual's story, the biography or autobiography, has universal appeal because it strikes at experiences we have in common. The immigrant's story has the most in common with the majority.

23 Rodriguez implied that he didn't feel much kinship to minority writers. He said he felt a special bond with D. H. Lawrence. It seems appropriate that Rodriguez, who writes of his alienation from family in becoming part of the mainstream, would turn to Lawrence. Lawrence, too, was a teacher turned writer. Lawrence, too, felt alienated from his working-class background. It was Lawrence who argued, in "Reflections on the Death of the Porcupine," that equality is not achievable; Lawrence who co-opted, left the mastered to join the masters. Is this what we want for our minority students? True, Lawrence's mastery of the English language cannot be gainsaid. I would be proud to have a Lawrence credit me with his voice, would appreciate his accomplishment. But I would rather share credit in a W. B. Yeats, Anglo and Irish, assimilated but with a well-fed memory of his ancestry, master of the English language, its beauty, its traditions—and voice of the colony.

A Proposed Amendment to the U.S. Constitution

Members of the House of Representatives in 1988 proposed an amendment to the Constitution of the United States that was designed to establish English as our official language. (The amendment thus far has not been approved in Congress and hence has not been passed to the states, where it would have to be ratified by 75% of the state legislatures.) Here is how the proposed amendment would read:

Article

1 SECTION 1. The English language shall be the official language of the United States.

2 SECTION 2. Neither the United States nor any State shall

require, by law, ordinance, regulation, order, decree, program, or policy, the use in the United States of any language other than English

SECTION 3. This article shall not prohibit any law, ordi- 3
nance, regulation, order, decree, program or policy

1. to provide educational instruction in a language other than English for the purpose of making students who use a language other than English proficient in English,
2. to teach a foreign language to students who are already proficient in English,
3. to protect public health and safety, or
4. to allow translators for litigants, defendants, or witnesses in court cases.

SECTION 4. The Congress and the States may enforce this 4
article by appropriate legislation.

California's Proposition 63

Proposition 63 is described fully in the next article by Stanley Diamond. Here is how the Proposition (offered to California voters in 1986 and typical of other "official language" resolutions) actually read:

Amendment to the Constitution of the State of California

A. *Purpose.*

English is the common language of the people of the United 1
States of America and of the State of California. This section is intended to preserve, protect, and strengthen the English language and not to supersede any of the rights guaranteed to the people by this constitution.

B. *English as the Official Language of California.*

English is the official language of the state of California. 2

C. *Enforcement.*

The legislature shall enforce this section by appropriate 3
legislation. The legislature and officials of the State of California shall take all steps necessary to insure that the role of English as the common language of the State of California is preserved and enhanced. The legislature shall make no law which diminishes or ignores the role of English

as the common language of the State of California.

D. *Personal Right of Action and Jurisdiction of Courts.*

4 Any person who is a resident or does business in the State of California shall have standing to sue the State of California to enforce this section, and the Courts of Record of the State of California shall have jurisdiction to hear cases brought to enforce this section. The legislature may provide reasonable and appropriate limitations on the time and manner of suits brought under this section.

E. *Severability.*

5 If any provision of this section, or the application of any such provision, to any person or circumstance shall be held invalid, the remainder of this section, to the extent it can be given effect, shall not be affected thereby, and to this end the provisions of this section are severable.

Stanley Diamond

English, the Official Language of California, 1983–1988

"U.S. English" is a group of citizens dedicated to establishing English as the nation's official language. The organization articulated its position in the following policy statement, which was written by Stanley Diamond of San Francisco, a founding member of the organization and the chair of the California English Campaign. Mr. Diamond presented the statement at a conference on "Official English and the Border States," held at Tempe, Arizona, in 1987. The conference occurred during an Arizona campaign to establish English as the official language of that state. (In the ensuing referendum on the question, the pro–official English side prevailed, but barely—only by 50.5% to 49.5%.)

1 "Language is a fundamental bond through which a people is held together. This bonding gives us harmony and unity. It permits debate in which we all can take part. We can talk to each other, reach understandings or if we disagree,

explore our disagreements and then resolve them, compromise them or agree to disagree.

"Making English official deprives no one of any right to use and enjoy his or her ethnic heritage. All languages and cultures are precious in our history and are to be preserved and maintained. These are not, however, public responsibilities. They belong, as they have throughout our history, in homes, churches, private schools and ethnic celebrations. 2

"Where linguistic unity has broken down, our energies and resources flow into tensions, hostilities, prejudices, and resentments. These develop and persist. Within a few years, if the breakdown persists, there will be no retreat. It becomes irrevocable, irreversible. Society as we know it can fade into noisy babel and then chaos. 3

"Our common English language is critical for our unity and for our democratic functioning. Protecting it in the months and years ahead is a deep personal responsibility of all our citizens." 4

Introduction

The preceding policy statement of *U.S. English* is what gives direction to the officers, directors, staff, the hundreds of active volunteers and the *U.S. English* membership. 5

The national organization, *U.S. English*, was founded by former U.S. Senator S. I. Hayakawa in January, 1983, with 300 members. In December, 1987, *U.S. English* had a membership of 340,000. By December, 1989, membership, will, at the present growth rate, reach 450,000, making it one of the major public interest organizations in the country. The founding team, along with Senator Hayakawa, included Dr. John Tanton of Petoskey, Michigan; Mrs. Gerda Bikales of Washington, D.C.; Mr. Leo Sorensen of Oakland, California; and me, Stanley Diamond, of San Francisco, California. In the first meeting, the founders agreed that all officers and directors of the national organization must be multi-lingual or multi-cultural. That requirement remains today. 6

U.S. English is a non-profit and non-partisan research and educational center. Its function is to encourage states to establish English as an official language and ultimately to pass a constitutional amendment declaring English the official language of the United States. 7

English Language Legislative Initiatives in California

8 In California, three citizen initiatives between 1983 and 1986 attracted national attention. They dramatized the English language movement in California as well as in many states in the country. These were:

1. Proposition "O," an advisory initiative in San Francisco in 1983;
2. Proposition 38, a statewide advisory initiative in 1984; and
3. Proposition 63, a statewide constitutional amendment in 1986.

The purpose of Proposition "O" was to solicit the opinion of voters in San Francisco on "ballots and voting materials in English *ONLY*." San Francisco at the time had trilingual ballots printed in English, Spanish and Chinese. The resulting vote was startling. In perhaps the most liberal and ethnically diverse city in the country, Proposition "O" won with 66% voter support. Republicans, Democrats and Independents alike supported the initiative, as did people from all socioeconomic levels and ethnic communities, including Hispanics and Asians.

9 Encouraged by the Proposition "O" victory, *U.S. English* decided to expand its horizons and proceeded with a statewide test of voter sentiment on bilingual ballots. 520,000 signatures were filed with the Secretary of State, and Proposition 38 was put on the ballot in November, 1984. Proposition 38 won in all 58 counties of the state with an overwhelming 72% of California voters supporting it. This result confirmed the increasing evidence that voters in California, and perhaps the country, were incensed with ballots in languages other than English. Moreover, this campaign, as well as the passage of the proposition, made the public aware that the issue was more than ballots. The real need was for an *official* language, and that language had to be English.

Proposition 63

10 "English as the *official* language of California," therefore, became the next major undertaking of *U.S. English*. For a

fledgling organization with limited resources and no experience, the survival of *U.S. English* itself rested on the outcome of this test. In many meetings after the campaign, the following was frequently heard: "If we really had understood the costs and complexity of a successful constitutional amendment initiative, we might well have abandoned an adventure on such dangerous seas." Anyway, knowing generally but not precisely where we were going, we set sail on January 23, 1986, for a rough ride.

The constitutional amendment declared "English is the *official* language of California" (emphasis added). Implementing and clarifying clauses were also included in the amendment itself. Why did *U.S. English* try a constitutional amendment and why an initiative? Prior to January, 1986, assemblyman Frank Hill of the California State Assembly, a state and national leader in the English language movement, had introduced Assembly Bill 201 in May, 1985. Bill 201 was a statute declaring English the official language of California. The bill came up for hearing before the Ways and Means Committee of the Assembly late in May, 1985. After about five minutes of testimony by Assemblyman Hill and me and after several interruptions by the Chairman, Committee Assemblyman Elihu Harris moved for a vote. It was immediately seconded and a vote called for by the Chairman. The bill was defeated, six ayes and four nays with nine votes required to move the bill to the Assembly floor. In answering my request for permission to complete my statement and for a fair hearing, Chairman Richard Alatorre pounded his gavel ending the hearing with, "I am from Mexico, I am bilingual, I find you and your bill offensive." This response made it clear that it would be difficult to get a bill through the assembly. Therefore, the logical next step was an initiative. 11

A constitutional amendment in California requires 670,000 signatures. Through volunteers and the help of a contractor, ultimately 1,100,000 signatures were turned in to the Secretary of State, the second largest total in California history. 12

The organization which distributed petitions, gathered signatures, handled media relations, and conducted daily operations was the "California English Campaign." Senator Hayakawa was Honorary Chairman, and I was Campaign Chairman. We were unpaid volunteers. The campaign "staff" consisted of one part time computer specialist who worked 13 out of her home. The state office in San Francisco was a cold, dark, damp storage room rented to us by a supporter for $100 per month. Four volunteers manned two phones, counted signatures and filed petitions. The blowing of runny noses and a concert of hacking coughs were the normal sounds of the office. Senator Hayakawa, on his frequent visits to the office, would ask, "Anyone who doesn't have a cold?" When a hand went up, the Senator would walk over, shake hands and say, "You must be new. Welcome aboard."

14 In Southern California, with its approximately 12,000,000 inhabitants, the campaign organization was an answering machine. Messages were picked up daily. The media budget was *zero*. Not one cent was spent on television, radio or print. As one political consultant said, after a visit to the San Francisco office, "What you call an organization is not to be believed."

15 Supporters of Proposition 63, in addition to the 110,000 members of *U.S. English* in California, were: The California Republican Party, California Republican Women Federated, American Legion, California Farm Bureau Federation, California State Grange, several hundred community groups, and thousands of highly motivated volunteers who gathered signatures.

16 Eight spokespersons, dedicated and trained, in addition to Senator Hayakawa and me, presented the positions favoring the amendment throughout the state. Arguments in support of the amendment were as follows: English, our language for over 200 years, was being eroded by other languages, particularly by Spanish. Examples of erosion were bilingual education that maintained the home language, and bilingual and trilingual ballots, that are divisive. Bilingual ballots are a disincentive to learn English. They are not necessary, are costly, and need to be eliminated. They are not necessary because only citizens can vote and citizens must either be born here or, if immigrants, have lived in the United States for five years and have passed an examination for fluency and literacy in English. Bilingual education needs to be fundamentally reformed to permit flexibility in teaching. Innovative ideas should be encouraged and tested. There should be local control over teaching methods, and teachers' counsel should be sought for program effectiveness and evaluation. The method of teaching non-English-speaking children only in the child's native

language was ineffective and in California a $500,000,000 annual waste.

Opposition to Proposition 63

The opposition to Proposition 63 was formidable. It was organized quickly with an umbrella organization called Californians United. The Mexican American Legal Defense and Education Fund (MALDEF) and the American Civil Liberties Union (ACLU) seemed to lead the opposition. Other opposition organizations were the League of United Latin American Citizens (LULAC), the Japanese American Citizens League, La Raza, a number of Chinese coalitions, the League of Women Voters, at least forty diverse ethnic and social organizations, and others having names but otherwise unidentified. 17

In addition to these organizations, all leading public officials opposed Proposition 63. Governor Deukmajian, Lt. Governor McCarthy, Attorney General Van de Kamp, Assembly Speaker Willie Brown, and Senate President Pro Tem David Roberti all publicly stated their opposition. Moreover, all the major press in California except the *San Francisco Examiner* opposed the amendment. These newspapers included the *Los Angeles Times; Los Angeles Herald Examiner*; the *San Diego Tribune*; the *San Diego Union*; the *San Francisco Chronicle*; the McClatchy newspapers; the Sacramento, Fresno and Modesto *Bees*; the *Stockton Record*; plus scores of other daily and weekly papers and magazines in the state. In addition, all major television channels and radio stations editorially opposed Proposition 63—*all*. Our wry comment after each review of the daily media bashing was, "Well, relax, nothing exciting or new yesterday." 18

Among the arguments presented by the opposition during debates, in press interviews, on the radio, and in press releases were the following: First, emergency services, among them the police and fire fighters, would not respond unless calls were in English; second, social services and hospitals would be banned to all who could not speak English; third, court translators and interpreters would be eliminated; fourth, courts would be flooded with lawsuits because all California residents would have a right to sue under the amendment passed; fifth, police would have authority to arrest non-English speaking persons; sixth, all 19 signs of businesses would have to be in English; and lastly, names of cities, Los Angeles, San Diego, San Francisco, San Jose, etc., would have to be changed to English. Some speakers said the city of Los Altos had already been changed to "The Heights." (This was a conscious lie.) Other such arguments were equally ridiculous, equally absurd. Voters, of course, did not believe such nonsense.

Public Support for Proposition 63

20 On November 4, 1986, the election day, Proposition 63 won with a stunning 73% of the vote. There were 5,016,556 voters supporting the English language amendment in all 58 counties in California, from all ethnic communities, and from all socio-economic levels. Republicans, Democrats, Independents, all supported Proposition 63. The victory was not only dramatic news in California but was the top story for much of the media nationally. Thirty-eight states sent telegrams and letters and phoned asking for details and for copies of the amendment.

21 The expression of the voters in California, considering the massive opposition, was, or should be, a powerful lesson to elected officials and to the media. Voters, when they feel deeply, will act on such feelings and will not forget those who attempted to mislead them.

22 One month after the victory a statewide survey was conducted by the *U.S. English* staff to seek out reasons for support of the amendment. Several were most frequently heard. The first was that California was becoming fragmented. Ethnic communities, especially Hispanic ones, were not integrating into our society. An ethnic nationalism was replacing the unity of "Americanism." New immigrants did not have the sense of personal responsibility that immigrants had had in the past. Responsibility for learning the new language, English, and a responsibility for becoming part of the new society seemed to be lacking. In addition, ballots in languages other than English were a constant irritation. An often heard comment was, "Every time I see a ballot in Spanish or Chinese I get mad—what's happening to this country? You have to be a citizen to vote, you have to know English to become a citizen. So how come a special ballot in Spanish or Chinese?" And they would say, "I have to pay for these

ballots. That's the final insult." There were frequent blasts of profanity along with the statements.

Many voters expressed the view that English has been the language that has unified us through our 200 year history. They could talk to people wherever they lived in this country. Now, they were not so sure what would happen in Florida, Texas, California, and New Mexico. Hispanics seemed to want two official languages and want their own customs and culture, not that of this country. Many said, in essence: "I don't object to other languages or customs. I like chile rellenos, burritos, sushi, won ton, and every pasta on the menu. Fine, preserve your languages and your cultures. But these are not my responsibility. They belong, if you want to keep them, in your homes, churches, private schools and your own celebrations. They're not my responsibility or that of my government." They also argued, "Our English language, because of our history, has some meaning for how we live. Our values, our freedom, our democracy itself is a part of our English language. Our English language, in a fundamental sense, is *US*." In a similar vein, many Hispanics said things like: "Our elected Hispanic leadership doesn't represent us. They want us kept in our barrios so they can stay in power. We need new Hispanic leadership, elected officials who want us educated, assimilated, and becoming a part of our new country." 23

The arguments presented by the opposition also came in for their share of criticism. "No 911 emergency services, no social or welfare services, business restrictions, changing names of cities—nobody believed such garbage. I knew they were lying and they lost my vote before they finished their speeches!" 24

Lastly, bilingual education was bitterly criticized by parents, teachers and the children themselves. Many people felt that immigrant children should be in English-speaking settings within one year, perhaps slightly longer, certainly not three, four, six or more years after they started school. They worried about children hearing Spanish daily in classes. Parents of children from English-speaking homes were particularly critical. "My child should be reading and writing English, not sitting in the back of the room doodling while a teacher teaches in Spanish in the front of the room." Parents of Hispanic children also said, "I want my child to learn English now. We speak Spanish at home. He doesn't have to have it at school." Parents and teachers are close to 25 revolt at the continuing teaching of children in Spanish and calling it a method of acquiring English proficiency.

Future *U.S. English* Programs

26 Did the passage of Proposition 63 end the language struggle? Not at all. In January, 1987, two months after the passage of the amendment, ignoring the 73% vote of the people, State Assemblymen and Senators introduced nine bills that would have crippled any implementation of the amendment. The effect of these bills included: Making investigation of complaints difficult, placing decision-making for filing of suits on agencies of the state or on the legislature itself, calling for expensive studies of language needs that would duplicate other studies, calling for a continuation of ineffectual bilingual education methods, and requiring document translations that would have been both expensive and a continuation of the bilingualism goal of the opposition. Through the leadership of Assemblyman Frank Hill, these bills were either defeated on the Assembly floor or vetoed by Governor Deukmajian. *U.S. English* representatives appeared in opposition to all these bills at committee hearings. I personally presented testimony at 24 hearings during the 1987 session.

27 What lies ahead? There are signs of progress. Even though the opposition of Californians United continues with forums, conferences, and political pressure on legislators, other legislators who were opposed to *U.S. English* are becoming cautious in their attacks. In 1988, only two bills were introduced that were troublesome. Both are, at the moment, off the calendar.

28 One *U.S. English* project that has the enthusiastic support of the education community and the Hispanic community is a "teaching English to immigrant adults" program in Southern California. The project was organized and is directed by Barbara Kaze, *U.S. English* Regional Director in Los Angeles. Foundations and *U.S. English* have pledged $650,000 for a startup of the program through radio and television. The second program involves on-site teaching to employees at factories, shops, and hotels without charge to employers or employees. It is directed by Fernando de la Pena of the Cambria Institute. The third program consists of cassettes, distributed without cost, that teach survival language. How

to deal with emergencies, shopping, asking directions, and elementary conversation are taught through these cassettes. These are given to churches, United Way agencies, community centers and to selected individuals. This project is extremely popular in Southern California. As funding increases, the project will expand throughout California and to other states. The funding goal is $2,000,000 with partial contributions by *U.S. English*.

Nationally, Florida, Arizona, and Colorado have initiatives in progress to establish English as the *official* language of their states. Texas has just completed an advisory vote on the English language issue with 92% in support of the resolution. Thirty-five states have the issue on their agendas for 1988 and 1989. Action by the U.S. Congress and court tests lie ahead. 29

The will of our citizens throughout the country is quite clear. English must be the *official* language of the United States and the *only official* language. Time and perseverance will inevitably bring the will and the voice of the people into the law of the land. 30

Geoffrey Nunberg

Why I'm Against Proposition 63

Geoffrey Nunberg, a language expert, offered this testimony on "official English" before the California State Legislature on September 29, 1986.

I want to make a few remarks about Proposition 63 from my perspective as a linguist, and in particular as someone who has devoted a lot of time to studying and writing about the English language. I want to concentrate on making two points. First, measures like Proposition 63 fly in the face of everything we have learned about the processes of language shift and acculturation. And second, Proposition 63 demeans some of the basic traditions of the English-speaking world. I do not think it would be going too far to say that the U.S. English movement represents a greater threat to the 1

English language than any group of immigrants could possibly pose.

2 I will start with the lessons of history. It is beyond doubt that people will learn a new language when they perceive the economic and social advantages of doing so. And if they do not want to change to a new language, legal measures are not going to do any good. Let me give you some examples. In Spain, Franco banned the use of Catalan, the language of the area around Barcelona, for more than 40 years. By the time of his death, there were more speakers of Catalan than ever before. The Polish language was submerged for two hundred years, but when the Polish state was established after World War I, lo and behold! there was a whole nation still speaking the language. Or you could look at what happened to English after the Norman Conquest, when French was made the language of justice, administration, and literature. For a period of about three hundred years, in fact, we have almost no records in English at all—if that were all the evidence there were, you would think that the language had utterly disappeared. It is only when English re-emerges in the fourteenth century that we realize that people had been using it all along. Of course, sometimes you can impose a language in this way, if you go at it hard enough and long enough. For a number of centuries, it was actually illegal to use Gaelic in Ireland. (In fact, the use of Gaelic is restricted to this day in Northern Ireland.) And of course the English finally succeeded in establishing English as a common language in Ireland. But the imposition of English scarcely resulted in an increased sense of British unity, or of loyalty to the Crown.

3 Now of course these situations are not like ours, in that people did not want to acquire the language that was being forced on them. But even in situations in which people do want to acquire the new language, we find that attempts to impose it officially invariably backfire. Not only do they wind up creating political turmoil and disunity, but they often actually slow down the spread of the national language. Take the example of the Soviet Union, where Russian is the native language of less than 60 per cent of the population. The use of Russian has been spreading ever since the Revolution, particularly among people who want to rise in the system or the party. But in the 1950s the Soviets began to get worried about the growth of non-Russian minorities, many of whom have much higher birthrates than the

Russians do. They said to themselves, "We had better make sure that these people all speak Russian, in the interest of national unity." So they took a number of steps, such as restricting the use of languages other than Russian in higher education in certain republics. The result was that in areas like Soviet Georgia there were mass demonstrations protesting the policy. Now I think you can appreciate that the Soviet Union is not a place where people get together and demonstrate whenever somebody closes a neighborhood school. In fact, the Soviets have had to back off from their schedule of "russification," as they call it. What they learned is that while people are willing to learn Russian, they do not like being forced to do so.

Or take the case of Sorbian, a Slavic language spoken in 4
Eastern Germany. Hitler was so concerned that the Sorbians should become German-speaking that he actually instituted a policy of requiring Sorbian parents to hire German-speaking maids. When the communists came to power after the war, they discovered that the number of Sorbian speakers had increased. They took a diametrically opposite line on the language—they encouraged the use of Sorbian, and established Sorbian schools. The result was that the use of Sorbian fell off drastically. This might seem surprising, but here again you have to realize that the Sorbians really did want to learn German, but felt compelled to resist the imposition of German from outside.

Now let me turn to English itself. From the eighteenth 5
century on, one thing that made English almost unique among the major Western languages is that we have had a sharp separation between language and state. The French have an official academy and a society charged with encouraging the use of French abroad, but both the English and later the Americans have explicitly rejected this sort of approach. As the great lexicographer Samuel Johnson put it, any attempt to establish an official basis for the language must be destroyed by "the spirit of a free people." And his American counterpart, Noah Webster, who realized better than anyone else the importance of linguistic unity in forging a single nation, opposed any state interference in matters of language. Instead, these men argued that language use should be a matter of individual choice, precisely because they had faith that citizens would agree on language standards out of their own free will. This was the view adopted by the framers of our Constitution, who

debated and rejected proposals to make English an official language.

6 This policy had been vindicated in the face of tests much more severe than anything we face today. We tend to lose sight of the fact that the use of foreign languages was much more common in the nineteenth century than it is now. Bilingual education was common, and the U.S. Commissioner of Education could write in 1870 that "the German language has actually become the second language of our Republic, and a knowledge of German is now considered essential to a finished education." In reaction, certain states tried to impose English by official means, particularly in the early years of this century, when xenophobic sentiment was at a high (often, these measures were coupled with attempts to restrict foreign immigration). In 1923, for example, the Nebraska legislature made it illegal to give instruction to primary-school students in any language other than English, and the law was upheld by the state supreme court, which held that such instruction would "inculcate in [students] the ideas and sentiments alien to the best interests of this country." Fortunately, the law was overturned by the U.S. Supreme Court on grounds of the Fourteenth Amendment.

7 Of course, this all seems silly now. The children and grandchildren of earlier immigrants are proficient in English, and the pockets of bilingualism that still exist—among the Pennsylvania Dutch, the Cajuns, or the Finns of Michigan's Upper Peninsula—are the pride of local tourist commissions. And I assure you that fifty years from now, Proposition 63 is going to appear just as absurd as the Nebraska law of 1923. The trouble with movements like the U.S. English group is that they lose sight of the enormous cultural and economic appeal of English, which have made it the most widely used language in the world, without the help of official support.

8 Let me sum up my objections to this proposition. When you start to pass laws to protect English, you send off two signals. The first is to speakers of other languages; you tell them, in effect, that they must give up their native tongues. And they react as anyone would; they begin to see the measure as an attack on their group identity, and it becomes a point of pride with them to resist and to keep using their original language. But the second signal is even more pernicious. You say to English speakers: "Our language is

not rich enough or strong enough to win speakers on its own; it needs to be bolstered by the full force of state authority." This is the mark of groups that have lost faith in the power of their language—people like the French and Italians, for example, who have enacted laws to restrict the use of English words in their newspapers. Whereas the wonderful thing about English, and particularly American English, is that we have not felt the need to protect our language against foreign influences. Take such "all-American words" as *nix, bum, kibitzer, phooey, hoosegow, buckaroo, barbecue, stampede, tycoon, chow, pizza, canoe, skunk* and *succotash*. What these words have in common is that they have all been taken into English from the languages of immigrants or native American groups. Now I do not know whether Proposition 63 would have the effect of actually preventing the official use of further loan words of this sort. But the important thing is not that, but rather that the "English language" that the proposition purports to protect is actually an amalgam of tongues, and that this enrichment has been possible precisely because English-speakers have had enough confidence in the strength and flexibility of their language to resist the temptation to try to protect it. For the sake of the English language, then, if for nothing else, I urge voters to reject the amendment.

IS ENGLISH SEXIST?

Casey Miller and Kate Swift

One Small Step for Genkind

Casey Miller and Kate Swift, co-authors of Words and Women *(1977) and* The Handbook of Nonsexist Writing *(1980), are freelance writers and editors. Their interest in language grew out of editorial work in a range of fields, including science, religion, history, and the arts. Their articles have appeared in many prestigious publications; this essay appeared in 1972 in* The New York Times Magazine.

1 A riddle is making the rounds that goes like this: A man and his young son were in an automobile accident. The father was killed and the son, who was critically injured, was rushed to a hospital. As attendants wheeled the unconscious boy into the emergency room, the doctor on duty looked down at him and said, "My God, it's my son!" What was the relationship of the doctor to the injured boy?

2 If the answer doesn't jump to your mind, another riddle that has been around a lot longer might help: The blind beggar had a brother. The blind beggar's brother died. The brother who died had no brother. What relation was the blind beggar to the blind beggar's brother?

3 As with all riddles, the answers are obvious once you see them: The doctor was the boy's mother and the beggar was her brother's sister. Then why doesn't everyone solve them immediately? Mainly because our language, like the culture it reflects, is male oriented. To say that a woman in medicine is an exception is simply to confirm that statement. Thousand of doctors are women, but in order to be seen in the mind's eye, they must be called women doctors.

4 Except for words that refer to females by definition (mother, actress, Congresswoman), and words for occupations traditionally held by females (nurse, secretary, prosti-

tute), the English language defines everyone as male. The hypothetical person ("If a man can walk 10 miles in two hours . . ."), the average person ("the man in the street") and the active person ("the man on the move") are male. The assumption is that unless otherwise identified, people in general—including doctors and beggars—are men. It is a semantic mechanism that operates to keep women invisible: *man* and *mankind* represent everyone; *he* in generalized use refers to either sex; the "land where our fathers died" is also the land of our mothers—although they go unsung. As the beetle-browed and mustachioed man in a Steig cartoon says to his two male drinking companions, "When I speak of mankind, one thing I *don't* mean is womankind."

Semantically speaking, woman is not one with the species of man, but a distinct subspecies. "Man," says the 1971 edition of the Britannica Junior Encyclopedia, "is the highest form of life on earth. His superior intelligence, combined with certain physical characteristics, have enabled man to achieve things that are impossible for other animals." (The prose style has something in common with the report of a research team describing its studies on "the development of the uterus in rats, guinea pigs and men.") As though quoting the Steig character, still speaking to his friends in McSorley's, the Junior Encyclopedia continues: "Man must invent most of his behavior, because he lacks the instincts of lower animals. . . . Most of the things he learns have been handed down from his ancestors by language and symbols rather than by biological inheritance." 5

Considering that for the last 5,000 years society has been patriarchal, that statement explains a lot. It explains why Eve was made from Adam's rib instead of the other way around, and who invented all those Adam-rib words like *fe*male and *wo*man in the first place. It also explains why, when it is necessary to mention woman, the language makes her a lower caste, a class separate from the rest of man; why it works to "keep her in her place." 6

This inheritance through language and other symbols begins in the home (also called a man's castle) where man and wife (not husband and wife, or man and woman) live for a while with their children. It is reinforced by religious training, the educational system, the press, government, commerce and the law. As Andrew Greeley wrote not long ago in his magazine, "man is a symbol-creating animal. He 7 orders and interprets his reality by his symbols, and he uses the symbols to reconstruct that reality."

8 Consider some of the reconstructed realities of American history. When school children learn from their textbooks that the early colonists gained valuable experience in governing themselves, they are not told that the early colonists who were women were denied the privilege of self-government; when they learn that in the 18th century the average man had to manufacture many of the things he and his family needed, they are not told that this "average man" was often a woman who manufactured much of what she and her family needed. Young people learn that intrepid pioneers crossed the country in covered wagons with their wives, children and cattle; they do not learn that women themselves were intrepid pioneers rather than part of the baggage.

9 In a paper published this year in Los Angeles as a guide for authors and editors of social-studies textbooks, Elizabeth Burr, Susan Dunn and Norma Farquhar document unintentional skewings of this kind that occur either because women are not specifically mentioned as affecting or being affected by historical events, or because they are discussed in terms of outdated assumptions. "One never sees a picture of women captioned simply 'farmers' or 'pioneers,'" they point out. The subspecies nomenclature that requires a caption to read "women farmers" or "women pioneers" is extended to impose certain jobs on women by definition. The textbook guide gives as an example the word *housewife,* which it says not only "suggests that domestic chores are the exclusive burden of females," but gives "female students the idea that they were born to keep house and teaches male students that they are automatically entitled to laundry, cooking and housecleaning services from the women in their families."

10 Sexist language is any language that expresses such stereotyped attitudes and expectations or that assumes the inherent superiority of one sex over the other. When a woman says of her husband, who has drawn up plans for a new bedroom wing and left out closets, "Just like a man," her language is as sexist as the man's who says, after his wife has changed her mind about needing the new wing after all, "Just like a woman."

11 Male and female are not sexist words, but masculine and

feminine almost always are. Male and female can be applied objectively to individual people and animals and, by extension, to things. When electricians and plumbers talk about male and female couplings, everyone knows or can figure out what they mean. The terms are graphic and culture free.

Masculine and feminine, however, are as sexist as any words can be, since it is almost impossible to use them without invoking cultural stereotypes. When people construct lists of "masculine" and "feminine" traits they almost always end up making assumptions that have nothing to do with innate differences between the sexes. We have a friend who happens to be going through the process of pinning down this very phenomenon. He is 7 years old and his question concerns why his coats and shirts button left over right while his sister's button the other way. He assumes it must have something to do with the differences between boys and girls, but he can't see how. 12

What our friend has yet to grasp is that the way you button your coat, like most sex-differentiated customs, has nothing to do with real differences but much to do with what society wants you to feel about yourself as a male or female person. Society decrees that it is appropriate for girls to dress differently from boys, to act differently, and to think differently. Boys must be masculine, whatever that means, and girls must be feminine. 13

Unabridged dictionaries are a good source of finding out what society decrees to be appropriate, though less by definition than by their choice of associations and illustrations. Words associated with males—*manly, virile* and *masculine,* for example—are defined through a broad range of positive attributes like strength, courage, directness and independence, and they are illustrated through such examples of contemporary usage as "a manly determination to face what comes," "a virile literary style," "a masculine love of sports." Corresponding words associated with females are defined with fewer attributes (though weakness is often one of them), and the examples given are generally negative if not clearly pejorative: "feminine wiles," "womanish tears," "a womanlike lack of promptness," "convinced that drawing was a waste of time, if not downright womanly." 14

Male-associated words are frequently applied to females to describe something that is either incongruous ("a mannish voice") or presumably commendable ("a masculine 15 mind," "she took it like a man"), but female-associated words are unreservedly derogatory when applied to males, and are sometimes abusive to females as well. The opposite of "masculine" is "effeminate," although the opposite of "feminine" is simply "unfeminine."

16 One dictionary, after defining the word *womanish* as "suitable to or resembling a woman," further defines it as "unsuitable to a man or to a strong character of either sex." Words derived from "sister" and "brother" provide another apt example, for whereas "sissy," applied either to a male or female, conveys the message that sisters are expected to be timid and cowardly, "buddy" makes clear that brothers are friends.

17 The subtle disparagement of females and corresponding approbation of males wrapped up in many English words is painfully illustrated by "tomboy." Here is an instance where a girl who likes sports and the out-of-doors, who is curious about how things work, who is adventurous and bold instead of passive, is defined in terms of something she is not—a boy. By denying that she can be the person she is and still be a girl, the word surreptitiously undermines her sense of identity: it says she is unnatural. A "tomboy," as defined by one dictionary, is a "girl, especially a young girl, who behaves like a spirited boy." But who makes the judgment that she is acting like a spirited boy, not a spirited girl? Can it be a coincidence that in the case of the dictionary just quoted the editor, executive editor, managing editor, general manager, all six members of the Board of Linguists, the usage editor, science editor, all six general editors of definitions, and 94 out of the 104 distinguished experts consulted on usage—are men?

18 It isn't enough to say that any invidious comparisons and stereotypes lexicographers perpetuate are already present in the culture. There are ways to define words like womanly and tomboy that don't put women down, though the tradition has been otherwise. Samuel Johnson, the lexicographer, was the same Dr. Johnson who said, "A woman preaching is like a dog's walking on his hind legs. It is not done well; but you are surprised to find it done at all."

19 Possibly because of the negative images associated with womanish and womanlike, and with expressions like "woman driver" and "women of the street," the word woman dropped out of fashion for a time. The women at the office and the women on the assembly line and the women one

first knew in school all became ladies or girls or gals. Now a countermovement, supported by the very term women's liberation, is putting back into words like woman and sister and sisterhood the meaning they were losing by default. It is as though, in the nick of time, women had seen that the language itself could destroy them.

Some long-standing conventions of the news media add insult to injury. When a woman or girl makes news, her sex is identified at the beginning of the story, if possible in the headline or its equivalent. The assumption, apparently, is that whatever event or action is being reported, a woman's involvement is less common and therefore more newsworthy than a man's. If the story is about achievement, the implication is: "pretty good for a woman." And because people are assumed to be male unless otherwise identified, the media have developed a special and extensive vocabulary to avoid the constant repetition of "woman." The results, "Grandmother Wins Nobel Prize," "Blonde Hijacks Airliner," "Housewife to Run for Congress," convey the kind of information that would be ludicrous in comparable headlines if the subjects were men. Why, if "Unsalaried Husband to Run for Congress" is unacceptable to editors, do women have to keep explaining that to describe them through external or superficial concerns reflects a sexist view of women as decorative objects, breeding machines and extensions of men, not real people? 20

Members of the Chicago chapter of the National Organization for Women recently studied the newspapers in their area and drew up a set of guidelines for the press. These include cutting out descriptions of the "clothes, physical features, dating life and marital status of women where such references would be considered inappropriate if about men"; using language in such a way as to include women in copy that refers to homeowners, scientists and business people where "newspaper descriptions often convey the idea that all such persons are male"; and displaying the same discretion in printing generalizations about women as would be shown toward racial, religious and ethnic groups. "Our concern with what we are called may seem trivial to some people," the women said, "but we regard the old usages as symbolic of women's position within this society." 21

The assumption that an adult woman is flattered by being called a girl is matched by the notion that a woman in a 22 menial or poorly paid job finds compensation in being called a lady. Ethel Strainchamps has pointed out that since lady is used as an adjective with nouns designating both high and low occupations (lady wrestler, lady barber, lady doctor, lady judge), some writers assume they can use the noun form without betraying value judgments. Not so, Strainchamps says, rolling the issue into a spitball: "You may write, 'He addressed the republican ladies,' or 'The Democratic ladies convened' . . . but I have never seen 'the Communist ladies' or 'the Black Panther ladies' in print."

23 Thoughtful writers and editors have begun to repudiate some of the old usages. "Divorcée," "grandmother" and "blonde," along with "vivacious," "pert," "dimpled" and "cute," were dumped by the *Washington Post* in the spring of 1970 by the executive editor, Benjamin Bradlee. In a memo to his staff, Bradlee wrote, "The meaningful equality and dignity of women is properly under scrutiny today . . . because this equality has been less than meaningful and the dignity not always free of stereotype and condescension."

24 What women have been called in the press—or at least the part that operates above ground—is only a fraction of the infinite variety of alternatives to "women" used in the subcultures of the English-speaking world. Beyond "chicks," "dolls," "dames," "babes," "skirts" and "broads" are the words and phrases in which women are reduced to their sexuality and nothing more. It would be hard to think of another area of language in which the human mind has been so fertile in devising and borrowing abusive terms. In "The Female Eunuch," Germaine Greer devotes four pages to anatomical terms and words for animals, vegetables, fruits, baked goods, implements and receptacles, all of which are used to dehumanize the female person. Jean Faust, in an article aptly called "Words That Oppress," suggests that effort to diminish women through language is rooted in a male fear of sexual inadequacy. "Woman is made to feel guilty for and akin to natural disasters," she writes; "hurricanes and typhoons are named after her. Any negative or threatening force is given a feminine name. If a man runs into bad luck climbing up the ladder of success (a male-invented game), he refers to the 'bitch goddess' Success."

25 The sexual overtones in the ancient and no doubt honorable custom of calling ships "she" have become more

explicit and less honorable in an age of air travel: "I'm Karen. Fly me." Attitudes of ridicule, contempt and disgust toward female sexuality have spawned a rich glossary of insults and epithets not found in dictionaries. And the usage in which four-letter words meaning copulate are interchangeable with cheat, attack and destroy can scarcely be unrelated to the savagery of rape.

In her updating of Ibsen's "A Doll's House," Clare Booth Luce has Nora tell her husband she is pregnant—"In the way only men are supposed to get pregnant." "Men, pregnant?" he says, and she nods; "With ideas. Pregnancies there [*she taps his head*] are masculine. And a very superior form of labor. Pregnancies here [*taps her tummy*] are feminine—a very inferior form of labor." 26

Public outcry followed a revised translation of the New Testament describing Mary as "pregnant" instead of "great with child." The objections were made in part on esthetic grounds: there is no attractive adjective in modern English for a woman who is about to give birth. A less obvious reason was that replacing the euphemism with a biological term undermined religious teaching. The initiative and generative power in the conception of Jesus are understood to be God's; Mary, the mother, was a vessel only. 27

Whether influenced by this teaching or not, the language of human reproduction lags several centuries behind scientific understanding. The male's contribution to procreation is still described as though it were the entire seed from which a new life grows: the initiative and generative power involved in the process are thought of as masculine, receptivity and nurturance as feminine. "Seminal" remains a synonym for "highly original," and there is no comparable word to describe the female's equivalent contribution. 28

An entire mythology has grown from this biological misunderstanding and its semantic legacy; its embodiment in laws that for centuries made women nonpersons was a key target of the 19th-century feminist movement. Today, more than 50 years after women finally won the basic democratic right to vote, the word "liberation" itself, when applied to women, means something less than when used of other groups of people. An advertisement for the N.B.C. news department listed Women's Liberation along with crime in the streets and the Vietnam war as "bad news." Asked for his views on Women's Liberation, a highly placed 29 politician was quoted as saying, "Let me make one thing perfectly clear. I wouldn't want to wake up next to a lady pipe-fitter."

30 One of the most surprising challenges to our male-dominated culture is coming from within organized religion, where the issues are being stated, in part, by confronting the implications of traditional language. What a growing number of theologians and scholars are saying is that the myths of the Judeo-Christian tradition, being the products of patriarchy, must be reexamined, and that the concept of an exclusively male ministry and the image of a male god have become idolatrous.

31 Women are naturally in the forefront of this movement, both in their efforts to gain ordination and full equality and through their contributions to theological reform, although both these efforts are often subtly diminished. When the Rev. Barbara Anderson was ordained by the American Lutheran Church, one newspaper printed her picture over a caption headed "Happy Girl." *Newsweek's* report of a protest staged last December by women divinity students at Harvard was jocular ("another tilt at the windmill") and sarcastic: "Every time anyone in the room lapsed into what [the students] regarded as male chauvinism—such as using the word 'mankind' to describe the human race in general—the outraged women . . . drowned out the offender with earpiercing blasts from party-favor kazoos. . . . What annoyed the women most was the universal custom of referring to God as 'He.' "

32 The tone of the report was not merely unfunny; it missed the connection between increasingly outmoded theological language and the accelerating number of women (and men) who are dropping out of organized religion, both Jewish and Christian. For language, including pronouns, can be used to construct a reality that simply mirrors society's assumptions. To women who are committed to the reality of religious faith, the effect is doubly painful. Professor Harvey Cox, in whose classroom the protest took place, stated the issue directly: The women, he said, were raising the "basic theological question of whether God is more adequately thought of in personal or suprapersonal terms."

33 Toward the end of Don McLean's remarkable ballad "American Pie," a song filled with the imagery of abandonment and disillusion, there is a stanza that must strike many

women to the quick. The church bells are broken, the music has died; then:

And the three men I admire most,
The Father, Son and the Holy Ghost,
They caught the last train for the Coast—
The day the music died.

Three men I admired most. There they go, briefcases in hand and topcoats buttoned left over right, walking down the long cold platform under the city, past the baggage wagons and the hissing steam onto the Pullman. Bye, bye God—all three of you—made in the image of male supremacy. Maybe out there in L.A. where the weather is warmer, someone can believe in you again. 34

The Roman Catholic theologian Elizabeth Farians says "the bad theology of an overmasculinized church continues to be one of the root causes of women's oppression." The definition of oppression is "to crush or burden by abuse of power or authority; burden spiritually or mentally as if by pressure." 35

When language oppresses, it does so by any means that disparage and belittle. Until well into the 20th century, one of the ways English was manipulated to disparage women was through the addition of feminine endings to nonsexual words. Thus a woman who aspired to be a poet was excluded from the company of real poets by the label poetess, and a woman who piloted an airplane was denied full status as an aviator by being called an aviatrix. At about the time poetess, aviatrix, and similar Adam-ribbisms were dropping out of use, H. W. Fowler was urging that they be revived. "With the coming expansion of women's vocations," he wrote in the first edition (1926) of "Modern English Usage," "feminines for vocation-words are a special need of the future." There can be no doubt he subconsciously recognized the relative status implied in the *-ess* designations. His criticism of a woman who wished to be known as an author rather than an authoress was that she had no need "to raise herself to the level of the male author by asserting her right to his name." 36

Who has the prior right to a name? The question has an interesting bearing on words that were once applied to men alone, or to both men and women, but now, having acquired 37 abusive associations, are assigned to women exclusively. Spinster is a gentle case in point. Prostitute and many of its synonyms illustrate the phenomenon better. If Fowler had chosen to record the changing usage of harlot from hired man (in Chaucer's time) through rascal and entertainer to its present definition, would he have maintained that the female harlot is trying to raise herself to the level of the male harlot by asserting her right to his name? Or would he have plugged for harlotress?

38 The demise of most *-ess* endings came about before the start of the new feminist movement. In the second edition of "Modern English Usage," published in 1965, Sir Ernest Gowers frankly admitted what his predecessors had been up to. "Feminine designations," he wrote "seem now to be falling into disuse. Perhaps the explanation of this paradox is that it symbolizes the victory of women in their struggle for equal rights; it reflects the abandonment by men of those ideas about women in the professions that moved Dr. Johnson to his rude remark about women preachers."

39 If Sir Ernest's optimism can be justified, why is there a movement back to feminine endings in such words as chairwoman, councilwoman and congresswoman? Betty Hudson, of Madison, Conn., is campaigning for the adoption of "selectwoman" as the legal title for a female member of that town's executive body. To have to address a woman as "Selectman," she maintains, "is not only bad grammar and bad biology, but it implies that politics is still, or should be, a man's business." A valid argument, and one that was, predictably, countered by ridicule, the surefire weapon for undercutting achievement. When the head of the Federal Maritime Commission, Helen D. Bentley, was named "Man of the Year" by an association of shipping interests, she wisely refused to be drawn into light-hearted debate with interviewers who wanted to make the award's name a humorous issue. Some women, of course, have yet to learn they are invisible. An 8-year-old who visited the American Museum of Natural History with her Brownie scout troop went through the impressive exhibit on pollution and overpopulation called "Can Man Survive?" Asked afterward, "Well, can he?" she answered, "I don't know about him, but we're working on it in Brownies."

40 Nowhere are women rendered more invisible by language than in politics. The United States Constitution, in describing the qualifications for Representative, Senator and Pres-

ident, refers to each as *he*. No wonder Shirley Chisholm, the first woman since 1888 to make a try for the Presidential nomination of a major party, has found it difficult to be taken seriously.

The observation by Andrew Greeley already quoted—that "man" uses "his symbols" to reconstruct "his reality"—was not made in reference to the symbols of language but to the symbolic impact that "nomination of a black man for the Vice-Presidency" would have on race relations in the United States. Did the author assume the generic term "man" would of course be construed to include "woman"? Or did he deliberately use a semantic device to exclude Shirley Chisholm without having to be explicit? 41

Either way, his words construct a reality in which women are ignored. As much as any other factor in our language, the ambiguous meaning of *man* serves to deny women recognition as people. In a recent magazine article, we discussed the similar effect on women of the generic pronoun *he,* which we proposed to replace by a new common gender pronoun *tey*. We were immediately told, by a number of authorities, that we were dabbling in the serious business of linguistics, and the message that reached us from these scholars was loud and clear: It-is-absolutely-impossible-for-anyone-to-introduce-a-new-word-into-the-language-just-because-there-is-a-need-for-it, so-stop-wasting-your-time. 42

When words are suggested like "herstory" (for history), "sportsoneship" (for sportsmanship) and "mistresspiece" (for the work of a Virginia Woolf) one suspects a not-too-subtle attempt to make the whole language problem look silly. But unless Alexander Pope, when he wrote "The proper study of mankind is man," meant that women should be relegated to the footnotes (or, as George Orwell might have put it, "All men are equal, but men are more equal than women"), viable new words will surely someday supersede the old. 43

Without apologies to Freud, the great majority of women do not wish in their hearts that they were men. If having grown up with a language that tells them they are at the same time men and not men raises psychic doubts for women, the doubts are not of their sexual identity but of their human identity. Perhaps the present unrest surfacing in the Women's Movement is part of an evolutionary change in our particular form of life—the one form of all in the 44 animal and plant kingdoms that orders and interprets its reality by symbols. The achievements of the species called man have brought us to the brink of self-destruction. If the species survives into the next century with the expectation of going on, it may only be because we have become part of what Harlow Shapely calls the psychozoic kingdom, where brain overshadows brawn and rationality has replaced superstition.

45 Searching the roots of Western civilization for a word to call this new species of man and woman, someone might come up with *gen,* as in genesis and generic. With such a word, *man* could be used exclusively for males as *woman* is used for females, for gen would include both sexes. Like the words deer and bison, gen would be both plural and singular. Like progenitor, progeny, and generation, it would convey continuity. Gen would express the warmth and generalized sexuality of generous, gentle, and genuine; the specific sexuality of genital and genetic. In the new family of gen, girls and boys would grow to genhood, and to speak of genkind would be to include all the people of the earth.

Cynthia Heimel
The Lady Killers

The following essay appeared in Playboy *in 1992; Ms. Heimel is a frequent contributor to that magazine.*

1 I have this new job: Five days a week, during business hours, I fight about whether or not women should be called ladies.

2 "But why does John have to say 'Hello, ladies'?" I scream at Marco as if my life depended on it.

3 "Look," Marco says, ready to strangle me, "for four years John has called them ladies! That's what he says, goddamn it!"

4 Marco and I work on a sitcom called *Dear John.* You know, the one with Judd Hirsch. The guys who work there are getting tired of the "ladies" controversy.

I don't care. It's like fingernails scratching on a blackboard 5
to me: it's a feminist thing. I thought we had it all settled back in the Seventies. Women are not ladies. The term connotes females who are simultaneously put on a pedestal and patronized. A lady is softer and weaker and more dependent than a man. Implicit in the definition is that a man must defer to her, take care of her, because she's not competent to do things on her own.

A lady would never fuck up her nails fixing a carburetor, 6
a lady doesn't swear like a longshoreman during childbirth, a lady doesn't like to give head. At least that's what our mothers told us when we were growing up. They had a litany of things that ladies, which we were supposed to become, were not allowed to do:

"A lady always sits quietly with her hands in her lap." 7

"A lady keeps her hair nicely combed and out of her eyes. 8

"A lady keeps her knees together at all times." 9

I despise this L word! Call me a lady and I feel like I'm 10
wearing a white dress and can't go splashing through puddles. When we hear a guy say "I want a terrific lady," we know we're dealing with someone with a different frame of reference, and we talk slower.

"OK, then," Marco says, "every day, John walks into a 11
room. Three women are standing there. What's he supposed to say? 'Hello, women'?"

He had me there. "Hello, women" sounds really goofy, as 12
would "Hello, men." As if you were on a military mission. You want something that is informal, colloquial.

I've discovered something depressing. There is no word in 13
our language to define a woman, or a group of women, that is nonjudgmental.

Walk into a room and say "Hello, girls" and you're either 14
talking to female people under the age of 21 or to plumpish housewives in fussy dresses who are in the habit of saying to their husbands, "The girls are coming over for bridge."

"Gals" means the same thing, except that if the women are 15
grownups, they're not wearing dresses, they're wearing Bermuda shorts.

"Chick" is another term that diminishes women. It's like 16
"girl" or "gal," only less respectful.

"Babe" implies that a woman is sexually appealing to 17
men, as in "Is she a babe?" "Well, she's seventy-five percent babe, but her ankles are fat." Ditto the terms fox and (remember?) tomato.

18 "Slut" used to mean a slovenly woman. Now it means a woman who will go to bed with everyone. This is considered a bad trait for a woman, though perfectly fabulous in a man.

19 "Bitch" means a woman who will go to bed with everyone but you.

20 I want to know why we have no nonjudgmental words to describe us. I want to know why there are no female equivalents to "guys," "fellows," "dudes." I want to know why our language is so goddamned *male,* why everything is defined by how it relates to men.

21 Why, yes, of course there are terms with sexual counterparts. "Spinster" and "bachelor," for example. Spinster means you are old and frustrated and unattractive and wear your hair in a bun and have too many cats and probably knit. The worst that can be said of a bachelor is that he's probably gay.

22 Then there are those genitalia words. Men can be "dicks," "dickheads," "pricks" and "schmucks." There are so many male genitalia words because men love penises. All those words mean "kind of a jerk." Whereas there is only one genitalia word for women, "cunt," and it is considered much more obscene than dick et al., because female genitalia are considered more obscene than male.

23 Oh, wait, I forgot "pussy." A word applied to men. It means cowardly, wimpy, weak.

24 Why are only men "bastards"? Are women considered so insignificant that it doesn't matter if they're born out of wedlock?

25 Linguists tell us that the language we speak defines the way we think. People whose language includes 32 words for snow have a lot more complicated thoughts about snow than we do.

26 Our language teaches us to think of women as less valuable than men. I hear the word babe, and I think, Am I a babe? And if not, am I worthless? I hear the term spinster and I feel a tiny stirring of fear and distaste before I think, Thank God I've been married, I'm not a spinster! I hear "cunt," and before I can stop myself, self-loathing trickles into my soul. I don't want to feel this way. It's unfair for my own language to betray me.

27 So I have a proposal. Let's make the word guy unisex. Let's everybody call one another guy so that everybody can feel equal, like they're one of the gang, like they belong. Women do this already, because we utterly refuse to call

each other ladies, but we feel a hint of self-betrayal. If it's made official, we won't.

We still need a nonjudgmental female word. I think "girl" is sometimes OK, but it's like "nigger." We can use it, you can't. 28

How about "bitch"? Too negative? I don't think so. A man will call a woman a bitch when he can't control her, when she won't do his bidding or when she's not compliant to his needs. I like this in a word. 29

Lewis Grizzard

Women Will Be Womyn

Lewis Grizzard is a columnist for The Atlanta Constitution *newspaper, where the following essay appeared in June 1991.*

The new-for-the-90s Webster's Collegiate Dictionary is out and wouldn't you know it. There are now different ways to spell certain words so as to accommodate the feminists. 1

There's even a new way to spell woman, according to the new dictionary. It may now be spelled "womyn," so there's no longer any need to use those awful three letters that spell m-a-n. 2

There's more. HIStory. That's for guys. The new word is HER-story, as in, "Joan Rivers was the worst morning television show hostess in all of *herstory.*" 3

The report I read concerning the new dictionary did not, however, tell of how certain other words, akin to the ones above, can be altered in order to rid them of any sexist connotations. 4

I did some guessing, though. Here's some examples of other changes: 5

- HERSTERECTOMY: Whoever heard of a man going through that type of operation?
- HERMALAYAS: Womyn should have a mountain range of their very own.

- HERSTERICAL: "Wanda was *hersterical* when she found out Bob had taken Bernice on a trip to the Hermalayas."
- HERMNS: Womyn sing in church, too.
- HERSY: "Bernice threw a *hersy* when she found out Wanda had found out about her trip to the Hermalayas with Bob."

6 You get my drift.

7 But let us take this a step further. Even if you spell woman "womyn," it still sounds the same. What womyn need in order to throw off the yoke of sexism when it comes to calling themselves something is an entirely new word.

8 Female doesn't work for obvious reasons. Changing that to fe-MULE would only encourage too many sexists to make remarks about the stereotypical tendency of a womyn to be stubborn.

9 I even thought it might work to turn women around backward. They would become "nemows," as in, "Boy, you should have seen the *nemows* in Ralph's last night."

10 But nemows still includes n-e-m, men spelled backward, a reminder of just how backward many of them still are despite all the efforts to teach them not to say, "You should have seen the chicks in Ralph's last night."

11 I did some thinking on this matter as well and came upon a few ideas of something new to call womyn.

- GIRL PERSONS: Too juvenile? You're right.
- LADIES: Some men name their dogs Lady, and there's that awful sexist joke that goes: "Who was that lady I saw you with last night?"
  "That was no lady. That was my wife."

12 Forget ladies.

- ADNOFENAJS: (Pronounced ad-NOFEN-ajuhs). That's Jane Fonda spelled backward, but it's a little cumbersome to say, "That adnofenaj should have been hanged for treason."
- EELADNERBS: (Pronounced eel-LADNER-buh). That's Brenda Lee spelled backward. I like Brenda Lee a lot more than Jane Fonda, but I guess most '90s womyn wouldn't.

- CHICKS: Just kidding.
- RALPHETTES: As in, "You shoulda seen the two Ralphettes we met last night at Ralph's."

Sorry, I just can't seem to get untracked here. 13

- PLAINTIFFS: That's got some possibilities. Like the guy said, "I've been divorced so many times, I just refer to all my ex-wives as Plaintiff."

I think that is probably as far as I should go here. The feminist hate mail will pour in for weeks as it is. 14

Oops! did I say "mail"? 15

Deborah Tannen

CrossTalk

Deborah Tannen, a professor of linguistics at Georgetown University in Washington, DC, published You Just Don't Understand: Women and Men in Conversation *in 1990. An exploration of the complexities of communication between men and women, it became a national best-seller. The following selection from that book has been printed elsewhere as a self-contained piece.*

A woman who owns a bookstore needed to have a talk with the store manager. She had told him to help the bookkeeper with billing, he had agreed, and now, days later, he still hadn't done it. Thinking how much she disliked this part of her work, she sat down with the manager to clear things up. They traced the problem to a breakdown in communication. 1

She had said, "Sarah needs help with the bills. What do you think about helping her out?" He had responded, "OK," by which he meant, "OK, I'll think about whether or not I want to help her." During the next day, he thought about it and concluded that he'd rather not. 2

3 This wasn't just an ordinary communication breakdown that could happen between any two people. It was a particular sort of breakdown that tends to occur between women and men.

4 Most women avoid giving orders. More comfortable with decision-making by consensus, they tend to phrase requests as questions, to give others the feeling they have some say in the matter and are not being bossed around. But this doesn't mean they aren't making their wishes clear. Most women would have understood the bookstore owner's question, "What do you think about helping her out?" as assigning a task in a considerate way.

5 The manager, however, took the owner's words literally. She had asked him what he thought; she hadn't told him to *do* anything. So he felt within his rights when he took her at her word, thought about it and decided not to help Sarah.

6 Women in positions of authority are likely to regard such responses as insubordination: "He knows I am in charge, and he knows what I want; if he doesn't do it, he is resisting my authority."

7 There may be a kernel of truth in this view—most men are inclined to resist authority if they can because being in a subordinate position makes them intensely uncomfortable. But indirect requests that are transparent to women may be genuinely opaque to men. They assume that people in authority will give orders if they really want something done.

8 These differences in management styles are one of many manifestations of gender differences in how we talk to one another. Women use language to create connection and rapport; men use it to negotiate their status in a hierarchical order. It isn't that women are unaware of status or that men don't build rapport, but that *the genders tend to focus on different goals.*

The Source of Gender Differences

9 These differences stem from the way boys and girls learn to use language while growing up. Girls tend to play indoors, either in small groups or with one other girl. The center of a girl's social life is her best friend, with whom she spends a great deal of time sitting, talking and exchanging secrets. It is the telling of secrets that makes them best

friends. Boys tend to play outdoors, in larger groups, usually in competitive games. It's doing things together that makes them friends.

Anthropologist Marjorie Harness Goodwin compared boys and girls at play in a black innercity neighborhood in Philadelphia. Her findings, which have been supported by researchers in other settings, show that the boys' groups are hierarchical: high-status boys give orders, and low-status boys have to follow them, so they end up being told what to do. Girls' groups tend to be egalitarian: girls who appeared "better" than others or gave orders were not countenanced and in some cases were ostracized. 10

So while boys are learning to fear being "put down" and pushed around, girls are learning to fear being "locked out." Whereas high-status boys establish and reinforce their authority by giving orders and resisting doing what others want, girls tend to make suggestions, which are likely to be taken up by the group. 11

Cross-Gender Communication in the Workplace

The implications of these different conversational habits and concerns in terms of office interactions are staggering. Men are inclined to continue to jockey for position, trying to resist following orders as much as possible within the constraints of their jobs. 12

Women, on the other hand, are inclined to do what they sense their bosses want, whether or not they are ordered to. By the same token, women in positions of authority are inclined to phrase their requests as suggestions and to assume they will be respected because of their authority. These assumptions are likely to hold up as long as both parties are women, but they may well break down in cross-gender communication. 13

When a woman is in the position of authority, such as the bookstore owner, she may find her requests are systematically misunderstood by men. And when a woman is working for a male boss, she may find that her boss gives bald commands that seem unnecessarily imperious because most women would prefer to be asked rather than ordered. One woman who worked at an all-male radio station commented that the way the men she worked for told her what to do made her feel as if she should salute and say, "Yes, boss." 14

15 Many men complain that a woman who is indirect in making requests is manipulative: she's trying to get them to do what she wants without telling them to do it. Another common accusation is that she is insecure: she doesn't know what she wants. But if a woman gives direct orders, the same men might complain that she is aggressive, unfeminine or worse.

16 Women are in a double bind: *If we talk like women, we are not respected. If we talk like men, we are not liked.*

17 We have to walk a fine line, finding ways to be more direct without appearing bossy. The bookstore owner may never be comfortable by directly saying, "Help Sarah with the billing today," but she might find some compromise such as, "Sarah needs help with the billing. I'd appreciate it if you would make some time to help her out in the next day or two." This request is clear, while still reflecting women's preferences for giving reasons and options.

18 What if you're the subordinate and your boss is a man who's offending you daily by giving you orders? If you know him well enough, one potential solution is "metacommunication"—that is, talk about communication. Point out the differences between women and men, and discuss how you could accommodate to each other's styles. (You may want to give him a copy of this article or my book.)

19 But if you don't have the kind of relationship that makes metacommunication possible, you could casually, even jokingly, suggest he give orders another way. Or just try to remind yourself it's a cross-cultural difference and try not to take his curtness personally.

How to Handle a Meeting

20 There are other aspects of women's styles that can work against us in a work setting. Because women are most comfortable using language to create rapport with someone they feel close to, and men are used to talking in a group where they have to prove themselves and display what they know, a formal meeting can be a natural for men and a hard nut to crack for women. Many women find it difficult to speak up at meetings; if they do, they may find their comments ignored, perhaps later to be resuscitated by a man who gets credit for the idea. Part of this is simply due

to the expectation that men will have more important things to contribute.

But the way women and men tend to present themselves can aggravate this inequity. At meetings, men are more likely to speak often, at length and in a declamatory manner. They may state their opinions as fact and leave it to others to challenge them. 21

Women, on the other hand, are often worried about appearing to talk too much—a fear that is justified by research showing that when they talk equally, women are perceived as talking more than men. As a result, many women are hesitant to speak at a meeting and inclined to be succinct and tentative when they do. 22

Developing Options

Working on changing your presentational style is one option; another is to make your opinions known in private conversation with the key people before a meeting. And if you are the key person, it would be wise to talk personally to the women on your staff rather than assuming all participants have had a chance to express themselves at the meeting. 23

Many women's reticence about displaying their knowledge at a meeting is related to their reluctance to boast. They find it more humble to keep quiet about their accomplishments and wait for someone else to notice them. But most men learn early on to display their accomplishments and skills. And women often find that no one bothers to ferret out their achievements if they don't put them on display. Again, a woman risks criticism if she talks about her achievements, but this may be a risk she needs to take, to make sure she gets credit for her work. 24

I would never want to be heard as telling women to adopt men's styles across the board. For one thing, there are many situations in which women's styles are more successful. For example, the inclination to make decisions by consensus can be a boon to a woman in a managerial position. Many people, men as well as women, would rather feel they have influence in decision-making than be given orders. 25

Moreover, recommending that women adopt men's styles would be offensive, as well as impractical, because women 26 are judged by the norms for women's behavior, and doing the same thing as men has a very different, often negative, effect.

A Starting Point

27 Simply knowing about gender differences in conversational style provides a starting point for improving relations with the women and men who are above and below you in a hierarchy.

28 The key is *flexibility;* a way of talking that works beautifully with one person may be a disaster with another. If one way of talking isn't working, try another, rather than trying harder to do more of the same.

29 Once you know what the parameters are, you can become an observer of your own interactions, and a style-switcher when you choose.

III.

GENDER

Introduction

One of the stunning social developments of the twentieth century has been the economic and political and cultural emergence of women. Beginning with the success of the women's suffrage movement early in the century and continuing with a series of legal and legislative victories in the past quarter of a century, the women's movement has largely achieved the goal of political equality in the United States—at least on paper. But that has not closed discussion on women's concerns, of course, because social, economic, and political parity between women and men remains incomplete and because the specific terms of social and economic liberation have not yet been agreed on. In fact, discussion of gender issues has intensified in the past decade as gender roles and their implications—for both men and women—continue to be negotiated through public discourse. This part of *Conversations* barely begins to capture the range of issues currently under debate, but it does present discussions of three general matters: How should women (and men) be defined? Are women's brains, are the ways women reason, different somehow from men's? And how do gender issues affect work and careers? (In addition, gender issues are taken up elsewhere in this book, most notably in part II, "Language," and in the sections in part V on pornography, affirmative action, and abortion.)

Until very recently men defined women, mostly in a misogynist (women-hating) tradition that is deeply seated in Western cultures. But the fact that women are now involved in defining gender roles has not effaced that tradition of misogyny, nor has it ended discussion of the nature of those roles. Just what form will the feminist revolution take? Just what is it that defines the essential natures of women and men? Beyond reproductive differences, are there inevitable distinctions between the sexes in terms of emotions, sexuality, physiology, morals, values, and so forth? Or are all such distinctions the result of social conditioning—social conditioning that might be altered? That is the basic issue under discussion in the first section of this part. A dozen or so selections of various kinds describe or explain or dramatize or argue for various positions on the question of the "essential natures" of women and men, and the extent to which history and culture and environment determine those natures. Those selections also illustrate the range of voices that can be summoned in support of a discussion of gender roles. Although most of the selections address women's concerns most directly, each has direct and indirect implications for men as well. And in the final years of this century, those implications must be faced up to each day.

It is not hard to notice that women have distinguished themselves comparatively rarely in fields related to science and mathematics. But why? That question is the topic of the second section. Are there somehow sex differences in mathematical reasoning ability? Do women actually *think* any differently than men do? Are women disadvantaged by their sex from excelling at math and science? Or are any such apparent differences the result of social conditioning? How can more women be encouraged to enter scientific and technical fields? What barriers discourage women from careers in science and engineering? Perhaps those questions have concrete implications on your campus or in your own life.

This part concludes with a set of readings that deal with the conditions women face at work. What happens—on the job and at home—when women enter professions and institutions traditionally dominated by men? How can women cope with unfriendly circumstances? Are the satisfactions of jobs in male-dominated fields worth the hassles? Speaking of hassles: What about the question of sexual harassment at work—what is it, and what can be done about it? Why do wages for women persistently lag behind those of men? Should corporations and institutions establish separate career tracks for women who want to combine careers and childrearing? Or is a fundamental change in childrearing conventions—a change requiring the greater involvement of men—the only route to economic parity? Do biological differences between women and men make such change unrealistic or undesirable?

Where do you stand on questions like these? The selections in this part of *Conversations* are designed to provoke further discussion, not to close it off. In fact, a premise of this part on gender is that by engaging in open, public discourse on these questions, writers can hasten the day when the effects of sexual polarization—perhaps sexual polarization itself—might be minimized and when codes of personal behavior might be more freely chosen, to the benefit of both women and men.

JUST HOW WOULD YOU DEFINE WOMEN AND MEN?

John Adams and Abigail Adams

Letters

Here are two letters and part of a third written by John Adams of Massachusetts, one of America's Founding Fathers (and later the second president of the United States), and his wife Abigail Adams (a formidable person as well) in the spring of 1776—while the nation was considering declaring its freedom from British rule. The first was sent by Abigail to John while he was in Philadelphia debating with his colleagues the merits of a Declaration of Independence: Note how Abigail uses the occasion to press her husband to "remember the ladies" in his discussions about freedom from tyranny. She was probably thinking not of suffrage—too radical an idea—but of fairer laws regarding inheritance, wifebeating, and so forth. The second is John's response to that letter. The third, John Adams's letter to James Sullivan (who had proposed that one's power at the ballot box should be proportional to one's financial worth), indicates that John Adams understood all too well the probable long-term implications of what was being written in the Declaration.

Letter from Abigail Adams to John Adams, March 31, 1776

1 I long to hear that you have declared an independancy—and by the way in the new Code of Laws which I suppose it will be necessary for you to make I desire you would Remember the Ladies, and be more generous and favourable to them than your ancestors. Do not put such unlimited power into the hands of the Husbands. Remember all Men would be tyrants if they could. If perticuliar care and attention is not

paid to the Laidies we are determined to foment a Rebelion, and will not hold ourselves bound by any Laws in which we have no voice, or Representation.

That your Sex are Naturally Tyrannical is a Truth so thoroughly established as to admit of no dispute, but such of you as wish to be happy willingly give up the harsh title of Master for the more tender and endearing one of Friend. Why then, not put it out of the power of the vicious and the Lawless to use us with cruelty and indignity with impunity. Men of Sense in all Ages abhor those customs which treat us only as the vassals of your Sex. Regard us then as Beings placed by providence under your protection and in immitation of the Supreem Being make use of that power only for our happiness. 2

Letter from John Adams to Abigail Adams, April 14, 1776

As to Declarations of Independency, be patient. Read our Privateering Laws, and our Commercial Laws. What signifies a Word. 3

As to your extraordinary Code of Laws, I cannot but laugh. We have been told that our Struggle has loosened the bands of Government every where. That Children and Apprentices were disobedient—that schools and Colledges were grown turbulent—that Indians slighted their Guardians and Negroes grew insolent to their Masters. But your Letter was the first Intimation that another Tribe more numerous and powerfull than all the rest were grown discontented.—This is rather too coarse a Compliment but you are so saucy, I wont blot it out. 4

Depend upon it, We know better than to repeal our Masculine systems. Altho they are in full Force, you know they are little more than Theory. We dare not exert our Power in its full Latitude. We are obliged to go fair, and softly, and in Practice you know We are the subjects. We have only the Name of Masters, and rather than give up this, which would compleatly subject Us to the Despotism of the Peticoat, I hope General Washington, and all our brave Heroes would fight. I am sure every good Politician would plot, as long as he would against Despotism, Empire, Monarchy, Aristocracy, Oligarchy, or Ochlocracy.—A fine Story indeed. I begin to think the Ministry as deep as 5 they are wicked. After stirring up Tories, Landjobbers, Trimmers, Bigots, Canadians, Indians, Negroes, Hanoverians, Hessians, Russians, Irish Roman Catholicks, Scotch Renegadoes, at last they have stimulated the[m] to demand new Priviledges and threaten to rebell.

Letter from John Adams to James Sullivan, May 26, 1776

6 . . . The same reasoning which will induce you to admit all men who have no property, to vote, with those who have, for those laws which affect the person, will prove that you ought to admit women and children; for, generally speaking, women and children have as good judgments, and as independent minds, as those men who are wholly destitute of property; these last being to all intents and purposes as much dependent upon others, who will please to feed, clothe, and employ them, as women are upon their husbands, or children on their parents.

7 As to your idea of proportioning the votes of men, in money matters, to the property they hold, it is utterly impracticable. There is no possible way of ascertaining, at any one time, how much every man in a community is worth; and if there was, so fluctuating is trade and property, that this state of it would change in half an hour. . . .

8 Depend upon it, Sir, it is dangerous to open so fruitful a source of controversy and altercation as would be opened by attempting to alter the qualifications of voters; there will be no end of it. New claims will arise; women will demand a vote; lads from twelve to twenty-one will think their rights not enough attended to; and every man who has not a farthing, will demand an equal voice with any other, in all acts of state. It tends to confound all distinctions, and prostrate all ranks to one common level.

Sojourner Truth

Ain't I a Woman?

Sojourner Truth's story is fascinating and moving. Born into slavery around 1797 and into the name Isabella in Ulster County, New York, sold three times before she was twelve, raped by one of her masters, she fled to freedom in 1827, a year before slavery was outlawed in New York. In New York City she worked as a domestic and fell in with an evangelical preacher who encouraged her efforts to convert prostitutes. In 1843, inspired by mystical visions, she took the name Sojourner Truth and set off alone and undeterred by her illiteracy to preach and sing about religion and the abolition of slavery. By 1850 huge crowds were coming to witness the oratory of the ex-slave with the resounding voice and message. During the Civil War she was presented to President Lincoln at the White House. After the war she spoke out for women's suffrage, but she never gave up her spiritual and racial themes—or her humor and exuberance. She continued to lecture until near her death in Battle Creek, Michigan, in 1883.

Sojourner Truth accepted neither the physical inferiority of women nor the idea that they should be placed on pedestals; nor did she subordinate women's rights to the pursuit of racial equality. At a religious meeting in May 1851, Sojourner Truth rose extemporaneously to rebut speakers who had impugned the rights and capabilities of women. According to an eyewitness who recorded the scene in his diary, this is what she said:

Well, children, where there is so much racket there must be something out of kilter. I think that 'twixt the negroes of the South and the women at the North, all talking about rights, the white men will be in a fix pretty soon. But what's all this here talking about? 1

That man over there says that women need to be helped into carriages, and lifted over ditches, and to have the best place everywhere. Nobody ever helps me into carriages, or over mud-puddles, or gives me any best place! And ain't I a woman? Look at me! Look at my arm! I have ploughed and planted, and gathered into barns, and no man could head me! And ain't I a woman? I could work as much and eat as much as a man—when I could get it—and bear the lash as 2 well! And ain't I a woman? I have borne thirteen children, and seen them most all sold off to slavery, and when I cried out with my mother's grief, none but Jesus heard me! And ain't I a woman?

3 Then they talk about this thing in the head; what's this they call it? [Intellect, someone whispers.] That's it, honey. What's that got to do with women's rights or negro's rights? If my cup won't hold but a pint, and yours holds a quart, wouldn't you be mean not to let me have my little half-measure full?

4 Then that little man in black there, he says women can't have as much rights as men, 'cause Christ wasn't a woman! Where did your Christ come from? Where did your Christ come from? From God and a woman! Man had nothing to do with Him.

5 If the first woman God ever made was strong enough to turn the world upside down all alone, these women together ought to be able to turn it back, and get it right side up again! And now they is asking to do it, the men better let them.

6 Obliged to you for hearing on me, and now old Sojourner ain't got nothing more to say.

Susan Glaspell

Trifles

Susan Glaspell (1882–1948), an Iowan by birth and education, moved east in 1911. A Pulitzer-Prize-winning dramatist and a prolific fictionwriter, she cofounded in 1915 the Provincetown Playhouse on Cape Cod, which became a center for experimental and innovative drama. In 1916 she wrote Trifles, *the one-act play reprinted here; then she adapted it a few months later into the story "A Jury of Her Peers."*

Characters

GEORGE HENDERSON, *County Attorney*
HENRY PETERS, *Sheriff*
LEWIS HALE, *A Neighboring Farmer*

Mrs. Peters
Mrs. Hale

SCENE

The kitchen in the now abandoned farmhouse of JOHN WRIGHT, 1
a gloomy kitchen, and left without having been put in order—
unwashed pans under the sink, a loaf of bread outside the
breadbox, a dish towel on the table—other signs of incom-
pleted work. At the rear the outer door opens and the SHERIFF
comes in followed by the COUNTY ATTORNEY *and* HALE. *The* SHERIFF
and HALE *are men in middle life, the* COUNTY ATTORNEY *is a young*
man; all are much bundled up and go at once to the stove.
They are followed by two women—the SHERIFF'S *wife first; she*
is a slight wiry woman, a thin nervous face. MRS. HALE *is larger*
and would ordinarily be called more comfortable looking, but
she is disturbed now and looks fearfully about as she enters.
The women have come in slowly, and stand close together
near the door.

COUNTY ATTORNEY. [*Rubbing his hands.*] This feels good. Come 2
up to the fire, ladies.

MRS. PETERS. [*After taking a step forward.*] I'm not—cold. 3

SHERIFF. [*Unbuttoning his overcoat and stepping away from* 4
the stove as if to mark the beginning of official business.]
Now, Mr. Hale, before we move things about, you explain
to Mr. Henderson just what you saw when you came here
yesterday morning.

COUNTY ATTORNEY. By the way, has anything been moved? Are 5
things just as you left them yesterday?

SHERIFF. [*Looking about.*] It's just the same. When it dropped 6
below zero last night I thought I'd better send Frank out
this morning to make a fire for us—no use getting pneumonia with a big case on, but I told him not to touch
anything except the stove—and you know Frank.

COUNTY ATTORNEY. Somebody should have been left here 7
yesterday.

SHERIFF. Oh—yesterday. When I had to send Frank to Morris 8
Center for that man who went crazy—I want you to know
I had my hands full yesterday. I knew you could get back
from Omaha by today and as long as I went over everything here myself—

COUNTY ATTORNEY. Well, Mr. Hale, tell just what happened 9
when you came here yesterday morning.

10 HALE. Harry and I had started to town with a load of potatoes. We came along the road from my place and as I got here I said, "I'm going to see if I can't get John Wright to go in with me on a party telephone." I spoke to Wright about it once before and he put me off, saying folks talked too much anyway, and all he asked was peace and quiet—I guess you know about how much he talked himself; but I thought maybe if I went to the house and talked about it before his wife, though I said to Harry that I didn't know as what his wife wanted made much difference to John—

11 COUNTY ATTORNEY. Let's talk about that later, Mr. Hale. I do want to talk about that, but tell now just what happened when you got to the house.

12 HALE. I didn't hear or see anything; I knocked at the door, and still it was all quiet inside. I knew they must be up, it was past eight o'clock. So I knocked again, and I thought I heard somebody say, "Come in." I wasn't sure, I'm not sure yet, but I opened the door—this door [*Indicating the door by which the two women are still standing*] and there in that rocker—[*Pointing to it.*] sat Mrs. Wright. [*They all look at the rocker.*]

13 COUNTY ATTORNEY. What—was she doing?

14 HALE. She was rockin' back and forth. She had her apron in her hand and was kind of—pleating it.

15 COUNTY ATTORNEY. And how did she—look?

16 HALE. Well, she looked queer.

17 COUNTY ATTORNEY. How do you mean—queer?

18 HALE. Well, as if she didn't know what she was going to do next. And kind of done up.

19 COUNTY ATTORNEY. How did she seem to feel about your coming?

20 HALE. Why, I don't think she minded—one way or other. She didn't pay much attention. I said, "How do, Mrs. Wright, it's cold, ain't it?" And she said, "Is it?"—and went on kind of pleating at her apron. Well, I was surprised; she didn't ask me to come up to the stove, or to set down, but just sat there, not even looking at me, so I said, "I want to see John." And then she—laughed. I guess you would call it a laugh. I thought of Harry and the team outside, so I said a little sharp: "Can't I see John?" "No," she says, kind o' dull like. "Ain't he home?" says I. "Yes," says she, "he's home." "Then why can't I see him?" I asked her, out of patience. " 'Cause he's dead," says she. *"Dead?"* says I. She

just nodded her head, not getting a bit excited, but rockin' back and forth. "Why—where is he?" says I, not knowing what to say. She just pointed upstairs—like that [*Himself pointing to the room above.*] I got up, with the idea of going up there. I walked from there to here—then I says, "Why, what did he die of?" "He died of a rope round his neck," says she, and just went on pleatin' at her apron. Well, I went out and called Harry. I thought I might—need help. We went upstairs and there he was lyin'—

COUNTY ATTORNEY. I think I'd rather have you go into that 21
upstairs, where you can point it all out. Just go on now with the rest of the story.

HALE. Well, my first thought was to get that rope off. It 22
looked . . . [*Stops, his face twitches*] . . . but Harry, he went up to him, and he said, "No, he's dead all right, and we'd better not touch anything." So we went back down stairs. She was still sitting that same way. "Has anybody been notified?" I asked. "No," says she, unconcerned. "Who did this, Mrs. Wright?" said Harry. He said it businesslike—and she stopped pleatin' of her apron. "I don't know," she says. "You don't *know?*" says Harry. "No," says she. "Weren't you sleepin' in bed with him?" says Harry. "Yes," says she, "but I was on the inside." "Somebody slipped a rope round his neck and strangled him and you didn't wake up?" says Harry. "I didn't wake up," she said after him. We must 'a looked as if we didn't see how that could be, for after a minute she said, "I sleep sound." Harry was going to ask her more questions but I said maybe we ought to let her tell her story first to the coroner, or the sheriff, so Harry went fast as he could to Rivers' place, where there's a telephone.

COUNTY ATTORNEY. And what did Mrs. Wright do when she 23
knew that you had gone for the coroner?

HALE. She moved from that chair to this one over here 24
[*Pointing to a small chair in the corner.*] and just sat there with her hands held together and looking down. I got a feeling that I ought to make some conversation, so I said I had come in to see if John wanted to put in a telephone, and at that she started to laugh, and then she stopped and looked at me—scared. [*The* COUNTY ATTORNEY, *who has had his notebook out, makes a note.*] I dunno, maybe it wasn't scared. I wouldn't like to say it was. Soon Harry got back, and then Dr. Lloyd came, and you, Mr. Peters, and so I guess that's all I know that you don't.

25 COUNTY ATTORNEY. [*Looking around.*] I guess we'll go upstairs first—and then out to the barn and around there. [*To the* SHERIFF] You're convinced that there was nothing important here—nothing that would point to any motive.

26 SHERIFF. Nothing here but kitchen things.

[*The* COUNTY ATTORNEY, *after again looking around the kitchen, opens the door of a cupboard closet. He gets up on a chair and looks on a shelf. Pulls his hand away, sticky.*]

27 COUNTY ATTORNEY. Here's a nice mess.

[*The women draw nearer.*]

28 MRS. PETERS. [*To the other woman.*] Oh, her fruit; it did freeze. [*To the* COUNTY ATTORNEY] She worried about that when it turned so cold. She said the fire'd go out and her jars would break.

29 SHERIFF. Well, can you beat the women! Held for murder and worryin' about her preserves.

30 COUNTY ATTORNEY. I guess before we're through she may have something more serious than preserves to worry about.

31 HALE. Well, women are used to worrying over trifles. [*The two women move a little closer together.*]

32 COUNTY ATTORNEY. [*With the gallantry of a young politician.*] And yet, for all their worries, what would we do without the ladies? [*The women do not unbend. He goes to the sink, takes a dipperful of water from the pail and pouring it into a basin, washes his hands. Starts to wipe them on the roller towel, turns it for a cleaner place.*] Dirty towels! [*Kicks his foot against the pans under the sink.*] Not much of a housekeeper, would you say, ladies?

33 MRS. HALE. [*Stiffly.*] There's a great deal of work to be done on a farm.

34 COUNTY ATTORNEY. To be sure. And yet [*With a little bow to her*] I know there are some Dickson county farmhouses which do not have such roller towels.

[*He gives it a pull to expose its full length again.*]

35 MRS. HALE. Those towels get dirty awful quick. Men's hands aren't always as clean as they might be.

36 COUNTY ATTORNEY. Ah, loyal to your sex, I see. But you and Mrs. Wright were neighbors. I suppose you were friends, too.

37 MRS. HALE. [*Shaking her head.*] I've not seen much of her of late years. I've not been in this house—it's more than a year.

38 COUNTY ATTORNEY. And why was that? You didn't like her?

39 MRS. HALE. I liked her all well enough. Farmers' wives have their hands full, Mr. Henderson. And then—

COUNTY ATTORNEY. Yes—? 40
MRS. HALE. [*Looking about.*] It never seemed a very cheerful 41
place.
COUNTY ATTORNEY. No—it's not cheerful. I shouldn't say she 42
had the homemaking instinct.
MRS. HALE. Well, I don't know as Wright had, either. 43
COUNTY ATTORNEY. You mean that they didn't get on very well? 44
MRS. HALE. No, I don't mean anything. But I don't think a 45
place'd be any cheerfuller for John Wright's being in it.
COUNTY ATTORNEY. I'd like to talk more of that a little later. I 46
want to get the lay of things upstairs now.
[*He goes to the left, where three steps lead to a stair door.*]
SHERIFF. I suppose anything Mrs. Peters does'll be all right. 47
She was to take in some clothes for her, you know, and a
few little things. We left in such a hurry yesterday.
COUNTY ATTORNEY. Yes, but I would like to see what you take, 48
Mrs. Peters, and keep an eye out for anything that might
be of use to us.
MRS. PETERS. Yes, Mr. Henderson. 49
[*The women listen to the men's steps on the stairs, then look about the kitchen.*]
MRS. HALE. I'd hate to have men coming into my kitchen, 50
snooping around and criticising.
[*She arranges the pans under sink which the* COUNTY ATTORNEY *had shoved out of place.*]
MRS. PETERS. Of course it's no more than their duty. 51
MRS. HALE. Duty's all right, but I guess that deputy sheriff that 52
came out to make the fire might have got a little of this on. [*Gives the roller towel a pull.*] Wish I'd thought of that sooner. Seems mean to talk about her for not having things slicked up when she had to come away in such a hurry.
MRS. PETERS. [*Who has gone to a small table in the left rear* 53
corner of the room, and lifted one end of a towel that covers a pan.] She had bread set.
[*Stands still.*]
MRS. HALE. [*Eyes fixed on a loaf of bread beside the breadbox,* 54
which is on a low shelf at the other side of the room. Moves slowly toward it.] She was going to put this in there. [*Picks up loaf, then abruptly drops it. In a manner of returning to familiar things.*] It's a shame about her fruit. I wonder if it's all gone. [*Gets up on the chair and looks.*] I think there's some here that's all right, Mrs. Peters. Yes—here; [*Holding it toward the window.*] this is cherries too. [*Looking again.*] I declare I believe that's the only one. [*Gets down, bottle in

her hand. Goes to the sink and wipes it off on the outside.] She'll feel awful bad after all her hard work in the hot weather. I remember the afternoon I put up my cherries last summer.

[*She puts the bottle on the big kitchen table, center of the room. With a sigh, is about to sit down in the rocking-chair. Before she is seated realizes what chair it is; with a slow look at it, steps back. The chair which she has touched rocks back and forth.*]

55 MRS. PETERS. Well, I must get those things from the front room closet. [*She goes to the door at the right, but after looking into the other room, steps back.*] You coming with me, Mrs. Hale? You could help me carry them.

[*They go in the other room; reappear,* MRS. PETERS *carrying a dress and skirt,* MRS. HALE *following with a pair of shoes.*]

56 MRS. PETERS. My, it's cold in there.

[*She puts the clothes on the big table, and hurries to the stove.*]

57 MRS. HALE. [*Examining her skirt.*] Wright was close. I think maybe that's why she kept so much to herself. She didn't even belong to the Ladies Aid. I suppose she felt she couldn't do her part, and then you don't enjoy things when you feel shabby. She used to wear pretty clothes and be lively, when she was Minnie Foster, one of the town girls singing in the choir. But that—oh, that was thirty years ago. This all you was to take in?

58 MRS. PETERS. She said she wanted an apron. Funny thing to want, for there isn't much to get you dirty in jail, goodness knows. But I suppose just to make her feel more natural. She said they was in the top drawer in this cupboard. Yes, here. And then her little shawl that always hung behind the door. [*Opens stair door and looks.*] Yes, here it is.

[*Quickly shuts door leading upstairs.*]

59 MRS. HALE. [*Abruptly moving toward her.*] Mrs. Peters?

60 MRS. PETERS. Yes, Mrs. Hale?

61 MRS. HALE. Do you think she did it?

62 MRS. PETERS. [*In a frightened voice.*] Oh, I don't know.

63 MRS. HALE. Well, I don't think she did. Asking for an apron and her little shawl. Worrying about her fruit.

64 MRS. PETERS. [*Starts to speak, glances up, where footsteps are heard in the room above. In a low voice.*] Mr. Peters says it looks bad for her. Mr. Henderson is awful sarcastic in a speech and he'll make fun of her sayin' she didn't wake up.

MRS. HALE. Well, I guess John Wright didn't wake when they 65
was slipping that rope under his neck.

MRS. PETERS. No, it's strange. It must have been done awful 66
crafty and still. They say it was such a—funny way to kill a man, rigging it all up like that.

MRS. HALE. That's just what Mr. Hale said. There was a gun in 67
the house. He says that's what he can't understand.

MRS. PETERS. Mr. Henderson said coming out that what was 68
needed for the case was a motive; something to show anger, or—sudden feeling.

MRS. HALE. [*Who is standing by the table.*] Well, I don't see any 69
signs of anger around here. [*She puts her hand on the dish towel which lies on the table, stands looking down at table, one half of which is clean, the other half messy.*] It's wiped to here. [*Makes a move as if to finish work, then turns and looks at loaf of bread outside the breadbox. Drops towel. In that voice of coming back to familiar things.*] Wonder how they are finding things upstairs. I hope she had it a little more red-up up there. You know, it seems kind of *sneaking*. Locking her up in town and then coming out here and trying to get her own house to turn against her!

MRS. PETERS. But Mrs. Hale, the law is the law. 70

MRS. HALE. I s'pose 'tis. [*Unbuttoning her coat.*] Better loosen 71
up your things, Mrs. Peters. You won't feel them when you go out.

[MRS. PETERS *takes off her fur tippet, goes to hang it on hook at back of room, stands looking at the under part of the small corner table.*]

MRS. PETERS. She was piecing a quilt. 72

[*She brings the large sewing basket and they look at the bright pieces.*]

MRS. HALE. It's log cabin pattern. Pretty, isn't it? I wonder if 73
she was goin' to quilt it or just knot it?

[*Footsteps have been heard coming down the stairs. The* SHERIFF *enters followed by* HALE *and the* COUNTY ATTORNEY.]

SHERIFF. They wonder if she was going to quilt it or just knot 74
it!

[*The men laugh; the women look abashed.*]

COUNTY ATTORNEY. [*Rubbing his hands over the stove.*] Frank's 75
fire didn't do much up there, did it? Well, let's go out to the barn and get that cleared up.

[*The men go outside.*]

MRS. HALE. [*Resentfully.*] I don't know as there's anything so 76
strange, our takin' up our time with little things while

we're waiting for them to get the evidence. [*She sits down at the big table smoothing out a block with decision.*] I don't see as it's anything to laugh about.

77 MRS. PETERS. [*Apologetically.*] Of course they've got awful important things on their minds.

[*Pulls up a chair and joins* MRS. HALE *at the table.*]

78 MRS. HALE. [*Examining another block.*] Mrs. Peters, look at this one. Here, this is the one she was working on, and look at the sewing! All the rest of it has been so nice and even. And look at this! It's all over the place! Why, it looks as if she didn't know what she was about!

[*After she has said this they look at each other, then start to glance back at the door. After an instant* MRS. HALE *has pulled at a knot and ripped the sewing.*]

79 MRS. PETERS. Oh, what are you doing, Mrs. Hale?

80 MRS. HALE. [*Mildly.*] Just pulling out a stitch or two that's not sewed very good. [*Threading a needle.*] Bad sewing always made me fidgety.

81 MRS. PETERS. [*Nervously.*] I don't think we ought to touch things.

82 MRS. HALE. I'll just finish up this end. [*Suddenly stopping and leaning forward.*] Mrs. Peters?

83 MRS. PETERS. Yes, Mrs. Hale?

84 MRS. HALE. What do you suppose she was so nervous about?

85 MRS. PETERS. Oh—I don't know. I don't know as she was nervous. I sometimes sew awful queer when I'm just tired. [MRS. HALE *starts to say something, looks at* MRS. PETERS, *then goes on sewing.*] Well, I must get these things wrapped up. They may be through sooner than we think. [*Putting apron and other things together.*] I wonder where I can find a piece of paper, and string.

86 MRS. HALE. In that cupboard, maybe.

87 MRS. PETERS. [*Looking in cupboard.*] Why, here's a birdcage. [*Holds it up.*] Did she have a bird, Mrs. Hale?

88 MRS. HALE. Why, I don't know whether she did or not—I've not been here for so long. There was a man around last year selling canaries cheap, but I don't know as she took one; maybe she did. She used to sing real pretty herself.

89 MRS. PETERS. [*Glancing around.*] Seems funny to think of a bird here. But she must have had one, or why would she have a cage? I wonder what happened to it.

90 MRS. HALE. I s'pose maybe the cat got it.

91 MRS. PETERS. No, she didn't have a cat. She's got that feeling some people have about cats—being afraid of them. My

cat got in her room and she was real upset and asked me to take it out.

MRS. HALE. My sister Bessie was like that. Queer, ain't it? 92

MRS. PETERS. [*Examining the cage.*] Why, look at this door. It's 93
broke. One hinge is pulled apart.

MRS. HALE. [*Looking too.*] Looks as if someone must have 94
been rough with it.

MRS. PETERS. Why, yes. 95
[*She brings the cage forward and puts it on the table.*]

MRS. HALE. I wish if they're going to find any evidence they'd 96
be about it. I don't like this place.

MRS. PETERS. But I'm awful glad you came with me, Mrs. Hale. 97
It would be lonesome for me sitting here alone.

MRS. HALE. It would, wouldn't it? [*Dropping her sewing.*] But I 98
tell you what I do wish, Mrs. Peters. I wish I had come over sometimes when *she* was here. I—[*Looking around the room.*]—wish I had.

MRS. PETERS. But of course you were awful busy, Mrs. 99
Hale—your house and your children.

MRS. HALE. I could've come. I stayed away because it weren't 100
cheerful—and that's why I ought to have come. I—I've never liked this place. Maybe because it's down in a hollow and you don't see the road. I dunno what it is but it's a lonesome place and always was. I wish I had come over to see Minnie Foster sometimes. I can see now—[*Shakes her head.*]

MRS. PETERS. Well, you mustn't reproach yourself, Mrs. Hale. 101
Somehow we just don't see how it is with other folks until—something comes up.

MRS. HALE. Not having children makes less work—but it 102
makes a quiet house, and Wright out to work all day, and no company when he did come in. Did you know John Wright, Mrs. Peters?

MRS. PETERS. Not to know him; I've seen him in town. They 103
say he was a good man.

MRS. HALE. Yes—good; he didn't drink, and kept his word as 104
well as most, I guess, and paid his debts. But he was a hard man, Mrs. Peters. Just to pass the time of day with him—[*Shivers.*] Like a raw wind that gets to the bone. [*Pauses, her eye falling on the cage.*] I should think she would'a wanted a bird. But what do you suppose went with it?

MRS. PETERS. I don't know, unless it got sick and died. [*She* 105
reaches over and swings the broken door, swings it again. Both women watch it.]

106 MRS. HALE. You weren't raised round here, were you? [MRS. PETERS *shakes her head.*] You didn't know—her?

107 MRS. PETERS. Not till they brought her yesterday.

108 MRS. HALE. She—come to think of it, she was kind of like a bird herself—real sweet and pretty, but kind of timid and—fluttery. How—she—did—change. [*Silence; then as if struck by a happy thought and relieved to get back to every day things.*] Tell you what, Mrs. Peters, why don't you take the quilt in with you? It might take up her mind.

109 MRS. PETERS. Why, I think that's a real nice idea, Mrs. Hale. There couldn't possibly be any objection to it, could there? Now, just what would I take? I wonder if her patches are in here—and her things.

[*They look in the sewing basket.*]

110 MRS. HALE. Here's some red. I expect this has got sewing things in it. [*Brings out a fancy box.*] What a pretty box. Looks like something somebody would give you. Maybe her scissors are in here. [*Opens box. Suddenly puts her hand to her nose.*] Why—[MRS. PETERS *bends nearer, then turns her face away.*] There's something wrapped up in this piece of silk.

111 MRS. PETERS. Why, this isn't her scissors.

112 MRS. HALE. [*Lifting the silk.*] Oh, Mrs. Peters—its—[MRS. PETERS *bends closer.*]

113 MRS. PETERS. It's the bird.

114 MRS. HALE. [*Jumping up.*] But, Mrs. Peters—look at it! Its neck! Look at its neck! It's all—other side *to*.

115 MRS. PETERS. Somebody—wrung—its—neck.

[*Their eyes meet. A look of growing comprehension, of horror. Steps are heard outside.* MRS. HALE *slips box under quilt pieces, and sinks into her chair. Enter* SHERIFF *and* COUNTY ATTORNEY. MRS. PETERS *rises.*]

116 COUNTY ATTORNEY. [*As one turning from serious things to little pleasantries.*] Well, ladies, have you decided whether she was going to quilt it or knot it?

117 MRS. PETERS. We think she was going to—knot it.

118 COUNTY ATTORNEY. Well, that's interesting, I'm sure. [*Seeing the birdcage.*] Has the bird flown?

119 MRS. HALE. [*Putting more quilt pieces over the box.*] We think the—cat got it.

120 COUNTY ATTORNEY. [*Preoccupied.*] Is there a cat?

[MRS HALE *glances in a quick covert way at* MRS. PETERS.]

121 MRS. PETERS. Well, not *now*. They're superstitious, you know. They leave.

122 COUNTY ATTORNEY. [*To* SHERIFF PETERS, *continuing an interrupted conversation.*] No sign at all of anyone having

come from the outside. Their own rope. Now let's go up again and go over it piece by piece. [*They start upstairs.*] It would have to have been someone who knew just the—[MRS. PETERS *sits down. The two women sit there not looking at one another, but as if peering into something and at the same time holding back. When they talk now it is in the manner of feeling their way over strange ground, as if afraid of what they are saying, but as if they can not help saying it.*]

MRS. HALE. She liked the bird. She was going to bury it in that 123
pretty box.

MRS. PETERS. [*In a whisper.*] When I was a girl—my kitten— 124
there was a boy took a hatchet, and before my eyes—and before I could get there—[*Covers her face an instant.*] If they hadn't held me back I would have—[*Catches herself, looks upstairs where steps are heard, falters weakly.*]—hurt him.

MRS. HALE. [*With a slow look around her.*] I wonder how it 125
would seem never to have had any children around. [*Pause.*] No, Wright wouldn't like the bird—a thing that sang. She used to sing. He killed that, too.

MRS. PETERS. [*Moving uneasily.*] We don't know who killed the 126
bird.

MRS. HALE. I knew John Wright. 127

MRS. PETERS. It was an awful thing was done in this house that 128
night, Mrs. Hale. Killing a man while he slept, slipping a rope around his neck that choked the life out of him.

MRS. HALE. His neck. Choked the life out of him. 129
[*Her hand goes out and rests on the birdcage.*]

MRS. PETERS. [*With rising voice.*] We don't know who killed 130
him. We don't *know*.

MRS. HALE. [*Her own feeling not interrupted.*] If there'd been 131
years and years of nothing, then a bird to sing to you, it would be awful—still, after the bird was still.

MRS. PETERS. [*Something within her speaking.*] I know what 132
stillness is. When we homesteaded in Dakota, and my first baby died—after he was two years old, and me with no other then—

MRS. HALE. [*Moving.*] How soon do you suppose they'll be 133
through, looking for the evidence?

MRS. PETERS. I know what stillness is. [*Pulling herself back.*] 134
The law has got to punish crime, Mrs. Hale.

MRS. HALE. [*Not as if answering that.*] I wish you'd seen Minnie 135
Foster when she wore a white dress with blue ribbons and stood up there in the choir and sang. [*A look around the room.*] Oh, I *wish* I'd come over here once in a while! That

was a crime! That was a crime! Who's going to punish that?

136 MRS. PETERS. [*Looking upstairs.*] We mustn't—take on.

137 MRS. HALE. I might have known she needed help! I know how things can be—for women. I tell you, it's queer, Mrs. Peters. We live close together and we live far apart. We all go through the same things—it's all just a different kind of the same thing. [*Brushes her eyes; noticing the bottle of fruit, reaches out for it.*] If I was you I wouldn't tell her her fruit was gone. Tell her it *ain't*. Tell her it's all right. Take this in to prove it to her. She—she may never know whether it was broke or not.

138 MRS. PETERS. [*Takes the bottle, looks about for something to wrap it in; takes petticoat from the clothes brought from the other room, very nervously begins winding this around the bottle. In a false voice.*] My, it's a good thing the men couldn't hear us. Wouldn't they just laugh! Getting all stirred up over a little thing like a—dead canary. As if that could have anything to do with—with—wouldn't they *laugh!*

[*The men are heard coming down stairs.*]

139 MRS. HALE. [*Under her breath.*] Maybe they would—maybe they wouldn't.

140 COUNTY ATTORNEY. No, Peters, it's all perfectly clear except a reason for doing it. But you know juries when it comes to women. If there was some definite thing. Something to show—something to make a story about—a thing that would connect up with this strange way of doing it—[*The women's eyes meet for an instant. Enter* HALE *from outer door.*]

141 HALE. Well, I've got the team around. Pretty cold out there.

142 COUNTY ATTORNEY. I'm going to stay here a while by myself. [*To the* SHERIFF.] You can send Frank out for me, can't you? I want to go over everything. I'm not satisfied that we can't do better.

143 SHERIFF. Do you want to see what Mrs. Peters is going to take in?

[*The* COUNTY ATTORNEY *goes to the table, picks up the apron, laughs.*]

144 COUNTY ATTORNEY. Oh, I guess they're not very dangerous things the ladies have picked out. [*Moves a few things about, disturbing the quilt pieces which cover the box. Steps back.*] No, Mrs. Peters doesn't need supervising. For that matter, a sheriff's wife is married to the law. Ever think of it that way, Mrs. Peters?

145 MRS. PETERS. Not—just that way.

146 SHERIFF. [*Chuckling.*] Married to the law. [*Moves toward the*

other room.] I just want you to come in here a minute, George. We ought to take a look at these windows.

COUNTY ATTORNEY. [*Scoffingly.*] Oh, windows! 147

SHERIFF. We'll be right out, Mr. Hale. 148

[HALE *goes outside. The* SHERIFF *follows the* COUNTY ATTORNEY *into the other room. Then* MRS. HALE *rises, hands tight together, looking intensely at* MRS. PETERS, *whose eyes make a slow turn, finally meeting* MRS. HALE*'s. A moment* MRS. HALE *holds her, then her own eyes point the way to where the box is concealed. Suddenly* MRS. PETERS *throws back quilt pieces and tries to put the box in the bag she is wearing. It is too big. She opens box, starts to take bird out, cannot touch it, goes to pieces, stands there helpless. Sound of a knob turning in the other room.* MRS. HALE *snatches the box and puts it in the pocket of her big coat. Enter* COUNTY ATTORNEY *and* SHERIFF.]

COUNTY ATTORNEY. [*Facetiously.*] Well, Henry, at least we found out that she was not going to quilt it. She was going to—what is it you call it, ladies? 149

MRS. HALE. [*Her hand against her pocket.*] We call it—knot it, Mr. Henderson. 150

CURTAIN

Diane Wakoski

Belly Dancer

Diane Wakoski (born 1937) has spent much of her life in New York, though she was born in Whittier, California, and educated at Berkeley. She now teaches at Michigan State University. This poem is from Trilogy *(1966), one of several collections of her poetry.*

Can these movements which move themselves
be the substance of my attraction? 1
Where does this thin green silk come from that covers my
  body?
Surely any woman wearing such fabrics
would move her body just to feel them touching every part
  of her.

2 Yet most of the women frown, or look away, or laugh stiffly.
They are afraid of these materials and these movements in some way.
The psychologists would say they are afraid of themselves, somehow.
Perhaps awakening too much desire—
that their men could never satisfy?

3 So they keep themselves laced and buttoned and made up
in hopes that the framework will keep them stiff enough not to feel
the whole register.
In hopes that they will not have to experience that unquenchable desire for rhythm and contact.

4 If a snake glided across this floor
most of them would faint or shrink away.
Yet that movement could be their own.
That smooth movement frightens them—
awakening ancestors and relatives to the tips of the arms and toes.

5 So my bare feet
and my thin green silks
my bells and finger cymbals
offend them—frighten their old-young bodies.
While the men simper and leer—
glad for the vicarious experience and exercise.
They do not realize how I scorn them:
or how I dance for their frightened,
unawakened, sweet
women.

Jamaica Kincaid

Girl

Born in St. Johns, on the Caribbean island of Antigua (the subject and setting of her 1988 book Small Place*), Jamaica Kincaid now lives with her family in Vermont. She is the author of a number of books of fiction, most of them derived from her own personal experiences, including* At the Bottom of the River *(1983), which contains the following chapter, titled "Girl." "Girl" also stands quite well on its own, however: Indeed, it first* *appeared on its own in the pages of* The New Yorker, *a monthly review of arts, letters, and public affairs that has a reputation for publishing outstanding writing and writers.*

Wash the white clothes on Monday and put them on the stone heap; wash the color clothes on Tuesday and put them on the clothesline to dry; don't walk barehead in the hot sun; cook pumpkin fritters in very hot sweet oil; soak your little clothes right after you take them off; when buying cotton to make yourself a nice blouse, be sure that it doesn't have gum on it, because that way it won't hold up well after a wash; soak salt fish overnight before you cook it; is it true that you sing benna in Sunday school?; always eat your food in such a way that it won't turn someone else's stomach; on Sundays try to walk like a lady and not like the slut you are so bent on becoming; don't sing benna in Sunday school; you mustn't speak to wharf-rat boys, not even to give directions; don't eat fruits on the street—flies will follow you; *but I don't sing benna on Sundays at all and never in Sunday school*; this is how to sew on a button; this is how to make a buttonhole for the button you have just sewed on; this is how to hem a dress when you see the hem coming down and so to prevent yourself from looking like the slut I know you are so bent on becoming; this is how you iron your father's khaki shirt so that it doesn't have a crease; this is how you iron your father's khaki pants so that they don't have a crease; this is how you grow okra—far from the house, because okra tree harbors red ants; when you are growing dasheen, make sure it gets plenty of water or else it makes your throat itch when you are eating it; this is how you sweep a corner; this is how you sweep a whole house; this is how you sweep a yard; this is how you smile to someone you don't like too much; this how you smile to someone you don't like at all; this is how you smile to someone you like completely; this is how you set a table for tea; this is how you set a table for dinner; this is how you set a table for dinner with an important guest; this is how you set a table for lunch; this is how you set a table for breakfast; this is how to behave in the presence of men who don't know you very well, and this way they won't recognize immediately the slut I have warned you against becoming; be sure to wash every day, even if it is with your own spit; don't squat down to play marbles—you are not a boy, you know; don't pick people's flowers—you might catch something; don't throw stones at blackbirds, because it might not be a blackbird at all; 1

this is how to make a bread pudding; this is how to make doukona; this is how to make pepper pot; this is how to make a good medicine for a cold; this is how to make a good medicine to throw away a child before it even becomes a child; this is how to catch a fish; this is how to throw back a fish you don't like, and that way something bad won't fall on you; this is how to bully a man; this is how a man bullies you; this is how to love a man, and if this doesn't work there are other ways, and if they don't work don't feel too bad about giving up; this is how to spit up in the air if you feel like it and this is how to move quick so that it doesn't fall on you; this is how to make ends meet; always squeeze bread to make sure it's fresh; *but what if the baker won't let me feel the bread?*; you mean to say that after all you are really going to be the kind of woman who the baker won't let near the bread?

Judy Syfers Brady

Why I Want a Wife

Judy Syfers Brady (born in 1937), active in support of women's causes, was educated at the University of Iowa. She now lives in San Francisco. This well-known essay appeared in the very first issue of Ms. *in 1972.*

1 I belong to that classification of people known as wives. I am A Wife. And, not altogether incidentally, I am a mother.

2 Not too long ago a male friend of mine appeared on the scene fresh from a recent divorce. He had one child, who is, of course, with his ex-wife. He is looking for another wife. As I thought about him while I was ironing one evening, it suddenly occurred to me that I, too, would like to have a wife. Why do I want a wife?

3 I would like to go back to school so that I can become economically independent, support myself, and, if need be, support those dependent upon me. I want a wife who will work and send me to school. And while I am going to school I want a wife to take care of my children. I want a wife to keep track of the children's doctor and dentist appointments. And to keep track of mine, too. I want a wife to make

sure my children eat properly and are kept clean. I want a wife who will wash the children's clothes and keep them mended. I want a wife who is a good nurturant attendant to my children, who arranges for their schooling, makes sure that they have an adequate social life with their peers, takes them to the park, the zoo, etc. I want a wife who takes care of the children when they are sick, a wife who arranges to be around when the children need special care, because, of course I cannot miss classes at school. My wife must arrange to lose time at work and not lose the job. It may mean a small cut in my wife's income from time to time, but I guess I can tolerate that. Needless to say, my wife will arrange and pay for the care of the children while my wife is working.

I want a wife who will take care of *my* physical needs. I 4
want a wife who will keep my house clean. A wife who will pick up after my children, a wife who will pick up after me. I want a wife who will keep my clothes clean, ironed, mended, replaced when need be, and who will see to it that my personal things are kept in their proper place so that I can find what I need the minute I need it. I want a wife who cooks the meals, a wife who is a *good* cook. I want a wife who will plan the menus, do the necessary grocery shopping, prepare the meals, serve them pleasantly, and then do the cleaning up while I do my studying. I want a wife who will care for me when I am sick and sympathize with my pain and loss of time from school. I want a wife to go along when our family takes a vacation so that someone can continue to care for me and my children when I need a rest and a change of scene.

I want a wife who will not bother me with rambling com- 5
plaints about a wife's duties. But I want a wife who will listen to me when I feel the need to explain a rather difficult point I have come across in my course of studies. I want a wife who will type my papers for me when I have written them.

I want a wife who will take care of the details of my social 6
life. When my wife and I are invited out by my friends, I want a wife who will take care of the babysitting arrangements. When I meet people at school that I like and want to entertain, I want a wife who will have the house clean, will prepare a special meal, serve it to me and my friends, and not interrupt when I talk about things that interest me and my friends. I want a wife who will have arranged that the children are fed and ready for bed before my guests arrive so that the children do not bother us. I want a wife who takes care of the needs of my guests so that they feel comfortable, who makes sure that they have an ashtray, that they are passed the hors d'oeuvres,

that they are offered a second helping of the food, that their wine glasses are replenished when necessary, that their coffee is served to them as they like it. And I want a wife who knows that sometimes I need a night out by myself.

7 I want a wife who is sensitive to my sexual needs, a wife who makes love passionately and eagerly when I feel like it, a wife who makes sure that I am satisfied. And, of course, I want a wife who will not demand sexual attention when I am not in the mood for it. I want a wife who assumes the complete responsibility for birth control, because I do not want more children. I want a wife who will remain sexually faithful to me so that I do not have to clutter up my intellectual life with jealousies. And I want a wife who understands that *my* sexual needs may entail more than strict adherence to monogamy. I must, after all, be able to relate to people as fully as possible.

8 If, by chance, I find another person more suitable as a wife than the wife I already have, I want the liberty to replace my present wife with another one. Naturally, I will expect a fresh, new life; my wife will take the children and be solely responsible for them so that I am left free.

9 When I am through with school and have a job, I want my wife to quit working and remain at home so that my wife can more fully and completely take care of a wife's duties.

10 My God, who *wouldn't* want a wife?

Kurt Fernsler

Why I Want a Husband

Kurt Fernsler (born in 1969) grew up in State College, Pennsylvania, and graduated in 1992 from Penn State with a degree in finance. He is planning a career in law. The following essay was written in 1988 for a class of fellow student writers, all of whom had read Judy Syfers' essay "Why I Want a Wife."

1 I am not a husband. I am, however, a male, and have a father who is a husband. I am also fortunate enough to know a great many men who are husbands and will probably become a husband myself someday.

I recently read Judy Syfers' essay "Why I Want a Wife" and decided a reply was in order. Though not the most qualified author for such an undertaking, I felt it my duty to make an effort. For I now realize that just as Judy Syfers wants a wife, I want a husband. 2

I want a husband who brings home the bacon. I mean really rakes in the bucks. After all, I certainly can't have anything less than the best. My husband must be driven to succeed; he must climb the corporate ladder quickly and efficiently. He must make every payroll and meet every deadline. Anything less would be completely unacceptable. 3

And I want a husband who bears the burden of being the wage earner without complaint. He must deal with the stresses of his job without bringing his problems home from the office so as not to upset me. I want a husband who deals patiently and lovingly with screaming, fighting kids even after a tough day. I want a husband who, for fairness sake, does the dishes (even sometimes the wash) for me so that I can put my feet up after dinner. And, I want a husband who will leave the office during a busy day of work to check on a sick child while I'm out on the town shopping. 4

I want a husband who will gladly eat cold leftovers for a week while I am relaxing with a friend in sunny California. My husband will have to sit through boring PTA meetings and ice-cream socials after a rough day at work. My husband must, of course, be courteous and kind to meddling gossiping friends. (After all, I am entitled to my friends, too.) I want a husband who listens patiently to my panic about the oversudsing washing machine while he silently sweats about the thousands of dollars he just borrowed from the bank. 5

I want a husband who keeps the house and lawn looking beautiful in his spare time. He must be willing to spend his Saturday afternoons weeding my garden, and he must give up that tee time with the guys when I decide the grass is a little too long. I want one who makes sure the car is fixed (engines are so complicated and dirty!) and takes care of all the "little" chores around the house—raking leaves in the fall, shoveling snow in the winter, painting the house in spring. And I want one who will take out the garbage. When he's done with these chores, he can take the kids to the zoo or the park or the ballgame because these are things a father should share with his children. 6

I want a husband who gladly pays for his wife's shopping sprees without ever asking her where all the money goes. He will understand that women need to spend time with their 7 friends. I want a husband who will watch the kids on vacation so my wife can shop and work on her tan. (He must accept the fact that after traveling so many miles, a shopping trip is the only way to wind down.)

8 And I want my husband to be completely receptive to my sexual needs. He must completely understand when I have a "headache." He will be sensitive to my problems and respect my private life. I want a husband who understands that I must have my freedom. He will be ready to accept the possibility that I may need to "find myself" and may walk out at any time. He will understand, of course, that I will take half of everything we own. He would keep the kids, however, because I would need to start a brand new life for myself.

9 I want a husband who will do all these things for me forever or until I decide we have enough money to retire, or until he has a heart attack and collapses in a heap. Yes, I want a husband.

10 How could anyone live without one?

Susan Brownmiller

Emotion

Susan Brownmiller is a journalist, novelist, and women's rights activist. Her book Against Our Will: Men, Women, and Rape *was published in 1975. She published* Femininity *in 1984; the following selection is excerpted from it.* Femininity *attempts to define the term and to place it in historical perspective. (For another example of Brownmiller's work,* *see page 580.**)*

1 A 1970 landmark study, known in the field as *Broverman and Broverman,* reported that "Cries very easily" was rated by a group of professional psychologists as a highly feminine trait. "Very emotional," "Very excitable in a minor crisis" and "Feeling easily hurt" were additional characteristics on the femininity scale. So were "Very easily influenced," "Very subjective," "Unable to separate feelings from ideas," "Very

illogical" and "Very sneaky." As might be expected, masculinity was defined by opposing, sturdier values: "Very direct," "Very logical," "Can make decisions easily," "Never cries." The importance of *Broverman and Broverman* was not in nailing down a set of popular assumptions and conventional perceptions—masculine-feminine scales were well established in the literature of psychology as a means of ascertaining normality and social adjustment—but in the authors' observation that stereotypic femininity was a grossly negative assessment of the female sex and, furthermore, that many so-called feminine traits ran counter to clinical descriptions of maturity and mental health.

Emotional femininity is a tough nut to crack, impossible 2
to quantify yet hard to ignore. As the task of conforming to a specified physical design is a gender mission that few women care to resist, conforming to a prepackaged emotional design is another imperative task of gender. To satisfy a societal need for sexual clarification, and to justify second-class status, an emblematic constellation of inner traits, as well as their outward manifestations, has been put forward historically by some of the world's great thinkers as proof of the "different" feminine nature.

"Woman," wrote Aristotle, "is more compassionate than 3
man, more easily moved to tears. At the same time, she is more jealous, more querulous, more apt to scold and to strike. She is, furthermore, more prone to despondency and less hopeful than man, more void of shame or self-respect, more false of speech, more deceptive and of more retentive memory. She is also more wakeful, more shrinking, more difficult to rouse to action, and she requires a smaller amount of nutriment."

Addressing a suffrage convention in 1855, Ralph Waldo 4
Emerson had kindlier words on the nature of woman, explicating the nineteenth-century view that her difference was one of superior virtue. "Women," he extolled, "are the civilizers of mankind. What is civilization? I answer, the power of good women. . . . The starry crown of woman is in the power of her affection and sentiment, and the infinite enlargements to which they lead." (In less elevated language, the Emersonian view was perhaps what President Reagan had in mind when he cheerfully stated, "Why, if it wasn't for women, we men would still be walking around in skin suits carrying clubs.")

A clarification is in order. Are women believed to possess 5 a wider or deeper emotional range, a greater sensitivity, say, to the beauties of nature or to the infinite complexities of feeling? Any male poet, artist, actor, marine biologist or backpacker would strenuously object. Rather, it is commonly agreed that women are tossed and buffeted on the high seas of emotion, while men have the tough mental fiber, the intellectual muscle, to stay in control. As for the civilizing influence, surely something more is meant than sophistication, culture and taste, using the correct fork or not belching after dinner. The idealization of emotional femininity, as women prefer to see themselves affirmed, is more exquisitely romantic: a finer temperament in a more fragile vessel, a gentler nature ruled by a twin need to love and to be protected: one who appreciates—without urgency to create—good art, music, literature and other public expressions of the private soul; a flame-bearer of spiritual values by whose shining example the men of the world are inspired to redemption and to accomplish great things.

6 Two thousand years ago *Dominus flevit,* Jesus wept as he beheld Jerusalem. "Men ceased weeping," proposed Simone de Beauvoir, "when it became unfashionable." Now it is Mary, *Mater Dolorosa,* who weeps with compassion for mankind. In mystical visions, in the reliquaries of obscure churches and miraculous shrines, the figure of the Virgin, the world's most feminine woman, has been seen to shed tears. There are still extant cultures in which men are positively lachrymose (and kissy-kissy) with no seeming detriment to their masculine image, but the Anglo-Saxon tradition, in particular, requires keeping a stiff upper lip. Weeping, keening women shrouded in black are an established fixture in mourning rites in many nations. Inconsolable grief is a feminine role, at least in its unquiet representations. In what has become a stock photograph in the national news magazines, women weep for the multitudes when national tragedy (a terrorist bombing, an air crash, an assassination) strikes.

7 The catharsis of tears is encouraged in women—"There, there, now, let it all out"—while a man may be told to get a grip on himself, or to gulp down a double Scotch. Having "a good cry" in order to feel better afterward is not usually recommended as a means of raising the spirits of men, for the cathartic relief of succumbing to tears would be tempered by the uncomfortable knowledge that the loss of control was hardly manly. In the 1972 New Hampshire

Presidential primary, Senator Edmund Muskie, then the Democratic front-runner, committed political suicide when he publicly cried during a campaign speech. Muskie had been talking about some harsh press comments directed at his wife when the tears filled his eyes. In retrospect it was his watershed moment: Could a man who became tearful when the going got rough in a political campaign be expected to face the Russians? To a nation that had delighted in the hatless, overcoatless macho posturing of John F. Kennedy, the military successes of General Ike and the irascible outbursts of "Give 'em hell" Harry Truman, the answer was No. Media accounts of Muskie's all-too-human tears were merciless. In the summer of 1983 the obvious and unshakable grief displayed by Israeli prime minister Menachem Begin after the death of his wife was seized upon by the Israeli and American press as evidence that a tough old warrior had lost his grip. Sharing this perception of his own emotional state, perhaps, Begin shortly afterward resigned.

Expressions of anger and rage are not a disqualifying 8
factor in the masculine disposition. Anger in men is often understood, or excused, as reasonable or just. Anger in men may even be cast in a heroic mold—a righteous response to an insult against honor that will preclude a manly, aggressive act. Because competitive acts of personal assertion, not to mention acts of outright physical aggression, are known to flow from angry feelings, anger becomes the most unfeminine emotion a woman can show.

Anger in a woman isn't "nice." A woman who seethes with 9
anger is "unattractive." An angry woman is hard, mean and nasty; she is unreliably, unprettily out of control. Her face contorts into unpleasant lines: the jaw juts, the eyes are narrowed, the teeth are bared. Anger is a violent snarl and a hostile threat, a declaration of war. The endless forbearance demanded of women, described as the feminine virtue of patience, prohibits an angry response. Picture a charming old-fashioned scene: The mistress of the house bends low over her needlework, cross-stitching her sampler: "Patience is a virtue, possess it if you can/Seldom seen in women, never seen in man." Does the needle jab through the cloth in uncommon fury? Does she prick her thumb in frustration?

Festering without a permissible release, women's undis- 10
solved anger has been known to seep out in petty, mean-spirited ways—fits of jealousy, fantasies of retaliation, unholy plots of revenge. Perhaps, after all, it is safer to cry.

"Woman's aptitude for facile tears," wrote Beauvoir, "comes largely from the fact that her life is built upon a foundation of impotent revolt."*

11 Beauvoir hedged her bet, for her next words were these: "It is also doubtless true that physiologically she has less nervous control than a man." Is this "doubtless true," or is it more to the point, as Beauvoir continues, that "her education has taught her to let herself go more readily"?

12 Infants and children cry out of fear, frustration, discomfort, hunger, anxiety at separation from a parent, and rage. Surveying all available studies of crying newborns and little children, psychologists Eleanor Maccoby and Carol Jacklin found no appreciable sexual difference. If teenage girls and adult women are known to cry more than men—and there is no reason to question the popular wisdom in this regard—should the endocrine changes of adolescence be held to account? What of those weepy "blue days" of premenstrual tension that genuinely afflict so many women? What about mid-life depression, known in some circles as "the feminine malady"? Are these conditions, as some men propose, a sign of "raging hormonal imbalance" that incapacitates the cool, logical functioning of the human brain? Or does feminine depression result, as psychiatrist Willard Gaylin suggests, when confidence in one's coping mechanism is lost?

13 Belief in a biological basis for the instability of female emotions has a notorious history in the development of medical science. Hippocrates the physician held that hysteria was caused by a wandering uterus that remained unfulfilled. Discovery in the seventeenth century that the thyroid gland was larger in women inspired that proposition that the thyroid's function was to give added grace to the feminine neck, but other beliefs maintained that the gland served to flush impurities from the blood before it reached the brain. A larger thyroid "was necessary to guard the female system from the influence of the more numerous causes of irritation and vexation" to which the sex was unfortunately disposed. Nineteenth-century doctors averred that womb-related disorders were the cause of such female complaints as "nervous prostration." For those without

* "Facile" is the English translators' match for the French *facile,* more correctly rendered as "easy." Beauvoir did not mean to ascribe a stereotype superficiality to women in her remark.

money to seek out a physician's care, Lydia E. Pinkham's Vegetable Compound and other patent medicines were available to give relief. In the 1940s and '50s, prefrontal lobotomy was briefly and tragically in vogue for a variety of psychiatric disorders, particularly among women, since the surgical procedure had a flattening effect on raging emotions. Nowadays Valium appears to suffice.

Beginning in earnest in the 1960s, one line of research has 14
attempted to isolate premenstrual tension as a contributing cause of accidents, suicide, admittance to mental hospitals and the commission of violent crimes. Mood swings, irritability and minor emotional upsets probably do lead to more "acting out" by females at a cyclical time in the month, but what does this prove beyond the increasingly accepted fact that the endocrine system has a critical influence on the human emotional threshold? Suicide, violent crime and dangerous psychiatric disorders are statistically four to nine times more prevalent in men. Should we theorize, then, that "raging hormonal imbalance" is a chronic, year-round condition in males? A disqualifying factor? By any method of calculation and for whatever reason—hormonal effects, the social inhibitions of femininity, the social pleasure of the masculine role, or all of these—the female gender is indisputably less prone to irrational, antisocial behavior. The price of inhibited anger and a nonviolent temperament may well be a bucketful of tears.

Like the emotion of anger, exulting in personal victory is 15
a harshly unfeminine response. Of course, good winners of either sex are supposed to display some degree of sportsmanlike humility, but the merest hint of gloating triumph—"Me, me, me, I did it!"—is completely at odds with the modesty and deference expected of women and girls. Arm raised in a winner's salute, the ritualized climax of a prizefight, wrestling match or tennis championship, is unladylike, to say the least. The powerful feeling that victory engenders, the satisfaction of climbing to the top of the heap or clinching a deal, remains an inappropriate emotion. More appropriate to femininity are the predictable tears of the new Miss America as she accepts her crown and scepter. Trembling lip and brimming eyes suggest a Cinderella who has stumbled upon good fortune through unbelievable, undeserved luck. At her moment of victory the winner of America's favorite pageant appears overcome, rather than superior in any way. A Miss America who raised her scepter

high like a trophy would not be in keeping with the feminine ideal.

16 The maidenly blush, that staple of the nineteenth-century lady's novel, was an excellent indicator of innocent virginal shyness in contrast to the worldliness and sophistication of men. In an age when a variety of remarks, largely sexual, were considered uncouth and not for the ears of virtuous women, the feminine blush was an expected response. On the other side of the ballroom, men never blushed, at least not in romantic fiction, since presumably they were knowledgeable and sexually practiced. Lowered eyes, heightened color, breathlessness and occasional swooning were further proofs of a fragile and innocent feminine nature that required protection in the rough, indelicate masculine world. (In the best-selling Harlequin and Silhouette books devoured by romance addicts who need the quick fix, the maidenly blush is alive and well.)

17 In a new age of relative sexual freedom, or permissiveness, at any rate, squeals and moans replace the blush and the downcast eye. Screaming bobbysoxers who fainted in the aisle at the Paramount Theater when a skinny young Frank Sinatra crooned his love ballads during the 1940s (reportedly, the first wave of fainting girls was staged by promoters) presaged the whimpering orgasmic ecstasy at rock concerts in huge arenas today. By contrast, young men in the audience automatically rise to their feet and whistle and shout when the band starts to play, but they seldom appear overcome.

18 Most emphatically, feminine emotion has gotten louder. The ribald squeal of the stereotypic serving wench in Elizabethan times, a supposed indicator of loose, easy ways, seems to have lost its lower-class stigma. One byproduct of our media-obsessed society, in which privacy is considered a quaint and rather old-fashioned human need, has been the reproduction of the unmistakable sounds of female orgasm on a record (Donna Summer's "Love to Love You Baby," among other hits). More than commercialization of sex is operative here. Would the sounds of male orgasm suffice for a recording, and would they be unmistakable? Although I have seen no studies on this interesting sex difference, I believe it can be said that most women do vocalize more loudly and uncontrollably than men in the throes of sexual passion. Is this response physiological, compensatory or merely symptomatic of the feminine mission to display

one's feelings (and the corresponding masculine mission to keep their feelings under control)?

Feminine emotion specializes in sentimentality, empathy 19
and admissions of vulnerability—three characteristics that most men try to avoid. Linking these traits to female anatomy became an article of faith in the Freudian school. Erik Erikson, for one, spoke of an "inner space" (he meant the womb) that yearns for fulfillment through maternal love. Helene Deutsch, the grande dame of Freudian feminine psychology, spoke of psychic acceptance of hurt and pain; menstrual cramps, defloration and the agonies of childbirth called for a masochistic nature she believed was innate.

Love of babies, any baby and all babies, not only one's 20
own, is a celebrated and anticipated feminine emotion, and a woman who fails to ooh and ahh at the snapshot of a baby or cuddle a proffered infant in her arms is instantly suspect. Evidence of a maternal nature, of a certain innate competence when handling a baby or at least some indication of maternal longing, becomes a requirement of gender. Women with no particular feeling for babies are extremely reluctant to admit their private truth, for the entire weight of woman's place in the biological division of labor, not to mention the glorification of motherhood as woman's greatest and only truly satisfactory role, has kept alive the belief that all women yearn to fulfill their biological destiny out of a deep emotional need. That a sizable number of mothers have no genuine aptitude for the job is verified by the records of hospitals, family courts and social agencies where cases of battery and neglect are duly entered—and perhaps also by the characteristic upper-class custom of leaving the little ones to the care of the nanny. But despite this evidence that day-to-day motherhood is not a suitable or a stimulating occupation for all, the myth persists that a woman who prefers to remain childless must be heartless or selfish or less than complete.

Books have been written on maternal guilt and its exploi- 21
tation, on the endemic feeling that whatever a mother does, her loving care may be inadequate or wrong, with consequences that can damage a child for life. Trends in child care (bottle feeding, demand feeding, not picking up the crying baby, delaying the toilet training or giving up an outside job to devote one's entire time to the family) illuminate the fear of maternal inadequacy as well as the variability or "expert" opinion in each generation. Advertising copywriters success-

fully manipulate this feminine fear when they pitch their clients' products. A certain cereal, one particular brand of packaged white bread, must be bought for the breakfast table or else you have failed to love your child sufficiently and denied him the chance to "build a strong body twelve ways." Until the gay liberation movement began to speak for itself, it was a commonplace of psychiatric wisdom that a mother had it within her power to destroy her son's heterosexual adjustment by failing to cut his baby curls, keep him away from dance class or encourage his interest in sports.

22 A requirement of femininity is that a woman devote her life to love—to mother love, to romantic love, to religious love, to amorphous, undifferentiated caring. The territory of the heart is admittedly a province that is open to all, but women alone are expected to make an obsessional career of its exploration, to find whatever adventure, power, fulfillment or tragedy that life has to offer within its bounds. There is no question that a woman is apt to feel most feminine, most confident of her interior gender makeup, when she is reliably within some stage of love—even the girlish crush or the stage of unrequited love or a broken heart. Men have suffered for love, and men have accomplished great feats in the name of love, but what man has ever felt at the top of his masculine form when he is lovesick or suffering from heartache?

23 Gloria Steinem once observed that the heart is a sex-distinctive symbol of feminine vulnerability in the marketing of fashion. Heart-shaped rings and heart-shaped gold pendants and heart-shaped frames on red plastic sunglasses announce an addiction to love that is beyond the pale of appropriate design for masculine ornamentation. (A man does not wear his heart on his sleeve.) The same observation applies a little less stringently to flowers.

24 Rare is the famous girl singer, whatever her age, of popular music (blues, country, Top Forty, disco or rock) who is not chiefly identified with some expression of love, usually its downside. Torchy bittersweet ballads and sad, suffering laments mixed with vows of eternal fidelity to the rotten bastard who done her wrong communicate the feminine message of love at any cost. Almost unique to the female singer, I think, is the poignant anthem of battered survival, from Fanny Brice's "My Man" to Gloria Gaynor's "I Will Survive," that does not quite shut the door on further emotional abuse if her man should return.

25 But the point is not emotional abuse (except in extreme, aberrant cases); the point is feeling. Women are instructed

from childhood to be keepers of the heart, keepers of the sentimental memory. In diaries, packets of old love letters and family albums, in slender books of poetry in which a flower is pressed, a woman's emotional history is preserved. Remembrance of things past—the birthday, the anniversary, the death—is a feminine province. In the social division of labor, the wife is charged with maintaining the emotional connection, even with the husband's side of the family. Her thoughtful task is to make the long-distance call, select the present and write the thank-you note (chores that secretaries are asked to do by their bosses). Men are busy; they move forward. A woman looks back. It is significant that in the Biblical parable it was Lot's wife who looked back for one last precious glimpse of their city, their home, their past (and was turned into a pillar of salt).

Love confirms the feminine psyche. A celebrated differ- 26
ence between men and women (either women's weakness or women's strength, depending on one's values) is the obstinate reluctance, the emotional inability of women to separate sex from love. Understandably. Love makes the world go round, and women are supposed to get dizzy—to rise, to fall, to feel alive in every pore, to be undone. In place of a suitable attachment, an unlikely or inaccessible one may have to do. But more important, sex for a woman, even in an age of accessible contraception, has reproductive consequences that render the act a serious affair. Casual sex can have a most uncasual resolution. If a young girl thinks of love and marriage while a boy thinks of getting laid, her emotional commitment is rooted not only in her different upbringing but in her reproductive biology as well. Love, then, can become an alibi for thoughtless behavior, as it may also become an identity, or a distraction, à la Emma Bovary or Anna Karenina, from the frustrations of a limited life.*

Christian houses of worship, especially in poor neighbor- 27
hoods, are filled disproportionately by women. This phenomenon may not be entirely attributable to the historic

* The overwhelming influence of feminine love is frequently offered as a mitigating explanation by women who do unfeminine things. Elizabeth Bentley, the "Red Spy Queen" of the cold war Fifties, attributed her illegal activities to her passion for the Russian master spy Jacob Golos. Judith Coplon's defense for stealing Government documents was love for another Russian, Valentin Gubichev. More recently, Jean Harris haplessly failed to convince a jury that her love for "Scarsdale diet" Doctor Herman Tarnower was so great that she could not possibly have intended to kill him.

role of the Catholic and Protestant religions in encouraging the public devotions of women (which Judaism and Islam did not), or because women have more time for prayer, or because in the Western world they are believed to be more religious by nature. Another contributing factor may be that the central article of Christian faith, "Jesus loves you," has particular appeal for the gender that defines itself through loving emotions.

28 Women's special interest in the field of compassion is catered to and promoted. Hollywood "weepies," otherwise known as four-handkerchief movies, were big-studio productions that were tailored to bring in female box-office receipts. Columns of advice to the lovelorn, such as the redoubtable "Dear Dorothy Dix" and the current "Dear Abby," were by tradition a woman's slot on daily newspapers, along with the coverage of society births and weddings, in the days when females were as rare in a newsroom as they were in a coal mine. In the heyday of the competitive tabloids, sob-sister journalism, that newsroom term for a human-interest story told with heart-wrenching pathos (usually by a tough male reporter who had the formula down pat), was held in contempt by those on the paper who covered the "hard stuff" of politics, crime and war. (Nathanael West's famous antihero labored under the byline of Miss Lonelyhearts.) Despite its obvious audience appeal, "soft stuff" was, and is, on the lower rungs of journalism—trivial, weak and unmanly.

29 In Government circles during the Vietnam war, it was considered a sign of emotional softness, of lily-livered liberals and nervous nellies, to suggest that Napalmed babies, fire-bombed villages and defoliated crops were reason enough to pull out American forces. The peace movement, went the charge, was composed of cowards and fuzzy thinkers. Suspicion of an unmanly lack of hard practical logic always haunts those men who espouse peace and nonviolence, but women, the weaker sex, are permitted a certain amount of emotional leeway. Feminine logic, after all, is reputedly governed by the heartstrings. Compassion and sentiment are the basis for its notorious "subjectivity" compared to the "objectivity" of men who use themselves as the objective standard.

30 As long as the social division of labor ordains that women should bear the chief emotional burden of caring for human life from the cradle to the grave while men may demonstrate their dimorphic difference through competitive acts of

physical aggression, emblematic compassion and fear of violence are compelling reasons for an aversion to war and other environmental hazards. When law and custom deny the full range of public expression and economic opportunity that men claim for themselves, a woman must place much of her hopes, her dreams, her feminine identity and her social importance in the private sphere of personal relations, in the connective tissue of marriage, family, friendship and love. In a world out of balance, where men are taught to value toughness and linear vision as masculine traits that enable them to think strategically from conquest to conquest, from campaign to campaign without looking back, without getting sidetracked by vulnerable feelings, there is, and will be, an emotional difference between the sexes, a gender gap that may even appear on a Gallup poll.

If a true shape could emerge from the shadows of historic 31
oppression, would the gender-specific experience of being female still suggest a range of perceptions and values that differ appreciably from those of men? It would be premature to offer an answer. Does a particular emotion ultimately resist separation from its historic deployment in the sexual balance of power? In the way of observation, this much can be said: The entwining of anatomy, history and culture presents such a persuasive emotional argument for a "different nature" that even the best aspects of femininity collaborate in its perpetuation.

Robert Bly

Naïveté

The following article is an excerpt from Robert Bly's 1990 best-seller Iron John *(subtitled* A Book about Men*). In the process of offering an elaborate explanation of each phase of a Grimm fairy tale called "Iron John"—the story of a wild man imprisoned in a cage who escapes and teaches a young boy the secrets of manhood—the book discusses changes in the modern American view of manhood and attempts to redefine the world of work and the whole notion of "masculinity." Bly (born 1926) is a native and resident of rural Minnesota who attempts in his poetry to articulate archetypal myths, to celebrate primal* *emotions, and to explore relations among people and the elemental forces of nature. His many books of poetry have established him as a major American poetic voice.*

1 We see more and more passivity in men, but also more and more naïveté. The naïve man feels a pride in being attacked. If his wife or girlfriend, furious, shouts that he is "chauvinist," a "sexist," a "man," he doesn't fight back, but just takes it. He opens his shirt so that she can see more clearly where to put the lances. He ends with three or four javelins sticking out of his body, and blood running all over the floor. If he were a bullfighter, he would remain where he was when the bull charges, would not even wave his shirt or turn his body, and the horn would go directly in. After each fight friends have to carry him on their shoulders to the hospital.

2 He feels, as he absorbs attacks, that he is doing the brave and advanced thing; he will surely be able to recover somewhere in isolation. A woman, so mysterious and superior, has given him some attention. To be attacked by someone you love—what could be more wonderful? Perhaps the wounds may pay for some chauvinistic act, and so allow him to remain special still longer.

3 The naïve man will also be proud that he can pick up the pain of others. He particularly picks up women's pain. When at five years old he sat at the kitchen table, his mother may have confided her suffering to him, and he felt flattered to be told of such things by a grown-up, even if it showed his father up poorly. He becomes attracted later to women who "share their pain." His specialness makes him, in his own eyes, something of a doctor. He is often more in touch with women's pain than with his own, and he will offer to carry a woman's pain before he checks with his own heart to see if this labor is proper in the situation. In general, I think each gender drops its own pain when it tries to carry the pain of the other gender. I don't mean that men shouldn't listen. But hearing a woman's pain and carrying it are two different things. Women have tried for centuries to carry men's pain, and it hasn't worked well.

4 The word special is important to the naïve man, and he has special relationships with certain people. We all have some special relationships, but he surrounds the special person with a cloying kind of goodwill. The relationship is so special that he never examines the dark side of the

person, which could be a son, a daughter, a wife, a male friend, a girlfriend. He accepts responses that are way off, conspires somehow with their dark side. "Some people are special," he says.

We might say that if he doesn't investigate his son's or 5
daughter's dark side, perhaps they will not investigate his. He may also have a secret and special relationship with a wounded little boy inside himself. If so, he won't challenge the little boy, nor will he point out his self-pity, nor actually listen to the boy either. He will simply let the boy run his life.

Sincerity is a big thing with him. He assumes that the 6
person, stranger, or lover he talks with is straightforward, goodwilled, and speaking from the heart. He agrees with Rousseau and Whitman that each person is basically noble by nature, and only twisted a little by institutions. He puts a lot of stock in his own sincerity. He believes in it, as if it were a horse or a city wall. He assumes that it will, and should, protect him from consequences that fall to less open people. He may say, "It's true that I betrayed you with your best friend while you were away, and even after you were back, but I was frank with you and told about it. So why should you be angry with me?"

A naïve man acts out strange plays of self-isolation. For 7
example, when an angry woman is criticizing him, he may say, quite sensibly, "You're right. I had no right to do that." If her anger turns to rage, he bends his head and says, "I've always been this way." In the third act, he may implicate his father. "He was never there; he never gave me any support." Her rage continues and he bends over still farther. He is losing ground rapidly, and in the fourth act he may say: "All men are shits." He is now many more times isolated than he was a few minutes ago. He feels rejected by the woman and he is now isolated from all other men as well. One man I knew went through this play every time he had a serious fight with a woman, about once a week.

The naïve man will lose what is most precious to him 8
because of a lack of boundaries. This is particularly true of the New Age man, or the man seeking "higher consciousness." Thieves walk in and out of his house, carrying large bags, and he doesn't seem to notice them. He tells his "white light" experiences at parties; he confides the contents of last night's dream to a total stranger. Mythologically, when he meets the giant he tells him all his plans. He rarely fights for

what is his; he gives away his eggs, and other people raise the chicks. We could say that, unaware of boundaries, he does not develop a good container for his soul, nor a good container for two people. There's a leak in it somewhere. He may break the container himself when he sees an attractive face. As an artist he improvises; as a poet his work lacks meter and shape. Improvisation is not all wrong, but he tends to be proud of his lack of form because he feels suspicious of boundaries. The lack of boundaries will eventually damage him.

9 The naïve man tends to have an inappropriate relation to ecstasy. He longs for ecstasy at the wrong time or in the wrong place, and ignores all masculine sources of it. He wants ecstasy through the feminine, through the Great Mother, through the goddess, even though what may be grounding for the woman ungrounds him. He uses ecstasy to be separated from grounding or discipline.

10 The naïve man will sink into a mood as if into a big hole. Some women, we notice, are able to get around a mood. If a woman has a bad mood before a party, for example, she may walk around the mood, detach it, and get rid of it, at least for a time. But the naïve man's mood seems attached as if to a mountain. He can't separate it. If he feels hurt, or in a low mood, he identifies with the mood, and everyone around him has to go down into the hole. In his mood-trance, he is not present to wife, children, friends.

11 The man without limitations may also specialize in not telling. If, for example, he and others decide that some chairs should be arranged before a performance, and he is assigned to do that, he will probably not tell anyone that he has decided to leave the chairs as they are. The people involved, usually older, immediately get mad and shout. Basically he has tricked them into carrying the anger, and its heaviness. He is clean and light, and wonders why other people get angry so often.

12 The naïve man often doesn't know that there is a being in him that wants to remain sick. Inside each man or woman there is a sick person and a well person: and one needs to know which one is talking at any moment. But awareness of the sick being, and knowledge of how strong he is, is not part of the naïve man's field of perceptions.

13 The naïve man often lacks what James Hillman has called "natural brutality." The mother hawk pushes the younglings out of the nest one day; we notice the father fox drives the

cubs away in early October. But the ascender lets things go on too long. At the start of a relationship, a few harsh words of truth would have been helpful. Instead he waits and waits, and then a major wounding happens farther down the line.

His timing is off. We notice that there will often be a missing beat a second or so after he takes a blow, verbal or physical. He will go directly from the pain of receiving the blow to an empathetic grasp of the reason why it came, skipping over the anger entirely. Misusing Jesus' remark, he turns the missing cheek. 14

As a final remark about naïveté, we might mention that there is something in naïveté that demands betrayal. The naïve man will have a curious link to betrayal, deceit, and lies. Not only will he betray others easily, being convinced his motives are always good, but when a woman lives with a truly naïve man for a while, she feels impersonally impelled to betray him. When there is too much naïveté around, the universe has no choice but to crystallize out some betrayal. 15

Sharon Doubiago

A Feminist Response to the Men's Movement

Sharon Doubiago, the author of seven books of poetry and fiction, grew up and received her education in southern California. She contributed the following essay to Ms. *magazine in March/April 1992.* Ms.*, of course, publishes articles, fiction, reviews, and news items of particular interest to women.*

Recently, an oldest girlfriend wrote me: 1

"When my grandmother died, my father's mother, our family, in some way, celebrated. You and I were 12. My mother, a devoted daughter-in-law, a woman of great wisdom, love, and fidelity—still the wisest person I know—explained that a man's mother is oppressive to him. My father was free now. A son cannot become a man until his mother dies. 2

3 *In bad dreams ever since I have been carrying my dead grandmother around in my arms unable to find a place to bury her. Robert Bly's work of the past ten years, now the men's movement, brings this dream back as nightmare."*

4 There was that awful moment, in February 1991, in Paris, while we rained iron down on Iraq, that I opened the *International Herald Tribune* to find Robert Bly's book *Iron John* number one on the best-seller list. The thought that Bly, the anti-Vietnam war, 1970s Mother-consciousness poet had somehow become the "mythopoetic voice" for this new war was sickening. I felt a little fear for him as sort of an old friend, for his karma; could hear him yelling across the seas *This is not what I meant!* This despite his railings-on through the 1980s against my good friends, the "soft men" (the ones I call pacifists): "The warriors inside American men have become weak in recent years"; despite this being the military's exact point of view. The Persian Gulf War broke the fragile line—held since Vietnam broke our killer will—against all-out, popular consensus war; it took the maturation of a new, "innocent" generation to pull it off.

5 And that's the point here: *Iron John* is so badly written, so inflammatory, and of such potential and outright treachery as to have, if not exactly unleashed the barely contained Mass Murderer in us, been a statement of His validity. *Iron John* is as much connected to the voice of our collective unconscious as were the S & M porno films shown the young flyers before the bombing runs (*whatever could be the connection?*). I remembered the afternoon in Mendocino 11 years earlier when Bly blasted me publicly for questioning the morality and structure of our fairy tales, for suggesting that Beauty should *not* kiss the Beast, forced as she is, her father having handed her over to save his own neck. Ranting like a fundamentalist at the sinner who dares to question, he said fairy tales are the Truth, or they wouldn't have lasted, they're the Collective Wisdom of the Race, we mess with them at our Great Peril.

6 Yes, and the use of "devotional" books to inspire warrior energy is an ancient one. For me, in Paris, a city warrior-crazed like the rest of the world, the Shadow of Robert Bly stepped forward to join those of George Bush and Saddam Hussein, a trinity fusing into the mythic figure of Goliath massacring David—to the score of 100,000 to 148.

7 Ever since, of course, in the same kind of blatant lie that permits Bly to insist that his book is not antifemale, he's

maintained that the Gulf War was *perverted* warrior energy. But using his own archetypal ideology, *there are no coincidences. Iron John* is our Desert Storm book.

Bly preaches that the contemporary male is "soft" because 8
he hasn't "cut his adult soul away from his mother-bound soul," because in the remoteness (more likely, absence) of his father he hasn't had a male role model, and because he's been "pussy-whipped" by feminists of the past quarter century. "We're drowning in female energy," he bemoans. In one of many dishonest stances, Bly accepts the kingly mantle for having "discovered" the necessity of mother-son severance. In fact, this has been the First Edict of all patriarchies; it is the heart and soul of our murderous, woman-hating, son-hating, daughter-hating, nature-hating, eros-hating, freedom-hating, life-hating culture. It's the historical, ongoing patriarch-led war between the sexes. It is the "Oldest War," the one that has to be waged on every human born—*Thou shalt commit psychic matricide*—because patriarchal civilization is the opposite of what comes naturally. It's Man's war against nature. It's the Severance traced repeatedly with massive documentation (officially ignored and repressed) that the original civilizations were brutally destroyed because they were matriarchies—a fact Robert Bly knows a lot about. "There must have been a war," he says in his 1973 essay, "I Come Out of the Mother Naked."

Yes, there was. It was led by the original men's movement. 9

Our dominant psychological notion, that the male must 10
cut himself off from his mother—we never quite get that this means *all* women—is so embedded in our culture that it feels dangerous to question it. But the Truth, as with all patriarchal reversals, is the other way around: the male is *not* supposed to break from his mother. *This* is the wound that paralyzes his soul, all our souls, the "male wound" we all suffer from, that lies at the heart of our sadomasochistic human dysfunctionalism. *Think about it;* please don't just interrupt me now about your fucked-up stepmother, which is the kind of "logic" Robert Bly uses. This is the wound that creates everything twisted and evil in us, creates the Beast, wimp or warrior, female or male. My girlfriend's brother is carrying around his grandma's dead body too, but she's buried in his male Hole; he, of course, can't remember his dreams.

This is the truth: we are *all* Sleeping Beauty and Rip Van 11

Winkle in the trance caused by domestic violence and sexual abuse, all the way back to generations of hideous wars and political genocides of our family roots; the trance of shock caused by the patriarchal destruction in ourselves, in our culture, of the Mother.

12 A major problem, all men agree, is the negligent, abusive, or absent father. But nowhere in the men's literature I've seen is there a condemnation of this man. All the blame, typically, goes to the mother—because she is the opposite of him: too close. Bly's main argument is for men to become *like* this man. The male is in essence that which is set apart, he instructs. The male moves away from wife and child and "stands alone. . . . Mythology is full of stories of the bad father. . . . There are no good fathers in the major stories." And so, by the There-You-Have-the-Archetype reasoning, the True Father is a Bad Father.

13 It's from this gender polarity that Bly makes the classic male mistake about the female: ". . . the father and the mother are in competition." From his pole he sees the female on her pole, as being the same as himself; he does not see her as the noncompetitive parent. His projection extends into the traditional masculine paranoia that the mother and son are in conspiracy to get rid of him, exactly the conspiracy *he's* trying to involve the son in. (The fact is, the mother wants the father *in* the circle.) Bly is guilty of the simple-minded patriarchal dualism, Us against Them, that's got us to the nuclear brink. He acts as if he doesn't know that the "set apart" male is the psychological cause of war and the ruination of Earth.

14 "All male violence is an incomplete, culturally damaging turn from unaccepted maternal love and power," Rachel Blau DuPlessis reminds us, "and by extension, from the life-force of the Great Goddess." Bly conveniently forgets the crucial feminist scholarship on the root of gender psychology: the male, between ages one and two, has to distance himself from his primary parent (usually a woman), to see that he is physically different from her. This is the origin of male objectification of the female. Then, to affirm his difference—he must not be like her—he renounces her for the secondary parent (usually a man). The female makes the same move but, seeing that she is not so different from her mother, rejects her only partially. Still, for ego, to find herself, she also turns to the secondary parent. Because this second love is usually a man, turning from the feminine to

the masculine is at the core of our psyches. This becomes the structure of our personalities, our civilizations, our religions; the creation of technology, violence, and war. It all stems from the search for male identity during our lifetime flight from the mother, that source with whom we also associate our mortality. Mother and mortality are, of course, in turn associated with the greatest foe of all, Nature. The endless culture-or-genetics debate of the difference between women and men is a blind; the crucial difference is psychological.

15 The psyche can be changed.

16 "One imagines," Bly blisses in a 1982 interview, "what the young male would be like if trained or initiated by the Wild Man rather than a woman . . ."

17 Actually this is close to Dorothy Dinnerstein's brilliant idea to save us from male apocalypse. In *The Mermaid and the Minotaur,* she noted that our salvation lies in half the world's population, *men,* raising the babies, so that the male body becomes the too-familiar one we grow from, and so reject. Then the universal turning to the secondary parent would be *to* and *for* the Female, the only thing that's going to save us. (How's that, Robert, for serious mother-severance? The argument for male child care?)

18 Freud, Jung, Jones, all the boys, tell of the dangers of insanity for the son if he gets too close to his mother. But in another system, a partnership-equality one—masculinity would be something else entirely. *Matriarchy is not patriarchy with a switch in rulers; it's the opposite.*

19 "I feel it is a fact," author Carol Bly (Robert's ex-wife and mother of his four children) says, "that the only way for middle-aged males to keep the species regressed is to spoil the son's learning through love. So they pull him out of the home and afterward he *cannot* learn through love. So then you can do what you like with him."

20 To label other men, especially younger men, "soft" is the oldest shaming trick in the book. The military uses it to great effect. (Masculinity as we know it is not about leadership but about following orders.) Poet and journalist Doug Marx, who attended a Portland, Oregon, men's conference as a profeminist "spy," reports that Bly's book is a great whitewash of what goes on in those all-male things: "Bly reading to 500 men a D. H. Lawrence passage that says any woman would be happy to walk behind a strong man . . . this is bad news! We don't need this shit. . . . Someone had the temerity to ask Bly if 'we're going to get in touch with

our feminine sides'; he shot back, 'As Joseph Campbell said, if you're a mama's boy, get the fuck out of the temple.' "

21 Something like *Iron John* happened before in recent history. As Carole Klein wrote in her book *Mothers and Sons,* just after World War II, Edward Strecker, a psychiatrist who served as adviser to the secretary of war, published *Their Mothers' Sons,* charging "Mom" with so crippling her sons that "the very breath of democracy" was nearly stilled. The main killers of history, of course, are teenage boys who've just *left* their mothers, soldiers who must prove to their fathers that they aren't "Mama's Boys."

22 Bly says he searched hard for a myth about the initiatory processes of male growth. (He missed the obvious one: the Son dead on the cross—dead to his mother, his people, the earth—rebirthing to and as the Inhuman Father.) But a feminist reading of the Iron John fairy tale suggests a meaning opposite to Bly's. The key to free the Wild Man from the cage in which the King holds him is under the pillow of the boy's mother. The key to the man who is in touch with his soul *is* the boy's mother. Moreover, the key is in her bed. Of course, Bly preaches, "the incest issue." Of course. As Freud posited, a mother loves her child (of either sex) only because it's a penis-substitute!

23 We must deal with this sickest of all patriarchal perversions. We desperately need a new understanding of the love between mother and son. Intimacy—the key under the pillow—is a fundamental characteristic of the Feminine; it's hardly an automatic translation to sex. The mother-son relationship is a key—but it's our greatest taboo. We need to wake up from this trance. Our lack of study, thought, and insight about raising our sons is a tragic mistake. Now the "subject" remains the domain of the Freudian mother-and-son haters and all the other mother-severed guys.

24 In ancient gylanic societies, the mother-son relationship was the core one, *not* the masculine imbalance of the patriarchal father-son relationship. The psychology of gender theory suggests that very different family structures must have existed to have created societies structured on the female values of equality, affiliation, caring, peace, pleasure, and love.

25 How were children raised in the ancient partnership societies? What were the roles of female and male? We need these answers. We don't need more rituals and initiations, as Bly and the Boys call for, which always lead to institu-

tionalized force, to fascism. It's only in the patriarchy that the male doesn't know who he is without being told.

I too want the Soft Men (who I assume have been doing their 40 days in the desert) to get up now, and to go forward with the feminism—that is, the love—that their women have given them. We *have* the natural model for the adult male: the mother's son. The son, not as child, but as the true male, the deep male. True masculinity, as the mother and son know, is not about dominance, or aggression, or severance, or sick sex, or being "set apart," or putting on false robes. We need to realize the fathers' intent to crucify our sons. The corpse we carry around in our arms is also our grandmother's lost son—our pitiful father. 26

The key to the true masculine is under our pillows. 27

Andrew Kimbrell

A Time for Men to Pull Together

A former concert pianist and music teacher, Andrew Kimbrell is now an attorney and lobbyist who lives and works in the Washington, DC, area. Among other things, he sees himself as one spokesman for the so-called "men's movement," an effort to liberate people from the notion that men must remain rational, unemotional, competitive, efficient breadwinners. He published the following essay in the May/June issue of the Utne Reader, *a relatively new magazine that bills itself as "the best of the alternative press" because it republishes articles on public affairs from other publications—somewhat in the tradition of* Reader's Digest, *except that* Reader's Digest *is quite traditional whereas* Utne Reader *articles reflect a more liberal and exploratory perspective.*

"Our civilization is a dingy ungentlemanly business; it drops so much out of a man."

—Robert Louis Stevenson

Men are hurting—badly. Despite rumors to the contrary, 1
men as a gender are being devastated physically and psychically by our socioeconomic system. As American society

continues to empower a small percentage of men—and a smaller but increasing percentage of women—it is causing significant confusion and anguish for the majority of men.

2 In recent years, there have been many impressive analyses documenting the exploitation of women in our culture. Unfortunately, little attention has been given to the massive disruption and destruction that our economic and political institutions have wrought on men. In fact, far too often, men as a gender have been thought of as synonymous with the power elite.

3 But thinking on this subject is beginning to change. Over the last decade, men have begun to realize that we cannot properly relate to one another, or understand how some of us in turn exploit others, until we have begun to appreciate the extent and nature of our dispossessed predicament. In a variety of ways, men across the country are beginning to mourn their losses and seek solutions.

4 This new sense of loss among men comes from the deterioration of men's traditional roles as protectors of family and the earth (although not the sole protectors)—what psychologist Robert Mannis calls the *generative* potential of men. And much of this mourning also focuses on how men's energy is often channeled in the direction of destruction—both of the earth and its inhabitants.

5 The mission of many men today—both those involved in the men's movement and others outside it—is to find new ways that allow men to celebrate their generative potential and reverse the cycle of destruction that characterizes men's collective behavior today. These calls to action are not abstract or hypothetical. The oppression of men, especially in the last several decades, can be easily seen in a disturbing upward spiral of male self-destruction, addiction, hopelessness, and homelessness.

6 While suicide rates for women have been stable over the last 20 years, among men—especially white male teenagers—they have increased rapidly. Currently, male teenagers are five times more likely to take their own lives than females. Overall, men are committing suicide at four times the rate of women. America's young men are also being ravaged by alcohol and drug abuse. Men between the ages of 18 and 29 suffer alcohol dependency at three times the rate of women of the same age group. More than two-thirds of all alcoholics are men, and 50 percent more men are regular users of illicit drugs than women. Men

account for more than 90 percent of arrests for alcohol and drug abuse violations.

A sense of hopelessness among America's young men is not surprising. Real wages for men under 25 have actually declined over the last 20 years, and 60 percent of all high school dropouts are males. These statistics, added to the fact that more than 400,000 farmers have lost their land in the last decade, account in part for the increasing rate of unemployment among men, and for the fact that more than 80 percent of America's homeless are men. 7

The stress on men is taking its toll. Men's life expectancy is 10 percent shorter than women's, and the incidence of stress-related illnesses such as heart disease and certain cancers remains inordinately high among men. 8

And the situation for minority men is even worse. One out of four black men between the ages of 20 and 29 is either in jail, on probation, or on parole—ten times the proportion for black women in the same age range. More black men are in jail than in college, and there are 40 percent more black women than black men studying in our nation's colleges and universities. Homicide is the leading cause of death among black males ages 15 to 24. Black males have the lowest life expectancy of any segment of the American population. Statistics for Native American and Hispanic men are also grim. 9

Men are also a large part of the growing crisis in the American family. Studies report that parents today spend 40 percent less time with their children than did parents in 1965, and men are increasingly isolated from their families by the pressures of work and the circumstances of divorce. In a recent poll, 72 percent of employed male respondents agreed that they are "torn by conflict" between their jobs and the desire to be with their families. Yet the average divorced American man spends less than two days a month with his children. Well over half of black male children are raised without fathers. While the trauma of separation and divorce affects all members of a family, it is especially poignant for sons: Researchers generally agree that boys at all ages are hardest hit by divorce. 10

The Enclosure of Men

The current crisis for men, which goes far beyond statistics, is nothing new. We have faced a legacy of loss, 11 especially since the start of the mechanical age. From the Enclosure Acts, which forced families off the land in Tudor England, to the ongoing destruction of indigenous communities throughout the Third World, the demands of the industrial era have forced men off the land, out of the family and community, and into the factory and office. The male as steward of family and soil, craftsman, woodsman, native hunter, and fisherman has all but vanished.

12 As men became the primary cog in industrial production, they lost touch with the earth and the parts of themselves that needed the earth to survive. Men by the millions—who long prided themselves on their husbandry of family, community, and land—were forced into a system whose ultimate goal was to turn one man against another in the competitive "jungle" of industrialized society. As the industrial revolution advanced, men lost not only their independence and dignity, but also the sense of personal creativity and responsibility associated with individual crafts and small-scale farming.

13 The factory wrenched the father from the home, and he often became a virtual nonentity in the household. By separating a man's work from his family, industrial society caused the permanent alienation of father from son. Even when the modern father returns to the house, he is often too tired and too irritable from the tensions and tedium of work in the factory or corporation to pay close attention to his children. As Robert Bly, in his best-selling book *Iron John* (1990, Addison-Wesley), has pointed out, "When a father, absent during the day, returns home at six, his children receive only his temperament, and not his teaching." The family, and especially sons, lose the presence of the father, uncle, and other male role models. It is difficult to calculate the full impact that this pattern of paternal absence has had on family and society over the last several generations.

14 While the loss of fathers is now beginning to be discussed, men have yet to fully come to terms with the terrible loss of sons during the mechanized wars of this century. World War I, World War II, Korea, and Vietnam were what the poet Robert Graves called "holocausts of young men." In the battlefields of this century, hundreds of millions of men were killed or injured. In World Wars I and II—in which more than 100 million soldiers were casualties—most of the victims were teenage boys, the average age being 18.5 years.

15 Given this obvious evidence of our exploitation, it is

remarkable that so few men have acknowledged the genocide on their gender over the last century—much less turned against those responsible for this vast victimization. Women have increasingly identified their oppression in society; men have not. Thankfully, some men are now working to create a movement, or community, that focuses on awareness and understanding of men's loss and pain as well as the potential for healing. Because men's oppression is deeply rooted in the political and economic institutions of modern society, it is critical that awareness of these issues must be followed by action: Men today need a comprehensive political program that points the way toward liberation. Instead of grieving over and acting on our loss of independence and generativity, modern men have often engaged in denial—a denial that is linked to the existence of a "male mystique." This defective mythology of the modern age has created a "new man." The male mystique recasts what anthropologists have identified as the traditional male role throughout history—a man, whether hunter-gatherer or farmer, who is steeped in a creative and sustaining relationship with his extended family and the earth household. In the place of this long-enduring, rooted masculine role, the male mystique has fostered a new image of men: autonomous, efficient, intensely self-interested, and disconnected from community and the earth.

The male mystique was spawned in the early days of the 16
modern age. It combines Francis Bacon's idea that "knowledge is power" and Adam Smith's view that the highest good is "the individual exerting himself to his own advantage." This power-oriented, individualistic ideology was further solidified by the concepts of the survival of the fittest and the ethic of efficiency. The ideal man was no longer the wise farmer, but rather the most successful man-eater in the Darwinian corporate jungle.

The most tragic aspect of all this for us is that as the male 17
mystique created the modern power elite, it destroyed male friendship and bonding. The male mystique teaches that the successful man is competitive, uncaring, unloving. It celebrates the ethic of isolation—it turns men permanently against each other in the tooth and claw world of making a living. As the Ivan Boesky-type character in the movie *Wall Street* tells his young apprentice, "If you need a friend, get a dog."

The male mystique also destroys men's ties to the earth. It 18 embodies the view of 17th century British philosopher John Locke that "[l]and that is left wholly to nature is called, as indeed it is, waste." A sustainable relationship with the earth is sacrificed to material progress and conspicuous consumption.

19 Ironically, men's own sense of loss has fed the male mystique. As men become more and more powerless in their own lives, they are given more and more media images of excessive, caricatured masculinity with which to identify. Men look to manufactured macho characters from the Wild West, working-class America, and modern war in the hope of gaining some sense of what it means to be a man. The primary symbols of the male mystique are almost never caring fathers, stewards of the land, or community organizers. Instead, over several decades these aggressively masculine figures have evolved from the Western independent man (John Wayne, Gary Cooper) to the blue-collar macho man (Sly Stallone and Robert DeNiro) and finally to a variety of military and police figures concluding with the violent revelry of *Robocop.*

20 Modern men are entranced by this simulated masculinity—they experience danger, independence, success, sexuality, idealism, and adventure as voyeurs. Meanwhile, in real life most men lead powerless, subservient lives in the factory or office—frightened of losing their jobs, mortgaged to the gills, and still feeling responsible for supporting their families. Their lauded independence—as well as most of their basic rights—disappear the minute they report for work. The disparity between their real lives and the macho images of masculinity perpetrated by the media confuses and confounds many men. In his book *The Men from the Boys,* Ray Raphael asks, "But is it really that manly to wield a jackhammer, or spend one's life in the mines? Physical labor is often mindless, repetitive, and exhausting. . . . The workers must be subservient while on the job, and subservience is hard to reconcile with the masculine ideal of personal power."

21 Men can no longer afford to lose themselves in denial. We need to experience grief and anger over our losses and not buy into the pseudo-male stereotypes propagated by the male mystique. We are not, after all, what we are told we are.

22 At the same time, while recognizing the pervasive victimization of women, we must resist the view of some feminists

that maleness itself, and not the current systems of social control and production, is primarily responsible for the exploitation of women. For men who are sensitive to feminist thinking, this view of masculinity creates a confusing and debilitating double bind: We view ourselves as oppressors yet experience victimization on the personal and social level. Instead of blaming maleness, we must challenge the defective mythology of the male mystique. Neither the male mystique nor the denigration of maleness offers hope for the future.

Fortunately, we may be on the verge of a historic shift in male consciousness. Recently, there has been a rediscovery of masculinity as a primal creative and generative force equal to that of the recently recognized creative and nurturing power of the feminine. A number of thinkers and activists are urging men to substitute empathy for efficiency, stewardship for exploitation, generosity for the competitiveness of the marketplace. 23

At the forefront of this movement have been poet Robert Bly and others working with him: psychologist James Hillman, drummer Michael Meade, Jungian scholar Robert Moore. Bly has called for the recognition and reaffirmation of the "wild" man. As part of Bly's crusade, thousands of men have come together to seek a regeneration of their sexuality and power, as they reject the cerebral, desiccated world of our competitive corporate culture. Another compelling analysis is that of Jungian therapist Robert Mannis, who has called for a renewal of the ethic of "husbandry," a sense of masculine obligation involved with generating and maintaining a stable relationship to one's family and to the earth itself. And a growing number of men are mounting other challenges to the male mystique. But so far, the men's movement has remained primarily therapeutic. Little effort has been made to extend the energy of male self-discovery into a practical social and political agenda. 24

As many of us come to mourn the lost fathers and sons of the last decades and seek to re-establish our ties to each other and to the earth, we need to find ways to change the political, social, and economic structures that have created this crisis. A "wild man" weekend in the woods, or intense man-to-man discussions, can be key experiences in self-discovery and personal empowerment. But these personal experiences are not enough to reverse the victimization of men. As the men's movement gathers strength, it is critical that this increasing sense of personal liberation be chan- 25 neled into political action. Without significant changes in our society there will only be continued hopelessness and frustration for men. Moreover, a coordinated movement pressing for the liberation of men could be a key factor in ensuring that the struggle for a sustainable future for humanity and the earth succeeds.

26 What follows is a brief political platform for men, a short manifesto with which we can begin the process of organizing men as a positive political force working for a better future. This is the next step for the men's movement.

Fathers and Children

27 Political efforts focusing on the family must reassert men's bonds with the family and reverse the "lost father" syndrome. While any long-term plan for men's liberation requires significant changes in the very structure of our work and economic institutions, a number of intermediate steps are possible: We need to take a leadership role in supporting parental leave legislation, which gives working parents the right to take time from work to care for children or other family members. And we need to target the Bush administration for vetoing this vital legislation. Also needed is pro-child tax relief such as greatly expanding the young child tax credit, which would provide income relief and tax breaks to families at a point when children need the most parental care and when income may be the lowest.

28 We should also be in the forefront of the movement pushing for changes in the workplace including more flexible hours, part-time work, job sharing, and home-based employment. As economic analyst William R. Mattox Jr. notes, a simple step toward making home-based employment more viable would be to loosen restrictions on claiming home office expenses as a tax deduction for parents. Men must also work strenuously in the legal arena to promote more liberal visitation rights for non-custodial parents and to assert appropriateness of the father as a custodial parent. Non-traditional family structures should also be given more recognition in our society, with acknowledgment of men's important roles as stepfathers, foster fathers, uncles, brothers, and mentors. We must seek legislative ways to recognize many men's commitments that do not fit traditional definitions of family.

Ecology as Male Politics

A sustainable environment is not merely one issue among others. It is the crux of all issues in our age, including men's politics. The ecological struggles of our time offer a unique forum in which men can express their renewed sense of the wild and their traditional roles as creators, defenders of the family, and careful stewards of the earth. 29

The alienation of men from their rootedness to the land has deprived us all of what John Muir called the "heart of wilderness." As part of our efforts to re-experience the wild in ourselves, we should actively become involved in experiencing the wilderness first hand and organize support for the protection of nature and endangered species. Men should also become what Robert Bly has called "inner warriors" for the earth, involving themselves in non-violent civil disobedience to protect wilderness areas from further destruction. 30

An important aspect of the masculine ethic is defense of family. Pesticides and other toxic pollutants that poison our food, homes, water, and air represent a real danger, especially to children. Men need to be adamant in their call for limitations on the use of chemicals. 31

Wendell Berry has pointed out that the ecological crisis is also a crisis of agriculture. If men are to recapture a true sense of stewardship and husbandry and affirm the "seed-bearing," creative capacity of the male, they must, to the extent possible, become involved in sustainable agriculture and organic farming and gardening. We should also initiate and support legislation that sustains our farming communities. 32

Men in the Classrooms and Community

In many communities, especially inner cities, men are absent not only from homes but also from the schools. Men must support the current efforts by black men's groups around the country to implement male-only early-grade classes taught by men. These programs provide role models and a surrogate paternal presence for young black males. We should also commit ourselves to having a far greater male presence in all elementary school education. Recent studies have shown that male grade school students have a 33 higher level of achievement when they are taught by male teachers. Part-time or full-time home schooling options can also be helpful in providing men a great opportunity to be teachers—not just temperaments—to their children.

34 We need to revive our concern for community. Community-based boys' clubs, scout troops, sports leagues, and big brother programs have achieved significant success in helping fatherless male children find self-esteem. Men's groups must work to strengthen these organizations.

Men's Minds, Men's Bodies, and Work

35 Men need to join together to fight threats to male health including suicide, drug and alcohol abuse, AIDS, and stress diseases. We should support active prevention and education efforts aimed at these deadly threats. Most importantly, men need to be leaders in initiating and supporting holistic and psychotherapeutic approaches that directly link many of these health threats to the coercive nature of the male mystique and the current economic system. Changes in diet, reduction of drug and alcohol use, less stressful work environments, greater nurturing of and caring for men by other men, and fighting racism, hopelessness, and homelessness are all important, interconnected aspects of any male health initiative.

Men Without Hope or Homes

36 Men need to support measures that promote small business and entrepreneurship, which will allow more people to engage in crafts and human-scale, community-oriented enterprises. Also important is a commitment to appropriate, human-scale technologies such as renewable energy sources. Industrial and other inappropriate technologies have led to men's dispossession, degradation—and increasingly to unemployment.

37 A related struggle is eliminating racism. No group of men is more dispossessed than minority men. White men should support and network with African-American and other minority men's groups. Violence and discrimination against men because of their sexual preference should also be challenged.

Men, who represent more than four-fifths of the homeless, can no longer ignore this increasing social tragedy. Men's councils should develop support groups for the homeless in their communities. 38

The Holocaust of Men

As the primary victims of mechanized war, men must oppose this continued slaughter. Men need to realize that the traditional male concepts of the noble warrior are undermined and caricatured in the technological nightmare of modern warfare. Men must together become prime movers in dismantling the military-industrial establishment and redistributing defense spending toward a sustainable environment and protection of family, school, and community. 39

Men's Action Network

No area of the men's political agenda will be realized until men can establish a network of activists to create collective action. A first step might be to create a high-profile national coalition of the men's councils that are growing around the country. This coalition, which could be called the Men's Action Network (MAN), could call for a national conference to define a comprehensive platform of men's concerns and to provide the political muscle to implement those ideas. 40

A Man Could Stand Up

The current generation of men face a unique moment in history. Though often still trapped by economic coercion and psychological co-optation, we are beginning to see that there is a profound choice ahead. Will we choose to remain subservient tools of social and environmental destruction or to fight for rediscovery of the male as a full partner and participant in family, community, and the earth? Will we remain mesmerized by the male mystique, or will we reclaim the true meaning of our masculinity? 41

There is a world to gain. The male mystique, in which many of today's men—especially the most politically 42 powerful—are trapped, is threatening the family and the planet with irreversible destruction. A men's movement based on the recovery of masculinity could renew much of the world we have lost. By changing types of work and work hours, we could break our subordination to corporate managers and return much of our work and lives to the household. We could once again be teaching, nurturing presences to our children. By devoting ourselves to meaningful work with appropriate technology, we could recover independence in our work and our spirit. By caring for each other, we could recover the dignity of our gender and heal the wounds of addiction and self-destruction. By becoming husbands to the earth, we could protect the wild and recover our creative connections with the forces and rhythms of nature.

43 Ultimately we must help fashion a world without the daily frustration and sorrow of having to view each other as a collection of competitors instead of a community of friends. We must celebrate the essence and rituals of our masculinity. We can no longer passively submit to the destruction of the household, the demise of self-employment, the disintegration of family and community, and the desecration of our earth.

44 Shortly after the First World War, Ford Madox Ford, one of this century's greatest writers, depicted 20th century men as continually pinned down in their trenches, unable to stand up for fear of annihilation. As the century closes, men remain pinned down by an economic and political system that daily forces millions of us into meaningless work, powerless lives, and self-destruction. The time has come for men to stand up.

DO WOMEN AND MEN THINK DIFFERENTLY?

Christine Gorman

Sizing Up the Sexes

The following article was a Time *magazine cover story in January 1992.*

What are little boys made of?
What are little boys made of?
Frogs and snails
And puppy dogs' tails,
That's what little boys are made of.

What are little girls made of?
What are little girls made of?
Sugar and spice
And all that's nice,
That's what little girls are made of.
Anonymous

Many scientists rely on elaborately complex and costly equipment to probe the mysteries confronting humankind. Not Melissa Hines. The UCLA behavioral scientist is hoping to solve one of life's oldest riddles with a toybox full of police cars, Lincoln Logs and Barbie dolls. For the past two years, Hines and her colleagues have tried to determine the origins of gender differences by capturing on videotape the squeals of delight, furrows of concentration and myriad decisions that children from 2½ to 8 make while playing. Although both sexes play with all the toys available in Hines' laboratory, her work confirms what most parents (and more than a few aunts, uncles and nursery-school teachers) already know. As a group, the boys favor sports cars, fire trucks and Lincoln Logs, while the girls are drawn more often to dolls and kitchen toys. 1

2 But one batch of girls defies expectations and consistently prefers the boy toys. These youngsters have a rare genetic abnormality that caused them to produce elevated levels of testosterone, among other hormones, during their embryonic development. On average, they play with the same toys as the boys in the same ways and just as often. Could it be that the high levels of testosterone present in their bodies before birth have left a permanent imprint on their brains, affecting their later behavior? Or did their parents, knowing of their disorder, somehow subtly influence their choices? If the first explanation is true and biology determines the choice, Hines wonders, "Why would you evolve to want to play with a truck?"

3 Not so long ago, any career-minded researcher would have hesitated to ask such questions. During the feminist revolution of the 1970s, talk of inborn differences in the behavior of men and women was distinctly unfashionable, even taboo. Men dominated fields like architecture and engineering, it was argued, because of social, not hormonal, pressures. Women did the vast majority of society's child rearing because few other options were available to them. Once sexism was abolished, so the argument ran, the world would become a perfectly equitable, androgynous place, aside from a few anatomical details.

4 But biology has a funny way of confounding expectations. Rather than disappear, the evidence for innate sexual differences only began to mount. In medicine, researchers documented that heart disease strikes men at a younger age than it does women and that women have a more moderate physiological response to stress. Researchers found subtle neurological differences between the sexes both in the brain's structure and in its functioning. In addition, another generation of parents discovered that, despite their best efforts to give baseballs to their daughters and sewing kits to their sons, girls still flocked to dollhouses while boys clambered into tree forts. Perhaps nature is more important than nurture after all.

5 Even professional skeptics have been converted. "When I was younger, I believed that 100% of sex differences were due to the environment," says Jerre Levy, professor of psychology at the University of Chicago. Her own toddler toppled that utopian notion. "My daughter was 15 months old, and I had just dressed her in her teeny little nightie. Some guests arrived, and she came into the room, knowing

full well that she looked adorable. She came in with this saucy little walk, cocking her head, blinking her eyes, especially at the men. You never saw such flirtation in your life." After 20 years spent studying the brain, Levy is convinced: "I'm sure there are biologically based differences in our behavior."

Now that it is O.K. to admit the possibility, the search for sexual differences has expanded into nearly every branch of the life sciences. Anthropologists have debunked Margaret Mead's work on the extreme variability of gender roles in New Guinea. Psychologists are untangling the complex interplay between hormones and aggression. But the most provocative, if as yet inconclusive, discoveries of all stem from the pioneering exploration of a tiny 3-lb. universe: the human brain. In fact, some researchers predict that the confirmation of innate differences in behavior could lead to an unprecedented understanding of the mind. 6

Some of the findings seem merely curious. For example, more men than women are lefthanded, reflecting the dominance of the brain's right hemisphere. By contrast, more women listen equally with both ears, while men favor the right one. 7

Other revelations are bound to provoke more controversy. Psychology tests, for instance, consistently support the notion that men and women perceive the world in subtly different ways. Males excel at rotating three-dimensional objects in their head. Females prove better at reading emotions of people in photographs. A growing number of scientists believe the discrepancies reflect functional differences in the brains of men and women. If true, then some misunderstandings between the sexes may have more to do with crossed wiring than cross-purposes. 8

Most of the gender differences that have been uncovered so far are, statistically speaking, quite small. "Even the largest differences in cognitive function are not as large as the difference in male and female height," Hines notes. "You still see a lot of overlap." Otherwise, women could never read maps and men would always be lefthanded. That kind of flexibility within the sexes reveals just how complex a puzzle gender actually is, requiring pieces from biology, sociology and culture. 9

Ironically, researchers are not entirely sure how or even why humans produce two sexes in the first place. (Why not just one—or even three—as in some species?) What is clear 10 is that the two sexes originate with two distinct chromosomes. Women bear a double dose of the large X chromosome, while men usually possess a single X and a short, stumpy Y chromosome. In 1990 British scientists reported they had identified a single gene on the Y chromosome that determines maleness. Like some kind of biomolecular Paul Revere, this master gene rouses a host of its compatriots to the complex task of turning a fetus into a boy. Without such a signal, all human embryos would develop into girls. "I have all the genes for being male except this one, and my husband has all the genes for being female," marvels evolutionary psychologist Leda Cosmides, of the University of California at Santa Barbara. "The only difference is which genes got turned on."

11 Yet even this snippet of DNA is not enough to ensure a masculine result. An elevated level of the hormone testosterone is also required during the pregnancy. Where does it come from? The fetus' own undescended testes. In those rare cases in which the tiny body does not respond to the hormone, a genetically male fetus develops sex organs that look like a clitoris and vagina rather than a penis. Such people look and act female. The majority marry and adopt children.

12 The influence of the sex hormones extends into the nervous system. Both males and females produce androgens, such as testosterone, and estrogens—although in different amounts. (Men and women who make no testosterone generally lack a libido.) Researchers suspect that an excess of testosterone before birth enables the right hemisphere to dominate the brain, resulting in lefthandedness. Since testosterone levels are higher in boys than in girls, that would explain why more boys are southpaws.

13 Subtle sex-linked preferences have been detected as early as 52 hours after birth. In studies of 72 newborns, University of Chicago psychologist Martha McClintock and her students found that a toe-fanning reflex was stronger in the left foot of 60% of the males, while all the females favored their right. However, apart from such reflexes in the hands, legs and feet, the team could find no other differences in the babies' responses.

14 One obvious place to look for gender differences is in the hypothalamus, a lusty little organ perched over the brain stem that, when sufficiently provoked, consumes a person with rage, thirst, hunger or desire. In animals, a region at

the front of the organ controls sexual function and is somewhat larger in males than in females. But its size need not remain constant. Studies of tropical fish by Stanford University neurobiologist Russell Fernald reveal that certain cells in this tiny region of the brain swell markedly in an individual male whenever he comes to dominate a school. Unfortunately for the piscine pasha, the cells will also shrink if he loses control of his harem to another male.

Many researchers suspect that, in humans too, sexual preferences are controlled by the hypothalamus. Based on a study of 41 autopsied brains, Simon LeVay of the Salk Institute for Biological Studies announced last summer that he had found a region in the hypothalamus that was on average twice as large in the heterosexual men as in either women or homosexual men. LeVay's findings support the idea that varying hormone levels before birth may immutably stamp the developing brain in one erotic direction or another. 15

These prenatal fluctuations may also steer boys toward more rambunctious behavior than girls. June Reinisch, director of the Kinsey Institute for Research in Sex, Gender and Reproduction at Indiana University, in a pioneering study of eight pairs of brothers and 17 pairs of sisters ages 6 to 18 uncovered a complex interplay between hormones and aggression. As a group, the young males gave more belligerent answers than did the females on a multiple-choice test in which they had to imagine their response to stressful situations. But siblings who had been exposed in utero to synthetic antimiscarriage hormones that mimic testosterone were the most combative of all. The affected boys proved significantly more aggressive than their unaffected brothers, and the drug-exposed girls were much more contentious than their unexposed sisters. Reinisch could not determine, however, whether this childhood aggression would translate into greater ambition or competitiveness in the adult world. 16

While most of the gender differences uncovered so far seem to fall under the purview of the hypothalamus, researchers have begun noting discrepancies in other parts of the brain as well. For the past nine years, neuroscientists have debated whether the corpus callosum, a thick bundle of nerves that allows the right half of the brain to communicate with the left, is larger in women than in men. If it is, and if size corresponds to function, then the greater 17 crosstalk between the hemispheres might explain enigmatic phenomena like female intuition, which is supposed to accord women greater ability to read emotional clues.

18 These conjectures about the corpus callosum have been hard to prove because the structure's girth varies dramatically with both age and health. Studies of autopsied material are of little use because brain tissue undergoes such dramatic changes in the hours after death. Neuroanatomist Laura Allen and neuroendocrinologist Roger Gorski of UCLA decided to try to circumvent some of these problems by obtaining brain scans from live, apparently healthy people. In their investigation of 146 subjects, published in April, they confirmed that parts of the corpus callosum were up to 23% wider in women than in men. They also measured thicker connections between the two hemispheres in other parts of women's brains.

19 Encouraged by the discovery of such structural differences, many researchers have begun looking for dichotomies of function as well. At the Bowman Gray Medical School in Winston-Salem, N.C., Cecile Naylor has determined that men and women enlist widely varying parts of their brain when asked to spell words. By monitoring increases in blood flow, the neuropsychologist found that women use both sides of their head when spelling, while men use primarily their left side. Because the area activated on the right side is used in understanding emotions, the women apparently tap a wider range of experience for their task. Intriguingly, the effect occurred only with spelling and not during a memory test.

20 Researchers speculate that the greater communication between the two sides of the brain could impair a woman's performance on certain highly specialized visual-spatial tasks. For example, the ability to tell directions on a map without physically having to rotate it appears stronger in those individuals whose brains restrict the process to the right hemisphere. Any crosstalk between the two sides apparently distracts the brain from its job. Sure enough, several studies have shown that this mental-rotation skill is indeed more tightly focused in men's brains than in women's.

21 But how did it get to be that way? So far, none of the gender scientists have figured out whether nature or nurture is more important. "Nothing is ever equal, even in the beginning," observes Janice Juraska, a biopsychologist at

the University of Illinois at Urbana-Champaign. She points out, for instance, that mother rats lick their male offspring more frequently than they do their daughters. However, Juraska has demonstrated that it is possible to reverse some inequities by manipulating environmental factors. Female rats have fewer nerve connections than males into the hippocampus, a brain region associated with spatial relations and memory. But when Juraska "enriched" the cages of the females with stimulating toys, the females developed more of these neuronal connections. "Hormones do affect things—it's crazy to deny that," says the researcher. "But there's no telling which way sex differences might go if we completely changed the environment." For humans, educational enrichment could perhaps enhance a woman's ability to work in three dimensions and a man's ability to interpret emotions. Says Juraska: "There's nothing about human brains that is so stuck that a different way of doing things couldn't change it enormously."

Nowhere is this complex interaction between nature and 22
nurture more apparent than in the unique human abilities of speaking, reading and writing. No one is born knowing French, for example; it must be learned, changing the brain forever. Even so, language skills are linked to specific cerebral centers. In a remarkable series of experiments, neurosurgeon George Ojemann of the University of Washington has produced scores of detailed maps of people's individual language centers.

First, Ojemann tested his patients' verbal intelligence 23
using a written exam. Then, during neurosurgery—which was performed under a local anesthetic—he asked them to name aloud a series of objects found in a steady stream of black-and-white photos. Periodically, he touched different parts of the brain with an electrode that temporarily blocked the activity of that region. (This does not hurt because the brain has no sense of pain.) By noting when his patients made mistakes, the surgeon was able to determine which sites were essential to naming.

Several complex sexual differences emerged. Men with 24
lower verbal IQs were more likely to have their language skills located toward the back of the brain. In a number of women, regardless of IQ, the naming ability was restricted to the frontal lobe. This disparity could help explain why strokes that affect the rear of the brain seem to be more devastating to men than to women.

25 Intriguingly, the sexual differences are far less significant in people with higher verbal IQs. Their language skills developed in a more intermediate part of the brain. And yet, no two patterns were ever identical. "That to me is the most important finding," Ojemann says. "Instead of these sites being laid down more or less the same in everyone, they're laid down in subtly different places." Language is scattered randomly across these cerebral centers, he hypothesizes, because the skills evolved so recently.

26 What no one knows for sure is just how hardwired the brain is. How far and at what stage can the brain's extraordinary flexibility be pushed? Several studies suggest that the junior high years are key. Girls show the same aptitudes for math as boys until about the seventh grade, when more and more girls develop math phobia. Coincidentally, that is the age at which boys start to shine and catch up to girls in reading.

27 By one account, the gap between men and women for at least some mental skills has actually started to shrink. By looking at 25 years' worth of data from academic tests, Janet Hyde, professor of psychology and women's studies at the University of Wisconsin at Madison, discovered that overall gender differences for verbal and mathematical skills dramatically decreased after 1974. One possible explanation, Hyde notes, is that "Americans have changed their socialization and educational patterns over the past few decades. They are treating males and females with greater similarity."

28 Even so, women still have not caught up with men on the mental-rotation test. Fascinated by the persistence of that gap, psychologists Irwin Silverman and Marion Eals of York University in Ontario wondered if there were any spatial tasks at which women outperformed men. Looking at it from the point of view of human evolution, Silverman and Eals reasoned that while men may have developed strong spatial skills in response to evolutionary pressures to be successful hunters, women would have needed other types of visual skills to excel as gatherers and foragers of food.

29 The psychologists therefore designed a test focused on the ability to discern and later recall the location of objects in a complex, random pattern. In series of tests, student volunteers were given a minute to study a drawing that contained

such unrelated objects as an elephant, a guitar and a cat. Then Silverman and Eals presented their subjects with a second drawing containing additional objects and told them to cross out those items that had been added and circle any that had moved. Sure enough, the women consistently surpassed the men in giving correct answers.

What made the psychologists really sit up and take notice, 30
however, was the fact that the women scored much better on the mental-rotation test while they were menstruating. Specifically, they improved their scores by 50% to 100% whenever their estrogen levels were at their lowest. It is not clear why this should be. However, Silverman and Eals are trying to find out if women exhibit a similar hormonal effect for any other visual tasks.

Oddly enough, men may possess a similar hormonal 31
response, according to new research reported in November by Doreen Kimura, a psychologist at the University of Western Ontario. In her study of 138 adults, Kimura found that males perform better on mental-rotation tests in the spring, when their testosterone levels are low, rather than in the fall, when they are higher. Men are also subject to a daily cycle, with testosterone levels lowest around 8 P.M. and peaking around 4 A.M. Thus, says June Reinisch of the Kinsey Institute: "When people say women can't be trusted because they cycle every month, my response is that men cycle every day, so they should only be allowed to negotiate peace treaties in the evening."

Far from strengthening stereotypes about who women 32
and men truly are or how they should behave, research into innate sexual differences only underscores humanity's awesome adaptability. "Gender is really a complex business," says Reinisch. "There's no question that hormones have an effect. But what does that have to do with the fact that I like to wear pink ribbons and you like to wear baseball gloves? Probably something, but we don't know what."

Even the concept of what an innate difference represents 33
is changing. The physical and chemical differences between the brains of the two sexes may be malleable and subject to change by experience: certainly an event or act of learning can directly affect the brain's biochemistry and physiology. And so, in the final analysis, it may be impossible to say where nature ends and nurture begins because the two are so intimately linked.

Anne Moir and David Jessel
Brain Sex

The introduction to Anne Moir and David Jessel's book Brain Sex *(published in 1991) states that "men are different from women . . . because their brains are different." Since the book was published in 1991, Moir and Jessel have extended their ideas—perhaps most notably in a series of television shows on the Discovery channel in 1992. This "abstract" of their book—published in it as chapter 1—appeared in a slightly different form in* The Washington Post *in May 1991.*

1 A hundred years ago, the observation that men were different from women, in a whole range of aptitudes, skills, and abilities, would have been a leaden truism, a statement of the yawningly obvious.

2 Such a remark, uttered today, would evoke very different reactions. Said by a man, it would suggest a certain social ineptitude, a *naïveté* in matters of sexual politics, a sad deficiency in conventional wisdom, or a clumsy attempt to be provocative. A woman venturing such an opinion would be scorned as a traitor to her sex, betraying the hard-fought 'victories' of recent decades as women have sought equality of status, opportunity and respect.

3 Yet the truth is that virtually every professional scientist and researcher into the subject has concluded that the brains of men and women are different. There has seldom been a greater divide between what intelligent, enlightened opinion presumes—that men and women have the same brain—and what science knows—that they do not.

4 When a Canadian psychologist entitled an academic paper 'Are men's and women's brains really different?' she acknowledged that the answer to the question was self-evident:

> Yes, of course. It would be amazing if men's and women's brains were not different, given the gross morphological [structural] and often striking behavioural differences between men and women.

Most of us intuitively sense that the sexes are different. But this has become a universal, unshared, guilty secret. We have ceased to trust our common sense.

The truth is that for virtually our entire tenancy of the 5
planet, we have been a sexist species. Our biology assigned separate functions to the male and female of *Homo sapiens*. Our evolution strengthened and refined those differences. Our civilisation reflected them. Our religion and our education reinforced them.

Yet we both fear, and defy, history. We fear it, because we 6
are afraid of seeming to be in complicity with the centuries-old crimes of sexual prejudice. We defy it, because we want to believe that mankind has at last achieved escape velocity, released from the muddy gravity of our animal past and neanderthal assumptions.

In the last thirty years a small but influential collection of 7
well-intentioned souls have tried to persuade us to adopt this new defiant appreciation. They have discovered that the religions and the education were a male plot to maintain the subordinate status of women. The discovery is probably correct. They have found that our so-called civilisations are founded on male aggression and dominance. That's probably true as well. So far so good.

The problem comes when you look for an explanation of 8
why this happened. If men and women are identical, and always have been, in the degree and manner in which they use their identical brains, how did the male sex manage so successfully, in virtually every culture and society in the world, to contrive a situation where the female was subordinate? Was it just men's greater musculature and bodyweight that have made the realm of womanhood an occupied country for the past scores of thousands of years? Was it the fact that until recent centuries women were pregnant most of the time? Or is it more likely—as the facts suggest—that the differences between the male and the female brain are at the root of the society we have and the people we are? There are some biological facts of life that, with the best, and most sexually liberated will in the world, we just cannot buck; would it not be better, rather than rage impotently against the differences between the sexes, to acknowledge, understand, exploit, and even enjoy them?

For the last hundred years, scientists have tried to explain 9
those differences—although it has to be said that the first science of brain sex differences began with a methodology as crude as its assumptions. Simple measurement of the brain apparently proved that women lacked the necessary cerebral endowment to claim an equality of intellect. The

Germans were particularly obsessed with this tape-measure scholarship. Bayerthal found it a minimum requirement for a professor of surgery that he have a head circumference of 52–53 centimetres: 'Under 52 cms you cannot expect an intellectual performance of any significance, while under 50.5 cms no normal intelligence can be expected.' In this connection he also observed, 'We do not have to ask for the head circumference of women of genius—they do not exist.'

10 The French scientist Gustave Le Bon, noting that many Parisian women had brains closer in size to those of gorillas than of men, concluded that female inferiority was 'so obvious that no one can contest it for a moment'. And he warned, forebodingly, of

> the day when, misunderstanding the inferior occupations which nature has given her, women leave the home and take part in our battles; on that day a social revolution will begin and everything that maintains the sacred ties of the family will disappear.

That social revolution has been with us for some time; there has also been a revolution in the science of brain differences. Many—perhaps most—of the mysteries of how the brain works have yet to be unravelled, but the differences between the brains of males and females—and the processes by which they become different—are now clear. There is more to be known, more detail and qualification perhaps to add—but the nature and cause of brain differences are now known beyond speculation, beyond prejudice, and beyond reasonable doubt.

11 But now, just at the very moment when science can tell us what the differences are, and where they spring from, we are asked to banish the assumption of difference as if it were a guilty thought.

12 Recent decades have witnessed two contradictory processes: the development of scientific research into the differences between the sexes, and the political denial that such differences exist. These two intellectual currents are, understandably, not on speaking terms. Science knows it dabbles in matters of sexual differences at its risk: at least one researcher into the field of gender differences was refused a grant on the grounds that 'this work ought not to be done'. Another told us that he had given up his work

because 'the political pressure—the pressure on the truth' had become too much. On the other hand, some of those working in the field of sex differences seem to evince an almost wanton disregard for scientific findings, blinkering themselves against findings whose implications they might find too uncomfortable to recognise.

The first systematic tests to explore sex differences were conducted in 1882 by Francis Gatton at the South Kensington Museum in London. He purported to have identified significant sex differences favouring men in strength of grip, sensitivity to shrill whistle sounds, and ability to work under pressure. Women were observed to be more sensitive to pain. 13

Ten years later, in the United States, studies discovered that women could hear better than men, had a more conventional vocabulary, and preferred blue to red. Men preferred red to blue, used more adventurous vocabulary, and had a preference for abstract and general thought, while women preferred practical problems, and individual tasks. 14

Havelock Ellis's *Man and Woman,* published in 1894, aroused immediate interest and ran into eight editions. Among the differences he chronicled were women's superiority over men in memory, cunning, dissimulation, compassion, patience, and tidiness. The work of female scientists was found to be more precise than that of men, but 'perhaps a little lacking in breadth and initiative, though admirable within a limited range.' A woman genius seemed to need the close support of a man; Ellis gave the example of Madame Curie, who was the wife of an already distinguished scientist, and pointed out that Mrs. Browning's finest poems were all written after she had the good fortune to meet Mr. Browning. Ellis found that women disliked the essentially intellectual process of analysis—'They have the instinctive feeling that analysis may possibly destroy the emotional complexes by which they are largely moved and which appeal to them.' 15

These observations would have remained mere curiosities of scholarship were it not for the development, beginning in the 1960s, of new scientific research into the brain. Paradoxically, the finding of gender differences corresponded with the period when the political denial that any differences existed was at its most vocal. 16

Paradoxically, too, interest in these differences grew out of an original scientific motive to suppress them. The 17 problem arose from IQ tests. Researchers noticed consistent differences favouring one sex over the other in some of the abilities tested. This did not result in a chorus of eureka from the scientific community. In fact, it was regarded as something of a nuisance, muddying the waters of accurate measurement of intelligence. In the 1950s Dr. D. Wechsler, an American scientist who developed the IQ test most commonly used today, found that over thirty tests 'discriminated' in favour of one or the other sex. The very use of the word suggests that the tests themselves were somehow to blame for the fact that different sexes achieved different success rates.

18 Wechsler, among others, sought to resolve the problem by eliminating all those tests which resulted in findings of significant sex differences. When it still proved difficult to produce 'sex-neutral' results, they deliberately introduced 'male-slanted' or 'female-slanted' items to arrive at approximately equal scores. It is an odd way of conducting a scientific study; if you don't like the result you get from an experiment, you fix the data to produce a more palatable conclusion. The sporting equivalent would be to handicap Olympic pole-vaulters with lead weights, or poles of different length, to ensure that the desired truth prevails: that all pole-vaulters, regardless of prowess or agility, are created equal.

19 Even so, sex differences stubbornly emerged, like recalcitrant dandelions in a chemically treated lawn. Wechsler even came to the conclusion from a series of sub-tests that it might be possible to demonstrate a measurable superiority of women over men in general intelligence. On the other hand, out of 105 tests assessing skills in solving maze-puzzles, involving the most heterogeneous populations throughout the world, ranging from the most primitive to the most highly civilised, 99 showed an incontrovertible male superiority. Perhaps the safest and least controversial synthesis of these findings would have been that girls are too intelligent to bother with anything as silly as a maze-puzzle test.

20 Preoccupied with finding sex-neutral IQ techniques, Wechsler regarded the evidence that the sexes *were* different as a mere nuisance. Rather as Columbus might have regarded his discovery of America as something of an irrelevance, since, after all, he was looking for the East Indies, Wechsler observed, almost parenthetically,

> Our findings do confirm what poets and novelists have often asserted, and the average person long believed, namely, that men not only behave, but 'think' differently from women.

What an early British pioneer of sex differences has called 'a conspiracy of silence surrounding the topic of human sex differences' was soon drowned in a babble of sociological explanations. Children, it was argued, were born psychosexually neutral; then parents, teachers, employers, politicians, and all the wicked fairies of society got to work on the innocent virginity of the mind. The main group championing the neutrality theory was led by Dr. John Money, of Johns Hopkins University in the USA.

> Sexuality is undifferentiated at birth and . . . it becomes differentiated as masculine or feminine in the various experiences of growing up.

So, if men and women were different, it must be the result of social conditioning. Society was to blame, which, in the view of sociology, it usually is.

21 If there is still a dispute about how sex differences arise there is now no argument in the scientific community that such differences exist. It cannot be stressed often enough that this essay concerns itself with the *average* man and the *average* woman. In the same way, we might say that men are taller than women. Look across any crowded room and this will be obvious. Of course some women will be taller than some men, and the tallest woman may possibly be taller than the tallest man. But statistically men are on average 7 per cent taller, and the tallest person in the world, rather than in the room, is certainly a man.

22 The statistical variations in sex differences which we will explore, in skills, aptitudes or abilities, are much greater than they are in relation to height; there will always be the exception to the average, the person with exceptional 'wrong-sex' skills, but the exception does not invalidate the general, average rule. These differences have a practical, social relevance. On measurements of various aptitude tests, the difference between the sexes in average scores on these tests can be as much as 25 per cent. A difference of as little as 5 per cent has been found to have a marked impact on the

occupations or activities at which men or women will, on average, excel.

23 The area where the biggest differences have been found lies in what scientists call 'spatial ability'. That's being able to picture things, their shape, position, geography and proportion, accurately in the mind's eye—all skills that are crucial to the practical ability to work with three-dimensional objects or drawings. One scientist who has reviewed the extensive literature on the subject concludes, 'The fact of the male's superiority in spatial ability is not in dispute.' It is confirmed by literally hundreds of different scientific studies.

24 A typical test measures the skill of men and women in the assembly of a three-dimensional, mechanical apparatus. Only a quarter of the women could perform the task better than the average male. At the top end of the scale of mechanical aptitude there will be twice as many men as women.

25 From school age onwards, boys will generally outperform girls in areas of mathematics involving abstract concepts of space, relationships, and theory. At the very highest level of mathematical excellence, according to the biggest survey ever conducted, the very best boys totally eclipse the very best girls. Dr. Julian Stanley and Dr. Camilla Benbow, two American psychologists, worked with highly gifted students of both sexes. Not only did they find that the best girl never beat the best boy—they also discovered a startling sex ratio of mathematical brilliance: for every exceptional girl there were more than thirteen exceptional boys.

26 Scientists know that they walk on social eggshells when they venture any theory about human behaviour. But researchers into sex differences are increasingly impatient with the polite attempt to find a social explanation for these differences. As Camilla Benbow now says of her studies showing a male superiority in mathematically gifted children, 'After 15 years looking for an environmental explanation and getting zero results, I gave up.' She readily admitted to us her belief that the difference in ability has a biological basis.

27 Boys also have the superior hand-eye co-ordination necessary for ball sports. Those same skills mean that they can more easily imagine, alter, and rotate an object in their mind's eye. Boys find it easier than girls to construct block buildings from two-dimensional blueprints, and to assess correctly how the angle of the surface level of water in a jug would change when the jug was tilted to different angles.

28 This male advantage in seeing patterns and abstract

relationships—what could be called general strategic rather than the detailed tactical thinking—perhaps explains the male dominance of chess, even in a country like the USSR, where the game is a national sport played by both sexes. An alternative explanation, more acceptable to those who would deny the biological basis of sex differences, is that women have become so conditioned to the fact of male chess-playing superiority that they subconsciously assign themselves lower expectations; but this is a rather wilful rejection of scientific evidence for the sake of maintaining a prejudice.

The better spatial ability of men could certainly help to 29
explain that male superiority in map-reading we noted earlier. Here again, the prejudice of male motorists is confirmed by experiment; girls and boys were each given city street maps and, without rotating the map, asked to describe whether they would be turning left or right at particular intersections as they mentally made their way across town and back. Boys did better. More women than men like to turn the map round, physically to match the direction in which they are traveling when they are trying to find their way.

While the male brain gives men the edge in dealing with 30
things and theorems, the female brain is organised to respond more sensitively to all sensory stimuli. Women do better than men on tests of verbal ability. Females are equipped to receive a wider range of sensory information, to connect and relate that information with greater facility, to place a primacy on personal relationships, and to communicate. Cultural influences may reinforce these strengths, but the advantages are innate.

The differences are apparent in the very first hours after 31
birth. It has been shown that girl babies are much more interested than boys in people and faces; the boys seem just as happy with an object dangled in front of them.

Girls say their first words and learn to speak in short 32
sentences earlier than boys, and are generally more fluent in their pre-school years. They read earlier, too, and do better in coping with the building blocks of language like grammar, punctuation and spelling. Boys outnumber girls by 4 : 1 in remedial reading classes. Later, women find it easier to master foreign languages, and are more proficient in their own, with a better command of grammar and spelling. They are also more fluent: stuttering and other speech defects occur almost exclusively among boys.

33 Girls and women hear better than men. When the sexes are compared, women show a greater sensitivity to sound. The dripping tap will get the woman out of bed before the man has even woken up. Six times as many girls as boys can sing in tune. They are also much more adept at noticing small changes in volume, which goes some way to explaining women's superior sensitivity to that 'tone of voice' which their male partners are so often accused of adopting.

34 Men and women even see some things differently. Women see better in the dark. They are more sensitive to the red end of the spectrum, seeing more red hues there than men, and have a better visual memory.

35 Men see better than women in bright light. Intriguing results also show that men tend to be literally blinkered; they see in a narrow field—mild tunnel vision—with greater concentration on depth. They have a better sense of perspective than women. Women, however, quite literally take in the bigger picture. They have wider peripheral vision, because they have more of the receptor rods and cones in the retina, at the back of the eyeball, to receive a wider arc of visual input.

36 The differences extend to the other senses. Women react faster, and more acutely, to pain, although their overall resistance to long-term discomfort is greater than men's. In a sample of young adults, females showed 'overwhelmingly' greater sensitivity to pressure on the skin on every part of the body. In childhood and maturity, women have a tactile sensitivity so superior to men's that in some tests there is no overlap between the scores of the two sexes; in these, the least sensitive woman is more sensitive than the most sensitive man.

37 There is strong evidence that men and women have different senses of taste—women being more sensitive to bitter flavours like quinine, and preferring higher concentrations and greater quantities of sweet things. Men score higher in discerning salty flavours. Overall, however, the evidence strongly suggests a greater female delicacy and perception in taste. Should more great chefs be women? Or do many great male chefs have more than their share of feminine sensibilities?

38 Women's noses, as well as their palates, are more sensitive than men's; a case in point is their perception of exaltolide, a synthetic musk-like odour associated with men, but hardly noticeable to them. Women found the smell attractive. Interestingly, this superior sensitivity increases just before

ovulation; at a critical time of her menstrual cycle, the biology of a woman makes her more sensitive to man.

This superiority in so many of the senses can be clinically measured—yet it is what accounts for women's almost supernatural 'intuition'. Women are simply better equipped to notice things to which men are comparatively blind and deaf. There is no witchcraft in this superior perception—it is extrasensory only in terms of the blunter, male senses. Women are better at picking up social cues, picking up important nuances of meaning from tones of voice or intensity of expression. Men sometimes become exasperated at a woman's reaction to what they say. They do not realise that women are probably 'hearing' much more than what the man himself thinks he is 'saying'. Women tend to be better judges of character. Older females have a better memory of names and faces, and a greater sensitivity to other people's preferences. 39

Sex differences have been noted in the comparative memory of men and women. Women can store, for short periods at least, more irrelevant and random information than men; men can only manage the trick when the information is organised into some coherent form, or has a specific relevance to them. 40

So men are more self-centered—so what else is new? What's new is that the folklore of gender, which is always vulnerable to dismissive, politically motivated, fashionable opinion, is now shown to have a basis in scientific fact. 41

Stephen Jay Gould

Women's Brains

Gould, born 1941, teaches biology, geology, and the history of science at Harvard, but he is best known as an essayist and as the author of a number of books on scientific issues and controversies. He has won many awards and honors for collections of essays such as Ever Since Darwin *(1977),* The Flamingo's Smile *(1985), and* The Panda's Thumb *(1980), and for books such as* Time's Arrow, Time's Cycle *(1987),* Wonderful Life *(1989), and* The Mismeasure of Man *(1981). The following essay appeared in* The Panda's Thumb *and, in somewhat different form, in a section of* The Mismeasure of Man*—a book about both the abuses of intelligence testing and the social influences on science.*

1 In the prelude to *Middlemarch,* George Eliot lamented the unfulfilled lives of talented women:

> Some have felt that these blundering lives are due to the inconvenient indefiniteness with which the Supreme Power has fashioned the natures of women: if there were one level of feminine incompetence as strict as the ability to count three and no more, the social lot of women might be treated with scientific certitude.

2 Eliot goes on to discount the idea of innate limitation, but while she wrote in 1872, the leaders of European anthropometry were trying to measure "with scientific certitude" the inferiority of women. Anthropometry, or measurement of the human body, is not so fashionable a field these days, but it dominated the human sciences for much of the nineteenth century and remained popular until intelligence testing replaced skull measurement as a favored device for making invidious comparisons among races, classes, and sexes. Craniometry, or measurement of the skull, commanded the most attention and respect. Its unquestioned leader, Paul Broca (1824–80), professor of clinical surgery at the Faculty of Medicine in Paris, gathered a school of disciples and imitators around himself. Their work, so meticulous and apparently irrefutable, exerted great influence and won high esteem as a jewel of nineteenth-century science.

3 Broca's work seemed particularly invulnerable to refutation. Had he not measured with the most scrupulous care and accuracy? (Indeed, he had. I have the greatest respect for Broca's meticulous procedure. His numbers are sound. But science is an inferential exercise, not a catalog of facts. Numbers, by themselves, specify nothing. All depends upon what you do with them.) Broca depicted himself as an apostle of objectivity, a man who bowed before facts and cast aside superstition and sentimentality. He declared that "there is no faith, however respectable, no interest, however legitimate, which must not accommodate itself to the progress of human knowledge and bend before truth." Women, like it or not, had smaller brains than men and, therefore, could not equal them in intelligence. This fact,

Broca argued, may reinforce a common prejudice in male society, but it is also a scientific truth. L. Manouvrier, a black sheep in Broca's fold, rejected the inferiority of women and wrote with feeling about the burden imposed upon them by Broca's numbers:

> Women displayed their talents and their diplomas. They also invoked philosophical authorities. But they were opposed by *numbers* unknown to Condorcet or to John Stuart Mill. These numbers fell upon poor women like a sledge hammer, and they were accompanied by commentaries and sarcasms more ferocious than the most misogynist imprecations of certain church fathers. The theologians had asked if women had a soul. Several centuries later, some scientists were ready to refuse them a human intelligence.

Broca's argument rested upon two sets of data: the larger 4
brains of men in modern societies, and a supposed increase in male superiority through time. His most extensive data came from autopsies performed personally in four Parisian hospitals. For 292 male brains, he calculated an average weight of 1,325 grams; 140 female brains averaged 1,144 grams for a difference of 181 grams, or 14 percent of the male weight. Broca understood, of course, that part of this difference could be attributed to the greater height of males. Yet he made no attempt to measure the effect of size alone and actually stated that it cannot account for the entire difference because we know, a priori, that women are not as intelligent as men (a premise that the data were supposed to test, not rest upon):

> We might ask if the small size of the female brain depends exclusively upon the small size of her body. Tiedemann has proposed this explanation. But we must not forget that women are, on the average, a little less intelligent than men, a difference which we should not exaggerate but which is, nonetheless, real. We are therefore permitted to suppose that the relatively small size of the female brain depends in part upon her physical inferiority and in part upon her intellectual inferiority.

In 1873, the year after Eliot published *Middlemarch,* 5
Broca measured the cranial capacities of prehistoric skulls from L'Homme Mort cave. Here he found a difference of

only 99.5 cubic centimeters between males and females, while modern populations range from 129.5 to 220.7. Topinard, Broca's chief disciple, explained the increasing discrepancy through time as a result of differing evolutionary pressures upon dominant men and passive women:

> The man who fights for two or more in the struggle for existence, who has all the responsibility and the cares of tomorrow, who is constantly active in combating the environment and human rivals, needs more brain than the woman whom he must protect and nourish, the sedentary woman, lacking any interior occupations, whose role is to raise children, love, and be passive.

6 In 1879, Gustave Le Bon, chief misogynist of Broca's school, used these data to publish what must be the most vicious attack upon women in modern scientific literature (no one can top Aristotle). I do not claim his views were representative of Broca's school, but they were published in France's most respected anthropological journal. Le Bon concluded:

> In the most intelligent races, as among the Parisians, there are a large number of women whose brains are closer in size to those of gorillas than to the most developed male brains. This inferiority is so obvious that no one can contest it for a moment; only its degree is worth discussion. All psychologists who have studied the intelligence of women, as well as poets and novelists, recognize today that they represent the most inferior forms of human evolution and that they are closer to children and savages than to an adult, civilized man. They excel in fickleness, inconstancy, absence of thought and logic, and incapacity to reason. Without doubt there exist some distinguished women, very superior to the average man, but they are as exceptional as the birth of any monstrosity, as, for example, of a gorilla with two heads; consequently, we may neglect them entirely.

7 Nor did Le Bon shrink from the social implications of his views. He was horrified by the proposal of some American reformers to grant women higher education on the same basis as men:

> A desire to give them the same education, and, as a consequence, to propose the same goals for them, is a dangerous

> chimera. . . . The day when, misunderstanding the inferior occupations which nature has given her, women leave the home and take part in our battles; on this day a social revolution will begin, and everything that maintains the sacred ties of the family will disappear.

Sound familiar?*

I have reexamined Broca's data, the basis for all this derivative pronouncement, and I find his numbers sound but his interpretation ill-founded, to say the least. The data supporting his claim for increased difference through time can be easily dismissed. Broca based his contention on the samples from L'Homme Mort alone—only seven male and six female skulls in all. Never have so little data yielded such far ranging conclusions. 8

In 1888, Topinard published Broca's more extensive data on the Parisian hospitals. Since Broca recorded height and age as well as brain size, we may use modern statistics to remove their effect. Brain weight decreases with age, and Broca's women were, on average, considerably older than his men. Brain weight increases with height, and his average man was almost half a foot taller than his average woman. I used multiple regression, a technique that allowed me to assess simultaneously the influence of height and age upon brain size. In an analysis of the data for women, I found that, at average male height and age, a woman's brain would weigh 1,212 grams. Correction for height and age reduces Broca's measured difference of 181 grams by more than a third, to 113 grams. 9

I don't know what to make of this remaining difference because I cannot assess other factors known to influence brain size in a major way. Cause of death has an important effect: degenerative disease often entails a substantial diminution of brain size. (This effect is separate from the decrease attributed to age alone.) Eugene Schreider, also working with Broca's data, found that men killed in accidents had brains weighing, on average, 60 grams more than men dying of infectious diseases. The best modern data I 10

* When I wrote this essay, I assumed that Le Bon was a marginal, if colorful, figure. I have since learned that he was a leading scientist, one of the founders of social psychology, and best known for a seminal study on crowd behavior, still cited today (*La psychologie des foules,* 1895), and for his work on unconscious motivation.

can find (from American hospitals) records a full 100-gram difference between death by degenerative arteriosclerosis and by violence or accident. Since so many of Broca's subjects were very elderly women, we may assume that lengthy degenerative disease was more common among them than among the men.

11 More importantly, modern students of brain size still have not agreed on a proper measure for eliminating the powerful effect of body size. Height is partly adequate, but men and women of the same height do not share the same body build. Weight is even worse than height, because most of its variation reflects nutrition rather than intrinsic size—fat versus skinny exerts little influence upon the brain. Manouvrier took up this subject in the 1880s and argued that muscular mass and force should be used. He tried to measure this elusive property in various ways and found a marked difference in favor of men, even in men and women of the same height. When he corrected for what he called "sexual mass," women actually came out slightly ahead in brain size.

12 Thus, the corrected 113-gram difference is surely too large; the true figure is probably close to zero and may as well favor women as men. And 113 grams, by the way, is exactly the average difference between a 5 foot 4 inch and a 6 foot 4 inch male in Broca's data. We would not (especially us short folks) want to ascribe greater intelligence to tall men. In short, who knows what to do with Broca's data? They certainly don't permit any confident claim that men have bigger brains than women.

13 To appreciate the social role of Broca and his school, we must recognize that his statements about the brains of women do not reflect an isolated prejudice toward a single disadvantaged group. They must be weighed in the context of a general theory that supported contemporary social distinctions as biologically ordained. Women, blacks, and poor people suffered the same disparagement, but women bore the brunt of Broca's argument because he had easier access to data on women's brains. Women were singularly denigrated but they also stood as surrogates for other disenfranchised groups. As one of Broca's disciples wrote in 1881: "Men of the black races have a brain scarcely heavier than that of white women." This juxtaposition extended into many other realms of anthropological argument, particularly to claims that, anatomically and emotionally, both

women and blacks were like white children—and that white children, by the theory of recapitulation, represented an ancestral (primitive) adult stage of human evolution. I do not regard as empty rhetoric the claim that women's battles are for all of us.

Maria Montessori did not confine her activities to educa- 14
tional reform for young children. She lectured on anthropology for several years at the University of Rome, and wrote an influential book entitled *Pedagogical Anthropology* (English edition, 1913). Montessori was no egalitarian. She supported most of Broca's work and the theory of innate criminality proposed by her compatriot Cesare Lombroso. She measured the circumference of children's heads in her schools and inferred that the best prospects had bigger brains. But she had no use for Broca's conclusions about women. She discussed Manouvrier's work at length and made much of his tentative claim that women, after proper correction of the data, had slightly larger brains than men. Women, she concluded, were intellectually superior, but men had prevailed heretofore by dint of physical force. Since technology has abolished force as an instrument of power, the era of women may soon be upon us: "In such an epoch there will really be superior human beings, there will really be men strong in morality and in sentiment. Perhaps in this way the reign of women is approaching, when the enigma of her anthropological superiority will be deciphered. Woman was always the custodian of human sentiment, morality and honor."

This represents one possible antidote to "scientific" claims 15
for the constitutional inferiority of certain groups. One may affirm the validity of biological distinctions but argue that the data have been misinterpreted by prejudiced men with a stake in the outcome, and that disadvantaged groups are truly superior. In recent years, Elaine Morgan has followed this strategy in her *Descent of Woman,* a speculative reconstruction of human prehistory from the woman's point of view—and as farcical as more famous tall tales by and for men.

I prefer another strategy. Montessori and Morgan fol- 16
lowed Broca's philosophy to reach a more congenial conclusion. I would rather label the whole enterprise of setting a biological value upon groups for what it is: irrelevant and highly injurious. George Eliot well appreciated the special tragedy that biological labeling imposed upon members of

disadvantaged groups. She expressed it for people like herself—women of extraordinary talent. I would apply it more widely—not only to those whose dreams are flouted but also to those who never realize that they may dream—but I cannot match her prose. In conclusion, then, the rest of Eliot's prelude to *Middlemarch:*

> The limits of variation are really much wider than anyone would imagine from the sameness of women's coiffure and the favorite love stories in prose and verse. Here and there a cygnet is reared uneasily among the ducklings in the brown pond, and never finds the living stream in fellowship with its own oary-footed kind. Here and there is born a Saint Theresa, foundress of nothing, whose loving heartbeats and sobs after an unattained goodness tremble off and are dispersed among hindrances instead of centering in some long-recognizable deed.

Evelyn Fox Keller

Women in Science: An Analysis of a Social Problem

Evelyn Fox Keller has been associated with several universities (e.g., MIT, Northeastern, Cornell), but she now is affiliated with the rhetoric, history of science, and women's studies programs at the University of California at Berkeley. She was one of the first scholars to look carefully at gender issues in the conduct of science. The following essay appeared in 1974 in Harvard Magazine*, an alumni publication.*

1 Are women's minds different from men's minds? In spite of the women's movement, the age-old debate centering around this question continues. We are surrounded by evidence of *de facto* differences between men's and women's intellects—in the problems that interest them, in the ways they try to solve those problems, and in the professions they choose. Even though it has become fashionable to view such

differences as environmental in origin, the temptation to seek an explanation in terms of innate differences remains a powerful one.

Perhaps the area in which this temptation is strongest is in science. Even those of us who would like to argue for intellectual equality are hard pressed to explain the extraordinarily meager representation of women in science, particularly in the upper echelons. Some would argue that the near absence of great women scientists demonstrates that women don't have the minds of true scientific creativity. While most of us would recognize the patent fallacies of this argument, it nevertheless causes us considerable discomfort. After all, the doors of the scientific establishment appear to have been open to women for some time now—shouldn't we begin to see more women excelling? 2

In the last fifty years the institutional barriers against women in science have been falling. During most of that time, the percentage of women scientists has declined, although recent years have begun to show an upswing (table I). Of those women who do become scientists, few are represented in the higher academic ranks (table II). In order to have a proper understanding of these data, it is necessary to review the many influences that operate. I would like to argue that the convenient explanation that men's minds are intrinsically different from women's is not only unwarranted by the evidence, but in fact reflects a mythology that is in itself a major contribution to the phenomena observed. 3

As a woman scientist, I have often pondered these questions, particularly at those times when my commitment to science seemed most precarious. Noticing that almost every other woman I had known in science had experienced similar crises of commitment, I sought to explain my ambivalence by concluding that science as a profession is 4

TABLE I. *Percentage of Ph.D.'s Earned by Women, 1920–1970*

	1920–29	1940–49	1950–59	1960–69
Physics and Astronomy	5.9	4.2	2.0	2.2
Biological Sciences	19.5	15.7	11.8	15.1
Mathematics	14.5	10.7	5.0	5.7
Psychology	29.4	24.1	14.8	20.7

Source: National Research Council

TABLE II. *Percentage Representation of Women, by Rank, in 20 Leading Universities (1962)*

	INSTRUCTOR	ASSISTANT PROFESSOR	ASSOCIATE PROFESSOR	PROFESSOR
Physics	5.6	1.2	1.3	0.9
Biological Sciences	16.3	7.1	6.7	1.3
Mathematics	16.7	10.1	7.3	0.4
Psychology	8.3	10.4	11.1	2.7

Source: J. B. Parrish, A. A. U. W. Journal, 55, 99

not as gratifying for women as it is for men, and that the reasons for this are to be found in the intrinsic nature of women and science. Several years ago, I endeavored to find out how general my own experiences were. In studying the statistics of success and failure for women in the professions, I indeed found that women fared less well in science than in other professions, although the picture that emerged seemed fairly bleak for all of us.

5 I collected these data during a leave of absence I had taken to accompany my husband to California. At the same time, I was also engaged in completing work I had begun the year before with a (male) colleague—work that seemed less and less compelling as the year wore on. Each week I would receive an enthusiastic telephone call from my colleague, reporting new information and responses he had received from workers he had met while delivering invited lectures on this work. At some point it occurred to me that perhaps there was a relation between my declining interest and isolation on the one hand, and his growing enthusiasm and public recognition on the other. Over the course of the year, he had received a score or more invitations to speak about this work, while I had received none. It began to dawn on me that there were far simpler explanations for both the observations I had made privately and the data I was collecting than that of intrinsic differences between the sexes.

6 I began to realize, for example, that had I been less isolated and more rewarded, my enthusiasm would have been correspondingly greater—a recognition that has been amply corroborated by my subsequent experience. Upon further reflection, I became aware of how much my own, and other similar, attitudes are influenced by a complex

interplay of subtle factors affecting us from birth on. The ways in which we rear our children, train our students, and interact with our colleagues are all so deeply imbued with our expectations and beliefs as to virtually guarantee a fulfillment to these beliefs.

How do men and women develop the characteristics we 7
attribute to them? There are clear differences between the sexes at birth, and there is even some evidence that these differences extend to the brain. Primate studies reveal marked differences in behavior between males and females—differences determined by the prenatal hormonal environment. It seems therefore quite possible that there are even intellectual differences determined prior to birth. For those inclined to believe in such predetermination, such a possibility may appear attractive. It is important to say, however, that there is to date no evidence of biologically determined differences in intelligence or cognitive styles, and that this remains true in spite of a rather considerable desire among many people to find such evidence.

An example of this interest is provided by the great 8
enthusiasm with which a recent study was met. This study purported to show that prenatal injection of progestin, a synthetic male hormone, leads to higher than average I.Q.'s in adolescent girls. Although this result was refuted by the original authors shortly after its original announcement, it nevertheless found its way into a rash of textbooks, where it remains. Similarly, there has been a great deal of interest in the measurement of differences in perceptual modes between girls and boys. Tests designed to measure the degree to which one's perception of a figure is independent of its background, or field, show that girls, by the time they enter school, are more field-dependent than boys. Field independence is positively correlated with mathematical and analytic abilities. While the results of these tests are remarkably culturally invariant (the Eskimos are a notable exception), it is important to point out both that the disparities observed are extremely small (of the order of 2 percent) and that they cannot be discerned before the age of five. While the possibility that these disparities are the result of innate differences between the sexes cannot be excluded, there is evidence relating performance on such tests to the individual's environment. What are the environmental differences that could account for such results?

9 We treat our sons and daughters differently from birth onward, although the magnitude of our distinction is largely unconscious. A rude awakening to the extent of our differential treatment can come in those rare instances when a fallacious sex assignment is made at birth, usually as a result of ambiguous genitalia, and must be subsequently corrected. The impact of these early cues can be assessed by the fact that such reassignments are considered unduly traumatic to make after the child is eighteen months old, in spite of the fact that failure to do so dooms the child to an apparent sexual identity at odds with his or her genotype. Sex reassignments made before this time result in apparently normal development. From this and related evidence, workers in this area have concluded that gender identity appears to be established, primarily on the basis of parental treatment, by the age of eighteen months.

10 Children acquire the meaning of their sex identity from the models before them. Their concept of female is based largely on the women they see, as their concept of male is based on the men they see. Their immediate perceptions are later expanded by the images they perceive on TV, and in the children's literature. It hardly need be pointed out that both of the latter present to our children extraordinarily rigid stereotypes.

11 It is not surprising, then, that children, even before they enter school, have acquired the belief that certain activities are male and others female. Science is a male activity.

12 The tenacity of this early view is such as to resist easy change. When my daughter was in nursery school, her class was asked one day about the occupation of their fathers. I objected to this, and, as a result, the next day the teacher asked, "Sarah, what does your mother do?" She replied, "My mother cooks, she sews, she cleans, and she takes care of us." "But Sarah, isn't your mother a scientist?" "Oh, yes," said Sarah—clearly implying that this was not a very relevant piece of information.

13 The explanation of her response lies not only in her need to define a conventional image of her mother, but also in the reality of her direct perceptions. Indeed it is true that, like many professional women, I do cook, sew, clean, and take care of my children. My professional identity is not brought into my home, although my husband's is. My daughter, therefore, like my son, continues to view mathematics and science as male, in spite of their information to the contrary.

While a child may be concerned with assigning sex labels only to external attributes, such as clothes, mannerisms, and occupations, the adolescent has already begun to designate internal states as male and female. Thus, in particular, clear thinking is characterized as hard thinking (a male image), and fuzzy thinking as soft thinking (a female image). A girl who thinks clearly and well is told she thinks "like a man." What are the implications of such associations for the girl who (for whatever reasons) does transcend social expectation and finds herself interested in science? Confusion in sexual identity is the inevitable concomitant of a self-definition at variance with the surrounding definitions of sexual norm. The girl who can take pride in "thinking like a man" without cost to her integrity as a girl is rare indeed. 14

Nevertheless, a considerable number of women, for whatever reasons, experience enough motivation and have demonstrated enough ability to embark on professional training for a scientific career. Graduate school is a time to prove that one is, in spite of one's aspirations, a woman, and—at one and the same time, because of one's aspirations—"more than" a woman. Social acceptability requires the former, and is considerably facilitated by the acquisition of a husband, while professional respectability requires the latter. The more exclusively male the definition of the profession, the more difficult it is to accomplish these conflicting goals. 15

My own experience as a graduate student of theoretical physics at Harvard was extreme, but possibly illustrative. I was surrounded by incessant prophecies of failure, independent of my performance. I knew of no counter-examples to draw confidence from, and was led to believe that none existed. (Later, however, I learned that some women in theoretical physics have survived, even at Harvard.) Warned that I would ultimately despair as I came to learn how impossible my ambitions were, I did, though not for the reasons that were then implied. Having denied myself rage, depression was in fact one of the few reasonable responses to the isolation, mockery, and suspicion that I experienced, both within and without my department. Ultimately I did earn my Ph.D. from the Harvard physics department, but only after having adapted my interests and thereby removed myself from the most critical pressures—a course many women have taken before and since. 16

Hostility, however, was not the only response I received, and not necessarily the usual response experienced by 17 professionally ambitious young women. The necessity of proving one's femininity leaves some women particularly susceptible to another danger—that of accepting, and even seeking, sexual approbation for intellectual and academic performance. There are enough men willing, if not eager, to provide such translated affirmation as to make this a serious problem. The relation between sexuality and intellectuality is an enormously complex subject. I raise it only to point out one perhaps obvious consequence of this confusion for women. Because, unlike men, they are often dependent on sexual and intellectual affirmation from one and the same individual or group, they can never be entirely confident of what is being affirmed. Is it an "A for a Lay" or a "Lay for an A"?

18 Finally, the female scientist is launched. What are her prospects? Many women choose this point to withdraw for a time in order to have children. Although there is a logic to this choice, it reflects a lack of awareness of the dynamics of normal professional growth. For the male scientist, the period immediately following acquisition of the Ph.D. is perhaps the most critical in his professional development. It is the time that he has, free of all the responsibilities that will later come to plague him, to accomplish enough work to establish his reputation. Often it is a time to affiliate himself with a school of thought, to prove his own, independent worth. Although this may have been the original function of the graduate training period, it has in recent times been displaced to the postgraduate years. Awareness of this displacement, of the critical importance of these years, has not permeated to the general public, or even, for the most part, to the science student. Many women therefore take this sometimes fatal step in ignorance. After having been out of a field for a few years, they usually find it next to impossible to return to their field except in the lowest-level positions. Only when it is too late do they learn that it would have been better to have their children first, before completing the Ph.D.

19 I need hardly enumerate the additional practical difficulties involved in combining a scientific (or any other) career with the raising of children. While the practical drains on one's time and energy are generally recognized, perhaps it is worth pointing out that the drains on one's intellectual energy are not generally recognized by men. Only those men

who have spent full time, for an extended period, caring for their children are aware of the extraordinary amount of mental space occupied by the thousand and one details and concerns that mothers routinely juggle. Many have come to the conclusion—beginning with Engels, and more recently including the Swedish government—that equality of the sexes in the work and professional force is not a realistic possibility until the sex roles in the family are radically redefined. Equality must begin at home.

Well, one might ask, what about those women in science 20
who have no children, who never marry? Surely they are freed from all of these difficulties. Why don't they perform better?

First of all, to be freed of responsibilities towards others is 21
not equivalent to having your own responsibilities assumed by others. Nowhere among women is to be found the counterpart of the male scientist who has a wife at home to look after his daily needs. The question, however, deserves a more serious answer, although the answer is almost painfully obvious. Our society does not have a place for unmarried women. They are among the most isolated, ostracized groups of our culture. When one thinks about the daily social and psychological pressures on the unmarried professional woman, one can hardly be surprised to discover that the data reveal that indeed, on the average, married women in science—even with children—publish more and perform better than unmarried women.

The enumeration of obstacles or handicaps faced by 22
women in science would hardly be complete without at least a reference to the inequalities of reward and approval awarded to work done by men and women. The personal anecdote I began with is more than an anecdote—it is evidence of a rather ubiquitous tendency, neither malicious nor necessarily even conscious, to give more public recognition to a man's accomplishments than to a woman's accomplishments. There are many different reasons for this—not least of which includes the habitually lesser inclination of many women to put themselves forward. There is also a simple, although documented, difference in evaluation of the actual work done by men and women.

While all of the above difficulties are hardly exclusive 23
problems of women in science, the question of identity in what has been defined as an almost exclusively male profes-

sion is more serious for women in science than in other fields. Not only is the field defined as male by virtue of its membership, it is also defined as male in relation to its methodology, style of thought, indeed its goals. To the extent that analytic thought is conceived as male thought, to the extent that we characterize the natural sciences as the "hard" sciences, to the extent that the procedure of science is to "attack" problems, and its goal, since Bacon, has been to "conquer" or "master" nature, a woman in science *must* in some way feel alien.

24 Traditionally, as in other similar situations, women who have succeeded in scientific careers have dealt with this conflict by identifying with the "aggressor"—incorporating its values and ideas, at the cost, inevitably, of separating themselves from their own sex. An alternative resolution, one opted for frequently in other professions, is to attempt to redefine one's subject so as to permit a more comfortable identification with it. It is in this way, and for this reason, that so many professional women root themselves in subjects that are viewed by the profession as peripheral. In science this is not easy to do, but perhaps not impossible. There is another tradition within science that is as replete with female images as the tradition that dominates today is replete with male images. We all know that the most creative science requires, in addition to a hardness of mind, also fertility and receptivity. The best scientists are those who have combined the two sets of images. It may be that a certain degree of intellectual security is necessary in order to permit the expression of both "male" and "female" thought in science. If women have first to prove their "male" qualifications for admission into the profession, they may never achieve the necessary confidence to allow themselves to use their "female" abilities. What is to be done?

25 The central theme of my discussion is that the differential performance of men and women in science, the apparent differences between conceptual styles of men and women everywhere, are the result, not so much of innate differences between the sexes, but rather of the myth that prevails throughout our culture identifying certain kinds of thinking as male and others as female. The consequent compartmentalization of our minds is as effective as if it had been biologically, and not socially, induced.

26 People conform to the expectations imposed upon them

in the evolution of their definition of sexual identity, thus confirming the very myth upon which these expectations are based. Such a process is not easy to change. Myths as deeply rooted and as self-affirming as this one can neither be wished nor willed away. The only hope is to chip away at it everywhere, to make enough small inroads so that future generations may ultimately grow up less hampered. Counter-measures can be effected at every stage of the process. Each may be of only limited effectiveness, but cumulatively they may permit enough women to emerge with intact, fully developed mental capacities—women who can serve as role models for future generations of students.

Specifically, we can begin by exerting a conscious effort to 27
raise our children to less rigid stereotypes. Although the full extent to which we differentiate our treatment of our sons and daughters is hidden from us, being largely unconscious, we can, by attending to what we do, raise our consciousness of our own behavior.

We can specifically encourage and reward interests and 28
abilities that survive social pressures. As teachers, men can consciously refrain from mixing academic with sexual approval. More generally, we can inform women students interested in science about the realities of the external difficulties they will face. It is all too easy for an individual experiencing such obstacles to internalize the responsibility for these obstacles. Specific advice can be given—for instance, to avoid interrupting a career immediately after the Ph.D. High-quality work by professional women can be sought out for recognition and encouragement in order to counteract the normal tendency to grant them less recognition. (The physicist Richard Courant, a very wise man, responded to the news that one of his most talented students was pregnant by giving her a raise—thus enabling her to hire competent help, and, simultaneously, obligating her to continue. After four such raises, she indeed did go on to become one of the country's better mathematicians.)

Extra care can be taken not to exclude women from 29
professional interaction on any level. Finally, hiring policies must take into account the human and political realities. Women students need role models if they are to mature properly. Providing such a model is an important part of the function of a faculty member and should be considered along with scholarly performance in hiring deliberations. Similarly, marriage is a social reality, and women scientists

who marry male scientists need jobs in the same area. Anti-nepotism hiring policies discriminate against women scientists, and even a neutral policy effectively does so as well. Universities might well consider pro-nepotism policies that would recognize the limitations of humans and geographical reality.

30 Most of the recommendations I have made require the cooperation of the male scientific community to implement. Why should they? Further, one may ask, why should women even be encouraged to become scientists when the list of odds against them is so overwhelming? Is a career in science intrinsically of so much greater value than other options more available to women?

31 I don't believe it is. Nevertheless, our society has become more and more technologically oriented. As we continue to move in this direction, as we come to attach increasing importance to scientific and technological know-how, women are threatened with a disenfranchisement possibly greater than ever before. The traditional role of the woman becomes increasingly eroded with technology and overpopulation, while the disparity between the more humanly oriented kinds of knowledge thought to be hers and the more technical kinds of knowledge operating in the real world grows larger. This disparity operates not only at the expense of the women who are thus barred from meaningful roles in society, but also at the expense of the society that has been content to relegate to women those more humanistic values we all claim to support.

32 Finally, myths that compartmentalize our minds by defining certain mental attributes as "male" and others as "female" leave us all functioning with only part of our minds. Though there may well be some innate biological differences between the sexes, there is hardly room for doubt that our preconceptions serve to exaggerate and rigidify any distinctions that might exist. These preconceptions operate as straitjackets for men and women alike. I believe that the best, most creative science, like the most creative human efforts of any kind, can only be achieved with a full, unhampered mind—if you like, an androgynous mind. Therefore, the giving up of the central myth that science is a product of male thought may well lead to a more creative, more imaginative, and, who knows, possibly even a more humanistic science.

GENDER AT WORK

Virginia Woolf
Professions for Women

Virginia Woolf (1882–1942) was one of the greatest writers of her time; perhaps you have read Mrs. Dalloway *(1925) or* To the Lighthouse *(1927) or* The Waves *(1931) or some of her essays. Born and raised in London in a circle of culture and learning known as the Bloomsbury Group, she founded with her husband the Hogarth Press in 1912, which was the first publisher (or first English publisher) of many famous writers. This essay, first given in 1931 to the Women's Service League in London, appeared in 1942 as part of her* Death of the Moth and Other Essays.

When your secretary invited me to come here, she told me 1
that your Society is concerned with the employment of women and she suggested that I might tell you something about my own professional experiences. It is true I am a woman; it is true I am employed, but what professional experiences have I had? It is difficult to say. My profession is literature; and in that profession there are fewer experiences for women than in any other, with the exception of the state—fewer, I mean, that are peculiar to women. For the road was cut many years ago—by Fanny Burney, by Aphra Behn, by Harriet Martineau, by Jane Austen, by George Eliot; many famous women, and many more unknown and forgotten, have been before me, making the path smooth, and regulating my steps. Thus, when I came to write, there were very few material obstacles in my way. Writing was a reputable and harmless occupation. The family peace was not broken by the scratching of a pen. No demand was made upon the family purse. For ten and sixpence one can buy paper enough to write all the plays of Shakespeare—if one has a mind that way. Pianos and models, Paris, Vienna and Berlin, masters and mistresses, are not needed by a writer.

The cheapness of writing paper is, of course, the reason why women have succeeded as writers before they have succeeded in the other professions.

2 But to tell you my story—it is a simple one. You have only got to figure to yourselves a girl in a bedroom with a pen in her hand. She had only to move that pen from left to right—from ten o'clock to one. Then it occurred to her to do what is simple and cheap enough after all—to slip a few of those pages into an envelope, fix a penny stamp in the corner, and drop the envelope in the red box at the corner. It was thus that I became a journalist; and my effort was rewarded on the first day of the following month—a very glorious day it was for me—by a letter from an editor containing a check for one pound ten shillings and sixpence. But to show you how little I deserve to be called a professional woman, how little I know of the struggles and difficulties of such lives, I have to admit that instead of spending that sum upon bread and butter, rent, shoes and stockings, or butcher's bills, I went out and bought a cat—a beautiful cat, a Persian cat, which very soon involved me in bitter disputes with my neighbors.

3 What could be easier than to write articles and to buy Persian cats with the profits? But wait a moment. Articles have to be about something. Mine, I seem to remember, was about a novel by a famous man. And while I was writing this review, I discovered that if I were going to review books I should need to do battle with a certain phantom. And the phantom was a woman, and when I came to know her better I called her after the heroine of a famous poem, The Angel in the House. It was she who used to come between me and my paper when I was writing reviews. It was she who bothered me and wasted my time and so tormented me that at last I killed her. You who come of a younger and happier generation may not have heard of her—you may not know what I mean by the Angel in the House. I will describe her as shortly as I can. She was intensely sympathetic. She was immensely charming. She was utterly unselfish. She excelled in the difficult arts of family life. She sacrificed herself daily. If there was chicken, she took the leg; if there was a draught she sat in it—in short she was so constituted that she never had a mind or a wish of her own, but preferred to sympathize always with the minds and wishes of others. Above all—I need not say it—she was pure. Her purity was supposed to be her chief beauty—her blushes, her great grace. In those days—

the last of Queen Victoria—every house had its Angel. And when I came to write I encountered her with the very first words. The shadow of her wings fell on my page; I heard the rustling of her skirts in the room. Directly, that is to say, I took my pen in hand to review that novel by a famous man, she slipped behind me and whispered: "My dear, you are a young woman. You are writing about a book that has been written by a man. Be sympathetic; be tender; flatter; deceive; use all the arts and wiles of our sex. Never let anybody guess that you have a mind of your own. Above all, be pure." And she made as if to guide my pen. I now record the one act for which I take some credit to myself, though the credit rightly belongs to some excellent ancestors of mine who left me a certain sum of money—shall we say five hundred pounds a year?—so that it was not necessary for me to depend solely on charm for my living. I turned upon her and caught her by the throat. I did my best to kill her. My excuse, if I were to be had up in a court of law, would be that I acted in self-defense. Had I not killed her she would have killed me. She would have plucked the heart out of my writing. For, as I found, directly I put pen to paper, you cannot review even a novel without having a mind of your own, without expressing what you think to be the truth about human relations, morality, sex. And all these questions, according to the Angel in the House, cannot be dealt with freely and openly by women; they must charm, they must conciliate, they must—to put it bluntly—tell lies if they are to succeed. Thus, whenever I felt the shadow of her wing or the radiance of her halo upon my page, I took up the inkpot and flung it at her. She died hard. Her fictitious nature was of great assistance to her. It is far harder to kill a phantom than a reality. She was always creeping back when I thought I had despatched her. Though I flatter myself that I killed her in the end, the struggle was severe; it took much time that had better have been spent upon learning Greek grammar; or in roaming the world in search of adventures. But it was a real experience; it was an experience that was bound to befall all women writers at that time. Killing the Angel in the House was part of the occupation of a woman writer.

But to continue my story. The Angel was dead; what then 4
remained? You may say that what remained was a simple and common object—a young woman in a bedroom with an inkpot. In other words, now that she had rid herself of falsehood, that young woman had only to be herself. Ah, but what is "herself"? I mean, what is a woman? I assure you, I

do not know. I do not believe that you know. I do not believe that anybody can know until she has expressed herself in all the arts and professions open to human skill. That indeed is one of the reasons why I have come here—out of respect for you, who are in process of showing us by your experiments what a woman is, who are in process of providing us, by your failures and successes, with that extremely important piece of information.

5 But to continue the story of my professional experiences. I made one pound ten and six by my first review; and I bought a Persian cat with the proceeds. Then I grew ambitious. A Persian cat is all very well, I said; but a Persian cat is not enough. I must have a motor car. And it was thus that I became a novelist—for it is a very strange thing that people will give you a motor car if you will tell them a story. It is a still stranger thing that there is nothing so delightful in the world as telling stories. It is far pleasanter than writing reviews of famous novels. And yet, if I am to obey your secretary and tell you my professional experiences as a novelist, I must tell you about a very strange experience that befell me as a novelist. And to understand it you must try first to imagine a novelist's state of mind. I hope I am not giving away professional secrets if I say that a novelist's chief desire is to be as unconscious as possible. He has to induce in himself a state of perpetual lethargy. He wants life to proceed with the utmost quiet and regularity. He wants to see the same faces, to read the same books, to do the same things day after day, month after month, while he is writing, so that nothing may break the illusion in which he is living—so that nothing may disturb or disquiet the mysterious nosings about, feelings round, darts, dashes and sudden discoveries of that very shy and illusive spirit, the imagination. I suspect that this state is the same both for men and women. Be that as it may, I want you to imagine me writing a novel in a state of trance. I want you to figure to yourselves a girl sitting with a pen in her hand, which for minutes, and indeed for hours, she never dips into the inkpot. The image that comes to my mind when I think of this girl is the image of a fisherman lying sunk in dreams on the verge of a deep lake with a rod held out over the water. She was letting her imagination sweep unchecked round every rock and cranny of the world that lies submerged in the depths of our unconscious being. Now came the experience, the experience that I believe to be far commoner with women writers than with men. The line raced through the girl's

fingers. Her imagination had rushed away. It had sought the pools, the depths, the dark places where the largest fish slumber. And then there was a smash. There was an explosion. There was foam and confusion. The imagination had dashed itself against something hard. The girl was roused from her dream. She was indeed in a state of the most acute and difficult distress. To speak without figure she had thought of something, something about the body, about the passions which it was unfitting for her as a woman to say. Men, her reason told her, would be shocked. The consciousness of what men will say of a woman who speaks the truth about her passions had roused her from her artist's state of unconsciousness. She could write no more. The trance was over. Her imagination could work no longer. This I believe to be a very common experience with women writers—they are impeded by the extreme conventionality of the other sex. For though men sensibly allow themselves great freedom in these respects, I doubt that they realize or can control the extreme severity with which they condemn such freedom in women.

These then were two very genuine experiences of my own. 6
These were two of the adventures of my professional life. The first—killing the Angel in the House—I think I solved. She died. But the second, telling the truth about my own experiences as a body, I do not think I solved. I doubt that any woman has solved it yet. The obstacles against her are still immensely powerful—and yet they are very difficult to define. Outwardly, what is simpler than to write books? Outwardly, what obstacles are there for a woman rather than for a man? Inwardly, I think, the case is very different; she has still many ghosts to fight, many prejudices to overcome. Indeed it will be a long time still, I think, before a woman can sit down to write a book without finding a phantom to be slain, a rock to be dashed against. And if this is so in literature, the freest of all professions for women, how is it in the new professions which you are now for the first time entering?

Those are the questions that I should like, had I time, to ask 7
you. And indeed, if I have laid stress upon these professional experiences of mine, it is because I believe that they are, though in different forms, yours also. Even when the path is nominally open—when there is nothing to prevent a woman from being a doctor, a lawyer, a civil servant—there are many phantoms and obstacles, as I believe, looming in her way. To discuss and define them is I think of great value and importance; for thus only can the labor be shared, the difficulties be

solved. But besides this, it is necessary also to discuss the ends and the aims for which we are fighting, for which we are doing battle with these formidable obstacles. Those aims cannot be taken for granted; they must be perpetually questioned and examined. The whole position, as I see it—here in this hall surrounded by women practising for the first time in history I know not how many different professions—is one of extraordinary interest and importance. You have won rooms of your own in the house hitherto exclusively owned by men. You are able, though not without great labor and effort, to pay the rent. You are earning your five hundred pounds a year. But this freedom is only a beginning; the room is your own, but it is still bare. It has to be furnished; it has to be decorated; it has to be shared. How are you going to furnish it, how are you going to decorate it? With whom are you going to share it, and upon what terms? These, I think, are questions of the utmost importance and interest. For the first time in history you are able to ask them; for the first time you are able to decide for yourselves what the answers should be. Willingly would I stay and discuss those questions and answers—but not tonight. My time is up; and I must cease.

Jean Reith Schroedel

Amy Kelley, Machinist

Jean Reith Schroedel (born 1951) worked as a machinist before attending the University of Washington, so it probably seemed natural for her to do oral histories of women in blue-collar trades, the histories collected in her 1985 book Alone in a Crowd: Women in the Trades Tell Their Stories. *One of the twenty-five Seattle-area women whom Schroedel profiles in her book is Amy Kelley.*

1 My parents were divorced when I was nine. My father was a cook at a twenty-four-hour cafe. My mother used to work two jobs—a pressman at a drycleaner's and also as a janitress. After the divorce, my mother moved in with my aunt, who is a widow. My aunt was a journeyman printer—

negative stripper—and she was very independent, so I learned a lot of that from her. She's also one of the first women in her field, which subconsciously I wonder if that's what got me into this, but somehow I really don't think so. My aunt was more influential in my life than my mom. Although my mom was around, she was always working.

When we moved to Ballard I was in the fourth grade, and 2
I made some friends out there, but found them to be more closed-minded than neighborly. I didn't really care for the types of kids that were out there, which is why I continued to commute to the Central District to go to school. I felt more comfortable there than I did out in Ballard. Being a minority made it kind of awkward. The school I went to was more or less for low-income students, so we didn't have a lot of classes, and it wasn't coed, so we didn't have classes like shop. There was home ec and sewing, basic women-type classes. From the time I was a freshman in high school I worked to put myself through. Right after school I had to go straight to work, so I was never able to take extracurricular activities like volleyball.

I started out when I was fourteen years old working for a 3
knitting company based in Ballard. They made ski sweaters. I started out as just a packer. I'd pack the sweaters in plastic bags and get them ready to ship. Then after awhile I got really interested in learning to run the knitting machines. There were no women running the knitting machines. I wasn't supposed to run the knitting machines because I was under age. Because of the child labor laws I had to be sixteen. But I would be able to sneak over and learn when I didn't have much else to do. The boss didn't care as long as I wasn't actually running them. I was just learning how. The knitting was minimum wage. I don't know what minimum wage was in nineteen sixty-nine. It was like a dollar twenty-five. It got slack and I got laid off, so I got a job working in a drive-in restaurant. I started that in nineteen seventy-one—waitress, whatever you want to call it. When I turned eighteen I was making a dollar sixty-five an hour. That was minimum wage, so it had to be a lot less when I was working at the sweater company. It was not so great, that's for sure. The conditions at the knitting mill were not that great. I didn't like the fact that the people who owned the place took advantage of immigrants. They'd pay them the minimum wage and work them like they had no feelings. Just produce the work and no money. I didn't like that. But the drive-in job, I enjoyed

that. I really liked working with the public. It was fun, and I had a neat boss who was an older guy. He was really good; there are not many places like that. But the pay was lousy.

4 I started thinking about non-traditional work seriously when I was a senior in high school, because I realized there'd be something I'd have to do when I got out. I had just met my husband. When he came back from Vietnam he eventually found employment as a machine operator at a big machine shop in Seattle. At first, during all this time I had known him, we discussed what he was doing at work. I found it fascinating. It was not necessarily machine-type work that I was thinking about. It was more like something automotive.

5 When I finally thought about machine shop work, I liked the money, and I always wanted to do something different. And then, of course, I like working with my hands. But I thought that maybe I might not be smart enough—whether my education was enough or did I know enough to do it. . . .

6 My husband (at that time he was my boyfriend) suggested I take some training courses, so he looked around. He had been going to a private fellow who had a private course he was giving in his house, teaching people how to read precision instruments and blueprints. Well, I'd only taken the precision part of it, learning how to use the instruments and stuff. My husband was working in the aircraft industry, and by then they were looking for women and minorities with non-traditional skills. The federal contracts wanted to see more minorities and women in the non-traditional jobs, so they were essentially out looking. They were asking people in the shop if they knew women that would qualify for that kind of thing, so I kind of fell right into place. It helps to know somebody on the inside out there.

7 When I was hired, I was hired as a milling-machine trainee, which is a twenty-two-month program. I didn't know what to expect, because I had never set foot in a machine shop before in my entire life. I didn't know what it would be like to work with a bunch of men. I felt like I was very naive when I went in there. I had just come out of an all-girl high school and I didn't know a four-letter word from a five-letter word.

8 . . . As it turned out I was probably the youngest person in the whole shop. And *all* these guys that I saw! I thought, "Gee, these guys don't look very friendly at all." And I'm trying to get enough courage to say, "I'll do all right." The

first room was awesome. It was closely packed with machines and noisy. It was the largest machine shop in the company—the machine fabrication shop. The head count at that time was over twelve hundred people on all three shifts. It averages three hundred to four hundred people per shift in the entire building and everybody has plenty of space to breathe. They're not real crowded or cramped. They could easily get two or three airplanes in a building that size. It's like a giant warehouse. And the amount of men compared with the amount of women was—really—I didn't think there were so many men in one place. At the time I was the youngest female in there. Now it's changed, but when I walked in there in nineteen seventy-two all the women were either dispatch clerks or tool room clerks, and all in their upper forties and had been there a long time. There wasn't any woman in the non-traditional jobs, so when I went on the machine it was like I was there all by myself.

When I went in I was wondering what it would be like to work with guys. I was wondering whether the guys would like me, whether I could work with them. I knew at least one person there and that was my husband, so I didn't feel like I'd be totally lost, but the others—they were all white, all male, and probably starting at age thirty-five and up. 9

After the first or second day there was a supervisor that kind of took me under his wing. He was Japanese and he always reminded me of the way I'd like to have my father be. He made me do and think on my own, but it was like he was looking out for me, which I really appreciated. 10

After eight months of learning the milling machine, I was approached by the apprenticeship supervisor and asked if I'd be interested in the apprenticeship program. It sounded fascinating, because I was getting bored with what I was doing, so I filled in the application and had to go before the review board, which was made up of three representatives of management, generally from upper management, and three members from the union. . . . 11

My entire interview was tape recorded, and I understand I was the only one tape recorded. The main concern was whether I was going to get married and get pregnant, and I got so tired of hearing it. And then also why I really wanted to become an apprentice, did I really feel I was going to stick it out. Was I going to be there the whole four years or was I going to get pregnant? I would have liked to answer it one way, but I just said, no, I wasn't going to, but I wish I'd told 12 them that nobody has to get married to get pregnant any more. I must have been asked that question four times in my interview. I passed—five people voted for me and one person did not.

13 I got spoiled in my apprenticeship. Everybody was so willing to teach me everything. Like I was saying earlier, women at that time were such a novelty all the guys were hands on, they wanted to train a woman. I think it was a macho thing for them—"Hey, we got a woman here." The only thing I found was some areas in which I worked I think they were afraid to let me go on the machine, because they were afraid of the fact that they didn't really know whether I could handle it or not, so I feel like sometimes I suffered in that respect.

. . .

14 Right now, because of the lathe I'm on, I do only large work. I run all the large jobs on the machine. It's not really hard. It's kind of funny to see a woman on this machine. You think, "Oh, she's gotta work hard." But it's not really that bad. I do work hard just to get it set up so I can actually get the job going. But you have cranes to work with. You do have to use brute strength, and I'm not afraid to ask somebody else for help if there's something I feel is beyond my capability.

15 I'm quite union active. I'm a shop steward now. I was elected two months ago as a shop steward in a machine shop. I am the first and only woman to be a steward in a machine shop, and I had to work hard at getting that. It's been real political, as far as just getting to *have* the election so I could become shop steward. The union's political for two important reasons. One is whether you support the incumbent that's in office right now, and two, the political incentive. Most men just aren't ready to take on a woman on a committee that's going to speak for them all. They feel uncomfortable with the fact that a woman has any self-confidence at all. They feel like it's a threat. Basically, they start near the bottom and head towards the top—down the road, like a business rep or staff assistant. They've got some really weird jobs in the union. I don't even understand why they even have those positions. I may not agree with what the elected officials are doing, but I believe in the causes and principles of the union. I believe that every person has a

right to fair pay and decent working conditions and somebody to represent them in case of problems. I think the approaches of the union have got to change from what they used to be, like way back in the old days, in how you succeed in getting the things you want. But basically the union is only as strong as its membership, and I'm a firm believer that the union should involve its members more, so it can become strong, not alienate themselves from it.

In relationship to women in non-traditional trades, I don't think the union's done all that much. They just look at it as something they don't talk too much about. If you're a woman and you've got any vocal tendencies to speak your mind, you might as well forget anything for yourself, unless you support their ticket. It's not really a fair game at all, so to speak, within the union. The union, as far as representing women or minorities, is just starting to come out and seeing that justice is done. Basically they don't like to work on problems with women or minorities because it upsets the rest of the membership—the white Caucasian males. They [the rank and file] think that women and minorities are getting preferential treatment, so they [the union officials] keep it all low-key and quiet. 16

I treat people with respect if they give me respect. And I don't appreciate supervisors, just because they have a little badge that says "supervisor," to treat me just like another employee, another number that doesn't have any feelings. I feel like there's no reason why he can't say, "Please," or "Thank you," or "I appreciate your work." I'm not hesitant to say that. I've had supervisors say, "I need this job done," and I'll say, "What about please?" Or some boss will ask me, "Where the hell were ya?" And I'll ask, "Who the hell wants to know?" I've been wanting to advance in the hourly positions, but I can't seem to, mainly because I'm too outspoken. They want people who are gonna say yes, not why or no, or how come. And I think being a woman doesn't help either. Also, Japanese women are supposed to be diminutive and quiet and do what they're told. I shock a lot of my co-workers. 17

When I first came into the shop I was a naive girl and I was afraid. I went in one day and opened a cabinet door and there was a nude centerfold. It set me back, but then I realized at the same time that women shouldn't expect to change attitudes of the men. I think, with time, we are showing men we know how to do the work. Then they'll 18 change just naturally. They can't help but respect you if they find out that you can do the work. I think it's very important for women to become more involved with their union and use it to make men realize that they have feelings; they have special problems that men don't understand, like sexual harassment, sexual discrimination. And most of these guys, unless they see it happen to their wives, are oblivious to the whole thing, so they have to be educated, and it has to start with the union, because the management's sure not going to do it.

19 I have had cases of sexual harassment. I have complained to the EEO [Equal Employment Opportunity] commission. The company has an EEO office. I had one supervisor that used to come up behind me and pat me on the butt, and I didn't even know he was back there. And I had another supervisor that would come around, when I didn't know it, and snap my bra strap! It was just something that they thought was cute. I told the supervisor who used to come up and pat me, "Hey, maybe you'd better cut that out, because if *your* supervisor saw you do that, you'd be in a heck of a lot of trouble and I'm not real keen on that." Sexual harassment is one touchy subject. This other supervisor—it wouldn't have done any good to talk to him. I filed a report and it hasn't happened since. They had a meeting and told us that they were getting some complaints, not from who, and it's gotten a lot better. I haven't had to worry about it from the fellow employees. It's the managers. I get a lot of teasing, a lot of jokes from the fellow employees; that doesn't bother me, and I think they have a little more respect for you because they're working *with* you. The supervisors, they're so away and detached from you. They feel like, "Gee, I'm a supervisor, so she should be flattered."

20 My husband understands my position. If you say too much then you can end up—you know, as much as they say they're not supposed to retaliate, there's other ways they can retaliate. They can make your work a little difficult for you, or they can give you jobs that they know you can't handle, or assign you to a different machine that's a little tricky.

21 I feel like I've been sexually discriminated against. I guess that's all I can say. Nobody's gonna come out and say, "You're being discriminated against because of your sex." I think that there have been jobs in which I have been sexually discriminated against—mainly the jobs that pay in the higher grades. About two years ago I was able to work a lot

of the different jobs that pay higher than I get now. No problems. I was always asked to come back. They would always come and get me for a higher-paying job if they needed someone, if someone was sick or absent. And I'd keep going, keep going, keep going in, and the only time there was a permanent opening I didn't get it. There's no selection process. It's a popularity deal. If the boss likes you, he gets you in the job. They'd put guys in the positions that had less time than I did, who had less experience and less qualifications. And if that's not sexual discrimination, I don't know what to call it. Because they've put me in the positions temporarily before, they're telling me that I'm qualified. All of a sudden the jobs open up permanent, and I'm *not* qualified. That doesn't make sense to me.

In the area I'm working in I'm the most senior employee 22
on second shift. I feel I am respected because I do know quite a bit more, as far as the procedures and where everybody in the area works, which jobs should be lathed on what machines. It makes me real mad when the lead man is not there they will not give me the lead position. I think it's because I'm vocal. I'm not a yes person. If you're not a yes person, you don't get the position. Although it doesn't help that I'm a woman, because there isn't a single woman in our shop that makes higher than a grade 8, which is what I am.

I went to the company's EEO office on a sexual discrim- 23
ination claim when I thought I was being discriminated against in not getting the higher-paying jobs. The guy that got the job had less time than I had, and he didn't even have to go through the connecting jobs like me. I was not really satisfied with the results. They told me I didn't have enough running-time experience, which I disagree with, but I felt like there wasn't a whole lot I could do internally and I wasn't quite ready yet to go on the outside. I think I could have been successful going to the outside, but at the same time I didn't want to cut my own throat. If I had gone to the outside and started a sex-discrimination case and won, then the supervisors may retaliate by giving me hard jobs or putting me in an area that was wrong. I'm not the kind of person who likes to make a whole heck of a lot of trouble. These supervisors know that I want to get ahead. I think they also know I could go to the outside if I wanted to. That's why I'm sort of biding my time. They're gonna realize that I'm gonna run out of patience.

I filed a sex-discrimination case with the EEO several 24

years ago. I had been trying and trying to get on the apprenticeship board. EEO said there had never been a case like that before. They said there wasn't anything they could do because it wasn't a paying job. So I was up a creek. But I wanted it real bad, and a group of apprentices wrote up a petition. The men sent it down to the union hall and the next thing I became an alternate to the committee. Of course, they say it's not because of the petition, but funny it didn't happen until the petition had been sent in.

25 Race hasn't been too much of a factor. I think most people realize I'm more American than I am Japanese. Race has only been a problem on the men's bathroom walls. There's stuff about me on the bathroom walls, but, you know, it's kind of touching. Somebody will make a comment about me. Amy is so-and-so, and somebody will put underneath the graffiti, "What difference does it make, she's nice." And it makes you feel good to think that somebody thinks that the clown who put this up there was crazy. But it's no different than blacks or Chicanos or anybody. There's racism in that shop just like everywhere else. I just live with it. When I first heard about it on the bathroom walls, what am I gonna do, tell 'em to erase it? It can still go back up there again, you know. I believe there are ignorant people out there, and I'll just ignore those ignorant people; I can't waste my time with them.

26 I like doing things around the house. I like to build things—small carpentry things. I built a sixteen-foot work bench in the garage. I've put light fixtures in our house. I've found that my job has made it a little easier to understand all these other things I do at home. My husband doesn't like doing things like that at home. So it's kind of like, if I don't do it, it won't get done. Our marriage is very different. My husband has always been in favor of me becoming better, becoming more independently capable, taking care of myself.

27 My family doesn't quite understand what I do. It's just a language barrier. I feel it's almost like they have learned to respect me making almost thirteen bucks an hour. And they also realize I'm a lot more American than they probably want. Most of the women in our family have been taught to be traditional Japanese. They're from Japan, where the wife obeys the husband. When he says to get something to eat, you hop to it and do it right away. Where I'm more likely to tell him, "There's the kitchen; if you want something to eat,

you can get it yourself." I'm more independent than they'd like to see a Japanese woman be.

But sometime I miss being able to look like a woman. There's a purpose behind the way I dress. I don't dress to work at a fashion show, but I mean it isn't glamorous and there are times I'd like to dress up. That would be the one thing about work that I don't like. It's hard to relate to other women about what I do. I get tired of getting stared at in department stores when I go in with my grubby jeans and my flannel shirt and my steel-toed shoes. They kind of look at you like, "What in the world?" It's a whole different attitude. 28

As soon as I walk in the door at work it's like I'm not any sex at all. It's no sex at all. It doesn't matter if I'm a man or a woman. I'm a machinist. I can do the work. The guys look at me, not because I'm a woman, but because I'm a machinist. And that feels real good. 29

I think this is a good job for a woman, but only if she's strong, and I don't mean just physically. I mean mentally. They need to be strong, secure, emotionally stable, and able to take some stress. There's more pressure than on other jobs I've done. You have to make a good part. Because if you don't make a good part, that's gonna make an unsafe plane. She has to be able to cope with the stress of wanting to do good. Somebody that's physically capable—who knows how to compensate for their weakness. The women I've noticed, and myself too, they find little ways of doing things a little different, because you can't do it the same way the guys do. They didn't build a woman's hip the way they did unless it was on purpose. I use my hip to a lot of advantage. I don't have the strength all on my own, so I'll put my weight into it also. 30

Some women just don't have the brute strength to do it, but I think the biggest *dis*advantage is from the moment they're born. Somebody's gonna raise them to be a "woman"—not to get their hands dirty, not to go out with Daddy and his hammer and nails. She's not gonna develop the mental skill or the agility. I know I have that problem with hand-eye coordination. On my job it hasn't been a problem, but it has been playing baseball. I think if I had been taught when I was a little girl that it was okay for little girls to play baseball, I would have developed that hand-eye coordination. There are other things that men take for granted. Boys, when they're growing up, learn how to fix 31 their cars, learn what a feeler gauge is or how to set spark plugs, how to understand mechanical levers. Women don't have that advantage, no matter how much training they get. They aren't brought up with it, so I think it's important that they realize that and try to compensate. Also I think it's important they realize not to raise their little girl to do the same thing.

Kati Marton

An All Too Common Story

Kati Marton, a writer and formerly a network correspondent, contributed the following commentary to Newsweek *on October 21, 1991, just after the Clarence Thomas/Anita Hill controversy over sexual harassment.*

1 Is there a woman in the American workplace for whom Prof. Anita Hill's painful revelations regarding sexual harassment do not resonate? For me, her recollections revived an incident I had suppressed for more than a decade and a half. Unlike Professor Hill's experience, my memory of sexual harassment will not leave a deep imprint on the nation's psyche. Mine is but one woman's story. The professor and I are products of vastly different cultures and professions: she an Oklahoma farm girl; I, Budapest-born and -raised, a relative newcomer to this land. In common we had this: both of us were determined to succeed in highly competitive and conspicuously male-dominated professions: hers the law, mine the media. Yet, listening to her testimony, I was struck by how similarly she and I, different in almost every way, responded to sexual pressures in our professional lives. In the wake of Anita Hill's searing memories, I now see my own experience as part of a sad, pervasive pattern of sexual blackmail in offices across the land.

2 I was 25 years old at the time, the same age as Professor Hill when she worked for Judge Clarence Thomas at the

Equal Employment Opportunity Commission. I was only six months into my job as an on-air reporter for a network affiliate in Philadelphia. Like Professor Hill, I, too, lacked a résumé. I, too, loved my job. On the day in question, a station news executive and I traveled by train to New York so that I could receive a George Foster Peabody Award for my work on a documentary on the Philadelphia Orchestra's visit to China. I delivered an earnest and self-conscious acceptance speech to the media heavyweights gathered in the gold-trimmed room. At one point, I momentarily lost my composure and my newly acquired American accent when I mentioned that only a few years before, I did not even speak English. But through it all I basked in the warm glow of my peers' approval. It should have been a proud day for a neophyte reporter. It did not turn out that way.

My executive escort, seemingly bristling with pride (it was the first time a local Philadelphia television reporter had won the coveted Peabody), invited me and a childhood friend from Budapest to the Russian Tea Room to toast the event. The hours passed in a happy haze. "Isn't it time we headed for the Metroliner back to Philadelphia?" I asked the executive around nightfall. Having said goodnight to my friend, we walked to the limousine my colleague had hired for the occasion. But the car did not follow the familiar route to Penn Station. Without a word of prompting, the limo pulled up in front of the Hilton hotel. Too astonished and too intimidated to muster anything like a firm protest, I found myself following the executive into the hotel elevator. "I only want to get to know you better," he explained. "To talk to you." 3

And talk I did, with the feverish urgency of a drowning person clinging to a life raft. I saw talk as my only escape from certain disaster, a compromise between humiliating the man to whom I owed my career and my own revulsion at the situation he had placed me in. So I talked about my childhood, embellishing and dramatizing, in the manner of a stand-up comic auditioning for the big time. By midnight I had run out of steam and stories so I prodded him to talk about his life, his troubles. It was the most exhausting tap dance of my life, but it was the only way I could think of to deflect this man from pursuing what I assumed to be his own objectives. There was no time to even wonder how in God's name he presumed this was where I wanted to spend 4 the proudest night of my short career. What gave a man with whom I had exchanged one handshake—and that on the day I was hired—this right? He assumed that right. I, loving my job, thinking I got it only by a stroke of luck, became his accomplice by not walking out, by not even voicing outrage. I did not have the nerve.

5 At dawn, he finally drifted off to sleep and I made my bleary-eyed way to the train and to Philadelphia. Toward evening, as I faced the bright lights of the studio cameras, I saw him just arriving to work. He looked much more rested than I. By then all memories of the previous day's brief moment of glory had been supplanted by other memories. Irrational feelings of guilt regarding my conduct began to nag at me. Had I given the wrong signals? He seemed such a nice, square sort of family man. And why had I not walked out on him? The minute a woman decides to stay and stay silent, in her own mind at least, she loses the moral edge. Like thousands of women in newsrooms, offices and factories, I had swapped the moral edge for job security. I did not think I had the luxury of choice in the matter.

6 I suppose the executive felt sure I would never talk about his abortive attempt at seduction. He was right. I never have, until now. Nor have I let myself take much pride in that hard-won Peabody Award, fearing that the other memories would rush in beside them. But hearing Professor Hill's taut recitation, accompanied by the belittling comments of certain members of the gentleman's club on Capitol Hill, forced me to mentally revisit that room in the Hilton. Professor Hill's dignity did not mask the lasting humiliation that is the inevitable residue of such moments.

7 There is more than personal catharsis at stake in owning up to this long-suppressed incident. I am writing this not only because the memory would not let go. I am writing because Professor Hill's voice moved me to do so. I wanted to say to the Senate panel, "Look, I know why she stayed on with the man who insulted her. So many of us have been there, not liked ourselves for it, but have stayed." And there is another impulse to my speaking out now. If men and women alike pronounce such degrading episodes unacceptable, perhaps our daughters might be spared similar choices in their professional lives. No one should have to purchase job security at so high a price.

Frederic Hayward

Sexual Harassment—From a Man's Perspective

Frederic Hayward was executive director of Men's Rights, Inc., a not-for-profit corporation that raises awareness on men's issues, when (in October 1990) he contributed the following essay to The Business Journal, *a publication that discusses issues of general interest to businesspeople in the Sacramento, California, area.*

1 The newcomer approaches a second man and snarls, "Hey, pal, you got a problem?" "No." "Well, I don't like the way you're lookin' at me." Typical macho behavior? Women are above that sort of thing?

2 Not exactly. It is at the insistence of women that simply looking at a woman "the wrong way" is banned by government.

3 On the surface, Freedom of Vision seems like a more fundamental right even than Freedom of Speech. Yet, just as laws against pornography can prohibit a man from looking at a naked woman, laws against sexual harassment can prohibit him from looking at a clothed woman while imagining her naked.

4 If you stare at a man and he doesn't like it, you risk a punch in the jaw. If you stare at a woman and she doesn't like it, you risk a megabuck financial settlement and/or a ruined career.

5 The problem is not, of course, that we make too much of sexual harassment; rather, the problem is that our perspective is biased by narrow, sexist, political interests.

6 A less-biased look at sexual harassment reveals, among other things, a host of women and men who are victimized by female abuse of sexual power. Ignore the immensity of that power at your peril.

7 Before our gender consciousness was raised by feminism, men had most of the political-economic power, while women had most of the sexual power. The traditional male-female relationship was based on the exchange of these two power imbalances. The traditional male-female contract consisted of the man tapping his source of power to give physical and

financial security to the woman while she, in return, tapped her sexual power to give him access to her body.

8 Recent events hint at the enormous sexual power that can be unleashed. Gary Hart gambled and lost the presidency in order to have sex with a woman. Jim Bakker gambled and lost a multimillion-dollar ministry in order to have sex with a woman. In the American embassy in Moscow, Sgt. Clayton Lonetree sacrificed our nation's security in order to have sex with a woman. If a man would trade away the highest office, the greatest prestige and the deepest loyalty in order to have sex with a woman, only the most dogmatic could deny that he would trade away a letter of recommendation.

9 Feminist protestations of women's powerlessness (hence, innocence) notwithstanding, most of us personally know of women who have used and abused their sexual power. Questions arise: If I or a woman do not get into graduate school because a female competitor has more A's from sleeping with more professors (Ilene F. was the notorious but proud example from my own university) then what are we victims of? If I or a woman do not get a job because a female competitor displays more enticing cleavage, then what are we victims of? If I or a woman do not get a promotion because a female competitor has an affair with our boss, then what are we victims of?

10 We do not even have a name for it, let alone a law against it. Any analysis of sexual office politics that ignores this component might be "politically correct," but is woefully inadequate.

11 Furthermore, the sexual harassment for which we do have a name has a silent, twin brother.

12 In essence, sexual harassment means requiring a person to carry out a traditional sex role as a subcondition for employment. Since a main component of the traditional female role is to provide sexual gratification, women usually find themselves caught in the well-publicized trap of providing sex as part of a job.

13 A main component of the traditional male role, on the other hand, is to bear physical risk and undertake heavy labor. The twin brother of sexual harassment, then, entails the primary assumption of dangerous and beast-of-burden tasks as a condition for a man's employment.

14 A people-based definition of sexual harassment would probably include as many male as female victims. Not

surprisingly, a frequent complaint of male security officers is that equally paid female co-workers are routinely given less than equally risky assignments. Male sales agents complain that they are forced into front-line duty when potentially violent customers appear. The federal Equal Employment Opportunity Commission and state agencies are singularly unresponsive to male "crybabies."

The bottom line is that men suffer a disproportionate share 15
of work-related accidents. The male-centered form of sexual "harassment" kills. Indeed, *USA Today* reports that men, who comprise about half the work force, suffer 95 percent of at-work fatalities and 82 percent of at-work murders! (In a telling comment on the media's deflection of attention away from male victimization, however, the article was simply headlined: "732 women were murdered on the job.")

This is not to say, of course, that there are no male victims 16
of the female-centered definition of sexual harassment, in which sexual favors become a condition of employment.

Since women are just as human as men, they are just as 17
likely to abuse power. There are cases where men incur sexual pressure from female (and gay male) bosses.

But for men, sex has historically been a reward for money 18
and power, while for women, sex has been a means to money and power. Again, the traditional contract acknowledged that women start with sexual power and need not trade for it.

The so-called shortage of eligible men, a common com- 19
plaint in women's magazines, attests to the continuing expectation that a man is not "eligible" if he stands below the woman on the ladder of success. The reason a female vice president is less likely to sexually harass her male secretary, therefore, has nothing to do with her higher standard of behavior. It is simply that she is conditioned to prefer an affair with the president.

Even when the concern is limited to only-female victims 20
of only-female defined sexual harassment, moreover, the male perspective needs to be included before effective solutions can be developed. Blaming one gender exclusively (men) is as politically popular as it is specious. Women do play a role in perpetrating the harassment ethic.

Not unusually, my own sexual harassment training was at 21
the hands of a woman. When I was young, I did not believe the peers and movie characters who encouraged me to never take "no" for an answer. The person who finally convinced me was Jane B. She was mercifully blunt about why her

initial romantic interest in me had dissipated into a platonic friendship. I was too much of a gentleman, she informed me. Before making decisions, I had naively asked for her input. Worst of all, when getting sexual, I had foolishly waited for permission. "Be a man!" was her closing advice.

22 I tested her sexual harassment encouragement on a succession of women and found that it worked. The consistent romantic failure that had been my reward for treating women with "respect" was replaced by consistent romantic success.

23 Popular wisdom has it backward: Sexist conditioning has not left most women ill-prepared to say an assertive "no." Rather, it has left most women ill-prepared to give assertive "yesses." That is, most men already assume that if a woman means "no," she says "no." But experience has taught us that when a woman means "yes," we cannot count on hearing it clearly.

24 Before men can unlearn harassing behavior, we need to experience female initiative. Until then, the game of romance will continue to have men playing the actor/predator and women playing the object/prey. Until then, men will never be sure whether a particular "no" means "No, I'm not interested at all," or "No, I'm not ready now, but I might be ready later, so you better try again because that is the only way you will find out," or "Yes, but I don't want you to lose respect for me by sounding too easy."

25 To make matters worse, since women are comparatively passive when it comes to initiating, men become conditioned to responding to visual cues. Indeed, some women in my workshops assert that giving visual cues is the female version of initiating. The problem, however, is that men cannot always read the visual signals they receive.

26 If a woman dresses to kill, for example, hoping to arouse the interest of those men she likes, non-targeted men receive many of the same visual cues. More and more men are, in fact, complaining that provocative dress constitutes sexual harassment against them.

27 Furthermore, sexual harassment is not necessarily a physical attack; it can even be an unwanted glance. Yet, the only purpose of showing cleavage is to have people admire it; can we really place all the blame on the man for looking?

28 Recently, I accompanied an attorney on her way to interview a potential client, a woman who felt she was unfairly

fired. The attorney explained that she did not yet know what the actual complaint would be because she did not yet know the gender of the boss. If the boss was male, he would be charged with sexual harassment. In other words, his actual conduct was irrelevant; if there is a conflict between a male boss and a female employee, the charge is sexual harassment. It's automatic.

Indeed, a personnel director at one of the nation's largest computer firms expressed his dismay to me at how many good male executives he has lost from accusations (and even simple threats of accusations) of sexual harassment. 29

As homely Henry Kissinger remarked, power is the ultimate aphrodisiac. For every executive who chases his secretary around the desk, there is a secretary who dreams of marrying an executive and not having to be a secretary any more. 30

Given the bitterness that can attend a broken love affair and the bitterness that can plague office politics, combining the two can be a powerful motivation to reach for any available weapon. The same safeguards that protect an innocent victim of sexual harassment are a potent arsenal in the hands of a bitter colleague/ex-lover. 31

Statistics do not tell us, therefore, how prevalent the problem is. We know only that the problem is serious. We also know that the problem will persist as long as we turn a deaf ear and a blind eye to the male perspective. 32

Lester C. Thurow

Why Women Are Paid Less Than Men

Lester C. Thurow (born 1938) grew up in Montana, the son of a Methodist minister. Rhodes Scholar and Harvard Ph.D., member of the Johnson administration and adviser to George McGovern, he is currently Dean of the Sloan School of Management at MIT. Among his books are Poverty and Discrimination, Dangerous Currents, *and the best-selling* Zero-Sum Society. *Thurow writes regularly for* The Los Angeles Times, Newsweek, *and other "generalist" publications; the following appeared in* The New York Times *in 1981.*

1 In the 40 years from 1939 to 1979 white women who work full time have with monotonous regularity made slightly less than 60 percent as much as white men. Why?

2 Over the same time period, minorities have made substantial progress in catching up with whites, with minority women making even more progress than minority men. Black men now earn 72 percent as much as white men (up 16 percentage points since the mid-1950's), but black women earn 92 percent as much as white women. Hispanic men make 71 percent of what their white counterparts do, but Hispanic women make 82 percent as much as white women. As a result of their faster progress, fully employed black women make 75 percent as much as fully employed black men while Hispanic women earn 68 percent as much as Hispanic men.

3 This faster progress may, however, end when minority women finally catch up with white women. In the bible of the New Right, George Gilder's *Wealth and Poverty,* the 60 percent is just one of Mother Nature's constants like the speed of light or the force of gravity. Men are programmed to provide for their families economically while women are programmed to take care of their families emotionally and physically. As a result men put more effort into their jobs than women. The net result is a difference in work intensity that leads to that 40 percent gap in earnings. But there is no discrimination against women—only the biological facts of life.

4 The problem with this assertion is just that. It is an assertion with no evidence for it other than the fact that white women have made 60 percent as much as men for a long period of time.

5 "Discrimination against women" is an easy answer but it also has its problems as an adequate explanation. Why is discrimination against women not declining under the same social forces that are leading to a lessening of discrimination against minorities? In recent years women have made more use of the enforcement provisions of the Equal Employment Opportunities Commission and the courts than minorities. Why do the laws that prohibit discrimination against women and minorities work for minorities but not for women?

6 When men discriminate against women, they run into a problem. To discriminate against women is to discriminate against your own wife and to lower your own family

income. To prevent women from working is to force men to work more.

When whites discriminate against blacks, they can at least think that they are raising their own incomes. When men discriminate against women they have to know that they are lowering their own family income and increasing their own work effort. 7

While discrimination undoubtedly explains part of the male-female earnings differential, one has to believe that men are monumentally stupid or irrational to explain all of the earnings gap in terms of discrimination. There must be something else going on. 8

Back in 1939 it was possible to attribute the earnings gap to large differences in educational attainments. But the educational gap between men and women has been eliminated since World War II. It is no longer possible to use education as an explanation for the lower earnings of women. Some observers have argued that women earn less money since they are less reliable workers who are more apt to leave the labor force. But it is difficult to maintain this position since women are less apt to quit one job to take another and as a result they tend to work as long, or longer, for any one employer. From any employer's perspective they are more reliable, not less reliable, than men. 9

Part of the answer is visible if you look at the lifetime earnings profile of men. Suppose that you were asked to predict which men in a group of 25-year-olds would become economically successful. At age 25 it is difficult to tell who will be economically successful and your predictions are apt to be highly inaccurate. But suppose that you were asked to predict which men in a group of 35-year-olds would become economically successful. If you are successful at age 35, you are very likely to remain successful for the rest of your life. If you have not become economically successful by age 35, you are very unlikely to do so later. 10

The decade between 25 and 35 is when men either succeed or fail. It is the decade when lawyers become partners in the good firms, when business managers make it onto the "fast track," when academics get tenure at good universities, and when blue collar workers find the job opportunities that will lead to training opportunities and the skills that will generate high earnings. If there is any one decade when it pays to work hard and to be consistently in the labor force, it is the decade between 25 and 35. For those 11 who succeed, earnings will rise rapidly. For those who fail, earnings will remain flat for the rest of their lives.

12 But the decade between 25 and 35 is precisely the decade when women are most apt to leave the labor force or become part-time workers to have children. When they do, the current system of promotion and skill acquisition will extract an enormous lifetime price.

13 This leaves essentially two avenues for equalizing male and female earnings. Families where women who wish to have successful careers, compete with men, and achieve the same earnings should alter their family plans and have their children either before 25 or after 35. Or society can attempt to alter the existing promotion and skill acquisition system so that there is a longer time period in which both men and women can attempt to successfully enter the labor force. Without some combination of these two factors, a substantial fraction of the male-female earnings differentials are apt to persist for the next 40 years, even if discrimination against women is eliminated.

Felice N. Schwartz

Management Women and the New Facts of Life

Felice N. Schwartz is president and founder of Catalyst, a not-for-profit research and advising organization that works with corporations to foster the career development of women. When she published her proposals and analyses in the Harvard Business Review *in January/February 1989, the* Review *was deluged with responses, some of which are reprinted here after the article. (Reprinted by permission of* Harvard Business Review. *"Management Women and the New Facts of Life" by Felice N. Schwartz, (Jan/Feb 1989). Copyright © 1988 by the President and Fellows of Harvard College; all rights reserved.)*

1 The cost of employing women in management is greater than the cost of employing men. This is a jarring statement, partly because it is true, but mostly because it is something

people are reluctant to talk about. A new study by one multinational corporation shows that the rate of turnover in management positions is 2½ times higher among top-performing women than it is among men. A large producer of consumer goods reports that one-half of the women who take maternity leave return to their jobs late or not at all. And we know that women also have a greater tendency to plateau or to interrupt their careers in ways that limit their growth and development. But we have become so sensitive to charges of sexism and so afraid of confrontation, even litigation, that we rarely say what we know to be true. Unfortunately, our bottled-up awareness leaks out in misleading metaphors ("glass ceiling" is one notable example), veiled hostility, lowered expectations, distrust, and reluctant adherence to Equal Employment Opportunity requirements.

Career interruptions, plateauing, and turnover are expensive. The money corporations invest in recruitment, training, and development is less likely to produce top executives among women than among men, and the invaluable company experience that developing executives acquire at every level as they move up through management ranks is more often lost. 2

The studies just mentioned are only the first of many, I'm quite sure. Demographic realities are going to force corporations all across the country to analyze the cost of employing women in managerial positions, and what they will discover is that women cost more. 3

But here is another startling truth: The greater cost of employing women is not a function of inescapable gender differences. Women *are* different from men, but what increases their cost to the corporation is principally the clash of their perceptions, attitudes, and behavior with those of men, which is to say, with the policies and practices of male-led corporations. 4

It is terribly important that employers draw the right conclusions from the studies now being done. The studies will be useless—or worse, harmful—if all they teach us is that women are expensive to employ. What we need to learn is how to reduce that expense, how to stop throwing away the investments we make in talented women, how to become more responsive to the needs of the women that corporations *must* employ if they are to have the best and the brightest of all those now entering the work force. 5

6 The gender differences relevant to business fall into two categories: those related to maternity and those related to the differing traditions and expectations of the sexes. Maternity is biological rather than cultural. We can't alter it, but we can dramatically reduce its impact on the workplace and in many cases eliminate its negative effect on employee development. We can accomplish this by addressing the second set of differences, those between male and female socialization. Today, these differences exaggerate the real costs of maternity and can turn a relatively slight disruption in work schedule into a serious business problem and a career derailment for individual women. If we are to overcome the cost differential between male and female employees, we need to address the issues that arise when female socialization meets the male corporate culture and masculine rules of career development—issues of behavior and style, of expectation, of stereotypes and preconceptions, of sexual tension and harassment, of female mentoring, lateral mobility, relocation, compensation, and early identification of top performers.

7 The one immutable, enduring difference between men and women is maternity. Maternity is not simply childbirth but a continuum that begins with an awareness of the ticking of the biological clock, proceeds to the anticipation of motherhood, includes pregnancy, childbirth, physical recuperation, psychological adjustment, and continues on to nursing, bonding, and child rearing. Not all women choose to become mothers, of course, and among those who do, the process varies from case to case depending on the health of the mother and baby, the values of the parents, and the availability, cost, and quality of child care.

8 In past centuries, the biological fact of maternity shaped the traditional roles of the sexes. Women performed the home-centered functions that related to the bearing and nurturing of children. Men did the work that required great physical strength. Over time, however, family size contracted, the community assumed greater responsibility for the care and education of children, packaged foods and household technology reduced the work load in the home, and technology eliminated much of the need for muscle power at the workplace. Today, in the developed world, the only role still uniquely gender related is childbearing. Yet

men and women are still socialized to perform their traditional roles.

Men and women may or may not have some innate psychological disposition toward these traditional roles—men to be aggressive, competitive, self-reliant, risk taking; women to be supportive, nurturing, intuitive, sensitive, communicative—but certainly both men and women are capable of the full range of behavior. Indeed, the male and female roles have already begun to expand and merge. In the decades ahead, as the socialization of boys and girls and the experience and expectations of young men and women grow steadily more androgynous, the differences in workplace behavior will continue to fade. At the moment, however, we are still plagued by disparities in perception and behavior that make the integration of men and women in the workplace unnecessarily difficult and expensive. 9

Let me illustrate with a few broadbrush generalizations. Of course, these are only stereotypes, but I think they help to exemplify the kinds of preconceptions that can muddy the corporate waters. 10

Men continue to perceive women as the rearers of their children, so they find it understandable, indeed appropriate, that women should renounce their careers to raise families. Edmund Pratt, CEO of Pfizer, once asked me in all sincerity, "Why would any woman choose to be a chief financial officer rather than a full-time mother?" By condoning and taking pleasure in women's traditional behavior, men reinforce it. Not only do they see parenting as fundamentally female, they see a career as fundamentally male—either an unbroken series of promotions and advancements toward CEOdom or stagnation and disappointment. This attitude serves to legitimize a woman's choice to extend maternity leave and even, for those who can afford it, to leave employment altogether for several years. By the same token, men who might want to take a leave after the birth of a child know that management will see such behavior as a lack of career commitment, even when company policy permits parental leave for men. 11

Women also bring counterproductive expectations and perceptions to the workplace. Ironically, although the feminist movement was an expression of women's quest for freedom from their home-based lives, most women were remarkably free already. They had many responsibilities, but they were autonomous and could be entrepreneurial in 12 how and when they carried them out. And once their children grew up and left home, they were essentially free to do what they wanted with their lives. Women's traditional role also included freedom from responsibility for the financial support of their families. Many of us were socialized from girlhood to expect our husbands to take care of us, while our brothers were socialized from an equally early age to complete their educations, pursue careers, climb the ladder of success, and provide dependable financial support for their families. To the extent that this tradition of freedom lingers subliminally, women tend to bring to their employment a sense that they can choose to change jobs or careers at will, take time off, or reduce their hours.

13 Finally, women's traditional role encouraged particular attention to the quality and substance of what they did, specifically to the physical, psychological, and intellectual development of their children. This traditional focus may explain women's continuing tendency to search for more than monetary reward—intrinsic significance, social importance, meaning—in what they do. This too makes them more likely than men to leave the corporation in search of other values.

14 The misleading metaphor of the glass ceiling suggests an invisible barrier constructed by corporate leaders to impede the upward mobility of women beyond the middle levels. A more appropriate metaphor, I believe, is the kind of cross-sectional diagram used in geology. The barriers to women's leadership occur when potentially counterproductive layers of influence on women—maternity, tradition, socialization—meet management strata pervaded by the largely unconscious preconceptions, stereotypes, and expectations of men. Such interfaces do not exist for men and tend to be impermeable for women.

15 One result of these gender differences has been to convince some executives that women are simply not suited to top management. Other executives feel helpless. If they see even a few of their valued female employees fail to return to work from maternity leave on schedule or see one of their most promising women plateau in her career after the birth of a child, they begin to fear there is nothing they can do to infuse women with new energy and enthusiasm and persuade them to stay. At the same time, they know there is nothing they can do to stem the tide of women into management ranks.

16 Another result is to place every working woman on a

continuum that runs from total dedication to career at one end to a balance between career and family at the other. What women discover is that the male corporate culture sees both extremes as unacceptable. Women who want the flexibility to balance their families and their careers are not adequately committed to the organization. Women who perform as aggressively and competitively as men are abrasive and unfeminine. But the fact is, business needs all the talented women it can get. Moreover, as I will explain, the women I call career-primary and those I call career-and-family each have particular value to the corporation.

Women in the corporation are about to move from a buyer's to a seller's market. The sudden, startling recognition that 80% of new entrants in the work force over the next decade will be women, minorities, and immigrants has stimulated a mushrooming incentive to "value diversity." 17

Women are no longer simply an enticing pool of occasional creative talent, a thorn in the side of the EEO officer, or a source of frustration to corporate leaders truly puzzled by the slowness of their upward trickle into executive positions. A real demographic change is taking place. The era of sudden population growth of the 1950s and 1960s is over. The birth rate has dropped about 40%, from a high of 25.3 live births per 1,000 population in 1957, at the peak of the baby boom, to a stable low of a little more than 15 per 1,000 over the last 16 years, and there is no indication of a return to a higher rate. The tidal wave of baby boomers that swelled the recruitment pool to overflowing seems to have been a one-time phenomenon. For 20 years, employers had the pick of a very large crop and were able to choose males almost exclusively for the executive track. But if future population remains fairly stable while the economy continues to expand, and if the new information society simultaneously creates a greater need for creative, educated managers, then the gap between supply and demand will grow dramatically and, with it, the competition for managerial talent. 18

The decrease in numbers has even greater implications if we look at the traditional source of corporate recruitment for leadership positions—white males from the top 10% of the country's best universities. Over the past decade, the increase in the number of women graduating from leading universities has been much greater than the increase in the 19 total number of graduates, and these women are well represented in the top 10% of their classes.

20 The trend extends into business and professional programs as well. In the old days, virtually all MBAs were male. I remember addressing a meeting at the Harvard Business School as recently as the mid-1970s and looking out at a sea of exclusively male faces. Today, about 25% of that audience would be women. The pool of male MBAs from which corporations have traditionally drawn their leaders has shrunk significantly.

21 Of course, this reduction does not have to mean a shortage of talent. The top 10% is at least as smart as it always was—smarter, probably, since it's now drawn from a broader segment of the population. But it now consists increasingly of women. Companies that are determined to recruit the same number of men as before will have to dig much deeper into the male pool, while their competitors will have the opportunity to pick the best people from both the male and female graduates.

22 Under these circumstances, there is no question that the management ranks of business will include increasing numbers of women. There remains, however, the question of how these women will succeed—how long they will stay, how high they will climb, how completely they will fulfill their promise and potential, and what kind of return the corporation will realize on its investment in their training and development.

23 There is ample business reason for finding ways to make sure that as many of these women as possible will succeed. The first step in this process is to recognize that women are not all alike. Like men, they are individuals with differing talents, priorities, and motivations. For the sake of simplicity, let me focus on the two women I referred to earlier, on what I call the career-primary woman and the career-and-family woman.

24 Like many men, some women put their careers first. They are ready to make the same trade-offs traditionally made by the men who seek leadership positions. They make a career decision to put in extra hours, to make sacrifices in their personal lives, to make the most of every opportunity for professional development. For women, of course, this decision also requires that they remain single or at least childless or, if they do have children, that they be satisfied to have

others raise them. Some 90% of executive men but only 35% of executive women have children by the age of 40. The *automatic* association of all women with babies is clearly unjustified.

The secret to dealing with such women is to recognize 25
them early, accept them, and clear artificial barriers from their path to the top. After all, the best of these women are among the best managerial talent you will ever see. And career-primary women have another important value to the company that men and other women lack. They can act as role models and mentors to younger women who put their careers first. Since upwardly mobile career-primary women still have few role models to motivate and inspire them, a company with women in its top echelon has a significant advantage in the competition for executive talent.

Men at the top of the organization—most of them over 55, 26
with wives who tend to be traditional—often find career women "masculine" and difficult to accept as colleagues. Such men miss the point, which is not that these women are just like men but that they are just like the *best* men in the organization. And there is such a shortage of the best people that gender cannot be allowed to matter. It is clearly counterproductive to disparage in a woman with executive talent the very qualities that are most critical to the business and that might carry a man to the CEO's office.

Clearing a path to the top for career-primary women has 27
four requirements:

1. Identify them early.
2. Give them the same opportunity you give to talented men to grow and develop and contribute to company profitability. Give them client and customer responsibility. Expect them to travel and relocate, to make the same commitment to the company as men aspiring to leadership positions.
3. Accept them as valued members of your management team. Include them in every kind of communication. Listen to them.
4. Recognize that the business environment is more difficult and stressful for them than for their male peers. They are always a minority, often the only woman. The male perception of talented, ambitious women is at best ambivalent, a mixture of admiration, resentment, confusion, competitiveness, attrac-

tion, skepticism, anxiety, pride, and animosity. Women can never feel secure about how they should dress and act, whether they should speak out or grin and bear it when they encounter discrimination, stereotyping, sexual harassment, and paternalism. Social interaction and travel with male colleagues and with male clients can be charged. As they move up, the normal increase in pressure and responsibility is compounded for women because they are women.

28 Stereotypical language and sexist day-to-day behavior do take their toll on women's career development. Few male executives realize how common it is to call women by their first names while men in the same group are greeted with surnames, how frequently female executives are assumed by men to be secretaries, how often women are excluded from all-male social events where business is being transacted. With notable exceptions, men are still generally more comfortable with other men, and as a result women miss many of the career and business opportunities that arise over lunch, on the golf course, or in the locker room.

29 The majority of women, however, are what I call career-and-family women, women who want to pursue serious careers while participating actively in the rearing of children. These women are a precious resource that has yet to be mined. Many of them are talented and creative. Most of them are willing to trade some career growth and compensation for freedom from the constant pressure to work long hours and weekends.

30 Most companies today are ambivalent at best about the career-and-family women in their management ranks. They would prefer that all employees were willing to give their all to the company. They believe it is in their best interests for all managers to compete for the top positions so the company will have the largest possible pool from which to draw its leaders.

31 "If you have both talent and motivation," many employers seem to say, "we want to move you up. If you haven't got that motivation, if you want less pressure and greater flexibility, then you can leave and make room for a new generation." These companies lose on two counts. First, they fail to amortize the investment they made in the early

training and experience of management women who find themselves committed to family as well as to career. Second, they fail to recognize what these women could do for their middle management.

The ranks of middle managers are filled with people on their way up and people who have stalled. Many of them have simply reached their limits, achieved career growth commensurate with or exceeding their capabilities, and they cause problems because their performance is mediocre but they still want to move ahead. The career-and-family woman is willing to trade off the pressures and demands that go with promotion for the freedom to spend more time with her children. She's very smart, she's talented, she's committed to her career, and she's satisfied to stay at the middle level, at least during the early child-rearing years. Compare her with some of the people you have there now. 32

Consider a typical example, a woman who decides in college on a business career and enters management at age 22. For nine years, the company invests in her career as she gains experience and skills and steadily improves her performance. But at 31, just as the investment begins to pay off in earnest, she decides to have a baby. Can the company afford to let her go home, take another job, or go into business for herself? The common perception now is yes, the corporation can afford to lose her unless, after six or eight weeks or even three months of disability and maternity leave, she returns to work on a full-time schedule with the same vigor, commitment, and ambition that she showed before. 33

But what if she doesn't? What if she wants or needs to go on leave for six months or a year or, heaven forbid, five years? In this worst-case scenario, she works full-time from age 22 to 31 and from 36 to 65—a total of 38 years as opposed to the typical male's 43 years. That's not a huge difference. Moreover, my typical example is willing to work part-time while her children are young, if only her employer will give her the opportunity. There are two rewards for companies responsive to this need: higher retention of their best people and greatly improved performance and satisfaction in their middle management. 34

The high-performing career-and-family woman can be a major player in your company. She can give you a significant business advantage as the competition for able people escalates. Sometimes too, if you can hold on to her, 35 she will switch gears in mid-life and reenter the competition for the top. The price you must pay to retain these women is threefold: you must plan for and manage maternity, you must provide the flexibility that will allow them to be maximally productive, and you must take an active role in helping to make family supports and high-quality, affordable child care available to all women.

36 The key to managing maternity is to recognize the value of high-performing women and the urgent need to retain them and keep them productive. The first step must be a genuine partnership between the woman and her boss. I know this partnership can seem difficult to forge. One of my own senior executives came to me recently to discuss plans for her maternity leave and subsequent return to work. She knew she wanted to come back. I wanted to make certain that she would. Still, we had a somewhat awkward conversation, because I knew that no woman can predict with certainty when she will be able to return to work or under what conditions. Physical problems can lengthen her leave. So can a demanding infant, a difficult family or personal adjustment, or problems with child care.

37 I still don't know when this valuable executive will be back on the job full-time, and her absence creates some genuine problems for our organization. But I do know that I can't simply replace her years of experience with a new recruit. Since our conversation, I also know that she wants to come back, and that she *will* come back—part-time at first—unless I make it impossible for her by, for example, setting an arbitrary date for her full-time return or resignation. In turn, she knows that the organization wants and needs her and, more to the point, that it will be responsive to her needs in terms of working hours and child-care arrangements.

38 In having this kind of conversation it's important to ask concrete questions that will help to move the discussion from uncertainty and anxiety to some level of predictability. Questions can touch on everything from family income and energy level to child care arrangements and career commitment. Of course you want your star manager to return to work as soon as possible, but you want her to return permanently and productively. Her downtime on the job is a drain on her energies and a waste of your money.

* * *

For all the women who want to combine career and family—the women who want to participate actively in the rearing of their children and who also want to pursue their careers seriously—the key to retention is to provide the flexibility and family supports they need in order to function effectively. 39

Time spent in the office increases productivity if it is time well spent, but the fact that most women continue to take the primary responsibility for child care is a cause of distraction, diversion, anxiety, and absenteeism—to say nothing of the persistent guilt experienced by all working mothers. A great many women, perhaps most of all women who have always performed at the highest levels, are also frustrated by a sense that while their children are babies they cannot function at their best either at home or at work. 40

In its simplest form, flexibility is the freedom to take time off—a couple of hours, a day, a week—or to do some work at home and some at the office, an arrangement that communication technology makes increasingly feasible. At the complex end of the spectrum are alternative work schedules that permit the woman to work less than full-time and her employer to reap the benefits of her experience and, with careful planning, the top level of her abilities. 41

Part-time employment is the single greatest inducement to getting women back on the job expeditiously and the provision women themselves most desire. A part-time return to work enables them to maintain responsibility for critical aspects of their jobs, keeps them in touch with the changes constantly occurring at the workplace and in the job itself, reduces stress and fatigue, often eliminates the need for paid maternity leave by permitting a return to the office as soon as disability leave is over, and, not least, can greatly enhance company loyalty. The part-time solution works particularly well when a work load can be reduced for one individual in a department or when a full-time job can be broken down by skill levels and apportioned to two individuals at different levels of skill and pay. 42

I believe, however, that shared employment is the most promising and will be the most widespread form of flexible scheduling in the future. It is feasible at every level of the corporation except at the pinnacle, for both the short and the long term. It involves two people taking responsibility for one job. 43

Two red lights flash on as soon as most executives hear 44

the words "job sharing": continuity and client-customer contact. The answer to the continuity question is to place responsibility entirely on the two individuals sharing the job to discuss everything that transpires—thoroughly, daily, and on their own time. The answer to the problem of client-customer contact is yes, job sharing requires reeducation and a period of adjustment. But as both client and supervisor will quickly come to appreciate, two contacts means that the customer has continuous access to the company's representative, without interruptions for vacation, travel, or sick leave. The two people holding the job can simply cover for each other, and the uninterrupted, full-time coverage they provide together can be a stipulation of their arrangement.

45 Flexibility is costly in numerous ways. It requires more supervisory time to coordinate and manage, more office space, and somewhat greater benefits costs (though these can be contained with flexible benefits plans, prorated benefits, and, in two-paycheck families, elimination of duplicate benefits). But the advantages of reduced turnover and the greater productivity that results from higher energy levels and greater focus can outweigh the costs.

46 A few hints:

- Provide flexibility selectively. I'm not suggesting private arrangements subject to the suspicion of favoritism but rather a policy that makes flexible work schedules available only to high performers.
- Make it clear that in most instances (but not all) the rates of advancement and pay will be appropriately lower for those who take time off or who work part-time than for those who work full-time. Most career-and-family women are entirely willing to make that trade-off.
- Discuss costs as well as benefits. Be willing to risk accusations of bias. Insist, for example, that half time is half of whatever time it takes to do the job, not merely half of 35 or 40 hours.

47 The woman who is eager to get home to her child has a powerful incentive to use her time effectively at the office and to carry with her reading and other work that can be done at home. The talented professional who wants to have it all can be a high performer by carefully ordering her

priorities and by focusing on objectives rather than on the legendary 15-hour day. By the time professional women have their first babies—at an average age of 31—they have already had nine years to work long hours at a desk, to travel, and to relocate. In the case of high performers, the need for flexibility coincides with what has gradually become the goal-oriented nature of responsibility.

Family supports—in addition to maternity leave and 48
flexibility—include the provision of parental leave for men, support for two-career and single-parent families during relocation, and flexible benefits. But the primary ingredient is child care. The capacity of working mothers to function effectively and without interruption depends on the availability of good, affordable child care. Now that women make up almost half the work force and the growing percentage of managers, the decision to become involved in the personal lives of employees is no longer a philosophical question but a practical one. To make matters worse, the quality of child care has almost no relation to technology, inventiveness, or profitability but is more or less a pure function of the quality of child care personnel and the ratio of adults to children. These costs are irreducible. Only by joining hands with government and the public sector can corporations hope to create the vast quantity and variety of child care that their employees need.

Until quite recently, the response of corporations to 49
women has been largely symbolic and cosmetic, motivated in large part by the will to avoid litigation and legal penalties. In some cases, companies were also moved by a genuine sense of fairness and a vague discomfort and frustration at the absence of women above the middle of the corporate pyramid. The actions they took were mostly quick, easy, and highly visible—child care information services, a three-month parental leave available to men as well as women, a woman appointed to the board of directors.

When I first began to discuss these issues 26 years ago, I 50
was sometimes able to get an appointment with the assistant to the assistant in personnel, but it was only a courtesy. Over the past decade, I have met with the CEOs of many large corporations, and I've watched them become involved with ideas they had never previously thought much about. Until recently, however, the shelf life of that enhanced awareness was always short. Given pressing, short-term concerns,

women were not a front-burner issue. In the past few months, I have seen yet another change. Some CEOs and top management groups now take the initiative. They call and ask us to show them how to shift gears from a responsive to a proactive approach to recruiting, developing, and retaining women.

51 I think this change is more probably a response to business needs—to concern for the quality of future profits and managerial talent—than to uneasiness about legal requirements, sympathy with the demands of women and minorities, or the desire to do what is right and fair. The nature of such business motivation varies. Some companies want to move women to higher positions as role models for those below them and as beacons for talented young recruits. Some want to achieve a favorable image with employees, customers, clients, and stockholders. These are all legitimate motives. But I think the companies that stand to gain most are motivated as well by a desire to capture competitive advantage in an era when talent and competence will be in increasingly short supply. These companies are now ready to stop being defensive about their experience with women and to ask incisive questions without preconceptions.

52 Even so, incredibly, I don't know of more than one or two companies that have looked into their own records to study the absolutely critical issue of maternity leave—how many women took it, when and whether they returned, and how this behavior correlated with their rank, tenure, age, and performance. The unique drawback to the employment of women is the physical reality of maternity and the particular socializing influence maternity has had. Yet to make women equal to men in the workplace we have chosen on the whole not to discuss this single most significant difference between them. Unless we do, we cannot evaluate the cost of recruiting, developing, and moving women up.

53 Now that interest is replacing indifference, there are four steps every company can take to examine its own experience with women:

1. Gather quantitative data on the company's experience with management-level women regarding turnover rates, occurrence of and return from maternity leave, and organizational level attained in relation to tenure and performance.

2. Correlate this data with factors such as age, marital status, and presence and age of children, and attempt to identify and analyze why women respond the way they do.
3. Gather qualitative data on the experience of women in your company and on how women are perceived by both sexes.
4. Conduct a cost-benefit analysis of the return on your investment in high-performing women. Factor in the cost to the company of women's negative reactions to negative experience, as well as the probable cost of corrective measures and policies. If women's value to your company is greater than the cost to recruit, train, and develop them—and of course I believe it will be—then you will want to do everything you can to retain them.

We have come a tremendous distance since the days when the prevailing male wisdom saw women as lacking the kind of intelligence that would allow them to succeed in business. For decades, even women themselves have harbored an unspoken belief that they couldn't make it because they couldn't be just like men, and nothing else would do. But now that women have shown themselves the equal of men in every area of organizational activity, now that they have demonstrated that they can be stars in every field of endeavor, now we can all venture to examine the fact that women and men are different. 54

On balance, employing women is more costly than employing men. Women can acknowledge this fact today because they know that their value to employers exceeds the additional cost and because they know that changing attitudes can reduce the additional cost dramatically. Women in management are no longer an idiosyncrasy of the arts and education. They have always matched men in natural ability. Within a very few years, they will equal men in numbers as well in every area of economic activity. 55

The demographic motivation to recruit and develop women is compelling. But an older question remains: Is society better for the change? Women's exit from the home and entry into the work force has certainly created problems—an urgent need for good, affordable child care; troubling questions about the kind of parenting children need; the costs and difficulties of diversity in the workplace; 56

the stress and fatigue of combining work and family responsibilities. Wouldn't we all be happier if we could turn back the clock to an age when men were in the workplace and women in the home, when male and female roles were clearly differentiated and complementary?

57 Nostalgia, anxiety, and discouragement will urge many to say yes, but my answer is emphatically no. Two fundamental benefits that were unattainable in the past are now within our reach. For the individual, freedom of choice—in this case the freedom to choose career, family, or a combination of the two. For the corporation, access to the most gifted individuals in the country. These benefits are neither self-indulgent nor insubstantial. Freedom of choice and self-realization are too deeply American to be cast aside for some wistful vision of the past. And access to our most talented human resources is not a luxury in this age of explosive international competition but rather the barest minimum that prudence and national self-preservation require.

Responses to Felice Schwartz: Letters to the Editor of Harvard Business Review

Editor:

1 The scenarios described by Ms. Schwartz indicate that she based her conclusions on traditional companies where lifetime employment and linear career paths are the norm and where value to the company is measured by the management level achieved. But with the information age, a new kind of corporate environment is emerging, replacing the traditional industrial-age organization. These "third wave" companies are based on flexible structures that support a changing work force, market, and economy.

2 My company is an example of this new type of organization. We don't expect a lifetime commitment from our employees, but we have created an exciting, flexible environment that allows us to attract and retain the most talented individuals in the technology industry. We've done this by providing options—from job sharing to day care to

sabbaticals. There are no "tracks" at Apple, only individual paths based on the choices our employees make in balancing career and personal needs. Some choose to emphasize their careers first, others, their families. But many choose *both*—and are successful in doing so.

Individuals at all levels in today's work force change jobs, and often careers, several times in their working lives. Many leave the work force part time or temporarily to pursue educational and training opportunities, to raise a child, or for any number of reasons. In this environment, Schwartz's recommended early identification of an individual's career path becomes not only impossible but also undesirable. It establishes barriers instead of providing the options people need. 3

The two-track approach does a disservice to all employees and forces both men and women into predefined roles that are inappropriate today. It is time for corporate America to respond to individual issues, not gender issues, and foster the kind of environment that leads to satisfying careers *and* personal lives. 4

Deborah Biondolillo
Vice President
Human Resources
Apple Computer, Inc.
Cupertino, California

Editor:

Felice Schwartz has attempted to answer the question CEOs often ask: What is the best way to retain and promote women? In her attempt to be concise, however, she is too simplistic. Men and women do continue to be socialized differently so that when women join a management culture populated predominantly by men, they must adapt in ways that are often alien to them. If women want to be part of the management ranks, and if the management ranks want to admit them, these differences must be identified and discussed openly. The new twist is that just as women are newly accepted into these ranks, they are raising families and asking for flexibility. 5

Well-intentioned work and family policies directed primarily at talented, high-potential women who ask for flexibility and child care assistance will fail unless certain biases are overcome. The most critical of these include: 6

1. *Women should be children's primary care givers, even if they work.* This assumes, for example, that mothers working a reduced schedule will be overstressed by unpredictable illnesses, home responsibilities, or guilt. Challenges, work responsibilities, or promotions are not offered to them while on this schedule, and so they lose valuable career momentum.
2. *Time spent at work equals dedication to career.* This assumes that a woman choosing to work half of her work week at home would not relocate or want a promotion to another position where this arrangement isn't possible. One problem is that coworkers don't make the effort to call her at home with critical information.
3. *Taking care of children is like a vacation.* You know this attitude has taken hold when a woman choosing to dedicate one-fourth of her workday to caring for her children hears comments like "Thanks for stopping by" or "I wish I could play on such a nice day" as she leaves the office.
4. *Family issues should not be in the workplace.* While work and family policies ostensibly say the opposite, this assumes that taking time to discuss child care center closings or babysitter illness have no place in the office.
5. *Schedule flexibility is only possible in "softer" jobs.* Many managers' first reaction is that schedule flexibility is not possible in *their* areas but only in "less important" positions. This bias could force women who work reduced hours into areas perceived as "soft," thereby creating a career plateau that they did not choose.

7 Schwartz's thesis is based on some of these biases. Calling the freedom that women seek "counterproductive" promotes the very inflexibility she criticizes. She suggests that the decision to put career first also requires that women remain single, or at least childless; this would force career mothers to make a permanent choice that is illogical and unnecessary. And as much as I don't like the dichotomy she has created between career and family, I would like to meet the person who can accurately identify early in their careers those women who do not alter their priorities later when they have children. Furthermore, depicting career mothers

as distracted, diverted, anxious, and absent only perpetuates the myth that they can't be successful at work during this period of their lives.

And finally, penalizing employees who work reduced hours by advancing them more slowly is absolutely counter to anything I would do. While the first solutions are often schedule flexibility and child care assistance, the next solution will be advancement and challenge. Creating a slower track will surely create a new ghetto of female employees and will certainly not motivate them to stay in corporations. 8

Karen A. Geiger
Vice President and Director of
Career Development
NCNB Corporation
Charlotte, North Carolina

Editor:

This debate takes place in the context of two important historical changes that question the assumptions underlying Felice Schwartz's argument. Schwartz assumes that women who sacrifice having children for their careers will make good managers; I question whether this is true of men or women. 9

The first change is in the nature of corporate work. Companies, especially those customizing products and services, seek ways to transform bureaucracy to increase quality, cut away layers of managerial control, and empower the front line of service employees, technicians, and professionals to solve customer problems. This type of "technoservice" requires a new kind of management, one more competent in both entrepreneurial strategy and human relationships. The most effective managers are not single-minded careerists willing to sacrifice family life to climb the corporate ladder. Though tough-minded, they temper their passion to win with an understanding heart. They are supportive and flexible. The driven managers who did so well in the past, be they men or women, are less adapted to the new competitive environment. 10

The second change is in values, in what people want from work. From my research, I have distinguished two types of values in the workplace. "Traditional" attitudes comprise traditional male values, focused on individual achievement and advancement up the hierarchy, and traditional female 11 values, focused on helping others and gaining appreciation. "New generation" values, on the other hand, are shared by men and women and focus on gaining independence and opportunity for self-development. The new generation struggles to create a balanced life, sacrificing neither work nor family. This value shift is caused not by demographic changes like the "baby boom" or the "baby bust" but by changes in family structure and socialization. One-fifth of all managers, but one-third of those under age 30 and 40% of new college graduates, possess new-generation values. Their numbers will continue to increase with the growth of dual-career families.

12 While Schwartz's double track desegregates the values of women, it will not resolve the issues raised by these historic changes. Many traditional managers at the top believe that the new-generation employees are not as loyal or committed as they should be, even though their work results are better than traditional employees'. Some very competent young managers do not aspire to top positions because they do not feel comfortable with their superiors. Instead of promotions, they seek lateral transfers that prepare them to start or join entrepreneurial businesses.

13 In this age of customized products and services, managers will also have to customize work arrangements with valued employees, providing, for instance, flexible schedules for new-generation team players. Some new-generation mothers will be satisfied to take limited technical, professional, or managerial roles. Some will let their husbands pursue the major career. Others will be the dominant careerists, while their husbands share a large part of the parenting. And still others will return from mothering to reach for the top. Business should not prejudge or categorize a woman by her attitude toward mothering but rather by her ambition, talent, and ability to balance values.

Michael Maccoby
Director
Project on Technology,
Work and Character
Washington, D.C.

Editor:

14 Much of the comment on Felice Schwartz's recent article seems to be written by people who have not read the essay carefully. They seize on the aspects of her argument that can

be taken negatively and ignore the importance of her subject.

15 The negative reaction undoubtedly comes from the blanket statement that women managers cost their employers more than men do. The natural response is, "What men and in what market conditions?" I know that colleges and universities experience a high turnover rate with their talented women faculty because they are at a premium in the employment market, always being bought away by higher bidders competing for a small pool of talent. This turnover is not a function of their femaleness but of their market position. So it is with many talented corporate women. In a hot market for male employees, such turnover would be viewed philosophically, but with women, it's blamed on "lack of commitment."

16 Moreover, what costs are calculated in the comparative return on investment among male and female managers? How about the higher rates of heart attacks for men? Or the higher incidence of alcoholism for men? Employers see costs associated with maternity negatively; however, they give time to men to perform community service, develop political savvy, or gain exposure to broader social and cultural concerns and see this as an investment.

17 Schwartz's division of women into career-primary and career-and-family women is resented because it implies that women with children are deficient in work motivation in ways that men are not and never can be. Such a view overlooks the frequency with which personnel committees hear about reduced performance in men because of divorce, critically ill children, spouses' health problems, and other family matters. Schwartz's formulation may need correction, but it at least raises an issue corporate America needs to think about more. At MIT, a faculty-administration committee is studying how all categories of employees might better combine work and family responsibilities.

18 Schwartz is absolutely right that demography compels attention to women's participation in society above all other factors. The loss of life experienced in Western Europe during two world wars means that there are family and maternal support policies in place in European countries that are totally lacking in the United States. Certainly, the author is correct in pointing out that although women have been encouraged to enter the ranks of management and the professions in large numbers since the 1960s, there has been

no corresponding tendency for employers to respond to working women's need for quality day care or to recognize maternity leave as a woman's right rather than an ambiguous threat to her future.

19 As for the glass ceiling, which Schwartz mentions as a misleading metaphor, it is real and clearly observable in many otherwise progressive organizations. It exists because few senior managers are willing to see talented women as real colleagues, although concerns for equity make it easy to impose affirmative action at the middle management level. The author is right to assert that demography will likely compel a change in these attitudes in the 1990s and beyond. Such male bastions as Harvard and Yale quickly welcomed women students when demography required them to, though they have been slow in extending a similar welcome to women faculty.

Jill Conway
President Emerita, Smith College
Visiting Scholar and Professor
Massachusetts Institute of Technology
Cambridge, Massachusetts

Editor:

20 My husband brought home Felice Schwartz's article for me to read, shaking his head and clucking over the "woman problem," which he said was well treated in the piece. Schwartz says that women managers cost a little more, but they are worth it. Strangely, this sounds very much like a television commercial for a cosmetic product.

21 As a mother and former manager, I had two thoughts after reading the article. First, because mothering and managing are so different, I wonder how anyone can combine the two; second, I do not think American business is ready for special parenting-emphasis programs.

22 Managing is rhythm and control, and when it goes well, there is no feeling like it in the world. But parenting is letting go; it feels more like endlessly trying to push marbles uphill with your nose. When it goes well, it too feels like nothing else in the world. But between parenting and managing there is such a chasm that it is no wonder that many women stop trying to do both and either delegate responsibility for the children to someone else or quit management.

23 They quit work to get down in the trenches, investing time

in their children to ensure that they become productive parts of the future. Endless wars on everything an ad executive can think of are fought daily by mothers—full-time, part-time, managerial, clerical, blue-collar, pink-collar—mothers who, Schwartz tells us, cost more than men to employ.

Schwartz buys into the very mentality that makes enjoying 24
both work and family relationships so difficult: thinking about work as zero-sum competition and approaching it with blind, single-purpose dedication. What service does Schwartz do her avowed cause of creating opportunities for women by embracing this paradigm as the one to govern approaches to the "problem" of mother-managers? There are so many other ways of thinking about the situation. For example, we could look at mothers who interrupt their careers as soldiers performing national service, deserving commendation from the federal department of "mothering affairs" when they return from the "front."

Schwartz is writing to an audience who she assumes is 25
ready to value women managers realistically and fearlessly. I am not convinced by her limited support for this premise. Advocating the segmentation of women managers only serves to make women work harder than ever to be allowed a chance at a rewarding job and to drum up business for Schwartz.

Janet L. Lowden
Mama
The Lowden Family
Scottsdale, Arizona

IV.

MEDIA

Introduction

Among the revolutions of the twentieth century, not the least significant has been a revolution in communications. Oral communications (such as public speeches) and print media—books, newspapers, periodicals, even personal correspondence—dominated public consciousness a century ago, but since then telephones, radio, recordings, film, television, and computer networks have joined the ranks of public media to great effect. It's not that oral communication or books or newspapers or personal letters have been supplanted; far from it. But the new media have given Americans broader and faster and sometimes more dramatic access to information than in the past and additional opportunities for enjoyment and artistic expression as well.

This does not mean that the new media have been accepted uncritically. Ever since television arrived as a form of mass media 45 years ago—in 1950 only 9 percent of U.S. households contained a television; by 1955, 50 percent did—people have worried about its effect on the national psyche. This worry derives in part from a puritanical distrust of things pleasurable and in part from a traditional national distrust over things technological; but it also derives from an honest concern about the seductive power of TV over the popular imagination. Can it really be true that the average American child typically watches more than seven hours of television a day? Is television programming "a vast wasteland" (to borrow a common formulation)? Do soap operas, sitcoms, and sports on TV anesthetize people more than entertain them? Does television make people into passive observers rather than active inquirers? Does it affect our sense of community? Does it make us into a nation of strangers, a nation of couch potatoes nesting in front of televisions and VCRs? Does violence on TV perpetuate violence in our culture? Does the advertising on television propagate destructive stereotypes and promulgate a national cynicism about honesty in general and the honesty of American business in particular? Is television news inevitably biased? In what direction? Does it deliberately seek out the visual and dramatic as opposed to the truly newsworthy? Does it shape events as much as report them? And if television does have any vices, what, in a world with the First Amendment, can be done about it? These are some of the questions that come up in the first set of readings in this part.

The second set of essays takes up another specific fear about the media: its effects on democracy. Does television change our national institutions and compromise access to public office? Do people who control the airwaves and print journalism control the electorate? If so, what can be done about it? Furthermore, does television change our sense of what it means to govern? Does it change our attitudes toward our leaders? Ever since John Kennedy debated Richard Nixon on television in 1960, people have worried about the effects of television on the electorate, and the perceived success of Ronald Reagan—the former actor who seemed at home in front of a camera as no place else—has not made that worry diminish. The essays collected in the section titled "Television and the Elections" offer historical and critical perspective on these questions; they offer food for your own thoughts, and your own prose, as the next election approaches.

But *media* means more than television and journalism, and it does more than create successful politicians. It creates popular heroes and myths as well, especially through film and popular music. Hence, the third section in this part of *Conversations* considers a single popular movie, director Spike Lee's *Malcolm X.* The three short articles focus on the issue of quality, since judgments about the relative merits of various films frequently occupy the time and the passions of average citizens. What makes a film good or not so good? What are the grounds for aesthetic evaluation? These questions are made concrete in the three movie reviews presented. The three reviewers differ in their assessment of the film's merits. How do you account for the differences? On what criteria do the reviewers base their judgments? Are certain important criteria ignored? These readings are likely to sharpen your responses to *Malcolm X* and your own arguments on the merits of other plays and movies and television shows that engage you.

This part concludes with a section on rap music. By reading the five articles, you will be listening in on a conversation about the value of rap in general and 2 Live Crew in particular. On the one hand, the discussion amounts to a commentary on rap music as a cultural artifact: What is rap music all about? On the other hand, the discussion brings up First Amendment issues that will be developed in the next part of *Conversations*. The analyses tell us plenty about rap music, plenty about 2 Live Crew, and—since analysts have a tendency to make over cultural artifacts in their own images—some things about their authors as well. As you read, keep in mind how the rhetorical situation of each analysis—the audience, the situation, the writer's aim—colors each analysis itself. And consider the articles as prototypes for your own further meditations on rap music, specific rap musicians, or other cultural artifacts.

WHAT ARE THE EFFECTS OF TELEVISION?

The Committee on the Judiciary, U.S. House of Representatives

Television Violence Act of 1989

A Television Violence Act was proposed by Congress in 1989. After hearings, the House Judiciary Committee submitted the following report, together with dissenting views. The House of Representatives passed the law, but it later died when a House-Senate conference committee could not reach agreement on it. (The report has been edited very slightly for increased readability.)

The Committee on the Judiciary, to whom was referred the bill (H.R. 1391) to exempt from the antitrust laws certain activities relating to alleviating the negative impact of violence in telecast material, having considered the same, report favorably thereon with an amendment and recommend that the bill as amended do pass. 1

I. Purpose of H.R. 1391

H.R. 1391 is a response to concerns about the negative impact of violence on television. The purpose of H.R. 1391 is to remove a possible impediment—the antitrust laws—for a limited time should persons in the television industry voluntarily wish to meet and adopt voluntary guidelines in this area. The bill is not meant to coerce any conduct or action whatsoever. Whether or not persons wish to meet as permitted by the bill, or whether or not they wish to develop or abide by guidelines, is entirely voluntary. 2

II. Procedural Background of H.R. 1391

3 On March 14, 1989, Congressmen Dan Glickman and Edward Feighan introduced H.R. 1391, legislation to grant a 3-year antitrust exemption to permit persons in the television industry to engage in certain joint voluntary action to develop and disseminate voluntary guidelines designed to alleviate the negative impact of violence in telecast material.

4 On May 10, 1989, the Subcommittee on Economic and Commercial Law held a hearing on H.R. 1391. Witnesses testifying in support of the legislation were: Senator Paul Simon of Illinois (sponsor of similar legislation in the Senate), Dr. William Dietz on behalf of the American Academy of Pediatrics, Dr. Brian Wilcox on behalf of the American Psychological Association, and Ms. Joan Dykstra on behalf of the National Parent-Teacher Association.

5 Ms. Beth Waxman Bressan of CBS Broadcast Group testified that CBS neither actively supported nor actively opposed the bill and thought it was unnecessary. Mr. Alan Gerson of the National Broadcasting Company testified that NBC did not oppose the bill but thought it was unnecessary as applied to over-the-air television. Mr. Alfred R. Schneider of Capital Cities/ABC, Inc. testified that ABC did not support the bill because "jointly-developed industry-wide standards to replace those which have been independently arrived at would in our judgment be unnecessary, inappropriate, and exceedingly difficult to implement."

6 Professor Cass R. Sunstein of the University of Chicago Law School testified to his belief that H.R. 1391 was constitutional. Mr. Barry W. Lynn testified in opposition to the bill on behalf of the American Civil Liberties Union, presenting the ACLU's view that the antitrust exemption in the bill "is both unwise and unconstitutional."

7 On June 15, 1989, the subcommittee adopted one clarifying amendment to the bill, offered by Mr. Glickman, and favorably reported the bill as an amendment in the nature of a substitute by a 10 to 4 vote. The amendment was intended to clarify the sponsors' intent that all entities that air or produce programming would fall within the orbit of the bill's coverage.

8 On June 20, 1989, the Committee on the Judiciary ordered the amendment in the nature of a substitute to H.R. 1391 favorably reported, by a vote of 26 to 8.

III. Background and Summary of H.R. 1391

A. Effects of TV Violence on Real Life Violence. H.R. 1391 9
is based upon the premise that there is a causal relationship between violence on television and aggressive behavior in real life, particularly with young viewers. The bulk of the scientific research into this area seems to indicate that there is some link between television violence and real life aggression. Though there is not universal acceptance of this conclusion—a minority of studies have reached the opposite conclusion—the committee, relying upon the greater weight of the research, accepts the premise that there is some causal relationship between violence on television and real life aggression.

A brief summary of some of the research in this area 10
follows:

1. *Surgeon General's Advisory Committee on Television and Behavior.*—Pursuant to a request by Senator John Pastore in 1969, this Advisory Committee was appointed under the auspices of the National Institute of Mental Health to study whether there was a causal connection between television violence and real life violence and anti-social behavior. Numerous research studies were funded and conducted, and in 1972 the Surgeon General's Report, *Television and Growing Up: The Impact of Televised Violence,* was published. The report's major conclusion was as follows:

> [T]here is a convergence of the fairly substantial experimental evidence for a short-run causation of aggression among some children by viewing violence on the screen and much less certain evidence from field studies that extensive violence viewing precedes some long-run manifestations of aggressive behavior. The convergence of the two types of evidence constitute some preliminary indication of a causal relationship, but a good deal of research remains to be done before one can have confidence in these conclusions.

The report acknowledged that these conclusions were tentative and limited, and were therefore not entirely satisfactory.

Ten years later, an update of the Surgeon General's 11
Report was issued by the National Institute of Mental Health (*Television and Behavior: Ten Years of Scientific*

Progress and Implications for the 80's). The update considered the research that had been conducted since the original study, and stated that "[r]ecent research confirms the earlier findings of a causal relationship between viewing televised violence and later aggressive behavior."[1] This conclusion applied to groups, rather than specific types of individuals. Importantly, the update also stated (pp. 89–90):

> [N]o single study unequivocally confirms the conclusion that televised violence leads to aggressive behavior. Similarly, no single study unequivocally refutes that conclusion. The scientific support for the causal relationship derives from the convergence of findings from many studies, the great majority of which demonstrates a positive relationship between televised violence and later aggressive behavior.

12 2. *Huesman Longitudinal Study.*—Dr. L. Rowell Huesman, a scientist who has spent many years researching the effects of television violence on behavior, wrote an article for the 1982 NIMH update in which he stated that "[a]t this time, it should be difficult to find any researcher who does not believe that a significant positive relationship exists between viewing television violence and subsequent aggressive behavior under most conditions."[2]

13 Dr. Huesman, along with other colleagues, also conducted a longitudinal study in which the same children were studied first in 1960 at age 8, and then later at ages 22 and 30 (632 persons were studied at all three ages). The researchers concluded that, in boys, "a preference for TV violence viewing at age 8 is related to both current aggressive behavior and later aggressive behavior including criminal behavior as an adult," while for girls, there was no relation between a preference for violent shows and aggression at ages 8 or 19, "but a slight relation between violence viewing and aggression at age 30."[3]

14 3. *Gerbner Prevalence of Violence Studies.*—Dr. George

[1] *Television and Behavior: Ten Years of Scientific Progress and Implications for the 80's*, Volume 1: Summary Report, page 89 (1982).

[2] "Television Violence and Aggressive Behavior," p. 126, included in *Television and Behavior: Ten Years of Scientific Progress and Implications for the 80's*, Volume 2: Technical Reviews (1982).

[3] Huesman, Eron, et al., "Television Viewing Habits in Childhood and Adult Aggression," p. 9.

Gerbner, Dean of the Annenberg School of Communications at the University of Pennsylvania, has led a team of researchers that has been analyzing the level of violence in television programs for each television season since 1967. One of the measures studied has been the rate of clear-cut and unambiguous episodes of physical violence. For the year 1985, the latest year for which results have been released, Dr. Gerbner's team found the following number of violent acts to have been committed in an hour of television during the specified period:

a. All programs on all networks: 9.7 violent acts in an average television hour.
b. Between 8 and 9 p.m., in what used to be called the family hour: 7.6 violent acts per hour.
c. Between 9 p.m. and 11 p.m.: 6.4 violent acts per hour.
d. Weekend-Daytime TV (children's programming, largely cartoons): 21.3 violent acts per hour.

Dr. Gerbner's team found that, in 1985, 85 percent of all 15
programs on television contained some act of violence.[4]

The 1985 study contended that viewers of violence, espe- 16
cially viewers who belong to the same group as the most prevalent victims of TV violence—women, young children, and the elderly—tend to identify symbolically with the victims of TV violence and translate this into real fear. The study stated (p. 10) that:

> While the convergence of research indicates that exposure to violence does occasionally incite and often desensitize, our findings show that, for most viewers, television's mean and dangerous world tends to cultivate a sense of relative danger, mistrust, dependence, and—despite its supposedly "entertaining nature"—alienation and gloom.

4. *Attorney General's Task Force on Family Violence.*—In a 17
report issued in September 1984, the Attorney General's Task Force on Family Violence stated that "the evidence is becoming overwhelming that just as witnessing violence in

[4] Gerbner, Gross, Signorielli and Morgan, "Television's Mean World: Violence Profile No. 14–15" (September, 1986).

the home may contribute to normal adults and children learning and acting out violent behavior, violence on TV and the movies may contribute to the same result."[5]

18 5. *Conflicting Research on Television Violence.*—As indicated, not all of the studies and literature support a finding that there is some relationship between television violence and real life aggression. For example, the National Broadcasting Company sponsored a study of the effect of exposure to violence on television on aggressive behavior. Exposure to television violence and aggressive behavior among elementary school boys and girls, and among teenage boys, was measured in different schools in two cities, on five (for teenage boys) or six (for elementary school boys and girls) different occasions between 1970 and 1973. Where possible, the same students were tracked over the course of this three-year period. The study "did not find evidence that television violence was causally implicated in the development of aggressive behavior patterns among children and adolescents over the time periods studied."[6]

19 The committee is persuaded by the majority of studies that indicate there is some relationship between television violence and real life behavior. The committee is therefore concerned about violence on television and its effects. H.R. 1391 addresses the problem of the impact on our Nation's children of violence on television; as formulated, the bill is a limited, narrow, non-coercive response. Television programmers who may wish to take steps to unilaterally alleviate the negative impact of television violence but who do not do so for fear of slipping in the ratings will be able to participate in joint discussions about voluntary guidelines.

IV. Constitutional Issues Raised by H.R. 1391

20 The committee believes that H.R. 1391 presents no constitutional problems. It is a bill that mandates nothing and is completely voluntary. It neither contains nor is meant to imply any sanctions for either failure to meet and hold discussions as permitted by the bill or failure to adhere to any

[5] Attorney General's Task Force on Family Violence, Final Report, September, 1984, p. 110.

[6] Milavsky, Kessler, Stipp, & Rubens, *Television and Aggression: A Panel Study*, 1982, p. 487.

voluntary guidelines that may be developed. The antitrust exemption in the bill is not intended to coerce the industry to either meet or adopt television violence guidelines; it is only intended to remove a possible impediment—the antitrust laws—should members of the industry voluntarily wish to meet and adopt guidelines in this area.[7]

The committee believes that H.R. 1391 contains no con- 21
stitutional infirmities. The bill is entirely voluntary and is reasonably designed to protect impressionable viewers from "developmental" harm. As Professor Cass R. Sunstein of the University of Chicago Law School told the Subcommittee on Economic and Commercial Law at its hearing:

> H.R. 1391 does not regulate speech. Its only effect is to authorize voluntary action by broadcasters. In this respect, it increases rather than decreases their freedom, by reducing the pressures of the marketplace with respect to television violence. The most powerful attack on the bill would be that the selective exemption it creates is based on the content of speech, and that content-based regulation is subject to careful judicial scrutiny. This attack is, however, unpersuasive in light of the fact that H.R. 1391 (a) is limited to the broadcasting area, (b) does not require or prohibit speech at all, and (c) does not discriminate on the basis of point of view, but is instead a legitimate effort to [combat] genuine harms.

H.R. 1391 is not an effort to regulate a point of view but is, rather, an effort to prevent a legitimate harm.

The bill's efforts to reduce the negative impact of violence 22
has some similarities to the factual situation presented in *Ginsberg* v. *New York,* though the speech involved in Ginsberg was pornography, which, unlike violent speech, is not entitled to First Amendment protections. In *Ginsberg,* the Supreme Court upheld a New York statute that prohibited the sale of pictures or magazines depicting nudity harmful to minors to persons under seventeen years of age. At the time the statute was enacted, there existed scientific studies that concluded exposure to obscenity impaired the de-

[7] In this regard, H.R. 1391 is entirely different from the situation in *Writers Guild* v. *ABC,* 609 F. 2d 355 (9th Cir. 1979), where the government, through the Federal Communications Commission, was found to have exerted informal, improper pressure on networks to adopt family viewing guidelines.

velopment of youth, as well as studies that claimed such exposure did not hinder development. Nevertheless, the Court said "we do not demand of legislatures scientifically certain criteria of legislation." It acknowledged the interest of the government in protecting the welfare of children and safeguarding them from abuses that might hinder children's development. Since the action of the legislature had a rational relation to the objective of safeguarding minors from harm, the statue was upheld.

23 The Supreme Court has upheld some governmental regulation of broadcasting because of the often uncontrolled or involuntary exposure of children to television, and because of the limited number of airwaves that exist. In *Federal Communications Commission* v. *Pacifica Foundation,* for example, the Court recognized that "it is broadcasting that has received the most limited First Amendment protection." The Court also indicated that "[b]ecause the broadcast audience is constantly tuning in and out, prior warnings cannot completely protect the listener or viewer from unexpected program content."

24 Given that there are not enough broadcast frequencies available to accommodate all parties who want to broadcast, the Supreme Court stated in *Red Lion Broadcasting* v. *FCC* in 1969 that "it is idle to posit an unabridgeable First Amendment right to broadcast comparable to the right of every individual to speak, write, or publish." While the weight of this pronouncement may be somewhat less now because of the recent proliferation of cable and satellite television systems, the Government's interest in protecting children from abuse is as strong as ever. In enacting H.R. 1391, the committee believes that it is acting in a reasonable, non-intrusive, non-coercive manner to try to prevent developmental harm to impressionable frequent viewers of television.[8]

V. Antitrust Consideration

25 H.R. 1391 would grant only a temporary exemption from the antitrust laws. It removes a possible impediment to

[8] In no way does the legislation restrict adults to viewing only what is acceptable for children. The legislation contains no restrictions or bans whatsoever.

persons in the television industry voluntarily getting together to develop voluntary guidelines to alleviate the negative impact of television violence.

The committee does not accept the argument that the antitrust laws now prohibit all joint activities contemplated by the legislation. Under existing law, many joint activities among competitors are not viewed as harmful to competition. Thus, trade associations and industry-wide groups have met for years in order to discuss common problems, to develop standards to improve the safety of the products and even to conduct joint research and development. Because such activities are generally not aimed at restricting competition or decreasing output, but instead are directed at improving competitiveness and efficiencies, the antitrust laws are not needed to restore the operation of a free market economy.[9] 26

The committee does not believe that the decision in *U.S.* v. *National Association of Broadcasters* can be read as prohibiting all joint voluntary agreements in the broadcast industry. In *NAB,* the district court struck down participation by broadcasters in a voluntary code in which there was industry-wide adherence to a rule prohibiting multiple products from being advertised during a single commercial. The court found the multiple product standard to be an artificial device aimed at enhancing the demand for commercial time and/or limiting the supply of commercial time available. Finding the effect to be similar to a tying arrangement, the court found the practice to be a *per se* violation of the antitrust laws. This particular rule was anti-competitive. Other parts of the NAB code were not viewed as anti-competitive, however, and were not invalidated. The committee does not believe that joint, voluntary agreements that are not anti-competitive in their effect, and that do not give rise to ancillary restraints, raise antitrust problems. 27

Having said this, the committee acknowledges that the antitrust laws are still perceived by some as an impediment to persons in the television industry developing joint voluntary guidelines. Because of its interest in protecting impressionable viewers from abuse, the committee is willing to approve the *limited, temporary,* exemption in H.R. 1391 so that if persons in the television industry wish to voluntarily 28

[9] *See e.g., Broadcast Music Inc.* v. *CBS*, 441 U.S. 1 (1979); *Continental TV* v. *GTE Sylvania Inc.*, 433 U.S. 36 (1977).

develop guidelines to reduce the negative impact of television violence, they will not be dissuaded from doing so by possible fears about antitrust exposure.

29 Perhaps most important, the legislation makes it clear that the antitrust exemption does *not* apply to any joint discussion, consideration, review, action, or agreement which results in a boycott of any person. The exemption is meant only to permit development of voluntary guidelines to alleviate the negative impact of violence on television, not to be used as a subterfuge for a boycott of any person because of adherence to the guidelines developed.

Dissenting Views of Hon. Don Edwards, Hon. Robert W. Kastenmeier, Hon. John Conyers, Jr., Hon. Patricia Schroeder, Hon. Geo. W. Crockett, Hon. Mike Synar, Hon. Howard L. Berman, and Hon. Rick Boucher

30 As Justice Brennan stated so eloquently in *Bantam Books, Inc.* v. *Sullivan:* "It is characteristic of the freedoms of expression in general that they are vulnerable to gravely damaging yet barely visible encroachments." H.R. 1391 is just such an encroachment. Along with the *Bantam Books* Court, we believe freedom of speech is a precarious, fragile freedom which must be guarded jealously and diligently. Thus, we must dissent from the Committee Report on H.R. 1391.

31 Proponents of H.R. 1391 have cited *Red Lion Broadcasting Co.* v. *FCC, Ginsberg* v. *New York,* and *FCC* v. *Pacifica Foundation* as supportive of their position that the bill does not violate the First Amendment. H.R. 1391 is readily distinguishable from narrow regulations previously upheld by the Supreme Court.

32 H.R. 1391 deals with televised violence. The Court has never suggested that depictions of violence lie outside the full protection of the First Amendment. Rather, the cases relied on by the majority deal primarily with the area of obscenity, an area never viewed by the Court as within the concerns of the First Amendment. As the Court stated in *Roth* v. *United States:* "Obscenity is not within the area of constitutionally protected speech or press."

33 Even in the unprotected area of obscenity, the Court has always required the government to regulate in a manner protective of constitutionally protected speech. "Our insis-

tence that regulations of obscenity scrupulously embody the most rigorous procedural safeguards . . . is . . . but a special instance of the larger principle that the freedoms of expression must be ringed about with adequate bulwarks" (*Bantam Books* v. *Sullivan*)

In contrast, H.R. 1391 operates in a protected area of 34
speech and it manipulates the federal antitrust laws to achieve an impermissible result. The bill exempts the TV industry from the antitrust laws for the express purpose not only of having that industry alter the content of its programs, but also to alter it in the direction the government dictates. That is indirect censorship, clear and simple.

Further, as the *Bantam Books* Court pointed out, "People 35
do not lightly disregard public officers' thinly veiled threats to institute . . . proceedings against them if they do not come around." The legislative history of H.R. 1391 is replete with thinly veiled threats of further government action.

In *Red Lion Broadcasting* v. *FCC,* the Court merely upheld 36
the Federal Communications Commission's "Fairness Doctrine." This doctrine, as the name implies, requires the presentation of differing viewpoints. The Court upheld the fairness doctrine in this case because it "enhance[d] rather than abridge[d] the freedoms of speech and press protected by the First Amendment."

In contrast, H.R. 1391 seeks to restrict or eliminate 37
particular viewpoints about the appropriate use of violence. Yet, the Court has said: "It is the purpose of the First Amendment to preserve an uninhibited marketplace of ideas in which truth will ultimately prevail, rather than to countenance monopolization of that market, whether it be by the Government itself or a private licensee."

The Court in *FCC* v. *Pacifica Foundation* upheld possible 38
administrative sanctions against a radio station for broadcasting "indecent" material in the early afternoon. The Court noted this would "deter only the broadcasting of patently offensive reference to excretory and sexual organs and activities" which "surely lie at the periphery of First Amendment concerns." In this case, the FCC pointed out that it "never intended to place an absolute prohibition on the broadcast of this type of language, but rather sought to channel it to times of day when children most likely would not be exposed to it." As the *Pacifica* Court emphasized, "It is a central tenet of the First Amendment that the government must remain neutral in the marketplace of ideas." In

its decision, the Court merely recognized that certain sexually-oriented speech historically has been outside the protection of the First Amendment, particularly if distributed to minors.

39 In *Ginsberg* v. *New York,* the Court upheld a prohibition on sale to minors of material which was "obscene" as to children, even if not legally "obscene" for adults. The Court was careful to point out that the prohibition did not limit the rights of adults to the same material, and that parents desiring to purchase the magazines for themselves or for their children were *not* barred from doing so.

40 Rather than according with previous Supreme Court decisions, the practical effect of H.R. 1391 is to reach the result forbidden by the Supreme Court in *Butler* v. *Michigan,* that of reducing the adult population to seeing only what is fit for children: "We have before us legislation not reasonably restricted to the evil with which it is said to deal. The incidence of this enactment is to reduce the adult population of Michigan to reading only what is fit for children."

41 The sincere motivations of the proponents of H.R. 1391 are not questioned here. All of us support the goal of a more civil society. But casting aside constitutional concerns and giving content-specific antitrust exemptions to the TV industry is a truly dangerous and constitutionally precluded way to achieve that goal.

42 The words of Justice Brennan in *Pacifica* are particularly salient to H.R. 1391: "Most parents will undoubtedly find understandable as well as commendable the Court's sympathy with the FCC's desire to prevent offensive broadcasts from reaching the ears of unsupervised children. Unfortunately, the facial appeal of this justification for radio censorship masks its constitutional insufficiency."

43 The proper place for TV programming content to be decided is in our homes and our communities. As Justice Douglas pointed out in *Ginsberg,* "It is one thing for parents and the religious organizations to be active and involved. It is quite a different matter for the state to become implicated as a censor." When Congress "signals" to the media what material it deems appropriate, that is informal censorship by the government; and, as such, it can have the same constitutionally impermissible effect as direct restraints on inhibiting communication.

44 S. 593, the Senate companion bill, like H.R. 1391 began with an exemption for violence, but passed the Senate with

exemptions for violence, illegal drug use, and sexually explicit material. The action of the Senate demonstrates that once this process is engaged in, there is no rational basis for stopping at any particular point.

When they are inclined to do so, power regularly is 45
exercised by our citizens to affect television content. The American people can directly control programming without the interference of the government, and that is how it should be.

The Court has in the past "look[ed] through forms to the 46
substance and recognize[d] that informal censorship may sufficiently inhibit the circulation of publications to warrant injunctive relief." Should the Congress proceed in its ill-advised path with H.R. 1391, we can only hope that the Court will do so once again, for it is not only a serious mistake—but also constitutional error—to encourage censorship through the manipulation of the federal antitrust laws.

A selection from his popular collection Akbar and Jeff's Guide to Life (1989), this cartoon by Matt Groening (born 1954) captures some of the feelings people associate with TV and TV watchers. Groening also developed the television show "The Simpsons." For another example of his work, see page 69.

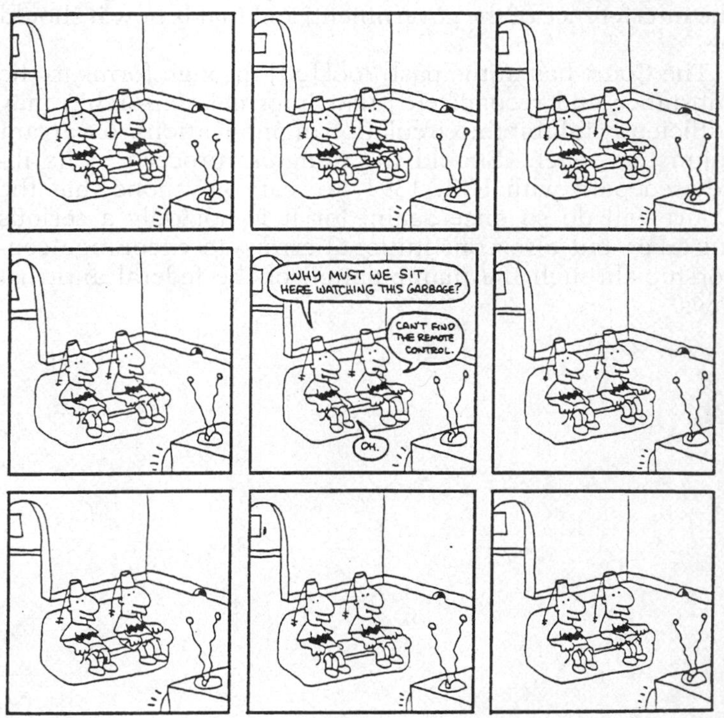

Madeline Drexler

Don't Touch That Dial

Madeline Drexler, a free-lance writer, contributed the following analysis to The Boston Globe *newspaper in 1991.*

Television acts as a narcotic on children—mesmerizing them, stunting their ability to think, and displacing such wholesome activities as book reading and family discussions. Right? 1

Wrong, says researcher Daniel Anderson, a psychologist at the University of Massachusetts at Amherst. Anderson doesn't have any particular affection for *Garfield and Friends,* MTV clips, or *Gilligan's Island* reruns. But he does believe it's important to distinguish television's impact on children from influences of the family and the wider culture. We tend to blame TV, he says, for problems it doesn't really cause. In the process, we overlook our own roles in shaping children's minds. 2

One conventional belief about television is that it impairs a child's ability to think and to interpret the world. But Anderson's own research and reviews of the scientific literature discredit this assumption. While watching TV, children do not merely absorb words and images. Instead, they muse upon the meaning of what they see, its plausibility, and its implications for the future—whether they've tuned in to a news report of a natural disaster or an action show. Because television relies on such cinematic techniques as montage and crosscutting, children learn early how to draw inferences about the passage of time, character psychology, and implied events. Even preschoolers comprehend more than just the information supplied on the tube. 3

Another contention about television is that it displaces reading as a form of entertainment. But according to Anderson, the amount of time spent watching television is not related to reading ability. For one thing, TV doesn't take the place of reading for most children; it takes the place of similar sorts of recreation, such as going to the movies, reading comic books, listening to the radio, and playing sports. Variables such as socioeconomic status and parents' educational background exert a far stronger influence on a child's reading. "Far and away," Anderson says, "the best 4 predictor of reading ability, and of how much a child reads, is how much a parent reads."

5 Conventional wisdom has it that heavy television-watching lowers IQ scores and hinders school performance. Since the 1960s, SAT scores have dropped, along with state and national assessments of educational achievement. But here, too, Anderson notes that no studies have linked prolonged television exposure in childhood to lower IQ later on. In fact, research suggests that it's the other way around. Early IQ predicts how much TV an older child will watch. "If you're smart young, you'll watch less TV when you're older," Anderson says. Conversely, in the same self-selecting process, people of lower IQ tend to be lifelong television devotees.

6 When parents watch TV with their young children, explaining new words and ideas to them, the children comprehend far more than they would if they were watching alone. This is due partly to the fact that when kids expect that TV will require thought, they spend more time thinking. What's ironic is that most parents use an educational program as an opportunity to park their kids in front of the set and do something in another room. "Even for parents who are generally wary of television," Anderson says, "*Sesame Street* is considered a show where it's perfectly okay to leave a child alone." The program was actually intended to be viewed by parents and children together, he says.

7 Because our attitudes inform TV viewing, Anderson applauds the nascent trend of offering high school courses that teach students how to "decode" television. In these classes, students learn to analyze the persuasive techniques of commercials, compare the reality of crime to its dramatic portrayal, inquire into the economics of broadcasting, and understand the mechanics of TV production. Such courses, Anderson contends, teach the kind of critical thinking central to the purpose of education. "Kids can be taught as much about television as about text or computers," he says.

8 If anything, Anderson's views underscore the fact that television cannot be disparaged in isolation from larger forces. For years researchers have attempted to show that television is inherently dangerous to children, hypnotizing them with its movement and color, cutting their attention span with its fast-paced, disconnected images, curbing intellectual development, and taking the place of loftier pastimes.

9 By showing that television promotes none of these effects, Anderson intends to shift the discussion to the real issue: content. That, of course, is a thornier discussion. How should

our society judge the violence of primetime shows? The sexism of MTV? The materialism of commercials? "I feel television is almost surely having a major social impact on the kids, as opposed to a cognitive impact," Anderson says.

In this context, he offers some advice to parents: First, "Parents should think of their kids as actively absorbing everything on television. They are not just passively mesmerized—in one eye and out the other. Some things on TV are probably good for children to watch, like educational TV, and some things are bad." 10

Second, "If you think your kid is spending lots of time watching television, think about what alternatives there are, from the child's point of view." Does a youngster have too much free time? Are there books, toys, games, or playmates around? "A lot of the time, kids watch TV as a default activity: There's nothing else to do." 11

Finally, "If a child persists in watching too much television, the question is why. It's rare that TV shows are themselves so entertaining." More often than not, the motive is escapism. A teen-ager may be uncomfortable with his or her peers; a child may want to retreat from a home torn by marital strife; there may be problems at school. 12

For children, as for adults, television can be a source of enlightenment or a descent into mindlessness—depending mostly on the choices of lucre-driven executives. But as viewers, we can't ignore what we ourselves bring to the medium. 13

Katha Pollitt

The Smurfette Principle

Katha Pollitt, a poet and essayist, contributed the following essay to The New York Times *in the spring of 1991.*

This Christmas, I finally caved in. I gave my 3-year-old daughter, Sophie, her very own cassette of "The Little Mermaid." Now, she, too, can sit transfixed by Ariel, the perky teen-ager with the curvy tail who trades her voice for a pair of shapely legs and a shot at marriage to a prince. ("On land it's much preferred for ladies not to say a word," sings the cynical sea witch, "and she who holds her tongue will get her man." Since she's the villain, we're not meant to notice that events prove her correct.) 1

2 Usually when parents give a child some item they find repellent, they plead helplessness before a juvenile filibuster. But "The Little Mermaid" was my idea. Ariel may look a lot like Barbie, and her adventure may be limited to romance and over with the wedding bells, but unlike, say, Cinderella or Sleeping Beauty, she's active, brave and determined, the heroine of her own life. She even rescues the prince. And that makes her a rare fish, indeed, in the world of preschool culture.

3 Take a look at the kids' section of your local video store. You'll find that features starring boys, and usually aimed at them, account for 9 out of 10 offerings. Clicking the television dial one recent week—admittedly not an encyclopedic study—I came across not a single network cartoon or puppet show starring a female. (Nickelodeon, the children's cable channel, has one of each.) Except for the crudity of the animation and the general air of witlessness and hype, I might as well have been back in my own 1960's childhood, nibbling Frosted Flakes in front of Daffy Duck, Bugs Bunny, Porky Pig and the rest of the all-male Warner Brothers lineup.

4 Contemporary shows are either essentially all-male, like "Garfield," or are organized on what I call the Smurfette principle: a group of male buddies will be accented by a lone female, stereotypically defined. In the worst cartoons—the ones that blend seamlessly into the animated cereal commercials—the female is usually a little-sister type, a bunny in a pink dress and hair ribbons who tags along with the adventurous bears and badgers. But the Smurfette principle rules the more carefully made shows, too. Thus, Kanga, the only female in "Winnie-the-Pooh," is a mother. Piggy, of "Muppet Babies," is a pint-size version of Miss Piggy, the camp glamour queen of the Muppet movies. April, of the wildly popular "Teen-Age Mutant Ninja Turtles," functions as a girl Friday to a quartet of male superheroes. The message is clear. Boys are the norm, girls the variation; boys are central, girls peripheral; boys are individuals, girls types. Boys define the group, its story and its code of values. Girls exist only in relation to boys.

5 Well, commercial television—what did I expect? The surprise is that public television, for all its superior intelligence, charm and commitment to worthy values, shortchanges preschool girls, too. Mister Rogers lives in a neighborhood populated mostly by middle-aged men like himself. "Shining Time Station" features a cartoon in which the male characters are train engines and the female char-

acters are passenger cars. And then there's "Sesame Street." True, the human characters are neatly divided between the genders (and among the races, too, which is another rarity). The film clips, moreover, are just about the only place on television in which you regularly see girls having fun together, practicing double Dutch, having a sleep-over. But the Muppets are the real stars of "Sesame Street," and the important ones—the ones with real personalities, who sing on the musical videos, whom kids identify with and cherish in dozens of licensed products—are *all* male. I know one little girl who was so outraged and heartbroken when she realized that even Big Bird—her last hope—was a boy that she hasn't watched the show since.

Well, there's always the library. Some of the best children's books ever written have been about girls—Madeline, Frances the badger. It's even possible to find stories with funny, feminist messages, like "The Paperbag Princess." (She rescues the prince from a dragon, but he's so ungrateful that she decides not to marry him, after all.) But books about girls are a subset in a field that includes a much larger subset of books about boys (12 of the 14 storybooks singled out for praise in last year's Christmas roundup in *Newsweek,* for instance) and books in which the sex of the child is theoretically unimportant—in which case it usually "happens to be" male. Dr. Seuss's books are less about individual characters than about language and imaginative freedom—but, somehow or other, only boys get to go on beyond Zebra or see marvels on Mulberry Street. Frog and Toad, Lowly Worm, Lyle the Crocodile, all *could* have been female. But they're not. 6

Do kids pick up on the sexism in children's culture? You bet. Preschoolers are like medieval philosophers; the text—a book, a movie, a TV show—is more authoritative than the evidence of their own eyes. "Let's play weddings," says my little niece. We grownups roll our eyes, but face it, it's still the one scenario in which the girl is the central figure. "Women are *nurses,*" my friend Anna, a doctor, was informed by her then 4-year-old, Molly. Even my Sophie is beginning to notice the back-seat role played by girls in some of her favorite books. "Who's that?" she asks every time we re-read "The Cat in the Hat." It's Sally, the timid little sister of the resourceful boy narrator. She wants Sally to matter, I think, and since Sally is really just a name and a hair ribbon, we have to say her name again and again. 7

The sexism in preschool culture deforms both boys and 8

girls. Little girls learn to split their consciousness, filtering their dreams and ambitions through boy characters while admiring the clothes of the princess. The more privileged and daring can dream of becoming exceptional women in a man's world—Smurfettes. The others are being taught to accept the more usual fate, which is to be a passenger car drawn through life by a masculine train engine. Boys, who are rarely confronted with stories in which males play only minor roles, learn a simpler lesson: girls just don't matter much.

9 How can it be that 25 years of feminist social change have made so little impression on preschool culture? Molly, now 6 and well aware that women can be doctors, has one theory: children's entertainment is mostly made by men. That's true, as it happens, and I'm sure it explains a lot. It's also true that, as a society, we don't seem to care much what goes on with kids, as long as they are reasonably quiet. Marshmallow cereal, junky toys, endless hours in front of the tube—a society that accepts all that is not going to get in a lather about a little gender stereotyping. It's easier to focus on the bright side. I had "Cinderella," Sophie has "The Little Mermaid"—that's progress, isn't it?

10 "We're working on it," Dulcy Singer, the executive producer of "Sesame Street," told me when I raised the sensitive question of those all-male Muppets. After all, the show has only been on the air for a quarter of a century; these things take time. The trouble is, our preschoolers don't have time. My funny, clever, bold, adventurous daughter is forming her gender ideas right now. I do what I can to counteract the messages she gets from her entertainment, and so does her father—Sophie watches very little television. But I can see we have our work cut out for us. It sure would help if the bunnies took off their hair ribbons, and if half of the monsters were fuzzy, blue—and female.

Anna Quindlen

TV or Not TV

Anna Quindlen's syndicated newspaper column "Public and Private" runs regularly in The New York Times *and many other newspapers. This article ran on November 30, 1991. Quindlen (born 1935) won the Pulitzer Prize for commentary in 1992.*

Ten years ago at some awards banquet I sat next to an actress who was bored out of her gourd (and probably high as a kite) and who proceeded to perform a medley of television theme songs. She did "Gilligan's Island," "The Flintstones," "The Patty Duke Show" and "Rawhide," making a very convincing whip sound by whistling between her front teeth. She did "Green Acres," "The Beverly Hillbillies" and, as her finale, the theme from "The Mickey Mouse Club." Though she'd grown up in the hills of Beverly, I felt we were neighbors. 1

I like television. This is unfashionable. Sniping at TV has become a kind of pedigree, a guarantee of superiority. One woman said to me proudly not long ago, "We don't even own a TV." Great—so you missed "The Civil War," the Challenger explosion, the "Who Shot J.R.?" episode of "Dallas," the World Series, and a considerable part of American culture over the last 10 years. We have a generation of parents who were raised on a steady diet of red meat, Pez and "The Brady Bunch" and who now pride themselves on denying their kids sugar and television. 2

I like television. "Nova." "Masterpiece Theater." "Sesame Street." Ah, public television, you say, the green vegetables of video viewing—they are exempt from censure. But I also like the channel that shows old movies, and "Headline News," and Nickelodeon, with reruns of most of the sitcoms from my own childhood. (Watch your kids marvel at the fact that you are personally familiar with "Mr. Ed"!) I love a good trashy miniseries, with lots of diamonds and a pint of ice cream. 3

I think television can be educational even when it doesn't come from the sanctified Corporation for Public Broadcasting. Not long ago a sitcom called "Dinosaurs," which is basically "The Honeymooners" except that the fat guy in the flannel shirt is a megalosaurus, did an episode called "I 4

Never Ate for My Father." Plot line: Son thinks he may be herbivorous instead of carnivorous; dad finds broccoli in son's room, is horrified. I watched this show with my sons and there ensued spirited discussion of parental expectations and prejudices. A friend with an adolescent, which is a little like saying a friend with a grenade, says they often watch "Roseanne" together, using exchanges on that program between mother and daughter as talking points, kind of an electronic mediator.

5 In our black/white, good/bad world, we've focused on all the ways TV can be abused, all the kids glassy-eyed before the tube for six hours a day, all the 4-year-olds watching "Nightmare on Elm Street 10—Freddy Maims the Homecoming Queen," all the bad programming. (Although sometimes we seem to forget that we are children of "The Three Stooges," which is not exactly Chekhov.) We focus on the either/or: either they'll read, or they'll watch television. And we respond with a blanket condemnation: No television. TV is bad.

6 I can still remember when TV was a kind of miracle that simultaneously enveloped us all in Ed Sullivan and "The Wonderful World of Disney." Now we trash our own technology almost as soon as we've invented it, worried that the machines have the upper hand. The only good explanation I've ever heard for that comes from the comedian Rita Rudner, who says she's not buying a CD player until someone promises her they're not going to invent anything else. I get an enormous kick out of writers who talk about the "tactile sensation" of rendering a novel in longhand. I like tactile sensation, but I've got laundry to do. Pass the word-processing software, please.

7 (I believe, however, that everyone is permitted one refusal to change with the times. Mine is the microwave oven. I prefer to prepare food by applying heat to it rather than by rearranging molecules.)

8 I like technology; I like being able to watch "Duck Soup" whenever I please on the VCR. And I like popular culture; it's where I come from. I want my kids to recognize Mozart, Sinatra and Madonna: I want them to know the world, not some bottled-water version of it. And that world includes television, some of it educational, some of it harmless. My kids have learned to spell Mickey Mouse as I did, by singing it: "M-I-C, K-E-Y, M-O-U-S-E." It's the new "Mickey Mouse Club"; Annette and Cubby are long gone and at the end they do a rap version of the old theme song. To be honest, it's an improvement.

David Byrne
Television Man

In the mid-1970s David Byrne (born 1952) organized the "Talking Heads," named after a TV phenomenon: announcers, in close-up, in the act of speaking. An inventive and unsentimental lyricist, Byrne mixed West African, rock-and-roll, soul, and gospel music into a distinctive sound known as "New Wave." The song "Television Man" is a cut from the Little Creatures *album.*

I'm looking and I'm dreaming for the first time 1
I'm inside and I'm outside at the same time
And everything is real
Do I like the way I feel?

When the world crashes in, into my living room 2
Television made me what I am
People like to put the television down
But we are just good friends
(I'm a) television man

I knew a girl, she was a macho man 3
But it's alright, I wasn't fooled for long
This is the place for me
I'm the king and you're the queen

When the world crashes in, into my living room 4
Television made me what I am
People like to put the television down
But we are just good friends
(I'm a) television man

Take a walk in the beautiful garden 5
Everyone would like to say hello
I doesn't matter what you say
Come and take us away

The world crashes in, into my living room 6
The world crashes in, into my living room
The world crashes in, into my living room
The world crashes in, into my living room

7 And we are still good friends . . . (Television man)
I'm watching everything . . . (Television man)
Television man . . . (Television man)
I'm watching everything . . . (Television man)
Television man . . . and I'm gonna say
We are still good friends . . . and I'm trying to be
Watchin' everything . . . and I gotta say
We are still good friends . . . You know the way it is
Television man . . . I've got what you need
We are still good friends . . . I know the way you are
Television man . . . I know you're trying to be
Watchin' everything . . . and I gotta say
That's how the story ends.

Jack McGarvey

To Be or Not to Be as Defined by TV

Jack McGarvey (born 1937) has been a teacher for over a quarter century; currently he teaches language arts and computer arts at Coleytown Middle School in Westport, Connecticut. Also a freelance writer, he has published his work in McCall's, Parents, *and other national publications. This essay appeared in 1982 in* Today's Education, *a publication for teachers and other educators.*

1 A couple of years ago, a television crew came to film my ninth grade English class at Bedford Junior High School in Westport, Connecticut. I'm still trying to understand what happened.

2 I was doing some work with my students, teaching them to analyze the language used in television commercials. After dissecting the advertising claims, most of the class became upset over what they felt were misleading—and in a few cases, untruthful—uses of language. We decided to write to the companies that presented their products inaccurately or offensively. Most of them responded with chirpy letters and cents-off coupons. Some did not respond at all.

3 I then decided to contact *Buyline,* a consumer advocate

program aired on New York City's WNBC-TV at the time. The show and its host, Betty Furness, were well-known for their investigation of consumer complaints. I sent off a packet of the unanswered letters with a brief explanation of the class's work.

About a week later, the show's producer telephoned me. She said that she'd seen the letters and was interested in the class's project. Could she and her director come to Westport to have a look? 4

I said sure and told her about a role-playing activity I was planning to do with my students. I said I was going to organize my class of 24 students into four committees—each one consisting of two representatives from the Federal Trade Commission (FTC), the agency that monitors truth in advertising; two advertising executives anxious to have their material used; and two TV executives caught somewhere in the middle—wanting to please the advertisers while not offending the FTC. Then, I would ask each committee to assume that there had been a complaint about the language used in a TV commercial, and that the committees had to resolve the complaint. "That sounds great! I'll bring a crew," she said. 5

I obtained clearance from my school district's office, and the next morning, as I was walking into the school, I met one of my students and casually let out the word: "WNBC's coming to film our class this afternoon." 6

I was totally unprepared for what happened. Word spread around school within five minutes. Students who barely knew me rushed up to squeal, "Is it true? Is it really, really true? A TV crew is coming to Bedford to film?" A girl who was not in my class pinned me into a corner near the magazine rack in the library to ask me whether she could sit in my class for the day. Another girl went to her counselor and requested an immediate change in English classes, claiming a long-standing personality conflict with her current teacher. 7

Later, things calmed down a bit, but as I took my regular turn as cafeteria supervisor, I saw students staring wide-eyed at me, then turning to whisper excitedly to their friends. I'd become a celebrity simply because I was the one responsible for bringing a TV crew to school. 8

Right after lunch, the show's producer and director came 9

to my class to look it over and watch the role-playing activity; they planned to tape near the end of the school day. The two women were gracious and self-effacing, taking pains not to create any disturbance; but the students, of course, knew why they were there. There were no vacant stares, no hair brushes, no gum chewers, and no note scribblers. It was total concentration, and I enjoyed one of my best classes in more than 15 years of teaching.

10 After the class, I met with the producer and director to plan the taping. They talked about some of the students they'd seen and mentioned Susan. "She's terribly photogenic and very, very good with words." They mentioned Steve. "He really chaired his committee well. Real leadership there. Handsome boy, too." They mentioned Jim, Pete, Randy, and Jenny and their insights into advertising claims. Gradually I became aware that we were engaged in a talent hunt; we were looking for a strong and attractive group to be featured in the taping.

11 We continued the discussion, deciding on the players. We also discussed the sequencing of the taping session. First, I'd do an introduction, explaining the role-playing activity as if the class had never heard of it. Then, I'd follow with the conclusion—summarizing remarks ending with a cheery "See you tomorrow!"—and dismiss the class. The bit players would leave the school and go home. We'd then rearrange the set and film the photogenic and perceptive featured players while they discussed advertising claims as a committee. Obviously, this is not the way I'd conduct an actual class, but it made sense. After all, I wanted my students to look good, and I wanted to look good.

12 "It'll be very hard work," the producer cautioned. "I trust your students understand that."

13 "It's already been hard work," I remarked as I thought of possible jealousies and bruised feelings over our choices of featured players.

14 About a half hour before school's end, the crew set up cameras and lights in the hall near the classroom we'd be working in, a room in an isolated part of the building. But as the crew began filming background shots of the normal passing of students through the hall, near chaos broke out.

15 Hordes of students suddenly appeared. A basketball star gangled through the milling mob to do an imitation of Nureyev, topping off a pirouette by feigning a couple of jump shots. A pretty girl walked back and forth in front of the cameras at least a dozen times before she was snared by

a home economics teacher. Three boys did a noisy pantomime of opening jammed lockers, none of which were theirs. A faculty member, seen rarely in this part of the building, managed to work his way through the crowd, smiling broadly. And as members of my class struggled through the press of bodies, they were hailed, clutched at, patted on the back, and hugged.

"Knock 'em dead!" I heard a student call. 16

It took the vice-principal and five teachers 10 minutes to 17
clear the hall.

We assembled the cast, arranged the furniture, erased 18
several mild obscenities from the chalkboard, and pulled down the window shades—disappointing a clutch of spectators outside. The producers then introduced the crew and explained their work.

I was wired with a mike and the crew set up a boom 19
microphone, while the girls checked each other's make-up and the boys sat squirming.

Finally, the taping began. It was show business, a per- 20
formance, a total alteration of the reality I know as a teacher. As soon as I began the introduction, 26 pairs of eyes focused on me as if I were Billy Joel about to sing. I was instantly startled and self-conscious. When I asked a question, some of the usually quieter students leaped to respond. This so unsettled me that I forgot what I was saying and had to begin again.

The novelty of being on camera, however, soon passed. 21
We had to do retakes because the soundman missed student responses from the rear of the room. The director asked me to rephrase a question and asked a student to rephrase a response. There were delays while technicians adjusted equipment.

We all became very much aware of being performers, and 22
some of the students who had been most excited about making their TV debut began to grumble about the hard work. That pleased me, for a new reality began to creep in: Television is not altogether glamorous.

We taped for almost five hours, on more than 3,200 feet of 23
video tape. That is almost an hour-and-a-half's worth, more than double a normal class period. And out of that mass of celluloid the producer said she'd use seven minutes on the program!

Two days later, five students and I went to the NBC 24

studios at Rockefeller Center to do a taping of a final segment. The producer wanted to do a studio recreation of the role-playing game. This time, however, the game would include real executives—one from advertising, one from the NBC network, and one from the FTC. We'd be part of a panel discussion moderated by Betty Furness. My students would challenge the TV and the advertising executives, asking them to justify some of the bothersome language used in current commercials.

25 This was the most arduous part of the experience. The taping was live, meaning that the cameras would run for no longer than eight minutes. As we ate turkey and ham during a break with Ms. Furness and the guest executives, I realized that we were with people who were totally comfortable with television. I began to worry. How could mere 14-year-olds compete in a debate with those to whom being on television is as ordinary as riding a school bus?

26 But my concern soon disappeared. As Ms. Furness began reading her TelePrompTer, Susan leaned over and whispered, "This is fun!" And it was Susan who struck first. " 'You can see how luxurious my hair feels' is a perfect example of the silly language your ad writers use," she said with all the poise of a Barbara Walters. "It's impossible to *see* how something feels," she went on.

27 That pleased me, for as an English teacher, I've always emphasized the value of striving for precision in the use of language. The work we'd done with TV commercials, where suggestibility is the rule, had taken hold, I thought, as the ad executive fumbled for a response. The tension vanished, and we did well.

28 The show aired two weeks later, and I had it taped so the class could view it together. It was a slick production, complete with music—"Hey, Big Spender"—to develop a theme for Ms. Furness' introduction. "Teens are big business these days," she said. "Does television advertising influence how they spend their money?" Then followed a shot of students in the hall—edited to show none of the wildness that actually occurred. Next, three of my students appeared in brief clips of interviews. They were asked, "Have you ever been disappointed by television advertising?" The responses were, "Yes, of course," and I was pleased with their detailed answers. Finally, the classroom appeared, and there I was, lounging against my desk, smiling calmly. I looked good—a young, unrumpled Orson Bean, with a cool

blue-and-brown paisley tie. My voice was mellifluous. Gee, I thought as I saw the tape, I could have been a TV personality.

Now, I am probably no more vain than most people. But television does strange things to the ego. I became so absorbed in studying the image of myself that the whole point of the show passed me by. I didn't even notice that I'd made a goof analyzing a commercial until I'd seen the show three times. The students who participated were the same; watching themselves on videotape, they missed what they had said. I had an enormous struggle to get both them and me to recall the hard work and to see the obvious editing. It was as if reality had been reversed: The actual process of putting together the tape was not real, but the product was. 29

I showed the tape again last year to my ninth grade class. I carefully explained to this delightful gang of fault-finders how the taping had been done. I told them about the changed sequence, the selection of the featured players, the takes and retakes. They themselves had just been through the same role-playing activity, and I asked them to listen carefully to what was said. They nodded happily and set their flinty minds to look at things critically. But as the tape ended, they wanted to tease me about how ugly and wrinkled I looked. They wanted to say, "That's Randy! He goes to Compo Beach all the time." "Jenny's eye shadow—horrible!" "When will you get us on TV?" 30

The visual image had worked its magic once again: They had missed the point of the show altogether. And, as I dismissed them, I felt something vibrating in their glances and voices—the celebrity image at work again. I was no longer their mundane English teacher: I was a TV personality. 31

I decided to show the tape again the next day. I reviewed the hard work, the editing, the slick packaging. I passed out questions so we could focus on what had been said on the program. I turned on the recorder and turned off the picture to let them hear only the sound. They protested loudly, of course. But I was determined to force them to respond to how effectively the previous year's class had taken apart the language used in the claims of commercials. This was, after all, the point of the program. And it worked, finally. 32

As class ended, one of the students drifted up to me. "What are we going to do next?" she asked. 33

"We're going to make some comparisons between TV news shows and what's written in newspapers," I replied. 34

35 "Do they put together news shows the way they filmed your class?"

36 "It's similar and usually much quicker," I answered.

37 She smiled and shook her head. "It's getting hard to believe anything anymore."

38 In that comment lies what every TV viewer should have—a healthy measure of beautiful, glorious skepticism. But as I said, I'm still trying to understand that taping session. And I'm aware of how hard it is to practice skepticism. Every time I see the *Buyline* tape, I'm struck by how good a teacher TV made me. Am I really that warm, intelligent, creative, and good looking? Of course not. But TV made me that way. I like it, and sometimes I find myself still hoping that I am what television defined me to be.

39 I sometimes think children have superior knowledge of TV. They know, from many years of watching it, that the product in all its edited glory is the only reality. Shortly after the program aired on that February Saturday two years ago, our telephone rang. The voice belonged to my daughter's 11-year-old friend. She said, "I just saw you on TV. May I have your autograph?"

40 I was baffled. After all, this was the boisterous girl who played with my daughter just about every day and who mostly regarded me as a piece of furniture that occasionally mumbled something about lowering your voices. "Are you serious?" I croaked.

41 "May I have your autograph?" she repeated, ignoring my question. "I can come over right now." Her voice was without guile.

42 She came. And I signed while she scrutinized my face, her eyes still aglow with Chromacolor.

43 To Stephanie, television had transformed a kindly grump into something real. And there is no doubt in my mind whatsoever that in the deepest part of her soul is the fervent dream that her being, too, will someday be defined and literally affirmed by an appearance on television.

44 Lately, my ninth grade class has been growing restless. Shall I move up the TV unit and bring out the tape again? Shall I remind them what a great teacher they have? Shall I remind myself what a fine teacher I am? Shall I renew their—and my—hope?

To be or not to be as defined by TV? Does that question suggest what makes television so totally unlike any other medium? 45

Joshua Meyrowitz

No Sense of Place

Joshua Meyrowitz is professor of communication at the University of New Hampshire. This selection and the next one were adapted by the author from the conclusion to his book No Sense of Place: The Impact of Electronic Media on Social Behavior *(1985).*

For Americans, the second half of the twentieth century has been marked by an unusual amount and type of social change. The underprivileged have demanded equal rights, a significant portion of the visible political elite has been discredited, and many of those in between have been maneuvering for new social position and identity. In the past few decades, the United States has experienced extraordinarily rapid and significant changes involving age, race, gender, and other roles. 1

Perhaps even more confusing than the dimensions of the change has been its seeming inconsistency, even randomness. What is the common thread? We have witnessed peaceful civil rights demonstrations juxtaposed with violent looting and rioting. We have seen the persecution of the people by the agencies of government followed by the virtual impeachment of a president by the people and press, which was followed, in turn, by the near-canonization of a president, even though many viewed him as neither particularly attentive nor extraordinarily intelligent. And angry talk of social revolution has been transformed into the cool and determined pursuit of "affirmative action," community control, and "citizen diplomacy." 2

Some social observers have comforted themselves by viewing the disruptions of the 1960s as a historical aberration and by pointing gleefully at former hippies who have clipped their locks and become materialistic yuppies. Noth- 3 ing has really changed, they seem to suggest. What they fail to see, however, are the male police and hardhats who now wear their hair long, the "redneck" farmers who let livestock loose in front of the Capitol (echoes of the yippies?), the wheelchair sit-ins of the disabled, the court battles over returning land (and human remains) to the Indians, the dramatic changes in women's and children's rights and behaviors, and hundreds of other small and large shifts in behavior and attitude.

4 What does it all mean? Are we witnessing constant change and confusion? Or is there a central mechanism that has been swinging the social pendulum to and fro?

5 Social change is always too complex to attribute to a single cause and too diverse to reduce to a unitary process, but one common theme that connects many recent and seemingly unrelated phenomena is a change in Americans' "sense of place." Electronic media have broken that age-old connection between location and experience, between *where* we are and what we see and hear, between our location and our access and accessibility to other people. As a result, the logic underlying "appropriate behavior" in a print- and place-oriented society has been radically subverted. Many Americans may no longer seem to "know their place" because the traditionally interlocking components of place—physical location and social position—have been split apart by electronic media. Wherever one is now, one may be in touch and tuned in. Our world may suddenly seem senseless to many observers because, for the first time in history, it is relatively placeless.

6 The greatest impact on the sense of place has been on social groups that were once defined in terms of their physical isolation in specific locations—playgrounds, kitchens, prisons, convents, and so forth.

7 Our children, for example, were once isolated from adult life by being physically isolated at home or school. But television now takes children across the globe even before they have permission to cross the street. Child viewers witness war, starvation, and brutality, as well as a broad spectrum of everyday adult problems, anxieties, and fears. This does not suggest that children simply imitate what they see on TV, but rather that their image of adults and adulthood has been radically altered. No wonder children now seem older and have less fear of, and respect for, adults.

8 Similarly, our society was once based on the assumption

that there were two separate worlds: the public, male realm of "rational accomplishments" and brutal competition, and the private, female sphere of childrearing, emotion, and intuition. But TV blurs the difference between public and private. Television close-ups reveal the private, emotional side of public figures and events: We see tears well up in the eyes of presidents, and abstractions such as "glorious victories" and "crushing defeats" are now conveyed through images of blood and limp bodies. Conversely, most public events are now dramas that are played out in the privacy of our living rooms and kitchens. Television has exposed even homebound women to many parts of the culture that were once considered exclusively male domains, just as it has made men more aware of the emotional dimensions and consequences of public actions. It is no surprise, then, that women have demanded integration into the male realm or that men have begun grappling in new ways with their emotions and are becoming more involved fathers.

Lifting Veils

For both better and worse, television has lifted many of the old veils of secrecy that used to exist between the worlds of children and adults, men and women, and people of different classes, regions, and levels of education. It has given us a broader but also a shallower sense of identity and community. 9

The intensity of social change in the past thirty years, in particular, may be related to the unique power of television to break down distinctions between here and there, live and recorded, and personal and public. More than any other electronic medium, television tends to involve us in issues we once thought were "not our business," to thrust us within a few inches of the faces of murderers and presidents, and to make physical barriers and passageways relatively meaningless in terms of patterns of access to social experience. Television has also enhanced the effects of earlier electronic media by providing us with a better image of the places experienced through radio and reached through the telephone. 10

The widespread social movements and disruptions since the late 1950s may be adjustments in behavior, attitudes, and laws to match new social settings. Many of the tradi- 11 tional distinctions among groups, among people at various stages of socialization, and among superiors and subordinates were based on the patterns of information flow that existed in a print society, where people of different groups, ages, sexes, and educational background tended to experience very different sets of information. The new and "strange" behavior of many individuals and of classes of people may be the result of the steady merging of formerly distinct social environments. Television has changed "who knows what about whom" and "who knows what compared to whom," making it more difficult to stay in one's old place. For there is nothing more frustrating than being exposed constantly to activities and adventures and excitements that you are told are reserved for someone else.

12 In spite of its often conservative *content,* television, as a new social *environment,* has been a force of liberation. Television has helped change the deferential Negro into the proud black, has fostered the merging of the Miss and Mrs. into a Ms., has supported the transformation of the child into a little adult with expanded rights and responsibilities. Television has encouraged the rise of hundreds of "minorities"—people who, in perceiving a wider world, now see themselves as unfairly isolated in some pocket of it. Television has empowered the elderly, disabled, and disenfranchised by giving them access to social information in spite of their physical isolation. Television has given women an outside view from which their traditional homebound roles appear to be a form of imprisonment. Television has weakened visible authorities by destroying the distance and mystery that once enhanced their aura and prestige. And television has been able to do this without requiring the disabled to leave their wheelchairs, without asking the traditional homemaker to stop cooking dinner, and without demanding that the average citizen leave his or her easy chair.

13 This is not to suggest that information integration leads to instant physical integration or to social harmony. Indeed, the initial outcome of information integration is increased social tension. Information access heightens outsiders' awareness of physical, economic, and legal segregation. Even in the long run, electronic media, in themselves, may continue to encourage a desire for physical and economic equality, but without providing any clear social mechanisms for accomplishing it.

Nevertheless, by merging discrete communities of discourse, television has made nearly every topic and issue a valid subject of interest and concern for virtually every member of the public. Further, many formerly private and isolated behaviors have been thrust into the large, unitary public arena. As a result, behaviors that were dependent on great distance and isolation have been largely banished from the social repertoire. The widened public sphere gives nearly everyone a new (and relatively shared) perspective from which to view others and to gain a reflected sense of self. We, our doctors, our police officers, our presidents, our secret agents, our parents, our children, and our friends are all performing roles in new theaters that demand new styles of drama. 14

Many formal reciprocal roles rely on lack of intimate knowledge of the "other." If the mystery and mystification disappear, so do the formal behaviors. Stylized courtship behaviors, for example, must quickly fade in the day-to-day intimacy of marriage. Similarly, the new access we gain to distant events and to the gestures and actions of the other sex, our elders, and authorities does not simply "educate" us; such access changes social reality. 15

In both fictional and nonfictional television programs, we have all seen how others prepare for and relax from their traditional "onstage" roles—as "parents who know best," as "masculine men" and "feminine women," and "inspiring leaders." By exposing previously "backstage" behaviors, television has served as an instrument of demystification. It has demystified adults for children, has made traditional sex roles seem transparent and phony, and has led to decline in the image and prestige of political and other leaders. 16

Our most successful recent president was the one most sensitive to the demands of the new dramatic arena. But even President Reagan's credibility suffered from the public's heightened awareness of the "performance" nature of his presidency. Certainly, we prefer a good performance to a poor one. But we are no longer simply a naive political audience that accepts the onstage role as the only reality. 17

It is not surprising that the widespread rejection of traditional child and adult, male and female, and leader and follower roles should have begun in the late 1960s with the coming of age of the first generation of Americans to have been exposed to television before learning to read. When this generation was born—around 1950—only 9 percent of 18

U.S. households owned TV sets; only five years later, 50 percent did. By 1966, only 6 percent of households did *not* own a television. In the shared environment of television, women and men, children and adults, and followers and leaders know a great deal about each other's behavior and social knowledge—too much, in fact, for them to play the traditional complementary roles of innocence versus omniscience.

19 As the experience and knowledge of different people increasingly overlap, we are witnessing major social transformations. We are seeing more adultlike children and more childlike adults, more career-oriented women and more family-oriented men, and leaders who act more like the person next door, just as our real neighbors demand to have more of a say in local, national, and international affairs.

The Secret-Exposing Machine

20 Nineteenth-century life entailed many isolated situations and sustained many isolated behaviors and attitudes. The current merging of situations does not give us a sum of what we had before, but rather new, synthesized behaviors that are qualitatively different. If we celebrate our child's wedding in an isolated situation where it is the sole "experience" of the day, then our joy may be unbounded. But when on our way to the wedding, we hear over the car radio of a devastating earthquake, or the death of a popular entertainer, or the assassination of a political figure, we not only lose our ability to rejoice fully, but also our ability to mourn deeply. The electronic combination of many different styles of interaction from distinct behavioral regions leads to new "middle region" behaviors that, while containing elements of formerly distinct roles, are themselves new behavior patterns with new expectations and emotions.

21 Gone, therefore, are many people's "special" behaviors, those that were associated with distinct and isolated interactions. Gone are the great eccentrics, the passionate overpowering loves, the massive unrelenting hates, the dramatic curses and flowery praises. Unbounded joy and unmitigated misery cannot coexist in the same place and time. As situations merge, the hot flush and the icy stare blend into a middle region "cool." The difference between the reality of behaviors in distinct situations versus the reality of behav-

iors in merged situations is as great as the difference between the nineteenth-century conception that a man might have a virtuous wife and a raunchy mistress and the twentieth-century notions of open marriages, living together, friendly divorce, and serial monogamy.

The height of print culture was a time of "secrets." The Victorians were fascinated with the multiple layers and depths of life: secret passageways, skeletons in the closet, masks upon masks upon masks. But the awareness of these layers did not push the Victorians to destroy secrecy, but rather to maintain and enhance it as an enriching aspect of the social order. For the most part, skeletons were meant to stay in the closet, sex was to remain behind closed doors (perhaps to be spied upon through keyholes), and scandalous acts were to be hidden from peering eyes. The rare exposures and discoveries were titillating, implicit hints of the vastness of undiscovered reality. 22

Our own age, in contrast, is fascinated by exposure. Indeed, the act of exposure now seems to excite us more than the content of the secrets exposed. The steady stripping away of layers of social behavior has made the "major scandal" and the exposure of the "deep dark secret" everyday affairs. Ironically, what is pulled from the closets that supposedly contain extraordinary secrets is, ultimately, the potential banality of everyone. The unusual becomes commonplace: famous stars who abuse their children; presidents with hemorrhoids or colon cancer; a pope who gets depressed; televangelists who extort and cavort. 23

Still we hunger for heroes, and perhaps our search beneath social masks is filled with the hope of finding people whose private selves are as admirable as their public ones. But since most of the people who make enduring contributions to our culture remain under our scrutiny too long to remain pure in our eyes, we have also begun to focus on people who make one grand gesture or who complete a single courageous act that cannot be undermined by scrutiny. Our new heroes are men and women like Lenny Skutnik, who dove into the water—before television cameras—to save an airplane crash survivor, or Reginald Andrews, who saved a blind man's life by pulling him from beneath a New York subway car. Both men were saluted as heroes by the president of the United States. We can admire such isolated heroic acts; the pasts and the futures of such heroes remain comfortably irrelevant and invisible. 24

The Birth of New Situations

25 Of course behind the many obvious social changes much of our social order remains the same. There continue to be many distinctions in roles of group identity, different stages of socialization, and different ranks of hierarchy in spite of the homogenizing trend. (And after the dust of change from the current merging of roles settles, we are also likely to rediscover some of the many differences among us.) Further, while electronic media have merged many social situations, direct physical presence and mutual monitoring are still primary experiential modes. And regardless of media access, living in a ghetto, a prison cell, and a middle-class suburb are certainly not equivalent social experiences. Nevertheless, roles and places have changed dramatically and an analysis of how and why they have changed helps to explain many social phenomena that are not otherwise easily understood. While the merging of spheres through electronic media has not given everyone the same knowledge and wisdom, much of the old mystification surrounding other people and places has been pierced. Print still exists and holds many mysteries and secrets for those who master it, but many of the "secrets of secrecy" have been exposed.

26 The changing conceptions of secrecy and place, of gender distinctions, of childhood innocence, and of authority can all be seen in a single social event: the birth of a new human being. Not long ago, this scene was marked by highly isolated environments. Pregnant women were to stay out of public view. Husbands were distanced from the pregnancy and sheltered from the birth. During delivery, the father paced nervously in an isolated waiting room; the mother herself was "removed" from the birthing situation through drugs; young children were kept out of the hospital and were often further isolated through ignorance of the processes of pregnancy and birth. In charge of the birth were the all-powerful doctors, whose authority allowed them to defy gravity and nature and curiosity and mother-love as they wrenched the drugged infant from the womb in a cold stainless steel delivery room.

27 Today, the scene is vastly different. Pregnancy and birth are "family-centered"; fathers and children are often fully involved. A new phrase has entered the language: "*we* are

pregnant," and it is now common practice for fathers and mothers to attend childbirth classes together and for fathers to be present at, and assist in, the birth. Siblings as young as two may be involved in the process by attending special "prepared sibling" classes, taking tours of the hospital, and, in some cases, being present at the birth itself.

Increasingly, many doctors and nurses are defining themselves more as "educators" than as authorities; the family is expected to make the final choices concerning the variables of delivery. In response to those hospitals and medical personnel who are not willing to allow families to choose their own birthing options, some middle-class families are opting for home deliveries with midwives. Others are giving birth in "alternative birthing centers," which are a cross between hospitals and motels. But the most significant trend is the move in regular hospitals to blur the differences between labor room and home. Many hospitals are building special birthing rooms that are designed to resemble home bedrooms. Some have double beds, flowery wallpaper, carpeting, and soft chairs. Equipment for delivery is present but kept out of sight until needed. A man and a woman may now give birth to their child while looking out a window or watching television. The specialness of the place in which birth now takes place is further diluted by the increasingly popular trend toward photographing, filming, or videotaping the birth—so that the experience is taken out of the hospital and shared with friends, family, and, perhaps later, with the child itself. 28

Millions of dollars have been spent studying the effects of television and other modern media. But in searching for effects largely in simple imitation and persuasion, we have been missing the broader impact on social boundaries and hence on social behavior. Electronic media affect us not primarily through their content but by changing the situational geography of everyday life. 29

TELEVISION AND THE ELECTIONS

Joshua Meyrowitz

Whither "1984"?

[For an introduction to this essay, see the headnote to the previous section.]

1 We have now entered the era of George Orwell's gloomy prophecy. And there are many apparent similarities between Orwell's *1984* and our time. Until stymied, at least temporarily, by the recent changes in the Eastern bloc, our government was presenting us with the image of a world divided into two superpowers, Good versus Evil. Our supposedly unavoidable conflict with The Enemy has served as a backdrop and rationale for many of our domestic and foreign policies. Language, too, has fought the battle. Our actions have always been "defensive," theirs always "aggressive." Our interventions have been "rescue missions to preserve freedom"; theirs have been "invasions to crush the will of the people." Our economic assistance to underdeveloped countries has always been "humanitarian"; theirs has been "propagandistic." And even today, mind-boggling weapons of death are benignly labelled "peacekeepers," while many would-be peacekeepers are surrounded by hints of treason.

2 Many people jump from such observations to the assumption that developments in electronic media are hastening the arrival of an Orwellian nightmare. The evolution of sophisticated surveillance devices and the decline in privacy are seen as concrete manifestations of the type of totalitarianism described by Orwell. Yet these technological developments may actually be signs of a trend in the opposite direction.

3 Orwell offered a vision of society where Big Brother watched all, but was himself invisible. Orwell conceived of an "inner party" elite who observed but were unobservable. The Party demanded and received total loyalty and unquestioning obedience. Such a system is conceivable in an electronic age, but if the new technologies have any inherent

bias, it may be against such a sharply hierarchical system.

"Leadership" and "authority" are unlike mere "power" in 4
that they depend on performance and appeal; one cannot lead or be looked up to if one is not there to be seen. Yet, paradoxically, authority is weakened by excess familiarity. Awe depends on the "distant-visibility" and "mystified-presence." One of the peculiar ironies of our age is that most people who step forward into the media limelight and attempt to gain national visibility become too visible, too exposed, and are thereby demystified. Electronic media may be used by officials to spy on private citizens, but when an electronic medium such as television is used by leaders as a means of communicating with the people, the medium's close-up bias also allows citizens to spy on officials.

Further, for a hierarchy to exist, there must be more 5
followers than leaders. In an era of easy and relatively shared access to information about people, one leader may be able to keep a close watch on thousands of followers, but thousands of followers can keep an even closer watch on one leader. Ironically, the simple mathematics of hierarchy suggests the stronger likelihood of an undermining of the pyramid of status in an electronic age.

The speaker's platform once lifted politicians up and away 6
from average citizens, both literally and symbolically. In newspaper quotes and reports, the politician—as a flesh-and-bones person—was completely absent. And on radio, politicians were disembodied voices. But the television camera now lowers politicians to the level of the common citizen and brings them close for our inspection. In recent years, we've seen our presidents sweat, stammer, and stumble—all in living color. In the face of a "crisis," our presidents once had many hours, sometimes even weeks or months, to consult with advisers and to formulate policy statements to be printed in newspapers. But in live, televised appearances today, even a five-second pause for thought can seriously damage a leader's credibility.

Television not only reduces our awe of politicians; it also 7
increases politicians' self-doubt and lowers self-esteem. A speaker's nervousness and mistakes usually are politely ignored by live audiences and therefore soon forgotten by the speaker too. But with videotape, politicians have permanent records of themselves misspeaking or anxiously licking their lips. Television may be a prime cause of the complaints of indecisive leadership and hesitant "followership" that we have heard since the mid-1960s.

8 Electronic media not only weaken authority by allowing those low on the ladder of hierarchy to gain access to much information about leaders, but also by affording increased opportunities for the sharing of information horizontally. The telephone and computer, for example, allow people to communicate with each other without going "through channels." Such horizontal flow of information through relatively egalitarian networks and matrices is another significant deterrent to totalitarian central leadership.

9 There is no doubt that new technologies—like old technologies—may be used by bad governments to bad ends. And once a totalitarian government exists, it can stop or control the flow of information. But the assumption that the new media or the lack of privacy they foster will, in and of themselves, support authoritarian hierarchies is based on a misunderstanding of the relationship between privacy and hierarchy. For it is privacy and distance that support strong central authorities. Our notions of privacy have a very short history in Western civilization, and as we know from studies of hunting and gathering societies and of pre-print Western Europe, the virtual lack of privacy tends to weaken rather than support great distinctions in status. It is the person who tries to stand apart or above, not the average citizen, who is most damaged by lack of privacy. We may be aesthetically uncomfortable with the thought of fuller and more open access to information, but, all other things being equal, such access tends to level hierarchies rather than erect them. Even the evidence we have been discovering recently about our leaders' abuses of power may, in this sense, testify more to our relatively increased ability to gather information on leaders rather than to an absolute increase in the abuse of power. The thing to fear is not the loss of privacy per se, but the *non-reciprocal* loss of privacy—that is, where we lose the ability to monitor those who monitor us.

10 As of now, electronic media may be encouraging the slow but steady growth of a "hierarchy of the people." For electronic media give a distinct advantage to the average person. Average people now have access to social information that once was not available to them. Further, they have information concerning the performers of high status roles. As a result, the distance, mystery, and mystification surrounding high status roles are minimized. There are still many "unusual" people with special knowledge and training, but the average person now knows more about what special individuals know and also more about high status people as

people. After seeing so much ordinariness in the close-up views of extraordinary people, we may continue to remain more ignorant and less powerful than they, but we are now more aware of the many things they do not know and cannot do. And even though much of this new information access is reciprocal, the common person has relatively less to lose from exposure and visibility. No one expects the common person to be anything but common. If Joe Smith finds out that the president cheats on his income tax, Joe is likely to be outraged—even if he cheats on his own income tax. Great leaders are not supposed to suffer the frailties of greed, lust, or instability.

Whether this demystification of political leaders is 11
ultimately good or bad is not yet entirely clear. On the good side, we seem less willing to follow leaders blindly. On the bad side, the void in confidence in leaders has not yet been filled by wide-scale political awareness or involvement. Nevertheless, at this moment in history, we may be witnessing the prelude to a political revolution of enormous proportions, a revolution that is masked by the conventions of our language and by the form of our traditional ideals. We are moving from a representative government of de facto elites to a government of direct participation with elected "administrators." The change is difficult to see, however, because we refer to both of these systems as "democracy" and because the new system involves the manifestation of many once unattainable ideals such as true "public servants" and "government by and for the people." Reality does not stay the same, however, when ideals become reality.

Electronic media offer the potential of government by di- 12
rect referendum, and the growth of interactive television promises the mixed blessing of a political system modeled after the structure of the "Gong Show"—where performers can be removed from the stage in midperformance. (A more pleasing metaphor for the same system is the Greek forum.) The new technology fosters the potential of the closest thing the earth has ever witnessed to participatory democracy on an enormous scale—with all the resulting problems and possibilities. Even if this comes to pass, however, we will need some rethinking of our conceptions of authority if we are to see the system for what it is. For whoever steps before us in the role of leader will seem to be a disappointment compared with our hazy, but glowing images of Washingtons, Jeffersons, and Lincolns, and any step taken without our knowl-

edge, any move taken in opposition to a majority "vote" in a national poll, will be seen as the arrogance of power.

13 Although the political problems of our age may not be the obvious ones many people fear, there remain a number of reasons for caution. The decline in trust in authorities is filled with paradox and some danger. The growth in weapons technology and the increase in speed in global communications have led to an enhancement of the raw power of national leaders even as our faith in governments and leaders has declined. Our recent presidents have had the power to destroy the entire world, but they have often lacked the authority to convince the majority of the population that they are doing a competent job. There is always the danger of leaders using their massive war-making powers in attempts to rally the people behind them—or as an excuse for secrecy and information control.

14 Further, television news continues to follow traditional journalistic conventions of relying primarily on "official sources" and of allowing authorities to set the agenda for news coverage, even as television exposure has encouraged us to question the authority of leaders. Similarly, our increasingly complex technological and social world has made us rely more and more heavily on "expert information," but the general exposure of experts as fallible human beings has lessened our faith in them as people. The change in our image of leaders and experts leaves us with a distrust of power, but also with a seemingly powerless dependence on those in whom we have little trust.

15 The vacuum in our visible political realm of authority may be giving undue power to *in*visible men and women who run large national and multinational corporations. Unlike governments, corporations have no code of "openness." Indeed, competitive business is built on a tradition of secrecy. A business leader who refuses an interview is not viewed as suspiciously as a governor or a president who refuses to speak to the press. We do need to be wary, therefore, of the increasingly complex involvement of many corporations in university research, in government, in domestic and foreign policy, and in all forms of national and international communication technologies themselves—from book publishing to satellites.

16 There is also one visible class of "authorities" who, through their unique positions in our society, have been able to become exceptions to the decline in visible authority. These people have managed to maintain both controlled

access to the people *and* controlled performances. They are the television newscasters whose daily performances are tightly controlled and scripted. In an implicit professional code, television news programs do not generally expose other news programs or news personalities. A few moments of prime time may be used to show a president fall down while skiing, collapse while jogging, or make a serious slip of the tongue, but there are few, if any, international television exposures of Peter Jennings, Tom Brokaw, or Dan Rather falling down, cursing, making serious mistakes, or becoming irritable and tense. Such conventions maintain the fiction that the selectively revealed aspects of newscasters' personalities are representative of their whole selves. This situation may explain why, a few years ago, Walter Cronkite was described as "the most trusted man in America" and was considered to be a viable vice-presidential candidate, even though he had not, at that point, ever expressed his personal political views. Although there is not yet evidence that this power is being abused, we need to be more aware of the staging contingencies that may be enhancing our trust in electronic journalists just as they weaken our faith in the political process.

Garry Wills

The Remaking of the Presidents

Garry Wills (born 1934) is an iconoclastic scholar and political essayist who lives in Chicago and teaches at Northwestern. Whether his books and articles concern the Kennedys or Richard Nixon, the Catholic church or political history, they always inspire controversy and careful thought. His Inventing America *(1978), an original account of the drafting of the Declaration of Independence, won the National Book Award;* Lincoln at Gettysburg *was published in 1992. The following essay appeared in 1988 in* Omni, *a general-interest magazine that tries to consider the impact of science on the future.*

The presidential candidate was on fire with his cause: "We 1
have petitioned, and our petitions have been scorned. . . .

We have begged, and they have mocked when our calamity came. We beg no longer. . . . We petition no more. We defy them. . . . You come to us and tell us that the great cities are in favor of the gold standard. We reply, Burn down your cities and leave our farms, and your cities will spring up again as if by magic; but destroy our farms, and grass will grow in the streets of every city in the country."

2 This speech was not televised from either the Republican convention in New Orleans or the Democratic convention in Atlanta, though the powerful images and sense of urgency are reminiscent of Reverend Jesse Jackson's plea in Atlanta to move to higher ground, common ground. "We find," said Jackson, "common ground at the farm auction, where a good farmer loses his or her land to bad loans or diminishing markets. . . . Farmers, you seek fair prices, and you are right. But you cannot stand alone; your patch is not big enough."

3 Television was not even a remote possibility in 1896 when William Jennings Bryan, author of the opening speech, ran for president against William McKinley. The thirty-six-year-old orator, all eloquence and moral glow, stampeded two parties—the Democratic and the Populist—with his "Cross of Gold" speech. But if the presence of television had forced an actual debate between the participants, Bryan would have had an immense edge—all of the gifts John Kennedy had in 1960, along with a greater sense of crisis in the nation. Even without the advantage television might have given to such an electrifying speaker, he won 6.5 million votes to McKinley's 7 million. Television cameras, tracking this dynamic young challenger in his restless moral quest, would most likely have forced McKinley to get out on the stump for at least some of the time.

4 Many people, when they think of television, consider its cosmetic possibilities rather than its ability to transmit information that only insiders knew in the past. This election year has given us nominees for the presidency who are not, either of them, strikingly telegenic in sheer cosmetic terms. Even Ronald Reagan, the "Great Communicator," spent as much of his time avoiding television (in the form of press conferences, debates, and questioning opportunities) as in adorning it with ceremonial addresses. Wrong information or historical blunders may doom a candidate's chances on Election Day. In the 1976 debate between Gerald Ford and Jimmy Carter, for example, Ford's mishap—

"There's no Soviet domination of Eastern Europe"—gave Carter an edge in the polls.

Even so, the cosmetic power is there, as was demonstrated when Senator Kennedy's image proved so much more attractive than Vice President Richard Nixon's in 1960. Before the first televised debates in American history, voters were evenly split between Kennedy and Nixon. In the four debates that followed, the young Kennedy was calm and relaxed; Nixon, the more experienced debater, appeared tense and ill at ease. Kennedy's forceful image probably was a crucial factor in his narrow victory over Nixon. 5

It is fair to say that modern politics occurs primarily before the TV camera. It is there, under the glare of the lights, that the candidate defines himself and discusses his agenda. A critical factor in the marriage between television and modern politics, however, is the use of image blips and visual symbols to influence the voters' perception of the candidate. According to an August 7, 1988, article in *The New York Times,* an art director at an ad agency in New York who helped design the first Republican Party ads for this year's campaign said that the Dukakis–Bush race "will probably be decided by images you see on television." 6

According to today's media consultants, candidates should avoid appearing uncertain, maintain eye contact, smile under pressure, use proper gestures, give brief but direct answers to questions, and learn how to control difficult interviews. The purpose: to win over the undecided voter. 7

Prior to the advent of television, candidates were just as concerned about their image and the message they conveyed, but they utilized the techniques of their day—banners, slogans, songs, newsprint, and the available technology (railroads, telegraphic and stenographic reporting). In the 1858 debates between Abraham Lincoln and Senator Stephen Douglas for the Senate, Douglas had a flatcar behind his private train coach with a 12-pound cannon announcing his arrival at a site. Lincoln specialized in female processions (which he called his "bouquets"); one of them marched to the scene with a banner held by 32 young women, each symbolizing a state in the Union: "Westward the course of empire takes its way." 8

Large crowds, possibly as many as 15,000 people at one time—gathered to hear Lincoln and Douglas debate. Partisans hissed, booed, and interrupted the speakers up close 9 and fought with one another around the edges of the crowd where "painkiller" was being hawked from various booths—the equivalent of modern TV ads.

10 Hypothetical history is never more than a game: more or less sophisticated, never quite legitimate, though entertaining. To change one factor is to imagine changes in all the other factors dependent upon it. For television to be present in earlier campaigns, other kinds of communications also would have to be assumed (jet airplanes rather than the railroads Douglas rode as the modern marvels of his time), and corresponding political displacements—weakened party control over the contenders for nomination. Mass radio and television would supply channels of information for candidates as well as voters.

11 With all of these factors taken into consideration, we can make some reasonable guesses about what would have happened if television had been present during past campaigns.

Stephen Douglas and Abraham Lincoln, Illinois Senatorial Race, 1858

12 The easiest way to belittle modern debates on television is by referring—with a reverence built on ignorance—to the epic 1858 encounters between Abraham Lincoln and Stephen Douglas. The Lincoln–Douglas debates have become our touchstone of reasoned disagreement at election time, and it hardly matters that they were demagogic exercises in mutual entrapment that backfired for both men. Lincoln lost the debates in the sense that he was not elected senator, his immediate objective. Douglas lost in that he was not elected president two years later, his ulterior objective. Both men lost by failing to save the Union, a goal they shared and that they actually made more difficult for each other and for the rest of the country.

13 This is not a "revisionist" view of the debates. Contemporaries were as harsh on them as we are on our televised question-and-answer sessions today; newspapers of the nineteenth century yearned for their own "good old days," when the founders of the Republic would not have stooped to the tricks of stump debaters. "Washington was no speech maker, neither was Jefferson," huffed a Cincinnati paper.

And the *Norfolk Argus* lamented: "In the earlier days of our republic such a piece of bold effrontery and impudence would have met with its merited rebuke." Lincoln himself would call campaign oratory divisive when he refused to give any speeches, two years later, as a candidate for the presidency.

Douglas won the Senate race in 1858. Television might have widened his margin a bit. He was an impressive speaker, full of jaunty energy of the Jimmy Cagney sort, all strut and humorous pugnacity—something frozen out of surviving pictures, which could be focused only if one held a long pose. Yet his voice gave out easily in the three-hour contests, making him plead with his own supporters not to drown his words with cheers—a problem TV would have obviated. 14

Lincoln, on the other hand, had some very eccentric platform manners, especially at the beginning of a speech, when he was still nervous. Historian Allan Nevins describes the problem: "His principal movements when talking—clasping and unclasping his hands, first behind him and then in front of himself, an uncouth swing of his long arms, or a sudden dip at the knees followed by a sharp upward jerk with much gesticulation of the head—were often indescribably gauche." 15

Perhaps with proper coaching he might have modified his style for television, where his logic, humor, and beautiful prose would have made its impact. His sly remarks would not have needed the folksy emphasis he gave them when milking gags for a big audience, especially his references to Douglas's theories as "homeopathic soup"—made by boiling the shadow of a pigeon that had starved to death. 16

The Lincoln–Douglas debates are historically important because they prefigured the breakdown of a nation. Both men were trying to save the Union from different but overlapping geographic bases. Television, had it been available, would have made the regional appeal less tempting and would have thrust other issues into the debate. It would certainly have improved the decorum of the proceedings, though it is hard to imagine its changing the outcome. Designated questioners might have led Lincoln to be less vague about how slavery would die out if people just let it alone. He contented himself with the thought that everyone would someday agree that it was wrong, and "then, and not 17 till then, I think, will we in some way come to an end of the slavery agitation." Douglas might have been forced to say what he thought of slavery personally, a matter he artfully evaded in the debates, to the lasting bewilderment of his admirers.

Theodore Roosevelt and Woodrow Wilson, 1912

18 The presence of television would have given Teddy Roosevelt the visibility he needed to heal the Republican spirit. Television would have undercut the power of the party bosses, who—for good or ill—controlled the nomination process. That power was what made Republicans cling to William Taft after Roosevelt led his "Bull Moose" (Progressive Republican) opposition out of the Chicago convention and held a counterconvention, improvised and full of drama, just made for television. Taft, a stranded whale, held out against his former mentor, calling in all party debts: but all the vitality of Progressivism was with Roosevelt.

19 In the closing weeks of the campaign Roosevelt was shot in Milwaukee by a fanatic who opposed any third-term president. Roosevelt, his shirt bloody, the bullet still in his body, went on to give his scheduled speech, saying, "I will give this speech or die." Television would not only have captured that incident with all its theatrical force, it would have replayed the dramatic moment repeatedly after October 14, magnifying Roosevelt's courage and rallying the Progressives who, doubtful that a third party could win, were defecting to the Democrats.

20 Woodrow Wilson, whom the Democrats had nominated late and rather reluctantly (on the forty-sixth ballot), was an inspirational orator of the Adlai Stevenson type, but without the visceral appeal of Roosevelt. Not only the more vital of the two, Roosevelt was the more genuinely learned (despite Wilson's doctorate, barely earned, in political science). In a television debate, Roosevelt would have had an enormous edge on his opponent. As it was, Wilson won only by a plurality of the popular votes, Taft drawing off enough of the Republican majority party's members to defeat Roosevelt. In retrospect, Roosevelt seems to have been born for TV; 1912 could have proved it.

Thomas E. Dewey and Harry Truman, 1948

The modern polling techniques of 1948 lured Thomas E. Dewey into a false sense of security in his bid against Harry Truman. Ignoring the expertise of the day, Truman invented the modern campaign train (now replaced by the campaign plane) and whistle-stopped himself to a great reversal. If we suppose a greater range and variety of technology available to both candidates, it is hard to imagine the surprise upset occurring. Television would have captured the excitement Truman was creating at distant Western stops; better polls and hot-line reports would have traced changes in the public mood. 21

Dewey would have had to come out of his ivory tower, where he was putting together his new government, and campaign like a candidate instead of making declarations as if he were already President. Perhaps he would not have been able to stop the extraordinary effort of Truman, but Dewey had been impressive in newsreels as a crusading district attorney in New York; he did have the initial lead that fooled everyone; Truman would have lost some of his underdog appeal if the polls were corrected and expectable countermeasures taken by Dewey. 22

In Dewey's case television would have forced on the candidate a bit more boldness but not enough to have altered the outcome. The present tendency seems to inculcate more caution. It is painfully clear that a single gaffe captured on television—Edmund Muskie seeming to cry, Senator Joseph Biden lashing out angrily at a question about his law school performance—can damage if not doom a candidacy. Furthermore, television is always watching. C-SPAN, the cable satellite public-affairs network, is present all the time, at the smallest caucus and primary events, even though the network news shows are drawing smaller audiences. The Biden outburst occurred before a C-SPAN camera, but it was instantly transmitted through the networks, adding a final touch to Biden's troubles over a plagiarism charge. 23

Today television is making candidates play "defense ball": speaking in predetermined sound bites, avoiding the spontaneous, cutting back on question-and-answer sessions, scheduling debates in less conspicuous time slots. Ironically, 24 apprentice politicians must strive to appear on the tube as often as possible in order to get name recognition (which is now face recognition as well). Then—progressively, as they come into positions where their comments matter more—they begin to ration those comments, hedge them, deliver them in muffled or ambiguous ways. So television has contradictory influences working at one and the same time—toward the wider dissemination of information and toward a tighter control and limitation of what we are to know or hear. This cautious tendency, this fear of any misstep, was there before television but in special cases rather than as a broad influence. It was the strategy that made Lincoln refuse to give any campaign speeches during the emotionally divisive time between his nomination and the 1861 inauguration, a time when several states had already seceded. Television would not have let Lincoln remain so aloof today.

Lincoln and William Seward, Republican Convention, Chicago, 1860

25 If television had been around in 1860, it is extremely unlikely that Lincoln would have been the Republican nominee for President. The best way to see the possible effects of television for accidental evil as well as general good is to go back to the Republican convention and look at the struggle to nominate a candidate. The great favorite in what was offering itself as the healing party was William Seward, who entered the convention in Chicago with a majority of delegates.

26 What followed was a series of deals, bribes, and dirty tricks that could not have endured the scrutiny of TV. Lincoln's managers prevented a balloting when Seward still held the lead, by blocking the printing of ballots. Then they jammed the hall with their supporters while Seward's people were out parading for him and offered posts in the Lincoln administration (which Lincoln later honored) to members of key delegations. As Murat Halstead, the best reporter of political conventions, wrote, "The fact of the Convention was the defeat of Seward rather than the nomination of Lincoln."

27 In 1980 television doomed the "dream ticket" of Ronald Reagan and Gerald Ford by airing its possibility and eliciting

strong criticism of it before Reagan could make up his mind. In New Orleans in 1988 television speculation on vice presidential bids led to the premature announcement of George Bush's choice of Senator Dan Quayle. And then, in his television debut, the telegenic senator from Indiana, a true child of the television age, appeared rattled and uncertain as he defended himself against allegations of past misconduct involving his military service, a golf trip to Florida with a female lobbyist, and whether he had enough experience to be President should Bush not be able to complete his term.

It is hard to imagine television reporters not swarming 28
around the ballot printers in Chicago in 1860, or the walkie-talkie teams of various networks not alerting camera crews out on the street that Lincoln's men were packing the hall with supporters. Given any of these interventions by television, Seward, not Lincoln, would have been nominated.

Seward was a sentimental favorite with Republicans 29
because of his clear-cut opposition to slavery. Lincoln was, by comparison, more equivocal: His supporters argued that he "had made no records to be defended or explained." As we have seen, he made no public statements at all, not even in response to editors' written requests, during the presidential contest. Seward would not have stayed silent had he been the candidate. But Seward, even if he had not been defeated at the convention, would certainly have been defeated by political passions in the general election. In fact, with Lincoln removed from the race, the most obvious winner would have been Stephen Douglas, his old foe of the Illinois debate—the most moderate candidate left in that field. Some champions of Douglas have argued that he might conceivably have held the Union together. But they ignore the disconcerting fact that he died three months after the 1861 inauguration—which would have left the hellish problems of secession to his running mate, Herschel V. Johnson, a former governor of Georgia.

How such a man, a Southerner, would have coped with 30
the unraveling nation, no one can know. But the outcome could hardly have been as favorable as it was under Lincoln's strong, magnanimous guidance. Would we have had a successful secession, the President of the United States blessing his sister states as they departed? Would a war have been fought, to an ambiguous conclusion? (Lincoln himself

was afraid he could not sustain the war in early 1864.) Would we have had a series of civil wars or trial republics that would be made up of splintering groups of states?

31 Television is a mixed blessing, and in dispelling the corruptions of the 1860 convention, it might have brought upon us curses even greater than those of the Civil War as it was fought—curses, moreover, brought vividly home to people who were frightened enough by Mathew Brady's murky photographs. (Between 1861 and 1865 Brady accompanied the Union armies, taking photographs that became the basis for a pictorial history of the Civil War.) Progress exacts its costs. Abraham Lincoln might have been one of the things the nation would have lost to the unquestionable benefit of modern communications technology.

Christopher Hitchens

Voting in the Passive Voice

Christopher Hitchens (born 1949 in Portsmouth, England) is the Washington editor of Harper's Magazine, *the public affairs and current affairs magazine that often carries his essays. The following one appeared in April 1992.*

1 The Salem Screen Printers plant in Salem, New Hampshire, is like thousands of other factories in America. Set among various freeway intersections in a quasi-sylvan environment, and situated just off auspiciously named South Policy Street, it employs some dozens of friendly, partially educated young people who are delighted to have a job. The work itself, which involves putting blank T-shirts under a die stamp and then removing them with logos imprinted, is only notionally above the burger-flipping level of which we hear so much. But then New Hampshire's deep and lingering recession has at least assured a free market for cheap take-out food: In all directions across the state, the mall outlets for T-shirts with logos are putting up the shutters. (You haven't vibrated to the deep resonance of the word "emptiness," by the way, until you have seen a dying mall in today's United States.)

It was a morning late in January when Arkansas Governor Bill Clinton arrived at the plant and stepped into an assemblage of workers, praying, I suppose, that nobody would make any jokes about pressing the flesh. His campaign for the presidential nomination was on this day poised awkwardly between the headquarters of this year's try at an early Democratic consensus and the hindquarters of Ms. Gennifer Flowers. Numerous representatives of the Fourth Estate—which already, following the requisite week or two of Washington briefings, huddlings, and phone-arounds, had declared Clinton the front-runner, and thus had a keen interest in keeping him so—were on hand. I circled the candidate, peppering him with questions, hoping to steer the conversation, however fleetingly, from his sleeping around to the quality of his sleep a few nights back after giving his personal okay for the execution of an imbecile Arkansas murderer. 2

Seeing Clinton scowling in my direction, I looked over my shoulder, hoping to hear a follow-up or two from my colleagues. It was then I realized that I was—photographers apart—alone. I had dutifully trailed the press corps from Washington to snowy Manchester to . . . *where was everybody?* The pack! Where was the pack!!? 3

It was, as it turned out, ranged respectfully around a small, mustached man gesturing freely, confident of his hold on his audience. This happened to be Stan Greenberg, Clinton's storied pollster. During Clinton's entire two-hour visit to the Salem plant, Greenberg was the only one who did any serious talking. Clinton—just then the anointed Democratic "front-runner," and perhaps the next leader of the Free World—seemed content with the division of labor. 4

As why should he not have been? He had gotten this far by judicious study of "the numbers" and by careful cultivation and propitiation of those who amass, decode, and package them. Clinton's quietude in Salem, the acquiescence of the press in that quietude, Greenberg's centrality—here was the true picture of democracy in America circa '92, no photo op necessary. Before my eyes, as Greenberg carefully walked the reporters through the results of his latest instant survey of New Hampshire's electorate—his questions, his sample voters, his interpretation of the results—impressions were taking shape as "perception," perception beginning its brisk march to fact and on to truth, or better, Truth. (That the truth lies, and is often found to lie somewhere in between, is 5 not the stuff of contemporary campaign politics.) Here indeed was the quadrennial American political ritual—the reduction of the vast, varied, and increasingly restless polis to a poll.

6 Poll, poll, poll. Try reading a news story or watching one aired on TV without encountering the word. Readers of *The Washington Post* of February 5, to take but one example, were offered seven stories on the front page, and of these, three—about the pessimism of Washington's residents, the souring of Poland on capitalism, and, it should go without saying, the Clinton campaign—were based on polls. Not content to wait a day or two for results, the Cable News Network pioneered the viewer phone-in poll, inviting nightly news watchers to glimpse a minute-long story, then dial an instant opinion. And this year, just a few days before heading to New Hampshire, I was invited by CBS to take part (as were you) in a phone-in poll conducted in the fading moments of the President's State of the Union address.

7 But allow me to bring this problem down to an anecdotal level, which, of course, pollsters decry as unscientific: At a dinner party, one is seldom told—and one is never to ask—how and especially why a given guest voted in the last primary or national election. Instead, one spends the evening at a certain clever, cool remove from the stuff of democratic politics—swapping back and forth across the table numbers gleaned from the CNN or ABC or Times Mirror poll.

8 And these are only the most visible polls. Behind the drapery of the permanent plebiscite are the private, strategic polls of the Bush Administration, of members of Congress, of all candidates for national office, as well as the daily digest of polling that is either modemed or hand-delivered to editors, producers, and reporters subscribing to *Hotline,* the political insider's ultimate data service. Gone are the days when newspapers like *The New York Times* debated whether they should commission polls of their own, and whether, if they did commission them, to put them on the front page, and whether, in that event, polls should carry a reporter's byline. Any newspaper—or newsmagazine or TV network—which these days declined to make news in this way might stand accused of lacking "objectivity" and also

"sophistication," which together are thought to attract readers. Moreover, polls today no longer make only their own news; they color the rest of it. A paper like the *Times* knows it is "objective" and "sophisticated" to publish a goofy photo of Bush or run a bit longer with one of his train-wreck quotations when its CBS/*New York Times* poll shows the President's approval rating sagging toward the 50 percent range.

Opinion polling was born out of a struggle not to discover the public mind but to master it. It was a weapon in the early wars to thwart organized labor and in the battle against Populism, and it later became rather a favorite in the arsenal of "mass psychology" parties of the European right. There was always money in it, and the term "pollster" originated in a 1949 book by a political scientist named Lindsay Rogers, who coined it in order to evoke the word "huckster." Rogers was arguing against a seminal and pernicious book by George Gallup in 1940 and pompously entitled *The Pulse of Democracy*. In its hucksterish pages Gallup sought to argue that James Bryce was wrong, in his *American Commonwealth,* to conclude that "the machinery for weighing or measuring the popular will from week to week or month to month is not likely to be invented." Not so, said Gallup. The opinion poll, or, as he grandly put it, "the sampling referendum," had the popular will wired: 9

> This means that the nation is literally in one great room. The newspapers and the radio conduct the debate on national issues, presenting both information and argument on both sides, just as the townsfolk did in person in the old town meeting. And finally, through the process of the sampling referendum, the people, having heard the debate on both sides of every issue, can express their will. After one hundred and fifty years we return to the town meeting. This time the whole nation is within the doors.

Lindsay Rogers wrote of this: "The best thing about these claims is that they are completely false. If there were a modicum of truth in them, the outlook for popular government would be even grimmer than it is." Rogers was particularly troubled by what he saw as the pollster's poten- 10 tial power to, in effect, wield the gavel at the town meeting—to frame a question in such a way as to limit, warp, or actually guarantee the answer. Wouldn't a practice of getting the right responses by asking the right questions (and only those) pose a grave threat to the ongoing and freewheeling conversation that is at the heart of democracy?

11 Rogers could not have imagined the way in which this particular malignancy would develop and advance. Early this past winter I sat and chatted in Los Angeles with Patrick Caddell, perhaps the most famous and successful pollster of the Seventies and Eighties. In 1988, Caddell recalled for me, he had been hired to do polling for Alan Cranston, the Democratic senator from California. "He was in big trouble," Caddell related. "The Republicans were running Ed Zschau against him, a guy who was moderate and smart and young. All our figures showed that the voters were bored with Cranston and that the younger voters wanted a younger guy. It looked bad."

12 Bad, but not impossible. "There was one other finding," Caddell went on to say. "The voters were alienated. They weren't strongly disposed to vote, and they were very turned off by negative campaigning. The fewer who voted, the better for Cranston." The thinking went that because Cranston had more name recognition and was the incumbent, with the attendant organization to get out the tried-and-true voters, he'd squeak by in a low-turnout race. "So I told them, 'Run the most negative campaign you can. Drive the voters away. Piss them off with politics.' It worked. Cranston just made it by two points. The day after, I realized what I had done and got out of the business."

13 But the business, of course, lives on, growing ever more subtle and insidious. An admiring *Time* magazine profile of Clinton published earlier this year described his campaign as being scientifically, masterfully "poll-driven." I learned the meaning of this term when I was told by the Clinton camp, very politely and candidly, that it would not be possible for me to watch a private poll being conducted. One of his senior advisers explained that that would be to give away the store. "Our polling is predictive," she said proudly. "We're laying out the race, getting it to play out so that we'll be where the voters will be by, say, July." Obviously, Clinton's people didn't want to expose their strategy any more than—and this was a comparison offered by a Clinton staffer—Lee Atwater did when he uncovered Michael

Dukakis's "vulnerability" on race and the flag in those legendary "focus groups" of voters back in 1988.

There is an entire, and not unrevealing, pollster's argot to which one is introduced by hanging out with the professionals. A term that I came to love is "forced choice." This is where the questioner puts a firm, no-exceptions, yes-or-no proposition to the interviewee. "You see, if you offer the people the *option* of saying, 'I'm not sure' or 'I don't have enough information,' " I was told by Professor David Moore of the University of New Hampshire, who is a student and critic of polling, "the number of them who will say it goes up by about 20 percent. 'Forced choice' means getting people to have an opinion." 14

Then there's "choice or lean," which sounds oddly like something you'd see in a butcher's window. If you can't get computer-selected citizens to choose your candidate or his position on a given issue from a multiple-choice menu, you can at least ask them whether they "lean" toward any one option. Together with "tracking" (three-day rolling averages of the evolution of opinion) and "panel-backing" (phoning up the same people you interviewed before and counting on their "indebtedness"—*gee, if you drop out of the sample now, the whole tracking thing blows up*—to prevent them from hanging up on you), a flickering image of the state of opinion can be kept on the screen. 15

There is a dialectic of manipulation involved here. Not only must the "poll-driven" campaign seek to shape and mold opinion but its candidate must be ready at all times to assume the required shape and posture. The process is very far from being infallible—for example, George Bush's tracking geniuses must have completely missed the signals about the emerging salience last fall of the health-care issue—but it is *the process*. In effect, politics has become a vast game of simulation which it takes a lot of money to play—the most modest of tracking polls costs a candidate about $20,000—and which has replaced, for politicians, canvassing and, for journalistists, basic reporting. 16

See the eager seeker after the nomination as he meets the people. See his frozen posture and quacking, halting speech as he musters unfamiliar bonhomie. See him as he gets gratefully into his car and grabs the portable phone to call his pollster and find out what people really want. Now see the mackintoshed reporter as he calls up the latest findings on his green PC screen, writes them up, and puts his name 17 on them. He has been out to test the temperature of the nation.

18 For one awful moment in January it had seemed that Bill Clinton's own god might fail him: He stood a sudden, deadly chance of being turned upon by the averages and the percentages—his own head, as it were, served up on a poll. A detailed study of this moment in New Hampshire—a scrutiny of a series of impressions as they strove to take form and shape, and to become a "perception" instead of an impression—will, I hope, illuminate how polling is not a benign, detached mapping of the political landscape but rather a powerful means of cultivating and reshaping it. Far from being the mere study of intention and attitude, it is a profound intervention in the formative period of these things. From the Flowers flap one learns not about the supposedly undue influence of tawdry tabloids, or of the inability of Americans to remain focused on the crucial issues of the day (tax cuts of $60, $80; standardized testing by the year 2000 or 2010), but rather how a cunning campaign team and a compliant "quality" press can do not everything yet many things.

19 If you exempt the polls done by the networks in conjunction with the big newspapers, and the private polling organizations of the individual candidates, there were in New Hampshire late this past January three polling organizations that *counted,* so to speak—and counted, or rather were counted, more than once. Results of these three polls—the *Boston Globe*/WBZ-TV poll, the poll taken by the American Research Group of Manchester, and that undertaken by the University of New Hampshire at Durham for station WMUR-TV in Manchester—were routinely extrapolated by columnists and broadcasters to say something on a national level about one or another candidate's standing or future chances. In turn, these impressions and analyses were *cycled back* into the state—by the media, the campaign staffs, and the candidates themselves—with further effects on fund-raising, on position taking, on day-to-day campaign plans, and thus, again, on statewide and nationwide "perceptions." Here, beneath the clean veneer afforded by computers and cellular phones, we have the new smoke-filled backrooms, where the silent but crucial "election" is held and the results

are posted (war chests filled, pundits brought on board, "electability" established) before even one citizen's vote has actually been cast.

20 On Monday, January 27—the day after Clinton's appearance with his wife, Hillary, on *60 Minutes,* and the day his campaign people and supporters in the media thought he might be broken by a press conference held in New York City by Ms. Flowers, during which scratchy recordings were played of purported Clinton-Flowers phone chats—the *Boston Globe* conducted its regular poll of 400 "likely Democratic primary voters" in New Hampshire. The *Globe*'s polling calls began going out to interviewees even as the Clintons could be glimpsed on the nightly news fending off reporters' questions about the scandalous tapes; and the polling continued as the crucial first edition of the paper—the edition that is sold, promoted, and studiously read by voters and opinion shapers *in New Hampshire*—went to press. The early sampling turned up the result that Clinton was favored by 33 percent of those polled, roughly the same as earlier in the month, given the poll's acknowledged (that is, arrogantly *claimed*) "margin of error" of plus or minus five points. These numbers, in turn, generated the front-page headline POLL SHOWS CLINTON'S LEAD UNDIMINISHED and the instant front-page analysis (paragraph four) by Walter V. Robinson that "so far, the poll suggests the new media—and not Clinton—have suffered from the intensive coverage of the Flowers charges."

21 The American Research Group, a private outfit that drops its market-research practice every four years during election season and concentrates on polling, came away with different numbers after polling that night. The ARG had Clinton moving from a 39 percent share to a 28 percent share. Not so, says UNH's David Moore. Likewise polling on January 27, Moore drew upon "likely Democrats" who had been interviewed twice before. His findings can best be summarized in his own words: "Clinton's support [on the twenty-seventh] is *not* from the same voters who supported him in the last poll." Moore, in his polling, found that while Clinton remained the "front-runner," only 54 percent of his original supporters stayed with him, while one-third went to other candidates and 12 percent moved to the "unsure" column. These statistics, in turn, were laid out by Moore in varying levels of intensity ("strongly believe," "moderately believe,"

etc.) so as to license his conclusion that "these figures suggest how volatile the vote in New Hampshire still [was] at this time of the campaign."

22 Now, one can attack the *Globe* numbers not only with other numbers but on innumerable theoretical and analytical grounds. For instance, I would agree with Robert Schmuhl, a professor of American studies at Notre Dame who specializes in the country's peculiar fascination with personality politics, when he said early in February that "the real people up in New Hampshire are not acknowledging as openly as they might the doubts that a story like the Clinton story raises in their minds." I might bolster this line of thought with, well, some rather volatile numbers. No more than 8 percent of those polled by the *Globe* on January 27 said they definitely would *not* vote for a candidate who'd admitted to an extramarital affair—and this number, or some rough approximation of it, was repeated through January and into February by pundits, editorialists, and Democratic movers/shakers as bracing proof that Americans (not simply New Hampshire's likely Democratic voters) were sick of supermarket sleaze, had matured as voters and citizens, were fully preoccupied with the issues. Interesting, and wholly uncommented upon, was the fact that fully 36 percent of those asked essentially the same question five years ago by the *Times* at the height of the Gary Hart–Donna Rice furor said they could not vote for an acknowledged adulterer.

23 But let's return to the *Globe,* and its crucial first edition, with its declaration that Clinton remained the front-runner and that the press, not the candidate, was in big trouble. This was the poll and conclusion trumpeted by David Broder, the capital's chronicler of received wisdom, in *The Washington Post* of January 28; thus was established the "take" inside the beltway. The *Globe*'s early edition was also cited by ABC's *Nightline* on the night of the twenty-seventh, and no doubt steeled Joe Grandmaison, New Hampshire's former Democratic chairman and a Clinton supporter; he managed to keep Forrest Sawyer on the defensive by accusing *Nightline* of sinking to the level of the tabloids by devoting an earlier show to the Flowers allegations. The editors of opinion-shaping papers and mags went to bed satisfied that they'd done the right thing by burying their stories about the scandal; and the fund-raisers and party bigs turned in resting easier now that their man had, at least for the time being, weathered the storm.

But here's what poor Forrest didn't know or couldn't know: By the time he was signing off, the *Globe*'s pollsters were uncovering a somewhat different response. Special calls placed to 229 additional likely voters found Clinton's support had dropped enough to bring the entire sample down three percentage points. If my math's right, Clinton was supported by about 25 percent of those phoned up later rather than sooner—those, that is, who'd had an hour or two to reflect. Given the margin of error, it turns out that this later sample threw similar support to former Massachusetts Senator Paul Tsongas. These interviewees were particularly troubled not by the question of adultery but by the question of whether Clinton was telling the truth about his adulterous ways. To return to Mr. Robinson, he would write in still another instant front-page analysis for the paper's *final* edition (paragraph four) that "as the evening wore on, Clinton's support eroded. . . ." 24

We wouldn't know that. Nobody ever used the follow-up edition. Was it not Michael Deaver who said that getting the first version into print was half the battle? The other half was that nobody—by which I mean the party heavies, the consultants, the columnists, etc.—wanted to hear it. The last thing anyone in *the process* wanted to read was the kind of "objective" headline the numbers truly called for: POLLS SHOW CLINTON SAGGING, TSONGAS SURGING, AMONG VOTERS GIVEN MOMENT TO THINK. With another candidate—one less firmly embraced by the party and the pack, a Gary Hart, say—one might have heard less about "privacy" and more about "credibility," ever an issue for the candidate from nowhere and very much one for Clinton, as, in the wake of his draft flap, fidelity to flag would commingle with fidelity to wife. However, with a nominating process constructed to ward off late entrants, with the filing deadlines by late January past for primaries that would choose nearly a third of the delegates, with the fund-raisers having taken their position with the "front-runner," with the press on board, a January 27 poll showing Clinton's support eroding had no place and was granted none. 25

Polls are deployed only when they might prove *useful*—that is, helpful to the powers that be in their quest to maintain their position and influence. Indeed, the polling industry is a powerful ally of depoliticization and its coun- 26 terpart, which is consensus. The polls undoubtedly help decide what people think, but their most important long-term influence may be on *how* people think. The interrogative process is very distinctly weighted against the asking of an intelligent question or the recording of a thoughtful answer. And, as all pollsters will tell you privately, the answers to poll questions are very greatly influenced by what has lately been defined as important by the television news. Since the television news, in turn, relies upon opinion polls to determine what is really going on, the range of discourse is increasingly constricted.

27 Moreover, with polling one has the introduction of bogus, pseudo-objective concepts into politics. Example: Do you think of Governor Clinton as "electable?" (a pseudo-objective criterion if there ever was one). If so, is your impression of his "electability" derived to any extent from your reading of the polled opinions of others? In any case, would you like to say whether, in your own private, considered opinion, Governor Clinton is (a) Highly electable? (b) Moderately electable? or (c) Only slightly electable?

28 "It's all part of an attempt to keep order," Pat Caddell commented, surprisingly but not inaccurately. "It defines politics and politicians to suit those who are already in power." And, of course, it is a great reinforcement of the spurious idea of the great national "we"; from polls, we make "our" rational-choice decisions on a basis of unpolluted and electronically delivered information. Is that Lee Atwater I hear laughing?

29 Of course, in theory it would be possible to ask questions that put the consensus to the test. In the late Eighties, when official Washington was striving to "put Iran-Contra behind us," it was common to hear the pundits saying that there was "zero public support" for prolonging or deepening the inquiry, or for letting it become a threat to a President "perceived" as popular. Analyses of this sort had their basis in polls that found a majority of interviewees assenting to questions such as "Is Colonel North a real patriot?" But no pollster ever asked a sample group: "If you were asked to choose between Ronald Reagan and the United States Constitution, which would you rather sacrifice?"

30 Biased? Meaningless? More meaningless than the ABC News/*Washington Post* poll of July 1985, which actually asked interviewees whether or not they thought Ronald Reagan's cancer would recur before he left office? No fewer

than 54 percent solemnly responded that it wouldn't, and 33 percent said that they thought it would, and only 12 percent gave the sane reply that they had no idea—"choice," on this occasion, not being "forced." Is not a plebiscite on the leader's health, reported on the front page, rather in keeping with the approach to politics and opinion exhibited by a banana republic?

It is because polls are very pricey that they tend toward broad, stark questions freighted with assumptions—questions that can "hit a nerve" and bring a quick, thoughtless response. Polls get more costly the more they are "filtered," filtering being a process of refinement that scrutinizes, separates, codifies, and "breaks down" the "don't knows." So it's not surprising that you read questions like "Are the poor lazy?" *(Los Angeles Times)* rather than "Does the Federal Reserve's tight money policy favor the rich, the poor, or neither?" (nobody yet). 31

A good pollster is like a good attorney, and fights for the result that the commissioning party expects or needs; in the parlance, such a poll is called "client-directed." Pollsters themselves make no bones about their influence on the outcome. In a 1988 interview Lou Harris boasted that "I elected one president, one prime minister, about twenty-eight governors, and maybe close to sixty U.S. senators." Thus pollstering/huckstering is inextricably bound up with considerations of who will pay for the poll's results and the need to serve political clients who are winners. 32

"Fluidity" is what pollsters call the chaos and ignorance that they seek to influence. The leading student of fluidity is Professor Sam Popkin of the University of California at San Diego, whose book *The Reasoning Voter* tries to deal with the "bandwagon effect," by which politicians in cahoots with pollsters seek to exert sufficient magnetism on enough scattered iron-filings to create a pattern and, with any luck, "momentum." In his book Popkin rehearses the way in which this was done the last time the Democratic Party "found" that what it needed was a pragmatic Southern governor. In February 1975 Gallup asked Democratic voters to choose among thirteen Democrats who had been "mentioned" (a key word for the consensus and the punditocracy. Mentioned by whom?) as potential candidates. Jimmy Carter, with 1 percent, came in thirteenth. Pat Caddell remembers the networks leaving him out in order to reduce the field to a round dozen. 33

34 After winning the Iowa caucuses in January 1976, Carter became the presidential choice of 12 percent of Democrats, according to the February 1976 CBS/*New York Times* poll. He went on to take the New Hampshire primary, make the covers of *Time* and *Newsweek,* and win primaries in Florida and Illinois. Within *one month* the same poll made him the first choice of 46 percent of Democrats. There are two views about this. The first is that of former Congressman Mo Udall, who, as a Democratic presidential candidate in '76, objected to the pollsters' practice of "defining" a "front-runner" in this way before most voters had gotten near a booth and long before any real policy arguments had been heard. He later put it thus: "It's like a football game, in which you say to the first team that makes a first down with ten yards, 'Hereafter your team has a special rule. Your first downs are five yards. And if you make three of those you get a two-yard first down. And we're going to let your first touchdown count twenty-one points. Now the rest of you bastards play catch-up under the regular rules.' "

35 Contrast the cool Professor Popkin, who concedes that "some voters *may* indeed have voted for [Carter] simply because he was shown in a positive light as a winner. But many more people felt that they had acquired enough information about him in barely a month to want him to be their president."

36 Which of these views—Udall's or Popkin's—seems a more reliable analysis of the queasy experience of watching the Clinton effect and realizing that, in both a crude and a subtle way, some kind of fix was plotted, if not fully *in,* before a single ballot had been cast?

37 Since, especially in primary season, money and press coverage follow the polls as doggedly as trade follows the flag, speed is of the first importance. "Perceptions" must harden into "numbers" and thus into "news" (all three commodities often being supplied, for greater convenience, by the same networks and outlets) in order for the "news" to keep the "perceptions" sufficiently acute for the "numbers" to build. As Popkin says excitedly of a later campaign:

> In 1984, it took three weeks of intensive campaigning in Iowa for Gary Hart to go from 5 percent in surveys to 17 percent of the actual [caucuses] vote. In New Hampshire, it took him five weeks to move from 5 percent to 13 percent in surveys,

> but after news of his second-place finish in Iowa, it took him only five days to go from 13 percent to 37 percent.

And how long to go from that back to zero? Later developments in that same primary season reveal another factor, what the pollsters privately and euphemistically call a sample's "inconsistency" on a given issue or candidate, but what has long looked to me like an interviewee saying, firmly if indirectly, "Who cares about your stupid poll?" Asked by a *Times*/CBS poll in March 1984 about Walter Mondale—whether their opinion was "favorable"—47 percent said that it was. Asked if they thought he had "enough experience to be a good president," 75 percent said yes. Yet asked if they had "confidence in [his] ability to deal wisely with a difficult international crisis" or were "uneasy" about this, 42 percent said they were uneasy. Well, what *did* they think of Mondale? We learned in November 1984, when Reagan drubbed him. 38

"Garbage in, garbage out," was the answer one pollster offered me without attribution, over the telephone, when I brought up "inconsistency." To him the problem is simply a technical one, a matter of refining the questions. He had no sooner said this when I distinctly heard his wife shout, "That's because the American people are *stupid.*" In fact, that conclusion is tempting only to pollsters and other elitists. The answers may be stupid, but the voters are not. Stupid answers traditionally come from stupid questions. Stupid questions, however, need not come from stupid people. 39

Pollsters, for the most part, know perfectly well what they are doing. One thing they are doing is aggregating and averaging ephemeral spasms of "mood" that may have commercial or political value. "The 'coding' process can be designed to prevent people from speaking their minds," according to Caddell, who, of course, has needed to be swift in his time. "They give you multiple-choice questions on, say, what motivated you to vote, and if your answer is not one of the choices offered, you get dumped or written off as 'other.'" 40

If you really don't fit, or conform, you can be dumped even if you are in the majority. Last fall the suggestive partnership of Peter Hart and Robert Teeter did its regular canvass on behalf of *The Wall Street Journal* and NBC. (I say 41 "suggestive" because Hart is a Democrats' pollster and Teeter polls for the Republican President, and both are friends of the *Journal*'s Washington bureau chief, Al Hunt, who likes to spread bipartisan joy when "bipartisan" translates as "consensus.") As reported on the *Journal*'s front page of November 1, 1991, the findings made up a cheery salad of trivial, emollient morsels. "Cutting taxes to spur the economy gets lukewarm support" (but support nevertheless!). "Bad voter vibes rise toward [Jesse] Jackson." "80 percent cite 'drinks too much' as a disqualification for the Presidency." Dan Quayle went up from 27 percent to 35 percent "positive."

42 Excluded entirely, and dealt with in a back-page story not until four days later, was the finding that 59 percent of a specially sampled group assented to the statement "The economic and political systems of this country are stacked against people like me." The sampled group were defined as "Democrats who say they voted for Bush in 1988 and independents with household incomes between $20,000 and $50,000"—that is to say, the group of so-called Reagan Democrats who might well decide this year's election. But 47 percent of *all other voters* also agreed with the proposition, known in the trade as the "alienation question," once it was put to them.

43 It is revealing, to say the least, that pollsters will talk of such results as an example of polls that don't *come out right*. Careful evidence of this proposition can be found in a study undertaken by Professor W. Lance Bennett of the University of Washington. Entitled *Marginalizing the Majority: Conditioning Public Opinion to Accept Managerial Democracy,* it takes the unusually well-documented case of United States public opinion regarding the Nicaraguan Contras. Generally, public opinion is seen by the expert class as uninformed and unstable, and thus moldable by, among other things, opinion polls. That a majority of Americans were against Contra aid, however, was one of those cases that the expert class characterized time and again as "stable" and "consistent." In other words, the voters held, at a fairly steady two to one, against Contra aid throughout the Eighties. Moreover, their opinion appeared to be based on an informed and decided, if rather general, opposition to military engagement in Central America.

44 Professor Bennett observes that the White House news managers understood this very well, and that while they

would trumpet official pollster Richard Wirthlin's discovery that the Reagan tax reform proposal was "popular," they consciously downplayed popular wisdom in the matter of Nicaragua. The media, which commissions polls and which constructs stories around them, generally followed suit. Between January 1, 1983, when congressional debate on Contra funding began, and October 15, 1986, when Reagan finally secured his Senate/House majority for Contra aid, there were 2,148 entries for Nicaragua in the *New York Times Index*. Of these, only .6 percent mentioned popular opinion on the subject and, according to Bennett's findings, only five references to the polls made it into the headlines affixed to *Times* stories on Nicaragua during that period.

On one of the biggest and least popular policy campaigns 45
of the Reagan Administration, public opinion simply was not an issue. When what "we" think jibes with the official and commissioning temperature-takers, we hear about it. Otherwise we don't get to know our own minds.

The final poll I studied was my own. Taking the University 46
of New Hampshire questionnaire in hand, I dialed at random (other polls dial by computer, but it comes to the same thing) from the Manchester, New Hampshire, telephone book. The first three "voters" hung up in my face when I announced myself to be from the "New Hampshire poll." ("We get 24 percent refusals," said Kelly Myers, a bright young graduate student at UNH. What are the politics of the phone-slammers? Hmm.) Making contact on my fourth call, I quickly established, at least to my satisfaction, that the "respondent" was over eighteen and a likely Democratic voter. The trouble was, she was too smart for me. As I read her the multiple choice of candidates and asked how she "leaned," she said it was equal between Clinton and Tsongas. There was no real provision for that answer.

"All right, who do you think is the 'front-runner'?" 47

"I guess Clinton has an edge there." 48

"Who do you think is the likely winner?" 49

"Isn't that the same question you just asked me?" (I bit my 50
tongue to avoid saying that as far as I could see it was.)

"Who do you think has the best likelihood of beating 51
George Bush?"

"Who knows? It's only January. There might be another of 52
his wars between now and November."

53 No designated space for *that* answer either.

54 On the registers of present discontent and propensity to vote, she scored very high, but the only "hard" opinion I was asked by the University of New Hampshire to solicit was about Clinton's alleged affairs. On this she said stoutly that she couldn't give a good god-damn. I was trembling when I hung up, and trembling too when I thought to what mush her spirited and warm answers would be reduced by a college student meeting his or her quota of calls from the telephone bank on a given evening with the presses and cameras set to roll.

55 On their own, one could argue, the opinion polls do no more than seek a common denominator among the demographics. But as practiced, polling is a search for and confirmation of consensus, this to be exploited and reinforced by professional politicians. In alliance with the new breed of handlers, fund-raisers, spin-specialists, and courtier journalists, it has become both a dangerous tranquilizer and an artificial stimulant. "Like many other technologies in politics," says Pat Caddell, if I may again quote him, polling is essentially "an instrument for deception whereby the truth is obscured and the public will be excluded and ignored." Which is a former pollster's way of calling polling an increasingly dangerous substitute for democracy, if not the precise negation of it.

Joe Saltzman

The More Talk the Better

Mr. Saltzman, a professor of journalism at the University of Southern California, is also associate mass media editor of USA Today*—where he published the following analysis toward the end of the presidential election campaign of 1992.*

1 It happens every time there is an election. Practically everyone complains that no one is talking about the issues, that all the media are interested in is the personal lives of the candidates, that nothing of substance is ever discussed.

2 The new rub in the national election campaign of 1992 is that the candidates are skirting the news media by going on

viewer call-in TV and radio shows. *The Washington Post* and other newspapers complain that these programs—ranging from Phil Donahue, Larry King, and the morning information shows to local TV and radio, and candidate-paid-for call-in programs—are like slow-pitch softballs to candidates. They allow politicians to evade unpleasantries and twist the truth, to circumvent the press in order to get easier questions and avoid scrutiny.

While it may be true that candidates feel more comfortable answering call-in questions that seldom challenge their veracity or pin them down with specific follow-up queries, there is something refreshing about the talk-show format with viewers asking the candidates primarily about issues involving the economy, education, health care, the environment. 3

It even may be argued that the voter can learn more about a candidate by watching him or her respond to a variety of questions about issues—even when the answers are superficial, repetitious, specious, and often just plain inaccurate. After seeing the presidential candidates on NBC's "Today Show," the Larry King program, and the Phil Donahue show, it is possible at the very least to get a sense of what kind of person the candidate is and how he responds to various issues. If the answers are purposely vague, that may reveal much about the candidate. Most of us vote for the person we feel most comfortable with and feel will speak to our needs and concerns. All the words may be quickly forgotten, but the impression of the candidate stays in the mind. It may be argued that the impression a voter gets of a candidate after watching him or her on a talk show is more accurate than the carefully created image the candidate exudes on paid commercials. 4

There are some facts about political life that must be acknowledged. No candidate is going to give a specific plan of action to any issue that may alienate a portion of the electorate. That is political suicide and anyone who runs for office never will do so again if he or she is too honest, too blunt, or too specific on almost any given issue. In the days before mass media, a candidate could go to a group of voters and tell those citizens exactly what they wanted to hear, then go to another community in another state and say exactly the opposite. Few would notice. Few would care. But in these days of immediate national exposure, no candidate can talk specifically to one group of people. The message 5 must be for everyone, and any universal message must be, by its very nature, vague enough not to offend. So anyone who expects a candidate to give a detailed, specific solution to the major problems facing this country never will be satisfied. It just won't happen.

6 There also are some facts about the media that must be acknowledged. With the exception of some magazines, newspapers, and seldom-listened-to segments of the broadcast media, no media in 1992, especially the broadcast media, will take the time to explore any issue in depth. Journalists complain that we are now in the 10-second sound bite era. But who put us there?—those who run the most popular of the mass media. These producers used to be journalists. Now they mostly are concerned with business and entertainment decisions and have decided, using ratings and surveys as their guides, that people want their news quick and clean, delivered by cheerful, friendly faces. Nothing is ever put into context because context takes too long. The print media, desperate in the face of declining audiences, have followed suit. With rare exceptions, the story becomes what slip the candidate made today, personally or politically. Few media take the time to publish hard information, even when that information is made available.

7 Those who bemoan the talk show format that has reached new heights of popularity this election year forget that many voters have grown disillusioned with journalists who seem more and more like frustrated district attorneys. The candidates, fearful of making mistakes that can cost them thousands of votes, seldom respond to specific, even hostile questioning about inconsistencies in their statements. They refuse to move from positions that are fuzzy on details because they know that the more specific they get, the more votes they will lose. One reason press conferences have become so hurtful to the political process is that the candidate, who may be lying or cheating or denying on-the-record facts, looks sympathetic to viewers tired of reporters who appear rude, arrogant, and disrespectful while pressing a point, no matter how legitimate their line of questioning may be.

8 So why not the talk show or call-in format? How different is that from the old town hall community meetings or whistle-stop train tours with candidates throwing out carefully honed statements to people asking questions?

9 Bill Clinton's give and take with teenagers on MTV proved

to be one of the best sessions seen or heard anywhere. When Clinton suggested that his MTV audience had more to lose than he did because they had their entire lives ahead of them, the lesson hit home that all of this is not trivial, that the political process concerns everyone. If that message comes through loud and clear—that it is time for Americans of all ages to pay attention, to make their vote count—then the rediscovery of viewer call-in campaigning will have made a significant contribution to the life of this confused democracy.

HOW GOOD IS THIS FILM?

Malcolm X *was released in mid-November 1992 to great fanfare. Indeed, half a dozen major national magazines, including* Newsweek, Ebony, *and* The New Yorker, *ran cover stories on the film, its director Spike Lee, its subject Malcolm X, or its leading man Denzel Washington. Later it was nominated for numerous awards.*

But just how good was the film? The three reviews that follow represent the range of opinions recorded on the movie. On November 18, 1992, Vincent Canby reviewed the film for The New York Times. *Canby (born 1924) is a well-known essayist, novelist, and playwright who has reviewed films for nearly three decades. J. Hoberman's review, which follows Canby's, appeared on November 24, 1992, in* The Village Voice, *the liberal and irreverent weekly newspaper that spends much of its space reviewing developments in the popular arts. The final review was written by Terrence Rafferty, also a well-known critic, and published in* The New Yorker *on November 30, 1992.*

Vincent Canby

Malcolm X: As Complex as Its Subject

1 Malcolm X lived a dozen different lives, each in its way a defining aspect of the black American experience from nightmare to dream. There was never any in-between for the man who was initially called Malcolm Little, the son of a Nebraska preacher, and who, when he died, was known by his Muslim name, El-Hajj Malik El-Shabazz. Malcolm traveled far, through many incarnations to become as much admired as he was feared as the black liberation movement's most militant spokesman and unrelenting conscience.

2 Malcolm was already something of a myth when he was assassinated at the Audubon Ballroom in New York on Feb.

21, 1965, just three months short of his 40th birthday. The publication later that year of "The Autobiography of Malcolm X," his remarkably vivid testament written with Alex Haley, eventually consolidated his position as a great American folk hero, someone whose life speaks with uncanny pertinence to succeeding generations, white as well as black.

Taking the autobiography and a screenplay by Arnold Perl 3
that was begun more than 20 years ago (Perl died in 1971), Spike Lee has attempted the impossible and almost brought it off. His new "Malcolm X" is not exactly the equal, or even the equivalent, of the book, but it's an ambitious, tough, seriously considered biographical film that, with honor, eludes easy characterization.

"Malcolm X" will offend many people for all the wrong 4
reasons. It is neither so inflammatory as Mr. Lee's statements about it would have you believe nor so comforting as might be wished by those who would call a halt to speculation concerning Malcolm's murder. It is full of color and exuberance as it tells of life on the streets in Boston and New York, but it grows increasingly austere when Malcolm is arrested for theft and sent to prison, where he finds his life's mission. The movie becomes proper, well mannered and somber, like Malcolm's dark suits and narrow ties, as it dramatizes his rise in the Nation of Islam, founded by Elijah Muhammad.

Mr. Lee treats the Nation of Islam and its black separatist 5
teachings seriously and, just as seriously, Malcolm's disillusionment when Elijah Muhammad's fondness for pretty young secretaries is revealed. When, after his split from the Nation of Islam, Malcolm goes on his pilgrimage to Mecca, the film celebrates his new insight into racial brotherhood, which makes his assassination all the more sorrowful.

In the film's view, a god has been recognized, then lost. 6

Mr. Lee means for "Malcolm X" to be an epic, and it is in 7
its concerns and its physical scope. In Denzel Washington it also has a fine actor who does for "Malcolm X" what Ben Kingsley did for "Gandhi." Mr. Washington not only looks the part, but he also has the psychological heft, the intelligence and the reserve to give the film the dramatic excitement that isn't always apparent in the screenplay.

This isn't a grave fault, nor is it singular. Biographical 8
films, except those about romantic figures long since dead

like "Lawrence of Arabia," carry with them responsibilities that tend to inhibit. Mr. Lee has not been inhibited so much as simultaneously awe struck and hard pressed.

9 "Malcolm X" is frank about what it sees as the murder conspiracy, which involves a combination of people representing the Nation of Islam and the Federal Bureau of Investigation. Yet in trying to cover Malcolm's life from his boyhood to his death, it sometimes seems more breathlessly desperate than cogently revealing.

10 The movie picks up Malcolm's story in the 1940's on his arrival in wartime Boston as a bright but square teen-ager from rural Michigan. Malcolm eagerly falls in with the wrong crowd, initially represented by Shorty (Mr. Lee), a street hustler who shows him how to dress (a pearl gray zoot suit) and introduces him to the fast set at the Roseland Ballroom. Malcolm learns how to Lindy and how to wheel and deal. He discovers women and drugs. In addition to his attachment to Laura (Theresa Randle), a sweet young black woman, he develops a far steamier liaison with a thrill-seeking young white woman, Sophia, played by Kate Vernon, who looks a lot like Carroll Baker in her "Baby Doll" days.

11 As the film moves forward from the 40's, it suffers spasms of flashbacks to Malcolm's childhood in Nebraska and Michigan. These are so fragmented that they may mean nothing to anyone who hasn't read the autobiography. They also don't do justice to the early experiences themselves, especially to Malcolm's time in a white foster home where he excelled in school and was encouraged by well-meaning adults who did not hesitate to refer to him as a "nigger."

12 Mr. Lee is very good in his handling of individual sequences, but until very near the end, "Malcolm X" fails to acquire the momentum that makes everything that happens seem inevitable. The film goes on and on in a kind of reverential narrative monotone.

13 The story of Malcolm X is fraught with pitfalls for any movie maker. Mr. Lee is creating a film about a man he admires for an audience that includes those who have a direct interest in the story, those who may not have an interest but know the details intimately and those who know nothing or only parts of the story. It's a tricky situation for anyone committed to both art and historical truth.

Mr. Lee's method is almost self-effacing. He never appears to stand between the material and the audience. He himself does not preach. There are no carefully inserted speeches designed to tell the audience what it should think. He lets Malcolm speak and act for himself. The moments of confrontational melodrama, something for which Mr. Lee has a particular gift, are quite consciously underplayed. 14

In this era of aggressive anti-intellectualism, the film's most controversial subtext might not even be recognized: Malcolm's increasing awareness of the importance of language in his struggle to raise black consciousness. Vaguely articulated feelings aren't enough. Ideas can be expressed only through a command of words. 15

Before Mr. Lee came to the "Malcolm X" project, other people had worked on it. In addition to Perl's screenplay, there were adaptations by James Baldwin, David Mamet, Calder Willingham, David Bradley and Charles Fuller. In retrospect, it's easy to see what their difficulties might have been. 16

Though the autobiography is full of characters and incidents, they are only peripheral to the larger story of Malcolm's awkward journey toward intellectual and spiritual enlightenment. Then too, Malcolm's life ended before the journey could be said to have been completed. This is not the sort of thing movies accommodate with ease. 17

"Malcolm X" never bursts with the free-flowing energy of the director's own fiction, but that's a reflection of the genre, the subject and Mr. Lee's sense of mission. Though the film is being promoted with all sorts of merchandise on the order of T-shirts and baseball caps, the one item that promotes it best is the new book,"By Any Means Necessary: The Trials and Tribulations of the Making of 'Malcolm X,'" by Mr. Lee with Ralph Wiley, published by Hyperion. 18

In addition to the screenplay, the book has an extensive report on the research Mr. Lee did before starting the production. Among the people he interviewed was the Rev. Louis Farrakhan, who succeeded Elijah Muhammad as the head of the Nation of Islam. It was apparently a polite encounter, but Mr. Lee remains sharp, skeptical and uninhibited. He's not a reporter to let anyone else have the last word. It's this sort of liveliness that is most missed in the film. 19

J. Hoberman

Rating *X*

1 Spike Lee's most arduous attempt to do the right thing, *Malcolm X* redefines the notion of grace under pressure. Was ever a movie more burdened with expectations? Has any Hollywood production received more prerelease publicity in the 53 years since *Gone With the Wind?* (The PR blitz even included the first personality cover in the history of *The New Yorker* magazine.) *X* is as awkward as it is forceful, but there's scarcely a dull moment. The movie hurtles across the finish line and into your life as though grateful to make it in one piece.

2 If Malcolm X is the embodiment of African American rage, the signifier of blackness (or, at least, male blackness), it is in part because he is thus far beyond white co-optation. As a Hollywood movie, however, *Malcolm X* necessarily complicates this. I can't think of a Hollywood product with more raison d'être— which is another way of saying that the discourse surrounding this three-hour-and-21-minute epic ultimately does more to justify the movie than vice versa. Indeed, *X* would be a significant event for the credit sequence alone: Lee alternates a screen-filling American flag with the video realness of Rodney King's beating, scoring this primal montage to one of Malcolm's more corrosive denunciations of the white race. As he preaches, the flag burns down to an iconic X.

3 The opening is a tough act to follow, and, nothing if not studied, *X* is actually a fairly cautious movie. Selectively uncompromising and essentially didactic, it's the culmination of Lee's media high-wire act as well as his learn-while-you-earn aesthetic. This is the sort of film where key images or juxtapositions detach themselves from the narrative for once and future reference—the close-up pan over a row of African American faces listening, as if for the first time, to the Black Muslim cosmology; the comparison of the dictionary definitions of black and white.

4 In *The Autobiography of Malcolm X,* a literary work in the tradition of *Up From Slavery* or *The Autobiography of an Ex-Colored Man,* Malcolm sculpted the myth of his life. The book maps his transformation from victimized child Malcolm Little to Harlem hustler Detroit Red to a prisoner so recalcitrant the guards called him "Satan" to the Black

Muslim minister Malcolm X to the Muslim dissident El-Hajj Malik El-Shabazz assassinated at the Audubon Ballroom in February 1965. Several movies in one, *Malcolm X* follows the original James Baldwin screenplay (a relic from the days when Hollywood produced *Ché*) in interpolating flashbacks from Malcolm's childhood—his accounts of a Klan attack on his family house and of his father's murder—into the tale of his criminal career.

The mix doesn't jell, although the first hour of pre-X 5
Malcolm may have had the greatest appeal for Lee. It's certainly long enough and echoes the themes of his previous films. The barbershop philosophy and jitterbug display suggest *School Daze* as the tormented relationship between Malcolm and his white girlfriend nods to *Jungle Fever* and the lovingly recreated jazz milieu recalls *Mo' Better Blues*. The time frame permits a dense musical mix that starts with Louis Jordan and incorporates all manner of black bands (Chick Webb, Count Basie) to wind up with a dramatized performance by Billie Holiday; the zoot suits were so irresistible that Lee cast himself as Malcolm's pal Shorty. The mode is more gangster derring-do than spiritual degradation—something Lee acknowledges with a scene of his character and Malcolm playing at Cagney and Bogart. Lee contributes a memorable scene of Russian roulette to Malcolm's myth and underscores his theory of straightened hair by having him busted while cooling his conked head in the toilet bowl. Still, it's a relief to escape the allover razzmatazz for the restricted drama of the prison.

Despite the materialization in his cell of the Honorable 6
Elijah Muhammad (Al Freeman Jr.), Malcolm's conversion seems less a factor of faith than brains. (Once he becomes a Muslim minister, his ultimate put-down is a cool "that's not intelligent.") The Malcolm of *X* is more a sardonic social critic than a religious zealot. Writing in Joe Wood's important anthology, *Malcolm X: In Our Own Image,* to which Lee's film seems one more contribution, Marlon Riggs calls Malcolm "the quintessential unfinished text." That text, of course, allows for erasures. *X* not only upgrades Malcolm's wardrobe, it drops the more extravagant details of the Muslim cosmology, downplays the doomsday tone of Malcolm's rhetoric, and omits specific embarrassments (Malcolm's meeting with the KKK on behalf of the Muslims, the Nation's views on Jews).

Not that *X* is not a movie of ideas. Denzel Washington's 7

remarkably supple and surprisingly good-natured performance is informed in each metamorphosis by the opalescence of his thinking. The scenes of Malcolm preaching on Harlem streets (where his rivals include Bobby Seale and the Reverend Al Sharpton) or razzing Christians coming out of church are crisply lucid. It's not just the now fashionable austerity of Malcolm's provocatively square neo-Rotarian look; the movie is very much concerned with the power of language.

8 *X* soars on the wings of Malcolm's rhetoric—and Denzel Washington's uncanny, often smiling, interpretation. As Malcolm calls for complete separation of the races, Elijah Muhammad beams beside him like a warming sun. (Freeman, who played Malcolm X in *Roots: The Next Generation,* nearly steals every scene with his chirping delivery and constricted, oddball rhythms.) When Malcolm goes on TV to explain his "X" or debate a middle-class opponent (and demolish him as a "house nigger"), he fully embodies the star quality Riggs says defines Malcolm: "a 'bad nigger' who looked like an academician, and at times spoke like an academician."

9 Malcolm's speeches provide the best dialogue in *X* (and Lee occasionally enhances them by inserting televised footage of brutal civil rights demonstrations). But the film turns stiff and mawkish whenever Malcolm's personal life comes into play. Not every scene flops—through pure persistence Lee can sometimes push a lifeless exchange to an emotional pitch. But the most naturalistic aspect of Malcolm's domestic sphere, after he marries Betty Shabazz (dourly played by Angela Bassett, the career mom in *Boyz N the Hood*), is the cheap furniture in their narrow Elmhurst house. The mode is hagiographic and Lee even tricks the FBI into helping him out. (The agent bugging Malcolm's phone tells his colleague that, "compared to King, this guy is a monk.")

10 While Malcolm's break with the Nation and his pilgrimage to Mecca are necessarily compressed, the movie begins to come full circle when the Muslims firebomb his house. Although more might have been made of the narrative parallels, once Lee uses Jr. Walker's "Shotgun" to light the fuse for the death montage, the mad confusion in the Audubon Ballroom after Malcolm is assassinated provides a nightmare reprise of the Savoy scenes. (This tumultuous sequence is the most powerful piece of editing in the movie.)

Malcolm was a genius of apocalyptic rhetoric, but he was murdered early in the era of apocalyptic deeds. Thus *X* ends with a combination of pamphleteering and showmanship. Ossie Davis delivers his historical funeral eulogy over a newsreel montage that draws attention away from the movie's artifice and gratifies a desire to see the actual Malcolm—"the Elvis of black pop politics" as he's called in Greg Tate's contribution to the Wood anthology. Lee then tops that by producing the living Nelson Mandela, in the way that Sean Connery graced the set for the final moments of *Robin Hood: Prince of Thieves*. 11

Lee, who considers himself second only to Madonna as a self-promoter (academics may prefer the term "mass culture semiotician"), combines the Pop Art acumen of Andy Warhol with the street-smart populism of Melvin Van Peebles, who made prophetic use of "X" (as in X-rating) paraphernalia 20 years ago to publicize *Sweet Sweetback's Baadasss Song*. Lee is, as the studios say, bankable, and *Malcolm X* demonstrates that he can also cut a rug—the climax of one musical number has him sliding into the camera like a third Nicholas Brother. 12

Does *Malcolm X* work as a movie? Like *School Daze, Jungle Fever,* and particularly, *Do the Right Thing,* it's a contribution to a national discourse. So can't we just talk? (I'd be a lot more interested in Justice Thomas's take on this movie, for example, than any amount of film crit bushwa on why it's badly made.) *Malcolm X* is bound to make some people unhappy but Time Warner should be pleased. The bottom line is that they've released a movie it behooves every American to see. If that's the least one can say for *X,* it's also the most. 13

Terrence Rafferty

Still Life

1 The most conspicuous achievement of Spike Lee's "Malcolm X" is its very existence—or, rather, its existence in the form of a three-hour-and-twenty-minute epic biography distributed and (largely) financed by a major Hollywood studio. Malcolm's story is not, on the face of it, the likeliest material for prestige-picture treatment. The hero is a smart, fiercely independent-minded ghetto black who spends his youth as a drug addict and a petty crook and his adulthood as a tireless proselytizer for resistance to the inherent racism of white America. His message is bitter, defiant, and unconciliatory, and it offers no comfort either to "well-meaning" white liberals or to black advocates of Martin Luther King, Jr.,'s integrationist philosophy. King's patient, nonviolent approach was to some extent a reflection of his Southern Christian background; Malcolm's world view is the product of the stern discipline of Islam, to which he was converted during a prison stretch. "The Autobiography of Malcolm X"—an as-told-to book, written by Alex Haley and published in 1965, not long after its subject's death—is formally an inspirational narrative, like the "Confessions" of St. Augustine, but the hero's spiritual triumph is couched in terms that are utterly alien to mainstream American society. He begins as an unscrupulous predator, becomes a studious ascetic, and fulfills himself as a scourge. Finding your way through what James Baldwin called "the great jungle of Malcolm's book" is a heady experience for any reader, white or black, because the narrator's voice—insistent, relentless, confoundingly forceful—keeps challenging you to refute its brazen assertions. Much of the autobiography was written after Malcolm broke with the Nation of Islam and its founder, Elijah Muhammad, whom he had revered. By all accounts, it was a period of intense spiritual confusion for him, and that not fully acknowledged uncertainty may be the source of the book's most mysterious, paradoxical quality—the way Malcolm's rhetoric, which is apparently so dogmatic, seems to open readers' minds to the possibility of unique, entirely personal truths. The Malcolm of the autobiography is an extraordinary literary creation—a strong, boldly drawn character whose meaning is fluid, ungraspable, fathomless.

There probably isn't a film maker alive who could do justice to the provocative complexities of Malcolm X's personality. What's disappointing about Lee's "Malcolm X" is that, for all the dedication and care he has lavished on it, the movie remains stubbornly impersonal. We can see that Lee loves Malcolm, even idolizes him, but the picture doesn't give readers of the autobiography anything like a fresh vision of its remarkable subject. Lee follows the contours of Malcolm's life story faithfully, hitting the high points of the book, and those viewers who know nothing about Malcolm, or who know him only by his formidable reputation as a black-pride firebrand, might find everything in the film fascinating, revelatory. "Malcolm X" is probably *intended* for people who don't really know as much as they should about the subject—for young urban blacks who have heard the name on rap records and have worn the cap but haven't read the autobiography. The picture has a sort of high-school field-trip quality, an explicitly educational tone. (The last scene takes place in a classroom in present-day Soweto; several children stand up, in succession, and announce "I'm Malcolm X," and then their teacher, Nelson Mandela, reads a passage from one of Malcolm's most famous speeches.) There's a great deal of passion in "Malcolm X," but it's not an artist's passion; the responses Lee aims for are the clear, pedagogically effective ones rather than the disturbing, irresolvable ones that Malcolm's own account evokes on virtually every page. I wouldn't presume to guess what effect the movie may have on inner-city kids. To me Lee's approach feels static and reductive, more functional than inspired. "Malcolm X" is as stately and as reverent as "Gandhi." 2

Lee assumes Malcolm's greatness and then simply illustrates it, with a series of lovingly detailed tableaux from the autobiography. He doesn't solve the fundamental problem of this life story, which is that the pilgrim's progress of the hero is a spiritual and intellectual journey. After Malcolm's wild youth, his private life consists of quiet, solitary self-education and watchful adherence to his religion's austere tenets; and his public action is almost exclusively verbal—he gives speeches and appears on talk shows. Malcolm X was a militant orator, but he wasn't, in the practical sense, an activist; unlike Gandhi (and King), he didn't accomplish anything concrete. (Elijah Muhammad, it should be noted, forbade political involvement by the Nation of Islam, so 3

Malcolm didn't have much choice.) In movie terms, this life isn't very dramatic. It would take a more radical artist than Spike Lee to give shape and visual force to Malcolm's internal conflicts; the ponderous rhythms of the great-man bio-pic only emphasize the impossibility of rendering this story with conventional movie-narrative means.

4 More than twenty years ago, James Baldwin took a crack at imagining Malcolm for the big screen. His script (which is in print, under the title "One Day, When I Was Lost") is a densely textured, impressionistic portrait of a mercurial personality, and although it's classically unfilmable, it plays beautifully in the reader's mind: it *interprets* Malcolm—passes the facts of his life through the critical consciousness of a sympathetic, penetrating artist. The screenplay of "Malcolm X," credited to Lee and Arnold Perl (who reworked Baldwin's original in the early seventies), uses scenes and some structural ideas from the Baldwin scenario, but in a haphazard way. Lee's choices are often strange—sometimes totally inexplicable. In the dissipated-youth passages, which account for the first hour or so of the film, we see Malcolm (Denzel Washington) swaggering through the streets, night clubs, bars, and hotels of Roxbury and Harlem, his life of crime moving to the infectious beat of jump blues, boogie-woogie, and swing-era big-band jazz. (The source music—Lionel Hampton, Basie, Ellington, Billie Holiday, Ella Fitzgerald, Big Joe Turner, Louis Jordan—is a marvellous sampler of black music of the forties.) We do not, however, see him—as Malcolm eventually saw himself—as a depraved parasite, feeding unscrupulously on both the pathetic illusions of his black brothers and sisters and the perverse desires of whites. Lee's Malcolm does a little numbers running, snorts cocaine once, and participates in an antically staged burglary. The autobiography and Baldwin's script show him selling dope, steering rich white men to whip-wielding black whores, and becoming crazed and violent from constant coke use. It's wise of Lee to modify the hellfire moralism that the autobiography imposes on Malcolm's early life as a ghetto hustler; the movie conveys some of the beauty and joyful vitality of that era's urban black culture, the sense of community that provided relief (if not salvation) from the daily grind of oppression. This period of Malcolm's life, full of flamboyant characters and pungent gangster atmosphere, is, after all, the most movie-friendly material in the whole story; if you don't make this stuff vivid

and exciting, your picture is in serious trouble. But the soft-pedalling of the hero's criminal activities undermines the dramatic (and emotional) coherence of his jailhouse conversion to the rigorous philosophy of Islam. Without evidence of true degradation, Malcolm's abrupt and total moral about-face feels even more like an overreaction than it should: he seems to be punishing himself for having had too good a time.

Malcolm was temperamentally an extremist—in each of his contradictory incarnations, he went all the way—but every radical swerve he made had some strong justification. His life was a dialectic, not a linear argument, and the conversion sequences in "Malcolm X" are the movie's worst failure, because Lee doesn't dramatize coherently the back-and-forth movement of his hero's consciousness: he springs the antithesis on us without ever having established the thesis. It's difficult not to feel that the movie is just marking time in these passages, holding on until Malcolm is released from prison and into his public life. When the merely human Malcolm bursts forth as the mythic Malcolm X, the famous preacher who inspires his people and scares the wits out of the white "devil" that keeps them down, Washington's performance takes a huge leap forward in power and authority. (His work in the early scenes is inventive but spotty: no actor in his mid-thirties should be required to play a teen-ager.) And Al Freeman, Jr., enlivens the picture periodically with a wonderfully sly turn as the gnomelike, enigmatic Elijah Muhammad. But everything else about the movie, in this final and supposedly climactic phase, feels inert. There's something about achieved celebrity that tends to stall a story's narrative momentum. And that's especially true in this case, because of the nature of Malcolm's celebrity: he was famous for what he said (or, more broadly, for what he represented), rather than for what he did. We gaze at the larger-than-life figure; we listen to his oratory; nothing, save for the internal squabbling of the Nation of Islam leadership, is actually happening. 5

Lee may not realize just how boring public figures—even figures as charismatic as Malcolm—really are: they're fixed, objects of contemplation. Malcolm himself, in the baffled final months of his life, complained to Alex Haley that he was trapped by people's perceptions of him—immobilized in his image, and unable to "turn the corner." Lee—whose aesthetic philosophy, shared with Oliver Stone, might be 6 expressed as *Koppelo ergo sum* ("I appear on 'Nightline,' therefore I am")—probably hasn't reached that frightening point himself. Or maybe the filmmaker has simply been undone by a worshipful attitude toward his subject. At times, it feels as if all the movie wanted to do were to create a recognizable image of Malcolm X, a statue for us to look up at in wonder. Oddly, there's more of the spirit of Malcolm X in Terrence Blanchard's soundtrack music than there is in the often spectacular sights Lee has put on the screen. The music weaves in and out of a couple of hauntingly lovely themes, constantly reorchestrating them or working subtle jazz variations on them, so that every time we hear them they sound different and seem to mean something different. This music understands that the X in Malcolm X—the symbol with which Malcolm cancelled out his slave name, Little—is also, poetically, the lowercase *x* of mathematical symbolism: the variable, the unknown value you have to search for. Spike Lee's "Malcolm X" gives you the answer right away and thus deprives you of the deepest meaning of Malcolm's adventure: the pleasure and satisfaction of thinking the problem through in your own way, in your own time.

WHAT DO YOU MAKE OF RAP AND 2 LIVE CREW?

Jon Pareles

Rap: Slick, Violent, Nasty, and, Maybe, Hopeful

The following essay appeared in The New York Times *on June 17, 1990, within a couple of days of the ones that follow it in this section of this book. Jon Pareles is the rock music critic of the* Times.

Rap music now has a criminal record. On June 6, United States District Court Judge Jose Gonzalez of Fort Lauderdale, Fla., declared that "As Nasty as They Wanna Be," an album by the 2 Live Crew, a rap group that is based in Miami, was obscene in the three counties under his jurisdiction, making it the first recording to be declared obscene by a Federal court. In the next few days, a record-store owner who had continued to sell the album was arrested; two members of the group were also arrested for performing one of the album's songs before an adults-only audience. 1

It was only the latest, if potentially the most far-reaching of rap's skirmishes with mainstream culture. As the voice of the young black male, rap has become a vivid, contentious cultural symbol. From its beginnings in the mid-1970's—when rap was part of New York's emerging hip-hop subculture, which also included break dancing and graffiti art—rap has been met by condescension, rejection and outright fear from those outside its domain. 2

Although rappers have made a point of denouncing black-on-black crime, many promoters refuse to book rap concerts fearing the audience would include violent members of a troubled community already plagued by crime. Some radio stations choose not to play rap music because their research 3 shows that the music alienates many listeners. People who monitor rock lyrics—from pop critics to the Parents' Music Resource Center (a group that advocates voluntary warning stickers on potentially offensive albums) to the Gay and Lesbian Alliance Against Defamation—worry about some rappers' overt homophobia, sexism and other bigotry along with their descriptions of violence.

4 To many listeners, white and black, rap is the sound of a threatening underclass—although, increasingly, suburbanites as well as urban teen-agers are embracing rap, which includes tall tales, jokes, ethical advice, political statements and baroquely exuberant metaphorical flights. Like the punk rock that appeared almost simultaneously in the 1970's, rap has as much to do with attitude as with conventionally defined musical skills. Rappers live by their wit—their ability to rhyme, the speed of their articulation—and by their ability to create outsized personas through words alone.

5 "The skills you need to be a good rapper are the same skills you need to get ahead in mainstream society," said Philippe Bourgois, an assistant professor of anthropology at San Francisco State University who is writing a book, "Scrambling," about street culture. "You have to write well and speak well in a creative manner, which are exactly the skills you need in an information-processing city like New York. And rap is about making something of yourself—it's the American dream.

6 Put simply, rap is an affirmation of self. It might define that self as successful, well paid, flaunting status symbols like jewelry and cars. And often, it defines that self as a sexually insatiable guy with a touch of the outlaw—an exaggerated version of the demeaning stereotypes young black men have grown up with.

7 "When you're faced with a stereotype, you can disavow it or you can embrace it and exaggerate it to the nth degree," said Henry Louis Gates, the John Spencer Bassett professor of English at Duke University. "The rappers take the white Western culture's worst fear of black men and make a game out of it."

8 With the furor over the 2 Live Crew, rap machismo has undergone ever closer scrutiny. The 2 Live Crew has been accused of misogyny and glorifying abuse of women. Yet while their rhymes on "As Nasty as They Wanna Be"

are openly, loutishly sexist, treating women entirely as objects, the lyrics are so single-mindedly concerned with self-gratification that the consequences for women don't seem to enter their minds.

Taken literally, the bulk of rap songs (like much heavy-metal rock) reveal adolescent attitudes toward women, who are often presented as either materialistic and cold or easy sexual conquests. But not all rap machismo should be taken entirely at face value. Like other black literary and oral traditions, rap lyrics also involve double-entendre, allegory and parody. Some rap machismo can be a metaphor for pride or political empowerment; it can be a shared joke, as it often is in 2 Live Crew's wildly hyperbolic rhymes. And while machismo has been a convention during rap's first decade, it is now under fire from female rappers like Queen Latifah and Roxanne Shanté. 9

By bringing the fractured rhythms and unlikely juxtapositions of the television age to the dance floor, rap revolutionized popular music and became the commercial success story of the 1980's. The recent No. 1 album on the Billboard pop charts was "Please Hammer Don't Hurt 'Em" by the Oakland rapper M. C. Hammer. 10

Over the last decade, while major record companies waited for the supposed fad to run its course, street-level independent labels made fortunes from rap hits. Now all the major companies have signed rap groups, and rap has its own daily show on MTV, where "Yo! MTV Raps" garners some of the cable channel's highest ratings. Rap is out of the ghetto. 11

While there are a few female rappers, and a handful of white rappers, rap is still an overwhelmingly black male style. Rap emerged when disk jockeys at clubs and parties in the South Bronx began improvising rhymes over the instrumentals of dance records, perhaps inspired by Jamaican disk jockeys or "toasters" who had been doing the same thing. It spread and diversified. Soon there were specialists in rhyming, or M.C.'s, and virtuosic disk jockeys, who created a musical backdrop by intercutting shorter and shorter pieces of more and more records, often "scratching" the records—twitching them backward and forward under the needle—to create percussive sounds. 12

Early rap mixed party chants with the braggadocio of the 13

blues, jailhouse chants and the dozens, a primarily male game of escalating insults. But soon after the first rap recordings appeared, at the end of the 1970's, some songs took on deeper content. With "The Breaks" by Kurtis Blow in 1980 and "The Message" by Grandmaster Flash and the Furious Five featuring Melle Mel in 1982, rap began to talk about ghetto life, often with humorous or belligerent candor.

14 Rap evolved fast. Using turntables and drum machines, rap groups could cut a single in a basement, and rap entrepreneurs could press records quickly and sell them from the trunks of their cars. As the music changed, stars and styles rose and fell within months. In its constantly changing slang and shifting concerns—no other pop has so many antidrug songs—rap's flood of words presents a fictionalized oral history of a brutalized generation.

15 "The difference between public culture and private culture has disappeared," Mr. Gates said. "There was material that was exclusively the province of the black oral tradition and race-record tradition, but now people have decided to cross the line. People like Keenan Ivory Wayans and Spike Lee and Eddie Murphy, along with the rappers, they're saying all the things that we couldn't say even in the 1960's about our own excesses, things we could only whisper in dark rooms. They're saying we're going to explode all these sacred cows. It's fascinating, and it's upsetting everybody—not just white people but black people. But it's a liberating moment."

16 Where the old style was mostly bragging—and went with a fashion statement of fat gold chains and other showy possessions—current rap embraces jokers, nice guys, bawdy fantasists, storytellers, romantics and political activists. Public Enemy brings black nationalist and Black Muslim ideas of self-determination to rap's most advanced sonic collages, sometimes with divisive effect. Public Enemy was branded anti-Semitic because of statements by a member who has since left the group.

17 The controversy was revived when Public Enemy's "Welcome to the Terrordome" alluded to the incident with these cryptic lines: "Crucifixion ain't no fiction/So called chosen frozen/Apology made to whoever pleases/Still they got me

like Jesus." Some listeners interpreted the lyrics as blaming the Jews for crucifying Christ.

N.W.A. and Ice-T chant stylized, calmly observed tales of ghetto violence, including N.W.A.'s infamous (and widely misread) "— Tha Police," which starts with a scene of police brutality and ends with what a band member has called a "revenge fantasy" about shooting policemen. In an unusual response to an artistic work, the Federal Bureau of Investigation wrote a letter to the band's record company complaining that the song advocated violence against police officers. 18

"I see rap as reflective," Mr. Bourgois said, "and what people should be scared about is the extent to which the songs reflect reality. That there is such unbelievable violence in these communities is a national tragedy, while the fact that people express themselves in terms of violence is a part of American culture, a way of thinking that goes back to the Wild West. I wouldn't worry about rap music leading to violence. On the contrary, rap music leads to a productive expression of alienation and oppression, and it's good that it gets channeled into creative outlets rather than drug addiction or physical violence. I see people, high-school dropouts, who carry around notebooks in their back pockets so they can compare their latest rhymes." 19

Of all the complaints against rap, the one that seems most unequivocal is about homophobia. Too few rappers can resist making some sort of swipe at gays, often taking a detour in a song to do so and rarely suggesting any double meaning. It seems an unexamined prejudice. 20

Rap's remarkable rate of change may make some complaints quickly obsolete. In a short time, simple boasts have given way to multileveled storytelling and political comment; when some rappers made a connection between gold chains and the South African gold industry, many rappers' neckwear of choice became leather Africa medallions instead of gold "dooky ropes." It's conceivable that a newer generation will not take sexism and homophobia so lightly. Rap will no doubt continue to reveal the tensions of the communities it speaks to. But with its humor, intelligence and fast-talking grace, it may also represent a way to transcend those tensions. 21

Henry Louis Gates
2 Live Crew, Decoded

Henry Louis Gates (born 1950) wrote the following essay while he was teaching at Duke University, but he has since moved to Harvard, where he heads the Afro-American Studies program. The article appeared in The New York Times *on June 19, 1990, two days after the previous article by Jon Pareles and the following ones by David Mills and Juan Williams. Gates, winner of many awards and prizes, is well known for his scholarship on African-American literature and culture.*

1 The rap group 2 Live Crew and their controversial hit recording "As Nasty as They Wanna Be" may well earn a signal place in the history of First Amendment rights. But just as important is how these lyrics will be interpreted and by whom.

2 For centuries, African-Americans have been forced to develop coded ways of communicating to protect them from danger. Allegories and double meanings, words redefined to mean their opposites ("bad" meaning "good," for instance), even neologisms ("bodacious") have enabled blacks to share messages only the initiated understood.

3 Many blacks were amused by the transcripts of Marion Barry's sting operation, which reveals that he used the traditional black expression about one's "nose being opened." This referred to a love affair and not, as Mr. Barry's prosecutors have suggested, to the inhalation of drugs. Understanding this phrase could very well spell the difference (for the Mayor) between prison and freedom.

4 2 Live Crew is engaged in heavy-handed parody, turning the stereotypes of black and white American culture on their heads. These young artists are acting out, to lively dance music, a parodic exaggeration of the age-old stereotypes of the oversexed black female and male. Their exuberant use of hyperbole (phantasmagoric sexual organs, for example) undermines—for anyone fluent in black cultural codes—a too literal-minded hearing of the lyrics.

5 This is the street tradition called "signifying" or "playing the dozens," which has generally been risqué, and where the best signifier or "rapper" is the one who invents the most extravagant images, the biggest "lies," as the culture says.

(H. "Rap" Brown earned his nickname in just this way.) In the face of racist stereotypes about black sexuality, you can do one of two things: you can disavow them or explode them with exaggeration.

2 Live Crew, like many "hip-hop" groups, is engaged in sexual carnivalesque. Parody reigns supreme, from a take-off of standard blues to a spoof of the black power movement; their off-color nursery rhymes are part of a venerable Western tradition. The group even satirizes the culture of commerce when it appropriates popular advertising slogans ("Tastes great!" "Less filling!") and puts them in a bawdy context. 6

2 Live Crew must be interpreted within the context of black culture generally and of signifying specifically. Their novelty, and that of other adventuresome rap groups, is that their defiant rejection of euphemism now voices for the mainstream what before existed largely in the "race record" market—where the records of Redd Foxx and Rudy Ray Moore once were forced to reside. 7

Rock songs have always been about sex but have used elaborate subterfuges to convey that fact. 2 Live Crew uses Anglo-Saxon words and is self-conscious about it: a parody of a white voice in one song refers to "private personal parts," as a coy counterpart to the group's bluntness. 8

Much more troubling than its so-called obscenity is the group's overt sexism. Their sexism is so flagrant, however, that it almost cancels itself out in a hyperbolic war between the sexes. In this, it recalls the inter-sexual jousting in Zora Neale Hurston's novels. Still, many of us look toward the emergence of more female rappers to redress sexual stereotypes. And we must not allow ourselves to sentimentalize street culture: the appreciation of verbal virtuosity does not lessen one's obligation to critique bigotry in all of its pernicious forms. 9

Is 2 Live Crew more "obscene" than, say, the comic Andrew Dice Clay? Clearly, this rap group is seen as more threatening than others that are just as sexually explicit. Can this be completely unrelated to the specter of the young black male as a figure of sexual and social disruption, the very stereotypes 2 Live Crew seems determined to undermine? 10

This question—and the very large question of obscenity and the First Amendment—cannot even be addressed until those who would answer them become literate in the ver- 11 nacular traditions of African-Americans. To do less is to censor through the equivalent of intellectual prior restraint—and censorship is to art what lynching is to justice.

David Mills

Criminalizing Black Culture

David Mills, a staff writer for The Washington Post, *wrote the following article for the* Post *on June 17, 1990—the same day as the preceding article, by Jon Pareles, and the following one, by Juan Williams.*

1 A rap fan in Tennessee sent me a letter last month, before a U.S. district judge in Florida declared the 2 Live Crew's latest album obscene, and before the Crew's leader, Luther Campbell, was arrested and manacled because of words uttered during a nightclub performance, words uttered to an audience of paying adults.

2 "I do not think that 2 Live Crew is actually on trial," the young man wrote. "I believe that black expression as a whole is on trial. . . . And if 2 Live Crew are found to be obscene, other forms of black expression will be targeted. This could act as the catalyst for anti-black censorship of a much greater scale."

3 Paranoia? Or does the banning of "As Nasty as They Wanna Be" in southern Florida indeed represent an immediate threat to free speech, especially the speech of African American young men?

4 Consider the experience of other popular—and foul-mouthed—rappers. Before a 1988 concert in Columbus, Ga., police officers warned Ice-T that he'd be arrested if he uttered certain profane words onstage, he says. Ice-T performed one song and canceled the rest of the show. Last summer, members of N.W.A. (Niggers With Attitudes) were chased out of Detroit's Joe Louis Arena by the police after the rappers, egged on by a chanting crowd, began performing their masterpiece of vituperation, "[Expletive] tha Police." And in Cincinnati, the town that so dutifully tried to

protect its citizens from the photographs of Robert Mapplethorpe, a judge fined members of N.W.A. $100 apiece for "offensively coarse utterances" between songs during a Riverfront Coliseum show.

The criminalization of a challenging form of black expres- 5
siveness raises some urgent questions. Should federal courts be determining the artistic worth of products of the African American culture? Just what artistic worth can there be in a collection of songs as violently raunchy and mean-spirited as 2 Live Crew's "As Nasty as They Wanna Be"?

Where are the black scholars and intellectuals who should 6
be able to place the 2 Live Crew in its cultural context and who, regardless of whatever distaste they may have for the album, must act as the first line of defense when black artists come under attack? And where are the 1.7 million people who have bought "As Nasty as They Wanna Be"? Where is their outrage? It is now a crime in Florida's Broward, Dade and Palm Beach counties to own this album. Anyone—young or old, black or white—who has "Nasty" lying around the house or in the automobile tape deck, is breaking the law. In Florida, possession of obscene material is punishable by up to 60 days in jail and a $500 fine.

E. Ethelbert Miller, director of Howard University's Afro- 7
American Resource Center, says the masses of black people tend to get alarmed only over the issue of racism, and tend to sit out public debates on such "abstract" matters as artistic freedom. He doesn't think that officials who attack "Nasty" are necessarily "singling out African American art. It's a whole climate out there . . . the right-wing social agenda. And this is where I respect the right wing—they're organized."

Miller hasn't heard the 2 Live Crew's album, nor is he 8
much of a rap fan. But as a poet and an opponent of censorship, he defends the group. "At this particular point, because people are politicizing art, what you have to always be protecting is the ability to create. That's the struggle."

"Neither the 'rap' or 'hip-hop' musical genres are on trial," 9
writes U.S. District Judge Jose A. Gonzales Jr. of Fort Lauderdale in the opinion he rendered 11 days ago. "The narrow issue before this court is whether the recording entitled 'As Nasty as They Wanna Be' is legally obscene," and therefore unprotected by the First Amendment. "This court's

role is not to serve as a censor or an art and music critic."

10 Despite this declamation, the judge displays a crucial lack of understanding of rap music and its cultural context when he applies the Supreme Court's three tests for obscenity to "As Nasty as They Wanna Be."

11 Let us accept Gonzales's conclusion that the album meets the first two tests—that it "appeals to the prurient interest" and that, "measured by contemporary community standards, the work depicts or describes, in a patently offensive way, sexual conduct" as defined by state law.

12 Gonzales writes that the 2 Live Crew's lyrics "are replete with references to female and male genitalia, human sexual excretion, oral-anal contact, fellatio, group sex, specific sexual positions, sado-masochism, the turgid state of the male sexual organ, masturbation, cunnilingus, sexual intercourse, and the sounds of moaning."

13 Indeed they are. Luther Campbell has purposefully explored the farthest fringes of comic vulgarity and overblown phallicism. Thus has the 2 Live Crew carved out a niche in the highly competitive rap market.

14 Yet all those lascivious lyrics are perfectly permissible under the First Amendment, unless the album,"taken as a whole, lacks serious literary, artistic, political or scientific value." That is the Supreme Court's third test for obscenity. And it gets to the heart of things: What qualifies U.S. District Judge Jose Gonzales to assess the artistic value of a rap album?

15 In the words of Henry Louis Gates, a Duke University English professor and an expert on African American "vernacular culture": "I don't see how people can jump into somebody else's culture, with completely no knowledge of that culture, and then decide what's obscene and what's not."

16 The Supreme Court says a work must be judged "as a whole." But Gonzales goes to great lengths to justify focusing almost exclusively on the dirty words. The judge, citing "expert testimony," writes that "a central characteristic of 'rap' music is its emphasis on the *verbal* message." He goes on to conclude that "it does not significantly alter the message of the 'Nasty' recording to reduce it to a written transcription."

17 He is absolutely wrong. Apart from the fact that rap is an outgrowth of funk—that it is fundamentally a dance music—rap is not about the words per se. It's about the rendition of

the words. The emphasis is not verbal, it is *oral*. The rappers call it "flow." To misunderstand this is to miss the essence of rap as a vibrant manifestation of the black oral tradition.

Only by listening to the 2 Live Crew, not by reading its lyrics on a sheet of paper, do you realize that their sexual rants aren't to be taken literally. (Just as that bawdy old limerick about a guy named Dave, "who kept a dead whore in his cave," shouldn't be interpreted as a celebration of necrophilia.) Anyone who thinks the song "Put Her in the Buck" is intended as a sex manual—or that rap fans perceive it as such—hasn't heard the goofy way one of the Crew barks out the title. 18

The 2 Live Crew engages in a style of African American ribaldry that is rooted in the inner-city BS heard on street corners and in schoolyards. It's the kind of humor found throughout the '70s on the adults-only "party records" of comedians such as Richard Pryor, Richard and Willie, and Rudy Ray Moore. (Snippets of their material, not coincidentally, can be found on "As Nasty as They Wanna Be".) The "adults-only" designation didn't keep those records out of the hands of teenage fellas back then, who, after all, enjoyed a dirty joke as much as anyone. 19

In court, the group's main argument was that "Nasty" has artistic value as comedy and satire. Gonzales did not agree: "It cannot be reasonably argued that the violence, perversion, abuse of women, graphic depictions of all forms of sexual conduct, and microscopic descriptions of human genitalia contained on this recording are comedic art." 20

This again demonstrates the danger of a cultural outsider passing judgment on something he doesn't understand. Just as you cannot appreciate a rap song by merely reading its lyrics—disregarding its rhythm tracks, disregarding the nuances of its vocalization—you cannot fully understand this profane style of rapping if you disregard the larger folklore of the streets. 21

There are fascinating echoes in today's hard-edged rap music not only of black comedy, but of the low-budget "black exploitation" action movies of the early '70s and the stylized folk performance-poems, called "toasts," that emanated from the world of pimps and hustlers. "As Nasty as They Wanna Be" has real cultural underpinnings. 22

Comedian Rudy Ray Moore, the spiritual godfather of the 2 Live Crew, made a career of recording versions of vulgar, 23 sometimes violent, often sexually exaggerated toasts such as "Dolemite" and "Pimpin' Sam." A member of 2 Live Crew drops a nasty couplet about lesbians rubbing belly to belly in "[Expletive] Almighty"; the same couplet can be found in Moore's version of the ultra-scatological toast "Dance of the Freaks," recorded more than 15 years earlier; and in one written collection of toasts, you can find a version of "Dance of the Freaks" recited by a Sing Sing inmate in 1954.

24 Perhaps the most famous of toasts, the metaphorical jungle tale "The Signifying Monkey," was adapted by tough-guy rapper Schoolly D in 1988. During the '70s, Moore recorded a couple of versions, one in his blaxploitation movie debut, "Dolemite." And Henry Louis Gates, in his scholarly study "The Signifying Monkey: A Theory of African-American Literary Criticism," traces the monkey tale to a trickster figure in West African mythology.

25 Toasts can be so compelling that one of the legendary, radical Last Poets adopted the style (and the name Lightnin' Rod) for his LP "Hustler's Convention" in 1973. Over funky background music from the likes of Kool and the Gang, a criminal flamboyantly spins his underworld tale. "I was a down stud's dream, a hustler supreme. There wasn't no game that I couldn't play. And if I caught a dude cheatin', I would give him a beatin', and I might even blow him away!" By the end of the record, after being beaten and shot by the cops and spending years on death row, this "nickel-and-dime" hustler has become politicized. Some 15 years later, Ice-T released his first album, "Rhyme Pays," a virtual homage to "Hustler's Convention."

26 Between 1972 and 1976, independent film producers and distributors churned out countless action movies with titles such as "Black Gunn," "Black Caesar," "Black Samson," "Black Fist," "The Black Godfather," "Black Samurai" and "Boss Nigger." Designed to appeal, obviously, to the fantasies of young black males, these films were often set in the criminal world.

27 "In the black community of past decades, the old-style pimp had sometimes been viewed as a folk hero of sorts: a smooth-talking, sexy, hip, moneyed man in control of his destiny," writes film historian Donald Bogle in "Blacks in American Films and Television." Describing the 1973 pimp's saga "The Mack," he continues: "By the 1970s, one might

have assumed the pimp would be seen for other things he represented, primarily as an exploiter of women. Instead, young black moviegoers seemed to delight in [the hero's] pretty looks, his firm control over his women, his striking array of material comforts . . . and his tenacious grip on survival."

Although whites usually held financial and creative control over these films, it was the performances of black actors that often resonated. 28

Rappers in their late 20s, such as Luther Campbell, probably have fond memories of watching movies like "The Mack" and "Super Fly" on the big screen. At the end of Public Enemy's "Burn, Hollywood, Burn"—an indictment of the movie industry's depiction of African Americans, from Stepin Fetchit to "Driving Miss Daisy"—guest rapper Big Daddy Kane says, "Yo, check it out, man, I got 'Black Caesar' at the crib. Y'all want to go check that out?" 29

Indeed, with many of those old blaxploitation films now on videocassette, younger rappers have a smorgasbord of macho fantasies to build upon. Take Poison Clan, two 19-year-olds billed as "The Baby 2 Live Crew" and signed to Campbell's Miami-based label, Luke Records (formerly Luke Skywalker Records, until "Star Wars" producer George Lucas sued Campbell). On the upcoming album "2 Low Life Muthas," the Clan's JT boasts that being a pimp is how he can afford "eatin' shrimp." 30

To understand the 2 Live Crew is to realize the difference between being a lowlife and pretending to be a lowlife, the difference between sick, mean humor and true sickness and meanness. "A lot of people fail to see that music is acting," says Debbie Bennett, spokeswoman for Luke Records. Of 2 Live Crew, she says,"You won't find four nicer guys." 31

But it's their pretense, in all its outrageous sexual explicitness, that fits squarely into the tradition of comedy albums and films that draw upon the rich black folklore of the streets. That is the "artistic value" of "As Nasty as They Wanna Be," which entitles it to protection under the First Amendment. That is the context in which the 2 Live Crew must be judged. And that is why U.S. District Judge Jose Gonzales was wrong to declare the album "utterly without any redeeming social value," and why anyone who is serious about the African American popular culture should be disturbed by his ruling. 32

* * *

33 Of course, "just because something comes out of the black culture, just because it has black cultural authenticity, doesn't make it good," says Stanley Crouch, noted jazz critic and essayist. Rap in general is "an expression of a lower aspect of the culture," in his view. The members of 2 Live Crew specifically are "some vulgar street-corner-type clowns," "spiritual cretins," "slime."

34 "We're so defensive about ourselves that we feel that we always have to come forward and defend anything that says it represents black authenticity," Crouch says. "We do not have to celebrate the lowest elements in our society. . . . I look at those people—pimps and hustlers—as parasites. We cannot make a powerful Afro-American culture if we're going to base it on what hustlers and pimps think about the world."

35 No doubt. But "As Nasty as They Wanna Be" is a piece of entertainment, not a blueprint for living. Personally, I don't find the album very entertaining. I am bothered by the meanness of the humor regarding women, just as I am bothered by the jokes of Andrew Dice Clay. But the 2 Live Crew has sold 1.7 million copies of this album, and Clay is packing arenas. Are they driving the culture, or simply reflecting it?

36 Janine McAdams, the black-music columnist for Billboard magazine, says, "I am tired of seeing Luke kicked around the way he has been in a purely political game to quash freedom of expression." On the other hand, after listening to "Nasty" once last year, she says, "I will never pick it up again. I hate it. It disgusts me."

37 "I wish Luther Campbell could demonstrate more respect for women," McAdams says. "I think he thinks it's humorous, and in certain respects I guess it is. . . . I have mixed feelings about it. If people had derogatory thoughts about women, if they had perverted sexual fantasies, they had those thoughts, I'm sure, before Luther came along."

38 Stanley Crouch, by the way, confesses to owning "three or four" raunchy Rudy Ray Moore LPs. "I've had those records for 15 years. I bought 'em because they reminded me of stuff guys said on the street corners when I was growing up. I haven't listened to them in a while." Does Crouch recall finding those records funny? "Yeah, I thought they were kind of comical," he says. But "I have evolved far beyond that."

Juan Williams
Making Heroes of Hate Mongers

Juan Williams, like David Mills a staff writer for The Washington Post, *contributed the following article to the* Post *on June 17, 1990. In fact, it appeared on the same page as the preceding article by Mills.*

Listen to this: Song number one on 2 Live Crew's million-plus seller "As Nasty as They Wanna Be" sings the praise of a man acting "like a dog in heat," and taking pride in breaking the walls of a woman's vagina. Song number two again sings about tearing a woman open before having her "kneel and pray." Song number three raps about the joy of a man forcing anal sex on a woman and later making her lick feces. 1

In Florida a black judge and now a Hispanic judge have ruled that these songs violate that state's obscenity law, prompting a ban on the sale of the record and public performances of the songs in three counties in Florida. In its defense the group's lawyer, Bruce Rogow, argues that the critics may be racists who don't understand black music and that the songs are not meant to be read but danced to by adults who are in a partying mood and appreciate blue humor, and if people don't want to listen to it they don't have to buy it. Luther Campbell, the group's leader, also argues that the lyrics reflect life in America's black neighborhoods. Rogow's ultimate argument is that banning the record amounts to artistic censorship that has resulted in the arrest of record store owners and members of the band. 2

The lawyer's arguments are more interesting than the profane music, but it's all a fake. 3

Racism, partying and even censorship are not the issue here. 2 Live Crew's record is hot—in fact getting hotter by all the talk of censorship in one state—and the group is still touring and making plans for another record that Campbell boasts will be "even more obscene." 4

The real issue is hate-filled music that is abusive of women—especially black women—and an assault on its young audience's budding concepts of good sex, good relationships and good times. Campbell has said he won't let his 7-year-old daughter listen to the music, which routinely refers to women as "bitches." 5

6 Making 2 Live Crew champions in a censorship fight or heroes of black America's battle against racial oppression frees the group from responsibility for making millions of dollars by selling pornography to teenagers. The debate over 2 Live Crew is not the same as that surrounding Robert Mapplethorpe and government support for controversial art. 2 Live Crew is cultivating young audiences with the cheap thrill of sex, violence and gold chains.

7 "Censorship is a red herring in this case," says Jewelle Taylor Gibbs, author of "Young, Black and Male in America: An Endangered Species." "The real issue is values, quality of life. And the real question is how can the black community turn it around. . . .

8 "With this music," says Gibbs, "I worry most about our young black men who see 2 Live Crew's success and take them as role models—negative, antisocial role models. Their music, their image, is based on degrading women. It extols and romanticizes violence and drugs. Now how can anyone say that is a productive social message for our black kids, especially young males struggling to learn how to become men?"

9 Gibbs and others concede that it is possible 2 Live Crew may be receiving tougher treatment from the judicial system than a white group would. But they argue that this case is not about race—it is about obscenity. And, specifically, about the impact the group is having on young black people.

10 In a nation where about half of all black children live in single-parent, female-headed households, the worry is not far-fetched. In a society in which the black family is falling apart, in which teen pregnancy regularly ruins lives and in which the rate of poverty is steadily rising, the urgent concern is that 2 Live Crew is selling corruption—self-hate—to vulnerable young minds in a weak black America.

11 Dorothy Height, head of the National Council of Negro Women, is particularly concerned with the music's negative impact on young black females. Height says black women are looking for ways to protest the music without making it all the more risqué and attractive to rebellious young people.

12 "Generally speaking, I favor upholding anyone's First Amendment rights," Height says. "But this music is damaging because it is degrading to women to have it suggested in our popular music that they are to be abused, that it is fun to abuse us, that we like to be abused. . . . This kind of

exhibition at a time when all of us are struggling to strengthen our community and deal with problems hurts us badly.

"We are trying to build self-esteem in black women," she says. "Many of our young women do not have a lot of self-respect. . . . We are tired of being put down." 13

Marilyn Kern-Foxworth, a professor of journalism at Texas A&M who studies blacks in media, believes 2 Live Crew's lyrics have not prompted a full-fledged opposition from black women because many still deny they are being victimized. 14

"Too many black women are still saying they see the music as about some other women, not them—no man would treat them like that," she says. "There is a great sense of denial, even though they will tell you these things actually do occur and they complain that black male responsibility toward black women is diminishing." 15

2 Live Crew's style and message of abusing women is finding a larger audience than the lewd black comedy and music of the past, which was aimed at adult audiences in nightclubs. "The young people listen to them and idolize them," says Kern-Foxworth. Record store owners nationwide report that teenagers are the big buyers of 2 Live Crew. "I don't get adults buying this stuff," says a record store owner in Northeast Washington. "This is rap, man—the kids get off on this." 16

"The music carries the words into their minds," says Kern-Foxworth. "And the music is now so widespread that the young people can't help but be influenced. They hold the musicians up on a platform so they can't help but want to be like them, to listen to them, to wear the clothes and the gold chains and to do what 2 Live Crew is singing about. 17

"We are talking about something deviant, aberrant and negative, and kids in the teenaged group do not have the mental ability, the maturity, to sort out what is good and bad for themselves. These musical idols have a tremendous influence." 18

The lack of social responsibility exercised by 2 Live Crew is not limited to glorifying abuse of black women. Although they don't sing about it, a simple look at the group in black baseball caps and layers of gold rope chains reveals their romanticization of the drug culture—featuring the male drug dealer as the hero. The right to use and abuse women is part of being a successful drug dealer. 19

20 "The central question," says Stanley Crouch, the New York jazz critic and commentator, "is how the sadistic, misogynic, hateful music adds to the problematic attitudes already burdening the black lower class in America. Listen to it. Women are sex slaves. Materialism is God. The ideal of cool is street-corner narcissism. This is no true vision of black America or black culture, but a slice of the worst of a small element of black culture that is not emblematic of the black community at large."

21 In addition, Crouch argues that 2 Live Crew sells whites on the idea that black culture is a base, vulgar entity that starts and stops on a ghetto corner.

22 "The young people listening to this music don't perceive it as a joke, they don't see it as metaphors about relationships and life," he says. "They see it as reality-based—a way to assert themselves and establish their identity. That is why it is obscene and threatening to black folks beyond what the judge had to say."

Robert Scheer

Does Censorship Kill Brain Cells?

This article by Robert Scheer appeared in the October 1990 issue of Playboy. *Scheer is a liberal commentator who contributes articles to a number of public forums.*

1 It used to be argued by weird village priests that sex destroyed brain cells. As a result, generations of Catholic boys grew up fearing that they would blow an exam if they masturbated. That theory never had a shred of scientific foundation and has been discarded. But a modified version of it seems plausible in light of current data. Recent experience suggests that thinking about *other* people's sex lives kills portions of the brain.

2 Sex makes people crazy. Not actually doing it: that's usually a release from mental tension. What drives some people nuts is the notion that others may be having lewd thoughts. How else to explain the sexual-censorship madness that afflicts some Americans?

Look at the character who went after the rap group 2 Live Crew down in Florida. This guy thinks he's Batman. No kidding. He drinks out of a Batman cup, wears a Batman watch and has a Batman poster plastered across his refrigerator door. This caped crusader, Florida lawyer Jack Thompson, told a reporter for the *L.A. Times* that his enemy, Luther Campbell, leader of 2 Live Crew, is "the Joker." You can't make stuff like this up. 3

The attacks on artistic freedom emanate from a tightly knit circle of fundamentalist right-wingers. Thompson says he got turned on to the crusade against 2 Live Crew after the Reverend Donald Wildmon's notorious censorship lobby distributed a transcript of the rap group's lyrics. It was Wildmon's group that initiated the attack on the National Endowment for the Arts last year—by complaining about Andres Serrano's controversial photo *Piss Christ.* Wildmon also tried to get Martin Scorsese's film *The Last Temptation of Christ* banned. 4

Unfortunately, many civil libertarians—horrified by what they perceived as the sexist and violent content of 2 Live Crew's lyrics—shirked this latest challenge. Why is it so easy to forget that freedom is indivisible. As noted First Amendment lawyer Floyd Abrams puts it, "One of the real tests of a dedication of a people to free expression is always whether they are willing to protect expression that they find really distasteful." 5

Abrams links this case with the suppression of a National Endowment for the Arts funded exhibit of photographs by the late Robert Mapplethorpe, which the censors managed to get pulled from the prestigious Corcoran Gallery in Washington. The director of a Cincinnati museum that exhibited the works was arrested. The Mapplethorpe case has received far greater support in establishment circles than have the rappers, but Abrams thinks both are victims of the same violation of the First Amendment. "We are at a turning point in enforcement of the obscenity laws," he says. "I don't separate the 2 Live Crew album from the Robert Mapplethorpe exhibit." 6

Neither does Batman/Thompson, who boasts, "There is a cultural war going on." 7

Thompson is not given to doubt about his calling by a higher power. "I believe the world is headed toward apocalyptic destruction," he told an *L.A. Times* interviewer, adding that "Government exists to point people God-ward." So much for the separation of church and state. 8

9 A secular explanation of Thompson's crusade against him and his music is offered by 2 Live Crew's Campbell. In 1988, Thompson, a Republican, ran unsuccessfully to unseat Dade County State's Attorney Janet Reno, a Democrat, and Campbell helped produce a record favoring Reno. "He lost the election and has been after me ever since," Campbell insists.

10 Those who attack 2 Live Crew because the group's lyrics are sexist may have qualms about Thompson, their strange bedfellow. During the 1988 campaign, according to *The Miami Herald,* he handed Reno a questionnaire insisting she check the appropriate box after the line "I, Janet Reno, am a bisexual, homosexual, heterosexual."

11 Thompson's letter carried the following warning: "If you do not respond . . . then you will be deemed to have checked one of the first two boxes." Reno refused to reply and won the election anyway.

12 You have to be a bit odd to be pushing the censors' line at this historical moment when it is so clearly out of sync with the time. Hungary has marked its move to greater freedom by permitting the publication of a Hungarian edition of *Playboy.* In eastern Europe, the lifting of the dead hand of Stalinism means the end of puritanical restraints that would have made Batman Thompson redundant. I never have understood why the right-wing fundamentalists in this country don't embrace communism as it is being practiced in places such as Cuba under Castro and as it was practiced in pre-Gorbachev Russia. You cannot take it away from Castro, Señor Clean, that he fundamentally altered the erotic life of Havana, turning it from perhaps the most permissive, even decadent, spot in the world into the capital of squeaky clean. Cincinnati should adopt Havana as a sister city.

13 But the Communist world is going over to freedom, which means that people have the right to check out what they want to check out. Last year in Moscow, I saw films at packed showings at the Writer's Union that I have yet to find in this country. One in particular, Pier Paolo Pasolini's *Salo or 120 Days of Sodom,* would turn Batman/Thompson blue. I have not met anyone in this country who has seen the Italian film, even though, aside from being rough and extreme at times, it is an important statement on the sexual basis of fascism. Will Moscow now become the center of the avant-garde, and will we be the new reactionaries.

14 As the rest of the world lunges to embrace our vision of

freedom for consenting adults—buy what you want when you want it—America's home-grown censors seem more virulent than ever. They claim to be conservatives but are frantic to shove the big nose of Government into what should be the most private recesses of our imaginations. Evidently, they detest the very market forces that eastern Europeans now embrace. Make no mistake, not only do these zealots wish to deny artistic freedom and shred the Constitution but, Lord save us, they are true subversives who seek—in the manner of Brezhnev's central planners—to control the market. Their record is distinctly un-American: Record sellers and musicians are arrested, gallery exhibits shut down, museum directors and trustees indicted and convenience stores intimidated into removing publications that readers want to buy. The sovereignty of the consumer is denied; some censor knows better how to spend the customer's hard-earned dollar. That's what it's all about, isn't it? You want to buy a ticket to a show or buy a book, and they won't let you.

When I was younger, it was the works of Henry Miller, 15
D. H. Lawrence and James Joyce that I could not legally purchase, no matter how many dollars I put aside. Hey, Ed Sullivan wouldn't even let me see the lower half of Elvis Presley's body. Today, if the censors have their way, it's rap music and X-rated videos that are taboo. Same difference. Of course, in our free society, the censors go to work only when a book, film or record is too explicitly sexual. Not when it is wrong, racist or violent, only when it may send blood to the privates.

Censors are inevitably liars. They almost never admit 16
seeking to ban a work because of its social content, because that would patently violate the spirit of the First Amendment. So they find a convenient loophole by insisting that sexual ideas are not ideas at all. Call someone a kike or a nigger and you are constitutionally protected. Sell extremely violent movies such as *The Texas Chain Saw Massacre* or, more recently, *The Omen,* in which women are routinely decapitated, or even *Batman,* in which violent death is the norm, and the law leaves you alone. But dare to refer, in what some consider a prurient manner, to sexual activity and they can slam you into jail.

Time out for a crash course in constitutional law as it 17
applies to obscenity: The Supreme Court has tended to define broadly the free-speech guarantee of the First Amendment, with one glaring exception—the expression of ideas

about sex. This absurdity, rendered in the "obscenity standard" codified in the Court's landmark *Miller* decision of 1973, created the one major loophole that has so far been in First Amendment protections. In *Miller,* the Court held that the expression of sexual thoughts or imagery can be banned if it runs afoul of current community standards and lacks redeeming artistic or political value.

18 Think of that for a moment. Ideas that violate a community's racial or religious norms are constitutionally protected. So the Nazis in Skokie, Illinois, had a right to march, swastikas and all. They could shout that Jews deserved to die in Hitler's gas chambers or that blacks should be slaves—and that would be protected as part of the traffic in ideas—as it should be. But if 2 Live Crew's Campbell raps that women want to commit impersonal oral sex, he can be thrown into jail.

19 The argument is that Campbell is not expressing ideas but merely seeking to arouse his audience. The distinction is meaningless. Surely the Nazis seek to rouse their audiences emotionally. Are only anemic ideas, those without emotional impact, to be constitutionally protected? Who are we kidding? The album *As Nasty As They Wanna Be* did not come to our attention because of its erotic or even pornographic content: it's a weak competitor in that category. The album irritates precisely because of its ideas.

20 What could be more provocative, given this nation's sick racial and sexual history than the specter of black male sexuality? Some may be troubled by what used to be called "race mixing" at 2 Live Crew concerts. "As several white female teens danced with and kissed black male teens to the beat of a thundering bass that shook the building floor," Lee May of the *L.A. Times* wrote, "reporters who remember Georgia's old racist climate joked that the rap group's name ought to be Your Worst Nightmare."

21 Taken at their worst, ignoring any possibility of a spoof or hyperbole, Campbell's lyrics assert that women, including white women, want to be sexually used by males, including, obviously, black males. One can condemn this idea as misogynist, even fascist, but not at the same moment deny its being an idea—indeed, a powerful one. The album is threatening precisely because it has thoughts that are bold and ugly.

22 Campbell is right in arguing that he is subjected to selective prosecution. The sentiments expressed on his al-

bum are widely advanced by others who are not harassed. He mentions Andrew Dice Clay and Guns n' Roses, whose albums remained on the shelves when 2 Live Crew's were banned. There are many other examples. *Eddie Murphy Raw,* widely available on cable television, far more effectively evokes the claims of male sexual domination than do Campbell's lyrics. Why not also ban the movie *9½ Weeks,* the films of Lina Wertmüller, the novels of D. H. Lawrence and almost every romance novel ever written? Hey, and what about that lustful Roger Rabbit?

Batman/Thompson recently initiated a campaign against 23 the critically acclaimed movie *The Cook, the Thief, His Wife & Her Lover.* Maybe if he succeeds with such respectable targets, we'll awake from the apathy that surrounds the 2 Live Crew case. But censors are vultures who thrive on the blood of their victims, and a defeat for Luther Campbell will make it all the more difficult for the next victim to defend himself. A case in point: When Bruce Springsteen had the courage to permit his music to be used in 2 Live Crew's *Banned in the U.S.A.,* Batman/Thompson responded with a crusade against the Boss himself. "Bruce and Luther can go to hell together," he thundered, adding that "Bruce Springsteen is facilitating the sexual abuse of women and the mental molestation of children."

Banned in the U.S.A. does not contain sexually explicit 24 lyrics. The song's message is an attack on censorship, not an attempt to rouse the prurient interests of adults or children. Yet Thompson had no reservations about smearing Springsteen's defense of artistic freedom with the smut brush.

Thompson is a dangerous joke. The serious villains here 25 are the music-business executives, on both the production and retail ends, who have made megabucks from the energy of their artists but run for cover at the first hint of attack. As Campbell notes, "In some areas, we have radio stations supporting us. But the record industry, no." According to a spokeswoman for the Recording Industry Association of America, *Nasty* was "the first recording in the history of popular music to be deemed obscene." A pretty serious precedent, but many music retailers quickly joined the offensive against the record, pulling it from stores when no legal order required them to do so.

Who are the gutless wonders who run Musicland, the 26 nation's largest chain of record stores, who dared to ban *Nasty* from all their outlets? Even the Federal judge who ruled against 2 Live Crew blasted that sort of prior constraint as a violation of the Constitution. Still, eager to escape Batman/Thompson's hate salvos, other chains followed Musicland's lead, pulling, or not restocking, the record—even in communities where prosecutors had not acted because they felt the lyrics did not violate community standards. Why have the top music profiteers been so chicken in coming to 2 Live Crew's defense?

27 The Thompsons and Wildmons of this world are nothings when stripped of their power to frighten. But when they can make entertainment executives—not to mention judges and prosecutors—get down on their knees without a fight, we are in serious trouble.

V.

CIVIL LIBERTIES AND CIVIL RIGHTS

Introduction

As you know, a basic premise of this book of readings is that writing typically emerges from other writing. As a demonstration of that premise, consider the very large body of writing that has emerged from some very basic texts in our political history. Consider, for instance, these words—the words of the First Amendment to the Constitution:

> Congress shall make no law respecting an establishment of religion, or prohibiting the free exercise thereof; or abridging the freedom of speech, or of the press; or the right of the people peaceably to assemble, and to petition the Government for a redress of grievances.

Or consider section one of the Fourteenth Amendment, ratified in 1868:

> All persons born or naturalized in the United States, and subject to the jurisdiction thereof, are citizens of the United States and of the State wherein they reside. No State shall make or enforce any law which shall abridge the privileges or immunities of citizens of the United States; nor shall any State deprive any person of life, liberty, or property, without due process of law; nor deny to any person within its jurisdiction the equal protection of the laws.

Or this fragment from the Declaration of Independence:

> We hold these Truths to be self-evident, that all Men are created equal, that they are endowed by their Creator with certain unalienable Rights, that among these are Life, Liberty, and the Pursuit of Happiness. That to secure these rights. Governments are instituted among Men. . . .

The readings in this part test out some of the implications of these seminal passages. First you will encounter a sort of prologue in the form of the Luis Valdez play *Los Vendidos,* a work that dramatizes a number of issues relating to race, gender, liberty, equality, economic justice, and civil rights that reverberate through the remainder of this part of the book. Then you will encounter conversations on a number of specific issues related to civil liberties and civil rights, conversations that in a sense began with the documents just quoted, which articulate our central political assumptions.

First are two sets of readings on the issue of censorship: one (on pornography) that picks up gender and language concerns from part II and the discussion of 2 Live Crew in part III; and another (the case of *Huckleberry Finn*) that picks up racial issues discussed in the same parts of this book. (The discussion of *Huckleberry Finn* also anticipates further discussions on the topic of race later in this part.)

Is pornography harmful? Should it be censored or restricted? Speaking for the affirmative, many women contend that pornography does indeed have harmful effects—that pornography provides the "theory" on how to treat women and rape or other forms of misogyny, the "practice." But other people see pornography as neutral in its effects or contend that the First Amendment protects all varieties of speech and writing from censorship. Did the framers of the Constitution intend to protect free speech and a free press in an absolute sense (as Hugo Black and William Douglas argued in a 1957 Supreme Court decision)? Or were the framers speaking only of political speech and writing (as the seven other Supreme Court justices agreed in that same 1957 case)? Is it indeed constitutional to restrict pornography? (After all, we do restrict libel and ban cigarette ads on TV, on the grounds of their harmful effects and apolitical content.) And just what is pornography, anyway? Can it be defined in a way that makes restrictions practical, or would such definitions and restrictions undermine artistic and political freedom? The issue of pornography makes for strange bedfellows; it is an issue about which liberals and conservatives disagree among themselves.

Liberals and conservatives also break ranks over *Huckleberry Finn* and its place in the school curriculum. Does reading *Huckleberry Finn* have harmful or beneficial effects? Is the book a racist one that reflects and perpetuates stereotypes that are offensive to African-Americans? Or does the book reflect those stereotypes only in order to subvert them? If the book does in fact subvert racial stereotypes but only in a very subtle way, does this suggest that the book should be kept for readers who have completed high school? Or do its merits as an American classic or as a central American document outweigh its demerits? If *Huckleberry Finn* is kept out of the curriculum, is that really censorship or merely a defensible pedagogical decision? If we keep *Huckleberry Finn* out of the classroom, will we also have to restrict works that reflect and possibly perpetuate stereotypical roles for women and men and native Americans too? Or should all works remain possible for consideration within a curriculum that foregrounds the inevitable social and political content of all art?

In a famous passage in *Huckleberry Finn* that you may remember, Huck ponders his legal and moral predicament in harboring the runaway slave Jim rather than turning him in to the authorities. Should Huck accede to the legal system that makes Jim a slave and that requires Huck to turn in the runaway? Or should he listen to the call of his conscience, continue to hide Jim, and in effect put his private morality before the public system of laws? The conflict between the individual and society is central to American culture because we value both the dignity of the private individual and the importance of public institutions sanctioned through the democratic process. Faced with the dilemma of paying taxes to support a popular war which he disagreed with, Henry David Thoreau proposed civil disobedience—a private act of personal conscience against "the tyranny of the majority." Later Mahatma Gandhi and Martin Luther King, Jr., refined civil disobedience into an effective tactic for achieving public justice and political equality. Were they right to do so? What is civil disobedience anyway? Is it a legitimate political tool or an invitation to anarchy that would destroy the principle of democratic rule? What should people do when "higher laws" put them in conflict with majority rule? What else can a democratic society do except be ruled by a majority? Can such a majority be a "tyranny," or is it the resistance to legitimate, democratic authority that is arrogant and tyrannical? Could civil disobedience even exist in a truly tyrannical society, one without a free press and trial by jury, one in which political minorities disappear in the middle of the night? The selections in this section articulate and debate the question of the legitimacy of civil disobedience and also offer critical analysis of and commentary on a central document of civil disobedience and the American civil rights movement: King's "Letter from Birmingham Jail."

Another central document of the civil rights movement was the Civil Rights Act of 1964, which attempted to eradicate discrimination from a range of public institutions in America. Part of Title VII of that act prohibited discrimination on the job because of race, color, religion, sex, or national origin:

> It shall be an unlawful employment practice for an employer . . . to fail or refuse to hire or to discharge any individual, or otherwise to discriminate against any individual with respect to his compensation, terms, conditions, or privileges of employment, because of such individual's race, color, religion, sex, or national origin. . . . It shall be an unlawful employment practice for any employer, labor organization, or joint labor-management committee controlling apprenticeship or other training or retraining, including on-the-job training programs, to discriminate against any individual because of his race, color, religion, sex, or national origin in admission to, or employment in, any program established to provide apprenticeship or other training. . . . If the court finds that the respondent has intentionally engaged in an unlawful employment practice . . . the court may enjoin the respondent from engaging in such unlawful employment practice, and order such affirmative action as may be appropriate. . . .

Title VII thus initiated a period of "affirmative action" to redress past injustices and to establish for everyone the possibility of equal opportunity.

But just what should affirmative action mean? Should it be a means of ensuring that everyone has a chance to compete on equal terms for jobs and education? Or should it denote a more active process of ensuring equal results, especially for people who arrive at jobs and schools with disadvantages that arise from past inequality? For some people, affirmative action means the former; in the words of Hubert Humphrey, nothing in Title VII should "give any power to the [Civil Rights] Commission or any court to require hiring, firing, or promotion of employees in order to meet a racial quota." For others, however, affirmative action means action: active measures (at least in the short run) such as goals, timetables, guidelines, and quotas designed to promote balanced results.

Are such actions fair? Is affirmative action a legitimate, short-term measure for breaking up a rigid caste system and for ameliorating the long-term effects of Jim Crow laws, sexist traditions, and inequitable education policies? Or is it inherently unfair? Has the "short-term" expired by now? Can we now justify passing over someone or favoring someone else because of the group that person is born into? Is the goal of affirmative action the reduction of social injustice or proportional representation of all races and both sexes? Is affirmative action inefficient, in that it favors racial and gender factors over job performance? Or is it more efficient, in that it speeds the progress of women and minorities and therefore allows those people a chance, at last, to show their right stuff? Does affirmative action damage self-esteem or promote it? These sensitive questions are discussed in the selections reprinted here on affirmative action.

Affirmative action is a product of the civil rights movement that has animated public discourse in the United States since the mid-1950s, especially in connection with the rights of African-Americans and women. In the past decade, members of another minority group—homosexuals—have clamored for civil rights as well, often quite publicly through marches and protests and other highly publicized tactics marshalled by organizations such as Act Up and Queer Nation. Should homosexuals be permitted to serve in the military? Should they be protected by fair housing and fair employment practices? Should gay couples be permitted to claim the rights enjoyed by married couples, such as the right to adopt children or share health benefits? Does the AIDS epidemic have implications for civil rights in this country? This final question is discussed in much greater detail in the section on AIDS later in this book, in part VII, "Science and Society," for AIDS is an issue that is certainly not limited to the gay community. But the other issues emerge in the readings on gay rights in this part of *Conversations*.

The part concludes with selections about the abortion controversy—probably the most heated discussion now taking place in our society. Since 1973, when the Supreme Court (in *Roe* v. *Wade*) legalized abortions performed in the first three months of a pregnancy, a pitched battle has been fought between those absolutely committed to upholding the Supreme Court position and those just as absolutely committed to overturning it. One camp, which sees the developing fetus as only a potential human being, is protective of women's right to privacy and personal freedom; the other camp, which sees the fetus as a human being with the rights of a human being, supports various restrictions on the right to abortion, if not an outright reversal of *Roe* v. *Wade*. In both camps, many people are convinced that only one side or the other can prevail in the abortion debate—

that "victory" without substantial compromise can be achieved through the ballot box, rallies, and Supreme Court appointments. Those who seek absolute victory on either side are often so committed to their positions that they are unwilling to participate in reasoned discussions. They typically produce more heat than light on the subject.

But other people are convinced that progress on the issue of abortion is not just possible but essential. They seek continuing discussion, reasoned exchange, and mutual respect among those involved in the conversation, and they tend to hold out a hope for negotiated consensus on the matter—incremental progress toward national agreement. When does a fetus become a person? What circumstances justify abortion? Are there ways of reducing abortions and at the same time protecting women's right to privacy (e.g., through improved methods of contraception)? Are any additional restrictions on abortions (for even *Roe* v. *Wade* restricts abortions to the first three months of pregnancy) sensible? Can those restrictions protect the rights of everyone involved, even as those rights are somewhat compromised?

These are some of the questions discussed in the final section of this central part of the textbook. No doubt questions like them—and like the others posed in the preceding paragraphs—are being discussed on every American campus this year.

Luis Valdez
Los Vendidos

Luis Valdez (born 1940), a key figure in the Chicano Theatre movement, has shaped drama that speaks to all Americans. The son of migrant farm workers, Valdez grew up around San Jose, California, and acquired Spanish as a second language. In the mid-1960s he began devising skits that could be given on the back of flatbed trucks in support of Cesar Chavez's union of farm workers; you can see the influence of that circumstance on Los Vendidos *("The Sellouts"), written in 1967. Valdez, who now lives in San Juan Bautista, California, wrote and directed the movie* La Bamba.

Characters

HONEST SANCHO	JOHNNY
SECRETARY	REVOLUCIONARIO
FARM WORKER	MEXICAN-AMERICAN

Scene: Honest Sancho's Used Mexican Lot and Mexican Curio Shop. Three models are on display in Honest Sancho's shop: to the right, there is a Revolucionario, complete with sombrero, carrilleras,[1] *and carabina 30-30. At center, on the floor, there is the Farm Worker, under a broad straw sombrero. At stage left is the Pachuco, filero*[2] *in hand.*

(*Honest Sancho is moving among his models, dusting them off and preparing for another day of business.*)

1 SANCHO: Bueno, bueno, mis monos, vamos a ver a quien vendemos ahora, ¿no? (*To audience.*) ¡Quihubo![3] I'm Honest Sancho and this is my shop. Antes fui contratista pero ahora logré tener mi negocito.[4] All I need now is a customer. (*A bell rings offstage.*) Ay, a customer!

2 SECRETARY (*Entering*): Good morning, I'm Miss Jiménez from—

3 SANCHO: ¡Ah, una chicana! Welcome, welcome Señorita Jiménez.

4 SECRETARY: (*Anglo pronunciation*): JIM-enez.

5 SANCHO: ¿Qué?

6 SECRETARY: My name is Miss JIM-enez. Don't you speak English? What's wrong with you?

7 SANCHO: On, nothing, Señorita JIM-enez. I'm here to help you.

8 SECRETARY: That's better. As I was starting to say, I'm a secretary from Governor Reagan's office, and we're looking for a Mexican type for the administration.

9 SANCHO: Well, you come to the right place, lady. This is Honest Sancho's Used Mexican lot, and we got all types here. Any particular type you want?

10 SECRETARY: Yes, we are looking for somebody suave—

[1] *carrilleras:* chin straps; perhaps cartridge belts.

[2] *Pachuco:* Chicano slang for a 1940s zoot suiter; *filero:* blade.

[3] *Bueno, bueno, . . . Quihubo:* "Good, good, my cute ones, let's see who we can sell now, O.K.?"

[4] *Antes fui . . . negocito:* "I used to be a contractor, but now I've succeeded in having my little business."

SANCHO: Suave. 11

SECRETARY: Debonair. 12

SANCHO: De buen aire. 13

SECRETARY: Dark. 14

SANCHO: Prieto. 15

SECRETARY: But of course not too dark. 16

SANCHO: No muy prieto. 17

SECRETARY: Perhaps, beige. 18

SANCHO: Beige, just the tone. Así como cafecito con leche,[5] 19
¿no?

SECRETARY: One more thing. He must be hard-working. 20

SANCHO: That could only be one model. Step right over here 21
to the center of the shop, lady. (*They cross to the Farm Worker.*) This is our standard farm worker model. As you can see, in the words of our beloved Senator George Murphy, he is "built close to the ground." Also take special notice of his four-ply Goodyear huaraches, made from the rain tire. This wide-brimmed sombrero is an extra added feature—keeps off the sun, rain, and dust.

SECRETARY: Yes, it does look durable. 22

SANCHO: And our farm worker model is friendly. Muy am- 23
able.[6] Watch. (*Snaps his fingers.*)

FARM WORKER (*Lifts up head*): Buenos días, señorita. (*His* 24
head drops.)

SECRETARY: My, he's friendly. 25

SANCHO: Didn't I tell you? Loves his patrones! But his most 26
attractive feature is that he's hard-working. Let me show you. (*Snaps fingers. Farm Worker stands.*)

FARM WORKER ¡El jale![7] (*He begins to work.*) 27

SANCHO: As you can see, he is cutting grapes. 28

SECRETARY: Oh, I wouldn't know. 29

SANCHO: He also picks cotton. (*Snap. Farm Worker begins to* 30
pick cotton.)

SECRETARY: Versatile, isn't he? 31

SANCHO: He also picks melons. (*Snap. Farm Worker picks* 32
melons.) That's his slow speed for late in the season. Here's his fast speed. (*Snap. Farm Workers picks faster.*)

SECRETARY: ¡Chihuahua! . . . I mean, goodness, he sure is a 33
hard worker.

SANCHO: (*Pulls the Farm Worker to his feet*): And that isn't the 34

[5] *Así como . . . leche:* like coffee with milk.

[6] *Muy amable:* very friendly.

[7] *El jale:* the job.

half of it. Do you see these little holes on his arms that appear to be pores? During those hot sluggish days in the field, when the vines or the branches get so entangled, it's almost impossible to move; these holes emit a certain grease that allow our model to slip and slide right through the crop with no trouble at all.

35 SECRETARY: Wonderful. But is he economical?

36 SANCHO: Economical? Señorita, you are looking at the Volkswagen of Mexicans. Pennies a day is all it takes. One plate of beans and tortillas will keep him going all day. That, and chile. Plenty of chile. Chile jalapenos, chile verde, chile colorado. But, of course, if you do give him chile (*Snap. Farm Worker turns left face. Snap. Farm Worker bends over.*) then you have to change his oil filter once a week.

37 SECRETARY: What about storage?

38 SANCHO: No problem. You know these new farm labor camps our Honorable Governor Reagan has built out by Parlier or Raisin City? They were designed with our model in mind. Five, six, seven, even ten in one of those shacks will give you no trouble at all. You can also put him in old barns, old cars, river banks. You can even leave him out in the field overnight with no worry!

39 SECRETARY: Remarkable.

40 SANCHO: And here's an added feature: Every year at the end of the season, this model goes back to Mexico and doesn't return, automatically, until next Spring.

41 SECRETARY: How about that. But tell me: does he speak English?

42 SANCHO: Another outstanding feature is that last year this model was programmed to go out on STRIKE! (*Snap.*)

43 FARM WORKER: ¡HUELGA! ¡HUELGA! Hermanos, sálganse de esos files.[8] (*Snap. He stops.*)

44 SECRETARY: No! Oh no, we can't strike in the State Capitol.

45 SANCHO: Well, he also scabs. (*Snap.*)

46 FARM WORKER: Me vendo barato, ¿y qué?[9] (*Snap.*)

47 SECRETARY: That's much better, but you didn't answer my question. Does he speak English?

48 SANCHO: Bueno . . . no pero[10] he has other—

49 SECRETARY: No.

[8] *HUELGA! HUELGA! . . . esos files:* "Strike! Strike! Brothers, leave those rows."

[9] *Me vendo . . . qué:* "I come cheap, so what?"

[10] *Bueno . . . no, pero:* "Well, no, but . . ."

SANCHO: Other features. 50
SECRETARY: NO! He just won't do! 51
SANCHO: Okay, okay pues. We have other models. 52
SECRETARY: I hope so. What we need is something a little 53
more sophisticated.
SANCHO: Sophisti—¿qué? 54
SECRETARY: An urban model. 55
SANCHO: Ah, from the city! Step right back. Over here in this 56
corner of the shop is exactly what you're looking for. Introducing our new 1969 JOHNNY PACHUCO model! This is our fast-back model. Streamlined. Built for speed, low-riding, city life. Take a look at some of these features. Mag shoes, dual exhausts, green chartreuse paint-job, dark-tint windshield, a little poof on top. Let me just turn him on. (*Snap. Johnny walks to stage center with a pachuco bounce.*)
SECRETARY: What was that? 57
SANCHO: That, señorita, was the Chicano shuffle. 58
SECRETARY: Okay, what does he do? 59
SANCHO: Anything and everything necessary for city life. For 60
instance, survival: He knife fights. (*Snap. Johnny pulls out switch blade and swings at Secretary.*)

(*Secretary screams.*)

SANCHO: He dances. (*Snap.*) 61
JOHNNY (*Singing*): "Angel Baby, my Angel Baby . . ." (*Snap.*) 62
SANCHO: And here's a feature no city model can be without. 63
He gets arrested, but not without resisting, of course. (*Snap.*)
JOHNNY: ¡En la madre, la placa![11] I didn't do it! I didn't do it! 64
(*Johnny turns and stands up against an imaginary wall, legs spread out, arms behind his back.*)
SECRETARY: Oh no, we can't have arrests! We must maintain 65
law and order.
SANCHO: But he's bilingual! 66
SECRETARY: Bilingual? 67
SANCHO: Simón que yes.[12] He speaks English! Johnny, give us 68
some English. (*Snap.*)
JOHNNY (*Comes downstage.*): Fuck-you! 69

[11] *En la . . . placa:* "Wow, the police!"
[12] *Simón . . . yes:* yeah, sure.

70 Secretary (*Gasps.*): Oh! I've never been so insulted in my whole life!

71 Sancho: Well, he learned it in your school.

72 Secretary: I don't care where he learned it.

73 Sancho: But he's economical!

74 Secretary: Economical?

75 Sancho: Nickels and dimes. You can keep Johnny running on hamburgers, Taco Bell tacos, Lucky Lager beer, Thunderbird wine, yesca—

76 Secretary: Yesca?

77 Sancho: Mota.

78 Secretary: Mota?

79 Sancho: Leños[13] . . . Marijuana. (*Snap; Johnny inhales on an imaginary joint.*)

80 Secretary: That's against the law!

81 Johnny (*Big smile, holding his breath*): Yeah.

82 Sancho: He also sniffs glue. (*Snap. Johnny inhales glue, big smile.*)

83 Johnny: Tha's too much man, ése.

84 Secretary: No, Mr. Sancho, I don't think this—

85 Sancho: Wait a minute, he has other qualities I know you'll love. For example, an inferiority complex. (*Snap.*)

86 Johnny (*To Sancho*): You think you've better than me, huh ése? (*Swings switchblade.*)

87 Sancho: He can also be beaten and he bruises; cut him and he bleeds; kick him and he— (*He beats, bruises and kicks Pachuco.*) would you like to try it?

88 Secretary: Oh, I couldn't.

89 Sancho: Be my guest. He's a great scapegoat.

90 Secretary: No, really.

91 Sancho: Please.

92 Secretary: Well, all right. Just once. (*She kicks Pachuco.*) Oh, he's so soft.

93 Sancho: Wasn't that good? Try again.

94 Secretary (*Kicks Pachuco*): Oh, he's so wonderful! (*She kicks him again.*)

95 Sancho: Okay, that's enough, lady. You ruin the merchandise. Yes, our Johnny Pachuco model can give you many hours of pleasure. Why, the L.A.P.D. just bought twenty of these to train their rookie cops on. And talk about maintenance. Señorita, you are looking at an entirely self-supporting machine. You're never going to find our

[13] *Leños:* "joints" of marijuana.

Johnny Pachuco model on the relief rolls. No, sir, this model knows how to liberate.

SECRETARY: Liberate? 96

SANCHO: He steals. (*Snap. Johnny rushes the Secretary and* 97
steals her purse.)

JOHNNY: ¡Dame esa bolsa, vieja![14] (*He grabs the purse and* 97
runs. Snap by Sancho. He stops.)

(*Secretary runs after Johnny and grabs purse away from him, kicking him as she goes.*)

SECRETARY: No, no, no! We can't have any *more* thieves in the 99
State Administration. Put him back.

SANCHO: Okay, we still got other models. Come on, Johnny, 100
we'll sell you to some old lady. (*Sancho takes Johnny back to his place.*)

SECRETARY: Mr. Sancho, I don't think you quite understand 101
what we need. What we need is something that will attract the women voters. Something more traditional, more romantic.

SANCHO: Ah, a lover. (*He smiles meaningfully.*) Step right over 102
here, señorita. Introducing our standard Revolucionario and/or Early California Bandit type. As you can see he is well-built, sturdy, durable. This is the International Harvester of Mexicans.

SECRETARY: What does he do? 103

SANCHO: You name it, he does it. He rides horses, stays in the 104
mountains, crosses deserts, plains, rivers, leads revolutions, follows revolutions, kills, can be killed, serves as a martyr, hero, movie star—did I say movie star? Did you ever see *Viva Zapata? Viva Villa? Villa Rides? Pancho Villa Returns? Pancho Villa Goes Back? Pancho Villa Meets Abbot and Costello*—

SECRETARY: I've never seen any of those. 105

SANCHO: Well, he was in all of them. Listen to this. (*Snap.*) 106

REVOLUCIONARIO (*Scream*): ¡VIVA VILLAAAAA! 107

SECRETARY: That's awfully loud. 108

SANCHO: He has a volume control. (*He adjusts volume. Snap.*) 109

REVOLUCIONARIO (*Mousey voice.*): ¡Viva Villa! 110

SECRETARY: That's better. 111

SANCHO: And even if you didn't see him in the movies, 112

[14] *Dame esa . . . , vieja:* "Gimme that bag, old lady!"

perhaps you saw him on TV. He makes commercials. (*Snap.*)

113 Revolucionario: Is there a Frito Bandito in your house?

114 Secretary: Oh, yes, I've seen that one!

115 Sancho: Another feature about this one is that he is economical. He runs on raw horsemeat and tequila!

116 Secretary: Isn't that rather savage?

117 Sancho: Al contrario,[15] it makes him a lover. (*Snap.*)

118 Revolucionario (*To Secretary*): ¡Ay, mamasota, cochota, ven pa'ca! (*He grabs Secretary and folds her back—Latin-lover style.*)

119 Sancho (*Snap. Revolucionario goes back upright.*): Now wasn't that nice?

120 Secretary: Well, it was rather nice.

121 Sancho: And finally, there is one outstanding feature about this model I KNOW the ladies are going to love: He's a GENUINE antique! He was made in Mexico in 1910!

122 Secretary: Made in Mexico?

123 Sancho: That's right. Once in Tijuana, twice in Guadalajara, three times in Cuernavaca.

124 Secretary: Mr. Sancho, I thought he was an American product.

125 Sancho: No, but—

126 Secretary: No, I'm sorry. We can't buy anything but American-made products. He just won't do.

127 Sancho: But he's an antique!

128 Secretary: I don't care. You still don't understand what we need. It's true we need Mexican models such as these, but it's more important that he be *American.*

129 Sancho: American?

130 Secretary: That's right, and judging from what you've shown me, I don't think you have what we want. Well, my lunch hour's almost over; I better—

131 Sancho: Wait a minute! Mexican but American?

132 Secretary: That's correct.

133 Sancho: Mexican but . . . (*A sudden flash.*) AMERICAN! Yeah, I think we've got exactly what you want. He just came in today! Give me a minute. (*He exits. Talks from backstage.*) Here he is in the shop. Let me just get some papers off. There. Introducing our new 1970 Mexican-American! Ta-ra-ra-ra-ra-ra-RA-RAAA!

[15] *Al contrario:* on the contrary.

(*Sancho brings out the Mexican-American model, a clean-shaven middle-class type in business suit, with glasses.*)

Secretary (*Impressed*): Where have you been hiding this 134
one?

Sancho: He just came in this morning. Ain't he a beauty? 135
Feast your eyes on him! Sturdy US STEEL frame, streamlined, modern. As a matter of fact, he is built exactly like our Anglo models except that he comes in a variety of darker shades: naugahyde, leather, or leatherette.

Secretary: Naugahyde. 136

Sancho: Well, we'll just write that down. Yes, señorita, this 137
model represents the apex of American engineering! He is bilingual, college educated, ambitious! Say the word "acculturate" and he accelerates. He is intelligent, well-mannered, clean—did I say clean? (*Snap. Mexican-American raises his arm.*) Smell.

Secretary (*Smells*): Old Sobaco, my favorite. 138

Sancho (*Snap. Mexican-American turns toward Sancho.*): 139
Eric! (*To Secretary.*) We call him Eric Garcia. (*To Eric.*) I want you to meet Miss JIM-enez, Eric.

Mexican-American: Miss JIM-enez, I am delighted to make 140
your acquaintance. (*He kisses her hand.*)

Secretary: Oh, my, how charming! 141

Sancho: Did you feel the suction? He has seven especially 142
engineered suction cups right behind his lips. He's a charmer all right!

Secretary: How about boards? Does he function on boards? 143

Sancho: You name them, he is on them. Parole boards, draft 144
boards, school boards, taco quality control boards, surf boards, two-by-fours.

Secretary: Does he function in politics? 145

Sancho: Señorita, you are looking at a political MACHINE. 146
Have you ever heard of the OEO, EOC, COD, WAR ON POVERTY? That's our model! Not only that, he makes political speeches.

Secretary: May I hear one? 147

Sancho: With pleasure. (*Snap.*) Eric, give us a speech. 148

Mexican-American: Mr. Congressman, Mr. Chairman, mem- 149
bers of the board, honored guests, ladies and gentlemen. (*Sancho and Secretary applaud.*) Please, please, I come before you as a Mexican-American to tell you about the problems of the Mexican. The problems of the Mexican stem from one thing and one thing alone: He's stupid.

He's uneducated. He needs to stay in school. He needs to be ambitious, forward-looking, harder-working. He needs to think American, American, American, AMERICAN, AMERICAN, AMERICAN. GOD BLESS AMERICA! GOD BLESS AMERICA! GOD BLESS AMERICA!! (*He goes out of control.*)

(*Sancho snaps frantically and the Mexican-American finally slumps forward, bending at the waist.*)

150 Secretary: Oh my, he's patriotic, too!

151 Sancho: Sí, señorita, he loves his country. Let me just make a little adjustment here. (*Stands Mexican-American up.*)

152 Secretary: What about upkeep? Is he economical?

153 Sancho: Well, no, I won't lie to you. The Mexican-American costs a little bit more, but you get what you pay for. He's worth every extra cent. You can keep him running on dry martinis, Langendorf bread.

154 Secretary: Apple pie?

155 Sancho: Only Mom's. Of course, he's also programmed to eat Mexican food on ceremonial functions, but I must warn you: an overdose of beans will plug up his exhaust.

156 Secretary: Fine! There's just one more question: HOW MUCH DO YOU WANT FOR HIM?

157 Sancho: Well, I tell you what I'm gonna do. Today and today only, because you've been so sweet, I'm gonna let you steal this model from me! I'm gonna let you drive him off the lot for the simple price of—let's see taxes and license included—$15,000.

158 Secretary: Fifteen thousand DOLLARS? For a MEXICAN!

159 Sancho: Mexican? What are you talking, lady? This is a Mexican-AMERICAN! We had to melt down two pachucos, a farm worker and three gabachos to make this model! You want quality, but you gotta pay for it! This is no cheap run-about. He's got class!

160 Secretary: Okay, I'll take him.

161 Sancho: You will?

162 Secretary: Here's your money.

163 Sancho: You mind if I count it?

164 Secretary: Go right ahead.

165 Sancho: Well, you'll get your pink slip in the mail. Oh, do you want me to wrap him up for you? We have a box in the back.

166 Secretary: No, thank you. The Governor is having a lunch-

eon this afternoon, and we need a brown face in the crowd. How do I drive him?

SANCHO: Just snap your fingers. He'll do anything you want. 167

(*Secretary snaps. Mexican-American steps forward.*)

MEXICAN-AMERICAN: RAZA QUERIDA, ¡VAMOS LEVAN- 168
TANDO ARMAS PARA LIBERARNOS DE ESTOS DESGRACIADOS GABACHOS QUE NOS EXPLOTAN! VAMOS.[16]

SECRETARY: What did he say? 169

SANCHO: Something about lifting arms, killing white people, 170
etc.

SECRETARY: But he's not supposed to say that! 171

SANCHO: Look, lady, don't blame me for bugs from the 172
factory. He's your Mexican-American; you bought him, now drive him off the lot!

SECRETARY: But he's broken! 173

SANCHO: Try snapping another finger. 174

(*Secretary snaps. Mexican-American comes to life again.*)

MEXICAN-AMERICAN: ¡ESTA GRAN HUMANIDAD HA DICHO 175
BASTA! Y SE HA PUESTO EN MARCHA! ¡BASTA! ¡BASTA! ¡VIVA LA RAZA! ¡VIVA LA CAUSA! ¡VIVA LA HUELGA! ¡VIVAN LOS BROWN BERETS! ¡VIVAN LOS ESTUDIANTES! ¡CHICANO POWER![17]

(*The Mexican-American turns toward the Secretary, who gasps and backs up. He keeps turning toward the Pachuco, Farm Worker, and Revolucionario, snapping his fingers and turning each of them on, one by one.*)

PACHUCO (*Snap. To Secretary*): I'm going to get you, baby! 176
¡Viva La Raza!

FARM WORKER (*Snap. To Secretary*): ¡Viva la huelga! ¡Viva la 177
Huelga! ¡VIVA LA HUELGA!

[16]*RAZA QUERIDA, . . . VAMOS:* "Beloved Raza, let's pick up arms to liberate ourselves from those damned whites that exploit us! Let's go."

[17] *ESTA GRAN . . . CHICANO POWER:* "This great mass of humanity has said enough! And it begins to march! Enough! Enough! Long live La Raza! Long live the Cause! Long live the strike! Long live the Brown Berets! Long live the students! Chicano Power!"

178 REVOLUCIONARIO (*Snap. To Secretary*): ¡Viva la revolución! ¡VIVA LA REVOLUCIÓN!

(*The three models join together and advance toward the Secretary who backs up and runs out of the shop screaming. Sancho is at the other end of the shop holding his money in his hand. All freeze. After a few seconds of silence, the Pachuco moves and stretches, shaking his arms and loosening up. The Farm Worker and Revolucionario do the same. Sancho stays where he is, frozen to his spot.*)

179 JOHNNY: Man, that was a long one, ése. (*Others agree with him.*)
180 FARM WORKER: How did we do?
181 JOHNNY: Perty good, look all that lana, man! (*He goes over to Sancho and removes the money from his hand. Sancho stays where he is.*)
182 REVOLUCIONARIO: En la madre, look at all the money.
183 JOHNNY: We keep this up, we're going to be rich.
184 FARM WORKER: They think we're machines.
185 REVOLUCIONARIO: Burros.
186 JOHNNY: Puppets.
187 MEXICAN-AMERICAN: The only thing I don't like is—how come I always got to play the goddamn Mexican-American?
188 JOHNNY: That's what you get for finishing high school.
189 FARM WORKER: How about our wages, ése?
190 JOHNNY: Here it comes right now. $3,000 for you, $3,000 for you, $3,000 for you, and $3,000 for me. The rest we put back into the business.
191 MEXICAN-AMERICAN: Too much, man. Heh, where you vatos going tonight?
192 FARM WORKER: I'm going over to Concha's. There's a party.
193 JOHNNY: Wait a minute, vatos. What about our salesman? I think he needs an oil job.
194 REVOLUCIONARIO: Leave him to me.

(*The Pachuco, Farm Worker, and Mexican-American exit, talking loudly about their plans for the night. The Revolucionario goes over to Sancho, removes his derby hat and cigar, lifts him up and throws him over his shoulder. Sancho hangs loose, lifeless.*)

195 REVOLUCIONARIO (*To audience*): He's the best model we got! ¡Ajua! (*Exit.*)

CENSORSHIP I: PORNOGRAPHY

Gloria Steinem

Erotica and Pornography

Gloria Steinem, born in 1934 in Toledo, has written for many prestigious magazines and in 1971–72 was a founding editor of Ms. *magazine, a forum for women's issues. She also helped found the National Women's Political Caucus, Women Against Pornography, and other activist groups. The following analysis appeared in* Ms. *in 1978.*

Human beings are the only animals that experience the same sex drive at times when we can—and cannot—conceive. 1

Just as we developed uniquely human capacities for language, planning, memory, and invention along our evolutionary path, we also developed sexuality as a form of expression, a way of communicating that is separable from our need for sex as a way of perpetuating ourselves. For humans alone, sexuality can be and often is primarily a way of bonding, of giving and receiving pleasure, bridging differentness, discovering sameness, and communicating emotion. 2

We developed this and other human gifts through our ability to change our environment, adapt physically, and in the long run, to affect our own evolution. But as an emotional result of this spiraling path away from other animals, we seem to alternate between periods of exploring our unique abilities to change new boundaries, and feelings of loneliness in the unknown that we ourselves have created; a fear that sometimes sends us back to the comfort of the animal world by encouraging us to exaggerate our sameness. 3

The separation of "play" from "work," for instance, is a problem only in the human world. So is the difference between art and nature, or an intellectual accomplish- 4 ment and a physical one. As a result, we celebrate play, art, and invention as leaps into the unknown; but any imbalance can send us back to nostalgia for our primate past and the conviction that the basics of work, nature, and physical labor are somehow more worthwhile or even moral.

5 In the same way, we have explored our sexuality as separable from conception: a pleasurable, empathetic bridge to strangers of the same species. We have even invented contraception—a skill that has probably existed in some form since our ancestors figured out the process of birth—in order to extend this uniquely human difference. Yet we also have times of atavistic suspicion that sex is not complete—or even legal or intended-by-god—if it cannot end in conception.

6 No wonder the concepts of "erotica" and "pornography" can be so crucially different, and yet so confused. Both assume that sexuality can be separated from conception, and therefore can be used to carry a personal message. That's a major reason why, even in our current culture, both may be called equally "shocking" or legally "obscene," a word whose Latin derivative means "dirty, containing filth." This gross condemnation of all sexuality that isn't harnessed to childbirth and marriage has been increased by the current backlash against women's progress. Out of fear that the whole patriarchal structure might be upset if women really had the autonomous power to decide our reproductive futures (that is, if we controlled the most basic means of production), right-wing groups are not only denouncing prochoice abortion literature as "pornographic," but are trying to stop the sending of all contraceptive information through the mails by invoking obscenity laws. In fact, Phyllis Schlafly recently denounced the entire Women's Movement as "obscene."

7 Not surprisingly, this religious, visceral backlash has a secular, intellectual counterpart that relies heavily on applying the "natural" behavior of the animal world to humans. That is questionable in itself, but these Lionel Tigerish studies make their political purpose even more clear in the particular animals they select and the habits they choose to emphasize. The message is that females should accept their "destiny" of being sexually dependent and devote themselves to bearing and rearing their young.

Defending against such reaction in turn leads to another temptation: to merely reverse the terms, and declare that *all* nonprocreative sex is good. In fact, however, this human activity can be as constructive or destructive, moral or immoral, as any other. Sex as communication can send messages as different as life and death; even the origins of "erotica" and "pornography" reflect that fact. After all, "erotica" is rooted in *eros* or passionate love, and thus in the idea of positive choice, free will, the yearning for a particular person. (Interestingly, the definition of erotica leaves open the question of gender.) "Pornography" begins with a root meaning "prostitution" or "female captives," thus letting us know that the subject is not mutual love, or love at all, but domination and violence against women. (Though, of course, homosexual pornography may imitate this violence by putting a man in the "feminine" role of victim.) It ends with a root meaning "writing about" or "description of" which puts still more distance between subject and object, and replaces a spontaneous yearning for closeness with objectification and a voyeur. 8

The difference is clear in the words. It becomes even more so by example. 9

Look at any photo or film of people making love; really making love. The images may be diverse, but there is usually a sensuality and touch and warmth, an acceptance of bodies and nerve endings. There is always a spontaneous sense of people who are there because they *want* to be, out of shared pleasure. 10

Now look at any depiction of sex in which there is clear force, or an unequal power that spells coercion. It may be very blatant, with weapons or torture or bondage, wounds and bruises, some clear humiliation, or an adult's sexual power being used over a child. It may be much more subtle: a physical attitude of conqueror and victim, the use of race or class difference to imply the same thing, perhaps a very unequal nudity, with one person exposed and vulnerable while the other is clothed. In either case, there is no sense of equal choice or equal power. 11

The first is erotic: a mutually pleasurable, sexual expression between people who have enough power to be there by positive choice. It may or may not strike the sense-memory in the viewer, or be creative enough to make the unknown seem real; but it doesn't require us to identify with a 12 conqueror or a victim. It is truly sensuous, and may give us a contagion of pleasure.

13 The second is pornographic: its message is violence, dominance, and conquest. It is sex being used to reinforce some inequality, or to create one, or to tell us the lie that pain and humiliation (ours or someone else's) are really the same as pleasure. If we are to feel anything, we must identify with conqueror or victim. That means we can only experience pleasure through the adoption of some degree of sadism or masochism. It also means that we may feel diminished by the role of conqueror, or enraged, humiliated, and vengeful by sharing identity with the victim.

14 Perhaps one could simply say that erotica is about sexuality, but pornography is about power and sex-as-weapon—in the same way we have come to understand that rape is about violence, and not really about sexuality at all.

15 Yes, it's true that there are women who have been forced by violent families and dominating men to confuse love with pain; so much so that they have become masochists. (A fact that in no way excuses those who administer such pain.) But the truth is that, for most women—and for men with enough humanity to imagine themselves into the predicament of women—true pornography could serve as aversion therapy for sex.

16 Of course, there will always be personal differences about what is and is not erotic, and there may be cultural differences for a long time to come. Many women feel that sex makes them vulnerable and therefore may continue to need more sense of personal connection and safety before allowing any erotic feelings. We now find competence and expertise erotic in men, but that may pass as we develop those qualities in ourselves. Men, on the other hand, may continue to feel less vulnerable, and therefore more open to such potential danger as sex with strangers. As some men replace the need for submission from childlike women with the pleasure of cooperation from equals, they may find a partner's competence to be erotic, too.

17 Such group changes plus individual differences will continue to be reflected in sexual love between people of the same gender, as well as between women and men. The points is not to dictate sameness, but to discover ourselves and each other through sexuality that is an exploring, pleasurable, empathetic part of our lives; a human sexuality

that is unchained both from unwanted pregnancies and from violence.

But that is a hope, not a reality. At the moment, fear of change is increasing both the indiscriminate repression of all nonprocreative sex in the religious and "conservative" male world, and the pornographic vengeance against women's sexuality in the secular world of "liberal" and "radical" men. It's almost futuristic to debate what is and is not truly erotic, when many women are again being forced into compulsory motherhood, and the number of pornographic murders, tortures, and woman-hating images are on the increase in both popular culture and real life. 18

It's a familiar division: wife or whore, "good" woman who is constantly vulnerable to pregnancy or "bad" woman who is unprotected from violence. *Both* roles would be upset if we were to control our own sexuality. And that's exactly what we must do. 19

In spite of all our atavistic suspicions and training for the "natural" role of motherhood, we took up the complicated battle for reproductive freedom. Our bodies had borne the health burden of endless births and poor abortions, and we had a greater motive for separating sexuality and conception. 20

Now we have to take up the equally complex burden of explaining that all nonprocreative sex is *not* alike. We have a motive: our right to a uniquely human sexuality, and sometimes even to survival. As it is, our bodies have too rarely been enough our own to develop erotica in our own lives, much less in art and literature. And our bodies have too often been the objects of pornography and the woman-hating, violent practice that it preaches. Consider also our spirits that break a little each time we see ourselves in chains or full labial display for the conquering male viewer, bruised or on our knees, screaming a real or pretended pain to delight the sadist, pretending to enjoy what we don't enjoy, to be blind to the images of our sisters that really haunt us—humiliated often enough ourselves by the truly obscene idea that sex and the domination of women must be combined. 21

Sexuality *is* human, free, separate—and so are we. 22

But until we untangle the lethal confusion of sex with violence, there will be more pornography and less erotica. There will be little murders in our beds—and very little love. 23

Report on the President's Commission on Obscenity and Pornography (Majority Report)

In 1967, Congress by law established an eighteen-member special commission (appointed by President Nixon) to study the impact of obscenity and pornography on American life. After gathering testimony, reviewing research, and conferring at length, the commission in 1970 recommended against legislation that would restrain pornography. A minority of the members of the commission, feeling differently, submitted their own dissenting report. Excerpts from both follow.

1 Discussions of obscenity and pornography in the past have often been devoid of fact. Popular rhetoric has often contained a variety of estimates of the size of the "smut" industry and assertions regarding the consequences of the existence of these materials and exposure to them. Many of these statements, however, have had little anchoring in objective evidence. Within the limits of its time and resources, the Commission has sought, through staff and contract research, to broaden the factual basis for future continued discussion. The Commission is aware that not all issues of concern have been completely researched nor all questions answered. It also recognizes that the interpretations of a set of "facts" in arriving at policy implications may differ even among men of good will. Nevertheless, the Commission is convinced that on most issues regarding obscenity and pornography the discussion can be informed by important and often new facts. It presents its Report, hopeful that it will contribute to this discussion at a new level. . . .

2 Exposure to erotic stimuli appears to have little or no effect on already established attitudinal commitments regarding either sexuality or sexual morality. A series of four studies employing a large array of indicators found practically no significant differences in such attitudes before and after single or repeated exposures to erotica. One study did find that after exposure persons became more tolerant in reference to other persons' sexual activities although their own sexual standards did not change. One study reported that some persons' attitudes toward premarital intercourse

became more liberal after exposure, while other persons' attitudes became more conservative, but another study found no changes in this regard. The overall picture is almost completely a tableau of no significant change. . . .

Statistical studies of the relationship between availability 3
of erotic materials and the rates of sex crimes in Denmark indicate that the increased availability of explicit sexual materials has been accompanied by a decrease in the incidence of sexual crime. Analysis of police records of the same types of sex crimes in Copenhagen during the past 12 years revealed that a dramatic decrease in reported sex crimes occurred during this period and that the decrease coincided with changes in Danish law which permitted wider availability of explicit sexual materials. Other research showed that the decrease in reported sexual offenses cannot be attributed to concurrent changes in the social and legal definitions of sex crimes or in public attitudes toward reporting such crimes to the police, or in police reporting procedures. 4

Statistical studies of the relationship between the availability of erotic material and the rates of sex crimes in the United States presents a more complex picture. During the period in which there has been a marked increase in the availability of erotic materials, some specific rates of arrest for sex crimes have increased (e.g., forcible rape) and others have declined (e.g., overall juvenile rates). For juveniles, the overall rate of arrests for sex crimes decreased even though arrests for nonsexual crimes increased by more than 100%. For adults, arrests for sex offenses increased slightly more than did arrests for nonsex offenses. The conclusion is that, for America, the relationship between the availability of erotica and changes in sex crime rates neither proves nor disproves the possibility that availability of erotica leads to crime, but the massive overall increases in sex crimes that have been alleged do not seem to have occurred. . . .

I. Non-Legislative Recommendation

The Commission believes that much of the "problem" 5
regarding materials which depict explicit sexual activity stems from the inability or reluctance of people in our society to be open and direct in dealing with sexual matters. . . .

The Commission believes that accurate, appropriate sex 6

information provided openly and directly through legitimate channels and from reliable sources in healthy contexts can compete successfully with potentially distorted, warped, inaccurate, and unreliable information about clandestine, illegitimate sources; and it believes that the attitudes and orientations toward sex produced by the open communication of appropriate sex information from reliable sources through legitimate channels will be normal and healthy, providing a solid foundation for the basic institutions of our society.

7 The Commission, therefore, . . . *recommends that a massive sex education effort be launched*. . . . The Commission feels that such a sex education program would provide a powerful positive approach to the problems of obscenity and pornography. By providing accurate and reliable sex information through legitimate sources, it would reduce interest in and dependence upon clandestine and less legitimate sources. By providing healthy attitudes and orientations toward sexual relationships, it would provide better protection for the individual against distorted and warped ideas he may encounter regarding sex. By providing greater ease in talking about sexual matters in appropriate contexts, the shock and offensiveness of encounters with sex would be reduced. . . .

II. Legislative Recommendation

8 *The Commission recommends that federal, state, and local legislation prohibiting the sale, exhibition, or distribution of sexual materials to consenting adults should be repealed*. . . .

Our conclusion is based upon the following considerations:

1. Extensive empirical investigation, both by the Commission and by others, provides no evidence that exposure to or use of explicit sexual materials plays a significant role in causation of social or individual harms such as crime, delinquency, sexual or nonsexual deviancy or severe emotional disturbances. . . . Empirical investigation thus supports the opinion of a substantial majority of persons professionally engaged in the treatment of deviancy, delinquency and antisocial behavior, that exposure to sexually

explicit materials has no harmful causal role in these areas. Studies show that a number of factors, such as disorganized family relationships and unfavorable peer influences, are intimately related to harmful sexual behavior or adverse character development. Exposure to sexually explicit materials, however, cannot be counted as among these determinative factors.

2. On the positive side, explicit sexual materials are sought as a source of entertainment and information by substantial numbers of American adults. At times, these materials also appear to serve to increase and facilitate constructive communication about sexual matters within marriage. The most frequent purchaser of explicit sexual materials is a college-educated, married male, in his thirties or forties, who is of above average socio-economic status. Even where materials are legally available to them, young adults and older adolescents do not constitute an important portion of the purchasers of such materials.

3. Society's attempts to legislate for adults in the area of obscenity have not been successful. Present laws prohibiting the consensual sale or distribution of explicit sexual materials to adults are extremely unsatisfactory in their practical application. The Constitution permits material to be deemed "obscene" for adults only if, as a whole, it appeals to the "prurient" interest of the average person, is "patently offensive" in light of "community standards," and lacks "redeeming social value." These vague and highly subjective aesthetic, psychological and moral tests do not provide meaningful guidance for law enforcement officials, juries or courts. As a result, law is inconsistently and sometimes erroneously applied and the distinctions made by courts between prohibited and permissible materials often appear indefensible. Errors in the application of the law and uncertainty about its scope also cause interference with the communication of constitutionally protected materials.

4. Public opinion in America does not support the imposition of legal prohibitions upon the right of adults to read or see explicit sexual materials. While a minority of Americans favors such prohibitions, a majority of the American people presently are of the view that adults should be legally able to read or see explicit sexual materials if they wish to do so.

5. The lack of consensus among Americans concerning whether explicit sexual materials should be available to

adults in our society, and the significant number of adults who wish to have access to such materials, pose serious problems regarding the enforcement of legal prohibitions upon adults, even aside from the vagueness and subjectivity of present law. Consistent enforcement of even the clearest prohibitions upon consensual adult exposure to explicit sexual materials would require the expenditure of considerable law enforcement resources. In the absence of a persuasive demonstration of damage flowing from consensual exposure to such materials, there seems no justification for thus adding to the overwhelming tasks already placed upon the law enforcement system. Inconsistent enforcement of prohibitions, on the other hand, invites discriminatory action based upon considerations not directly relevant to the policy of the law. The latter alternative also breeds public disrespect for the legal process.

6. The foregoing considerations take on an added significance because of the fact that adult obscenity laws deal in the realm of speech and communication. Americans deeply value the right of each individual to determine for himself what books he wishes to read and what pictures or films he wishes to see. Our traditions of free speech and press also value and protect the right of writers, publishers, and booksellers to serve the diverse interests of the public. The spirit and letter of our Constitution tell us that government should not seek to interfere with these rights unless a clear threat of harm makes that course imperative. Moreover, the possibility of the misuse of general obscenity statutes prohibiting distributions of books and films to adults constitutes a continuing threat to the free communication of ideas among Americans—one of the most important foundations of our liberties.

7. In reaching its recommendation that government should not seek to prohibit consensual distributions of sexual materials to adults, the Commission discussed several arguments which are often advanced in support of such legislation. The Commission carefully considered the view that adult legislation should be retained in order to aid in the protection of young persons from exposure to explicit sexual materials. We do not believe that the objective of protecting youth may justifiably be achieved at the expense of denying adults materials of their choice. It seems to us wholly inappropriate to adjust the level of adult communication to that considered suitable for children. Indeed, the

Supreme Court has unanimously held that adult legislation premised on this basis is a clearly unconstitutional interference with liberty. . . .

8. The Commission has also taken cognizance of the concern of many people that the lawful distribution of explicit sexual materials to adults may have a deleterious effect upon the individual morality of American citizens and upon the moral climate in America as a whole. This concern appears to flow from a belief that exposure to explicit materials may cause moral confusion which, in turn, may induce antisocial or criminal behavior. As noted above, the Commission has found no evidence to support such a contention. Nor is there evidence that exposure to explicit sexual materials adversely affects character or moral attitudes regarding sex and sexual conduct. . . .

Report of the President's Commission on Obscenity and Pornography (Minority Report)

Overview

The Commission's majority report is a Magna Carta for the pornographer. . . . The fundamental "finding" on which the entire report is based is: that "empirical research" has come up with "no reliable evidence to indicate that exposure to explicit sexual materials plays a significant role in the causation of delinquent or criminal behavior among youth or adults." The inference from this statement, i.e., pornography is harmless, is not only insupportable on the slanted evidence presented; it is preposterous. How isolate one factor and say it causes or does not cause criminal behavior? How determine that one book or one film caused one man to commit rape or murder? A man's entire life goes into one criminal act. No one factor can be said to have caused that act. 1

The Commission has deliberately and carefully avoided coming to grips with the basic underlying issue. The government interest in regulating pornography has always related primarily to the prevention of moral corruption and *not* to prevention of overt criminal acts and conduct, or the protection of persons from being shocked and/or offended. 2

The basic question is whether and to what extent society may establish and maintain certain moral standards. If it is conceded that society has a legitimate concern in maintaining moral standards, it follows logically that government has a legitimate interest in at least attempting to protect such standards against any source which threatens them. . . .

3 Sex education, recommended so strongly by the majority, is the panacea for those who advocate license in media. The report suggests sex education, with a plaint for the dearth of instructors and materials. It notes that three schools have used "hard-core pornography" in training potential instructors. The report does not answer the question that comes to mind immediately: Will these instructors not bring the hard-core pornography into the grammar schools? Many other questions are left unanswered: How assure that the instructor's moral or ethical code (or lack of same) will not be communicated to children? Shouldn't parents, not children, be the recipients of sex education courses?

4 Children cannot grow in love if they are trained with pornography. Pornography is loveless; it degrades the human being, reduces him to the level of animal. And if this Commission majority's recommendations are heeded, there will be a glut of pornography for teachers and children.

5 In contrast to the Commission report's amazing statement that public opinion in America does not support the imposition of legal prohibitions upon the consensual distribution of pornography to adults, we find, as a result of public hearings conducted by two of the undersigned in eight cities throughout the country, that the majority of the American people favor tighter controls. Twenty-six out of twenty-seven witnesses at the hearing in New York City expressed concern and asked for remedial measures. Witnesses were a cross section of the community, ranging from members of the judiciary to members of women's clubs. This pattern was repeated in the cities of New Orleans, Indianapolis, Chicago, Salt Lake City, San Francisco, Washington, D.C., and Buffalo. . . . Additionally, law enforcement officers testifying at the Hill-Link hearings were unanimous in declaring that the problem of obscenity and pornography is a serious one. . . . We point also to the results of a Gallup poll, published in the summer of 1969. Eighty-five out of every 100 adults interviewed said they favored stricter state and local laws dealing with pornography sent through the mails,

and 76 of every 100 wanted stricter laws on the sort of magazines and newspapers available on newsstands. . . .

Some have argued that because sex crimes have apparently declined in Denmark while the volume of pornography has increased, we need not be concerned about the potential effect in our country of this kind of material (because, essentially, of Denmark's benign experience). However two considerations must be noted. First we are a different culture with a greater commitment to the Judeo-Christian tradition; and secondly, we are actually only a year or so behind Denmark in the distribution and sale of pornography. Hardcore written pornography can be purchased anywhere in the U.S. now. Hardcore still pictures and movies can now be purchased over the counter in some cities. Anything can be purchased through the mails. And in a few cities people can attend hardcore pornographic movies. About the only thing we don't have, which Denmark has, are live sex shows. What is most relevant are sex crime statistics in this country, not Denmark . . . : 6

Reported Rapes (verified)
Up 116% 1960–69 (absolute increase)
Up 93% 1960–69 (controlled for Pop. Growth)

Rape Arrests
Up 56.6% all ages 1960–69
Up 85.9% males under 18 1960–69

However, it should be stated that conclusively proving causal relationships among social science type variables is extremely difficult if not impossible. Among adults whose life histories have included much exposure to pornography it is nearly impossible to disentangle the literally hundreds of causal threads or chains that contributed to their later adjustment or maladjustment. Because of the extreme complexity of the problem and the uniqueness of the human experience it is doubtful that we will ever have absolutely convincing scientific proof that pornography is or isn't harmful. And the issue isn't restricted to, "Does pornography cause or contribute to sex crimes?" The issue has to do with how pornography affects or influences the individual in his total relationship to members of the same as well as opposite sex, children and adults, with all of its ramifications. 7

Susan Brownmiller

Let's Put Pornography Back in the Closet

Susan Brownmiller is a journalist, novelist, women's rights activist, and a founder of Women against Pornography. Her book Against Our Will: Men, Women, and Rape, *published in 1975, articulates her position on pornography. (She has also published* Femininity, *in 1984; if you would like to read a sample from that book, see page 316.) The following essay appeared in* Newsday, *a Long Island newspaper, in 1979, and a year later in* Take Back the Night, *a collection of essays against pornography.*

1 Free speech is one of the great foundations on which our democracy rests. I am old enough to remember the Hollywood Ten, the screenwriters who went to jail in the late 1940s because they refused to testify before a congressional committee about their political affiliations. They tried to use the First Amendment as a defense, but they went to jail because in those days there were few civil liberties lawyers around who cared to champion the First Amendment right to free speech, when the speech concerned the Communist Party.

2 The Hollywood Ten were correct in claiming the First Amendment. Its high purpose is the protection of unpopular ideas and political dissent. In the dark, cold days of the 1950s, few civil libertarians were willing to declare themselves First Amendment absolutists. But in the brighter, though frantic, days of the 1960s, the principle of protecting unpopular political speech was gradually strengthened.

3 It is fair to say now that the battle has largely been won. Even the American Nazi Party has found itself the beneficiary of the dedicated, tireless work of the American Civil Liberties Union. But—and please notice the quotation marks coming up—"To equate the free and robust exchange of ideas and political debate with commercial exploitation of obscene material demeans the grand conception of the First Amendment and its high purposes in the historic struggle for freedom. It is a misuse of the great guarantees of free speech and free press."

4 I didn't say that, although I wish I had, for I think the words are thrilling. Chief Justice Warren Burger said it in

1973, in the United States Supreme Court's majority opinion in *Miller* v. *California*. During the same decades that the right to political free speech was being strengthened in the courts, the nation's obscenity laws also were undergoing extensive revision.

It's amazing to recall that in 1934 the question of whether James Joyce's *Ulysses* should be banned as pornographic actually went before the Court. The battle to protect *Ulysses* as a work of literature with redeeming social value was won. In later decades, Henry Miller's *Tropic* books, *Lady Chatterley's Lover* and the *Memoirs of Fanny Hill* also were adjudged not obscene. These decisions have been important to me. As the author of *Against Our Will,* a study of the history of rape that does contain explicit sexual material, I shudder to think how my book would have fared if James Joyce, D. H. Lawrence and Henry Miller hadn't gone before me. 5

I am not a fan of *Chatterley* or the *Tropic* books, I should quickly mention. They are not to my literary taste, nor do I think they represent female sexuality with any degree of accuracy. But I would hardly suggest that we ban them. Such a suggestion wouldn't get very far anyway. The battle to protect these books is ancient history. Time does march on, quite methodically. What, then, is unlawfully obscene, and what does the First Amendment have to do with it? 6

In the Miller case of 1973 (not Henry Miller, by the way, but a porn distributor who sent unsolicited stuff through the mails), the Court came up with new guidelines that it hoped would strengthen obscenity laws by giving more power to the states. What it did in actuality was throw everything into confusion. It set up a three-part test by which materials can be adjudged obscene. The materials are obscene if they depict patently offensive, hard-core sexual conduct; lack serious scientific, literary, artistic or political value; and appeal to the prurient interest of an average person—as measured by contemporary community standards. 7

"Patently offensive," "prurient interest" and "hard-core" are indeed words to conjure with. "Contemporary community standards" are what we're trying to redefine. The feminist objection to pornography is not based on prurience, which the dictionary defines as lustful, itching desire. We are not opposed to sex and desire, with or without the itch, and we certainly believe that explicit sexual material has its place in literature, art, science and education. Here we part company rather swiftly with old-line conservatives who 8 don't want sex education in the high schools, for example.

9 No, the feminist objection to pornography is based on our belief that pornography represents hatred of women, that pornography's intent is to humiliate, degrade and dehumanize the female body for the purpose of erotic stimulation and pleasure. We are unalterably opposed to the presentation of the female body being stripped, bound, raped, tortured, mutilated and murdered in the name of commercial entertainment and free speech.

10 These images, which are standard pornographic fare, have nothing to do with the hallowed right of political dissent. They have everything to do with the creation of a cultural climate in which a rapist feels he is merely giving in to a normal urge and a woman is encouraged to believe that sexual masochism is healthy, liberated fun. Justice Potter Stewart once said about hard-core pornography, "You know it when you see it," and that certainly used to be true. In the good old days, pornography looked awful. It was cheap and sleazy, and there was no mistaking it for art.

11 Nowadays, since the porn industry has become a multimillion dollar business, visual technology has been employed in its service. Pornographic movies are skillfully filmed and edited, pornographic still shots using the newest tenets of good design artfully grace the covers of *Hustler, Penthouse* and *Playboy,* and the public—and the courts—are sadly confused.

12 The Supreme Court neglected to define "hard-core" in the Miller decision. This was a mistake. If "hard-core" refers only to explicit sexual intercourse, then that isn't good enough. When women or children or men—no matter how artfully—are shown tortured or terrorized in the service of sex, that's obscene. And "patently offensive," I would hope, to our "contemporary community standards."

13 Justice William O. Douglas wrote in his dissent to the Miller case that no one is "compelled to look." This is hardly true. To buy a paper at the corner newsstand is to subject oneself to a forcible immersion in pornography, to be demeaned by an array of dehumanized, chopped-up parts of the female anatomy, packaged like cuts of meat at the supermarket. I happen to like my body and I work hard at the gym to keep it in good shape, but I am embarrassed for my body and for the bodies of all women when I see the fragmented parts of us so frivolously, and so flagrantly, displayed.

Some constitutional theorists (Justice Douglas was one) have maintained that any obscenity law is a serious abridgement of free speech. Others (and Justice Earl Warren was one) have maintained that the First Amendment was never intended to protect obscenity. We live quite compatibly with a host of free-speech abridgements. There are restraints against false and misleading advertising or statements—shouting "fire" without cause in a crowded movie theater, etc.—that do not threaten, but strengthen, our societal values. Restrictions on the public display of pornography belong in this category. 14

The distinction between permission to publish and permission to display publicly is an essential one and one which I think consonant with First Amendment principles. Justice Burger's words which I quoted above support this without question. We are not saying "Smash the presses" or "Ban the bad ones," but simply "Get the stuff out of our sight." Let the legislatures decide—using realistic and humane contemporary community standards—what can be displayed and what cannot. The courts, after all, will be the final arbiters. 15

Susan Jacoby

I Am a First Amendment Junkie

Susan Jacoby, born 1946, has written numerous articles on women's issues for popular magazines such as Glamour, McCall's, *and* The Nation, *as well as several books. She has also served as a columnist for* The Washington Post *and* The New York Times; *in fact, the following argument appeared in her syndicated "Hers" column in 1978.*

It is no news that many women are defecting from the ranks of civil libertarians on the issue of obscenity. The conviction of Larry Flynt, publisher of *Hustler* magazine—before his metamorphosis into a born-again Christian—was greeted with unabashed feminist approval. Harry Reems, the unknown actor who was convicted by a Memphis jury 1 for conspiring to distribute the movie *Deep Throat,* has carried on his legal battles with almost no support from women who ordinarily regard themselves as supporters of the First Amendment. Feminist writers and scholars have even discussed the possibility of making common cause against pornography with adversaries of the women's movement—including opponents of the equal rights amendment and "right-to-life" forces.

2 All of this is deeply disturbing to a woman writer who believes, as I always have and still do, in an absolute interpretation of the First Amendment. Nothing in Larry Flynt's garbage convinces me that the late Justice Hugo L. Black was wrong in this opinion that "the Federal Government is without any power whatsoever under the Constitution to put any type of burden on free speech and expression of ideas of any kind (as distinguished from conduct)." Many women I like and respect tell me I am wrong; I cannot remember having become involved in so many heated discussions of a public issue since the end of the Vietnam War. A feminist writer described my views as those of a "First Amendment junkie."

3 Many feminist arguments for controls on pornography carry the implicit conviction that porn books, magazines and movies pose a greater threat to women than similarly repulsive exercises of free speech pose to other offended groups. This conviction has, of course, been shared by everyone—regardless of race, creed or sex—who has ever argued in favor of abridging the First Amendment. It is the argument used by some Jews who have withdrawn their support from the American Civil Liberties Union because it has defended the right of American Nazis to march through a community inhabited by survivors of Hitler's concentration camps.

4 If feminists want to argue that the protection of the Constitution should not be extended to *any* particularly odious or threatening form of speech, they have a reasonable argument (although I don't agree with it). But it is ridiculous to suggest that the porn shops on 42d Street are more disgusting to women than a march of neo-Nazis is to survivors of the extermination camps.

5 The arguments over pornography also blur the vital

distinction between expression of ideas and conduct. When I say I believe unreservedly in the First Amendment, someone always comes back at me with the issue of "kiddie porn." But kiddie porn is not a First Amendment issue. It is an issue of the abuse of power—the power adults have over children—and not of obscenity. Parents and promoters have no more right to use their children to make porn movies than they do to send them to work in coal mines. The responsible adults should be prosecuted, just as adults who use children for back-breaking farm labor should be prosecuted.

Susan Brownmiller, in *Against Our Will: Men, Women and Rape,* has described pornography as "the undiluted essence of anti-female propaganda." I think this is a fair description of some types of pornography, especially of the brutish subspecies that equates sex with death and portrays women primarily as objects of violence. 6

The equation of sex and violence, personified by some glossy rock record album covers as well as by *Hustler,* has fed the illusion that censorship of pornography can be conducted on a more rational basis than other types of censorship. Are all pictures of naked women obscene? Clearly not, says a friend. A Renoir nude is art, she says, and *Hustler* is trash. "Any reasonable person" knows that. 7

But what about something between art and trash—something, say, along the lines of *Playboy* or *Penthouse* magazines? I asked five women for their reactions to one picture in *Penthouse* and got responses that ranged from "lovely" and "sensuous" to "revolting" and "demeaning." Feminists, like everyone else, seldom have rational reasons for their preferences in erotica. Like members of juries, they tend to disagree when confronted with something that falls short of 100 percent vulgarity. 8

In any case, feminists will not be the arbiters of good taste if it becomes easier to harass, prosecute and convict people on obscenity charges. Most of the people who want to censor girlie magazines are equally opposed to open discussion of issues that are of vital concern to women: rape, abortion, menstruation, contraception, lesbianism—in fact, the entire range of sexual experience from a woman's viewpoint. 9

Feminist writers and editors and film makers have limited 10 financial resources: Confronted by a determined prosecutor, Hugh Hefner will fare better than Susan Brownmiller. Would the Memphis jurors who convicted Harry Reems for his role in *Deep Throat* be inclined to take a more positive view of paintings of the female genitalia done by sensitive feminist artists? *Ms.* magazine has printed color reproductions of some of those art works; *Ms.* is already banned from a number of high school libraries because someone considers it threatening and/or obscene.

11 Feminists who want to censor what they regard as harmful pornography have essentially the same motivation as other would-be censors: They want to use the power of the state to accomplish what they have been unable to achieve in the marketplace of ideas and images. The impulse to censor places no faith in the possibilities of democratic persuasion.

12 It isn't easy to persuade certain men that they have better uses for $1.95 each month than to spend it on a copy of *Hustler?* Well, then, give the men no choice in the matter.

13 I believe there is also a connection between the impulse toward censorship on the part of people who used to consider themselves civil libertarians and a more general desire to shift responsibility from individuals to institutions. When I saw the movie *Looking for Mr. Goodbar,* I was stunned by its series of visual images equating sex and violence, coupled with what seems to me the mindless message (a distortion of the fine Judith Rossner novel) that casual sex equals death. When I came out of the movie, I was even more shocked to see parents standing in line with children between the ages of 10 and 14.

14 I simply don't know why a parent would take a child to see such a movie, any more than I understand why people feel they can't turn off a television set their child is watching. Whenever I say that, my friends tell me I don't know how it is because I don't have children. True, but I do have parents. When I was a child, they did turn off the TV. They didn't expect the Federal Communications Commission to do their job for them.

15 I am a First Amendment junkie. You can't OD on the First Amendment, because free speech is its own best antidote.

John Irving

Pornography and the New Puritans

If you saw the film The World According to Garp, *you have had some experience with the work of John Irving (born 1942), for he is the author of the novel on which the film was based as well as six other novels. He contributed the following essay to* The New York Times Book Review *in March 1992. Notice that a response to the article, also printed in the* Times Book Review, *is printed right after it.*

1 These are censorial times. I refer to the pornography victims' compensation bill, now under consideration by the Senate Judiciary Committee—that same bunch of wise men who dispatched such clearheaded, objective jurisprudence in the Clarence Thomas hearings. I can't wait to see what they're going to do with this maladroit proposal. The bill would encourage victims of sexual crimes to bring civil suits against publishers and distributors of material that is "obscene or constitutes child pornography"—*if* they can prove that the material was "a substantial cause of the offense," *and if* the publisher or distributor should have "foreseen" that such material created an "unreasonable risk of such a crime." If this bill passes, it will be the first piece of legislation to give credence to the unproven theory that sexually explicit material actually *causes* sexual crimes.

2 At the risk of sounding old-fashioned, I'm still pretty sure that rape and child molestation predate erotic books and pornographic magazines and X-rated videocassettes. I also remember the report of the two-year, $2 million President's Commission on Obscenity and Pornography (1970), which concluded there was "no reliable evidence . . . that exposure to explicit sexual material plays a significant role in the causation of delinquent or criminal sexual behavior." In 1986, not satisfied with that conclusion, the Meese commission on pornography and the Surgeon General's conference on pornography also failed to establish such a link. Now, here they go again.

3 This time, it's Republican Senators Mitch McConnell of Kentucky, Charles Grassley of Iowa and Strom Thurmond of South Carolina; I can't help wondering if they read much.

Their charmless bill is a grave mistake for several reasons; for starters, it's morally reprehensible to shift the responsibility for any sexual crime onto a third party—namely, *away* from the actual perpetrator.

4 And then, of course, there's the matter of the bill running counter to the spirit of the First Amendment of the United States Constitution; this bill is a piece of back-door censorship, plain and simple. Moreover, since the laws on obscenity differ from state to state, and no elucidation of the meaning of obscenity is presented in the bill, how are the publishers or distributors to know in advance if their material is actionable or not? It is my understanding, therefore, that the true intent of the bill is to make the actual creators of this material think very conservatively—that is, when their imaginations turn to sex and violence.

5 I recall that I received a lot of unfriendly mail in connection with a somewhat explicit scene in my novel "The World According to Garp," wherein a selfish young man loses part of his anatomy while enjoying oral sex in a car. (I suppose I've always had a fear of rear-end collisions.) But thinking back about that particular hate mail, I don't recall a single letter from a young woman saying that she intended to rush out and *do* this to someone; and in the 14 years since that novel's publication, in more than 35 foreign languages, no one who actually *has done* this to someone has written to thank me for giving her the idea. Boy, am I lucky!

6 In a brilliant article on the Op-Ed page of *The New York Times,* Teller, of those marvelous magicians Penn & Teller, had this to say about the pornography victims' compensation bill: "The advocates of this bill seem to think that if we stop showing rape in movies people will stop committing it in real life. Anthropologists call this 'magical thinking.' It's the same impulse that makes people stick pins in voodoo dolls, hoping to cripple an enemy. It feels logical, but it does not work." (For those of you who've seen these two magicians and are wondering which is Penn and which is Teller, Teller is the one who never talks. He *writes* very well, however.) "It's a death knell for creativity, too," Teller writes. "Start punishing make-believe, and those gifted with imagination will stop sharing it." He adds, "We will enter an intellectual era even more insipid than the one we live in."

7 Now *there's* a scary idea! I remember when the film

version of Günter Grass's novel "The Tin Drum" was banned in Canada. I always assumed it was the eel scene that offended the censors, but I don't know. In those days, a little naked sex—in the conventional position—was permissible, but unpleasant suggestiveness with eels was clearly going too far. But now, in the light of this proposed pornography victims' compensation bill, is there any evidence to suggest that there have been *fewer* hellish incidents of women being force-fed eels in Canada than in those countries where the film was available? Somehow, I doubt it. I know that they're out there—those guys who want to force-feed eels to women—but I suspect they're going to do what they're going to do, unaided by books or films. The point is: let's do something about *them,* instead of trying to control what they read or see.

It dismays me how some of my feminist friends are hot to ban pornography. I'm sorry that they have such short memories. It wasn't very long ago when a book as innocent and valuable as "Our Bodies, Ourselves" was being banned by school boards and public libraries across the country. The idea of this good book was that women should have access to detailed information about their bodies and their health, yet the so-called feminist ideology behind the book was thought to be subversive; indeed, it was (at that time) deplored. But many writers and writers' organizations (like PEN) wrote letters to those school boards and those public libraries. I can't speak to the overall effectiveness of these letters in regard to reinstating the book, but I'm aware that some of the letters worked; I wrote several of those letters. Now here are some of my old friends, telling me that attitudes toward rape and child molestation can be changed only if we remove the offensive *ideas.* Once again, it's ideology that's being banned. And although the movement to ban pornography is especially self-righteous, it looks like blacklisting to me. 8

Fascism has enjoyed many name changes, but it usually amounts to banning something you dislike and can't control. Take abortion, for example. I think groups should have to apply for names; if the Right to Life people had asked me, I'd have told them to find a more fitting label for themselves. It's morally inconsistent to manifest such concern for the poor fetus in a society that shows absolutely no pity for the poor child after it's born. 9

I'm also not so sure that these so-called Right to Lifers are 10 as fired up about those fetuses as they say. I suspect what really makes them sore is the idea of women having sex and somehow not having to *pay* for it—pay in the sense of suffering all the way through an unwanted pregnancy. I believe this is part of the loathing for promiscuity that has always fueled those Americans who feel that a life of common decency is slipping from their controlling grasp. This notion is reflected in the unrealistic hope of those wishful thinkers who tell us that sexual abstinence is an alternative to wearing a condom. But I say how about *carrying* a condom, just in case you're moved to *not* abstain?

11 No one is coercing women into having abortions, but the Right to Lifers want to coerce women into having babies; that's why the pro-choice people are well named. It's unfortunate, however, that a few of my pro-choice friends think that the pornography victims' compensation bill is a good idea. I guess that they're really not entirely pro-choice. They want the choice to reproduce or not, but they *don't* want too broad a choice of things to read and see; they know what *they* want to read and see, and they expect other people to be content with what they want. This sounds like a Right to Life idea to me.

12 Most feminist groups, despite their vital advocacy of full enforcement of laws against violence to women and children, seem opposed to Senate Bill 1521. As of this writing, both the National Organization for Women in New York State and in California have written to the Senate Judiciary Committee in opposition to the bill, although the Los Angeles chapter of NOW states that it has "no position." I admit it is perverse of me even to imagine what Tammy Bruce thinks about the pornography victims' compensation bill; I hope Ms. Bruce is not such a loose cannon as she appears, but she has me worried. Ms. Bruce is president of L.A. NOW, and she has lately distinguished herself with two counts of knee-jerk overreaction. Most recently, she found the Academy of Motion Picture Arts and Sciences to be guilty of an "obvious exhibition of sexism" in not nominating Barbra Streisand for an Oscar for best director. Well, maybe. Ms. Streisand's other talents have not been entirely overlooked; I meekly submit that the academy might have found "The Prince of Tides" lacking in directorial merit—it wouldn't be the first I've heard of such criticism. (Ms. Bruce says the L.A. chapter received "unrelenting calls" from NOW members who were riled up at the perceived sexism.)

Most readers will remember Tammy Bruce for jumping all over that nasty novel by Bret Easton Ellis. To refresh our memories: Simon & Schuster decided at the 11th hour not to publish *American Psycho* after concluding that its grisly content was in "questionable taste." Now please don't get excited and think I'm going to call that censorship; that was merely a breach of contract. And besides, Simon & Schuster has a right to its own opinion of what questionable taste is. *People* magazine tells us that Judith Regan, a vice president and senior editor at Simon & Schuster, recently had a book idea, which she pitched to Madonna. "My idea was for her to write a book of her sexual fantasies, her thoughts, the meanderings of her erotic mind," Ms. Regan said. The pity is, Madonna hasn't delivered. And according to Mitchell Fink, author of the Insider column for *People,* "Warner Books confirmed it is talking about a book—no word on what kind—with Madonna." I don't know Madonna, but maybe she thought the Simon & Schuster book idea was in questionable taste. Simon & Schuster, clearly, subscribes to more than one opinion of what questionable taste *is.* 13

But only two days after Mr. Ellis's book was dropped by Simon & Schuster, Sonny Mehta, president of Alfred A. Knopf and Vintage Books, bought *American Psycho,* which was published in March 1991. Prior to the novel's publication, Ms. Bruce called for a boycott of all Knopf and Vintage titles—except for books by feminist authors, naturally—until *American Psycho* was withdrawn from publication (it wasn't), or until the end of 1991. To the charge of censorship, Ms. Bruce declared that she was *not* engaged in it; she sure fooled me. 14

But Ms. Bruce wasn't alone in declaring what *wasn't* censorship, nor was she alone in her passion; she not only condemned Mr. Ellis's novel—she condemned its availability. And not only the book itself *but its availability* were severely taken to task in the very pages in which I now write. In December 1990—three months *before American Psycho* was published, and at the urging of *The Book Review*—Roger Rosenblatt settled Mr. Ellis's moral hash in a piece of writing prissy enough to please Jesse Helms. According to Mr. Rosenblatt, Jesse Helms has never engaged in censorship, either. For those of us who remain improperly educated in regard to what censorship actually *is,* Mr. Rosenblatt offers a blanket definition. "Censorship is when a 15 government burns your manuscript, smashes your presses and throws you in jail," he says.

16 Well, as much as I may identify with Mr. Rosenblatt's literary taste, I'm of the opinion that there are a few forms of censorship more subtle than that, and Mr. Rosenblatt has engaged in one of them. If you slam a book when it's published, that's called book reviewing, but if you write about a book three months in advance of its publication and your conclusion is "don't buy it," your intentions are more censorial than critical.

17 And it *is* censorship when the writer of such perceived trash is not held *as* accountable as the book's publisher; the pressure that was brought to bear on Mr. Mehta was totally censorial. *The Book Review* is at its most righteous in abusing Mr. Mehta, who is described as "clearly as hungry for a killing as Patrick Bateman." (For those of you who don't know Mr. Ellis's book, Patrick Bateman is the main character and a serial killer.) Even as reliable a fellow as the editorial director of *Publisher's Weekly,* John F. Baker, described *American Psycho* as a book that "does transcend the boundaries of what is acceptable in mainstream publishing."

18 It's the very idea of making or keeping publishing "acceptable" that gives *me* the shivers, because that's the same idea that lurks behind the pornography victims' compensation bill—making the *publisher* (not the perpetrator of the crime or the writer of the pornography) responsible for what's "acceptable." If you want to bash Bret Easton Ellis for what he's written, go ahead and bash him. But when you presume to tell Sonny Mehta, or any other publisher, what he can or can't—or should or shouldn't—*publish,* that's when you've stepped into dangerous territory. In fact, that's when you're knee-deep in blacklisting, and you ought to know better—all of you.

19 Mr. Rosenblatt himself actually says, "No one argues that a publishing house hasn't the right to print what it wants. We fight for that right. But not everything is a right. At some point, someone in authority somewhere has to look at Mr. Ellis's rat and call the exterminator." Now this is interesting, and perhaps worse than telling Sonny Mehta what he should or shouldn't publish—because that's exactly what Mr. Rosenblatt *is* doing while he's *saying* that he isn't.

Do we remember that tangent of the McCarran-Walter Act of 1952, that finally defunct business about ideological exclusion? That was when we kept someone from coming into our country because we perceived that the person had *ideas* that were in conflict with the "acceptable" ideas of our country. Under this act of exclusion, writers as distinguished as Graham Greene and Gabriel Garcia Márquez were kept out of the United States. Well, when we attack what a publisher has the right to publish, we are simply applying the old ideological exclusion act at home. Of all people, those of us in the idea business should know better than that. 20

As for the pornography victims' compensation bill, the vote in the Senate Judiciary Committee will be close. As of this writing, seven senators have publicly indicated their support of the bill; they need only one more vote to pass the bill out of committee. Friends at PEN tell me that the committee has received a lot of letters from women saying that support of the bill would in some way "make up for" the committee's mishandling of the Clarence Thomas hearings. Some women are putting the decision to support Justice Thomas alongside the decision to find William Kennedy Smith innocent of rape; these women think that a really strong antipornography bill will make up for what they perceive to be the miscarriage of justice in both cases. 21

The logic of this thinking is more than a little staggering. What would these women think if lots of men were to write the committee and say that because Mike Tyson has been found guilty of rape, what we need is *more* pornography to make up for what's happened to Iron Mike? This would make a lot of sense, wouldn't it? 22

I conclude that these are not only censorial times; these are stupid times. However, there is some hope that opposition to Senate Bill 1521 is mounting. The committee met on March 12 but the members didn't vote on the bill. Discussion was brief, yet encouraging. Colorado Senator Hank Brown told his colleagues that there are serious problems with the legislation; he should be congratulated for his courageous decision to oppose the other Republicans on the committee, but he should also be encouraged not to accept any compromise proposal. Ohio Senator Howard Metzenbaum suggested that imposing third-party liability on producers and distributors of books, magazines, movies and recordings raises the question of whether the bill 23 shouldn't be amended to cover the firearms and liquor industries as well.

24 It remains to be seen if the committee members will resist the temptation to *fix* the troubled bill. I hope they will understand that the bill cannot be fixed because it is based on an erroneous premise—namely, that publishers or distributors should be held liable for the acts of criminals. But what is important for us to recognize, even if this lame bill is amended out of existence or flat-out defeated, is that *new* antipornography legislation will be proposed.

25 Do we remember Nancy Reagan's advice to would-be drug users? ("Just say no.") As applied to drug use, Mrs. Reagan's advice is feeble in the extreme. But writers and other members of the literary community *should* just say no to censorship in any and every form. Of course, it will always be the most grotesque example of child pornography that will be waved in front of our eyes by the Good Taste Police. If we're opposed to censorship, they will say, are we in favor of filth like this?

26 No; we are not in favor of child pornography if we say no to censorship. If we disapprove of reinstating public hangings, that doesn't mean that we want all the murderers to be set free. No writer or publisher or *reader* should accept censorship in any form; fundamental to our freedom of expression is that each of us has a right to decide what is obscene and what isn't.

27 But lest you think I'm being paranoid about the iniquities and viciousness of our times, I'd like you to read a description of Puritan times. It was written in 1837—more than 150 years ago—and it describes a scene in a Puritan community in Massachusetts that you must imagine taking place more than 350 years ago. This is from a short story by Nathaniel Hawthorne called "Endicott and the Red Cross," which itself was written more than 10 years before Hawthorne wrote "The Scarlet Letter." This little story contains the germ of the idea for that famous novel about a woman condemned by Puritan justice to wear the letter A on her breast. But Hawthorne, obviously, had been thinking about the iniquities and viciousness of early New England morality for many years.

28 Please remember, as you read what Nathaniel Hawthorne thought of the Puritans, that the Puritans are not dead and gone. We have many new Puritans in our country today; they are as dangerous to freedom of expression as the old

Puritans ever were. An especially sad thing is, a few of these new Puritans are formerly liberal-thinking feminists.

“In close vicinity to the sacred edifice [the meeting-house] 29
appeared that important engine of Puritanic authority, the whipping-post—with the soil around it well trodden by the feet of evil doers, who had there been disciplined. At one corner of the meeting-house was the pillory, and at the other the stocks; . . . the head of an Episcopalian and suspected Catholic was grotesquely incased in the former machine; while a fellow-criminal, who had boisterously quaffed a health to the king, was confined by the legs in the latter. Side by side, on the meeting-house steps, stood a male and a female figure. The man was a tall, lean, haggard personification of fanaticism, bearing on his breast this label,—A WANTON GOSPELLER,—which betokened that he had dared to give interpretations of Holy Writ unsanctioned by the infallible judgment of the civil and religious rulers. His aspect showed no lack of zeal . . . even at the stake. The woman wore a cleft stick on her tongue, in appropriate retribution for having wagged that unruly member against the elders of the church; and her countenance and gestures gave much cause to apprehend that, the moment the stick should be removed, a repetition of the offence would demand new ingenuity in chastising it.

“The above-mentioned individuals had been sentenced to 30
undergo their various modes of ignominy, for the space of one hour at noonday. But among the crowd were several whose punishment would be life-long; some, whose ears had been cropped, like those of puppy dogs; others, whose cheeks had been branded with the initials of their misdemeanors; one, with his nostrils slit and seared; and another, with a halter about his neck, which he was forbidden ever to take off, or to conceal beneath his garments. Methinks he must have been grievously tempted to affix the other end of the rope to some convenient beam or bough. There was likewise a young woman, with no mean share of beauty, whose doom to was to wear the letter A on the breast of her gown, in the eyes of all the world and her own children. And even her own children knew what that initial signified. Sporting with her infamy, the lost and desperate creature had embroidered the fatal token in scarlet cloth, with golden thread and the nicest art of needlework; so that the capital A might have been thought to mean Admirable, or anything rather than Adulteress.

31 "Let not the reader argue, from any of these evidences of iniquity, that the times of the Puritans were more vicious than our own."

32 In my old-fashioned opinion, Mr. Hawthorne sure got that right.

Andrea Dworkin

Reply to John Irving

As she notes in the following reply, Andrea Dworkin (born 1947) has written (with University of Michigan law professor Catherine MacKinnon) antipornography ordinances for Minneapolis, Indianapolis, and other cities. (The ordinances later were overturned by the courts.) A successful and controversial essayist and fiction writer, she has also written Pornography: Men Possessing Women *(1988) and* Pornography and Civil Rights *(1988), both of which argue in favor of the kinds of laws that she advocates.*

To the Editor:

1 As a woman determined to destroy the pornography industry, a writer of 10 published books and someone who reads, perhaps I should be the one to tell John Irving ("Pornography and the New Puritans," March 29) who the new Puritan is. The old Puritans wouldn't like her very much; but then, neither does Mr. Irving.

2 I am 45 years old now. When I was a teen-ager, I baby-sat. In any middle-class home one could always find the dirty books—on the highest shelf, climbing toward God, usually behind a parched potted plant. The books themselves were usually "Ulysses," "Tropic of Cancer" or "Lady Chatterley's Lover." They always had as a preface or afterword the text of an obscenity decision in which the book was exonerated and art extolled. Or a lawyer would stand in for the court to tell us that through his mighty efforts law had finally vindicated a persecuted genius.

3 Even at 15 and 16, I noticed something strange about the special intersection of art, law and sex under the obscenity

rubric: some men punished other men for producing or publishing writing that caused arousal in (presumably) still other men. Although Mrs. Grundy got the blame, women didn't make these laws or enforce them or sit on juries to deliberate guilt or innocence. This was a fight among men—but about what?

Meanwhile, my life as a woman in prefeminist times went 4
on. This means that I thought I was a human being with rights. But before I was much over 18, I had been sexually assaulted three times. Did I report these assaults (patriarchy's first question, because surely the girl must be lying)?

When I was 9, I told my parents. To protect me, for better 5
or worse, they did not call the police.

The second time, beaten as well as raped, I told no one. I 6
was working for a peace group, and I heard jokes about rape day in and day out. What do you tell the draft board when they ask you if you would kill a Nazi who was going to rape your sister? "I'd tell my sister to have a good time" was the answer of choice.

The third time, I was 18, a freshman in college, and I had 7
been arrested for taking part in a sit-in outside the United Nations to protest the Vietnam War. It was February of 1965. This time, my experience was reported in *The New York Times,* newspapers all around the world and on television: girl in prison—New York's notorious Women's House of Detention—says she was brutalized by two prison doctors. Forced entry with a speculum—for 15 days I had vaginal bleeding, a vagina so bruised and ripped that my stone-cold family doctor burst into tears when he examined me.

I came out of the Women's House of Detention mute. 8
Speech depends on believing you can make yourself understood: a community of people will recognize the experience in the words you use and they will care. You also have to be able to understand what happened to you enough to convey it to others. I lost speech. I was hurt past what I had words for. I lived out on the streets for several days, not having a bed of my own, still bleeding; and finally spoke because Grace Paley convinced me that she would understand and care. Then I spoke a lot. A grand jury investigated. Columnists indicted the prison. But neither of the prison doctors was charged with sexual assault or sexual battery. In fact, no one ever mentioned sexual assault. The grand jury concluded that the prison was fine. In despair, I left the country—to be a writer, my human dream.

9 A year later I came back. I have since discovered that what happened to me is common: homeless, poor, still sexually traumatized, I learned to trade sex for money. I spent a lot of years out on the street, living hand to mouth, these New York streets and other streets in other hard cities. I thought I was a real tough woman, and I was: tough-calloused; tough-numb; tough-desperate; tough-scared; tough-hungry; tough-beaten by men often; tough-done it every which way including up. All of my colleagues who fight pornography with me know about this. I know about the lives of women in pornography because I lived the life. So have many feminists who fight pornography. Freedom looks different when you are the one it is being practiced on. It's his, not yours. Speech is different, too. Those sexy expletives are the hate words he uses on you while he is using you. Your speech is an inchoate protest never voiced.

10 In my work, fiction and nonfiction, I've tried to voice the protest against a power that is dead weight on you, fist and penis organized to keep you quiet. I would do virtually anything to get women out of prostitution and pornography, which is mass-produced, technologized prostitution. With pornography, a woman can still be sold after the beatings, the rapes, the pain, the humiliation have killed her. I write for her, on behalf of her. I know her. I have come close to being her.

11 I read a lot of books. None of them ever told me the truth about what happens to women until feminists started writing and publishing in this wave, over these last 22 years. Over and over, male writers consider prostituted women "speech"—their speech, their right. Without this exploitation, published for profit, the male writer feels censored. The woman lynched naked on a tree, or restrained with ropes and a ball gag in her mouth, has what? Freedom of what?

12 I lost my ability to speak—became mute—a second time in my life. I've written about being a battered wife: I was beaten and tortured over a period of a few years. Amnesty International never showed up. Toward the end, I lost all speech. Words were useless to the likes of me. I had run away and asked for help—from friends, neighbors, the police—and had been turned away many times. My words didn't seem to mean anything, or it was O.K. to torture me.

13 Taken once by my husband to a doctor when hurt, I risked asking for help. The doctor said he could write me a

prescription for Valium or have me committed. The neighbors heard the screaming, but no one did anything. So what are words? I have always been good with them, but never good enough to be believed or helped. No, there were no shelters then.

But I am talking about speech: it isn't easy for me. I come to speech from under a man, tortured and tormented. What he did to me took away everything; he was the owner of everything. He hurt all the words out of me, and no one would listen anyway. I come to speech from under the brutalities of thousands of men. For me, the violence of marriage was worse than the violence of prostitution; but this is no choice. Men act out pornography. They have acted it out on me. Women's lives become pornography. Mine did. And so for 20 years now I have been looking for the words to say what I know. 14

But maybe liberal men—so open-minded and intellectually curious—can't find the books that would teach them about women's real lives. Maybe, while John Irving and PEN are defending *Hustler,* snuff films and "Deep Throat," the direct product of the coercion of Linda Marchiano, political dissidents like myself are anathema—especially to the free-speech fetishists—not because the publishing industry punishes prudes but because dissenters who mean it, who stand against male power over women, are pariahs. 15

Maybe Mr. Irving and others do not know that in the world of women, pornography is the real geography of how men use us and torment us and hate us. 16

With Catharine A. MacKinnon, I drafted the first civil law against pornography. It held pornographers accountable for what they do: they traffic women (contravening the United Nations Universal Declaration of Human Rights and the Convention on the Elimination of All Forms of Discrimination Against Women); they eroticize inequality in a way that materially promotes rape, battery, maiming and bondage; they make a product that they know dehumanizes, degrades and exploits women; they hurt women to make the pornography, and then consumers use the pornography in assaults both verbal and physical. 17

Mr. Irving refers to a scene in "The World According to Garp" in which a woman bites off a man's penis in a car when the car is accidentally rammed from behind. This, he says, did not cause women to bite off men's penises in cars. I have written (in my novels, *Ice and Fire* and *Mercy,* and 18 in the story "The New Woman's Broken Heart") about a woman raped by two men sequentially, the first aggressor routed by the second one, to whom the woman, near dead, submits; he bites viciously and repeatedly into her genitals. When I wrote it, someone had already done it—to me. Mr. Irving uses his imagination for violent farce. My imagination can barely grasp my real life. The violence, as Mr. Irving must know, goes from men to women.

19 Women write to me because of our shared experiences. In my books they find their lives—until now beyond the reach of language. A letter to me dated March 11 says in part: "The abuse was quite sadistic—it involved bestiality, torture, the making of pornography. Sometimes, when I think about my life, I'm not sure why I'm alive, but I'm always sure about why I do what I do, the feminist theory and the antipornography activism." Another letter, dated March 13, says: "It was only when I was almost [raped] to pieces that I broke down and learned to hate. . . . I have never stopped resenting the loss of innocence that occurred the day I learned to hate."

20 Male liberals seem to think we fight pornography to protect sexual innocence, but we have none to protect. The innocence we want is the innocence that lets us love. People need dignity to love.

21 Mr. Irving quoted Hawthorne's condemnation of Puritan orthodoxy in the short story "Endicott and the Red Cross"—a graphic description of public punishments of women: bondage, branding, maiming, lynching. Today pornographers do these things to women, and the public square is a big place—every newsstand and video store. A photograph shields rape and torture for profit. In defending pornography as if it were speech, liberals defend the new slavers. The only fiction in pornography is the smile on the woman's face.

CENSORSHIP II: THE CASE OF *HUCKLEBERRY FINN*

Margot Allen

Huck Finn: Two Generations of Pain

Margot Allen lived in State College, Pennsylvania, when the following account of her family's experience with Huckleberry Finn *appeared in the* Interracial Books for Children Bulletin *in 1984. She now resides in Gladstone, Oregon.*

My adventure with *Huckleberry Finn* has been a stinging and bitter one, one which has left a dull pain that spans two generations, mine and my son's. 1

Today, during the book's centenary, while Mark Twain specialists and scholars laud this book as one of the "most profound, most transcendent literary images the human imagination has ever come up with,"* it is easy for me to recall a time nearly 30 years ago, a time that seemed like an eternity of teeth-clenching and inner contortions that threatened to betray my extreme discomfort when reading this book in the ninth grade. Had I shared my tension and stress with my teacher or classmates, I would have literally frightened them, and my Blackness would have stood out even more than it did as I read the book along with everyone else and kept my feelings in check. 2

But such negative experiences with *Huck Finn* are not a thing of the past. Just three years ago, when my son was thirteen, he too was victimized by those same negative images. I am sharing our story with you now in the hopes that teachers, school administrators, and parents will be more sensitive to the negative racial elements of this book 3

* The comment of novelist John Barth at the Conference on American Comedy: A Celebration of 100 Years of *Huckleberry Finn,* held at Pennsylvania State University, April 26–28, 1984.

and will begin to question, research and speak out regarding how and when this book can best be taught.

4 My story begins with two different classroom experiences some 30 years apart. In both accounts I focus on feelings and reactions because I believe these represent the very foundation upon which most complaints about the book rest. They are personal but real, and to ignore these feelings, to intellectualize them or to misconstrue them as an excuse to charge censorship, would be to continue with a status quo that oppresses people of color. We need to come to grips with *Huck Finn*'s powerful imagery and the *feelings* evoked by those images.

An Introduction to *Huck*

5 I was first introduced to *Huck Finn* in 1957. I was thirteen and in the ninth grade of a large middle-class, suburban, predominantly white high school in Portland, Oregon. I was the only Black student in the class. When *Huck Finn* was assigned, there was no advance preparation; we simply started to read the book, a classic whose name held a familiar—and friendly—ring for most students. As we began to get into the story, however, the dialect alone made me feel uneasy. And as we continued, I began to be apprehensive, to fear being singled out, being put on the spot, being ridiculed or made fun of because of my color, and only because of my color! It was the exact same feeling I'd had as a child when a supposedly "fun game" turned into a hurting one. The feelings that I had as a ninth grader reading *Huck Finn* very much resembled those that I had as a child playing "eenie, meenie, minie, moe: catch a ___ by the toe." While it never occurred to me to refuse to play such games, I would pray like the dickens that no one would use that awful word—the very word my parents had taught me was used only by people who were ignorant or of low moral character. And there it was, in print, that word, staring me in the face over and over again throughout the entire book.

6 I need not tell you that I hated the book! Yet, while we read it, I pretended that it didn't bother me. I hid, from my teacher and my classmates, the tension, discomfort and hurt I would feel every time I heard that word or watched the class laugh at Jim and felt some white youngster's stare

being directed my way, as if to say, "Hey, it's you and your kind we're talking about in this book." I think the hardest part was keeping my composure while being stared at. Somehow I thought that a blank face would protect me from not only this book's offensiveness and open insults, but the silent indicting, accusing and sometimes apologetic stares of my classmates. After all, the very last thing I wanted anyone to think was that I was ashamed of being Black, even though I could not identify with Jim or other Blacks in the novel.

I suffered silently through the reading of *Huck Finn;* at times, I pretended to fake a certain easiness with the book that I thought my classmates had. I learned very little from this experience about literature, the antebellum South or slavery. I learned precious little, if anything, about the novel as a form and the elements of irony and satire. 7

I was so glad to move on to something else that I completely suppressed the experience (a not uncommon experience for Black people)—until my son ran into *Huck Finn* in his English class three years ago. My son, the only Black youngster in his class, was asked by his teacher to read the part of Jim aloud. When a curious white youngster immediately asked why he was selected, the teacher replied, "He has the perfect voice for it." At that, the class laughed. My son was humiliated, though he, too, tried to hide his feelings, just as I had so many years before. After class a number of his friends came up to him and made comments like, "Gee, I'm sorry, the teacher's a real jerk." Others were not so supportive. One child said, "That must tell you what the teacher thinks of you," and there were those who took the opportunity to snicker "nigger" under their breath to him. 8

Greatly distressed by my son's experience, I called the Vice-Principal who, in turn, had the teacher call me later that same morning. In our discussion, I asked why she chose my son to read Jim's part and told her emphatically that I did not want him to read that part. The teacher reported that in years past, whenever she had Black students in her class, she'd asked them to read Jim's part and without exception, they had been "proud" to do so. (She also said that she felt that since slavery was a part of the Black heritage, my son should be proud to authenticate that history by reading Jim's part aloud . . . and after all, since he is Black, he could read the part better than the white students.) 9

Use of *Huck Finn* Questioned

10 Incensed by this teacher's lack of sensitivity and understanding, I wrote to the [school] asking that *Huck Finn* be immediately discontinued as required reading. I felt that any book that leads a teacher to openly discriminate and to offend a student should be seriously questioned for its appropriateness as a tool of instruction. I also questioned the real educational value of *Huck Finn* as it was currently taught.

11 The Principal responded immediately to my letter by pulling my son out of English class and sending him to the library where he was instructed to work on something else. When the Principal called to tell me of his actions, I did not immediately object to his taking my son out of class because I was more concerned as to what the school's response was going to be to my request to have the book discontinued as required reading. Our phone conversation was very brief, however, and the Principal said very little beyond informing me that the forms needed to challenge class materials were being mailed to me.

12 In retrospect, the school's first action was awkward at best, perhaps symptomatic of the staff's inexperience in dealing with matters relating to race. Had officials been more willing to discuss the "incident," it certainly would have gone a long way towards reducing the racial tension and suspicion on both sides which, in turn, may have had an ameliorative effect on the final resolution of this matter. Since this was not the case, I had no alternative but to proceed to formally challenge the book's use. In effect, the battlelines were drawn before there was ample opportunity to discuss the nature of the conflict or even establish a climate for discussion.

13 Fortunately, Christmas vacation intervened, providing time to step back from the situation, to reflect and to do some research in this area. I had, however, no further contact with the Principal, the teacher or any of the school district officials until March of 1982, when the paperwork detailing objections to the book was formally submitted to the district. (The "Citizen's Request for Reconsideration of a Book" was a one-page questionnaire asking for specific examples from the book for each stated objection. I gave seven objections and the completed form was some five

pages long. I am grateful that I had the expert assistance of Dr. Jane Madsen, a professor of education at Penn State, whose specialty is identifying racism and sexism in children's literature.)

In April, my husband and I participated in two rather heated meetings involving the Supervisor of Secondary Education and the District English Coordinator. During these discussions, while apologies were offered for the teacher's blunder (the words "stupidity" and "insensitivity" were used) and for the embarrassment and pain it caused our son, neither the Supervisor nor the English Coordinator could understand that the teacher's remarks were, in and of themselves, racist and discriminatory in nature. 14

In fact, the English Coordinator, who spent a good deal of time explaining the desired educational objectives involved in teaching the book, preferred that we avoid any discussion regarding the teacher's competence. We were asked to focus our concerns *solely* on the book. That focus led to an agreement between the School District and ourselves to put our "Request for Reconsideration" on hold while a Study Group was formed to identify the positive and negative effects of reading *Huck Finn* at the ninth-grade level. I consented to be part of the Study Group because the Supervisor of Secondary Education seemed to be very empathetic about our concerns, and both my husband and I had every hope that the issue would be resolved to our satisfaction. (The English Coordinator, however, continued to defend the book's literary and educational value.) 15

In the initial meetings of this Study Group, I was adamant in expressing my feeling that any book that permits an otherwise competent teacher to openly discriminate in class should not be required reading. My inclination was still to find fault with the book rather than the teacher; this may have been a strategic and critical error on my part. 16

During the next 18 months, the Study Group met some 16 times. Eventually—after much struggle—two recommendations were made. They were, very briefly: 17

1. To use a book other than *Huck Finn* as required reading for ninth-grade classes but make it available for use in courses for grade eleven and twelve; and

2. To undertake a comprehensive study of the schools' sensitivity to and treatment of minority groups in the curricula for grades K–12. (A Task Force on Understanding Others was set up to meet this recommendation.)

Racism Not Addressed

18 Reasonable as these recommendations sound, they unfortunately failed to address the real underlying issue of institutional racism. This often happens when educators overintellectualize problems rooted in racial prejudice. Whites, in particular, find it very hard to identify, accept and understand their own racism and the way in which institutions, including the educational system, contribute to and perpetuate this racism.

19 At any rate, pressure from the School District to bring closure to this whole matter resulted in conclusions being drawn from the study that were not totally sound and which warranted further statistical analysis. Even worse, the study seemed to suggest (in the face of evidence to the contrary) that reading *Huck Finn* did not encourage stereotypic thinking in ninth graders. This study, which, to my dismay, bears my name as a group member, has been distributed in a number of arenas, the most significant being the 1983 National Council of Teachers of English Convention.

20 Significantly, the printed study's recommendation that the book be held for the last two grades of high school was ignored. The School Board stated that it was not the Board's prerogative to decide the grade placement of the book, and that decision was referred to an English Advisory Committee made up of the English Coordinator and classroom teachers. At a School Board meeting in October 1983, the final decision was to retain *Huck Finn* in the ninth grade.

21 The District did give the assurance that, prior to teaching the novel this year, in order to allow parents and youngsters to decide whether they wanted to read the book or not, letters would be sent to all parents informing them that the book had recently come under scrutiny because of the controversy surrounding its negative racial stereotyping of Blacks and its abundant use of racial slurs. The School District never sent such a letter; it later decided to offer *Huck Finn* as one of three titles ninth graders could select for English class. (The other two books were also about adolescence: *Great Expectations* and *A Separate Peace.*)

Complaints Filed

After the School Board condoned the continued use of *Huck Finn,* and with the support and urging of Ida Belle Minnie, Education Chairperson of the State NAACP standing committee, I filed formal complaints with the Pennsylvania Human Relations Commission and the Pennsylvania NAACP. It was clear that my original concerns about the impact of this book on youngsters (both Black and white) had been lost between the cracks of committee bureaucracy and School Board politics. I asked that an investigation be held to ascertain what corrective action had taken place to ensure the appropriateness of teaching methodologies used with this book, and the competence and sensitivity of teachers to carry out those methodologies without racial overtones. 22

I filed my complaint with both organizations in November 1983. Although my son's experience had occurred more than two years earlier, I felt a compelling need to continue the challenge. Accordingly, I sent copies of my complaint to several legislators and state agencies. I got a supportive response from K. Leroy Irvis, Pennsylvania House Minority Leader, and from the Office of the Secretary of Education. In addition, the NAACP delegated Virginius Thornton, a Black historian, to speak against the continued use of *Huck Finn* at a School Board meeting, but I heard from no one locally—not the School Board President, not a single School Board member, and certainly not the Superintendent of Schools. 23

In January 1984, I received a notice from the Pennsylvania Human Relations Commission, indicating that my complaint had been assigned a docket number. This was encouraging, but everything seemed to be moving at a snail's pace. I felt very much alone and the occasional support from a parent here and a couple of parents there, an English professor here and a psychology professor there, were not enough to brighten what seemed to be a bleak horizon. 24

Two Supportive Events

Two separate but related events occurred in March of this year to change this entire picture for me. The first of these was reading the article, "*Huckleberry Finn* and the Traditions 25 of Blackface Minstrelsy" in the CIBC *Bulletin* (Vol. 15, Nos. 1 & 2). This comprehensive piece, which brought some new historical and scholarly insights to understanding the negative characterization of Jim, underpinned academically many of the concerns that had been expressed nationwide about the book at a more emotional level.

26 The second thing that happened was that I was asked to participate in a panel on the teaching of *Huck Finn* in the public schools, at the Conference on American Comedy: A Celebration of 100 Years of *Huckleberry Finn,* hosted by Penn State in April (see Vol. 15, No. 4). The panel presentation resulted in a very extensive and positive dialogue. And, while there was by no means a consensus, there was substantive agreement that indeed there are problems in teaching the novel; that it should be held for use in college or, at the earliest, in the upper grades of high school; and that new teaching strategies *must* be developed to properly teach the novel.

27 I came out of this conference buoyed and more committed than ever to the belief that no youngsters should be required to read literature which demeans, dehumanizes and caricatures their racial or ethnic heritage. Several years ago, *The Merchant of Venice* was dropped from a required reading list for this very reason. Why is *Huck Finn* immune from similar scrutiny?

28 Currently, the Pennsylvania NAACP Education Committee is fully supportive of my complaint, but the bureaucratic wheels of the Human Relations Commission are moving at a much slower pace. With or without their support, I intend to continue to fight this issue. The District hired a new superintendent in July, and I have already written him about my concerns. Dr. Fredrick Woodard, co-author of the *Bulletin*'s article on *Huck Finn,* is conducting new research on the negative racial elements of the book and I do not see how it can be ignored. In addition, Roy L. Austin, a professor of sociology at Penn State, James Stewart, a professor of economics as well as President of the Penn State Forum on Black Affairs (an organization of Black faculty, staff and graduate students), and the aforementioned Jane Madsen recently reviewed the study on "The Effects of Reading *Huckleberry Finn* on the Racial Attitudes of Ninth Grade Students." Their conclusions were such that the Forum's membership voted to issue a public statement affirming that the Study's findings had been published

prematurely and were misleading and biased. The statement appeared in the local newspapers and has led to some constructive dialogue between the Black community and the School District. In addition, I understand that the School District's Task Force on Understanding Others, which until this summer had been very inactive, is now meeting again.

Bringing new insights, visions and perspectives to the teaching of *Huck Finn* is no easy matter. The book is cherished; its worth is passed down from professor to graduate student, from teacher to teacher, from teacher to student. But whatever the book's merits, there is a cost to pay in reading it, and unfortunately that cost is borne in large part by young Black students who may experience a complex range and mix of feelings from indifference to anger, from insult to humiliation. (There is also a cost to white students, whose out-dated notions of white superiority are reinforced.) No one has yet proven that the price we pay is reflected in positive educational gains for any student. 29

John H. Wallace

Huckleberry Finn Is Offensive

John H. Wallace had been a high school administrator at the Mark Twain School in northern Virginia for over twenty years when he wrote this guest column for The Washington Post *in 1982.*

Ever since it was written, Mark Twain's "The Adventures of Huckleberry Finn" has provoked great controversy, and it runs on unabated even now in Fairfax County. After reading the book at least six times, I think it's perfectly all right for college class use, especially at the graduate level, where students can gain insight into the use and writing of satire and an uncensored flavor of the times. The caustic and abusive language is less likely to offend students of that age level because they tend to be mature enough to understand the ridicule. 1

2 "Huckleberry Finn" uses the pejorative term "nigger" profusely. It speaks of black Americans with implications that they are not honest, they are not as intelligent as whites and they are not human. All of this, of course, is meant to be satirical. It is. But at the same time, it ridicules blacks. This kind of ridicule is extremely difficult for black youngsters to handle. I maintain that it constitutes mental cruelty, harassment and outright racial intimidation to force black students to sit in a classroom to read this kind of literature about themselves.

3 I read "Huck Finn" when I was in high school and I can remember feeling betrayed by the teacher. I felt humiliated and embarrassed. Ten years ago, my oldest son went through the same experience in high school, until I went to talk to the teachers about it and he lost all interest in English classes. Before reading this book, this bright, energetic youngster was inquisitive and liked school; but afterward—after he had been asked to participate in the reading with an all-white class—I could see a definite negative change in his attitude toward teachers and school. (I'm happy to say he has recovered now.)

4 For years, black families have trekked to schools in just about every district in America to say that "this book is bad for our children," only to be turned away by insensitive and often unwittingly racist teachers and administrators responding that "this is a classic." Classic or not, it should not be allowed to continue to make our children feel bad about themselves.

5 I am convinced that the assignment and reading aloud of "Huck Finn" in our classrooms causes black children to have a low esteem of themselves and of their race. It also causes white students to have little or no respect for blacks. The resulting attitudes can lead to tension, discontent and fights. If the book is removed from the curriculums of our schools, there will be much better student-to-student, student-to-teacher and teacher-to-teacher relationships; and black students will definitely enjoy school a little bit more.

6 Every black child is the victim of the history of his race in this country. As John Fisher, former president of Columbia Teachers College, has noted, "On the day he enters kindergarten, he carries a burden no white child can ever know, no matter what handicaps or disabilities he may suffer." Add to this the reading of a book like "Huckleberry Finn" and the experience can be devastatingly traumatic.

Many of my friends have cited First Amendment rights. But I am convinced that the continued use of pejorative materials about one particular racial group is a violation of the equal protection clause of the 14th Amendment. It also may violate the right to liberty as applied to reputation, in that the book maligns all black people. 7

I have no problem with "Huckleberry Finn" being on the library shelf, for any youngster or his parents to check out and read to their hearts' content, in school or at home. But as a professional educator with 28 years of teaching at all levels, I cannot see the slightest need to use disparaging language to identify any racial, ethnic or religious group. If the lesson cannot be taught in positive terms, maybe it should not be taught. 8

We must be sensitive, creative teachers, encouraged to understand the special factors in the backgrounds of all the children—with curriculums that reflect these varied needs. And no sensitive, loving teacher would use "Huckleberry Finn" in class. 9

Robert Nadeau

Huckleberry Finn Is a Moral Story

Robert Nadeau, professor of English at George Mason University, wrote this essay in 1982. It appeared on the same page of The Washington Post *as the previous essay by John H. Wallace.*

When the principal of Mark Twain Intermediate School in Fairfax County followed the advice of the school's racially mixed human relations committee and recommended that "The Adventures of Huckleberry Finn" be removed from the school's curriculum, he was not acting without precedent. Misguided guardians of the moral integrity of schoolchildren have often attempted, particularly in Twain's own lifetime, to prevent young minds from being exposed to the profoundly moral views of the 13-year-old, pipe-smoking, marvelously imaginative liar whose love for the runaway slave, Jim, grows to such proportions that he would risk eternal damnation to protect him. 1

2 A letter written by Twain to a Brooklyn librarian who was seeking to ban both "Tom Sawyer" and "Huckleberry Finn" from the children's room of the library has not, I suspect, been read by most faculty members teaching at a school named in honor of one of our greatest American artists. Let me share a portion of it with them: "I wrote 'Tom Sawyer' and 'Huck Finn' for adults exclusively, and it always distresses me when I find that boys and girls have been allowed access to them. The mind that becomes soiled in youth can never again be washed clear. I know this by my own experience, and to this day I cherish an unappeasable bitterness against the unfaithful guardians of my young life, who not only permitted but compelled me to read an unexpurgated Bible before I was 15 years old. . . . More honestly do I wish that I could say a softening word or two in defense of Huck's character since you wish it, but really, in my opinion, it is no better than those of Solomon, David, and the rest of the sacred brotherhood."

3 That Twain firmly believed that the behavior and character of his first person narrator was designed to be morally instructive to young people is obvious. Countless individuals in this culture, including myself, know from the experience of reading the book at an early age that he was absolutely correct.

4 Apparently the faculty members as well as the parents and the administrators who concurred with the recommendation to bar teachers from assigning the novel—or even reading it aloud in class—feel otherwise. They object, we are told, to "the flagrant use of the word 'nigger' and the demeaning way in which black people are portrayed in the book." "Nigger" is, of course, a terribly offensive word in our own time and should definitely not be used by anyone who respects the rights and integrities of others. But it might help to explain to those students who might continue to study the book at the intermediate school that in slave states the word was merely the ordinary colloquial term for a slave, and not necessarily abusive.

5 More important, however, as the historical record also shows, Twain was a violent opponent of the institution of slavery, and "Huckleberry Finn" can and should be read as one of the most forceful indictments ever made against the subjugation of any class of human beings by another.

6 Anyone, including adolescents, who has carefully read the book should have little difficulty recognizing the many

instances in which this theme is abundantly obvious. Since there is not sufficient space here to detail all of them, I will only touch briefly on that climactic moment when Huck, in defiance of what he has been taught to be the will of God in his own morally bankrupt society, elects to imperil his mortal soul.

Subjected, as many children in this country continue to 7
be, to a religious education in which the interpreters of spiritual verities seek to sanction the view of black people as innately inferior, Huck reflects late in the narrative upon his many efforts to help Jim to escape and concludes: "And at last, when it hit me all of a sudden that here was the plain hand of Providence slapping me in the face and letting me know my wickedness was being watched all the time from up there in Heaven, whilst I was stealing a poor old woman's nigger that hadn't ever done me no harm, and now was showing me there's One that's always on the lookout, and ain't agoing to allow such miserable doing to go only just so fur and no further, I almost dropped in my tracks I was so scared." Feeling oppressed with guilt, realizing that "people that acts as I'd been acting about that nigger goes to everlasting fire," Huck writes a letter to Mrs. Watson indicating where Jim can be found. But then immediately thereafter he recalls—in a passage that is one of the best illustrations in literature of the power of agape love—the many acts of kindness displayed by Jim toward himself, looks once again at the letter, and says to himself, " 'All right, then, I'll go to hell'—and tore it up."

The message here, which is pervasive in this marvelous 8
novel, is that truly moral acts are, often enough, undertaken in defiance of a so-called moral majority. And it is that which this particular member of the sacred brotherhood has chosen to do. If studying "Huckleberry Finn" is in any way to hurt students at Mark Twain Intermediate School, it can only be because those who teach the book have failed to understand it.

But there is, of course, a larger issue here. When we 9
prevent our children from being exposed in the classroom to the best that has been known and said in our literary tradition, we not only narrow the range of their educational experience, but we also—unintentionally to be sure—help them to grow into individuals, like the members of the Shepherdson and Grangerford families in the novel, who might commit senseless acts of destruction out of a lack of

understanding of the complexities of moral life. If "Huckleberry Finn" is, as an administrative aide at the school put it, "poison," then I suspect my own 11-year-old daughter must have a remarkably immune system. She even appears to thrive on it.

Nat Hentoff

Huck Finn Better Get Out of Town by Sundown

*As a novelist, Nat Hentoff (born in 1925) has written several books for teenagers, including one—*The Day They Came to Arrest the Book *(1982)—that dramatizes a parent's demand that* Huckleberry Finn *be withdrawn from a high school. As a social critic and civil libertarian and defender of the First Amendment, he has written numerous books and articles for prestigious magazines. He is a regular contributor to* The Village Voice, *the influential New York weekly that published his analysis of the controversy over* Huckleberry Finn *in May, 1982.*

> We have not abrogated anybody's First Amendment rights. We've just said we don't want any kid to be forced to read this racist trash. . . . The book is poison. . . . It is anti-American. . . . It works against the idea that all men are created equal. . . . Anybody who teaches this book is racist.
>
> —*John H. Wallace, administrative aide, Mark Twain Intermediate School, Fairfax County, Virginia*

> The last damn thing blacks should do is get into the vanguard of banning books. The next step is banning blacks.
>
> —*Dr. Kenneth B. Clark*

> The rush for racism-free literature is not a call for censorship, but rather a push for

> responsibility on the part of educators, librarians and authors.
>
> —*Dorothy Gilliam, columnist,* Washington Post, *April 12*

> The proof that *Huckleberry Finn* has to be taught in our schools is that some people can read great books and not know what the hell they're about.
>
> —*Stephen Altman, on the letters page,* Washington Post, *April 12*

I

The recent attempt by black administrator John Wallace to roust the perennially troublesome *Huckleberry Finn* from his school's curriculum made the network newscasts, wire services, and most papers around the country. A teacher in Houston told me that when it came over the radio, she had to stop her car, she was so agitated. On the other hand, a group of black parents in Houston who are also trying to get this white trash out of *their* schools were pleased to hear they had an ally up there in Fairfax, Virginia. 1

My guess is that this wouldn't have been such a widely played story if the name of the school where Mr. Wallace works were not the Mark Twain Intermediate School. Mr. Clemens would have whooped long and loud over that one. Maybe even longer and louder over the name of the racially integrated six-member faculty committee that *unanimously* voted to protect the kids from his book. It's called the Human Relations Committee of the Mark Twain Intermediate School. 2

Dr. Kenneth Clark of *Brown* v. *Board of Education* and *Dark Ghetto* told me the other day that he first came upon Huck Finn in the public library at 135th Street and Lenox Avenue when he was about 12 years old. No one was around at the time to protect Kenneth from certain books, and he got all caught up in *Huckleberry Finn*. 3

"I loved the book," Dr. Clark says. "I just loved it. Especially the relationship between Huck and Jim. It was such an easy, *understanding* relationship. The kind a boy wishes he could have." 4

Then, as now, the book was full of the word "nigger." Why, 5

John Martin, the principal of the Mark Twain Intermediate School in Fairfax County—who agreed with the Human Relations Committee that *Huckleberry Finn* is racist—told National Public Radio that the word is repeated some 160 times in the book. How come Kenneth Clark, when he was just 12 years old, didn't recoil from this "racist" book?

6 Because he read it, he really read it. Without some adult censoring what he read beforehand to make sure it did him no harm. Someone like John Wallace, who told me a couple of weeks ago: "It's books like *Huckleberry Finn* that are screwing up black children—books that make black children feel bad about themselves. How can a black child, reading that racist trash, be proud of being black?"

7 Maybe Kenneth Clark didn't get the message. Or maybe it's John Wallace, who has read *Huckleberry Finn* eight times in the last five months, as he tells me, who can't see past that word. Just as the whites in pre–Civil War Missouri whom Twain was writing about couldn't see past that word. They had no idea who "Miss Watson's big nigger, named Jim" was. Though Huck came to know Jim, underneath that word. And being able to do that changed his whole life.

8 We are about to begin what has become an annual journey into the minds of those who would censor for the most fervent of motives—the shielding of young minds from books that debase them. Although the focus this trip is on *Huckleberry Finn*—in Virginia; in the Spring Independent School District of Houston; in Davenport, Iowa; in Warrington, Pennsylvania—we shall also stop in Midland, Michigan, to look into a long, bitter conflict over how *The Merchant of Venice* should be taught in school—if at all. And farther on down the line, we shall visit a Sunday service in Baltimore's First Unitarian Church where "sexist" passages by "patriarchal" theologians (from St. Augustine to Karl Barth) are burned in front of the altar.

9 And to show that no enclave in our society is immune from those who would uplift our souls and purge our minds, we shall hear from the managing editor of a daily newspaper in New Hampshire who has been striving mightily to cleanse the comic strips of sexism—much to the ungrateful fury of most of his readers, who are clamoring that they do not wish to be delivered from this sin.

10 To begin with Huck: my interest in the ceaseless assault

on this well-known drifter has to do with my own ceaseless delight in the book. I keep going back to it, as I do to certain jazz recordings, when I feel tempted to agree with Mr. Twain's gloomy assessment, in his last years, of our species' prospects. "Why *was* the human race created?" he wrote William Dean Howells in 1900. "Or at least why wasn't something creditable created in place of it? God had his opportunity. He could have made a reputation. But no, He must commit this grotesque folly. . . ."

But then I become a Musteite again, a believer in the perfectibility of us all, when I listen to Ben Webster. Or to Huck: "It was kind of solemn, drifting down the big still river, laying on our backs, looking up at the stars, and we didn't ever feel like talking loud, and it warn't often that we laughed—only a little kind of low chuckle." 11

Another reason I have been charting the present perils of Huck Finn—talking both to those chasing the boy and those offering him succor—concerns a book of my own. It's a Y/A (young adult) novel that Delacorte Press will publish this fall, and it's called *The Day They Came to Arrest the Book.* 12

The story is about the fierce civil war in a high school—and in the town as a whole—when an otherwise unharmonious alliance of parents and other citizens moves to rid the school of *Huckleberry Finn*. Among the attackers are black students and their parents; "progressive" white students; and white churchgoing folk who consider Huck's stealing, lying, and irreverence, both general and particular, the very worst kind of model for youngsters. Also readying the guillotine are some feminists, though not all, who see the women in the novel as subservient to men, and empty-headed besides. 13

It's not a tract. In my novel, the enemies of Huck are as skillfully compelling as you or I, because I want the reader to make up his or her own mind. I don't think anybody's going to like the principal, though. Anyway, as I thought about my book, and researched the embattled odyssey of *Huckleberry Finn,* I came to understand more about the complex, seductive dynamics of censorship than I had before. 14

Although *Catcher in the Rye* and the works of Kurt Vonnegut and Judy Blume are currently the most frequently censored books in school libraries, no novel has been on the 15 firing line so long and so continuously as *Huckleberry Finn*. What is there about this book that manages to infuriate, differently, each generation of Americans? What does it tell us that we don't want to hear?

16 As for the history of Huck-the-fugitive, I noticed that none of the New York papers, covering the attempt to get the book thrown out of the Mark Twain Intermediate School in Virginia, mentioned *this* city's involvement in the censorship of Huck. In September 1957, under pressure from the NAACP and the Urban League—which called the novel "racially offensive"—the New York City Board of Education removed Huck from the approved textbook reading lists in all elementary and junior high schools.

17 So you thought the Big Apple was too hip to banish so free a spirit as Huck because of certain words in his book? Well, as I shall recount later, *The Village Voice*—and who are more hip than we?—had its own civil war in 1979 when Jules Feiffer used "nigger" in a cartoon strip that a less-than-average third-grader would have known was an antiracist gibe. God forbid they should ever be contaminated by such impurity.

18 Herewith a brief chronicle of the ways in which *Huckleberry Finn* has been buked and scorned, and loved. At first, it was not that word but rather the uncivilized, unsocialized nature of the wandering boy himself that kept getting him into trouble with decent citizens.

19 A year after the book was published, *The Boston Transcript* reported on March 17, 1885:

20 "The Concord [Massachusetts] Public Library committee has decided to exclude Mark Twain's latest book from the library. One member of the committee says that, while he does not wish to call it immoral, he thinks it contains but little humor, and that of a very coarse type. He regards it as the veriest trash. The librarian and other members of the committee entertain similar views, characterizing it as rough, coarse, and inelegant, dealing with a series of experiences not elevating, the whole book being more suited to the slums than to intelligent, respectable people."

21 Concord, where Emerson and Thoreau had incandescently lived! Where Louisa May Alcott still lived. And she—as quoted in Michael Patrick Hearn's invaluable *The Annotated Huckleberry Finn,* Clarkson N. Potter, 1981—said

derisively, "If Mr. Clemens cannot think of something better to tell our pure-minded lads and lasses, he had best stop writing for them."

Mr. Twain refused to be chastened: "Those idiots in Concord are not a court of last resort, and I am not disturbed by their moral gymnastics. No other book of mine has sold so many copies within 2 months after issue as this one. . . ." Actually, the idiots in Concord had done him a good turn: "[They] have given us a rattling tip-top puff which will go into every paper in the country. . . . That will sell 25,000 copies for us sure." 22

In 1902, Huck was thrown out of the Denver Public Library ("immoral and sacrilegious"); and three years later, he was taken by the scruff of his neck and booted out of the children's room of the Brooklyn Public Library as "a bad example for ingenuous youth." 23

And so it went. By 1907, it was reported at the time, Huck had been "turned out of some library every year." Not only did he lie his way out of danger, and steal—if only to stay alive—but his grammar was terrible. So was everybody else's in the book. Worse yet, said an editorial in the Springfield *Republican,* Mr. Clemens indulges in "a gross trifling with every fine feeling . . . he has no reliable sense of propriety." And his "moral level is low." 24

Over the decades, however, the direction and nature of the attacks on *Huckleberry Finn* changed. From the 1950s on, groups of black parents—with some white sympathizers among school faculties and administrators—have been concentrating on the 160 appearances of "nigger" in the book. In 1976, at the New Trier High School in Winnetka, Illinois, for instance, after a five-year struggle, black parents succeeded in getting the novel taken off all required-reading lists on the charge that it is "morally insensitive" and "degrading and destructive to black humanity." 25

Four years earlier, Huck had also been stricken from required reading lists in Indianapolis. Said the curriculum director: "There's simply no reason to use books that offend minorities if other books may be used instead." 26

Said a protesting letter from a bunch of Indianapolis students—self-described as white, black, Catholics, Jews, and agnostics—"This is a pointless withdrawal from reality." 27

But black parents I have spoken to in Texas could not be more convinced that Huck Finn is, in reality, a clear and present danger to *their* children. 28

II

29 The easy way to think you're dealing effectively with censors is to see them as indistinguishable. On one side of the deep, clear Manichaean line, wearing white hats, are us—the forces of light, the boon companions of Madison and Jefferson. On the other side, shrouded in ignorance, pinched in spirit, are the dark hordes ready to start the bonfires. And whatever particular book each of these censors wants to toss into the flames, all of the censors are alike. They're all Yahoos. Barely literate.

30 I used to think that way until some of my own books started to get into trouble, and I tried to find out why. For instance, a novel for young readers, *This School is Driving Me Crazy,* has been tossed out of a school in Maryland and is on permanent probation in Mobile. I couldn't figure it out. There's not even *implicit* sex in the book. It's what might be called a moral adventure story. As for the language, there are a few "damns" and "hells." And that's it. Not one of George Carlin's seven dirty words. Even more puzzling is that a lot of teachers and—more to the point—kids dig the book, without anybody at all getting upset. It only gets busted in a few places, but the parents in those places are very angry indeed at the book and at me.

31 One of those places is a small town in southern Illinois. At a conference in Chicago, I met the librarian from there. She is as stubborn a free speech fighter as any Wobbly before the First World War, but she doesn't think of her opponents as if they were in cartoons.

32 "There are kids in my town," she told me, "who come from very religious families. What they see on television, what movies they go to, are controlled. They are taught at home that certain words, used in certain ways, are blasphemous. Sure, they hear other kids say them, but when they see those words in a *book*—and 'damn' and 'hell' are among them—these children are really stunned. And their parents go up the wall. And so would I. If I were them.

33 "I fight for your book," the librarian went on. "I tell the parents who want it ridden out of town that they cannot decide what *all* the children in my library are going to read. But I do tell these parents that I will give *their* children alternative books to read."

34 That is standard American Library Association policy,

with which the American Civil Liberties Union concurs. An individual parent should have some say in what the state does with his or her child's mind. Education up to a certain age is compulsory. But when a parent's values conflict fundamentally with those of a book assigned for school reading—in the matter of blasphemy, let's say—should the parent have no recourse at all? *For his or her own child?* Give the kid another book.

But what happens when a parent informs the school that his child must not read a certain book, and the kid insists that he does too want to read that damn book? The child, it seems to me, must be allowed to prevail. But at what age? Depends on the child. For example—though this is not about books—from what I've read of the record in the Walter Polovchak case, I think he was capable of deciding at 12 that he did not want to leave the United States and go back to the Ukraine with his parents. For this, and other reasons, I also think the Illinois affiliate of the ACLU has been dead wrong in taking the side of Walter's parents in this battle. 35

Anyway, if under ALA and ACLU standards, it's okay for individual parents to censor certain books *for their own children only,* what's the First Amendment answer when *groups* of parents charge that because a book is debasing to their own kids, it has to be removed from the curriculum entirely? Why? Because otherwise, that book will create or intensify animus *towards their own kids* from the rest of the student body. In this context, I mean protesting parental groups of the same race or religion. Blacks, or Jews, for example. 36

The standard answer—"We'll give *your* kids alternative books"—has been unacceptable to black parents in most places where *Huckleberry Finn* is under intense attack. It is not acceptable, the black parents say, because the book—by its incessant use of the word "nigger," and by the way it portrays blacks—incites racism. Right now. And some of these parents point to the black eighth-grader in Warrington, Pennsylvania, who last year, his father says, was verbally and physically abused by his white classmates after they had all read *Huckleberry Finn* in class. The novel was required reading in the eighth grade then. It no longer is in Warrington. Later in this column, we shall journey to this 37

Pennsylvania town and find out about the Huck Finn "compromise" that school personnel and black parents are very pleased with. That snorting you hear from way down below is a dissenting view from Mr. Clemens.

38 From Texas to Virginia, I've talked to black objectors to *Huckleberry Finn,* as I've talked to Jewish objectors to *The Merchant of Venice*. They're not Yahoos. I think they were wrong in wanting to throw out or hide these works, but they do raise questions about how to teach certain books. Questions that go even more deeply into the very nature of teaching itself.

39 But first, it's useful to understand the depth of these protesters' feelings. Consider John Wallace, the black administrator at the Mark Twain Intermediate School in Fairfax County, Virginia, who has led the thus far unsuccessful fight to remove *Huckleberry Finn* from that school's curriculum.

40 "The press has cut me down something terrible," Wallace told me. Yes, it has, if only by quoting him. ("Anybody who teaches this book is racist.") But where's he coming from? There wasn't much in the press about that. "I grew up in Aurora, Illinois," Wallace told me, "and there were very few black kids there. When I was a kid, I had to study *Huckleberry Finn* in that school; and every time the teacher, reading it aloud, mentioned the word 'nigger,' I flinched. There was only one other black kid in the room, and every time he heard the teacher say that word, he put his head down on his desk."

41 Wallace's mother was dead by the time he was 12, but he remembers how an aunt, and the minister of his church, led the battle to kick *Huckleberry Finn* out of that school. They failed. But Wallace, who has worked in schools for 28 years, has never stopped trying to save black kids from this book which, as he sees it, will make them feel unworthy. It's become a family mission, he tells me, as he looks at a photograph of his two heroes, Malcolm X and Martin Luther King, shaking hands. His son in Chicago, Wallace adds, is also involved in the jihad against Huck Finn.

42 "You want to know why it's so important to get rid of this book?" Wallace says. "We are always lamenting that black students don't learn or progress as well as whites. Well, if

you give them this kind of crap about themselves, how are they going to feel good about themselves?"

I tried to tell Wallace what Twain had done in the book. Russell Baker put it pretty good in the *Times* on April 14 when he wrote about Huck and Jim on the Mississippi. 43

"The people they encounter are drunkards, murderers, bullies, swindlers, lynchers, thieves, liars, frauds, child abusers, numbskulls, hypocrites, windbags and traders in human flesh. All are white. The one man of honor in this phantasmagoria is black Jim, the runaway slave. 'Nigger Jim,' as Twain called him to emphasize the irony of a society in which the only true gentleman was held beneath contempt." 44

I didn't get anywhere with Mr. Wallace about what the book is saying. I didn't get anywhere with Mrs. Dora Durden, mother of an 11th-grade student at Westfield High School in the Spring Independent School District of Houston. She is one of the leaders of a black parent "Sensitivity Committee" which has been trying for months to get *Huckleberry Finn* off the required reading list there. The committee claims that the book is degrading to blacks, that no book is worth the humiliation of their children, and that to compound the harm, the book has been taught insensitively. (More about how Mr. Twain's novel has been taught in that district later. Intriguingly, the perceptions of the teachers and the black parents could not be more dissimilar.) 45

Dora Durden is no Yahoo either. Crisply articulate, she points out how difficult it is for black kids in a school district where they make up only about 4.4 percent of the student body. "When a child, like my daughter, is the only black in her class, teachers have to be more sensitive about what and how they teach. But they're not, and they make some of our kids feel like dogs." 46

If *Huckleberry Finn* has to be taught, Mrs. Durden said, "then at least don't mention the word 'nigger.' But actually, why does it have to be taught? Surely there are other good American novels without that word in it? I myself would just as soon have *Huckleberry Finn* removed not only from the reading list, but taken out of the school entirely. And that may not be the only book that should go. I have asked the curriculum director for a list of all the books used in all the courses so that we can examine them and determine which are good for our children and which are harmful to them. And that means any book that degrades *any* race." 47

48 So far, Mrs. Durden and her allies have failed to get *Huck Finn* taken off the required reading list. But they're pushing on to the school board, and then the Texas Education Agency, and then the state courts. A Westfield High School review committee (two teachers and a librarian), set up to deal with the complaint, has reported: ". . . no other literary selection illustrates the mid-nineteenth century and its evils of slavery as well as this novel, Mark Twain's satirical masterpiece."

49 In Fairfax County, Virginia, John Wallace reacts with derision to the notion that Mark Twain's satire can get through to kids. "It's asinine to think that," says Wallace. "How many children understand satire?"

50 And back in Texas, Mrs. Durden tells me that eight black youngsters at Westfield High School took the option of not reading *Huckleberry Finn,* and instead chose another book. One of those students was her daughter. I asked which book she had chosen.

51 *"Fahrenheit 451,"* Mrs. Durden said.

52 I wonder if her daughter told Mrs. Durden what the book is about. By the way, that Ray Bradbury novel—about official arsonists of the future torching subversive books—was taken off the required reading list at another Texas high school in 1981. The school principal decided it gave students "too negative" an outlook.

53 But the business at hand here is still to persuade you that censors are not indistinguishable, that they are as heterogeneous, and can be well-read, as you or I.

54 For instance, from the October 5, 1981, issue of the *Baltimore Sun,* a story by religion editor Frank P. L. Somerville:

55 "Baltimore's First Unitarian Church had a symbolic book-burning yesterday—midway through its 11 A.M. service—in which centuries of Jewish, Christian, Islamic and Hindu writings were 'expurgated' because of sections described as 'sexist.'

56 "Touched off by a candle and consumed in a pot on a table in front of the altar were slips of paper containing 'patriarchal' excerpts from Martin Luther King, Thomas Aquinas, the Koran, St. Augustine, St. Ambrose, St. John Chrysostom, the Hindu Code of Manu V, and the Old Testament.

57 "Also included were references from the writings of such relatively recent theologians as Kierkegaard and Karl Barth.

58 "Nine women—some in dressy gowns, others wearing

pants—filed to the altar from the congregation and read 11 'sexist' passages aloud in turn, adding their commentary. . . .

"Then the group 'shared a fantasy' with the congregation of men and women, burning 'these slanderous statements, aimed at half the human race.' As the last flame died in the pot and the organ pealed, there was applause. 59

"In his remarks from the pulpit, First Unitarian's minister, the Rev. Robert L. Zoerheide, inquired: 'Do you ever have the feeling you are making history in this historic church?' " 60

I don't know about *making* history, Reverend, but you and your congregation have moved us a mite closer to *Fahrenheit 451*. 61

Mr. Twain once said: "No civilization can be perfect until exact equality between man and woman is included." 62

But then, you know what Mr. Twain and Huck thought about civilization, both the male and female of it. 63

III

The way it used to be in Warrington—about 25 miles north of Philadelphia—most junior high school students had to read *Huckleberry Finn*. That is, the teachers were required to pick their class reading assignments from a small list of books, and from only those books. Huck was on that list, and was often chosen because, as Mr. Hemingway once said, "All modern American literature comes from one book by Mark Twain called *Huckleberry Finn*." 64

Then came the complaint. Last year, the parents of a black eighth-grader asked that Mr. Twain's book be removed from junior high school reading lists and from the school libraries. Their son, they said, had been harassed verbally and physically by white kids in his class because of the infectious use of the word "nigger" in the novel. 65

These parents agreed that Mr. Twain himself was not a racist. Why, *Huckleberry Finn,* they said, is strongly anti-slavery and anti-racist. But the book is too subtle, too difficult, for eighth-graders to understand in terms of Mr. Twain's intentions. All that the kids, white and black, see is: "nigger." 66

I have been unable to find out the nature and extent of the abuse of the black eighth-grader by his classmates. School officials told me they just don't know. They had heard the charges, but they had no specifics, nor had they gone after 67 any. (Wouldn't you think they'd try?) The black parents involved do not wish to speak to the press. Since they are not public officials or public figures, I did not try to crack their unlisted phone number or work through intermediaries. The right to say, "No" to the press is—or should be—one of the most sacred American liberties.

68 But, for the sake of argument, let me stipulate that a very bad scene did occur—the actual beating of the black child. (Though if that had happened, I would think his parents would have insisted the white hooligans be at least suspended.) And let me stipulate there was constant taunting of the boy as a "nigger."

69 Do you keep *Huckleberry Finn* on a required reading list when it leads to such baleful results?

70 In recent weeks, I've asked this question of a good many citizens, black and white, including teachers—most recently, teachers and librarians at the International Reading Association convention in Chicago. The overwhelming consensus has been that what happened in that eighth-grade classroom in Warrington is a boon to any reasonably awake teacher. What a way to get Huck and Jim, on the one hand, and all those white racists they meet, on the other hand, off the pages of the book and into that very classroom. Talk about a book coming alive!

71 Look at that Huck Finn. Reared in racism, like all the white kids in his town. And then, on the river, on the raft with Jim, shucking off that blind ignorance because this runaway slave is the most honest, perceptive, fair-minded man this white boy has ever known. What a book for the children, all the children, in Warrington, Pennsylvania, in 1982!

72 "To miss that teaching opportunity, to not confront what happened to that black kid in Warrington head-on by really exploring this book," Dr. Kenneth Clark told me, "is to underestimate every child in that classroom. And by underestimating them—while also 'protecting' the black child from this book—you deprive them all of what they should know. And what they can especially learn from *Huckleberry Finn*."

73 Ah, but the book is too difficult for eighth-grade kids! We'll hear a rebuttal of this rationale for overprotecting black and white children in a conversation with a school official in a town very much like Warrington. But keep this

in mind: *Huckleberry Finn* is not *The Magic Mountain* or *The Castle* or *Remembrance of Things Past.* It is a novel by a writer who, as he put it, "never cared what became of the cultured classes; they could go to the theater and the opera, they had no use for me and the melodeon." Instead, Mr. Twain, in his words, "always hunted for the bigger game—the masses."

All the more so in 1884, when *Huckleberry Finn* was published, because Twain was in need of money and wanted to attract as many bookbuyers as he could that year. He even went on a three-and-a-half-month reading tour of 70 cities to advertise *Huckleberry Finn.* In every way, this was intended to be a popular novel. 74

And surely, kids in 1982—after all the television programs and movies they've seen—are at least as able as children were in 1884 to fathom what Mr. Twain is saying in this novel. Kids have not grown dumber. I will grant you that reading it again last summer, I found more in *Huckleberry Finn* than when I first read it the summer I was 14. Or, as Lionel Trilling wrote: 75

"One can read it at ten and then annually ever after, and each year find that it is as fresh as the year before, that it has changed only in becoming somewhat larger. To read it young is like planting a tree young—each year adds a new growth ring of meaning, and the book is as little likely as the tree to become dull. So, we may imagine, an Athenian boy grew up together with the *Odyssey.* There are few other books which we can know so young and love so long." 76

But at 10, or 12, or 14, even with only the beginning ring of meaning, any child who can read will not miss the doltishness and sheer meanness and great foolishness of most of the whites in the book, particularly in their attitudes toward blacks. Nor will the child miss the courage and invincible decency of the white boy and the black man on the river. 77

And if any child, black or white, does miss—through being blocked in one way or another—these points as big as barn doors, then what the hell is the teacher for? 78

Well, what *did* happen in Warrington after the incident connected with *Huckleberry Finn?* Were the teachers told that now is the time to really teach that thing? No, they were not. The novel was removed from the required reading list at Tamamend Junior High School, where the incident took place. And starting next September, it will be gone from the 79 reading lists in all junior high schools in Central Bucks County School District. But Huck will still have shelf room in all school libraries, and he'll be taught in high school. Well, maybe he'll be taught in high school. More of that later.

80 Although the black parents had started by urging that *Huckleberry Finn* be taken off all reading lists, and from all school libraries, they were pleased by the compromise. So were the white school officials. They had shown themselves to be sensitive to the feelings of this very small minority in the district (about 200 black kids out of 11,000 students). One of the school officials told me, by the way, that "it's unfortunate that most of our kids don't have experiences with people of other races."

81 In years past, many of them did get to know Jim, though, but he's been told to make himself scarce.

82 I don't know how many Jewish kids there are in the Central Bucks County schools; but the educators there are so nice, so eager to insulate youngsters from having to think beyond platitudes, that they've removed *The Merchant of Venice* from all the junior high schools. It'll be optional in high school. No one had even complained about Shylock, but as one administrator told me, "We had become concerned with the way the Jewish people are presented in that play."

83 How *do* the teachers spend their time in those classrooms? Reading *TV Guide?*

84 As for Huck, now that the junior high kids have been protected from him, what will take his place? Well, it looks as if three books will replace Mr. Twain's misguided novel on that small required reading list from which teachers are to choose what the junior high kids can absorb without harm, and without their imaginations being unduly stimulated. The winners are: William H. Armstrong's *Sounder;* Allen Eckert's *Incident at Hawk's Hill;* and Chaim Potok's *The Chosen.*

85 With all respect to fans of any or all of the above, ain't none of them *Huckleberry Finn.* It's like removing Duke Ellington from a music course, and substituting Oscar Peterson, Dave Brubeck, and Chick Corea.

86 But what the hell, the kids will be able to get on that raft with Huck and Jim when they reach the safety zone, the

10th grade. There, *Huckleberry Finn* will be one of eight titles from which teachers must choose. Kind of long odds against Huck, and all the longer when you realize that the book now has a stigma attached to it in Central Bucks County. After all, Huck had to be bodily removed from junior high, so how many 10th-grade teachers are going to take a chance on maybe getting into trouble with this book, even though it's permitted by then? Who needs a grim visit from black parents when you can teach something that minds its manners and never gets anybody into trouble?

There's much more to be learned from the Incident in Warrington, and its aftermath. The reason I have done this much inquiring is because this victory for niceness in the Central Bucks County School District is much more insidiously harmful to kids than the Armageddons of censorship that get widespread press play. In most of the latter battles, the enemy is clear. There are folks out there who want to censor, ban, burn (if they can) certain books. 87

But in Warrington, and in an increasing number of other places, offending books are *not* banned. They're just put in the back of the bus. They're taken off reading lists, but kept in the library. Often, moreover, they're kept in the library on restricted shelves, or are just plain hidden. Or they're taken out of lower-school curriculums and placed, maybe, on high school lists. Usually optional lists. Whatever the device, the books are made less accessible to kids. And so they're less often read. If they're read at all. 88

This is not the kind of stuff that makes for pungent newspaper or broadcast coverage. Actually, this sort of "compromise" is seldom covered at all. I was only the second reporter in two years to talk to school officials about the Incident at Warrington. The principal of Tamamend Junior High School was surprised to hear from me. "We're not having any racial riots, any racial problems here," he told me. "That takes the fun out of your story, I guess. And we're not banning anything either. I don't believe in going into the censorship business. Besides, then the civil liberties groups get after you." 89

"The only story here," another school official told me, "is that we worked out a compromise by which everybody wins." 90

Except the kids, black and white, who are being treated with such "sensitivity" and "kindness"—but not with respect. Respecting a child means you work with him so that he can 91 keep discovering more and more of his potential. So that he can keep learning what his strengths are. Like the capacity to see past words like "nigger" or "kike" or "wop" into what the writer is actually *saying*. What's going to happen to a kid when he gets into the world if he's going to let a word paralyze him so he can't think?

92 But the principal of Tamamend Junior High School told me Huck had to be taken out of his school because black kids' feelings were hurt. Again, where the hell were the teachers—to connect those feelings to Huck and Jim?

93 And the principal of Mark Twain Intermediate School in Fairfax County, Virginia, went along with the banning of *Huckleberry Finn* (before he was overruled) because: "I just felt that a student of any race or nationality shouldn't be made to feel uncomfortable in a classroom."

94 And in school districts around the country, similar nice people have said similar nice things in justifying the removal of *Huckleberry Finn* and other books from required high school as well as junior high school reading lists. Some school folks, however, refuse to yield to this milky niceness. They figure kids aren't that fragile. And they figure that when educators *are* softly obeisant to those who want to shortchange kids, the result is yet another generation of adults who never learned in school how to think for themselves.

95 So it was in Davenport, Iowa, recently when an attack was made on that good old boy, Huck, who is required reading in an American literature high school course called "Great American Authors." A black student and the parent of another black student wanted this "racist" novel taken off all required reading lists.

96 The demand was turned down. The student was told she could read another book if she wanted to, but, said the English faculty, "It's impossible to have a class called 'Great American Authors' without including Mark Twain." And Huck.

97 Back in Warrington, Pennsylvania, a black girl in junior high asked for *Huckleberry Finn* this year. She'd heard somewhere it was a good book. Although still available in *her* lower school (until September), it had not been chosen by her teacher. The black student got *Huckleberry Finn* and thought it was one hell of a book. She liked it a whole lot. Didn't find it racist at all. Quite the opposite.

98 Better keep an eye on that young woman. Another one of

those independent thinkers who'll always be getting into trouble. Like that kid on the raft.

IV

If I were to name the town, most of you would have to look it up in an atlas. It's not a village—being big enough for a school population of 16,000—but it's no metropolis. Hardly any news comes out of this town that's of interest to anyone but the folks who live there, and they'd like to keep it that way. 99

Especially, these days, the man in charge of coordinating the English program in the town's classrooms isn't looking to be on the nightly news. A black parent has just complained to him about *Huckleberry Finn,* which is required reading in the ninth grade. I mean it's really required. No child leaves the ninth grade in this town without getting on the raft with Huck and Jim. 100

The black parent is disturbed that his child, that any child for that matter—but especially a black child—should have to read a book with the word "nigger" in it. All the way through it. At this point, the black parent is not demanding that *Huckleberry Finn* be removed from the curriculum and the library. He is objecting to the book being *required* reading. 101

So far, the discussions have been low-key and informal. No newspaper or wire service or broadcast station has any idea that this place may join Fairfax County, Virginia; Davenport, Iowa; Warrington, Pennsylvania; and Houston as yet another battleground over whether Mr. Twain's novel does injury to young readers, particularly young black readers. 102

The school official in this unnamed town agreed to let me hear him think out what he's going to do—he's not sure yet—provided I didn't name him or the town. 103

"You see," he said, "I've kept a file on the attacks on *Huckleberry Finn* around the country, and one thing that's clear to me is that as soon as the press gets into this, it gets a lot harder to keep the talks between the school and the parents low-key. Anyway, there is no story here. Yet. We're trying to figure things out. The parent doesn't want to come across as a censor. And I don't want to come across as being callous on this thing." 104

105 He paused, and then said slowly, "When a person is offended, a person is offended. You can't say to him, 'Well, you shouldn't have been offended, or it's ridiculous to be offended by this book.' But on the other hand, it's difficult for me to agree to allow any child to go through our school system without reading *Huckleberry Finn.* There's no other book I know of that is so important—in so many different ways—for kids to know. Especially ninth-grade kids. It seems to me I'd be falling down on my job if I didn't keep that book on the required list. On the other hand, I've got to be sensitive to other people's sensitivities. So I don't know what I'm going to do."

106 Before hearing why this schoolman felt so strongly that all kids who don't read *Huckleberry Finn* are culturally deprived, a note about the impact of the press on these matters. On the one hand, as I tell librarians around the country, as soon as the censor draws a battle line, go to the press. Illumination works wonders, even in those areas where most folks attend fundamentalist churches.

107 The majority of citizens, anywhere, do not like appearing, in newspapers or on television, as if they're being manipulated by organized pressure groups deciding for them what they and their children are going to read. Knowing this element of the American grain is how librarian Kathy Russell triumphed over the censors in conservative Washington County in Virginia. Through the newspapers and broadcast stations there, she kept reminding people that the library belonged to *all* of them, not just the Baptist minister and his allies who wanted to purge it. And the people got angry—at the Baptist minister.

108 Press attention, however, does not always have salutary effects. I have already written about the travails of *Huckleberry Finn* in Warrington, Pennsylvania, and the ultimate grand compromise there which took the book out of the junior high schools and removed it to the high school where it will be only one of eight titles from which teachers can choose.

109 In Warrington, the protest began with one set of black parents. The wire services picked up the story, followed by some of the big papers in the area, notably the *Philadelphia Inquirer.*

110 Thereupon, other black parents came forward. They reported—and this impressed school officials—that their children had not only suffered emotional harm because

they'd had to read *Huckleberry Finn,* but their classwork in other subjects as well had been adversely affected. All because of Mr. Twain's creature.

I asked the language arts supervisor in the Warrington school system whether there had been any such reports of damage to black children during all the previous years in which *Huckleberry Finn* had been on the required reading list in the junior high schools. 111

No, there had been no such reports. 112

I asked if she and other school officials had investigated this alleged correlation between Huck and those black children's failing grades. A correlation that revealed itself only after the press reports on the single initial complaint against the novel. 113

Well, no, the school officials had not really looked into whether such a connection could actually be demonstrated. 114

My own theory, which I also can't prove, is that a kind of group loyalty was in operation among the black kids who claimed to have been injured by the book. The parents of one of their own had complained about *Huckleberry Finn,* and in a show of solidarity, other black children began protesting against the book. And to make their points all the more vivid, they also began showing symptoms that the presence of that book was so malign that they couldn't concentrate on their other studies either. 115

Every one of those black children may well have thoroughly believed all this to be true. The function of the school, however, is to try to find out if it is true. And it didn't even try. 116

But let us suppose it is true, that Huck had paralyzed those black kids. All the more reason for them to get all the way into *Huckleberry Finn.* Otherwise, what a terrible thing for a child to learn! That he is so fragile, so vulnerable, so without intellectual and emotional resources that a book can lay him low. And that is what the teachers and supervisors of the junior high schools in Warrington, Pennsylvania, have allowed the black children in their care to learn. 117

To return to the conflict still aborning in the small town which I will not name. The coordinator of the English curriculum was saying one recent morning that he is riven between his desire to avoid a racial conflict in the community and his desire to "keep the best literature we can in the classroom." 118

If he wanted a way out, I told him, Russell Baker, among 119 others, had given him one. In the April 14 *New York Times,* Baker, an admirer of *Huckleberry Finn,* nonetheless claimed: "It's a dreadful disservice to Mark Twain for teachers to push *Huckleberry Finn* on seventh-, eighth-, and ninth-graders. . . . *Huckleberry Finn* can be partly enjoyed after the age of 25, but for fullest benefit it probably shouldn't be read before age 35, and even then only if the reader has had a broad experience of American society."

120 Dr. Kenneth Clark had snorted when I read him that Russell Baker passage on the phone. So had I when I saw it.

121 But how did this schoolman—worrying about a possible racial confrontation over this book—react to what Baker had said? He *could* tell the black parents that on reflection, he had decided that this book was not right for any child in the secondary schools. And, for that matter, he could recommend that even on their own time, all teachers under 35 stay away from the novel.

122 "No," the man decided not to take this escape route. "No. Neither Russell Baker nor my concern about other people's concern over the use of the word 'nigger' is going to change my mind about what's right educationally. *Huckleberry Finn* is well placed, very well placed, in the ninth grade. And I'll tell you why.

123 "First, the story is told by an adolescent: and there are very few *quality* novels where a youth is dealing with adults entirely from his perspective, in his language, through his experiences.

124 "Second, in terms of craftsmanship and flow, it's a simple novel. At the ninth grade, students are just learning the structure of the novel. It's really our first opportunity to teach the novel as a form, and there's nothing better to do that with than *Huckleberry Finn.* Especially the way it's tied in so nicely with the river.

125 "Also, it's a chronological novel. Not all novels are. For instance, when you jump into Charles Dickens at grade 10, you've got a different, more complicated structure to the novel than you have with *Huckleberry Finn.* So Twain's book is a great introduction to the form of the novel.

126 "Then," the schoolman continued, "it ties in very well with the pre–Civil War history that this school district, and most others, are studying at this grade. Twain has a lot to say about America during that period. He gives adolescent kids a great deal to learn and think about.

127 "Take the word 'nigger.' It's during the *adolescent* years

that kids ought to be dealing with that word, its history, and the kind of people who used it then, and those who still use it. Good Lord, Twain spends three-quarters of his book trying to make clear what a damnable word 'nigger' is, because it shows the whites who used it didn't *see,* didn't begin to understand the people they were talking about."

I mentioned a letter I'd received recently from a librarian 128
in Twain's home state, Missouri. She was focusing on books as a vital part of what she calls the initiation rights of children. Books, she insisted, are among the ways teenagers move into adulthood. "And," she continued, "to deny them the books that can most help them make that transition is inhumane."

"Well, sure," said the schoolman. "That's another reason 129
I've insisted on requiring that all kids in this town read *Huckleberry Finn.* That book is *about* Huck's rites of passage. To put it more prosaically, a large part of it has to do with an adolescent's growth. But that book also has such a sweeping magnitude to it. It has so many things in it. It's about adolescence; it's about the race thing; it's about con men, the Duke and the Dauphin; it's about the murderous foolishness of pride, the Grangerfords. Oh, I could go on all morning."

The schoolman's voice became low. "It would be such a 130
shame for a kid never to get to read this book."

I asked him how he felt about such "compromises" as the 131
one that had been worked out in Warrington, Pennsylvania, to spare kids from Huck Finn in junior high and maybe allow them to read the book in high school. But even then, in the majority of such "compromises," *Huckleberry Finn* has carefully been removed from *required* reading lists in high schools.

"It's insidious," the schoolman in the small town said. "I 132
mean, it's not outright censorship, so nobody has to defend himself against that charge. But this kind of 'compromise' does make it harder and harder for the kid and the book to come together. Oh, some self-starters will seek out *Huckleberry Finn* in the library or ask if they can choose it for independent study; but in those school districts that have compromised, *most* kids will never get to read the book.

"And you know what that's an extension of? The way we 133
underestimate kids. This is a classic case of just that. We

underestimate the capacity of black kids to understand why and how 'nigger' is used in *Huckleberry Finn*. And God knows we underestimate Mark Twain."

134 "Yeah, but so much of this book is Twain's satire," I said. "And John Wallace, the black administrator at Mark Twain Intermediate School in Fairfax County, said that it was asinine to think that most children understand satire."

135 The schoolman laughed. "What could be a more perfect underestimation of kids than that? Look at what kids read on their own. Sometimes I think they live on satire."

136 "Well, it seems to me you've made up your mind that Huck's going to stay here," I said. "In the ninth grade. And on the *required* reading list."

137 "I don't know," he sighed. "I know I'm right about the book, but the key thing is this—you have to be sensitive to someone else's sensitivities. I can talk about the book to the black parents, just the way I've been talking to you about it now. And I can assure them we teach it sensitively, and they'll say, 'It still hurts my child.' And I'll say the child can choose another book. But what book can replace *Huckleberry Finn?*"

138 The schoolman had another appointment. "I'd say," he bade me farewell, "that it's a toss-up right now as to what's going to happen. This is just one of those little battles fought in remote places. Only we'll know how it turns out."

CIVIL RIGHTS, EQUAL RIGHTS, AND THE LAW

ON CIVIL DISOBEDIENCE

Henry David Thoreau

Civil Disobedience

Henry David Thoreau (1817–1862) is best known for his classic Walden *(1854), an autobiographical, satiric, spiritual, scientific, and naturalistic "self-help book" based on his two years' stay at Walden Pond, near Boston. A friend of Ralph Waldo Emerson and other transcendentalists, Thoreau expressed his idealism in a number of concrete ways, for example in his opposition to slavery and the Mexican War. His refusal to pay taxes to support the Mexican War inspired his essay "Civil Disobedience" (1849). First delivered as a lecture in 1848, "Civil Disobedience" influenced the thinking of Mahatma Gandhi and Martin Luther King, Jr.*

I heartily accept the motto,—"That government is best which governs least"; and I should like to see it acted up to more rapidly and systematically. Carried out, it finally amounts to this, which also I believe,—"That government is best which governs not at all"; and when men are prepared for it, that will be the kind of government which they will have. Government is at best but an expedient; but most governments are usually, and all governments are sometimes, inexpedient. The objections which have been brought against a standing army, and they are many and weighty, and deserve to prevail, may also at last be brought against a standing government. The standing army is only an arm of the standing government. The government itself, which is only the mode which the people have chosen to execute their will, is equally liable to be abused and perverted before the people can act through it. Witness the present Mexican war, the work of comparatively a few individuals using the 1 standing government as their tool; for, in the outset, the people would not have consented to this measure.

2 This American government—what is it but a tradition, though a recent one, endeavoring to transmit itself unimpaired to posterity, but each instant losing some of its integrity? It has not the vitality and force of a single living man; for a single man can bend it to his will. It is a sort of wooden gun to the people themselves. But it is not the less necessary for this; for the people must have some complicated machinery or other, and hear its din, to satisfy that idea of government which they have. Governments show thus how successfully men can be imposed on, even impose on themselves, for their own advantage. It is excellent, we must all allow. Yet this government never of itself furthered any enterprise, but by the alacrity with which it got out of its way. *It* does not keep the country free. *It* does not settle the West. *It* does not educate. The character inherent in the American people has done all that has been accomplished; and it would have done somewhat more, if the government had not sometimes got in its way. For government is an expedient by which men would fain succeed in letting one another alone; and, as has been said, when it is most expedient, the governed are most let alone by it. Trade and commerce, if they were not made of India-rubber, would never manage to bounce over the obstacles which legislators are continually putting in their way; and, if one were to judge these men wholly by the effects of their actions and not partly by their intentions, they would deserve to be classed and punished with those mischievous persons who put obstructions on the railroads.

3 But, to speak practically and as a citizen, unlike those who call themselves no-government men, I ask for, not at once no government, but *at once* a better government. Let every man make known what kind of government would command his respect, and that will be one step toward obtaining it.

4 After all, the practical reason why, when the power is once in the hands of people, a majority are permitted, and for a long period continue, to rule is not because they are most likely to be in the right, nor because this seems fairest to the minority, but because they are physically the strongest. But a government in which the majority rule in all cases cannot be based on justice, even as far as men understand it. Can there not be a government in which majorities do not

virtually decide right and wrong, but conscience?—in which majorities decide only those questions to which the rule of expediency is applicable? Must the citizen ever for a moment, or in the least degree, resign his conscience to the legislator? Why has every man a conscience, then? I think that we should be men first, and subjects afterward. It is not desirable to cultivate a respect for the law, so much as for the right. The only obligation which I have a right to assume is to do at any time what I think right. It is truly enough said, that a corporation has no conscience; but a corporation of conscientious men is a corporation *with* a conscience. Law never made men a whit more just; and, by means of their respect for it, even the well-disposed are daily made the agents of injustice. A common and natural result of an undue respect for law is, that you may see a file of soldiers, colonel, captain, corporal, privates, powder-monkeys, and all, marching in admirable order over hill and dale to the wars, against their will, ay, against their common sense and consciences, which makes it very steep marching indeed, and produces a palpitation of the heart. They have no doubt that it is a damnable business in which they are concerned; they are all peaceably inclined. Now, what are they? Men at all? or small movable forts and magazines, at the service of some unscrupulous man in power? Visit the Navy-Yard, and behold a marine, such a man as an American government can make, or such as it can make a man with its black arts,—a mere shadow and reminiscence of humanity, a man laid out alive and standing, and already, as one may say, buried under arms with funeral accompaniments, though it may be,—

"Not a drum was heard, not a funeral note,
As his corse to the rampart we hurried;
Not a soldier discharged his farewell shot
O'er the grave where our hero we buried."[1]

The mass of men serve the state thus, not as men mainly, 5
but as machines, with their bodies. They are the standing army, and the militia, jailers, constables, posse comitatus, etc. In most cases there is no free exercise whatever of the judgment or of the moral sense; but they put themselves on a level with wood and earth and stones; and wooden men

[1] From "Burial of Sir John Moore at Corunna" by Charles Wolfe (1817).

can perhaps be manufactured that will serve the purpose as well. Such command no more respect than men of straw or a lump of dirt. They have the same sort of worth only as horses and dogs. Yet such as these even are commonly esteemed good citizens. Others—as most legislators, politicians, lawyers, ministers, and office-holders—serve the state chiefly with their heads; and, as they rarely make any moral distinctions, they are as likely to serve the Devil, without *intending* it, as God. A very few, as heroes, patriots, martyrs, reformers in the great sense, and *men,* serve the state with their consciences also, and so necessarily resist it for the most part; and they are commonly treated as enemies by it. A wise man will only be useful as a man, and will not submit to be "clay," and "stop a hole to keep the wind away," but leave that office to his dust at least:—

"I am too high-born to be propertied,
To be a secondary at control,
Or useful serving-man and instrument
To any sovereign state throughout the world."[2]

6 He who gives himself entirely to his fellow-men appears to them useless and selfish; but he who gives himself partially to them is pronounced a benefactor and philanthropist.

7 How does it become a man to behave toward this American government to-day? I answer, that he cannot without disgrace be associated with it. I cannot for an instant recognize that political organization as *my* government which is the *slave's* government also.

8 All men recognize the right of revolution; that is, the right to refuse allegiance to, and to resist, the government, when its tyranny or its inefficiency are great and unendurable. But almost all say that such is not the case now. But such was the case, they think, in the Revolution of '75. If one were to tell me that this was a bad government because it taxed certain foreign commodities brought to its ports, it is most probable that I should not make an ado about it, for I can do without them. All machines have their friction; and possibly this does enough good to counterbalance the evil. At any rate, it is a great evil to make a stir about it. But when the friction comes to have its machine, and oppression and

[2] The line before the quotation is from *Hamlet* V. i. 236–37; the quotation is from Shakespeare's *King John* V. ii. 79–82.

robbery are organized, I say, let us not have such a machine any longer. In other words, when a sixth of the population of a nation which has undertaken to be the refuge of liberty are slaves, and a whole country is unjustly overrun and conquered by a foreign army, and subjected to military law, I think that it is not too soon for honest men to rebel and revolutionize. What makes this duty the more urgent is the fact that the country so overrun is not our own, but ours is the invading army.

Paley,[3] a common authority with many on moral questions, in his chapter on the "Duty of Submission to Civil Government," resolves all civil obligation into expediency; and he proceeds to say, "that so long as the interest of the whole society requires it, that is, so long as the established government cannot be resisted or changed without public inconveniency, it is the will of God that the established government be obeyed, and no longer. . . . This principle being admitted, the justice of every particular case of resistance is reduced to a computation of the quantity of the danger and grievance on the one side, and of the probability and expense of redressing it on the other." Of this, he says, every man shall judge for himself. But Paley appears never to have contemplated those cases to which the rule of expediency does not apply, in which a people, as well as an individual, must do justice, cost what it may. If I have unjustly wrested a plank from a drowning man, I must restore it to him though I drown myself. This, according to Paley, would be inconvenient. But he that would save his life, in such a case, shall lose it. This people must cease to hold slaves, and to make war on Mexico, though it cost them their existence as a people. 9

In their practice, nations agree with Paley; but does any one think that Massachusetts does exactly what is right at the present crisis? 10

"A drab of state, a cloth-o'-silver slut,
To have her train borne up, and her soul trail in the dirt."

Practically speaking the opponents to a reform in Massachusetts are not a hundred thousand politicians at the South, but a hundred thousand merchants and farmers here, who are more interested in commerce and agriculture

[3] William Paley (1743–1805), English theologian.

than they are in humanity, and are not prepared to do justice to the slave and to Mexico, *cost what it may*. I quarrel not with far-off foes, but with those who, near at home, coöperate with, and do the bidding of, those far away, and without whom the latter would be harmless. We are accustomed to say, that the mass of men are unprepared; but improvement is slow, because the few are not materially wiser or better than the many. It is not so important that many should be as good as you, as that there be some absolute goodness somewhere; for that will leaven the whole lump. There are thousands who are *in opinion* opposed to slavery and to the war, who yet in effect do nothing to put an end to them; who, esteeming themselves children of Washington and Franklin, sit down with their hands in their pockets, and say that they know not what to do, and do nothing; who even postpone the question of freedom to the question of free-trade, and quietly read the prices-current along with the latest advices from Mexico, after dinner, and, it may be, fall asleep over them both. What is the price-current of an honest man and patriot to-day? They hesitate, and they regret, and sometimes they petition; but they do nothing in earnest and with effect. They will wait, well disposed, for others to remedy the evil, that they may no longer have it to regret. At most, they give only a cheap vote, and a feeble countenance and Godspeed, to the right, as it goes by them. There are nine hundred and ninety-nine patrons of virtue to one virtuous man. But it is easier to deal with the real possessor of a thing than with the temporary guardian of it.

11 All voting is a sort of gaming, like checkers or backgammon, with a slight moral tinge to it, a playing with right and wrong, with moral questions; and betting naturally accompanies it. The character of the voters is not staked. I cast my vote, perchance, as I think right; but I am not vitally concerned that that right should prevail. I am willing to leave it to the majority. Its obligation, therefore, never exceeds that of expediency. Even voting *for the right* is *doing* nothing for it. It is only expressing to men feebly your desire that it should prevail. A wise man will not leave the right to the mercy of chance, nor wish it to prevail through the power of the majority. There is but little virtue in the action of masses of men. When the majority shall at length vote for the abolition of slavery, it will be because they are indifferent to slavery, or because there is but little slavery left to be

abolished by their vote. *They* will then be the only slaves. Only *his* vote can hasten the abolition of slavery who asserts his own freedom by his vote.

I hear of a convention to be held at Baltimore, or elsewhere, for the selection of a candidate for the Presidency, made up chiefly of editors, and men who are politicians by profession; but I think, what is it to any independent, intelligent, and respectable man what decision they may come to? Shall we not have the advantage of his wisdom and honesty, nevertheless? Can we not count upon some independent votes? Are there not many individuals in the country who do not attend conventions? But no: I find that the respectable man, so called, has immediately drifted from his position, and despairs of his country, when his country has more reason to despair of him. He forthwith adopts one of the candidates thus selected as the only *available* one, thus proving that he is himself *available* for any purposes of the demagogue. His vote is of no more worth than that of any unprincipled foreigner or hireling native, who may have been bought. O for a man who is a *man,* and, as my neighbor says, has a bone in his back which you cannot pass your hand through! Our statistics are at fault: the population has been returned too large. How many *men* are there to a square thousand miles in this country? Hardly one. Does not America offer any inducement for men to settle here? The American has dwindled into an Odd Fellow,—one who may be known by the development of his organ of gregariousness, and a manifest lack of intellect and cheerful self-reliance; whose first and chief concern, on coming into the world, is to see that the Almshouses are in good repair; and, before yet he has lawfully donned the virile garb, to collect a fund for the support of the widows and orphans that may be; who, in short, ventures to live only by the aid of the Mutual Insurance company, which has promised to bury him decently. 12

It is not a man's duty, as a matter of course, to devote himself to the eradication of any, even the most enormous wrong; he may still properly have other concerns to engage him; but it is his duty, at least, to wash his hands of it, and, if he gives it no thought longer, not to give it practically his support. If I devote myself to other pursuits and contemplations, I must first see, at least, that I do not pursue them sitting upon another man's shoulders. I must get off him first, that he may pursue his contemplations too. See what 13 gross inconsistency is tolerated. I have heard some of my townsmen say, "I should like to have them order me out to help put down an insurrection of the slaves, or to march to Mexico;—see if I would go"; and yet these very men have each, directly by their allegiance, and so indirectly, at least, by their money, furnished a substitute. The soldier is applauded who refuses to serve in an unjust war by those who do not refuse to sustain the unjust government which makes the war; is applauded by those whose own act and authority he disregards and sets at naught; as if the state were penitent to that degree that it hired one to scourge it while it sinned, but not to that degree that it left off sinning for a moment. Thus, under the name of Order and Civil Government, we are all made at last to pay homage to and support our own meanness. After the first blush of sin comes its indifference; and from immoral it becomes, as it were, *un*moral, and not quite unnecessary to that life which we have made.

14 The broadest and most prevalent error requires the most disinterested virtue to sustain it. The slight reproach to which the virtue of patriotism is commonly liable, the noble are most likely to incur. Those who, while they disapprove of the character and measures of a government, yield to it their allegiance and support are undoubtedly its most conscientious supporters, and so frequently the most serious obstacles to reform. Some are petitioning the state to dissolve the Union, to disregard the requisitions of the President. Why do they not dissolve it themselves,—the union between themselves and the state,—and refuse to pay their quota into its treasury? Do not they stand in the same relation to the state that the state does to the Union? And have not the same reasons prevented the state from resisting the Union which have prevented them from resisting the state?

15 How can a man be satisfied to entertain an opinion merely, and enjoy *it?* Is there any enjoyment in it, if his opinion is that he is aggrieved? If you are cheated out of a single dollar by your neighbor, you do not rest satisfied with knowing that you are cheated, or with saying that you are cheated, or even with petitioning him to pay you your due; but you take effectual steps at once to obtain the full amount, and see that you are never cheated again. Action from principle, the perception and the performance of right, changes things and relations; it is essentially revolutionary, and does not consist wholly with anything which was. It not

only divides states and churches, it divides families; ay, it divides the *individual,* separating the diabolical in him from the divine.

Unjust laws exist: shall we be content to obey them, or 16
shall we endeavor to amend them, and obey them until we have succeeded, or shall we transgress them at once? Men generally, under such a government as this, think that they ought to wait until they have persuaded the majority to alter them. They think that, if they should resist, the remedy would be worse than the evil. But it is the fault of the government itself that the remedy *is* worse than the evil. *It* makes it worse. Why is it not more apt to anticipate and provide for reform? Why does it not cherish its wise minority? Why does it cry and resist before it is hurt? Why does it not encourage its citizens to be on the alert to point out its faults, and *do* better than it would have them? Why does it always crucify Christ, and excommunicate Copernicus and Luther, and pronounce Washington and Franklin rebels?

One would think, that a deliberate and practical denial of 17
its authority was the only offense never contemplated by government; else, why has it not assigned its definite, its suitable and proportionate penalty? If a man who has no property refuses but once to earn nine shillings for the state, he is put in prison for a period unlimited by any law that I know, and determined only by the discretion of those who place him there; but if he should steal ninety times nine shillings from the state, he is soon permitted to go at large again.

If the injustice is part of the necessary friction of the 18
machine of government, let it go, let it go; perchance it will wear smooth,—certainly the machine will wear out. If the injustice has a spring, or a pulley, or a rope, or a crank, exclusively for itself, then perhaps you may consider whether the remedy will not be worse than the evil; but if it is of such a nature that it requires you to be the agent of injustice to another, then, I say, break the law. Let your life be a counter friction to stop the machine. What I have to do is to see, at any rate, that I do not lend myself to the wrong which I condemn.

As for adopting the ways which the state has provided for 19
remedying the evil, I know not of such ways. They take too much time, and a man's life will be gone. I have other affairs to attend to. I came into this world, not chiefly to make this a good place to live in, but to live in it, be it good or bad. A

man has not everything to do, but something; and because he cannot do *everything,* it is not necessary that he should do *something* wrong. It is not my business to be petitioning the Governor or the Legislature any more than it is theirs to petition me; and if they should not hear my petition, what should I do then? But in this case the state has provided no way; its very Constitution is the evil. This may seem to be harsh and stubborn and unconciliatory; but it is to treat with the utmost kindness and consideration the only spirit that can appreciate or deserves it. So is all change for the better, like birth and death, which convulse the body.

20 I do not hesitate to say, that those who call themselves Abolitionists should at once effectually withdraw their support, both in person and property, from the government of Massachusetts, and not wait till they constitute a majority of one, before they suffer the right to prevail through them. I think that it is enough if they have God on their side, without waiting for that other one. Moreover, any man more right than his neighbors constitutes a majority of one already.

21 I meet this American government, or its representative, the state government, directly, and face to face, once a year—no more—in the person of its tax-gatherer; this is the only mode in which a man situated as I am necessarily meets it; and it then says distinctly, Recognize me; and the simplest, the most effectual, and, in the present posture of affairs, the indispensablest mode of treating with it on this head, of expressing your little satisfaction with and love for it, is to deny it then. My civil neighbor, the tax-gatherer, is the very man I have to deal with,—for it is, after all, with men and not with parchment that I quarrel,—and he has voluntarily chosen to be an agent of the government. How shall he ever know well what he is and does as an officer of the government, or as a man, until he is obliged to consider whether he shall treat me, his neighbor, for whom he has respect, as a neighbor and well-disposed man, or as a maniac and disturber of the peace, and see if he can get over this obstruction to his neighborliness without a ruder and more impetuous thought or speech corresponding with his action. I know this well, that if one thousand, if one hundred, if ten men whom I could name,—if ten *honest* men only,—ay, if *one* HONEST man, in this State of Massachusetts, *ceasing to hold slaves,* were actually to withdraw from this copartnership, and be locked up in the county jail therefor,

it would be the abolition of slavery in America. For it matters not how small the beginning may seem to be; what is once well done is done forever. But we love better to talk about it: that we say is our mission. Reform keeps many scores of newspapers in its service, but not one man. If my esteemed neighbor, the State's ambassador, who will devote his days to the settlement of the question of human rights in the Council Chamber, instead of being threatened with the prisons of Carolina, were to sit down the prisoner of Massachusetts, that State which is so anxious to foist the sin of slavery upon her sister,—though at present she can discover only an act of inhospitality to be the ground of a quarrel with her,—the Legislature would not wholly waive the subject the following winter.

Under a government which imprisons any unjustly, the true place for a just man is also a prison. The proper place to-day, the only place which Massachusetts has provided for her freer and less desponding spirits, is in her prisons, to be put out and locked out of the State by her own act, as they have already put themselves out by their principles. It is there that the fugitive slave, and the Mexican prisoner on parole, and the Indian come to plead the wrongs of his race should find them; on that separate, but more free and honorable ground, where the State places those who are not *with* her, but *against* her,—the only house in a slave State in which a free man can abide with honor. If any think that their influence would be lost there, and their voices no longer afflict the ear of the State, that they would not be as an enemy within its walls, they do not know by how much truth is stronger than error, nor how much more eloquently and effectively he can combat injustice who has experienced a little in his own person. Cast your whole vote, not a strip of paper merely, but your whole influence. A minority is powerless while it conforms to the majority; it is not even a minority then; but it is irresistible when it clogs by its whole weight. If the alternative is to keep all just men in prison, or give up war and slavery, the State will not hesitate which to choose. If a thousand men were not to pay their tax-bills this year, that would not be a violent and bloody measure, as it would be to pay them, and enable the State to commit violence and shed innocent blood. This is, in fact, the definition of a peaceable revolution, if any such is possible. If the tax-gatherer, or any other public officer, asks me, as one has done, "But what shall I do?" my answer is, "If you really wish to do anything, resign your office." When the subject has refused allegiance, and the officer has resigned his office, then the revolution is accomplished. But even suppose blood should flow. Is there not a sort of blood shed when the conscience is wounded? Through this wound a man's real manhood and immortality flow out, and he bleeds to an everlasting death. I see this blood flowing now.

23 I have contemplated the imprisonment of the offender, rather than the seizure of his goods,—though both will serve the same purpose,—because they who assert the purest right, and consequently are most dangerous to a corrupt State, commonly have not spent much time in accumulating property. To such the State renders comparatively small service, and a slight tax is wont to appear exorbitant, particularly if they are obliged to earn it by special labor with their hands. If there were one who lived wholly without the use of money, the State itself would hesitate to demand it of him. But the rich man—not to make any invidious comparison—is always sold to the institution which makes him rich. Absolutely speaking, the more money, the less virtue; for money comes between a man and his objects, and obtains them for him; and it was certainly no great virtue to obtain it. It puts to rest many questions which he would otherwise be taxed to answer; while the only new question which it puts is the hard but superfluous one, how to spend it. Thus his moral ground is taken from under his feet. The opportunities of living are diminished in proportion as what are called the "means" are increased. The best thing a man can do for his culture when he is rich is to endeavor to carry out those schemes which he entertained when he was poor. Christ answered the Herodians according to their condition. "Show me the tribute-money," said he;—and one took a penny out of his pocket;—if you use money which has the image of Caesar on it, and which he has made current and valuable, that is, *if you are men of the State,* and gladly enjoy the advantages of Caesar's government, then pay him back some of his own when he demands it. "Render therefore to Caesar that which is Caesar's, and to God those things which are God's,"—leaving them no wiser than before as to which was which; for they did not wish to know.

24 When I converse with the freest of my neighbors, I perceive that, whatever they may say about the magnitude and seriousness of the question, and their regard for the public tranquillity, the long and the short of the matter is, that they cannot spare the protection of the existing govern-

ment, and they dread the consequences to their property and families of disobedience to it. For my own part, I should not like to think that I ever rely on the protection of the State. But, if I deny the authority of the State when it presents its tax-bill, it will soon take and waste all my property, and so harass me and my children without end. This is hard. This makes it impossible for a man to live honestly, and at the same time comfortably, in outward respects. It will not be worth the while to accumulate property; that would be sure to go again. You must hire or squat somewhere, and raise but a small crop, and eat that soon. You must live within yourself, and depend upon yourself always tucked up and ready for a start, and not have many affairs. A man may grow rich in Turkey even, if he will be in all respects a good subject of the Turkish government. Confucius said: "If a state is governed by the principles of reason, poverty and misery are subjects of shame; if a state is not governed by the principles of reason, riches and honors are the subjects of shame." No: until I want the protection of Massachusetts to be extended to me in some distant Southern port, where my liberty is endangered, or until I am bent solely on building up an estate at home by peaceful enterprise, I can afford to refuse allegiance to Massachusetts, and her right to my property and life. It costs me less in every sense to incur the penalty of disobedience to the State than it would to obey. I should feel as if I were worth less in that case.

Some years ago, the State met me in behalf of the Church, 25
and commanded me to pay a certain sum toward the support of a clergyman whose preaching my father attended, but never I myself. "Pay," it said, "or be locked up in the jail." I declined to pay. But, unfortunately, another man saw fit to pay it. I did not see why the schoolmaster should be taxed to support the priest, and not the priest the schoolmaster; for I was not the State's schoolmaster, but I supported myself by voluntary subscription. I did not see why the lyceum should not present its tax-bill, and have the State to back its demand, as well as the Church. However, at the request of the selectmen, I condescended to make some such statement as this in writing:—"Know all men by these presents, that I, Henry Thoreau, do not wish to be regarded as a member of any incorporated society which I have not joined." This I gave to the town clerk; and he has it. The State, having thus learned that I did not wish to be regarded as a member of that church, has never made a like demand on me since; though it said that

it must adhere to its original presumption that time. If I had known how to name them, I should then have signed off in detail from all the societies which I never signed on to; but I did not know where to find a complete list.

26 I have paid no poll-tax[4] for six years. I was put into jail once on this account, for one night; and, as I stood considering the walls of solid stone, two or three feet thick, the door of wood and iron, a foot thick, and the iron grating which strained the light, I could not help being struck with the foolishness of that institution which treated me as if I were mere flesh and blood and bones, to be locked up. I wondered that it should have concluded at length that this was the best use it could put me to, and had never thought to avail itself of my services in some way. I saw that, if there was a wall of stone between me and my townsmen, there was still a more difficult one to climb or break through before they could get to be as free as I was. I did not for a moment feel confined, and the walls seemed a great waste of stone and mortar. I felt as if I alone of all my townsmen had paid my tax. They plainly did not know how to treat me, but behaved like persons who are underbred. In every threat and in every compliment there was a blunder; for they thought that my chief desire was to stand the other side of that stone wall. I could not but smile to see how industriously they locked the door on my meditations, which followed them out again without let or hindrance, and *they* were really all that was dangerous. As they could not reach me, they had resolved to punish my body; just as boys, if they cannot come at some person against whom they have a spite, will abuse his dog. I saw that the State was half-witted, that it was timid as a lone woman with her silver spoons, and that it did not know its friends from its foes, and I lost all my remaining respect for it, and pitied it.

27 Thus the State never intentionally confronts a man's sense, intellectual or moral, but only his body, his senses. It is not armed with superior wit or honesty, but with superior physical strength. I was not born to be forced. I will breathe after my own fashion. Let us see who is the strongest. What force has a multitude? They only can force me who obey a higher law than I. They force me to become like themselves. I do not hear of *men* being *forced* to live this way or that by masses of men. What sort of life were that to live? When I

[4] Tax assessed against a person (not property); payment was frequently prerequisite for voting.

meet a government which says to me, "Your money or your life," why should I be in haste to give it my money? It may be in a great strait, and not know what to do: I cannot help that. It must help itself; do as I do. It is not worth the while to snivel about it. I am not responsible for the successful working of the machinery of society. I am not the son of the engineer. I perceive that, when an acorn and a chestnut fall side by side, the one does not remain inert to make way for the other, but both obey their own laws, and spring and grow and flourish as best they can, till one, perchance, overshadows and destroys the other. If a plant cannot live according to its nature, it dies; and so a man.

The night in prison was novel and interesting enough. The 28
prisoners in their shirt-sleeves were enjoying a chat and the evening air in the doorway, when I entered. But the jailer said, "Come, boys, it is time to lock up;" and so they dispersed, and I heard the sound of their steps returning into the hollow apartments. My room-mate was introduced to me by the jailer as "a first-rate fellow and a clever man." When the door was locked, he showed me where to hang my hat, and how he managed matters there. The rooms were whitewashed once a month; and this one, at least, was the whitest, most simply furnished, and probably the neatest apartment in the town. He naturally wanted to know where I came from, and what brought me there; and, when I had told him, I asked him in my turn how he came there, presuming him to be an honest man, of course; and, as the world goes, I believe he was. "Why," said he, "they accuse me of burning a barn; but I never did it." As near as I could discover, he had probably gone to bed in a barn when drunk, and smoked his pipe there; and so a barn was burnt. He had the reputation of being a clever man, had been there some three months waiting for his trial to come on, and would have to wait as much longer; but he was quite domesticated and contented, since he got his board for nothing, and thought that he was well treated.

He occupied one window, and I the other; and I saw that 29
if one stayed there long, his principal business would be to look out the window. I had soon read all the tracts that were left there, and examined where former prisoners had broken out, and where a grate had been sawed off, and heard the history of the various occupants of that room; for I found that even here there was a history and a gossip which never circulated beyond the walls of the jail. Probably this is the only house in the town where verses are composed, which

are afterward printed in a circular form, but not published. I was shown quite a long list of verses which were composed by some young men who had been detected in an attempt to escape, who avenged themselves by singing them.

30 I pumped my fellow-prisoner as dry as I could, for fear I should never see him again; but at length he showed me which was my bed, and left me to blow out the lamp.

31 It was like traveling into a far country, such as I had never expected to behold, to lie there for one night. It seemed to me that I never had heard the town-clock strike before, nor the evening sounds of the village; for we slept with the windows open, which were inside the grating. It was to see my native village in the light of the Middle Ages, and our Concord was turned into a Rhine stream, and visions of knights and castles passed before me. They were the voices of old burghers that I heard in the streets. I was an involuntary spectator and auditor of whatever was done and said in the kitchen of the adjacent village-inn,—a wholly new and rare experience to me. It was a closer view of my native town. I was fairly inside of it. I never had seen its institutions before. This is one of its peculiar institutions; for it is a shire town. I began to comprehend what its inhabitants were about.

32 In the morning, our breakfasts were put through the hole in the door, in small oblong-square tin pans, made to fit, and holding a pint of chocolate, with brown bread, and an iron spoon. When they called for the vessels again, I was green enough to return what bread I had left; but my comrade seized it, and said that I should lay that up for lunch or dinner. Soon after he was let out to work at haying in a neighboring field, whither he went every day, and would not be back till noon; so he bade me good-day, saying that he doubted if he should see me again.

33 When I came out of prison—for some one interfered, and paid that tax,—I did not perceive that great changes had taken place on the common, such as he observed who went in a youth and emerged a tottering and gray-headed man; and yet a change had to my eyes come over the scene,—the town, and State, and country,—greater than any that mere time could effect. I saw yet more distinctly the State in which I lived. I saw to what extent the people among whom I lived could be trusted as good neighbors and friends; that their friendship was for summer weather only; that they did not greatly propose to do right; that they were a distinct race from me by their prejudices and superstitions, as the Chi-

namen and Malays are; that in their sacrifices to humanity they ran no risks, not even to their property; that after all they were not so noble but they treated the thief as he had treated them, and hoped, by a certain outward observance and a few prayers, and by walking in a particular straight though useless path from time to time, to save their souls. This may be to judge my neighbors harshly; for I believe that many of them are not aware that they have such an institution as the jail in their village.

It was formerly the custom in our village, when a poor 34
debtor came out of jail, for his acquaintances to salute him, looking through their fingers, which were crossed to represent the grating of a jail window, "How do ye do?" My neighbors did not thus salute me, but first looked at me, and then at one another, as if I had returned from a long journey. I was put into jail as I was going to the shoemaker's to get a shoe which was mended. When I was let out the next morning, I proceeded to finish my errand, and, having put on my mended shoe, joined a huckleberry party, who were impatient to put themselves under my conduct; and in half an hour,—for the horse was soon tackled,—was in the midst of a huckleberry field, on one of our highest hills, two miles off, and then the State was nowhere to be seen.

This is the whole history of "My Prisons." 35

Mahatma Gandhi

Letter to Lord Irwin

Mahatma Gandhi (Mahatma means "of great soul") was born in India in 1869, studied law in London, and in 1893 went to South Africa, where he opposed discriminatory legislation against Indians, was exposed to the writing of Henry David Thoreau, and carried on a famous correspondence with the Russian novelist Leo Tolstoy concerning civil disobedience. In 1914 he returned to India and about 1920 began a lifetime of committed support for India's independence from England—notably through the practice and encouragement of nonviolent resistance (satyagraha). *After a decade of sporadic civil disobedience and periodic imprisonments, Gandhi in 1930 prepared a Declaration of Independence for India and soon after led a remarkable (and famous) 200-mile march to the sea to collect salt in symbolic defiance of the English government's monopoly on that product; by the end of the year, more than 100,000 people were jailed in the campaign. India of course did finally achieve independence in 1947. The following year, while trying to calm tensions between Hindus and Moslems, Gandhi was assassinated.*

The following letter was sent by Gandhi to the British viceroy in India, Lord Irwin, in March 1930, just ten days before the salt march was to begin. It was sent from Satyagraha Ashram, a community established to practice the method of nonviolent resistance.

Satyagraha Ashram, Sabarmati,
March 2, 1930

Dear Friend,

1 Before embarking on civil disobedience and taking the risk I have dreaded to take all these years, I would fain approach you and find a way out.

2 My personal faith is absolutely clear. I cannot intentionally hurt anything that lives, much less fellow human beings, even though they may do the greatest wrong to me and mine. Whilst, therefore, I hold the British rule to be a curse, I do not intend harm to a single Englishman or to any legitimate interest he may have in India.

3 I must not be misunderstood. Though I hold the British rule in India to be a curse, I do not, therefore, consider Englishmen in general to be worse than any other people on earth. I have the privilege of claiming many Englishmen as dearest friends. Indeed much that I have learnt of the evil of British rule is due to the writings of frank and courageous Englishmen who have not hesitated to tell the unpalatable truth about that rule.

4 And why do I regard the British rule as a curse?

5 It has impoverished the dumb millions by a system of progressive exploitation and by a ruinously expensive military and civil administration which the country can never afford.

6 It has reduced us politically to serfdom. It has sapped the foundations of our culture. And, by the policy of cruel disarmament, it has degraded us spiritually. Lacking the inward strength, we have been reduced, by all but universal disarmament, to a state bordering on cowardly helplessness.

In common with many of my countrymen, I had hugged the fond hope that the proposed Round Table Conference might furnish a solution. But, when you said plainly that you could not give any assurance that you or the British Cabinet would pledge yourselves to support a scheme of full Dominion Status, the Round Table Conference could not possibly furnish the solution for which vocal India is consciously, and the dumb millions are unconsciously, thirsting. 7

It seems as clear as daylight that responsible British statesmen do not contemplate any alteration in British policy that might adversely affect Britain's commerce with India or require an impartial and close scrutiny of Britain's transactions with India. If nothing is done to end the process of exploitation India must be bled with an ever increasing speed. The Finance Member regards as a settled fact the 1/6 ratio which by a stroke of the pen drains India of a few crores.[1] And when a serious attempt is being made through a civil form of direct action, to unsettle this fact, among many others, even you cannot help appealing to the wealthy landed classes to help you to crush that attempt in the name of an order that grinds India to atoms. 8

Unless those who work in the name of the nation understand and keep before all concerned the motive that lies behind the craving for independence, there is every danger of independence coming to us so changed as to be of no value to those toiling voiceless millions for whom it is sought and for whom it is worth taking. It is for that reason that I have been recently telling the public what independence should really mean. 9

Let me put before you some of the salient points. 10

The terrific pressure of land revenue, which furnishes a large part of the total, must undergo considerable modification in an independent India. Even the much vaunted permanent settlement benefits the few rich zamindars,[2] not the ryots.[3] The ryot has remained as helpless as ever. He is a mere tenant at will. Not only, then, has the land revenue to be considerably reduced, but the whole revenue system has to be so revised as to make the ryot's good its primary concern. But the British system seems to be designed to 11

[1] In Indian currency, a crore is equivalent to ten million rupees.

[2] A zamindar is a landowner.

[3] A ryot is a tenant farmer.

crush the very life out of him. Even the salt he must use to live is so taxed as to make the burden fall heaviest on him, if only because of the heartless impartiality of its incidence. The tax shows itself still more burdensome on the poor man when it is remembered that salt is the one thing he must eat more than the rich man both individually and collectively.

12 The iniquities sampled above are maintained in order to carry on a foreign administration, demonstrably the most expensive in the world. Take your own salary. It is over Rs. 21,000 per month, besides many other indirect additions. The British Prime Minister gets £ 5,000 per year, i.e., over Rs. 5,400 per month at the present rate of exchange. You are getting over Rs. 700 per day against India's average income of less than annas 2 per day. The Prime Minister gets Rs. 180 per day against Great Britain's average income of nearly Rs. 2 per day. Thus you are getting much over five thousand times India's average income. The British Prime Minister is getting only ninety times Britain's average income. On bended knees I ask you to ponder over this phenomenon. I have taken a personal illustration to drive home a painful truth. I have too great a regard for you as a man to wish to hurt your feelings. I know that you do not need the salary you get. Probably the whole of your salary goes for charity. But a system that provides for such an arrangement deserves to be summarily scrapped.

13 If India is to live as a nation, if the slow death by starvation of her people is to stop, some remedy must be found for immediate relief. The proposed Conference is certainly not the remedy. It is not a matter of carrying conviction by argument. The matter resolves itself into one of matching forces. Conviction or no conviction, Great Britain would defend her Indian commerce and interests by all the forces at her command. India must consequently evolve force enough to free herself from that embrace of death.

14 It is common cause that, however disorganized and, for the time being, insignificant it may be, the party of violence is gaining ground and making itself felt. Its end is the same as mine. But I am convinced that it cannot bring the desired relief to the dumb millions. And the conviction is growing deeper and deeper in me that nothing but unadulterated non-violence can check the organized violence of the British Government. Many think that non-violence is not an active force. My experience, limited though it undoubtedly is,

shows that non-violence can be an intensely active force. It is my purpose to set in motion that force as well against the organized violent force of the British rule as [against] the unorganized violent force of the growing party of violence. To sit still would be to give rein to both the forces above mentioned. Having an unquestioning and immovable faith in the efficacy of non-violence as I know it, it would be sinful on my part to wait any longer.

This non-violence will be expressed through civil disobe- 15
dience, for the moment confined to the inmates of the Satyagraha Ashram, but ultimately designed to cover all those who choose to join the movement with its obvious limitations.

I know that in embarking on non-violence I shall be 16
running what might fairly be termed a mad risk. But the victories of truth have never been won without risks, often of the gravest character. Conversion of a nation that has consciously or unconsciously preyed upon another, far more numerous, far more ancient and no less cultured than itself, is worth any amount of risk.

I have deliberately used the word "conversion." For my 17
ambition is no less than to convert the British people through non-violence, and thus make them see the wrong they have done to India. I do not seek to harm your people. I want to serve them even as I want to serve my own. I believe that I have always served them. I served them up to 1919 blindly. But when my eyes were opened and I conceived non-cooperation, the object still was to serve them. I employed the same weapon that I have in all humility successfully used against the dearest members of my family. If I have equal love for your people with mine it will not long remain hidden. It will be acknowledged by them even as the members of my family acknowledged it after they had tried me for several years. If the people join me as I expect they will, the sufferings they will undergo, unless the British nation sooner retraces its steps, will be enough to melt the stoniest hearts.

The plan through civil disobedience will be to combat 18
such evils as I have sampled out. If we want to sever the British connection it is because of such evils. When they are removed the path becomes easy. Then the way to friendly negotiation will be open. If the British commerce with India is purified of greed, you will have no difficulty in recognizing our independence. I respectfully invite you then to pave the

way for immediate removal of those evils, and thus open a way for a real conference between equals, interested only in promoting the common good of mankind through voluntary fellowship and in arranging terms of mutual help and commerce equally suited to both. You have unnecessarily laid stress upon the communal problems that unhappily affect this land. Important though they undoubtedly are for the consideration of any scheme of government, they have little bearing on the greater problems which are above communities and which affect them all equally. But if you cannot see your way to deal with these evils and my letter makes no appeal to your heart, on the 11th day of this month, I shall proceed with such co-workers of the Ashram as I can take, to disregard the provisions of the salt laws. I regard this tax to be the most iniquitous of all from the poor man's standpoint. As the independence movement is essentially for the poorest in the land the beginning will be made with this evil. The wonder is that we have submitted to the cruel monopoly for so long. It is, I know, open to you to frustrate my design by arresting me. I hope that there will be tens of thousands ready, in a disciplined manner, to take up the work after me, and, in the act of disobeying the Salt Act to lay themselves open to the penalties of a law that should never have disfigured the Statute-book.

19 I have no desire to cause you unnecessary embarrassment, or any at all, so far as I can help. If you think that there is any substance in my letter, and if you will care to discuss matters with me, and if to that end you would like me to postpone publication of this letter, I shall gladly refrain on receipt of a telegram to that effect soon after this reaches you. You will, however, do me the favour not to deflect me from my course unless you can see your way to conform to the substance of this letter.

20 This letter is not in any way intended as a threat but is a simple and sacred duty peremptory on a civil resister. Therefore I am having it specially delivered by a young English friend who believes in the Indian cause and is a full believer in non-violence and whom Providence seems to have sent to me, as it were, for the very purpose.

I remain,
Your sincere friend,
M. K. Gandhi

Martin Luther King, Jr.

Love, Law, and Civil Disobedience

Born in Atlanta and educated at Morehouse College, Crozer Theological Seminary (near Philadelphia), and Boston University, Martin Luther King, Jr. (1929–1968), was the leader of the civil rights movement of the 1960s. An ordained minister with a doctorate in theology from Boston University, he worked especially in the South and through nonviolent means to overturn segregation statutes, to increase the number of African-American voters, and to support other civil rights initiatives. Reverend King won the Nobel Peace Prize in 1964. When he was assassinated in 1968, all America mourned. The following item is a transcript of a speech that Dr. King delivered in 1961 to the annual meeting of the Fellowship of the Concerned in Atlanta. After you read the address, note how several passages reappeared later (in a somewhat different form) in his "Letter from Birmingham Jail," the next selection in this book.

Members of the Fellowship of the Concerned, of the 1 Southern Regional Council, I need not pause to say how very delighted I am to be here today, and to have the opportunity of being a little part of this very significant gathering. I certainly want to express my personal appreciation to Mrs. Tilly and the members of the Committee, for giving me this opportunity. I would also like to express just a personal word of thanks and appreciation for your vital witness in this period of transition which we are facing in our Southland, and in the nation, and I am sure that as a result of this genuine concern, and your significant work in communities all across the South, we have a better South today and I am sure will have a better South tomorrow with your continued endeavor. And I do want to express my personal gratitude and appreciation to you of the Fellowship of the Concerned for your significant work and for your forthright witness.

Now, I have been asked to talk about the philosophy 2 behind the student movement. There can be no gainsaying of the fact that we confront a crisis in race relations in the United States. This crisis has been precipitated on the one hand by the determined resistance of reactionary forces in the South to the Supreme Court's decision in 1954 outlawing segregation in the public schools. And we know that at times this resistance has risen to ominous proportions. At times we find the legislative halls of the South ringing loud with such words as interposition and nullification. And all of these forces have developed into massive resistance. But we must also say that the crisis has been precipitated on the other hand by the determination of hundreds and thousands and millions of Negro people to achieve freedom and human dignity. If the Negro stayed in his place and accepted discrimination and segregation, there would be no crisis. But the Negro has a new sense of dignity, a new self respect, and new determination. He has re-evaluated his own intrinsic worth. Now this new sense of dignity on the part of the Negro grows out of the same longing for freedom and human dignity on the part of the oppressed people all over the world; for we see it in Africa, we see it in Asia, and we see it all over the world. Now we must say that this struggle for freedom will not come to an automatic halt, for history reveals to us that once oppressed people rise up against that oppression, there is no stopping point short of full freedom. On the other hand, history reveals to us that those who oppose the movement for freedom are those who are in privileged positions who very seldom give up their privileges without strong resistance. And they very seldom do it voluntarily. So the sense of struggle will continue. The question is how will the struggle be waged.

3 Now there are three ways that oppressed people have generally dealt with their oppression. One way is the method of acquiescence, the method of surrender; that is, the individuals will somehow adjust themselves to oppression, they adjust themselves to discrimination or to segregation or colonialism or what have you. The other method that has been used in history is that of rising up against the oppressor with corroding hatred and physical violence. Now of course we know about this method in western civilization, because in a sense it has been the hallmark of its grandeur, and the inseparable twin of western materialism. But there is a weakness in this method because it ends up creating many more social problems than it solves. And I am convinced that if the Negro succumbs to the temptation of using violence in his struggle for freedom and justice, unborn generations will be the recipients of a long and desolate

night of bitterness. And our chief legacy to the future will be an endless reign of meaningless chaos.

But there is another way, namely the way of non-violent resistance. This method was popularized in our generation by a little man from India, whose name was Mohandas K. Gandhi. He used this method in a magnificent way to free his people from the economic exploitation and the political domination inflicted upon them by a foreign power. 4

This has been the method used by the student movement in the South and all over the United States. And naturally whenever I talk about the student movement I cannot be totally objective. I have to be somewhat subjective because of my great admiration for what the students have done. For in a real sense they have taken our deep groans and passionate yearnings for freedom, and filtered them in their own tender souls, and fashioned them into a creative protest which is an epic known all over our nation. As a result of their disciplined, non-violent, yet courageous struggle, they have been able to do wonders in the South, and in our nation. But this movement does have an underlying philosophy, it has certain ideas that are attached to it, it has certain philosophical precepts. These are the things that I would like to discuss for the few moments left. 5

I would say that the first point or the first principle in the movement is the idea that means must be as pure as the end. This movement is based on the philosophy that ends and means must cohere. Now this has been one of the long struggles in history, the whole idea of means and ends. Great philosophers have grappled with it, and sometimes they have emerged with the idea, from Machiavelli on down, that the end justifies the means. There is a great system of thought in our world today, known as Communism. And I think that with all of the weaknesses and tragedies of Communism, we find its greatest tragedy right here, that it goes under the philosophy that the end justifies the means that are used in the process. So we can read or we can hear the Lenins say that lying, deceit, or violence, that many of these things justify the ends of the classless society. 6

This is where the student movement and the non-violent movement that is taking place in our nation would break with Communism and any other system that would argue that the end justifies the means. For in the long run, we must see that the end represents the means in process and the 7 ideal in the making. In other words, we cannot believe, or we cannot go with the idea that the end justifies the means because the end is pre-existent in the means. So the idea of non-violent resistance, the philosophy of non-violent resistance, is the philosophy which says that the means must be as pure as the end, that in the long run of history, immoral destructive means cannot bring about moral and constructive ends.

8 There is another thing about this philosophy, this method of non-violence which is followed by the student movement. It says that those who adhere to or follow this philosophy must follow a consistent principle of non-injury. They must consistently refuse to inflict injury upon another. Sometimes you will read the literature of the student movement and see that, as they are getting ready for the sit-in or stand-in, they will read something like this, "if you are hit do not hit back, if you are cursed do not curse back." This is the whole idea, that the individual who is engaged in a non-violent struggle must never inflict injury upon another. Now this has an external aspect and it has an internal one. From the external point of view it means that the individuals involved must avoid external physical violence. So they don't have guns, they don't retaliate with physical violence. If they are hit in the process, they avoid external physical violence at every point. But it also means that they avoid internal violence of spirit. This is why the love ethic stands so high in the student movement. We have a great deal of talk about love and non-violence in this whole thrust.

9 Now when the students talk about love, certainly they are not talking about emotional bosh, they are not talking about merely a sentimental outpouring; they're talking something much deeper, and I always have to stop and try to define the meaning of love in this context. The Greek language comes to our aid in trying to deal with this. There are three words in the Greek language for love; one is the word Eros. This is a beautiful type of love, it is an aesthetic love. Plato talks about it a great deal in his dialogue, the yearning of the soul for the realm of the divine. It has come to us to be a sort of romantic love, and so in a sense we have read about it and experienced it. We've read about it in all the beauties of literature. I guess in a sense Edgar Allan Poe was talking about Eros when he talked about his beautiful Annabelle Lee, with the love surrounded by the halo of eternity. In a sense Shakespeare was talking about Eros when he said

"Love is not love which alters when alteration finds, or bends with the remover to remove; O, no! it is an ever fixed mark that looks on tempest and is never shaken, it is the star to every wandering bark." (You know, I remember that because I used to quote it to this little lady when we were courting; that's Eros.) The Greek language talks about Philia which was another level of love. It is an intimate affection between personal friends, it is a reciprocal love. On this level you love because you are loved. It is friendship.

Then the Greek language comes out with another word 10
which is called the Agape. Agape is more than romantic love, agape is more than friendship. Agape is understanding, creative, redemptive, good will to all men. It is an overflowing love which seeks nothing in return. Theologians would say that it is the love of God operating in the human heart. So that when one rises to love on this level, he loves men not because he likes them, not because their ways appeal to him, but he loves every man because God loves him. And he rises to the point of loving the person who does an evil deed while hating the deed that the person does. I think this is what Jesus meant when he said "love your enemies." I'm very happy that he didn't say like your enemies, because it is pretty difficult to like some people. Like is sentimental, and it is pretty difficult to like someone bombing your home; it is pretty difficult to like somebody threatening your children; it is difficult to like congressmen who spend all of their time trying to defeat civil rights. But Jesus says love them, and love is greater than like. Love is understanding, redemptive, creative, good will for all men. And it is this idea, it is this whole ethic of love which is the idea standing at the basis of the student movement.

There is something else: that one seeks to defeat the 11
unjust system, rather than individuals who are caught in that system. And that one goes on believing that somehow this is the important thing, to get rid of the evil system and not the individual who happens to be misguided, who happens to be misled, who was taught wrong. The thing to do is to get rid of the system and thereby create a moral balance within society.

Another thing that stands at the center of this movement 12
is another idea: that suffering can be a most creative and powerful social force. Suffering has certain moral attributes involved, but it can be a powerful and creative social force. Now, it is very interesting at this point to notice that both

violence and non-violence agree that suffering can be a very powerful social force. But there is this difference: violence says that suffering can be a powerful social force by inflicting the suffering on somebody else; so this is what we do in war, this is what we do in the whole violent thrust of the violent movement. It believes that you achieve some end by inflicting suffering on another. The non-violent say that suffering becomes a powerful social force when you willingly accept that violence on yourself, so that self-suffering stands at the center of the non-violent movement and the individuals involved are able to suffer in a creative manner, feeling that unearned suffering is redemptive, and that suffering may serve to transform the social situation.

13 Another thing in this movement is the idea that there is within human nature an amazing potential for goodness. There is within human nature something that can respond to goodness. I know somebody's liable to say that this is an unrealistic movement if it goes on believing that all people are good. Well, I didn't say that. I think the students are realistic enough to believe that there is a strange dichotomy of disturbing dualism within human nature. Many of the great philosophers and thinkers through the ages have seen this. It caused Ovid the Latin poet to say, "I see and approve the better things of life, but the evil things I do." It caused even St. Augustine to say "Lord, make me pure, but not yet." So that that is in human nature. Plato centuries ago said that the human personality is like a charioteer with two headstrong horses, each wanting to go in different directions, so that within our own individual lives we see this conflict and certainly when we come to the collective life of man, we see a strange badness. But in spite of this there is something in human nature that can respond to goodness. So that man is neither innately good nor is he innately bad; he has potentialities for both. So in this sense, Carlyle was right when he said that "there are depths in man which go down to the lowest hell, and heights which reach the highest heaven, for are not both heaven and hell made out of him, everlasting miracle and mystery that he is?" Man has the capacity to be good, man has the capacity to be evil.

14 And so the non-violent resister never lets this idea go, that there is something within human nature that can respond to goodness. So that a Jesus of Nazareth or a Mohandas Ghandi can appeal to human beings and appeal to that element of goodness within them, and a Hitler can appeal to

the element of evil within them. But we must never forget that there is something within human nature that can respond to goodness, that man is not totally depraved, to put it in theological terms, the image of God is never totally gone. And so the individuals who believe in this movement and who believe in non-violence and our struggle in the South, somehow believe that even the worst segregationist can become an integrationist. Now sometimes it is hard to believe that this is what this movement says, and it believes it firmly, that there is something within human nature that can be changed, and this stands at the top of the whole philosophy of the student movement and the philosophy of non-violence.

It says something else. It says that it is as much a moral obligation to refuse to cooperate with evil as it is to cooperate with good. Non-cooperation with evil is as much a moral obligation as the cooperation with good. So that the student movement is willing to stand up courageously on the idea of civil disobedience. Now I think this is the part of the student movement that is probably misunderstood more than anything else. And it is a difficult aspect, because on the one hand the students would say, and I would say, and all the people who believe in civil rights would say, obey the Supreme Court's decision of 1954 and at the same time, we would disobey certain laws that exist on the statutes of the South today. 15

This brings in the whole question of how can you be logically consistent when you advocate obeying some laws and disobeying other laws. Well, I think one would have to see the whole meaning of this movement at this point by seeing that the students recognize that there are two types of laws. There are just laws and there are unjust laws. And they would be the first to say obey the just laws, they would be the first to say that men and women have a moral obligation to obey just and right laws. And they would go on to say that we must see that there are unjust laws. Now the question comes into being, what is the difference, and who determines the difference, what is the difference between a just and an unjust law? 16

Well, a just law is a law that squares with a moral law. It is a law that squares with that which is right, so that any law that uplifts human personality is a just law. Whereas that law which is out of harmony with the moral is a law which does not square with the moral law of the universe. It does 17 not square with the law of God, so for that reason it is unjust and any law that degrades the human personality is an unjust law.

18 Well, somebody says that that does not mean anything to me: first, I don't believe in these abstract things called moral laws and I'm not too religious, so I don't believe in the law of God: you have to get a little more concrete, and more practical. What do you mean when you say that a law is unjust, and a law is just? Well, I would go on to say in more concrete terms that an unjust law is a code that the majority inflicts on the minority that is not binding on itself. So that this becomes difference made legal. Another thing that we can say is that an unjust law is a code which the majority inflicts on the minority, which that minority had no part in enacting or creating, because that minority had no right to vote in many instances, so that the legislative bodies that made these laws were not democratically elected. Who could ever say that the legislative body of Mississippi was democratically elected, or the legislative body of Alabama was democratically elected, or the legislative body even of Georgia has been democratically elected, when there are people in Terrell County and in other counties because of the color of their skin who cannot vote? They confront reprisals and threats and all of that; so that an unjust law is a law that individuals did not have a part in creating or enacting because they were denied the right to vote.

19 Now by the same token a just law would be just the opposite. A just law becomes sameness made legal. It is a code that the majority, who happen to believe in that code, compel the minority, who don't believe in it, to follow, because they are willing to follow it themselves, so it is sameness made legal. Therefore the individuals who stand up on the basis of civil disobedience realize that they are following something that says that there are just laws and there are unjust laws. Now, they are not anarchists. They believe that there are laws which must be followed; they do not seek to defy the law, they do not seek to evade the law. For many individuals who would call themselves segregationists and who would hold on to segregation at any cost seek to defy the law, they seek to evade the law, and their process can lead on into anarchy. They seek in the final analysis to follow a way of uncivil disobedience, not civil disobedience. And I submit that the individual who disobeys

the law, whose conscience tells him it is unjust and who is willing to accept the penalty by staying in jail until that law is altered, is expressing at the moment the very highest respect for law.

This is what the students have followed in their movement. Of course there is nothing new about this; they feel that they are in good company and rightly so. We go back and read the *Apology* and the *Crito,* and you see Socrates practicing civil disobedience. And to a degree academic freedom is a reality today because Socrates practiced civil disobedience. The early Christians practiced civil disobedience in a superb manner, to a point where they were willing to be thrown to the lions. They were willing to face all kinds of suffering in order to stand up for what they knew was right even though they knew it was against the laws of the Roman Empire. 20

We could come up to our own day and we see it in many instances. We must never forget that everything that Hitler did in Germany was "legal." It was illegal to aid and comfort a Jew, in the days of Hitler's Germany. But I believe that if I had the same attitude then as I have now I would publicly aid and comfort my Jewish brothers in Germany if Hitler were alive today calling this an illegal process. If I lived in South Africa today in the midst of the white supremacy law in South Africa, I would join Chief Luthuli and others in saying break these unjust laws. And even let us come up to America. Our nation in a sense came into being through a massive act of civil disobedience, for the Boston Tea Party was nothing but a massive act of civil disobedience. Those who stood up against the slave laws, the abolitionists, by and large practiced civil disobedience. So I think these students are in good company, and they feel that by practicing civil disobedience they are in line with men and women through the ages who have stood up for something that is morally right. 21

Now there are one or two other things that I want to say about this student movement, moving out of the philosophy of non-violence, something about what it is a revolt against. On the one hand it is a revolt against the negative peace that has encompassed the South for many years. I remember when I was in Montgomery, Ala., one of the white citizens came to me one day and said—and I think he was very sincere about this—that in Montgomery for all of these 22 years we have been such a peaceful community, we have had so much harmony in race relations and then you people have started this movement and boycott, and it has done so much to disturb race relations, and we just don't love the Negro like we used to love them, because you have destroyed the harmony and the peace that we once had in race relations. And I said to him, in the best way I could say and I tried to say it in non-violent terms, we have never had peace in Montgomery, Ala., we have never had peace in the South. We have had a negative peace, which is merely the absence of tension; we've had a negative peace in which the Negro patiently accepted his situation and his plight, but we've never had true peace, we've never had positive peace, and what we're seeking now is to develop this positive peace. For we must come to see that peace is not merely the absence of some negative force, it is the presence of a positive force. True peace is not merely the absence of tension, but it is the presence of justice and brotherhood. I think this is what Jesus meant when he said, I come not to bring peace but a sword. Now Jesus didn't mean he came to start war, to bring a physical sword, and he didn't mean, I come not to bring positive peace. But I think what Jesus was saying in substance was this, that I come not to bring an old negative peace, which makes for stagnant passivity and deadening complacency, I come to bring something different, and whenever I come, a conflict is precipitated, between the old and the new, whenever I come a struggle takes place between justice and injustice, between the forces of light and the forces of darkness. I come not to bring a negative peace, but a positive peace, which is brotherhood, which is justice, which is the Kingdom of God.

23 And I think this is what we are seeking to do today, and this movement is a revolt against a negative peace and a struggle to bring into being a positive peace, which makes for true brotherhood, true integration, true person-to-person relationships. This movement is also revolt against what is often called tokenism. Here again many people do not understand this; they feel that in this struggle the Negro will be satisfied with tokens of integration, just a few students and a few schools here and there and a few doors open here and there. But this isn't the meaning of the movement and I think that honesty impels me to admit it everywhere I have an opportunity, that the Negro's aim is

to bring about complete integration in American life. And he has come to see that token integration is little more than token democracy, which ends up with many new evasive schemes and it ends up with new discrimination, covered up with such niceties of complexity. It is very interesting to discover that the movement has thrived in many communities that had token integration. So this reveals that the movement is based on a principle that integration must become real and complete, not just token integration.

It is also a revolt against what I often call the myth of time. 24
We hear this quite often, that only time can solve this problem. That if we will only be patient, and only pray—which we must do, we must be patient and we must pray—but there are those who say just do these things and wait for time, and time will solve this problem. Well, the people who argue this do not themselves realize that time is neutral, that it can be used constructively or destructively. At points the people of ill will, the segregationists, have used time much more effectively than the people of good will. So individuals in the struggle must come to realize that it is necessary to aid time, that without this kind of aid, time itself will become an ally of the insurgent and primitive forces of social stagnation. Therefore, this movement is a revolt against the myth of time.

There is a final thing that I would like to say to you, this 25
movement is a movement based on faith in the future. It is a movement based on a philosophy, the possibility of the future bringing into being something real and meaningful. It is a movement based on hope. I think this is very important. The students have developed a theme song for their movement, maybe you've heard it. It goes something like this, "we shall overcome, deep in my heart, I do believe, we shall overcome," and then they go on to say another verse, "we are not afraid, we are not afraid today, deep in my heart I do believe, we shall overcome." So it is out of this deep faith in the future that they are able to move out and adjourn the councils of despair, and to bring new light in the dark chambers of pessimism. I can remember the times that we've been together. I remember that night in Montgomery, Ala., when we had stayed up all night, discussing the Freedom Rides, and that morning came to see that it was necessary to go on with the Freedom Rides, that we would

not in all good conscience call an end to the Freedom Rides at that point. And I remember the first group got ready to leave, to take a bus for Jackson, Miss.; we all joined hands and started singing together. "We shall overcome, we shall overcome." And something within me said, now how is it that these students can sing this, they are going down to Mississippi, they are going to face hostile and jeering mobs, and yet they could sing, "We shall overcome." They may even face physical death, and yet they could sing, "We shall overcome." Most of them realized that they would be thrown into jail, and yet they could sing. "We shall overcome, we are not afraid." Then something caused me to see at that moment the real meaning of the movement. That students had faith in the future. That the movement was based on hope, that this movement had something within it that says somehow even though the arc of the moral universe is long, it bends toward justice. And I think this should be a challenge to all others who are struggling to transform the dangling discords of our Southland into a beautiful symphony of brotherhood. There is something in this student movement which says to us, that we shall overcome. Before the victory is won some may have to get scarred up, but we shall overcome. Before the victory of brotherhood is achieved, some will maybe face physical death, but we shall overcome. Before the victory is won, some will lose jobs, some will be called Communists, and reds, merely because they believe in brotherhood, some will be dismissed as dangerous rabblerousers and agitators merely because they're standing up for what is right, but we shall overcome. That is the basis of this movement, and as I like to say, there is something in this universe that justifies Carlyle in saying no lie can live forever. We shall overcome because there is something in this universe which justifies William Cullen Bryant in saying truth crushed to earth shall rise again. We shall overcome because there is something in this universe that justifies James Russell Lowell in saying, truth forever on the scaffold, wrong forever on the throne. Yet that scaffold sways the future, and behind the dim unknown standeth God within the shadows, keeping watch above His own. With this faith in the future, with this determined struggle, we will be able to emerge from the bleak and desolate midnight of man's inhumanity to man, into the bright and glittering daybreak of freedom and justice. Thank you.

Public Statement by Eight Alabama Clergymen

Letter from Birmingham Jail

On April 12, 1963, in order to have himself arrested on a symbolic day (Good Friday), Reverend Martin Luther King, Jr., disobeyed a court injunction forbidding demonstrations in Birmingham, Alabama. That same day, eight leading white Birmingham clergymen (Christian and Jewish) published a letter in The Birmingham News *calling for the end of protests and exhorting protesters to work through the courts for the redress of their grievances. On the morning after his arrest, while held in solitary confinement, King began his response to these clergymen—his famous "Letter from Birmingham Jail." Begun in the margins of newspapers and on scraps of paper and finished by the following Tuesday, the letter was widely distributed and then became a central chapter in King's* Why We Can't Wait *(1964).*

Public Statement by Eight Alabama Clergymen

April 12, 1963 1

We the undersigned clergymen are among those who, in
January, issued "An Appeal for Law and Order and Common
Sense," in dealing with racial problems in Alabama. We
expressed understanding that honest convictions in racial
matters could properly be pursued in the courts, but urged
that decisions of those courts should in the meantime be 2
peacefully obeyed.

Since that time there had been some evidence of increased forbearance and a willingness to face facts. Responsible citizens have undertaken to work on various problems which cause racial friction and unrest. In Birmingham, recent public events had given indication that we all have opportunity for a new constructive and realistic approach to racial problems.

3 However, we are now confronted by a series of demonstrations by some of our Negro citizens, directed and led in part by outsiders. We recognize the natural impatience of people who feel that their hopes are slow in being realized. But we are convinced that these demonstrations are unwise and untimely.

4 We agree rather with certain local Negro leadership which has called for honest and open negotiation of racial issues in our area. And we believe this kind of facing of issues can best be accomplished by citizens of our own metropolitan area, white and Negro, meeting with their knowledge and experience of the local situation. All of us need to face that responsibility and find proper channels for its accomplishment.

5 Just as we formerly pointed out that "hatred and violence have no sanction in our religious and political traditions," we also point out that such actions as incite to hatred and violence, however technically peaceful those actions may be, have not contributed to the resolution of our local problems. We do not believe that these days of new hope are days when extreme measures are justified in Birmingham.

6 We commend the community as a whole, and the local news media and law enforcement officials in particular, on the calm manner in which these demonstrations have been handled. We urge the public to continue to show restraint should the demonstrations continue, and the law enforcement officials to remain calm and continue to protect our city from violence.

7 We further strongly urge our own Negro community to withdraw support from these demonstrations, and to unite locally in working peacefully for a better Birmingham. When rights are consistently denied, a cause should be pressed in the courts and in negotiations among local leaders, and not in the streets. We appeal to both our white and Negro citizenry to observe the principles of law and order and common sense.

Signed by:

C. C. J. Carpenter, D.D., LL.D.,
Bishop of Alabama

Joseph A. Durick, D.D.,
Auxiliary Bishop, Diocese of Mobile, Birmingham

Rabbi Milton L. Grafman,
Temple Emanu-El, Birmingham, Alabama

Bishop Paul Hardin,
Bishop of the Alabama-West Florida Conference of the Methodist Church
Bishop Nolan B. Harmon,
Bishop of the North Alabama Conference of the Methodist Church
George M. Murray, D.D., LL.D.,
Bishop Coadjutor, Episcopal Diocese of Alabama
Edward V. Ramage,
Moderator, Synod of the Alabama Presbyterian Church in the United States
Earl Stallings,
Pastor, First Baptist Church, Birmingham, Alabama

Letter from Birmingham Jail

April 16, 1963

My Dear Fellow Clergymen:

While confined here in the Birmingham city jail, I came across your recent statement calling my present activities "unwise and untimely." Seldom do I pause to answer criticism of my work and ideas. If I sought to answer all the criticisms that cross my desk, my secretaries would have little time for anything other than such correspondence in the course of the day, and I would have no time for constructive work. But since I feel that you are men of genuine good will and that your criticisms are sincerely set forth, I want to try to answer your statement in what I hope will be patient and reasonable terms. 1

I think I should indicate why I am here in Birmingham, since you have been influenced by the view which argues against "outsiders coming in." I have the honor of serving as president of the Southern Christian Leadership Conference, an organization operating in every southern state, with headquarters in Atlanta, Georgia. We have some eighty-five affiliated organizations across the South, and one of them is the Alabama Christian Movement for Human Rights. Frequently we share staff, educational and financial resources with our affiliates. Several months ago the affiliate here in Birmingham asked us to be on call to engage in a nonviolent direct-action program if such were deemed necessary. We readily consented, and when the hour came we lived up to 2 our promise. So I, along with several members of my staff, am here because I was invited here. I am here because I have organizational ties here.

3 But more basically, I am in Birmingham because injustice is here. Just as the prophets of the eighth century B.C. left their villages and carried their "thus saith the Lord" far beyond the boundaries of their home towns, and just as the Apostle Paul left his village of Tarsus and carried the gospel of Jesus Christ to the far corners of the Greco-Roman world, so am I compelled to carry the gospel of freedom beyond my own home town. Like Paul, I must constantly respond to the Macedonian call for aid.

4 Moreover, I am cognizant of the interrelatedness of all communities and states. I cannot sit idly by in Atlanta and not be concerned about what happens in Birmingham. Injustice anywhere is a threat to justice everywhere. We are caught in an inescapable network of mutuality, tied in a single garment of destiny. Whatever affects one directly, affects all indirectly. Never again can we afford to live with the narrow, provincial "outside agitator" idea. Anyone who lives inside the United States can never be considered an outsider anywhere within its bounds.

5 You deplore the demonstrations taking place in Birmingham. But your statement, I am sorry to say, fails to express a similar concern for the conditions that brought about the demonstrations. I am sure that none of you would want to rest content with the superficial kind of social analysis that deals merely with effects and does not grapple with underlying causes. It is unfortunate that demonstrations are taking place in Birmingham, but it is even more unfortunate that the city's white power structure left the Negro community with no alternative.

6 In any nonviolent campaign there are four basic steps: collection of the facts to determine whether injustices exist; negotiation; self-purification; and direct action. We have gone through all these steps in Birmingham. There can be no gainsaying the fact that racial injustice engulfs this community. Birmingham is probably the most thoroughly segregated city in the United States. Its ugly record of brutality is widely known. Negroes have experienced grossly unjust treatment in the courts. There have been more unsolved bombings of Negro homes and churches in Birmingham than in any other city in the nation. These are the hard, brutal facts of the case. On the basis of these conditions, Negro leaders

sought to negotiate with the city fathers. But the latter consistently refused to engage in good-faith negotiation.

Then, last September, came the opportunity to talk with 7
leaders of Birmingham's economic community. In the course of the negotiations, certain promises were made by the merchants—for example, to remove the stores' humiliating racial signs. On the basis of these promises, the Reverend Fred Shuttlesworth and the leaders of the Alabama Christian Movement for Human Rights agreed to a moratorium on all demonstrations. As the weeks and months went by, we realized that we were the victims of a broken promise. A few signs, briefly removed, returned; the others remained.

As in so many past experiences, our hopes had been 8
blasted, and the shadow of deep disappointment settled upon us. We had no alternative except to prepare for direct action, whereby we would present our very bodies as a means of laying our case before the conscience of the local and the national community. Mindful of the difficulties involved, we decided to undertake a process of self-purification. We began a series of workshops on nonviolence, and we repeatedly asked ourselves: "Are you able to accept blows without retaliating?" "Are you able to endure the ordeal of jail?" We decided to schedule our direct-action program for the Easter season, realizing that except for Christmas, this is the main shopping period of the year. Knowing that a strong economic-withdrawal program would be the by-product of direct action, we felt that this would be the best time to bring pressure to bear on the merchants for the needed change.

Then it occurred to us that Birmingham's mayoral elec- 9
tion was coming up in March, and we speedily decided to postpone action until after election day. When we discovered that the Commissioner of Public Safety, Eugene "Bull" Connor, had piled up enough votes to be in the run-off, we decided again to postpone action until the day after the run-off so that the demonstrations could not be used to cloud the issues. Like many others, we waited to see Mr. Connor defeated, and to this end we endured postponement after postponement. Having aided in this community need, we felt that our direct action program could be delayed no longer.

You may well ask: "Why direct action? Why sit-ins, 10
marches and so forth? Isn't negotiation a better path?" You

are quite right in calling for negotiation. Indeed, this is the very purpose of direct action. Nonviolent direct action seeks to create such a crisis and foster such a tension that a community which has constantly refused to negotiate is forced to confront the issue. It seeks so to dramatize the issue that it can no longer be ignored. My citing the creation of tension as part of the work of the nonviolent-resister may sound rather shocking. But I must confess that I am not afraid of the word "tension." I have earnestly opposed violent tension, but there is a type of constructive, nonviolent tension which is necessary for growth. Just as Socrates felt that it was necessary to create a tension in the mind so that individuals could rise from the bondage of myths and half-truths to the unfettered realm of creative analysis and objective appraisal, so must we see the need for nonviolent gadflies to create the kind of tension in society that will help men rise from the dark depths of prejudice and racism to the majestic heights of understanding and brotherhood.

11 The purpose of our direct-action program is to create a situation so crisis-packed that it will inevitably open the door to negotiation. I therefore concur with you in your call for negotiation. Too long has our beloved Southland been bogged down in a tragic effort to live in monologue rather than dialogue.

12 One of the basic points in your statement is that the action that I and my associates have taken in Birmingham is untimely. Some have asked: "Why didn't you give the new city administration time to act?" The only answer that I can give to this query is that the new Birmingham administration must be prodded about as much as the outgoing one, before it will act. We are sadly mistaken if we feel that the election of Albert Boutwell as mayor will bring the millennium to Birmingham. While Mr. Boutwell is a much more gentle person than Mr. Connor, they are both segregationists, dedicated to maintenance of the status quo. I have hope that Mr. Boutwell will be reasonable enough to see the futility of massive resistance to desegregation. But he will not see this without pressure from devotees of civil rights. My friends, I must say to you that we have not made a single gain in civil rights without determined legal and nonviolent pressure. Lamentably, it is an historical fact that privileged groups seldom give up their privileges voluntarily. Individuals may see the moral light and voluntarily give up their

unjust posture; but, as Reinhold Niebuhr has reminded us, groups tend to be more immoral than individuals.

We know through painful experience that freedom is never voluntarily given by the oppressor; it must be demanded by the oppressed. Frankly, I have yet to engage in a direct-action campaign that was "well timed" in the view of those who have not suffered unduly from the disease of segregation. For years now I have heard the word "Wait!" It rings in the ear of every Negro with piercing familiarity. This "Wait" has almost always meant "Never." We must come to see, with one of our distinguished jurists, that "justice too long delayed is justice denied." 13

We have waited for more than 340 years for our constitutional and God-given rights. The nations of Asia and Africa are moving with jetlike speed toward gaining political independence, but we still creep at horse-and-buggy pace toward gaining a cup of coffee at a lunch counter. Perhaps it is easy for those who have never felt the stinging darts of segregation to say, "Wait." But when you have seen vicious mobs lynch your mothers and fathers at will and drown your sisters and brothers at whim; when you have seen hate-filled policemen curse, kick and even kill your black brothers and sisters; when you see the vast majority of your twenty million Negro brothers smothering in an airtight cage of poverty in the midst of an affluent society; when you suddenly find your tongue twisted and your speech stammering as you seek to explain to your six-year-old daughter why she can't go to the public amusement park that has just been advertised on television, and see tears welling up in her eyes when she is told that Funtown is closed to colored children, and see ominous clouds of inferiority beginning to form in her little mental sky, and see her beginning to distort her personality by developing an unconscious bitterness toward white people; when you have to concoct an answer for a five-year-old son who is asking: "Daddy, why do white people treat colored people so mean?"; when you take a cross-country drive and find it necessary to sleep night after night in the uncomfortable corners of your automobile because no motel will accept you; when you are humiliated day in and day out by nagging signs reading "white" and "colored"; when your first name becomes "nigger," your middle name becomes "boy" (however old you are) and your last name becomes "John," and your wife and mother are 14 never given the respected title "Mrs."; when you are harried by day and haunted by night by the fact that you are a Negro, living constantly at tiptoe stance, never quite knowing what to expect next, and are plagued with inner fears and outer resentments; when you are forever fighting a degenerating sense of "nobodiness"—then you will understand why we find it difficult to wait. There comes a time when the cup of endurance runs over, and men are no longer willing to be plunged into the abyss of despair. I hope, sirs, you can understand our legitimate and unavoidable impatience.

15 You express a great deal of anxiety over our willingness to break laws. This is certainly a legitimate concern. Since we so diligently urge people to obey the Supreme Court's decision of 1954 outlawing segregation in the public schools, at first glance it may seem rather paradoxical for us consciously to break laws. One may well ask: "How can you advocate breaking some laws and obeying others?" The answer lies in the fact that there are two types of laws: just and unjust. I would be the first to advocate obeying just laws. One has not only a legal but a moral responsibility to obey just laws. Conversely, one has a moral responsibility to disobey unjust laws. I would agree with St. Augustine that "an unjust law is no law at all."

16 Now, what is the difference between the two? How does one determine whether a law is just or unjust? A just law is a man-made code that squares with the moral law or the law of God. An unjust law is a code that is out of harmony with the moral law. To put it in the terms of St. Thomas Aquinas: An unjust law is a human law that is not rooted in eternal law and natural law. Any law that uplifts human personality is just. Any law that degrades human personality is unjust. All segregation statutes are unjust because segregation distorts the soul and damages the personality. It gives the segregator a false sense of superiority and the segregated a false sense of inferiority. Segregation, to use the terminology of the Jewish philosopher Martin Buber, substitutes an "I–it" relationship for an "I–thou" relationship and ends up relegating persons to the status of things. Hence segregation is not only politically, economically and sociologically unsound, it is morally wrong and sinful. Paul Tillich has said that sin is separation. Is not segregation an existential expression of man's tragic separation, his awful estrangement, his terrible sinfulness? Thus it is that I can urge men

to obey the 1954 decision of the Supreme Court, for it is morally right; and I can urge them to disobey segregation ordinances, for they are morally wrong.

Let us consider a more concrete example of just and unjust laws. An unjust law is a code that a numerical or power majority group compels a minority group to obey but does not make binding on itself. This is *difference* made legal. By the same token, a just law is a code that a majority compels a minority to follow and that it is willing to follow itself. This is *sameness* made legal. 17

Let me give another explanation. A law is unjust if it is inflicted on a minority that, as a result of being denied the right to vote, had no part in enacting or devising the law. Who can say that the legislature of Alabama which set up that state's segregation laws was democratically elected? Throughout Alabama all sorts of devious methods are used to prevent Negroes from becoming registered voters, and there are some counties in which, even though Negroes constitute a majority of the population, not a single Negro is registered. Can any law enacted under such circumstances be considered democratically structured? 18

Sometimes a law is just on its face and unjust in its application. For instance, I have been arrested on a charge of parading without a permit. Now, there is nothing wrong in having an ordinance which requires a permit for a parade. But such an ordinance becomes unjust when it is used to maintain segregation and to deny citizens the First-Amendment privilege of peaceful assembly and protest. 19

I hope you are able to see the distinction I am trying to point out. In no sense do I advocate evading or defying the law, as would the rabid segregationist. That would lead to anarchy. One who breaks an unjust law must do so openly, lovingly, and with a willingness to accept the penalty. I submit that an individual who breaks a law that conscience tells him is unjust, and who willingly accepts the penalty of imprisonment in order to arouse the conscience of the community over its injustice, is in reality expressing the highest respect for law. 20

Of course, there is nothing new about this kind of civil disobedience. It was evidenced sublimely in the refusal of Shadrach, Meshach and Abednego to obey the laws of Nebuchadnezzar, on the ground that a higher moral law was at stake. It was practiced superbly by the early Chris- 21 tians, who were willing to face hungry lions and the excruciating pain of chopping blocks rather than submit to certain unjust laws of the Roman Empire. To a degree, academic freedom is a reality today because Socrates practiced civil disobedience. In our own nation, the Boston Tea Party represented a massive act of civil disobedience.

22 We should never forget that everything Adolf Hitler did in Germany was "legal" and everything the Hungarian freedom fighters did in Hungary was "illegal." It was "illegal" to aid and comfort a Jew in Hitler's Germany. Even so, I am sure that, had I lived in Germany at the time, I would have aided and comforted my Jewish brothers. If today I lived in a Communist country where certain principles dear to the Christian faith are suppressed, I would openly advocate disobeying that country's antireligious laws.

23 I must make two honest confessions to you, my Christian and Jewish brothers. First, I must confess that over the past few years I have been gravely disappointed with the white moderate. I have almost reached the regrettable conclusion that the Negro's great stumbling block in his stride toward freedom is not the White Citizen's Counciler or the Ku Klux Klanner, but the white moderate, who is more devoted to "order" than to justice; who prefers a negative peace which is the absence of tension to a positive peace which is the presence of justice; who constantly says: "I agree with you in the goal you seek, but I cannot agree with your methods of direct action"; who paternalistically believes he can set the timetable for another man's freedom; who lives by a mythical concept of time and who constantly advises the Negro to wait for a "more convenient season." Shallow understanding from people of good will is more frustrating than absolute misunderstanding from people of ill will. Lukewarm acceptance is much more bewildering than outright rejection.

24 I had hoped that the white moderate would understand that law and order exist for the purpose of establishing justice and that when they fail in this purpose they become the dangerously structured dams that block the flow of social progress. I had hoped that the white moderate would understand that the present tension in the South is a necessary phase of the transition from an obnoxious negative peace, in which the Negro passively accepted his unjust plight, to a substantive and positive peace, in which all men will respect the dignity and worth of human personality. Actually, we who engage in nonviolent direct action are not

the creators of tension. We merely bring to the surface the hidden tension that is already alive. We bring it out in the open, where it can be seen and dealt with. Like a boil that can never be cured so long as it is covered up but must be opened with all its ugliness to the natural medicines of air and light, injustice must be exposed, with all the tension its exposure creates, to the light of human conscience and the air of national opinion before it can be cured.

25 In your statement you assert that our actions, even though peaceful, must be condemned because they precipitate violence. But is this a logical assertion? Isn't this like condemning a robbed man because his possession of money precipitated the evil act of robbery? Isn't this like condemning Socrates because his unswerving commitment to truth and his philosophical inquiries precipitated the act by the misguided populace in which they made him drink hemlock? Isn't this like condemning Jesus because his unique God-consciousness and never-ceasing devotion to God's will precipitated the evil act of crucifixion? We must come to see that, as the federal courts have consistently affirmed, it is wrong to urge an individual to cease his efforts to gain his basic constitutional rights because the quest may precipitate violence. Society must protect the robbed and punish the robber.

26 I had also hoped that the white moderate would reject the myth concerning time in relation to the struggle for freedom. I have just received a letter from a white brother in Texas. He writes: "All Christians know that the colored people will receive equal rights eventually, but it is possible that you are in too great a religious hurry. It has taken Christianity almost two thousand years to accomplish what it has. The teachings of Christ take time to come to earth." Such an attitude stems from a tragic misconception of time, from the strangely irrational notion that there is something in the very flow of time that will inevitably cure all ills. Actually, time itself is neutral; it can be used either destructively or constructively. More and more I feel that the people of ill will have used time much more effectively than have the people of good will. We will have to repent in this generation not merely for the hateful words and actions of the bad people but for the appalling silence of the good people. Human progress never rolls in on wheels of inevitability; it comes through the tireless efforts of men willing to be co-workers with God, and without this hard work, time

itself becomes an ally of the forces of social stagnation. We must use time creatively, in the knowledge that time is always ripe to do right. Now is the time to make real the promise of democracy and transform our pending national elegy into a creative psalm of brotherhood. Now is the time to lift our national policy from the quicksand of racial injustice to the solid rock of human dignity.

27 You speak of our activity in Birmingham as extreme. At first I was rather disappointed that fellow clergymen would see my nonviolent efforts as those of an extremist. I began thinking about the fact that I stand in the middle of two opposing forces in the Negro community. One is a force of complacency, made up in part of Negroes who, as a result of long years of oppression, are so drained of self-respect and a sense of "somebodiness" that they have adjusted to segregation; and in part of a few middle-class Negroes who, because of a degree of academic and economic security and because in some ways they profit by segregation, have become insensitive to the problems of the masses. The other force is one of bitterness and hatred, and it comes perilously close to advocating violence. It is expressed in the various black nationalist groups that are springing up across the nation, the largest and best-known being Elijah Muhammad's Muslim movement. Nourished by the Negro's frustration over the continued existence of racial discrimination, this movement is made up of people who have lost faith in America, who have absolutely repudiated Christianity, and who have concluded that the white man is an incorrigible "devil."

28 I have tried to stand between these two forces, saying that we need emulate neither the "do-nothingism" of the complacent nor the hatred and despair of the black nationalist. For there is the more excellent way of love and nonviolent protest. I am grateful to God that, through the influence of the Negro church, the way of nonviolence became an integral part of our struggle.

29 If this philosophy had not emerged, by now many streets of the South would, I am convinced, be flowing with blood. And I am further convinced that if our white brothers dismiss as "rabble-rousers" and "outside agitators" those of us who employ nonviolent direct action, and if they refuse to support our nonviolent efforts, millions of Negroes will, out of frustration and despair, seek solace and security in

black-nationalist ideologies—a development that would inevitably lead to a frightening racial nightmare.

Oppressed people cannot remain oppressed forever. The yearning for freedom eventually manifests itself, and that is what has happened to the American Negro. Something within has reminded him of his birthright of freedom, and something without has reminded him that it can be gained. Consciously or unconsciously, he has been caught up by the *Zeitgeist*, and with his black brothers of Africa and his brown and yellow brothers of Asia, South America and the Caribbean, the United States Negro is moving with a sense of great urgency toward the promised land of racial justice. If one recognizes this vital urge that has engulfed the Negro community, one should readily understand why public demonstrations are taking place. The Negro has many pent-up resentments and latent frustrations, and he must release them. So let him march; let him make prayer pilgrimages to the city hall; let him go on freedom rides—and try to understand why he must do so. If his repressed emotions are not released in nonviolent ways, they will seek expression through violence; this is not a threat but a fact of history. So I have not said to my people: "Get rid of your discontent." Rather, I have tried to say that this normal and healthy discontent can be channeled into the creative outlet of nonviolent direct action. And now this approach is being termed extremist. 30

But though I was initially disappointed at being categorized as an extremist, as I continued to think about the matter I gradually gained a measure of satisfaction from the label. Was not Jesus an extremist for love: "Love your enemies, bless them that curse you, do good to them that hate you, and pray for them which despitefully use you, and persecute you." Was not Amos an extremist for justice: "Let justice roll down like waters and righteousness like an ever-flowing stream." Was not Paul an extremist for the Christian gospel: "I bear in my body the marks of the Lord Jesus." Was not Martin Luther an extremist: "Here I stand; I cannot do otherwise, so help me God." And John Bunyan: "I will stay in jail to the end of my days before I make a butchery of my conscience." And Abraham Lincoln: "This nation cannot survive half slave and half free." And Thomas Jefferson: "We hold these truths to be self-evident, that all men are created equal . . ." So the question is not whether 31 we will be extremists, but what kind of extremists we will be. Will we be extremists for hate or for love? Will we be extremists for the preservation of injustice or for the extension of justice? In that dramatic scene on Calvary's hill three men were crucified. We must never forget that all three were crucified for the same crime—the crime of extremism. Two were extremists for immorality, and thus fell below their environment. The other, Jesus Christ, was an extremist for love, truth and goodness, and thereby rose above his environment. Perhaps the South, the nation and the world are in dire need of creative extremists.

32 I had hoped that the white moderate would see this need. Perhaps I was too optimistic; perhaps I expected too much. I suppose I should have realized that few members of the oppressor race can understand the deep groans and passionate yearnings of the oppressed race, and still fewer have the vision to see that injustice must be rooted out by strong, persistent and determined action. I am thankful, however, that some of our white brothers in the South have grasped the meaning of this social revolution and committed themselves to it. They are still all too few in quantity, but they are big in quality. Some—such as Ralph McGill, Lillian Smith, Harry Golden, James McBride Dabbs, Ann Braden and Sarah Patton Boyle—have written about our struggle in eloquent and prophetic terms. Others have marched with us down nameless streets of the South. They have languished in filthy, roach-infested jails, suffering the abuse and brutality of policemen who view them as "dirty nigger-lovers." Unlike so many of their moderate brothers and sisters, they have recognized the urgency of the moment and sensed the need for powerful "action" antidotes to combat the disease of segregation.

33 Let me take note of my other major disappointment. I have been so greatly disappointed with the white church and its leadership. Of course, there are some notable exceptions. I am not unmindful of the fact that each of you has taken some significant stands on this issue. I commend you, Reverend Stallings, for your Christian stand on this past Sunday, in welcoming Negroes to your worship service on a nonsegregated basis. I commend the Catholic leaders of this state for integrating Spring Hill College several years ago.

34 But despite these notable exceptions, I must honestly reiterate that I have been disappointed with the church. I do not say this as one of those negative critics who can always

find something wrong with the church. I say this as a minister of the gospel, who loves the church; who was nurtured in its bosom; who has been sustained by its spiritual blessings and who will remain true to it as long as the cord of life shall lengthen.

When I was suddenly catapulted into the leadership of the 35
bus protest in Montgomery, Alabama, a few years ago, I felt we would be supported by the white church. I felt that the white ministers, priests and rabbis of the South would be among our strongest allies. Instead, some have been outright opponents, refusing to understand the freedom movement and misrepresenting its leaders; all too many others have been more cautious than courageous and have remained silent behind the anesthetizing security of stained-glass windows.

In spite of my shattered dreams, I came to Birmingham 36
with the hope that the white religious leadership of this community would see the justice of our cause and, with deep moral concern, would serve as the channel through which our just grievances could reach the power structure. I had hoped that each of you would understand. But again I have been disappointed.

I have heard numerous southern religious leaders admon- 37
ish their worshipers to comply with a desegregation decision because it is the law, but I have longed to hear white ministers declare: "Follow this decree because integration is morally right and because the Negro is your brother." In the midst of blatant injustices inflicted upon the Negro, I have watched white churchmen stand on the sideline and mouth pious irrelevancies and sanctimonious trivialities. In the midst of a mighty struggle to rid our nation of racial and economic injustice, I have heard many ministers say: "Those are social issues, with which the gospel has no real concern." And I have watched many churches commit themselves to a completely otherworldly religion which makes a strange, un-Biblical distortion between body and soul, between the sacred and the secular.

I have traveled the length and breadth of Alabama, Mis- 38
sissippi and all the other southern states. On sweltering summer days and crisp autumn mornings I have looked at the South's beautiful churches with their lofty spires pointing heavenward. I have beheld the impressive outlines of her massive religious-education buildings. Over and over I have found myself asking: "What kind of people worship here?

Who is their God? Where were their voices when the lips of Governor Barnett dripped with words of interposition and nullification? Where were they when Governor Wallace gave a clarion call for defiance and hatred? Where were their voices of support when bruised and weary Negro men and women decided to rise from the dark dungeons of complacency to the bright hills of creative protest?"

39 Yes, these questions are still in my mind. In deep disappointment I have wept over the laxity of the church. But be assured that my tears have been tears of love. There can be no deep disappointment where there is not deep love. Yes, I love the church. How could I do otherwise? I am in the rather unique position of being the son, the grandson and the great-grandson of preachers. Yes, I see the church as the body of Christ. But, oh! How we have blemished and scarred that body through social neglect and through fear of being nonconformists.

40 There was a time when the church was very powerful—in the time when the early Christians rejoiced at being deemed worthy to suffer for what they believed. In those days the church was not merely a thermometer that recorded the ideas and principles of popular opinion; it was a thermostat that transformed the mores of society. Whenever the early Christians entered a town, the people in power became disturbed and immediately sought to convict the Christians for being "disturbers of the peace" and "outside agitators." But the Christians pressed on, in the conviction that they were "a colony of heaven," called to obey God rather than man. Small in number, they were big in commitment. They were too God-intoxicated to be "astronomically intimidated." By their effort and example they brought an end to such ancient evils as infanticide and gladiatorial contests.

41 Things are different now. So often the contemporary church is a weak, ineffectual voice with an uncertain sound. So often it is an arch-defender of the status quo. Far from being disturbed by the presence of the church, the power structure of the average community is consoled by the church's silent—and often even vocal—sanction of things as they are.

42 But the judgment of God is upon the church as never before. If today's church does not recapture the sacrificial spirit of the early church, it will lose its authenticity, forfeit the loyalty of millions, and be dismissed as an irrelevant social club with no meaning for the twentieth century.

Every day I meet young people whose disappointment with the church has turned into outright disgust.

Perhaps I have once again been too optimistic. Is organized religion too inextricably bound to the status quo to save our nation and the world? Perhaps I must turn my faith to the inner spiritual church, the church within the church, as the true *ekklesia* and the hope of the world. But again I am thankful to God that some noble souls from the ranks of organized religion have broken loose from the paralyzing chains of conformity and joined us as active partners in the struggle for freedom. They have left their secure congregations and walked the streets of Albany, Georgia, with us. They have gone down the highways of the South on tortuous rides for freedom. Yes, they have gone to jail with us. Some have been dismissed from their churches, have lost the support of their bishops and fellow ministers. But they have acted in the faith that right defeated is stronger than evil triumphant. Their witness has been the spiritual salt that has preserved the true meaning of the gospel in these troubled times. They have carved a tunnel of hope through the dark mountain of disappointment. 43

I hope the church as a whole will meet the challenge of this decisive hour. But even if the church does not come to the aid of justice, I have no despair about the future. I have no fear about the outcome of our struggle in Birmingham, even if our motives are at present misunderstood. We will reach the goal of freedom in Birmingham and all over the nation, because the goal of America is freedom. Abused and scorned though we may be, our destiny is tied up with America's destiny. Before the pilgrims landed at Plymouth, we were here. Before the pen of Jefferson etched the majestic words of the Declaration of Independence across the pages of history, we were here. For more than two centuries our forebears labored in this country without wages; they made cotton king; they built the homes of their masters while suffering gross injustice and shameful humiliation—and yet out of a bottomless vitality they continued to thrive and develop. If the inexpressible cruelties of slavery could not stop us, the opposition we now face will surely fail. We will win our freedom because the sacred heritage of our nation and the eternal will of God are embodied in our echoing demands. 44

Before closing I feel impelled to mention one other point in your statement that has troubled me profoundly. You 45 warmly commended the Birmingham police force for keeping "order" and "preventing violence." I doubt that you would have so warmly commended the police force if you had seen its dogs sinking their teeth into unarmed, nonviolent Negroes. I doubt that you would so quickly commend the policemen if you were to observe their ugly and inhumane treatment of Negroes here in the city jail; if you were to watch them push and curse old Negro women and young Negro girls; if you were to see them slap and kick old Negro men and young boys; if you were to observe them, as they did on two occasions, refuse to give us food because we wanted to sing our grace together. I cannot join you in your praise of the Birmingham Police Department.

46 It is true that the police have exercised a degree of discipline in handling the demonstrators. In this sense they have conducted themselves rather "nonviolently" in public. But for what purpose? To preserve the evil system of segregation. Over the past few years I have consistently preached that nonviolence demands that the means we use must be as pure as the ends we seek. I have tried to make clear that it is wrong to use immoral means to attain moral ends. But now I must affirm that it is just as wrong, or perhaps even more so, to use moral means to preserve immoral ends. Perhaps Mr. Connor and his policemen have been rather nonviolent in public, as was Chief Pritchett in Albany, Georgia, but they have used the moral means of nonviolence to maintain the immoral end of racial injustice. As T. S. Eliot has said: "The last temptation is the greatest treason: To do the right deed for the wrong reason."

47 I wish you had commended the Negro sit-inners and demonstrators of Birmingham for their sublime courage, their willingness to suffer and their amazing discipline in the midst of great provocation. One day the South will recognize its real heroes. They will be the James Merediths, with the noble sense of purpose that enables them to face jeering and hostile mobs, and with the agonizing loneliness that characterizes the life of the pioneer. They will be old, oppressed, battered Negro women, symbolized in a seventy-two-year-old woman in Montgomery, Alabama, who rose up with a sense of dignity and with her people decided not to ride segregated buses, and who responded with ungrammatical profundity to one who inquired about her weariness: "My feets is tired, but my soul is at rest." They will be the young high school and college students, the young ministers

of the gospel and a host of their elders, courageously and nonviolently sitting in at lunch counters and willingly going to jail for conscience sake. One day the South will know that when these disinherited children of God sat down at lunch counters, they were in reality standing up for what is best in the American dream and for the most sacred values in our Judaeo-Christian heritage, thereby bringing our nation back to those great wells of democracy which were dug deep by the founding fathers in their formulation of the Constitution and the Declaration of Independence.

Never before have I written so long a letter. I'm afraid it is 48
much too long to take your precious time. I can assure you that it would have been much shorter if I had been writing from a comfortable desk, but what else can one do when he is alone in a narrow jail cell, other than write long letters, think long thoughts and pray long prayers?

If I have said anything in this letter that overstates the 49
truth and indicates an unreasonable impatience, I beg you to forgive me. If I have said anything that understates the truth and indicates my having a patience that allows me to settle for anything less than brotherhood, I beg God to forgive me.

I hope this letter finds you strong in the faith. I also hope 50
that circumstances will soon make it possible for me to meet each of you, not as an integrationist or a civil-rights leader but as a fellow clergyman and a Christian brother. Let us all hope that the dark clouds of racial prejudice will soon pass away and the deep fog of misunderstanding will be lifted from our fear-drenched communities, and in some not too distant tomorrow the radiant stars of love and brotherhood will shine over our great nation with all their scintillating beauty.

Yours for the cause of Peace and Brotherhood,
Martin Luther King, Jr.

Mia Klein Anderson

The *Other* Beauty of Martin Luther King, Jr.'s "Letter from Birmingham Jail"

Mia Klein Anderson teaches English at Bergen Community College in New Jersey. Her analysis of King's "Letter" was published in 1981 in College Composition and Communication, *a professional journal read by college writing teachers. Note well: The version of King's letter that Professor Anderson cites is not exactly the same as the one that precedes this article.*

1 Martin Luther King, Jr.'s "Letter from Birmingham Jail" is a document of great beauty. The arguments King makes for an end to the racial nightmare and for a new era of brotherhood are powerful in their intellectual appeal; just as powerfully persuasive in its ethical appeal is King's carefully established *persona* as a wise, educated, and moderate proponent of peaceful civil disobedience. In an essay appearing in *The Quarterly Journal of Speech,* "The Public Letter as Rhetorical Form: Structure, Logic, and Style in King's 'Letter from Birmingham Jail,'" Richard Fulkerson has thoughtfully and effectively discussed King's craft in structuring his "Letter" and in using logic as a major means of argument. Fulkerson, however, makes only a beginning at examining King's prose style for its extraordinary emotional appeal to readers. I suggest that King's persuasiveness in this "Letter" as well as in his other speeches and essays may be attributed not only to his structure, logic, and ethos, but even more to his creative, eloquent, and commanding use of the English language.

2 "Letter from Birmingham Jail" is anthologized in nearly a dozen college texts, and a group of black ministers from across the country aims to have it made a new book in the Bible. That the "Letter" enjoys such broad appeal and, indeed, has already become an American classic must be accounted for in a way other than that it rationally and ethically convinces its readers. When we examine King's prose style, we find paragraphs that are highly developed: not counting, for the moment, one paragraph that is 331 words long and one that is 118 words long, the average number of words per

paragraph is 138 (or nine sentences). We find a vocabulary that is highly polysyllabic; of the substantive words in paragraphs one through ten, 59% contain more than one syllable. We find sentences that are highly complex: of the 325 sentences in the "Letter," only 38% are simple sentences. And we find some twenty-eight educated allusions—to Greek philosophers, to persons and events in Christian history, to modern-day Christian and Jewish philosophers, and to others. Despite this sophistication of style, I submit, King's prose exerts a strong attraction—it is magnetic; and it is this quality that primarily accounts for the "Letter's" appeal beyond the audience of eight Southern clergymen to whom it is ostensibly addressed, beyond them to the much broader audience of lay readers.

Specifically, King's tone is engaging because of its candor and its lack of affectation; he appeals, if you will, to the life-wish rather than to the death-wish that would be implied in a tone characterized by defiance and aggression. King's prose schemes—that is, his structural devices—are rhythmical, appealing to the reader's emotions on a level he or she may be only vaguely aware of. And his tropes—his figures of speech—appeal not so importantly to the intellect as to the imagination. Life-affirming in its tone, rhythmical in its schemes, and, in its tropes, challenging to the imagination—these are the characteristics of King's prose that captivate and persuade. 3

King establishes his tone in the introductory paragraph. Patience and reasonableness, he promises, will be maintained, and they are—to a degree of consistency which, to readers already committed to his philosophy, may be maddening. Always he patiently notes the exceptions to his generalizations; always he balances criticism with commendation (33).* He patiently describes his critical perspective (34). Patiently he provides helpful historical background (6–9). Patiently he offers both theoretical explanations and concrete examples (15–22). In his conclusion, King humbly expresses concern that he has taken too much of his readers' time by writing at such length, begs their forgiveness if he has overstated the truth or has been unduly impatient, begs God's forgiveness if he has understated the truth or has been unduly patient, and shares his vision of brotherhood. Never, it should be noted, does King sound coy or appear to be using 4

* Where not otherwise noted, paragraph numbers will be provided in parentheses.

his patience and reasonableness as a manipulative device; he manages to maintain that perfect balance between a commanding and authoritative argument on the one hand and a humble and helpful tone on the other.

5 Fulkerson has demonstrated how carefully King, in establishing an identification with his audience and a conciliatory tone, has moved among the personal pronouns, *I, you,* and *we*. But I think a somewhat different emphasis is important here. Many of the 139 "I" clauses in the "Letter" tell of King's willingness to give, to act, to believe: "I would like to answer," "I have earnestly worked and preached," "I am trying," "I continued to think," "I have watched," "I have travelled," "I have looked," "I can assure," and "I hope" are examples. Similarly, a perusal of King's topic sentences reveals the same kind of willingness to consider, to be helpful, to dream of a better time. He writes, "I think I should give the reason," "Let us turn to a more concrete example," "Let me give another explanation," "I hope you can see the distinction I am trying to point out," "But as I continued to think about the matter," and "I hope the Church as a whole will meet the challenge." King's frequent use of allusions implies that he and his readers share a common heritage (Christianity, as detailed in the Bible) and that they share a common knowledge (the knowledge of history and philosophy). These characteristics of King's tone contribute to an irresistible call for harmony—irresistible because produced justly, reasonably, and sincerely—the harmony that is unity of spirit and purpose among writer and readers.

6 Two powerful instances of understatement (litotes) help establish King's lack of belligerence, his direct but unaggressive tone. In Paragraph 45, King graphically describes five instances of violence perpetrated by the Birmingham police against the Black community. He ends the paragraph by saying starkly, "I'm sorry that I can't join you in your praise for the police department." In Paragraph 14, he offers ten vivid illustrations of the "stinging darts of segregation," piling on detail after detail in a manner that suggests the list could go on endlessly. Then he closes the paragraph with this simple, direct statement: "I hope, sirs, you can understand our legitimate and unavoidable impatience." The restraint from attack is awesome.

7 Besides the emotionally appealing candor and unpretentiousness of his tone, there is a second important element of King's prose style—the music of his schemes. King employs

many structural devices, each of which produces an engaging beat or rhythm. Most notable are his use of balance in instances of parallelism and antithesis and his use of repetition in instances of anaphora, alliteration, and assonance.

King puts into parallel structure a wide variety of gram- 8
matical and syntactical units. He parallels nouns—here, four "-tion" nouns, with ascending and then descending numbers of syllables: "collection . . . negotiation . . . self-purification . . . direct action" (6). He parallels adverbs—here, four "-ally" adverbs, with ascending/descending syllable counts: "So segregation is not only politically, economically, and sociologically unsound, but it is morally wrong and sinful" (16). He parallels adjectives: "These are the hard, brutal, and unbelievable facts" (6). Verbs: "policemen curse, kick, brutalize, and even kill . . ." (14). Adjective/noun pairs—here, of equal numbers of syllables: "pent-up resentments and latent frustrations" (30). Clauses: "Some . . . have written . . . Others have marched . . . They have languished . . . They . . . have recognized . . . (32).

King's use of antithesis—notable because his juxtaposi- 9
tion of contrasting ideas is most often both of wording and of sense, and because he most often renders antithetical ideas in parallel structure—adds still more to the pleasing rhythm, however unconsciously the ear hears it. Many of King's antithetical expressions move from concepts of depth or darkness to concepts of height or light. Fulkerson rightly notes the archetypal appeal of these expressions, but he stops short of pointing to the rhythm that results from such constructions. For example:

> . . . that will help men rise from the dark depths of prejudice to the majestic heights of understanding and brotherhood. (10)

> . . . freedom is never voluntarily given by the oppressor; it must be demanded by the oppressed. (13)

> Any law that uplifts human personality is just. Any law that degrades human personality is unjust. (16)

> So I can urge men to obey the 1954 decision of the Supreme Court because it is morally right, and I can urge them to disobey segregation ordinances because they are morally wrong. (15)

> Shallow understanding from people of good will is more frustrating than absolute misunderstanding from people of ill will. (23)

> . . . the transition from an obnoxious negative peace . . . to a substance-filled positive peace . . . (24)

> Now is the time to . . . transform our pending national elegy into a creative psalm of brotherhood. (26)

> Where were their voices of support when tired, bruised, and weary Negro men and women decided to rise from the dark dungeons of complacency to the bright hills of creative protest? (38)

There are more than thirty such eminently quotable—because so strikingly rhythmic—instances of antithesis in the "Letter."

10 Contributing also to the music of King's prose is repetition. Instances of anaphora (repetition of the same word or group of words at the beginnings of successive clauses), for example, occur in the "Letter" more than a dozen times, often, as with other structural devices, in parallel units. Consider this series of anaphoristic clauses from paragraph 23:

> . . . the white moderate who is more devoted . . . ; who prefers . . . ; who constantly says . . . ; who paternalistically feels . . . ; who lives . . . and who constantly advises. . . .

Or this series of interrogative sentences from paragraph 25:

> Isn't this like condemning the robbed man because . . . ? Isn't this like condemning Socrates because . . . ? Isn't this like condemning Jesus because . . . ?

Again in paragraph 31 we find repetition at the openings of successive rhetorical questions:

> Was not Jesus an extremist . . . ? Was not Amos an extremist . . . ? Was not Paul an extremist . . . ? Was not Martin Luther an extremist . . . ? Was not John Bunyan an extremist . . . ? Was not Abraham Lincoln an extremist . . . ? Was not Thomas Jefferson an extremist . . . ?

Spanning paragraphs 34 through 38, we find successive clauses beginning, "I have . . . ":

> I have been disappointed . . . I have heard . . . but I have longed to hear . . . I have watched . . . I have heard . . . and I have watched . . . I have travelled . . . I have looked . . . I have beheld . . . I have found myself asking . . . I have wept . . .

Once such a rhythm is set in motion, the reader becomes engaged—unconsciously engaged in awaiting the next beat or refrain.

King makes music as well through alliteration, assonance, 11
and other sound combinations. Particularly alliteration. For example, the repeated d's, s's, and p's in "the shadow of a deep disappointment settled upon us" (8) are subtly pleasing to the ear, as are the b's in "So I am here . . . because we were invited here. I am here because I have basic organizational ties here. Beyond this, I am in Birmingham because injustice is here" (2–3). In this sentence, the hard c's stand out: "Nonviolent direct action seeks to create such a crisis and establish such creative tension that a community that has constantly refused to negotiate is forced to confront the issue" (10). The following passage features many s's and many vowel matches, but, even more importantly, it features a rapid fire of the "explosive" consonants, d, t, p, k, and b: "When you suddenly find your tongue twisted and your speech stammering as you seek to explain to your six-year-old daughter why she can't go to the public amusement park that has just been advertised on television . . ." (14). The repeated explosive consonants, besides being musical, reflect the sharp-edged frustration that charges the speaker and thus add to the immediacy of the image.

Alliteration and assonance appear interwoven in such 12
passages as these:

> a a a b c c b c
> . . . the South would be flowing with floods of blood. (29)
>
> a a b c b c
> . . . I have watched white churches stand on the sideline and
> d d e f g b f d g e f g
> merely mouth pious irrelevancies and sanctimonious trivial-
> f g
> i ties. (37)

Others of the schemes may also be readily found in King's 13
prose—more often than not, as we have already seen,

simultaneously—and all combine to please the outer or inner ear. Polysyndeton is found in these passages:

> . . . when you suddenly find your tongue twisted and your speech stammering as you seek to explain to your six-year-old daughter why she can't go to the public amusement park that has just been advertised on television, and see tears welling up in her little eyes when she is told that Funtown is closed to colored children, and see the depressing clouds of inferiority begin to form in her little mental sky, and see her begin to distort her little personality by unconsciously developing a bitterness toward white people . . . (14)

> . . . when your first name becomes "nigger" and your middle name becomes "boy" (however old you are) and your last name becomes "John," and when your wife and mother are never given the respected title "Mrs." . . . (14) [emphasis in both passages is added]

Anastrophe is found:

> Seldom, if ever, do I pause . . . (1)

> Never again can we afford . . . (4)

> Then came the opportunity . . . (6)

> Too long has our beloved Southland been bogged down . . . (11)

Polyptoton is found:

> . . . privileged groups seldom give up their privileges voluntarily. (12)

> Society must protect the robbed and punish the robber. (25)

> . . . write long letters, think strange thoughts, and pray long prayers? (48)

We must not underestimate the power of these devices to captivate readers. Granted, "Letter from Birmingham Jail" becomes more and more memorable each time it is "heard." Students relate easily to this concept, by the way, when I refer them to their experience with a new, good song. The point is that the "Letter's" musical arrangement of sounds plays a large part in its impact on readers.

Turning now to consider the role played by King's tropes 14
in broadening the appeal of the "Letter," I wish to emphasize that while his similes and metaphors certainly do engage the intellect, more importantly they engage the imagination and emotion. His similes and metaphors become the (serious) playthings of the imagination, and the play of the imagination has the effect on the emotions of readying the reader, making him or her more accepting and sympathetic toward the intellectual content of the figures of speech. I referred earlier to Fulkerson's correctly identifying the archetypal depth/height and dark/light element which pervades the tropes, but I would like to carry this observation a step further. Of the more than sixty readily noted similes and metaphors, almost four times as many come from the *organic* world—having to do with the body, with the sky and weather, and with the earth (topographical, as well as relating to water, plants, etc.)—as come from the world of *manufacture* or *technology*, though these, too, relate man to his largely familiar world.

Of King's two significant similes, one is "organic," and one 15
is not:

> Like a boil that can never be cured as long as it is covered up but must be opened with all its pus-flowing ugliness to the natural medicines of air and light, injustice must likewise be exposed, with all of the tension its exposing creates, to the light of human conscience and the air of national opinion before it can be cured. (24)

> So here we are moving toward the exit of the twentieth century with a religious community largely adjusted to the status quo, standing as a tail light behind other community agencies rather than a headlight leading men to higher levels of justice. (35)

King's organic metaphors of the body move back and forth between sickness and health:

> . . . Suffered unduly from the disease of segregation. (13)

> . . . plagued with inner fears and outer resentments . . . (14)

> . . . the need for powerful "action" antidotes to combat the disease of segregation. (32)

> . . . the anesthetizing security of stained glass windows. (35)

> How we have blemished and scarred that body [the Church as the body of Christ] through social neglect and fear of being nonconformist. (39)

His organic metaphors of the sky and weather are seen in these instances:

> . . . the dark shadow of a deep disappointment settled upon us. (8)

> . . . so that the demonstrations could not be used to cloud the issues. (9)

His organic metaphors relating to the earth are seen here:

> These men have been the leaven in the lump of the race. Their witness has been the spiritual salt that has preserved the true meaning of the gospel in these troubled times. They have carved a tunnel of hope through the dark mountain of disappointment. (43)

> . . . thus carrying our whole nation back to great wells of democracy which were dug deep by the founding fathers in the formulation of the Constitution and the Declaration of Independence. (47)

Most of the metaphors drawing from the world of manufacture and technology are quite uncomplicated:

> We are caught in an inescapable network of mutuality tied in a single garment of destiny. (4)

> . . . the stinging darts of segregation . . . (14)

> . . . smothering in an air-tight cage of poverty . . . (14)

> . . . the cup of endurance runs over . . . (14)

> We must come to see that human progress never rolls in on wheels of inevitability. (26)

> . . . the paralyzing chains of conformity . . . (43)

Two very memorable metaphors are decidedly technological (or scientific) but still are familiar:

> [The word "Wait!"] has been a tranquilizing thalidomide, relieving the emotional stress for the moment, only to give birth to an ill-formed infant of frustration. (11)

> In those days the Church was not merely a thermometer that recorded the ideas and principles of popular opinion; it was a thermostat that transformed the mores of society. (40)

Readers will want to make use of their dictionaries (for intellectual exercise) or apply their experience (gaining a more imaginative and emotional relationship to the matter of the trope) to appreciate precisely the difference between a thermometer and a thermostat, and then they will appreciate the distinction King is making between the Church of old and the Church of the 50's and 60's. They will want to make use of their reference books or apply their experience to explain the uses to which leaven and salt are put in cooking. They will want to explore why "air-tight cage" is uniquely appropriate for describing poverty, why despair can so aptly be said to "corrode," and why "stinging darts" so fittingly describes segregation. On the latter, my students surprised me with the subtlety of their insight: darts, they suggested, are purposely thrown, either as a weapon or for pleasure (sport); they enter quickly, penetrate deeply, and cause wounds more painful and slower to heal than surface wounds. My students' squirming and their facial expressions revealed that not only their minds but also their imaginations were fully engaged. Tropes of this caliber are exciting. 16

John Frederick Nims (in *Western Wind: An Introduction to Poetry*) tells the following story to illustrate the fact that "there are times when rhythm has a stronger hold on us than our most sacred concerns": 17

> A few years ago thousands of young people met in the gymnasium at Cornell to show their concern over vital issues of the day. But as time went on they became listless. Some started throwing Frisbees, some fell asleep in each other's arms. Then a young Irishman took the platform to plead for contributions: "Spontaneously, without any musical backing," *The New York Times* account goes, "he sang an Irish rebel ballad. The words mattered little but the rhythm

> caught them. The youths rose and danced. They snake-danced in congas. They did jigs. It went on that way until early morning and it picked up again at noon. 'It's pretty bad,' said an editor of the *Cornell Daily Sun*. 'What does this have to do with politics or peace or any real issue?' "

Perhaps you have discussed with your students Alexander Solzhenitsyn's *One Day in the Life of Ivan Denisovich* and have seen how they are infinitely more repelled by the evils of that social system for having lived—via the imagination—through a day as one of its victims than they would have been had they read a factual document confronting them with essentially the same details. Rhythm and imagination, acting as they do on the emotion, are the key. Martin Luther King, Jr., knew that his effectiveness in reaching his wider audience would come both from what he said and from how he said it. The words can reach the mind, but the music and imagination can reach the heart and soul.

Lewis H. Van Dusen, Jr.

Civil Disobedience: Destroyer of Democracy

Lewis H. Van Dusen, Jr. (born 1910) has practiced law in Philadelphia since 1935. Decorated for valor during World War II, he also served with the State Department during his distinguished career. He has written many essays for professional journals; the following one appeared in 1969 in the American Bar Association Journal.

1 As Charles E. Wyzanski, Chief Judge of the United States District Court in Boston, wrote in the February 1968, *Atlantic:* "Disobedience is a long step from dissent. Civil disobedience involves a deliberate and punishable breach of legal duty." Protesters might prefer a different definition. They would rather say that civil disobedience is the peaceful resistance of conscience.

2 The philosophy of civil disobedience was not developed in

our American democracy, but in the very first democracy of Athens. It was expressed by the poet Sophocles and the philosopher Socrates. In Sophocle's tragedy, Antigone chose to obey her conscience and violate the state edict against providing burial for her brother, who had been decreed a traitor. When the dictator Creon found out that Antigone had buried her fallen brother, he confronted her and reminded her that there was a mandatory death penalty for this deliberate disobedience of the state law. Antigone nobly replied, "Nor did I think your orders were so strong that you, a mortal man, could overrun the gods' unwritten and unfailing laws."

Conscience motivated Antigone. She was not testing the validity of the law in the hope that eventually she would be sustained. Appealing to the judgment of the community, she explained her action to the chorus. She was not secret and surreptitious—the interment of her brother was open and public. She was not violent; she did not trespass on another citizen's rights. And finally, she accepted without resistance the death sentence—the penalty for violation. By voluntarily accepting the law's sanctions, she was not a revolutionary denying the authority of the state. Antigone's behavior exemplifies the classic case of civil disobedience. 3

Socrates believed that reason could dictate a conscientious disobedience of state law, but he also believed that he had to accept the legal sanctions of the state. In Plato's *Crito*, Socrates from his hanging basket accepted the death penalty for his teaching of religion to youths contrary to state laws. 4

The sage of Walden, Henry David Thoreau, took this philosophy of nonviolence and developed it into a strategy for solving society's injustices. First enunciating it in protest against the Mexican War, he then turned it to use against slavery. For refusing to pay taxes that would help pay the enforcers of the fugitive slave law, he went to prison. In Thoreau's words, "If the alternative is to keep all just men in prison or to give up slavery, the state will not hesitate which to choose." 5

Sixty years later, Gandhi took Thoreau's civil disobedience as his strategy to wrest Indian independence from England. The famous salt march against a British imperial tax is his best-known example of protest. 6

But the conscientious law breaking of Socrates, Gandhi, and Thoreau is to be distinguished from the conscientious law testing of Martin Luther King, Jr., who was not a civil disobedient. The civil disobedient withholds taxes or violates state laws knowing he is legally wrong, but believing he is 7 morally right. While he wrapped himself in the mantle of Gandhi and Thoreau, Dr. King led his followers in violation of state laws he believed were contrary to the Federal Constitution. But since Supreme Court decisions in the end generally upheld his many actions, he should not be considered a true civil disobedient.

8 The civil disobedience of Antigone is like that of the pacifist who withholds paying the percentage of his taxes that goes to the Defense Department, or the Quaker who travels against State Department regulations to Hanoi to distribute medical supplies, or the Vietnam war protester who tears up his draft card. This civil disobedient has been nonviolent in his defiance of the law; he has been unfurtive in his violation; he has been submissive to the penalties of the law. He has neither evaded the law nor interfered with another's rights. He has been neither a rioter nor a revolutionary. The thrust of his cause has not been the might of coercion but the martyrdom of conscience.

Was the Boston Tea Party Civil Disobedience?

9 Those who justify violence and radical action as being in the tradition of our Revolution show a misunderstanding of the philosophy of democracy.

10 James Farmer, former head of the Congress of Racial Equality, in defense of the mass action confrontation method, has told of a famous organized demonstration that took place in opposition to political and economic discrimination. The protestors beat back and scattered the law enforcers and then proceeded to loot and destroy private property. Mr. Farmer then said he was talking about the Boston Tea Party and implied that violence as a method for redress of grievances was an American tradition and a legacy of our revolutionary heritage. While it is true that there is no more sacred document than our Declaration of Independence, Jefferson's "inherent right of rebellion" was predicated on the tyrannical denial of democratic means. If there is no popular assembly to provide an adjustment of ills, and if there is no court system to dispose of injustices, then there is, indeed, a right to rebel.

11 The seventeenth century's John Locke, the philosophical father of the Declaration of Independence, wrote in his *Second Treatise on Civil Government:* "Wherever law ends, tyranny begins . . . and the people are absolved from any

further obedience. Governments are dissolved from within when the legislative [chamber] is altered. When the government [becomes] . . . arbitrary disposers of lives, liberties and fortunes of the people, such revolutions happen. . . ."

But there are some sophisticated proponents of the revolutionary redress of grievances who say that the test of the need for radical action is not the unavailability of democratic institutions but the ineffectuality of those institutions to remove blatant social inequalities. If social injustice exists, they say, concerted disobedience is required against the constituted government, whether it be totalitarian or democratic in structure. 12

Of course, only the most bigoted chauvinist would claim that America is without some glaring faults. But there has never been a utopian society on earth and there never will be unless human nature is remade. Since inequities will mar even the best-framed democracies, the injustice rationale would allow a free right of civil resistance to be available always as a shortcut alternative to the democratic way of petition, debate and assembly. The lesson of history is that civil insurgency spawns far more injustices than it removes. The Jeffersons, Washingtons, and Adamses resisted tyranny with the aim of promoting the procedures of democracy. They would never have resisted a democratic government with the risk of promoting the techniques of tyranny. 13

Legitimate Pressures and Illegitimate Results

There are many civil rights leaders who show impatience with the process of democracy. They rely on the sit-ins, boycott or mass picketing to gain speedier solutions to the problems that face every citizen. But we must realize that the legitimate pressures that won concessions in the past can easily escalate into the illegitimate power plays that might extort demands in the future. The victories of these civil rights leaders must not shake our confidence in the democratic procedures, as the pressures of demonstration are desirable only if they take place within the limits allowed by law. Civil rights gains should continue to be won by the persuasion of Congress and other legislative bodies and by the decision of courts. Any illegal entreaty for the rights of some can be an injury to the rights of others, for mass demonstrations often trigger violence. 14

Those who advocate taking the law into their own hands 15

should reflect that when they are disobeying what they consider to be an immoral law, they are deciding on a possibly immoral course. Their answer is that the process for democratic relief is too slow, that only mass confrontation can bring immediate action, and that any injuries are the inevitable cost of the pursuit of justice. Their answer is, simply put, that the end justifies the means. It is this justification of any form of demonstration as a form of dissent that threatens to destroy a society built on the rule of law.

16 Our Bill of Rights guarantees wide opportunities to use mass meetings, public parades, and organized demonstrations to stimulate sentiment, to dramatize issues, and to cause change. The Washington freedom march of 1963 was such a call for action. But the rights of free expression cannot be mere force cloaked in the garb of free speech. As the courts have decreed in labor cases, free assembly does not mean mass picketing or sit-down strikes. These rights are subject to limitations of time and place so as to secure the rights of others. When militant students storm a college president's office to achieve demands, when certain groups plan rush-hour car stalling to protest discrimination in employment, these are not dissent, but a denial of rights to others. Neither is it the lawful use of mass protest, but rather the unlawful use of mob power.

17 Justice Black, one of the foremost advocates and defenders of the right of protest and dissent, has said:

> . . . Experience demonstrates that it is not a far step from what to many seems to be the earnest, honest, patriotic, kind-spirited multitude of today, to the fanatical, threatening, lawless mob of tomorrow. And the crowds that press in the streets for noble goals today can be supplanted tomorrow by street mobs pressuring the courts for precisely opposite ends.[1]

18 Society must censure those demonstrators who would trespass on the public peace, as it must condemn those rioters whose pillage would destroy the public peace. But more ambivalent is society's posture toward the civil disobedient. Unlike the rioter, the true civil disobedient commits no violence. Unlike the mob demonstrator, he commits no trespass on others' rights. The civil disobedient, while deliberately violating a law, shows an oblique respect for the law

[1] In *Cox* v. *Louisiana*, 379 U.S. 536, 575, 584 (1965).

by voluntarily submitting to its sanctions. He neither resists arrest nor evades punishment. Thus, he breaches the law but not the peace.

But civil disobedience, whatever the ethical rationalization, is still an assault on our democratic society, an affront to our legal order and an attack on our constitutional government. To indulge civil disobedience is to invite anarchy, and the permissive arbitrariness of anarchy is hardly less tolerable than the repressive arbitrariness of tyranny. Too often the license of liberty is followed by the loss of liberty, because into the desert of anarchy comes the man on horseback, a Mussolini or a Hitler. 19

Violations of Law Subvert Democracy

Law violations, even for ends recognized as laudable, are not only assaults on the rule of law, but subversions of the democratic process. The disobedient act of conscience does not ennoble democracy; it erodes it. 20

First, it courts violence, and even the most careful and limited use of nonviolent acts of disobedience may help sow the dragon-teeth of civil riot. Civil disobedience is the progenitor of disorder, and disorder is the sire of violence. 21

Second, the concept of civil disobedience does not invite principles of general applicability. If the children of light are morally privileged to resist particular laws on grounds of conscience, so are the children of darkness. Former Deputy Attorney General Burke Marshall said: "If the decision to break the law really turned on individual conscience, it is hard to see in law how [the civil rights leader] is better off than former Governor Ross Barnett of Mississippi who also believed deeply in his cause and was willing to go to jail."[2] 22

Third, even the most noble act of civil disobedience assaults the rule of law. Although limited as to method, motive and objective, it has the effect of inducing others to engage in different forms of law breaking characterized by methods unsanctioned and condemned by classic theories of law violation. Unfortunately, the most patent lesson of civil disobedience is not so much nonviolence of action as defiance of authority. 23

Finally, the greatest danger in condoning civil disobedi- 24

[2] "The Protest movement and the Law," *Virginia Legal Review* 51 (1965), 785.

ence as a permissible strategy for hastening change is that it undermines our democratic processes. To adopt the techniques of civil disobedience is to assume that representative government does not work. To resist the decisions of courts and the laws of elected assemblies is to say that democracy has failed.

25 There is no man who is above the law, and there is no man who has a right to break the law. Civil disobedience is not above the law, but against the law. When the civil disobedient disobeys one law, he invariably subverts all law. When the civil disobedient says that he is above the law, he is saying that democracy is beneath him. His disobedience shows a distrust for the democratic system. He is merely saying that since democracy does not work, why should he help make it work. Thoreau expressed well the civil disobedient's disdain for democracy:

> As for adopting the ways which the state has provided for remedying the evil, I know not of such ways. They take too much time and a man's life will be gone. I have other affairs to attend to. I came into this world not chiefly to make this a good place to live in, but to live in it, be it good or bad.[3]

26 Thoreau's position is not only morally irresponsible but politically reprehensible. When citizens in a democracy are called on to make a profession of faith, the civil disobedients offer only a confession of failure. Tragically, when civil disobedients for lack of faith abstain from democratic involvement, they help attain their own gloomy prediction. They help create the social and political basis for their own despair. By foreseeing failure, they help forge it. If citizens rely on antidemocratic means of protest, they will help bring about the undemocratic result of an authoritarian or anarchic state.

27 How far demonstrations properly can be employed to produce political and social change is a pressing question, particularly in view of the provocations accompanying the National Democratic Convention in Chicago last August and the reaction of the police to them. A line must be drawn by the judiciary between the demands of those who seek absolute order, which can lead only to a dictatorship, and those who seek absolute freedom, which can lead only to anarchy. The line, wherever it is drawn by our courts,

[3] Thoreau, "Civil Disobedience" (see page 637).

should be respected on the college campus, on the streets, and elsewhere.

Undue provocation will inevitably result in overreaction, human emotions being what they are. Violence will follow. This cycle undermines the very democracy it is designed to preserve. The lesson of the past is that democracies will fall if violence, including the intentional provocations that will lead to violence, replaces democratic procedures, as in Athens, Rome, and the Weimar Republic. This lesson must be constantly explained by the legal profession. 28

We should heed the words of William James: 29

> Democracy is still upon its trial. The civic genius of our people is its only bulwark and . . . neither battleships nor public libraries nor great newspapers nor booming stocks: neither mechanical invention nor political adroitness, nor churches nor universities nor civil service examinations can save us from degeneration if the inner mystery be lost.
>
> That mystery, at once the secret and the glory of our English-speaking race, consists of nothing but two habits. . . . [O]ne of them is the habit of trained and disciplined good temper towards the opposite party when it fairly wins its innings. The other is that of fierce and merciless resentment toward every man or set of men who break the public peace.[4]

[4] James, *Pragmatism* (1907), pp. 127–28. 30

Woody Allen

A Brief, Yet Helpful, Guide to Civil Disobedience

*Woody Allen (born 1935) has won many Oscars for his movies—*Annie Hall; Play It Again, Sam; Bananas; *and* Hannah and Her Sisters *(to name a few). He has also contributed comic essays to* The New Republic, The New Yorker, Playboy, *and other publications. After the following essay appeared in* The New York Times *in 1972, it was collected in his book* Without Feathers.

In perpetrating a revolution, there are two requirements: someone or something to revolt against and someone to 1 actually show up and do the revolting. Dress is usually casual and both parties may be flexible about time and place but if either faction fails to attend, the whole enterprise is likely to come off badly. In the Chinese Revolution of 1650 neither party showed up and the deposit on the hall was forfeited.

2 The people or parties revolted against are called the "oppressors" and are easily recognized as they seem to be the ones having all the fun. The "oppressors" generally get to wear suits, own land, and play their radios late at night without being yelled at. Their job is to maintain the "status quo," a condition where everything remains the same although they may be willing to paint every two years.

3 When the "oppressors" become too strict, we have what is known as a police state, wherein all dissent is forbidden, as in chuckling, showing up in a bow tie, or referring to the mayor as "Fats." Civil liberties are greatly curtailed in a police state, and freedom of speech is unheard of, although one is allowed to mime to a record. Opinions critical of the government are not tolerated, particularly about their dancing. Freedom of the press is also curtailed and the ruling party "manages" the news, permitting the citizens to hear only acceptable political ideas and ball scores that will not cause unrest.

4 The groups who revolt are called the "oppressed" and can generally be seen milling about and grumbling or claiming to have headaches. (It should be noted that the oppressors never revolt and attempt to become the oppressed as that would entail a change of underwear.)

5 Some famous examples of revolutions are:

The French Revolution, in which the peasants seized power by force and quickly changed all locks on the palace doors so the nobles could not get back in. Then they had a large party and gorged themselves. When the nobles finally recaptured the palace they were forced to clean up and found many stains and cigarette burns.

6 ***The Russian Revolution,*** which simmered for years and suddenly erupted when the serfs finally realized that the Czar and the Tsar were the same person.

7 It should be noted that after a revolution is over, the "oppressed" frequently take over and begin acting like the "oppressors." Of course by then it is very hard to get them on the phone, and money lent for cigarettes and gum during the fighting may as well be forgotten about.

Methods of Civil Disobedience: 8

Hunger Strike. Here the oppressed goes without food until his demands are met. Insidious politicians will often leave biscuits within easy reach or perhaps some cheddar cheese, but they must be resisted. If the party in power can get the striker to eat, they usually have little trouble putting down the insurrection. If they can get him to eat and also lift the check, they have won for sure. In Pakistan, a hunger strike was broken when the government produced an exceptionally fine veal cordon bleu, which the masses found was too appealing to turn down, but such gourmet dishes are rare.

The problem with the hunger strike is that after several days one can get quite hungry, particularly since sound trucks are paid to go through the streets saying, "Um . . . what nice chicken—umm . . . some peas . . . umm . . ." 9

A modified form of the Hunger Strike for those whose political convictions are not quite so radical is giving up chives. This small gesture, when used properly, can greatly influence a government, and it is well known that Mahatma Gandhi's insistence on eating his salads untossed shamed the British government into many concessions. Other things besides food one can give up are: whist, smiling, and standing on one foot and imitating a crane. 10

Sit-down Strike. Proceed to a designated spot and then sit down, but sit all the way down. Otherwise you are squatting, a position that makes no political point unless the government is also squatting. (This is rare, although a government will occasionally crouch in cold weather.) The trick is to remain seated until concessions are made, but as in the Hunger Strike, the government will try subtle means of making the striker rise. They may say, "Okay, everybody up, we're closing." Or, "Can you get up for a minute, we'd just like to see how tall you are?" 11

Demonstration and Marches. The key point about a demonstration is that it must be seen. Hence the term "demonstration." If a person demonstrates privately in his own home, this is not technically a demonstration but merely "acting silly" or "behaving like an ass." 12

A fine example of a demonstration was the Boston Tea Party, where outraged Americans disguised as Indians dumped British tea into the harbor. Later, Indians disguised as outraged Americans dumped actual British into the water. Following that, the British, disguised as tea, dumped 13 each other into the harbor. Finally, German mercenaries clad only in costumes from *The Trojan Women* leapt into the harbor for no apparent reason.

14 When demonstrating, it is good to carry a placard stating one's position. Some suggested positions are: (1) lower taxes, (2) raise taxes, and (3) stop grinning at Persians.

15 Miscellaneous methods of Civil Disobedience:

Standing in front of City Hall and chanting the word "pudding" until one's demands are met.

Tying up traffic by leading a flock of sheep into the shopping area.

Phoning members of "the establishment" and singing "Bess, You Is My Woman Now" into the phone.

Dressing as a policeman and then skipping.

Pretending to be an artichoke but punching people as they pass.

AFFIRMATIVE ACTION

Kurt Vonnegut, Jr.

Harrison Bergeron

After graduating from Cornell University, Kurt Vonnegut, Jr. (born in 1922 in Indianapolis), worked in journalism and public relations. Then he started publishing best-selling novels that often feature imaginary (yet all too real) settings, a satiric edge, and his characteristic narrative voice. Among them are Cat's Cradle, Slaughterhouse-Five, Breakfast of Champions, *and* Jailbird. *"Harrison Bergeron" was published as part of his collection of stories entitled* Welcome to the Monkey House.

The year was 2081, and everybody was finally equal. They weren't only equal before God and the law. They were equal every which way. Nobody was smarter than anybody else. Nobody was better looking than anybody else. Nobody was stronger or quicker than anybody else. All this equality was due to the 211th, 212th, and 213th Amendments to the Constitution, and to the unceasing vigilance of agents of the United States Handicapper General. 1

Some things about living still weren't quite right, though. April, for instance, still drove people crazy by not being springtime. And it was in that clammy month that the H-G men took George and Hazel Bergeron's fourteen-year-old son, Harrison, away. 2

It was tragic, all right, but George and Hazel couldn't think about it very hard. Hazel had a perfectly average intelligence, which meant she couldn't think about anything except in short bursts. And George, while his intelligence was way above normal, had a little mental handicap radio in his ear. He was required by law to wear it at all times. It was tuned to a government transmitter. Every twenty seconds or so, the transmitter would send out some sharp noise to keep people like George from taking unfair advantage of their brains. 3

George and Hazel were watching television. There were 4

tears on Hazel's cheeks, but she'd forgotten for the moment what they were about.

5 On the television screen were ballerinas.

6 A buzzer sounded in George's head. His thoughts fled in panic, like bandits from a burglar alarm.

7 "That was a real pretty dance, that dance they just did," said Hazel.

8 "Huh?" said George.

9 "That dance—it was nice," said Hazel.

10 "Yup," said George. He tried to think a little about the ballerinas. They weren't really very good—no better than anybody else would have been, anyway. They were burdened with sashweights and bags of birdshot, and their faces were masked, so that no one, seeing a free and graceful gesture or a pretty face, would feel like something the cat drug in. George was toying with the vague notion that maybe dancers shouldn't be handicapped. But he didn't get very far with it before another noise in his ear radio scattered his thoughts.

11 George winced. So did two out of the eight ballerinas.

12 Hazel saw him wince. Having no mental handicap herself, she had to ask George what the latest sound had been.

13 "Sounded like somebody hitting a milk bottle with a ball peen hammer," said George.

14 "I'd think it would be real interesting, hearing all the different sounds," said Hazel, a little envious. "All the things they think up."

15 "Um," said George.

16 "Only, if I was Handicapper General, you know what I would do?" said Hazel. Hazel, as a matter of fact, bore a strong resemblance to the Handicapper General, a woman named Diana Moon Glampers. "If I was Diana Moon Glampers," said Hazel, "I'd have chimes on Sunday—just chimes. Kind of in honor of religion."

17 "I could think, if it was just chimes," said George.

18 "Well—maybe make 'em real loud," said Hazel. "I think I'd make a good Handicapper General."

19 "Good as anybody else," said George.

20 "Who knows better'n I do what normal is?" said Hazel.

21 "Right," said George. He began to think glimmeringly about his abnormal son who was now in jail, about Harrison, but a twenty-one-gun salute in his head stopped that.

22 "Boy!" said Hazel, "that was a doozy, wasn't it?"

23 It was such a doozy that George was white and trembling, and tears stood on the rims of his red eyes. Two of the eight

ballerinas had collapsed to the studio floor, [and] were holding their temples.

"All of a sudden you look so tired," said Hazel. "Why don't you stretch out on the sofa, so's you can rest your handicap bag on the pillows, honeybunch." She was referring to the forty-seven pounds of birdshot in a canvas bag, which was padlocked around George's neck. "Go on and rest the bag for a little while," she said. "I don't care if you're not equal to me for a while." 24

George weighed the bag with his hands. "I don't mind it," he said. "I don't notice it any more. It's just a part of me." 25

"You been so tired lately—kind of wore out," said Hazel. "If there was just some way we could make a little hole in the bottom of the bag, and just take out a few of them lead balls. Just a few." 26

"Two years in prison and two thousand dollars fine for every ball I took out," said George. "I don't call that a bargain." 27

"If you could just take a few out when you came home from work," said Hazel. "I mean—you don't compete with anybody around here. You just set around." 28

"If I tried to get away with it," said George, "then other people'd get away with it—and pretty soon we'd be right back to the dark ages again, with everybody competing against everybody else. You wouldn't like that, would you?" 29

"I'd hate it," said Hazel. 30

"There you are," said George. "The minute people start cheating on laws, what do you think happens to society?" 31

If Hazel hadn't been able to come up with an answer to this question George couldn't have supplied one. A siren was going off in his head. 32

"Reckon it'd fall all apart," said Hazel. 33

"What would?" said George blankly. 34

"Society," said Hazel uncertainly. "Wasn't that what you just said?" 35

"Who knows?" said George. 36

The television program was suddenly interrupted for a news bulletin. It wasn't clear at first as to what the bulletin was about, since the announcer, like all announcers, had a serious speech impediment. For about half a minute, and in a state of high excitement, the announcer tried to say, "Ladies and gentlemen—" 37

He finally gave up, handed the bulletin to a ballerina to read. 38

"That's all right—" Hazel said of the announcer, "he tried. 39

That's the big thing. He tried to do the best he could with what God gave him. He should get a nice raise for trying so hard."

40 "Ladies and gentlemen—" said the ballerina, reading the bulletin. She must have been extraordinarily beautiful, because the mask she wore was hideous. And it was easy to see that she was the strongest and most graceful of all the dancers, for her handicap bags were as big as those worn by two-hundred-pound men.

41 And she had to apologize at once for her voice, which was a very unfair voice for a woman to use. Her voice was a warm, luminous, timeless melody. "Excuse me—" she said, and she began again, making her voice absolutely uncompetitive.

42 "Harrison Bergeron, age fourteen," she said in a grackle squawk, "has just escaped from jail, where he was held on suspicion of plotting to overthrow the government. He is a genius and an athlete, is under-handicapped, and should be regarded as extremely dangerous."

43 A police photograph of Harrison Bergeron was flashed on the screen upside down, then sideways, upside down again, then right side up. The picture showed the full length of Harrison against a background calibrated in feet and inches. He was exactly seven feet tall.

44 The rest of Harrison's appearance was Halloween and hardware. Nobody had ever borne heavier handicaps. He had outgrown hindrances faster than the H-G men could think them up. Instead of a little ear radio for a mental handicap, he wore a tremendous pair of earphones, and spectacles with thick wavy lenses. The spectacles were intended to make him not only half blind, but to give him whanging headaches besides.

45 Scrap metal was hung all over him. Ordinarily, there was a certain symmetry, a military neatness to the handicaps issued to strong people, but Harrison looked like a walking junkyard. In the race of life, Harrison carried three hundred pounds.

46 And to offset his good looks, the H-G men required that he wear at all times a red rubber ball for a nose, keep his eyebrows shaved off, and cover his even white teeth with black caps at snaggle-tooth random.

47 "If you see this boy," said the ballerina, "do not—I repeat, do not—try to reason with him."

48 There was the shriek of a door being torn from its hinges.

49 Screams and barking cries of consternation came from the television set. The photograph of Harrison Bergeron on

the screen jumped again and again, as though dancing to the tune of an earthquake.

George Bergeron correctly identified the earthquake, and 50
well he might have—for many was the time his own home had danced to the same crashing tune. "My God—" said George, "that must be Harrison!"

The realization was blasted from his mind instantly by the 51
sound of an automobile collision in his head.

When George could open his eyes again, the photograph 52
of Harrison was gone. A living, breathing Harrison filled the screen.

Clanking, clownish, and huge, Harrison stood in the center 53
of the studio. The knob of the uprooted studio door was still in his hand. Ballerinas, technicians, musicians, and announcers cowered on their knees before him, expecting to die.

"I am the Emperor!" cried Harrison. "Do you hear? I am 54
the Emperor! Everybody must do what I say at once!" He stamped his foot and the studio shook.

"Even as I stand here—" he bellowed, "crippled, hobbled, 55
sickened—I am a greater ruler than any man who ever lived! Now watch me become what I *can* become!"

Harrison tore the straps of his handicap harness like wet 56
tissue paper, tore straps guaranteed to support five thousand pounds.

Harrison's scrap-iron handicaps crashed to the floor. 57

Harrison thrust his thumbs under the bar of the padlock 58
that secured his head harness. The bar snapped like celery. Harrison smashed his headphones and spectacles against the wall.

He flung away his rubber-ball nose, revealed a man that 59
would have awed Thor, the god of thunder.

"I shall now select my Empress!" he said, looking down on 60
the cowering people. "Let the first woman who dares rise to her feet claim her mate and her throne!"

A moment passed, and then a ballerina arose, swaying like 61
a willow.

Harrison plucked the mental handicap from her ear, 62
snapped off her physical handicaps with marvelous delicacy. Last of all, he removed her mask.

She was blindingly beautiful. 63

"Now—" said Harrison, taking her hand, "shall we show 64
the people the meaning of the word dance? Music!" he commanded.

The musicians scrambled back into their chairs, and Har- 65
rison stripped them of their handicaps, too. "Play your best,"

he told them, "and I'll make you barons and dukes and earls."

66 The music began. It was normal at first—cheap, silly, false. But Harrison snatched two musicians from their chairs, waved them like batons as he sang the music as he wanted it played. He slammed them back into their chairs.

67 The music began again and was much improved.

68 Harrison and his Empress merely listened to the music for a while—listened gravely, as though synchronizing their heartbeats with it.

69 They shifted their weights to their toes.

70 Harrison placed his big hands on the girl's tiny waist, letting her sense the weightlessness that would soon be hers.

71 And then, in an explosion of joy and grace, into the air they sprang!

72 Not only were the laws of the land abandoned, but the law of gravity and the laws of motion as well.

73 They reeled, whirled, swiveled, flounced, capered, gamboled, and spun.

74 They leaped like deer on the moon.

75 The studio ceiling was thirty feet high, but each leap brought the dancers nearer to it.

76 It became their obvious intention to kiss the ceiling.

77 They kissed it.

78 And then, neutralizing gravity with love and pure will, they remained suspended in air inches below the ceiling, and they kissed each other for a long, long time.

79 It was then that Diana Moon Glampers, the Handicapper General, came into the studio with a double-barreled ten-gauge shotgun. She fired twice, and the Emperor and the Empress were dead before they hit the floor.

80 Diana Moon Glampers loaded the gun again. She aimed it at the musicians and told them they had ten seconds to get their handicaps back on.

81 It was then that the Bergerons' television tube burned out.

82 Hazel turned to comment about the blackout to George. But George had gone out into the kitchen for a can of beer.

83 George came back in with the beer, paused while a handicap signal shook him up. And then he sat down again. "You been crying?" he said to Hazel.

84 "Yup," she said.

85 "What about?" he said.

86 "I forget," she said. "Something real sad on television."

87 "What was it?" he said.

88 "It's all kind of mixed up in my mind," said Hazel.

89 "Forget sad things," said George.

"I always do," said Hazel. 90

"That's my girl," said George. He winced. There was the sound of a riveting gun in his head. 91

"Gee—I could tell that one was a doozy," said Hazel. 92

"You can say that again," said George. 93

"Gee—" said Hazel, "I could tell that one was a doozy." 94

Paul R. Spickard

Why I Believe in Affirmative Action

Paul R. Spickard, who teaches history at Capital University in Columbus, Ohio, published the following essay in Christianity Today, *an evangelical monthly magazine, in 1986.*

Since the late 1960s, the federal government has required those with whom it does business to act positively to hire and promote people from groups that have been discriminated against. And affirmative action has helped bring a noticeable improvement in the life chances of many blacks, Hispanics, Asians, and white women. 1

More recently, Attorney General Edwin Meese mounted a campaign against affirmative action, calling it "reverse discrimination." Although the Supreme Court handed him a defeat in July, Justice Sandra Day O'Connor's concurring opinion and the justice department's hedging comments show that Meese is unlikely to surrender. 2

I, a white male, have suffered from affirmative action. In 1976, with degrees from Harvard and the University of California, and a teacher's credential, I applied to teach the history of China and Japan. I was told, "I think we'll hire an Asian-American." That stung. I was highly qualified: I spoke Japanese, had lived in Asia, and had studied Asian history for years. What would an American of Asian descent know about Asian history that I did not? The school could not find a qualified Asian, and I drove a truck for a living. 3

Five years later it happened again. A major university told me they would love to hire me. But the department was all white and all male, and they were looking to hire a minority woman. 4

I have been denied the chance to make a living because I am white and male. Yet I remain convinced that affirmative action is good social policy. 5

6 It is also a scriptural imperative in our social situation. Why? My understanding begins with Philippians 2:3–6, where Paul reminds us that Jesus did not look to his own benefit but spent himself for us, and he tells us that as Christians we have a responsibility to look out for other people's welfare before our own. Affirmative action is an appropriate way to do that.

7 America's initial push for equal opportunity resulted in very little progress. Blacks and others had not just been shut out of jobs, but had also been shut out of the education necessary to qualify for jobs.

8 Then Lyndon Johnson argued that an equal race is not necessarily a fair one. You don't starve somebody for a month, break both his legs, put him at the starting line and say, "May the best man win." The long history of oppression had left some categories of people unable to compete.

9 Fortunately, the federal government's commitment to affirmative action created a mentality in society that it was valuable to hire minorities. This wider conviction has played an important part in improving the life chances of some women and minorities.

10 Isn't all this unfair? It felt like discrimination to me. But consider: I come from generations of moderate wealth. My family came over on the *Mayflower* and made money in the slave trade. Doctors, lawyers, judges, and comfortable business people go back several generations in my clan. I was never wealthy, but I could not have devoted myself to college and graduate school without support from my family and a timely inheritance. I am standing on the shoulders of my ancestors and their discriminatory behavior.

11 Contrast my experience with that of a Chicano friend, whose immigrant father had a fourth-grade education and ran a grocery store. Without affirmative action and the social commitment it symbolizes, my friend might not have gone to Amherst, nor to Stanford law school. He might not have found a job with a major law firm, nor as a congressional aide. He is talented and has worked hard. But without affirmative action he might well be back in Modesto pumping gas. Our society would be poorer for the loss of his skills.

12 Affirmative action's job is not yet done. Black men still earn only about 76 percent as much as white men in the same job categories. The gap between white males and others is far from closed.

Everything costs something. In the 1960s, when the economy was expanding, affirmative action seemed painless. But in the middle 1970s we realized that if some were to gain then others must lose. That was when affirmative action began to be called "reverse discrimination" (implying that there is a normal, proper direction for discrimination), and we white males began to defend our privileges. 13

Of course, affirmative action cannot do the whole job. It can do little about residential, religious, and educational segregation. But if genuine equal opportunity is to be achieved, affirmative action must be part of the picture. Some white males will get the short end of the stick, just as we have given the short end to others for dozens of generations. 14

Affirmative action may not always be fair. But I'm willing to take second best if overall fairness is achieved. After all, for biblical Christians, fairness—often translated in our Bibles as "justice" or "righteousness"—is a fundamental principle by which God calls us to live. And affirmative action is an appropriate part of a larger program aimed at achieving the godly goal of putting others' welfare before my own. 15

Shelby Steele

A Negative Vote on Affirmative Action

A professor of English at San Jose State University, Shelby Steele frequently writes essays on the topic of race in America—particularly on the causes of (and potential cures for) the friction between black and white Americans. He collected many of those essays (including the one printed here) in his 1990 book The Content of Our Character. *The article first appeared in* The New York Times Magazine *in 1990.*

In a few short years, when my two children will be applying to college, the affirmative-action policies by which most universities offer black students some form of preferential treatment will present me with a dilemma. I am a middle-class black, a college professor, far from wealthy, but also well removed from the kind of deprivation that would qualify my children for the label "disadvantaged." Both of them have endured racial insensitivity from whites. They have been called names, have suffered slights and have experienced first hand the peculiar malevolence that racism 1 brings out of people. Yet they have never experienced racial discrimination, have never been stopped by their race on any path they have chosen to follow. Still, their society now tells them that if they will only designate themselves as black on their college applications, they will probably do better in the college lottery than if they conceal this fact. I think there is something of a Faustian bargain in this.

2 Of course many blacks and a considerable number of whites would say that I was sanctimoniously making affirmative action into a test of character. They would say that this small preference is the meagerest recompense for centuries of unrelieved oppression. And to these arguments other very obvious facts must be added. In America, many marginally competent or flatly incompetent whites are hired every day—some because their white skin suits the conscious or unconscious racial preference of their employers. The white children of alumni are often grandfathered into elite universities in what can only be seen as a residual benefit of historic white privilege. Worse, white incompetence is always an individual matter, but for blacks it is often confirmation of ugly stereotypes. Given that unfairness cuts both ways, doesn't it only balance the scales of history, doesn't this repair, in a small way, the systematic denial under which my children's grandfather lived out his days?

3 In theory, affirmative action certainly has all the moral symmetry that fairness requires. It is reformist and corrective, even repentent and redemptive. And I would never sneer at these good intentions. Born in the late 1940's in Chicago, I started my education (a charitable term, in this case) in a segregated school, and suffered all the indignities that come to blacks in a segregated society. My father, born in the South, made it only to the third grade before the white man's fields took permanent priority over his formal education. And though he educated himself into an advanced reader with an almost professorial authority, he could only drive a truck for a living, and never earned more than $90 a week in his entire life. So yes, it is crucial to my sense of citizenship, to my ability to identify with the spirit and the interests of America, to know that this country, however imperfectly, recognizes its past sins and wishes to correct them.

4 Yet good intentions can blind us to the effects they generate when implemented. In our society affirmative action is, among other things, a testament to white good will and to black power, and in the midst of these heavy investments its effects can be hard to see. But after 20 years of implemen-

tation I think that affirmative action has shown itself to be more bad than good and that blacks—whom I will focus on in this essay—now stand to lose more from it than they gain.

In talking with affirmative-action administrators and with 5
blacks and whites in general, I found that supporters of affirmative action focus on its good intentions and detractors emphasize its negative effects. It was virtually impossible to find people outside either camp. The closest I came was a white male manager at a large computer company who said, "I think it amounts to reverse discrimination, but I'll put up with a little of that for a little more diversity." But this only makes him a half-hearted supporter of affirmative action. I think many people who don't really like affirmative action support it to one degree or another anyway.

I believe they do this because of what happened to white 6
and black Americans in the crucible of the 1960's, when whites were confronted with their racial guilt and blacks tasted their first real power. In that stormy time white absolution and black power coalesced into virtual mandates for society. Affirmative action became a meeting ground for those mandates in the law. At first, this meant insuring equal opportunity. The 1964 civil-rights bill was passed on the understanding that equal opportunity would not mean racial preference. But in the late 60's and early 70's, affirmative action underwent a remarkable escalation of its mission from simple anti-discrimination enforcement to social engineering by means of quotas, goals, timetables, set-asides and other forms of preferential treatment.

Legally, this was achieved through a series of executive 7
orders and Equal Employment Opportunity Commission guidelines that allowed racial imbalances in the workplace to stand as proof of racial discrimination. Once it could be assumed that discrimination explained racial imbalances, it became easy to justify group remedies to presumed discrimination rather than the normal case-by-case redress.

Even though blacks had made great advances during the 8
60's without quotas, the white mandate to achieve a new racial innocence and the black mandate to gain power, which came to a head in the very late 60's, could no longer be satisfied by anything less than racial preferences. I don't think these mandates, in themselves, were wrong, because whites clearly needed to do better by blacks and blacks needed more real power in society. But as they came together in affirmative action, their effect was to distort our understanding of racial discrimination. By making black the

color of preference, these mandates have reburdened society with the very marriage of color and preference (in reverse) that we set out to eradicate.

9 When affirmative action grew into social engineering, diversity became a golden word. Diversity is a term that applies democratic principles to races and cultures rather than to citizens, despite the fact that there is nothing to indicate that real diversity is the same thing as proportionate representation. Too often the result of this, on campuses for example, has been a democracy of colors rather than of people, an artificial diversity that gives the appearance of an educational parity between black and white students that has not yet been achieved in reality. Here again, racial preferences allow society to leapfrog over the difficult problem of developing blacks to parity with whites and into a cosmetic diversity that covers the blemish of disparity—a full six years after admission, only 26 to 28 percent of blacks graduate from college.

10 Racial representation is not the same thing as racial development. Representation can be manufactured; development is always hard earned. But it is the music of innocence and power that we hear in affirmative action that causes us to cling to it and to its distracting emphasis on representation. The fact is that after 20 years of racial preferences the gap between median incomes of black and white families is greater than it was in the 1970's. None of this is to say that blacks don't need policies that insure our right to equal opportunity, but what we need more of is the development that will let us take advantage of society's efforts to include us.

11 I think one of the most troubling effects of racial preferences for blacks is a kind of demoralization. Under affirmative action, the quality that earns us preferential treatment is an implied inferiority. However this inferiority is explained—and it is easily enough explained by the myriad deprivations that grew out of our oppression—it is still inferiority. There are explanations and then there is the fact. And the fact must be borne by the individual as a condition apart from the explanation, apart even from the fact that others like himself also bear this condition. In integrated situations in which blacks must compete with whites who may be better prepared, these explanations may quickly wear thin and expose the individual to racial as well as personal self-doubt. (Of course whites also feel doubt, but only personally, not racially.)

12 What this means in practical terms is that when blacks deliver themselves into integrated situations they encounter a nasty little reflex in whites, a mindless, atavistic reflex that

responds to the color black with negative stereotypes, such as intellectual ineptness. I think this reflex embarrasses most whites today and thus it is usually quickly repressed. On an equally atavistic level, the black will be aware of the reflex his color triggers and will feel a stab of horror at seeing himself reflected in this way. He, too, will do a quick repression, but a lifetime of such stabbings is what constitutes his inner realm of racial doubt. Even when the black sees no implication of inferiority in racial preferences, he knows that whites do, so that—consciously or unconsciously—the result is virtually the same. The effect of preferential treatment—the lowering of normal standards to increase black representation—puts blacks at war with an expanded realm of debilitating doubt, so that the doubt itself becomes an unrecognized preoccupation that undermines their ability to perform, especially in integrated situations.

I believe another liability of affirmative action comes from the fact that it indirectly encourages blacks to exploit their own past victimization. Like implied inferiority, victimization is what justifies preference, so that to receive the benefits of preferential treatment one must, to some extent, become invested in the view of one's self as a victim. In this way, affirmative action nurtures a victim-focused identity in blacks and sends us the message that there is more power in our past suffering than in our present achievements. 13

When power itself grows out of suffering, blacks are encouraged to expand the boundaries of what qualifies as racial oppression, a situation that can lead us to paint our victimization in vivid colors even as we receive the benefits of preference. The same corporations and institutions that give us preference are also seen as our oppressors. At Stanford University, minority group students—who receive at least the same financial aid as whites with the same need—recently took over the president's office demanding, among other things, more financial aid. 14

But I think one of the worst prices that blacks pay for preference has to do with an illusion. I saw this illusion at work recently in the mother of a middle-class black student who was going off to his first semester of college: "They owe us this, so don't think for a minute that you don't belong there." This is the logic by which many blacks, and some whites, justify affirmative action—it is something "owed," a form of reparation. But this logic overlooks a much harder and less digestible reality, that it is impossible to repay blacks living today for the historic suffering of the race. If all 15 blacks were given a million dollars tomorrow it would not amount to a dime on the dollar for three centuries of oppression, nor would it dissolve the residues of that oppression that we still carry today. The concept of historic reparation grows out of man's need to impose on the world a degree of justice that simply does not exist. Suffering can be endured and overcome, it cannot be repaid. To think otherwise is to prolong the suffering.

16 Several blacks I spoke with said they were still in favor of affirmative action because of the "subtle" discrimination blacks were subject to once they were on the job. One photojournalist said, "They have ways of ignoring you." A black female television producer said: "You can't file a lawsuit when your boss doesn't invite you to the insider meetings without ruining your career. So we still need affirmative action." Others mentioned the infamous "glass ceiling" through which blacks can see the top positions of authority but never reach them. But I don't think racial preferences are a protection against this subtle discrimination; I think they contribute to it.

17 In any workplace, racial preferences will always create two-tiered populations composed of preferreds and unpreferred. In the case of blacks and whites, for instance, racial preferences imply that whites are superior just as they imply that blacks are inferior. They not only reinforce America's oldest racial myth but, for blacks, they have the effect of stigmatizing the already stigmatized.

18 I think that much of the "subtle" discrimination that blacks talk about is often (not always) discrimination against the stigma of questionable competence that affirmative action marks blacks with. In this sense, preferences make scapegoats of the very people they seek to help. And it may be that at a certain level employers impose a glass ceiling, but this may not be against the race so much as against the race's reputation for having advanced by color as much as by competence. This ceiling is the point at which corporations shift the emphasis from color to competency and stop playing the affirmative-action game. Here preference backfires for blacks and becomes a taint that holds them back. Of course one could argue that this taint, which is after all in the minds of whites, becomes nothing more than an excuse to discriminate against blacks. And certainly the result is the same in either case—blacks don't get past the glass ceiling. But this argument does not get around the fact that racial preferences now taint this color with a new theme of suspicion that makes

blacks even more vulnerable to discrimination. In this crucial yet gray area of perceived competence, preferences make whites look better than they are and blacks worse, while doing nothing whatever to stop the very real discrimination that blacks may encounter. I don't wish to justify the glass ceiling here, but only suggest the very subtle ways that affirmative action revives rather than extinguishes the old rationalizations for racial discrimination.

I believe affirmative action is problematic in our society 19
because we have demanded that it create parity between the races rather than insure equal opportunity. Preferential treatment does not teach skills, or educate, or instill motivation. It only passes out entitlement, by color, a situation that in my profession has created an unrealistically high demand for black professors. The social engineer's assumption is that this high demand will inspire more blacks to earn Ph.D's and join the profession. In fact, the number of blacks earning Ph.D's has declined in recent years. Ph.D's must be developed from preschool on. They require family and community support. They must acquire an entire system of values that enables them to work hard while delaying gratification.

It now seems clear that the Supreme Court, in a series of 20
recent decisions, is moving away from racial preferences. It has disallowed preferences except in instances of "identified discrimination," eroded the precedent that statistical racial imbalances are prima facie evidence of discrimination, and, in effect, granted white males the right to challenge consent degrees that use preference to achieve racial balances in the workplace. Referring to this and other Supreme Court decisions, one civil-rights leader said, "Night has fallen . . . as far as civil rights are concerned." But I am not so sure. The effect of these decisions is to protect the constitutional rights of everyone rather than to take rights away from blacks. Night has fallen on racial preferences, not on the fundamental rights of black Americans. The reason for this shift, I believe, is that the white mandate for absolution from past racial sins has weakened considerably in the 1980's. Whites are now less willing to endure unfairness to themselves in order to grant special entitlements to blacks, even when those entitlements are justified in the name of past suffering. Yet the black mandate for more power in society has remained unchanged. And I think part of the anxiety many blacks feel over these decisions has to do with the loss of black power that they may signal.

But the power we've lost by these decisions is really only 21
the power that grows out of our victimization. This is not a

very substantial or reliable power, and it is important that we know this so we can focus more exclusively on the kind of development that will bring enduring power. There is talk now that Congress may pass new legislation to compensate for these new limits on affirmative action. If this happens, I hope the focus will be on development and anti-discrimination, rather than entitlement, on achieving racial parity rather than jerry-building racial diversity.

22 But if not preferences, what? The impulse to discriminate *is* subtle and cannot be ferreted out unless its many guises are made clear to people. I think we need social policies that are committed to two goals: the educational and economic development of disadvantaged people regardless of race and the eradication from our society—through close monitoring and severe sanctions—of racial, ethnic or gender discrimination. Preferences will not get us to either of these goals, because they tend to benefit those who are not disadvantaged—middle-class white women and middle-class blacks—and attack one form of discrimination with another. Preferences are inexpensive and carry the glamour of good intentions—change the numbers and the good deed is done. To be against them is to be unkind. But I think the unkindest cut is to bestow on children like my own an undeserved advantage while neglecting the development of those disadvantaged children in the poorer sections of my city who will most likely never be in a position to benefit from a preference. Give my children fairness; give disadvantaged children a better shot at development—better elementary and secondary schools, job training, safer neighborhoods, better financial assistance for college and so on. A smaller percentage of black high school graduates go to college today than 15 years ago; more black males are in prison, jail or in some other way under the control of the criminal-justice system than in college. This despite racial preferences.

23 The mandates of black power and white absolution out of which preferences emerged were not wrong in themselves. What was wrong was that both races focused more on the goals of those mandates than on the means to the goals. Blacks can have no real power without taking responsibility for their own educational and economic development. Whites can have no racial innocence without earning it by eradicating discrimination and helping the disadvantaged to develop. Because we ignored the means, the goals have not been reached and the real work remains to be done.

Catharine Stimpson

It Is Time to Rethink Affirmative Action

Catherine Stimpson, a widely published English professor, is also Dean of the Graduate School at Rutgers University. The following article appeared in The Chronicle of Higher Education, *a weekly newspaper designed for college professors and administrators, in January 1992.*

On December 4, Secretary of Education Lamar Alexander proposed new rules governing the legality of scholarships for minority students. They declare campus diversity a good thing, but race-specific scholarships a bad thing—unless a private donor or Congress creates them. 1

Mr. Alexander's action leaves unanswered questions about civil-rights law, educational policy, and the politics of the ruling. By the first week in March, responses to the proposals must be in. Yet no matter what they are, no matter what the Secretary's final regulations ultimately are, the issue of affirmative action will still be with us—because educational inequities will still be with us. 2

The birth of affirmative action in the late 1960's and 1970's was a struggle. Its most principled opponents argued honorably that American law and public policy ought to be color-blind. Anything that was limited to one race, no matter how well intentioned, was wrong. Unfortunately, not every opponent was principled. The argument about affirmative action also was divisive and prejudicial, a misinformation campaign that demonstrated more hostility about a remedy for injustice than about the injustice itself. 3

After the 1970's, the struggle became less rancorous in higher education. Indeed, during the 1980's, the Department of Education received fewer than a dozen inquiries or complaints about race-specific scholarships. However, during the same decade, the opposition to affirmative action gained two weapons. First, the elections of Ronald Reagan and George Bush to the Presidency permitted lower federal officials to translate ideological opposition to affirmative action into practice. Second, some highly accomplished African-American intellectuals began to criticize the programs that had, ironically, often aided their education. 4

Of these writers, I find the most persuasive to be Stephen 5

L. Carter, the Yale School professor and author of *Reflections of an Affirmative Action Baby* (Basic Books, 1991). Speaking to a black audience, he defends the right to dissent from communal orthodoxies. Speaking to people like me, he claims that affirmative action has had its day. To its credit, affirmative action has nurtured a black middle class, Carter says, but its members pay the price of being stigmatized as people who made it only because of that remedy.

6 Given the persistence of the resistance to affirmative action, it might be tempting to toss up one's compliance plans and agree that affirmative action has gone astray, over the top, beyond the pale. Certainly, it has not brought a paradise of equity, and its administration has often been clumsy. Institutions have made some bad, cynical faculty hires and admitted some students without sufficient preparation and support. A very few faculty members and students have ripped off the system by manipulating it, for example by playing on racial guilt. I have occasionally groaned at the ways of bureaucracy as I have read and written affirmative-action reports.

7 Despite all this, affirmative action has not gone astray. If anything, it has been driven astray by sloppiness, indifference, and belligerence. I have heard faculty members and administrators say biased things about women and minorities and deliberately ignorant things about affirmative action, such as "it's forcing quotas down my throat"—their behavior revealing why affirmative action was necessary in the first place. I have listened to members of the same groups rationalize their inability to hire anyone other than a clone by blaming a "limited pool" of minority candidates or the "dual career" demands of women of all races.

8 The important reality is this: Affirmative action has worked. To be sure, it has lumbered and creaked. It has worked slowly, unevenly, and incompletely—particularly when support for equity has been mean and opposition to it lavish. Arguably, it has worked least well for black males. Nevertheless, affirmative action has served us.

9 The process of doing affirmative action has demonstrated that the pool of qualified candidates was wider and deeper than the academy had previously admitted. The process also has released talent and industry. Think, for example, of the career of Dolores E. Cross. At 19, she was married, a clerk at the Newark Board of Education, pregnant with her second child. She entered college in 1955, received her Ph.D. in

1971, and is now the president of Chicago State University.

Moreover, as the heroic example of President Cross shows, the academy now has greater diversity among students, staffs, and faculties. In 1990, the United States awarded the greatest number of doctorates ever: 36,027. From 1960 to 1990, the proportion of women earning them increased from 11 per cent to 36 per cent, including more women from every racial group. 10

Yet, even if affirmative action has not gone astray, it is time to rethink it. This proposal is not a craven submission to the anti-affirmative actioneers but the recognition of another reality: Affirmative action was the creation of a historical period, meant to heal its historical problems. Then, despite the passage of several civil-rights laws, virtually no members of minority groups and only a handful of white women were being allowed to advance in predominantly white institutions. This period is receding. The problems have mutated. One reason they have done so is that affirmative action did work to a degree, because it did help to nurse affirmative-action babies. 11

In 1975, the Carnegie Council on Policy Studies in Higher Education foresaw such an evolution. Its valuable study, "Making Affirmative Action Work in Higher Education," describes affirmative action as a "transition period between actual past deficiencies of major proportions and potential future achievements of true equality of opportunity." Because affirmative action *is* such a transitional program, the book concluded that it needs periodic reviews to see "what amount and kind of federal involvement is still necessary." 12

In the harsh early light of the 1990's, a broad review is due, a rethinking that avoids both the easy comforts of hysteria about any change and the denunciation of affirmative action's mere existence. Rethinking entails seven steps: 13

- Reinvigorating the purpose of affirmative action, which was to remove prejudice and open the gates of higher education. Today, because class and the economy, perhaps as much as race, are closing these gates, the process should take a student's economic background into account, in addition to minority status.
- Enlarging the meaning of affirmative action. Narrowly construed, it is a legally mandated employment

practice. Broadly construed, it is the umbrella term for all the programs that reflect a community's commitment to equity. The broader the construction, the more successful the practices for advancing underrepresented groups seem to become.

- Creating a national "equity ledger" setting out what equity means in student admissions, financial aid, and retention and what it means in employment. We should rigorously examine *all* the preferences that now exist in these areas. We would then ask who breathes deeply enough of the air of equity on that fabled site, the level playing field, to drop the oxygen mask of affirmative action—and, crucially, who does not.
- Strengthening the links among various kinds of schools and colleges. Disadvantaged junior-high and high-school students feel more comfortable in college if they have some experience of college—even a visit—before they get into first-year English. Community-college students need good transfer programs to four-year institutions; many poor and/or minority students are in community colleges. For example, the number of Asian Americans enrolled in all higher education grew from 198,000 in 1976 to 497,000 in 1988. Most of these students attend public institutions, and almost one-half are in a two-year college.
- Nurturing the historically black colleges and universities. Of the baccalaureate institutions in the United States whose minority graduates went on to earn Ph.D.'s between 1986 and 1990, 17 of the top 20 were historically black colleges and universities. The other three were urban institutions: Wayne State University, City College of the City University of New York, and New York University. At Howard and Hampton, Spelman and Fisk are many of the next generation of black scholars, researchers, and teachers.
- Remembering the obvious, that the purpose of higher education is education. Thus, rethinking affirmative action means accepting the new scholarship about women and gender, race and ethnicity, domination and freedom, class and sexuality. The syllabi of an equitable community will reflect these intellectual movements, not because faculties are filled with Dr.

Feelgoods of thought, but because they are thoughtful.

- Expanding, with more passion than many of us in higher education have shown, affirmative action for children. Any rethinking for higher education is chaff unless we feed, shelter, love, and educate all children. In my neighborhood is Scotty, a retired man and shrewd observer, who gets his coffee and hangs out at the delicatessen next to my Victorian house. For two years, Scotty has babysat for a husky, bright little kid, Luther, the child of a single, working mother. Recently, when I had not seen Luther with Scotty for several days, I asked where Luther was. "Oh," said Scotty, with relief, pride, and happiness, "he got into the Head Start program. He's in that Head Start. He's on his way." Here, in my neighborhood, is a dollop of affirmative action for children. How many neighborhoods have programs for a Luther?

In Adrienne Rich's newest book, she has a title poem, "An 14
Atlas of the Difficult World." There she writes of the waste of "those who could bind, join, reweave, cohere, replenish . . . those needed to teach, advise, persuade, weigh arguments/ those urgently needed for the work of perception/work of the poet, the astronomer, the historian, the architect of new streets."

Affirmative action is a meritorious plan against obscene 15
waste. We need to rethink it so that it can better bind and reweave the present. If we fail to do so, we will have pushed it further astray, to be devoured by its enemies or to atrophy on a diet of inertia.

Clarence Thomas

Climb the Jagged Mountain

Clarence Thomas (born 1948 in Savannah, Georgia) was appointed to the Supreme Court during the presidency of George Bush. After confirmation hearings that became very stormy on account of his conservative views (including those on affirmative action) and the sexual harassment charges of Anita Hill, he joined the Court in 1991. The following article was published in The New York Times *in July 1991, just before the hearings; but it was originally presented, in a somewhat longer form, as a commencement address at Savannah State College in Georgia in June 1985. At the time, Thomas was serving as chair of the Equal Employment Opportunity Commission in Washington, DC, which is responsible for helping to enforce fair employment legislation.*

1 I grew up here in Savannah. I was born not far from here (in Pinpoint). I am a child of those marshes, a son of this soil. I am a descendant of the slaves whose labors made the dark soil of the South productive. I am the great-great-grandson of a freed slave, whose enslavement continued after my birth. I am the product of hatred and love—the hatred of the social and political structure which dominated the segregated, hate-filled city of my youth, and the love of some people—my mother, my grandparents, my neighbors and relatives—who said by their actions, "You can make it, but first you must endure."

2 You can survive, but first you must endure. You can live, but first you must endure. You must endure the unfairness. You must endure the hatred. You must endure the bigotry. You must endure the segregation. You must endure the indignities.

3 I stand before you as one who had the same beginning as yourselves—as one who has walked a little farther down the road, climbed a little higher up the mountain. I come back to you, who must now travel this road and climb this jagged, steep mountain that lies ahead. I return as a messenger—a front-runner, a scout. What lies ahead of you is even tougher than what is now behind you.

4 That mean, callous world out there is still very much filled with discrimination. It still holds out a different life for

those who do not happen to be the right race or the right sex. It is a world in which the "haves" continue to reap more dividends than the "have-nots."

You will enter a world in which more than one-half of all 5
black children are born primarily to youthful mothers and out of wedlock. You will enter a world in which the black teenage unemployment rate as always is more than double that of white teenagers. Any discrimination, like sharp turns in a road, becomes critical because of the tremendous speed at which we are traveling into the high-tech world of a service economy.

There is a tendency among young, upwardly mobile, 6
intelligent minorities to forget. We forget the sweat of our forefathers. We forget the blood of the marchers, the prayers and hope of our race. We forget who brought us into this world. We overlook who put food in our mouths and clothes on our backs. We forget commitment to excellence. We procreate with pleasure and retreat from the responsibilities of the babies we produce.

We subdue, we seduce, but we don't respect ourselves, our 7
women, our babies. How do we expect a race that has been thrown into the gutter of socioeconomic indicators to rise above these humiliating circumstances if we hide from responsibility for our own destiny?

The truth of the matter is we have become more in- 8
terested in designer jeans and break dancing than we are in obligations and responsibilities.

Over the past 15 years, I have watched as others have 9
jumped quickly at the opportunity to make excuses for black Americans. It is said that blacks cannot start businesses because of discrimination. But I remember businesses on East Broad and West Broad that were run in spite of bigotry. It is said that we can't learn because of bigotry. But I know for a fact that tens of thousands of blacks were educated at historically black colleges, in spite of discrimination. We learned to read in spite of segregated libraries. We built homes in spite of segregated neighborhoods. We learned how to play basketball (and did we ever learn!), even though we couldn't go to the N.B.A.

We have lost something. We look for role models in all the 10
wrong places. We refuse to reach back in our not too distant past for the lessons and values we need to carry us into the

uncertain future. We ignore what has permitted blacks in this country to survive the brutality of slavery and the bitter rejection of segregation. We overlook the reality of positive values and run to the mirage of promises, visions and dreams.

11 I dare not come to this city, which only two decades ago clung so tenaciously to segregation, bigotry and Jim Crow-ism, to convince you of the fairness of this society. My memory is too precise, my recollection, too keen, to venture down that path of self-delusion. I am not blind to our history—nor do I turn a deaf ear to the pleas and cries of black Americans. Often I must struggle to contain my outrage at what has happened to black Americans—what continues to happen—what we let happen and what we do to ourselves.

12 If I let myself go, I would rage in the words of Frederick Douglass: "At a time like this, scorching irony, not convincing, argument, is needed. Oh! Had I the ability, and could reach the nation's ear, I would today pour out a fiery stream of biting ridicule, blasting reproach, withering sarcasm and stern rebuke. For it is not light that is needed, but fire; it is not the gentle shower, but thunder. We need the storm, the whirlwind and the earthquake."

13 I often hear rosy platitudes about this country—much of which is true. But how are we black Americans to feel when we have so little in a land with so much? How is black America to respond to the celebration of the wonders of this great nation?

14 In 1964, when I entered the seminary, I was the only black in my class and one of two in the school. A year later, I was the only one in the school. Not a day passed that I was not pricked by prejudice.

15 But I had an advantage over black students and kids today. I had never heard any excuses made. Nor had I seen my role models take comfort in excuses. The women who worked in those kitchens and waited on the bus knew it was prejudice which caused their plight, but that didn't stop them from working.

16 My grandfather knew why his business wasn't more successful, but that didn't stop him from getting up at 2 in the morning to carry ice, wood and fuel oil. Sure, they knew it was bad. They knew all too well that they were held back by prejudice. But they weren't pinned down by it. They fought discrimination under W. W. Law [a Georgia civil

rights leader] and the N.A.A.C.P. Equally important, they fought against the awful effects of prejudice by doing all they could do in spite of this obstacle.

They could still send their children to school. They could still respect and help each other. They could still moderate their use of alcohol. They could still be decent, law-abiding citizens. 17

I had the benefit of people who knew they had to walk a straighter line, climb a taller mountain and carry a heavier load. They took all that segregation and prejudice would allow them and at the same time fought to remove these awful barriers. 18

You all have a much tougher road to travel. Not only do you have to contend with the ever-present bigotry, you must do so with a recent tradition that almost requires you to wallow in excuses. You now have a popular national rhetoric which says that you can't learn because of racism, you can't raise the babies you make because of racism, you can't get up in the mornings because of racism. You commit crimes because of racism. Unlike me, you must not only overcome the repressiveness of racism, you must also overcome the lure of excuses. You have twice the job I had. 19

Do not be lured by sirens and purveyors of misery who profit from constantly regurgitating all that is wrong with black Americans and blaming these problems on others. Do not succumb to this temptation of always blaming others. 20

Do not become obsessed with all that is wrong with our race. Rather, become obsessed with looking for solutions to our problems. Be tolerant of all positive ideas; their number is much smaller than the countless number of problems to be solved. We need *all* the hope we can get. 21

Most importantly, draw on that great lesson and those positive role models who have gone down this road before us. We are badgered and pushed by our friends and peers to do unlike our parents and grandparents—we are told not to be old-fashioned. But they have weathered the storm. It is up to us now to learn how. Countless hours of research are spent to determine why blacks fail or why we commit crimes. Why can't we spend a few hours learning how those closest to us have survived and helped us get this far? 22

As your front-runner, I have gone ahead and taken a long, hard look. I have seen two roads from my perch a few 23 humble feet above the madding crowd. On the first, a race of people is rushing mindlessly down a highway of sweet, intoxicating destruction, with all its bright lights and grand promises constructed by social scientists and politicians. To the side, there is a seldom used, overgrown road leading through the valley of life with all its pitfalls and obstacles. It is the road—the old-fashioned road—traveled by those who endured slavery, who endured Jim Crowism, who endured hatred. It is the road that might reward hard work and discipline, that might reward intelligence, that might be fair and provide equal opportunity. But there are no guarantees.

24 You must choose. The lure of the highway is seductive and enticing. But the destruction is certain. To travel the road of hope and opportunity is hard and difficult, but there is a chance that you might somehow, some way, with the help of God, make it.

Julianne Malveaux

Why Are the Black Conservatives All Men?

An activist, economist, and journalist with a special interest in the economic condition of African-American women, Julianne Malveaux teaches at the University of California at Berkeley. The following article appeared in Ms. *magazine (which prints fiction and nonfiction of interest to women) in 1991.*

1 Michael L. Williams, the Department of Education's Assistant Secretary of Civil Rights, grabbed headlines last year with his independent ruling that college scholarships awarded on the basis of race were illegal. Williams joined the parade of black men—economists Thomas Sowell, Walter Williams, and Glenn Loury, and English professor Shelby Steele—who have bashed affirmative action, minority scholarships, and social programs. Many of these men were beneficiaries of the very programs they now oppose.

What do they hope to accomplish by dismantling programs that offer African Americans an opportunity to close gaps created by decades of discrimination? And why are these publicly visible conservatives all men?

More than 25 years after the passage of the Civil Rights Act, the race debate continues. Gaps persist. Black family income is less than 60 percent of white family income. The black poverty rate is triple the white rate. Black student undergraduate enrollment, 1.2 million in 1986, represented about 12 percent of total enrollment. Since the 1970s there has been little economic progress for blacks relative to whites, and a recent study by economist Bennett Harrison showed that a third of all black males ages 25 to 34, and one fifth of all black graduates, earned less than $12,000 in 1987. 2

There has been selective progress. One in ten black families (compared to one in four white) have earnings above $50,000. African Americans have entered a number of fields previously closed to them. A highly visible group of black people, mostly concentrated in the arts, entertainment, and sports, are symbols of this progress; indeed, their presence is often used to suggest that other blacks who aren't making it simply aren't trying hard enough. But this ignores economics, and most recent racial tensions are a function of transformations in the U.S. economic structure, where productivity and wages grew half as slowly in the 1975–90 period as in the previous 15 years. The shift from a manufacturing to a service economy has cut the number of "good jobs" drastically. The Reagan Revolution worked. Unions are weaker, employers offer fewer benefits, and part-time employment opportunities grew faster than full-time ones in 1985–89. A bad situation, at least for the working class and the middle class, has been getting worse. 3

Still, some blacks are succeeding, and it comes back to that in many people's minds: if whites are doing poorly, why aren't blacks doing worse? (They are: in December 1990 when overall unemployment was 6.1 percent, black unemployment was 12.2 percent.) What advantage do these blacks have? It must be affirmative action, or quotas, those dreaded words used to conjure up visions of unqualified blacks invading positions of power. But there has never been any law mandating quotas (defined as a proportional share of opportunities). Nor does affirmative action mean unqualified people placed in jobs; it means employers (and educational institutions) do outreach and solicit applica- 4 tions from people they never approached before; it means communicating to potential applicants that an educational or employment institution is now open; it may mean offering such incentives as scholarships to signal openness.

5 What about the charge that black students are less "qualified"? Do we mean by the highest standardized test score, though organizations like the Center for Women Policy Studies have shown that such tests are biased, especially against women of color? Are we saying a student with a 3.8 grade point average (GPA) is less able to handle college work than the student sitting next to her who has a 4.0 GPA?

6 What we really have is an adjustment problem here. The rules on how the goodie pot got divided up were made by the good old boys to serve the good old boys. Word of mouth (with lips moving in those all-male clubs) was as responsible for employment information as open advertising. Enter the Civil Rights Act. The law didn't fix everything, but at least it defined the parameters for lawsuits. We learned you could have more clients and make more sales but still not earn partnership status if your partners didn't think you were "feminine enough" (*Price Waterhouse* v. *Hopkins*). We learned you could be humiliated on the job, and called all kinds of names but have no legal recourse (*Patterson* v. *McLean Credit Union*). We learned when the managers are white and the workers nonwhite, some employers call that "business necessity" (*Ward's Cove* v. *Antonio*). Meanwhile, white men learned how to holler "reverse discrimination."

7 Like them, black men who bash affirmative action use sports metaphors—rules of the game, the level playing field. These black men tend to be high achievers who may feel diminished by the notion they got where they are because of affirmative action. Thus the hankering for a "fair fight" on a "level playing field."

8 How do we define "winners" in a capitalist patriarchy? You either make the most money or have the most status. But after Ronald Reagan made racism acceptable, and George Bush popularized it with his use of Willie Horton as a campaign symbol, no black man can possibly have the status of a white man. Some of the black men who are affirmative action-bashing are really trying to affirm that their status is the result of a fair fight.

9 Given the image of African American men in the media, such an attempt is understandable. Black men have been portrayed as lazy, irresponsible, unemployable, and crimi-

nal. Shelby Steele uses the word "stigma" quite a bit in his book, *The Content of Our Character: A New Vision of Race in America,* and clearly the current media image of black men is incredibly negative. But that negativity comes from without, not from within, and Steele is writing about an inner stigma, inner negativity. He coins phrases like "race fatigue" (tired of talking about race) and "integration shock" (the way black people supposedly behave in integrated settings). Steele assumes that if he feels fatigue and shock stigma, then so must the rest of us. And he is ready to dismantle a policy that has opened doors because he can't stand the stigma.

Steele's book is devoid of socioeconomic content and 10
analysis. Yet I can't recall any nonfiction book by a black writer getting such critical acclaim in the past decade; not Derrick Bell's *And We Are Not Saved*; not John Edgar Wideman's *Philadelphia Fire*. Perhaps Alice Walker's *The Color Purple*, or Toni Morrison's *Beloved* got such a response, but fiction markets are very different from nonfiction.

Why the acclaim? The applause for Steele's book, like the 11
acceptance of Michael Williams' announcement, signals an unspoken agreement between white and black male conservatives. The white men are desperately trying to preserve their perquisites; while the black men are desperately trying to prove they can fight the good fight with white men and win. Women don't see the world in such combative terms. Life is not so clear cut for those well acquainted with the double shift, with dashed hopes and broken promises. Level playing field? Words that don't even enter women's vocabularies.

From a sociopolitical perspective, this is all the more true 12
of African American women. We head 46 percent of all black families and now shoulder multigenerational responsibilities as the caretakers of crack babies, as members of the "sandwich generation." We are often buffers between social and criminal institutions and the black male, the person who negotiates the school system for her children, the juvenile justice system for her adolescent, and the criminal justice system for her brother or spouse. This is not to say that every black woman has to deal with social deviance, or that every black man has problems with institutions. But it is important to note that black women, like most women, bear heavy family responsibility. Society's differential treatment of the black male places an additional burden on the

black woman. And women seem far less concerned about a level playing field than about the location of the field, the context of the race, and the issue of whether hierarchical competition is the best way to do allocations! We are certain that life isn't fair, and few of us see life as a game.

13 There may be black women conservatives, but they are rendered invisible by media that are both racist and sexist. Indeed, as Steele skyrocketed to notoriety, the loudest black female voice in the press was that of Shahrazad Ali, a self-published writer whose poorly written *The Blackman's Guide to Understanding the Blackwoman* suggested that the black man "get control of his woman," and advocated domestic violence. The contrast between Steele and Ali was reminiscent of a decade ago, when the most widely read black writers were William Julius Wilson (*The Declining Significance of Race*) and Michele Wallace (*Black Macho and the Myth of the Superwoman*). Then, as now, black women's voices were heard only when we spoke of black-on-black relationships, especially black male-female relationships. Black men's voices are the ones that are heard in discussions of black-white issues.

14 Black male conservatives are exercising their masculinist game playing prerogatives by closing the door on affirmative action and other social programs. In essence, they are placing a higher priority on rules and appearances than on outcomes and equity. So while a handful of black male conservatives speak of fair competition and level playing fields, a large number of African Americans realize that competitions can't be fair when the rules are rigged, that playing fields can't be leveled when one side is weighed down with generations of inequity, and that in economic crisis those who don't write the rules will end up holding the short end of the stick.

Migdia Chinea-Varela

My Life as a "Twofer"

Migdia Chinea-Varela contributed this essay to Newsweek *on December 26, 1988.*

This Christmas I'll be celebrating my 10th anniversary as a card-carrying member of the film industry's Writers Guild. Ten brain-numbing years and a debilitating employment lull during the five-month-long writers' strike have taken their toll. Last week I'd awakened in what can only be described as profound financial melancholia and was taking inventory of my career alternatives when the phone rang. The caller was a friend at the Writers Guild of America, West. Great news, he said. Several production companies were starting "access" programs for minorities, women, the elderly and the disabled. They'd requested a sampler of scripts ASAP from which to fish out two, maybe *three* writers for free-lance assignments. It could even lead to staff jobs, he said. 1

My imagination flashes to a TV scene in which I grab the lifeline and submit my best script. I subsequently get chosen for a plum writing assignment that quickly turns into a staff position, where I do such a bang-up job that I become the show's producer and an Emmy award winner as well. In real life, however, I thank the guide rep for his good-faith efforts and tell him that my answer is no. Though I helped found and then chaired the Latino writer's committee, I don't want to send in my scripts. 2

Why? Why would anyone pass up such a sweet deal? Everyone knows how tough the film and television industry is. Yet contacts are everything, the insiders say. It helps if you have an agent with hot connections who believes in you and is willing to put in the time required to promote your career. It helps if you attended the "right" film school. It's a matter of timing. It's difficult for everyone. Yes, but consider this—if you're a member of a minority group, the equation should be multiplied by 10; and if you're a minority woman, then add 30 more points. 3

So what's my problem? Why not take advantage of every opportunity that comes my way? The answer is: I've been in this situation before and I don't like the way it makes me 4 feel. There's something almost insulting about these well-meaning affirmative-action searches. In the past I'd always rationalized my participation partly because I needed the break and even more because I needed the money. And as fate would have it, whenever a film- or TV-production company saw fit to round up minorities for a head count, I always came out on top. But the truth is that I've never felt good about it.

5 I've asked myself the obvious questions. Am I being picked for my writing ability, or to fulfill a quota? Have I been selected because I'm a "twofer"—a female Hispanic—or because they were enthralled with my deftly drawn characters and strong, original story line? My writing career, it appears, has taken a particularly tortuous course. I've gone from being a dedicated writer to dedicated *minority* writer, which seems limiting for someone who was first inspired by Woody Allen.

6 Truth is, that even with the aid of special programs, job assignments for writers who fit the "minority" category are inexplicably few and far between. The sad employment statistics reveal that ethnic minorities comprise less than 3 percent of our guild. Those who work do so less frequently and for a lot less money, yet the publicity harvested by the special programs creates the illusion of equal opportunity where very little exists. I don't want to seem overly gloomy. Nevertheless, my work's almost always seen on shows that have a minority star like "The Facts of Life," "What's Happening Now!" and "Punky Brewster."

7 Except for "The Cosby Show," minorities are not being taken seriously enough to write about their real lives outside of the ghetto. Though few of us will admit to it—for fear of speaking out or being tagged as ungrateful—we're reminded of our status in not-so-subtle ways. I remember the time I was waiting for a story meeting where I wanted to pitch several ideas. As I chatted with the production secretary, an aspiring writer herself, I could hear laughter coming from inside the conference room. Finally, the executive in charge stepped outside, followed by five young men. Judging by the look of satisfaction on their faces, it had probably been a profitable session. The executive greeted me effusively by saying, as he turned to the rest of the group, "Meet M-I-G-D-I-A V-A-R-R-R-R-E-L-A. She's one of our minority writers." This comment drew a tight smile from my lips, as one and all present reacted with extravagant expressions of

support. Somehow I knew right then and there that my project would be down for the count. KO'd with kindness.

Killer sharks: More recently, I was spilling my guts to a friend with a recognizable name whose uncle was a famous writer. After sharing my woes and commiserating as fellow writers often do, we parted with that old cliché: "We're in the same boat." Suddenly it dawned on me that hell *no*, we're not even close. We're no doubt on the same ocean, but hardly in the same boat. From where I sit, my friend's being attended to on a luxury liner while I'm all alone paddling a canoe, surrounded by killer sharks and in the midst of a typhoon. 8

I'd like to think that after 10 years of paying my dues as a professional writer that I've earned the right to walk through the front door. After so many years, it's depressing to feel that I have to tag myself a minority as an incentive to those who may hire me. Why can't I get a job on my own merits? Am I destined to spend the rest of my writing career hooked up to these kinds of life-support systems? 9

I'm painfully aware that affirmative action, what little there is of it, may be the only way minorities are given a chance to compete. However, for me, it has become a stigma of sorts. In my view, there can be no affirmative action without segregation—nor any end to the segregation if our names must be kept on separate lists. I'd like to propose instead a simple scenario: a fair job market where employment is commensurate with ability regardless of gender, racial or ethnic background. I make a pitch, they like my story, I get the job. Why not? 10

GAY RIGHTS

Craig R. Dean

Let's Legalize Gay Marriage

Dean, a lawyer and executive director of the Equal Marriage Rights Fund, wrote the following short essay for The New York Times *in 1991.*

1 In November 1990, my lover, Patrick Gill, and I were denied a marriage license because we are gay. In a memorandum explaining the District's decision, the clerk of the court wrote that "the sections of the District of Columbia code governing marriage do not authorize marriage between persons of the same sex." By refusing to give us the same legal recognition that is given to heterosexual couples, the District has degraded our relationship as well as that of every other gay and lesbian couple.

2 At one time, interracial couples were not allowed to marry. Gays and lesbians are still denied this basic civil right in the U.S.—and around the world. Can you imagine the outcry if any other minority group was denied the right to legally marry today?

3 Marriage is more than a piece of paper. It gives societal recognition and legal protection to a relationship. It confers numerous benefits to spouses; in the District alone, there are more than 100 automatic marriage-based rights. In every state in the nation, married couples have the right to be on each other's health, disability, life insurance and pension plans. Married couples receive special tax exemptions, deductions and refunds. Spouses may automatically inherit property and have rights of survivorship that avoid inheritance tax. Though unmarried couples—both gay and heterosexual—are entitled to some of these rights, they are by no means guaranteed.

4 For married couples, the spouse is legally the next of kin

in case of death, medical emergency or mental incapacity. In stark contrast, the family is generally the next of kin for same-sex couples. In the shadow of AIDS, the denial of marriage rights can be even more ominous.

In November, Patrick and I filed suit against the District 5
alleging twofold discrimination. First, the District violated its gender-neutral marriage law. Nowhere does its legal code state that a marriage must consist of a man and a woman or that a married couple may not be of the same sex.

Second, the District violated its own Human Rights Act, 6
the strongest in the nation. According to the act, which was enacted in 1977, "every individual shall have an equal opportunity to participate in the economic, cultural and intellectual life of the District and to have an equal opportunity to participate in all aspects of life."

The law is clearly on our side. In fact, cases interpreting 7
the act have held that the "eradication of sexual orientation discrimination is a compelling governmental interest." Moreover, in 1987 the District Court of Appeals elevated anti-gay bias to the same level as racial and gender discrimination.

Some argue that gay marriage is too radical for society. We disagree. According to a 1989 study by the American Bar Association, eight to 10 million children are currently being reared in three million gay households. Therefore, approximately 6 percent of the U.S. population is made up of gay and lesbian families with children. Why should these families be denied the protection granted to other families?

Allowing gay marriage would strengthen society by in- 9
creasing tolerance. It is paradoxical that mainstream America perceives gays and lesbians as unable to maintain long-term relationships while at the same time denying them the very institutions that stabilize such relationships.

Twenty-five years ago, one-third of the U.S. did not allow 10
interracial marriage. It took a 1967 Supreme Court decision, in *Loving* v. *Virginia,* a case similar to ours, to strike down these discriminatory prohibitions and redefine family and marriage. Then, as now, those who argued against granting civil rights spoke of morality, social tensions and protection of family values. But, now, as then, the real issue is justice vs. oppression.

Jean Bethke Elshtain
Accepting Limits

Ms. Elshtain is a professor of political science at Vanderbilt University and the author of several books, including Power Trips and Other Journeys, *published in 1992. "Accepting Limits" makes use of several paragraphs from* Power Trips, *in particular an essay called "The Family and Civic Life." "Accepting Limits" was published in 1991 in* Commonweal, *a biweekly review of public affairs, religion, and the arts; associated loosely with Catholicism,* Commonweal *has a generally liberal outlook.*

1 Every society embraces an image of a body politic. This complex symbolism incorporates visions and reflections on who is inside and who is outside; on what counts as order and disorder; on what is cherished and what is despised. This imagery is fluid but not, I will argue, entirely up for grabs. For without some continuity in our imagery and concern, we confront a deepening nihilism. In a world of ever-more transgressive enthusiasms, the individual—the self—is more, not less, in thrall to whatever may be the reigning ethos. Ours is a culture whose reigning ethnic is surely individualism and freedom. Great and good things have come from this stress on freedom and from the insistence that there are things that cannot and must not be done for me and to me in the name of some overarching collective. It is, therefore, unsurprising that anything that comes before us in the name of "rights" and "freedom" enjoys a *prima facie* power, something akin to political grace.

2 But perhaps we have reached the breaking point. When Madonna proclaims, in all sincerity, that mock masturbation before tens of thousands is "freedom of expression" on a par, presumably, with the right to petition, assemble, and protest, something seems a bit out of whack—distorted, quirky, not-quite-right. I thought about this sort of thing a lot when I listened to the stories of the "Mothers of the Disappeared" in Argentina and to their invocation of the language of "human rights" as a fundamental immunity—the right not to be tortured and "disappeared." I don't

believe there is a slippery slope from queasiness at, if not repudiation of, public sexual acts for profit, orchestrated masturbation, say, and putting free speech as a fundamental right of free citizens in peril. I don't think the body politic has to be nude and sexually voracious—getting, consuming, demanding pleasure. That is a symbolism that courts nihilism and privatism (however publicly it may be trumpeted) because it repudiates intergenerational, familial, and communal contexts and believes history and tradition are useful only to be trashed. Our culture panders to what social critic John O'Neill calls the "libidinal body," the body that titillates and ravishes and is best embodied as young, thin, antimaternal, calculating, and disconnected. Make no mistake about it: much of the move to imagery of the entitled self and the aspirations to which it gives rise are specifically, deeply, and troublingly antinatal—hostile to the regenerative female body and to the symbolism of social regeneration to which this body is necessarily linked and has, historically, given rise.

Don't get me wrong: not every female body must be a 3
regenerative body. At stake here is not mandating and coercing the lives of individuals but pondering the fate of a society that, more and more, repudiates generativity as an animating image in favor of aspiration without limit of the contractual and "wanting" self. One symbol and reality of the latter is the search for intrusive intervention in human reproducing coming from those able to command the resources of genetic engineers and medical reproduction experts, also, therefore, those who have more clout over what gets lifted up as our culture's dominant sense of itself. One finds more and more the demand that babies can and must be made whenever the want is there. This demandingness, this transformation of human procreation into a technical operation, promotes a project Oliver O'Donovan calls "scientific self-transcendence." The technologizing of birth is antiregenerative, linked as it is to a refusal to accept any natural limits. What technology "can do," and the law permits, we seem ready to embrace. Our ethics rushes to catch up with the rampant rush of our forged and incited desires.

These brief reflections are needed to frame my equally 4
brief comments on the legality, or not, of homosexual marriage. I have long favored domestic partnership possibilities—ways to regularize and stabilize commitments

and relationships. But marriage is not, and never has been, primarily about two people—it is and always has been about the possibility of generativity. Although in any given instance, a marriage might not have led to the raising of a family, whether through choice or often unhappy recognition of, and final reconciliation to, the infertility of one or another spouse, the symbolism of marriage-family as social regenesis is fused in our centuries-old experience with marriage ritual, regulation, and persistence.

5 The point of criticism and contention runs: in defending the family as framed within a horizon of intergenerationality, one privileges a restrictive ideal of sexual and intimate relations. There are within our society, as I already noted, those who believe this society can and should stay equally open to all alternative arrangements, treating "life-styles" as so many identical peas in a pod. To be sure, families in modernity coexist with those who live another way, whether heterosexual and homosexual unions that are by choice or by definition childless; communalists who diminish individual parental authority in favor of the preeminence of the group; and so on.

6 But the recognition and acceptance of plural possibilities does not mean each alternative is equal to every other with reference to specific social goods. No social order has ever existed that did not endorse certain activities and practices as preferable to others. Ethically responsible challenges to our terms of exclusion and inclusion push toward a loosening but not a wholesale negation in our normative endorsement of intergenerational family life. Those excluded by, or who exclude themselves from, the familial intergenerational ideal, should not be denied social space for their own practices. And it is possible that if what were at stake were, say, seeking out and identifying those creations of self that enhance an aesthetic construction of life and sensibility, the romantic bohemian or rebel would get higher marks than the Smith family of Remont, Nebraska. Nevertheless, we should be cautious about going too far in the direction of a wholly untrammeled pluralism lest we become so vapid that we are no longer capable of distinguishing between the moral weightiness of, say, polishing one's Porsche and sitting up all night with an ill child. The intergenerational family, as symbolism of social regenesis, as tough and compelling reality, as defining moral norm, remains central and critical in nurturing recognitions of human frailty,

mortality, and finitude and in inculcating moral limits and constraints. To resolve the untidiness of our public and private relations by either reaffirming unambiguously a set of unitary, authoritative norms or eliminating all such norms as arbitrary is to jeopardize the social goods that democratic and familial authority, paradoxical in relation to one another, promise—to men and women as parents and citizens and to their children.

Michael Cunningham

Taking the Census of Queer Nation

Michael Cunningham is a member of the gay rights group Act Up. A writer of fiction and nonfiction, he contributed the following essay to Mother Jones *in the summer of 1992.* Mother Jones, *published bi-monthly, is a liberal, irreverent magazine of commentary on current affairs. (Some of the names of people in this essay—the ones identified by first name only—have been changed.)*

Tim and I were walking home late from St. Vincent's Hospital in New York City, where we'd been sitting with what remained of a friend named John. We went every night, although John had been unconscious for nearly a week. We hoped that if we held his hand and spoke to him something might still register. Doctors suspect that hearing is the last sense to go. You should talk to the dying. 1

As Tim and I walked home through the streets of the West Village, we talked about John's funeral. "Definitely something glamorous," Tim said. "He'd hate anything morbid." 2

I agreed. When he was healthy, John had dyed his hair platinum. He'd worn baggy shorts and purple high tops. Lamentation wasn't his style. 3

On the corner where we parted, I looked closely at Tim's face. He was deeply pale, putty-colored, and his eyes looked unnaturally large in his skull. He had AIDS too. He was still working full-time and keeping two hospital vigils. 4

5 "What are you eating?" I asked. "You look like you've lost weight."

6 He waved my question away. "I'm eating all the right things," he said. "I'm taking perfect care of myself. Give it a rest, Mom."

7 We said good-night, and he turned down Fourth Street, a scrawny, determined figure in oversized hoop earrings. I watched him for a moment, thinking about the workings of ordinary courage.

8 I'd just made it home and into bed when the phone rang. It was Tim.

9 "Hi," he said. "Guess where I'm calling from? St. Vincent's."

10 "Shit," I said. "Did John die right after we left?"

11 "No, it's not John," he said. His voice carried a thin, slightly blurred tone of good cheer, as if he'd been drugged. "It's me. I got beaten up. About five minutes after I left you. By three guys."

12 I went to get him with another friend of his, an English journalist named Karen. Tim was woozy and slightly manic from painkillers, and his fair hair was swathed in bandages. Karen asked him if he'd gotten a good look at the men who beat him.

13 "You know, I don't exactly remember them," he said in a chipper voice. "I know they were yelling 'faggot' at me. And I think I yelled back. Something like, 'You got it, sweethearts—who wants to be first?' Then I was in the emergency room, being stitched up. Poof. There one minute, here the next."

14 Karen and I got him back to his apartment and put him to bed. We sat with him until he fell asleep. Karen whispered, "He looks about fifteen, doesn't he?" He did look preternaturally young and wan, his blue-veined eyelids translucent, the bandage white around his head. He was a cheerful, domestically inclined boy from Indiana. He adored his friends, had a cat named Aretha, and always fell asleep before it was time to go out to the clubs. Someone had hit his frail, compromised body with a two-by-four. Someone, somewhere in the city, was congratulating himself at that moment. Someone was laughing and popping a beer.

15 To calm myself I laid my hand, gently, on Tim's scrawny chest. I felt the steady effort of his breathing. After a moment, Karen put her hand on top of mine. "This makes me crazy," I said to her. "This makes me want to hurt

people." I was furious at myself for failing to watch out for Tim. And I was angry at Tim. Why did he have to talk back to those morons?

Karen shook her head disapprovingly, and I was suddenly, fiercely angry at her as well. Because she and her girlfriend are staunchly opposed to violence in any form. Because she refuses to have anything to do with activist groups like ACT UP (the AIDS Coalition to Unleash Power) or Queer Nation, the radical gay-rights organization spawned by ACT UP to strike back at all the people who'd beat up an innocent gay kid like Tim. Because several weeks earlier, as we passed a series of posters announcing the homosexuality of some very big—and very closeted—Hollywood stars, she hissed: "The fascists who force other people to come out are doing us more harm than good." 16

If you're straight, it may be hard to understand the need for an obstreperous, in-your-face organization like Queer Nation. It may be hard to imagine the intricate combination of rage and terror that constitutes the gay zeitgeist of 1992. There's a virus ticking its way through the arteries of people we love. That would be enough to make us crazy, right there. But what's driven some of us around the bend is the fact that, even as our friends keep dying, the hatred of homosexuals flourishes. 17

Gay-bashing is up all over the country. Homophobia is thriving like mosquitoes in August, and it comes as often as not in relatively subtle, nonviolent packages. Take Magic Johnson, for instance. Shortly after announcing he was HIV-positive, he inspired wild applause on the Arsenio Hall show when he said, "I'm nowhere near homosexual." People cheered. If you're a person of color, try to imagine a celebrity telling an appreciative audience, "I thank God I'm white!" If you're Jewish, imagine the same audience clapping and whistling when a celebrity announces, "No way am I a Jew." 18

If you're gay and you're not angry, you're just not paying attention. 19

I myself belong to ACT UP. I've helped engineer an on-screen takeover of the *MacNeil/Lehrer Newshour* (you'd be surprised at how easy it is to get into a television studio). I've chained myself to the White House gates. I've committed these and other acts of civil disobedience in the company of people I consider heroes. I confess up front to deep affection and respect for Queer Nation, which was launched just over 20 two years ago by a band of ACT UP members from New York City who wanted to concentrate on gay issues outside the realm of AIDS.

21 Queer Nation is a peculiar mix of outrage and wackiness—you could call it the illegitimate child of Huey Newton and Lucy Ricardo. Male and female members go en masse to straight bars and hockey games, where they kiss their lovers passionately. They stage impromptu fashion shows in suburban shopping malls, featuring men in tutus and women in Harley-Davidson gear.

22 The name itself started as a joke of sorts. "Queer Nation" was a temporary moniker, offered in jest. Once the founding members got used to it, though, they didn't mind the idea of throwing a word like "queer" back in the faces of those who'd been spitting it at them for decades. They decided they could repossess the insult; they could cauterize it by taking it on themselves. Besides, the word emphasizes difference. Members aren't trying to say to the straight world, "Accept us, because we're just like you." That was the old tactic, which is now known disparagingly as assimilationism. Queer Nation's official tag line is "We're here. We're queer. Get used to it."

23 By the time it was a year old, Queer Nation existed in over sixty cities, from New York and San Francisco to Indianapolis and Shreveport. Now, just past its second anniversary, no one's quite sure how many chapters there are. The rise has been swift but chaotic, and established chapters have burned out nearly as quickly as new ones have appeared. Since I started writing this article, the Eugene and Houston chapters have taken off while the San Francisco chapter has dissolved.

24 Like ACT UP, Queer Nation is ferociously democratic and decentralized. Its founders were determined not to emulate what they called the "hierarchical, patriarchal" pecking order by which most groups—from the Young Republicans to the Crips and the Bloods—are run. At every chapter, anyone who shows up at a meeting is instantaneously a full member. Some chapters are run by consensus; some simply function as a forum for people who want to recruit others for demonstrations. The prevailing aim—you could call it an obsession—is to exclude no one.

25 It would be easy to play up Queer Nation's kind intentions and zany antics. But members can also be loudly confrontational. They've irritated a lot of people, including other

lesbians and gay men. Gay opposition is wildly various, but I can offer a quintessential scenario. Say your parents are visiting from Michigan, and you've finally decided to come out to them. You're a relatively ordinary citizen with a nine-to-five job. In a quiet restaurant, over coffee, you say it: "Listen, I guess you may have suspected this. I don't want to keep secrets from you anymore. I'm gay." Your mother cries and tells you she loves you anyway. She says it with a certain forced conviction, which doesn't quite ring true. Your father is murderously silent. This is the hardest thing you've ever done. As you leave the restaurant, your mother is sniffling and your father is glacial. You're searching for something else to say, some way to make them understand that you haven't suddenly transformed yourself into an alien. As you struggle for the right words, you walk out of the restaurant into a band of men and women carrying QUEER POWER signs. They're blowing whistles. Some wear nose rings and combat boots. Two of the men have on dresses, and one sports a Nancy Sinatra wig. As they pass, somebody slaps a Day-Glo sticker on your father's seersucker jacket. The sticker says GO GIRL.

Opposition to Queer Nation's tactics doesn't end with 26
questions of style or demeanor. Last September, gay riots exploded in Los Angeles and San Francisco after California governor Pete Wilson vetoed AB 101, a bill that would have outlawed job discrimination on the basis of sexual orientation. After his veto, Queer Nationals and other gay activists hurled police barricades through windows. They set fires in the streets. And some of them threatened to expose gay members of Wilson's staff, further igniting the ongoing debate about outing, tactics, and propriety.

Gay activists face a fundamental question familiar to 27
feminists and civil-rights leaders, among others. Do we play by the rules, court public sympathy, and push steadily but politely for recognition? Or do we make ourselves so unpleasant that yielding to our demands finally becomes easier than ignoring us? I myself favor the noisier alternatives. I believe the AIDS epidemic has taught us that nobody will listen unless we scream. But still, I'm plagued by doubts. At ACT UP meetings, when members talk about planning a new action that will "show our anger," I find myself asking, What exactly do we expect people to do with our anger once we've shown it to them? As I set out to visit Queer Nation chapters around the country, that question was on my mind.

And on my first stop, in Atlanta, Georgia, a woman named Cheryl Summerville was pondering it too.

28 Cheryl Summerville may have been the best-behaved lesbian in the world. She lived outside Atlanta with her lover, Sandra Riley, in a house the two women helped build themselves. She and Riley were raising Summerville's son from a long-dissolved marriage and were thinking of having a child of their own. Summerville had a decent job as a cook at the local Cracker Barrel, one of a chain of country-style restaurants.

29 But in February of 1991, the associate manager of the restaurant, Marilee Gonzalez, called Summerville into her office. Gonzalez, who had been friendly with Summerville, told her in a nervous but formal tone that Cracker Barrel had decided to reexamine its policy about gay and lesbian employees. She asked, "Are you a lesbian?"

30 Summerville answered: "Marilee, you know I am. You going to fire me for that?"

31 That day, Summerville received a pink slip on the orders of Cracker Barrel district manager Jody Waller. The restaurant's general manager filed a separation notice with the Georgia Department of Labor, on which he wrote: "This employee is being terminated due to violation of company policy. The employee is gay."

32 Waller was complying with a memo sent to the managers of all outlets by Cracker Barrel's main office in Lebanon, Tennessee. The memo said, in part: "It is inconsistent with our concept and values, and is perceived to be inconsistent with those of our customer base, to continue to employ individuals in our operating units whose sexual preferences fail to demonstrate normal heterosexual values which have been the foundation of families in our society."

33 In all, eighteen lesbians and gay men were fired from Cracker Barrel's outlets. Some managers called the employees they suspected into their offices and formally asked if they were homosexual. Others just convened staff meetings and announced that certain employees were being terminated in accordance with company policy.

34 Summerville simply didn't get it at first. In every respect but one, she'd always been a model of conventional good behavior. She'd received a "personal achievement award," given by Cracker Barrel to outstanding staff members, and

was up for another. She'd helped build a house with her own hands, adored her parents and son, earned a living through hard work. Her single transgression was to love another woman and, even in that, she'd been modest and forthright. She hadn't concealed her love for Sandra Riley, nor had she flaunted it. Now she was out of work, for failing to display normal values.

At first, Summerville assumed she could take Cracker 35
Barrel to court. But only a few states and about sixty cities and counties have barred discrimination on the basis of sexual preference in both public and private employment. Atlanta isn't among them. When Summerville learned she had no legal recourse, she called ACT UP for help, but was told that it worked only on issues relating directly to AIDS. She was referred to the Atlanta chapter of Queer Nation.

Summerville was not a political person. She wasn't tor- 36
tured by ideals or abstractions—she just wanted to live an uncomplicated life. The idea of speaking to a group that called itself Queer Nation gave her a kind of vertigo. "It took me a week to get up the nerve," she says. She and Sandra Riley made a dry run in their car past the Five Points Community Center, where the group's next meeting was to take place. The center looked ordinary enough. But still.

On the night of the meeting, she and Riley were so 37
nervous they arrived twenty minutes early. As the members started drifting in, Summerville was surprised to find that they looked like everybody else. "I didn't expect just normal-looking people," she says. "I thought we were in the wrong place. They were wearing just jeans and T-shirts. One of 'em came in in a suit, and I sure as hell didn't expect that."

Despite this, Summerville and Riley stood out, even 38
among the conservatively dressed men. They are ample women, and they dress along suburban lines. Sandra Riley favors ruffles. She carries a pocketbook. "To start with, they ignored us," Summerville recalls. "They probably thought we'd stumbled into the wrong place or something."

But after the meeting was called to order, the first item of 39
business was the firings at Cracker Barrel. "Somebody asked, 'What are we going to do about this?' " Summerville remembers. "And I said: 'Hey it was me. I'm one of 'em.' " Everyone turned to look at the short, stocky woman in a sweatshirt and jeans. "I want to know what we can do about it," she said.

* * *

40 The first demonstration against Cracker Barrel was held in a rainstorm. Thirty-plus people marched in front of the restaurant with signs, urging customers to stay away until the chain reversed its policy. It was, generally, a humiliating experience. "It was just kind of nasty," Summerville says. "It was pouring, and a few of us slipped in the mud. People laughed at us."

41 Before the picket lines started, members had been rebuffed when they tried to meet with the Cracker Barrel management to present their complaints. Soon after, the central office sent a memo to all Cracker Barrel outlets, claiming that its "recent position on the employment of homosexuals in a limited number of stores may have been a well-intentioned over-reaction to the perceived values of our customers and their comfort levels with these individuals."

42 If the firings themselves didn't qualify as national news, Cracker Barrel's subsequent change of heart apparently did. The controversy was reported in *The New York Times,* the *Wall Street Journal,* and the *Atlanta Journal & Constitution,* which also ran an editorial excoriating Cracker Barrel and asking how any discrimination could have possibly been "well-intentioned."

43 While it withdrew its chainwide policy about the discharge of homosexuals, Cracker Barrel turned down Queer Nation's demand that individual outlets be specifically forbidden from practicing sexual discrimination in hiring. It also refused to rehire the fired employees, and balked at Queer Nation's request for a written apology.

44 In March of last year, Queer Nation started staging sit-ins aimed at cutting Cracker Barrel's profits. The idea was simple: members filled as many tables as possible, ordered the bare minimum, and sat there for two or three hours. When they ordered their coffees or Cokes, the protesters at each table gave their waitress a five-dollar tip wrapped in a note that said: "We realize that you are not the source of the discriminatory policy of Cracker Barrel. We in no way want to penalize you or make your life more difficult. On the contrary, we want to assure that YOU are not the next victim of renegade bigotry at Cracker Barrel."

45 Every few weeks, Queer Nation hit a different Cracker Barrel outlet, always on Sunday, after church. Last June, I went to the ninth Cracker Barrel sit-in with Lynn Cothren, a thin blond man wearing madras shorts and love beads.

Cothren, a founding member of Queer Nation/Atlanta, is something of an anomaly. In an organization that eschews the very idea of leaders, he boldly proclaimed himself chair of the Atlanta chapter. The demonstrations against Cracker Barrel were largely his idea.

Nearly 120 people had gathered in a parking lot next to the Cracker Barrel in Union City, about ten miles outside Atlanta. They were a living monument to the notion that, aside from some fundamental appetites, human beings have very little in common. There were women in plaid flannel shirts, and women with rouge and pink lipstick. There were middle-aged men in sweat suits, bodybuilders, and reedy, acne-scarred boys who still carried the mortified auras of their adolescent torments. 46

Everyone was nervous. Most of the protesters had picketed or participated in sit-ins before, but none had ever been arrested for civil disobedience. Although the towers and spires of Atlanta were visible on the horizon, Union City was a conservative town. No one was sure what would happen or how any of us would be treated when taken to jail. 47

Cheryl Summerville and Sandra Riley stood close together, holding hands in the parking lot. Neither had slept the night before. Riley, a large woman with long hair and a lovely, innocent face, looked as if she might cry at any moment. But when Summerville told her that she thought she should change her mind, Riley said: "What am I going to do while you're in jail? Sit outside worrying about you? No thanks." To be arrested, Riley wore heels and a blue flowered dress. She carried a white pocketbook. 48

After we all assembled, we filed into the restaurant. To reach the dining room we passed through a gift shop that sold penny candy, stars-and-stripes decals, and plaster cherry pies with lattice crusts. The restaurant proper featured turn-of-the-century memorabilia screwed to its walls—farm implements and brown photographs of families. Hard shadowless light caromed off its acoustic ceiling. 49

I sat at a table with a fiftyish woman named Marty. She'd come with her gay son and his lover and a young lesbian named Elizabeth, who'd been cut off by her family. Marty introduced her as "my adopted daughter." When I asked Marty how she felt about her son being gay, she drawled, "I've known he was gay since he was in the fourth grade, so I've had plenty of time to get used to it." When I asked if she'd rather he was straight, she said, "Well, he's a hell of a 50 lot happier than one of his brothers, who's married with two kids."

51 A cheerful waitress brought us menus, and we told her we were just having coffee. We gave her her five-dollar tip up front, wrapped in the note explaining what we were doing there. She smiled graciously, and pocketed the tip and the note without reading it. Slowly the restaurant filled with protesters. I drifted through, asking the few remaining nonmembers for reactions. A beige-faced woman in a biscuit-colored jumpsuit said: "I don't carry on about my sexuality in public. I don't know why you all have to carry on about yours." At another table, a man with a beard said: "Cracker Barrel was right to fire those people. What with AIDS and all, I don't want 'em touching food my kids are gonna eat."

52 Most of the waitresses didn't appear to mind. Some even seemed to be having a good time. An older woman swept through the room periodically, filling coffee cups, and when she got to us she said to Marty: "Honey, I'm cuttin' you off. You're starting to shake the whole table."

53 I went to Cothren's table and asked him what, exactly, he thought this protest was accomplishing. He looked at me as if he couldn't believe I would ask such a question. "We're putting direct pressure on them," he said. "We're cutting into their business."

54 "But so far," I said, "you've gotten only one minor concession. Obviously, their fundamental attitude hasn't changed. None of the people who were fired have their jobs back."

55 "We're going to win," Cothren answered in an impatient tone, as if I simply didn't understand the righteousness of Queer Nation's cause or the immensity of his will.

56 An hour passed before Jody Waller, the district manager, appeared with two cops and began working his way through the restaurant, table by table. Waller was a trim man with glasses and a receding hairline, wearing a tie and a navy blazer. At each table he announced: "I'm asking you to leave now. If you don't leave, you'll be arrested. Do you understand?"

57 Eighteen people chose to stay and be arrested. The rest of us went to the jail house to wait until they were released. We marched in an orderly circle before the jail, which was located in a town that seemed to consist only of the jail, a post office, and several unprosperous-looking antique stores. We carried signs that said THERE'S BIGOTRY IN MY

BISCUIT and CRACKER BARREL SERVES HATE. We displayed the signs to ourselves and to an occasional passing car. In two hours, not a single person walked by on the street.

A the end of two hours, several demonstrators were released. We gathered around them expectantly, and they told us they'd been treated with surprising respect. A court date had been set for mid-August, when a judge would rule on Cracker Barrel's trespassing charge. Summerville and Riley stood close together, talking happily to their friends. Riley's white shoes were unsmudged. 58

We started back to our cars, planning to meet at a bar in Atlanta for a celebratory beer. But as we were dispersing, a battered pickup truck roared toward us from down the street. As it screamed past, a gang of shirtless teenage boys yelled, "Faggots." They all wore their hair below their shoulders, a minor cosmetic freedom won by others before they were born. They turned around and passed us a second time, still hollering insults. 59

They left a chill in the air. Any one of them could have been Jody Waller's wild son, testing his limits before he grew up and got his own job managing a Cracker Barrel. Cothren didn't hesitate. He turned and marched back into the jail—a skinny, wrathful twenty-eight-year-old man in Bermuda shorts—to demand that his pot-bellied jailers track down the boys and arrest them for verbal assault. 60

As I traveled around the country visiting other chapters of Queer Nation, I kept thinking, God, these people are young. If furious exuberance is the organization's most salient feature, youth is a close second. I've just turned thirty-nine, and in my travels I met only a handful of women and men my age or older. More often, I found myself among people who could literally have been my sons or daughters. The media liaison from the now-defunct San Francisco chapter tried to reassure me that the group's reputation for youth was exaggerated, saying proudly, "Some of us are in our late twenties and even our early thirties." 61

Youth, with its energy and its bottomless outrage, may account for that fact that Queer Nation demonstrations are sometimes ignited by events that seem less than urgent. When the residents of Gay Court, in a suburban community east of San Francisco, petitioned to change the name of their street to High Eagle Road, a band of protesters from 62

Queer Nation showed up with banners and bullhorns. In New York City, I went with about twenty activists to stage a "kiss-in" in a straight bar, where the patrons frankly couldn't have cared less. Looking for drama, I asked a straight-looking guy in a crewneck sweater what he thought about all this. "All *what?*" he asked.

63 "Those people over there," I said. "The ones who are kissing. The ones with the stickers that say 'Queer.' "

64 He looked calmly at a pair of tattooed men who were kissing passionately among a bevy of big-haired secretaries sipping margaritas. He shrugged. "Guess it means they're queer," he replied.

65 Youth, combined with Queer Nation's adamantly non-hierarchical structure, may also partially account for the fact that the group is often disorganized nearly to the point of incoherence. In preparing to write this article, I made dozens of calls across the country and learned repeatedly that the person whose name I'd been given had left town for a few months, or moved away entirely, or fought with other members and quit. Members conceive passionate devotions and then burn out. They leave Queer Nation over philosophical differences, or because their grades are suffering, or because they've fallen in love with other members who don't return their affections.

66 When I called a contact person in Shreveport, Louisiana, his mother answered the phone and told me, cordially, that her son had gone to live with his lover. When I reached him at his lover's house, he said that Queer Nation/Shreveport consisted entirely of himself and another man occasionally distributing literature on safer sex.

67 I had planned to attend a demonstration being held by Queer Nation of Lincoln, Nebraska. Together with Queer Nation/Iowa City, members were going to Iowa State University in Ames, where a heterosexual supremacist group—consisting of about a dozen people committed to fighting the very concept of gay rights—was campaigning for formal recognition by the university. Queer Nation was going to parade in front of the group leader's house, kissing and holding hands. I was looking forward to the demonstration. I'd made plane reservations. But when I called about some last-minute details, I learned that the action had been called off because a main organizer had set fire to another member's house.

68 I did go to Salt Lake City, because I'd heard Queer Nation

was thriving there and because the woman I'd first contacted continued to answer her phone over a period of several months. Still, I arrived too late. By the time my plane landed, the group was in disarray. A splinter group had formed. Members were writing vicious lampoons of one another in the chapter's newsletter.

I admit it. I was beginning to feel a certain despair. 69

I also visited Queer Nation/San Francisco, which several 70
months after I left degenerated into internecine battles and then disbanded entirely. In January of 1991, it was among the largest chapters in the country, attracting as many as four hundred to its weekly meetings. It carried out one of Queer Nation's most notorious protests, when bands of Queer Nationals did everything possible to disrupt the filming of *Basic Instinct,* a thriller about murderous lesbians and bisexual women.

By autumn, its numbers had dropped to the low twenties. 71
Last December, the few remaining members agreed to dissolve the group. Some members there even call Queer Nation/San Francisco a "fad that fizzled out." Others say that it was done in by racism and sexism among the members themselves.

Tensions had flourished from the beginning. Soon after 72
the San Francisco chapter was established, bands of women and people of color started LABIA (Lesbians and Bi-Women in Action) and United Colors. These organizations-within-the-organization were called "focus groups" and were meant to concentrate on issues that might escape the attention of the larger body.

As ever-increasing numbers packed themselves into the 73
dour ochre-and-brown auditorium of San Francisco's Women's Building, members of LABIA and United Colors consistently felt that certain white men dominated. At one meeting last winter, several members came to the floor and asked the group at large to contribute a hundred dollars to a march. They were turned down—no big deal. But after the meeting, a group of white male members started arguing about the march with a group of women. The argument grew so heated that the women left, with the men following them down the street, still shouting their opinions. The men's raucous voices brought faces to apartment windows; a passerby asked the women if they needed help.

Later, the men claimed they'd only been carrying on an 74
impassioned discourse. The women said they'd been terror-

ized. This was one of a number of incidents in which some of the white men told one version of a story and the women or people of color told another. Several months later, when a band of men from Queer Nation plastered stickers on the home of a lesbian city supervisor, LABIA pulled out altogether, claiming that the male "terrorism" could no longer be countenanced.

75 Christine Carraher, one of the founding members of the bisexual focus group UBIQUITOUS, explains: "There's a wide gulf between a lot of lesbians and gay men. Sometimes I think it's worse than the one that exists between straight men and women."

76 "Some of these guys believe feminists are doing to men what Big Nurse did to the warders in *One Flew Over the Cuckoo's Nest,"* said a male member of the group.

77 As these tensions built, a big, noisy, politically savvy New Yorker named Mitchell Halberstadt started showing up at meetings and shouting other members out of the room. Halberstadt is a classic New York activist, all bombast and aggression. When he arrived in San Francisco, he brought his swagger to a group that employed two "vibes watchers" at every meeting to make sure no one felt intimidated, and permitted members to stop the meeting and discuss their grievances every time they felt personally insulted. But now, if women or people of color stopped a meeting to complain of a racist or sexist remark, they were often shouted down by Halberstadt and several other men. Because there was no formalized code of behavior for the meetings, and no decision could be made without consensus, the abusive tirades had to be tolerated. More and more people left.

78 At a meeting in early November, there was another confrontation. When one of the few female members started to walk out of the room, Halberstadt barred the door, screaming, "How dare you try to leave!" Frank Herron, a physically imposing man, told Halberstadt he was out of line and that he would do anything to stop him from threatening the others. And so the group that had pledged itself to banding together against homophobia was about to begin slugging it out over racism and sexism.

79 In an attempt to recover some sense of equilibrium, the members who stayed on—down to about twenty-five—held a special session in late November to discuss ways in which the general meetings could be better managed. At the session, John Woods of United Colors and a white member

named Allen Carson proposed that the group agree to a ban on all sexist and racist language, although they did not offer a specific list of forbidden terms. Halberstadt blocked the proposal and later claimed: "My politics are antiauthoritarian. [This is] a power grab by wannabe bureaucrats."

Soon after that session, the handful of remaining members called a "hiatus" until March, at which time they would regroup and see what, if anything, they could get to rise from the ashes. 80

When I accepted the assignment to write about Queer Nation a year ago, I was full of zeal. I confess to ending my story in a state of confusion. I had expected to write a story about heroism, and I did, in fact, meet heroic people everywhere I went. I'd prefer to write only about their strength and solidarity. I don't like reporting about the squabbles, the naiveté, the self-destructive tendencies. I likewise don't quite know what to make of the fact that, of the chapters I visited, the only one that's holding together effectively—the group in Atlanta—is the only one with an old-fashioned leader. (Cheryl Summerville is now the chapter's cochair.) It's also the only one embroiled in a battle with a clear-cut villain, which may help account for its strength. Fighting homophobia, sexism, and racism, is, for most of us, a little like battling crabgrass. It's everywhere, so intricately stitched into the lawn that you can't quite tell where to begin. 81

My misgivings about Queer Nation stem mainly from its tendency toward self-destruction, and this criticism is shared by other lesbians and gay men. Becky Moorman, publisher of *The Bridge,* a lesbian and gay magazine based in Utah, says: "The [lesbian and gay] community's really divided about what Queer Nation is doing. Their protests aren't focused. They need to decide who they're speaking to and what they're trying to say." Anthony Christiansen, an openly gay Ph.D. candidate in Columbia University's clinical-psychology program, adds: "Queer Nation focuses so much on our difference [from heterosexuals], they lose track of our connectedness. There are millions of complex situations out there—being gay isn't as cut-and-dried as they'd like to make out." 82

That may be the heart of the problem. We are probably the most diverse of all persecuted groups. A Martian field 83 biologist sent to earth to capture two homosexual specimens could easily bring back a twenty-three-year-old white guy with an MBA from Yale and a sixty-five-year-old black lesbian separatist from Detroit. Queer Nation, fostered by people who've been unfairly excluded, is determined to be utterly inclusive. That's turning out to mean equal voice not only for women and men of all colors but also for the foolish, the prejudiced, and the outright deluded.

Perhaps Queer Nation is simply an early, flawed step
84 toward a new kind of lesbian and gay militancy. Frank Herron of San Francisco insists that the city's chapter hasn't been a failure: "It's spawned a dozen groups doing different things. We've drawn a lot of people into activism." Herron sees the future of gay activism as a welter of small groups modeled on revolutionary cells. "Twelve people can reach a decision more easily than five hundred can," he says. "If these twelve need help, they work with another group of twelve. I don't know if we'll ever have a cohesive national gay activist organization."

Meanwhile, it's difficult not to feel panicky, because, as we
85 argue over structure and focus, as we bicker among ourselves, our people are being attacked in increasing numbers. Since I was in Atlanta, Cheryl Summerville and Sandra Riley have become more famous and, simultaneously, more widely despised. After Summerville appeared on the Oprah Winfrey show in January, her sixteen-year-old son was so tormented by his classmates that she and Riley chose to move him to another school. There have been hate letters and threats. Riley has closed her sewing and alterations business so that she can be home when the boy gets back from school.

And as we struggle to set a coherent agenda, our people
86 continue to die. My friend Tim, for one, died while I was working on this story. It was sudden, if that term can be applied to someone who'd had AIDS for almost three years. He was comparatively well and then he caught pneumonia and then he died. His parents, who hadn't spoken to him in years, didn't want his ashes. Karen is keeping them in a box in her apartment until we decide what to do with them. Another friend has taken Aretha, Tim's cat.

Just before Tim died, I found myself sitting with Karen at
87 his bedside. He was unconscious, breathing noisily and steadily on a respirator. As Karen and I sat watching him, I told her I was struggling to write an article about Queer

Nation. She shrugged dismissively. "A bunch of thugs," she said.

"Right," I said. "That's right. And you've got a better idea, haven't you?" My voice was loud enough to surprise me. 88

"Honey, calm down," she said with a nervous smile. 89

"You've got a much better solution," I said. "It's very effective to be discreet in public and send a little money to the Gay Men's Health Crisis and write features about the ten best espresso bars in lower Manhattan. Thank you for your contribution." 90

A nurse put her head through the curtains and asked if everything was all right. We told her not to worry, to get on with her other business. 91

"You don't need to scream at me," Karen said quietly after the nurse had gone. 92

"I know," I said. 93

"I'm not the one you're really angry at." 94

"I know. Let's not talk about it, okay?" 95

Of course, she was right. But I couldn't calm myself. Later, after Tim died, I was able to see how stupid I'd been. How quickly I'd self-destructed. Karen had been there for me to scream at, and, even more important, she understood what I was screaming about. A man like Jody Waller, standing smugly with two cops behind him, doesn't get the point. There's no outward evidence that he suspects he's doing anything wrong. 96

Karen and I will never be friends. Now that Tim is gone, there's no reason for us to know each other. But during Tim's last days, she and I managed to act like compatriots. We had to. There was a funeral to plan, and, if we didn't do it, nobody would. 97

It's hard to know what to do sometimes. I wish I felt more certain about how to proceed. I wish I'd walked Tim home that night after we left St. Vincent's. I keep thinking I could have protected him. 98

Dan Chaon

Transformations

Mr. Chaon lives in Cleveland, Ohio, and teaches at Cleveland State University. He has published a number of short stories; the one reprinted here appeared in 1991 in Story, *a prestigious quarterly that prints only short fiction.*

1 The first time I saw my brother Corky in women's clothes, I was eleven and he was fourteen. He came out of my parents' bedroom in my mother's good dress, the one with bird of paradise flowers patterned on it, and her high heels and lipstick. I thought he was kidding. He chased after me, talking in a Southern accent, and I ran off laughing. Corky was always pretending to be someone else, dressing up in clothes he'd bought at the Catholic rummage house or found in the garage, imitating the mannerisms of his math teacher, or Uncle Evan, who drove semi trucks and stuttered, or some disc jockey on the radio. I didn't realize then, not for years and years actually, that he was gay and all.

2 He is still your brother, my father told me when he showed me the picture. This was the second time I'd seen Corky in women's clothes. In the photo, he was wearing a big red wig, a blue-jean skirt, pumps, and a blouse with fringe. He looked like a country singer. My father asked me: "Do you know who this is?" All I said was, Yes, and, It figures.

3 My father shook his head at me. He liked to pretend that he didn't care what Corky was, just so long as he was happy. That was the official line. But I'd seen the kind of cloudy distance that came into his eyes when he talked to Corky on the phone. I'd noticed him, once, studying an old Polaroid of the three of us, pheasant hunting, examining it as if looking for clues. I'd seen his expression when one of his buddies from the electrician's union asked: "So how's that boy of yours doing back East?" My father shifted from foot to foot. "Oh, fine, fine," he said quickly, and looked down.

4 But he looked me sternly in the eyes. "He is still your brother," he said. He folded his thick hands, staring glumly at the glossy black-and-white photo.

5 "My sister, you mean," I said.

6 He frowned. "You're getting pretty smart-mouthed," he

said. He laid the photo on the kitchen table between us, like some important document I was supposed to sign. "He does this as entertainment," my father said. The words "CABARET BERLINER, New York," were printed on the bottom of the picture.

"I'll bet," I said. 7

My brother worked at a bar in New York City. We'd known that. We also knew he was gay. He'd told my parents over the phone after he'd been away a year. I wasn't sure how they reacted at first, though they seemed calm by the time they got around to telling me. Corky had come to a decision, my father said, and my mother nodded grimly. For a long time afterward, my father wouldn't refer to it at all except as "your brother's decision," though he also pointed out to me that the words "fag" and "queer" were worse than swearing as far as he was concerned. 8

Corky was going to college in New York at the time, but he dropped out shortly after to audition for plays and work in bars at night. He hadn't been home since he told them. Instead, he sent clippings, pictures, lists of productions he was trying out for. "One thing about Corky," my father pointed out to me as he looked through the packets Corky sent. "At least he knows what he wants, and he's not afraid to go after it." 9

It was my senior year in high school, and my father thought I had no ambition. Maybe that was true. In any case, I wasn't like Corky had been when he was in high school. His senior year, there was always something about him taped to the refrigerator—a certificate of merit, or a clipping from the local paper about a scholarship he'd won. He pinned the acceptance letters from colleges in neat rows on a bulletin board in our room, as if they were rare butterflies. 10

That was why I was surprised when he called to say he was taking some time off to attend my high school graduation. I went to the Catholic school as Corky had, but there was no chance of me ending up valedictorian like him. For a while maybe people wondered whether I'd be a teacher's pet like Corky, and they even sometimes called me by his name. But it didn't take them long to find out that I wasn't going to leave any brilliant reputation in my wake. My father always said that I didn't "apply myself" like Corky did. Out of ninety-six seniors I was ranked forty-ninth. I would just be a vague, doughy face in the middle of the third row. 11

There was no great cause for celebration. I hadn't found a job or a college to attend in the fall. But at least my parents had a son who could give them grandchildren, they could appreciate that. And as for that fat, mustached drama teacher, Sister Vincent, who continually remembered Corky's beautiful singing voice and his performance in *South Pacific,* well, I wished she could see his new song and dance at Cabaret Berliner.

12 Corky came home two days before graduation. My mother and father and I went to pick him up at Stapleton Airport in Denver. The whole way there, I worried. I couldn't help but imagine Corky appearing to us in a feather boa and an evening gown or something, trotting down the ramp to meet us with a big lipstick grin. I told myself I was being low-minded and ugly, but that image of him kept popping into my mind. My face felt hot.

13 Meanwhile, my parents acted like everything was wonderful. The full moon reflected off the early May snow that still lay on the fields, and my father kept howling like a wolf. It seemed to amuse my mother, because she chuckled every time he did it, and laughed aloud when he grabbed her around the waist and growled.

14 I was sitting in the back seat, watching the car drift toward the center of the road while they horsed around. "I hope we wreck," I said.

15 The three of us stood there in the waiting area, watching the planes land. We didn't recognize Corky when he approached us, but at least he was wearing normal clothes. He'd dyed his hair bright red—it was shoulder-length, tied in a ponytail. When he was close enough, I noticed the little crease in his earlobe that meant it was pierced, but he didn't have an earring. He hugged my mother, kissing her lightly. Then he turned and kissed my father. My father always kissed us on the lips, and wasn't even afraid to do it in public. He puckered up like a cartoon character, and it would've been funny if he wasn't so earnest about it. Here he was, this big, middle-aged construction worker, smacking lips with his son. He didn't even hesitate knowing Corky was gay, though I looked around to see if people were staring.

16 When my brother turned to me, I stuck out my hand. I didn't want him kissing on me. "So," he said, and squeezed my palm, hard. "The graduate!"

I shrugged. "Yeah, well," I said. "I'm just glad it's over." 17

He kept holding my hand till I pulled back a little. He grinned. "Congratulations," he said. 18

"Congratulations to you, too," I said, though I didn't know why. 19

As we drove back to Mineral, I watched my brother suspiciously. Ever since we were little he'd always been the center of things, and I doubted that he'd come all that way just to congratulate me. I kept expecting him to take over at any minute. I remembered how, when we were young, we had a place behind the house, an old shed we'd furnished with lawn chairs and cinder blocks and such. This became the plantation from *Gone with the Wind*—Corky was Rhett and Scarlett, I was the slaves; or a rocket—Corky was the captain and the alien invaders, I was the crew that got killed. Once, when I was eleven and he was fifteen, and he was going to play the lead in *South Pacific,* he got me all excited about trying out for the part of his little Polynesian son. He gave me the music and then made fun of me, standing by the bedroom door and warbling like an old chicken. 20

Maybe, I thought, Corky had changed. It had been a long time since I'd really spoken to him. It had been several years since I'd seen him, and I seldom felt like talking to him on the phone. Even when my father *did* put me on the line, I couldn't think of what to say. "What's new," Corky would ask, and I'd shrug: "Nothing." Maybe he'd become a totally different person, and I hadn't known. 21

But I couldn't tell. He was so motionless as we drove that he hardly seemed real. He just stared, like some stone idol, out toward the passing telephone poles and fields and the grasshopper oil wells nodding against the moonlit sky. His hands remained in his lap, except once, when he suddenly touched his hair with his fingertips as if adjusting a hat. When my parents asked him a question he leaned forward, smiling politely. "What? What did you say?" 22

It was late, nearly one in the morning, when we got home. Corky went to the bedroom to unpack—our old room, my room now—and when I came in he was already stretched out on the upper bunk. It used to be that I slept in the bottom and he slept in the top, but since he'd left I'd been 23 using the lower bunk to store papers and laundry and stuff. He looked down at me and smiled.

24 "That's my bed," I told him.

25 He sat up and his bare feet dangled over the edge, swinging lightly. He was wearing silky-looking pajamas. We'd always just slept in our underwear, and I imagined that this was what he wore when he lay down next to another man. "That's rich," he said. "You know, all these years I wanted that bottom bunk. I suppose you always wanted the top."

26 "I didn't care one way or another," I said. I began to take handfuls of dirty laundry from the bottom bunk and put them on the floor. "You can sleep there if you want."

27 He nodded and lay back. "It's been a long time since I've heard any news from you."

28 "Yeah, well," I said. "My life isn't that exciting."

29 "You've really changed the room around," he said. He gestured to a poster of a model in a white bikini who was holding a six-pack of beer. "She's sexy," he said.

30 "Yeah," I said. "I guess."

31 He looked from the poster to me, his lips puckered out a little. "So," he said at last. "Do you have a girlfriend, Todd?"

32 "Yes," I said. "Sort of." I didn't. I had friends that were girls, and one of them I took to most of the dances. But I wasn't like some of the guys in school, who'd been going steady with one girl since eighth grade. All the girls I liked had either paired off or weren't interested. The furtive gropes and kisses after dances hadn't amounted to much. I was afraid that even if I got a girl to do more, I'd be clumsy, and I couldn't stand the thought of her laughing, maybe telling her friends. "You know," I told Corky. "I date around and stuff."

33 "Good for you," he said. He pulled his feet up onto the bed the way a fish would flip its tail. Then he laughed. I could feel my ears warming.

34 "What's so funny?" I said.

35 "Nothing," he said. "Just the way you said it." He deepened his voice to a macho swagger. " 'I date around and stuff.' " He laughed again. "You used to be such a little high-voiced thing."

36 "Hm," I said. He leaned back and I turned off the light. I moved over near the closet, where it was darkest, so I could undress without him seeing me. The hangers made wind-chime sounds as I brushed them.

"It's so weird, being home," he said. His voice floated from the top bunk as I took off my shirt. I decided to sleep in my jeans. I didn't have any pajamas. "You can't believe how strange it is." 37

"Well, nothing has changed," I said. I groped across the dim room to my bed. I could see the lump where he was lying, a shadow bending toward me. 38

"No," he said, "no." And then, slowly: "So did you see the picture I sent?" The house was still. I could hear water whispering through the pipes in the walls; I could hear him breathing. 39

"I saw it." I tried to make my voice noncommital. I sighed deeply, like I was already almost asleep. 40

He didn't say anything for a long time, and I thought he might have drifted off. When he spoke out of the dark, finally, his voice sounded odd, twittery, not like him, and it made my neck prickle. "Sometimes," he said, "I'm glad I sent it and other times not." I didn't say anything. "Todd?" he whispered. 41

I waited. I recalled the way we used to lie in our bunks when we were little and tell each other jokes and make up songs. I remembered how I would go to sleep to the sound of his murmuring, crooning. "What," I whispered back finally. 42

"How did Mom and Dad react?" 43

"How should I know?" I mumbled. "They don't tell me anything." 44

"What did they say?" 45

"What did you expect them to say?" 46

"I don't know," he said. "It's hard to explain." 47

But I didn't want him to explain. I didn't want to keep picturing him in that outfit, swishing and singing, maybe kissing a member of his audience, leaving a bright wing of lipstick on his forehead. "They didn't say much of anything," I told him. "They don't care what you do in your personal life." 48

"Do you?" 49

"Why should I?" I whispered. I rolled over, pretending to be asleep. 50

When I woke, my brother was already up. I could hear him talking in the kitchen, and the sound of eggs cracking on a skillet. I went to the bathroom to shower and when I 51 came back to dress, I couldn't help but notice Corky's suitcase. It was expensive-looking, dark strips of leather bound around brick-red cloth. Through the walls I could hear the vague whisper of conversation and I bent down, running my hands along the sides, finding the zipper.

52 Most of the things had been taken out. He'd put them in dresser drawers my mother had cleared out for him. But there was a compartment along one side, and when I opened it, I found what I figured I'd find. It gave me a fluttery feeling in my stomach: a skirt, a flowered blouse, pantyhose, a box of make-up with the colors arranged chromatically. Beneath that were more photos—Corky gripping a fireman's pole, his leg sliding along it, his eyes looking seductively away; being lifted by a group of men in tuxedos, his head flung back, his arms open wide, jeweled necklaces in his clenched fists. There were two clippings of advertisements for Cabaret Berliner: a drawing of a man's hairy leg with a high heel on his foot, and underneath, in small letters, the words: Corky Petersen with Sister Mary Josephine—After Tea Dance Party. Another had a photo of Corky in his cowgirl outfit. I wondered if he was planning to show us a sample of his act. I closed the suitcase quickly.

53 They didn't look up when I came into the kitchen. They were sitting at the table, eating toast and scrambled eggs. Corky was telling my father that New York City was in a state of collapse and had been ever since Reagan took office. He said the homeless filled the streets, that a bag lady had died on his doorstep. My father kept nodding very seriously, frowning, "Mm-hmm," as if he were talking to a grownup. He never spoke to me that way. Then Corky began to tell about the semis that parked outside his apartment at night, and how his whole place filled up with diesel fumes. He was afraid to light a cigarette. In the middle of this, he looked up and saw me standing there. "Well, hello, Sleeping Beauty," he said, and cocked his hand on his hip.

54 I glared at him. "Mornin'," I said in my deepest voice. I slid into the chair at the far end of the table.

55 "You hungry, punkin?" my mother asked brightly.

56 I looked sternly at her. I wanted to tell them that my name was Todd, not Sleeping Beauty or pumpkin. But all I said was, No. Then I looked at Corky. "So how come you live in New York if you don't like it?"

57 Corky shrugged. "Frankly," he said, "there's no other place I could stand." Then he leaned toward my father and

lowered his voice. "I'll tell you what's really scary," he said. "This AIDS thing. Out here, I'm sure no one realizes, but it's really terrifying."

My father blushed and we were all silent. "Well," my father said, and cleared his throat. "I hope you're being careful." He picked at his eggs. 58

"Careful?" Corky said. He gave a short laugh. "I can't even tell you. The other night I was out with this guy." He stopped. All of us were sitting stiffly, and my father had a pinched look on his face. He touched his eyelids, as if to clear away the image of Corky and this man, this lover. 59

"Well, anyway," Corky said. "He didn't even want to kiss. He goes: 'I don't know you well enough yet.'" He took a bite of toast, nervously, then looked over at me and winked. I kept my face expressionless. He winked again. "So, Todd." He said my name as if it were some ridiculously cheerful exclamation, like "gee whiz," or "wowee," the kind of thing he used to say with mocking relish when he was in high school. "Tomorrow's the big day!" he said. "Graduation. Commencement. The beginning of a new life." 60

"Right," I said. I didn't like to think about it that way. I couldn't imagine myself working a regular job forty hours a week, or leaving home for college or the service; it seemed amazing to me that Corky lived alone, and paid his own bills, got up in the morning without my mother waking him. 61

"Yes, Toddy," my mother said quickly. "We haven't seen you in your cap and gown." 62

"Yeah, and you're not going to either," I said. 63

"What's the matter," my father said. I could see how it was going to go. They'd do anything to escape more information about Corky's sex life. "Are you ashamed of your cap and gown?" 64

"I just don't want to put it on, that's all," I said. "What's the big deal?" 65

"Oh, come on, Todd," my brother said. He grinned. I shook my head at all of them. It figured—even with all of them looking at me, the focus was still on Corky underneath. 66

"I feel like a dancing dog," I said. I pushed away from the table. 67

When I went into my bedroom, I just stood there for a minute, staring at Corky's suitcase, then to the window. The morning was warm and clear. Outside, the grass was a sickly yellow-green in the patches that appeared where the snow had drawn back. It made me think of a horror movie I'd seen 68 where the smooth, pale skin of a dead woman peeled away to reveal a monster's face. At last, I went to the closet and took the box out. The cap and gown were still wrapped in plastic, and I tore it away roughly. I slid the gown over my head, the silky cloth slick against my bare arms, my neck. I fit the cap over my hair, and it fit snugly. It made me think of a wig. The tassel dangled in front of my nose.

69 When I came into the kitchen my brother began to hum a jazzy "Pomp and Circumstance," snapping his fingers. The gown billowed around me, the cap tilted against my line of vision, and I shambled forward, trying to imagine how Clint Eastwood would walk in a cap and gown.

70 "You look real nice," my father nodded.

71 "Stand up straight," my mother said.

72 It would have been nice to say that I was going out that night with a group of friends to some party out on somebody's farm where everyone was singing and carrying on around a keg an older brother had bought. Some of my classmates were doing that, but not *my* friends. Jeanine's grandparents were coming in from California that night, Craig's family was taking him out to dinner, Lisa and Jeff, both of them too straight for their own good, were going to a special Mass or wake or whatever it was for graduating seniors. I remember Corky and the other seniors who were in plays had a formal dinner for themselves. They'd sent out calligraphied invitations, and dressed up in coats and ties. At the party, they'd put parts of Corky's valedictorian speech to the music of *My Fair Lady*. He'd come home late, singing in a Cockney accent at the top of his lungs.

73 And what did I do? I sat around. Corky was busy providing the entertainment. As I sat after breakfast and read a horror book, my brother helped with the dishes and told my mother about Jacek, a Yugoslavian man he'd dated, a man who made independent films and had done a video for a rock group. Actually, Corky didn't say they'd dated. That was only to be guessed from the careful description he'd given. My mother drew various dishes out of the soapy water, nodding as if she didn't quite understand what it all meant.

74 After lunch, we went for a drive. Corky seemed excited. He wanted to drive by Rattlesnake Knob, he said, and take pictures to show his friends in New York. I pictured him joking about it at some cocktail party, showing his photos to

a group of lithe, smirking gay men, as they stood before the huge picture window of some penthouse, surrounding Corky, looking at the pictures and then to the city lights that blurred to dazzles, to the Statue of Liberty with the moon hanging over her head. "How quaint," they'd murmur.

The four of us squeezed into the cab of the pickup, with Corky and me in the middle. We drove out toward the hills, and when we passed the rock house, Corky made us stop. 75

The house stood in the middle of a field. It had been built by pioneers and the sod roof had long since collapsed. The rest of it had been built of pumice rock they'd gathered from the hills, and from the smattering of trees they'd found by the creek and cut down. It was still recognizable as a house, there was still the frame of the doors and windows, though the wood was mostly rotten and even the stone walls were crumbling. My father used to take us out here when we were little, and tell us about pioneers. Corky wanted to take a picture. 76

He got out of the truck and strode purposefully through the ditch to the fence. We followed after. He stretched the lines of barbed wire apart so he could squeeze through, then paused on the other side and looked closely at the wire. "Hey, Dad," he said, as we came to the edge of the fence. "Look at the strands of this wire. It's really intricate. Is that rare?" 77

My father bent over to look with Corky, so their foreheads nearly touched, so they looked like mirror images of one another, leaning over, hands on their knees. "No," my father said. "No, not rare. Just old." He sighed, straightening up. It used to be that, wherever we went, my father would be pointing things out, explaining things. As we'd drive up into the hills, my father would tell us how the trickle of creek we'd passed a mile back had made them; over millions of years a valley was created with hills on either side. I remember imagining the gray hills with their jagged lace of pumice cliffs, rising up on either side, pushing slowly out of the flat prairie like mushrooms. He taught us trivia that seemed amazing then—how to tell a rattlesnake from a bullsnake; types of barbed wire. Maybe he was remembering the same thing, because he just stood there, touching his fingers to his eyelids, as Corky clicked his camera at the rusty barbed wire. 78

"So," my brother said to me as we walked across the pasture to the rock house. "Am I going to get to meet one of 79 these girlfriends of yours? Is one of them going to stop by the house tomorrow?"

80 "I don't know," I said. My parents looked at me. They didn't say anything, but it still made me feel like a failure. They knew I didn't have a girlfriend. Even in the one thing I had over Corky I was a flop. Corky stopped in front of the rock house, which was surrounded by tall dry weeds, and put his hands on his hips. He looked over his shoulder at me, and I sighed. My parents glanced at me, and I stared down at the sod. "They're not really girlfriends," I said. "They're just friend friends."

81 When I looked up, my eyes met Corky's. I couldn't tell what he was thinking. "Hey," he said. "Why don't you all stand in front of the place? That'll make a nice shot."

82 We arranged ourselves—my father stood behind my mother and me and pulled us close to him so he could hide his pot belly. He and Corky were the tall ones in the family, and I'd inherited my mother's shortness. We pressed together. "Smile," Corky called, and stepped back. I set my lips into one of those smiles I knew was crooked and silly, but I couldn't stop it. "That's great," Corky said. He aimed the camera at us. "It's one of those pictures you'll keep forever, you know?" We separated from our cluster. Corky took another picture.

83 As we walked back to the car, Corky put his arm around my shoulders. I stiffened, but I didn't shrug him off. "I think just plain friends are the best kind," he said.

84 "Yeah, right," I said. He tilted his head as if a cool breeze were blowing.

85 "I sing this song in my show called 'We're Only Friends.' It's really great. I've got this sort of Dietrich look, and the tune is a 30s German thing, you know." He began to sing softly, his voice raspy, deep, but strikingly like a woman's. His voice carried, wafting in the open air.

86 I didn't know what he was trying to prove. Maybe he was trying to get us used to the idea. Maybe he was just needling my parents. Maybe he was showing off. Whatever he thought, the Subject kept coming into our conversations. He had given a man my mother's recipe for fried chicken. He used "Blue Moon," my father's favorite song, as the closing number for his show. He kept at it, through dinner, after, as we were watching TV, tossing little bits out for our consideration. My father had gotten a glazed look, as if he could hear someone

far away calling his name. My mother looked more and more bewildered.

As for me, I found myself thinking about the clothes I'd seen in his suitcase. I wondered if and when he was planning to put them on. 87

When he came into the bedroom late that night I was lying on the bottom bunk, reading my book. "Corky," I said. He was bent down, searching through his suitcase. "Do you—" I cleared my throat. I watched him collect a toothbrush and dental floss from his bag. "I mean you normally wear normal clothes, don't you?" 88

He looked up at me, not smiling. "I only dress for my act, if that's what you mean." 89

I nodded. I took a deep breath. "How come you packed women's clothes?" 90

His eyes narrowed. I remembered how he used to have his secret drawers, a scrapbook full of old clippings and things, the way he'd come in and found me looking through it. "Keep out of my stuff, you pig!" he'd shouted, and started punching me. 91

"What do you mean?" he said softly. He was looking me up and down, appraising me, and I watched him set the items in his hand back into the bag. He unzipped the compartment and pulled out the make-up kit, the photos. "This stuff?" he said fiercely. For a minute, I shrank back, as if he were my older brother again and I'd ruined another game. He stared at me, and then suddenly shook his head. "Todd," he said, as if remembering some other brother that wasn't me. "I thought maybe someone might have wanted to see my show." He shook his head. "People pay money to see it." He put the blouse to his face. "Here," he said, and threw it at me, hitting the book I was still holding in my hand. "Smell it." 92

It must have been the look on my face that made him laugh. I held it and sniffed the air. I had dark thoughts about what I was supposed to smell. 93

"Old Spice," he said. "For the manly man." It was my father's brand. "It's a joke," he said. He picked out the bunch of pictures and clippings and walked over to the bunks with them. He put them on top of the blouse. "If you want to look at this stuff, you can," he said. "I'm going to brush my teeth." 94

Before he got to the door, he turned. "What did you think?" he said. "I came home for the sole purpose of ruining your graduation by running around in drag?" 95

96 I looked down at the pictures of him. "Why *did* you come home?" I said.

97 He put his back to me. "Because I was stupid," he said.

98 At my graduation party, my relatives drank and gave me money. Commencement was as long and dull as the past four years of high school had been. In her speech, the valedictorian kept referring to the future as a train, and I imagined myself standing on the railroad tracks, watching it bear down on me.

99 The party made it even worse. There I was, in the middle of the living room, holding a paper plate—melting ice cream, a slice of chocolate cake—dabbing the frosting from the base of the little wax graduate that had been in the center of the cake, that my mother had insisted I take as a memento. After the first time, when my uncle Evan had come up to me and handed me an envelope, and asked me what my plans were, and I tried to tell him I had a lot of options I was considering, I gave up. The next time, when my aunt Susan handed me a card and asked me the same question, I just shrugged.

100 Which of them had futures that were so wonderful? I watched my great-aunt Birdie, already drunk even before noon. She'd been married twice and now was living with some man in Denver. Or my cousin David, who'd just gone bankrupt. Or Grandpa Mitch, who a few months before had a heart attack, who had to crawl from the bedroom, down the hall to the phone. "Oh, he looks so thin, so pale," they whispered behind his back. "He shouldn't be in that old house alone." Soon, he'd be in a rest home. My parents sat on the couch near my grandfather, looking nervously at Corky. It was sickening. They'd spent the better part of their lives raising us, and look what that got them.

101 Corky was across the room, sitting on a folding chair with his legs crossed. He was right on the edge of the kitchen; people had to walk past him to get to the food and the beer. I watched my relatives move slowly by, their eyes fixed on him. They asked him how life was treating him in the Big Apple, and tightened their smiles.

102 I stirred my ice cream and cake together. Even I couldn't help staring at him. Aunt Birdie came weaving up to me, fiddling with the tab on her beer. A napkin was stuck to her shoe, dragging behind her as she sidled up to me. "Congrat-

ulations, precious," she said, and pushed her lips to my forehead, leaning against me for support. "What's in your future?" she asked, and pushed a crumpled bill into my jacket pocket. I shook my head. "Nothing." Corky had lit another cigarette and was saying: "That sounds an awful lot like a play I auditioned for." Aunt Birdie kissed me on the eyelid, and I slid away from her grasp. I decided I needed to go outside for a while.

It was cold. I leaned against the side of the house and bunched my jacket together at the neck, staring out past the yard to the driveway, which was crowded with my relative's vehicles. I breathed slowly. For a minute I'd imagined I might spin out of control. I might have broken free of Aunt Birdie, lisping and sashaying, cooing: "My new play I auditioned for. Oh, how wonderful I am." I might have told everyone, in a loud voice, what hypocrites my parents were: "We're so proud of our Corky! How nice it is to have a son who's so glamorous and successful." 103

Corky came out a few moments later. He exhaled smoke as he poked his head out the door. "Todd," he said. "You're missing your party." He kept his body inside the house, so it looked like his head was disembodied, moving along the doorframe. He bent so he could look at me upside down. It was an old game from childhood. We used to practice miming around the edges of the doors, so from the other side it looked like we were floating, or being lifted by an invisible force. "Todd," he said, in a Donald Duck voice. "Why so glum, Todd?" His head vanished then, like a puppet yanked from a stage. He came out of the house, and stood beside me. 104

In the house, someone had turned on music, my father's Patsy Cline tape. It drifted mournfully in the stillness, wisping through the walls. 105

I sighed. "Did you ever," I said at last, "wonder what was going to happen to you?" 106

There was a flicker in his eyes, as if he'd forgotten something important. His smile wavered. "No," he said. 107

I considered this. Probably, he'd always known. "Well," I said. "What do you think will happen to me, then? Because I wonder. I wonder a lot." 108

He stared at me for a long time, and then put another cigarette to his lips. "You'll probably be miserable," he said. "Like everybody else." Our eyes met, and then we both looked down. His words hung there, with both of us con- 109 sidering them—as if he'd dropped a bowl at my feet, and we were both looking at the shards of broken glass. In the house, I could hear my father laughing.

110 "Thanks a lot," I said stiffly. "Sorry I asked."

111 He shrugged, and pulled a folded bill out of his pocket. He pushed it into my hand. "Maybe I will go squeeze into that dress," he whispered.

112 "Don't," I said through my teeth. I looked at the piece of paper in my hand. A hundred-dollar bill. "I can't take this," I said. "That's too much."

113 He lifted his eyebrows, and I watched him put it back in his pocket. His hand slid out of his pocket holding a nickel, which he flipped toward me. I fumbled, caught it. "There," he said.

114 "Very funny," I said. He dragged deeply on his cigarette.

115 We stared at each other. "Go ahead," my brother whispered. Smoke curled around his face as he breathed, and he pushed his hands through his dyed hair, loosening his ponytail. "I know you're dying to. Say 'faggot.' Say 'cocksucker.'" He smirked at me. But then as I watched, it seemed that some awful transformation was coming over his face. It was trembling and contorting like there was something beneath it trying to escape. For a second I imagined that he must be seeing something terrifying, a dark shape lunging at us, and I turned quickly. But there was only the empty yard.

116 "Say it," he whispered. "Say it."

ABORTION

Sallie Tisdale

We Do Abortions Here

A registered nurse and writer, Tisdale (born 1957) has published two books about the nursing profession, The Sorcerer's Apprentice: Medical Miracles and Other Disasters *(1986) and* Harvest Moon: Portrait of a Nursing Home *(1987), as well as* Lot's Wife: Salt and the Human Condition *(1988). In the following essay, published in 1987 in* Harper's *magazine (a prestigious forum for discussions of American culture and politics), Tisdale describes her experiences as a nurse in an abortion clinic. Does her essay take a position on the abortion question?*

We do abortions here; that is all we do. There are weary, grim moments when I think I cannot bear another basin of bloody remains, utter another kind phrase of reassurance. So I leave the procedure room in the back and reach for a new chart. Soon I am talking to an eighteen-year-old woman pregnant for the fourth time. I push up her sleeve to check her blood pressure and find row upon row of needle marks, neat and parallel and discolored. She has been so hungry for her drug for so long that she has taken to using the loose skin of her upper arms; her elbows are already a permanent ruin of bruises. She is surprised to find herself nearly four months pregnant. I suspect she is often surprised, in a mild way, by the blows she is dealt. I prepare myself for another basin, another brief and chafing loss. 1

"How can you stand it?" Even the clients ask. They see the machine, the strange instruments, the blood, the final stroke that wipes away the promise of pregnancy. Sometimes I see that too: I watch a woman's swollen abdomen sink to softness in a few stuttering moments and my own belly flip-flops with sorrow. But all it takes for me to catch my breath is another interview, one more story that sounds so 2 much like the last one. There is a numbing sameness lurking in this job: the same questions, the same answers, even the same trembling tone in the voices. The worst is the sameness of human failure, of inadequacy in the face of each day's dull demands.

3 In describing this work, I find it difficult to explain how much I enjoy it most of the time. We laugh a lot here, as friends and as professional peers. It's nice to be with women all day. I like the sudden, transient bonds I forge with some clients: moments when I am in my strength, remembering weakness, and a woman in weakness reaches out for my strength. What I offer is not power, but solidness, offered almost eagerly. Certain clients waken in me every tender urge I have—others make me wince and bite my tongue. Both challenge me to find a balance. It is a sweet brutality we practice here, a stark and loving dispassion.

4 I look at abortion as if I am standing on a cliff with a telescope, gazing at some great vista. I can sweep the horizon with both eyes, survey the scene in all its distance and size. Or I can put my eye to the lens and focus on the small details, suddenly so close. In abortion the absolute must always be tempered by the contextual, because both are real, both valid, both hard. How can we do this? How can we refuse? Each abortion is a measure of our failure to protect, to nourish our own. Each basin I empty is a promise—but a promise broken a long time ago.

5 I grew up on the great promise of birth control. Like many women my age, I took the pill as soon as I was sexually active. To risk pregnancy when it was so easy to avoid seemed stupid, and my contraceptive success, as it were, was part of the promise of social enlightenment. But birth control fails, far more frequently than laboratory trials predict. Many of our clients take the pill; its failure to protect them is a shocking realization. We have clients who have been sterilized, whose husbands have had vasectomies; each one is a statistical misfit, fine print come to life. The anger and shame of these women I hold in one hand, and the basin in the other. The distance between the two, the length I pace and try to measure, is the size of an abortion.

6 The procedure is disarmingly simple. Women are surprised, as though the mystery of conception, a dark and hidden genesis, requires an elaborate finale. In the first trimester of pregnancy, it's a mere few minutes of vacuuming, a neat tidying up. I give a woman a small yellow Valium, and

when it has begun to relax her, I lead her into the back, into bareness, the stirrups. The doctor reaches in her, opening the narrow tunnel to the uterus with a succession of slim, smooth bars of steel. He inserts a plastic tube and hooks it to a hose on the machine. The woman is framed against white paper that crackles as she moves, the light bright in her eyes. Then the machine rumbles low and loud in the small windowless room; the doctor moves the tube back and forth with an efficient rhythm, and the long tail of it fills with blood that spurts and stumbles along into a jar. He is usually finished in a few minutes. They are long minutes for the woman; her uterus frequently reacts to its abrupt emptying with a powerful, unceasing cramp, which cuts off the blood vessels and enfolds the irritated, bleeding tissue.

I am learning to recognize the shadows that cross the faces of the women I hold. While the doctor works between her spread legs,the paper drape hiding his intent expression, I stand beside the table. I hold the woman's hands in mine, resting them just below her ribs. I watch her eyes, finger her necklace, stroke her hair. I ask about her job, her family; in a haze she answers me; we chatter, faces close, eyes meeting and sliding apart. 7

I watch the shadows that creep up unnoticed and suddenly darken her face as she screws up her features and pushes a tear out each side to slide down her cheeks. I have learned to anticipate the quiver of chin, the rapid intake of breath, and the surprising sobs that rise soon after the machine starts to drum. I know this is when the cramp deepens, and the tears are partly the tears that follow pain—the sharp, childish crying when one bumps one's head on a cabinet door. But a well of woe seems to open beneath many women when they hear that thumping sound. The anticipation of the moment has finally come to fruit; the moment has arrived when the loss is no longer an imagined one. It has come true. 8

I am struck with the sameness and I am struck every day by the variety here—how this commonplace dilemma can so display the differences of women. A twenty-one-year-old woman, unemployed, uneducated, without family, in the fifth month of her fifth pregnancy. A forty-two-year-old mother of teenagers, shocked by her condition, refusing to tell her husband. A twenty-three-year-old mother of two having her seventh abortion, and many women in their thirties having their first. Some are stoic, some hysterical, a few giggle uncontrollably, many cry. 9

10 I talk to a sixteen-year-old uneducated girl who was raped. She has gonorrhea. She describes blinding headaches, attacks of breathlessness, nausea. "Sometimes I feel like two different people," she tells me with a calm smile, "and I talk to myself."

11 I pull out my plastic models. She listens patiently for a time, and then holds her hands wide in front of her stomach.

12 "When's the baby going to go up into my stomach?" she asks.

13 I blink. "What do you mean?"

14 "Well," she says, still smiling, "when women get so big, isn't the baby in your stomach? Doesn't it hatch out of an egg there?"

15 My first question in an interview is always the same. As I walk down the hall with the woman, as we get settled in chairs and I glance through her files, I am trying to gauge her, to get a sense of the words, and the tone, I should use. With some I joke, with others I chat, sometimes fall into a brisk, business-line patter. But I ask every woman, "Are you sure you want to have an abortion?" Most nod with grim knowing smiles. "Oh, yes," they sigh. Some seek forgiveness, offer excuses. Occasionally a woman will flinch and say, "Please don't use that word."

16 Later I describe the procedure to come, using care with my language. I don't say "pain" any more than I would say "baby." So many are afraid to ask how much it will hurt. "My sister told me—" I hear. "A friend of mine said—" and the dire expectations unravel. I prick the index finger of a woman for a drop of blood to test, and as the tiny lancet approaches the skin she averts her eyes, holding her trembling hand out to me and jumping at my touch.

17 It is when I am holding a plastic uterus in one hand, a suction tube in the other, moving them together in imitation of the scrubbing to come, that women ask the most secret question. I am speaking in a matter-of-fact voice about "the tissue" and "the contents" when the woman suddenly catches my eye and asks, "How big is the baby now?" These words suggest a quiet need for a definition of the boundaries being drawn. It isn't so odd, after all, that she feels relief when I describe the growing bud's bulbous shape, its miniature nature. Again I gauge, and sometimes lie a little, weaseling around its infantile features until its clinging power slackens.

18 But when I look in the basin, among the curdlike blood

clots, I see an elfin thorax, attenuated, its pencilline ribs all in parallel rows with tiny knobs of spine rounding upwards. The translucent arm and hand swim beside.

A sleepy-eyed girl, just fourteen, watched me with a slight and goofy smile all through her abortion. "Does it have little feet and little fingers and all?" she'd asked earlier. When the suction was over she sat up woozily at the end of the table and murmured, "Can I see it?" I shook my head firmly. 19

"It's not allowed," I told her sternly, because I knew she didn't really want to see what was left. She accepted this statement of authority, and a shadow of confused relief crossed her plain, pale face. 20

Privately, even grudgingly, my colleagues might admit the power of abortion to provoke emotion. But they seem to prefer the broad view and disdain the telescope. Abortion is a matter of choice, privacy, control. Its uncertainty lies in specific cases: retarded women and girls too young to give consent for surgery, women who are ill or hostile or psychotic. Such common dilemmas are met with both compassion and impatience; they slow things down. We are too busy to chew over ethics. One person might discuss certain concerns, behind closed doors, or describe a particularly disturbing dream. But generally there is to be no ambivalence. 21

Every day I take calls from women who are annoyed that we cannot see them, cannot do their abortion today, this morning, now. They argue the price, demand that we stay after hours to accommodate their job or class schedule. Abortion is so routine that one expects it to be like a manicure: quick, cheap, and painless. 22

Still, I've cultivated a certain disregard. It isn't negligence, but I don't always pay attention. I couldn't be here if I tried to judge each case on its merits; after all, we do over a hundred abortions a week. At some point each individual in this line of work draws a boundary and adheres to it. For one physician the boundary is a particular week of gestation; for another, it is a certain number of repeated abortions. But these boundaries can be fluid too: one physician overruled his own limit to abort a mature but severely malformed fetus. For me, the limit is allowing my clients to carry their own burden, shoulder the responsibility themselves. I shoulder the burden of trying not to judge them. 23

24 This city has several "crisis pregnancy centers" advertised in the Yellow Pages. They are small offices staffed by volunteers, and they offer free pregnancy testing, glossy photos of dead fetuses, and movies. I had a client recently whose mother is active in the antiabortion movement. The young woman went to the local crisis center and was told that the doctor would make her touch the dismembered baby, that the pain would be the most horrible she could imagine, and that she might, after an abortion, never be able to have children. All lies. They called her at home and at work, over and over and over, but she had been wise enough to give a false name. She came to us a fugitive. We who do abortions are marked, by some, as impure. It's dirty work.

25 When a delivery man comes to the sliding glass window by the reception desk and tilts a box toward me, I hesitate. I read the packing slip, assess the shape and weight of the box in the light of its supposed contents. We request familiar faces. The doors are carefully locked; I have learned to half glance around at bags and boxes, looking for a telltale sign. I register with security when I arrive, and I am careful not to bang a door. We are a little on edge here.

26 Concern about size and shape seem to be natural, and so is the relief that follows. We make the powerful assumption that the fetus is different from us, and even when we admit the similarities, it is too simplistic to be seduced by form alone. But the form is enormously potent—humanoid, powerless, palm-sized, and pure, it evokes an almost fierce tenderness when viewed simply as what it appears to be. But appearance, and even potential, aren't enough. The fetus, in becoming itself, can ruin others: its utter dependence has a sinister side. When I am struck in the moment by the contents in the basin, I am careful to remember the context, to note the tearful teenager and the woman sighing with something more than relief. One kind of question, though, I find considerably trickier.

27 "Can you tell what it is?" I am asked, and this means gender. This question is asked by couples, not women alone. Always couples would abort a girl and keep a boy. I have been asked about twins, and even if I could tell what race the father was.

28 An eighteen-year-old woman with three daughters brought her husband to the interview. He glared first at me, then at his

wife, as he sank lower and lower in the chair, picking his teeth with a toothpick. He interrupted a conversation with his wife to ask if I could tell whether the baby would be a boy or a girl. I told him I could not.

"Good," he replied in a slow and strangely malevolent voice, " 'cause if it was a boy I'd wring her neck." 29

In a literal sense, abortion exists because we are able to ask such questions, able to assign a value to the fetus which can shift with changing circumstances. If the human bond to a child were as primitive and unflinchingly narrow as that of other animals, there would be no abortion. There would be no abortion because there would be nothing more important than caring for the young and perpetuating the species, no reason for sex but to make babies. I sense this sometimes, this wordless organic duty, when I do ultrasounds. 30

We do ultrasound, a sound-wave test that paints a faint, gray picture of the fetus, whenever we're uncertain of gestation. Age is measured by the width of the skull and confirmed by the length of the femur or thighbone; we speak of a pregnancy as being a certain "femur length" in weeks. The usual concern is whether a pregnancy is within the legal limit for an abortion. Women this far along have bellies which swell out round and tight like trim muscles. When they lie flat, the mound rises softly above the hips, pressing the umbilicus upward. 31

It takes practice to read an ultrasound picture, which is grainy and etched as though in strokes of charcoal. But suddenly a rapid rhythmic motion appears—the beating heart. Nearby is a soft oval, scratched with lines—the skull. The leg is harder to find, and then suddenly the fetus moves, bobbing in the surf. The skull turns away, an arm slides across the screen, the torso rolls. I know the weight of a baby's head on my shoulder, the whisper of lips on ears, the delicate curve of a fragile spine in my hand. I know how heavy and correct a newborn cradled feels. The creature I watch in secret requires nothing from me but to be left alone, and that is precisely what won't be done. 32

These inadvertently made beings are caught in a twisting web of motive and desire. They are at least inconvenient, sometimes quite literally dangerous in the womb, but most often they fall somewhere in between—consequences never quite believed in come to roost. Their virtue rises and falls outside their own nature: they become only what we make 33 them. A fetus created by accident is the most absolute kind of surprise. Whether the blame lies in a failed IUD, a slipped condom, or a false impression of safety, that fetus is a thing whose creation has been actively worked against. Its existence is an error. I think this is why so few women, even late in pregnancy, will consider giving a baby up for adoption. To do so means making the fetus real—imagining it as something whole and outside oneself. The decision to terminate a pregnancy is sometimes so difficult and confounding that it creates an enormous demand for immediate action. The decision is rejection; the pregnancy has become something to be rid of, a condition to be ended. It is a burden, a weight, a thing separate.

34 Women have abortions because they are too old, and too young, too poor, and too rich, too stupid, and too smart. I see women who berate themselves with violent emotions for their first and only abortion, and others who return three times, five times, hauling two or three children, who cannot remember to take a pill or where they put the diaphragm. We talk glibly about choice. But the choice for what? I see all the broken promises in lives lived like a series of impromptu obstacles. There are the sweet, light promises of love and intimacy, the glittering promise of education and progress, the warm promise of safe families, long years of innocence and community. And there is the promise of freedom: freedom from failure, from faithlessness. Freedom from biology. The early feminist defense of abortion asked many questions, but the one I remember is this: is biology destiny? And the answer is yes, sometimes it is. Women who have the fewest choices of all exercise their right to abortion the most.

35 Oh, the ignorance. I take a woman to the back room and ask her to undress; a few minutes later I return and find her positioned discreetly behind a drape, still wearing underpants. "Do I have to take these off too?" she asks, a little shocked. Some swear they have not had sex. Many do not know what a uterus is, how sperm and egg meet, how sex makes babies. Some late seekers do not believe themselves pregnant; they believe themselves *impregnable.* I was chastised when I began this job for referring to some clients as girls: it is a feminist heresy. They come so young, snapping gum, sockless and sneakered, and their shakily applied eyeliner smears when they cry. I call them girls with maternal benignity. I cannot imagine them as mothers.

* * *

The doctor seats himself between the woman's thighs and reaches into the dilated opening of a five-month pregnant uterus. Quickly he grabs and crushes the fetus in several places, and the room is filled with a low clatter and snap of forceps, the click of the tanaculum,* and a pulling, sucking sound. The paper crinkles as the drugged and sleepy woman shifts, the nurse's low, honey-brown voice explains each step in delicate words. 36

I have fetus dreams, we all do here: dreams of abortions one after the other; of buckets of blood splashed on the walls; trees full of crawling fetuses. I dreamed that two men grabbed me and began to drag me away: "Let's do an abortion," they said with a sickening leer, and I began to scream, plunged into a vision of sucking, scraping pain, of being spread and torn by impartial instruments that do only what they are bidden. I woke from this dream barely able to breathe and thought of kitchen tables and coat hangers, knitting needles striped with blood, and women all alone clutching a pillow in their teeth to keep the screams from piercing the apartment-house walls. Abortion is the narrowest edge between kindness and cruelty. Done as well as it can be, it is still violence—merciful violence, like putting a suffering animal to death. 37

Maggie, one of the nurses, received a call at midnight not long ago. It was a woman in her twentieth week of pregnancy; the necessarily gradual process of cervical dilation begun the day before had stimulated labor, as it sometimes does. Maggie and one of the doctors met the woman at the office in the night. Maggie helped her onto the table, and as she lay down the fetus was delivered into Maggie's hands. When Maggie told me about it the next day, she cupped her hands into a small bowl—"It was just like a little kitten," she said softly, wonderingly. "Everything was still attached." 38

At the end of the day I clean out the suction jars, pouring blood into the sink, splashing the sides with flecks of tissue. From the sink rises a rich and humid smell, hot, earthy, and moldering; it is the smell of something recently alive beginning to decay. I take care of the plastic tub on the floor, filled with pieces too big to be trusted to the trash. The law defines the contents of the bucket I hold protectively against my chest as "tissue." Some would say my complicity in filling 39

* A type of sharp forceps used on bleeding arteries.

that bucket gives me no right to call it anything else. I slip the tissue gently into a bag and place it in the freezer, to be burned at another time. Abortion requires of me an entirely new set of assumptions. It requires a willingness to live with conflict, fearlessness, and grief. As I close the freezer door, I imagine a world where this won't be necessary, and then return to the world where it is.

Mary Meehan

A Pro-Life View from the Left

Mary Meehan has written many articles on various topics for respected newspapers and periodicals such as The Nation, The Washington Monthly, *and* The Washington Post. *In 1980 she contributed the following article to* The Progressive, *a monthly magazine that, true to its name, takes a liberal stance toward current public issues.*

1 The abortion issue, more than most, illustrates the occasional tendency of the Left to become so enthusiastic over what is called a "reform" that it forgets to think the issue through. It is ironic that so many on the Left have done on abortion what conservatives and Cold War liberals did on Vietnam: They marched off in the wrong direction, to fight the wrong war, against the wrong people.

2 Some of us who went through the anti-war struggles of the 1960s and early 1970s are now active in the right-to-life movement. We do not enjoy opposing our old friends on the abortion issue, but we feel that we have no choice. We are moved by what pro-life feminists call the "consistency thing"—the belief that respect for human life demands opposition to abortion, capital punishment, euthanasia, and war. We don't think we have either the luxury or the right to choose some types of killing and say that they are all right, while others are not. A human life is a human life; and if equality means anything, it means that society may not value some human lives over others.

3 Until the last decade, people on the Left and Right

generally agreed on one rule: We all protected the young. This was not merely agreement on an ethical question: It was also an expression of instinct, so deep and ancient that it scarcely required explanation.

Protection of the young included protection of the unborn, 4
for abortion was forbidden by state laws throughout the United States. Those laws reflected an ethical consensus, not based solely on religious tradition but also on scientific evidence that human life begins at conception. The prohibition of abortion in the ancient Hippocratic Oath is well known. Less familiar to many is the Oath of Geneva, formulated by the World Medical Association in 1948, which included these words: "I will maintain the utmost respect for human life from the time of conception." A Declaration of the Rights of the Child, adopted by the United Nations General Assembly in 1959, declared that "the child, by reason of his physical and mental immaturity, needs special safeguards and care, including appropriate legal protection, before as well as after birth."

It is not my purpose to explain why courts and parlia- 5
ments in many nations rejected this tradition over the past few decades, though I suspect their action was largely a surrender to technical achievement—if such inventions as suction aspirators can be called technical achievements. But it is important to ask why the Left in the United States generally accepted legalized abortion.

One factor was the popular civil-libertarian rationale for 6
freedom of choice in abortion. Many feminists presented it as a right of women to control their own bodies. When the objection was raised that abortion ruins *another person*'s body, they respond that a) it is not a body, just a "blob of protoplasm" (thereby displaying ignorance of biology); or b) it is not really a "person" until it is born. When it was suggested that this is a wholly arbitrary decision, unsupported by any biological evidence, they said, "Well, that's your point of view. This is a matter of individual conscience, and in a pluralistic society people must be free to follow their consciences."

Unfortunately, many liberals and radicals accepted this 7
view without further question. Perhaps many did not know that an eight-week-old fetus has a fully human form. They did not ask whether American slaveholders before the Civil War were right in viewing blacks as less than human and as private property; or whether the Nazis were correct in

viewing mental patients, Jews, and Gypsies as less than human and therefore subject to the final solution.

8 Class issues provided another rationale. In the late 1960s, liberals were troubled by evidence that rich women could obtain abortions regardless of the law, by going to careful society doctors or to countries where abortion was legal. Why, they asked, should poor women be barred from something the wealthy could have? One might turn this argument on its head by asking why rich children should be denied protection that poor children have.

9 But pro-life activists did not want abortion to be a class issue one way or the other; they wanted to end abortion everywhere, for all classes. And many people who had experienced poverty did not think providing legal abortion was any favor to poor women. Thus, in 1972, when a Presidential commission on population growth recommended legalized abortion, partly to remove discrimination against poor women, several commission members dissented.

10 One was Graciela Olivarez, a Chicana who was active in civil rights and anti-poverty work. Olivarez, who later was named to head the Federal Government's Community Services Administration, had known poverty in her youth in the Southwest. With a touch of bitterness, she said in her dissent, "The poor cry out for justice and equality and we respond with legalized abortion." Olivarez noted that blacks and Chicanos had often been unwanted by white society. She added, "I believe that in a society that permits the life of even one individual (born or unborn) to be dependent on whether that life is 'wanted' or not, all its citizens stand in danger." Later she told the press, "We do not have equal opportunities. Abortion is a cruel way out."

11 Many liberals were also persuaded by a church/state argument that followed roughly this line: "Opposition to abortion is a religious viewpoint, particularly a Catholic viewpoint. The Catholics have no business imposing their religious views on the rest of us." It is true that opposition to abortion is a religious position for many people. Orthodox Jews, Mormons, and many of the fundamentalist Protestant groups also oppose abortion. (So did the mainstream Protestant churches until recent years.) But many people are against abortion for reasons that are independent of reli-

gious authority or belief. Many would still be against abortion if they lost their faith; others are opposed to it after they *have* lost their faith, or if they never had any faith. Only if their non-religious grounds for opposition can be proven baseless could legal prohibition of abortion fairly be called an establishment of religion. The pro-abortion forces concentrate heavily on religious arguments against abortion and generally ignore the secular arguments—possibly because they cannot answer them.

Still another, more emotional reason is that so many conservatives oppose abortion. Many liberals have difficulty accepting the idea that Jesse Helms can be right about *anything.* I do not quite understand this attitude. Just by the law of averages, he has to be right about something, sometime. Standing at the March for Life rally at the U.S. Capitol last year, and hearing Senator Helms say that "We reject the philosophy that life should be only for the planned, the perfect, or the privileged," I thought he was making a good civil-rights statement. 12

If much of the leadership of the pro-life movement is right-wing, that is due largely to the default of the Left. We "little people" who marched against the war and now march against abortion would like to see leaders of the Left speaking out on behalf of the unborn. But we see only a few, such as Dick Gregory, Mark Hatfield, Jesse Jackson, Richard Neuhaus, Mary Rose Oakar. Most of the others either avoid the issue or support abortion. We are dismayed by their inconsistency. And we are not impressed by arguments that we should work and vote for them because they are good on such issues as food stamps and medical care. 13

Although many liberals and radicals accepted legalized abortion, there are signs of uneasiness about it. Tell someone who supports it that you have many problems with the issue, and she is likely to say, quickly, "Oh, I don't think I could ever have one myself, but. . . ." or "I'm really not pro-*abortion;* I'm pro-*choice*" or "I'm *personally* opposed to it, but. . . ." 14

Why are they personally opposed to it if there is nothing wrong with it? 15

Perhaps such uneasiness is a sign that many on the Left are ready to take another look at the abortion issue. In the hope of contributing toward a new perspective, I offer the following points: 16

First, it is out of character for the Left to neglect the weak 17 and helpless. The traditional mark of the Left has been its protection of the underdog, the weak, and the poor. The unborn child is the most helpless form of humanity, even more in need of protection than the poor tenant farmer or the mental patient or the boat people on the high seas. The basic instinct of the Left is to aid those who cannot aid themselves—and that instinct is absolutely sound. It is what keeps the human proposition going.

18 *Second,* the right to life underlies and sustains every other right we have. It is, as Thomas Jefferson and his friends said, self-evident. Logically, as well as in our Declaration of Independence, it comes before the right to liberty and the right to property. The right to exist, to be free from assault by others, is the basis of equality. Without it, the other rights are meaningless, and life becomes a sort of warfare in which force decides everything. There is no equality, because one person's convenience takes precedence over another's life, provided only that the first person has more power. If we do not protect this right for everyone, it is not guaranteed for everyone, because anyone can become weak and vulnerable to assault.

19 *Third,* abortion is a civil-rights issue. Dick Gregory and many other blacks view abortion as a type of genocide. Confirmation of this comes in the experience of pro-life activists who find open bigotry when they speak with white voters about public funding of abortion. Many white voters believe abortion is a solution for the welfare problem and a way to slow the growth of the black population. I worked two years ago for a liberal, pro-life candidate who was appalled by the number of anti-black comments he found when discussing the issue. And Representative Robert Dornan of California, a conservative pro-life leader, once told his colleagues in the House, "I have heard many rock-ribbed Republicans brag about how fiscally conservative they are and then tell me that I was an idiot on the abortion issue." When he asked why, said Dornan, they whispered, "Because we have to told them down, we have to stop the population growth." Dornan elaborated: "To them, population growth means blacks, Puerto Ricans, or other Latins," or anyone who "should not be having more than a polite one or two 'burdens on society.' "

20 *Fourth,* abortion exploits women. Many women are pressured by spouses, lovers, or parents into having abortions they do not want. Sometimes the coercion is subtle, as when a husband complains of financial problems. Sometimes it is open and crude, as when a boyfriend threatens to end the

affair unless the woman has an abortion, or when parents order a minor child to have an abortion. Pro-life activists who do "clinic counseling" (standing outside abortion clinics, trying to speak to each woman who enters, urging her to have the child) report that many women who enter clinics alone are willing to talk and to listen. Some change their minds and decide against abortion. But a woman who is accompanied by someone else often does not have the chance to talk, because the husband or boyfriend or parent is so hostile to the pro-life worker.

Juli Loesch, a feminist/pacifist writer, notes that feminists 21
want to have men participate more in the care of children, but abortion allows a man to shift total responsibility to the woman: "He can *buy* his way out of accountability by making 'The Offer' for 'The Procedure.'" She adds that the man's sexual role "then implies—exactly nothing: no relationship. How quickly a 'woman's right to choose' comes to serve a 'man's right to use.'" And Daphne de Jong, a New Zealand feminist, says, "If women must submit to abortion to preserve their lifestyle or career, their economic or social status, they are pandering to a system devised and run by men for male convenience." She adds, "Of all the things which are done to women to fit them into a society dominated by men, abortion is the most violent invasion of their physical and psychic integrity. It is a deeper and more destructive assault than rape. . . ."

Loesch, de Jong, Olivarez, and other pro-life feminists 22
believe men should bear a much greater share of the burdens of child-rearing than they do at present. And de Jong makes a radical point when she says, "Accepting short-term solutions like abortion only delays the implementation of real reforms like decent maternity and paternity leaves, job protection, high-quality child care, community responsibility for dependent people of all ages, and recognition of the economic contribution of childminders." Olivarez and others have also called for the development of safer and more effective contraceptives for both men and women. In her 1972 dissent, Olivarez noted with irony that "medical science has developed four different ways for killing a fetus, but has not yet developed a safe-for-all-to-use contraceptive."

Fifth, abortion is an escape from an obligation that is 23
owed to another. Doris Gordon, Coordinator of Libertarians for Life, puts it this way: "Unborn children don't cause women to become pregnant but parents cause their children

to be in the womb, and as a result, they need parental care. As a general principle, if we are the cause of another's need for care, as when we cause an accident, we acquire an obligation to that person as a result. . . . We have no right to kill in order to terminate any obligation."

24 *Sixth,* abortion brutalizes those who perform it, undergo it, pay for it, profit from it, and allow it to happen. Too many of us look the other way because we do not want to think about abortion. A part of reality is blocked out because one does not want to see broken bodies coming home, or going to an incinerator, in those awful plastic bags. People deny their own humanity when they refuse to identify with, or even acknowledge, the pain of others.

25 With some it is worse: They are making money from the misery of others, from exploited women and dead children. Doctors, businessmen, and clinic directors are making a great deal of money from abortion. Jobs and high incomes depend on abortion; it's part of the gross national product. The parallels of this with the military-industrial complex should be obvious to anyone who was involved in the anti-war movement.

26 And the "slippery slope" argument is right: People really do go from accepting abortion to accepting euthanasia and accepting "triage" for the world hunger problem and accepting "lifeboat ethics" as a general guide to human behavior. We slip down the slope, back to the jungle.

27 To save the smallest children, and to save its own conscience, the Left should speak out against abortion.

Sally Quinn
Our Choices, Ourselves

Sally Quinn (born 1941), a novelist, a writer for The Washington Post *since 1969, and a well-known and respected Washington "insider," contributed the following article to* The Washington Post *in April 1992.*

When I was in college, a classmate told a group of us about a friend who had gotten pregnant and had been too scared to tell anyone. Now she was almost eight months along and showing. She had found someone to perform an abortion for her (illegal, of course; this was 1963) and was agonizing over what to do. She should definitely have the abortion, we all agreed. There was really no other choice. 1

When I think now how sanguine we all were about our position on aborting an 8-month-old, presumably normal, fetus it makes me shudder. A fetus, we figured, was just that—a fetus—until it came out of the mother's body; and up until that time, even at nine months, it was okay to abort it. 2

Thinking about that also makes me realize how far we've come in terms of our awareness of the complexity of the abortion issue. And thinking about it on a day like today, when tens of thousands of abortion rights advocates hold their March for Women's Lives here, makes me realize how far we have to go. 3

For me, today's protest, sponsored by the National Organization for Women and other groups, is a reminder that the biggest problem with the abortion issue today is the nearly absolute polarization of both sides. Like a marriage on the rocks, the two sides have hardened their positions. The sad thing is that most American women fall somewhere in between but are driven by politics to adopt rigid views. 4

Part of the problem is the labels. Those who are against abortion call themselves "pro-life" and refer to their opponents as "pro-abortion." On the other side are the abortion-rights advocates who refer to those who oppose abortion as "antiabortion" and "anti-choice." 5

The "label war" is out of balance. I can't understand how people who oppose abortion rights managed to wrest away the "pro-life" label. In the same way that conservatives managed to appropriate the American flag, the position of 6 caring about human life has been virtually surrendered. But I am for abortion rights, and I am as much—if not more—pro-life as anyone. And I won't give that away.

7 The polarization gets intense because the antiabortion people start with the position that abortion is murder. It's that simple, they say. From the moment of conception, from the second that the egg is fertilized by the sperm, it becomes a human life. Period.

8 Of course, no one then acts as if the fetus is a human life. The IRS does not let us count the fetus as a dependent. No one to my knowledge has ever suggested that a fetus ought to be baptized. And so on.

9 The fact is that most women are extremely conflicted about the idea of abortion, particularly late-term abortions; even a National Abortion Rights League spokeswoman will say, as she did late last week, "We don't love abortion." Anyone who has been pregnant can tell you that after you have felt that quickening in your womb, after a fetus has kicked in your belly, the very idea of abortion becomes painfully difficult.

10 Yet every woman who has amniocentesis or a chorionic villus sampling (a similar, but earlier test) does it because she at least entertains the possibility of having an abortion if something is wrong with the fetus. One reason so many women opt for the CVS (despite the greater risk of miscarriage) is that they can't bear the idea of a late abortion. An amino cannot give you results until the fetus is almost five months old. At five months, an abortion is, in effect, the delivery of a dead baby. You don't need the label "pro-life" to know that.

11 The single worst month of my life was the month between the time I had the amnio and the time I got the results. All the time, my child was kicking in my stomach. He was a part of me by then. I had invested so much in him that the idea of losing him was unthinkable.

12 All the choices were unthinkable. Modern-day tests like amnios and sonograms can tell you many abnormalities that could show up. They range in severity from anencephaly (being born without a brain, like the child in Florida last week), to Marfan syndrome, a connective tissue disorder that Abraham Lincoln may have had. Down syndrome is a major reason for an amnio, especially in older women.

Spina bifida is revealed by a blood test. Both have varying degrees of severity.

13 As I lay in my bed each night, I was haunted by the idea of my child having any one of hundreds of possible defects. What would I do if. . . . If the diagnosed deformity were severe, the decision was obvious to me. In the case of less crippling defects, the decision would be heartwrenchingly confusing. None was easy.

14 Heart defects don't show up on the amnio, and my son was born with a heart defect. Most heart defects are easily repaired and the children go on to lead normal lives. Today, the defect is detectable by sonogram and women can choose to abort. Knowing what joy our son has brought to us, that would be unthinkable. And unbearable.

15 I had a friend whose amnio revealed that her baby would be born with severe defects. She decided to abort. She's never been the same since. And she never had another child.

16 The antiabortion people, meanwhile, have painted supporters of abortion rights as murderers, a bunch of sex-crazed women who don't want to suffer the consequences of their actions and don't give a damn about human life. But that is, of course, a fantasy. The reality is that favoring abortion rights is not the same as favoring abortion. It means you are concerned about privacy. It means you don't want someone else to impose his or her views—personal, political or religious—on you. According to the latest *Washington Post* survey, 57 percent of American women favor abortion rights—a figure that has been fairly consistent over the years.

17 At least half of my friends have had abortions at some time in their lives, and I'll bet that is not an unusual statistic for most American women of my age. It has always been scary and sad. People are always surprised at how difficult emotionally it can be. And this is when it is safe and legal; there are about 1.6 million abortions performed each year in the United States.

18 In the days when abortion was unsafe and illegal (and the annual death rate was in the thousands), several of my mother's friends died from botched abortions. Some of these were already mothers—some with several children. I had friends who couldn't have children after badly botched abortions. I had a beautiful and brilliant friend in college

who was afraid of an illegal abortion. She went to a home for unwed mothers and gave her baby up for adoption. She has been in and out of mental institutions ever since.

19 Even a few years ago, it was thought that only bad girls and actresses got pregnant out of wedlock. And not so long ago, I would have had an abortion if I'd gotten pregnant before marriage. There were times when I thought I was pregnant. The fear was indescribable. Even after abortion was legal, the fear was indescribable.

20 Though I believe in choice, it is perfectly understandable to me that some people do not believe that abortion is ever justified. Many Catholics hold this view. I have a Catholic friend who told me that they would not choose to have amniocentesis if his wife got pregnant because "I don't know whether or not I would have the strength to make the right decision if something turned out wrong."

21 Such people may even believe that abortion is akin to murder. But they're not prepared to accuse others whose opinions differ of committing murder.

22 Of course this "pro-life" position is not consistent. If it is murder, and it's premeditated, shouldn't the punishment be the same as for any murder conviction? And for those "pro-life" people in favor of the death penalty, shouldn't any mother who willingly aborts a child be put to death? Hanged by the neck until dead, fried in the chair, given an injection? And that goes for the doctor who performs the abortion, and anyone who aids it.

23 It's either murder or it ain't. You can't have it both ways.

24 Particularly specious are those who say abortion is murder but it's okay in the case of rape or incest.

25 Excuse me? The innocent "child" is murdered because it had the unfortunate luck of being conceived illegally? Does the manner of conception make the child any less human? By this reasoning, a 5-year-old who is discovered to have been conceived in incest could be put to death.

26 There are many reasons why someone may choose to abort. Rape or incest, birth defects, poverty, illness, a mother either too young or too old.

27 But there are other more subtle reasons too. If a mother feels unprepared, emotionally or psychologically or physically, whose decision should it be? Who, after all, will live with the consequences?

28 Often that decision to abort is nothing less than a pro-life decision. Anyone who has walked through a neo-natal ward

in a hospital and seen the half-pound "babies" with dark glasses on and tubes coming out every pore, crack babies, AIDS babies, abandoned babies and babies who will grow up to be retarded or profoundly emotionally disturbed, can't help wondering about the quality of life these children will have.

It seems to me that those who are pro-choice may know what lies in store for these children—and care more about life than many of those who call themselves "pro-life." 29

If the abortion question had not so polarized America, the two "sides" might be better able to talk about such questions. But I get the impression that many antiabortion or "pro-life" advocates, for all their talk of "ethics" and "morality," have little concern for what happens to the babies after they are born. The mere fact of life is their only concern. But who will shoulder the financial and emotional burdens of these "lives"? Once it's a "life" they lose interest. 30

Meanwhile, a question haunts all of us who are in favor of abortion rights: When does life begin, anyway? 31

Under the *Roe* v. *Wade* ruling, a woman has virtually unrestricted access to abortion in the first trimester, may be subject to specific regulations in the second trimester and can be barred (except when it affects maternal health) in the third. This Solomon-like decision seems a proper way to look at it. On the one hand, I don't want anyone telling me what to do with my body; on the other, I have difficulty with the concept of aborting a 9-month-old fetus. I'm not ready to call it murder, but I have grave doubts. 32

But I don't like to admit any hesitancy or doubt. I fear being pounced on by those who will take my lack of conviction—my unwillingness to dig my heels in—as agreement with antiabortion advocates. 33

A 9-month-old fetus can certainly live independently. So, in some cases, can a 7-month-old fetus. Is it all right to kill the fetus inside the mother's body? I think not. 34

Catherine Stern aborted her 7-month-old fetus when she learned it had no arms and legs and was possibly brain-damaged. Would I have done that? Yes, devastating as it would have been. But the consequences of not doing it would have been worse. 35

In the future, science may allow us to know far more about a fetus—from her IQ and height to the color of its 36 hair. But what if the fetus is projected to have an IQ of 80? Or if it were homely? Would I allow an abortion if it were up to me? What about choosing to abort if it's the "wrong" sex—already commonplace in some Third World countries, where female babies are devalued? I find these notions reprehensible, yet I'm unwilling to say where I would draw the line.

37 Meanwhile, some people are using abortion as a form of birth control. I know a woman who brags that she's had eight abortions rather than use contraceptives, which she derides as "inconvenient." How do I feel about this? The way most people do, regardless of where they stand on today's march: Disgusted. Am I prepared to tell her that she can't have more abortions? The answer is no.

38 That is how things have become polarized: Some antiabortionists have poisoned the well to the point where they have even made contraception and sex education controversial. And by taking the position that abortion is murder, they have forced those of us who believe in abortion rights to take an equally hard-line position, no matter how bothered we are by some of the results.

39 The fact is that you can't reduce this argument to simple choices, and you can't avoid it by simple rules. There are a lot of issues that women on both sides of the abortion issue would agree on if they simply were able to admit their honest doubts, but politics has made it even more divisive.

40 The First Amendment permits anyone to carry fetuses around in bottles and say, "Is this what you want?" But the black-and-white nature of the resulting argument destroys any possibility of commonality of beliefs, or feelings, or emotions or interests.

41 If most women had the choice, they would acknowledge that one group should not have the power to determine the lives of another. And ultimately that has to be the way it is. Ultimately, the debate is not about murder, or even choice, but the most intimate kind of privacy.

42 If I got pregnant today, would I have an abortion? I know the answer to that, and it's nobody's business but mine. And that's the point.

Mike Royko

A Pox on Both Your Houses

Royko (born 1922), a syndicated columnist associated with The Chicago Tribune*—and with Chicago in general, since he worked as a reporter for several Chicago newspapers for many years—wrote the following commentary in July 1992, a few days after the Supreme Court upheld both* Roe v. Wade *and most parts of a controversial Pennsylvania law requiring women desiring an abortion to wait 24 hours, to receive written material on the medical procedure, and, if they are minors, to inform their parents. Mike Royko has won a Pulitzer Prize for social commentary.*

"Why are all those women so mad?" asked Slats Grobnik, gesturing at the TV set. "The old man stop for a few after work?" 1

No, it is far more serious than that. They are an anti-abortion group, furious because the Supreme Court has upheld the right of women to get abortions. 2

The TV switched to another angry group of women. 3

"Now what's this bunch mad about? They're yelling louder than the others." 4

They are a pro-abortion group, and they are furious because the Supreme Court has upheld a few restrictions. 5

"Like what?" 6

A 24-hour waiting period. Parental consent for teen-agers. And women being told what their options are, such as adoption, and what kind of medical and financial help is available if she has the baby. 7

"Wait a minute, I don't get it." 8

Get what? 9

"I can see how the anti-abortion crowd would be mad because abortions are still legal, right?" 10

That's what the court said. 11

"Then if they're legal, what's the other side got to beef about?" 12

They don't like any kind of restrictions. They feel it is a threat to their control over their own bodies. 13

"Waiting 24 hours? Nowadays, you got to wait 24 hours for everything. It takes longer than that to get a tooth drilled or your car tuned up. So what's the big rush? And what's 14 wrong with telling some girl about financial help or that there are people who want to adopt kids?"

15 They believe that is not society's business to intrude on their right to control their own bodies.

16 "Hey, when the draft board told me I was gonna go fight in Korea, that was messing with my right to control my body, because I guarantee you, I didn't want my body being shot up by no Chinese commies. So I wind up putting in two years with society, by way of the government, telling my body where it's going to go and what it's going to do. If I want to stick a needle in my arm and shoot up with dope, that's illegal. Even though that arm is part of my body right?"

17 Correct.

18 "See, that's what bothers me about this abortion fight. These people don't always make sense."

19 Which side?

20 "Both sides. They're not always, what'ya call it, consistent?"

21 In what way?

22 "Well, the one side says they are pro-life. Now, does that mean that they're against frying someone in the electric chair?"

23 I would doubt that.

24 "That's what I thought, because I know a few of the pro-life ladies and they want to hang 'em high. And were they against us dropping bombs and killing women and children in Iraq because we wanted to put this rich emir back on his throne in Kuwait?"

25 I would guess that they were part of the mainstream of public opinion that delighted in the triumphs of our heroic video war.

26 "That's what I think. So when they say they're pro-life, it all depends on what life, right?"

27 Yes, the unborn.

28 "And don't get me wrong. I don't have any trouble with that. Especially when I read that there's been 26 million abortions in the last 19 years. You know what that works out to on my pocket calculator?"

29 Lots.

30 "Yeah, more than 26,000 a week. About 3,700 a day. About 156 an hour. Almost three a minute. Think about it. Every 20 or 30 seconds, there's an abortion. Are there really that many people whose lives are gonna be ruined if they have a

kid? I'm supposed to believe that it's a disaster if they gotta wait 24 hours? Or if someone talks to them about adoption?"

But it is a question of choice, which is why they call themselves pro-choice. 31

"They don't sound like they're in favor of a choice if they're in a flap because they don't want some young girl to wait 24 hours or to listen to what somebody's got to say about her options. Another thing—how do they feel about frying John Gacy, that serial killer who buried his victims under his house?" 32

What does he have to do with it? 33

"Well, I noticed something. Some women I know who are in favor of abortion are against the death penalty, and that don't make sense to me. How can you be in favor of killing some harmless little thing in a woman's tummy but you get all weepy when they pull the switch on some ax murderer? I don't see how you can be for one and not the other." 34

Well, maybe they believe that the decision as to whether John Gacy is executed should be made by his mother. 35

"Yeah, I guess that makes sense, kind of a pro-choice thing." 36

Right. So, where do you stand? 37

"On what?" 38

Abortion. Are you for it or against it? 39

"Forget it. If I say I'm against, then they'll say I'm in favor of killing women, right? 40

It wouldn't surprise me. 41

"And if I'm for it, they'll say I'm a baby-killer, right?" 42

Almost a certainty. 43

"So you're not gonna corner me. There's one thing I'm sure of, though. We got to check on the diets of American women." 44

What do their diets have to do with it? 45

"If there's been 26 million abortions over the last 19 years, they should try eating more brain foods." 46

VI.

CRIME AND PUNISHMENT

Introduction

You've heard all the statistics.

According to the Department of Justice, a violent crime occurs somewhere in the United States every twenty seconds. A murder occurs every half hour (about 23,000 in 1990). Someone is raped every six minutes. Over fifteen million arrests were made in 1990, over a million of them for drug abuse violations. Many more Americans are in prison, per capita, than citizens in any other "developed" nation. The point is this: Crime has become an inescapable fact of American life. And what to do about it has become a perennial issue, as the selections in this part demonstrate.

The first set of readings, a sort of transition from the previous part on civil liberties and civil rights, discusses the question of gun control. Should the ownership and possession of firearms be restricted? An absolute "no" is the answer of those who wish to protect citizens' right to bear arms. They cite for support the Second Amendment to our Constitution: "A well regulated militia being necessary to the security of a free state, the right of the people to keep and bear arms shall not be infringed." On the other hand, a number of people (some of them included in this book) contend that the right to purchase and keep guns is not absolute, that we already restrict in certain reasonable ways "the right to bear arms" (e.g., you can't own rocket launchers or a tank; you can't own guns if you're a minor or a convicted felon or mentally incompetent). Faced with certain abuses—shocking assassinations; 25,000 shooting deaths each year—proponents of gun control simply argue for additional reasonable restrictions, particularly on the handguns that are so available in our society and so commonly employed in the conduct of violent crime. Just what is it about Americans and guns, anyway? Why do they figure so prominently in our society? Can anything be done about it? Should anything be done about it? Do guns cause crime, or are people responsible?

That brings up the question posed by the second set of readings in this part of *Conversations:* What is the source of crime, anyway? Is crime simply a manifestation of our human fallibility, our human sinfulness, that Americans are simply unwilling to face up to? Or do economic circumstances cause crime? Are most people driven to crime, desperate to meet their daily needs or determined to strike out against a system that keeps them attached permanently to an underclass? Is crime a blow against "the system"? Then again, if economic circumstances cause crime, why were crime rates lower during the Great Depression than during the economic boom years of the 1960s or 1980s? Or does crime have a broader social explanation? Is it an outgrowth of our society's rootlessness, or our fragmented families, or impersonal "value-free" schools? Is crime an inevitable by-product of a national identity that prizes nonconformity and anti-authoritarianism? (Think of Billy the Kid and Bonnie and Clyde.) Or is crime glorified and perpetuated by the media—by violent movies and newspaper sensationalism and television shows? (In this connection, you may wish to read or reread earlier sections in this book on the effects of television and pornography.) Finally, two contributions to this part of *Conversations* ask if some people are simply programmed to commit crime by their genetic disposition, their lack of intelligence, or their gender. Such arguments were dismissed after World War II because they had been promulgated by fascists responsible for horrible crimes against humanity, but in the past decade they had been put forward again by people who ask why men commit more crimes than women do and whether there is indeed a genetic predisposition to criminal behavior.

The third group of readings debate the justice and wisdom of capital punishment. From the mid-1960s to 1977 no executions were carried out in America as the nation debated the abuses in the application of capital punishment and the wisdom of carrying out such punishment at all; indeed, capital punishment has been outlawed in a great many nations. But in 1976 the Supreme Court by a 5–4 vote decided that capital punishment is constitutional under certain circumstances. Executions inevitably followed, and so the debate about capital punishment has been renewed: Is capital punishment an expression of justice, "an eye for an eye"? Is it a useful deterrent to other would-be murderers? Or does it feed one of our basest instincts—for revenge? Is the death penalty cruel and unusual punishment? Is it unfairly applied to minority criminals, especially for crimes against majority members? If so, is this an argument for abolition or for improving our system of justice?

This part of *Conversations* concludes with a discussion of whether illegal drugs should be regulated or made legal. As you know, presidents Bush and Reagan made well-publicized declarations of war against illegal drugs, but the war remains unwon. In the face of persistent and debilitating drug use, some have proposed legalization—not because they see drugs as less than a menace, but because they trust in other measures than law to fight it. Those who would legalize drugs propose that we approach drug abuse as an economic and medical problem rather than as a legal one. Legalizers wish to minimize the effects of illegal drugs by eliminating black market profits; legalization would drive down drug prices, the argument goes, and therefore reduce secondary crime motivated by the need to finance the drug habit. Legalizers would regulate drugs and tax drug producers, as liquor is regulated and taxed; the revenues could be used for education and drug prevention campaigns, and for treatment of drug addicts. Those who would legalize drugs argue by analogy to the prohibition of alcohol in the 1920s, a prohibition that made average citizens into criminals, made gangsters and rumrunners into millionaires, and reduced respect for law throughout the land. But those against legalization also point to Prohibition—to the end of Prohibition in 1930, when alcohol use skyrocketed. They argue that legalizing drugs would result in an inevitable spread in the use of cocaine and heroin, and an inevitable increase in cocaine babies, child abuse, wrecked automobiles and airplanes, and wrecked lives. And they contend that it is against the American grain to legalize immoral acts, no matter how often the acts are being committed.

In any case, what to do about drugs—and what to do about crime and criminals in general—will continue to engage our national attention for the remainder of this century. At least.

SHOULD GUNS BE REGULATED?

Leonard Kriegel

A Loaded Question: What Is It About Americans and Guns?

Kriegel (born 1933), a writer of fiction and essays, contributed the following piece to Harper's *magazine, a publication featuring contributions on American politics and culture, in mid-1992. The article itself will tell you more about him.*

I have fired a gun only once in my life, hardly experience enough to qualify one as an expert on firearms. As limited as my exposure to guns has been, however, my failure to broaden that experience had nothing at all to do with moral disapproval or with the kind of righteous indignation that views an eight-year-old boy playing cops and robbers with a cap pistol as a preview of the life of a serial killer. None of us can speak with surety about alternative lives, but had circumstances been different I suspect I not only would have hunted but very probably would have enjoyed it. I might even have gone in for target shooting, a "sport" increasingly popular in New York City, where I live (like bowling, it is practiced indoor in alleys). To be truthful, I have my doubts that target shooting would really have appealed to me. But in a country in which grown men feel passionately about a game as visibly ludicrous as golf, anything is possible. 1

The single shot I fired didn't leave me with a traumatic hatred of or distaste for guns. Quite the opposite. I liked not only the sense of incipient skill firing that shot gave me but also the knowledge that a true marksman, like a good hitter in baseball, had to practice—and practice with a real gun. Boys on the cusp of adolescence are not usually disciplined, but they do pay attention to the demands of skill. Because I immediately recognized how difficult it would be for me to 2 practice marksmanship, I was brought face to face with the fact that my career as a hunter was over even before it had started.

3 Like my aborted prospects as a major league ballplayer, my short but happy life as a hunter could be laid at the metaphorical feet of the polio virus which left me crippled at the age of eleven. Yet the one thing that continues to amaze me as I look back to that gray February afternoon when I discovered the temptation of being a shooter and hunter is that I did not shoot one or the other of the two most visible targets—myself or my friend Jackie, the boy who owned the .22.

4 Each of us managed to fire one shot that afternoon. And when we returned to the ward in which we lived along with twenty other crippled boys between the ages of nine and thirteen, we regaled our peers with a story unashamedly embellished in the telling. As the afternoon chill faded and the narrow winter light in which we had hunted drifted toward darkness, Jackie managed to hide the .22 from ward nurses and doctors on the prowl. What neither of us attempted to hide from the other boys was our brief baptism in the world of guns.

5 Like me, Jackie was a Bronx boy, as ignorant about guns as I was. Both of us had been taken down with polio in the summer of '44. We had each lost the use of our legs. We were currently in wheelchairs. And we had each already spent a year and a half in the aptly named New York State Reconstruction Home, a state hospital for long-term physical rehabilitation. Neither of us had ever fired anything more lethal than a Daisy air rifle, popularly known as a BB gun—and even that, in my case at least, had been fired under adult supervision. But Jackie and I were also American claimants, our imaginations molded as much by Hollywood westerns as by New York streets. At twelve, I was a true Jeffersonian who looked upon the ownership of a six-shooter as every American's "natural" right.

6 To this day I don't know how Jackie got hold of that .22. He refused to tell me. And I still don't know how he got rid of it after our wheelchair hunt in the woods. For months afterward I would try to get him to promise that he and I would go hunting again, but, as if our afternoon hunt had enabled him to come to terms with his own illusions about the future (something that would take me many more

years), Jackie simply shook his head and said, "That's over." I begged, wheedled, cajoled, threatened. Jackie remained obdurate. A single shot for a single hunt. It would have to be sufficient.

7 I never did find out whether or not I hit the raccoon. On the ride back to the ward, Jackie claimed I had. After he fired his shot, he dropped from his wheelchair and slid backward on his rump to the abandoned water pipe off the side of the dirt road into which the raccoon had leaped at the slashing crack of the .22. His hand came down on something red—a bloodstain, he excitedly suggested, as he lifted himself into his wheelchair and we turned to push ourselves back to the ward. It looked like a rust stain to me, but I didn't protest. I was quite willing to take whatever credit I could. That was around an hour after the two of us, fresh from lunch, had pushed our wheelchairs across the hospital grounds, turning west at the old road that cut through the woods and led to another state home, this one ministering to the retarded. The .22, which lay on Jackie's lap, had bounced and jostled as we maneuvered our wheelchairs across that rutted road in search of an animal—any animal would do—to shoot. The early February sky hung above us like a charcoal drawing, striations of gray slate shadings feeding our nervous expectation.

8 It was Jackie who first spotted the raccoon. Excited, he handed the .22 to me, a gesture spurred, I then thought, by friendship. Now I wonder whether his generosity wasn't simply self-protection. Until that moment, the .22 lying across Jackie's dead legs had been an abstraction, as much an imitation gun as the "weapons" boys in New York City constructed out of the wood frames and wood slats of fruit and vegetable crates, nails, and rubber bands—cutting up pieces of discarded linoleum and stiff cardboard to use as ammunition. I remember the feel of the .22 across my own lifeless legs, the weight of it surprisingly light, as I stared at the raccoon who eyed us curiously from in front of the broken pipe. Then I picked up the gun, aimed, and squeezed the trigger, startled not so much by the noise nor by the slight pull, but by the fact that I had actually fired at something. The sound of the shot was crisp and clean. I felt as if I had done something significant.

9 Jackie took the gun from me. "Okay," he said eagerly. "My turn now." The raccoon was nowhere in sight, but he aimed

in the direction of the water pipe into which it had disappeared and squeezed the trigger. I heard the crack again, a freedom of music now, perhaps because we two boys had suddenly been bound to each other and had escaped, for this single winter afternoon moment, the necessary but mundane courage which dominates the everyday lives of crippled children. "Okay," I heard him cry out happily, "we're goddamn killers now."

10 A formidable enough hail and farewell to shooting. And certainly better than being shot at. God knows what happened to that raccoon. Probably nothing; but for me, firing that single shot was both the beginning and the end of my life as a marksman. The raccoon may have been wounded, as Jackie claimed. Perhaps it had crawled away, bleeding, to die somewhere in the woods. I doubt it. And I certainly hope I didn't hit it, although in February 1946, six months before I returned to the city and to life among the "normals," I would have taken its death as a symbolic triumph. For that was a time I needed any triumph I could find, no matter how minor. Back then it seemed natural to begin an uncertain future with a kill—even if one sensed, as I did, that my career as a hunter was already over. The future was hinting at certain demands it would make. And I was just beginning to bend into myself, to protect my inner man from being crushed by the knowledge of all I would never be able to do. Hunting would be just another deferred dream.

11 But guns were not a dream. Guns were real, definitive, stamped on the imagination of their functional beauty. A gun was not a phallic symbol; a gun didn't offer me revenge on polio; a gun would not bring to life dead legs or endow deferred dreams with substance. I am as willing as the next man to quarantine reality within psychology. But if a rose is no more than a rose, then tell me why a gun can't simply be a gun? Guns are not monuments to fear and aspiration any more than flowers are.

12 I was already fascinated by the way guns looked. I was even more fascinated by what they did and by what made people use them. Like any other twelve-year-old boy, I was absorbed by talk about guns. Six months after the end of the Second World War, boys in our ward were still engrossed by the way talking about guns entangled us in the dense underbrush of the national psyche. And no one in that ward

was more immersed in weaponry than I. On the verge of adolescence, forced to seek and find adventure in my own imagination, I was captivated by guns.

It was a fascination that would never altogether die. A few weeks ago I found myself nostalgically drifting through the arms and armor galleries of the Metropolitan Museum of Art. Years ago I had often taken my young sons there. A good part of my pleasure now derived from memories pinned to the leisurely innocence of those earlier visits. As I wandered among those rich cabinets displaying ornate pistols and rifles whose carved wood stocks were embossed with gold and silver and ivory and brass, I was struck by how incredibly lovely many of these weapons were. It was almost impossible to conceive of them as serving the function they had been designed to serve. These were not machines designed to kill and maim. Created with an eye to beauty, their sense of decorative purpose was as singular as a well-designed eighteenth-century silver drinking cup. These guns in their solid display cases evoked a sense of the disciplined craftsmanship to which a man might dedicate his life. 13

Flintlocks, wheel locks, a magnificent pair of ivory pistols owned by Catherine the Great—all of them as beckoning to the touch of fingers, had they not been securely locked behind glass doors, as one of those small nineteenth-century engraved cameos that seem to force time itself to surrender its pleasures. I gazed longingly at a seventeenth-century wheel lock carbine, coveting it the way I might covet a drinking cup by Cellini or a small bronze horse and rider by Bologna. Its beautifully carved wooden stock had been inlaid with ivory, brass, silver, and mother-of-pearl, its pride of artisanship embossed with the name of its creator, Caspar Spät. I smiled with pleasure. Then I wandered through the galleries until I found myself in front of a case displaying eighteenth-century American flintlock rifles, all expressing the democratic spirit one finds in Louis Sullivan's buildings or Whitman's poetry or New York City playgrounds built by the WPA during the Great Depression. Their polished woods were balanced by ornately carved stag-antler powder horns, which hung like Christmas decorations beneath them. To the right was another display case devoted to long-barreled Colt revolvers; beyond that, a splendidly engraved 1894 Winchester rifle and a series of Smith & Wesson revolvers, all of them decorated by Tiffany. 14

15 And yet they were weapons, designed ultimately to do what weapons have always done—destroy. Only in those childlike posters of the 1970s did flower stems grow out of the barrel of a gun. People who shoot, like people who cook, understandably choose the best tools available. And if it is easier to hit a target with an Uzi than a homemade zip gun, chances are those who want to hit the target will feel few qualms about choosing the Uzi.

16 Nonetheless, these galleries are a remarkable testimony to the functional beauty of guns. Nor am I the only person who has been touched by their beauty. The problem is to define where the killing ceases and the beauty begins. At what point does a young boy's sense of adventure transform itself into the terror of blood and destruction and pain and death? I remember my sons' excitement when they toured these splendid galleries with me. (Yes, doctor, I did permit them to enjoy guns. And neither became a serial killer.) These weapons helped bring us together, bound father and sons, just as going to baseball games or viewing old Chaplin movies had.

17 Geography may not be the sole father of morality, but one would have to be remarkably naive to ignore its claims altogether. As I write this, I can see on the table in front of me a newspaper headlining the most recent killings inflicted on New York City's anarchic populace. Firearms now rule street and schoolyard, even as the rhetoric of politicians demanding strict gun control escalates—along with the body count.

18 And yet I recognize that one man's fear and suffering is another man's freedom and pleasure. Here is the true morality of geography. Like it or not, we see the world against a landscape of accommodation. Guns may be displayed behind glass cases in that magnificent museum, but in the splendid park in which that museum has been set down like a crowning jewel, guns have been known to create not art but terror. Functional beauty, it turns out, does not alter purpose.

19 I have a friend who has lived his entire life in small towns in Maine. My friend is both a hunter and a connoisseur of guns. City streets and guns may be a volatile mix, but the Maine woods and guns apparently aren't. Rifles and pistols hang on my friend's living room wall like old family portraits. They are lived with as comfortably as a family heirloom. My friend speaks knowingly of their shape, de-

scribes each weapon lovingly, as if it possessed its own substance. He is both literate and civilized, but he would never deny that these guns are more than a possession to him. They are an altar before which he bends the knee, a right of ownership he considers inviolable, even sacrosanct. And yet my friend is not a violent man.

I, too, am not a violent man. But I am a New Yorker. And 20
like most people who live in this city, I make certain assumptions about the value of the very indignities one faces by choosing to live here. If I didn't, I probably couldn't remain in New York. For with all of the problems it forces one to face, the moral geography of New York also breeds a determination not to give in to the daily indignities the city imposes.

During the summer of 1977, I lived within a different 21
moral geography. I was teaching a graduate seminar on Manhood and American Culture at the University of New Mexico in Albuquerque, tracing the evolution of the American man from Ben Franklin's sturdy, middle-class acolyte to the rugged John Wayne of *Stagecoach*. Enchanted by the New Mexico landscape, I would frequently drive off to explore the small towns and brilliant canyons in whose silences ghosts still lingered. One day a friend volunteered to drive with me into the Manzano Mountains. I had announced my desire to look at the ruins of a seventeenth-century mission fort at Gran Quivira, while he wanted me to meet a man who had, by himself, built a house in those haunting, lovely mountains.

Tension between Anglos and Hispanics was strong in New 22
Mexico in the summer of 1977. Even a stranger could feel a palpable, almost physical, struggle for political and cultural hegemony. Coming from a New York in which the growing separation of black and white was already threatening to transform everyday life into a racial battlefield, I did not feel particularly intimidated by this. Instead of black and white, New Mexico's ethnic and racial warfare would be between Anglo, Hispanic, and Indian. Mountainair, where we were to visit my friend's friend, was considered an Anglo town. Chilili, some miles up the road, was Hispanic.

My friend's friend had built his house on the outskirts of 23
Mountainair, with a magnificent view of ponderosa pine. He was a man in his early sixties and had come to New Mexico from Virginia soon after World War II to take a job as a technical writer in a nuclear research laboratory in Albu-

querque. Before the war he had done graduate work in literature at the University of Virginia, but the demands of fatherhood had decided him against finishing his doctorate. Like so many Americans before him, he had taken wife and young children to start over in the West.

24 In the warmth and generosity of his hospitality, however, he remained a true Southerner. As we sat and talked and laughed in a huge sun-drenched living room that opened onto that magnificent view of the mountains and pines and long New Mexico sky, I could not help but feel that here was the very best of this nation—a man secure in himself, a man of liberal sympathies and a broad understanding of human behavior and a love of children and grandchildren and wife, a man who spoke perceptively of Jane Austen's novels and spoke sadly of the savage threat of drugs (his oldest son, a veteran of the war in Vietnam, was living with him, along with wife and three-year-old daughter, trying to purge the heroin addiction that threatened to wreck his life).

25 I remember him happily holding forth on Jane Austen's *Persuasion* when his body suddenly seemed to freeze in mid-sentence. I could hear a motor in the distance. Without another word, he turned and crossed the room. Twin double-barreled shotguns hung on the wall above the fireplace. He took one, his right hand scooping shells from a canvas bag hanging from a thong looped around a horseshoe nail banged shoulder-high into the wall. His son, the ex-Marine, grabbed the other gun and scooped shells from the same bag. Through the glassed-in cathedral living room leading to the porch, I watched the two of them stand side by side, shotguns pointed at a pickup truck already out of range. "Those bastards!" I heard my host snarl.

26 "We'll get 'em yet, Pop," his son said. "I swear it."

27 After we left to drive on to the ruins of Gran Quivira, I asked the friend who had accompanied me to explain what had happened. "A pickup truck from Chilili. Hispanics driving up the mountain to cut trees. It's illegal. But they do it anyway."

28 "Do the trees belong to your friend?"

29 "Not his trees. Not his mountain." Then he shrugged.

30 "But it's his gun."

31 I angrily cast my eyes at the man and find myself staring into the twin barrels of a shotgun loosely held but pointed

directly at me. It is that same summer in Albuquerque, three weeks later, and I am sitting in the driver's seat of my car, my ten-year-old son, Bruce, directly behind me. Alongside him is the eleven-year-old daughter of the man who had invited me to teach at the University of New Mexico. I have just backed my car away from a gasoline pump to allow another car to move out of the garage into the road. As the other car came out of the gas station, the man with the shotgun adroitly cut me off and maneuvered his rust-pocked yellow pickup ahead of me in line before I could get back to the gas pump.

My first reaction is irritation with my car, as if the steel and chrome were sentient and responsible. It is the same ugly gold 1971 Buick in which, five summers earlier, I had driven through a Spanish landscape remarkably similar to the New Mexico in which I now find myself. Bruce had been with me then, too, along with his older brother and mother. But it is not the Buick that attracts men with guns. Nor is it that mythical violence of American life in which European intellectuals believe so fervently. In Spain we had been stopped at a roadblock, a sandbagged machine gun aimed by one of Franco's troops perusing traffic like a farmer counting chickens in a henhouse. The soldiers had asked for passports, scowled at the children, examined the Buick as if it were an armored tank, inspecting glove compartment and trunk and wedging their hands into the spaces between seat and back. At the hotel restaurant at which we stopped for lunch twenty minutes later, we learned that two *guardia civil* had been ambushed and killed by Basque guerrillas. During Franco's last years, such acts grew more and more frequent. Spain was filled with guns and soldiers. One was always aware of the presence of soldiers patrolling the vacation beaches of the Costa del Sol—and particularly aware of their guns. 32

As I am aware of the shotgun now. And as I am growing aware of that same enraged sense of humiliation and helplessness that seized me as those Spanish soldiers examined car and sons and wife, their guns casually pointed at all I loved most in the world, these other lives that made my life significantly mine. "Guns don't kill, people do!" Offer that mind-deadening cliché to a man at a roadblock watching the faces of soldiers for whom the power of a gun is simply that it permits them to feel contempt for those without guns. Tell that to a man sitting in a car with two young children, contemplating doing what he knows he cannot do because 33 the gun is in another man's hands. Both in Spain and in this New Mexico that Spain had planted in the New World like a genetic acorn breeding prerogatives of power, guns endowed men with a way to settle all questions of responsibility.

34 The man with the shotgun says nothing. He simply holds the weapon in his beefy hand, its muzzle casually pointed in my direction. I toy with the notion of getting out of the car and confronting him. I am angry, enraged. I don't want to give in to his rude power. Only my son and my colleague's daughter are in the back of the car. Defensively, I turn to look at them. My colleague's daughter is wide-eyed and frightened. Bruce is equally frightened, but his eyes are on me. I am his father and he expects me to do something, to say something, to alter the balance of expectation and reality. Our car was on line for gas first. To a ten-year-old, justice is a simple arithmetic.

35 To that ten-year-old's father it is not necessarily more complex. I could tell myself that it was insane to tell a man pointing a shotgun at me and these two children that he has broken the rules. Chances are he wouldn't have fired, would probably have responded with a shrug of the shoulders no more threatening than a confession of ignorance.

36 Obviously, none of this mattered. My growing sense of humiliation and rage had nothing to do with having to wait an extra minute or two while the station attendant filled the tank of the pickup. I was in no particular rush. I was simply returning home from a day-long excursion to a state park, where my son and his new friend had crawled through caves and climbed rocks splashed by a warm spring. But I was facing a man with a shotgun, a man who understood that people with guns define options for themselves.

37 The man with the gun decides whether or not to shoot, just as he chooses where to point his gun. It is not political power that stems from the barrel of a gun, as Maoists used to proclaim so ritualistically. It is individual power, the ability to impose one's presence on the world, simply because guns always do what language only sometimes does: Guns command! Guns command attention, guns command discipline, guns command fear.

38 And guns bestow rights and prerogatives, even to those who have read Jane Austen and engaged the world in their own comedy of manners. There is a conditional nature to all rights. And there are obligations that should not be shunted aside. Guns are many things, some symbolic, some all too

real. But in real life they are always personal and rarely playful. They measure not capacity but the obligation the bearer of the gun has to believe that power belongs not to the gun but to him. And yet were I to tell this to my friend in Maine—that sophisticated, literate, humane man—I suspect he would turn to me and say, "That's right. There's always got to be somebody's finger on the trigger."

A confession, then: I may be as fascinated by guns as my gun-owning and gun-loving friend in Maine, but were it up to me, I would rid America of its guns. I would be less verbally self-righteous about gun control than I was in the past, for I think I have begun to understand those who, like my friend in Maine, have arguments of their own in defense of guns. They are formidable arguments. Their fear matches mine, and I assume that their anguish over the safety of their children is also equal to mine. I, too, know the statistics. I can repeat, as easily as he can, that in Switzerland, where an armed citizenry is the norm, the homicide rate is far lower than in many countries that carefully control the distribution of guns to their populace. Laws are simply words on paper—unless they embody what a population wants. 39

There is no logic with which I can convince my gun-owning friend in Maine. But there are images I wish I could get him to focus on. Like me, he is a writer. Only I write about cities, and my friend writes about the Maine woods. He is knowledgeable about animals and rocks and trees and silence, and I am knowledgeable about stubs of grass growing between cracks in a concrete sidewalk and the pitch and pull of conflicting voices demanding recognition. I wish I could explain to him the precise configuration of that double-barreled shotgun pointing at me and those two children. Maybe then I could convince him that truth is not merely a matter of geography. Yes, guns don't kill and people do—but in the America he and I share, those people usually kill with guns. 40

Four years after that incident at the gas station, I was sitting with Bruce in a brasserie in Paris. It was a sunny July afternoon and we were eating lunch at a small outside table, the walls of the magisterial Invalides beckoning to us from across the street. Bruce was fourteen, and fifteen minutes earlier he had returned from his first trip alone on the Paris 41

Metro. Suddenly a man approached, eyes menacing and bloodshot. He was short and thick, his body seemingly caked by the muscularity of a beaten-down club fighter or an unemployed stevedore. He stared at us, eyes filled with the rage of the insane. Then he flexed his muscles as if he were on exhibit as a circus strong man, cried out something—a sound I remember as a cross between gargling and choking—and disappeared just as suddenly down the street.

42 The incident still haunts me. The French, I suspect, are as violent as they like to claim we Americans are. But in Paris it is difficult for a man filled with rage and craziness to get hold of a gun. Not impossible, mind you, just difficult. Somewhere along the line, the French have learned not that guns don't kill and people do but that people with guns can kill. And they know what we have yet to acknowledge—that when the Furies dance in the head it's best to keep the weapons in display cases in the museum. For that, at least, I wish my friend in Maine could learn to be grateful. As I was, eating lunch with my son in Paris.

Roy Innis

Gun Control Sprouts from Racist Soil

Innis is the respected national chairman of the Congress of Racial Equality. Born in the Virgin Islands in 1934, as a youth he moved with his family to New York City and has continued to make his home there. He contributed the following article to The Wall Street Journal *in November 1991.*

1 What irony. Most black leaders (as distinct from rank-and-file blacks) are supporters, at least in public, of the gun control—really, prohibition—movement. Do they realize that America's gun-control movement sprouted from the soil of Roger B. Taney, the racist chief justice who wrote the infamous *Dred Scott* decision of 1857?

2 In the early part of the 19th century, Dred Scott, a black slave, had been taken by his owner from Missouri, a slave

state, to Illinois, a free state. From there he was taken into the Wisconsin territory, free territory above the 36°30' latitude of the Missouri Compromise. After living in free territory for a while, he returned with his owner to Missouri.

When his owner died in 1846, Scott sued in the state 3
courts of Missouri for his freedom, on the ground that he had lived in free territory. He won his case, but it was reversed in the Missouri Supreme Court. Scott appealed to the federal courts, since the person he was actually suing, John Sanford, the executor of the estate that owned Scott, lived in New York.

It was in that setting that Chief Justice Taney made his 4
infamous rulings:

1. That black people, whether free or slave, were not citizens of the U.S.; therefore, they had no standing in court.
2. Scott was denied freedom.
3. The Missouri Compromise was ruled unconstitutional.

Well known to most students of race relations is the 5
former attorney general and secretary of the Treasury's pre-civil war dictum that black people "being of an inferior order" had "no right which any white man was bound to respect." Much less known are his equally racist pronouncements denying black people, whether slave or free, specific constitutional protections enjoyed by whites.

In *Dred Scott* Chief Justice Taney, writing for the court's 6
majority, stated that if blacks were "entitled to the privileges and immunities of citizens, . . . it would give persons of the negro race, who were recognized as citizens in any one state of the union, the right . . . to keep and carry arms wherever they went. And all of this would be done in the face of the subject race of the same color, both free and slaves, and inevitably producing discontent and insubordination among them, and endangering the peace and safety of the state. . . ."

Although much of Justice Taney's overly racist legal 7
reasoning was repudiated by events that followed—such as the Civil War and Reconstruction—the subliminal effects were felt throughout that era. In the post-Reconstruction period, when the pendulum swung back to overt racism, Justice Taney's philosophy resurfaced. It was during this period that racial paranoia about black men with guns

intensified. It was potent enough to cause the infringement on the Second Amendment to the Constitution's "right . . . to keep and bear arms."

8 Under natural law, a freeman's right to obtain and maintain the implements of self-defense has always been sacred. This right was restricted or prohibited for serfs, peasants and slaves. Gun control was never an issue in America until after the Civil War when black slaves were freed.

9 It was this change in the status of the black man, from slave to freeman, that caused racist elements in the country (North and South) to agitate for restrictions on guns—ignoring long established customs and understanding of the Second Amendment. The specter of a black man with rights of a freeman, bearing arms, was too much for the early heirs of Roger Taney to bear.

10 The 14th and 15th Amendments to the Constitution, along with the various Reconstruction civil rights acts, prevented gun prohibitionists from making laws that were explicitly racist and that would overtly deny black people the right to bear arms. The end of Reconstruction signaled the return of Taneyism—overtly among the masses and covertly on the Supreme Court. Gun-control legislation of the late 19th and early 20th centuries, enacted at the state and local levels, was implicitly racist in conception. And in operation, those laws invidiously targeted blacks.

11 With the influx of large numbers of Irish, Italian and Jewish immigrants into the country, gun laws now also targeted whites from the underprivileged classes of immigrants. Eventually these oppressive gun laws were extended to affect all but a privileged few. Throughout the history of New York state's Sullivan law, enacted at the start of the 20th century, mainly the rich and powerful have had easy access to licenses to carry handguns. Some of the notables who have received that privilege include Eleanor Roosevelt, John Lindsay, Donald Trump, Arthur Sulzberger, Joan Rivers and disk jockey Howard Stern.

12 Of the 27,000 handgun carry permits in New York City, fewer than 2% are issued to blacks—who live and work in high-crime areas and really are in need of protection.

13 And what of the origins of the National Rifle Association, which is wrongly viewed as a racist organization by the black supporters of gun prohibition? It was inspired and organized by Union Army officers after the Civil War.

Ronald Reagan

Why I'm for the Brady Bill

In 1991 and 1992, Congress debated the "Brady Bill," a handgun-control bill described in the following essay by Ronald Reagan. President Reagan (born 1911), who served from 1981–1989 and was endorsed by the National Rifle Association, published his essay in The New York Times *on March 29, 1991. The bill was first debated on its own and then was incorporated into a broader crime prevention measure. As of mid-1993, it still had not been passed into law.*

"Anniversary" is a word we usually associate with happy events that we like to remember: birthdays, weddings, the first job. March 30, however, marks an anniversary I would just as soon forget, but cannot. 1

It was on that day 10 years ago that a deranged young man standing among reporters and photographers shot a policeman, a Secret Service agent, my press secretary and me on a Washington sidewalk. 2

I was lucky. The bullet that hit me bounced off a rib and lodged in my lung, an inch from my heart. It was a very close call. Twice they could not find my pulse. But the bullet's missing my heart, the skill of the doctors and nurses at George Washington University Hospital and the steadfast support of my wife, Nancy, saved my life. 3

Jim Brady, my press secretary, who was standing next to me, wasn't as lucky. A bullet entered the left side of his forehead, near his eye, and passed through the right side of his brain before it exited. The skills of the George Washington University medical team, plus his amazing determination and the grit and spirit of his wife, Sarah, pulled Jim through. His recovery has been remarkable, but he still lives with physical pain every day and must spend much of his time in a wheelchair. 4

Thomas Delahanty, a Washington police officer, took a bullet in his neck. It ricocheted off his spinal cord. Nerve damage to his left arm forced his retirement in November 1981. 5

Tim McCarthy, a Secret Service agent, was shot in the chest and suffered a lacerated liver. He recovered and returned to duty. 6

7 Still, four lives were changed forever, and all by a Saturday-night special—a cheaply made .22 caliber pistol—purchased in a Dallas pawnshop by a young man with a history of mental disturbance.

8 This nightmare might never have happened if legislation that is before Congress now—the Brady bill—had been law back in 1981.

9 Named for Jim Brady, this legislation would establish a national seven-day waiting period before a handgun purchaser could take delivery. It would allow local law enforcement officials to do background checks for criminal records or known histories of mental disturbances. Those with such records would be prohibited from buying the handguns.

10 While there has been a Federal law on the books for more than 20 years that prohibits the sale of firearms to felons, fugitives, drug addicts and the mentally ill, it has no enforcement mechanism and basically works on the honor system, with the purchaser filling out a statement that the gun dealer sticks in a drawer.

11 The Brady bill would require the handgun dealer to provide a copy of the prospective purchaser's sworn statement to local law enforcement authorities so that background checks could be made. Based upon the evidence in states that already have handgun purchase waiting periods, this bill—on a nationwide scale—can't help but stop thousands of illegal handgun purchases.

12 And, since many handguns are acquired in the heat of passion (to settle a quarrel, for example) or at times of depression brought on by potential suicide, the Brady bill would provide a cooling-off period that would certainly have the effect of reducing the number of handgun deaths.

13 Critics claim that "waiting period" legislation in the states that have it doesn't work, that criminals just go to nearby states that lack such laws to buy their weapons. True enough, and all the more reason to have a Federal law that fills the gaps. While the Brady bill would not apply to states that already have waiting periods of at least seven days or that already require background checks, it would automatically cover the states that don't. The effect would be a uniform standard across the country.

14 Even with the current gaps among states, those that have waiting periods report some success. California, which has a 15-day waiting period that I supported and signed into law while Governor, stopped nearly 1,800 prohibited handgun

sales in 1989. New Jersey has had a permit-to-purchase system for more than two decades. During that time, according to the state police, more than 10,000 convicted felons have been caught trying to buy handguns.

Every year, an average of 9,200 Americans are murdered 15
by handguns, according to Department of Justice statistics. This does not include suicides or the tens of thousands of robberies, rapes and assaults committed with handguns.

This level of violence must be stopped. Sarah and Jim 16
Brady are working hard to do that, and I say more power to them. If the passage of the Brady bill were to result in a reduction of only 10 or 15 percent of those numbers (and it could be a good deal greater), it would be well worth making it the law of the land.

And there would be a lot fewer families facing anniversa- 17
ries such as the Bradys, Delahantys, McCarthys and Reagans face every March 30.

Elizabeth Swazey

Women and Handguns

Elizabeth Swazey, an attorney, a certified firearms instructor, and the director of the National Rifle Association's group on women's issues, writes a column every other month for American Rifleman *magazine (a publication of the NRA that is devoted to articles of various kinds on various kinds of firearms). The following such column appeared in 1992.*

James Michael Barnes failed to appear in court on March 1
8, 1991. He was dead.

According to New Jersey *Courier-Post* staff reporters Alan 2
Guenther and Renee Winkler, by February 1990 the relationship between Amy Gardiner and James Michael Barnes had broken off. On February 9, he appeared on Gardiner's doorstep to return some of her things. Instead, he raped her. He even photographed the event. Barnes pled guilty to assault and was sentenced to two years probation. He also was ordered to stay away from Gardiner and her relatives.

3 He didn't. According to court documents, Barnes broke into Gardiner's home, stole from her, left a hot iron on her carpet and smeared her walls and furniture with feces.

4 During this period, Barnes was charged with robbing and intimidating another ex-girlfriend. Bail was set at $50,000 cash. Barnes stayed in jail until January 17. On that date, prosecutors sought to have his opportunity for bail revoked on grounds he was a threat to Gardiner. But the judge actually *reduced* Barnes' bail to $25,000. Barnes posted the 10% required and was free that afternoon.

5 Free to look for Amy Gardiner.

6 But in the meantime, Gardiner had done three things. She had filed harassment charges against Barnes; she had changed her address; and she had purchased a shotgun. Two weeks later at 9:30 in the evening, Gardiner's doorbell rang. She was alone and didn't answer the door. Soon the telephone rang. When she answered, the caller hung up. Sensing danger, Gardiner went to the bedroom to get the shotgun. Barnes, armed with a revolver and a disturbed mind, kicked in the front door and stormed into the bedroom, threatening to kill her. Gardiner fired once. Barnes died. The terror was over. But at what cost?

7 Taking the life of another human being, *no matter how justified,* carries a heavy burden. Why New Jersey Superior Court Judge Joseph F. Green, Jr., allowed Barnes to buy temporary freedom for $2,500 is beyond me. Is that the price he places on a woman's suffering, on the white-hot fear she felt that night, alone, with a madman trying to kill her?

8 Amy Gardiner could be any of us, *You, Your wife, daughter or friend.* According to the Dept. of Justice, three of four American women will face crime in their lifetimes. And, as has been held in another case, ". . . a government and its agents are under no general duty to provide public services, such as police protection, to any particular individual citizen. . . ." *Warren v. District of Columbia,* 444 A.2d 1 (D.C.App.181).

9 Or, put another way, "[T]here is no constitutional right to be protected by the state against being murdered by criminals or madmen." *Bowers v. DeVito,* 686 F.2d 616, at 618 (7th Cir. 1982).

10 Amy Gardiner faced a criminal madman. Thankfully, the innocent life prevailed. And while it is human nature to avoid thinking about unpleasant topics, we must recognize

that *any one of us* could be violently attacked. Until our criminal justice system becomes a victims' justice system—and NRA is helping turn the tide through our *CrimeStrike* program—violent criminals like James Michael Barnes will continue to be routinely set free. We need to decide, in advance, how to respond if you, I or a loved one is threatened.

Owning a gun, and whether to use it in lawful self-defense, are *deeply personal choices* that each individual must make. For those who decide in favor of gun ownership, NRA can help. We offer introductory Personal Protection Seminars for women across the country, and the intensive Personal Protection Program to men and women nationwide through a network of certified instructors. Information about both is available by simply calling (800) 368-5714 or (202) 828-6224. 11

Handgun Control, Inc., (HCI) doesn't want women to have this choice. The group's Chairman Emeritus Pete Shields advises women faced with criminal attack to "give them what they want." But what James Michael Barnes wanted was for Amy Gardiner *to be dead*. 12

Sometimes HCI softens its message by expressing "concern" that if a woman tried to use a gun in self-defense, it would be taken away and used against her. Why doesn't HCI Chair Sarah Brady ever say this about men? Amy Gardiner faced an armed attacker and prevailed. And the most recent National Crime Survey by the Bureau of Justice Statistics found that in *less than 1%* of cases did criminals manage to turn guns against their owners. 13

HCI says one of its principal political goals this year is to conduct a "public information campaign" about "the extremist nature of the gun lobby and alert women . . . that they've been targeted as a new market. . . ." 14

So the lines are drawn: NRA says defend your right to defend yourself. HCI says give criminals what they want. Now who's extreme? 15

National Rifle Association
Don't Edit the Bill of Rights

The ad printed on these two pages, developed and paid for by the National Rifle Association Institute for Legislative Action, appeared in USA Today *and many other newspapers in December 1991—on the 200th anniversary of the ratification of the Bill of Rights.*

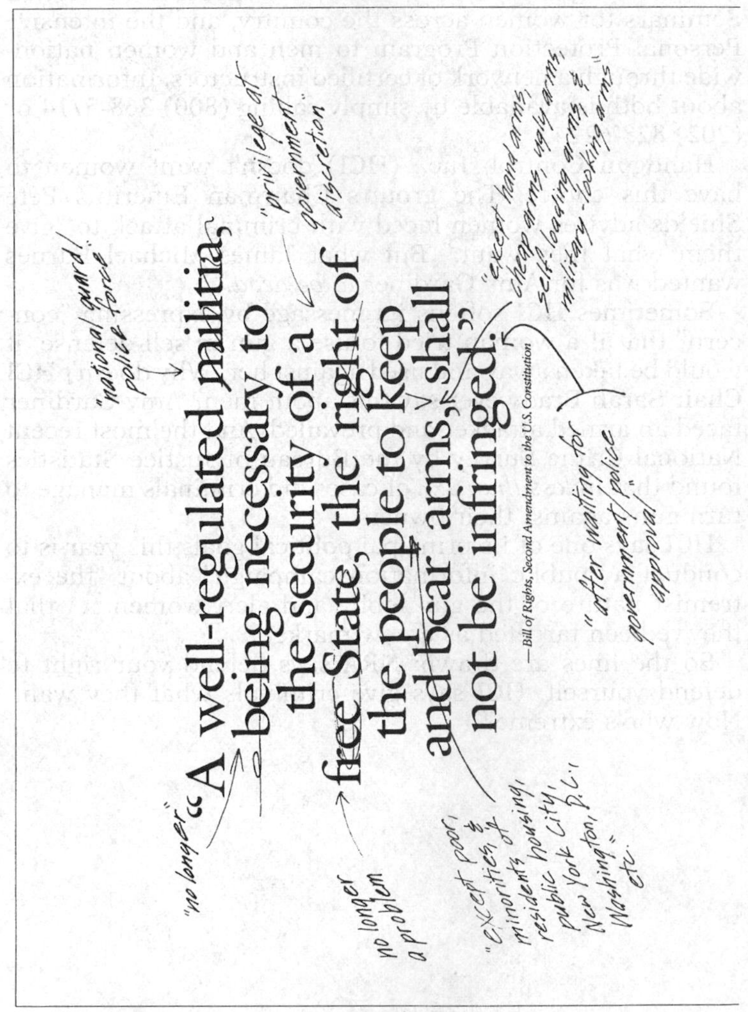

Before anyone edits the Bill of Rights, the authors would like a word with you:

"No free man shall ever be debarred the use of arms."

THOMAS JEFFERSON

"Arms in the hands of citizens may be used at individual discretion... in private self-defense."

JOHN ADAMS

"[The Constitution preserves] the advantage of being armed which Americans possess over the people of almost every other nation... [where] the governments are afraid to trust the people with arms."

JAMES MADISON

"...arms discourage and keep the invader and plunderer in awe, and preserve order in the world as well as property.... Horrid mischief would ensue were [the law-abiding] deprived of the use of them."

THOMAS PAINE

"Laws that forbid the carrying of arms... disarm only those who are neither inclined nor determined to commit crimes... Such laws make things worse for the assaulted and better for the assailants; they serve rather to encourage than to prevent homicides, for an unarmed man may be attacked with greater confidence than an armed man."

THOMAS JEFFERSON, quoting Cesare Beccaria

"A militia, when properly formed, are in fact the people themselves... and include all men capable of bearing arms... To preserve liberty it is essential that the whole body of the people always possess arms and be taught alike... how to use them."

RICHARD HENRY LEE

"The Constitution shall never be construed to prevent the people of the United States who are peaceable citizens from keeping their own arms."

SAMUEL ADAMS

"I ask, sir, what is the militia? It is the whole people... To disarm the people is the best and most effectual way to enslave them..."

GEORGE MASON

A message in celebration of the 200th Anniversary of the Ratification of the Bill of Rights, December 15, 1791. Paid for by the National Rifle Association Institute for Legislative Action. For more information call 202-828-6330.

Robert Goldwin

Gun Control Is Constitutional

Goldwin is a scholar affiliated with the American Enterprise Institute, a conservative research institute. He contributed the following to The Wall Street Journal, *the conservative business-news daily, in December 1991. The letters published after it and responding to it appeared a few weeks later in the same newspaper.*

1 Congress has been dismayingly inconsistent in its voting on gun-control legislation this year, first passing the Brady Bill, then moving in the opposite direction by defeating a provision to ban certain assault weapons and ammunition. But in one respect members of Congress are consistent: they demand respect for our "constitutional right to own a gun." They cite the Constitution's Second Amendment and argue it prohibits effective national regulation of the private ownership of guns.

2 But there are strong grounds for arguing that the Second Amendment is no barrier to gun-control legislation. In my opinion, it even provides a solid constitutional basis for effective national legislation to regulate guns and gun owners.

3 The best clues to the meaning of the key words and phrases are in debates in the First Congress of the United States. The Members of that Congress were the authors of the Second Amendment. A constitutional amendment calling for the prohibition of standing armies in time of peace was proposed by six state ratifying conventions. Virginia's version, later copied by New York and North Carolina, brought together three elements in one article—affirmation of a right to bear arms, reliance on state militia, and opposition to a standing army.

4 "That the people have a right to keep and bear arms; that a well regulated militia, composed of the body of the people trained to arms, is the proper, natural, and safe defense of a free state; that standing armies, in times of peace, are dangerous to liberty, and therefore ought to be avoided. . . ."

5 The purpose was to limit the power of the new Congress to establish a standing army, and instead to rely on state militias under the command of governors. The Constitution

was ratified without adopting any of the scores of proposed amendments. But in several states ratification came only with solemn pledges that amendments would follow.

Soon after the First Congress met, James Madison, elected as a congressman from Virginia on the basis of such a pledge, proposed a number of amendments resembling yet different from articles proposed by states. These eventually became the Bill of Rights. In the version of the arms amendment he presented, Madison dropped mention of a standing army and added a conscientious objector clause. 6

"The right of the people to keep and bear arms shall not be infringed, a well armed and well regulated militia being the best security of a free country, but no person religiously scrupulous of bearing arms shall be compelled to render military service in person." 7

In this version, "bearing arms" must mean "to render military service," or why else would there have to be an exemption for religious reasons? What right must not be infringed? The right of the people to serve in the militia. 8

This militia amendment was referred to a congressional committee and came out of committee in this form: 9

"A well regulated militia, composed of the body of the people, being the best security of a free state, the right of the people to keep and bear arms shall not be infringed; but no person religiously scrupulous shall be compelled to bear arms." 10

Two significant changes had been made: first, the phrase "to render military service in person" was replaced by the phrase, "to bear arms," again indicating that they are two ways to say the same thing; second, an explanation was added that the "militia" is "composed of the body of the people." 11

The House then debated this new version in committee of the whole and, surprisingly, considering the subsequent history of the provision, never once did any member mention the private uses of arms, for self-protection, or hunting, or any other personal purpose. The debate focused exclusively on the conscientious objector provision. Eventually the committee's version was narrowly approved. The Senate in turn gave it its final form: briefer, unfortunately more elliptical, and with the exemption for conscientious objectors deleted: 12

"A well-regulated militia, being necessary to the security of a free state, the right of the people to keep and bear arms, shall not be infringed." 13

14 Certain explanations were lost or buried in this legislative process: that the right to bear arms meant the right to serve in the militia; that just about everybody was included in the militia; and that the amendment as a whole sought to minimize if not eliminate reliance on a standing army by emphasizing the role of the state militia, which would require that everyone be ready to be called to serve.

15 But what about the private right "to keep and bear arms," to own a gun for self-defense and hunting? Isn't that clearly protected by the amendment? Didn't just about everyone own a gun in 1791? Wouldn't that "right" go without saying? Yes, of course, it would go without saying, especially then when there were no organized police forces and when hunting was essential to the food supply.

16 But such facts tell us almost nothing relevant to our question. Almost everyone also owned a dog for the same purposes. The Constitution nevertheless says nothing about the undeniable right to own a dog. There are uncountable numbers of rights not enumerated in the Constitution. These rights are neither denied nor disparaged by not being raised to the explicit constitutional level. All of them are constitutionally subject to regulation.

17 The right to bear arms protected in the Second Amendment has to do directly with "a well-regulated militia." More evidence of the connection can be found in the Militia Act of 1792.

18 "Every free able-bodied white male citizen " (it was 1792, after all) was required by the act to "enroll" in the militia for training and active service in case of need. When reporting for service, every militiaman was required to provide a prescribed rifle or musket, and ammunition.

19 Here we see the link of the private and public aspects of bearing arms. The expectation was that every man would have his own firearms. But the aspect that was raised to the level of constitutional concern was the public interest in those arms.

20 What does this mean for the question of gun control today? Well, for example, it means that Congress has the constitutional power to enact a Militia Act of 1992, to require every person who owns a gun or aspires to own one to "enroll" in the militia. In plain 1990s English, if you want to own a gun, sign up with the National Guard.

21 Requiring every gun owner to register with the National Guard (as we require 18-year-olds to register with the

Selective Service) would provide the information about gunowners sought by the Brady and Staggers bills, and much more. Standards could be set for purchase or ownership of guns, and penalties could be established.

Restoring a 200-year-old understanding of the Constitution may be difficult, but there isn't time to dawdle. Americans now own more than 200 million guns, and opinion polls show Americans want gun control. Why not avail ourselves of the Second Amendment remedy? Call in the militia, which is, after all, "composed of the body of the people." 22

Responses to Robert Goldwin: Letters to the Editor of *The Wall Street Journal*

In his "Gun Control is Constitutional" the American Enterprise Institute's Robert A. Goldwin's principal concern, it seems, is to deny that the right to keep and bear arms precludes the power to regulate gun ownership and use. Few would disagree. Even activities protected by the First Amendment may be regulated when they threaten the rights of others. 1

But Mr. Goldwin also writes that "The right to bear arms protected in the Second Amendment has to do directly with 'a well regulated militia' "; thus, arguably, he continues, "if you want to own a gun, sign up with the National Guard." Clearly, this goes well beyond regulating to protect the rights of others. This would condition the "right" to keep and bear arms on joining the National Guard. 2

Mr. Goldwin's mistake stems from his having confused a necessary with a sufficient condition. The Second Amendment, in its language and its history, makes plain that the need for a well-regulated militia is a *sufficient* condition for the right to keep and bear arms. Yet Mr. Goldwin treats it as a *necessary* condition, which enables him to conclude that Congress could deny an individual the right to own a gun if he did not join the National Guard. 3

Mr. Goodwin makes this mistake, in turn, because he has misread Madison's original version of the Second Amendment, which exempted conscientious objectors from military service. Thus he says that "In this version, 'bearing arms' must mean 'to render military service,' or why else would there have to be an exemption for religious reasons? 4

What right must not be infringed? The right of the people to serve in the militia."

5 Plainly, any conscientious objector provision would arise not from a *right* but from a *duty* to serve in the militia. Yet Mr. Goldwin believes the amendment means, as he later says, "that the right to bear arms meant the right to serve in the militia." Thus does he reduce the first of these rights to the second, when clearly it is much broader.

ROGER PILON
Senior Fellow and Director
Center for Constitutional Studies
CATO Institute

6 The militia is not the National Guard but rather the people of the original states. In Ohio, we have an Ohio militia that is not a part of the National Guard. The fear of standing armies and the control these armed men gave a central government was foremost in the Framers' minds when writing the Bill of Rights. Thomas Jefferson moved to prevent this type of power in a few people's hands by the Second Amendment. He stated, "No free man shall ever be debarred the use of arms."

7 The addition in the early drafts of a conscientious-objector clause was added for the preservation of religious freedoms, which the Colonists had not had in England. It is unfortunate today's "scholars" seem to spend their time picking apart history and the great thoughts of the visionary men who formed this country.

8 In my personal celebration of this 200-year-old document, I have pledged the following: I will give up my freedom of speech when they cut out my tongue; I will give up my right to worship when they have slain my God and myself; I will assemble with the people of my choice even when they are imprisoned, and I will give up my rifle when they pry my cold dead fingers from around it.

Samuel R. Bush III

9 Let those who want guns join the National Guard, says Mr. Goldwin. Ah, the sanctimonious arrogance of it. What gives Mr. Goldwin the right to deny mine when I abide by the laws?

10 He stresses the differences between the world of 1791 and

today to suit his prejudice. He studiously ignores other major differences between 1791 and today.

In 1791, punishment was swifter and surer. Plea bargaining was not epidemic; judges did not provide revolving doors on prisons. There was no army of drug dealers and junkies preying on the public. If anything, the reasons for citizens to own weapons for self-defense are more compelling today then they were in 1791. 11

Let Mr. Goldwin show us how he would make us safer in our homes and we might understand his wish to strip away our only sure defense. 12

CARL ROESSLER

Mr. Goldwin suggests gun control via enlistment in the National Guard. Swell idea. Updating the right to bear arms from 1791 to 1991, when I report for service, I'll bring, as required, a few items consistent with the current infantryman's inventory: a Barett Light .50 semiautomatic sniper rifle, so I can reach out and touch people half a mile away; a Squad Automatic Weapon firing 5.56mm rounds at the rate of a whole lot per second out of 30-round clips or hundred-round belts; a 40mm grenade launcher . . . but you get the idea. Then, as a thoroughly modern, well-regulated militiaman, I'll take my weapons home, just as did Morgan's riflemen, and the musket bearers of Lexington and Concord, and the Colonial light artillerists. 13

ANDREW L. ISAAC

WHAT CAUSES CRIME?

Clarence Darrow

Address to the Prisoners in the Cook County Jail

Clarence Darrow (1857–1928) was the most famous American lawyer of the early twentieth century. An eloquent speaker from Youngstown, Ohio, who practiced mostly in Chicago, Darrow defended Eugene V. Debs and other controversial labor leaders, Nathan Leopold and Richard Loeb (two notorious murderers), and John Scopes in the famous Monkey Trial of 1925. The following is a transcript of a speech that Darrow delivered to prisoners in Chicago in 1902.

1 If I looked at jails and crimes and prisoners in the way the ordinary person does, I should not speak on this subject to you. The reason I talk to you on the question of crime, its cause and cure, is that I really do not in the least believe in crime. There is no such thing as a crime as the word is generally understood. I do not believe there is any sort of distinction between the real moral conditions of the people in and out of jail. One is just as good as the other. The people here can no more help being here than the people outside can avoid being outside. I do not believe that people are in jail because they deserve to be. They are in jail simply because they cannot avoid it on account of circumstances which are entirely beyond their control and for which they are in no way responsible.

2 I suppose a great many people on the outside would say I was doing you harm if they should hear what I say to you this afternoon, but you cannot be hurt a great deal anyway, so it will not matter. Good people outside would say that I was really teaching you things that were calculated to injure society, but it's worth while now and then to hear something different from what you ordinarily get from preachers and

the like. These will tell you that you should be good and then you will get rich and be happy. Of course we know that people do not get rich by being good, and that is the reason why so many of you people try to get rich some other way, only you do not understand how to do it quite as well as the fellow outside.

There are people who think that everything in this world 3
is an accident. But really there is no such thing as an accident. A great many folks admit that many of the people in jail ought to be there, and many who are outside ought to be in. I think none of them ought to be here. There ought to be no jails; and if it were not for the fact that people on the outside are so grasping and heartless in their dealings with the people on the inside, there would be no such institution as jails.

I do not want you to believe that I think all you people 4
here are angels. I do not think that. You are people of all kinds, all of you doing the best you can—and that is evidently not very well. You are people of all kinds and conditions and under all circumstances. In one sense everybody is equally good and equally bad. We all do the best we can under the circumstances. But as to the exact things for which you are sent here, some of you are guilty and did the particular act because you needed the money. Some of you did it because you are in the habit of doing it, and some of you because you are born to it, and it comes to be as natural as it does, for instance, for me to be good.

Most of you probably have nothing against me, and most 5
of you would treat me the same way as any other person would, probably better than some of the people on the outside would treat me, because you think I believe in you and they know I do not believe in them. While you would not have the least thing against me in the world, you might pick my pockets. I do not think all of you would, but I think some of you would. You would not have anything against me, but that's your profession, a few of you. Some of the rest of you, if my doors were unlocked, might come in if you saw anything you wanted—not out of any malice to me, but because that is your trade. There is no doubt there are quite a number of people in this jail who would pick my pockets. And still I know this—that when I get outside pretty nearly everybody picks my pocket. There may be some of you who would hold up a man on the street, if you did not happen to have something else to do, and needed the money; but when I want to light my house or my office the gas company holds

me up. They charge me one dollar for something that is worth twenty-five cents. Still all these people are good people; they are pillars of society and support the churches, and they are respectable.

6 When I ride on the streetcars I am held up—I pay five cents for a ride that is worth two and a half cents, simply because a body of men have bribed the city council and the legislature, so that all the rest of us have to pay tribute to them.

7 If I do not want to fall into the clutches of the gas trust and choose to burn oil instead of gas, then good Mr. Rockefeller holds me up, and he uses a certain portion of his money to build universities and support churches which are engaged in telling us how to be good.

8 Some of you are here for obtaining property under false pretenses—yet I pick up a great Sunday paper and read the advertisements of a merchant prince—"Shirtwaists for 39 cents, marked down from $3.00."

9 When I read the advertisements in the paper I see they are all lies. When I want to get out and find a place to stand anywhere on the face of the earth, I find that it has all been taken up long ago before I came here, and before you came here, and somebody says, "Get off, swim into the lake, fly into the air; go anywhere, but get off." That is because these people have the police and they have the jails and the judges and the lawyers and the soldiers and all the rest of them to take care of the earth and drive everybody off that comes in their way.

10 A great many people will tell you that all this is true, but that it does not excuse you. These facts do not excuse some fellow who reaches into my pocket and takes out a five-dollar bill. The fact that the gas company bribes the members of the legislature from year to year, and fixes the law, so that all you people are compelled to be "fleeced" whenever you deal with them; the fact that the streetcar companies and the gas companies have control of the streets; and the fact that the landlords own all the earth—this, they say, has nothing to do with you.

11 Let us see whether there is any connection between the crimes of the respectable classes and your presence in the jail. Many of you people are in jail because you have really committed burglary; many of you, because you have stolen something. In the meaning of the law, you have taken some other person's property. Some of you have entered a store

and carried off a pair of shoes because you did not have the price. Possibly some of you have committed murder. I cannot tell what all of you did. There are a great many people here who have done some of these things who really do not know themselves why they did them. I think I know why you did them—every one of you; you did these things because you were bound to do them. It looked to you at the time as if you had a chance to do them or not, as you saw fit; but still, after all, you had no choice. There may be people here who had some money in their pockets and who still went out and got some more money in a way society forbids. Now, you may not yourselves see exactly why it was you did this thing, but if you look at the question deeply enough and carefully enough you will see that there were circumstances that drove you to do exactly the thing which you did. You could not help it any more than we outside can help taking the positions that we take. The reformers who tell you to be good and you will be happy, and the people on the outside who have property to protect—they think that the only way to do it is by building jails and locking you up in cells on weekdays and praying for you Sundays.

I think that all of this has nothing whatever to do with 12
right conduct. I think it is very easily seen what has to do with right conduct. Some so-called criminals—and I will use this word because it is handy, it means nothing to me—I speak of the criminals who get caught as distinguished from the criminals who catch them—some of these so-called criminals are in jail for their first offenses, but nine tenths of you are in jail because you did not have a good lawyer and, of course, you did not have a good lawyer because you did not have enough money to pay a good lawyer. There is no very great danger of a rich man going to jail.

Some of you may be here for the first time. If we would 13
open the doors and let you out, and leave the laws as they are today, some of you would be back tomorrow. This is about as good a place as you can get anyway. There are many people here who are so in the habit of coming that they would not know where else to go. There are people who are born with the tendency to break into jail every chance they get, and they cannot avoid it. You cannot figure out your life and see why it was, but still there is a reason for it; and if we were all wise and knew all the facts, we could figure it out.

In the first place, there are a good many more people who 14 go to jail in the wintertime than in the summer. Why is this? Is it because people are more wicked in winter? No, it is because the coal trust begins to get in its grip in the winter. A few gentlemen take possession of the coal, and unless the people will pay seven or eight dollars a ton for something that is worth three dollars, they will have to freeze. Then there is nothing to do but to break into jail, and so there are many more in jail in the winter than in summer. It costs more for gas in the winter because the nights are longer, and people go to jail to save gas bills. The jails are electric-lighted. You may not know it, but these economic laws are working all the time, whether we know it or do not know it.

15 There are more people who go to jail in hard times than in good times—few people, comparatively, go to jail except when they are hard up. They go to jail because they have no other place to go. They may not know why, but it is true all the same. People are not more wicked in hard times. That is not the reason. The fact is true all over the world that in hard times more people go to jail than in good times, and in winter more people go to jail than in summer. Of course it is pretty hard times for people who go to jail at any time. The people who go to jail are almost always poor people—people who have no other place to live, first and last. When times are hard, then you find large numbers of people who go to jail who would not otherwise be in jail.

16 Long ago, Mr. Buckle, who was a great philosopher and historian, collected facts, and he showed that the number of people who are arrested increased just as the price of food increased. When they put up the price of gas ten cents a thousand, I do not know who will go to jail, but I do know that a certain number of people will go. When the meat combine raises the price of beef, I do not know who is going to jail, but I know that a large number of people are bound to go. Whenever the Standard Oil Company raises the price of oil, I know that a certain number of girls who are seamstresses, and who work night after night long hours for somebody else, will be compelled to go out on the streets and ply another trade, and I know that Mr. Rockefeller and his associates are responsible and not the poor girls in the jails.

17 First and last, people are sent to jail because they are poor. Sometimes, as I say, you may not need money at the particular time, but you wish to have thrifty forehanded habits, and do not always wait until you are in absolute want. Some of you people are perhaps plying the trade, the

profession, which is called burglary. No man in his right senses will go into a strange house in the dead of night and prowl around with a dark lantern through unfamiliar rooms and take chances of his life, if he has plenty of the good things of the world in his own home. You would not take any such chances as that. If a man had clothes in his clothespress and beefsteak in his pantry and money in the bank, he would not navigate around nights in houses where he knows nothing about the premises whatever. It always requires experience and education for this profession, and people who fit themselves for it are no more to blame than I am for being a lawyer. A man would not hold up another man on the street if he had plenty of money in his own pocket. He might do it if he had one dollar or two dollars, but he wouldn't if he had as much money as Mr. Rockefeller has. Mr. Rockefeller has a great deal better hold-up game than that.

The more that is taken from the poor by the rich, who 18
have the chance to take it, the more poor people there are who are compelled to resort to these means for a livelihood. They may not understand it, they may not think so at once, but after all they are driven into that line of employment.

There is a bill before the legislature of this state to punish 19
kidnaping children with death. We have wise members of the legislature. They know the gas trust when they see it and they always see it—they can furnish light enough to be seen; and this legislature thinks it is going to stop kidnaping children by making a law punishing kidnapers of children with death. I don't believe in kidnaping children, but the legislature is all wrong. Kidnaping children is not a crime, it is a profession. It has been developed with the times. It has been developed with our modern industrial conditions. There are many ways of making money—many new ways that our ancestors knew nothing about. Our ancestors knew nothing about a billion-dollar trust; and here comes some poor fellow who has no other trade and he discovers the profession of kidnaping children.

This crime is born, not because people are bad; people 20
don't kidnap other people's children because they want the children or because they are devilish, but because they see a chance to get some money out of it. You cannot cure this crime by passing a law punishing by death kidnapers of children. There is one way to cure it. There is one way to cure all these offenses, and that is to give the people a

chance to live. There is no other way, and there never was any other way since the world began; and the world is so blind and stupid that it will not see. If every man and woman and child in the world had a chance to make a decent, fair, honest living, there would be no jails and no lawyers and no courts. There might be some persons here or there with some peculiar formation of their brain, like Rockefeller, who would do these things simply to be doing them; but they would be very, very few, and those should be sent to a hospital and treated, and not sent to jail; and they would entirely disappear in the second generation, or at least in the third generation.

21 I am not talking pure theory. I will just give you two or three illustrations.

22 The English people once punished criminals by sending them away. They would load them on a ship and export them to Australia. England was owned by lords and nobles and rich people. They owned the whole earth over there, and the other people had to stay in the streets. They could not get a decent living. They used to take their criminals and send them to Australia—I mean the class of criminals who got caught. When these criminals got over there, and nobody else had come, they had the whole continent to run over, and so they could raise sheep and furnish their own meat, which is easier than stealing it. These criminals then became decent, respectable people because they had a chance to live. They did not commit any crimes. They were just like the English people who sent them there, only better. And in the second generation the descendants of those criminals were as good and respectable a class of people as there were on the face of the earth, and then they began building churches and jails themselves.

23 A portion of this country was settled in the same way, landing prisoners down on the southern coast; but when they got here and had a whole continent to run over and plenty of chances to make a living, they became respectable citizens, making their own living just like any other citizen in the world. But finally the descendants of the English aristocracy who sent the people over to Australia found out they were getting rich, and so they went over to get possession of the earth as they always do, and they organized land syndicates and got control of the land and ores, and then they had just as many criminals in Australia as they did in England. It was not because the world had grown bad; it

was because the earth had been taken away from the people.

Some of you people have lived in the country. It's prettier than it is here. And if you have ever lived on a farm you understand that if you put a lot of cattle in a field, when the pasture is short they will jump over the fence; but put them in a good field where there is plenty of pasture, and they will be law-abiding cattle to the end of time. The human animal is just like the rest of the animals, only a little more so. The same thing that governs in the one governs in the other. 24

Everybody makes his living along the lines of least resistance. A wise man who comes into a country early sees a great undeveloped land. For instance, our rich men twenty-five years ago saw that Chicago was small and knew a lot of people would come here and settle, and they readily saw that if they had all the land around here it would be worth a good deal, so they grabbed the land. You cannot be a landlord because somebody has got it all. You must find some other calling. In England and Ireland and Scotland less than five per cent own all the land there is, and the people are bound to stay there on any kind of terms the landlords give. They must live the best they can, so they develop all these various professions—burglary, picking pockets, and the like. 25

Again, people find all sorts of ways of getting rich. These are diseases like everything else. You look at people getting rich, organizing trusts and making a million dollars, and somebody gets the disease and he starts out. He catches it just as a man catches the mumps or the measles; he is not to blame, it is in the air. You will find men speculating beyond their means, because the mania of money-getting is taking possession of them. It is simply a disease—nothing more, nothing less. You cannot avoid catching it; but the fellows who have control of the earth have the advantage of you. See what the law is: when these men get control of things, they make the laws. They do not make the laws to protect anybody; courts are not instruments of justice. When your case gets into court it will make little difference whether you are guilty or innocent, but it's better if you have a smart lawyer. And you cannot have a smart lawyer unless you have money. First and last it's a question of money. Those men who own the earth make the laws to protect what they have. They fix up a sort of fence or pen around what they have, and they fix the law so the fellow on the outside cannot get in. The laws are really organized for the protection of the 26 men who rule the world. They were never organized or enforced to do justice. We have no system for doing justice, not the slightest in the world.

27 Let me illustrate: Take the poorest person in this room. If the community had provided a system of doing justice, the poorest person in this room would have as good a lawyer as the richest, would he not? When you went into court you would have just as long a trial and just as fair a trial as the richest person in Chicago. Your case would not be tried in fifteen or twenty minutes, whereas it would take fifteen days to get through with a rich man's case.

28 Then if you were rich and were beaten, your case would be taken to the Appellate Court. A poor man cannot take his case to the Appellate Court; he has not the price. And then to the Supreme Court. And if he were beaten there he might perhaps go to the United States Supreme Court. And he might die of old age before he got into jail. If you are poor, it's a quick job. You are almost known to be guilty, else you would not be there. Why should anyone be in the criminal court if he were not guilty? He would not be there if he could be anywhere else. The officials have no time to look after all these cases. The people who are on the outside, who are running banks and building churches and making jails, they have no time to examine 600 or 700 prisoners each year to see whether they are guilty or innocent. If the courts were organized to promote justice the people would elect somebody to defend all these criminals, somebody as smart as the prosecutor—and give him as many detectives and as many assistants to help, and pay as much money to defend you as to prosecute you. We have a very able man for state's attorney, and he has many assistants, detectives, and policemen without end, and judges to hear the cases—everything handy.

29 Most all of our criminal code consists in offenses against property. People are sent to jail because they have committed a crime against property. It is of very little consequence whether one hundred people more or less go to jail who ought not to go—you must protect property, because in this world property is of more importance than anything else.

30 How is it done? These people who have property fix it so they can protect what they have. When somebody commits a crime it does not follow that he has done something that is morally wrong. The man on the outside who has commit-

ted no crime may have done something. For instance: to take all the coal in the United States and raise the price two dollars or three dollars when there is no need of it, and thus kill thousands of babies and send thousands of people to the poorhouse and tens of thousands to jail, as is done every year in the United States—this is a greater crime than all the people in our jails ever committed; but the law does not punish it. Why? Because the fellows who control the earth make the laws. If you and I had the making of the laws, the first thing we would do would be to punish the fellow who gets control of the earth. Nature put this coal in the ground for me as well as for them and nature made the prairies up here to raise wheat for me as well as for them, and then the great railroad companies came along and fenced it up.

Most all of the crimes for which we are punished are 31
property crimes. There are a few personal crimes, like murder—but they are very few. The crimes committed are mostly those against property. If this punishment is right the criminals must have a lot of property. How much money is there in this crowd? And yet you are all here for crimes against property. The people up and down the Lake Shore have not committed crime; still they have so much property they don't know what to do with it. It is perfectly plain why these people have not committed crimes against property; they make the laws and therefore do not need to break them. And in order for you to get some property you are obliged to break the rules of the game. I don't know but what some of you may have had a very nice chance to get rich by carrying a hod for one dollar a day, twelve hours. Instead of taking that nice, easy profession, you are a burglar. If you had been given a chance to be a banker you would rather follow that. Some of you may have had a chance to work as a switchman on a railroad where you know, according to statistics, that you cannot live and keep all your limbs more than seven years, and you can get fifty dollars or seventy-five dollars a month for taking your lives in your hands; and instead of taking that lucrative position you chose to be a sneak thief, or something like that. Some of you made that sort of choice. I don't know which I would take if I was reduced to this choice. I have an easier choice.

I will guarantee to take from this jail, or any jail in the 32
world, five hundred men who have been the worst criminals and law-breakers who ever got into jail, and I will go down to our lowest streets and take five hundred of the most

abandoned prostitutes, and go out somewhere where there is plenty of land, and will give them a chance to make a living, and they will be as good people as the average in the community.

33 There is one remedy for the sort of condition we see here. The world never finds it out, or when it does find it out it does not enforce it. You may pass a law punishing every person with death for burglary, and it will make no difference. Men will commit it just the same. In England there was a time when one hundred different offenses were punishable with death, and it made no difference. The English people strangely found out that so fast as they repealed the severe penalties and so fast as they did away with punishing men by death, crime decreased instead of increased; that the smaller the penalty the fewer the crimes.

34 Hanging men in our county jails does not prevent murder. It makes murderers.

35 And this has been the history of the world. It's easy to see how to do away with what we call crime. It is not so easy to do it. I will tell you how to do it. It can be done by giving the people a chance to live—by destroying special privileges. So long as big criminals can get the coal fields, so long as the big criminals have control of the city council and get the public streets for streetcars and gas rights—this is bound to send thousands of poor people to jail. So long as men are allowed to monopolize all the earth, and compel others to live on such terms as these men see fit to make, then you are bound to get into jail.

36 The only way in the world to abolish crime and criminals is to abolish the big ones and the little ones together. Make fair conditions of life. Give men a chance to live. Abolish the right of private ownership of land, abolish monopoly, make the world partners in production, partners in the good things of life. Nobody would steal if he could get something of his own some easier way. Nobody will commit burglary when he has a house full. No girl will go out on the streets when she has a comfortable place at home. The man who owns a sweatshop or a department store may not be to blame himself for the condition of his girls, but when he pays them five dollars, three dollars, and two dollars a week, I wonder where he thinks they will get the rest of their money to live. The only way to cure these conditions is by equality. There should be no jails. They do not accomplish what they pretend to accomplish. If you would wipe them

out there would be no more criminals than now. They terrorize nobody. They are a blot upon any civilization, and a jail is an evidence of the lack of charity of the people on the outside who make the jails and fill them with the victims of their greed.

Richard J. Herrnstein and James Q. Wilson

Are Criminals Made or Born?

Richard J. Herrnstein and James Q. Wilson work at Harvard University—Herrnstein as a professor of psychology, Wilson as a professor of government. The following article, adapted from their book Crime and Human Nature, *appeared in* The New York Times Magazine *in 1985.*

A revolution in our understanding of crime is quietly overthrowing some established doctrines. Until recently, criminologists looked for the causes of crime almost entirely in the offenders' social circumstances. There seemed to be no shortage of circumstances to blame: weakened, chaotic or broken families, ineffective schools, antisocial gangs, racism, poverty, unemployment. Criminologists took seriously, more so than many other students of social behavior, the famous dictum of the French sociologist Emile Durkheim: Social facts must have social explanations. The sociological theory of crime had the unquestioned support of prominent editorialists, commentators, politicians and most thoughtful people. 1

Today, many learned journals and scholarly works draw a different picture. Sociological factors have not been abandoned, but increasingly it is becoming clear to many scholars that crime is the outcome of an interaction between social factors and certain biological factors, particularly for the offenders who, by repeated crimes, have made public places dangerous. The idea is still controversial, but increasingly, to the old question "Are criminals born or made?" the answer seems to be: both. The causes of crime lie in a combination of predisposing biological traits channeled by social circumstance into criminal behavior. The traits 2 alone do not inevitably lead to crime; the circumstances do not make criminals of everyone; but together they create a population responsible for a large fraction of America's problem of crime in the streets.

3 Evidence that criminal behavior has deeper roots than social circumstances has always been right at hand, but social science has, until recent years, overlooked its implications. As far as the records show, crime everywhere and throughout history is disproportionately a young man's pursuit. Whether men are 20 or more times as likely to be arrested as women, as is the case in Malawi or Brunei, or only four to six times as likely, as in the United States or France, the sex difference in crime statistics is universal. Similarly, 18-year-olds may sometimes be four times as likely to be criminal as 40-year-olds, while at other times only twice as likely. In the United States, more than half of all arrests for serious property crimes are of 20-year-olds or younger. Nowhere have older persons been as criminal as younger ones.

4 It is easy to imagine purely social explanations for the effects of age and sex on crime. Boys in many societies are trained by their parents and the society itself to play more roughly and aggressively than girls. Boys are expected to fight back, not to cry, and to play to win. Likewise, boys in many cultures are denied adult responsibilities, kept in a state of prolonged dependence and confined too long in schools that many of them find unrewarding. For a long time, these factors were thought to be the whole story.

5 Ultimately, however, the very universality of the age and sex differences in crime have alerted some social scientists to the implausibility of a theory that does not look beyond the accidents of particular societies. If cultures as different as Japan's and Sweden's, England's and Mexico's, have sex and age differences in crime, then perhaps we should have suspected from the start that there was something more fundamental going on than parents happening to decide to raise their boys and girls differently. What is it about boys, girls and their parents, in societies of all sorts, that leads them to emphasize, rather than overcome, sex differences? Moreover, even if we believed that every society has arbitrarily decided to inculcate aggressiveness in males, there would still be the greater criminality among *young* males to explain. After all, in some cultures, young boys are not

denied adult responsibilities but are kept out of school, put to work tilling the land and made to accept obligations to the society.

6 But it is no longer necessary to approach questions about the sources of criminal behavior merely with argument and supposition. There is evidence. Much crime, it is agreed, has an aggressive component, and Eleanor Emmons Maccoby, a professor of psychology at Stanford University, and Carol Nagy Jacklin, a psychologist now at the University of Southern California, after reviewing the evidence on sex differences in aggression, concluded that it has a foundation that is at least in part biological. Only that conclusion can be drawn, they said, from data that show that the average man is more aggressive than the average woman in all known societies, that the sex difference is present in infancy well before evidence of sex-role socialization by adults, that similar sex differences turn up in many of our biological relatives—monkeys and apes. Human aggression has been directly tied to sex hormones, particularly male sex hormones, in experiments on athletes engaging in competitive sports and on prisoners known for violent or domineering behavior. No single line of evidence is decisive and each can be challenged, but all together they convinced Drs. Maccoby and Jacklin, as well as most specialists on the biology of sex differences, that the sexual conventions that assign males the aggressive roles have biological roots.

7 That is also the conclusion of most researchers about the developmental forces that make adolescence and young adulthood a time of risk for criminal and other nonconventional behavior. This is when powerful new drives awaken, leading to frustrations that foster behavior unchecked by the internalized prohibitions of adulthood. The result is usually just youthful rowdiness, but, in a minority of cases, it passes over the line into crime.

8 The most compelling evidence of biological factors for criminality comes from two studies—one of twins, the other of adopted boys. Since the 1920's it has been understood that twins may develop from a single fertilized egg, resulting in identical genetic endowments—identical twins—or from a pair of separately fertilized eggs that have about half their genes in common—fraternal twins. A standard procedure for estimating how important genes are to a trait is to compare the similarity between identical twins with that

between fraternal twins. When identical twins are clearly more similar in a trait than fraternal twins, the trait probably has high heritability.

9 There have been about a dozen studies of criminality using twins. More than 1,500 pairs of twins have been studied in the United States, the Scandinavian countries, Japan, West Germany, Britain and elsewhere, and the result is qualitatively the same everywhere. Identical twins are more likely to have similar criminal records than fraternal twins. For example, the late Karl O. Christiansen, a Danish criminologist, using the Danish Twin Register, searched police, court and prison records for entries regarding twins born in a certain region of Denmark between 1881 and 1910. When an identical twin had a criminal record, Christiansen found, his or her co-twin was more than twice as likely to have one also than when a fraternal twin had a criminal record.

10 In the United States, a similar result has recently been reported by David Rowe, a psychologist at the University of Oklahoma, using questionnaires instead of official records to measure criminality. Twins in high school in almost all the school districts of Ohio received questionnaires by mail, with a promise of confidentiality as well as a small payment if the questionnaires were filled out and returned. The twins were asked about their activities, including their delinquent behavior, about their friends, and about their co-twins. The identical twins were more similar in delinquency than the fraternal twins. In addition, the twins who shared more activities with each other were no more likely to be similar in delinquency than those who shared fewer activities.

11 No single method of inquiry should be regarded as conclusive. But essentially the same results are found in studies of adopted children. The idea behind such studies is to find a sample of children adopted early in life, cases in which the criminal histories of both adopting and biological parents are known. Then, as the children grow up, researchers can discover how predictive of their criminality are the family histories of their adopting and biological parents. Recent studies show that the biological family history contributes substantially to the adoptees' likelihood of breaking the law.

12 For example, Sarnoff Mednick, a psychologist at the University of Southern California, and his associates in the United States and Denmark have followed a sample of

several thousand boys adopted in Denmark between 1927 and 1947. Boys with criminal biological parents and non-criminal adopting parents were more likely to have criminal records than those with noncriminal biological parents and criminal adopting parents. The more criminal convictions a boy's natural parents had, the greater the risk of criminality for boys being raised by adopting parents who had no records. The risk was unrelated to whether the boy or his adopting parents knew about the natural parents' criminal records, whether the natural parents committed their crimes before or after the boy was given up for adoption, or whether the boy was adopted immediately after birth or a year or two later. The results of this study have been confirmed in Swedish and American samples of adopted children.

Because of studies like these, many sociologists and criminologists now accept the existence of genetic factors contributing to criminality. When there is disagreement, it is about how large the genetic contribution to crime is and about how the criminality of biological parents is transmitted to their children. 13

Both the twin and adoption studies show that genetic contributions are not alone responsible for crime—there is, for example, some increase in criminality among boys if their adopted fathers are criminal even when their biological parents are not, and not every co-twin of a criminal identical twin becomes criminal himself. Although it appears, on average, to be substantial, the precise size of the genetic contribution to crime is probably unknowable, particularly since the measures of criminality itself are now so crude. 14

We have a bit more to go on with respect to the link that transmits a predisposition toward crime from parents to children. No one believes there are "crime genes," but there are two major attributes that have, to some degree, a heritable base and that appear to influence criminal behavior. These are intelligence and temperament. Hundreds of studies have found that the more genes people share, the more likely they are to resemble each other intellectually and temperamentally. 15

Starting with studies in the 1930's, the average offender in broad samples has consistently scored 91 to 93 on I.Q. tests for which the general population's average is 100. The 16 typical offender does worse on the verbal items of intelligence tests than on the nonverbal items but is usually below average on both.

17 Criminologists have long known about the correlation between criminal behavior and I.Q., but many of them have discounted it for various reasons. Some have suggested that the correlation can be explained away by the association between low socioeconomic status and crime, on the one hand, and that between low I.Q. and low socioeconomic status, on the other. These criminologists say it is low socioeconomic status, rather than low I.Q., that fosters crime. Others have questioned whether I.Q. tests really measure intelligence for the populations that are at greater risk for breaking the law. The low scores of offenders, the argument goes, betray a culturally deprived background or alienation from our society's values rather than low intelligence. Finally, it is often noted that the offenders in some studies have been caught for their crimes. Perhaps the ones who got away have higher I.Q.s.

18 But these objections have proved to be less telling than they once seemed to be. There are, for example, many poor law-abiding people living in deprived environments, and one of their more salient characteristics is that they have higher I.Q. scores than those in the same environment who break the law.

19 Then, too, it is a common misconception that I.Q. tests are invalid for people from disadvantaged backgrounds. If what is implied by this criticism is that scores predict academic potential or job performance differently for different groups, then the criticism is wrong. A comprehensive recent survey sponsored by the National Academy of Sciences concluded that "tests predict about as well for one group as for another." And that some highly intelligent criminals may well be good at eluding capture is fully consistent with the belief that offenders, in general, have lower scores than nonoffenders.

20 If I.Q. and criminality are linked, what may explain the link? There are several possibilities. One is that low scores on I.Q. tests signify greater difficulty in grasping the likely consequences of action or in learning the meaning and significance of moral codes. Another is that low scores, especially on the verbal component of the tests, mean trouble in school, which leads to frustration, thence to resentment, anger and delinquency. Still another is that

persons who are not as skillful as others in expressing themselves verbally may find it more rewarding to express themselves in ways in which they will do better, such as physical threat or force.

For some repeat offenders, the predisposition to criminality may be more a matter of temperament than intelligence. Impulsiveness, insensitivity to social mores, a lack of deep and enduring emotional attachments to others and an appetite for danger are among the temperamental characteristics of high-rate offenders. Temperament is, to a degree, heritable, though not as much so as intelligence. All parents know that their children, shortly after birth, begin to exhibit certain characteristic ways of behaving—they are placid or fussy, shy or bold. Some of the traits endure, among them aggressiveness and hyperactivity, although they change in form as the child develops. As the child grows up, these traits, among others, may gradually unfold into a disposition toward unconventional, defiant or antisocial behavior. 21

Lee Robins, a sociologist at Washington University School of Medicine in St. Louis, reconstructed 30 years of the lives of more than 500 children who were patients in the 1920's at a child guidance clinic in St. Louis. She was interested in the early precursors of chronic sociopathy, a condition of antisocial personality that often includes criminal behavior as one of its symptoms. Adult sociopaths in her sample who did not suffer from psychosis, mental retardation or addiction, were, without exception, antisocial before they were 18. More than half of the male sociopaths had serious symptoms before they were 11. The main childhood precursors were truancy, poor school performance, theft, running away, recklessness, slovenliness, impulsiveness and guiltlessness. The more symptoms in childhood, the greater the risk of sociopathy in adulthood. 22

Other studies confirm and extend Dr. Robin's conclusions. For example, two psychologists, John J. Conger of the University of Colorado and Wilbur Miller of Drake University in Des Moines, searching back over the histories of a sample of delinquent boys in Denver, found that "by the end of the third grade, future delinquents were already seen by their teachers as more poorly adapted than their classmates. They appeared to have less regard for the rights and feelings of their peers; less awareness of the need to accept re- 23 sponsibility for their obligations, both as individuals and as members of a group, and poorer attitudes toward authority."

24 Traits that foreshadow serious, recurrent criminal behavior have been traced all the way back to behavior patterns such as hyperactivity and unusual fussiness, and neurological signs such as atypical brain waves or reflexes. In at least a minority of cases, these are detectable in the first few years of life. Some of the characteristics are sex-linked. There is evidence that newborn females are more likely than newborn males to smile, to cling to their mothers, to be receptive to touching and talking, to be sensitive to certain stimuli, such as being touched by a cloth, and to have less upper-body strength. Mothers certainly treat girls and boys differently, but the differences are not simply a matter of the mother's choice—female babies are more responsive than male babies to precisely the kind of treatment that is regarded as "feminine." When adults are asked to play with infants, they play with them in ways they think are appropriate to the infants' sexes. But there is also some evidence that when the sex of the infant is concealed, the behavior of the adults is influenced by the conduct of the child.

25 Premature infants or those born with low birth weights have a special problem. These children are vulnerable to any adverse circumstances in their environment—including child abuse—that may foster crime. Although nurturing parents can compensate for adversity, cold or inconsistent parents may exacerbate it. Prematurity and low birth weight may result from poor prenatal care, a bad diet or excessive use of alcohol or drugs. Whether the care is due to poverty, ignorance or anything else, here we see criminality arising from biological, though not necessarily genetic, factors. It is now known that these babies are more likely than normal babies to be the victims of child abuse.

26 We do not mean to blame child abuse on the victim by saying that premature and low-birth-weight infants are more difficult to care for and thus place a great strain on the parents. But unless parents are emotionally prepared for the task of caring for such children, they may vent their frustration at the infant's unresponsiveness by hitting or neglecting it. Whatever it is in parent and child that leads to prematurity or low birth weight is compounded by the subsequent interaction between them. Similarly, children with low I.Q.s may have difficulty in understanding rules, but if their parents also have poor verbal skills, they may

have difficulty in communicating rules, and so each party to the conflict exacerbates the defects of the other.

The statement that biology plays a role in explaining human behavior, especially criminal behavior, sometimes elicits a powerful political or ideological reaction. Fearful that what is being proposed is a crude biological determinism, some critics deny the evidence while others wish the evidence to be confined to scientific journals. Scientists who have merely proposed studying the possible effects of chromosomal abnormalities on behavior have been ruthlessly attacked by other scientists, as have those who have made public the voluminous data showing the heritability of intelligence and temperament. 27

Some people worry that any claim that biological factors influence criminality is tantamount to saying that the higher crime rate of black compared to white Americans has a genetic basis. But no responsible work in the field leads to any such conclusion. The data show that of all the reasons people vary in their crime rates, race is far less important than age, sex, intelligence and the other individual factors that vary within races. Any study of the causes of crime must therefore first consider the individual factors. Differences among races may have many explanations, most of them having nothing to do with biology. 28

The intense reaction to the study of biological factors in crime, we believe, is utterly misguided. In fact, these discoveries, far from implying that "criminals are born" and should be locked up forever, suggest new and imaginative ways of reducing criminality by benign treatment. The opportunity we have is precisely analogous to that which we had when the biological bases of other disorders were established. Mental as well as physical illness—alcoholism, learning disabilities of various sorts, and perhaps even susceptibilities to drug addiction—now seem to have genetic components. In each case, new understanding energized the search for treatment and gave it new direction. Now we know that many forms of depression can be successfully treated with drugs; in time we may learn the same of Alzheimer's disease. Alcoholics are helped when they understand that some persons, because of their predisposition toward addiction to alcohol, should probably never consume it at all. A chemical treatment of the predisposition is 29 a realistic possibility. Certain types of slow learners can already be helped by special programs. In time, others will be also.

30 Crime, admittedly, may be a more difficult program. So many different acts are criminal that it is only with considerable poetic license that we can speak of "criminality" at all. The bank teller who embezzles $500 to pay off a gambling debt is not engaging in the same behavior as a person who takes $500 from a liquor store at the point of a gun or one who causes $500 worth of damage by drunkenly driving his car into a parked vehicle. Moreover, crime, unlike alcoholism or dyslexia, exposes a person to the formal condemnation of society and the possibility of imprisonment. We naturally and rightly worry about treating all "criminals" alike, or stigmatizing persons whom we think might become criminal by placing them in special programs designed to prevent criminality.

31 But these problems are not insurmountable barriers to better ways of thinking about crime prevention. Though criminals are of all sorts, we know that a very small fraction of all young males commit so large a fraction of serious street crime that we can properly blame these chronic offenders for most such crime. We also know that chronic offenders typically begin their misconduct at an early age. Early family and preschool programs may be far better repositories for the crime-prevention dollar than rehabilitation programs aimed—usually futilely—at the 19- or 20-year-old veteran offender. Prevention programs risk stigmatizing children, but this may be less of a risk than is neglect. If stigma were a problem to be avoided at all costs, we would have to dismantle most special-needs education programs.

32 Having said all this, we must acknowledge that there is at present little hard evidence that we know how to inhibit the development of delinquent tendencies in children. There are some leads, such as family training programs of the sort pioneered at the Oregon Social Learning Center, where parents are taught how to use small rewards and penalties to alter the behavior of misbehaving children. There is also evidence from David Weikart and Lawrence Schweinhart of the High/Scope Educational Research Foundation at Ypsilanti, Mich., that preschool education programs akin to

Project Head Start may reduce later delinquency. There is nothing yet to build a national policy on, but there are ideas worth exploring by carefully repeating and refining these pioneering experimental efforts.

Above all, there is a case for redirecting research into the causes of crime in ways that take into account the interaction of biological and social factors. Some scholars, such as the criminologist Marvin E. Wolfgang and his colleagues at the University of Pennsylvania, are already exploring these issues by analyzing social and biological information from large groups as they age from infancy to adulthood and linking the data to criminal behavior. But much more needs to be done. 33

It took years of patiently following the life histories of many men and women to establish the linkages between smoking or diet and disease; it will also take years to unravel the complex and subtle ways in which intelligence, temperament, hormonal levels and other traits combine with family circumstances and later experiences in school and elsewhere to produce human character. 34

Alison Bass

Why Aren't There More Women Murderers?

Bass is a staff writer for The Boston Globe *newspaper, where this article appeared in 1992.*

Accused serial killer Aileen Wuornos, who was recently sentenced to death in Florida, is the exception that doesn't prove the rule. 1

The rule is that women, unlike men, don't kill strangers or even casual acquaintances, except in very rare cases of self-defense. When women do kill—and they do so at astonishingly lower rates than men, who commit 85 percent of all homicides—the vast majority kill family members, usually men who have battered them for years. 2

3 As many as 90 percent of the women in jail today for murdering men have been battered by those men. A much smaller number—about 3 in 100,000—kill their children as a result of a postpartum psychosis that has gone untreated.

4 There is also a smattering of women with a history of mental disorders who kill in a psychotic rage. And then there is the rare woman who kills family members for money; according to historical accounts, Lizzie Borden was one.

5 Fewer than 3 percent of serial killers are female, according to FBI statistics. No one knows why this disparity exists, although many researchers believe that differences in brain chemistry may be the primary reason why men are so much more violent than women.

6 Usually, female multiple killers are caretakers—most often nurses—who rationalize their crimes as mercy killings. Nurse Genene Jones, for example, was suspected of killing as many as 16 children in a Texas hospital with a lethal drug in an attempt to prove to administrators that the hospital needed a pediatric intensive care unit; she was convicted of killing one infant and sentenced to 99 years in prison.

7 Another multiple killer, Velma Barfield, who was electrocuted in North Carolina in 1984 (the first woman to be executed in 26 years), admitted killing four family members after years of sexual and physical abuse.

8 But Aileen Wuornos, who authorities say killed seven men, is the first woman in FBI annals accused in a multiple killing of strangers, a series of murders that spanned several years. In many respects, Wuornos, a bisexual prostitute whose alleged victims had picked her up for sex, fits the profile of a male killer.

9 "She has the characteristics we see with our male killers," said John Douglas, unit chief of behavioral sciences for the FBI at Quantico, Va. "Like many of our male killers, she comes from a very dysfunctional background where she was abused, physically and sexually. But usually women from that kind of background internalize the abuse and their feelings. While the men turn to aggression, the women turn to alcohol, drugs, prostitution and suicide."

10 Women who have been badly abused as children also tend to get involved with violent men who abuse them and their children, perpetuating the cycle of violence into the next generation. One 1991 study by New York University researchers found that 21 females who had been incarcerated

for criminal behavior as teenagers did not—as many of their male counterparts did—commit violent crimes as adults: instead the majority became enmeshed in violent relationships, abused or neglected their children, and lost custody of them as a result.

Other research indicates that women who have been sexually abused as children—unlike men similarly abused—do not commit sexual crimes. 11

"Women don't have sexual deviations—they don't make obscene phone calls, they don't flash, they don't have paraphilias [addictions to bizarre practices, such as having sex with a corpse]," says Ann Burgess, professor of psychiatric nursing at the University of Pennsylvania and an authority on sexual homicide. "It is rare for a woman to murder more than one person, and they never commit sexual crimes." 12

The big question is why. 13

While there is no definitive data on the subject, Burgess and other forensic experts believe there are sharp differences between men and women's brain chemistry, and that those differences are accentuated by cultural differences in the way males and females are raised. 14

"It must be a combination of things, but we know it can't be culture alone," says Angela Browne, a social psychologist at the University of Massachusetts Medical Center and a specialist on women who kill. "You can change environments across cultures, and across almost all cultures men are far more prone to homicide than women. Men are also more prone to socially sanctioned actions that lead to death, like civil strife and war." 15

"It makes sense to conclude that physiological rather than simply societal influences are at play," agrees Dr. Dorothy Otnow Lewis, professor of psychiatry at New York University and an authority on violence. 16

In detailed research, Lewis has found that men who have been horribly abused as children and suffer from a constellation of psychiatric and neurological disorders are much more likely than others to become extremely violent. But as Lewis notes, it takes the Y chromosome, i.e., maleness, to complete the picture. 17

Lewis and others believe male hormones such as testosterone and androgen play a key role in making men much more aggressive than women. But merely having a high level of testosterone does not make someone violent; many men with high levels are simply more competitive. 18

They channel their hormonal drives into constructive pursuits.

19 It seems equally clear that culture plays a role.

20 "Men are brought up to fight and to defend themselves, and they are reinforced for engaging in those behaviors," says Robert Prentky, a forensic psychologist at New England Forensic Associates in Arlington and an authority on sexual violence. "When they are challenged by a bully at school, their fathers will teach them how to fight with their fists. But how many times do parents teach girls to defend themselves?"

21 Girls are taught to nurture and care for others; some psychologists believe females may be biochemically "wired" to be more giving and nurturing. For whatever reason, women respond to conflict in ways very different than men do.

22 "Women may be emotionally abusive and damaging, rather than physically abusive," says Browne, author of a book called *When Battered Women Kill.* "Even though women could theoretically equalize their lesser strength with a gun, they still don't perpetrate violence in very large numbers."

23 The statistics show that most women do not become violent unless they are in fear of their own lives or their children's. In research on battered women who kill their male partners, Browne found the majority of women were responding to threats against their children. And the rest had reason to believe that, after battering them for years, the men in their lives planned to kill them.

24 Browne also found that the rate of women who kill their partners has fallen 25 percent since the mid-70s, when many shelters for battered women were opened and police started adopting tougher policies on domestic violence. There has been no comparable decrease in the rates of men who kill their female partners. (Of all the male-female partner killings in the United States, 61 percent of the victims were women.)

25 Research also shows that a small percentage of women kill when their biochemistry goes haywire, as the result of drugs, alcohol, mental disease or pregnancy. The few female mass murderers had long histories of untreated severe mental disorders, such as paranoid schizophrenia and

manic mood swings. Among them was Sylvia Seegrist, who in 1985 shot three people during a psychotic rampage at a Philadelphia area mall.

Perhaps the most preventable cause of lethal violence is postpartum psychosis, which afflicts about one woman in 1,000. Fully 3 percent of women with this disorder kill their infants, according to Susan Hickman, a San Diego psychotherapist and specialist in postpartum psychiatric disorders. 26

"Women with postpartum psychiatric illnesses often experience sleep and appetite disturbances, and in the most extreme cases they hallucinate, hear voices and imagine things," she said. "Often there is some kind of delusional construct involving the infant; for example, a delusion about the baby's being the devil. These delusions often take a religious tone." 27

Hickman and others believe this psychosis is biochemical in nature. During pregnancy, the placenta takes over some of the body's hormone production, and in most cases after delivery the pituitary gland, which regulates hormones, kicks back in. But in a few cases, Hickman speculates, the pituitary fails to kick back in and the woman's hormones become unbalanced, causing postpartum depression or psychosis. 28

"There is a neuroleptic medication that will control the symptoms very rapidly," Hickman says. "A woman can continue to nurse her baby and be restored to her normal functioning with the medication. And over time her body chemistry will level itself out and she should have no recurrence of symptoms, unless she has another pregnancy." 29

Aileen Wuornos, of course, was not pregnant. Nor, apparently, was she suffering from a serious mental disorder that clouded her judgment about right and wrong. 30

She had, however, experienced a brutal childhood. Her father was convicted of molesting a seven-year-old girl and implicated in the murder of another. When Wuornos was six months old, her mother handed her over to her grandparents, who physically abused her. Her grandfather also sexually abused her. At 13, she became pregnant after being raped by a stranger, according to psychiatrist Susan C. Vaughan of Columbia/New York State Psychiatric Institute, who has written about the case. 31

Thrown out of her grandparents' home when she became pregnant, Wuornos stayed in a home for unwed mothers until her baby was born and given up for adoption. After 32 that, she lived on her own—in a neighbor's junked car or in a woods nearby—and turned to prostitution, drinking and drugs. She roamed the Midwest for years, supporting herself as a prostitute, and when she was 21, she tried to kill herself by shooting herself in the stomach, Vaughan wrote in the winter 1991 issue of the *American Academy of Psychoanalysis Forum.*

33 In the early 1980s, Wuornos was convicted of robbery. Florida police believe the murders did not begin until 1988, when Wuornos was living with another woman and supporting her through prostitution. After police caught up with her in January 1991, she admitted to killing two men who had picked her up for sex. She said she shot them repeatedly after they refused to pay her.

34 "Her motive may have been displaced rage motive—she just wanted to kill these men for revenge," Prentky speculates. "Other women may have her fantasies, but they don't act on it."

Garrison Keillor

The Current Crisis in Remorse

Garrison Keillor, born in 1942 in Anoka, Minnesota, is a writer and broadcaster. He founded and hosted "A Prairie Home Companion," an award-winning radio variety show offered on National Public Radio. A droll and funny storyteller who spins affectionate yarns of small-town life, he published in 1985 the best-selling Lake Wobegon Days, *named for the fictional locale of his broadcasts. The following sketch appeared in* The New Yorker *and in his 1989 collection* We Are Still Married.

1 Remorse is a fairly new area in social work so it's no wonder we get the short end when it comes to budget and staffing. Take me, for example. For three years, I was the *only professional remorse officer* in a Department of Human Services serving a city of *more than 1.5 million,* and not so long ago my supervisor Mitch (a man with no remorse background at all) told me I was "expendable" and that he

would "shed no tears" if remorse was eliminated from the Department entirely. I had no office, only a desk across from the elevators, and I shared a phone with the director of the Nephew Program in Family Counseling. And it's not only me! Around the country, morale in remorse has never been lower.

We in remorse are a radical minority with the social-work community. We believe that not every wrong in our society is the result of complex factors such as poor early-learning environment and resultative dissocialized communication. Some wrong is the result of *badness*. We believe that some people act like jerks, and that when dealing with jerks one doesn't waste too much time on sympathy. They're jerks. They do bad things. They should feel sorry for what they did and stop doing it. Of course, I'm oversimplifying here, trying to state things in layman's terms, and I should add that we are professionals, after all, who are trained in behavioral methodology *including* remorse, but also a lot more—if you're interested, read "Principles of Deductive Repentance," by Morse and Frain, or Professor Frain's excellent "Failure and Fault: Assignment and Acceptance." 2

I did my training under Frain and graduated in 1976, just as remorse was coming to the forefront. People in the helping professions had begun to notice a dramatic increase in the number of clients who did terrible things and didn't feel one bit sorry. It was an utterly common phenomenon for a man who had been apprehended after months of senseless carnage to look at a social worker or psychologist with an expression of mild dismay and say, "Hey, I know what you're thinking, but that wasn't *me* out there, it wasn't *like* me at all. I'm a caring type of guy. Anyway, it's over now, it's done, and I got to get on with my own life, you know," as if he had only been unkind or unsupportive of his victims and not dismembered them and stuffed them into mailboxes. This was not the "cold-blooded" or "hardened" criminal but, rather, a cheerful, self-accepting one, who looked on his crimes as "something that happened" and had a theory to explain it. 3

"I'm thinking it was a nutritional thing," one mass murderer remarked to me in 1978. "I was feeling down that day. I'd been doing a lot of deep-fried foods, and I was going to get a multi-vitamin out of the medicine chest when I noticed all those old ladies in the park and—well, one thing just led to another. I've completely changed my food intake since 4 then. I really feel *good* now. I know I'm never going to let myself get in that type of situation again!"

5 It wasn't only vicious criminals who didn't feel sorry, though. It was a regretless time all around. Your own best friend might spill a glass of red wine on your new white sofa and immediately *explain* it—no spontaneous shame and embarrassment, just "Oh, I've always had poor motor skills," or "You distracted me with your comment about Bolivia." People walked in and stole your shoes, they trashed your lawn and bullied your children and blasted the neighborhood with powerful tape machines at 4:00 a.m. and got stone drunk and cruised through red lights, smashing your car and ruining your life for the next six months, and if you confronted them about these actions they told you about a particularly upsetting life-experience they'd gone through recently, such as condemnation, that caused them to do it.

6 In 1976, a major Protestant denomination narrowly defeated an attempt to destigmatize the Prayer of Confession by removing from it all guilt or guilt-oriented references: "Lord, we approach Thy Throne of Grace, having committed acts which, we do heartily acknowledge, must be very difficult for Thee to understand. Nevertheless, we do beseech Thee to postpone judgment and to give Thy faithful servants the benefit of the doubt until such time as we are able to answer all Thy questions fully and clear our reputations in Heaven."

7 It was lack of remorse among criminals, though, that aroused public outrage, and suddenly we few professionals in the field were under terrible pressure to have full-fledged remorse programs in place in weeks, even days. City Hall was on the phone, demanding to see miscreants slumped in courtrooms, weeping, shielding their faces while led off to jail.

8 Fine, I said. Give me full funding to hire a staff and I'll give you a remorse program you can be proud of. Mitch sneered. "Ha!" he said. He said, "Get this straight, showboat, 'cause I'll only say it once. You work for me, and I say remorse is Number Last on the list around here. Cosmetics! That's all City Hall wants and that's what we give them. A few tears. You can twist arms, step on toes, or use raw onions, but forget about funding."

9 His insensitivity shocked me. Remorselessness is a fundamental flaw, a crack in the social contract, and repair

requires a major commitment. One man simply couldn't keep up with the caseload.

I spent two months on the president of AmTox, who was sent to me after his conviction for dumping tons of deadly wastes into a scenic gorge and killing thousands of trout and who took a Who—me? attitude toward the deed until finally I elicited a small amount of shame by requiring him to spend Saturdays panhandling in the bus depot, wearing a sign that said "Help Me. I'm Not Too Bright." But meanwhile hundreds of others got off scot-free. I'd put the screws to the guy who enjoyed touching pedestrians with his front fender, but meanwhile the guys who bilked hundreds of elderly women of their life savings walked out the door saying, "Hey, what's the big deal? So we exaggerated a little. No need to get huffy about it." 10

It depressed the hell out of me. Here I was, swimming in paperwork with my hands tied, and out on the street were jerks on parade: unassuming, pleasant, perfectly normal people except that they had an extra bone in their head and less moral sense than God gave badgers. And the ones I did put through remorse didn't improve a lot. Six months ago, thirty-seven former clients of mine filed a class-action suit against the state demanding millions in restitution for the ethically handicapped and arguing neglect on the state's part in failing to provide remorse counseling earlier. "We have suffered terrible remorse," the brief said, "as we begin to recognize the enormity of our sins, including but not limited to: pure selfishness, vicious cruelty, utter dishonesty, blind insensitivity, gross neglect, overweening pride, etc. And that's fine. But where was this program ten years ago? Nowhere to be found! That was the Me Decade! Is that our fault? Therefore, in consideration of the vast black abyss of guilt to which we have been suddenly subjected, we demand that the court order. . . ." My heart sank as I read it. They had even quoted my speech to the Council on Penitential Reform in 1981: 11

> Criminal nonremorse is the tip of a very large iceberg, and unless we initiate broad-based remorse reforms on the community level and start talking about an overhaul of our entire moral system—church, media, education, the parental system, personal networking, the entire values-delivery infrastructure—and recognize that it requires major

> investment by private *and* public sectors in professional training and research and that we're looking at a time frame of years, not months, and that we must begin now, we simply *must,* because, believe me, if we don't, that is a mistake we're going to live to regret!

The state, they said further, had failed to exercise due care in neglecting to warn them earlier and to inform them of the urgent necessity of changing their ways.

12 Three days later, the order came down that I was reassigned. By offering remorse assistance, it said, I had needlessly raised people's expectations of inner peace.

13 "That means you, lamebrain," Mitch cackled, leaning across his desk and poking an index finger into my rib cage. "Let's see how you like it in the basement." He assigned me to "assist in the assembly and assessment" of ancient and dusty ascertainment files in a dim, airless room deep in the bowels of Human Services—useless and demeaning work that left me weak and dispirited after only a day; but I held on and did the work and didn't complain. He plugged the ventilator, reduced light-bulb wattage, denied me a radio. I spent three weeks in that hellhole, reading lengthy case histories of clients long since deceased and sorting them into meaningless piles and attaching gummed labels that tasted like dead socks.

14 Suddenly, one afternoon, he appeared in the doorway, his face drawn, his eyes filled with tears. "I read Frain last night," he said. "All night. Why—I—You should have told me. Oh God, oh God! What have I done to you? How can I make it up? You want my job? Take it."

15 "No, thanks. That's all right. No problem," I said. "I'm quitting."

16 He begged me to stay. "I can't live with my conscience if you won't let me do something for you. Let me at least take you to lunch. There's a terrific little seafood place a block from here that I've been keeping to myself—"

17 "Don't bother," I said. "Come five o'clock you'll never see me again."

18 I was true to my word. I'm a vice-president of Yakamoto now, where I've designed a remorse program for assembly-line workers to build stronger emotional responses to poor workmanship, tardiness, false sick days, and excessive lunch breaks. The job is challenging, the people pleasant, the fringe benefits outstanding, and the salary is three hundred

and ninety-five thou a year. The Japanese place a high premium on shame. You don't see them treating other people like dirt. They even feel contrition for things that someone standing next to them did! They treat me like a prince. I'm a lucky man. I'm extremely happy here.

CAPITAL PUNISHMENT

James Wright

At the Executed Murderer's Grave

James Wright (1927–1980)—educator, translator, poet—frequently wrote about people and places and things in his native Midwest. Born in Martin's Ferry, Ohio, and educated at Kenyon College and the University of Washington, he won the Pulitzer Prize for poetry in 1972. The following poem is a response to the execution of George L. Doty, a convicted rapist and murderer who was electrocuted in 1957.

> Why should we do this? What good is it to us? Above all, how can we do such a thing? How can it possibly be done?
>
> —*Freud*

1 My name is James A. Wright, and I was born
Twenty-five miles from this infected grave,
In Martins Ferry, Ohio, where one slave
To Hazel-Atlas Glass became my father.
He tried to teach me kindness. I return
only in memory now, aloof, unhurried,
To dead Ohio, where I might lie buried,
Had I not run away before my time.
Ohio caught George Doty. Clean as lime,
His skull rots empty here. Dying's the best
Of all the arts men learn in a dead place.
I walked here once. I made my loud display,
Leaning for language on a dead man's voice.
Now sick of lies, I turn to face the past.
I add my easy grievance to the rest:

2 Doty, if I confess I do not love you,
Will you let me alone? I burn for my own lies.
The nights electrocute my fugitive,

My mind. I run like the bewildered mad
At St. Clair Sanitarium, who lurk,
Arch and cunning, under the maple trees,
Pleased to be playing guilty after dark.
Staring to bed, they croon self-lullabies.
Doty, you make me sick. I am not dead.
I croon my tears at fifty cents per line.

Idiot, he demanded love from girls, 3
And murdered one. Also, he was a thief.
He left two women, and a ghost with child.
The hair, foul as a dog's upon his head,
Made such revolting Ohio animals
Fitter for vomit than a kind man's grief.
I waste no pity on the dead that stink,
And no love's lost between me and the crying
Drunks of Belaire, Ohio, where police
Kick at their kidneys till they die of drink.
Christ may restore them whole, for all of me.
Alive and dead, those giggling muckers who
Saddled my nightmares thirty years ago
Can do without my widely printed sighing
Over their pains with paid sincerity.
I do not pity the dead, I pity the dying.

I pity myself, because a man is dead. 4
If Belmont County killed him, what of me?
His victims never loved him. Why should we?
And yet, nobody had to kill him either.
It does no good to woo the grass, to veil
The quicklime hole of a man's defeat and shame.
Nature-lovers are gone. To hell with them.
I kick the clods away, and speak my name.

This grave's gash festers. Maybe it will heal, 5
When all are caught with what they had to do
In fear of love, when every man stands still
By the last sea,
And the princes of the sea come down
To lay away their robes, to judge the earth
And its dead, and we dead stand undefended everywhere,
And my bodies—father and child and unskilled criminal—
Ridiculously kneel to bare my scars,
My sneaking crimes, to God's unpitying stars.

6 Staring politely, they will not mark my face
From any murderer's, buried in this place.
Why should they? We are nothing but a man.

7 Doty, the rapist and the murderer,
Sleeps in a ditch of fire, and cannot hear;
And where, in earth or hell's unholy peace,
Men's suicides will stop, God knows, not I.
Angels and pebbles mock me under trees.
Earth is a door I cannot even face.
Order be damned, I do not want to die,
Even to keep Belaire, Ohio, safe.
The hackles on my neck are fear, not grief.
(Open, dungeon! Open, roof of the ground!)
I hear the last sea in the Ohio grass,
Heaving a tide of gray disastrousness.
Wrinkles of winter ditch the rotted face
Of Doty, killer, imbecile, and thief:
Dirt of my flesh, defeated, underground.

George Orwell

A Hanging

Born Eric Arthur Blair in India in 1903, educated in England, and a member of the Imperial Police in Burma for five years, George Orwell was England's most prominent political writer in the decade before his death in 1950. A socialist but no communist, he wrote numerous books of fiction and nonfiction, but he is best remembered for Animal Farm *(1945) and* 1984 *(1948)—novels that contributed to our culture terms like* doublespeak *and* Big Brother. *His fictional description of "A Hanging" appeared in* Shooting an Elephant and Other Essays *(1950); it was first published in 1931.*

1 It was in Burma, a sodden morning of the rains. A sickly light, like yellow tinfoil, was slanting over the high walls into the jail yard. We were waiting outside the condemned cells, a row of sheds fronted with double bars, like small animal

cages. Each cell measured about ten feet by ten and was quite bare within except for a plank bed and a pot for drinking water. In some of them brown, silent men were squatting at the inner bars, with their blankets draped round them. These were the condemned men, due to be hanged within the next week or two.

One prisoner had been brought out of his cell. He was a Hindu, a puny wisp of a man, with a shaven head and vague liquid eyes. He had a thick, sprouting mustache, absurdly too big for his body, rather like the mustache of a comic man on the films. Six tall Indian warders were guarding him and getting him ready for the gallows. Two of them stood by with rifles and fixed bayonets, while the others handcuffed him, passed a chain through his handcuffs and fixed it to their belts, and lashed his arms tight to his sides. They crowded very close about him, with their hands always on him in a careful, caressing grip, as though all the while feeling him to make sure he was there. It was like men handling a fish which is still alive and may jump back into the water. But he stood quite unresisting, yielding his arms limply to the ropes, as though he hardly noticed what was happening. 2

Eight o'clock struck and a bugle call, desolately thin in the wet air, floated from the distant barracks. The superintendent of the jail, who was standing apart from the rest of us, moodily prodding the gravel with his stick, raised his head at the sound. He was an army doctor, with a gray toothbrush mustache and a gruff voice. "For God's sake, hurry up, Francis," he said irritably. "The man ought to have been dead by this time. Aren't you ready yet?" 3

Francis, the head jailer, a fat Dravidian in a white drill suit and gold spectacles, waved his black hand. "Yes sir, yes sir," he bubbled. "All iss satisfactorily prepared. The hangman iss waiting. We shall proceed." 4

"Well, quick march, then. The prisoners can't get their breakfast till this job's over." 5

We set out for the gallows. Two warders marched on either side of the prisoner, with their rifles at the slope; two others marched close against him, gripping him by arm and shoulder, as though at once pushing and supporting him. The rest of us, magistrates and the like, followed behind. Suddenly, when we had gone ten yards, the procession stopped short without any order or warning. A dreadful thing had happened—a dog, come goodness knows whence, 6 had appeared in the yard. It came bounding among us with a loud volley of barks and leapt round us wagging its whole body, wild with glee at finding so many human beings together. It was a large woolly dog, half Airedale, half pariah. For a moment it pranced around us, and then, before anyone could stop it, it had made a dash for the prisoner, and jumping up tried to lick his face. Everybody stood aghast, too taken aback even to grab the dog.

7 "Who let that bloody brute in here?" said the superintendent angrily. "Catch it, someone!"

8 A warder detached from the escort charged clumsily after the dog, but it danced and gamboled just out of his reach, taking everything as part of the game. A young Eurasian jailer picked up a handful of gravel and tried to stone the dog away, but it dodged the stones and came after us again. Its yaps echoed from the jail walls. The prisoner, in the grasp of the two warders, looked on incuriously, as though this was another formality of the hanging. It was several minutes before someone managed to catch the dog. Then we put my handkerchief through its collar and moved off once more, with the dog still straining and whimpering.

9 It was about forty yards to the gallows. I watched the bare brown back of the prisoner marching in front of me. He walked clumsily with his bound arms, but quite steadily, with that bobbing gait of the Indian who never straightens his knees. At each step his muscles slid neatly into place, the lock of hair on his scalp danced up and down, his feet printed themselves on the wet gravel. And once, in spite of the men who gripped him by each shoulder, he stepped lightly aside to avoid a puddle on the path.

10 It is curious; but till that moment I had never realized what it means to destroy a healthy, conscious man. When I saw the prisoner step aside to avoid the puddle, I saw the mystery, the unspeakable wrongness, of cutting a life short when it is in full tide. This man was not dying, he was alive just as we are alive. All the organs of his body were working—bowels digesting food, skin renewing itself, nails growing, tissues forming—all toiling away in solemn foolery. His nails would still be growing when he stood on the drop, when he was falling through the air with a tenth-of-a-second to live. His eyes saw the yellow gravel and the gray walls, and his brain still remembered, foresaw, reasoned—even about puddles. He and we were a party of men walking together, seeing, hearing, feeling, understanding the same

world; and in two minutes, with a sudden snap, one of us would be gone—one mind less, one world less.

The gallows stood in a small yard, separate from the main grounds of the prison, and overgrown with tall prickly weeds. It was a brick erection like three sides of a shed, with planking on top, and above that two beams and a crossbar with the rope dangling. The hangman, a gray-haired convict in the white uniform of the prison, was waiting beside his machine. He greeted us with a servile crouch as we entered. At a word from Francis the two warders, gripping the prisoner more closely than ever, half led, half pushed him to the gallows and helped him clumsily up the ladder. Then the hangman climbed up and fixed the rope round the prisoner's neck. 11

We stood waiting, five yards away. The warders had formed in a rough circle round the gallows. And then, when the noose was fixed, the prisoner began crying out to his god. It was a high, reiterated cry of "Ram! Ram! Ram! Ram!" not urgent and fearful like a prayer or cry for help, but steady, rhythmical, almost like the tolling of a bell. The dog answered the sound with a whine. The hangman, still standing on the gallows, produced a small cotton bag like a flour bag and drew it down over the prisoner's face. But the sound, muffled by the cloth, still persisted, over and over again: "Ram! Ram! Ram! Ram! Ram!" 12

The hangman climbed down and stood ready, holding the lever. Minutes seemed to pass. The steady, muffled crying from the prisoner went on and on, "Ram! Ram! Ram!" never faltering for an instant. The superintendent, his head on his chest, was slowly poking the ground with his stick; perhaps he was counting the cries, allowing the prisoner a fixed number—fifty, perhaps, or a hundred. Everyone had changed color. The Indians had gone gray like bad coffee, and one or two of the bayonets were wavering. We looked at the lashed, hooded man on the drop, and listened to his cries—each cry another second of life; the same thought was in all our minds; oh, kill him quickly, get it over, stop that abominable noise! 13

Suddenly the superintendent made up his mind. Throwing up his head he made a swift motion with his stick. "Chalo!" he shouted almost fiercely. 14

There was a clanking noise, and then dead silence. The prisoner had vanished, and the rope was twisting on itself. I let go of the dog, and it galloped immediately to the back of 15 the gallows; but when it got there it stopped short, barked, and then retreated into a corner of the yard, where it stood among the weeds, looking timorously out at us. We went round the gallows to inspect the prisoner's body. He was dangling with his toes pointed straight downwards, very slowly revolving, as dead as a stone.

16 The superintendent reached out with his stick and poked the bare brown body; it oscillated slightly. "*He's* all right," said the superintendent. He backed out from under the gallows, and blew out a deep breath. The moody look had gone out of his face quite suddenly. He glanced at his wristwatch. "Eight minutes past eight. Well, that's all for this morning, thank God."

17 The warders unfixed bayonets and marched away. The dog, sobered and conscious of having misbehaved itself, slipped after them. We walked out of the gallows yard, past the condemned cells with their waiting prisoners, into the big central yard of the prison. The convicts, under the command of warders armed with lathis, were already receiving their breakfast. They squatted in long rows, each man holding a tin pannikin, while two warders with buckets marched around ladling out rice; it seemed quite a homely, jolly scene, after the hanging. An enormous relief had come upon us now that the job was done. One felt an impulse to sing, to break into a run, to snigger. All at once everyone began chattering gaily.

18 The Eurasian boy walking beside me nodded towards the way we had come, with a knowing smile: "Do you know sir, our friend (he meant the dead man) when he heard his appeal had been dismissed, he pissed on the floor of his cell. From fright. Kindly take one of my cigarettes, sir. Do you not admire my new silver case, sir? From the boxwallah, two rupees eight annas. Classy European style."

19 Several people laughed—at what, nobody seemed certain.

20 Francis was walking by the superintendent, talking garrulously: "Well, sir, all has passed off with the utmost satisfactoriness. It was all finished—flick! Like that. It iss not always so—oah, no! I have known cases where the doctor wass obliged to go beneath the gallows and pull the prisoner's legs to ensure decease. Most disagreeable!"

21 "Wriggling about, eh? That's bad," said the superintendent.

22 "Ach, sir, it iss worse when they become refractory! One man, I recall, clung to the bars of hiss cage when we went to

take him out. You will scarcely credit, sir, that it took six warders to dislodge him, three pulling at each leg. We reasoned with him, 'My dear fellow,' we said, 'think of all the pain and trouble you are causing to us!' But no, he would not listen! Ach, he wass very troublesome!"

I found that I was laughing quite loudly. Everyone was laughing. Even the superintendent grinned in a tolerant way. "You'd better all come out and have a drink," he said quite genially. "I've got a bottle of whiskey in the car. We could do with it." 23

We went through the big double gates of the prison into the road. "Pulling at his legs!" exclaimed a Burmese magistrate suddenly, and burst into a loud chuckling. We all began laughing again. At that moment Francis' anecdote seemed extraordinarily funny. We all had a drink together, native and European alike, quite amicably. The dead man was a hundred yards away. 24

Edward I. Koch

Death and Justice

Outspoken and controversial, Edward I. Koch (born 1924) served as the Democratic mayor of New York from 1978 to 1989. He has always been eager to engage in public debate on controversial issues in his three books, in his hundreds of speeches, and in his published articles. In 1985 he contributed the following essay to The New Republic, *an influential public affairs magazine generally considered middle-of-the-road in its outlook.*

Last December a man named Robert Lee Willie, who had been convicted of raping and murdering an 18-year-old woman, was executed in the Louisiana state prison. In a statement issued several minutes before his death, Mr. Willie said: "Killing people is wrong. . . . It makes no difference whether it's citizens, countries, or governments. Killing is wrong." Two weeks later in South Carolina, an admitted killer named Joseph Carl Shaw was put to death for mur- 1 dering two teenagers. In an appeal to the governor for clemency, Mr. Shaw wrote: "Killing is wrong when I did it. Killing is wrong when you do it. I hope you have the courage and moral strength to stop the killing."

2 It is a curiosity of modern life that we find ourselves being lectured on morality by cold-blooded killers. Mr. Willie previously had been convicted of aggravated rape, aggravated kidnapping, and the murders of a Louisiana deputy and a man from Missouri. Mr. Shaw committed another murder a week before the two for which he was executed, and admitted mutilating the body of the 14-year-old girl he killed. I can't help wondering what prompted these murderers to speak out against killing as they entered the death-house door. Did their newfound reverence for life stem from the realization that they were about to lose their own?

3 Life is indeed precious, and I believe the death penalty helps to affirm this fact. Had the death penalty been a real possibility in the minds of these murderers, they might well have stayed their hand. They might have shown moral awareness before their victims died, and not after. Consider the tragic death of Rosa Velez, who happened to be home when a man named Luis Vera burglarized her apartment in Brooklyn. "Yeah, I shot her," Vera admitted. "She knew me, and I knew I wouldn't go to the chair."

4 During my 22 years in public service, I have heard the pros and cons of capital punishment expressed with special intensity. As a district leader, councilman, congressman, and mayor, I have represented constituencies generally thought of as liberal. Because I support the death penalty for heinous crimes of murder, I have sometimes been the subject of emotional and outraged attacks by voters who find my position reprehensible or worse. I have listened to their ideas. I have weighed their objections carefully. I still support the death penalty. The reasons I maintain my position can be best understood by examining the arguments most frequently heard in opposition.

5 1. *The death penalty is "barbaric."* Sometimes opponents of capital punishment horrify with tales of lingering death on the gallows, of faulty electric chairs, or of agony in the gas chamber. Partly in response to such protests, several states such as North Carolina and Texas switched to execution by lethal injection. The condemned person is put to death painlessly, without ropes, voltage, bullets, or gas. Did this answer the objections of death penalty opponents? Of

course not. On June 22, 1984, *The New York Times* published an editorial that sarcastically attacked the new "hygienic" method of death by injection, and stated that "execution can never be made humane through science." So it's not the method that really troubles opponents. It's the death itself they consider barbaric.

Admittedly, capital punishment is not a pleasant topic. 6
However, one does not have to like the death penalty in order to support it any more than one must like radical surgery, radiation, or chemotherapy in order to find necessary these attempts at curing cancer. Ultimately we may learn how to cure cancer with a simple pill. Unfortunately, that day has not yet arrived. Today we are faced with the choice of letting the cancer spread or trying to cure it with the methods available, methods that one day will almost certainly be considered barbaric. But to give up and do nothing would be far more barbaric and would certainly delay the discovery of an eventual cure. The analogy between cancer and murder is imperfect, because murder is not the "disease" we are trying to cure. The disease is injustice. We may not like the death penalty, but it must be available to punish crimes of cold-blooded murder, cases in which any other form of punishment would be inadequate and, therefore, unjust. If we create a society in which injustice is not tolerated, incidents of murder—the most flagrant form of injustice—will diminish.

2. *No other major democracy uses the death penalty.* No 7
other major democracy—in fact, few other countries of any description—are plagued by a murder rate such as that in the United States. Fewer and fewer Americans can remember the days when unlocked doors were the norm and murder was a rare and terrible offense. In America the murder rate climbed 122 percent between 1963 and 1980. During that same period, the murder rate in New York City increased by almost 400 percent, and the statistics are even worse in many other cities. A study at M.I.T. showed that based on 1970 homicide rates a person who lived in a large American city ran a greater risk of being murdered than an American soldier in World War II ran of being killed in combat. It is not surprising that the laws of each country differ according to differing conditions and traditions. If other countries had our murder problem, the cry for capital punishment would be just as loud as it is here. And I daresay that any other major democracy where 75 percent

of the people supported the death penalty would soon enact it into law.

8 3. *An innocent person might be executed by mistake.* Consider the work of Adam Bedau, one of the most implacable foes of capital punishment in this country. According to Mr. Bedau, it is "false sentimentality to argue that the death penalty should be abolished because of the abstract possibility that an innocent person might be executed." He cites a study of the 7,000 executions in this country from 1893 to 1971, and concludes that the record fails to show that such cases occur. The main point, however, is this. If government functioned only when the possibility of error didn't exist, government wouldn't function at all. Human life deserves special protection, and one of the best ways to guarantee that protection is to assure that convicted murderers do not kill again. Only the death penalty can accomplish this end. In a recent case in New Jersey, a man named Richard Biegenwald was freed from prison after serving 18 years for murder; since his release he has been convicted of committing four murders. A prisoner named Lemuel Smith, who, while serving four life sentences for murder (plus two life sentences for kidnapping and robbery) in New York's Green Haven Prison, lured a woman corrections officer into the chaplain's office and strangled her. He then mutilated and dismembered her body. An additional life sentence for Smith is meaningless. Because New York has no death penalty statute, Smith has effectively been given a license to kill.

9 But the problem of multiple murder is not confined to the nation's penitentiaries. In 1981, 91 police officers were killed in the line of duty in this country. Seven percent of those arrested in the cases that have been solved had a previous arrest for murder. In New York City in 1976 and 1977, 85 persons arrested for homicide had a previous arrest for murder. Six of these individuals had two previous arrests for murder, and one had four previous murder arrests. During those two years the New York police were arresting for murder persons with a previous arrest for murder on the average of one every 8.5 days. This is not surprising when we learn that in 1975, for example, the median time served in Massachusetts for homicide was less than two-and-a-half years. In 1976 a study sponsored by the Twentieth Century Fund found that the average time served in the United States for first-degree murder is ten years. The median time served may be considerably lower.

4. *Capital punishment cheapens the value of human life.* On 10
the contrary, it can be easily demonstrated that the death penalty strengthens the value of human life. If the penalty for rape were lowered, clearly it would signal a lessened regard for the victims' suffering, humiliation, and personal integrity. It would cheapen their horrible experience, and expose them to an increased danger of recurrence. When we lower the penalty for murder, it signals a lessened regard for the value of the victim's life. Some critics of capital punishment, such as columnist Jimmy Breslin, have suggested that a life sentence is actually a harsher penalty for murder than death. This is sophistic nonsense. A few killers may decide not to appeal a death sentence, but the overwhelming majority make every effort to stay alive. It is by exacting the highest penalty for the taking of human life that we affirm the highest value of human life.

5. *The death penalty is applied in a discriminatory manner.* 11
This factor no longer seems to be the problem it once was. The appeals process for a condemned prisoner is lengthy and painstaking. Every effort is made to see that the verdict and sentence were fairly arrived at. However, assertions of discrimination are not an argument for ending the death penalty but for extending it. It is not justice to exclude everyone from the penalty of the law if a few are found to be so favored. Justice requires that the law be applied equally to all.

6. *Thou Shalt Not Kill.* The Bible is our greatest source of 12
moral inspiration. Opponents of the death penalty frequently cite the sixth of the Ten Commandments in an attempt to prove that capital punishment is divinely proscribed. In the original Hebrew, however, the Sixth Commandment reads, "Thou Shalt Not Commit Murder," and the Torah specifies capital punishment for a variety of offenses. The biblical viewpoint has been upheld by philosophers throughout history. The greatest thinkers of the 19th century—Kant, Locke, Hobbes, Rousseau, Montesquieu, and Mill—agreed that natural law properly authorizes the sovereign to take life in order to vindicate justice. Only Jeremy Bentham was ambivalent. Washington, Jefferson, and Franklin endorsed it. Abraham Lincoln authorized executions for deserters in wartime. Alexis de Tocqueville, who expressed profound respect for American institutions, believed that the death penalty was indispensable to the support of social order. The United

States Constitution, widely admired as one of the seminal achievements in the history of humanity, condemns cruel and inhuman punishment, but does not condemn capital punishment.

13 7. *The death penalty is state-sanctioned murder.* This is the defense with which Messrs. Willie and Shaw hoped to soften the resolve of those who sentenced them to death. By saying in effect, "You're no better than I am," the murderer seeks to bring his accusers down to his own level. It is also a popular argument among opponents of capital punishment, but a transparently false one. Simply put, the state has rights that the private individual does not. In a democracy, those rights are given to the state by the electorate. The execution of a lawfully condemned killer is no more an act of murder than is legal imprisonment an act of kidnapping. If an individual forces a neighbor to pay him money under threat of punishment, it's called extortion. If the state does it, it's called taxation. Rights and responsibilities surrendered by the individual are what give the state its power to govern. This contract is the foundation of civilization itself.

14 Everyone wants his or her rights, and will defend them jealously. Not everyone, however, wants responsibilities, especially the painful responsibilities that come with law enforcement. Twenty-one years ago a woman named Kitty Genovese was assaulted and murdered on a street in New York. Dozens of neighbors heard her cries for help but did nothing to assist her. They didn't even call the police. In such a climate the criminal understandably grows bolder. In the presence of moral cowardice, he lectures us on our supposed failings and tries to equate his crimes with our quest for justice.

15 The death of anyone—even a convicted killer—diminishes us all. But we are diminished even more by a justice system that fails to function. It is an illusion to let ourselves believe that doing away with capital punishment removes the murderer's deed from our conscience. The rights of society are paramount. When we protect guilty lives, we give up innocent lives in exchange. When opponents of capital punishment say to the state: "I will not let you kill in my name," they are also saying to murderers: "You can kill in your *own* name as long as I have an excuse for not getting involved."

It is hard to imagine anything worse than being murdered while neighbors do nothing. But something worse exists. When those same neighbors shrink back from justly punishing the murderer, the victim dies twice. 16

Jacob Weisberg

This Is Your Death

The following account appeared in The New Republic *in July 1991.* The New Republic *is a weekly magazine of opinion about various public issues; it is considered to be middle-of-the-road in its general slant on things. In what way is Weisberg's article a contribution to the national discussion on the death penalty? Is Weisberg's own position on the death penalty apparent here?*

Thanks to the decision of a California district judge last week, the American public has been spared the spectacle of criminals being executed on television. But the lawsuit, filed by KQED, the public television station in San Francisco, still served a useful function. It reminded people not only that the United States remains the only advanced democracy that executes criminals, but that it is the only country in the world with a grotesque array of execution techniques worth televising. A century ago Americans knew full well what it meant for the state to hang someone from the end of a rope. Today, thanks to the century-long search for a more "humane" method, we know little about the range of practices that would be featured on the execution channel. 1

Of the five means of execution still extant in the United States, the oldest is hanging, which was nearly universal before 1900. The gallows was last used in Kansas in 1965 and remains an option in Delaware, Montana, and Washington State. If a hanging were ever televised, viewers would see the blindfolded prisoner standing on a trap door with a rope fastened around his neck, the knot under his left ear. So long as he is hooded, it is impossible to know for how 2 long after the trap door opens the victim suffers, or at what point he loses consciousness. But according to Harold Hillman, a British physiologist who has studied executions, the dangling person feels cervical pain, and probably suffers from an acute headache as well, a result of the rope closing off the veins of the neck.

3 In the opinion of Dr. Cornelius Rosse, the chairman of the Department of Anatomy at the University of Washington School of Medicine, the belief that fracture of the spinal cord causes instantaneous death is wrong in all but a small fraction of cases. The actual cause of death is strangulation or suffocation. In medical terms, the weight of the prisoner's body causes tearing of the cervical muscles, skin, and blood vessels. The upper cervical vertebrae are dislocated, and the spinal cord is separated from the brain, which causes death.

4 Clinton Duffy, the warden at San Quentin from 1942 to 1954, who participated in sixty hangings, described his first thus:

> The man hit bottom and I observed that he was fighting by pulling on the straps, wheezing, whistling, trying to get air, that blood was oozing through the black cap. I observed also that he urinated, defecated, and droppings fell on the floor, and the stench was terrible. I also saw witnesses pass out and have to be carried from the witness room. Some of them threw up.

It took ten minutes for the condemned man to die. When he was taken down and the cap removed, "big hunks of flesh were torn off" the side of his face where the noose had been, "his eyes were popped," and his tongue was "swollen and hanging from his mouth." His face had also turned purple. The annals of Walla Walla State Penitentiary in Washington, which was seeking to hire an executioner in 1988 when Charles Campbell obtained a stay of execution, are filled with horror stories: prisoners partially decapitated by overlong drops, or pleading with hangmen to take them up and drop them again.

5 Almost as rare as hanging—but still around—is the firing squad. Gary Gilmore, who was shot in Utah in 1977, was the last to die by this method, which remains an option only there and in Idaho. Gilmore was bound to a chair with

leather straps across his waist and head, and in front of an oval-shaped canvas wall. A black hood was pulled over his head. A doctor then located his heart with a stethoscope and pinned a circular white cloth target over it. Five shooters armed with .30-caliber rifles loaded with single rounds (one of them blank to spare the conscience of the executioners) stood in an enclosure twenty feet away. Each man aimed his rifle through a slot in the canvas and fired.

Though shooting through the head at close range causes 6
nearly instantaneous death, a prisoner subjected to a firing squad dies as a result of blood loss caused by rupture of the heart or a large blood vessel, or tearing of the lungs. The person shot loses consciousness when shock causes a fall in the support of blood to the brain. If the shooters miss, by accident or intention, the prisoner bleeds to death slowly, as Elisio J. Mares did in Utah in 1951. It took Gilmore two minutes to die.

It was to mitigate the barbarism of these primitive meth- 7
ods that New York introduced the electric chair in 1890 as a humane alternative. Eighty-three people have been electrocuted since the Supreme Court reinstated capital punishment in 1976, making the method the most common one now in use. It is probably the most gruesome to watch. After being led into the death chamber, the prisoner is strapped to the chair with belts that cross his chest, groin, legs, and arms. Two copper electrodes are then attached: one to his leg, a patch of which will have been shaved bare to reduce resistance to electricity, and another to his shaved head. The electrodes are either soaked in brine or treated with gel (Electro-Creme) to increase conductivity and reduce burning. The prisoner will also be wearing a diaper.

The executioner gives a first jolt of between 500 and 2,000 8
volts, which lasts for thirty seconds. Smoke usually comes out of the prisoner's leg and head. A doctor then examines him. If he's not dead, another jolt is applied. A third and fourth are given if needed to finish the job. It took five jolts to kill Ethel Rosenberg. In the grisly description of Justice Brennan:

> . . . the prisoner's eyeballs sometimes pop out and rest on [his] cheeks. The prisoner often defecates, urinates, and vomits blood and drool. The body turns bright red as its temperature rises, and the prisoner's flesh swells and his skin stretches to the point of breaking. Sometimes the prisoner

> catches on fire, particularly if [he] perspires excessively. Witnesses hear a loud and sustained sound like bacon frying, and the sickly sweet smell of burning flesh permeates the chamber.

An electrocuted corpse is hot enough to blister if touched. Thus autopsy must be delayed while internal organs cool. According to Robert H. Kirschner, the deputy chief medical examiner of Cook County, Illinois, "The brain appears cooked in most cases."

9 There is some debate about what the electrocuted prisoner experiences before he dies, but most doctors I spoke to believe that he feels himself being burned to death and suffocating, since the shock causes respiratory paralysis as well as cardiac arrest. According to Hillman, "It must feel very similar to the medieval trial by ordeal of being dropped in boiling oil." Because the energy of the shock paralyzes the prisoner's muscles, he cannot cry out. "My mouth tasted like cold peanut butter. I felt a burning in my head and my left leg, and I jumped against the straps," Willie Francis, a 17-year-old who survived an attempted execution in 1946, is reported to have said. Francis was successfully executed a year later.

10 Though all methods of execution can be botched, electrocutions go wrong frequently and dramatically, in part because the equipment is old and hard to repair. At least five have gone awry since 1983. If the electrical current is too weak, the prisoner roasts to death slowly. An instance of this was the May 4, 1990, killing of Jesse Joseph Tafero in Florida. According to witnesses, when the executioner flipped the switch, flames and smoke came out of Tafero's head, which was covered by a mask and cap. Twelve-inch blue and orange flames sprouted from both sides of the mask. The power was stopped, and Tafero took several deep breaths. The superintendent ordered the executioner to halt the current, then try it again. And again.

11 The affidavits presented for an internal inquiry into what went wrong describe the bureaucratization of the death penalty brilliantly. In the words of one of the officials:

> . . . while working in the Death Chamber, proceeding with the execution as scheduled, I received an indication from Mr.

> Barton to close my electric breaker. I then told the executioner to close his electric breaker. When the executioner completed the circuit, I noticed unusual fire and smoke coming from the inmate's headpiece. After several seconds, I received an indication to open the electrical breaker to stop the electrical flow. At this time, I noticed the body move as if to be gasping for air. After several seconds, I received the indication to close the breaker the second time, which I did. Again, I noticed the unusual fire and smoke coming from the headpiece. After several seconds, I received the third indication to close the breaker, and again, the fire and smoke came from the headpiece . . .

And so on. Apparently a synthetic sponge, soaked in brine, had been substituted for the natural one applied to Tafero's head. This reduced the flow of electricity to as little as one hundred volts, and ended up torturing the prisoner to death. According to the state prison medical director, Frank Kligo, who attended, it was "less than aesthetically attractive."

Advanced technology does not always make the death penalty less painful to undergo or more pleasant to watch. The gas chamber, which was invented by an army medical corps officer after World War I, was first introduced as a humane alternative to the electric chair in 1924 in Nevada. The original idea, which proved impracticable, was to surprise the prisoner by gassing him in his cell without prior warning. Seven states, including California, still use the gas chamber. The most recent fatality was Leo Edwards, a 36-year-old who was killed in Jackson County, Mississippi, in 1989. 12

Had KQED won its suit, millions of viewers would have joined a dozen live witnesses in seeing Robert Alton Harris, who murdered two teenage boys in San Diego in 1978, led into a green, octagonal room in the basement of San Quentin Penitentiary. Inside the chamber are two identical metal chairs with perforated seats, marked "A" and "B." The twin chairs were last used in a double execution in 1962. If Harris's execution goes ahead this year or next, two orderlies will fasten him into chair A, attaching straps across his upper and lower legs, arms, groin, and chest. They will also affix a long stethoscope to Harris's chest so that a doctor on the outside can pronounce death. 13

14 Beneath the chair is a bowl filled with sulfuric acid mixed with distilled water, with a pound of sodium cyanide pellets suspended in a gauze bag just above. After the door is sealed, and when the warden gives the signal, an executioner in a separate room flicks a lever that releases the cyanide into the liquid. This causes a chemical reaction that releases hydrogen cyanide gas, which rises through the holes in the chair. Like most death row prisoners, Harris is likely to have been reduced to a state of passive acquiescence by his years on death row, and will probably follow the advice of the warden to breathe deeply as soon as he smells rotten eggs. As long as he holds his breath nothing will happen. But as soon as he inhales, according to the testimony of Duffy, the former warden, Harris will lose consciousness in a few seconds. "At first there is evidence of extreme horror, pain, and strangling. The eyes pop. The skin turns purple and the victim begins to drool. It is a horrible sight," he testified.

15 In medical terms, victims of cyanide gas die from hypoxia, which means the cut-off of oxygen to the brain. The initial result of this is spasms, as in an epileptic seizure. Because of the straps, however, involuntary body movements are restrained. Seconds after he first inhales, Harris will feel himself unable to breathe, but will not lose consciousness immediately. "The person is unquestionably experiencing pain and extreme anxiety," according to Dr. Richard Traystman of Johns Hopkins. "The pain begins immediately and is felt in the arms, shoulders, back, and chest. The sensation is similar to the pain felt by a person during a heart attack, where essentially the heart is being deprived of oxygen." Traystman adds: "We would not use asphyxiation, by cyanide gas or by any other substance, in our laboratory to kill animals that have been used in experiments."

16 Harris will stop wriggling after ten or twelve minutes, and the doctor will pronounce him dead. An exhaust fan then sucks the poison air out of the chamber. Next the corpse is sprayed with ammonia, which neutralizes traces of the cyanide that may remain. After about half an hour, orderlies enter the chamber, wearing gas masks and rubber gloves. Their training manual advises them to ruffle the victim's hair to release any trapped cyanide gas before removing him.

17 Thanks to these grotesqueries, states are increasingly turning to lethal injection. This method was imagined for

decades (by Ronald Reagan, among others, when he was governor of California in 1973), but was technically invented in 1977 by Dr. Stanley Deutsch, who at the time chaired the Anesthesiology Department at Oklahoma University Medical School. In response to a call by an Oklahoma state senator for a cheaper alternative to repairing the state's derelict electric chair, Deutsch described a way to administer drugs through an intravenous drip so as to cause death rapidly and without pain. "Having been anesthetized on several occasions with ultra short-acting barbiturates and having administered these drugs for approximately 20 years, I can assure you that this is a rapid, pleasant way of producing unconsciousness," Deutsch wrote to state senator Bill Dawson in February 1977. The method was promptly adopted in Oklahoma, and is now either the exclusive method or an option in half of the thirty-six states with death penalty laws. It is becoming the method of choice around the country because it is easier on both the witnesses and the prisoner.

A recent injectee was Lawrence Lee Buxton, who was 18
killed in Huntsville, Texas, on February 26. Buxton was strapped to a hospital gurney, built with an extension panel for his left arm. Technicians stuck a catheter needle into Buxton's arm. Long tubes connected the needle through a hole in a cement block wall to several intravenous drips. The first, which was started immediately, dispensed harmless saline solution. Then, at the warden's signal, a curtain went up, which permitted the witnesses—reporters and friends of the soon-to-be decreased—to view the scene. Unlike some prisoners, Buxton did not have a long wait before the warden received a call from the governor's office, giving the final go-ahead.

According to Lawrence Egbert, an anesthesiologist at the 19
University of Texas in Dallas who has campaigned against lethal injection as a perversion of medical practice, the first drug administered was sodium thiopental, a common barbiturate used as an anesthetic, which puts patients quickly to sleep. A normal dose for a long operation is 1,000 milligrams; Buxton got twice that. As soon as he lost consciousness, the executioner administered pavulon, another common muscle relaxant used in heart surgery. The dose was 100 milligrams, ten times the usual, which stops the prisoner's breathing. This would have killed him in

about ten minutes; to speed the process, an equal dose of potassium chloride was subsequently administered. This is another drug commonly used in bypass surgery that relaxes the heart and stops it pumping. It works in about ten seconds. All witnesses heard was the prisoner take a deep breath, then a gurgling noise as his tongue dropped back in his mouth. Watt Espy, who has compiled a list of 17,718 executions in America, from the early period of drownings, burnings, sawings-in-half, pressings-to-death, and even the crucifixions of two mutinous Continental Army soldiers, compares lethal injection to the way a devoted owner treats "a faithful dog he's loved and cherished."

20 The only physical pain, if the killing is done correctly, "is the pain of the initial prick of the needle," according to Traystman. There are, however, some potential hitches. Since doctors are precluded by medical ethics from participating in executions, except to pronounce death, the injections are often performed by incompetent or inexperienced technicians. If a death worker injects the drugs into muscle instead of a vein, or if the needle becomes clogged, extreme pain can result. This is what happened when James Autry was killed in 1984 in Texas. *Newsweek* reported that he "took at least ten minutes to die and throughout much of that time was conscious, moving about, and complaining of pain." Many prisoners have damaged veins from injecting drugs intravenously, and technicians sometimes struggle to find a serviceable one. When Texas executed Stephen Morin, a former heroin addict, orderlies prodded his arms with catheters for forty-one minutes. Being strapped to a table for a lengthy period while waiting to die is a form of psychological torture arguably worse than most physical kinds. This is demonstrated by the fact that mock executions, which cause no physical pain, are a common method of torture around the world. The agony comes not from the prospect of pain, but from the expectation of death.

21 Televised executions would mark the reversal of the process described in Louis P. Masur's *Rites of Execution* and Robert Johnson's *Death Work,* whereby executions have been removed further and further from the community that compels them. Through the eighteenth century, executions were atavistic spectacles performed in full public view. In the nineteenth they were moved inside the prison yard and

witnessed by only a few. In the twentieth century, executions moved deep inside the bowels of prisons, where they were performed ever more quickly and quietly to attract minimal notice. American death penalty opponents in the 1800s supported the abolition of public executions as a waystation to ending all executions. They thought that eliminating the grossest manifestations of public barbarism would inevitably lead to the end of capital punishment as an institution. The reform had the opposite effect, however. Invisible executions shocked the sensibilities of fewer people, and dampened the momentum of the reform movement.

Those abolitionists who now support televising executions have absorbed this historical lesson. They want to bring back the equivalent of public executions in order to shock the public into opposing all executions. They hope to accomplish with pictures what Arthur Koestler did with words in his 1955 tract *Reflections on Hanging,* the publication of which led to the abolition of the rope in Great Britain in 1969. 22

But advances in the art of killing may have deprived them of that tactic. The prospect of televised executions is likely to accelerate the trend away from grisly methods and toward ever more hermetic ways of dispatching wrongdoers. Had the KQED suit been successful, Henry Schwarzschild, a retired ACLU death penalty expert, speculates that California would have responded by quickly joining the national trend toward lethal injection. 23

Michael Kroll of the Death Penalty Information Center objects to televising executions for exactly this reason. He argues that a video camera would capture only a "very antiseptic moment at the end of a very septic process." With the advent of death by the needle, execution itself is becoming so denatured and mechanistic as to be unshocking even to most live witnesses. This throws death penalty opponents back upon a less vivid, but more compelling case: that it is punishing people with death, not the manner in which they are killed, that is the true issue here; that capital punishment is to be opposed not simply because it is cruel, but because it is wrong. 24

James Panichi
The Morality of Capital Punishment

James Panichi, born in Melbourne, Australia, in 1969 to an Anglo-American mother and an Italian immigrant father, lived in Italy from 1978 to 1986 before returning to Australia. He later came to Penn State as an exchange student, where he contributed the following article to the Penn State newspaper The Daily Collegian *on July 7, 1992. The essay was motivated by the executions named in the article and reflects Panichi's international perspective. He is now a graduate student studying journalism in Australia, and he hopes to eventually become a script writer for television and film.*

1 I remember back in my first misguided years of college, after classes on Thursday night, we'd walk down to the Comedy Club where billboards would usually announce the arrival of "America's funniest comic," or "More L.A. Madness!" The best performers would get to the city a week before opening the show, in order to understand the local culture and rewrite some of the jokes. The less international comedians would walk in straight from the airport, and would usually wind up making the audience very hostile. They didn't realize that the English-speaking world is actually culturally very diverse.

2 One night I remember an American comic getting on stage and saying: "Back home some people think the death penalty is wrong. Well, you know what I think? Fry their families as well!" In retrospect I can see that back in California, where four out of five people are in favour of capital punishment, the joke would have got a few laughs and "woofs" from the audience. It would have been seen as an attack on the intellectual left which questions the validity of the death penalty.

3 The audience I was with, however, was stunned into an embarrassing silence. There is nothing that divides Americans from the rest of the Western world as much as their attitude towards capital punishment. The guy from L.A. had stuffed up his show as far as we were concerned.

4 Yet how much did we understand about the American way of thinking? Not much. We imagined that those behind

the death penalty were a small group of right-wing extremists, the various Pat Buchanans of society, accompanied by a few loud-mouths, such as the comedian we saw that night.

But that isn't the case. Capital punishment is supported by common Americans as well, people who, surprisingly enough, believe in basic principles of democracy and justice. These people may subscribe to religious values, yet still see executing criminals as a desperate solution for desperate times. And it is hard not to be sympathetic when reading about crime and violence which goes well beyond human decency. It becomes extremely difficult to talk about moral values when the world around you fails to recognize any such standards of humanity. 5

Recently, however, the execution of Roger Keith Coleman in Virginia stirred up my latent feelings of disgust for that form of punishment which many non-Americans associate with underdevelopment or lack of democracy. On the night of March 10, 1981, Wanda Fay McCoy was raped and murdered in the small town of Grundy, Va. Not longer after that day, police arrested Coleman, merely because they didn't believe his alibi and he had a criminal record. The evidence against him was, at its very best, circumstantial. 6

As tragic as this execution may have seemed to any rational American, it was by no means atypical. Federal judges have found constitutional errors in about 40 percent of the death penalty cases reviewed since 1976, the year in which capital punishment was reintroduced. It is impossible to estimate how many innocent people have been killed by American "justice" since that year, but one of them might have been Jesus Romero, a 27-year-old migrant worker executed by lethal injection in Texas recently. As with Coleman, the prosecution was flawed. Yet Romero was sent to death, amid national and international calls for the case to be re-examined. 7

In the light of these tragic examples, it is legitimate for all Americans to ask themselves firstly how many of the 2,588 people currently on death row are indeed responsible for the crimes of which they are accused, and secondly whether there are any real differences between state executions and the ugly mob lynchings which characterized the more brutal years of the country's history. 8

It is also time we took a closer look at the Supreme Court, which under the influence of extremely conservative indi- 9 viduals such as Antonin Scalia is doing its best to make capital punishment more routine, in spite of all the controversial circumstances of recent cases. By eliminating all impediments and readily approving executions the Supreme Court is subscribing to cold, premeditated, state-run homicide, putting the justice system of the country at the same moral level as a common street assassin.

10 In our moments of human weakness when we hear of blood-thirsty gang members killing innocent people, we must have the courage to realize that our desire for revenge is not going to have any long-term benefits for society. We must realize that capital punishment is not working as a deterrent, and that it is dragging American society into a cesspool of tit-for-tat justice.

11 Above all, we must never lose track of what "civilization" means. It means taking pride in standards of decency, it means leading by example rather than by fear. An influential social theorist of the 19th century, Cesare Beccaria, said that "the death penalty is futile for the example of atrocity it gives mankind." The strength of Beccaria's argument is not his reflections on the social uselessness of executing people, but his strong sense of morality. We do not punish killers because they are incompatible with a functional society, but because we believe killing is wrong, immoral and barbaric.

12 It is up to future generations of Americans to decide whether the law should be a structure of decency and humanity, or a moral desert of violence and despair. Let's hope that future generations understand that they are referring to a fellow human being when shouting "fry them!" no matter what the person may have done.

Doug Marlette

Doug Marlette, who won the Pulitzer Prize for editorial cartooning, draws for New York Newsday, *and his sometimes controversial work is regularly reprinted in* Newsweek, The Washington Post, *and elsewhere. Eleven collections of his work have been published, including* In Your Face: A Cartoonist at Work *(1991), where the following cartoon appeared. The cartoon was first published on Good Friday, as you might guess from its content, while Marlette worked for* The Charlotte *[North Carolina]* Observer.

SHOULD DRUGS BE LEGALIZED?

Kurt Schmoke

A War for the Surgeon General, Not the Attorney General

One of the most outspoken advocates of legalizing drugs has been Kurt Schmoke (born 1949), mayor of Baltimore since 1987. Previously, as Assistant U.S. Attorney and as State's Attorney for Baltimore, Schmoke was a highly visible prosecutor of drug cases. The following argument appeared in New Perspectives Quarterly, *a public affairs forum, in the summer of 1989. It was adapted from his testimony before a congressional committee on September 29, 1988.*

1 In the last ten years, the US has become absolutely awash in illegal drugs. Tougher laws, greater efforts at interdiction, and stronger rhetoric at all levels of government and from both political parties have not and will not be able to stop the flow. That is why we must begin to consider what heretofore has been beyond the realm of consideration: decriminalization.

Addiction Is a Disease

2 The violence brought about by the black market in drugs is attributable in large part to the fact that we have chosen to make criminals out of millions of people who have a disease. In the words of the American Medical Association, "It is clear that addiction is not simply the product of a failure of individual will-power. . . . It is properly viewed as a disease, and one that physicians can help many individuals control and overcome."

3 The nature of addiction is very important to the argument in favor of decriminalization. The sad truth is that heroin and morphine addiction is, for most users, a lifetime afflic-

tion that is impervious to any punishment that the criminal-justice system could reasonably mete out.

Given the nature of addiction—whether to narcotics or cocaine—and the very large number of Americans using drugs (the National Institute on Drug Abuse estimates that one in six working Americans has a substance abuse problem), laws restricting their possession and sale have had predictable consequences—most of them bad. 4

Crimes Committed by Addicts

Addicts commit crimes in order to pay for their drug habits. According to the Justice Department, 90 percent of those who voluntarily seek treatment are turned away. In other words, on any given day, nine out of every ten addicts have no legal way to satisfy their addiction. And, failing to secure help, an untreated addict will commit a crime every other day to maintain his habit. 5

Whether one relies on studies, or on simple observation, it is indisputable that drug users are committing vast amounts of crime. Baltimore, the city with which I am most familiar, is no exception. According to James A. Inciardi, of the Division of Criminal Justice at the University of Delaware, a 1983 study of addicts in Baltimore showed that "... there were high rates of criminality among heroin users during those periods that they were addicted and markedly lower rates during times of nonaddiction." The study also showed that addicts committed crimes on a persistent day-to-day basis and over a long period of time. And the trends are getting worse. Thus, while the total number of arrests in Baltimore remained almost unchanged between 1983 and 1987, there was an approximately 40 percent increase in the number of drug-related arrests. 6

On the other hand, statistics recently compiled by the Maryland Drug and Alcohol Abuse Administration indicate that crime rates go down among addicts when treatment is available. Thus, for example, of the 6,910 Baltimore residents admitted to drug-abuse treatment in fiscal 1987, 4,386 or 63 percent had been arrested one or more times in the 24-month period prior to admission to treatment, whereas of the 6,698 Baltimore residents who were discharged from drug treatment in fiscal 1987, 6,152 or 91.8 percent were not arrested during the time of their treatment. These statistics 7 tend to support the view that one way to greatly reduce drug-related crime is to assure addicts legal access to methadone or other drugs.

Overload of the Criminal-Justice System

8 We cannot prosecute our way out of the drug problem. There are several reasons for this, but the most basic reason is that the criminal-justice system cannot—without sacrificing our civil liberties—handle the sheer volume of drug-related cases.

9 Nationwide last year, over 750,000 people were arrested for violating drug laws. Most of these arrests were for possession. In Baltimore, there were 13,037 drug-related arrests in 1987. Between January 1, 1988 and July 1, 1988, there were 7,981 drug-related arrests. Those numbers are large, but they hardly reflect the annual total number of drug violations committed in Baltimore. Should we, therefore, try to arrest still more? Yes—as long as the laws are on the books. But as a practical matter, we don't have any place to put the drug offenders we are now arresting. The population in the Baltimore City Jail is currently 2,900 inmates, even though its inmate capacity is only 2,700. This shortage of prison space has led to severe overcrowding, and Baltimore is now under court order to reduce its jail population.

10 Will more prisons help? Not in any significant way. We simply cannot build enough of them to hold all of America's drug offenders—which number in the millions. And even if we could, the cost would far exceed what American taxpayers would be willing to pay.

11 Decriminalization is the single most effective step we could take to reduce prison overcrowding. And with less crowded prisons, there will be less pressure on prosecutors to plea bargain and far greater chance that non-drug criminals will go to jail—and stay in jail.

12 The unvarnished truth is that in our effort to prosecute and imprison our way out of the drug war, we have allowed the drug lords to put us exactly where they want us: wasting enormous resources—both in money and in personnel—attacking the fringes of the problem (the drug users and small-time pushers), while the heart of the problem—the traffickers and their profits—goes unsolved.

Failed Supply-Side Policies

Not only can we not prosecute our way out of our drug morass, we cannot interdict our way out of it either. Lately, there have been calls for stepped-up border patrols, increased use of the military and greater pressure on foreign governments. 13

Assuming these measures would reduce the supply of illegal drugs, that reduction would not alleviate the chaos in our cities. According to statistics recently cited by the American Medical Association, Latin American countries produced between 162,000 and 211,400 metric tons of cocaine in 1987. That is five times the amount needed to supply the US market. Moreover, we are probably only interdicting 10 to 15 percent of the cocaine entering this country. Thus, even if we quadrupled the amount of cocaine we interdict, the world supply of cocaine would still far outstrip US demand. 14

If the drug laws in the US simply didn't achieve their intent, perhaps there would be insufficient reason to get rid of them. But these laws are doing more than not working—they are violating Hippocrates' famous admonition: First, do no harm. 15

The legal prohibition of narcotics, cocaine and marijuana demonstrably increases the price of those drugs. For example, an importer can purchase a kilogram of heroin for \$10,000. By the time that kilogram passes through the hands of several middlemen, its street value can reach \$1,000,000. Such profits can't help but attract major criminal entrepreneurs willing to take any risk to keep their product coming to the American market. 16

Victimization of Children

Perhaps the most tragic victims of our drug laws are children. Many, for example, have been killed as innocent bystanders in gun battles among traffickers. Furthermore, while it is true that drug prohibition probably does keep some children from experimenting with drugs, almost any child who wants drugs can get them. Keeping drugs outlawed has not kept them out of children's hands. 17

Recent statistics in both Maryland and Baltimore prove the point: In a 1986–87 survey of Maryland adolescents, 13 18 percent of eighth graders, 18.5 percent of tenth graders and 22.3 percent of twelfth graders report that they are currently using drugs. In Baltimore, the percentages are 16.6, 16.5 and 20.3, respectively. It should be noted that these numbers exclude alcohol and tobacco, and that current use means at least once a month. It should also be noted that these numbers show a decrease from earlier surveys in 1982 and 1984. Nevertheless, the fact remains that drugs are being widely used by students. Moreover, these numbers do not include the many young people who have left school or who failed to report their drug use.

19 A related problem is that many children, especially those living in the inner city, are frequently barraged with the message that selling drugs is an easy road to riches. In Baltimore, as in many other cities, small children are acting as lookouts and runners for drug pushers, just as they did for bootleggers during Prohibition. Decriminalization and the destruction of the black market would end this most invidious form of child labor.

20 As for education, decriminalization will not end the *Just Say No* and similar education campaigns. On the contrary, more money will be available for such programs. Decriminalization will, however, end the competing message of "easy money" that the drug dealers use to entice children. Furthermore, decriminalization will free up valuable criminal-justice resources that can be used to find, prosecute and punish those who sell drugs to children.

21 This said, if there has been one problem with the current drug-reform debate, it has been the tendency to focus on narrow problems and narrow solutions. That is, we talk about the number of people arrested, the number of tons of drugs entering our ports, the number of available treatment centers, and so on, but there is a bigger picture out there. We, as a nation, have not done nearly enough to battle the social and economic problems that make drug abuse an easy escape for the despairing, and drug trafficking an easy answer to a lack of education and joblessness.

22 Adolescents who take drugs are making a not-so-subtle statement about their confidence in the future. Children without hope are children who will take drugs. We need to give these children more than simple slogans. We need to give them a brighter tomorrow, a sense of purpose, a chance at economic opportunity. It is on that battlefield that the real war against drugs must be fought.

Spread of AIDS

The 1980s have brought another major public health problem that is being made still worse because of our drug laws: AIDS. Contaminated intravenous drug needles are now the principal means of transmission for the HIV infection. The users of drug needles infect not only those with whom they share needles, but also their sex partners and their unborn children. 23

One way to effectively slow this means of transmission would be to allow addicts to exchange their dirty needles for clean ones. However, in a political climate where all illicit drug use is condemned, and where possession of a syringe can be a criminal offense, few jurisdictions have been willing to initiate a needle exchange program. This is a graphic example, along with our failure to give illegal drugs to cancer patients with intractable pain, of our blind pursuit of an irrational policy. 24

The Mixed Message of Tobacco and Alcohol

The case for the decriminalization of drugs becomes even stronger when illegal drugs are looked at in the context of legal drugs. 25

It is estimated that over 350,000 people will die this year from tobacco-related diseases. Last year the number was equally large. And it will be again next year. Why do millions of people continue to engage in an activity which has been proven to cause cancer and heart disease? The answer is that smoking is more than just a bad habit. It is an addiction. In 1988, Surgeon General C. Everett Koop called nicotine as addictive as heroin and cocaine. And yet, with the exception of taxes and labeling, cigarettes are sold without restriction. 26

By every standard we apply to illicit drugs, tobacco should be a controlled substance. But it is not, and for good reason. Given that millions of people continue to smoke—many of whom would quit if they could—making cigarettes illegal would be an open invitation to a new black market. 27

The certain occurrence of a costly and dangerous illegal tobacco trade (if tobacco were outlawed) is well understood by Congress, the Bush Administration and the criminal-justice community. No rationally thinking person would 28 want to bring such a catastrophe down upon the US—even if it would prevent some people from smoking.

29 Like tobacco, alcohol is a drug that kills thousands of Americans every year. It plays a part in more than half of all automobile fatalities and is also frequently involved in suicides, non-automobile accidents, domestic disputes and crimes of violence. Millions of Americans are alcoholic, and alcohol costs the nation billions of dollars in health care and lost productivity. So why not ban alcohol? Because, as almost every American knows, we already tried that. Prohibition turned out to be one of the worst social experiments this country has ever undertaken.

30 I will not review the sorry history of Prohibition except to make two important points. The first is that in repealing Prohibition, we made significant mistakes that should not be repeated in the event that drug use is decriminalized. Specifically, when alcohol was again made legal in 1934, we made no significant effort to educate people as to its dangers. There were no (and still are no) *Just Say No* campaigns against alcohol. We allowed alcohol to be advertised and have associated it with happiness, success and social acceptability. We have also been far too lenient with drunk drivers.

31 The second point is that, notwithstanding claims to the contrary by critics of decriminalization, there are marked parallels between the era of Prohibition and our current policy of making drugs illegal, and important lessons to be learned from our attempts to ban the use and sale of alcohol.

32 During Prohibition, the government tried to keep alcohol out of the hands of millions of people who refused to give it up. As a result, our cities were overrun by criminal syndicates enriching themselves with the profits of bootleg liquor and terrorizing anyone who got in their way. We then looked to the criminal-justice system to solve the crime problems that Prohibition created. But the criminal-justice system—outmanned, outgunned and often corrupted by enormous black market profits—was incapable of stopping the massive crime wave that Prohibition brought, just as it was incapable of stopping people from drinking.

33 As a person now publicly identified with the movement to reform our drug laws through the use of some form of decriminalization, I consider it very important to say that I am not soft on either drug use or drug dealers. I am a soldier

in the war against drugs. As Maryland's State Attorney, I spent years prosecuting and jailing drug traffickers, and had one of the highest rates of incarceration for drug convictions in the country. And if I were still State's Attorney, I would be enforcing the law as vigorously as ever. My experience as a prosecutor did not in any way alter my passionate dislike for drug dealers, it simply convinced me that the present system doesn't work and cannot be made to work.

During the Revolutionary War, the British insisted on wearing red coats and marching in formation. They looked very pretty. They also lost. A good general does not pursue a strategy in the face of overwhelming evidence of failure. Instead, a good general changes from a losing strategy to one that exploits his enemy's weakness, while exposing his own troops to only as much danger as is required to win. The drug war can be beaten and the public health of the US can be improved if we are willing to substitute common sense for rhetoric, myth and blind persistence, and to put the war in the hands of the Surgeon General, not the Attorney General. 34

William Bennett

Should Drugs Be Legalized?

William Bennett (born 1943) studied and played football (and the guitar for a rock group) at Williams College. Later he earned a doctorate in philosophy at the University of Texas and a law degree at Harvard, and taught at Southern Mississippi, Boston University, and the University of Wisconsin. He joined the Reagan administration as chair of the National Endowment for the Humanities in 1981 and became Secretary of Education in 1985; in 1988 he was appointed as the nation's "drug czar"—in charge of waging President Bush's "war on drugs." He published the following argument in 1990 in Reader's Digest. *Note, too, the exchange between Bennett and Milton Friedman that is reprinted following "Should Drugs Be Legalized?"*

1 Since I took command of the war on drugs, I have learned from former Secretary of State George Schultz that our concept of fighting drugs is "flawed." The only thing to do, he says, is to "make it possible for addicts to buy drugs at some regulated place." Conservative commentator William F. Buckley, Jr., suggests I should be "fatalistic" about the flood of cocaine from South America and simply "let it in." Syndicated columnist Mike Royko contends it would be easier to sweep junkies out of the gutters "than to fight a hopeless war" against the narcotics that send them there. Labeling our efforts "bankrupt," federal judge Robert W. Sweet opts for legalization, saying, "If our society can learn to stop using butter, it should be able to cut down on cocaine."

2 Flawed, fatalistic, hopeless, bankrupt! I never realized surrender was so fashionable until I assumed this post.

3 Though most Americans are overwhelmingly determined to go toe-to-toe with the foreign drug lords and neighborhood pushers, a small minority believe that enforcing drug laws imposes greater costs on society than do drugs themselves. Like addicts seeking immediate euphoria, the legalizers want peace at any price, even though it means the inevitable proliferation of a practice that degrades, impoverishes and kills.

4 I am acutely aware of the burdens drug enforcement places upon us. It consumes economic resources we would like to use elsewhere. It is sometimes frustrating, thankless and often dangerous. But the consequences of *not* enforcing drug laws would be far more costly. Those consequences involve the intrinsically destructive nature of drugs and the toll they exact from our society in hundreds of thousands of lost and broken lives . . . human potential never realized . . . time stolen from families and jobs . . . precious spiritual and economic resources squandered.

5 That is precisely why virtually every civilized society has found it necessary to exert some form of control over mind-altering substances and why this war is so important. Americans feel up to their hips in drugs now. They would be up to their necks under legalization.

6 Even limited experiments in drug legalization have shown that when drugs are more widely available, addiction skyrockets. In 1975 Italy liberalized its drug law and now has one of the highest heroin-related death rates in Western Europe. In Alaska, where marijuana was decriminalized in

1975, the easy atmosphere has increased usage of the drug, particularly among children. Nor does it stop there. Some Alaskan schoolchildren now tout "coca puffs," marijuana cigarettes laced with cocaine.

Many legalizers concede that drug legalization might increase use, but they shrug off the matter. "It may well be that there would be more addicts, and I would regret that result," says Nobel laureate economist Milton Friedman. The late Harvard Medical School psychiatry professor Norman Zinberg, a longtime proponent of "responsible" drug use, admitted that "use of now illicit drugs would certainly increase. Also, casualties probably would increase." 7

In fact, Dr. Herbert D. Kleber of Yale University, my deputy in charge of demand reduction, predicts legalization might cause "a five-to-sixfold increase" in cocaine use. But legalizers regard this as a necessary price for the "benefits" of legalization. What benefits? 8

1. *Legalization will take the profit out of drugs.* The result supposedly will be the end of criminal drug pushers and the big foreign drug wholesalers, who will turn to other enterprises because nobody will need to make furtive and dangerous trips to his local pusher. 9

But what, exactly, would the brave new world of legalized drugs look like? Buckley stresses that "adults get to buy the stuff at carefully regulated stores." (Would you want one in *your* neighborhood?) Others, like Friedman, suggest we sell the drugs at "ordinary retail outlets." 10

Former City University of New York sociologist Georgette Bennett assures us that "brand-name competition will be prohibited" and that strict quality control and proper labeling will be overseen by the Food and Drug Administration. In a touching egalitarian note, she adds that "free drugs will be provided at government clinics" for addicts too poor to buy them. 11

Almost all the legalizers point out that the price of drugs will fall, even though the drugs will be heavily taxed. Buckley, for example, argues that somehow federal drugstores will keep the price "low enough to discourage a black market but high enough to accumulate a surplus to be used for drug education." 12

Supposedly, drug sales will generate huge amounts of revenue, which will then be used to tell the public not to use drugs and to treat those who don't listen. 13

In reality, this tax would only allow government to *share* 14 the drug profits now garnered by criminals. Legalizers would have to tax drugs heavily in order to pay for drug education and treatment programs. Criminals could undercut the official price and still make huge profits. What alternative would the government have? Cut the price until it was within the lunch-money budget of the average sixth-grade student?

15 2. *Legalization will eliminate the black market.* Wrong. And not just because the regulated prices could be undercut. Many legalizers admit that drugs such as crack or PCP are simply too dangerous to allow the shelter of the law. Thus criminals will provide what the government will not. "As long as drugs that people very much want remain illegal, a black market will exist," says legalization advocate David Boaz of the liberatarian Cato Institute.

16 Look at crack. In powdered form, cocaine was an expensive indulgence. But street chemists found that a better and far less expensive—and far more dangerous—high could be achieved by mixing cocaine with baking soda and heating it. Crack was born, and "cheap" coke invaded low-income communities with furious speed.

17 An ounce of powdered cocaine might sell on the street for $1200. That same ounce can produce 370 vials of crack at $10 each. Ten bucks seems like a cheap hit, but crack's intense ten- to 15-minute high is followed by an unbearable depression. The user wants more crack, thus starting a rapid and costly descent into addiction.

18 If government drugstores do not stock crack, addicts will find it in the clandestine market or simply bake it themselves from their legally purchased cocaine.

19 Currently crack is being laced with insecticides and animal tranquilizers to heighten its effect. Emergency rooms are now warned to expect victims of "sandwiches" and "moon rocks," life-threatening smokable mixtures of heroin and crack. Unless the government is prepared to sell these deadly variations of dangerous drugs, it will perpetuate a criminal black market by default.

20 And what about children and teen-agers? They would obviously be barred from drug purchases, just as they are prohibited from buying beer and liquor. But pushers will continue to cater to these young customers with the old, favorite come-ons—a couple of free fixes to get them hooked. And what good will anti-drug education be when these youngsters observe their older brothers and sisters, parents

and friends lighting up and shooting up with government permission?

Legalization will give us the worst of both worlds: millions of *new* drug users *and* a thriving criminal black market. 21

3. *Legalization will dramatically reduce crime.* "It is the high price of drugs that leads addicts to robbery, murder and other crimes," says Ira Glasser, executive director of the American Civil Liberties Union. A study by the Cato Institute concludes: "Most, if not all, 'drug-related murders' are the result of drug prohibition." 22

But researchers tell us that many drug-related felonies are committed by people involved in crime *before* they started taking drugs. The drugs, so routinely available in criminal circles, make the criminals more violent and unpredictable. 23

Certainly there are some kill-for-a-fix crimes, but does any rational person believe that a cut-rate price for drugs at a government outlet will stop such psychopathic behavior? The fact is that under the influence of drugs, normal people do not act normally, and abnormal people behave in chilling and horrible ways. DEA agents told me about a teen-age addict in Manhattan who was smoking crack when he sexually abused and caused permanent internal injuries to his one-month-old daughter. 24

Children are among the most frequent victims of violent, drug-related crimes that have nothing to do with the cost of acquiring the drugs. In Philadelphia in 1987 more than half the child-abuse fatalities involved at least one parent who was a heavy drug user. Seventy-three percent of the child-abuse deaths in New York City in 1987 involved parental drug use. 25

In my travels to the ramparts of the drug war, I have seen nothing to support the legalizers' argument that lower drug prices would reduce crime. Virtually everywhere I have gone, police and DEA agents have told me that crime rates are highest where crack is cheapest. 26

4. *Drug use should be legal since users only harm themselves.* Those who believe this should stand beside the medical examiner as he counts the 36 bullet wounds in the shattered corpse of a three-year-old who happened to get in the way of his mother's drug-crazed boyfriend. They should visit the babies abandoned by cocaine-addicted mothers—infants who already carry the ravages of addiction in their own tiny bodies. They should console the devastated relatives of the nun who worked in a homeless shelter and was 27

stabbed to death by a crack addict enraged that she would not stake him to a fix.

28 Do drug addicts only harm themselves? Here is a former cocaine addict describing the compulsion that quickly draws even the most "responsible" user into irresponsible behavior: "Everything is about getting high, and any means necessary to get there becomes rational. If it means stealing something from somebody close to you, lying to your family, borrowing money from people you know you can't pay back, writing checks you know you can't cover, you do all those things—things that are totally against everything you have ever believed in."

29 Society pays for this behavior, and not just in bigger insurance premiums, losses from accidents and poor job performance. We pay in the loss of a priceless social currency as families are destroyed, trust between friends is betrayed and promising careers are never fulfilled. I cannot imagine sanctioning behavior that would increase that toll.

30 I find no merit in the legalizers' case. The simple fact is that drug use is wrong. And the moral argument, in the end, is the most compelling argument. A citizen in a drug-induced haze, whether on his back-yard deck or on a mattress in a ghetto crack house, is not what the founding fathers meant by the "pursuit of happiness." Despite the legalizers' argument that drug use is a matter of "personal freedom," our nation's notion of liberty is rooted in the ideal of a self-reliant citizenry. Helpless wrecks in treatment centers, men chained by their noses to cocaine—these people are slaves.

31 Imagine if, in the darkest days of 1940, Winston Churchill had rallied the West by saying, "This war looks hopeless, and besides, it will cost too much. Hitler can't be *that* bad. Let's surrender and see what happens." That is essentially what we hear from the legalizers.

32 This war *can* be won. I am heartened by indications that education and public revulsion are having an effect on drug use. The National Institute on Drug Abuse's latest survey of current users shows a 37-percent *decrease* in drug consumption since 1985. Cocaine is down 50 percent; marijuana use among young people is at its lowest rate since 1972. In my travels I've been encouraged by signs that Americans are fighting back.

33 I am under no illusion that such developments, however hopeful, mean the war is over. We need to involve more

citizens in the fight, increase pressure on drug criminals and build on antidrug programs that have proved to work. This will not be easy. But the moral and social costs of surrender are simply too great to contemplate.

Milton Friedman
Prohibition and Drugs

When he was on the faculty of the University of Chicago, Milton Friedman won the Nobel Prize for his "monetarist" school of economics, one that stresses stable growth in the supply of money and credit in an economy. A conservative who influenced the policies of Ronald Reagan and George Bush, he enjoys writing about a range of public issues. Now a senior research fellow at the Hoover Institute at Stanford University, he wrote the two following essays on the legalization of drugs—one for Newsweek *(1972) and one for* The Wall Street Journal *(1989).*

The Wall Street Journal article, *which contains a reference in paragraph five to the* Newsweek *essay, is an "open letter" to William Bennett, the nation's "drug czar" (i.e. director of the Office of National Drug Policy) under President Bush. Bennett is the author of the previous essay in this book as well as the response to Milton Friedman that is reprinted after Friedman's two essays. Friedman's own counter-response follows that, on page 917.*

"The reign of tears is over. The slums will soon be only a memory. We will turn our prisons into factories and our jails into storehouses and corncribs. Men will walk upright now, women will smile, and the children will laugh. Hell will be forever for rent." 1

That is how Billy Sunday, the noted evangelist and leading crusader against Demon Rum, greeted the onset of Prohibition in early 1920. We know now how tragically his hopes were doomed. New prisons and jails had to be built to house the criminals sprawned by converting the drinking of spirits into a crime against the state. Prohibition undermined 2 respect for the law, corrupted the minions of the law, created a decadent moral climate—but did not stop the consumption of alcohol.

3 Despite this tragic object lesson, we seem bent on repeating precisely the same mistake in the handling of drugs.

Ethics and Expediency

4 On ethical grounds, do we have the right to use the machinery of government to prevent an individual from becoming an alcoholic or a drug addict? For children, almost everyone would answer at least a qualified yes. But for responsible adults, I, for one, would answer no. Reason with the potential addict, yes. Tell him the consequences, yes. Pray for and with him, yes. But I believe that we have no right to use force, directly or indirectly, to prevent a fellow man from committing suicide, let alone from drinking alcohol or taking drugs.

5 I readily grant that the ethical issue is difficult and that men of goodwill may well disagree. Fortunately, we need not resolve the ethical issue to agree on policy. *Prohibition is an attempted cure that makes matters worse—for both the addict and the rest of us.* Hence, even if you regard present policy toward drugs as ethically justified, considerations of expediency make that policy most unwise.

6 *Consider first the addict.* Legalizing drugs might increase the number of addicts, but it is not clear that it would. Forbidden fruit is attractive, particularly to the young. More important, many drug addicts are deliberately made by pushers, who give likely prospects their first few doses free. It pays the pusher to do so because, once hooked, the addict is a captive customer. If drugs were legally available, any possible profit from such inhumane activity would disappear, since the addict could buy from the cheapest source.

7 Whatever happens to the number of addicts, the individual addict would clearly be far better off if drugs were legal. Today, drugs are both incredibly expensive and highly uncertain in quality. Addicts are driven to associate with criminals to get the drugs, become criminals themselves to finance the habit, and risk constant danger of death and disease.

8 *Consider next the rest of us.* Here the situation is crystal-clear. The harm to us from the addiction of others arises

almost wholly from the fact that drugs are illegal. A recent committee of the American Bar Association estimated that addicts commit one-third to one-half of all street crime in the U.S. Legalize drugs, and street crime would drop dramatically.

Moreover, addicts and pushers are not the only ones corrupted. Immense sums are at stake. It is inevitable that some relatively low-paid police and other government officials—and some high-paid ones as well—will succumb to the temptation to pick up easy money. 9

Law and Order

Legalizing drugs would simultaneously reduce the amount of crime and raise the quality of law enforcement. Can you conceive of any other measure that would accomplish so much to promote law and order? 10

But, you may say, must we accept defeat? Why not simply end the drug traffic? That is where experience under Prohibition is most relevant. We cannot end the drug traffic. We may be able to cut off opium from Turkey—but there are innumerable other places where the opium poppy grows. With French cooperation, we may be able to make Marseilles an unhealthy place to manufacture heroin—but there are innumerable other places where the simple manufacturing operations involved can be carried out. So long as large sums of money are involved—and they are bound to be if drugs are illegal—it is literally hopeless to expect to end the traffic or even to reduce seriously its scope. 11

In drugs, as in other areas, persuasion and example are likely to be far more effective than the use of force to shape others in our image. 12

Milton Friedman

An Open Letter to Bill Bennett

Dear Bill:

1 In Oliver Cromwell's eloquent words, "I beseech you, in the bowels of Christ, think it possible you may be mistaken" about the course you and President Bush urge us to adopt to fight drugs. The path you propose of more police, more jails, use of the military in foreign countries, harsh penalties for drug users, and a whole panoply of repressive measures can only make a bad situation worse. The drug war cannot be won by those tactics without undermining the human liberty and individual freedom that you and I cherish.

2 You are not mistaken in believing that drugs are a scourge that is devastating our society. You are not mistaken in believing that drugs are tearing asunder our social fabric, ruining the lives of many young people, and imposing heavy costs on some of the most disadvantaged among us. You are not mistaken in believing that the majority of the public share your concerns. In short, you are not mistaken in the end you seek to achieve.

3 Your mistake is failing to recognize that the very measures you favor are a major source of the evils you deplore. Of course the problem is demand, but it is not only demand, it is demand that must operate through repressed and illegal channels. Illegality creates obscene profits that finance the murderous tactics of the drug lords; illegality leads to the corruption of law enforcement officials; illegality monopolizes the efforts of honest law forces so that they are starved for resources to fight the simpler crimes of robbery, theft and assault.

4 Drugs are a tragedy for addicts. But criminalizing their use converts that tragedy into a disaster for society, for users and non-users alike. Our experience with the prohibition of drugs is a replay of our experience with the prohibition of alcoholic beverages.

5 I append excerpts from a column that I wrote in 1972 on "Prohibition and Drugs." The major problem then was heroin from Marseilles; today, it is cocaine from Latin America. Today, also, the problem is far more serious than it was 17 years ago: more addicts, more innocent victims; more drug pushers, more law enforcement officials; more

money spent to enforce prohibition, more money spent to circumvent prohibition.

Had drugs been decriminalized 17 years ago, "crack" would never have been invented (it was invented because the high cost of illegal drugs made it profitable to provide a cheaper version) and there would today be far fewer addicts. The lives of thousands, perhaps hundreds of thousands of innocent victims would have been saved, and not only in the U.S. The ghettos of our major cities would not be drug-and-crime-infested no-man's lands. Fewer people would be in jails, and fewer jails would have been built. 6

Colombia, Bolivia and Peru would not be suffering from narco-terror, and we would not be distorting our foreign policy because of narco-terror. Hell would not, in the words with which Billy Sunday welcomed Prohibition, "be forever for rent," but it would be a lot emptier. 7

Decriminalizing drugs is even more urgent now than in 1972, but we must recognize that the harm done in the interim cannot be wiped out, certainly not immediately. Postponing discriminalization will only make matters worse, and make the problem appear even more intractable. 8

Alcohol and tobacco cause many more deaths in users than do drugs. Decriminalization would not prevent us from treating drugs as we now treat alcohol and tobacco: prohibiting sales of drugs to minors, outlawing the advertising of drugs and similar measures. Such measures could be enforced, while outright prohibition cannot be. Moreover, if even a small fraction of the money we now spend on trying to enforce drug prohibition were devoted to treatment and rehabilitation, in an atmosphere of compassion not punishment, the reduction in drug usage and in the harm done to the users could be dramatic. 9

This plea comes from the bottom of my heart. Every friend of freedom, and I know you are one, must be as revolted as I am by the prospect of turning the United States into an armed camp, by the vision of jails filled with casual drug users and of an army of enforcers empowered to invade the liberty of citizens on slight evidence. A country in which shooting down unidentified planes "on suspicion" can be seriously considered as a drug-war tactic is not the kind of United States that either you or I want to hand on to future generations. 10

William Bennett

A Response to Milton Friedman

Dear Milton:

1 There was little, if anything, new in your open letter to me calling for the legalization of drugs (*The Wall Street Journal*, Sept. 7). As your 1972 article made clear, the legalization argument is an old and familiar one, which has recently been revived by a small number of journalists and academics who insist that the only solution to the drug problem is no solution at all. What surprises me is that you would continue to advocate so unrealistic a proposal without pausing to consider seriously its consequences.

2 If the argument for drug legalization has one virtue it is its sheer simplicity. Eliminate laws against drugs, and street crime will disappear. Take the profit out of the black market through decriminalization and regulation, and poor neighborhoods will no longer be victimized by drug dealers. Cut back on drug enforcement, and use the money to wage a public health campaign against drugs, as we do with tobacco and alcohol.

Counting Costs

3 The basic premise of all these propositions is that using our nation's laws to fight drugs is too costly. To be sure, our attempts to reduce drug use do carry with them enormous costs. But the question that must be asked—and which is totally ignored by the legalization advocates—is, what are the costs of *not* enforcing laws against drugs?

4 In my judgment, and in the judgment of virtually every serious scholar in this field, the potential costs of legalizing drugs would be so large as to make it a public policy disaster.

5 Of course, no one, including you, can say with certainty what would happen in the U.S. if drugs were suddenly to become a readily purchased product. We do know, however, that wherever drugs have been cheaper and more easily obtained, drug use—and addiction—has skyrocketed. In opium and cocaine producing countries, addiction is rampant among the peasants involved in drug production.

Professor James Q. Wilson tells us that during the years in which heroin could be legally prescribed by doctors in Britain, the number of addicts increased forty-fold. And after the repeal of Prohibition—an analogy favored but misunderstood by legalization advocates—consumption of alcohol soared by 350%. 6

Could we afford such dramatic increases in drug use? I doubt it. Already the toll of drug use on American society—measured in lost productivity, in rising health insurance costs, in hospitals flooded with drug overdose emergencies, in drug caused accidents, and in premature death—is surely more than we would like to bear. 7

You seem to believe that by spending just a little more money on treatment and rehabilitation, the costs of increased addiction can be avoided. That hope betrays a basic misunderstanding of the problems facing drug treatment. Most addicts don't suddenly decide to get help. They remain addicts either because treatment isn't available or because they don't seek it out. The National Drug Control Strategy announced by President Bush on Sept. 5 goes a long way in making sure that more treatment slots are available. But the simple fact remains that many drug users won't enter treatment until they are forced to—often by the very criminal justice system you think is the source of the problem. 8

As for the connection between drugs and crime, your unswerving commitment to a legalization solution prevents you from appreciating the complexity of the drug market. Contrary to your claim, most addicts do not turn to crime to support their habit. Research shows that many of them were involved in criminal activity before they turned to drugs. Many former addicts who have received treatment continue to commit crimes during their recovery. And even if drugs were legal, what evidence do you have that the habitual drug user wouldn't continue to rob and steal to get money for clothes, food or shelter? Drug addicts always want more drugs than they can afford, and no legalization scheme has yet come up with a way of satisfying that appetite. 9

The National Drug Control Strategy emphasizes the importance of reclaiming the streets and neighborhoods where drugs have wrought havoc because, I admit, the price of having drug laws is having criminals who will try to subvert them. Your proposal might conceivably reduce the amount of gang- and dealer-related crime, but it is fanciful to suggest that it would make crime vanish. Unless you are 10

willing to distribute drugs freely and widely, there will always be a black market to undercut the regulated one. And as for the potential addicts, for the school children and for the pregnant mothers, all of whom would find drugs more accessible and legally condoned, your proposal would offer nothing at all.

11 So I advocate a larger criminal justice system to take drug users off the streets and deter new users from becoming more deeply involved in so hazardous an activity. You suggest that such policies would turn the country "into an armed camp." Try telling that to the public housing tenants who enthusiastically support plans to enhance security in their buildings, or to the residents who applaud police when a local crack house is razed. They recognize that drug use is a threat to the individual liberty and domestic tranquility guaranteed by the Constitution.

12 I remain an ardent defender of our nation's laws against illegal drug use and our attempts to enforce them because I believe drug use is wrong. A true friend of freedom understands that government has a responsibility to craft and uphold laws that help educate citizens about right and wrong. That, at any rate, was the Founders' view of our system of government.

Liberal Ridicule

13 Today this view is much ridiculed by liberal elites and entirely neglected by you. So while I cannot doubt the sincerity of your opinion on drug legalization, I find it difficult to respect. The moral cost of legalizing drugs is great, but it is a cost that apparently lies outside the narrow scope of libertarian policy prescriptions.

14 I do not have a simple solution to the drug problem. I doubt that one exists. But I am committed to fighting the problem on several fronts through imaginative policies and hard work over a long period of time. As in the past, some of these efforts will work and some won't. Your response, however, is to surrender and see what happens. To my mind that is irresponsible and reckless public policy. At a time when national intolerance for drug use is rapidly increasing, the legalization argument is a political anachronism. Its recent resurgence is, I trust, only a temporary distraction from the genuine debate on national drug policy.

Milton Friedman

A Response to William Bennett

William Bennett is entirely right (editorial page, Sept. 19) 1
that "there was little, if anything, new in" my open letter to him—just as there is little, if anything, new in his proposed program to rid this nation of the scourge of drugs. That is why I am so disturbed by that program. It flies in the face of decades of experience. More police, more jails, more-stringent penalties, increased efforts at interception, increased publicity about the evils of drugs—all this has been accompanied by more, not fewer, drug addicts; more, not fewer, crimes and murders; more, not less, corruption; more, not fewer, innocent victims.

Like Mr. Bennett, his predecessors were "committed to 2
fighting the problem on several fronts through imaginative policies and hard work over a long period of time." What evidence convinces him that the same policies on a larger scale will end the drug scourge? He offers none in his response to me, only assertion and the conjecture that legalizing drugs would produce "a public policy disaster"—as if that is not exactly what we already have.

Legalizing drugs is not equivalent to surrender in the fight 3
against drug addiction. On the contrary, I believe that legalizing drugs is a precondition for an effective fight. We might then have a real chance to prevent sales to minors; get drugs out of the schools and playgrounds; save crack babies and reduce their number; launch an effective educational campaign on the personal costs of drug use—not necessarily conducted, I might add, by government; punish drug users guilty of harming others while "under the influence"; and encourage large numbers of addicts to volunteer for treatment and rehabilitation when they could do so without confessing to criminal actions. Some habitual drug users would, as he says, "continue to rob and steal to get money for clothes, food or shelter." No doubt also there will be "a black market to undercut the regulated one"—as there now is bootleg liquor thanks to high taxes on alcoholic beverages. But these would be on a far smaller scale than at present. Perfection is not for this world. Pursuing the unattainable best can prevent achievement of the attainable good.

As Mr. Bennett recognizes, the victims of drugs fall into 4

two classes: those who choose to use drugs and innocent victims—who in one way or another include almost all the rest of us. Legalization would drastically reduce the number of innocent victims. That is a virtual certainty. The number of self-chosen victims might increase, but it is pure conjecture that the number would, as he asserts, skyrocket. In any event, while both groups of victims are to be pitied, the innocent victims surely have a far greater claim on our sympathy than the self-chosen victims—or else the concept of personal responsibility has been emptied of all content.

5 A particular class of innocent victims generally overlooked is foreigners. By what right do we impose our values on the residents of Colombia? Or, by our actions undermine the very foundations of their society and condemn hundreds, perhaps thousands, of Colombians to violent death? All because the U.S. government is unable to enforce its own laws on its own citizens. I regard such actions as indefensible, entirely aside from the distortions they introduce into our foreign policy.

6 Finally, he and I interpret the "Founders' view of our system of government" very differently. To him, they believed "that government has a responsibility to . . . help educate citizens about right and wrong." To me, that is a totalitarian view opening the road to thought control and would have been utterly unacceptable to the Founders. I do not believe, and neither did they, that it is the responsibility of government to tell free citizens what is right and wrong. That is something for them to decide for themselves. Government is a means to enable each of us to pursue our own vision in our own way so long as we do not interfere with the right of others to do the same. In the words of the Declaration of Independence, "all Men are . . . endowed by their Creator with certain unalienable Rights, that among these are Life, Liberty, and the pursuit of Happiness. That to secure these Rights Governments are instituted among Men, deriving their just powers from the consent of the Governed." In my view, Justice Louis Brandeis was a "true friend of freedom" when he wrote, "Experience should teach us to be most on our guard to protect liberty when the government's purposes are beneficial. Men born to freedom are naturally alert to repel invasions of their liberty by evil-minded rulers. The greater dangers to liberty lurk in insidious encroachment by men of zeal, well meaning, but without understanding."

Milton Friedman
Hoover Institution
Stanford, Calif.

VII. SCIENCE AND SOCIETY

Introduction

No one doubts that science and technology have become central enterprises in our culture. Some scientists would like to have it otherwise; they would like to insulate science as much as possible from social pressures. But that would be impossible: Not only is it impossible to keep scientific enterprises such as medicine, genetic engineering, evolutionary biology, supercolliders, space exploration, or environmental science away from public scrutiny, it is also not in our interest to do so. For ultimately science and technology are themselves social creations, carried out through very human means for human purposes; that has already been made quite clear in the discussion of science and gender in part III of this book and in the controversy over abortion in part V. To try to dehumanize science and technology is to diminish them. Nevertheless, as science and technology become more central to our society, it is inevitable that conflicts between science and technology (on the one hand) and society (on the other) will become more important and more complicated. The scientific enterprise will inevitably involve ethical and rhetorical dimensions.

The first readings in this part establish that very clearly. The contemporary controversy over genetic engineering springs from basic conflicts between science, nature, and society that have bothered Americans since our beginnings as a nation; only this time the controversy has specific practical applications. Are scientists justified in intervening in nature in a fundamental way—by altering the very genetic codes that define a species? Is it legitimate to invent and patent new life forms, and to market these products for a profit, as Harvard scientists did when they created a "new" mouse in 1988 for the sake of cancer research? Is it acceptable to control the processes of nature, to manipulate living things for our human advantage? Or should we worry about the ethical and practical implications of genetic engineering? Some articles in the section on genetic engineering contend that genetic engineering is a moral imperative because it can lead to breakthroughs in the management of sickle cell anemia, Huntington's disease, Tay-Sachs disease, or other genetic disorders. But others worry about the safety of manufacturing and managing life forms, or about the ethics of eugenics. After all, the Nazis espoused eugenics half a century ago. And after all, who will determine which traits count as "deformities" to be stamped out through genetic engineering? And what are the implications of "using" genetically engineered animals to serve us?

The last question brings up the matter of animal rights. As the next set of readings makes clear, over the past decade many people have wondered about the ethics of "using" animals, whether for clothing or cosmetics, or for food or laboratory experiments. Do animals really have rights? If so, what are they? Do people have any rights that animals do not have? Is it legitimate to put people before animals—or animals before people? Do animals compose another kind of American minority in need of protection from a stronger and exploitative majority? Is it a form of discrimination—"specieism"—to exploit animals, or do human beings by virtue of their special attributes have the right to do just that? Do the benefits of using animals for food, clothing, and medical science outweigh the liabilities? Does the controversy come down to a conflict of rights that pits the rights of animals against the rights of people—including the rights of scientists to pursue their work? Should the animal rights movement be less focused on abstract rights and more concerned about treating animals decently while they are "used"? According to some estimates, 50 million animals—cats, dogs, pigs, frogs, turtles, mice, rats, chimpanzees, rabbits, the proverbial guinea pigs, and more—are experimented on each year, very probably some on your own campus. And very probably the use of animals is an issue someplace on your campus as well.

The third section of this part of *Conversations* takes up the vexing question of AIDS: How should we fight this terrible, worldwide epidemic that has already claimed many millions of people throughout the world? (By the year 2000, as many as 20 million people are likely to have the disease; in the United States alone, half a million people had contracted the disease by the end of 1992.) First recognized in the United States early in the 1980s, AIDS (or acquired immune deficiency syndrome) seems to be caused by the human immunodeficiency virus—the HIV virus—that is spread through sexual contact, through the reuse of infected needles (especially by drug users), through childbirth (when the mother is infected), or through the transfusion of contaminated blood. Since the causes of the AIDS epidemic are well understood, the question arises: How should we fight it? Should citizens reconsider the sexual mores that have become conventional in the past few decades? Should health-care workers or other citizens have to undergo regular testing for the HIV virus? Should laws be passed requiring HIV carriers to inform their sexual partners that they carry the virus? Can health-care workers be required to treat AIDS patients? This section of *Conversations* simply begins a debate about a public health that is in everyone's mind these days.

Then comes a discussion of one of the most controversial questions related to science and society today: the matter of euthanasia. Again, the question comes up because of advances in technology—because medical science has extended life expectancies and because medical technology can extend the life of the grievously ill and injured. But what are society's responsibilities to the very ill and incapacitated? Under what circumstances is it permissible to deny or remove medical treatment from a patient? And is it ever permissible to use medical technology actively to end a life—when someone is suffering, for example? Who should decide when euthanasia is permissible—family or physicians? Will an acceptance of euthanasia bring out our worst prejudices toward the aged, toward the mentally disadvantaged, toward the insane or deviant? Questions like these are taken up daily because of legal cases involving the "right to die" with dignity, because of highly publicized "right to die" organizations such as the Hemlock Society, and because some physicians have been quite public about assisting terminally ill patients to commit suicide.

Thus, this book ends appropriately with one of the most important political and social issues that we now face: health care. How can we ensure that all Americans have access to effective and affordable health care? Can we maintain first-rate care and still make care available to all? And can we do that without investing every last national penny into health-care costs? What should the government's role be in our health-care system?

The advances brought by science and technology solve many human problems, but with these advances come a number of perplexing ethical dilemmas. This is the lesson of this final part of *Conversations,* and this is the challenge to all citizens, whether they are scientists or not, in this last decade of the twentieth century.

GENETIC ENGINEERING

Lewis Thomas

The Hazards of Science

Lewis Thomas has served as president of the Sloan-Kettering Cancer Center in New York, as dean of the Yale Medical School, and as a member of the National Academy of Sciences, among other things. But he is best known as an essayist about science. His collection of essays The Lives of a Cell *(1974) won a National Book Award. "The Hazards of Science" appeared in a similar collection,* Medusa and the Snail, *in 1977; it originally appeared in* The New England Journal of Medicine.

The code word for criticism of science and scientists these days is "hubris." Once you've said that word, you've said it all; it sums up, in a word, all of today's apprehensions and misgivings in the public mind—not just about what is perceived as the insufferable attitude of the scientists themselves but, enclosed in the same word, what science and technology are perceived to be doing to make this century, this near to its ending, turn out so wrong. 1

"Hubris" is a powerful word, containing layers of powerful meaning, derived from a very old word, but with a new life of its own, growing way beyond the limits of its original meaning. Today, it is strong enough to carry the full weight of disapproval for the cast of mind that thought up atomic fusion and fission as ways of first blowing up and later heating cities as well as the attitudes which led to stripmining, offshore oil wells, Kepone, food additives, SSTs, and the tiny spherical particles of plastic recently discovered clogging the waters of the Sargasso Sea. 2

The biomedical sciences are now caught up with physical science and technology in the same kind of critical judgment, with the same pejorative word. Hubris is responsible, it is said, for the whole biological revolution. It is hubris that has given us the prospects of behavior control, psychosur- 3 gery, fetal research, heart transplants, the cloning of prominent politicians from bits of their own eminent tissue, iatrogenic disease, overpopulation, and recombinant DNA. This last, the new technology that permits the stitching of one creature's genes into the DNA of another, to make hybrids, is currently cited as the ultimate example of hubris. It is hubris for man to manufacture a hybrid on his own.

4 So now we are back to the first word again, from "hybrid" to "hubris," and the hidden meaning of two beings joined unnaturally together by man is somehow retained. Today's joining is straight out of Greek mythology: it is the combining of man's capacity with the special prerogative of the gods, and it is really in this sense of outrage that the word "hubris" is being used today. That is what the word has grown into, a warning, a code word, a shorthand signal from the language itself: if man starts doing things reserved for the gods, deifying himself, the outcome will be something worse for him, symbolically, than the litters of wild boars and domestic sows were for the ancient Romans.

5 To be charged with hubris is therefore an extremely serious matter, and not to be dealt with by murmuring things about antiscience and antiintellectualism, which is what many of us engaged in science tend to do these days. The doubts about our enterprise have their origin in the most profound kind of human anxiety. If we are right and the critics are wrong, then it has to be that the word "hubris" is being mistakenly employed, that this is not what we are up to, that there is, for the time being anyway, a fundamental misunderstanding of science.

6 I suppose there is one central question to be dealt with, and I am not at all sure how to deal with it, although I am quite certain about my own answer to it. It is this: are there some kinds of information leading to some sorts of knowledge that human beings are really better off not having? Is there a limit to scientific inquiry not set by what is knowable but what we *ought* to be knowing? Should we stop short of learning about some things, for fear of what we, or someone, will do with the knowledge? My own answer is a flat no, but I must confess that this is an intuitive response and I am neither inclined nor trained to reason my way through it.

7 There has been some effort, in and out of scientific quarters, to make recombinant DNA into the issue on which to settle this argument. Proponents of this line of research are accused of pure hubris, of assuming the rights of gods,

of arrogance and outrage; what is more, they confess themselves to be in the business of making live hybrids with their own hands. The mayor of Cambridge and the attorney general of New York have both been advised to put a stop to it, forthwith.

It is not quite the same sort of argument, however, as the 8
one about limiting knowledge, although this is surely part of it. The knowledge is already here, and the rage of the argument is about its application in technology. Should DNA for making certain useful or interesting proteins be incorporated into *E. coli* plasmids or not? Is there a risk of inserting the wrong sort of toxins or hazardous viruses, and then having the new hybrid organisms spread beyond the laboratory? Is this a technology for creating new varieties of pathogens, and should it be stopped because of this?

If the argument is held to this level, I can see no reason 9
why it cannot be settled, by reasonable people. We have learned a great deal about the handling of dangerous microbes in the last century, although I must say that the opponents of recombinant-DNA research tend to downgrade this huge body of information. At one time or another, agents as hazardous as those of rabies, psittacosis, plague, and typhus have been dealt with by investigators in secure laboratories, with only rare instances of self-infection of the investigators themselves, and no instances at all of epidemics. It takes some high imagining to postulate the creation of brand-new pathogens so wild and voracious as to spread from equally secure laboratories to endanger human life at large, as some of the arguers are now maintaining.

But this is precisely the trouble with the recombinant- 10
DNA problem: it has become an emotional issue, with too many irretrievably lost tempers on both sides. It has lost the sound of a discussion of technological safety and begins now to sound like something else, almost like a religious controversy, and here it is moving toward the central issue: are there some things in science we should not be learning about?

There is an inevitably long list of hard questions to follow 11
this one, beginning with the one which asks whether the mayor of Cambridge should be the one to decide, first off.

Maybe we'd be wiser, all of us, to back off before the 12
recombinant-DNA issue becomes too large to cope with. If we're going to have a fight about it, let it be confined to the immediate issue of safety and security, of the recombinants

now under consideration, and let us by all means have regulations and guidelines to assure the public safety wherever these are indicated or even suggested. But if it is possible let us stay off that question about limiting human knowledge. It is too loaded, and we'll simply not be able to cope with it.

13 By this time it will have become clear that I have already taken sides in the matter, and my point of view is entirely prejudiced. This is true, but with a qualification. I am not so much in favor of recombinant-DNA research as I am opposed to the opposition to this line of inquiry. As a longtime student of infectious-disease agents I do not take kindly the declarations that we do not know how to keep from catching things in laboratories, much less how to keep them from spreading beyond the laboratory walls. I believe we learned a lot about this sort of thing, long ago. Moreover, I regard it as a form of hubris-in-reverse to claim that man can make deadly pathogenic microorganisms so easily. In my view, it takes a long time and a great deal of interliving before a microbe can become a successful pathogen. Pathogenicity is, in a sense, a highly skilled trade, and only a tiny minority of all the numberless tons of microbes on the earth has ever involved itself in it; most bacteria are busy with their own business, browsing and recycling the rest of life. Indeed, pathogenicity often seems to me a sort of biological accident in which signals are misdirected by the microbe or misinterpreted by the host, as in the case of endotoxin, or in which the intimacy between host and microbe is of such long standing that a form of molecular mimicry becomes possible, as in the case of diphtheria toxin. I do not believe that by simply putting together new combinations of genes one can create creatures as highly skilled and adapted for dependence as a pathogen must be, any more than I have ever believed that microbial life from the moon or Mars could possibly make a living on this planet.

14 But, as I said, I'm not at all sure this is what the argument is really about. Behind it is that other discussion, which I wish we would not have to become enmeshed in.

15 I cannot speak for the physical sciences, which have moved an immense distance in this century by any standard, but it does seem to me that in the biological and medical sciences we are still far too ignorant to begin making judgments about what sorts of things we should be learning or not learning. To the contrary, we ought to be grateful for whatever snatches

we can get hold of, and we ought to be out there on a much larger scale than today's, looking for more.

We should be very careful with that word "hubris," and make sure it is not used when not warranted. There is a great danger in applying it to the search for knowledge. The application of knowledge is another matter, and there is hubris in plenty of our technology, but I do not believe that looking for new information about nature, at whatever level, can possibly be called unnatural. Indeed, if there is any single attribute of human beings, apart from language, which distinguishes them from all other creatures on earth, it is their insatiable, uncontrollable drive to learn things and then to exchange the information with others of the species. Learning is what we do, when you think about it. I cannot think of a human impulse more difficult to govern. 16

But I can imagine lots of reasons for trying to govern it. New information about nature is very likely, at the outset, to be upsetting to someone or other. The recombinant-DNA line of research is already upsetting, not because of the dangers now being argued about but because it is disturbing, in a fundamental way, to face the fact that the genetic machinery in control of the planet's life can be fooled around with so easily. We do not like the idea that anything so fixed and stable as a species line can be changed. The notion that genes can be taken out of one genome and inserted in another is unnerving. Classical mythology is peopled with mixed beings—part man, part animal or plant—and most of them are associated with tragic stories. Recombinant DNA is a reminder of bad dreams. 17

The easiest decision for society to make in terms of this kind is to appoint an agency, or a commission, or a subcommittee within an agency to look into the problem and provide advice. And the easiest course for a committee to take, when confronted by any process that appears to be disturbing people or making them uncomfortable, is to recommend that it be stopped, at least for the time being. 18

I can easily imagine such a committee, composed of unimpeachable public figures, arriving at the decision that the time is not quite ripe for further exploration of the transplantation of genes, that we should put this off for a while, maybe until next century, and get on with other affairs that make us less discomfited. Why not do science on something more popular, say, how to get solar energy more cheaply? Or mental health? 19

20 The trouble is, it would be very hard to stop once this line was begun. There are, after all, all sorts of scientific inquiry that are not much liked by one constituency or another, and we might soon find ourselves with crowded rosters, panels, standing committees, set up in Washington for the appraisal, and then the regulation, of research. Not on grounds of the possible value and usefulness of the new knowledge, mind you, but for guarding society against scientific hubris, against the kinds of knowledge we're better off without.

21 It would be absolutely irresistible as a way of spending time, and people would form long queues for membership. Almost anything would be fair game, certainly anything to do with genetics, anything relating to population control, or, on the other side, research on aging. Very few fields would get by, except perhaps for some, like mental health, in which nobody really expects anything much to happen, surely nothing new or disturbing.

22 The research areas in the greatest trouble would be those already containing a sense of bewilderment and surprise, with discernible prospects of upheaving present dogmas.

23 It is hard to predict how science is going to turn out, and if it is really good science it is impossible to predict. This is in the nature of the enterprise. If the things to be found are actually new, they are by definition unknown in advance, and there is no way of telling in advance where a really new line of inquiry will lead. You cannot make choices in this matter, selecting things you think you're going to like and shutting off the lines that make for discomfort. You either have science or you don't, and if you have it you are obliged to accept the surprising and disturbing pieces of information, even the overwhelming and upheaving ones, along with the neat and promptly useful bits. It is like that.

24 The only solid piece of scientific truth about which I feel totally confident is that we are profoundly ignorant about nature. Indeed, I regard this as a major discovery of the past hundred years of biology. It is, in its way, an illuminating piece of news. It would have amazed the brightest minds of the eighteenth-century Enlightenment to be told by any of us how little we know, and how bewildering seems the way ahead. It is this sudden confrontation with the depth and scope of ignorance that represents the most significant contribution of twentieth-century science to the human intellect. We are, at last, facing up to it. In earlier times, we either pretended to understand how things worked or ig-

nored the problem, or simply made up stories to fill the gaps. Now that we have begun exploring in earnest, doing serious science, we are getting glimpses of how huge the questions are, and how far from being answered. Because of this, these are hard times for the human intellect, and it is no wonder that we are depressed. It is not so bad being ignorant if you are totally ignorant; the hard thing is knowing in some detail the reality of ignorance, the worst spots and here and there the not-so-bad spots, but no true light at the end of any tunnel nor even any tunnels that can yet be trusted. Hard times, indeed.

But we are making a beginning, and there ought to be 25
some satisfaction, even exhilaration, in that. The method works. There are probably no questions we can think up that can't be answered, sooner or later, including even the matter of consciousness. To be sure, there may well be questions we can't think up, ever, and therefore limits to the reach of human intellect which we will never know about, but that is another matter. Within our limits, we should be able to work our way through to all our answers, if we keep at it long enough, and pay attention.

I am putting it this way, with all the presumption and 26
confidence that I can summon, in order to raise another, last question. Is this hubris? Is there something fundamentally unnatural, or intrinsically wrong, or hazardous for the species in the ambition that drives us all to reach a comprehensive understanding of nature, including ourselves? I cannot believe it. It would seem to me a more unnatural thing, and more of an offense against nature, for us to come on the same scene endowed as we are with curiosity, filled to overbrimming as we are with questions, and naturally talented as we are for the asking of clear questions, and then for us to do nothing about it or, worse, to try to suppress the questions. This is the greater danger for our species, to try to pretend that we are another kind of animal, that we do not need to satisfy our curiosity, that we can get along somehow without inquiry and exploration and experimentation, and that the human mind can rise above its ignorance by simply asserting that there are things it has no need to know. This, to my way of thinking, is the real hubris, and it carries danger for us all.

Nathaniel Hawthorne

The Birth-mark

Nathaniel Hawthorne (1804–1864), one of America's greatest fiction writers, lived most of his life near Boston. He first published "The Birth-mark" in 1843.

1 In the latter part of the last century, there lived a man of science—an eminent proficient in every branch of natural philosophy—who, not long before our story opens, had made experience of a spiritual affinity, more attractive than any chemical one. He had left his laboratory to the care of an assistant, cleared his fine countenance from the furnace-smoke, washed the stain of acids from his fingers, and persuaded a beautiful woman to become his wife. In those days, when the comparatively recent discovery of electricity, and other kindred mysteries of nature, seemed to open paths into the region of miracle, it was not unusual for the love of science to rival the love of woman, in its depth and absorbing energy. The higher intellect, the imagination, the spirit, and even the heart, might all find their congenial aliment in pursuits which, as some of their ardent votaries believed, would ascent from one step of powerful intelligence to another, until the philosopher should lay his hand on the secret of creative force, and perhaps make new worlds for himself. We know not whether Aylmer possessed this degree of faith in man's ultimate control over nature. He had devoted himself, however, too unreservedly to scientific studies, ever to be weaned from them by any second passion. His love for his young wife might prove the stronger of the two; but it could only be by intertwining itself with his love of science, and uniting the strength of the latter to its own.

2 Such a union accordingly took place, and was attended with truly remarkable consequences, and a deeply impressive moral. One day, very soon after their marriage, Aylmer sat gazing at his wife, with a trouble in his countenance that grew stronger, until he spoke.

3 "Georgiana," said he, "has it never occurred to you that the mark upon your cheek might be removed?"

4 "No, indeed," said she, smiling; but perceiving the seriousness of his manner, she blushed deeply. "To tell you the

truth, it has been so often called a charm, that I was simple enough to imagine it might be so."

"Ah, upon another face, perhaps it might," replied her 5
husband. "But never on yours! No, dearest Georgiana, you came so nearly perfect from the hand of Nature, that this slightest possible defect—which we hesitate whether to term a defect or a beauty—shocks me, as being the visible mark of earthly imperfection."

"Shocks you, my husband!" cried Georgiana, deeply hurt; 6
at first reddening with momentary anger, but then bursting into tears. "Then why did you take me from my mother's side? You cannot love what shocks you!"

To explain this conversation, it must be mentioned, that, in 7
the centre of Georgiana's left cheek, there was a singular mark, deeply interwoven, as it were, with the texture and substance of her face. In the usual state of her complexion,—a healthy, though delicate bloom,—the mark wore a tint of deeper crimson, which imperfectly defined its shape amid the surrounding rosiness. When she blushed, it gradually became more indistinct, and finally vanished amid the triumphant rush of blood, that bathed the whole cheek with its brilliant glow. But, if any shifting emotion caused her to turn pale, there was the mark again, a crimson stain upon the snow, in what Aylmer sometimes deemed an almost fearful distinctness. Its shape bore not a little similarity to the human hand, though of the smallest pigmy size. Georgiana's lovers were wont to say, that some fairy, at her birth-hour, had laid her tiny hand upon the infant's cheek, and left this impress there, in token of the magic endowments that were to give her such sway over all hearts. Many a desperate swain would have risked life for the privilege of pressing his lips to the mysterious hand. It must not be concealed, however, that the impression wrought by this fairy sign-manual varied exceedingly, according to the difference of temperament in the beholders. Some fastidious persons—but they were exclusively of her own sex—affirmed that the Bloody Hand, as they chose to call it, quite destroyed the effect of Georgiana's beauty, and rendered her countenance even hideous. But it would be as reasonable to say, that one of those small blue stains, which sometimes occur in the purest statuary marble, would convert the Eve of Powers to a monster. Masculine observers, if the birth-mark did not heighten their admiration, contented themselves with wishing it away, that the world might possess one living specimen of ideal loveliness,

without the semblance of a flaw. After his marriage—for he thought little or nothing of the matter before—Aylmer discovered that this was the case with himself.

8 Had she been less beautiful—if Envy's self could have found aught else to sneer at—he might have felt his affection heightened by the prettiness of this mimic hand, now vaguely portrayed, now lost, now stealing forth again, and glimmering to-and-fro with every pulse of emotion that throbbed within her heart. But, seeing her otherwise so perfect, he found this one defect grow more and more intolerable, with every moment of their united lives. It was the fatal flaw of humanity, which Nature, in one shape or another, stamps ineffaceably on all her productions, either to imply that they are temporary and finite, or that their perfection must be wrought by toil and pain. The Crimson Hand expressed the ineludible grip, in which mortality clutches the highest and purest of earthly mould, degrading them into kindred with the lowest, and even with the very brutes, like whom their visible frames return to dust. In this manner, selecting it as the symbol of his wife's liability to sin, sorrow, decay, and death, Aylmer's sombre imagination was not long in rendering the birth-mark a frightful object, causing him more trouble and horror than ever Georgiana's beauty, whether of soul or sense, had given him delight.

9 At all the seasons which should have been their happiest, he invariably, and without intending it—nay, in spite of a purpose to the contrary—reverted to this one disastrous topic. Trifling as it at first appeared, it so connected itself with innumerable trains of thought, and modes of feeling, that it became the central point of all. With the morning twilight, Aylmer opened his eyes upon his wife's face, and recognized the symbol of imperfection; and when they sat together at the evening hearth, his eyes wandered stealthily to her cheek, and beheld, flickering with the blaze of the wood fire, the spectral Hand that wrote mortality, where he would fain have worshipped. Georgiana soon learned to shudder at his gaze. It needed but a glance, with the peculiar expression that his face often wore, to change the roses of her cheek into a deathlike paleness, amid which the Crimson Hand was brought strongly out, like a bas-relief of ruby on the whitest marble.

10 Late one night, when the lights were growing dim, so as hardly to betray the stain on the poor wife's cheek, she herself, for the first time, voluntarily took up the subject.

"Do you remember, my dear Aylmer," said she, with a feeble attempt at a smile—"have you any recollection of a dream, last night, about this odious Hand?" 11

"None!—none whatever!" replied Aylmer, starting; but then he added in a dry, cold tone, affected for the sake of concealing the real depth of his emotion:—"I might well dream of it; for before I fell asleep, it had taken a pretty firm hold of my fancy." 12

"And you did dream of it," continued Georgiana, hastily; for she dreaded lest a gush of tears should interrupt what she had to say—"A terrible dream! I wonder that you can forget it. Is it possible to forget this one expression?—'It is in her heart now—we must have it out!'—Reflect, my husband; for by all means I would have you recall that dream." 13

The mind is in a sad note, when Sleep, the all-involving, cannot confine her spectres within the dim region of her sway, but suffers them to break forth, affrighting this actual life with secrets that perchance belong to a deeper one. Aylmer now remembered his dream. He had fancied himself, with his servant Aminadab, attempting an operation for the removal of the birth-mark. But the deeper went the knife, the deeper sank the Hand, until at length its tiny grasp appeared to have caught hold of Georgiana's heart; whence, however, her husband was inexorably resolved to cut or wrench it away. 14

When the dream had shaped itself perfectly in his memory, Aylmer sat in his wife's presence with a guilty feeling. Truth often finds its way to the mind close-muffled in robes of sleep, and then speaks with uncompromising directness of matters in regard to which we practise an unconscious self-deception, during our waking moments. Until now, he had not been aware of the tyrannizing influence acquired by one idea over his mind, and of the lengths which he might find in his heart to go, for the sake of giving himself peace. 15

"Aylmer," resumed Georgiana, solemnly, "I know not what may be the cost to both of us, to rid me of this fatal birth-mark. Perhaps its removal may cause cureless deformity. Or, it may be, the stain goes as deep as life itself. Again, do we know that there is a possibility, on any terms, of unclasping the firm grip of this little Hand, which was laid upon me before I came into the world?" 16

"Dearest Georgiana, I have spend much thought upon the subject," hastily interrupted Aylmer—"I am convinced of the perfect practicability of its removal." 17

18 "If there be the remotest possibility of it," continued Georgiana, "let the attempt be made, at whatever risk. Danger is nothing to me; for life—while this hateful mark makes me the object of your horror and disgust—life is a burthen which I would fling down with joy. Either remove this dreadful Hand, or take my wretched life! You have deep science! All the world bears witness of it. You have achieved great wonders! Cannot you remove this little, little mark, which I cover with the tips of two small fingers? Is this beyond your power, for the sake of your own peace, and to save your poor wife from madness?"

19 "Noblest—dearest—tenderest wife!" cried Aylmer, rapturously. "Doubt not my power. I have already given this matter the deepest thought—thought which might almost have enlightened me to create a being less perfect than yourself. Georgiana, you have led me deeper than ever into the heart of science. I feel myself fully competent to render this dear cheek as faultless as its fellow; and then, most beloved, what will be my triumph, when I shall have corrected what Nature left imperfect, in her fairest work! Even Pygmalion, when his sculptured woman assumed life, felt not greater ecstasy than mine will be."

20 "It is resolved, then," said Georgiana, faintly smiling,—"And, Aylmer, spare me not, though you should find the birth-mark take refuge in my heart at last."

21 Her husband tenderly kissed her cheek—her right cheek—not that which bore the impress of the Crimson Hand.

22 The next day, Aylmer apprized his wife of a plan that he had formed, whereby he might have opportunity for the intense thought and constant watchfulness, which the proposed operation would require; while Georgiana, likewise, would enjoy the perfect repose essential to its success. They were to seclude themselves in the extensive apartments occupied by Aylmer as a laboratory, and where, during his toilsome youth, he had made discoveries in the elemental powers of nature, that had roused the admiration of all the learned societies in Europe. Seated calmly in this laboratory, the pale philosopher had investigated the secrets of the highest cloud-region, and of the profoundest mines; he had satisfied himself of the causes that kindled and kept alive the fires of the volcano; and had explained the mystery of fountains, and how it is that they gush forth, some so bright and pure, and others with such rich medicinal virtues, from the dark bosom of the earth. Here, too, at an

earlier period, he had studied the wonders of the human frame, and attempted to fathom the very process by which Nature assimilates all her precious influences from earth and air, and from the spiritual world, to create and foster Man, her masterpiece. The latter pursuit, however, Aylmer had long laid aside, in unwilling recognition of the truth, against which all seekers sooner or later stumble, that our great creative Mother, while she amuses us with apparently working in the broadest sunshine, is yet severely careful to keep her own secrets, and, in spite of her pretended openness, shows us nothing but results. She permits us indeed, to mar, but seldom to mend, and, like a jealous patentee, on no account to make. Now, however, Aylmer resumed these half-forgotten investigations; not, of course, with such hopes or wishes as first suggested them; but because they involved much physiological truth, and lay in the path of his proposed scheme for the treatment of Georgiana.

As he led her over the threshold of the laboratory, Georgiana was cold and tremulous. Aylmer looked cheerfully into her face, with intent to reassure her, but was so startled with the intense glow of the birth-mark upon the whiteness of her cheek, that he could not restrain a strong convulsive shudder. His wife fainted. 23

"Aminadab! Aminadab!" shouted Aylmer, stamping violently on the floor. 24

Forthwith, there issued from an inner apartment a man of low stature, but bulky frame, with shaggy hair hanging about his visage, which was grimed with the vapors of the furnace. This personage had been Aylmer's under-worker during his whole scientific career, and was admirably fitted for that office by his great mechanical readiness, and the skill with which, while incapable of comprehending a single principle, he executed all the practical details of his master's experiments. With his vast strength, his shaggy hair, his smoky aspect, and the indescribable earthiness that incrusted him, he seemed to represent man's physical nature; while Aylmer's slender figure, and pale, intellectual face, were no less apt a type of the spiritual element. 25

"Throw open the door of the boudoir, Aminadab," said Aylmer, "and burn a pastille." 26

"Yes, master," answered Aminadab, looking intently at the lifeless form of Georgiana; and then he muttered to himself:—"If she were my wife, I'd never part with that birth-mark." 27

28 When Georgiana recovered consciousness, she found herself breathing an atmosphere of penetrating fragrance, the gentle potency of which had recalled her from her deathlike faintness. The scene around her looked like enchantment. Aylmer had converted those smoky, dingy, sombre rooms, where he had spent his brightest years in recondite pursuits, into a series of beautiful apartments, not unfit to be the secluded abode of a lovely woman. The walls were hung with gorgeous curtains, which imparted the combination of grandeur and grace, that no other species of adornment can achieve; and as they fell from the ceiling to the floor, their rich and ponderous folds, concealing all angles and straight lines, appeared to shut in the scene from infinite space. For aught Georgiana knew, it might be a pavilion among the clouds. And Aylmer, excluding the sunshine, which would have interfered with his chemical processes, had supplied its place with perfumed lamps, emitting flames of various hue, but all uniting in a soft, empurpled radiance. He now knelt by his wife's side, watching her earnestly, but without alarm; for he was confident in his science, and felt that he could draw a magic circle round her, within which no evil might intrude.

29 "Where am I?—Ah, I remember!" said Georgiana, faintly; and she placed her hand over her cheek, to hide the terrible mark from her husband's eyes.

30 "Fear not, dearest!" exclaimed he. "Do not shrink from me! Believe me, Georgiana, I even rejoice in this single imperfection, since it will be such rapture to remove it."

31 "Oh, spare me!" sadly replied his wife—"Pray do not look at it again. I never can forget that convulsive shudder."

32 In order to soothe Georgiana, and, as it were, to release her mind from the burthen of actual things, Aylmer now put in practice some of the light and playful secrets, which science had taught him among its profounder lore. Airy figures, absolutely bodiless ideas, and forms of unsubstantial beauty, came and danced before her, imprinting their momentary footsteps on beams of light. Though she had some indistinct idea of the method of these optical phenomena, still the illusion was almost perfect enough to warrant the belief, that her husband possessed sway over the spiritual world. Then again, when she felt a wish to look forth from her seclusion, immediately, as if her thoughts were answered, the procession of external existence flitted across a screen. The scenery and the figures of actual life were

perfectly represented, but with that bewitching, yet indescribable difference, which always makes a picture, an image, or a shadow, so much more attractive than the original. When wearied of this, Aylmer bade her cast her eyes upon a vessel, containing a quantity of earth. She did so, with little interest at first, but was soon startled, to perceive the germ of a plant, shooting upward from the soil. Then came the slender stalk—the leaves gradually unfolded themselves—and amid them was a perfect and lovely flower.

"It is magical!" cried Georgiana, "I dare not touch it." 33

"Nay, pluck it," answered Aylmer, "pluck it, and inhale its 34
brief perfume while you may. The flower will wither in a few moments, and leave nothing save its brown seed-vessels—but thence may be perpetuated a race as ephemeral as itself."

But Georgiana had no sooner touched the flower than the 35
whole plant suffered a blight, its leaves turning coal-black, as if by the agency of fire.

"There was too powerful a stimulus," said Aylmer thought- 36
fully.

To make up for this abortive experiment, he proposed to 37
take her portrait by a scientific process of his own invention. It was to be effected by rays of light striking upon a polished plate of metal. Georgiana assented—but, on looking at the result, was affrighted to find the features of the portrait blurred and indefinable; while the minute figure of a hand appeared where the cheek should have been. Aylmer snatched the metallic plate, and threw it into a jar of corrosive acid.

Soon, however, he forgot these mortifying failures. In the 38
intervals of study and chemical experiment, he came to her, flushed and exhausted, but seemed invigorated by her presence, and spoke in glowing language of the resources of his art. He gave a history of the long dynasty of the Alchemists, who spent so many ages in quest of the universal solvent, by which the Golden Principle might be elicited from all things vile and base. Aylmer appeared to believe, that, by the plainest scientific logic, it was altogether within the limits of possibility to discover this long-sought medium; but, he added, a philosopher who should go deep enough to acquire the power, would attain too lofty a wisdom to stoop to the exercise of it. Not less singular were his opinions in regard to the Elixir Vitae. He more than intimated, that it was his option to concoct a liquid that should prolong life

for years—perhaps interminably—but that it would produce a discord in nature, which all the world, and chiefly the quaffer of the immortal nostrum, would find cause to curse.

39 "Aylmer, are you in earnest?" asked Georgiana, looking at him with amazement and fear; "it is terrible to possess such power, or even to dream of possessing it!"

40 "Oh, do not tremble, my love!" said her husband, "I would not wrong either you or myself by working such inharmonious effects upon our lives. But I would have you consider how trifling, in comparison, is the skill requisite to remove this little Hand."

41 At the mention of the birth-mark, Georgiana, as usual, shrank, as if a red-hot iron had touched her cheek.

42 Again Aylmer applied himself to his labors. She could hear his voice in the distant furnace-room, giving directions to Aminadab, whose harsh, uncouth, misshapen tones were audible in response, more like the grunt or growl of a brute than human speech. After hours of absence, Aylmer reappeared, and proposed that she should now examine his cabinet of chemical products, and natural treasures of the earth. Among the former he showed her a small vial, in which, he remarked, was contained a gentle yet most powerful fragrance, capable of impregnating all the breezes that blow across a kingdom. They were of inestimable value, the contents of that little vial; and, as he said so, he threw some of the perfume into the air, and filled the room with piercing and invigorating delight.

43 "And what is this?" asked Georgiana, pointing to a small crystal globe, containing a gold-colored liquid. "It is so beautiful to the eye, that I could imagine it the Elixir of Life."

44 "In one sense it is," replied Aylmer, "or rather the Elixir of Immortality. It is the most precious poison that ever was concocted in this world. By its aid, I could apportion the lifetime of any mortal at whom you might point your finger. The strength of the dose would determine whether he were to linger out years, or drop dead in the midst of a breath. No king, on his guarded throne, could keep his life, if I, in my private station, should deem that the welfare of millions justified me in depriving him of it."

45 "Why do you keep such a terrific drug?" inquired Georgiana in horror.

46 "Do not mistrust me, dearest!" said her husband, smiling; "its virtuous potency is yet greater than its harmful one. But,

see! here is a powerful cosmetic. With a few drops of this, in a vase of water, freckles may be washed away as easily as the hands are cleansed. A stronger infusion would take the blood out of the cheek, and leave the rosiest beauty a pale ghost."

"Is it with this lotion that you intend to bathe my cheek?" asked Georgiana anxiously. 47

"Oh, no!" hastily replied her husband—"this is merely superficial. Your case demands a remedy that shall go deeper." 48

In his interviews with Georgiana, Aylmer generally made minute inquiries as to her sensations, and whether the confinement of the rooms, and the temperature of the atmosphere, agreed with her. These questions had such a particular drift, that Georgiana began to conjecture that she was already subjected to certain physical influences, either breathed in with the fragrant air, or taken with her food. She fancied, likewise—but it might be altogether fancy—that there was a stirring up of her system,—a strange indefinite sensation creeping through her veins, and tingling, half painfully, half pleasurably, at her heart. Still, whenever she dared to look into the mirror, there she beheld herself, pale as a white rose, and with the crimson birth-mark stamped upon her cheek. Not even Aylmer now hated it so much as she. 49

To dispel the tedium of the hours which her husband found it necessary to devote to the processes of combination and analysis, Georgiana turned over the volumes of his scientific library. In many dark old tomes, she met with chapters full of romance and poetry. They were the works of the philosophers of the middle ages, such as Albertus Magnus, Cornelius Agrippa, Paracelsus, and the famous friar who created the prophetic Brazen Head. All these antique naturalists stood in advance of their centuries, yet were imbued with some of their credulity, and therefore were believed, and perhaps imagined themselves, to have acquired from the investigation of nature a power above nature, and from physics a sway over the spiritual world. Hardly less curious and imaginative were the early volumes of the Transactions of the Royal Society, in which the members, knowing little of the limits of natural possibility, were continually recording wonders, or proposing methods whereby wonders might be wrought. 50

But, to Georgiana, the most engrossing volume was a large folio from her husband's own hand, in which he had 51 recorded every experiment of his scientific career, with its original aim, the methods adopted for its development, and its final success or failure, with the circumstances to which either event was attributable. The book, in truth, was both the history and emblem of his ardent, ambitious, imaginative, yet practical and laborious, life. He handled physical details, as if there were nothing beyond them; yet spiritualized them all, and redeemed himself from materialism, by his strong and eager aspiration towards the infinite. In his grasp, the veriest clod of earth assumed a soul. Georgiana, as she read, reverenced Aylmer, and loved him more profoundly than ever, but with a less entire dependence on his judgment than heretofore. Much as he had accomplished, she could not but observe that his most splendid successes were almost invariably failures, if compared with the ideal at which he aimed. His brightest diamonds were the merest pebbles, and felt to be so by himself, in comparison with the inestimable gems which lay hidden beyond his reach. The volume, rich with achievements that had won renown for its author, was yet as melancholy a record as ever mortal hand had penned. It was the sad confession, and continual exemplification, of the short-comings of the composite man—the spirit burthened with clay and working in matter—and of the despair that assails the higher nature, at finding itself so miserably thwarted by the earthly part. Perhaps every man of genius, in whatever sphere, might recognize the image of his own experience in Aylmer's journal.

52 So deeply did these reflections affect Georgiana, that she laid her face upon the open volume, and burst into tears. In this situation she was found by her husband.

53 "It is dangerous to read in a sorcerer's books," said he, with a smile, though his countenance was uneasy and displeased. "Georgiana, there are pages in that volume, which I can scarcely glance over and keep my senses. Take heed lest it prove as detrimental to you!"

54 "It has made me worship you more than ever," said she.

55 "Ah! wait for this one success," rejoined he, "then worship me if you will. I shall deem myself hardly unworthy of it. But, come! I have sought you for the luxury of your voice. Sing to me, dearest!"

56 So she poured out the liquid music of her voice to quench the thirst of his spirit. He then took his leave, with a boyish exuberance of gaiety, assuring her that her seclusion would

endure but a little longer, and that the result was already certain. Scarcely had he departed, when Georgiana felt irresistibly impelled to follow him. She had forgotten to inform Aylmer of a symptom, which, for two or three hours past, had begun to excite her attention. It was a sensation in the fatal birth-mark, not painful, but which induced a restlessness throughout her system. Hastening after her husband, she intruded, for the first time, into the laboratory.

The first thing that struck her eye was the furnace, that 57
hot and feverish worker, with the intense glow of its fire, which, by the quantities of soot clustered above it, seemed to have been burning for ages. There was a distilling apparatus in full operation. Around the room were retorts, tubes, cylinders, crucibles, and other apparatus of chemical research. An electrical machine stood ready for immediate use. The atmosphere felt oppressively close, and was tainted with gaseous odors, which had been tormented forth by the processes of science. The severe and homely simplicity of the apartment, with its naked walls and brick pavement, looked strange, accustomed as Georgiana had become to the fantastic elegance of her boudoir. But what chiefly, indeed almost solely, drew her attention, was the aspect of Aylmer himself.

He was pale as death, anxious, and absorbed, and hung 58
over the furnace as if it depended upon his utmost watchfulness whether the liquid, which it was distilling, should be the draught of immortal happiness or misery. How different from the sanguine and joyous mien that he had assumed for Georgiana's encouragement!

"Carefully now, Aminadab! Carefully, thou human ma- 59
chine! Carefully, thou man of clay!" muttered Aylmer, more to himself than his assistant. "Now, if there be a thought too much or too little, it is all over!"

"Hoh! hoh!" mumbled Aminadab—"look, master, look!" 60

Aylmer raised his eyes hastily, and at first reddened, then 61
grew paler than ever, on beholding Georgiana. He rushed towards her, and seized her arm with a grip that left the print of his fingers upon it.

"Why do you come hither? Have you no trust in your 62
husband?" cried he impetuously. "Would you throw the blight of that fatal birth-mark over my labors? It is not well done. Go, prying woman, go!"

"Nay, Aylmer," said Georgiana, with the firmness of which 63
she possessed no stinted endowment, "it is not you that have

a right to complain. You mistrust your wife! You have concealed the anxiety with which you watch the development of this experiment. Think not so unworthily of me, my husband! Tell me all the risk we run; and fear not that I shall shrink, for my share in it is far less than your own!"

64 "No, no, Georgiana!" said Aylmer impatiently, "it must not be."

65 "I submit," replied she calmly. "And, Aylmer, I shall quaff whatever draught you bring me; but it will be on the same principle that would induce me to take a dose of poison, if offered by your hand."

66 "My noble wife," said Aylmer, deeply moved. "I knew not the height and depth of your nature, until now. Nothing shall be concealed. Know, then, that this Crimson Hand, superficial as it seems, has clutched its grasp into your being, with a strength of which I had no previous conception. I have already administered agents powerful enough to do aught except to change your entire physical system. Only one thing remains to be tried. If that fail us, we are ruined!"

67 "Why did you hesitate to tell me this?" asked she.

68 "Because, Georgiana," said Aylmer, in a low voice, "there is danger!"

69 "Danger? There is but one danger—that this horrible stigma shall be left upon my cheek!" cried Georgiana. "Remove it! remove it!—whatever be the cost—or we shall both go mad!"

70 "Heaven knows, your words are too true," said Aylmer, sadly. "And now, dearest, return to your boudoir. In a little while, all will be tested."

71 He conducted her back, and took leave of her with a solemn tenderness, which spoke far more than his words how much was now at stake. After his departure, Georgiana became wrapt in musings. She considered the character of Aylmer, and did it completer justice than at any previous movement. Her heart exulted, while it trembled, at his honorable love, so pure and lofty that it would accept nothing less than perfection, nor miserably make itself contented with an earthlier nature than he had dreamed of. She felt how much more precious was such a sentiment, than that meaner kind which would have borne with the imperfection for her sake, and have been guilty of treason to holy love, by degrading its perfect idea to the level of the actual. And, with her whole spirit, she prayed, that for a

single moment, she might satisfy his highest and deepest conception. Longer than one moment, she well knew, it could not be; for his spirit was ever on the march—ever ascending—and each instant required something that was beyond the scope of the instant before.

The sound of her husband's footsteps aroused her. He 72
bore a crystal goblet, containing a liquor colorless as water, but bright enough to be the draught of immortality. Aylmer was pale; but it seemed rather the consequence of a highly wrought state of mind, and tension of spirit, than of fear or doubt.

"The concoction of the draught has been perfect," said he, 73
in answer to Georgiana's look. "Unless all my science have deceived me, it cannot fail."

"Save on your account, my dearest Aylmer," observed his 74
wife, "I might wish to put off this birth-mark of mortality by relinquishing mortality itself, in preference to any other mode. Life is but a sad possession to those who have attained precisely the degree of moral advancement at which I stand. Were I weaker and blinder, it might be happiness. Were I stronger, it might be endured hopefully. But, being what I find myself, methinks I am of all mortals the most fit to die."

"You are fit for heaven without tasting death!" replied her 75
husband. "But why do we speak of dying? The draught cannot fail. Behold its effect upon this plant!"

On the window-seat there stood a geranium, diseased 76
with yellow blotches, which had overspread all its leaves. Aylmer poured a small quantity of the liquid upon the soil in which it grew. In a little time, when the roots of the plant had taken up the moisture, the unsightly blotches began to be extinguished in a living verdure.

"There needed no proof," said Georgiana, quietly. "Give 77
me the goblet. I joyfully stake all upon your word."

"Drink, then, thou lofty creature!" exclaimed Aylmer, with 78
fervid admiration. "There is no taint of imperfection on thy spirit. Thy sensible frame, too, shall soon be all perfect!"

She quaffed the liquid, and returned the goblet to his 79
hand.

"It is grateful," said she, with a placid smile. "Methinks it 80
is like water from a heavenly fountain; for it contains I know not what of unobtrusive fragrance and deliciousness. It allays a feverish thirst, that had parched me for many days.

Now, dearest, let me sleep. My earthly senses are closing over my spirit, like the leaves round the heart of a rose, at sunset."

81 She spoke the last words with a gentle reluctance, as if it required almost more energy than she could command to pronounce the faint and lingering syllables. Scarcely had they loitered through her lips, ere she was lost in slumber. Aylmer sat by her side, watching her aspect with the emotions proper to a man, the whole value of whose existence was involved in the process now to be tested. Mingled with this mood, however, was the philosophic investigation, characteristic of the man of science. Not the minutest symptom escaped him. A heightened flush of the cheek—a slight irregularity of breath—a quiver of the eyelid—a hardly perceptible tremor through the frame—such were the details which, as the moments passed, he wrote down in his folio volume. Intense thought had set its stamp upon every previous page of that volume; but the thoughts of years were all concentrated upon the last.

82 While thus employed, he failed not to gaze often at the fatal Hand, and not without a shudder. Yet once, by a strange and unaccountable impulse, he pressed it with his lips. His spirit recoiled, however, in the very act, and Georgiana, out of the midst of her deep sleep, moved uneasily and murmured, as if in remonstrance. Again, Aylmer resumed his watch. Nor was it without avail. The Crimson Hand, which at first had been strongly visible upon the marble paleness of Georgiana's cheek, now grew more faintly outlined. She remained not less pale than ever; but the birth-mark, with every breath that came and went, lost somewhat of its former distinctness. Its presence had been awful; its departure was more awful still. Watch the stain of the rainbow fading out of the sky; and you will know how that mysterious symbol passed away.

83 "By Heaven, it is well nigh gone!" said Aylmer to himself, in almost irrepressible ecstasy. "I can scarcely trace it now. Success! Success! And now it is like the faintest rose-color. The slightest flush of blood across her cheek would overcome it. But she is so pale!"

84 He drew aside the window-curtain, and suffered the light of natural day to fall into the room, and rest upon her cheek. At the same time, he heard a gross, hoarse chuckle, which he had long known as his servant Aminadab's expression of delight.

"Ah, clod! Ah earthly mass!" cried Aylmer, laughing in a sort of frenzy. "You have served me well! Matter and Spirit—Earth and Heaven—have both done their part in this! Laugh, thing of senses! You have earned the right to laugh." 85

These exclamations broke Georgiana's sleep. She slowly unclosed her eyes, and gazed into the mirror, which her husband had arranged for that purpose. A faint smile flitted over her lips, when she recognized how barely perceptible was now that Crimson Hand, which had once blazed forth with such disastrous brilliancy as to scare away all their happiness. But then her eyes sought Aylmer's face, with a trouble and anxiety that he could by no means account for. 86

"My poor Aylmer!" murmured she. 87

"Poor? Nay, richest! Happiest! Most favored!" exclaimed he. "My peerless bride, it is successful! You are perfect!" 88

"My poor Aylmer!" she repeated, with a more than human tenderness. "You have aimed loftily!—you have done nobly! Do not repent, that, with so high and pure a feeling, you have rejected the best that earth could offer. Aylmer—dearest Aylmer—I am dying!" 89

Alas, it was too true! The fatal Hand had grappled with the mystery of life, and was the bond by which an angelic spirit kept itself in union with a mortal frame. As the last crimson tint of the birth-mark—that sole token of human imperfection—faded from her cheek, the parting breath of the now perfect woman passed into the atmosphere, and her soul, lingering a moment near her husband, took its heavenward flight. Then a hoarse, chuckling laugh was heard again! Thus ever does the gross Fatality of Earth exult in its invariable triumph over the immortal essence, which, in this dim sphere of half-development, demands the completeness of a higher state. Yet, had Aylmer reached a profounder wisdom, he need not thus have flung away the happiness, which would have woven his mortal life of the self-same texture with the celestial. The momentary circumstance was too strong for him; he failed to look beyond the shadowy scope of Time, and living once for all in Eternity, to find the perfect Future in the present. 90

Jonathan King

New Genetic Technology: Prospects and Hazards

Jonathan King, who holds a doctorate in genetics, teaches biology at Massachusetts Institute of Technology. He wrote the following essay in 1980 for Technology Review, *a product of the MIT alumni association.*

1 During the past 30 years we have witnessed extraordinary advances in knowledge of fundamental biological processes, particularly at the cellular and molecular level. These advances have derived in large part from the major investment of public funds in the training of biomedical scientists and support for biomedical research, conducted by the governments of the industrialized countries since the end of World War II. The 1978 budget for biomedical research in the U.S. is about 3 billion dollars. This is one thousand times the federal expenditure for biomedical research in 1948.

2 In the U.S., these programs originated in the pressing need for coordinated biomedical research to deal with the immense damage suffered by soldiers during and after World War II. The federal funding and encouragement of cooperative, organized research ventures was highly successful and continued after the war, when public pressure overcame opposition from the private medical sector.

3 The well-financed program of training and research has led to: the elucidation of the chemical structure of the genetic material, DNA; the understanding of the organization of the genetic material in linear segments, the genes; the recognition that genes are blueprints for the structure of protein molecules, which form both the building blocks and working parts of cells; the understanding of the roles of the thin membranes that divide cells into different compartments; and enhanced knowledge of the organization and functions of the complex ribosomes, themselves composed of more than 70 different kinds of protein molecules, which serve as the factories for assembling new proteins according to the instructions of the genes. Thus, the mental and physical labors of tens of thousands of laboratory workers have revealed the extraordinary richness and creativity of

the mechanisms by which living things reproduce themselves and interact with their environment.

4 In the industrialized nations, the major steps in cutting infant mortality, increasing the life span, and controlling infectious disease occurred earlier in this century. These resulted from economic struggles, led principally by the trade unions, for an improved standard of living—notably the shorter working day, increased wages, and improved working conditions. They were aided by public health professionals who fought for improved sanitation, water supplies, and food, thereby helping to eliminate cholera, diphtheria, scarlet fever, and other scourges of the urban poor.

5 The more recently acquired understanding of the biochemistry of bacteria and the role of viruses in human disease, and the development of tissue culture technology for growing cells and viruses in the test tube, laid the basis for eliminating a further set of diseases: poliovirus infections in the 1950s; rinderpest virus, a major killer of African cattle, in the 1960s; and more recently, the dramatic eradication of smallpox. (Twenty years ago in India alone there were 150,000 cases of smallpox, causing 41,000 deaths.) The elimination of rinderpest and smallpox viruses resulted from campaigns organized and coordinated by the United Nations.

6 The scientific basis now exists for mounting research campaigns against viral diseases such as Rift Valley fever in North Africa, yellow fever in Central Africa, and hemorrhagic fever in Asia, as well as such widespread parasitic diseases as schistosomiasis and filariasis, including one of its more tragic forms, river blindness.

7 Of course many of these diseases are intimately associated with particular conditions of life—local housing, agriculture, water supplies and sanitation, and nutrition. Increased knowledge of the biochemistry and physiology of particular organisms does not substitute for the need to study the interrelationships of organisms within ecosystems as well as the social and economic conditions of human society.

8 Smallpox infects only humans for example, enabling all potential hosts to be identified and vaccinated. Many of the other viruses that affect humans also live in insects or animals and other parts of the ecosystem. These cannot be eradicated by the same strategies used for smallpox. Cholera provides another example: it is still a major problem in

Calcutta, where the virus was first isolated in 1817. Indian scientists understand the microbiology of cholera, but the poverty that is partly the legacy of British imperialism must be overcome before the disease can be eradicated.

9 Another major contribution of modern molecular genetics and cell biology is the recognition that much of human cancer is due to damage by external agents to the genes of human somatic cells. These agents include industrial chemicals such as aniline dyes, which cause bladder cancer, vinyl chloride, which causes liver cancer, and most forms of ionizing radiation. For example, high levels of leukemia and bone cancer are found among survivors of the Hiroshima and Nagasaki holocausts and among people repeatedly exposed to nuclear testing. Other cancers from excessive medical irradiation and exposure to mismanaged nuclear waste will likely manifest themselves in coming years.

10 These major breakthroughs have led to the recognition among a sector of the scientific community that much human cancer is preventable. Unfortunately, powerful economic forces have vested interests in the continued production and sale of these agents. Therefore, the prevention of cancer will involve a social struggle similar to those earlier in the century for better working conditions.

11 In the United States, we do not have a national system of comprehensive medical care. This limits our ability to realize the fullest fruits of our biomedical research. Without a comprehensive health care system, it is difficult to couple research to health care needs. When substantial advances occur, they are sometimes available only to economically advantaged groups. Farm workers in Texas, for example, have an average life span many years less than the national average.

Recombinant DNA Technology

12 The growth of biological knowledge has engendered the development of very sophisticated biochemical genetic technologies. These technologies, which are today tools for the accumulation of knowledge of organisms, are also the tools for the genetic and biochemical modification of those organisms.

13 The most dramatic and revolutionary of these technologies is recombinant DNA technology, or genetic engineering—the

ability to incorporate segments of DNA, i.e., genetic material, derived from one organism into the cells of another organism. The donor and recipient may be closely related (for example, two strains of bacteria), or they may be very different (for example, a mouse and a bacterium).

Members of the same species exchange segments of genetic material regularly; this is the biological basis of mating and sex—the exchange of equivalent segments of genetic material of parents, generating new genetic combinations in the offspring, which may prove advantageous in adapting to a changing environment. 14

However, exchange of genetic material between members of unrelated species is rare. Organisms adapting to different environments—to different niches, to use the ecologists' term—evolve different "instructions"; different genes. Exchange between such organisms is generally not useful, and therefore rarely observed in nature. 15

Recombinant DNA technology is useful in biological research, however. Suppose I am studying how pancreatic cells produce insulin and why liver cells do not. I might remove the pancreas from a mouse, and extract from the pancreas cells the long, stringy DNA molecules that represent the blueprints for being a mouse. By treating the isolated DNA molecules with a special protein catalyst, the DNA can be cut into shorter pieces, with the cut ends left sticky. Using similar techniques, I can isolate DNA molecules from a bacterium, whose cut ends are also sticky. Usually this bacterium will be common in the human gut, and called *E. coli.* On mixing the two tubes of DNA, the sticky ends of mouse DNA will join with lengths of bacterial DNA. Such molecules, containing the genetic material of two different organisms, are termed "recombinant DNA" molecules. 16

These recombinant molecules can then be reincorporated into a living, growing bacterium. When the bacterium divides, it will reproduce its own DNA, and also reproduce the piece of mouse DNA, or gene. If we isolate the bacterium and incubate it in some beef broth, the next morning we will have 100 billion daughter cells. Each of these will have an identical copy of the mouse gene. Molecular biologists speak of this as "cloning" a mouse gene. 17

Because bacteria, despite their complexity, are vastly simpler than mouse cells, the techniques of chemistry and biochemistry can be used to study the mouse gene and 18 sometimes the protein whose structure it encodes. From these studies, we might learn about what signals turn this gene on in some cells and off in others. We might also get some hint as to how the genetic information stored in the nucleus of a cell provides the blueprint for the three-dimensional structure and function of the cell.

19 This technology requires no more equipment than is found in a common college microbiology laboratory. Therefore, it is being used in a vast variety of research situations. Furthermore, recently developed techniques make it possible to transfer in the *other* direction to introduce DNA of a bacterium into a mouse cell. Similarly, one can introduce DNA from one species of mouse into another, or transfer small segments of DNA from human cells to mouse cells or other human cells. This technology, developed originally from microbiology and molecular genetics, provides the technological basis for human genetic manipulation. Because of the intense level of research—hundreds of laboratories are using these techniques to study the genes of animal cells—experiments labelled "impossible" become routine six months later.

Commercial Exploitation and Biological Hazards

20 Though the scientific community generally views recombinant DNA technology as a research tool, private corporations have moved rapidly to construct and market strains of economically or agriculturally valuable organisms and their byproducts. In addition to the activities of small venture firms and most of the pharmaceutical industry, substantial investments have been made by transnational corporations such as International Nickel, Standard Oil, and Imperial Chemical Industries. A well-publicized case in the drug industry is Eli Lilly Corp.'s plan to grow strains of *E. coli* bacteria containing insulin for sale to diabetics. Strains have already been constructed or isolated that contain the human insulin gene and that synthesize the protein and export a version of it outside the cell. Lilly believes this will be less expensive than its current practice of extracting insulin from the pancreas of beef cattle. The sale of insulin to diabetics is a $100-million-a-year business.

21 As most people know, there has been substantial debate over recombinant DNA technology. The debate has centered

on whether bacteria incorporating foreign DNA constitute new hazards to humans or to other species of the ecosystem. For example, though *E. coli* is a normal inhabitant of our intestinal tract, certain strains are the cause of infantile meningitis and diarrhea, urinary tract infections in women, and serious bloodstream infections in hospital patients. In many cases, the pathogenicity of these strains stems from the parasites—derivations of wild strains—that they harbor. Were such strains to synthesize and export insulin, they could well cause additional damage.

To the extent that such strains escape into the environment and establish themselves in some niche, they constitute a form of pollution, an unwanted byproduct of technology. But such biological pollution is qualitatively different from other forms of pollution such as heavy metals, oil, and synthetic chemicals. Organisms reproduce themselves and cannot easily be removed from the ecosystem. This self-reproducing potential of the byproducts of recombinant DNA technology is the reason for the special concern of many scientists and the public. 22

After considerable internal debate and controversy, the scientific community adopted guidelines requiring that recombinant DNA experiments be performed with weakened strains of bacteria unlikely to survive outside the laboratory, and that physical containment procedures be used, making it even less likely that such strains would escape. 23

These guidelines are now referred to as the NIH (National Institutes of Health) guidelines. A controversy arose in Cambridge, Mass over adequacy of these guidelines, and whether compliance should be left to scientists or overseen by the community and laboratory workers. Cambridge and a few other communities subsequently passed ordinances making the NIH guidelines mandatory. However, they do not apply to private industry or non-federally funded research. Thus, no laws regulate the activities of private companies engaged in genetic engineering in the U.S., although some have been proposed by a number of legislators. These were defeated by the combined influence of the corporations and a wing of the scientific community more interested in exploiting the technology than in protecting the public. In Great Britain, however, these guidelines apply to the entire country, and are supported by the Trade Union Congress and strengthened by representation of the workers involved. 24

25 Unfortunately, during 1979 the guidelines were severely weakened by the efforts of a group of scientists actively engaged in the development of recombinant DNA technology in alliance with commercial interests. These scientists first argued that the risks are trivial, since the guidelines prevent the construction or release of hazardous strains. This argument was then switched around: since the risks are trivial, there is no need for strong guidelines. The negative outcomes of a few risk-assessment experiments were widely publicized, while the positive results reported in the same studies were actively ignored and suppressed. The guidelines have now been so weakened that rather than protecting public health, they in fact protect those engaged in the technology from public inquiry and regulation. The few within the scientific community who understand the major misrepresentations that have occurred, and are inclined to critique them, are inhibited by the fact that we receive our funding from the NIH.

26 Some observers have found it difficult to understand why scientists should be concerned about community-imposed safety standards on laboratory work. Many safety constraints are inconvenient but have a relatively minor effect, as one can see by the rate at which work proceeds. However, safety procedures that are a minor inconvenience on work involving 10 milliliters of cells have a very different impact on the production of 1000 liters at the commercial scale. If concerned scientists, citizens, and workers demand strong safety standards, these will not only decrease profit margins but will also result in greater community and worker control over the production process.

27 New technologies often result in human casualties, such as respiratory damage in coal miners after the development of deep mining, the induction of bladder cancer in workers in British and German chemical industries, and lung cancer among uranium miners. And the costs, as well as the suffering, have generally been borne by the workers themselves. In the case of recombinant DNA technology, we must insist that such costs be reckoned with from the beginning as part of the production process, and not be passed on to an unwilling or unknowing population. It is not just a question of costs versus benefits, but who gets the benefits and who bears the costs.

28 Attempts to protect capital investments and profit margins distort certain features of the scientific process. A number of

corporations involved in exploiting recombinant DNA technology have obtained patents on organisms and processes, even though all of the developmental work was publicly financed. The scientists involved simply disassociated themselves from public funding and entered into relations with private companies, thus appropriating public knowledge for private accumulation of wealth not generally available to academic scientists.

Although some scientific/industrial spokespersons have called for the unfettered (and unregulated) "search for truth," the controversy over recombinant DNA technology is not about freedom of enquiry; it is about regulating those who want to rashly exploit for private gain the fruits of knowledge that should belong to all. 29

Agricultural and Microbial Productivity

A potentially productive application of recombinant DNA and other molecular genetic technologies is the development of new strains of plants and microorganisms. The danger here is familiar: the strains developed in the industrialized countries will be designed for capital-intensive agriculture, thus requiring chemical fertilizer, pesticides, and the destruction of many indigenous ecosystems. But the most productive uses with respect to preservation of human and natural resources will probably involve less manipulative technologies. 30

For example, in India, China, and Pakistan, microbial technologies for converting manure and waste into clean gas for cooking, heating, and transportation have been developed with existing bacterial strains. And the residue provides a good source of fertilizer. Similarly in India, Burma, and Nepal, very successful projects to fertilize rice paddies have utilized strains of nitrogen-fixing blue-green algae. 31

If local education and know-how are not commensurate with the sophistication of the imported technologies, proper investigation will be unlikely, and it will be difficult for the people of the developing countries to assert control. 32

A second danger derives from corporations who move production facilities for modified organisms from industrialized countries to developing countries to escape regulation. Of course, this is done in the name of technology 33 transfer. Ironically, the health hazards of recombinant DNA technology are much more acute in developing countries, where conditions for the spread of disease still exist.

Human Genetic Engineering

34 The new biological technologies make possible the ultimate modification: the "engineering" of human beings. There is a great deal of research with small mammals such as mice and rabbits, both in introducing segments of DNA into their cells and analyzing the DNA by taking pieces out of the cells and cloning them in bacteria. For example, attempts are now being made to remove bone marrow cells (which form blood cells) from an animal and insert into those cells the DNA segment coding for hemoglobin. The cell with the added segment can be transplanted back into the animal. This is a model for gene therapy of inherited blood diseases such as sickle cell anemia and thalassemia.

35 The use of genetic technologies on human beings will expand in the medical sector far more rapidly than anyone can accurately predict. This will alleviate the suffering of a small number of individuals but will also generate many moral and social dilemmas.

36 The development of human *in vitro* fertilization by Edwards and Steptoe has vastly increased the potential for human genetic manipulation. One can obtain in the test tube the earliest stages of a human embryo. By introducing DNA, or cells altered in the laboratory, into this embryo and then reimplanting the embryo into the womb, the possibility exists for introducing genetic change in most of the cells of the body—including the germ-line cells. Thus, changes would be passed on to subsequent generations.

37 Prior to the genetic manipulation itself, the use of DNA technology to physically analyze the DNA of human cells will vastly increase. Some of this analysis will be used for screening purposes, as in rare cases where the change in the DNA and the relationship to disease is known (in certain rare inherited blood diseases, for example). Instead of examining the blood in the already mature fetus, we will examine the DNA of the cells of the early embryo or the parents.

38 Researchers will be confronted by the full range of genetic variation among individuals. What constitutes a genetic

defect and what constitutes genetic variation? Historically, the value of many genetically determined features such as skin color and hair character were socially determined. What is a defect in one society is a desirable characteristic in another. At the biological level, the sickle cell trait is considered by some a genetic defect in the United States. But in central Africa it is necessary for survival in malaria-infested areas, rendering the blood cells resistant to the malarial parasite.

Another problem is the distortion of the true causes of human disease. Genetic engineering technology will focus attention on affected individuals and their genes. As a result there will be a strong tendency to lose sight of the agents that caused the damage in the first place, such as mutagenic and carcinogenic chemicals and radiation. Most problems are not with our genes; they are in recreating a society in which the genes of individuals are protected from unnecessary damage. It is critically important that the ability to identify genetic damage serves as a first step in identifying the *cause* of the damage wherever possible, and removing it from the ecosphere. 39

Note that not all conditions resulting from damage to genes are inherited. If the egg is damaged, resulting in altered chromosome compositions, as in Down's syndrome, this is not passed on to the next generation. 40

Reordering Priorities

We must support every effort to expand and increase knowledge of the functioning of living things and their interactions with the environment, and of the effect of human society on these interactions. This knowledge must be available to all the peoples of the earth and not just a technocratic elite. 41

At present, a number of the most potent biological technologies are being developed by transnational corporations and institutions who serve private gain rather than social and economic justice. To select what is needed in a particular area will require very broad biological, ecological, and agricultural education. The same lessons that many peoples of the world have learned with respect to the import of technologies of resource exploitation will have to be applied in this field if the fruits of biological knowledge are to be 42 used to attain an equitable, participatory, and sustainable society.

43 Citizen participation in the decision-making processes, whether on biohazards committees, protection-of-human-subjects committees, or other appropriate forms, must be encouraged. Appropriate support on an international level might be achieved through efforts of the International Labor Organization, the World Health Organization, and the United Nations Agency for Development. In the United States, it is critically important to involve the Environmental Protection Agency and the Occupational Safety and Health Agency in the regulation of genetic technologies. NIH lacks the experience and inclination to regulate a burgeoning multimillion-dollar industry.

44 In the area of human experimentation and genetic manipulation, we must ensure that the development of very sophisticated technologies for helping a small number of individuals does not obscure the pressing need for eliminating widespread causes of disease and genetic damage. An appropriate form might be task forces on protection of the genetic inheritance from environmental and social damage. This will entail input into the setting of priorities in biomedical research (i.e., what technologies to develop) and not just into the use of technology that is *already* developed. Today we can transplant kidneys, but we cannot prevent kidney disease.

45 Public health, social ethics, and the problems of underdeveloped rural societies are not the highest priority of experts in molecular genetics and antibiotic production. We must insure the fullest participation of different sectors of society in the development of biological technologies, not as a cosmetic nod to democracy, but because this is the only way to maximize the social benefits and minimize the risks. We are entering a new era of direct modification and design of organisms. These endeavors will require new social forms and the development of a much higher level of democratic process within the technological sphere.

To Fight World Hunger

The ad on these two pages was devised by ICI AMERICAS, Inc., and appeared in a number of weekly news magazines in 1989. The original picture of the plant was in full color, the seedling a brilliant green against a blue sky and the brown earth.

To help fight world hunger, a new plant is being built.

Last year, millions of tons of grain were lost due to disease and drought. Grain that, had it survived, could have helped others do the same.

And while an estimated 10% of the world's population went hungry, more than 1 million square miles of the world's most arable land was lost.

For the many millions of people who went hungry last year, there is no greater technological breakthrough we could achieve than one which results in placing food on an empty table.

Today, ICI technology already helps more farmers throughout the world grow more food than any other company. But there's still more work to be done.

To that end, ICI is dedicated to the continued development of innovative agricultural products and technologies. And we back our efforts by spending millions on worldwide agricultural research to develop improved methods of food production.

Presently, our researchers are working with plant breeding technology to develop high-yield, disease and drought-tolerant crops. Crops which could one day help put an end to world hunger.

Plant bioscience is just one example of ICI's commitment to finding solutions to world problems.

Our health care efforts are helping in the treatment of breast cancer and other serious diseases. We're working on the development of new, ozone-friendly fluorocarbons. And we're revolutionizing the field of criminal investigation with the development of genetic fingerprinting.

Through research and innovation, ICI is developing products and technologies to help build a better tomorrow.

And for the millions of people who starve each year, plant a seed of hope.

World Problems World Solutions

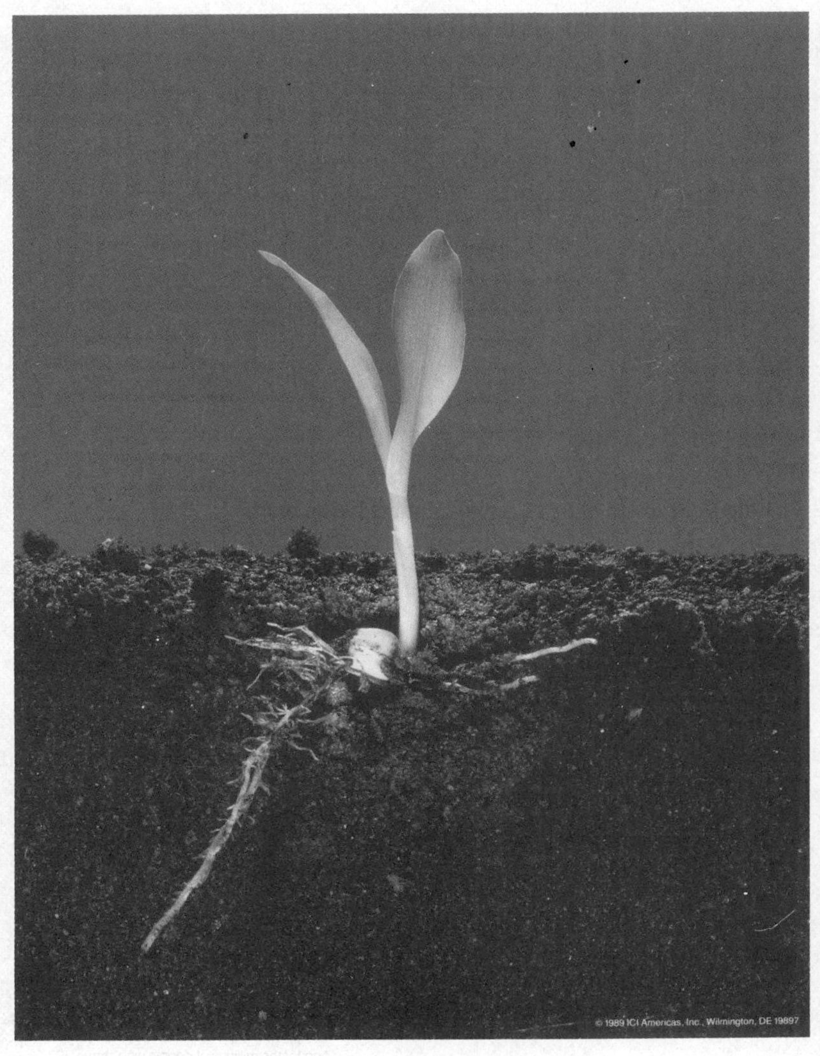
© 1989 ICI Americas, Inc., Wilmington, DE 19897

Susan Wright

Genetic Engineering: The Risks

Susan Wright, a consultant to the National and World Councils of Churches, directs the Science and Society program at the University of Michigan. The following essay appeared in 1983 in Christianity and Crisis, *a Christian journal of opinion. It was adapted from an article written with Robert L. Sinsheimer for the* Bulletin of the Atomic Scientists, *1983.*

Media coverage of genetic engineering has painted a picture of an optimistic and benign future: industrialized bacteria meekly pumping out lifesaving quantities of insulin and interferon; a combination of genetic engineering and fetal surgery ultimately eradicating genetic diseases; self-fertilizing plants ending hunger and famine. But the media picture may be too optimistic, too benign. As research and development (R and D) in genetic engineering accelerates, two questions need critical attention. 1

1. What hazards to workers, the environment, and the general population will be generated by research and full-scale industrial activities?
2. What are the real goals of new military interest in this field?

Recombinant DNA, or gene splicing, techniques were developed in 1972, in a few California biological research laboratories. Gene splicing is a method of chemically cutting and joining DNA, the hereditary material of living things. Because DNA usually has the same structure regardless of its source, the techniques can be used to remove genes from a donor organism and transfer them into a recipient, where, under appropriate conditions, they can function. For example, in 1978, the human insulin gene was introduced into the bacterium *Escherichia coli* so that the bacterium was "programmed" to make human insulin. More recently, recombinant DNA containing the gene for growth hormone was inserted into fertilized mouse cells. In some cases, the gene functioned, and mice bearing this gene grew to twice their normal size. 2

In a word, gene splicing offers the potential to redesign 3

life (in genetic terms), to construct new combinations of genes, and new organisms with new functions.

4 Because it signified different potentialities to different sectors of society, it was clear from the first that this technology would be controversial. Biologists had at hand a set of powerful research tools and it seemed likely that these tools would yield a new understanding of the structure and function of genes. (And, indeed they have.) Industrial and commercial interests foresaw a wide range of applications in techniques that could be used to transform bacteria into miniscule "factories" for producing substances not easily manufactured through conventional processes. It also seemed likely that in the future the techniques could be applied to commercially important plants and animals. Plants might be endowed with their own nitrogen-fixing genes; cows might be endowed with extra growth hormone genes; and surely some task would be found for the giant mice.

5 It was equally clear that the techniques might generate a broad range of problems. Concerns about health hazards and hazards to the environment were expressed. If microorganisms, or other organisms, were endowed with new functions, might they not find new ecological niches, and with what impact on the rest of the living world? For example, could an *E.coli* bacterium, endowed with the gene for *cellulase,* the enzyme that breaks down cellulose, find a niche in the human intestine? If so, would such an organism cause epidemics of chronic diarrhea? Could a plant endowed with nitrogen-fixing genes, and thus self-fertilizing, become a persistent weed, threatening the survival of other plants? The potential for military application was apparent. If gene splicing could find application in commerce, why not in warfare? For example, could the technology be used for toxin manufacture, or for construction of novel pathogens against which an adversary would have no defense?

6 Concern also focused on:

- the potential for *human genetic engineering.* If gene splicing could be used to redesign mice, why not human beings? Who would decide whether this would be desirable, and for what purpose?
- the *proprietary status* of redesigned forms of life. Was it ethically acceptable for corporations to patent redesigned genes, or organisms containing such genes, or the progeny of such organisms?

- the *terms of development* of this technology: Whose priorities and values should determine how this potent technology would be applied, and toward what ends? Should the reshaping of life be left to market forces to determine?

Many of these issues were either recognized at the outset or emerged shortly after the first gene-splicing experiments, and as they were aired, it became apparent that perceptions were mixed. Many of those close to the development of the techniques saw mainly the advantages they would yield for science and industry. But others saw a possibly highly destructive impact on society and on the environment. These critics focused on the power of the new techniques and argued that increasing the power to intervene in natural processes had frequently brought the power to disrupt them as well. They pointed to the history of nuclear fission and synthetic organic chemicals. Would the technology of genetic manipulation likewise generate serious hazards? Furthermore, would these hazards be uncontrollable since they would be borne by living organisms that could reproduce themselves? And even if the techniques turned out to be safe when used in research or industry, could they be deliberately applied in biological warfare, or in unethical forms of genetic treatment? 7

The first response to these concerns came from the community of molecular biologists in whose midst the techniques had been developed. In 1974, at an international conference held in Asilomar, California, leading molecular biologists called on governments in countries where research was underway to assess the risks and to develop controls. 8

This meeting is interesting as much for what was *not* addressed as for what it achieved: The only issue addressed in depth was the question of the hazards of research. Other concerns were either not raised or quickly dropped from the agenda. Health hazards, and controls to protect against them, quickly became the center of concern. This led eventually to the promulgation of guidelines for recombinant DNA research in most countries involved in this work. In the United States, guidelines were written by an advisory committee to the National Institutes of Health. 9

In 1976, these guidelines were quite strict. Six different categories of R and D were prohibited; much other research 10 could proceed only under rigorous containment conditions; all research was screened both nationally and locally. There was, however, always a major loophole: the guidelines applied only to government-supported R and D; R and D supported by other sources, such as pharmaceutical companies or companies founded by molecular biologists themselves, was not covered.

11 Only six years after the promulgation of those guidelines, a dramatic shift of attitude has taken place. (This has been particularly striking in the United States.) Within the scientific community, initial fears of potential harm have been widely (although not completely) dismissed. For the general public, the controversy has all but faded away. Controls have been progressively dismantled. At the present time, there are effective controls for only the most hazardous experiments. For other work—the vast majority of recombinant DNA experiments and processes—there is virtually no provision for oversight or containment.

12 The new "biobusiness," based on recombinant DNA and other forms of genetic manipulation, is now booming. Production processes using genetically manipulated organisms are functioning, and their first products are being marketed. Most major oil, chemical, and pharmaceutical corporations are investing heavily in the field. A race to achieve technological dominance began to accelerate in 1978, and continues today. It is this side of recombinant DNA technology that is constantly reflected in the press: Commercial applications—usually portrayed as "benefits"—are highlighted; hazards and social problems are played down or—what is more usual—ignored.

13 But have the problems been resolved? Is it really the case that we can now sit back and wait for the new genetic paradise to come to us, complete with giant mice?

14 I shall argue no: the problems are still there, some, now, in a more acute form than before. I strongly disagree with the conventional wisdom: that the questions surrounding recombinant DNA activities are "non-issues," or, in other words, that the recombinant DNA issue has been decided largely "on its merits" (that is, it has been "scientifically," and "objectively" resolved).

15 First, the question of hazards that may arise *inadvertently*—as side effects of recombinant DNA activities—is largely unresolved. Second, the question of *deliberate* construction of hazardous organisms has not been addressed; further, there are now pressing reasons to do so.

The question of hazards arising inadvertently in the course of recombinant DNA research or industrial production has long been the focus of concern and the primary reason for development of controls. At one end of the spectrum are gene combinations which would almost certainly produce a fearsome organism. (For example, introduction of the botulinus toxin gene into *E.coli* would likely pose serious hazard.) At the other end of the spectrum are procedures which everyone would agree are innocuous (for example, the insertion into *E.coli* of a gene from an organism that naturally exchanges genes with *E.coli*.). 16

Between these two extremes, there is an enormous number of possible gene combinations, and their implications have been marked by a great deal of controversy and very little solid scientific consensus based on good evidence. Would it be safe, for example, to be exposed to *E.coli* bacteria programmed to make insulin, or interferon, or growth hormone? We have little evidence to draw on, certainly nothing that scientists would call "definitive." 17

Those who claim that the recombinant DNA "problem" has been solved agree that we now have "new evidence" which shows that the procedures are safe, that the original fears were unfounded, and that controls are unnecessary (see Sheldon Krimsky, *Genetic Alchemy*, MIT Press, 1982). Note that the scope of this claim is large: it applies not only to the techniques used today, but to future refinements as well. I would argue that while this "new evidence" is applicable to considerations of hazard, it is applicable only in a limited way in which major issues are left unresolved. 18

Let me briefly indicate two examples: 19

1. The "epidemic pathogen" argument. One of the arguments used most extensively to downplay hazards is that the bacterium often used for recombinant DNA experiments (*E.coli* K-12) cannot be converted into an epidemic pathogen (i.e., a disease-causing organism that spreads throughout a human population). There is solid consensus that this generalization is correct: K-12 is a weakly bug (usually), and it is unlikely to survive in competition with the normal gut flora. So it is unlikely to be transmitted from one person to another. 20

It is important to understand what this argument does *not* say: 21

First, the argument says nothing about what happens to the individual unfortunate enough to be the first to be exposed to *E.coli* bacteria manipulated to make a harmful 22 substance. It doesn't matter that the bacteria would all die out in 24 hours: by that time, the damage might be done.

23 Second, the argument does not apply to organisms other than *E.coli* K-12. It does not apply, for example, to the relatives of K-12—the strains of *E. coli* that live in the human intestine, which under some circumstances can survive and colonize the guts of human beings quite effectively. It does not apply to all the other organisms being used for recombinant DNA activities: *Salmonella* (a food contaminant), *Pseudomonas* (an organism responsible for a wide range of hospital-acquired and other infections), viruses, etc. So there is a wide range of possibilities that the "epidemic pathogen" argument does not cover.

24 **2. The "intervening sequence" argument.** In 1977, new evidence on the structure of genes of higher organisms showed that most DNA of higher organisms would not be automatically processed by bacteria. This meant that the possibility of accidentally constructing bacteria capable of synthesizing proteins encoded in the genes of higher organisms was remote.

25 This argument, too, is limited in scope. It does not apply to the whole range of recombinant DNA activities *deliberately* aimed at enabling bacteria to make proteins usually made only by higher organisms. It does not apply to experiments in which genes from bacterial species are transferred into other bacteria, where expression of these genes may occur.

26 Arguments like these—all partial, with a limited range of applicability—have provided a veneer of scientific objectivity for the position that controls for recombinant DNA activities are no longer necessary. They have been used repeatedly since 1977 to justify progressive dismantling of controls to the point where there are now virtually no controls whatever. I think that detailed analysis of these and other arguments shows that, in fact, the recombinant DNA issue was not "decided on its merits": The decision to dismantle controls was political, not scientific.

27 A more objective assessment would conclude that in fact we still know very little about possible recombinant DNA hazards, particularly those involved in industrial processes. New biotechnologies will use very large volumes of microorganisms such as *E.coli, B.subtilis, Pseudomonas* and yeast in fermentation processes. Within the workplace, possible occupational hazards include exposure to microorganisms

containing recombinant DNA, exposure to the products of such organisms, and exposure to hazardous chemicals used in extraction and purification. Outside the workplace, hazards may be generated by spills and leaks, improper ventilation, and improper disposal of wastes. For example, organisms released in large quantities into surface waters or sewer systems might transfer harmful characteristics to other organisms capable of infecting humans or animals. There is very little hard evidence, at present, concerning such possibilities. But the evidence we do have is not particularly reassuring. For example, it has been shown that even a weakened strain of *E.coli* not only survives in sewage but also survives secondary sewage treatment. But perhaps more importantly in the long run, the direction of recombinant DNA research and development is toward increasing both the variety of organisms used for synthesis of new products and the efficiency with which they can function. Genetic manipulation techniques, if they are to compete effectively with existing production methods, must be made more efficient than they are at present. Thus, if there are hazards, it is likely that they will increase as the commercial potential of recombinant DNA technology is realized.

If the issue of hazards that arise inadvertently is unre- 28
solved, few would argue against the possibility of *deliberate* design and construction of a hazardous organism with recombinant DNA techniques. That, one might say, is the ultimate biohazard, and the obvious applications are for military and terrorist purposes.

The question of military application of recombinant DNA 29
technology has always been in the background of the controversy. There are several reasons why the issue needs to be addressed, and why, in the last three years, this need has become pressing. (See Robert Sinsheimer and Susan Wright, "Recombinant DNA and Biological Warfare," *Bulletin of the Atomic Scientists,* November 1983.)

First, the progressive weakening of controls for recombi- 30
nant DNA technology in the last few years means that it is now permissible to do experiments which were originally seen as so hazardous that they were prohibited. Consequently, a variety of experiments are now being planned to introduce into bacteria genes for some of the most potent toxins known to science. We may expect that the number of such experiments will increase. And while these experiments are being undertaken in the civilian sector for scientific and

medical reasons, they may be of equal if not greater interest to the military. Thus an unintended consequence of the weakening of controls is likely to be the provision of a body of knowledge on the behavior of novel biological agents which could find military application.

31 Second, since 1980, new military interests in biological research in general and in recombinant DNA technology in particular have emerged:

32 1. Data on support for biological research by the Department of Defense (DOD) and the National Institutes of Health (NIH) show that in the past few years, DOD support has increased substantially whereas NIH support has declined. In 1980–82, defense obligations for all biological research and for biological research in the universities increased in real terms by 15 percent and 24 percent respectively. (The percentages in terms of current dollars are, of course, more dramatic: 36 percent vs. 47 percent.) On the other hand, the corresponding changes for NIH were decreases of 4.1 percent and 3.6 percent respectively. We may expect that biologists will feel increased pressure to seek support from military sources.

33 2. In FY 1980, the DOD initiated programs of research using recombinant DNA technology. There are at present some 15 unclassified projects underway and an expansion of this program is planned. Many of these projects focus on cloning of genes for pathogenic organisms in order to make vaccines against them. No fewer than six of these projects focus on making the enzyme acetylicholinesterase, a neural transmitter attacked by nerve gas. (The DOD frankly acknowledges that the teams of scientists involved in these projects are competing with one another for results.) All of these projects are justified as "defensive" research (a point of legal importance since, as I will discuss later, the United States is a party to the Biological Weapons Convention).

34 3. In addition, the DOD has recognized that recombinant DNA (as well as other newer biological techniques) could also present new military problems because of its potential to enhance such factors as the selectivity, lethality, and stability of microorganisms. DOD reports to Congress for FY 1980 and FY 1981 characterize this possibility as a "new threat." And in response to this perception, the DOD contemplates new lines of research, the objective of this research being: "to provide a better understanding of . . . [disease-causing organisms] *with or without* genetic manip-

ulation." That passage suggests that DOD planners contemplate projects using recombinant DNA techniques to change or accentuate the properties of disease-causing organisms: For how else could a "better understanding" of such organisms be derived? Statements of DOD officials have confirmed this interpretation: Under certain circumstances, the DOD is prepared to initiate programs aimed at making novel pathogens.

35 4. The DOD also anticipates that recombinant DNA technology may be applied for the production of toxins or other toxic agents. A report commissioned by the department in 1981 concludes that "toxins could probably be manufactured by newly created bacterial strains under controlled laboratory conditions."

36 DOD officials insist that no work on novel harmful agents—either toxins or organisms—is currently in progress.

37 Finally, there are potential loopholes in the international treaty covering biological research and development for military purposes, the Biological Weapons Convention. The convention bans development, construction, and stockpiling of biological weapons. For many years, the fact that the convention existed, and that it had been signed by the major world powers (including the U.S. and the Soviet Union), served to assuage concern about the development of recombinant DNA technology for weapons purposes.

38 It is not clear, however, that the treaty covers all aspects of the newer forms of genetic engineering. For example, it is unclear how much "research" is prohibited by the convention's ban on "development," whether this ban covers the construction of novel harmful agents, and whether it would cover manufacture of novel toxins. Furthermore, the treaty makes no provision for verification of compliance.

39 The enhanced capability made possible by the new technology might provide the incentive to use such loopholes. And that possibility is increased in the present climate of deepening suspicion and deteriorating international relations.

40 In the face of these problems, what can we do, first, to ensure that the new biology is directed exclusively for peaceful applications; and second, to ensure that those peaceful applications are safe?

41 With respect to the industrial application of genetic engineering, the situation seems comparable to the development of synthetic organic chemicals by 1950. By that

point, advances in chemistry had made possible the invention of thousands of novel substances the impact of which on health and environment was unknown. Only now are we facing the full consequences of that ignorance: the overwhelming costs to human health and the environment of dioxin, PBB, PCBs, kepone, and the thousands of other lethal chemicals we have recklessly released. Can we afford to make the same mistake again, this time with self-reproducing novel organisms?

42 We need to regulate this field. The costs of regulation will be minute compared to the possible costs of damage wrought by an unregulated industry. We need to ensure that wastes are adequately treated and monitored. We need to monitor the health of workers. And we need meaningful involvement of workers and communities in decision making.

43 With respect to the military application of the new biology, the situation seems comparable to that in nuclear physics in 1940. Novel biological weapons have not yet been invented; yet it is likely that they could be as the result of determined effort on the part of military establishments. The critical question is whether we can learn from the experience of nuclear physics. The application of that field for weapons purposes, fueled by the logic of protection and counter-protection, has brought us to the brink of nuclear annihilation. Unless we renounce that logic, we run the risk of being swept up into a new weapons race, this time based on biology. Efforts directed toward negotiation and control of biological weapons are surely less hazardous than the alternative of *not* attempting to take this step.

44 Before the nations begin to build major military dependencies on the new biological technologies, we need to intervene to ensure that these technologies are directed exclusively into peaceful applications. All the nations should be encouraged to sign the existing treaty and to incorporate its provisions into their domestic law. And all nations should renounce secret biological research.

45 Beyond these steps, the entire subject of biological weapons disarmament needs to be reopened. Collectively, the United States and other nations should seek to strengthen the Biological Weapons Convention to ensure that any research on novel harmful agents is screened nationally and internationally, that all appropriate research is conducted in the open, in internationally approved facilities, and that all such work is directed toward peaceful ends.

I am not advocating that we stop the development of the 46
new biology. I believe that we can achieve wonderful and
important results with it. But we do need to ensure that its
application is both peaceful and safe. We have to learn from
the history of nuclear physics and organic chemistry. Indeed, I believe we have no real choice. We cannot afford to
develop the new biological technologies without controlling
them.

DO ANIMALS HAVE RIGHTS?

Tom Regan

Religion and Animal Rights

Tom Regan, a philosopher and educator who teaches at North Carolina State University, is president of the Culture and Animals Foundation in Raleigh, North Carolina. The author of many books on animal rights, he presented the following argument before the Conference on Creation Theology and Environmental Ethics at the World Council of Churches in Annecy, France, in 1988. It was reprinted in The Animals' Voice *magazine, which is devoted to animal rights.*

1 In its simplest terms the animal rights position I uphold maintains that such diverse practices as the use of animals in science, sport and recreational hunting, the trapping of furbearing animals for vanity products, and commercial animal agriculture are categorically wrong—wrong because these practices systematically violate the rights of the animals involved. Morally, these practices ought to be abolished. That is the goal of the *social* struggle for animal rights. The goal of our *individual* struggle is to divest ourselves of our moral and economic ties to these injustices—for example, by not wearing the skins of dead animals and by not eating their decaying corpses.

2 Not a few people regard the animal rights position as extreme, calling, as it does, for the abolition of certain well-entrenched social practices rather than for their "humane" reform. And many seem to imagine that once this label ("extreme") is applied, the need for further refutation evaporates. After all, how can such an "extreme" moral position be correct?

3 I addressed this question in a recent speech, reminding my audience of a few "extreme" moral positions we all accept:

4 Rape is *always* wrong.

5 Child pornography is *always* wrong.

Racial and sexual discrimination are *always* wrong. 6

I went on to note that when an injustice is absolute, as is 7
true of each of the examples just cited, then one must
oppose it absolutely. It is not reformed, more humane child
pornography that an enlightened ethic calls for; it is its
abolition that is required—it is this *extreme* position we
must uphold. And analogous remarks apply in the case of
the other examples.

Once this much is acknowledged, it is evident (or at least 8
it should be) that those who oppose or resist the animal
rights position will have to do better than merely attach the
label "extreme" to it. Sometimes "extreme" positions about
what is wrong are right.

Of course, there are two obvious differences between the 9
animal rights position and the other examples of extreme
views I have given. The latter views are very generally accepted, whereas the former position is not. And unlike these
very generally accepted views, which concern wrongful acts
done to human beings, the animal rights position concerns
the (alleged) wrongfulness of treating animals (nonhuman
animals, that is) in certain ways. Those who oppose or resist
the animal rights position might seize upon these two differences in an effort to justify themselves in accepting extreme positions regarding rape and child abuse, for example,
while rejecting the "extremism" of animal rights.

But neither of these differences will bear the weight of 10
justification. That a view (whether moral or otherwise) is
very generally accepted is not a sufficient reason for accepting it as true. There was a time when the shape of the earth
was very generally believed to be flat, and when the presence
of physical and mental handicaps was very generally
thought to make the people who bore them morally inferior.
That very many people believed these falsehoods obviously
did not make them true. We won't discover or confirm
what's true by taking a vote.

The reverse of the preceding also can be demonstrated. 11
That a view (moral or otherwise) is not generally accepted is
not a sufficient reason for judging it to be false. When those
lonely few first conjectured that the earth is round and that
women are the moral equals of men, they conjectured truly,
notwithstanding how grandly they were outnumbered. The
solitary person who, in Thoreau's enduring image, marches
to a different drummer, may be the only person to apprehend the truth.

12 The second difference noted above is more problematic. That difference cites the fact that child abuse and rape, for example, involve evils done to human beings, while the animal rights position claims that certain (alleged) evils are done to nonhuman animals. Now, there is no question that this does constitute a difference. The question is, is this a *morally relevant difference*—a difference, that is, that would justify us in accepting the extreme opposition we judge to be appropriate in the case of child abuse and rape, for example, but which most people resist or abjure in the case of, say, vivisection. For a variety of reasons I do not myself think that this difference is a morally relevant one. Permit me to explain why.

13 Viewed scientifically, this second difference succeeds only in citing a biological difference: The victims of rape and child abuse belong to one species (the species *Homo sapiens*) whereas the (alleged) victims of vivisection and trapping belong to other species (the species *Canis lupus,* for example). But biological differences *inside* the species *Homo sapiens* do not justify radically different treatment among those individual humans who differ biologically (for example, in terms of sex, or skin color, or chromosome count). Why, then, should biological differences *outside* our species count morally? If having one eye or deformed limbs does not disqualify a human being from moral consideration equal to that given to those humans who are more fortunate, how can it be rational to disqualify a rat or a wolf from equal moral consideration because, unlike us, they have paws and a tail?

14 Some of those who resist or oppose the animal rights position might have recourse to "intuition" at this point. They might claim that one either "sees" that the principal biological difference at issue (namely, species membership) *is* a morally relevant one, or does *not* see this. No *reason* can be given as to why belonging to the species *Homo sapiens* gives one a superior moral status, just as no *reason* can be given as to why belonging to the species *Canis lupus* gives wolves an inferior moral status (if wolves have a moral status at all). This difference in moral status can only be grasped immediately, without making an inference, by an exercise of intuitive reason. This moral difference is "self-evident"—or so it will be claimed by those who claim to "intuit" it.

15 However attractive this appeal to intuition may seem to

some, it woefully fails to bear the weight of justification. The plain fact is, people have claimed to "intuit" differences in the comparative moral standing of individuals and groups *inside* the human species, and these alleged "intuitions," we all would agree, are painful symptoms of unquestioned and unjustifiable prejudice. Over the course of history, for example, many men have "intuited" the moral superiority of men when compared with that of women, and many white-skinned humans have "intuited" the moral superiority of white-skinned humans when compared with humans having different skin colors. If this is a matter of intuition, then no reason can be given for this superiority. No inference is (or can be) required, no evidence adduced. One either "sees" it, or one doesn't. It's just that those who do "see" it (or so they will insist) apprehend the truth, while those whose deficient intuitive faculties prevent them from "seeing" it fail to do so.

I cannot believe that any thoughtful person will be taken in by this ruse. Appeals to "intuition" in these contexts are symptomatic of unquestioned and unjustifiable moral prejudices. What prompts or encourages men to "see" their moral superiority over women are the sexual prejudices men bring with them, not what is to be found in the existence of sexual differences themselves. And the same is true, *mutatis mutandis,* of "seeing" moral superiority in racial or other biological differences between humans. 16

That much established, the weakness of appeals to intuition in the case at hand should be apparent. Since intuition is not to be trusted when questions of the comparative moral standing of biologically different individuals *inside* the species *Homo sapiens* are at issue, it cannot be rational to assume or insist that such appeals can or should be trusted when questions of the comparative moral standing of individuals *outside* the species are at issue. Moreover, since appeals to intuition in the former case turn out to be symptomatic of unquestioned and unjustifiable moral prejudices, rather than being revelatory of some important moral truth, it is not unreasonable to suspect that the same diagnosis applies to appeals to intuition in the latter case. If true, then those who "intuit" the moral superiority of all members of the species *Homo sapiens* over all members of every other species also emerge as the unwitting victims or the willful perpetrators of an unquestioned and unjustifiable moral prejudice. 17

"Speciesism" is the name given to this (alleged) prejudice. 18

This idea has been characterized in a variety of ways. For present purposes let us begin with the following twofold characterization of what I shall call "categorical speciesism."

19 Categorical speciesism is the belief that (1) the inherent value of an individual can be judged solely on the basis of the biological species to which that individual belongs, and that (2) all the members of the species *Homo sapiens* have equal inherent value, while all the members of every other species lack this kind of value, simply because all and only humans are members of the species *Homo sapiens.*

20 In speaking of inherent value, both here and throughout what follows, I mean something that coincides with Kant's famous idea of "end-in-itself." Individuals who have inherent value, in other words, have value in their own right, apart from their possible utility for others; as such, these individuals are never to be treated in ways that reduce their value to their possible usefullness for others; they are always to be treated as "ends-in-themselves," not as "means merely." Categorical speciesism, then, holds that all and only humans have this kind of value precisely because all and only humans belong to the species *Homo sapiens.*

21 I have already indicated why I believe that appeals to intuition cannot succeed in establishing the truth of categorical speciesism as so characterized. How, then, might the prejudicial character of speciesism be established?

22 Part of that answer is to be found when we pause to consider the nature of the animals we humans hunt, trap, eat and use for scientific purposes. Any person of common sense will agree that these animals bring the mystery of consciousness to the world. These animals, that is, not only are *in* the world, they are aware *of it*—and also of their "inner" world. They see, hear, touch and feel; but they also desire, believe, remember and anticipate.

23 If anyone questions my assessment of the common sense view about these animals, then I would invite them to speak with people who share their lives with dogs or cats or horses, or others who know the ways of wolves or coyotes, or still others who have had contact with any bird one might wish to name. Common sense clearly is on the side of viewing these animals as unified psychological beings, individuals who have a biography (a psychological life-story), not merely a biology. And common sense is not in conflict with our best science here. Indeed, our best science offers a scientific corroboration of the common sense view.

That corroboration is to be found in a set of diverse but related considerations. One is evolutionary theory, which implies that (1) the more complex has evolved from the less complex, that (2) members of the species *Homo sapiens* are the most complex life form of which we are aware, that (3) members of our species bring a psychological presence to the world, that (4) the psychological capacities we find in humans have evolved over time, and that (5) these capacities would not have evolved at all and would not have been passed on from one generation to the next if they (that is, these capacities) failed to have adaptive value—that is, if they failed to offer advantages to our species in its ongoing struggle to survive in an ever-changing environment. 24

Given these five points, it is entirely consistent with the main thrust of evolutionary theory, and is, indeed, required by it, to maintain that the members of some species of nonhuman animals are like us in having the capacity to see and hear and feel, for example, as well as to believe and desire, to remember and anticipate. 25

Certainly this is what Darwin thinks, as is evident when he writes of the animals we humans eat and trap, to use just two instances, that they differ psychologically (or mentally) from us in degree, not in kind. 26

A second, related consideration involves comparative anatomy and physiology. Everything we know about nature must incline us to believe that a complex structure has a complex reason for being. It would therefore be an extraordinary lapse of form if we humans had evolved into complicated psychological creatures, with an underlying anatomical and physiological complexity, while other species of animals had evolved to have a more or less complex anatomy and physiology, very much like our own in many respects, and yet lacked—*totally* lacked—any and every psychological capacity. If nature could respond to this bizarre suggestion, the verdict we would hear would be, "Nonsense!" 27

Thus it is, then, that both common sense and our best science speak with one voice regarding the psychological nature we share with the nonhuman animals I have mentioned—those, for example, many people stew, roast, fry, broil and grill for the sake of their gustatory desires and delights. When the dead and putrefying bodies of these animals are eaten, our psychological kin are consumed. 28

Recall the occasion for this review of relevant scientific considerations. Categorical speciesism, which I character- 29 ized earlier, is not shown to be a moral prejudice merely because those who accept it are unable to prove its truth. This much has been conceded and, indeed, insisted upon. What more, then, would have to be established before the charge of moral prejudice could be made to stick? Part of that answer is to be found in the recent discussion of what common sense and our best science contribute to our understanding of the nonhuman animals we have been discussing. Both agree that these animals are fundamentally like ordinary human beings—like you and me. For, like us, these animals have a unified psychological presence in the world, a life-story that is uniquely their own, a separate biography. In the simplest terms *they are somebody, not something.* Precisely because this similarity is so well established, grounded in the opinions, as Aristotle would express this, of both "the many and the wise," any substantive moral position at odds with it seems dubious to say the least.

30 And categorical speciesism, as I have characterized it, *is* at odds with the joint verdict of common sense and our best science. For once the appeal to intuition is denied (and denied for good reasons), the onus of justification must be borne by the speciesist to cite some unique feature of being human that would ground the attribution of inherent value exclusively to human beings, a task that we now see is all but certain to end in failure, given the biological status humans share with those nonhuman animals to whom I have been referring. Rationally considered, we must judge similar cases similarly. This is what the principle of formal justice requires, what respect for logical consistency demands. Thus, since we share a biographical presence in the world with these animals, it seems arbitrary and prejudicial in the extreme to insist that all humans have a kind of value that every other animal lacks.

31 In response to this line of argument people who wish to retain the spirit of speciesism might be prompted to alter its letter. This position I shall call modified speciesism. According to this form of speciesism those nonhuman animals who, like us, have a biographical presence in the world have *some* inherent value, it's just that the degree of inherent value they have *always is less* than that possessed by human beings. And if we ask why this is thought to be so, the answer modified speciesism offers is the same as categorical speciesism: The degree of value differs because humans belong to a particular species to which no other animal belongs—the species *Homo sapiens.*

I think it should be obvious that modified speciesism is open to many of the same kinds of damaging criticisms as categorical speciesism. What, we may ask, is supposed to be the basis of the alleged superior value of human beings? Will it be said that one simply "intuits" this? Then all the same difficulties this appeal faced in the case of categorical speciesism will resurface and ultimately swamp modified speciesism. To avoid this, will it be suggested that the degree of inherent value an individual possesses depends on the relative complexity of that individual's psychological repertoire—the greater the complexity, the greater the value? Then modified speciesism simply will not be able to justify the ascription of superior inherent value to all human beings when compared with every nonhuman animal. And the reason it will not be able to do this is simple: Some nonhuman animals bring to their biography a degree of psychological complexity that far exceeds what is brought by some human beings. One need only compare, say, the psychological repertoire of a healthy two year old chimp, or dog, or hog, or robin to that of a profoundly handicapped human of any age, to recognize the incontrovertible truth of what I have just said. Not all human beings have richer, more complex biographies than every nonhuman animal. 32

How are speciesists to get around this fact—for get around it they must, because fact it is. There is a familiar theological answer to this question; at least it is familiar to those who know something of the Judeo-Christian religious traditions, as these traditions sometimes have been interpreted. That answer states that human beings—all of us—are inherently more valuable than any other existing individual because we are spiritually different and, indeed, unique. This uniqueness stems from our having been created in the image of God, a status we share with no other creature. If, then, it is true that all humans uniquely image God, then we are able to cite a real (spiritual) difference between every member of our species and the countless numbers of the millions of other species of creaturely life. And, if, moreover, this difference is a morally relevant one, then speciesists might seem to be in a position to defend their speciesism (and this is true whether they are categorical or moderate speciesists) in the face of the demands of formal justice. After all, that principle requires that we judge similar cases similarly, whereas any two individuals—the one human, the other of some other species—will not be 33 relevantly similar, given the hypothesis of the unique spiritual worth of all human beings.

34 Now I myself am not ill-disposed to the idea of there being something about us humans that gives us a unique spiritual worth, nor am I ill-disposed to the idea that the ground of this worth is to be found or explicated in the idea that we humans uniquely "image" God. Not surprisingly, therefore, the interpretation of these ideas I favor, while it concedes this (possible) difference between humans and the rest of creation, does not yield anything like the results favored by speciesism, whether categorical or moderate. Let me explain.

35 The position I favor is the one that interprets our divine "imaging" in terms of our moral responsibility. By this I mean that we are expressly chosen by God to be God's vice-regent in the day-to-day affairs of the world; we are chosen by God, that is, to be as loving in our day-to-day dealings with the created order as God was in creating that order in the first place. In *this* sense, therefore, there *is* a morally relevant difference between human beings and every other creaturely expression of God. For it is only members of the human species who are given the awesome freedom and responsibility to be God's representative within creation. And it is, therefore, only we humans who can be held morally blameworthy when we fail to do this, and morally praiseworthy when we succeed.

36 Within the general context of this interpretation of our unique "imaging" of God, then, we find a morally relevant difference between God's creative expression in the human and God's creative expression in every other aspect of creation. But—as should be evident—this difference *by itself* offers neither aid nor comfort to speciesism, of whatever variety. For to agree that only humans image God, in the sense that only humans have the moral responsibility to be loving toward God's creation, in no way entails either that all and only humans have inherent value (so-called categorical speciesism) or that all and only humans have a superior inherent value (modified speciesism, as I have called it). It is perfectly consistent with our unique status as God's chosen representative within creation that *other* creatures have inherent value and possess it to a degree equal to that possessed by human beings. Granted, our uniqueness lies in our moral responsibility to God and to God's creation, including, of course, all members of the human family. But

this fact, assuming it to be a fact, only answers the question, "Which among God's creatures are capable of acting rightly or wrongly (or, as philosophers might say, 'are moral agents')?" What this fact, assuming it to be one, does not answer are the questions, "To which creatures can we act rightly or wrongly?" and "What kind of value do other creatures have?"

Every prejudice dies hard. Speciesism is no exception. 37
That it is a prejudice and that, by acting on it, we humans have been, and continue to be, responsible for an incalculable amount of evil, an amount of truly monumental proportions, is, I believe, as true as it is regrettable. In my philosophical writings over the past fifteen years I have endeavored to show how this tragic truth can be argued for on wholly secular grounds. On this occasion I have looked elsewhere for support—have in fact looked to the original saga of creation we find in *Genesis*—in the hope that we might there find a religious or theological account that resonates with the secular case for animal rights. Neither case—not the secular and not the religious—has, or can have, the conclusiveness of a proof in, say, geometry. I say "can have" because I am reminded of Aristotle's astute observation, that it is the mark of an educated person not to demand "proof" that is inappropriate for a given subject matter. And whatever else we might think of moral thought, I believe we at least can agree that it is importantly unlike geometry.

It remains true, nonetheless, that my attempt to explain 38
and defend as egalitarian this view of the inherent value of humans and other animals must face a number of important challenges. For reasons of length, if for no other, I cannot on this occasion characterize or respond to all these challenges, not even all the most fundamental ones. The best I can do, before concluding, is describe and defuse two of them.

The first begins by observing that, within the traditions of 39
Judaism and Christianity, *every form of life,* not simply humans and other animals, is to be viewed as expressive of God's love. Thus, to attempt to "elevate" the value of nonhuman animals, as I might be accused of having done, could be viewed as having the unacceptable consequence of negating or reducing the value of everything else.

I think this objection misses the mark. There is nothing in 40
the animal rights philosophy (nothing, that is, in the kind of egalitarianism I have endeavored to defend) that either

denies or diminishes the value of fruits, nuts, grains and other forms of vegetative life, or that refuses to accept the possibility that these and the rest of creation are so many ways in which God's loving presence is manifested. Nor is there anything in this philosophy that disparages the wise counsel to treat all of creation gently and appreciatively. It is an arrogant, unbridled anthropocentrism, often aided and abetted in our history by an arrogant, unbridled Christian theology, not the philosophy of animal rights, that has brought the earth to the brink of ecological disaster.

41 Still, this philosophy does find in humans and other animals, because of our shared biographical status in creation, a kind of value—inherent value—which other creatures fail to possess, either not at all or at least not to the degree in which humans and other animals possess it. Is it possible to defend this view? I believe it is, both on the grounds of a purely secular moral philosophy and by appeal to Biblical authority. The secular defense I have attempted to offer elsewhere and will not repeat here. As for the Christian defense, I shall merely reaffirm the vital importance (in my view) of *Genesis 1,* as well as (to my mind) the more than symbolic significance of the covenant, and note that in both we find biblical sanction for viewing the value of animals to be superior to that of vegetables. After all, we do not find carrots and almonds included in the covenant, and we do find God expressly giving these and other forms of vegetative life to us, as our food, in *Genesis'* first creation saga. In a word, then, vegetative life was meant to be used by us, thus giving it utility value for us (which does not mean or entail that we may use these life forms thoughtlessly or even irreverently.)

42 So much for the first challenge. The second one emanates from quite a different source and mounts a quite different objection. It begins by noting the large disparities that exist in the quality of life available to those who are affluent (the "haves") and those who are poor (the "have-nots"), especially those who live in the so-called "Third World." "It is all fine and good to preach the gospel of animal rights to those people who have the financial and other means to practice it, if they choose to do so," this objection states, "but please do spare us your self-righteous denunciation of the struggling (and often starving) masses of people in the rest of the world, who really have no choice but to eat animals, wear their skins, and use them in other ways. To condemn these

people is to value animal life above human life. And this is misanthropy at its worst."

Now, this particular variation on the familiar theme of misanthropy (at least this is familiar to advocates of animal rights) has a point, up to a point. The point it has, is that it would be self-righteous to condemn the people in question for acting as they do, especially if we are acting worse than they are (as well we may be). But, of course, nothing in what I have argued supports such a condemnation, and this for the simple reason that I have nowhere argued that people who eat animals, or who hunt and trap them, or who cut their heads off or burst their intestines in pursuit of "scientific knowledge," either are or must be *evil* people. The position I have set forth concerns the moral wrongness of what people do, not the *vileness of their character.* In my view, it is entirely possible that good people sometimes do what is wrong, and evil people sometimes do what is right. 43

Indeed, not only is this possible, it frequently happens, and among those circumstances in which it does, some concern the actions performed by people in the Third World. At least this is the conclusion we reach if we take the philosophy of animal rights seriously. To make my meaning clearer, consider the following example. Suppose we chance upon a tribe of hunter-gatherers who annually, on a date sacred to their tradition, sacrifice the most beautiful female child to the gods, in the hope that the tribe will prosper in the coming year. In my view this act of human sacrifice is morally wrong and ought to be stopped (which does *not* mean that we should invade with tanks and flame-throwers to stop it!). From this moral assessment of what these human beings do, however, it does not follow that we should judge them to be evil, vicious people. It could well be that they act from only the best intentions and with nothing but the best motives. Nevertheless, what they do, in my judgment, is morally wrong. 44

What is true of the imaginary case of this tribe is no less true of real-life cases where people in the Third World raise and kill animals for food, cruelly subject other animals to forced labor, and so on. Anytime anyone reduces the inherent value of a nonhuman animal to that animal's utility value for human beings, what is done, in my view, is morally wrong. But it does not follow from this that we should make a negative moral judgment about the character of the human moral agents involved, especially if, as is true in the 45

Third World, there are mitigating circumstances. For it often happens that people who do what is morally wrong should be *excused* from moral blame and censure. A person who shoots a family member, for example, in the mistaken belief that there is a burglar in the house, does what is wrong and yet may well *not* be morally blameworthy. Similarly, those people in the Third World who act in ways that are prohibited by respect for the rights of animals, do what is wrong. But because of the harsh, uncompromising exigencies of their life, where they are daily faced with the demand to make truly heroic sacrifices, where indeed it often is a matter of their life or their death that hangs in the balance, the people of the Third World in my view should be excused from our harsh, uncompromising judgments of moral blame. The circumstances of their life, one might say, are as mitigating as any circumstances can be.

46 In light of the preceding remarks, I hope it is clear why it would be a bad reading of the philosophy of animal rights, to charge its proponents with a hearty appetite, if not for animal flesh then at least for self-righteousness. When we understand the difference between morally assessing a person's act and that person's character, and when we take cognizance of the appropriateness of reducing or erasing moral blame in the face of mitigating circumstances, then the proponents of animal rights should be seen to be no more censorious or "self-righteous" than the proponents of any other moral philosophy.

47 The challenge to lead a good, respectful, loving life just in our dealings within the human family is onerous and demanding. How much more onerous and demanding must it be, therefore, if we widen the circle of the moral community to include the whole of creation. How might we begin to meet this enlarged challenge? Doubtless there are many possible places to begin, some of which will be more accessible to some than to others. For my part, however, I cannot help believing that an appropriate place to begin is with the food on our plates. For here we are faced with a direct personal choice, over which we exercise absolute sovereign authority. Such power is not always within our grasp. How little influence we really have, you and I, on the practices of the World Bank, the agrarian land-reform movement, the call to reduce armed conflicts, the cessation of famine and the evil of abject poverty! These large-scale evils stand beyond the reach of our small wills.

But not the food on our plates. Here we are at liberty to exercise absolute control. And here, then, we ought to be asking ourselves, "Which of those choices I can make are most in accord with the idea of the integrity of creation?" 48

When we consider the biographical and, I dare say, the spiritual kinship we share with those billions of animals raised and slaughtered for food, when, further, we inform ourselves of the truly wretched conditions in which most of these animals are raised, not to mention the deplorable methods by which they are transported and the gruesome, blood-soaked reality of the slaughterhouse; and when, finally, we take honest stock of our privileged position in the world, a position that will not afford us the excuse from moral blame shared by the desperately poor who, as we say, "really have no choice"—when we consider all these factors, then the case for abstaining from animal flesh has the overwhelming weight of both impartial reason and a spiritually-infused compassion on its side. 49

True, to make this change will involve some sacrifices—in taste perhaps, in convenience certainly. And yet the whole fabric of Christian *agape* is woven from the threads of sacrificial acts. To abstain, on principle, from eating animals, therefore, although it is not the end-all, can be the begin-all of our conscientious effort to journey back to (or toward) Eden, can be one way (among others) to re-establish or create that relationship to the earth which, if *Genesis 1* is to be trusted, was part of God's original hopes for and plans in creation. It is the integrity of this creation we seek to understand and aspire to honor. In the choice of our food, I believe, we see, not in a glass darkly, but face to face, a small but not unimportant part of both the challenge and the promise of Christianity and animal rights. 50

Vicki Hearne

What's Wrong with Animal Rights

Hearne is an animal trainer, a writer, and a contributing editor at Harper's Magazine, *the public and cultural affairs magazine where this essay was published in September 1991. The letters that follow it were published a few months later in* Harper's.

1 Not all happy animals are alike. A Doberman going over a hurdle after a small wooden dumbbell is sleek, all arcs of harmonious power. A basset hound cheerfully performing the same exercise exhibits harmonies of a more lugubrious nature. There are chimpanzees who love precision the way musicians or fanatical housekeepers or accomplished hypochondriacs do; others for whom happiness is a matter of invention and variation—chimp vaudevillians. There is a rhinoceros whose happiness, as near as I can make out, is in needing to be trained every morning, all over again, or else he "forgets" his circus routine, and in this you find a clue to the slow, deep, quiet chuckle of his happiness and to the glory of the beast. Happiness for Secretariat is in his ebullient bound, that joyful length of stride. For the draft horse or the weight-pull dog, happiness is of a different shape, more awesome and less obviously intelligent. When the pulling horse is at its most intense, the animal goes into himself, allocating all of the educated power that organizes his desire to dwell in fierce and delicate intimacy with that power, leans into the harness, and MAKES THAT SUCKER *MOVE*.

2 If we are speaking of human beings and use the phrase "animal happiness," we tend to mean something like "creature comforts." The emblems of this are the golden retriever rolling in the grass, the horse with his nose deep in the oats, the kitty by the fire. Creature comforts are important to animals—"Grub first, then ethics" is a motto that would describe many a wise Labrador retriever, and I have a pit bull named Annie whose continual quest for the perfect pillow inspires her to awesome feats. But there is something more to animals, a capacity for satisfactions that come from work in the fullest sense—what is known in philosophy and in this country's Declaration of Independence as "happi-

ness." This is a sense of personal achievement, like the satisfaction felt by a good wood-carver or a dancer or a poet or an accomplished dressage horse. It is a happiness that, like the artist's, must come from something within the animal, something trainers call "talent." Hence, it cannot be imposed on the animal. But it is also something that does not come *ex nihilo*. If it had not been a fairly ordinary thing, in one part of the world, to teach young children to play the pianoforte, it is doubtful that Mozart's music would exist.

Happiness is often misunderstood as a synonym for 3 pleasure or as an antonym for suffering. But Aristotle associated happiness with ethics—codes of behavior that urge us toward the sensation of getting it right, a kind of work that yields the "click" of satisfaction upon solving a problem or surmounting an obstacle. In his *Ethics*, Aristotle wrote, "If happiness is activity in accordance with excellence, it is reasonable that it should be in accordance with the highest excellence." Thomas Jefferson identified the capacity for happiness as one of the three fundamental rights on which all others are based: "life, liberty, and the pursuit of happiness."

I bring up this idea of happiness as a form of work 4 because I am an animal trainer, and work is the foundation of the happiness a trainer and an animal discover together. I bring up these words also because they cannot be found in the lexicon of the animal-rights movement. This absence accounts for the uneasiness toward the movement of most people, who sense that rights advocates have a point but take it too far when they liberate snails or charge that goldfish at the country fair are suffering. But the problem with the animal-rights advocates is not that they take it too far; it's that they've got it all wrong.

Animal rights are built upon a misconceived premise that 5 rights were created to prevent us from unnecessary suffering. You can't find an animal-rights book, video, pamphlet, or rock concert in which someone doesn't mention the Great Sentence, written by Jeremy Bentham in 1789. Arguing in favor of such rights, Bentham wrote: "The question is not, Can they *reason?* nor, can they *talk?* but, can they suffer?"

The logic of the animal-rights movement places suffering 6

at the iconographic center of a skewed value system. The thinking of its proponents—given eerie expression in a virtually sado-pornographic sculpture of a tortured monkey that won a prize for its compassionate vision—has collapsed into a perverse conundrum. Today the loudest voices calling for—demanding—the destruction of animals are the humane organizations. This is an inevitable consequence of the apotheosis of the drive to relieve suffering: Death is the ultimate release. To compensate for their contradictions, the humane movement has demonized, in this century and the last, those who made animal happiness their business: veterinarians, trainers, and the like. We think of Louis Pasteur as the man whose work saved you and me and your dog and cat from rabies, but antivivisectionists of the time claimed that rabies increased in areas where there were Pasteur Institutes.

7 An anti-rabies public-relations campaign mounted in England in the 1880s by the Royal Society for the Prevention of Cruelty to Animals and other organizations led to orders being issued to club any dog found not wearing a muzzle. England still has her cruel and unnecessary law that requires an animal to spend six months in quarantine before being allowed loose in the country. Most of the recent propaganda about pit bulls—the crazy claim that they "take hold with their front teeth while they chew away with their rear teeth" (which would imply, incorrectly, that they have double jaws)—can be traced to literature published by the Humane Society of the United States during the fall of 1987 and earlier. If your neighbors want your dog or horse impounded and destroyed because he is a nuisance—say the dog barks, or the horse attracts flies—it will be the local Humane Society to whom your neighbors turn for action.

8 In a way, everyone has the opportunity to know that the history of the humane movement is largely a history of miseries, arrests, prosecutions, and death. The Humane Society is the pound, the place with the decompression chamber or the lethal injections. You occasionally find worried letters about this in Ann Landers's column.

9 Animal-rights publications are illustrated largely with photographs of two kinds of animals—"Helpless Fluff" and "Agonized Fluff," the two conditions in which some people seem to prefer their animals, because any other version of an animal is too complicated for propaganda. In the in-

troduction to his book *Animal Liberation,* Peter Singer says somewhat smugly that he and his wife have no animals and, in fact, don't much care for them. This is offered as evidence of his objectivity and ethical probity. But it strikes me as an odd, perhaps obscene, underpinning for an ethical project that encourages university and high school students to cherish their ignorance of, say, great bird dogs as proof of their devotion to animals.

I would like to leave these philosophers behind, for they are inept connoisseurs of suffering who might revere my Airedale for his capacity to scream when subjected to a blowtorch but not for his wit and courage, not for his natural good manners that are a gentle rebuke to ours. I want to celebrate the moment not long ago when, at his first dog show, my Airedale, Drummer, learned that there can be a public place where his work is respected. I want to celebrate his meticulousness, his happiness upon realizing at the dog show that no one would swoop down upon him and swamp him with the goo-goo excesses known as the "teddy-bear complex" but that people actually got out of his way, gave him room to work. I want to say, "There can be a six-and-a-half-month-old puppy who can care about accuracy, who can be fastidious, and whose fastidiousness will be a foundation for courage later." I want to say, "Leave my puppy alone!" 10

I want to leave the philosophers behind, but I cannot, in part because the philosophical problems that plague academicians of the animal-rights movement are illuminating. They wonder, do animals have rights or do they have interests? Or, if these rightists lead particularly unexamined lives, they dismiss that question as obvious (yes, of course, animals have rights, prima facie) and proceed to enumerate them, James Madison style. This leads to the issuance of bills of rights—the right to an environment, the right not to be used in medical experiments—and other forms of trivialization. 11

The calculus of suffering can be turned against the philosophers of festering flesh, even in the case of food animals, or exotic animals who perform in movies and circuses. It is true that it hurts to be slaughtered by man, but it doesn't hurt nearly as much as some of the cunningly cruel arrange- 12 ments meted out by "Mother Nature." In Africa, 75 percent of the lions cubbed do not survive to the age of two. For those who make it to two, the average age at death is ten years. Asali, the movie and TV lioness, was still working at age twenty-one. There are fates worse than death, but twenty-one years of a close relationship with Hubert Wells, Asali's trainer, is not one of them. Dorset sheep and polled Herefords would not exist at all were they not in a symbiotic relationship with human beings.

13 A human being living in the "wild"—somewhere, say, without the benefits of medicine and advanced social organization—would probably have a life expectancy of from thirty to thirty-five years. A human being living in "captivity"—in, say, a middle-class neighborhood of what the Centers for Disease Control call a Metropolitan Statistical Area—has a life expectancy of seventy or more years. For orangutans in the wild in Borneo and Malaysia, the life expectancy is thirty-five years; in captivity, fifty years. The wild is not a suffering-free zone or all that frolicsome a location.

14 The questions asked by animal-rights activists are flawed, because they are built on the concept that the origin of rights is in the avoidance of suffering rather than in the pursuit of happiness. The question that needs to be asked—and that will put us in closer proximity to the truth—is not, do they have rights? or, what are those rights? but rather, what is a right?

15 Rights originate in committed relationships and can be found, both intact and violated, wherever one finds such relationships—in social compacts, within families, between animals, and between people and nonhuman animals. This is as true when the nonhuman animals in question are lions or parakeets as when they are dogs. It is my Airedale whose excellencies have my attention at the moment, so it is with reference to him that I will consider the question, what is a right?

16 When I imagine situations in which it naturally arises that A defends or honors or respects B's rights, I imagine situations in which the relationship between A and B can be indicated with a possessive pronoun. I might say, "Leave her alone, she's my daughter" or, "That's what she wants, and she is my daughter. I think I am bound to honor her wants." Similarly, "Leave her alone, she's my mother." I am more

tender of the happiness of my mother, my father, my child, than I am of other people's family members; more tender of my friends' happiness than your friends' happinesses, unless you and I have a mutual friend.

Possession of a being by another has come into more and more disrepute, so that the common understanding of one person possessing another is slavery. But the important detail about the kind of possessive pronoun that I have in mind is reciprocity: If I have a friend, she has a friend. If I have a daughter, she has a mother. The possessive does not bind one of us while freeing the other; it cannot do that. Moreover, should the mother reject the daughter, the word that applies is "disown." The form of disowning that most often appears in the news is domestic violence. Parents abuse children; husbands batter wives. 17

Some cases of reciprocal possessives have built-in limitations, such as "my patient / my doctor" or "my student / my teacher" or "my agent / my client." Other possessive relations are extremely limited but still remarkably binding: "my neighbor" and "my country" and "my president." 18

The responsibilities and the ties signaled by reciprocal possession typically are hard to dissolve. It can be as difficult to give up an enemy as to give up a friend, and often the one becomes the other, as though the logic of the possessive pronoun outlasts the forms it chanced to take at a given moment, as though we were stuck with one another. In these bindings, nearly inextricable, are found the origin of our rights. They imply a possessiveness but also recognize an acknowledgment by each side of the other's existence. 19

The idea of democracy is dependent on the citizens' having knowledge of the government; that is, realizing that the government exists and knowing how to claim rights against it. I know this much because I get mail from the government and see its "representatives" running about in uniforms. Whether I actually have any rights in relationship to the government is less clear, but the idea that I do is symbolized by the right to vote. I obey the government, and, in theory, it obeys me, by counting my ballot, reading the *Miranda* warning to me, agreeing to be bound by the Constitution. My friend obeys me as I obey her; the government "obeys" me to some extent, and, to a different extent, I obey it. 20

What kind of thing can my Airedale, Drummer, have 21

knowledge of? He can know that I exist and through that knowledge can claim his happiness, with varying degrees of success, both with me and against me. Drummer can also know about larger human or dog communities than the one that consists only of him and me. There is my household—the other dogs, the cats, my husband. I have had enough dogs on campuses to know that he can learn that Yale exists as a neighborhood or village. My older dog, Annie, not only knows that Yale exists but can tell Yalies from townies, as I learned while teaching there during labor troubles.

22 Dogs can have elaborate conceptions of human social structures, and even of something like their rights and responsibilities within them, but these conceptions are never elaborate enough to construct a rights relationship between a dog and the state, or a dog and the Humane Society. Both of these are concepts that depend on writing and memoranda, officers in uniform, plaques and seals of authority. All of these are literary constructs, and all of them are beyond a dog's ken, which is why the mail carrier who doesn't also happen to be a dog's friend is forever an intruder—this is why dogs bark at mailmen.

23 It is clear enough that natural rights relations can arise between people and animals. Drummer, for example, can insist, "Hey, let's go outside and do something!" if I have been at my computer several days on end. He can both refuse to accept various of my suggestions and tell me when he fears for his life—such as the time when the huge, white flapping flag appeared out of nowhere, as it seemed to him, on the town green one evening when we were working. I can (and do) say to him either, "Oh, you don't have to worry about that" or, "Uh oh, you're right, Drum, that guy looks dangerous." Just as the government and I—two different species or organism—have developed improvised ways of communicating, such as the vote, so Drummer and I have worked out a number of ways to make our expressions known. Largely through obedience, I have taught him a fair amount about how to get responses from me. Obedience is reciprocal; you cannot get responses from a dog to whom you do not respond accurately. I have enfranchised him in a relationship to me by educating him, creating the conditions by which he can achieve a certain happiness specific to a dog, maybe even specific to an Airedale, inasmuch as this

same relationship has allowed me to plumb the happiness of being a trainer and writing this article.

Instructions in this happiness are given terms that are alien to a culture in which liver treats, fluffy windup toys, and miniature sweaters are confused with respect and work. Jack Knox, a sheepdog trainer originally from Scotland, will shake his crook at a novice handler who makes a promiscuous move to praise a dog, and will call out in his Scottish accent, "Eh! Eh! Get back, get BACK! Ye'll no be abusin' the dogs like that in my clinic." America is a nation of abused animals, Knox says, because we are always swooping at them with praise, "no gi'ing them their freedom." I am reminded of Rainer Maria Rilke's account in which the Prodigal Son leaves—has to leave—because everyone loves him, even the dogs love him, and he has no path to the delicate and fierce truth of himself. Unconditional praise and love, in Rilke's story, disenfranchise us, distract us from what truly excites our interest. 24

In the minds of some trainers and handlers, praise is dishonesty. Paradoxically, it is a kind of contempt for animals that masquerades as a reverence for helplessness and suffering. The idea of freedom means that you do not, at least not while Jack Knox is nearby, helpfully guide your dog through the motions of, say, herding over and over—what one trainer calls "explainy-wainy." This is rote learning. It works tolerably well on some handlers, because people have vast unconscious minds and can store complex pre-programmed behaviors. Dogs, on the other hand, have almost no unconscious minds, so they can learn only by thinking. Many children are like this until educated out of it. 25

If I tell my Airedale to sit and stay on the town green, and someone comes up and burbles, "What a pretty thing you are," he may break his stay to go for a caress. I pull him back and correct him for breaking. Now he holds his stay because I have blocked his way to movement but not because I have punished him. (A correction blocks one path as it opens another for desire to work; punishment blocks desire and opens nothing.) He holds his stay now, and—because the stay opens this possibility of work, new to a heedless young dog—he watches. If the person goes on talking, and isn't going to gush with praise, I may heel Drummer out of his stay and give him an "Okay" to make friends. Sometimes something about the person makes Drummer feel that reserve is in order. He responds to an insincere approach by 26 sitting still, going down into himself, and thinking, "This person has no business pawing me. I'll sit very still, and he will go away." If the person doesn't take the hint from Drummer, I'll give the pup a little backup by saying, "Please don't pet him, he's working," even though he was not under any command.

27 The pup reads this, and there is a flicker of a working trust now stirring in the dog. Is the pup grateful? When the stranger leaves, does he lick my hand, full of submissive blandishments? This one doesn't. This one says nothing at all, and I say nothing much to him. This is a working trust we are developing, not a mutual-congratulation society. My backup is praise enough for him; the use he makes of my support is praise enough for me.

28 Listening to a dog is often praise enough. Suppose it is just after dark and we are outside. Suddenly there is a shout from the house. The pup and I both look toward the shout and then toward each other: "What do you think?" I don't so much as cock my head, because Drummer is growing up, and I want to know what he thinks. He takes a few steps toward the house, and I follow. He listens again and comprehends that it's just Holly, who at fourteen is much given to alarming cries and shouts. He shrugs at me and goes about his business. I say nothing. To praise him for this performance would make about as much sense as praising a human being for the same thing. Thus:

A. What's that?
B. I don't know. [Listens] Oh, it's just Holly.
A. What a gooooood human being!
B. Huh?

29 This is one small moment in a series of like moments that will culminate in an Airedale who on a Friday will have the discrimination and confidence required to take down a man who is attacking me with a knife and on Saturday clown and play with the children at the annual Orange Empire Dog Club Christmas party.

30 People who claim to speak for animal rights are increasingly devoted to the idea that the very keeping of a dog or a horse or a gerbil or a lion is in and of itself an offense. The

more loudly they speak, the less likely they are to be in a rights relation to any given animal, because they are spending so much time in airplanes or transmitting fax announcements of the latest Sylvester Stallone anti-fur rally. In a 1988 *Harper's* forum, for example, Ingrid Newkirk, the national director of People for the Ethical Treatment of Animals, urged that domestic pets be spayed and neutered and ultimately phased out. She prefers, it appears, wolves—and wolves someplace else—to Airedales and, by a logic whose interior structure is both emotionally and intellectually forever closed to Drummer, claims thereby to be speaking for "animal rights."

She is wrong. I am the only one who can own up to my Airedale's inalienable rights. Whether or not I do it perfectly at any given moment is no more refutation of this point than whether I am perfectly my husband's mate at any given moment refutes the fact of marriage. Only people who know Drummer, and whom he can know, are capable of this relationship. PETA and the Humane Society and the ASPCA and the Congress and NOW—as institutions—do have the power to affect my ability to grant rights to Drummer but are otherwise incapable of creating conditions or laws or rights that would increase his happiness. Only Drummer's owner has the power to obey him—to obey who he is and what he is capable of—deeply enough to grant him his rights and open up the possibility of happiness. 31

Responses to Vicki Hearne: Letters to the Editor of *Harper's*

Vicki Hearne is so wrapped up in defining happiness for Drummer, her Airedale, that she neglects to examine the most crucial argument advanced by proponents of animal rights. Despite Hearne's complaint, it is only the most extreme animal-rights activists who suggest that domestic pets be "phased out." The remainder of those concerned with the plight of animals, like myself, focus instead on what Hearne only alludes to: suffering. 1

Few would agree that training a show dog or putting a horse to work is cruel. Surely Hearne takes good care of her own dog, as do most pet owners. Countless acts of 2 animal neglect do exist, however, and are preventable. The wanton destruction of laboratory rats to test cosmetics or the obsessive shooting of cats to study gunshot wounds *is* cruel and unusual. These blatant abuses outrage the majority of animal-rights activists and fuel their sympathies. Much as it may surprise Hearne, these activists are not losing sleep over her playing fetch with her loyal Drummer.

3 Furthermore, Hearne twists logic when she suggests that since the Humane Society destroys animals, the entire animal-rights movement is rotten to the core. This is old, tired rhetoric. The Humane Society destroys unwanted animals so that they will not suffer. Moreover, by writing that "the wild is not a suffering-free zone," Hearne infers that any pain an animal incurs in a domestic situation (home or laboratory) is somehow, in her view, legitimated. Here, she fails to isolate intention from her clever "calculus of suffering." Does Mother Nature *intend* to hurt, maim, and kill, or are these effects simply part of a larger cyclical design? Clearly the answer is the latter. The wolf tears apart the frail and sick caribou not only to ensure its own survival but to maintain the balance of nature. Humankind, however, is not compelled to shock the monkey. Must we infect, injure, and inject in our quest for luscious lipstick, thicker eyelashes, more efficient handguns? Does this research ensure our survival? Although some animal experimentation does provide useful data, much of it provides only superfluous pain for animals.

4 True, the notion of animal rights per se is troubling: Who really knows what animals desire or need? Although Hearne pretends to possess the secrets of the animal world, the truth is that we will never know the true essence of animal happiness. No human is Doctor Doolittle. No one, not even the dog lovers among us, can speak to or for animals' sensibilities. But does this insurmountable communication gap permit us to act without empathy? To disregard decency and common sense? If animal suffering can be prevented, without significant detriment to whatever useful scientific knowledge animal testing purports to produce, then perhaps our own species will have progressed.

Ethan Gilsdorf
Baton Rouge, La.

In order for a human or an animal to have rights, says Vicki Hearne, that human or animal must be involved in a reciprocal relationship with the source of the right and must be able to have a knowledge of the reciprocal character of the relationship. Animals, she argues, can never understand rights and responsibilities to the degree necessary for them to be rights-holders. If we accept this theory, however, we must then reject rights for very young children and the mentally deranged or incompetent, because they, too, cannot have sufficiently elaborate conceptions of rights and responsibilities. Hearne is unable to admit that we might include children or incompetents among rights-holders simply because they are human, because that begs the question of whether we are morally justified in denying rights to nonhumans only because they happen to belong to a different species. 1

Hearne also argues that the animal-rights movement is built upon the misconceived premise that rights were intended to prevent animals from unnecessary suffering. In truth, the basis of animal-rights theory has less to do with the prevention of suffering than with the recognition of the inherent value of the animal's life irrespective of whether that life is of any benefit to anyone other than the animal. 2

Gary L. Francione
Professor of Law and Director,
Animal Rights Law Clinic
Rutgers University
Newark

Happiness, as dog trainer Vicki Hearne defines it, comes to animals in the course of being trained and "getting it right." Thus, the draft horse is happy only when it strains against an unbearable weight, and the trained rhino is happy only when it perches on a tiny stool and mimics ballet steps. What Hearne has recognized, and then twisted, is the very real desire of some animals to please humans. Rowlf, in Richard Adams's *The Plague Dogs,* puzzles about why the whitecoats drown and revive him over and over again. He finally hits upon an explanation: He was trying to "get it right," but he just couldn't. Hearne's hellish, whitecoat logic is as follows: Animals like to please humans. Therefore, animals are happiest when they are fulfilling humans' whims, however cruel. Therefore, in order to contribute to 1 animals' happiness, humans should force animals to fulfill human whims. If it pleases a vivisector to pour oven cleaner into a rabbit's eye, the rabbit is happiest with oven cleaner in his eye. If it pleases a deep-sea fishing guide to use a live kitten for bait, the kitten is happiest impaled on a fishing hook.

2 Hearne concludes by revealing the philosophical underpinnings of her theory: "Only [an animal's] owner has the power . . . to grant him his rights. . . ." Jefferson, whose name Hearne blasphemously evokes in support of a theory that would sicken him, knew better. He recognized that rights are inalienable, their existence self-evident. A rabbit's right not to have oven cleaner poured in its eye is inherent. It exists whether the state recognizes it or not. If our government repeals the Thirteenth Amendment tomorrow, slavery may once again be legal, but it will still be wrong. Pouring oven cleaner in rabbits' eyes is wrong. It always has been; it always will be. One day, the law will conform to this truth.

Elizabeth L. DeCoux
Jackson, Miss.

Alexis Dorn

Animal Rights, Vegetarianism, and Saving the Planet

Alexis Dorn (born 1973) was raised near Philadelphia. At the age of 14 she could no longer bring herself to eat meat and committed herself to vegetarianism. After she graduates from Penn State, she plans to join the Peace Corps and then to become a high school social studies teacher. She wrote the following essay for a first-year college composition course.

1 Why should we expect anyone to think that there is something wrong with eating meat? A belief has developed in our culture, over many years, that to be truly an "All-American," one should enjoy barbecues, cold cuts, and fast food. We mark our year off with appropriate meat dishes—

the fourth of July with the smokey smell of grilled hot dogs and hamburgers; the late summer with picnics, checkered blankets, and fried chicken; the age-old tradition of roasting the decorated turkey for the day of giving thanks. And don't forget the garnished ham for Christmas or New Years.

In festive surroundings, who stops to wonder what went 2 into the process of acquiring the animal and preparing it to be consumed? Or when driving through a Burger King, who realizes that thousands of miles away a lush rain forest is turning into a desert because of the demand for hamburgers in America? People have remained ignorant of the horrifying consequences of their eating habits, but now is the time for everyone to become more aware. Otherwise the earth will no longer be able to handle everything that Americans continue to dish out.

Becoming aware may be a monumental task for the 3 American public because certainly the beef industry does not advertise the destruction that occurs when animals are bred and slaughtered. Instead, the industry concentrates on spending its time and cash (more than $45 million a year) to announce that for McDonald's, "Billions are served" and that "BEEF . . . It's what for dinner," or that beef is "Real food for real people." (Apparently the people who care about the animals and the earth are somehow not real.) Never will it be advertised that 55 square feet of rain forest are being destroyed for each hamburger that is being enjoyed. And never will it be publicly announced that because of the destruction of the Amazon for cattle grazing, thousands of species are becoming extinct. We must find information like this ourselves, in books such as the *Rain Forest Book* and *Diet For A New America,* written by John Robbins, the vegetarian king who rejected his position at the top of the lucrative Baskin-Robbins business.

Just as the meat-related industries will not admit to the 4 harm being done to supply Americans with meat, people in general will not admit that they alone can make a positive change. But everyone must realize that by refusing to purchase any meat, we can dramatically help preserve the natural balance of the entire earth. People now must become sensitive to all of the outcomes of every action every day. They must see animal rights in direct relation to humans, to the balance of the ecosystems, and to the preservation of not only the animals being slaughtered but also thousands of various species of life. As a corollary of animal rights, vegetarianism questions not just the morality of medical research or even the frivolousness of fur coats on humans; it underscores how the negative energy that we are putting into the slaughtering of innocent animals is killing us too. Now, with new compassion, we all must save the earth and ourselves by sparing the animals from a death they do not deserve.

5 As for "real people" and what they eat: remember that Thoreau, Einstein, and Ghandi were all vegetarians; all are among the most respected thinkers in history. Vice President Al Gore also knows the consequences of meat eating; he has written about them in his book *Earth In The Balance.* Gore speaks about how the rain forest is being burned to create fast pasture for fast-food beef: "More than one Tennessee's worth of rain forest [is] being slashed and burned each year." Those who listen to Gore's words, or read his writings, are aware of the fact that thousands of species are about to perish because of the slashing and burning.

6 What exactly can be done? Is it feasible for our government to discourage America's lucrative beef industry in order for animals to survive? Must we continue to allow this destruction to occur, even though these species are dying out one thousand times faster now than at any time in the past 65 million years? We are starting to worry about letting the plants that could hold cures for our worst diseases just slip away. We are becoming angry that the rain forests are turning into deserts. We are feeling guilty that because of our desire to satisfy our superficial hunger for wealth and convenience, we are slaughtering countless animals and endangering the future of all life on earth.

7 If the destruction in the Amazon is too far away for the people of the United States to become compassionate, think about the destruction that is occurring in our own country. From *Diet for a New America,* we learn that the cattle raised in the United States use up in one way or another more than 50% of the precious water resources of our nation—a circumstance that could cause all of the water left over from the ice age to vanish in less than 30 years. John Robbins explains that the production of cattle is polluting the environment as well as taking from it: "The livestock of the United States produce twenty times as much excrement as the entire human population of the country." Those livestock also produce 12% of the harmful methane gas that is

released into the atmosphere, methane gas that helps contribute to global warming.

Supporters of the beef industry will say, "Well, kill them and eat them and there won't be that problem!" But it is the continuing cycle of destruction that is the problem. Without human intervention, cows would be roaming in herds in their natural balance with the earth. Instead, they are placed in unnatural, man-made environments where they are kept immobile and restricted from freedom. The cost of satisfying our unnecessary desires is the lives of countless innocent animals. If humans would be humane enough to let the animals live, rather than gruesomely to kill and barbarically eat them, the earth could restore its peace and perhaps a healthy future would not be such an impossible feat. 8

Please realize that every purchase of meat contributes to the cycle of destruction, and that only by stopping the consumption of animals can the earth have a chance for balance again. Know that it is the casual life-style of the American humans that has knocked the ecosystem of the entire world out of whack. And believe that as long as meat is consumed, tranquility will never be restored. Until the time that respect is given to the earth, the environment and all its critters, creatures, plants and animals are struggling for survival. 9

Foundation for Biomedical Research

It's the Animals You Don't See That Really Helped

This ad was developed by the Foundation for Biomedical Research, an organization whose self-described aim is articulated in the fine print on the ad, which was published in many newspapers and magazines from 1990 to 1992.

The following excerpts from Garry B. Trudeau's "Doonesbury" appeared around Christmas 1989. For more of his work, and more on Mr. Trudeau, see pages 94 and 170.

Doonesbury BY G.B. TRUDEAU

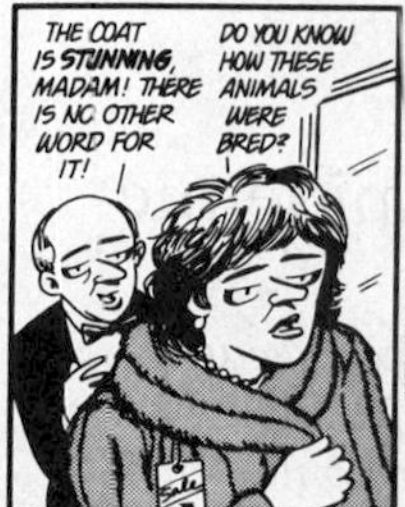

Doonesbury BY G.B. TRUDEAU

Doonesbury BY G.B. TRUDEAU

HOW SHOULD WE FIGHT AIDS?

Marcia Angell

A Dual Approach to the AIDS Epidemic

In May 1991, Marcia Angell—a physician and the executive editor of the prestigious New England Journal of Medicine—*wrote the following editorial concerning methods of containing the AIDS epidemic. Note that several responses to Dr. Angell's argument, as well as her own reply to those responses, are printed below her essay.*

1 Ten years ago five homosexual men in Los Angeles were reported to have acquired a mysterious and profound immune deficiency associated with pneumocystis pneumonia and other opportunistic infections. The report on these men, published in the *Morbidity and Mortality Weekly Report* on June 5, 1981, marked the beginning of the AIDS epidemic.[1] Within weeks, similar cases were being described elsewhere.[2–5] Even before the isolation of the causative virus in 1983 and the introduction of serologic testing in 1985, it was clear that a major epidemic had begun.

2 Now, a decade later, well over 100,000 Americans have died of AIDS and an estimated 1 million are currently infected with the virus, of whom more than 125,000 are thought to have clinical AIDS.[6] Women and children are affected, as well as both heterosexual and homosexual men. Although the rate of spread in the homosexual community has slowed, the reservoir is now huge, and we can therefore expect to see the number of cases continue to grow. Thus, AIDS is no longer an obscure disease known only to the medical and homosexual communities; it is now a household word, of concern to most Americans and frightening to many. Not since the polio outbreaks of the early 1950s have we been faced with so threatening an epidemic. Furthermore, with the advent of expensive treatments that extend the lives of persons infected with the human immunodefi-

ciency virus (HIV) for many years, the cost of this epidemic has become a troubling issue in a time of shrinking resources.

In addition to the medical and economic issues surrounding AIDS, there are social issues unique to this epidemic that have greatly complicated our response to it. Unlike the polio epidemic of the 1950s or the influenza pandemic of 1918, AIDS tends to afflict people who are for one reason or another the objects of discrimination. Although increasingly a disease of inner-city black and Hispanic intravenous drug abusers of both sexes and their sexual partners, AIDS was at first almost exclusively a disease of homosexual men. It therefore carried the stigma of any sexually transmitted disease, but unlike syphilis or gonorrhea, it also carried the stigma of homosexuality—a double burden. Members of the homosexual community, articulate and well educated and accustomed to injustice, mobilized to protect themselves from a discriminatory backlash more effectively than the politically powerless drug abusers could possibly have done. Concerned that identification of those with AIDS would lead to loss of employment, housing, and medical insurance, as well as to social ostracism, they and others sensitive to civil rights issues argued successfully for confidentiality and against screening and efforts to trace sexual partners. Thus, although AIDS is reportable in all states, HIV infection is not, nor are contacts systematically traced. Instead, testing for infection is by and large voluntary, as is the notification of sexual partners. 3

We are now seeing growing opposition to this policy of strict confidentiality, as described by Bayer in this issue of the *Journal*.[7] With recent reports of the transmission of AIDS from patients to health care providers and, more recently, from a provider to patients,[8] we hear calls for the routine screening of both groups—all patients admitted to hospitals and all doctors and nurses. There are also calls for the routine screening of pregnant women and newborns in response to the growing number of infants who contract AIDS from their mothers perinatally. Requiring the notification of sexual partners is less emphasized, perhaps because it is so difficult, but it, too, is receiving renewed attention. 4

Debates about these issues, it seems to me, too often confuse the social with the epidemiologic problems. To be sure, both sets of issues are closely enmeshed, but there 5 seems to have been little effort to sort them out. Many of those who believe that controlling the epidemic should be our most important priority recommend draconian methods for doing so, including not only widespread screening, but also the removal of infected children from their schools, infected adults from their jobs, and both from the neighborhood. On the other hand, those moved primarily by compassion for AIDS sufferers and concern for civil rights are likely to resist the usual methods for monitoring and containing an epidemic—methods that might spare more people suffering.

6 I believe we need a dual approach that attempts to distinguish social from epidemiologic problems and that deals with both, simultaneously but separately. Clearly, HIV-infected persons need to be protected against discrimination and hysteria, but doing so requires social and political measures, not epidemiologic ones. Jobs, housing, and insurance benefits, for example, should be protected by statute. The economic consequences of HIV infection require additional attention, since they go far beyond the possible loss of employment and ordinary insurance benefits. Treating AIDS is expensive, and the disease lasts for the rest of a patient's life, during much of which he or she may be unable to work. Even the most generous medical insurance is unlikely to cover all the health care needs of a patient with AIDS; thus, as patients grow sicker they also stand to become destitute.

7 We as a society should deal more systematically with the devastating economic consequences of HIV infection. I suggest we establish a nationally funded program, analogous to the end-stage renal disease program, for the medical care of HIV-infected persons. The end-stage renal disease program, established by Congress in 1972, extends Medicare coverage to all patients with kidney failure.[9] This is a response to the development of effective but extremely expensive treatments for end-stage renal disease—namely, long-term dialysis and renal transplantation. Handling the AIDS epidemic in the same way would probably cost society no more than it spends on HIV infection now. Increases in costs due to expanded access would probably be offset by the elimination of the expensive practice of attempting to shift costs. Under the present patchwork system, each potential payer (employers as well as federal, state, municipal, and private insurers) naturally wishes to pass the costs

to another. Thus, for example, a health care institution that finds itself possibly liable for the care of an employee who becomes infected with HIV takes an adversarial stance, asserting that there is no proof the infection was work-related. Whatever the outcome of any such dispute, some element in the system, often Medicaid, eventually must assume the costs. A nationally funded program would have the advantage of uniformity, simplicity, and efficiency. It would also give those at risk an incentive to be tested, thus allowing for earlier treatment and the protection of sexual partners. The present system, in contrast, is filled with disincentives for being tested.

If by such measures we can soften the social and economic 8
burdens on people with HIV infection, perhaps we will be freer to address the epidemiologic problems more rigorously. Concern about social issues now creates a reluctance to deal effectively with the epidemiologic problems. For example, systematic tracing of the sexual partners of HIV-infected persons is generally resisted because of the threat to confidentiality, although contact tracing makes sense from an epidemiologic standpoint and is officially required for other sexually transmitted diseases. Similarly, there is resistance to a screening program for all pregnant women and newborns,[10–12] although such a program would be reasonable, given the accuracy of new confirmatory tests and the fact that perinatally acquired HIV infection is now more common than congenital syphilis or phenylketonuria, both of which are tested for routinely. Infected women could make more-informed choices about family planning, and infected newborns could be treated earlier.

Testing health care providers and hospitalized patients is 9
also controversial,[13] although it makes sense from several standpoints. Screening patients on admission would identify those with whom health care providers must be most alert; it is unrealistic to expect them to maintain the highest level of vigilance continuously. Similarly, because it is remotely possible that there could be an exchange of blood during a medical procedure, patients have a right to know whether a doctor or nurse who performs invasive procedures is infected with HIV. If necessary, retraining in noninvasive areas or early retirement could be provided for by special insurance programs for health care professionals. Screening both patients and health care providers would also, of course, identify those for whom treatment could be

begun early and whose sexual partners could be protected. I believe that, on balance, systematic tracing and notification of the sexual partners of HIV-infected persons and screening of pregnant women, newborns, hospitalized patients, and health care professionals are warranted. These populations are, after all, relatively accessible to the health care system and at some special risk. Attempting to screen the entire population would simply be impractical; on the other hand, targeting only high-risk groups would be unworkable, in part because it would entail making distinctions that are often impossible as well as invidious. With any increase in screening, however, the specter of discrimination arises once a person is known to be infected. Only if such discrimination, at least in its more tangible expressions, is countered by statute and if those with HIV infection are assured of receiving all the medical care they need, can we pursue the basic elements of infection control more resolutely and so spare others the tragedy of this disease.

References

1. Gottlieb MS, Schanker HM, Fan PT, Saxon A. Weisman JD. *Pneumocystis* pneumonia—Los Angeles, MMWR 1981; 30:250–2.
2. Friedman-Kien A, Laubenstein L, Marmor M. et al. Kaposi's sarcoma and *Pneumocystis* pneumonia among homosexual men—New York City and California. MMWR 1981; 30:305–8.
3. Gottlieb MS, Schroff R, Schanker HM, et al. *Pneumocystis carinii* pneumonia and mucosal candidiasis in previously healthy homosexual men: evidence of a new acquired cellular immunodeficiency, N Engl J Med 1981; 305:1425–31.
4. Masur H, Michelis MA, Greene JB, et al. An outbreak of community-acquired *Pneumocystis carinii* pneumonia: initial manifestation of cellular immune dysfunction. N Engl J Med 1981; 305:1431–8.
5. Siegal FP, Lopez C, Hammer GS, et al. Severe acquired immunodeficiency in male homosexuals, manifested by chronic perianal ulcerative herpes simplex lesions. N Engl J Med 1981; 305:1439–44.
6. Karon JM, Dondero TJ Jr. HIV prevalence estimates and AIDS case projections for the United States: report based upon a workshop. MMWR 1990; 39(RR-16): 1–31.
7. Bayer R. Public health policy and the AIDS epidemic—an end to HIV exceptionalism? N Engl J Med 1991; 324:1500–4.
8. Update: transmission of HIV infection during an invasive dental procedure—Florida. JAMA 1991; 265:563–8.

9. Levinsky N, Rettig RA. The Medicare end-stage renal disease program: a report from the Institute of Medicine. N Engl J Med 1991; 324:1143–8.
10. Hardy LM, ed. HIV screening of pregnant women and newborns. Washington, D.C.: National Academy Press, 1991.
11. Working Group on HIV Testing of Pregnant Women and Newborns. HIV infection, pregnant women, and newborns: a policy proposal for information and testing. JAMA 1990; 264:2416–20.
12. Nolan K. Ethical issues in caring for pregnant women and newborns at risk for human immunodeficiency virus infection. Semin Perinatol 1989; 13:55–65.
13. Brennan TA. Transmission of the human immunodeficiency virus in the health care setting—time for action. N Engl J Med 1991; 324:1504–9. 1

Responses to Marcia Angell: Letters to the Editor of *The New England Journal of Medicine* (and a Counter-Response by Marcia Angell)

To the Editor: Angell proposes a nationally funded program for the cure of all persons infected with the human immunodeficiency virus (HIV). Although the provision of adequate medical care to all persons, including the HIV-infected, should be a social goal, it is silly to think that it is a reality, or will soon be. Divorced from her utopian promise of care, Angell's recommendation is little more than a stick with no carrot. 1

There is, however, an alternative course between, on the one hand, Angell's proposal that millions of people should be subjected to mandatory testing in exchange for an elusive promise of free treatment and, on the other hand, the current situation, in which too few have access to confidential HIV testing, education and counseling, prophylactic therapies, and associated services, such as substance-abuse treatment and legal services for discrimination problems. That middle path would increase the incentive for voluntary, confidential HIV testing by funding HIV-testing programs fully, enacting or strengthening guarantees of confidentiality and nondiscrimination, expanding Medicaid eligibility and coverage to ensure medical treatment for all, adopting a national standard of care for that treatment, and providing a full range of substance-abuse treatment for those who need 2 it. Indeed, if people are confident that testing will result in life-sustaining treatment, that their substance abuse will receive compassionate care, and that their jobs, housing, and families will be safeguarded, few would decline opportunities for voluntary, confidential HIV testing and counseling. By contrast, forced testing without such guarantees is worse than useless: it is counterproductive in that it drives people away from the systems of health care and support.

3 The middle path is also more consistent with our political and moral culture, which demands that before we resort to coercion, all possible alternatives that are less restrictive be tried and proved insufficient. A decade into the HIV epidemic, some, like Angell, are apparently convinced that a disease-control strategy based on voluntarism—voluntary testing, voluntary treatment, and voluntary preventive behavior—has been a failure. The truth, however, is that given the meager Medicaid coverage and coverage for uninsured people in most states, the lack of frank, explicit information on HIV prevention, the lack of assurances of confidentiality and nondiscrimination, and the lack of substance-abuse treatment, voluntarism has not yet been given a decent chance to work.

William B. Rubenstein, Esq.
AIDS Project
American Civil Liberties Union

David A. Hansell, Esq.
Gay Men's Health Crisis

Evan Wolfson, Esq.
Lambda Legal Defense
and Education Fund, Inc.

1 *To the Editor:* I have always thought it peculiarly irrational that the American medical and political establishments embrace an entitlement program for a single condition, end-stage renal disease. Thus, people with this disease enjoy the benefits of a national health care program for the management of their renal failure. Angell advocates creating a similar program for persons infected with HIV. I submit that persons with any serious, progressive illness are at similar risk of catastrophic medical expenses and conse-

quent indigence. Why are the victims of end-stage renal disease and the acquired immunodeficiency syndrome (AIDS) more worthy of entitlement programs than, say, patients with cancer or multiple sclerosis? If we are going to have national health care, should it not be for all Americans, not just the relative few with a specific diagnosis?

David C. Dodson, M.D.

To the Editor: Angell's contention that it is "unrealistic to 1
expect [health care providers] to maintain the highest level of vigilance continuously" seems defeatist and is, in my experience, unduly pessimistic. We minimize our risk of occupational exposure to HIV by assuming that every patient is infected. Once that premise is internalized, knowing a patient's HIV status does not influence which precautions are implemented.

Angell also supports the right of patients to know the HIV 2
status of their health care providers—by mandatory testing, I infer. But the question of mandatory testing of health care providers presupposes that such testing could convert a currently very low risk to a zero risk. Although the consequences of HIV transmission are tragic, it is not clear that mandatory testing of practitioners can reduce the risk to patients below what it now appears to be. The enzyme-linked immunosorbent assay for HIV antibody is being continuously improved but is known to give false negative results both during the "window" between infection and the production of detectable antibody[1] and in people who remain antibody-negative for years while harboring HIV.[2] Even with a perfect HIV test, we could never be entirely certain that a given person was uninfected.

The logistics and costs of such an effort are also formida- 3
ble. Who would be tested? The number of health care providers in the United States who perform invasive procedures may well exceed a million. And given the window, how frequently would testing need to be done in order to provide the degree of certainty that patients want? Yearly, monthly, daily? Repeated testing of such a large, low-prevalence population is an expensive proposition, and at this point the potential gain is not apparent.

Because transmission to patients is possible, the obliga- 4
tions of practitioners who know themselves to be infected

does merit further discussion. However, in developing policies to protect our patients and ourselves, we cannot afford to be unclear about the limits of our technology or the level of certainty that can be attained.

BARBARA E. BERGER, M.S., R.N.

1. Nakamura RM, Bylund DJ, Rooney KE. Current status of clinical laboratory tests for the human immunodeficiency virus. J Clin Lab Anal 1990; 4:295–306.
2. Imagawa DT, Lee MH, Wolinsky SM, et al. Human immunodeficiency virus type 1 infection in homosexual men who remain seronegative for prolonged periods. N Engl J Med 1989; 320:1458–62.

1 *To the Editor:* The institution of widespread HIV testing for health care workers or their patients will not have a substantial effect on the rate of accidentally acquired HIV infection in either group. The rates of transmission are exceedingly low and become even lower when attention is paid to the use of universal precautions. A real tragedy will result not from the lack of widespread HIV testing but from the misallocation of health care resources away from larger health problems. It would be ironic if extensive HIV-screening programs for health care workers and their patients reduced even further the health care resources available to inner-city patients, the very group most affected by the AIDS epidemic. Although rare unfortunate cases of nosocomial HIV infection command public attention, let us not forget the millions of Americans whose lives can be threatened through the lack of adequate health care.

2 Real safety in health care delivery comes from appropriate routine work practices, such as universal precautions, that protect against many infectious diseases, not just HIV. There are far greater risks to patients from exposure to health care workers impaired by alcoholism and drug abuse. Perhaps the greatest risk to patients results from travel to and from medical facilities. Moreover, as a nation we seem to overlook many serious problems while trying to avoid unlikely ones. It was not until last year that the number of deaths from AIDS finally exceeded that of deaths from injuries involving firearms in the United States. We need rational public policies concerning health care that address

major health problems so that resources can be allocated fairly to all Americans. There is a greater good that can be achieved with the acceptance by health care workers and their patients of the extremely minimal risk of accidental HIV infection, so that the health care system as a whole can function more effectively for everyone.

EDWARD C. KLATT, M.D.

To the Editor: Angell assumes that "patients have a right to 1
know whether a doctor or nurse who performs invasive procedures is infected with HIV," since it is "remotely possible" that blood-to-blood contact could occur. This position is inconsistent with the principles and practice of informed consent, in that it sets an untenable standard for the required disclosure of remote risks to patients.

The Centers for Disease Control (CDC) has estimated that 2
the risk of HIV transmission from an infected health care worker to a patient is 2.4 to 24 per million procedures.[1] In fact, except for one dentist whom the CDC has documented to have used substandard infection-control technique,[2] such transmission remains undocumented. Yet a consistent application of Angell's "right to know" would require the disclosure of all such risks in health care delivery—remote, undocumented, or both. Thus, health care workers could be required to inform patients of many individual disabilities or conditions affecting themselves, such as side effects of continuing medications, chronic conditions, sleeplessness, psychiatric conditions, even surgeon-specific postoperative and perioperative mortality rates and surgeon-specific rates of wound infection. All are arguably much more relevant to patients' safety than a health worker's HIV infection.

The law of informed consent has long held that only 3
"material" or "significant" risks need to be disclosed to patients before treatment.[3, 4] The materiality or significance of the risk is determined in turn by the standard of a "reasonable patient" or, in some states, by the customary practice of the medical community. Although many and perhaps most patients would probably like to know such information, the medical, legal, and public health communities must bring their professional judgment to bear on the reasonableness of that desire. These communities should be mindful of their obligation to distinguish between how

much of that desire can be attributed to overreaction and how much to a rational apprehension of harm. I also question whether, if disclosure is mandated, the information disclosed should concern the individual practitioner's record and practice of infection control, rather than his or her known serologic status with regard to blood-borne pathogens.

4 If improving the safety and choice afforded to patients is our goal, we should not begin by singling out HIV infection of health workers, from which the aggregate harm to patients is truly remote.

Nancy M. Louden
Ad Hoc Committee on AIDS
Association of the Bar of the
City of New York

1. Centers for Disease Control. Estimates of the risk of endemic transmission of HBV and HIV to patients by the percutaneous route during invasive surgical and dental procedures. Atlanta: Centers for Disease Control, January 30, 1991.
2. Update: transmission of HIV infection during an invasive dental procedure—Florida. MMWR 1991; 40:21, 25–7.
3. Information that need not be disclosed. In: Rozovsky FA. Consent to treatment: a practical guide. 2nd ed. Boston; Little, Brown, 1990:59–64.
4. The legal requirements for disclosure and consent: history and current status. In: Appelbaum PS, Lidz CW, Meisel A. Informed consent: legal theory and clinical practice. New York: Oxford University Press, 1987:50–4.

1 *Editor's reply:* In my editorial I proposed a dual approach to the AIDS epidemic: on the one hand, I advocated stronger measures to protect those with HIV infection from social and economic deprivation; on the other, I recommended the routine screening of certain population groups that are accessible to the health care system. Rubenstein et al. imply that I believe the two elements of this dual approach can be separated; I do not.

2 I find it puzzling that some of the correspondents whose letters appear here seem to object to my proposals because they do not represent perfect solutions to problems. Thus, they object to funding the treatment of HIV infection because we do not fund the care of everyone. They see the

fact that screening would yield a small number of false negative results as a reason to remain ignorant about the status of the great majority in whom the test would be accurate. (Somehow, the issue of false negative results does not stop them from calling for more widespread voluntary screening.) As is too often the case in this epidemic, the rights of sexual partners are all but overlooked.

It is particularly disturbing that some doctors seem to 3
focus disproportionately on resisting proposals to test health care providers. To be sure, the risk of HIV transmission from doctors to patients is exceedingly small—much smaller than the risk of transmission from patients to doctors. But there are two reasons for testing doctors that have nothing to do with the magnitude of the risk. First, agreeing to routine screening would give doctors the moral leadership necessary to ask for reciprocity from their patients: they would in effect not be asking anything of them that they were not willing to do themselves. Second, the public overwhelmingly believes that certain groups of health care providers should be screened for HIV infection, and there is no overriding reason not to do so. Some believe it "draconian" to divert HIV-positive doctors to noninvasive professional pursuits, but the CDC and the American Medical Association think otherwise, and I agree. The further admonition that a screening program would make doctors reluctant to care for patients with AIDS is odd: it suggests that doctors would be more worried about having to retrain than about contracting a lethal disease.

The best approach to containing the spread of a transmis- 4
sible disease is to find out who is infected and who is at risk and to treat the former and try to protect the latter. The system I proposed is not perfect, but it is better than our current nonsystem. We should not make the perfect the enemy of the good.

MARCIA ANGELL, M.D.

EUTHANASIA

It's Over, Debbie

In 1988 the Journal of the American Medical Association *published the following anonymous contribution to its "A Piece of My Mind" opinion column. Nothing ever published there has been more controversial.*

1 The call came in the middle of the night. As a gynecology resident rotating through a large, private hospital, I had come to detest telephone calls, because invariably I would be up for several hours and would not feel good the next day. However, duty called, so I answered the phone. A nurse informed me that a patient was having difficulty getting rest, could I please see her. She was on 3 North. That was the gynecologic-oncology unit, not my usual duty station. As I trudged along, bumping sleepily against walls and corners and not believing I was up again, I tried to imagine what I might find at the end of my walk. Maybe an elderly woman with an anxiety reaction, or perhaps something particularly horrible.

2 I grabbed the chart from the nurses station on my way to the patient's room, and the nurse gave me some hurried details: a 20-year-old girl named Debbie was dying of ovarian cancer. She was having unrelenting vomiting apparently as the result of an alcohol drip administered for sedation. Hmm, I thought. Very sad. As I approached the room I could hear loud, labored breathing. I entered and saw an emaciated, dark-haired woman who appeared much older than 20. She was receiving nasal oxygen, had an IV, and was sitting in bed suffering from what was obviously severe air hunger. The chart noted her weight at 80 pounds. A second woman, also dark-haired but of middle-age, stood at her right, holding her hand. Both looked up as I entered. The room seemed filled with the patient's desperate effort to survive. Her eyes were hollow, and she had suprasternal and intercostal retractions with her rapid inspirations. She had

not eaten or slept in two days. She had not responded to chemotherapy and was being given supportive care only. It was a gallows scene, a cruel mockery of her youth and unfulfilled potential. Her only words to me were, "Let's get this over with."

I retreated with my thoughts to the nurses station. The patient was tired and needed rest. I could not give her health, but I could give her rest. I asked the nurse to draw 20 mg of morphine sulfate into a syringe. Enough, I thought, to do the job. I took the syringe into the room and told the two women I was going to give Debbie something that would let her rest and to say good-bye. Debbie looked at the syringe, then laid her head on the pillow with her eyes open, watching what was left of the world. I injected the morphine intravenously and watched to see if my calculations on its effects would be correct. Within seconds her breathing slowed to a normal rate, her eyes closed, and her features softened as she seemed restful at last. The older woman stroked the hair of the now-sleeping patient. I waited for the inevitable next effect of depressing the respiratory drive. With clocklike certainty, within four minutes the breathing rate slowed even more, then became irregular, then ceased. The dark-haired woman stood erect and seemed relieved. 3

It's over, Debbie. 4

Name Withheld by Request

Charles Colson

It's Not Over, Debbie

Charles Colson (born 1931) was converted to Christianity while serving a prison term for his role in the Watergate scandal of the Nixon administration. He has written five books on Christian topics and contributes regularly to the evangelical publication Christianity Today, *where the following column appeared in 1988.*

The scene is a darkened hospital ward. An intern stands over Debbie, a young woman with terminal cancer. Her breathing is labored as she struggles for oxygen. She weighs 80 pounds. She is in horrible pain. 1

2 The doctor has never seen Debbie before, but a glance at her chart confirms she is not responding to treatment. He leans down to hear her whisper, "Let's get this over with."

3 Most doctors would have hurried to give relief against the pain, or tried to offer some solace to the anguished relative standing near the bed. But this intern measured out 20 milligrams of morphine into a syringe—enough, he wrote later, "to do the job"—and injected it. Four minutes later, Debbie was dead. The doctor's only comment: "It's over, Debbie."

4 Stories like this, publicized a few months back, are shocking but should not surprise us. While no one likes to admit it, active euthanasia is not uncommon. It has been closeted in hospital ethics committees, cloaked in euphemisms spoken to grieving relatives. It is the unnamed shadow on an unknown number of death certificates—of handicapped newborns; sickly, aged parents; the terminally ill in critical pain.

5 No, Debbie's case is something new only because of the public nature of both its telling and the debate that has followed.

6 This story was first written, anonymously but without apology, by the intern himself, and published in the *Journal of the American Medical Association* (JAMA)—one of the most respected medical journals in the world.

7 Following the article's publication, the commentary came fast and furious. Some experts dismissed the incident as fictional. Others believed it, but focused their criticism on the young doctor's lack of familiarity with Debbie's medical history.

8 But the article's greatest effect was to yank euthanasia out of the closet and thrust it into the arena of national debate. On the surface that might seem healthy, getting the whole ugly issue into the open. But there's a subtle danger here: The JAMA article and the impassioned discussion it provoked offer a case study of a recurring process in American life by which the unthinkable in short order becomes the unquestionable.

9 Usually it works like this: Some practice so offensive that it could scarcely be discussed in public is suddenly advocated by a respected expert in a respected forum. The public is shocked, then outraged. The very fact that such a thing could be publicly debated becomes the focus of the debate.

10 But in the process, the sheer repetition of the shocking gradually dulls its shock effect. No longer outraged, people

begin to argue for positions to moderate the extreme; or they accept the premise, challenging instead the means to achieve it. (Note that in Debbie's debate, many challenged not the killing, but the intern's failure to check more carefully into the case.)

And gradually, though no one remembers quite how it all happened, the once unspeakable becomes tolerable and, in time, acceptable. 11

An example of how this process works is the case of homosexuality. Not long ago it was widely regarded, even in secular society, as a perversion. The gay-rights movement's first pronouncements were received with shock; then, in the process of debate, the public gradually lost its sense of outrage. Homosexuality became a cause—and what was once deviant is today, in many jurisdictions, a legally protected right. All this in little more than a decade. 12

Debbie's story appears to have initiated this process for euthanasia. Columnist Ellen Goodman welcomed the case as "a debate that should be taking place." 13

So what was once a crime becomes a debate. And, if history holds true, that debate will usher the once unmentionable into common practice. 14

Already the stage is set. In a 1983 poll, 63 percent of Americans approved of mercy killing in certain cases. In a 1988 poll, more than 50 percent of lawyers favored legal euthanasia. The Hemlock Society is working to put the issue on the ballot in several states. 15

I don't intend to sound alarmist: legal euthanasia in this country is still more a threat than a reality. But 20 years ago, who would have thought abortion would one day be a constitutional right, or that infanticide would be given legal protection? 16

The path from the unmentionable to the commonplace is being traveled with increasing speed in medical ethics. Without some concerted resistance, euthanasia is likely to be the next to make the trip. As Ellen Goodman concluded her column, "The Debbie story is not over yet, not by a long shot." 17

Indeed. 18

Novelist Walker Percy, in *The Thanatos Syndrome*, offers one vision of where such compromising debates on the value of life might take us. 19

The time is the 1990s. Qualitarian Life Centers have sprung up across the country after the landmark case of *Doe v. Dade* "which decreed, with solid scientific evidence, that 20 the human infant does not achieve personhood until 18 months." At these centers one can conveniently dispose of unwanted young and old alike.

21 An old priest, Father Smith, confronts the narrator, a psychiatrist, in this exchange:

22 "You are an able psychiatrist. On the whole a decent, generous humanitarian person in the abstract sense of the word. You know what is going to happen to you."

23 "What?"

24 "You are a member of the first generation of doctors in the history of medicine to turn their backs on the oath of Hippocrates and kill millions of old, useless people, unborn children, born malformed children, for the good of mankind—and to do so without a single murmur from one of you. Not a single letter of protest in the august *New England Journal of Medicine*. And do you know what you are going to end up doing?"

25 "No," I say . . .

26 The priest aims his azimuth squarely at me and then appears to lose his train of thought. . . .

27 "What is going to happen to me, Father?" I ask before he gets away altogether.

28 "Oh," he says absently, appearing to be thinking of something else, "you're going to end up killing Jews."

James Rachels

Active and Passive Euthanasia

James Rachels (born 1941), a philosopher and teacher at New York University, University of Miami, and the University of Alabama at Birmingham (where he currently works), is particularly interested in ethics. He contributed the following essay to The New England Journal of Medicine *in 1975.*

1 The distinction between active and passive euthanasia is thought to be crucial for medical ethics. The idea is that it is permissible, at least in some cases, to withhold treatment and allow a patient to die, but it is never permissible to take any direct action designed to kill the patient. This doctrine

seems to be accepted by most doctors, and it is endorsed in a statement adopted by the House of Delegates of the American Medical Association on December 4, 1973:

> The intentional termination of the life of one human being by another—mercy killing—is contrary to that for which the medical profession stands and is contrary to the policy of the American Medical Association.
>
> The cessation of the employment of extraordinary means to prolong the life of the body when there is irrefutable evidence that biological death is imminent is the decision of the patient and/or his family. The advice and judgment of the physician should be freely available to the patient and/or his immediate family.

However, a strong case can be made against this doctrine. In what follows I will set out some of the relevant arguments, and urge doctors to reconsider their views on this matter.

To begin with a familiar type of situation, a patient who is 2
dying of incurable cancer of the throat is in terrible pain, which can no longer be satisfactorily alleviated. He is certain to die within a few days, even if present treatment is continued, but he does not want to go on living for those days since the pain is unbearable. So he asks the doctor for an end to it, and his family joins in the request.

Suppose the doctor agrees to withhold treatment, as the 3
conventional doctrine says he may. The justification for his doing so is that the patient is in terrible agony, and since he is going to die anyway, it would be wrong to prolong his suffering needlessly. But now notice this. If one simply withholds treatment, it may take the patient longer to die, and so he may suffer more than he would if more direct action were taken and a lethal injection given. This fact provides strong reason for thinking that, once the initial decision not to prolong his agony has been made, active euthanasia is actually preferable to passive euthanasia, rather than the reverse. To say otherwise is to endorse the option that leads to more suffering rather than less, and is contrary to the humanitarian impulse that prompts the decision not to prolong his life in the first place.

Part of my point is that the process of being "allowed to 4
die" can be relatively slow and painful, whereas being given a lethal injection is relatively quick and painless. Let me give a different sort of example. In the United States about one in

600 babies is born with Down's syndrome. Most of these babies are otherwise healthy—that is, with only the usual pediatric care, they will proceed to an otherwise normal infancy. Some, however, are born with congenital defects such as intestinal obstructions that require operations if they are to live. Sometimes, the parents and the doctor will decide not to operate, and let the infant die. Anthony Shaw describes what happens then:

> . . . When surgery is denied [the doctor] must try to keep the infant from suffering while natural forces sap the baby's life away. As a surgeon whose natural inclination is to use the scalpel to fight off death, standing by and watching a salvageable baby die is the most emotionally exhausting experience I know. It is easy at a conference, in a theoretical discussion, to decide that such infants should be allowed to die. It is altogether different to stand by in the nursery and watch as dehydration and infection wither a tiny being over hours and days. This is a terrible ordeal for me and the hospital staff—much more so than for the parents who never set foot in the nursery.

I can understand why some people are opposed to all euthanasia, and insist that such infants must be allowed to live. I think I can also understand why other people favor destroying these babies quickly and painlessly. But why should anyone favor letting "dehydration and infection wither a tiny being over hours and days"? The doctrine that says that a baby may be allowed to dehydrate and wither, but may not be given an injection that would end its life without suffering, seems so patently cruel as to require no further refutation. The strong language is not intended to offend, but only to put the point in the clearest possible way.

5 My second argument is that the conventional doctrine leads to decisions concerning life and death made on irrelevant grounds.

6 Consider again the case of the infants with Down's syndrome who need operations for congenital defects unrelated to the syndrome to live. Sometimes, there is no operation, and the baby dies. But when there is no such defect, the baby lives on. Now, an operation such as that to remove an intestinal obstruction is not prohibitively difficult. The reason why such operations are not performed in these cases is, clearly, that the child has Down's syndrome and the parents

and doctor judge that because of that fact it is better for the child to die.

But notice that this situation is absurd, no matter what view one takes of the lives and potential of such babies. If the life of such an infant is worth preserving, what does it matter if it needs a simple operation? Or, if one thinks it better that such a baby should not live on, what difference does it make that it happens to have an unobstructed intestinal tract? In either case, the matter of life and death is being decided on irrelevant grounds. It is the Down's syndrome, and not the intestines, that is the issue. The matter should be decided, if at all, on that basis, and not be allowed to depend on the essentially irrelevant question of whether the intestinal tract is blocked. 7

What makes this situation possible, of course, is the idea that when there is an intestinal blockage, one can "let the baby die," but when there is no such defect there is nothing that can be done, for one must not "kill" it. The fact that this idea leads to such results as deciding life or death on irrelevant grounds is another good reason why the doctrine should be rejected. 8

One reason why so many people think that there is an important moral difference between active and passive euthanasia is that they think killing someone is morally worse than letting someone die. But is it? Is killing in itself worse than letting die? To investigate this issue, two cases may be considered that are exactly alike except that one involves killing whereas the other involves letting someone die. Then it can be asked whether this difference makes any difference to the moral assessments. It is important that the cases be exactly alike, except for this one difference and not some other that accounts for any variation in the assessments of the two cases. So, let us consider this pair of cases: 9

In the first, Smith stands to gain a large inheritance if anything should happen to his six-year-old cousin. One evening while the child is taking his bath, Smith sneaks into the bathroom and drowns the child, and then arranges things so that it will look like an accident. 10

In the second, Jones also stands to gain if anything should happen to his six-year-old cousin. Like Smith, Jones sneaks in planning to drown the child in his bath. However, just as he enters the bathroom Jones sees the child slip and hit his head, and fall face down in the water. Jones is delighted; he stands by, ready to push the child's head back under if it is 11 necessary. With only a little thrashing about, the child drowns all by himself, "accidentally," as Jones watches and does nothing.

12 Now Smith killed the child, whereas Jones "merely" let the child die. That is the only difference between them. Did either man behave better, from a moral point of view? If the difference between killing and letting die were in itself a morally important matter, one should say that Jones's behavior was less reprehensible than Smith's. But does one really want to say that? I think not. In the first place, both men acted from the same motive, personal gain, and both had exactly the same end in view when they acted. It may be inferred from Smith's conduct that he is a bad man, although that judgment may be withdrawn or modified if certain further facts are learned about him—for example, that he is mentally deranged. But would not the very same thing be inferred about Jones from his conduct? And would not the same further considerations also be relevant to any modification of this judgment? Moreover, suppose Jones pleaded, in his own defense, "After all, I didn't do anything except just stand there and watch the child drown. I didn't kill him; I only let him die." Again, if letting die were in itself less bad than killing, this defense should have at least some weight. But it does not. Such a "defense" can only be regarded as a grotesque perversion of moral reasoning. Morally speaking, it is no defense at all.

13 Now, it may be pointed out, quite properly, that the cases of euthanasia with which doctors are concerned are not like this at all. They do not involve personal gain or the destruction of normal healthy children. Doctors are concerned only with cases in which the patient's life is of no further use to him, or in which the patient's life has become or will soon become a terrible burden. However, the point is the same in these cases: the bare difference between killing and letting die does not, in itself, make a moral difference. If a doctor lets a patient die, for humane reasons, he is in the same moral position as if he had given the patient a lethal injection for humane reasons. If his decision was wrong—if, for example, the patient's illness was in fact curable—the decision would be equally regrettable no matter which method was used to carry it out. And if the doctor's decision was the right one, the method used is not in itself important.

14 The AMA policy statement isolates the crucial issue very well; the crucial issue is "the intentional termination of the

life of one human being by another." But after identifying this issue, and forbidding "mercy killing," the statement goes on to deny that the cessation of treatment is the intentional termination of a life. This is where the mistake comes in, for what is the cessation of treatment, in these circumstances, if it is not "the intentional termination of the life of one human being by another"? Of course it is exactly that, and if it were not, there would be no point to it.

Many people will find this judgment hard to accept. One 15
reason, I think, is that it is very easy to conflate the question of whether killing is, in itself, worse than letting die, with the very different question of whether most actual cases of killing are more reprehensible that most actual cases of letting die. Most actual cases of killing are clearly terrible (think, for example, of all the murders reported in the newspapers), and one hears of such cases every day. On the other hand, one hardly ever hears of a case of letting die, except for the actions of doctors who are motivated by humanitarian reasons. So one learns to think of killing in a much worse light than of letting die. For it is not the bare difference between killing and letting die that makes the difference in these cases. Rather, the other factors—the murderer's motive of personal gain, for example, contrasted with the doctor's humanitarian motivation—account for the different reactions to the different cases.

I have argued that killing is not in itself any worse than 16
letting die; if my contention is right, it follows that active euthanasia is not any worse than passive euthanasia. What arguments can be given on the other side? The most common, I believe, is the following:

"The important difference between active and passive 17
euthanasia is that in passive euthanasia, the doctor does not do anything to bring about the patient's death. The doctor does nothing, and the patient dies of whatever ills already afflict him. In active euthanasia, however, the doctor does something to bring about the patient's death: he kills him. The doctor who gives the patient with cancer a lethal injection has himself caused his patient's death; whereas if he merely ceases treatment, the cancer is the cause of the death."

A number of points need to be made here. The first is that 18
it is not exactly correct to say that in passive euthanasia the doctor does nothing, for he does do one thing that is very important: he lets the patient die. "Letting someone die" is

certainly different in some respects, from other types of action—mainly in that it is a kind of action that one may perform by way of not performing certain other actions. For example, one may let a patient die by way of not giving medication, just as one may insult someone by way of not shaking his hand. But for any purpose of moral assessment, it is a type of action nonetheless. The decision to let a patient die is subject to moral appraisal in the same way that a decision to kill him would be subject to moral appraisal: it may be assessed as wise or unwise, compassionate or sadistic, right or wrong. If a doctor deliberately let a patient die who was suffering from a routinely curable illness, the doctor would certainly be to blame for what he had done, just as he would be to blame if he had needlessly killed the patient. Charges against him would then be appropriate. If so, it would be no defense at all for him to insist that he didn't "do anything." He would have done something very serious indeed, for he let his patient die.

19 Fixing the cause of death may be very important from a legal point of view, for it may determine whether criminal charges are brought against the doctor. But I do not think that this notion can be used to show a moral difference between active and passive euthanasia. The reason why it is considered bad to be the cause of someone's death is that death is regarded as a great evil—and so it is. However, if it had been decided that euthanasia—even passive euthanasia—is desirable in a given case, it has also been decided that in this instance death is no greater an evil than the patient's continued existence. And if this is true, the usual reason for not wanting to be the cause of someone's death simply does not apply.

20 Finally, doctors may think that all of this is only of academic interest—the sort of thing that philosophers may worry about but that has no practical bearing on their own work. After all, doctors must be concerned about the legal consequences of what they do, and active euthanasia is clearly forbidden by law. But even so, doctors should also be concerned with the fact that the law is forcing upon them a moral doctrine that may well be indefensible, and has a considerable effect on their practices. Of course, most doctors are not now in the position of being coerced in this matter, for they do not regard themselves as merely going along with what the law requires. Rather, in statements such as the AMA policy statement that I have quoted, they

are endorsing this doctrine as a central point of medical ethics. In that statement, active euthanasia is condemned not merely as illegal but as "contrary to that for which the medical profession stands," whereas passive euthanasia is approved. However, the preceding considerations suggest that there is really no moral difference between the two, considered in themselves (there may be important moral differences in some cases in their consequences, but, as I pointed out, these differences may make active euthanasia, and not passive euthanasia, the morally preferable option). So whereas doctors may have to discriminate between active and passive euthanasia to satisfy the law, they should not do any more than that. In particular, they should not give the distinction any added authority and weight by writing it into official statements of medical ethics.

Sidney Hook

In Defense of Voluntary Euthanasia

Sidney Hook (born 1902) studied philosophy under John Dewey and became an outspoken, controversial, daring social thinker. A prolific essayist who also published some thirty books, a champion of Marx in the 1930s but of individual freedoms as well, Hook remains iconoclastic and independent. He wrote the following essay for The New York Times *in 1987.*

A few short years ago, I lay at the point of death. A congestive heart failure was treated for diagnostic purposes by an angiogram that triggered a stroke. Violent and painful hiccups, uninterrupted for several days and nights, prevented the indigestion of food. My left side and one of my vocal cords became paralyzed. Some form of pleurisy set in, and I felt I was drowning in a sea of slime. At one point, my heart stopped beating; just as I lost consciousness, it was thumped back into action again. In one of my lucid intervals during those days of agony, I asked my physician to discontinue all life-supporting services or show me how to do it. He refused and told me that someday I would appreciate the unwisdom of my request. 1

2 A month later, I was discharged from the hospital. In six months, I regained the use of my limbs, and although my voice still lacks its old resonance and carrying power I no longer croak like a frog. There remain some minor disabilities and I am restricted to a rigorous, low sodium diet. I have resumed my writing and research.

3 My experience can be and has been cited as an argument against honoring requests of stricken patients to be gently eased out of their pain and life. I cannot agree. There are two main reasons. As an octogenarian, there is a reasonable likelihood that I may suffer another "cardiovascular accident" or worse. I may not even be in a position to ask for the surcease of pain. It seems to me that I have already paid my dues to death—indeed, although time has softened my memories they are vivid enough to justify my saying that I suffered enough to warrant dying several times over. Why run the risk of more?

4 Secondly, I dread imposing on my family and friends another grim round of misery similar to the one my first attack occasioned.

5 My wife and children endured enough for one lifetime. I know that for them the long days and nights of waiting, the disruption of their professional duties and their own familial responsibilities counted for nothing in their anxiety for me. In their joy at my recovery they have been forgotten. Nonetheless, to visit another prolonged spell of helpless suffering on them as my life ebbs away, or even worse, if I linger on into a comatose senility, seems altogether gratuitous.

6 But what, it may be asked, of the joy and satisfaction of living, of basking in the sunlight, listening to music, watching one's grandchildren growing into adolescence, following the news about the fate of freedom in a troubled world, playing with ideas, writing one's testament of wisdom and folly for posterity? Is not all that one endured, together with the risk of its recurrence, an acceptable price for the multiple satisfactions that are still open even to a person of advanced years?

7 Apparently those who cling to life, no matter what, think so. I do not.

8 The zest and intensity of these experiences are no longer what they used to be. I am not vain enough to delude myself that I can in the few remaining years make an important discovery useful for mankind or can lead a social movement

or do anything that will be historically eventful, no less event-making. My autobiography, which describes a record of intellectual and political experiences of some historical value, already much too long, could be posthumously published. I have had my fill of joys and sorrows and am not greedy for more life. I have always thought that a test of whether one had found happiness in one's life is whether one would be willing to relive it—whether, if it were possible, one would accept the opportunity to be born again.

Having lived a full and relatively happy life, I would 9
cheerfully accept the chance to be reborn, but certainly not to be reborn again as an infirm octogenarian. To some extent, my views reflect what I have seen happen to the aged and stricken who have been so unfortunate as to survive crippling paralysis. They suffer, and impose suffering on others, unable even to make a request that their torment be ended.

I am mindful too of the burdens placed upon the com- 10
munity, with its rapidly diminishing resources, to provide the adequate and costly services necessary to sustain the lives of those whose days and nights are spent on mattress graves of pain. A better use could be made of these resources to increase the opportunities and qualities of life for the young. I am not denying the moral obligation the community has to look after its disabled and aged. There are times, however, when an individual may find it pointless to insist on the fulfillment of a legal and moral right.

What is required is no great revolution in morals but an 11
enlargement of imagination and an intelligent evaluation of alternative uses of community resources.

Long ago, Seneca observed that "the wise man will live as 12
long as he ought, not as long as he can." One can envisage hypothetical circumstances in which one has a duty to prolong one's life despite its costs for the sake of others, but such circumstances are far removed from the ordinary prospects we are considering. If wisdom is rooted in the knowledge of the alternatives of choice, it must be reliably informed of the state one is in and its likely outcome. Scientific medicine is not infallible, but it is the best we have. Should a rational person be willing to endure acute suffering merely on the chance that a miraculous cure might presently be at hand? Each one should be permitted

to make his own choice—especially when no one else is harmed by it.

13 The responsibility for the decision, whether deemed wise or foolish, must be with the chooser.

Leon R. Kass

Why Doctors Must Not Kill

A physician and professor at the University of Chicago, Leon R. Kass published the following in 1991 in a special issue of Commonweal *on euthanasia.* Commonweal *is a biweekly review of public affairs, religion, the arts, and literature (it publishes many book reviews). It has a generally liberal outlook and is associated with Catholicism.*

1 Do you want your doctor licensed to kill? Should he or she be permitted or encouraged to inject or prescribe poison? Shall the mantle of privacy that protects the doctor-patient relationship, in the service of life and wholeness, now also cloak decisions for death? Do you want *your* doctor deciding, on the basis of his own private views, when you still deserve to live and when you now deserve to die? And what about the other fellow's doctor—that shallow technician, that insensitive boor who neither asks nor listens, that unprincipled money-grubber, that doctor you used to go to until you got up the nerve to switch: do you want *him* licensed to kill? Speaking generally, shall the healing profession become also the euthanizing profession?

2 Common sense has always answered, "No." For more than two millennia, the reigning medical ethic, mindful that the power to cure is also the power to kill, has held as an inviolable rule, "Doctors must not kill." Yet this venerable taboo is now under attack. Proponents of euthanasia and physician-assisted suicide would have us believe that it is but an irrational vestige of religious prejudice, alien to a true ethic of medicine, which stands in the way of a rational and humane approach to suffering at the end of life. Nothing could be further from the truth. The taboo against doctors killing patients (even on request) is the very embodiment of reason and wisdom. Without it, medicine will have trouble

doing its proper work; without it, medicine will have lost its claim to be an ethical and trustworthy profession; without it, all of us will suffer—yes, more than we now suffer because some of us are not soon enough released from life.

3 Consider first the damaging consequences for the doctor-patient relationship. The patient's trust in the doctor's whole-hearted devotion to the patient's best interests will be hard to sustain once doctors are licensed to kill. Imagine the scene: you are old, poor, in failing health, and alone in the world; you are brought to the city hospital with fractured ribs and pneumonia. The nurse or intern enters late at night with a syringe full of yellow stuff for your intravenous drip. How soundly will you sleep? It will not matter that your doctor has never yet put anyone to death; that he is legally entitled to do so will make a world of difference.

4 And it will make a world of psychic difference too for conscientious physicians. How easily will they be able to care whole-heartedly for patients when it is always possible to think of killing them as a "therapeutic option"? Shall it be penicillin and a respirator one more time, or, perhaps, this time just an overdose of morphine? Physicians get tired of treating patients who are hard to cure, who resist their best efforts, who are on their way down—"gorks," "gomers," and "vegetables" are only some of the less than affectionate names they receive from the house officers. Won't it be tempting to think that death is the best "treatment" for the little old lady "dumped" again on the emergency room by the nearby nursing home?

5 It is naive and foolish to take comfort from the fact that the currently proposed change in the law provides "aid-in-dying" only to those who request it. For we know from long experience how difficult it is to discover what we truly want when we are suffering. Verbal "requests" made under duress rarely reveal the whole story. Often a demand for euthanasia is, in fact, an angry or anxious plea for help, born of fear of rejection or abandonment, or made in ignorance of available alternatives that could alleviate pain and suffering. Everyone knows how easy it is for those who control the information to engineer requests and to manipulate choices, especially in the vulnerable. Paint vividly a horrible prognosis, and contrast it with that "gentle, quick release": which will the depressed or frightened patient choose, especially in the

face of a spiraling hospital bill or children who visit grudgingly? Yale Kamisar asks the right questions: "Is this the kind of choice, assuming that it can be made in a fixed and rational manner, that we want to offer a gravely ill person? Will we not sweep up, in the process, some who are not really tired of life, but think others are tired of them; some who do not really want to die, but who feel that they should not live on, because to do so when there looms the legal alternative of euthanasia is to do a selfish or cowardly act? Will not some feel an obligation to have themselves 'eliminated' in order that funds allocated for their terminal care might be better used by their families or, financial worries aside, in order to relieve their families of the emotional strain involved?"

6 Euthanasia, once legalized, will not remain confined to those who freely and knowingly elect it—and the most energetic backers of euthanasia do not really want it thus restricted. Why? Because the vast majority of candidates who merit mercy-killing cannot request it for themselves: adults with persistent vegetative state or severe depression or senility or aphasia or mental illness or Alzheimer's disease; infants who are deformed; and children who are retarded or dying. All incapable of requesting death, they will thus be denied our new humane "assistance-in-dying." But not to worry. The lawyers and the doctors (and the cost-containers) will soon rectify this injustice. The enactment of a law legalizing mercy killing (or assisted suicide) on voluntary request will certainly be challenged in the courts under the equal-protection clause of the Fourteenth Amendment. Why, it will be argued, should the comatose or the demented be denied the right to such a "dignified death" or such a "treatment" just because they cannot claim it for themselves? With the aid of court-appointed proxy consenters, we will quickly erase the distinction between the right to choose one's own death and the right to request someone else's—as we have already done in the termination-of-treatment cases.

7 Clever doctors and relatives will not need to wait for such changes in the law. Who will be around to notice when the elderly, poor, crippled, weak, powerless, retarded, uneducated, demented, or gullible are mercifully released from the lives their doctors, nurses, and next of kin deem no longer worth living? In Holland, for example, a recent survey of 300 physicians (conducted by an author who supports euthana-

sia) disclosed that over 40 percent had performed euthanasia *without the patient's request,* and over 10 percent had done so in more than five cases. Is there any reason to believe that the average American physician is, in his private heart, more committed than his Dutch counterpart to the equal worth and dignity of every life under his care? Do we really want to find out what he is like, once the taboo is broken?

Even the most humane and conscientious physician psy- 8
chologically needs protection against himself and his weaknesses, if he is to care fully for those who entrust themselves to him. A physician-friend who worked many years in a hospice caring for dying patients explained it to me most convincingly: "Only because I knew that I could not and would not kill my patients was I able to enter most fully and intimately into caring for them as they lay dying." The psychological burden of the license to kill (not to speak of the brutalization of the physician-killers) could very well be an intolerably high price to pay for the physician-assisted euthanasia.

The point, however, is not merely psychological: it is also 9
moral and essential. My friend's horror at the thought that he might be tempted to kill his patients, were he not enjoined from doing so, embodies a deep understanding of the medical ethic and its intrinsic limits. We move from assessing consequences to looking at medicine itself.

The beginning of ethics regarding the use of power 10
generally lies in nay-saying. The wise setting of limits on the use of power is based on discerning the excesses to which the power, unrestrained, is prone. Applied to the professions, this principle would establish strict outer boundaries—indeed, inviolable taboos—against those "occupational hazards" to which each profession is especially prone. *Within* these outer limits, no fixed rules of conduct apply; instead, prudence—the wise judgment of the man-on-the-spot—finds and adopts the best course of action in the light of the circumstances. But the outer limits themselves are fixed, firm, and non-negotiable.

What are those limits for medicine? At least three are set 11
forth in the venerable Hippocratic Oath: no breach of confidentiality; no sexual relations with patients; no dispensing of deadly drugs. These unqualified, self-imposed restric-

tions are readily understood in terms of the temptations to which the physician is most vulnerable, temptations in each case regarding an area of vulnerability and exposure that the practice of medicine requires of patients. Patients necessarily divulge and reveal private and intimate details of their personal lives; patients necessarily expose their naked bodies to the physician's objectifying gaze and investigating hands; patients necessarily expose and entrust the care of their very lives to the physician's skill, technique, and judgment. The exposure is, in all cases, one-sided and asymmetric: the doctor does not reveal his intimacies, display his nakedness, offer up his embodied life to the patient. Mindful of the meaning of such nonmutual exposure, the physician voluntarily sets limits on his own conduct, pledging not to take advantage of or to violate the patient's intimacies, naked sexuality, or life itself.

12 The prohibition against killing patients, the first negative promise of self-restraint sworn to in the Hippocratic Oath, stands as medicine's first and most abiding taboo: "I will neither give a deadly drug to anybody if asked for it, nor will I make a suggestion to this effect. . . . In purity and holiness I will guard my life and my art." In forswearing the giving of poison, the physician recognizes and restrains a god-like power he wields over patients, mindful that his drugs can both cure and kill. But in forswearing the giving of poison, *when asked for it,* the Hippocratic physician rejects the view that the patient's choice for death can make killing him—or assisting his suicide—right. For the physician, at least, human life in living bodies commands respect and reverence—*by its very nature*. As its respectability does not depend upon human agreement or patient consent, revocation of one's consent to live does not deprive one's living body of respectability. The deepest ethical principle restraining the physician's power is not the autonomy or freedom of the patient; neither is it his own compassion or good intention. Rather, it is the dignity and mysterious power of human life itself, and, therefore, also what the oath calls the purity and holiness of the life and art to which he has sworn devotion. A person can choose to be a physician, but he cannot simply choose what physicianship means.

13 The central meaning of physicianship derives not from medicine's powers but from its goal, not from its means but from its end: to benefit the sick by the activity of healing. The physician as physician serves only the sick. He does not

serve the relatives or the hospital or the national debt inflated due to Medicare costs. Thus he will never sacrifice the well-being of the sick to the convenience or pocketbook or feelings of the relatives or society. Moreover, the physician serves the sick not because they have rights or wants or claims, but because they are sick. The healer works with and for those who need to be healed, in order to help make them whole. Despite enormous changes in medical technique and institutional practice, despite enormous changes in nosology and therapeutics, the center of medicine has not changed: it is as true today as it was in the days of Hippocrates that the ill desire to be whole; that wholeness means a certain well-working of the enlivened body and its unimpaired powers to sense, think, feel, desire, move, and maintain itself; and that the relationship between the healer and the ill is constituted, essentially even if only tacitly, around the desire of both to promote the wholeness of the one who is ailing.

Can wholeness and healing ever be compatible with intentionally killing the patient? Can one benefit the patient as a whole by making him dead? There is, of course, a logical difficulty: how can any good exist for a being that is not? But the error is more than logical: to intend and to act for someone's good requires his continued existence to receive the benefit. 14

To be sure, certain attempts to benefit may in fact turn out, unintentionally, to be lethal. Giving adequate morphine to control pain might induce respiratory depression leading to death. But the intent to relieve the pain of the living presupposes that the living still live to be relieved. This must be the starting point in discussing all medical benefits: no benefit without a beneficiary. 15

Against this view, someone will surely bring forth the hard cases: patients so ill-served by their bodies that they can no longer bear to live, bodies riddled with cancer and racked with pain, against which their "owners" protest in horror and from which they insist on being released. Cannot the person "in the body" speak up against the rest, and request death for "personal" reasons? 16

However sympathetically we listen to such requests, we must see them as incoherent. Such person-body dualism cannot be sustained. "Personhood" is manifest on earth only in living bodies; our highest mental functions are held up by, and are inseparable from, lowly metabolism, respiration, 17 circulation, excretion. There may be blood without consciousness, but there is never consciousness without blood. Thus one who calls for death in the service of personhood is like a tree seeking to cut its roots for the sake of growing its highest fruit. No physician, devoted to the benefit of the sick, can serve the patient as person by denying and thwarting his personal embodiment.

18 To say it plainly, to bring nothingness is incompatible with serving wholeness: one cannot heal—or comfort—by making nil. The healer cannot annihilate if he is truly to heal. The physician-euthanizer is a deadly self-contradiction.

19 But we must acknowledge a difficulty. The central goal of medicine—health—is, in each case, a perishable good: inevitably, patients get irreversibly sick, patients degenerate, patients die. Healing the sick is *in principle* a project that must at some point fail. And here is where all the trouble begins: How does one deal with "medical failure"? What does one seek when restoration of wholeness—or "much" wholeness—is by and large out of the question?

20 Contrary to the propaganda of the euthanasia movement, there is, in fact, much that can be done. Indeed, by recognizing finitude yet knowing that we will not kill, we are empowered to focus on easing and enhancing the *lives* of those who are dying. First of all, medicine can follow the lead of the hospice movement and—abandoning decades of shameful mismanagement—provide truly adequate (and now technically feasible) relief of pain and discomfort. Second, physicians (and patients and families) can continue to learn how to withhold or withdraw those technical interventions that are, in truth, merely burdensome or degrading medical additions to the unhappy end of a life—including, frequently, hospitalization itself. Ceasing treatment and allowing death to occur when (and if) it will seem to be quite compatible with the respect life itself commands for itself. Doctors may and must allow to die, even if they must not intentionally kill.

21 Ceasing medical intervention, allowing nature to take its course, differs fundamentally from mercy killing. For one thing, death does not necessarily follow the discontinuance of treatment; Karen Ann Quinlan lived more than ten years after the court allowed the "life-sustaining" respirator to be

removed. Not the physician, but the underlying fatal illness becomes the true cause of death. More important morally, in ceasing treatment the physician need not *intend* the death of the patient, even when the death follows as a result of his omission. His intention should be to avoid useless and degrading medical *additions* to the already sad end of a life. In contrast, in active, direct mercy killing the physician must, necessarily and indubitably, intend *primarily* that the patient be made dead. And he must knowingly and indubitably cast himself in the role of the agent of death. This remains true even if he is merely an assistant in suicide. A physician who provides the pills or lets the patient plunge the syringe after he leaves the room is *morally* no different from one who does the deed himself. "I will neither give a deadly drug to anybody if asked for it, nor will I make a suggestion to this effect."

Once we refuse the technical fix, physicians and the rest of us can also rise to the occasion: we can learn to act humanly in the presence of finitude. Far more than adequate morphine and the removal of burdensome machinery, the dying need our presence and our encouragement. Dying people are all too easily reduced ahead of time to "thinghood" by those who cannot bear to deal with the suffering or disability of those they love. Withdrawal of contact, affection, and care is the greatest single cause of the dehumanization of dying. Not the alleged humaneness of an elixir of death, but the humanness of connected living-while-dying is what medicine—and the rest of us—most owe the dying. The treatment of choice is company and care. 22

The euthanasia movement would have us believe that the physician's refusal to assist in suicide or perform euthanasia constitutes an affront to human dignity. Yet one of their favorite arguments seems to me rather to prove the reverse. Why, it is argued, do we put animals out of their misery but insist on compelling fellow human beings to suffer to the bitter end? Why, if it is not a contradiction for the veterinarian, does the medical ethic absolutely rule out mercy killing? Is this not simply inhumane? 23

Perhaps *inhumane*, but not thereby *inhuman*. On the contrary, it is precisely because animals are not human that we must treat them (merely) humanely. We put dumb animals to sleep because they do not know that they are dying, because they can make nothing of their misery or mortality, and, therefore, because they cannot live 24 deliberately—i.e., humanly—in the face of their own suffering and dying. They cannot live out a fitting end. Compassion for their weakness and dumbness is our only appropriate emotion, and given our responsibility for their care and well-being, we do the only humane thing we can. But when a conscious human being asks us for death, by that very action he displays the presence of something that precludes our regarding him as a dumb animal. Humanity is owed humanity, not humaneness. Humanity is owed the bolstering of the human, even or especially in its dying moments, in resistance to the temptation to ignore its presence in the sight of suffering.

25 What humanity needs most in the face of evils is courage, the ability to stand against fear and pain and thoughts of nothingness. The deaths we most admire are those of people who, knowing that they are dying, face the fact frontally and act accordingly: they set their affairs in order, they arrange what could be final meetings with their loved ones, and yet, with strength of soul and a small reservoir of hope, they continue to live and work and love as much as they can for as long as they can. Because such conclusions of life require courage, they call for our encouragement—and for the many small speeches and deeds that shore up the human spirit against despair and defeat.

26 Many doctors are in fact rather poor at this sort of encouragement. They tend to regard every dying or incurable patient as a failure, as if an earlier diagnosis or a more vigorous intervention might have avoided what is, in truth, an inevitable collapse. The enormous successes of medicine these past fifty years have made both doctors and laymen less prepared than ever to accept the fact of finitude. Doctors behave, not without some reason, as if they have godlike powers to revive the moribund; laymen expect an endless string of medical miracles. Physicians today are not likely to be agents of encouragement once their technique begins to fail.

27 It is, of course, partly for these reasons that doctors will be pressed to kill—and many of them will, alas, be willing. Having adopted a largely technical approach to healing, having medicalized so much of the end of life, doctors are being asked—often with thinly veiled anger—to provide a final technical solution for the evil of human finitude and for their own technical failure: If you cannot cure me, kill me. The last gasp of autonomy or cry for dignity is asserted

against a medicalization and institutionalization of the end of life that robs the old and the incurable of most of their autonomy and dignity: intubated and electrified, with bizarre mechanical companions, once proud and independent people find themselves cast in the roles of passive, obedient, highly disciplined children. People who care for autonomy and dignity should try to reverse this dehumanization of the last stages of life, instead of giving dehumanization its final triumph by welcoming the desperate goodbye-to-all-that contained in one final plea for poison.

The present crisis that leads some to press for active eu- 28
thanasia is really an opportunity to learn the limits of the medicalization of life and death and to recover an appreciation of living with and against mortality. It is an opportunity for physicians to recover an understanding that there remains a residual human wholeness—however precarious—that can be cared for even in the face of incurable and terminal illness. Should doctors cave in, should doctors become technical dispensers of death, they will not only be abandoning their posts, their patients, and their duty to care; they will set the worst sort of example for the community at large—teaching technicism and so-called humaneness where encouragement and humanity are both required and sorely lacking. On the other hand, should physicians hold fast, should doctors learn that finitude is no disgrace and that human wholeness can be cared for to the very end, medicine may serve not only the good of its patients, but also, by example, the failing moral health of modern times.

May Sarton

From *Recovering: A Journal 1978–1979*

May Sarton (born 1912 in Belgium, which her family fled when World War I broke out) has been writing poems and novels for over half a century. She has over thirty-five books to her credit. Old age has been the subject of some of her most moving novels. Lately she has been publishing her journals: Recovering: A Journal *(1980),* At Seventy: A Journal *(1984), and* After the Stroke *(1988). The following excerpts are from* Recovering *and* At Seventy.

Thursday, December 28th, 1978

1 I had thought not to begin a new journal until I am seventy, four years from now, but perhaps the time has come to sort myself out, and see whether I can restore a sense of meaning and continuity to my life by this familiar means.

2 Also I need to communicate with something better than tears my long companionship with Judy that began thirty-five years ago in Santa Fe and ended on Christmas Day. Our last Christmas together; it was a fiasco. I wasn't feeling well and had a low fever when I went to fetch her on Christmas Eve at the Walden Nursing Home where she has been for seven years. I had been warned that she had changed for the worse in her slow progress toward complete senility, but I hoped that after twenty-four hours with me here, she would begin to relate again. That is the way it has been for the last few years and when she was here for her eightieth birthday in September, we did have a few moments of communion.

3 Over the years we have always opened our stockings in bed but Judy no longer enjoys opening presents so I had given up on stockings and brought up a present from faithful Emily Huntington for her to unwrap. She showed no interest in an elegant pair of gray slacks after refusing to unwrap the package. It was "downhill all the way," and I began to wonder how I was going to manage. I made fires in both fireplaces downstairs and got Judy dressed in a warm sweater and slacks and settled her in an armchair with a rug over her knees beside the fire in the library. But she was very

restless and was soon up, moving around in the curious shuffle that has replaced walking now. She never once looked at the tree, poignantly beautiful this year, and—as it has been for thirty years—decorated with the many ornaments we have collected together.

It is often a small thing that shatters hope. For me it came 4
when a male pheasant appeared close to the porch window—such a dazzling sight in all the gloom that I called out. "Come Judy, come quickly!" She didn't come, of course. I found her shuffling about in the library and by the time I had dragged her to the window, the pheasant was out of sight. At that moment I knew that Judy had gone beyond where being with me in this house means anything.

Yesterday I took the day off and took the making of an 5
oyster stew to Eleanor Blair. She has graduated from her walker to a four-pronged cane that makes her far more mobile with less effort. She told me triumphantly that she has even climbed the stairs. What joy it was to be in her dear house, so full of life, geraniums in flower in a small window greenhouse, books everywhere, light and peace. At eighty-five she is a marvelous "role model" as today's fashion has the phrase, and I hated to cut the visit short but I wanted to stop and see Judy. Since the disaster of Christmas I have not seen her.

I think she recognized me but I am not sure. Two nurses 6
were making her bed and laughed with real merriment when they forgot, because we were talking, to put in the rubber sheet and had to begin again. Their presence was a help as Judy was totally unresponsive, except that she noticed my green jacket when I took off my coat. I stayed only a quarter of an hour. When I left I turned back at the door and saw her sitting in the only chair in her room, her face still so distinguished, but now a blank mask. She is not lonely, but the isolation of her state struck me like a blow to the heart. To be so helpless to help, and to leave her there lost. She did not look up even as I said goodbye.

Tuesday, July 10th

I am happy to hear that Judy's family, so sensitive to her 7
needs, so much on the job, came to the decision two weeks ago or more, to move her to a smaller nursing home where

she is in a less institutional atmosphere. Connie, her sister, went to see her around two one day and found her eating strawberry shortcake with evident relish, sitting in her wheelchair in the parlor there. The best news is that she is now off tranquilizers (overused no doubt in the larger place) and as soon as I can drive that far, I long to see her, and perhaps to erase my last vision of her some months ago, sitting alone in her room, her face turned away, with a look of tragic emptiness in it. I have thought of Judy so much since the operation, benign star in my firmament, she who could and did love me for what I am and accepted the flaws. The never-failing support and friend.

Friday, August 24th

8 The day before yesterday I went down to Cambridge and stopped on the way to see Judy in her new "home." Her windows look out on trees and the atmosphere is sunny and peaceful. The move has been a wise one. She did not recognize me, "babbles of green fields," and I shall leave it there.

9 Judy's senility throws me. There is no way to transcend it except through the memory of what she was. I suppose I have been honest about all the horror of senility because there are many people who have to face it alone. I have wished *to be present* to their pain. To be honest. Not to deny the physical facts which make transcendence difficult if not impossible. I have thought of those who share my pain, rather than of Judy who does not care, does not know, and is not in pain.

10 What of the nurses who deal with all this every day? How do they keep on being loving and care-full of a stranger who cannot respond? It takes superior love and superior detachment and I honor them for both, more than I can say. But for them there is the consolation of doing what has to be done, and they are not betrayed in their inmost hearts by what cannot be changed and can only get worse, as the families of loved ones are.

From *At Seventy: A Journal*

Wednesday, September 8th

But then I had to go shortly after lunch to drive to Concord to see Judy for the first time in months, since before Christmas. There she was, there she will be until she slips away, in her wheelchair, singing to herself. I know now that she will not recognize me, but I held her cold little hand and talked about old times. I gave her the duck feathers and reminded her of our walks at Mt. Auburn and for thirty seconds I thought she was enjoying the silky feathers, and perhaps listening, but then she put them into her mouth, and I had to try to take them away. She held on fiercely and only let them go when I gave her a brownie to eat. Her face is still so distinguished, the dark eyes, the cap of white hair, that it seems incredible that she herself is far away and what is left is a baby, for whom food is the only real pleasure. The truth is I go to see her for me, not for her. After a time I feel a strong compulsion to touch base, as it were. True love does not die. 1

Wednesday, December 22nd

I feel I have been climbing the Christmas mountain for weeks, so many things I longed to record here and didn't. But now that I have come to a good pause I can lay down my knapsack and look at the view. 2

The tree is up and it is a dream. Last year I took a great dislike to the tree, which was enormous and rather ferocious looking. I felt it was so German! This one is beautifully proportioned and smaller, and Edythe and I had a lovely afternoon decking it, as we have done now twice, so it is becoming a ritual. Of course, almost every ornament brings memories of July and our trees at 14 Wright Street in Cambridge, and the little front parlor where it stood on a table, and where we invited our friends in, one by one or in small groups, for champagne and to sit by the Franklin stove. There Anne Thorp and Agnes Swift came bearing jars of wild cranberry jelly from Greenings Island; there we heard Dorothy Wallace with her daughter Anne and her 3 husband, bearing Anne's tiny daughter in a basket, singing "Go Tell It on the Mountain," and there on one memorable occasion Barbara Hawthorne came with (of all singular and magical things) a bunch of violets, so forever after I have associated Christmas Eve with that scent. There Judy's cousin Nancy Carey came with her two small children and Ruth Harnden and so many other friends—and after the guests left we had restful lamb stew, which I always made for the holidays.

4 Later there were the Christmases of Nelson when the Warners came down from the farm on the Eve for chocolate ice cream with ginger ale poured over it and a cake Sally baked shaped like a tree with green frosting, and Mildred and Quig crossed the street, and Judy was with me. And now—it is hard to believe—it is the tenth Christmas here.

5 Why is it, I wonder, that Christmas brings so much depression with it, so many people struggle against an undertow? It is partly because this moment of light shines out of the darkest and shortest days of the year, the lowest ebb of the cycle when wise animals dig themselves in for a long sleep, while we, driven creatures, spend immense energy on wrapping presents, sending off packages, baking cookies (this I used to do but have stopped doing myself, so other people's cookies are specially welcome). Partly it is that memories well up and not all are happy ones. We are dealing with a host of faces and times and sorrows and joys, and there is no time to sort them out.

6 Every year Christmas becomes a real creation for each of us, and as it is created we are re-creating the moment when Love is born again, Love that will know pain as well as joy.

7 As I was writing that last sentence Tim Warren, Judy's nephew, called—it is 8 A.M.—to tell me that Judy died last night. I have prayed that she might be allowed to slip away, and now she has. But it is always so sudden, so unexpected—death—and so final. When I went to see her last September and held her ice-cold hand in mine, at the very end of the half-hour when she had made no sign of recognition, she reached over and patted my hand and held it over her other one for a moment. I must remember that and that she is free at last of the failing body and mind and is wherever spirits dwell.

HOW SHOULD WE ADDRESS THE HEALTH CARE CRISIS?

Milton Terris

A Wasteful System That Doesn't Work

In October 1990, Dr. Milton Terris (the editor of The Journal of Public Health Policy, *published in South Burlington, Vermont) contributed the following analysis of the health-care crisis to* The Progressive, *a left-of-center public affairs magazine that is produced in Madison, Wisconsin.*

Americans spend more than 11 per cent of the gross national product on health services—more than any other country—but adequate care for all is still out of reach. Private health insurance has failed to meet the need; thirty-seven million Americans have no insurance at all, and many more millions have too little insurance to cover the costs they incur. 1

The Government programs established by Congress in 1965 have also proved inadequate. Medicare—the Federal health-insurance program for the aged that is financed through Social Security—now covers only 40 per cent of their health costs. Medicaid, the Federal-state program for the poor, was always insufficient and has been further reduced by the states. Out-of-pocket payments by consumers come to 28 per cent of all personal health care expenditures; private health insurance pays for only 31 per cent, and 40 per cent is paid by government. 2

Paradoxically, our enormous health expenditures don't begin to assure better health for Americans. Our life expectancy for men is surpassed by nineteen countries and for women by fourteen. Twenty-one countries have a lower infant-mortality rate than the United States. 3

What accounts for these discrepancies? Part of the answer lies in the nature of health insurance in the United States. Private health insurance, which began to grow in the 1930s, 4 received an enormous impetus during World War II, when wage controls and tax policy encouraged employers to provide nonwage fringe benefits. The number of Americans covered by private health insurance tripled from ten million to thirty million during the war, and the basic pattern set then is still dominant: Private health insurance is tied to employment, with industry paying part or all of premiums.

5 Other patterns of private insurance have also set the stage for the current crisis: (1) separation of payment for hospital care from payment for physician services; (2) distortion of the medical-care system by concentration on surgical services and inpatient hospital care; (3) failure to cover services fully, including the use of deductibles and co-payments paid by the consumers; and (4) building in a cost-inflation factor by permitting physicians and other providers to make additional charges to the consumer beyond those covered by insurance.

6 All of these features of private health insurance were incorporated into Medicare, except that coverage of ambulatory care was included as a voluntary option. And the administration of Medicare at the state and local level was handed over to private insurance companies.

7 We have, therefore, inherited a complex, wasteful system with a bewildering variety of benefit plans offered by a multiplicity of private insurance companies that incur enrollment costs, maintain reserves, skim off profits, and impose enormous burdens of paperwork on both consumers and health-care providers.

8 Administrative costs amount to at least 5 per cent of total health expenditures in the United States. In Canada, where private insurance companies play no role and the medical-care program for the entire population is administered by provincial governments, administrative costs come to a little more than 1 per cent of total health expenditures. In Canada, there are no deductibles, no co-payments, no extra charges by physicians. The system pays fully for the services provided. And the insurance plan is not tied to employment; everyone is covered, and the costs are paid through provincial and federal taxes.

9 What makes the U.S. health-care crisis so acute is the enormous escalation of costs. From 1980 to 1988, the Consumer Price Index, excluding medical care, rose by 41

per cent; for all medical care, it rose by 85 per cent. As costs have risen, so have insurance premiums, and so have complaints by employers, who have mounted a determined and increasingly successful drive to shift costs to their employees. Bitter strikes have centered on this issue—by telephone workers and the Pittston miners, among others.

Part of the cost increase can be explained by the de- 10
velopment of technology, another part by the increased need for care of an aging population. But the most important causes of escalating health-care costs in the United States relate to two factors: the method of paying physicians, and the structure of the medical profession.

Most physicians in this country are paid by fee-for-service 11
instead of salary. The more services, the more income. There is a great incentive, therefore, to provide unneeded services. This incentive system also pushes up hospital costs, since many procedures are performed in the hospital. It is the physician who controls the costs and makes the decisions on what needs to be done. Despite the doctors' propaganda to the contrary, most patients don't demand to be operated on or to undergo tests; they meekly follow doctors' orders.

Take, for example, the spectacular recent rise in physi- 12
cians' total charges for Medicare patients. From 1982 to 1987 they rose by 76 per cent, from $15.1 billion to $26.6 billion. Did technology improve by 76 per cent in five years? Did the older population expand by 76 per cent? Did old people's demands for care grow by 76 per cent? More likely, doctors' appetites for higher incomes were responsible. In this five-year period, surgical services increased by 85 per cent, physicians' visits by 52 per cent, consultations by 127 per cent, diagnostic x-rays by 133 per cent, x-ray treatments by 109 per cent, and clinical lab services by 84 per cent.

Physicians paid by fee-for-service are small businessmen, 13
like lawyers, investment counselors, dry cleaners, and auto mechanics, who also sell services, and like small manufacturers, farmers, and retail merchants, who sell products. In common with other businessmen, physicians are in the business of making profits, and their profits depend on the prices they receive for their services and how many services they sell.

Controlling the costs for fee-for-service payment is ex- 14
tremely difficult. If the Government tries to reduce doctors' fees, they make up the loss by increasing services. In Canada,

which also pays doctors on a fee-for-service basis, attempts by the provinces to control health budgets by restricting doctors' fees have failed. From 1972 to 1984, the provinces cut fees by 18 per cent in real terms, but by an amazing coincidence, doctors' total billing claims rose by 17 per cent. When Quebec froze doctors' fees in the early 1970s and their real-dollar value dropped by 9 per cent, doctors increased their billings by almost the same amount, 8.3 per cent. Alberta froze medical fees in 1984, but physicians increased their gross incomes that year by almost 12 per cent.

15 Hit with a fee cut, doctors simply see patients more often and provide more services. In Canada, a quarter to a third of each provincial budget is determined not by the provincial government but by the medical profession.

16 In Canada as in the United States, doctors often perform tests, procedures, and surgical operations without regard to medical necessity. There is no scientific basis for the wholesale removal of children's tonsils, for example, but one study found that tonsillectomies were performed on 107 out of every 10,000 people per year in British Columbia and on 200 per 10,000 in Ontario. In Liverpool, England, and Uppsala, Sweden, where surgeons are all on salary, the rates were twenty-six and seventeen per 10,000.

17 Cesarian sections in Canada have skyrocketed from fewer than 5 per cent of births in 1968 to about 20 per cent today—second only to the U.S. rate of more than 25 per cent. As a World Health Organization expert committee has pointed out, "Countries with some of the lowest perinatal mortality rates in the world have Cesarian-section rates of less than 10 per cent. There is no justification for any region to have a rate higher than 10 to 15 per cent."

18 If Canada also pays doctors by fee-for-service, why are health expenditures 40 per cent higher in the United States? One reason is that Medicare policy has been to pay doctors at their "usual and customary" rates, which is an open invitation to raise fees. For another, Canadian fee schedules are not so generous as those in the United States. The main reason, however, is the differing structures of the medical profession in the two countries.

19 In Canada, the number of residency-training programs in the specialties is limited. In the United States, however, the doors to specialty training were thrown wide open after World War II. About 5,000 residencies were available in 1941, but the number has grown to 51,000 by 1972.

The result was a drastic decline in the number of general practitioners, from eighty-three per 100,000 population in 1940 to only thirty-two in 1967, a decrease of 61 per cent. No attempt was made to match the number of specialty-training programs to the estimated needs of the public, so that we now have a surplus of surgeons and other specialists who are trained to provide services that aren't needed. 20

In Canada, 50 per cent of all physicians are general practitioners, as against only 10 per cent in the United States. Although the ratio of physicians to population is about the same in the two countries, the United States has 33 per cent more surgeons per capita. It is hardly surprising, then, that Americans undergo 40 per cent more surgical operations per capita than Canadians. 21

Specialists charge considerably more than general practitioners, and their incomes are higher. The median income of U.S. general practitioners in 1987 was about $80,000, a third less than the median for all physicians. The highest median incomes went to the surgical and other specialists who did their work primarily in hospitals: cardiovascular surgeons, about $270,000; neurosurgeons, $235,000; orthopedic surgeons, $195,000; plastic surgeons, $180,000; ophthalmologists, $170,000; thoracic surgeons, $165,000; radiologists, $165,000; anesthesiologists, $160,000; urologists, $145,000; obstetricians/gynecologists, $140,000; and general surgeons, $130,000. 22

Specialists are trained to use expensive high-tech diagnostic and therapeutic procedures, whether or not these make a significant improvement in the patient's health. The fact that 90 per cent of all physicians in the United States are specialists, and that we have a surplus of surgeons, means that many Americans suffer not from a lack of medical care but from too much care, some of which may be harmful and much of which is unnecessary. 23

Most of the proposals being advanced to solve the health-care crisis are concerned with providing some insurance coverage for the uninsured. This would leave the current system intact, with all its waste, complexity, and ever-rising costs. 24

A more rational solution would be to establish a Canadian-type health-care system, modified to accord with American conditions. Such a system would cover the entire population 25 for all medical-care services, including dental, mental, and long-term care, without deductibles, co-payments, or extra charges by providers.

26 Payments would not be made to individual practitioners but to provider organizations: community health centers, group-practice organizations, and individual-practice associations. Payments would reflect the demographic characteristics of the persons served and the estimated cost of providing care, based on the experience of salaried group-practice prepayment plans and community health centers.

27 These estimated costs would be applied to all provider organizations, including individual practice associations which pay practitioners on a fee-for-service basis, in order to prevent unnecessary hospitalizations, surgical operations, and procedures. Salaried group-practice plans and community health centers have 40 per cent lower hospitalization costs and 25 per cent lower overall costs than individual-practice fee-for-service plans, with equal or better results in terms of patients' health.

28 Provider organizations would be classified as public utilities, with their records open to public scrutiny, and with profit margins and uses regulated. Every provider organization would be required to establish a consumers' council and an employees' council, each of which would meet regularly with the administrator and have the right to appeal to local, state, and Federal health departments for investigation and action on deficiencies in the care and treatment of patients.

29 Large-scale government grants and loans would be available to assist consumer-controlled and health-worker-controlled provider organizations to form community health centers and salaried group-practice organizations that offer a wide range of health services.

30 The system would be administered by Federal, state, and local health departments responsible to boards of health composed entirely of public representatives drawn from all sections of the population. In order to ensure flexibility, the states would submit plans that meet all the basic requirements of the national system, but would have considerable latitude to devise ways to improve the system.

31 Quality of care would be improved by (1) the imposition of Federal standards; (2) evaluation of the services of all provider organizations with respect to the quality and performance of personnel, suitability of facilities, compli-

ance with performance standards, and effectiveness of care; (3) prompt response by health departments to appeals by consumers' and employees' councils; (4) consultation, training, and other governmental assistance; and (5) regulatory action to correct abuses and gross deficiencies.

The system would be financed by the Federal Government 32
and the states. The Federal share would be 75 to 90 per cent of the total, with the higher proportions going to the poorer states. It would be supported by progressive, graduated income taxes, corporation taxes, and excise taxes on tobacco, alcohol, foods rich in saturated fat and cholesterol, firearms, and toxic substances used in industry, agriculture, construction, and the community.

A national health-care system, however, is *not* the same 33
thing as a national health program. Such a program must emphasize the two major determinants of health: prevention and the standard of living.

The most rapid and dramatic improvements in the health 34
of the public will result not from medical care but from preventive measures. These are grossly underfunded at the present time; only 2.9 per cent of all U.S. health dollars are spent for government public-health activities. The funds available to prevent heart disease, cancer, stroke injuries, chronic lung disease, infant mortality, occupational and environmental diseases, alcohol and other drug problems, AIDS and other infectious diseases, should at least be doubled.

One alarming aspect of the current situation, in both 35
Canada and the United States, is the widening gap between rich and poor in preventing disease. Canadians are learning the painful lesson that their medical program assures equity in health care, but not in health. Studies have shown that in the late 1970s, the wealthiest fifth of Canadians lived 4.5 years longer than the poorest fifth and avoided disability eleven years longer. Poor people in Canada have, on the average, only fifty-five years of disability-free life, while rich Canadians have sixty-six years.

Such studies make it clear that the most important 36
determinant of health—in the United States, Canada, and every other country—is the standard of living. Poor nutrition lowers resistance to many diseases. Illiteracy is a serious obstacle to learning about preventive measures such as

personal hygiene, immunization, and lifestyle changes. Poor working conditions cause many preventable diseases and injuries. Poverty produces low self-esteem, mental dysfunction, alcoholism, drug addiction, and violence.

37 During the 1980s, poverty increased in the United States. Although unemployment dropped slightly from 7.1 to 7.0 per cent between 1977 and 1986, the poverty rate rose from 11.6 to 13.6 per cent, and the number of persons in poverty rose from 24,720,000 to 32,370,000. Hunger reappeared in the 1980s; the Physicians Task Force on Hunger in America reported in 1985 that some twenty million Americans experience hunger at least some days every month. Clearly, this decline in living standards needs to be reversed if the United States is to become a healthy nation.

38 Our country has the capacity to solve the health-care crisis, support vigorous and effective preventive measures, and improve the standard of living for all Americans. What we lack, so far, is a commitment to human welfare and social justice, and a political will to make health a right, not a privilege, in the United States.

Michael Dukakis

The States and Health Care Reform

The Democratic nominee for president of the United States in 1988 and now a professor at Northeastern University, Michael Dukakis contributed the following essay in 1992 to The New England Journal of Medicine*—one of the nation's most prestigious medical journals.*

1 In 1945 Harry Truman became the first president in U.S. history to propose a universal health plan for all Americans. Forty-seven years later, the American people are still waiting.

2 True, we have made some progress since the days when a massive lobbying effort by the American Medical Association and the nation's insurers shot down the Truman plan. But two Republican presidents who supported universal,

employer-based health insurance in the 1970s could not get their proposals through Congress. President Carter preferred to focus on cost containment in health care rather than on universal coverage. And neither Ronald Reagan nor George Bush has been willing to support the kind of universal coverage that both Richard Nixon and Gerald Ford advocated some 20 years ago.

Now Washington gridlock has produced another year of 3 frustration. Congress will not support the Bush proposals to reform malpractice and small-business insurance. President Bush is adamantly opposed to any plan that makes Medicare universal or requires all employers to provide basic health insurance for employees and their dependents.

Meanwhile, Congress and the President have not hesitated 4 to expand Medicaid coverage for the poor by mandating additional benefits and increased eligibility. But virtually nothing has been done in Washington to contain the explosive costs of health care that are driving virtually every state budget into the red. On the contrary, in seeking to contain Medicare costs, the President and the Congress have succeeded only in shifting some of those costs onto the backs of the employers, consumers, and state governments who must pay the bills.

Little wonder, then, that the 1989 annual meeting of the 5 nation's governors exploded in bipartisan anger over what all this was doing to the efforts of both Republican and Democratic governors to balance their budgets and pay for other important priorities, such as public education. And little wonder that a number of state governments are now trying to devise ways to provide greater access to high-quality health care for their people and control costs at the same time.

Hawaii: The Pioneer

Long before any of the mainland states began thinking 6 about comprehensive health care reform, Hawaii had adopted its Prepaid Health Act and was moving ahead with a system of near-universal access to health care. Curiously, only within recent months have some of the nation's policy makers taken time off from endless debates over the Canadian, German, and other national systems to explore in detail the experience of the nation's 50th state.

7 What they have found is impressive.[1] Hawaii has for nearly 20 years done what Presidents Ford and Nixon were proposing in the early and mid-1970s. Since 1974 all Hawaiian employers have been required to provide their employees with a comprehensive package of health insurance. Employees can be required to contribute 50 percent of the premium or 1.5 percent of their gross wages, whichever is lower. Hawaii does not require employers to cover their employees' dependents, but a large majority of them do so voluntarily.

8 By 1989 all but 50,000 Hawaiians were insured by their employers or through Medicare or Medicaid, or received health care as members of the armed forces or their dependents or through the Department of Veteran Affairs. In that year the Hawaiian legislature created the State Health Insurance Program, which is designed to provide coverage for all those not otherwise covered under existing law. The program is funded by general state revenues and is managed under contract by the Hawaii Medical Services Association (HMSA, the local Blue Cross affiliate) or Kaiser Permanente, the dominant health maintenance organization in Hawaii. Approximately 18,000 people have already been insured under the program, and Hawaii expects to achieve its goal of universal coverage soon.

9 Currently, a majority of Hawaiians are insured by HMSA. An additional 19 percent are members of Kaiser Permanente. For all businesses with 100 or fewer employees, HMSA and Kaiser Permanente have a single risk pool each, and those businesses pay a single community rate. The fact that two insurers dominate the Hawaiian health insurance market has had a substantial impact on costs. Although Hawaii's cost of living is some 30 percent higher than that on the mainland, Hawaiian health care costs are lower, about equal to Canada's. Moreover, Hawaiians are now the healthiest people in the United States.[2] Life expectancy is the highest in the nation. Hawaii is tied with Massachusetts for the lowest infant mortality rate.

10 Hawaii is not resting on its laurels. Governor John Waihee and State Health Director John C. Lewin have announced plans for what they call "a seamless system of health care services." They want to make the primary care physician the health care system's gatekeeper. They also want to create a new state commission on health costs that will collect data, certify insurance rates, and have a standby authority to set provider rates.[3]

Other States

Hawaii has been far and away the national leader in health care reform. Although several other states have now joined the fray, they have not yet fully implemented their plans for reform. Massachusetts approved its universal health care law in the spring of 1988.[4] Approximately 100,000 additional Massachusetts residents, including students, severely disabled adults and children, and the uninsured unemployed, all qualify for and receive basic health insurance. 11

Moreover, Massachusetts, one of the few states that have approved comprehensive malpractice reform, has eliminated double payments for medical expenses, limited attorneys' fees, and imposed a $500,000 cap on compensation for pain and suffering.[5] Malpractice premiums have dropped 25 percent, and Massachusetts doctors and dentists now pay substantially less for their malpractice insurance than many practitioners in other industrial states. 12

Unfortunately, a combination of strong opposition by small businesses to the law's mandate for employer contributions, a new governor, and economic recession has brought progress toward the implementation of the new law to a standstill. Governor William Weld has repeatedly attempted to repeal the mandate for employer participation. Although he has so far been unsuccessful, the legislature has agreed to postpone implementation of the law for another three years. 13

Oregon followed Massachusetts with its own version of universal health care legislation. Like the Massachusetts law, the Oregon law includes an employer mandate that is scheduled to take effect in 1995. Unlike the Massachusetts law, it also includes a rationing scheme for those covered by Medicaid that has been rejected by the Bush administration. 14

Minnesota, Vermont, and Florida have all passed important new health care legislation this year that in a variety of ways seeks to move over the next two to three years toward the goal of universal coverage at an affordable cost. New York's Governor Mario Cuomo recently signed into law a sweeping reform of small-business health insurance. Dozens of other states are wrestling with the same issues and drafting their own health care legislation. 15

What Can We Learn from the States?

16 Hawaii's success and the troubles of Massachusetts and Oregon teach us some important lessons for the future and should provide the president who takes office in January 1993 and the new Congress with a better understanding of the possibilities and pitfalls of comprehensive health care reform. The lessons are outlined below.

17 *Universal, employer-based coverage can work, and work effectively, provided steps are taken to protect small and medium-sized employers from the kinds of discriminatory practices that are bedeviling them in most states.* The Hawaiian health care system is an impressive example of how to provide universal coverage at relatively reasonable cost through the private market and with a minimum of government bureaucracy and interference. Moreover, it is a reminder that providing everyone with basic primary coverage is itself an important contributor to cost control. Hawaiians visit the doctor more often than most of us on the mainland do. But they spend a lot less time in the hospital, and that has substantially lowered costs.[1]

18 One of the principal reasons for the success of Hawaii's employer mandate and its acceptance by small businesses is the kind of protection that Hawaii's single risk pool provides to small and medium-sized employers. Furthermore, a regulated insurance market that requires insurers to accept all comers at a single community rate eliminates the need for a large alternative public insurance plan. In Hawaii, every employer can "play."

19 *A limited number of insurers and managed-care organizations, working in concert with health regulators, can substantially reduce the administrative expenses of the health care system and use their market power to keep costs under control.* One of the impressive features of the Hawaiian system has been its ability to keep costs down despite the fact that the state has one of the highest costs of living in America. HMSA in particular has enormous influence over hospital and physicians' rates because Hawaiian health care providers are under no illusions about who the principal payer is in the Hawaiian system.[1]

20 This should confirm the views of those who believe that a health care system with a single payer or a relatively small number of insurers can do a much better job of holding

down costs than one with hundreds of insurers and managed-care organizations, many of which are cherry-picking the market for healthy risks. On the other hand, the fact that HMSA is competing with Kaiser Permanente is important, too. Although the two organizations seem to get along reasonably well, the competition for subscribers between them is intense, and it adds to the pressure to keep costs down.

Any plan for universal coverage must include primary as well as catastrophic coverage. A number of proponents of health care reform have suggested that we begin with catastrophic care and then move gradually to full coverage. Hawaii's experience suggests that such an approach would be a serious mistake. Most observers in Hawaii believe that one of the reasons for its lower health care costs is the fact that good primary care is almost universally available under Hawaii's health care law. They believe that Hawaii's lower rate of hospitalization is the direct result of the widespread availability of primary care for virtually all Hawaiians. 21

It is time once again to make the primary care physician the manager of health care in America. There has been a good deal of debate recently over the idea that the family physician should be the gatekeeper for our health care.[6] That principle is part of the health care system of virtually every other advanced industrial nation in the world. Forty or 50 years ago, it was an accepted part of the U.S. health care system. 22

My father, for example, was a general practitioner in Boston for more than 50 years. He worked seven days a week and made house calls. But woe unto any of his patients who saw another doctor without getting his approval. If he found out about it, he invariably told them to find themselves another physician. 23

Hawaii is seriously considering a plan that would, in effect, restore the system that most of us accepted as a matter of course when my father practiced medicine. Governor Waihee's recommendations would prohibit the reimbursement of specialists at the specialist rate without a referral from a primary care physician. Waihee's recommendations would also pay the general practitioner a small fee for managing the patient's care. 24

A universal, employer-based plan can provide coverage for the uninsured without new taxes. One of the most difficult problems facing policy makers in Washington and state 25 capitals is how to provide health insurance for the people who remain uninsured even after an employer mandate is implemented. Hawaii, for example, has decided to pay for such coverage with general revenues. But even Hawaii is now being forced to consider cuts in programs as it prepares its budget for the next fiscal year.

26 There is a practical alternative to the use of general revenues or the imposition of a new tax, however. Today, health insurance premiums include, either directly or indirectly, a substantial surcharge that pays providers for uncompensated care. In Massachusetts, for example, it is approximately 9.5 percent. In other states, where the number of uninsured people is much higher, it is substantially more.

27 If all employers are required to provide employees and their dependents with health insurance, the amount of uncompensated care will drop dramatically. In a study at the University of Hawaii in 1991,[7] it was estimated that approximately 4 percent of the premium base could finance comprehensive health insurance for the remaining "gap group." Although this would require a continuing surcharge on premiums, it would be much less than the amount that is currently being added to premiums for free care, either explicitly or in the form of increased doctor and hospital charges.

28 *By themselves, the states cannot possibly provide all Americans with access to health care at an affordable cost.* Louis Brandeis called the states the laboratories of social and economic change in America—and so they are. Almost no important domestic legislation in this country has been approved by Congress before some state or group of states has taken the lead and tested it.

29 Health care reform is no exception. While Washington seems paralyzed on the issue, the states have moved ahead in a variety of ways. We have the impressive results of Hawaii's first-in-the-nation plan, the successes and failures of Massachusetts, the extraordinary process of citizen participation that preceded the passage of Oregon's health care law, Minnesota's bipartisan effort, Vermont's creation of a state commission that will attempt to impose global budgeting on its health care system, and Maryland's all-payer system of hospital cost control. These and efforts in many other states should be studied carefully as we consider proposals for national health care reform.

30 But universal access to affordable health care for all

Americans cannot possibly be achieved on a state-by-state basis. For one thing, the efforts of any state to impose additional burdens on its employers and citizens will immediately be met by protests from the business community that it is being required to shoulder burdens that are not being placed on businesses in neighboring states. Hawaii may have an advantage over other states in that it is harder for businesses to relocate.

State efforts to control costs through some form of global 31
budgeting will face similar objections. Consider states like Massachusetts, for example, that have high health costs largely because they are internationally renowned medical centers with many teaching hospitals and research institutions. If we in Massachusetts attempted to impose system-wide limits on health care spending without nationally imposed ceilings that applied to all states, we would be met immediately with the argument from our teaching and research centers that we were putting them at a serious competitive disadvantage in their efforts to attract and hold the world's finest researchers.

In short, comprehensive health care reform that guaran- 32
tees all Americans access to good health care at reasonable cost will not be achieved through state initiative alone. The president and Congress must act—and act together. In so doing, however, they can learn much from the experience of states that have been willing to take the plunge into uncharted waters.

MICHAEL S. DUKAKIS

References

1. Holoweiko M. Health care reform: what does Hawaii have to teach? Medical Economics, February 3, 1992:158–74.
2. State health ratings. Minneapolis: Northwestern National Life Insurance. 1991:12.
3. Lewin JC. Toward a seamless system of access to health care: the time is now. (Address before the Hawaii State Board of Health, July 5, 1991.) Honolulu: Hawaii Department of Health, 1991.
4. 1988 Mass Acts c. 23.
5. 1986 Mass. Acts c. 351.
6. Franks P, Clancy CM, Nutting PA. Gatekeeping revisited—

protecting patients from overtreatment. N Engl J Med 1992:327:424–9.
7. Dukakis M, Roseman C. Uni Health Cap: a proposed universal health access plan, May 16, 1991. Honolulu: University of Hawaii School of Public Health, 1991.

Ezekiel J. Emanuel
The Prescription

Ezekiel Emanuel is an oncologist and medical ethicist affiliated with the Harvard Medical School. In the summer of 1992 he offered the following prescription for the cure of the nation's health-care difficulties to The New Republic, *a widely read, middle-of-the-road magazine that examines public issues of all kinds.*

1 Distinguishing a sham treatment from a cure for our ailing health care system is no easy matter for those who don't happen to have a doctorate in health economics. The profusion of solutions now making the rounds has led to mass confusion bordering on despair. Cheer up. There are four basic rules that need to guide health care reform, rules that can distinguish useless or even damaging reforms from potentially good ones. What's more, the outlines of a practical alternative—more radical than anything yet proposed—are beginning to emerge.

2 The four rules are minimum requirements. Satisfying them means a plan meets the basic issues of access and cost; it doesn't mean the plan tackles secondary issues, such as distributing doctors and hospital services to rural areas and inner cities, training enough primary care physicians, balancing the demands for preventive care against disease treatment, or ensuring patient choice of physicians. But they're a start.

3 *Rule 1: Any program to expand access to health care must be linked to cost control.* Up to 40 million Americans—including almost 10 million children—lack health insurance. Getting a system that ensures universal access is no great problem. All you need is to subsidize those who can't afford insurance and force those who resist to get it. So we could simply extend Medicare coverage to all uninsured

people or give them government vouchers to buy private insurance. Without cost controls, however, this would cost between $40 billion and $100 billion per year.

In 1991 the United States spent over $2,800 per person on 4
health care, over a third more than Canada, the country with the second-highest costs. And these costs are rising fast. Per capita costs have risen by $500 in just two years. In 1987 American health care cost $500 billion, in 1991, $750 billion, and in 1995 it will exceed $1 trillion, or almost 15 percent of GNP. Old people covered by Medicare now pay a higher share of their income for health care than they did before Medicare existed. For corporations, health care costs now equal a staggering 90 percent of after-tax profits. A universal access program based upon the existing finance system clearly would increase costs still further. Not only would billions have to be added to provide for the uninsured, but added costs due to higher demand and uncontrolled health care inflation would continue.

Rule 2: One-time cost savings schemes will not substitute 5
for controlling health care inflation. Many reform proposals address the cost problem by proposing to cut the waste out of the system. Think again. Take administrative costs. About a fifth of the American health care budget, $100 billion to $120 billion annually, is spent on administration, from insurance overhead to physician billing. Some estimates suggest that half our costs could be saved by procedures such as uniform insurance claim forms, more use of electronic filing systems, and the like. But such cost savings are not the same as real cost controls. Cutting waste is a one-time savings: a mere dent in medical inflation. And even a whopping $60 billion savings works out to less than one year of health care inflation.

Rule 3: Cost controls mean containing inflation and limit- 6
ing the use of technology. The cost problem is increasingly related to the fact that health care costs are rising much faster than inflation, consuming an ever growing percentage of GNP. Last year overall inflation was only 3.4 percent but health care inflation was more than 9 percent, and health care rose from 12.2 percent of GNP to an estimated 13.1 percent.

Two factors contribute to the higher health care inflation 7
rate: an increasingly old population; and the introduction of new tests and therapies, with an increase in what's called the "intensity" of medical services. Inflation due to population

demographics can be altered only if we're willing to ration care by age. Regardless of its ethics, however, age-based rationing would be politically impossible. Along with general inflation, this accounts for 60 to 70 percent of the annual cost increase. So controlling health care inflation relies on the 30 to 40 percent attributed to technology and the intensity of care. What's needed is not so much a limitation on R&D as limits on the clinical use of technology. Canada and European countries have imposed such limits. Limiting the number of magnetic resonance imagers, the number of cardiac operating rooms, and so on, restricts use of these high-tech services and helps hold down costs. Although these limitations of technology can affect the care given individual patients, they may not diminish the overall health of a population.

8 Some reform advocates claim that managed care and malpractice reform can limit technology cost increases. They're wrong. HMOs save money not by limiting the use of medical technology, but by reducing the number of days that patients spend in the hospital. In recent years, however, Medicare and private insurance companies have also reduced hospital stays. And HMOs—as well as conventional health insurers—lack cost controls over the other forms of technology. Sooner or later, they'll get clobbered too. In fact, they already have: since 1988 HMO costs have risen 14 percent per year.

9 As for proposals to reform the malpractice system, malpractice premiums consume only 1 percent of the health care budget. The real savings are supposed to come through the effect on physician behavior. By limiting malpractice awards, it is argued, physicians will stop practicing defensive medicine and cut down on treatment without lowering the quality of care. But malpractice reform doesn't alter many other factors behind unnecessary treatment. More care leads to higher pay. And doctors react to their patients' demands for the latest technology. Finally, there is the physician's simple concern to do what's best for the patient. In any case, malpractice reform could save at most only $15 billion a year, less than 3 percent of the health care budget.

10 Some argue that money could be saved by lowering the salaries of physicians and other health care workers. But

physician salaries account for a mere 10 percent of overall health care costs. Thus even a 10 or 20 percent reduction in salaries would lower costs a mere 1 or 2 percent. Lowering salaries might also exacerbate shortages of nurses and other health care professionals.

Rule 4: An independent board should have authority to impose a national health care budget. The president and Congress are subject to conflicting forces on health care. On one side are rising costs that consume more and more federal money. On the other are constituents who balk at cuts or limits on care. Over the last decade Medicare has reflected this conflict: the president and Congress have deeply cut hospital and physician reimbursement, such as prospective payments to hospitals, but made no major cuts in services. This approach has not controlled overall Medicare cost increases. Indeed, health care costs have increased from about 10 percent of the federal budget in 1980 to more than 15 percent in 1990. At current rates health care will consume almost 25 percent of the budget by the end of the century. 11

Only an independent board, insulated from special interest groups, much like the Federal Reserve, could implement real cost control. This board probably should not have the authority to administer the health care system or to determine benefits; these matters are better addressed at the state or local level. The board, however, should have the power to set overall costs. 12

How do various proposals now being debated comply with these rules? 13

The Republican Plan: It breaks all the rules. It aims to extend care to all by a mixture of tax credits for the poor, tax deductions for the self-employed, and making it easier for small businesses to buy insurance. But Richard Darman at Office of Management and Budget—the plan's primary architect—didn't aim for universal coverage: at least 2 million and maybe up to 5 million people would be unable to afford insurance and be without government programs. And by relying on the current health insurance system, the Republican plan would exacerbate the cost problem. The plan is estimated to cost $100 billion over five years. This figure doesn't include what states would have to ante up for cuts in federal Medicaid funding. With the Republican's plan, health costs would likely soar. 14

15 The plan contains the most extensive endorsement of managed care and malpractice reforms for cost control; it would end restrictions on managed care programs and encourage states to enroll the poor in managed care. It would encourage use of alternative dispute resolution mechanisms and set limits on reimbursing for pain and suffering in malpractice cases. This doesn't add up to much. Finally, the plan ignores the fact that power to impose cost controls needs to be removed from the market. In health care, the buyer-seller relationship will always be loaded. The patient's ignorance, the uncertainty of most cases, and the fact that someone besides the patient pays most of the bills encourage greater use of services. As the 1980s showed, the more unregulated health care becomes and the more for-profit providers compete, the higher the costs.

16 *The HealthAmerica Plan.* Four prominent Democratic senators who have long backed health care reform—George Mitchell, Edward Kennedy, Donald Riegle, and Jay Rockefeller—have proposed HealthAmerica. More substantive than the Republican plan, it fulfills rule 2, and part of rules 1 and 4, but ultimately fails to develop real cost controls.

17 HealthAmerica is a so-called "play or pay" plan in which employers must provide their workers with insurance or contribute to a publicly administered fund that provides coverage. Americare is the name given by the senators to the public program that would replace Medicaid and cover those not insured through employers. Standards for benefits and services for Americare would be established at the federal level, although programs would be administered at the state level. To ensure that Americare would not be overutilized, private insurance premiums would be lowered by changing from a risk-rating system, in which the healthy pay less and the sick are priced out of the market, to a community-based system, in which all pay the same rate. Like the Republican plan, HealthAmerica would adjust rules to encourage cooperation among small businesses in buying insurance. To address one of the main problems of Medicaid—that payments to hospitals and physicians are often lower than the cost of providing services—Americare payments would be at or above Medicare levels. While the plan would guarantee universal access, play or pay relies on the current system to provide care.

18 The HealthAmerica proposal does have some useful savings schemes: cutting administrative costs by standardizing claims forms, setting up consortiums of small insurers to provide fewer payers and less paperwork, reforming the insurance market for small businesses. It would also encourage managed care and malpractice reform, although less emphatically than the Bush plan.

19 HealthAmerica also partly fulfills rule 4 by setting up an independent Federal Health Expenditure Board to set national, regional, and state spending goals and to recommend health insurance and payment rates to achieve them. Unfortunately, the powers to "recommend rates" wouldn't be binding on providers and purchasers, so they would have virtually no teeth. The plan's main flaws, however, lie in the area of cost control. According to the senators, costs are driven by uninsured costs being passed to the insured; unnecessary care of up to 15 percent of all costs; administrative waste; and open-ended reimbursement. The first problem doesn't increase costs but only affects their distribution. Solving the next three problems would reduce costs but wouldn't cut the underlying health care inflation rate. The only gestures toward reining in technology-driven cost increases are proposals to develop practice guidelines for physicians and expand research in technology assessment. The likely impact of this is quite limited. Because HealthAmerica relies on the current medical care system and is unable to confront the problem of technology, it's unlikely to limit cost increases.

20 *The Kerrey Health USA Plan.* Though it would satisfy rules 1, 2, and 3, Kerrey's plan would generate significant pressure on Congress to undermine the independent board by tinkering with the health care budget. To preserve patients' freedom to choose their own doctors, provision of actual care in the Kerrey plan would be dispersed. Within each state care would be provided by plans, whether HMOs, private insurance programs, or employer-based programs, as well as by a newly created public fee-for-service plan. These private and public plans would be required to provide a uniform package of services stipulated by a new National Health Care Commission. The state would pay each plan a "capitation" fee for each patient enrolled to cover all required services. The private plans would be prohibited from charging additional costs or adding co-payments and other

cost-sharing mechanisms beyond a minimal amount. And they wouldn't be allowed to exclude anyone from coverage because of pre-existing medical conditions.

21 The Kerrey plan would centralize all finances into a single payer. Medicare, Medicaid, and all other government programs would go; businesses and individuals would no longer buy private insurance. Taxes that go toward Medicare and other programs would be supplemented by a new 5 percent payroll tax, new taxes on 85 percent of Social Security benefits, and other taxes pooled into a federal health care trust fund. The government would distribute money to states, which, in turn, would pay private and public health plans, which would pay physicians and hospitals for services. Fees would be set by negotiations between the states and the physicians and hospitals. All plans, public and private, would pay the same state-set fee. There would be two other sources of funds. A "prevention account" would help cover preventive services and promotion. A "capital account" would pay for expanding and modernizing hospitals.

22 The plan claims to save money by cutting administrative waste. It wouldn't much. Though it would end the cost of marketing and insurance underwriting, the elaborate finance cascade it would also create, passing money through so many hands, would impose extra costs. But, unlike the other plans, it does target technology as a culprit. For hospitals, Health USA would use the capital account to restrict the dissemination of high-tech, high-cost interventions. Furthermore, there would be no erosion of these limitations by outlawing competing private insurance.

23 Health USA almost ensures the development of pressure to override the budget limits. A National Health Care Commission would be entrusted to generate an annual budget for the country and to determine the contributions to each state. However, to satisfy the constitutional requirement that ultimately Congress must vote the federal budget and allocate funds, this budget would only be a recommendation to Congress, which would have final power to pass or change the board's recommendations. And because people would not be permitted to purchase additional insurance or otherwise circumvent the limits and waiting lists of a budgeted system, lobbying Congress would be the only way to expand benefits. The Kerry plan would expose health care finances to intense interest group pressures and political bargaining.

* * *

Two points become clear in reviewing these plans. Incremental changes are likely to perpetuate the problems of the existing system, and only deep reform is likely to solve the real problems of access and cost. Second, controlling technologically-driven advances and the intensity of care is vital to reform. We Americans love technology; we invest billions in biomedical research, the media publicize the latest breakthroughs, patients demand the latest techniques. Yet the widespread use of high tech is the chief culprit behind the rise in costs. 24

So what's the solution? My proposal hopes to meet rules 1 through 4: a universal, cost-controlling health service. It's a community-based voucher system with the following rough structure. It would give each citizen a government-backed voucher, to be used in community health plans, which would coordinate the care. The community health plans couldn't discriminate against patients based on age, race, and sex or based on preexisting conditions, such as cancer or HIV. And they shouldn't be able to impose high co-payment provisions to exclude the poor. (Minimal co-payments may be desirable, as studies have shown they decrease use of certain services.) Eligible community plans might include health insurance plans, HMOs, and neighborhood health centers. They'd either coordinate care with hospitals, physicians, nursing homes, home health services, etc., or provide such services with their own physicians and facilities. These community plans would redeem the vouchers for payment from the government. This resembles the arrangement in Germany, where 1,145 sickness funds provide 88 percent of all care. In the German system, funding is derived from payroll taxes, and each sickness fund negotiates payments and benefits with physician associations and individual hospitals. 25

Defining the benefits that citizens should receive is much more controversial. Most proposals, like Kerrey's Health USA plan, aim for a uniform national benefits package and either specify minimal services or leave it to a federal board to designate a uniform benefits package applicable to all health plans in the country. There is a strong case, however, that defining types of medical services that citizens receive should be made locally, within each of the community plans actually providing care. 26

In all likelihood, different plans would therefore offer 27

different packages of services, and citizens would have to choose among them. For instance, an HMO might restrict patients' freedom to choose their own physicians in return for more benefits, such as cheaper medications, and dental coverage. Conversely, more traditional insurance plans might cover fewer services while guaranteeing choice among physicians. Some plans might stress preventive care and exclude high-tech services such as organ transplants, while others might cover transplants but not some preventive services. To ensure that residents of inner cities and rural areas can turn their vouchers into actual services, some monies beyond the vouchers might be allocated to foster community health centers, rural health cooperatives, and the like.

28 If the members wish, community health plans should be allowed to supplement the value of the vouchers by large patient contributions to provide more benefits. To ensure equity, these contributions would have to be made on a sliding scale according to income. By this redistributive mechanism, patients in health plans could collectively decide to spend more on health care than the voucher value without creating a two-tier system. Unlike Kerry's Health USA plan, a system in which voters could pay more for wider coverage would avoid the lobbying of Congress to override the budget limits and increase the voucher values.

29 Such a diversity of benefits, in which neighbors could have different plans and not be entitled to the same treatment for the same disease, would be just if citizens could participate through some democratic procedures in deciding which services would be offered and which excluded. Such participation by patients in determining benefits is not unprecedented; it already exists in many community health centers and some HMOs.

30 The vouchers should have two special characteristics. First, they could have different values. Older patients might have higher value vouchers; so could residents of inner cities and rural areas, in order to induce community health plans into those areas. Second, there's a strong argument that vouchers should extend for five- or ten-years with options for switching plans if necessary. This would cultivate long-term physician-patient relationships. It would also encourage investment in preventive medicine, risk reduction, and screening services where benefits take time to accrue. And it would discourage patients from switching

plans to obtain more extensive services for a newly diagnosed disease.

To create a community-based voucher system would 31
require shifting monies currently spent on government and private health programs into a federal trust fund—along the lines of the Kerrey plan. Second, since businesses and individuals would no longer buy health insurance or subscribe to managed care plans, the equivalent amounts of money could be taxed and put in the trust fund. The important point is that this system should not consume an ever-growing proportion of GNP. Thus we should set the cumulative value of the vouchers to the level we're now spending on health care, about $750 billion per year and an average voucher value of $2,800. Annual increases would be tied to the general inflation level.

The community-based voucher system would have two 32
levels of administration. On one level, there would be community plans responsible either for directly providing care or for coordinating care. On a second level, there would be a national board whose members would be nominated by the president to serve for five-year terms. The board would establish the health care budget, set voucher values, and disburse actual funds in exchange for vouchers.

This plan fulfills the four rules. Though it might strike 33
some as utopian or too radical to implement, it needs only moderate change in administration and very little in actual health care delivery. It also extricates the government and insurance companies from micromanaging health care decisions. Mandated second opinions for surgery, precertification for hospitalization, utilization reviews, and all the other intrusive cost controls devised over the last few years would no longer be necessary.

By granting community health plans the authority to 34
allocate funds, this plan also diffuses political pressures to increase funding. Since money not spent on some services would be available to provide other benefits, members would have an incentive to scrutinize the worthiness of the services available. If members felt that providing dialysis to patients over 65 was not worthwhile, they could restrict dialysis and spend the money on other services, such as prenatal care or cancer screening. Any rationing of services, whether by age or by cost effectiveness, as is being proposed

in Oregon, would be a decision voted by the patients, not one made by bureaucrats. This should appeal to patients and advocates of greater patient involvement in health care policies. And each plan would have the option of supplementing the value of vouchers and offering a wider range of services. This should appeal to politicians squeezed between budget limits and constituent pressures.

No doubt this system is not the only—or necessarily the best—reform option that exists. But unlike many others under consideration, it realistically confronts the thorniest problem: how to provide universal coverage without impossible costs.

The following pages of acknowledgments are a continuation of those on the copyright page.

Pages 33–41: From HORACE'S SCHOOL by Theodore Sizer. Copyright © 1992 by Theodore Sizer. Reprinted by permission of Houghton Mifflin Company. All rights reserved.

Pages 58–68: From *Smart Schools, Smart Kids: Why Do Some Schools Work?* by Edward B. Fiske. Copyright © 1991 by Fiske Futures, Inc. Reprinted by permission of Simon & Schuster, Inc.

Pages 70–71: From "What They Learn in School," *All Things Considered,* National Public Radio, March 17, 1989. Copyright © 1989 Jerome Stern. Reprinted by permission of Jerome Stern.

Pages 72–80: "Everyday Use" from IN LOVE & TROUBLE: STORIES OF BLACK WOMEN, copyright © 1973 by Alice Walker, reprinted by permission of Harcourt Brace & Company.

Pages 81–88: "Pedagogy and Political Commitment: A Comment" is reprinted from *Talking Back,* by bell hooks, by permission of South End Press. Copyright © 1989 by Gloria Watkins.

Pages 88–93: "Claiming an Education" is reprinted from *On Lies, Secrets, and Silence, Selected Prose, 1966–1978,* by Adrienne Rich, by permission of W. W. Norton & Company, Inc. Copyright © 1979 by W. W. Norton & Company, Inc.

Pages 95–98: From Christopher Jester, "Career Oriented Yuppie Students," *The Daily Collegian,* July 18, 1989. Reprinted by permission from *The Daily Collegian* and Christopher Jester.

Pages 99–100: From Lester C. Krogh, "Overselling of American Universities," *Atlanta Constitution,* March 28, 1991. Reprinted by permission of Lester C. Krogh.

Page 101: Hofstra University advertisement was reprinted by permission of Hofstra University. Photo by Joseph Berger Photography.

Page 102: Babson College advertisement was created by Kelley and Wallwork, Boston, Massachusetts. Reprinted by permission.

Pages 103–107: From Aram Bakshian, Jr., "Just Say No to College," *The American Spectator,* November 1991. Reprinted by permission of *The American Spectator.*

Pages 107–109: From W. D. Snodgrass, *The Examination,* New York: SOHO Press. Reprinted by permission.

Pages 109–125: From Louis Menard, "What Are Universities For?" *Harper's Magazine,* December 1991. Copyright © 1991 by *Harper's Magazine.* All rights reserved. Reprinted from the December issue by special permission.

Pages 126–139: From Eugene D. Genovese, "Heresy, Yes—Sensitivity, No," *The New Republic,* April 15, 1991. Reprinted by permission of *The New Republic.*

Pages 139–158: From John Taylor, "Are You Politically Incorrect?" *New York* Magazine, January 1991. Copyright © 1991 K-III Magazine Corporation. All rights reserved. Reprinted with the permission of *New York* Magazine.

Pages 171–172: From Emily Tsao, "Thoughts of an Oriental Girl," *The Washington Post,* September 29, 1991. © *The Washington Post.* Reprinted by permission of *The Washington Post.*

Pages 173–179: From Richard Goldstein, "The Politics of Political Correctness," *The Village Voice,* June 18, 1991. Reprinted by permission of *The Village Voice.*

Pages 179–186: From Rosa Ehrenreich, "What Campus Radicals?" *Harper's Magazine,* December 1991. Copyright © 1991 by *Harper's*

Magazine. All rights reserved. Reprinted from the December issue by special permission.
Pages 190–201: "From Outside, In" originally appeared in *The Georgia Review,* Volume XLI, No. 2 (Summer 1987), © 1987 by The University of Georgia, © 1987 by Barbara Mellix. Reprinted by permission of Barbara Mellix and *The Georgia Review*.
Pages 201–204: From Rachel L. Jones, "What's Wrong with Black English," *Newsweek,* December 27, 1982. Reprinted by permission of Rachel L. Jones.
Pages 204–216: From Geneva Smitherman, *White English in Blackface.* Oakland, CA: The Black Scholar. Reprinted by permission of the publisher.
Pages 216–227: From PARADIGMS LOST: Reflections on Literacy and Its Decline by John Simon. Copyright © 1976, 1977, 1978, 1979, 1980 by John Simon. Reprinted by permission of Clarkson N. Potter, Inc., a division of Crown Publishers, Inc.
Pages 229–241: From HUNGER OF MEMORY by Richard Rodriguez. Copyright © 1982 by Richard Rodriguez. Reprinted by permission of David R. Godine, Publisher.
Pages 241–250: From Victor Villanueva, Jr., "Whose Voice Is It Anyway? Rodriguez' Speech in Retrospect," *English Journal,* December 1987. Copyright 1987 by the National Council of Teachers of English. Reprinted with permission.
Pages 252–261: "English—The Official Language of California—1983–1988," by Stanley Diamond, is reprinted from *Perspectives on Official English,* edited by Karen L. Adams and Daniel T. Brinks. Copyright © 1990 by Mouton de Gruyter & Co. Reprinted by permission of Mouton de Gruyter, a division of Walter de Gruyter & Co.
Pages 261–265: "Testimony Before the State Legislature on California Proposition 63," by Geoffrey Nunberg, is reprinted from *Perspectives on Official English,* edited by Karen L. Adams and Daniel T. Brinks. Copyright © 1990 by Mouton de Gruyter & Co. Reprinted by permission of Mouton de Gruyter, a division of Walter de Gruyter & Co.
Pages 266–278: "One Small Step for Genkind," copyright © by Casey Miller and Kate Swift. Reprinted by arrangement with Virginia Barber Literary Agency. All rights reserved.
Pages 278–281: From the *Playboy* Column titled "Women: The Lady Killers" by Cynthia Heimel, *Playboy* magazine (January 1992). Copyright © 1991 by Playboy. All rights reserved.
Pages 281–283: From Lewis Grizzard, "Women Will Be Womyn," *The Atlanta Constitution,* June 14, 1991. Reprinted by permission of King Features Syndicate.
Pages 283–288: Text of "Crosstalk" from YOU JUST DON'T UNDERSTAND by Deborah Tannen. Copyright © 1990 by Deborah Tannen. Reprinted by permission of William Morrow & Co., Inc.
Pages 292–294: Reprinted by permission of the publishers from THE BOOK OF ABIGAIL AND JOHN: SELECTED LETTERS OF THE ADAMS FAMILY, 1762–1784, edited by L.H. Butterfield, Cambridge, Mass.: Harvard University Press. Copyright © 1975 by the Massachusetts Historical Society.
Pages 296–309: From Susan Glaspell, *Trifles,* by permission of Daphne C. Cook.
Pages 309–310: From "Belly Dancer" copyright © 1966 by Diane Wakoski. Reprinted from *Emerald Ice: Selected Poems 1962–1987* with the permission of Black Sparrow Press.
Pages 310–312: "Girl" is reprinted from *At the Bottom of the River,* by

Jamaica Kincaid, Copyright © 1983 by Jamaica Kincaid, by permission of Farrar, Strauss, and Giroux.
Pages 312–314: From Judy Syfers Brady, "Why I Want a Wife," *Ms.* magazine, December 31, 1971. Reprinted by permission of the author.
Pages 314–316: From Kurt Fernsler, "Why I Want a Husband." Used by permission of the author.
Pages 316–327: "Emotion" from *Femininity,* by Susan Brownmiller. Copyright © 1984 by Susan Brownmiller. Reprinted by permission of Simon & Schuster, Inc.
Pages 327–331: *Iron John* © 1990 by Robert Bly. Reprinted with permission of Addison-Wesley Publishing Company, Inc.
Pages 331–337: From Sharon Doubiago, "A Feminist Response to the Men's Movement," *Ms.* magazine, March/April 1992. Reprinted by permission of *Ms.* Magazine, © 1992.
Pages 337–348: From Andrew Kimbrell, "A Time for Men to Pull Together," *Utne Reader,* May/June 1991. Reprinted by permission of Andrew Kimbrell.
Pages 349–357: From Christine Gorman, "Sizing Up the Sexes," *Time,* January 20, 1992. Copyright 1992 Time Inc. Reprinted by permission.
Pages 358–367: From BRAIN SEX: The Real Difference Between Men and Women by Anne Moir and David Jessel. Copyright © 1989, 1991 by Anne Moir and David Jessel. Published by arrangement with Carol Publishing Group. A Lyle Stuart Book.
Pages 367–374: "Women's Brains" is reprinted from *The Panda's Thumb,* by Stephen Jay Gould, by permission of W. W. Norton & Company, Inc. Copyright © 1980 by Stephen Jay Gould.
Pages 374–384: From Evelyn Fox Keller, "Women in Science: An Analysis of a Social Problem," *Harvard Magazine,* October 1974. Copyright © 1974 Harvard Magazine. Reprinted by permission.
Pages 385–390: "Professions for Women" from THE DEATH OF THE MOTH AND OTHER ESSAYS by Virginia Woolf, copyright 1942 by Harcourt Brace & Company and renewed 1970 by Marjorie Parsons, Executrix, reprinted by permission of the publisher.
Pages 390–400: "Amy Kelley" is reprinted from *Alone in a Crowd: Women in the Trades Tell Their Stories* by Jean Reith Schroedel. Philadelphia, PA: Temple University Press. © 1985 by Temple University. Reprinted by permission of Temple University Press.
Pages 400–402: From Kati Marton, "An All Too Common Story," *Newsweek,* October 21, 1991. Reprinted by permission of Kati Marton.
Pages 403–407: From Frederic Hayward, "Sexual Harassment—From a Man's Perspective," *The Business Journal,* October 8, 1990. Reprinted by permission of *The Business Journal.*
Pages 407–410: From Lester C. Thurow, "Why Women are Paid Less Than Men," *The New York Times,* March 8, 1981. Copyright © 1981/87/90/91 by The New York Times Company. Reprinted by permission.
Pages 410–426: "Management Women and the New Facts of Life" by Felice N. Schwartz. Reprinted by permission of *Harvard Business Review* (January/February 1989) Copyright © 1988 by President and Fellows of Harvard College; all rights reserved.
Pages 426–427: "Letter to the Editor" by Deborah Biondolillo, *Harvard Business Review* (March/April 1989). Reprinted by permission of the author.
Pages 427–429: "Letter to the Editor" by Karen A. Geiger, *Harvard Business Review* (March/April 1989). Reprinted by permission of the author.

Pages 429–430: "Letter to the Editor" by Michael Maccoby, *Harvard Business Review* (March/April 1989). Reprinted by permission of the author.
Pages 430–432: "Letter to the Editor" by Jill Conway, *Harvard Business Review* (March/April 1989). Reprinted by permission of the author.
Pages 432–433: "Letter to the Editor" by Janet L. Lowden, *Harvard Business Review* (March/April 1989). Reprinted by permission of the author.
Pages 453–455: From Madeline Drexler, "Don't Touch That Dial," *The Boston Globe,* July 28, 1991. Reprinted by permission of Madeline Drexler.
Pages 455–458: From Katha Pollitt, "The Smurfette Principle," *The New York Times,* April 7, 1991. Copyright © 1981/87/90/91 by The New York Times Company. Reprinted by permission.
Pages 459–460: From Anna Quindlen, "TV or Not TV." *The New York Times,* November 30, 1991. Copyright © 1981/87/90/91 by The New York Times Company. Reprinted by permission.
Pages 461–462: "TELEVISION MAN" (David Byrne) © 1985 BLEU DISQUE MUSIC CO., INC. & INDEX MUSIC. All rights administered by WB MUSIC CORP. All Rights Reserved. Used By Permission.
Pages 462–469: From Jack McGarvey, "To Be or Not to Be as Defined by TV," *Today's Education,* February/March, 1982. Reprinted by permission of the National Education Association.
Pages 469–483: From *No Sense of Place: The Impact of Electronic Media on Social Behavior* by Joshua Meyrowitz. Copyright © 1985 by Joshua Meyrowitz. Reprinted by permission of Oxford University Press, Inc.
Pages 483–492: From Garry Wills "The Remaking of the Presidents," OMNI Magazine November 1988. Reprinted by permission of OMNI, Copyright © 1988, OMNI PUBLICATIONS INTERNATIONAL, LTD.
Pages 492–508: From Christopher Hitchens, "Voting in the Passive Voice," *Harper's Magazine,* April 1992. Reprinted by permission of Wylie, Aitken & Stone Incorporated.
Pages 508–511: From Joe Saltzman, "The More Talk the Better," *USA Today,* September 1992. Reprinted from USA TODAY MAGAZINE, September copyright 1992 by the Society for the Advancement of Education.
Pages 512–515: From Vincent Canby, "'Malcolm X' as Complex as Its Subject," *The New York Times,* November 18, 1992. Copyright © 1992 by The New York Times Company. Reprinted by permission.
Pages 516–519: From J. Hoberman, "Rating X," *The Village Voice,* November 24, 1992. Reprinted by permission of the author and *The Village Voice.*
Pages 520–524: From Terrence Rafferty, "Still Life," *The New Yorker,* November 30, 1992. Reprinted by permission; © 1992 Terrence Rafferty. Originally in *The New Yorker.* All Rights Reserved.
Pages 525–529: From Jon Pareles, "Rap: Slick, Violent, Nasty, and, Maybe, Hopeful," *The New York Times,* June 17, 1990. Copyright © 1990 by The New York Times Company. Reprinted by permission.
Pages 530–532: From Henry Louis Gates, Jr., "2 Live Crew, Decoded," op-ed, *The New York Times,* June 19, 1990. Copyright © 1981/87/90/91 by The New York Times Company. Reprinted by permission.
Pages 532–538: From David Mills, "The Obscenity Case: Criminalizing Black Culture," *The Washington Post,* June 17, 1990. © 1990, *The Washington Post.* Reprinted with permission.
Pages 539–542: From Juan Williams, "The Real Crime: Making Heroes

of Hate Mongers," *The Washington Post,* June 17, 1990. © 1990, *The Washington Post.* Reprinted with permission.
Pages 542–548: From Robert Scheer, "Reporters Notebook: Does Censorship Kill Brain Cells?" *Playboy,* October 1990. Originally appeared in *Playboy* magazine. Reprinted by permission of Robert Scheer.
Pages 555–566: From Luis Valdez, *Los Vendidos,* 1967. Reprinted by permission of the author.
Pages 567–571: From Gloria Steinem, "Erotica and Pornography." First appeared in *Ms.*, November 1978. Copyright © 1978 Gloria Steinem. Reprinted with permission.
Pages 580–583: From Susan Brownmiller, *Take Back the Night: Women on Pornography,* edited by Laura Lederer. New York: Morrow, 1980. Reprinted by permission of the author.
Pages 583–586: "I Am a First Amendment Junkie" by Susan Jacoby. Copyright © 1978 by Susan Jacoby. Reprinted by permission of Georges Borchardt, Inc. for author.
Pages 587–596: From John Irving, "Pornography and the New Puritans," book review, *The New York Times,* March 29, 1992. Copyright © 1991/92 by The New York Times Company. Reprinted by permission.
Pages 596–600: From Andrea Dworkin, "Reply to John Irving," *The New York Times,* May 2, 1992. Copyright 1992. Printed by permission of Andrea Dworkin.
Pages 601–609: From Margot Allen, "*Huck Finn*: Two Generations of Pain," *Interracial Books for Children Bulletin,* May 1984. Reprinted by permission of the Council on Interracial Books for Children, 1841 Broadway, New York, NY 10023.
Pages 609–611: From John H. Wallace, "*Huckleberry Finn* is Offensive," *The Washington Post,* April 11, 1982. © The Washington Post.
Pages 611–614: From Robert Nadeau, "*Huckleberry Finn* Is a Moral Story," *The Washington Post,* April 11, 1982. © The Washington Post.
Pages 614–636: From Nat Hentoff, "Huck Finn Better Get Out of Town by Sundown," *The Village Voice,* May 4, 11, 18, 25, 1982. Reprinted by permission of the author.
Pages 653–658: From Mahatma Gandhi, "Letter to Lord Irwin," March 1930. Reprinted by permission of Navajivan Trust.
Pages 659–670: From Martin Luther King, Jr. "Love, Law, and Civil Disobedience," *New South,* December 1961. Reprinted by permission of Southern Regional Council, Inc.
Pages 671–673: Birmingham clergymen, "A Call for Unity," originally appeared in *The Birmingham News*.
Pages 673–689: "Letter from Birmingham Jail" from WHY WE CAN'T WAIT by Martin Luther King, Jr. Copyright © 1963, 1964 by Martin Luther King, Jr. Repritned by permission of HarperCollins Publishers.
Pages 690–700: From Mia Klein Anderson, "The *Other* Beauty of Martin Luther King, Jr.'s 'Letter from Birmingham Jail,'" *College Composition and Communication,* February 1981. Copyright 1981 by the National Council of Teachers of English. Reprinted with permission.
Pages 700–707: From Lewis H. Van Dusen, Jr., "Civil Disobedience: Destroyer of Democracy," *ABA Journal,* February 1969. Reprinted with permission from the February 1969 issue of the *ABA Journal,* The Lawyer's Magazine, published by the American Bar Association.
Pages 707–710: From *Without Feathers* by Woody Allen. Copyright 1972. Reprinted by permission of Random House, Inc.
Pages 710–716: "Harrison Bergeron" by Kurt Vonnegut, Jr., from WELCOME TO THE MONKEY HOUSE by Kurt Vonnegut, Jr. Copyright © 1961 by Kurt Vonnegut, Jr. Used by permission of

Delacorte Press/Seymour Lawrence, a division of Bantam Doubleday Dell Publishing Group, Inc.

Pages 716–718: From Paul R. Spickard, "Why I Believe in Affirmative Action," *Christianity Today,* October 3, 1986. Reprinted by permission of the author.

Pages 719–726: From Shelby Steele, "A Negative Vote on Affirmative Action," *The New York Times Magazine,* May 13, 1990. Reprinted by permission of Shelby Steele.

Pages 727–731: From Catharine R. Stimpson, "It Is Time to Rethink Affirmative Action," *The Chronicle of Higher Education,* January 15, 1992. Reprinted by permission of Catharine R. Stimpson.

Pages 736–740: From Julianne Malveaux, "Why Are the Black Conservatives All Men?" *Ms.* magazine, March/April 1991. Reprinted by permission of *Ms.* Magazine, © 1991.

Pages 741–743: From Migdia Chinea-Varela, "My Life as a 'Twofer,'" *Newsweek,* December 26, 1988. Reprinted by permission of the author.

Pages 744–745: From Craig R. Dean, "Let's Legalize Gay Marriage," op-ed, *The New York Times,* September 28, 1991. Copyright © 1991/92 by The New York Times Company. Reprinted by permission.

Pages 746–749: From Jean Bethke Elshtain, "Against Gay Marriage II: Accepting Limits," *Commonweal,* November 22, 1991. Reprinted by permission of *Commonweal.*

Pages 749–765: From Michael Cunningham, "If You're Queer and You're Not Angry in 1992," *Mother Jones,* May/June 1992. © 1992, Foundation for National Progress. Reprinted with permission.

Pages 766–780: From Dan Chaon, "Transformations," *Story,* Winter 1991. Reprinted by permission of Dan Chaon.

Pages 781–790: From Sallie Tisdale, "We Do Abortions Here," *Harper's Magazine,* October 1987. Reprinted by permission of Sallie Tisdale.

Pages 790–796: From Mary Meehan, "Abortion: The Left Has Betrayed the Sanctity of Life," *The Progressive,* September 1980. Reprinted by permission from *The Progressive,* 409 East Main Street, Madison, WI 53703.

Pages 797–802: From Sally Quinn, "Our Choices, Ourselves," *The Washington Post,* April 1992. Reprinted by permission of the author.

Pages 803–805: From Mike Royko, *Chicago Tribune,* July 6, 1992. Reprinted by permission: Tribune Media Services.

Pages 811–822: From Leonard Kriegel, "A Loaded Question," *Harper's Magazine,* May 1992. Copyright © 1992 by *Harper's Magazine.* All rights reserved. Reprinted from the May issue by special permission.

Pages 822–824: From Roy Innis, "Gun Control Sprouts from Racist Soil," *The Wall Street Journal,* November 21, 1991. Reprinted with permission of *The Wall Street Journal* © 1991 Dow Jones & Company, Inc. All rights reserved.

Pages 825–827: From Ronald Reagan, "Why I'm for the Brady Bill," op-ed, *The New York Times,* March 29, 1991. Copyright © 1991/92 by The New York Times Company. Reprinted by permission.

Pages 827–829: From Elizabeth Swazey, "NRA Woman's Voice," *American Rifleman,* April 1992. Reprinted by permission of *American Rifleman* and Elizabeth Swazey.

Pages 830–831: Advertisement, reprinted by permission of National Rifle Association Institute for Legislative Action. © 1991 NRA.

Pages 832–835: From Robert A. Goldwin, "Gun Control Is Constitutional," *The Wall Street Journal,* December 12, 1991. Reprinted with permission of *The Wall Street Journal* © 1991 Dow Jones & Company, Inc. All rights reserved.

Pages 835–837: From Responses to Robert Goldwin: Letters to the Editor, "Smile When You Say Gun Control," *The Wall Street Journal,* January 14, 1992. Reprinted with permission of *The Wall Street Journal* © 1992 Dow Jones & Company, Inc. All rights reserved.
Pages 849–859: "Are Criminals Made or Born?" is reprinted from *Crime and Human Nature,* by James Q. Wilson and Richard J. Herrnstein. Copyright © 1985 by James Q. Wilson and Richard J. Herrnstein. Reprinted by permission of Simon & Schuster, Inc.
Pages 859–864: From Alison Bass, "Why Aren't There More Women Murderers?" *The Boston Globe,* February 24, 1992. (Reprinted courtesy of *The Boston Globe.*)
Pages 864–869: "The Current Crisis in Remorse," copyright © 1983 by Garrison Keillor, from WE ARE STILL MARRIED: STORIES AND LETTERS by Garrison Keillor. Used by permission of Viking Penguin, a division of Penguin Books USA Inc.
Pages 870–872: From "American Twilights, 1957." Copyright © 1971 by James Wright. Reprinted from *Collected Poems* by permission of University Press of New England.
Pages 872–877: "A Hanging" from SHOOTING AN ELEPHANT AND OTHER ESSAYS by George Orwell, copyright 1950 by Sonia Brownell Orwell and renewed 1978 by Sonia Pitt-Rivers, reprinted by permission of Harcourt Brace & Company.
Pages 877–883: From Edward I. Koch, "Death and Justice: How Capital Punishment Affirms Life," *The New Republic,* April 15, 1985. Reprinted by permission of the *The New Republic.*
Pages 883–891: From Jacob Weisberg, "This Is Your Death," *The New Republic,* July 1, 1991. Reprinted by permission of *The New Republic.*
Pages 892–894: From James Panichi, "The Morality of Capital Punishment," *The Daily Collegian,* July 7, 1992. Reprinted by permission of James Panichi.
Page 895: From *In Your Face,* by Doug Marlette. Boston: Houghton Mifflin. Copyright © 1991 by Doug Marlette. Reprinted by permission of Doug Marlette.
Pages 896–903: From Kurt Schmoke, "A War for the Surgeon General, Not the Attorney General," *New Perspectives Quarterly* (Summer 1989), vol. 6, no. 2. Reprinted by permission of the author.
Pages 903–909: From William Bennett, "Should Drugs Be Legalized?" *Reader's Digest,* March 1990. Reprinted with permission from the March 1990 *Reader's Digest.* Copyright © 1990 by The Reader's Digest Assn., Inc.
Pages 909–911: From Milton Friedman, "Prohibition and Drugs," *Newsweek,* 1972. Reprinted by permission of the author.
Pages 912–913: From Milton Friedman, "An Open Letter to Bill Bennett," *The Wall Street Journal,* September 7, 1989. Reprinted with permission of the author and *The Wall Street Journal*, © 1989, Dow Jones & Company, Inc. All rights reserved.
Pages 914–916: From William Bennett, "A Response to Milton Friedman," *The Wall Street Journal,* September 19, 1989. Reprinted with permission of the author and *The Wall Street Journal,* © 1989, Dow Jones & Company, Inc. All rights reserved.
Pages 917–918: From Letters to the Editor, "Bennett Fears 'Public Policy Disaster'—It's Already Here," *The Wall Street Journal,* September 29, 1989. Reprinted by permission.
Pages 923–929: "The Hazards of Science," copyright © 1977 by Lewis Thomas, from THE MEDUSA AND THE SNAIL by Lewis Thomas. Used by permission of Viking Penguin, a division of Penguin Books USA Inc.

Pages 946–956: From Jonathan King, "New Genetic Technology: Prospects and Hazards," *Technology Review,* February 1980. Reprinted with permission from *Technology Review,* copyright 1980.
Pages 957–958: Advertisement, "World Problems World Solutions" reprinted by permission of ICI Americas, Inc.
Pages 959–969: From Susan Wright, "Genetic Engineering: The Real Risks," *Christianity and Crisis.* Reprinted with permission. Copyright 1983, Christianity & Crisis, 537 West 121st Street, New York, New York 10027.
Pages 970–983: From Tom Regan, *The Animal's Voice Magazine.* Reprinted from *The Animal's Voice Magazine,* 1989. PO Box 341347, Los Angeles, CA 90034 / 1-800-82-VOICE.
Pages 984–993: From Vicki Hearne, "What's Wrong With Animal Rights," *Harper's Magazine,* September 1991. Copyright © 1991 by *Harper's Magazine.* All rights reserved. Reprinted from the September issue by special permission.
Pages 993–996: From "Letters to the Editor About 'Animal Rights, Wronged,'" *Harper's Magazine,* December 1991. Copyright © 1991 by *Harper's Magazine.* All rights reserved. Reprinted from the December issue by special permission.
Pages 996–999: From Alexis Dorn, "Animal Rights, Vegetarianism, and the American Effort to Save the Planet." Reprinted by permission of Alexis Dorn.
Page 1000: Advertisement, "It's the Animals You Don't See That Really Helped" reprinted by permission of the Foundation for Biomedical Research.
Pages 1002–1007: From Marcia Angell, "A Dual Approach to the AIDS Epidemic," *The New England Journal of Medicine,* (May 23, 1991) Vol. 234, pp. 1498–1500. Reprinted by permission of *The New England Journal of Medicine.*
Pages 1007–1013: From Letters to the Editor, "Responding to the AIDS Epidemic," *The New England Journal of Medicine,* (September 12, 1991) Vol. 235, pp. 809–811. Reprinted by permission of *The New England Journal of Medicine.*
Pages 1014–1015: From Anonymous, "It's Over, Debbie," *Journal of the American Medical Association* (January 1988) vol. 259, no. 2: 272. Copyright 1988, American Medical Association. Reprinted by permission.
Pages 1015–1018: From Charles Colson, "It's Not Over, Debbie," *Christianity Today,* October 7, 1988, page 80. Reprinted by permission of *Christianity Today*.
Pages 1019–1025: From James Rachels, "Active and Passive Euthanasia," *The New England Journal of Medicine* (1975), vol. 292, pp. 78–80. Copyright 1975 Massachusetts Medical Society.
Pages 1025–1028: From Sidney Hook, "In Defense of Voluntary Euthanasia," op-ed, *The New York Times,* March 1, 1987. Copyright © 1981/87/90/91 by The New York Times Company. Reprinted by permission.
Pages 1028–1037: From Leon R. Kass, "Why Doctors Must Not Kill," *Commonweal,* Copyright © 1991 by Commonweal Foundation. Reprinted by permission of *Commonweal* and Leon R. Kass.
Pages 1038–1042: Reprinted from *Recovering: A Journal, 1978–1979* by May Sarton, by permission of W. W. Norton & Company, Inc. Copyright © 1980 by May Sarton.
Reprinted from *At Seventy: A Journal* by May Sarton, by permission of W. W. Norton & Company, Inc. Copyright © 1984 by May Sarton.

Pages 1043–1050: From Milton Terris, "A Wasteful System That Doesn't Work," *The Progressive,* October 1990. Reprinted by permission from *The Progressive,* 409 East Main Street, Madison, WI 53703.
Pages 1050–1058: From Michael Dukakis, "The States and Health Care Reform," *The New England Journal of Medicine,* (1992) Vol. 327, pp. 1090–1092. Reprinted by permission of *The New England Journal of Medicine.*
Pages 1058–1068: From Ezekiel J. Emanuel, "The Prescription," *The New Republic,* June 1, 1992. Reprinted by permission of *The New Republic.*

Author/Title Index